# PERFORMANCE MEASUREMENT & CONTROL SYSTEMS FOR IMPLEMENTING STRATEGY

## Text & Cases

## Robert Simons
Harvard Business School, Boston

*Contributors:*

**Antonio Dávila**
IESE, University of Navarra, Barcelona

**Robert S. Kaplan**
Harvard Business School, Boston

Prentice Hall
Upper Saddle River, New Jersey 07458

| Executive Editor: | Annie Todd |
| Editorial Assistant: | Fran Toepfer |
| Editor-in-Chief: | PJ Boardman |
| Executive Marketing Manager: | Beth Toland |
| Production Editor: | Marc Oliver |
| Manufacturing Buyer: | Lisa DiMaulo |
| Senior Manufacturing Supervisor: | Paul Smolenski |
| Senior Manufacturing/Prepress Manager: | Vincent Scelta |
| Designer: | Jill Little |
| Design Manager: | Patricia Smythe |
| Cover Illustration/Photo: | Tony Stone Images |
| Composition: | Progressive Information Technologies |

Case material of the Harvard Graduate School of Business Administration is made possible by the cooperation of business firms and other organizations which may wish to remain anonymous by having names, quantities, and other identifying details disguised while maintaining basic relationships. Cases are prepared as the basis for class discussion rather than to illustrate either effective or ineffective handling of an administrative situation.

**Library of Congress Cataloging-in-Publication Data**

Simons, Robert.
　Performance measurement & control systems for implementing strategy: text & cases / Robert Simons; contributors, Antonio Dávila, Robert S. Kaplan.
　　p.　cm.
　Includes bibliographical references and index.
　**ISBN 0-13-234006-2**
　1. Managerial accounting.　2. Managerial accounting--Case studies.
　3. Controllership.　4. Cost control.　5. Strategic planning.
　6. Industrial efficiency--Evaluation.　7. Industrial management--Evaluation.　8. Organizational effectiveness--Evaluation.
　I. Dávila, Antonio.　II. Kaplan, Robert S.
　III. Title.　IV. Title: Performance measurement and control systems for implementing strategy.
　HF5657.4.S527　1999
　658.15'11--dc21

99-21129
CIP

Prentice-Hall International (UK) Limited, London
Prentice-Hall of Australia Pty. Limited, Sydney
Prentice-Hall Canada, Inc., Toronto
Prentice-Hall Hispanoamericana, S.A., Mexico
Prentice-Hall of India Private Limited, New Delhi
Prentice-Hall of Japan, Inc., Tokyo
Pearson Education Asia Pte. Ltd., Singapore
Editora Prentice-Hall do Brasil, Ltda., Rio de Janeiro

Printed in the United States of America

20　19　18　17　16　15　14

*To Judy*

# C O N T E N T S

# PREFACE

New accounting and control tools are needed to implement strategy in the 21st century. Rapid innovation, entrepreneurial competitors, and increasingly demanding customers have radically altered competitive dynamics. This book integrates the latest performance measurement and control techniques with the new realities of competition, strategy, and organization design. Anyone interested in running a business—either experienced managers or students—will benefit from understanding these new concepts and approaches to implementing strategy.

All the materials in the book have been rigorously pre-tested both in and out of the classroom. Students enrolled in Harvard Business School's MBA course, *Achieving Profit Goals & Strategies,* have used early versions of the book for three years. Selected chapters have been used in executive education programs at Harvard Business School and in a variety of corporate training programs. Case studies have been classroom tested at Harvard and many other business schools. Well-known U.S. and international companies have successfully implemented these new concepts. The result of this pre-testing and refinement is a coherent body of practical theory coupled with the latest application techniques.

The book is divided into four parts. Part I sets out the foundations for strategy implementation. Part II teaches quantitative tools for performance measurement and control. Part III illustrates the use of these techniques by managers to achieve profit goals and strategies. Part IV offers action-oriented case studies to illustrate key ideas and management techniques.[1] Throughout the book, concepts are illustrated with current, real-life examples. The reader is encouraged to refer to the glossary at the end of the text to gain a further overview of the broad range of concepts and techniques covered. An extensive bibliography is provided at the end of the book for those interested in additional references for specific topics.

Chapter 1 sets the stage for Part I—Foundations for Implementing Strategy—by highlighting the *tensions* that are the essence of successful strategy implementation. We discuss the challenges of balancing profit, growth, and control; the tensions between short-term results and long-term capabilities; the differing expectations of a firm's constituents; and the motives of human behavior.

Chapter 2 explores the basics of formulating and implementing *business strategy.* We discuss how to analyze competitive dynamics and the capabilities of a business. We then view strategy from four different angles: strategy as perspective, strategy as market

---

[1] Part IV is included only in the Text & Cases format of this book (ISBN 0-13-234006-2)

position, strategy as goals and plans, and strategy as patterns of emerging activities. We demonstrate that each of these approaches to strategy implementation requires distinct performance measurement and control techniques.

Chapter 3 introduces the essentials of *organization design*. In this chapter, we explore the implications of grouping business units by function as opposed to grouping business units by geography, products, or customers. We introduce key concepts that are essential to the effective design of performance measurement systems such as span of control, span of accountability, and span of attention.

Chapter 4 rounds out the introductory part of the book. In this chapter, we study how managers use *information* to control critical outputs. We discuss the technical feasibility of monitoring and measurement, the cost of information, and the effects of performance measurement and control on innovation. We end the chapter by discussing how managers use information not only for decision-making and control, but also for signaling, learning, and external communication.

Part II of the book—Creating Performance Measurement Systems—begins with Chapter 5, in which we show how to build effective *profit plans*. Using a profit wheel model, we illustrate how to develop accurate estimates for sales, profit, cash flow, investment in new assets, return-on-equity, profitability, and asset turnover. We illustrate how to gather and analyze data and assumptions, and demonstrate the effects of sensitivity analysis on predictions. We end this chapter by illustrating how to use a profit plan to test a strategy's validity.

Chapter 6 shows how to use *strategic profitability analysis* to calculate profit from competitive effectiveness and profit from operating efficiencies. Formulas and examples are provided for variance calculations related to profit plans, market share, revenue, and efficiency and costs.

Chapter 7 provides tools for *allocating resources*. For assets that enhance operating efficiencies or increase revenue, we review well-known techniques such as discounted cash flow and internal rate of return. For assets designed to enhance competitive effectiveness, we review the necessary analyses to ensure that resources are aligned with strategic initiatives.

Chapter 8 shows how to link profit plans and other performance measurement systems to internal and external *markets*. We discuss how to design an internal transfer pricing system. In addition, we discuss how to create financial and nonfinancial measures to link corporate performance to capital markets, supplier markets, and customer markets. Finally, we illustrate how to use residual income techniques such as economic value added.

Chapter 9 completes Part II by describing how to build a *balanced scorecard*. Using an internal value chain model, we discuss how the balanced scorecard can support and enable innovation, operations, and post-sale service processes. We describe how to build performance indicators to monitor the achievement of financial goals, customer goals, internal process goals, and learning and growth goals.

Part III of the book—Achieving Profit Goals and Strategies—focuses on how managers actually use these techniques to achieve business goals.

Chapter 10 introduces *diagnostic* and *interactive* control systems. We illustrate how managers use these systems to implement top-down intended strategy and guide bottom-up emergent strategy. In addition, we explore the special risks that are introduced through the use of performance measurement and control systems.

Chapter 11 focuses on *goal setting* and the aligning of *incentives*. We learn how to use goals to communicate strategy, the importance of targets and benchmarks for motivation, and the multiple purposes for which goals are used, including planning, coordination, motivation, and evaluation.

Chapter 12 provides the tools to identify *strategic risks*. We illustrate how performance measurement and control systems can be used to monitor operations risk, asset impairment risk, competitive risk, and franchise risk. We introduce the risk exposure calculator—a tool to measure the type and magnitude of pressures that can lead to failures or breakdowns. Finally, we consider the possibility of misrepresentation and fraud.

Chapter 13 provides an overview of the design and use of business conduct and strategic *boundaries* to control risk. We present a framework for designing *internal control systems* to safeguard information and assets. We review the behavioral and motivational assumptions that underlie these systems.

Chapter 14 ends the book by pulling together key concepts into an integrated model—the *levers of control*. The power of this approach is illustrated in two contexts: the introduction of performance measurement and control systems over the life cycle of the business, and the use of the levers of control by managers taking charge of a new business.

As I look back over the scope of the book, I realize that I could not have completed such an ambitious project without the help of many people. Robert Kaplan, my friend and colleague for the past 15 years, contributed Chapter 9 on the balanced scorecard. An acknowledged expert and one of the innovators of this important performance measurement tool, Bob was generous to allow me to include this chapter as well as several of his cases in the book. Antonio Dávila, a former doctoral student at Harvard Business School and now an assistant professor at the University of Navarra in Spain, worked closely with me on this project during his four years at Harvard. Tony helped write Chapters 5 and 6 (Building a Profit Plan and Strategic Profitability Analysis), prepared initial drafts of the bibliography, provided detailed commentary and suggestions on many of the chapters, and was a joint author for several of the case studies. Ken Koga, another doctoral student now at Waseda University in Japan, provided helpful comments and input. My colleagues Thomas Piper, who teaches *Achieving Profit Goals & Strategies* with me in the MBA program, William Bruns, the author of a number of cases in the book, and Marc Epstein and John Waterhouse, both of whom visited Harvard while I was developing the manuscript, helped me work through ideas and approaches. Professor William Fruhan generously allowed me to include one of his cases in the book.

I also gratefully acknowledge the willingness of Harvard Business School Press and Harvard Business School Publishing to allow me to use material from my book *Levers of Control* and to reproduce the Harvard case studies. Audrey Barrett, permissions editor at Harvard Business School Publishing, was especially helpful in researching all the cases and granting the necessary permissions.

I have benefited from comments on early drafts provided by Michael Alles (University of Texas at Austin), Shahid Ansari (California State University, Northridge), Howard Armitage (University of Waterloo), Jacob Birnberg (University of Pittsburgh), Len Brooks (University of Toronto), Clifton Brown (University of Illinois, Urbana-Champaign), Kung Chen (University of Nebraska, Lincoln), Chee Chow (San Diego State University), Kenneth Euske (Naval Postgraduate School), Neil Fargher (University of Oregon), Severin Grabski (Michigan State University), Harriette Griffin (North Carolina State University), Sanford Gunn (SUNY at Buffalo), Susan Haka (Michigan State University), Raffi Indjejikian (University of Michigan), Christopher Ittner (University of Pennsylvania, Wharton School), Stephen Jablonsky (Penn State University), Douglas Johnson (Arizona State University), Charles Klemstine (University of Michigan), Laureen Maines (Indiana University), Steve Reimer (University of Iowa), Alan Richardson (Queen's University), Toshi Shibano (University of Chicago), Michael Shields (Michigan State University), and John Vogel (Lockheed Martin).

Students in Harvard Business School's *Achieving Profit Goals & Strategies* course responded with good humor and perceptive suggestions as I tested and revised various versions of the manuscript. Many students, including Nicole DeHoratius, Timothy Dornan, Kenneth Gonzalez, Uchechi Orji, Yungwook Shin, and Kirsten Steward, made substantive suggestions that are reflected in the current text. Special mention must go to Michael Mahoney, who worked with me over several months revising and refining the manuscript prior to publication. Mike made many suggestions, drafted the initial version of the glossary, prepared clarifying paragraphs to the text, and identified many of the business examples.

Research associate Indra Reinbergs also made important contributions finding company examples to support the text material, as did Jeff Cronin, information analyst at Baker Library. Luz Velazquez, my assistant for the past two years, coordinated the submission of the manuscript and cases, and was characteristically efficient and cheerful in the face of deadline pressures. Jenny Tsoulos also provided invaluable assistance in checking page proofs and managing the submission of final changes.

At Prentice Hall, I am indebted to Annie Todd, executive editor, who has patiently and professionally shepherded the project to completion, PJ Boardman, editor-in-chief, who gave critical support throughout the project, and Marc Oliver, production editor, and Fran Toepfer, editorial assistant, both of whom kept the flow of the project on schedule. Ann Koonce made helpful suggestions in copyediting the manuscript. Beth Toland, executive marketing manager, provided the skill to communicate the essence of these new ideas to potential readers.

Developing the concepts, cases, and course upon which this book is based has filled my professional life over the past three years. I hope that you, the reader, will find the effort worthwhile.

Robert Simons
Boston

# PART I

## Foundations for Implementing Strategy

C H A P T E R

# 1

# Organizational Tensions to be Managed

Imagine that you are the owner of a small clothing chain in suburban Boston. You started with one small store and a novel idea: to offer cheap but fashionable clothing, along with a selection of decorative merchandise, to college students who attend Boston's many universities.

By focusing on the college market and staying in tune with youthful fashion and lifestyle changes, you have successfully built up a company with six stores. Your business now employs more than 100 employees. Innovation—focusing on the local youth market—differentiates your merchandise from the big department stores in the area. The key to success is your employees—young and in tune with the college clientele. They experiment continually with new products and fashion fads and recommend changes in merchandising mix.

However, as the company has grown larger, unanticipated problems have surfaced. Profitability among the six stores has been uneven. Two of the units are especially profitable, but it is not clear what causes them to be more profitable than the others. Another store seems to consistently underperform. Moreover, if you are not always in a store, you suspect that sloppy financial controls may be eroding profits.

Other issues have absorbed a lot of your time. You worry about missing the next fad. In one store, employees began experimenting with nontraditional products such as vegetarian foods. Some of the new products sold briskly, but overall store sales declined.

You are considering expanding into New York state, but you worry about how much to invest in new facilities and inventory. As the business becomes larger and more dispersed, you wonder how to set direction and ensure common goals for the business. The strength of your business has been in letting employees suggest new products to meet their local customers' needs. They know their customers best. On the other hand, some of their ideas have been failures. As the number of stores increases—especially in other states—greater geographical distance will make it harder for you to communicate your vision for the business and to get information to allow you to manage the business effectively.

To resolve these issues, effective managers rely on **performance measurement and control systems** to set direction, make strategic decisions, and achieve desired goals. Setting direction and achieving desired goals is relatively easy for a small business in which all employees work together in one location. Informal discussions and direct supervision can be used to ensure that the business is being managed effectively. As businesses become larger and more dispersed, however, these techniques become more difficult.

At the heart of the problem is a series of tensions—between innovation and control; between profitability and growth; between your goals and those of your employees (and others who have an interest in the business); and between the various opportunities to create value in the marketplace and the scarce amount of time and attention available to you.

This book describes the techniques that effective managers use to set direction and achieve desired strategic goals for the organizations they lead. The issues to be addressed in succeeding chapters can be broken down into the following questions:

1. How can managers leverage the potential for innovation in their businesses and, at the same time, ensure adequate control and protection from unpleasant surprises by employees?
2. How can managers drive growth that enhances, rather than dilutes, profitability?
3. How can managers communicate business strategy and performance goals effectively to all employees?
4. How can managers organize and dedicate various kinds of resources to support the implementation of business strategies?
5. How do managers measure and track performance toward strategically important goals?
6. How can managers ensure that their businesses are not exposed to unacceptable levels of risk?
7. How can senior managers move information from employees, who are in day-to-day contact with customers, back up the hierarchy to those who are responsible for formulating and supporting new strategies?

Throughout the book, we focus primarily on performance measurement and control systems for business organizations. However, the principles and techniques discussed are applicable to all goal-oriented organizations whose managers are interested in maximizing performance. Such organizations include non-profit educational institutions, charities, government departments and agencies, the military, and many others.

## SYSTEMS FOR PERFORMANCE MEASUREMENT AND CONTROL

This book focuses on performance measurement and control systems, which are the *formal, information-based routines and procedures managers use to maintain or alter patterns in organizational activities.*[1] Four aspects of this definition are important:

1. The purpose of any performance measurement and control system is to *convey information.* These systems focus on *data*—financial and nonfinancial information that influences decision making and managerial action.

---

[1] Robert Simons, *Levers of Control* (Boston: Harvard Business School Press, 1995): 5.

2. Performance measurement and control systems represent *formal routines and procedures.* Information is written down or entered into computer systems and captured in standard formats, either on paper documents or in computer-based systems. The recording, analyzing, and distributing of this information is embedded in the rhythm of the organization, and is often based on predetermined practices and at preset times in the business cycle.

3. The performance measurement and control systems that we study in this book are designed specifically to be *used by managers.* Organizations create massive amounts of information, not all of which is directly relevant to managers in their day-to-day work. A profit statement for a division or data on customer satisfaction is part of a manager's control system; information received by shipping clerks to allow them to pick merchandise from inventory for specific customers is not.

4. Managers use performance measurement and control systems *to maintain or alter patterns in organizational activities.* Desirable patterns of activity may relate to efficiency and error-free processing, such as yield rates in a manufacturing process. In other instances, they may relate to patterns of ongoing creativity and innovation in products or internal processes, such as the percentage of sales from new products or year-over-year improvement in processing speed.

We can think of performance measurement and control systems in a business in much the same way that we think of controls in a car. The steering, accelerator, and brakes allow the driver to control direction and speed; instrumentation on the dashboard provides critical information about actual speed and early warning about potential problems with the car's key operating systems. Like a racing car operating at top speed, high-performance organizations need excellent performance measurement and control systems to allow managers to operate their organizations to their highest potential.

In the next section, we introduce profit planning systems. These systems are the foundation for performance measurement and control in all high-performing businesses, and we will refer to them repeatedly throughout the book.

## Profit Planning Systems

Every business seeks to make a *profit.* For a business to survive and prosper over time, the inflow of resources must exceed the outflow. Revenue from goods and services provided to customers must be greater than the expenditures needed to manufacture and supply those goods and services on an ongoing basis.

**Accounting systems** collect information about the transactions of a business. Accounts (such as the T accounts that you studied in financial accounting classes) are ultimately summarized in financial statements such as balance sheets, income statements, and cash flow statements. **Internal control systems**—the set of procedures that dictate how and by whom information should be recorded and verified—provide the checks and balances to ensure that assets are safeguarded and the information collected and processed by the accounting system is accurate.

Accounting systems report actual, or historical, data. In addition to understanding how a business has performed in past accounting periods, however, managers must *plan* how much profit the business will (or needs to) make in future accounting periods. A **profit plan** is a summary of future financial inflows and outflows for a specified future accounting period. It is usually prepared in the familiar format of an income statement (similar to the one used in financial accounting). Managers must plan in order to (1) determine the quantity and type of resources that should be committed to a business and to (2) estimate the resources that will be provided by the business. Analyzing resource requirements—such as cash needs, machinery and equipment, and distribution facilities—is necessary because funding for resources must be lined up in advance and the acquisition and installation of resources may take considerable lead time. Estimating the level of resources that will be provided by the business—accounts receivable, cash flow, inventory stocks—is necessary to predict the business's ability to cover its obligations and invest in future productive capacity.

Profit planning involves analyzing past trends, making assumptions concerning cause and effect (e.g., what is the effect of advertising on revenue growth?), and predicting expected outcomes. In a seasonal ski-manufacturing business, for example, past trends might include looking at how revenues expanded and contracted each month over the past three years. Assumptions need to be made about anticipated interest costs and the availability and cost of purchased materials and services. Predictions must also be made about customer demand and the effects of competitor pricing.

Profit plans are supported by **planning systems**—recurring procedures to routinely disseminate planning assumptions, gather market information, provide details about relevant analyses, and prompt managers to estimate resource needs and performance goals and milestones. These systems are essential in providing the frameworks or templates for complete and careful trend analysis, consistent assumptions, and thoughtful predictions. In subsequent chapters, we will study how managers use these systems to implement their objectives.

## Performance Measurement Systems

Profit is earned by success in a competitive marketplace. Firms compete for customers by offering goods and services that customers are willing to buy after comparing available alternatives. Profit is an outcome of successful performance against competitors. Thus, the starting point in our analysis must be understanding how a business chooses to compete in its market—that is, the strategies and goals that managers set for the business. It is the successful implementation of these strategies and goals that provide profit.

**Business strategy** refers to how a company creates value for customers and differentiates itself from competitors in the marketplace. Strategy necessarily involves decisions about how a company will compete and what types of opportunities employees should be encouraged to exploit. The clothing store in Boston, described at the beginning of this chapter, may choose to compete on fashion and selection, drawing customers away from competitors because of a superior array of up-to-the-minute fashion clothing. In this store, employees are encouraged to keep in touch with the latest fashions and adjust retail displays to ensure that they attract fashion-conscious shoppers. Alternatively, a competing store several blocks away may choose to attract customers by offering lower prices. In this store, fashions are less current. The store is still profitable, however, because the customers attracted to this outlet are more price conscious.

Employees are constantly reminded of how to keep the store's costs to a minimum to ensure adequate profits in spite of low prices.

**Business goals** are the measurable aspirations that managers set for a business. Goals are determined by reference to business strategy. Goals may be financial, for example, achieve 14% return on sales; or nonfinancial, for example, to increase market share from 6% to 9%. The business goals for the clothing store following a fashion strategy will be different than the goals of the store following the low-price strategy. As we will discuss in later chapters, goals can be set for any entity that can be held accountable for performance: individual managers, departments, divisions, and stand-alone businesses.

**Performance measurement systems** assist managers in tracking the implementation of business strategy by comparing actual results against strategic goals and objectives. A performance measurement system typically comprises systematic methods of setting business goals together with periodic feedback reports that indicate progress against those goals. Performance goals may be either short-term or long-term. Short-term performance usually focuses on time frames of one year or less. Longer-term performance goals include the ability to innovate and adapt to changing competitive dynamics over periods of several years. Successful competitors are able to recognize or create opportunities and turn them into advantage over both the short term and long term. Performance measurement systems can play a critical role in helping managers adapt and learn.

Two types of decisions must be made by the designer of a performance measurement system. The first decisions are about *design features:* What types of information should be collected and with what frequency of feedback? Second, decisions must be made about how to *use* the performance measurement systems. Who should receive the data and what should they do and not do with it?

How to make each of these types of decisions will be covered in subsequent chapters. First, we must acknowledge briefly the inherent challenge of employing performance measurement and management control systems in any complex organization.

## BALANCING ORGANIZATIONAL TENSIONS

Organizations are complex entities in which managers must balance a variety of forces. There are five major tensions to be balanced in implementing performance measurement and control systems effectively:

### 1. Balancing Profit, Growth, and Control

Managers of high-performance companies constantly seek profitable growth. To do so, they are continually innovating. Innovation may take many forms. It may be in developing new products or services, or it may appear as new ways of doing internal tasks related to order-processing and manufacturing. Over time, successful innovation finds its way into sustained profitability and growth.

However, an excessive emphasis on profit and growth can lead to danger. Employees may engage in behaviors that put the business at risk. They may misconstrue management's intentions and "innovate" in ways that present unnecessary risks to the business. Recent debacles at Barings Bank, Kidder Peabody, and other financial institutions are chilling examples of employee behavior putting the entire organization in jeopardy.

A wise manager knows that control is the foundation of any healthy business. Only when adequate controls are in place can managers focus their energies on creating profit. Only when a business is profitable can managers focus on growing the business.

In all businesses, there is a constant tension between profit, growth, and control (see Figure 1-1). A profitable business that lacks adequate controls can quickly collapse. Control weaknesses inevitably allow error and risk to creep into operations and transaction processing. Managers can fool themselves into thinking that because the business is profitable, controls must be adequate. (Over the next month, make a point of looking at the front page of *The Wall Street Journal* for stories that describe businesses that have gotten into trouble because managers ignored the adequacy of controls and focused their attention elsewhere.)

Similarly, attempting to grow a business that is not profitable can only be described as foolhardy. Adding incremental revenues that do not generate profits can only lower the returns to stockholders. Managers in a poorly performing business might ask, "What is worse than 20% market share?" (Answer: 30% market share!)

Thus, as we consider how to design and use performance measurement and control techniques to implement strategy, it is important that we constantly assess whether or not managers have struck the right balance between profit, growth, and control. So far, we have alluded to several types of formal management systems: accounting systems, internal control systems, profit planning systems, and performance measurement systems. There are others to be covered later in the book that are important for managers in achieving profit goals and strategies. Collectively, these systems and techniques allow managers to balance the organizational tensions created by striving for profit and growth.

**FIGURE 1–1   Tension of Profit, Growth, and Control**

*Source:* Robert Simons, "Templates for Profit Planning," Boston: Harvard Business School Case 199-032, 1998.

---

### Tension of Profit and Growth at America Online

When America Online (AOL) went public in 1992, it pursued an aggressive growth strategy. AOL "rained diskettes" by direct mail to millions of computer owners, offering them free trials of AOL. It distributed free disks in music CDs, in boxes of Rice Chex cereal, with video rentals at Blockbuster Video, and even with meals on United Airlines. Membership soared from 155,000 in 1992 to more than 4.6 million in 1996.

However, this growth came at the expense of profitability and control. Subscriber-acquisition costs soared to $400 per new subscriber. AOL decided to treat these enormous marketing costs as capital expenses, amortizing them over 12 to 18 months. However, after negative publicity over its accounting practices, AOL abandoned its amortization policy and wrote off $385 million, an amount that exceeded the sum of all prior earnings. Then, when AOL changed its pricing policy from an hourly charge to a flat-rate plan, its systems could not handle the explosive growth in subscriber demand, leading to well-publicized outages and breakdowns in service access.

AOL's refocus on profitability started in 1997. Having established a well-recognized brand name for Internet access, managers slashed marketing costs. AOL's subscriber-acquisition costs were reduced to $90 per new subscriber and more than 3 million new subscribers were added to the system. It leveraged its scale to cut access costs by nearly 50%. AOL exploited its dominant market position by signing lucrative advertising deals with online retailers such as N2K music, 1-800-FLOWERS, Preview Travel, and CUC International. For example, Tel-Save paid AOL $100 million to become the exclusive retailer of telecommunication services on AOL. By 1998, AOL reported profits once again. It even increased monthly subscriber charges, a clear sign that it did not intend to sacrifice profitability for growth in the future.

---

*Source:* Adapted from Marc Gunther, "The Internet is Mr. Case's Neighborhood," *Fortune,* March 30, 1998, 69–80.

## 2. Balancing Short-Term Results Against Long-Term Capabilities and Growth Opportunities

Businesses must deliver financial performance—not tomorrow, or the year after, but today. The stock market, representing shareowners, rewards managers who can produce earnings in the current period. However, producing earnings consistently—period after period—is often difficult, especially in cyclical businesses, or when significant up-front investment is necessary to launch a new product or invest in a new plant.

Managers must also manage for the long term. They must renew production facilities, enter new markets with new products, and invest in research and development to stay current with competitors and meet changing customer needs.

Performance measurement and control systems play a critical role in managing the tension between short-term profit demands and the necessity for long-term investment in capabilities and growth opportunities. These systems do this by serving the following objectives:

- communicating to the organization the strategic goals of the business and the performance drivers critical to achieving those goals
- providing a framework for ensuring that adequate resources are available for the achievement of long-term goals and strategies
- specifying the cause-and-effect relationship between business goals and profit
- providing a yardstick for systematic growth in key performance indicators
- establishing and monitoring short-term profit goals
- establishing a framework for allocating resources to build long-term organizational capabilities

We will say more about each of these objectives in later chapters.

## 3. Balancing Performance Expectations of Different Constituencies

Managers strive to achieve a variety of goals: financial, nonfinancial, short-term, and long-term. However, we must stop and ask the question, "Whose goals are we seeking to achieve?" A business entity is comprised of many different constituencies. Different parties may have different stakes in the success of a business and desire different things from the people who manage it. Important constituencies might include:

- owners, including both small and large stockholders
- managers and employees of the business
- customers
- suppliers
- lenders such as banks
- government agencies (e.g., the Internal Revenue Service) and regulators such as the National Labor Relations Board

Each of these constituencies may be interested in different aspects of performance. *Owners and stockholders* may seek growth in earnings or stability in dividend payments. *Managers,* in addition to profit, may value growth in the size of the business to allow the opportunity for promotion and advancement. *Employees* may desire steady earnings and employment and the opportunity to participate in the business's success. *Customers* will be interested in product quality, service, and price. *Suppliers* appreciate ease of doing business and reliability in order and payment processing. *Lenders* will look for indicators of financial strength and liquidity to pay debt obligations as they become due. *Government agencies* will be interested in compliance with laws and regulations.

Thus, when managers design and use performance measurement and control systems, they must be aware of the different interests of each of these constituencies.[2] Managers must strike a balance between these expectations because they will sometimes collide. For example, customers may want high quality and low prices; managers may want

[2] For further elaboration of this argument, see Anthony A. Atkinson, John H. Waterhouse, and Robert B. Wells, "A Stakeholder Approach to Strategic Performance Measurement," *Sloan Management Review* (Spring 1997): 25–37.

to increase prices and profit margins, but pay low taxes; employees may be interested in salary increases and generous post-retirement benefits. Well-designed performance measurement and control systems provide a fundamental way of recognizing and balancing these trade-offs.

## 4. Balancing Opportunities and Attention

Another tension in organizations relates to having too much of one thing and too little of another. What do managers today have too much of? The answer is "opportunity." Think of all the things that any modern business might choose to do: new products, new services, branching into other industries, striking alliances, and opening global markets. Consider MCI Communications Corporation, started by a young Harvard M.B.A. in 1968 to compete with AT&T's monopoly in long-distance telephone communications. MCI's managers recognized many untapped opportunities to create value for customers, and they have created many opportunities themselves. Today, MCI has entered into a long-term alliance with Microsoft Corporation to develop an array of on-line and Internet services. MCI is also collaborating with News Corporation to deliver satellite television using high-powered orbital satellites. Recently, MCI agreed to merge with World-Com, another communications company. What is the limit to the opportunities that MCI WorldCom might pursue?

To answer that question, think about what businesses have too little of. The answer is management time and attention. Think of all the constraints facing a modern business: financial constraints, production constraints, information constraints, and technology constraints. Still, the most critical constraint is *management attention.* If enough smart people focus their attention on a set of problems, there are very few opportunities that cannot be turned to advantage and very few problems that cannot be solved. However, there are only 24 hours in a day. Yet, there are so many things to do, and so many issues to focus on, that managers must ration their time and attention wisely. There is too little to go around.

Thus, an important issue in designing performance measurement and control systems is ensuring that these systems are valuable tools in leveraging scarce management time and attention. In the chapters that follow, we will be focusing on various types of measurement techniques and financial ratio measures such as Return on Assets (ROA) and Return on Investment (ROI). We should note, however, that we need to pay attention always to how performance measurement and control systems can enhance **Return on Management (ROM),** which we can define as:

$$\text{Return on Management} = \frac{\text{Amount of productive organizational energy released[3]}}{\text{Amount of management time and attention invested}}$$

Effective managers have learned how to leverage this scarcest of all resources. In this book we will study how managers can use performance measurement and control systems to maximize their ROM by driving up the numerator (amount of productive

---

[3] Robert Simons and Antonio Dávila, "How High is Your Return on Management?" *Harvard Business Review* 76 (January–February 1998): 70–80.

organizational energy released) and driving down the denominator (amount of management time and attention invested).

## 5. Balancing the Motives of Human Behavior

One of the principal reasons that managers use performance measurement and control systems is to influence the behavior of subordinate managers and other employees of the business. To do so successfully, managers (and designers of performance measurement and control systems) must have a clear sense of what motivates people to work effectively toward the goals of any business. Every manager—and each of us—makes assumptions about how people in organizations will act in particular circumstances. These assumptions are critical in determining the best designs for performance measurement and control systems.

What are your assumptions about human nature? One possibility is that people are fundamentally self-interested and put their own interests ahead of the interests of the firm. Individuals calculate what will make them personally better or worse off and act accordingly to maximize their personal utility. In most cases, they can be expected to *minimize effort* devoted to achieving business objectives that do not pay off for them

---

### Values at Allied Signal

Lawrence Bossidy helped Jack Welch turn around General Electric Company. Then in 1991, he became CEO of AlliedSignal, a $13 billion supplier of aerospace systems and automotive parts. When he arrived at AlliedSignal, the company was facing a severe cash drain. Bossidy approached the problem with his "burning platform" theory of change—he believed that employees would be willing to change only if top management was open with employees about the company's situation so they could see the problem for themselves. To this end, he spoke to 5,000 employees in his first 60 days.

The company's cost problem stemmed from a bloated bureaucracy of 58 strategic business units, with managers of each business unit protecting their own turf. Once the organization had been slimmed down, Bossidy described how he attempted to achieve cohesion of values throughout the business. "I think that you coach people to win. Basically, people want to be successful. They want to go home at night and feel that they've made a contribution. . . . But we had to unite ourselves with vision and values. And that effort begins with the team at the top. In November 1991, we had an off-site meeting with the top 12 managers of the company. We spent two days arguing—and I mean arguing—about values. That was helpful because, at the end of the meeting, we not only had the values, we also had a specific definition of each of those values. The seven values we settled on are simple: customers, integrity, people, teamwork, speed, innovation, and performance."

---

*Source:* Noel M. Tichy and Ram Charan, "The CEO as Coach: An Interview with AlliedSignal's Lawrence A. Bossidy," *Harvard Business Review* 73 (March–April 1995): 68–78.

personally. This is the view that is prevalent in economic models of organization: Employees and managers are viewed as rational, calculating, maximizing individuals who dislike work, attempt to do the minimum that is demanded of them, and can be expected to act in opportunistic ways to enhance their own well-being at the expense of the organization to which they belong. To the extent these assumptions are true, performance measurement and control systems must be designed to ensure that people will work hard and do what managers expect of them.

Although these assumptions are undoubtedly true in specific circumstances for all of us, they can sometimes be too limiting. For example, they fail to explain people's sense of commitment and responsibility to others—why people often try to help someone else without inducement or possibility for future payoff. They fail to explain why people join organizations in which they think that they can make a difference, such as charities and benevolent organizations that help the poor and indigent. They fail to explain the importance of deeply held convictions about values, core beliefs, and religion. They fail to explain the role of conscience in personal decisions. They fail to explain the sense of pride and accomplishment that is often a sufficient reward for a job well done.

To design a performance measurement and control systems effectively, therefore, managers need a more holistic and rounded view of human nature. In this book, we make the following assumptions about the nature of human activity in organizations operating in modern economies.[4]

1. People in organizations *want to contribute* to an organization of which they can be proud. All of us have a need to contribute. We want to feel that we are making a difference. The organizations to which we belong can be vehicles to express that need. Many of us join churches and synagogues or work for volunteer organizations. In our work life, as well, we want to feel that "our business" is doing something worthwhile and that we are playing a productive role in that mission. In many businesses, our value is easy to appreciate. We can see our contribution and how we make a difference. In other circumstances, however, employees may be unsure of the mission of the business or its value to society. (The *New York Times* recently carried a feature story on the personal turmoil that is presented to executives of cigarette manufacturing firms.)[5]

2. People employed by business organizations know the difference between right and wrong and generally *choose to do right*. Our society has complex mechanisms for teaching people the difference between right and wrong, such as social groups, churches and synagogues, benevolent associations, and scouting. These organizations transmit norms of acceptable behavior. Also, educated citizens are aware of the laws that govern behavior and generally act accordingly. Our actions become guided by our conscience.

3. People *strive to achieve*. All of us work for a variety of reasons. In many instances, we work to capture extrinsic rewards such as money, promotion, and praise. These are always valuable and must be considered carefully in the design of reward and compensation systems. However, there are also innate drives in all of us to feel a sense of satis-

---

[4] A modern economy is one in which there is both economic freedom and institutions to effectively legislate and enforce laws. See S. H. Hanke, "The Curse of Corruption," *Forbes*, July 29, 1996, 103 for a summary of countries that satisfy these requirements based on a 1996 report *Economic Freedom of the World* by Transparency International.

[5] J. Goldberg, "Big Tobacco's Endgame," *New York Times Magazine*, June 21, 1998.

faction from personal achievement. Even in the absence of external inducements, people often set a personal goal for themselves, whether it be sailing around the world or learning a new skill.

4. People *like to innovate.* The basic urge to experiment is a powerful human instinct that has allowed mankind to continually improve our standard of living over time. Men and women in organizations also have innate desires to experiment by creating new technologies and new ways of doing things. In many companies, the so-called "bootleg project" refers to the secret experiment by employees who are trying something new without the express consent or knowledge of senior management. This is a powerful inner force that can successfully be harnessed by organizations.

5. People *want to do competent work.* Many, if not most, individuals take pride in their abilities. A job well done allows us to exercise our skills and receive satisfaction from our competence. In addition, people would rather do something right than have to go back later to fix it.

Now that we have made these somewhat heroic assumptions—that people want to contribute, achieve, innovate, and do competent work—we must confront reality. Although we can find examples of these behaviors in many circumstances, oftentimes people do not act like this in businesses that we know. What are the reasons?

Organizations—especially large ones—often make it hard for people to reach their potential. To understand why, we must examine the **organizational blocks** that organizations unwittingly create for the men and women who work in them.

First, business organizations often make it *difficult for people to understand* how they can contribute and make a difference. Employees may not understand the strategy and direction of the business. They may not be sure of the larger purpose—or mission—of the business, or how they can fit into that purpose.

Second, businesses often create *pressure and temptation* for employees. Performance pressures ("If you can't do it, I'll find someone who can!") may cause people to bend the rules or hide information, even though they know what they are doing is wrong. Also, temptation in the form of lucrative bonuses and performance awards—as well as access to company assets—may cause employees to step over the line between what they know to be right and wrong.

Third, achievement can be difficult either because individuals *lack resources* to get the job done, or because they face so many *competing demands* that they are unable to focus on any single objective with enough intensity to achieve the desired outcomes. Productive energy becomes scattered and diffused, making it difficult to achieve strategically important goals.

Fourth, people may fail to innovate because they *lack the resources* or are *afraid of the risk* of challenging the status quo. How many times do we hesitate when attempting to voice opinions that may seem novel or radical and may not be supported by our superiors and colleagues?

The qualities of human nature are inextricably bound up in the organizational tensions that affect all of us who work in organizations. Performance measurement and control systems cannot be designed without taking into account both human behavior and the causes and effects of these organizational blocks.

In the following chapters, we will study how effective managers utilize performance measurement and control systems to balance the organization tensions that are the keys to unlocking profitable growth through the successful implementation of business strategy.

## CHAPTER SUMMARY

Performance measurement and control systems are essential tools used by all effective managers in achieving their desired profit goals and strategies. These systems comprise profit planning and a variety of performance-management techniques that we will discuss later. These systems also allow managers to balance the tensions between: profit, growth, and control; short-term versus long-term performance; expectations of different constituencies; opportunities and attention; and the differing motives of human behavior. Properly applied, performance measurement and control systems can be used to overcome the organizational blocks that impede the true potential of all people who work in modern organizations.

# 2

# Basics for Successful Strategy

This chapter reviews the underpinnings for a successful business strategy. Some readers may have already studied parts of this material in a business-strategy or business-policy course. For others, the ideas and concepts will be new. Whatever your level of familiarity with this topic, we recommend that you review this chapter because the remainder of our analysis in the book builds on concepts that we introduce here.

Business strategy is at the root of effective performance measurement and control for two reasons. First, performance measurement and control systems provide the analytic discipline and communication channels to formalize business strategy and ensure that strategic goals are communicated throughout the business. Second, performance measurement and control systems are the primary vehicle to monitor the implementation of these strategies.

The techniques and systems that we discuss in this book help managers of all organizations answer two critical questions:

1. How can we be sure that people understand what we are trying to achieve?
2. How can we ensure that we are reaching our strategic goals?

## CORPORATE STRATEGY AND BUSINESS STRATEGY

Strategy is a word that is used in many different ways in business and other organizational settings. The first distinction that is important for our purposes is the distinction between corporate strategy and business strategy.

**Corporate strategy** defines the way that a firm attempts to maximize the value of the resources it controls. Corporate strategy decisions focus on *where* corporate resources will be invested. Questions such as "What businesses should we compete in?" or "What level of resources should we invest across our portfolio of businesses?" are typical of corporate-level resource allocation decisions. For example, managers at Boston Retail can choose to compete in women's clothing or in some entirely different product category. They may wish to branch out into men's clothing, or even to home furnishings. In time, it may be possible to leverage existing distribution resources to enter an entirely unrelated business, such as apparel manufacturing or wholesale distribution. These decisions—which businesses and segments of the market to compete in—are necessary whenever a corporation decides to expand its scope beyond a single product market.

*Business strategy,* by contrast, is concerned with *how* to compete in defined product markets. Once managers have decided to compete in the women's clothing market in Boston, they must attract customers and build market share. How will they differentiate themselves from competitors to create value in the marketplace? How can they offer something unique and valuable to their targeted customers? These are the questions that we tackle in this chapter.

Figure 2–1 illustrates the distinction between corporate strategy and business strategy.

Performance measurement and control techniques are important for the successful implementation of both corporate strategies and business strategies. The majority of topics in this book focus on creating value in specific product markets, which is the major issue for managers who run businesses. However, for firms operating in multiple markets, special measurement and control systems are needed to implement corporate-level strategy effectively. We cover these techniques and systems as well in later chapters.

The formal processes for formulating and implementing business strategy can be captured in the cascading hierarchy illustrated in Figure 2–2. Strategy formulation and implementation are multifaceted concepts. The cascading hierarchy of Figure 2–2 illustrates that a mission—the broad purpose for which an organization exists—guides the formation of business strategy. Business strategy, in turn, determines performance goals and measures, and, ultimately, patterns of action.

**FIGURE 2–1   Corporate and Business Strategy**

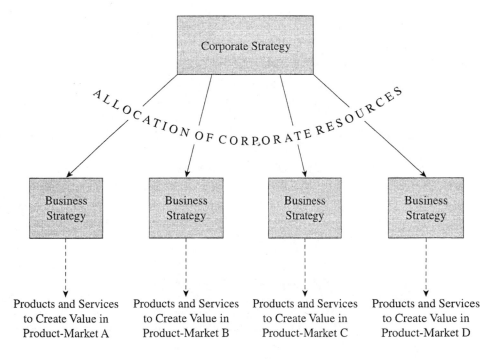

FIGURE 2-2    **Hierarchy of Business Strategy**

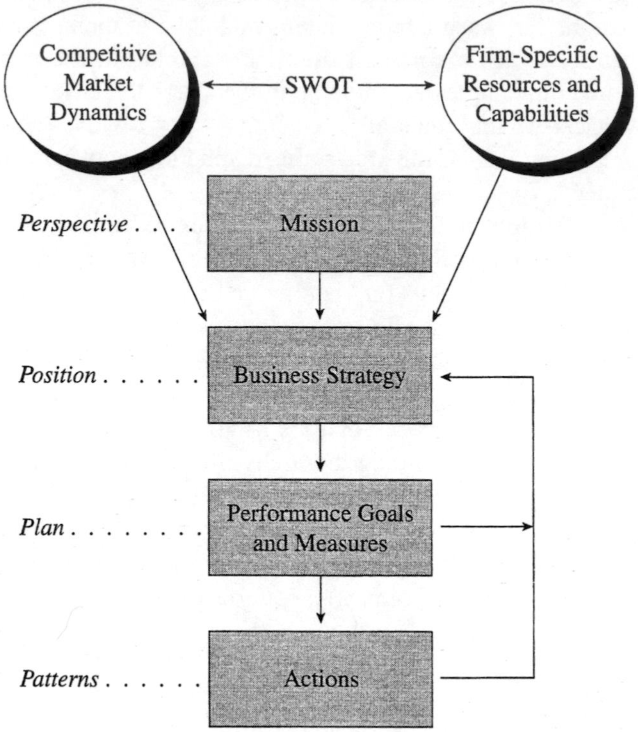

Before they develop specific business strategies, managers must analyze and understand (1) the competitive market dynamics in their industry and (2) their own firm's resources and capabilities. Thus, the first stage of our analysis must relate the *internal* strengths and weaknesses of the firm to *external* opportunities and threats in the marketplace. These two inputs to the strategy process are illustrated as ovals at the top of Figure 2-2.

**SWOT** is a useful acronym to remember the purpose of this analysis. SWOT stands for: **S**trengths, **W**eaknesses, **O**pportunities, and **T**hreats. The purpose of a SWOT analysis is to relate firm-specific strengths and weakness back to the industry opportunities and threats. Only then can we understand the context within which successful strategies can be formulated.

## COMPETITIVE MARKET DYNAMICS

What is the nature of the market? Who are the major competitors? What are the rules of the game? How great is the potential for profit? These are questions that all managers must answer as they seek to create competitive advantage in specific markets. The "five-forces" analysis provides a useful framework and checklist for analyzing the competitive dynamics of any given industry.[1]

The **five forces** that determine the degree and nature of competition (as shown in Figure 2–3) are (1) customers, (2) suppliers, (3) substitute products, (4) new entrants, and (5) competitive rivalry. In any industry, these forces individually and collectively influence competitive dynamics and potentially create opportunities for or constraints to effective competition.

In attempting to understand market dynamics at the industry level, the following questions must be analyzed in detail to fully understand opportunities and threats:

**Customers**
- Who are our customers? How much does each buy from us? Would they be willing to buy more? Under what circumstances?
- Is any customer or customer group particularly important to us?
- How do we appeal to different segments of the market? Why do they buy our product or services? What advantages does it offer them?
- How sensitive are they to price? To quality? To service? To other factors?

**FIGURE 2–3    Five Forces of Competitive Markets**

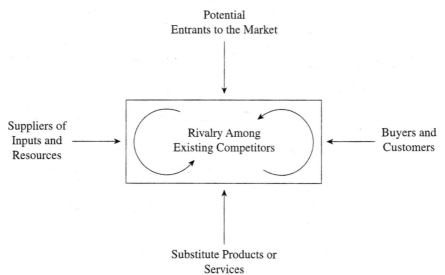

*Source:* Adapted from Michael E. Porter, *Competitive Strategy* (New York: The Free Press, 1980), 4.

---

[1] For a complete treatment, see Michael E. Porter, *Competitive Strategy* (New York: The Free Press, 1980).

### Suppliers

- Who are our major suppliers? How much do we buy from each? Would we be willing to buy more or less? Under what circumstances?
- Is any supplier or supplier group particularly important to us?
- What supply factors are critical to us — quality, price, reliability, service, and so forth?
- How costly is it for us to switch to alternate suppliers or sources?

### Substitute Products

- What substitutes for our products or services exist in the market?
- How are they different from our offerings in terms of price, quality, and performance?
- How likely are our customers to switch to competitors' products or services?

### New Entrants

- What are the barriers to entry to deter new competitors from entering our markets?
- How strong is our brand franchise?
- How difficult would it be for a new competitor to imitate the way we do business?

### Competitive Rivalry

- Is the industry growing or shrinking?
- Are there few or many competitors?
- Is there overcapacity?
- What are the switching costs for customers who might consider purchasing goods and services from competing firms?
- What is the ownership structure of competing firms? How important is our market to each of them?

At Boston Retail, managers have targeted a specific customer segment: young, fashion-conscious students. However, because of limited incomes, many of these customers are price sensitive, so merchandise must be both up-to-date and price competitive. To reach this goal, Boston Retail has found non-traditional suppliers — some of whom are themselves start-ups — who are willing to supply fashionable goods at reasonable prices. These suppliers are critical to Boston Retail's strategy.

There are many substitutes in the market and competition is intense. To prosper, managers at Boston Retail have decided to follow a niche strategy and expand only to regions that have similar customer demographics, but they must choose their battlefields carefully. Fortunately, the failure of a competitor — a business that offered a full line of women's and men's clothes throughout New England — has opened up the possibility for enlarging the business.

Armed with insight about *opportunities* and *threats* in a specific market, managers are ready to set strategy. However, before they can make definitive recommendations for a successful strategy, they must assess the internal *strengths* and *weaknesses* of the business. It is useless to enter a competitive arena unless a firm has the resources to fight for market share and a reasonable chance of earning profit.

## RESOURCES AND CAPABILITIES OF A BUSINESS

Accordingly, the next stage of a SWOT analysis, shown at the top of Figure 2–2, is to analyze the *resources and capabilities* of the firm to determine what a business does well and what it does not do well.

As a first step in analyzing internal strengths and weaknesses, we can look at a firm's balance sheet to learn more about the resources that are available for competition. (In this discussion, we focus only on the asset side of the balance sheet, leaving consideration of the debt and equity side of the balance sheet to finance and financial-statement-analysis courses.) As we perform this analysis, we need to remember that accountants apply a series of tests to determine which resources can be recorded on the balance sheet. In accounting, an **asset** is defined as *a resource, owned or controlled by the entity, that will yield future economic benefits.* Examples include plant, equipment, cash in the bank, and inventory. For purposes of strategy formulation, a **resource** is more broadly defined as *a strength of the business embodied in the tangible or intangible assets that are tied semipermanently to the firm.*[2] As we shall see, a resource may or may not appear as an asset on the balance sheet.

### Balance Sheet Assets

The following assets are customarily recorded on the balance sheet. These accounting assets are employed by the firm to generate revenues and will be the focus, in later chapters, of analytic techniques for performance measurement and control of strategy.

#### Current Assets

The first category on the balance sheet is current assets. **Current assets** include cash and other assets that will be turned into cash during the course of an accounting cycle — normally one year. Current assets include:

- cash
- marketable securities
- accounts receivable
- inventory
- prepaid expenses

Any strategy requires sufficient cash flow to fund it. Cash is needed to pay bills, purchase inventory, pay service providers, and meet current debt obligations. Cash flows, based on sales and the conversion of inventory to cash, must be planned carefully in advance to ensure that cash levels will be adequate, especially in a growing business. A large cash reserve may provide the freedom to fund growth or acquisition strategies. Our profit planning and performance measurement techniques must, therefore, include analysis of cash flows, cash reserves, and forecasts of the cash needed to fund specific strategies.

---

[2] B. Wernerfelt, "A Resource-Based View of the Firm," *Strategic Management Journal* 5 (1984): 171–180.

### Productive Assets

The second major category of assets on the balance sheet is **productive assets.** These assets are used to produce goods and services for customers. Productive assets represent the technology, machinery, and infrastructure necessary to compete. Some of these assets contribute directly to production—such as a machine in the manufacturing process. Other productive assets contribute indirectly to production—such as the computer hardware and software used to support gate agents at an airline terminal.

Examples of productive assets include:

- computers and information-technology equipment
- buildings
- manufacturing equipment

Productive assets must be sufficient—both in quantity and type—to support a business's strategy. As part of our performance measurement and control toolkit, we will discuss techniques to analyze the acquisition of productive assets and measure their effective utilization.

### Intangible Assets

The final category of assets on the balance sheet is **intangible assets.** These include:

- copyrights, patents, and trademarks
- goodwill
- valuable licenses (e.g., broadcast rights)
- leases

For any asset—either tangible or intangible—to be recognized on the balance sheet, accountants impose two tests. First, an asset must have *future value* to the firm. Second, that value must be *quantifiable with reasonable precision.* Tangible assets, such as buildings and equipment, or financial assets, such as cash and notes receivable, easily pass these tests and, therefore, are included on a firm's balance sheet. For intangible assets, however, the second condition—the ability to quantify value with precision—is typically met only when that value is priced independently through a third-party transaction. Examples of arm's length transactions that implicitly price the value of an intangible asset include the purchase of a broadcast license, the signing of a lease agreement, the granting of a patent based on past investment in proprietary research, or the creation of goodwill on the purchase of a subsidiary. Other intangible assets that may build up over time, such as reputation or dealer contacts, are much more problematic for accounting purposes. Their monetary value is difficult to measure, so these resources rarely appear on a firm's balance sheet.

## Intangible Resources

Intangible resources are often among a business's most valuable assets. These intangible resources may include, for example:

- distinctive internal capabilities
- market franchises
- networks and relationships with suppliers and customers

In highly competitive markets, it is these three categories of resources that provide the essential difference between success and failure. They are critical to achieving profit goals and strategies, yet they are not recognized on a firm's financial statements. Because intangible resources are a central focus of management's attention, our analysis of performance measurement and control systems must take into account the quality and nature of these intangible resources. Let's review briefly the nature of these three categories of resources.

### Distinctive Internal Capabilities

Distinctive business capabilities—sometimes called **core** or **distinctive competencies**—refer to the *special resources and know-how possessed by a firm that give it competitive advantage in the marketplace.* **Distinctive capabilities** include the ability to perform world-class research (e.g., Merck & Company), excellence in product design (e.g., Apple Computer), superior marketing skills (e.g., Coca-Cola Company), the ability to manage costs (e.g., Vanguard Mutual Funds), proprietary information technology (e.g., American Airlines), proprietary manufacturing skills (e.g., Intel Corporation), and so on. Distinctive capabilities are of three types: functional skills, market skills, and embedded resources.

**Functional skills** refer to strengths (and weaknesses) in the major functional areas of a business, such as research and development, information technology, production and manufacturing, and marketing and sales. Each of these functions can be an important source of opportunity in the marketplace. Research and development creates value at Minnesota Mining & Manufacturing (3M), manufacturing quality allows differentiation in the marketplace for many Japanese automobile companies, and marketing skills at consumer packaged-goods companies such as General Mills allow successful competition. As the name suggests, functional skills reside in the internal functions of a business. Functional vice presidents—such as vice presidents of marketing or manufacturing—are usually responsible for managing these critical competencies.

**Market skills** refer to a business's ability to respond quickly and effectively to market needs. Rather than analyzing resources and competencies by function, the appropriate unit of analysis is the customer or market segment. Here, the analysis focuses on (1) understanding what attributes of a product or service create value for a customer and (2) assessing the business's ability to provide those attributes. Responsiveness is key— to demands of price, quality, flexibility, reliability, service, or whatever else may be important in creating value in the eyes of a defined customer or market segment. Examples of well-known companies with strong market skills include American Express Company (travel and financial services), Johnson & Johnson (health care products), and Nordstrom (fashion retail).

The final category of distinctive capability is **embedded resources**—tangible resources that are difficult to acquire and/or replace. Physical plant, distribution channels, and information technology are all embedded assets that represent potential strengths and weaknesses. Although their historical transaction prices may appear on a balance sheet, these assets are far more valuable than a balance sheet would suggest because of the distinctive capability that they provide. A plant may be new or old—efficient or inefficient—yielding a competitive strength or weakness in the market. Similarly, information-technology advantages over competitors may be strengths (or weaknesses if old and outdated), as may a long-standing network of dealer contracts.[3]

Distinctive business capabilities—whether from functional skills, market skills, or embedded resources—often build up over long periods of time. Think of the firms listed above and ask yourself how long it took these firms to acquire their distinctive capabilities. How long did it take Merck to build up its world-class research capabilities? Or Coca-Cola to acquire its awesome marketing prowess?

Note also how difficult these capabilities are to copy. How difficult would it be to imitate any of these firms in what they do so well? Imagine attempting to "out-market" Coca-Cola, or to beat Merck at developing the next generation of hypertension drugs? Possessing distinct capabilities is a unique resource that often gives a business substantial competitive advantage (and puts competitors at a substantial disadvantage).

In some instances, capabilities are created by being first at something—a "first-mover"—and locking out competitors. For example, many U.S. airlines built efficient distribution networks in the early 1980s by creating regional hubs to serve as gateways for all their connecting domestic routes. By obtaining contractual rights to the majority of gates in these hubs, major airlines were able to gain significant first-mover advantages over regional competitors in the same markets. Thus, Delta Air Lines has a 72% market share in Atlanta, Northwest has an 80% share in Minneapolis, and United has a 70% market share in Denver.[4]

Business capabilities are the lifeblood of any firm operating in a competitive market and are among its most valuable assets. Although business capabilities sometimes appear on the balance sheet—such as large-scale distribution centers or investments in proprietary information technology—most business capabilities represent intangible assets that are not normally valued on a firm's balance sheet. They are "invisible assets."[5]

Managers must understand the existence and nature of these invisible resources if they are to measure their effectiveness in achieving profit goals and strategies. Performance measures must focus on the key drivers of success. Moreover, these capabilities are dynamic; they are constantly changing. New capabilities are developed, previous competencies atrophy, people and skills come and go, new technologies emerge, and new alliances are formed. Performance measurement and control systems provide the essential feedback to allow managers to monitor the health of these distinctive resources.

---

[3] For a complete treatment of this topic, see Pankaj Ghemawat, *Commitment: The Dynamic of Strategy* (New York: The Free Press, 1991).

[4] Michael J. McCarthy, "Major Airlines Find Their 'Fortress' Hubs Aren't Impenetrable," *Wall Street Journal*, February 6, 1996, A1.

[5] Hiroyuki Itami, *Mobilizing Invisible Assets* (Boston: Harvard University Press, 1987).

---

### Unilever vs. Mars

Since the late 1980s, Unilever plc, the Anglo Dutch consumer-goods company, and Mars, the U.S. company, have been battling over the Irish market for impulse-bought ice cream. Mars entered the Irish market in the late 1980s, at which time Unilever had 85% market share. Unilever's commanding market share was due to its ownership of freezers in retail shops. Most retailers were willing to carry only one ice-cream freezer because of limited floor space, so Unilever had the power over retailers to tell them which products to carry (either directly or by filling the freezer with Unilever ice creams). To protect its market share, and preempt Mars' entrance in the Irish market, Unilever tried to exclude Mars products from its freezers. As a result, Mars was able to sell its products through only 400 of a possible 1,920 outlets.

Mars interpreted this policy as an anti-competitive use of market power and successfully petitioned for an investigation on the "freezer exclusivity" issue by the European Commission. Mars' objective was to gain freezer space in Unilever's freezers to allow it to compete on an equal footing.

---

*Source:* J. Willman, "Seized Unilever Papers Show Strategy to Freeze Out Mars," *Financial Times,* June 22, 1998, 22.

---

### Market Franchises

**Market franchises** is the second category of intangible resources. The term franchise is used two ways in business. In a strict sense, a franchise is a *contractual agreement that allows an independent party to use a trade name or to sell a specific product owned by someone else.* A franchise agreement names the *franchisor*—the owner of the brand name—and the *franchisee*—who purchases the right to use the brand name under conditions set out in the franchise agreement (e.g., standards related to quality control, pricing, etc.). The ubiquitous North American fast food restaurants, such as McDonald's and Burger King, are typically operated as franchises. So too are auto repair centers (e.g., Midas) and rental car agencies (e.g., Budget Group). In each of these instances, an independent owner/operator of the retail unit is the franchisee who has purchased the right to sell products or services under the brand name of the franchisor.

A franchisee is willing to pay a fee and be bound by the strict terms of the franchise agreement because he or she is receiving something valuable in return—a recognized brand name and set of products or services ("a franchise") that can be expected to draw in customers.

Thus, the more general use of the term **franchise** among business managers refers to a *business's distinctive ability to attract customers who are willing to purchase the business's products and services based on marketwide perceptions of value.* A business is said to "own a franchise" when a brand name itself is an important source of revenue and value to the business. For example, consumers may seek out and be willing to pay a premium for an IBM computer, Johnson & Johnson Band-Aids, a Citibank credit card, Cheerios breakfast cereal, a Coke, Calvin Klein perfume, or any number of products that have created market franchises through customer awareness and brand loyalty.

Needless to say, franchises are among the most important and valuable assets of a business. Healthy franchises produce long-lived streams of revenue and profitability. As a result, the stock of companies with strong franchises often trade at high price/earnings multiples. Managers jealously guard their brand franchises and invest heavily in their brands to ensure a continuing perception of value in the eyes of current and potential customers. Accordingly, it is common in consumer companies for the highest levels of management—often the CEO—to personally review all new brand advertising to ensure that misguided advertising does not dilute or harm the brand image.

Unfortunately, a balance sheet, which is based on the accounting for historical cost transactions, is of little help in determining the value of a company's brand franchise. Because the value of a brand cannot be measured with precision, financial accounting standards in North America do not allow the recognition of franchise value on a firm's financial statements. How much is the L. L. Bean brand name worth? It clearly has great value, but you won't find its value reported in its financial statements.[6]

The exception to this rule occurs when businesses are bought and sold by corporate owners. When one firm buys another, it is buying more than the physical assets of the business, such as its buildings and equipment. It is also buying its franchise—the brand name, the customer base, and the goodwill in the marketplace. Thus, the purchase price of an acquisition is often significantly higher than the assessed value of its tangible assets. To make the debits equal the credits, accountants must somehow reconcile the difference between the purchase price of the business, which includes franchise value, and the historical cost shown on the balance sheet, which omits it. This residual—the difference between purchase price and the value of identifiable assets—is classified as "goodwill," an intangible asset recorded on the balance sheet to be amortized against income over some arbitrary period.

Notwithstanding the limitations of financial accounting, effective performance measurement and control systems must monitor the effective use of *all* significant business assets. Accordingly, as we think about techniques for achieving profit goals and strategies, we must pay special care to ensure that our performance measurement and control systems capture and protect the value of brand franchises.

### Relationships and Networks

In addition to distinctive capabilities and market franchises, successful businesses must also create and nurture long-term relationships with important suppliers and customers. These relationships are critical intangible resources for successful strategies.

Suppliers of factor inputs—raw materials, technical services, parts, and administrative support—are essential to the success of any business. Relationships with suppliers can be especially important if:

---

[6] In countries such as Britain that depart from the cost-based accounting model favored in North America, the value of a franchise can be estimated and shown explicitly on the balance sheet.

- there are few suppliers from which to choose
- there are few substitutes for the product or service that the supplier provides
- the supplier's product or service is important to the competitive success of the business
- switching to alternative sources of supply is expensive[7]

In these situations, good relations with suppliers is an essential resource to be monitored and managed carefully.

Similarly, relationships with buyers become important to competitive success if:

- a customer buys large quantities relative to the business's total sales
- products or services are standard or undifferentiated (allowing customers to easily purchase from someone else)
- a buyer can switch to alternative suppliers with little cost[8]

In many industries, distribution access is a prerequisite for success. Products are sold to wholesalers who warehouse and deliver products to retail stores; retailers in turn sell the product to customers. This is true in the brewing industry, for example, where Miller Breweries sells beer in large quantity to regional wholesalers. Sales representatives who are employees of the wholesaler visit retail establishments (restaurants and liquor stores) on a weekly basis to deliver product, stock shelves, and take orders for later delivery. Without these distributors, the nature of Miller's competitive position would be severely damaged. In industries such as this, access to efficient distribution channels that facilitate the flow of goods and services from the producer to the end consumer is an extremely valuable resource.

Like everything else in our modern world, electronic media has changed dramatically the nature of customer relationships. It is now commonplace to electronically link producers, distributors, and customers so that orders can be instantly transmitted from buyer to seller, with real-time updating of purchase orders, inventory records, and shipment dates. These electronic linkages can be extremely valuable intangible resources providing competitive advantage.

## THE 4 Ps OF STRATEGY

Look back at Figure 2–2. Our SWOT analysis has now considered the strengths, weaknesses, opportunities, and threats created by the interplay of competitive market dynamics and firm-specific resources and capabilities. This is the background or context for the formation and implementation of business strategy. Next, to formulate and implement strategy effectively, we must understand the design implications of each of the four cascading boxes shown in Figure 2–2. Understanding these different views of strategy will be essential to the performance measurement and control techniques developed later. In the remainder of this chapter, we analyze strategy from these four different angles: strategy as perspective, strategy as position, strategy as plan, and strategy as patterns of action. These are the four Ps of strategy.[9]

---

[7] Porter, *Competitive Strategy,* 27–28.

[8] *ibid,* 24–26.

[9] Henry Mintzberg, "Five Ps for Strategy," *California Management Review* (fall 1987). The fifth "P," not covered in this chapter, is strategy as ploy.

---

### Information Technology at Wal-Mart

Wal-Mart, the $100 billion U.S. retailing giant, continually searches for ways to boost its profits through advanced use of information technology. With 65 million retail transactions a week, even incremental improvements can have a significant impact.

Wal-Mart keeps information-technology spending lean (0.5% of sales as compared with competitors' 1.0% to 1.4% of sales) and develops applications in-house. Wal-Mart typically has 350 new IT applications in the pipeline, requiring retraining of 600,000 cashiers every two weeks. For example, Wal-Mart's SMART information system, (Store Merchandising through Applied Retail Technology), encompasses more than 1,000 applications that store employees can access through handheld units.

Wal-Mart's proprietary "Store Manager Workbench" system provides up-to-the-minute profitability analysis and "what-if" scenarios for store-based decision making. These systems enable headquarters to calculate profitability down to the individual shopping-cart level and combine it with data on weekend sales, gross margins, and payroll—all available for its 3,017 stores in seven countries by 6 a.m. on Mondays.

To maintain profitability under its "Everyday Low Prices" strategy, Wal-Mart uses its purchasing power to extract favorable terms from vendors. In turn, it integrates them into its information-technology systems. With the promise of lower inventory costs, Wal-Mart provides weekly sales forecasting data to more than 3,500 of its 5,000 suppliers.

---

*Source:* Bruce Calwell, "Wal-Mart Ups the Pace," *Informationweek,* December 9, 1996, 37–51.

## Creating a Mission—Strategy as Perspective

Mission is the starting point for our analysis of the formulation and implementation of business strategy. **Mission** refers to the broad purpose, or reason, that a business exists. At the most basic level, a firm's mission is recorded in its legal charter or articles of incorporation. However, senior managers usually draft their own versions of the business's mission to communicate their personal views of ideals and core values to employees throughout the organization.

Good missions supply both inspiration and a sense of direction for the future. Sony Corporation, for example, was founded in 1945 with the following purpose:

- To establish a place of work where engineers can feel the joy of technological innovation, be aware of their mission to society, and work to their heart's content.
- To pursue dynamic activities in technology and production for the reconstruction of Japan and the elevation of the nation's culture.
- To apply advanced technology to the life of the general public.[10]

---

[10] James C. Collins and Jerry I. Porras, *Built to Last* (New York: Harper Business, 1994), 50.

Sony's mission is intended to inspire employees to patriotic effort and make each employee proud of his or her association with the company and its values.

Missions are often written down in formal documents known as **mission statements** that are circulated widely throughout a firm. A mission statement communicates the core values of the business. Some firms may adopt different names for their mission statements such as *credo,* or *statement of purpose,* but they all serve the same objective: *to communicate the larger purpose of the organization and inspire pride in participants.*

Johnson & Johnson's Credo is reproduced in Exhibit 2–1. Note that in both the Sony and Johnson & Johnson examples—as well as the missions of most high-performance companies—maximizing profit is *not* the principal reason for existence. Earning profit is never a sufficient definition of a firm's mission; higher ideals are necessary to instill pride and motivate productive effort from employees. Of course, every company has to earn profit—just as each of us needs oxygen and water to survive. However, breathing and quenching our thirst are not the primary purposes by which we define our human existence. Like profit, they are necessary, but not sufficient, conditions for success.

A firm's mission provides an overarching *perspective* to all its activities. Rooted in a business's history, its culture, and the values of its senior managers, a mission statement provides the guideposts that allow all employees to understand how the firm responds to the opportunities that surround it. Can you imagine Jaguar introducing a low-priced entry level car to compete with Hyundai Motor Company? Or McDonald's Corporation opening a fashionable French restaurant? Or Rolex Watch Company producing cheap plastic watches? Or Swatch Group AG offering a $5,000 watch? Of course not. In each of these firms, an overarching perspective frames the opportunities that managers pursue and the types of decisions they make when faced with competing choices. This perspective is the lens through which business strategy is defined.

The mission of Boston Retail is reproduced in Exhibit 2–2. What do you think of it? What are its strengths and weaknesses? (Remember, its purpose is to inspire, instill pride, and give an overarching sense of direction and perspective to employees at all levels of the business.)

## Choosing How to Compete—Strategy as Position

With the mission of the business providing overall perspective—a backdrop for formulating strategy—the next step is to focus on two key questions about the **position of a business** in its competitive marketplace: (1) How do we create value for our customers? and (2) how do we differentiate our products and services from those of our competitors?

Managers of competing firms might answer these questions in very different ways. Some firms may choose to create value by offering their goods and services at *low cost,* hoping to draw customers who are price sensitive; other firms may compete by *differentiating* their products and services in a way that adds unique benefits for customers, or by *customizing* product offerings to respond to the specialized needs of specific customer segments. In the mutual fund industry, for example, Fidelity Investments has suc-

**EXHIBIT 2–1**
Johnson & Johnson Credo

# Our Credo

We believe our first responsibility is to the doctors, nurses and patients,
to mothers and fathers and all others who use our products and services.
In meeting their needs everything we do must be of high quality.
We must constantly strive to reduce our costs
in order to maintain reasonable prices.
Customers' orders must be serviced promptly and accurately.
Our suppliers and distributors must have an opportunity
to make a fair profit.

We are responsible to our employees,
the men and women who work with us throughout the world.
Everyone must be considered as an individual.
We must respect their dignity and recognize their merit.
They must have a sense of security in their jobs.
Compensation must be fair and adequate,
and working conditions clean, orderly and safe.
We must be mindful of ways to help our employees fulfill
their family responsibilities.
Employees must feel free to make suggestions and complaints.
There must be equal opportunity for employment, development
and advancement for those qualified.
We must provide competent management,
and their actions must be just and ethical.

We are responsible to the communities in which we live and work
and to the world community as well.
We must be good citizens—support good works and charities
and bear our fair share of taxes.
We must encourage civic improvements and better health and education.
We must maintain in good order
the property we are privileged to use,
protecting the environment and natural resources.

Our final responsibility is to our stockholders.
Business must make a sound profit.
We must experiment with new ideas.
Research must be carried on, innovative programs developed
and mistakes paid for.
New equipment must be purchased, new facilities provided
and new products launched.
Reserves must be created to provide for adverse times.
When we operate according to these principles,
the stockholders should realize a fair return.

*Johnson & Johnson*

**EXHIBIT 2–2**
**Boston Retail Mission**

> *Boston Retail Clothing was founded to offer young-at-heart customers*
> *the best in fashion, value, and fun. Our employees work together as a team*
> *to listen, learn, and serve to the very best of our ability.*
> *We will not sell products that we would not be proud to own and wear*
> *ourselves.*
> *We anticipate fashion trends and ensure that our products lead the way.*

cessfully differentiated itself by providing high levels of service and excellent invest-ment returns on its actively managed funds. The ability of its fund managers to outper-form market indexes is critical to its differentiation strategy. Because of its history of su-perior returns and high service levels, many customers are willing to pay Fidelity a fee that is higher than some other competitors in the industry. By contrast, Vanguard Mutual Funds competes on the basis of price and attracts its customer by offering the lowest possible management fees. Vanguard does not attempt to outperform the market, but in-stead specializes in index funds that mirror the rise and fall of the stock market. Finally, some specialized mutual funds target their offerings only at specified customer groups, such as the Teachers Income and Annuity fund, which tailors its services to college pen-sion funds.

---

### Perspective and Position at British Petroleum

John Browne, CEO of British Petroleum, described the key aspects for success in his business:

> A business has to have a clear purpose. A clear purpose allows a company to fo-cus its learning efforts in order to increase its competitive advantage. What do we mean by purpose? Our purpose is who we are and what makes us distinctive. It's what we as a company exist to achieve, and what we're willing to do to achieve it. We are in *only* four components of the energy business: oil and gas exploration and production; refining and marketing; petrochemicals; and photovoltaics, or solar. We're a public company that has to compete for capital, which means that we have to deliver a com-petitive return to shareholders. But, in our pursuit of exceptional performance and sus-tained growth, there are certain financial boundaries we will not cross and values we will not violate. The values concern ethics; health, safety, and the environment; the way we treat employees; and external relations.

*Source:* Steven E. Prokesch, "Unleashing the Power of Learning: An Interview with British Petroleum's John Browne," *Harvard Business Review* 75 (September/October 1997): 146–168.

## Setting Performance Goals—Strategy as Plan

After determining the mission and desired strategic position for the business (by analyzing competitive dynamics and resources and capabilities), the preparation of plans and goals represents the formal means by which managers (a) communicate a business's strategy to the organization and (b) coordinate the internal resources to ensure that the strategy can be achieved. When managers are asked, "What is your strategy?," they will often refer to their strategic plans—the documents where strategy is written down.

A major purpose of preparing plans is to communicate **intended strategy.** With agreement among top managers about how to compete in the marketplace, it is essential that they communicate this direction to the organization at large. Plans and goals can be used to communicate strategies and coordinate action. The linkage can be visualized as shown in Figure 2–4.

**Goals,** as reflected in profit plans and operating plans, are the *ends or results that management desires to achieve in implementing the business strategy.* Examples of goals for Boston Retail might include:

- increase market share
- open new stores
- launch a new product line
- reduce expenses
- develop information-technology capabilities
- improve customer satisfaction

However, goals become actionable only when time frames and quantitative indicators of success are added. Without performance indicators and time frames, managers cannot track progress and evaluate their success in achieving goals. For example, to be actionable, the performance goals listed above could be rewritten as follows:

- increase market share by 4% within 18 months
- open two new stores during the next year
- launch a new product line by July 1
- reduce expenses by 5% over the next year
- install a new automated inventory system in the next six months
- improve customer satisfaction by 12%

**FIGURE 2–4    Linking Strategy with Action**

Mission
↓
Intended Strategy
↓
Goals and Plans
↓
Performance Measure
↓
Actions

The final requirement for effective communication and implementation of goals is a *measure or scale* that can be used by managers to monitor progress toward these goals. For example, when driving your car on a long trip, you may set a goal of covering 100 more miles before stopping for gas. However, without an odometer and fuel gauge, you have no way of tracking your success in achieving that goal. Measures are equally important for every business. For the business goals and objectives listed above, we might measure:

- number of units of product shipped
- number of new store openings
- number of new product launches
- spending levels in dollars
- customer satisfaction ratings on a scale of 1 to 10

Plans can be used to communicate strategy, set goals, and coordinate resources. In subsequent chapters we will discuss the nature of information used for performance measurement and control, and then we will study in detail how to: build profit plans, evaluate performance against those plans, ensure that adequate resources are on hand to support successful implementation of strategies, link performance goals with markets, and design balanced measurement systems to communicate and monitor the achievement of strategic goals.

## Feedback and Adjustment—Strategy as Patterns in Action

The hierarchy of *mission → strategy → goals → measures → action* (shown in Figure 2–4) illustrates a cascading concept—from a general inspirational mission to specific quantitative measures of success. As we have discussed briefly, this hierarchy is supported by strategic plans based on a series of analytic techniques such as SWOT. However, this is an incomplete picture of the strategy process. Not all successful strategies are planned. Many arise spontaneously. Consider the following story:

> Robert Stage, president of Hamilton Bank, was addressing a group of M.B.A. students at Harvard Business School. Hamilton Bank was an important competitor in the private banking industry. The bank specialized in meeting the personal and corporate banking needs of wealthy individuals who owned their own businesses.
>
> A student raised her hand and asked, "Mr. Stage, you've told us that your private banking strategy is new. Where did it come from? Whose idea was it?"
>
> Stage responded, "Denise, that's an excellent question. You probably think that a group of us—Hamilton's executive committee—got together and worked it out based on market opportunities and an assessment of our own capabilities. But it didn't happen like that. As I explained to you, our earlier strategy was much broader . . . and not very successful. We had scheduled a series of performance review meetings with key managers around the world—country heads of major markets. Each came to the meeting to review their profit plans for the coming year and discuss year-to-date performance.
>
> "What surprised us was how many country managers described profitable niches they had created catering to wealthy business owners in their local countries. During the meetings, we started to question how much of this type of business we had around the world. No one had a clue. So we commissioned a study to find out.

"After a couple of months' hard work, we were stunned to discover that, in country after country, our local managers had built up very solid and profitable franchises catering to this market segment. After digesting this for a time, and looking at the momentum that had already been built, we decided that this could be the key to a successful strategy in the future. After further analysis and a lot of thought, we threw out the old strategy and adopted this new one. We're still in the process of rolling it out. This strategy didn't come from the top—it emerged from the bottom of the organization as local managers independently figured out how to create value in their markets."

This story is not unusual. Many successful strategies arise from local experimentation and replication. New approaches are tried—and many fail. However, some initiatives work in unexpected ways and suggest new ideas to managers about how to reposition the business. Experiments, trial and error, and sometimes just plain luck lead to new tactics and ways of competing. If these innovations are replicated, managers can learn over time how to change and/or improve their strategy. This "bottom-up" strategy is illustrated in Figure 2–5.

The importance of **emergent strategy** and learning is as true in life in general as it is in business. Read the biography of any successful business person (or any person, for that matter) and ask yourself how much of their success was planned and how much was due to serendipity and a willingness to embrace new circumstances that were emerging around them.

Thus, strategy can be planned—as we have discussed at length in our analysis of strategy as position and plan—but it can also emerge in unexpected and unanticipated ways. At Boston Retail, the decision to focus on college students was not planned. The company's first store stocked a wide variety of merchandise: clothing for both men and women, as well as an assortment of household goods. However, the female college students who worked in the store attracted friends who enjoyed mixing unusual fashion accessories to create bold statements. Over time, the store became known among local college women as a unique source of fashion accessories. Without a lot of forethought by

**FIGURE 2–5   Bottom-Up or Emergent Strategy**

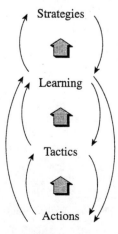

the owners, volume in this category grew steadily. In time, a decision was made by the owner/president to specialize in the college-fashion niche and eliminate other product lines. Replicating this formula, the business prospered and additional stores were opened.

Professor Henry Mintzberg describes how this can happen in other unpredictable ways:

> Out in the field, a salesman visits a customer. The product isn't quite right, and together they work on some modifications. The salesman returns to his company and puts the changes through; after two or three more rounds, they finally get it right. A new product

---

## Emergent Strategy at 3M

Innovation is the driving force in 3M's strategy. In 1997, 30% of sales came from products less than four years old, up from 26% in 1994. However, innovation, by its nature, cannot be planned in advance. Over the years, 3M has created a unique culture and set of processes that promote its prolific inventiveness.

All 3M employees are trained in risk-taking, and all scientists are expected to devote 15% of their time to projects outside of their current responsibilities. If a project fails to win approval within a business unit, scientists routinely find funding outside of their own organization. 3M is determined to follow where its scientists and customers lead them. 3M scientists work closely with major-customer teams to address expressed requirements and to identify and solve unarticulated needs. 3M promotes cross-fertilization of knowledge and ideas by frequent job changes. For example, when the "Post-It Note" product was being launched, 3M temporarily assigned the Post-It note product manager to develop a new fly-fishing line.

3M pursues a corporate program of investing in emerging technologies with limited current commercial application but with the potential for changing the basis of competition in an industry. In 1961, for example, 3M developed a technology called "microreplication" for covering surfaces with millions of precisely made structures such as cubes or spheres. By 1981, microreplication was used in one small 3M business for making lenses for lighting systems, but many more business units were experimenting with this technology for new applications. Recognizing its broader applicability, 3M made substantial investments in the technology. Microreplication is now responsible for more than $1 billion in sales, with explosive growth predicted.

Being a patient investor is not without its risks. For example, 3M continued to invest in innovation in its magnetic-storage business while the technology followed steep downward cost curves that quickly turned the high-tech product into a commodity. In 1994, 3M wrote off $600 million, laid off thousands of workers, and spun off operations related to this investment.

---

*Source:* Adapted from Thomas A. Stewart, "3M Fights Back," *Fortune,* February 5, 1996, 94–99; 3M 1997 Annual Report Chairman's Letter.

emerges, which eventually opens up a new market. The company has changed strategic course.[11]

The potential for new strategies to emerge in unexpected ways requires managers to be constantly aware of changing *patterns of action* in their businesses. For example, in the 1980s, Intel Corporation changed its strategy from a manufacturer of commodity computer memory to a manufacturer of high-value-added microprocessors. This change was not planned from the top; instead it was driven by mid-level managers and operations people who were making day-to-day decisions aimed at maximizing the value of scarce production capacity. However, top managers were ready to *learn*. They were alert for changing patterns in the business and were able to embrace the new strategy when it became evident from the actions of lower-level employees that this new approach could pave a profitable pathway to the future.[12]

To capture the benefits of emerging strategy, managers must foster **organizational learning**—the ability of an organization to monitor changes in its environment and adjust its processes, products, and services to capitalize on those changes. They must use their performance measurement and control systems to encourage employees to constantly innovate and search for signs of change in the business. Managers must encourage employees to experiment, to find new opportunities, and test new ideas. And, perhaps most importantly, they must ensure that performance measurement and control systems create effective communication channels to move this information up the line from employees to senior managers at headquarters. Feedback becomes critical for learning: it allows managers to fine-tune and, sometimes, radically change their business strategies.

## CHAPTER SUMMARY

Getting strategy right is not simple—if it was, top managers would not command the high salaries and bonuses that are the rewards of success. Implementing successful strategies requires the ability to conduct SWOT analysis of market dynamics and internal capabilities. Then, managers must be able to control the multiple dimensions of strategy reflected in the four Ps of strategy implementation (see Figure 2–6).

Ideals, values, and history must be woven together into an overall perspective that provides a lens through which to view the opportunities that surround the business. This is strategy as *perspective*. Managers must also have a deep understanding—a gut-level intimacy—of the market dynamics in their industry. They must use a five-forces analysis to understand customers, suppliers, products, and competitors. Based on a SWOT assessment of their own business's strengths and weaknesses, they must choose how to create value for customers. Will they compete on price? On quality? On service? On product features? This is strategy as *position*. Once strategy is set, managers must possess the tools to implement it. They must prepare plans, communicate goals, coordinate

---

[11] Henry Mintzberg, "Crafting Strategy," *Harvard Business Review* (July–August, 1987).
[12] Robert Burgelman, "A Process View of Strategic Business Exit: Implications for an Evolutionary Perspective on Strategy," *Strategic Management Journal* 17 (Summer 1996): 193–214.

**FIGURE 2–6    Basics for Successful Strategy Implementation**

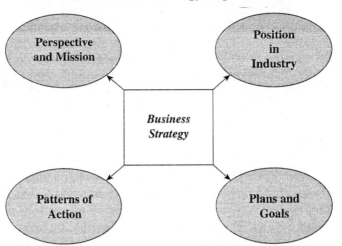

resources, motivate people, and measure and monitor implementation. This is strategy as *plan*. Finally, to succeed over the long term, managers must keep their eyes focused on customers and competitors and their ears to the ground. They must listen and learn. They must encourage employees to experiment and constantly challenge subordinates to share their ideas and successes so this information can be used to realign strategy over time. This is strategy as emerging *patterns* of actions.

The remainder of this book is devoted to learning how to use performance measurement and control systems to achieve profit goals and strategies. To do so, we introduce the tools and techniques that allow managers to take charge of *all* the aspects of successful strategy.

# 3

# Organizing for Performance

After business strategy has been set, managers must decide how to organize people and resources to achieve that strategy. As we shall see, there are many potential ways of organizing a business, but some ways are preferable to others. In this chapter, we tackle the questions, How do managers organize people and resources into work units? and What are the implications of this choice for implementing strategy?

We start by looking at the basic building block of organization design—the work unit. Then we explore different accountability structures and the criteria by which managers can choose one structure over another. Understanding organization design is important because performance measurement and management control systems must be aligned with the underlying structure of organizations.

Organizations are comprised of individuals who work together in groups. Groups may be large or small, including teams, task forces, shifts, departments, functions, plants, divisions, business units, and so on. Each of these groups performs specific functions that support the strategy of the firm.

## PURPOSE OF STRUCTURE

A dictionary defines structure as the way in which individual parts or elements are arranged or put together to form a whole. When designing **organizational structure,** the "parts" are the basic building blocks of the organization—that is, the groupings of people into work units—and the "whole" is the working relationships among these groups that collectively comprise a business.

In organizations, managers seek to impose structure for two principal reasons: (1) to facilitate work flows and (2) to focus attention. The former relates to the physical flow of materials and information, the latter to where people focus their time and energy.

Patterns in work flows are achieved by the structuring of *activities.* For example, managers must choose what assembly steps to put in a specific production line and in what order. They must also decide where information about new orders should be routed as it is received from salespeople. In both of these cases, the design of work flows—in one case the flow of products down an assembly line; in the other case, the flow of information through a networked computer system—determines how value will be added at each specific stage of the production, billing, and collection processes.

Managers must also structure the *attention* of the people who work in their organizations. In this case, rather than dealing with work flows per se, managers attempt to influence what people think about, worry about, gather information on, and make decisions about. This aspect of organization structure recognizes that the creativity and energy of managers and workers throughout the business must be channeled so that all energy can be as productive as possible.

Structuring of attention is achieved by three primary levers: the design of work units, span of control, and span of accountability.

## DESIGN OF WORK UNITS

The basic building block for organizational design is the clustering of related work activity in a work unit. A **work unit** represents *a grouping of individuals who utilize the firm's resources and are accountable for performance.* A maintenance facility, a production team, and a university history department are all examples of work units.

Individuals are grouped into work units to perform specific tasks. On the machine floor of a factory, for example, clusters of workers are organized around a production line; in the controller's department of a gas utility, accounting staff are grouped together to provide transaction processing and accounting services; in an international consumer-products firm, separate business units are created to produce and deliver products into specific geographic markets.

**Accountability** defines (1) the outputs that a work unit is expected to produce and (2) the performance standards that managers and employees of that unit are expected to meet. Most firms create a picture, or diagram, of their accountability units called an **organization chart.** Organization charts are useful visual reference tools because they allow members of the organization to understand how people and resources are grouped and who is responsible for directing activities and receiving accountability information—that is, information for performance measurement and control.

As we move from the smallest work unit (a team) to the largest work unit (a business), we see a hierarchy of organizing that reflects the foundation of organization design. Small work units are grouped together into larger work units; team-based production lines are grouped together into a plant; three plants are grouped together into a production division; the production division is grouped with marketing and sales into a geographic unit serving the Canadian market; the Canadian unit is grouped with other international units to form the international division; the international division is grouped with the U.S. division to form the highest level grouping—the entire business.

## BASIC DESIGN CHOICES

There are two basic types of work units: (1) groups of people and resources engaged in a similar *work-process,* and (2) groups of people and resources focused on a specific *market.* The former is often called a function; the latter is often called a division or business unit.

## Units Clustered by Work-Process

When new organizations are created, and are therefore quite small, employees typically work as "jacks-of-all-trades." When the first Boston Retail stores opened, for example, each employee pitched in to do whatever needed to be done with little regard for titles or specialization of duties. Think of anyone you know who has started his or her own business. At first, they have to do everything themselves—from selling, to purchasing, to record keeping, to negotiating contracts and obtaining permits. As the business grows and employees are hired, however, this approach becomes increasingly inefficient for two reasons. First, some people are better at certain tasks than others. This means that efficiencies can be gained by **specialization**—matching specific individuals with tasks that they enjoy and at which they can excel. It does not make sense to ask talented salespeople to spend their time bookkeeping, and vice versa. To maximize their productivity and contribution, certain people should spend all their time selling; others should spend all their time keeping records. Second, the constant switching back and forth between different tasks can result in wasted time and a **diffusion of attention** as employees refocus on a new set of activities. With employees frequently changing their attention to the latest demand or crisis, no single activity receives the full attention and expertise it deserves.

Accordingly, as businesses grow, it is common for managers to streamline work flows and focus attention by clustering workers by work-process or function. A **function** is the most basic organizational component, comprising a group of managers and employees who specialize in a specific work process.

Examples of functions based on work-process include:

- a marketing and sales unit
- a controller's department
- an information technology department
- a production unit

In a "functional" organization—where work units are grouped by activity—specific groups of individuals specialize in ordering merchandise and maintaining adequate inventory, others specialize in selling to customers, and others specialize in accounting and keeping records. In each case, the work unit performs a specialized function (hence the name) needed by the business: generating revenue (sales and marketing), designing new products (research and development), providing transaction processing and accounting services (the controller's department), supplying networked computing power (information technology), or manufacturing goods for sale (production department).

Managers organize by function to leverage the benefits of specialization and thereby create economies of scale in production, research and development (R&D), and marketing. With specialization, large-scale resources can be effectively deployed to maximize efficiency and effectiveness. Specialized resources, specialized knowledge, and dedicated support functions can all focus on achieving maximum outputs for predetermined levels of inputs.

In cases where specialization is carried to an extreme, organizations often group work processes by knowledge.[1] In hospitals and universities, for example, highly trained experts are organized by specialty. In a hospital, each medical specialty is clustered as a separate work unit: obstetricians are organized together; cardiologists are grouped separately, and so on. Similarly, in a university business school, the finance faculty are clustered as a unit, as are the accounting and control faculty. In these cases, professional postgraduate training and apprenticeship (of a physician or a professor) impart specific specialized knowledge that can be best exploited by clustering experts who work together on common sets of tasks using similar methods and techniques.

Functional work units typically receive both financial and nonfinancial goals and are held accountable for specific lines on a business's profit and loss statement. For example, the marketing and sales organization may be held accountable for successfully launching a new product (a nonfinancial goal) and the amount of sales revenue that it

---

### PSA Rationalizes Manufacturing

On October 1, 1997, Jean-Martin Folz became CEO of PSA Peugeot Citroën, the French car company formed in the 1970s when Peugeot and Citroën merged to create one of Europe's largest car makers. For more than 20 years, the company had kept manufacturing for the two brands virtually separate. Folz believed that the company could reduce costs by combining production for the two brands. Folz's aim was to reduce the number of platforms (groups of similar components) from seven to three for cars and one platform for car parts. At the same time, Folz intended to differentiate the marketing, sales, and style autonomy of each brand.

Peugeot and Citroën already shared such functions as finance, information systems, engineering, purchasing, and manufacturing of major components including engines. Furthermore, a precedent for rationalizing manufacturing facilities existed among PSA's competitors like Volkswagen and Fiat. To implement his new strategy, Folz reorganized the company into three functional divisions: one group manufacturing operation (in charge of all of the group's factories) and two separate sales divisions, one for Citroën and the other for Peugeot.

The full corporate reorganization, completed six months later, created three additional divisions to support PSA's product-development strategy: a new innovation and quality division to revamp and separate the Citroën brand identity from Peugeot, a platform division with responsibility for managing costs and quality, and an engineering and purchasing division.

---

*Sources:* Stephane Farhi, "PSA Managers to Enter the Folz Era," *Automotive News Europe,* March 2, 1998, 8; "Peugot Starts Revamp to Boost Image and Sales," *Wall Street Journal Europe,* January 22, 1998, 3; "France's Peugot Merging Production of Core Auto Brands," *Dow Jones Online News,* January 21, 1998.

---

[1] Henry Mintzberg, *The Structuring of Organizations* (Englewood Cliffs, N.J.: Prentice Hall, 1979), 108.

generates (a financial goal representing the top line of the income statement). The manufacturing department is held accountable for product quality indexes (nonfinancial goals), as well as cost of goods sold and relevant production variances on the income statement. Even in hospitals and health maintenance organizations (HMOs), physicians are held accountable for indices of patient care as well as expense control and resource utilization.

## Units Clustered by Market Focus

The second principal way of clustering individuals and firm resources is by market. Market-focused work units are normally found in one of three basic configurations: units clustered by product, units clustered by customer, and units clustered by geography.

### Units Clustered by Product

At the level of the firm, companies that have only one product are already clustered by product: All the energies of the organization—both people and resources—are focused on producing and marketing a single product category. Boston Retail, for example, competes in only one market segment—young women's fashion clothing.

However, the strategy of many companies leads them to produce products for multiple market segments. These multiproduct companies often choose to cluster workers and facilities according to a defined subset of products so employees in each unit focus their attention exclusively on their range of products. Thus, IBM Corporation has created a separate unit for its mainframe computer products, another unit for its personal computer products, another unit for its networking products, and so on. In such cases, each work unit, comprising dedicated production facilities and employees, is called a **product division.**

Firms choose to organize by product for two reasons. First, product specialization can create *economies in production* (for example, by allowing dedicated and specialized plant facilities for personal computer products), *economies in R&D* (scientists and engineers can spend all of their time working on enhancing existing software products or creating new products for defined target markets), and *economies in distribution and marketing* (distribution channels and marketing campaigns can be focused on meeting the needs of defined retail customer segments). These economies may be due to either **economies of scale**—allowing the business to utilize efficient large-scale resources to drive down unit costs—or **economies of scope**—utilizing the same resources (such as distribution channels) across multiple products or activities to increase the throughput for a given fixed amount of that resource. Economies of scale are achieved when Ford Motor Company builds all its Windstar minivans in one plant and can therefore install and dedicate efficient, high-volume production equipment to this single purpose. Economies of scope can be seen in the distribution trucks that bring fresh stock to convenience stores. Companies like PepsiCo are able to use their vast and highly efficient distribution networks to deliver multiple product categories (such as soft drinks and potato chips) in one truck. Because of these potential economies, many firms reorganized their businesses around product lines during the wave of "downsizing" that occurred in the 1990s.

The second reason for product-based clusters is to increase *return on management* when product knowledge and specialization are key to competitive success. Without undue distraction, managers can devote their full attention to understanding the competitive threats and opportunities related to a narrow, defined set of product-market opportunities and work to create value in the eyes of target customers. They can devote all their energy to understanding customers and competitors and implementing strategies with the utmost effectiveness and efficiency.

Thus, even though Fidelity Investments owns a limousine service—Boston Coach—and a large portfolio of community newspapers, these operations are segregated into separate product divisions that do not distract the attention of investment managers from Fidelity's primary mutual fund business. Similarly, many U.S. auto manufacturers have moved away from functional organizations that emphasized efficiency to product division structures to ensure adequate focus on differentiated product markets (for example, small front-wheel drive, rear-wheel drive, and recreational trucks).

Unlike a function, where managers are held accountable only for those revenues or costs relating to their specific activities—typically a single line on the income statement—a product division manager is held accountable for an entire profit and loss statement. Often, product divisions are also responsible for managing assets on their balance sheet.

## Units Clustered by Customer

A second common clustering based on market focus occurs when a business is grouped according to customer or customer type. This type of organizational arrangement is found most often when firms have a small number of large, important customers, each

---

### Reorganization at Compaq Computers

In 1991, Compaq was losing market share due to its inability to compete in a new, price-sensitive market for personal computers (PCs). In the third quarter, it reported a loss of $70 million and its CEO was fired. A new management team, lead by Eckhard Pfeiffer, had to turn the company around and bring costs back under control. Pfeiffer changed Compaq's structure from a functional structure (based on manufacturing, sales, etc.) to a product division structure to focus each business on its key competencies. Each product division was given profit and loss responsibilities. PC operations, where low cost was paramount for success, became one of the new divisions. The objective for the PC division was to cut costs by 35% to 50%. Pfeiffer sent this message again and again to ensure that people understood clearly the new strategy. Products with higher technological content were grouped in another division. When expertise was not available within the organization, partnerships were formed, including the server division's union with Corollary, whose software enabled eight processors to run simultaneously.

*Source:* C. Arnst and S.A. Forest, "Compaq: How It Made Its Impressive Move Out of the Doldrums," *Business Week,* November 4, 1992, 146 and E. Nee, "Compaq Computer," *Forbes,* January 12, 1998, 90.

with distinct needs and attributes. Businesses like General Electric Corporation that sell to both industrial and government customers often organize their people and resources so that one organizational unit specializes in production and sales to the government, and another specializes in production and sales to industrial customers. Similarly, textbook publishers cluster their activities into separate customer-focused business units that specialize in producing and marketing books for elementary schools, four-year colleges, graduate schools, and so on.

Customer-based work units can take two forms. The first is a separate sales and marketing organization dedicated to serving the needs of large, important customers. IBM has followed this approach by creating a separate unit of "Client Executives" who receive specialized training and are dedicated to meeting the needs of the specific, large corporate customers to whom each is assigned. The second, and larger scale, approach is to carve out an entire organization—from procurement, to production, to sales and marketing—that is dedicated to a single customer or category of customer. This is most often encountered in businesses like General Dynamics that do a substantial amount of work with the U.S. government and set up dedicated business units to serve the specialized needs of this important customer. Similarly, the Internal Revenue Service is changing from an organizational structure based on region to one based on serving its three main constituencies: individual filers, small businesses, and big corporations.[2]

Firms cluster by customer type when the market needs of each customer segment are sufficiently unique that *specialized expertise and knowledge* about that customer are essential to competitive success in the marketplace. To serve a large customer effec-

---

### Structuring for Customer Service at Ford Motor Company

Customer demands are forcing managers of traditional hierarchical, functional organizations to group units horizontally around key customer-oriented processes. At Ford Motor Company's Customer Service Department, managers realized that they were behind both American and Japanese competitors in customer satisfaction ratings. Accordingly, the 6,200-employee division was reorganized around four key processes: (1) fixing it right the first time on time; (2) supporting dealers and handling customers; (3) engineering cars with ease of service in mind; and (4) developing service fixes more quickly. Changes in dealer relations were especially dramatic. Through the introduction of field teams, the number of Ford people a dealer had to contact to resolve a customer problem dropped from 25 to three—a divisional operations manager, a field engineer, and a customer service representative.

*Source:* Rahul Jacob and Rajiv M. Rao, "The Struggle to Create an Organization for the 21st Century," *Fortune,* April 3, 1995, 90–99.

---

[2] Richard W. Stevenson, "Senate Votes 96–2 On Final Approval for Changing I.R.S.," *New York Times,* July 10, 1998, A1.

tively may require a dedicated sales forces, specialized distribution channels, or special attention to laws and regulations that only a separate and distinct organizational unit can provide. Customer-focused work units provide this attention and specialization. Managers who wish to increase revenue growth (particularly after a cost-driven downsizing) often reorganize their businesses to create customer-based units. By focusing work units around various customer segments (by industry, customers size, etc.), the organization becomes more knowledgeable about the needs of specific customers and the strengths and weaknesses of its competitors in each market segment. This customer intimacy can lead to more opportunities to do business with these customers (but often at the cost of corporate efficiencies previously described).

## Units Clustered by Geography

The final type of market-focused cluster occurs when firms organize by region or geography. Businesses venturing abroad for the first time often do so by creating regionally-based work units that focus on specific regions. For example, a U.S.-based firm may set up separate organizations to serve Canada, Europe, and Asia-Pacific. The task of each of these business units, often referred to as a **regional business,** is to market and sell (and sometimes produce) the company's products in their defined geographic territory. Again, specialization is necessary to understand and respond to local languages, tastes and

---

### Organizing for Global Service

When expanding outside their "home countries," service firms often adopt different organizing approaches depending on management's analysis of competitive industry dynamics and SWOT. Managers in these firms generally employ three types of organizing structures or "networks":

- Brand networks—Used when the brand is relatively strong, customer needs are local, and strategy can be customized to specific geographies. Units are organized by geography with core operational systems copied from the home country. Examples: McDonald's and Blockbuster Video.
- Distribution networks—Used when customers who travel to different regions or countries desire the same products or services in each of those locations with the same consistently high standards. Units are organized with centralized services providing global consistency. Examples: British Airways and Marriott Hotels.
- Knowledge networks—Used when the firm competes by its ability to transfer knowledge globally and to offer best-practice solutions to clients around the world. Global organization structures require significant coordination on two dimensions: lines of business and geography. Organizational practices and policies such as recruiting and compensation are centrally determined. Example: McKinsey & Company and Citibank.

---

*Source:* Gary Loveman, "The Internationalization of Services: Four Strategies that Drive Growth Across Borders," Boston: Harvard Business School, Note 897–081, 1996.

preferences, packaging laws, and business regulations. In addition, unique arrangements are often necessary to support product distribution in countries where the firm has no infrastructure of its own. As with all market-focused units, all the energies of the cluster are focused on serving the defined geography and its local markets.

## A HIERARCHY OF ACCOUNTABILITY

From the previous discussion, it should be clear that the grouping of people and resources into work units entails choice. Managers must choose, for example, whether to cluster business activities by function, by customer, or by geography. However, this question is complicated because it is typically embedded in a hierarchy of organization design. At one level in any organization, units are grouped by function; at another level, they are grouped by market focus.

The most basic design is the functional organization, with distinct work units that are accountable for marketing, sales, production, accounting, R&D, and so forth. For example, the organization chart in Figure 3–1 for a medium-sized business that produces consumer radios reflects its functional groupings.

Inside this functional organization, however, the marketing function may in turn be grouped into three distinct units, each serving a different geographical area. Thus, separate units may be accountable for North American sales and marketing, European sales and marketing, and Asia-Pacific sales and marketing. The organization chart now looks as shown in Figure 3–2.

Figures 3–1 and 3–2 represent a stand-alone business. However, in a larger, more diversified firm, this business might be one of several businesses, each organized around discrete products or sets of products. Thus, the organization chart in Figure 3–3 depicts a company with three product divisions (consumer radios, avionics, and cellular telephones), each of which is organized functionally. Within each organization, the sales and marketing function is further subdivided as before into separate units focusing on distinct geographic regions.

**FIGURE 3–1   Organization Chart for a Functional Organization**

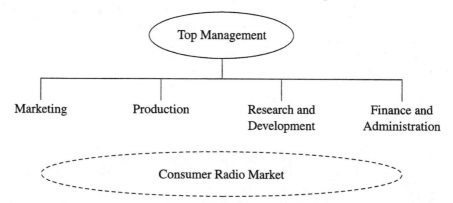

**FIGURE 3–2  Functional Organization with Expansion of Sales and Marketing**

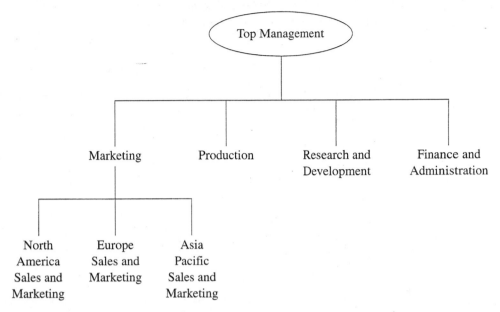

Hybrids on these basic designs are also possible. For example, Ford Europe has organized to create a national sales company in each separate country (market-focused), but it retains one large, centralized manufacturing division that produces cars and trucks for all European markets (functional specialization).

After a brief review of the design possibilities in terms of clustering organizations—by function or market focus—and the hierarchy of work units, the question

**FIGURE 3–3  Organization Chart of Product Division Organization**

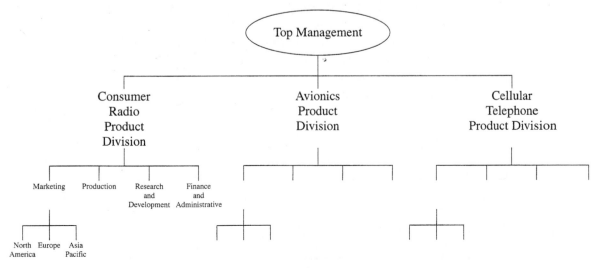

arises, "How do managers decide on the optimal organizational design?" As these examples illustrate, there are many different ways of grouping people and resources. Yet, there are systematic ways of evaluating these choices.

## SPECIALIZATION AND MARKET RESPONSIVENESS

As a starting point in our analysis, there are two generalizations about work-unit design that are true in virtually all cases. First, any firm—whatever the structure—*when taken as a whole* is a market-focused entity. As discussed in the previous chapter, a firm's mission and strategy focus on creating value for customers and differentiating products and services in a defined market. Thus, the consumer radio company illustrated in Figure 3–1 is organized by function, but, at the firm level, all its activities focus on producing and selling radios to consumers. As a total firm, it is market focused.

Second, it should also be clear that, at the lowest organizational level, all activity is grouped by function to allow specialization. This is true in even the largest firms. For example, at the center of any billion-dollar diversified firm you will find dedicated functions for production, research, accounting, and so on. Thus, the basic choices for managers relate to the structuring of intermediate organization levels—those between the top of the organization and the bottom. For these intermediate levels, we must ask: when do managers choose to group people and resources based on *work-process,* and when do they choose groupings based on *market focus*?

Each choice—clustering by function or clustering by market focus—brings different benefits and costs. The benefits of grouping by work-process derive primarily from the benefits of specialization: economies of scale and scope in production, R&D, and marketing and distribution. These economies can bring improved effectiveness and efficiencies that are reflected in lower costs and/or higher quality.

The benefits of clustering by market derive from increased responsiveness to customers and competitors. Many consumer products companies such as Colgate–Palmolive Company are extremely responsive to changing market conditions and can launch new products and adjust pricing, promotion, and packaging extremely quickly to defend market share. If everyone in a unit—regardless of function—is focusing only on one type of product, one type of customer, or one geographic region, then all energy in the unit can be devoted to gathering information about that product, customer, or region. This information can then be used to deploy resources rapidly and respond quickly to changing threats and opportunities.

However, there is an important trade-off to be made here. *A unit can be either as efficient as possible or as responsive as possible—but, unfortunately, not both.* Except under the difficult circumstances of a matrix organization, managers must choose one over the other.[3] How do they choose?

*Managers cluster units by function when the benefits of specialization are greater than the benefits of market responsiveness.* If the strategy of a firm relies on economies

---

[3] Readers interested in the workings of a matrix organization can refer to Chris Bartlett and Robert Simons, "Asea Brown Boveri," Boston: Harvard Business School, Case No. 192–139, 1992.

of scale and scope—to drive such critical performance variables as low price, high quality, capital-intensive R&D, or standardized distribution—then managers will choose a functional organization. Thus, major pharmaceutical companies such as Merck are invariably organized by function to obtain economies of specialization in R&D, production, and marketing. This specialization is critical to the success of their strategy.

We can generalize and apply this rule to all organizations: *Working from the core of any organization outward, work units are grouped by function as long as the benefits of specialization are greater than the benefits of market responsiveness.* In general, the benefits of specialization outweigh the benefits of market-focused feedback at the lowest organizational levels. Thus, most manufacturing plants are organized as functional units—the benefits of bringing specialized knowledge and resources together in one group outweigh the benefits of focusing on market intelligence and responsiveness. Individuals in the core of the organization do not generally interact directly with customers and markets. Instead, everyone in the manufacturing division can focus their full attention on producing the highest quality goods for the lowest cost. Imagine what would happen if the assembly line supervisors were required to spend 50% of their time meeting with customers and research scientists: The benefits of specialization would be lost, and the potential gains in customer responsiveness would be slight. Instead, other units are better suited to the task of interacting with customers and scientists. The trade-off in favor of the relative importance of specialization is true also for staff functions. Because the benefits of specialized knowledge and training outweigh the benefits of market responsiveness, staff units such as accounting, legal, and human relations are invariably clustered by work activity.

At some point as we move higher in any organization, however, the demands of market forces must prevail. *Managers cluster work units by market focus (i.e., products, customers, or geography) when the benefits of market responsiveness outweigh the benefits of specialization.* (For this reason, the overall firm itself—the organization that interacts with its competitive environment—is always a market-focused unit.) The benefits of grouping by market derive principally from enhanced focus on the customer and the ability to create value through product and service differentiation. Market-focused units devote all their energies to aligning internal resources to respond to customer needs and changing competitive conditions. For example, worldwide food companies such as Nestlé are organized by geography because the taste and packaging requirements for food products differ widely around the world. Managers of these businesses must be able to respond to local market demands. Market-focused units are designed to scan and process competitive market information quickly—and to act on that information.

The benefits of each of these choices—specialization and market responsiveness—are not without corresponding costs. These costs accrue primarily from the need to create and use information for coordination, control, and learning. For units that are clustered by function, specialization creates the need to integrate highly interdependent processes: sales forecasts must be integrated with production plans; R&D expenditures must be coordinated with production prototypes; marketing programs must be coordinated with inventory levels to ensure that surges in demand can be handled. Literally thousands of day-to-day decisions and actions must be coordinated between functional work units that each focus primarily on performing their specialized work processes with maximum efficiency. In these businesses, higher level managers must ensure that performance measurement and control systems can effectively coordinate inputs and outputs between the different specialized units inside each business.

Also, with separate functions managed as stand-alone units, cross-fertilization of ideas and innovation may be stifled. Creativity and learning may be sacrificed in the pursuit of efficiency.

Coordination of the inputs, outputs, and information flows of independent functions is achieved primarily through formal *operating plans and budgets*. Performance targets — both financial and nonfinancial — are set by senior managers to define acceptable levels of performance. Because the outputs of marketing, R&D, procurement, and production departments are transferred internally and cannot easily be translated into corresponding market prices, managers must monitor expense levels to gain assurance that each functional unit is delivering value in accordance with the resources consumed. These monitoring systems are costly, however, both in terms of the cost of creating information, and in the management attention consumed to ensure that the units are working effectively in support of the business strategy.

For units that are clustered by market, there is less need to invest in systems for internal coordination. Performance standards are created naturally by selling goods or services into the market (for example, market share, revenue growth, gross margins), so performance evaluation can be based on achieving acceptable levels of profit from the assets employed in running the business. Instead of monitoring line-by-line expense statements, managers can review overall profit plans and accomplishments to assure themselves that the business is producing adequate returns.

However, market-focused units make performance measurement and control costly in two ways. First, there is a critical need to transmit market intelligence and best-practice information to other units within the firm so they can learn from it. If there is no possibility for learning or transferring best practice from one market-based unit to the next, there is little reason for these units to be in the same firm. Accordingly, an investment must be made in transferring information vertically — to higher management levels — and horizontally to other organizational units.

Second, to the extent there are product flows between market-focused units (i.e., the outputs of one unit are inputs to another), a system of internal transfer prices must be created and administered. (These transfer-pricing mechanisms are described in Chapter 8.)

## ACCOUNTABILITY AND SPAN OF CONTROL

So far in this chapter, we have discussed the organizational arrangements that are depicted in a business's organization chart — how the parts are put together to form the whole. These reporting relationships are illustrated by solid lines connecting functions or business units. However, we have not yet introduced the most important part of organization structure — the *managers* who are responsible for achieving profit goals and strategies. After all, we must remember that we are talking about groupings of people. It is important, therefore, to understand that the solid vertical lines represent *accountabil-*

*ity* of individual managers—those who have the formal authority to direct subordinates in their activities and who are ultimately responsible for the success of their efforts in creating value for the firm.

Thus, instead of focusing on functions or business units, we can redraw these diagrams to show more precisely the reporting relationships of individual managers. For example, Figure 3–4 shows that the regional director of the European Sales and Marketing unit reports to the vice president of marketing, who in turn reports to the company's president.

Hidden within any organization chart are three related "spans" that are important in understanding the role of performance measurement and control systems. They are span of control, span of accountability, and span of attention. As we shall see, unit grouping (discussed in the pervious sections), span of control, and span of accountability are the key levers that influence a manager's span of attention (i.e., what he or she pays attention to).

## Span of Control and Span of Accountability

When organization charts are drawn on the basis of the reporting relationships of individual managers, the solid lines connecting individuals depict the **span of control** for each manager in the organization chart. Span of control indicates how many (and which) subordinates and functions report to each manager in the organization. Span of control, in effect, describes the resources—in terms of people and work units—*directly* under a manager's control. Span of control can be broad, with many people and a wide range of resources reporting to a manager, or narrow, with few people and a narrow range of resources under a manager's direct control (see Figure 3–5).

However, span of control as shown on an organization chart is only part of the story. It outlines reporting relationships—*who* is accountable to whom—but span of control does not tell us *what* they are accountable for. For this, we need another

**FIGURE 3–4    Organization Chart Showing Accountability of Individual Managers**

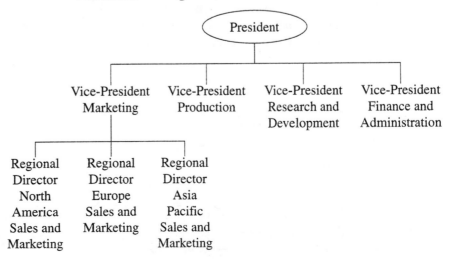

**FIGURE 3–5   Comparison of Two Different Spans of Control**

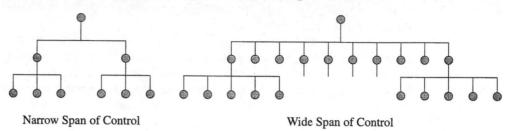

Narrow Span of Control                    Wide Span of Control

concept—**span of accountability.** *Span of accountability describes the range of performance measures used to evaluate a manager's achievements.* At its most basic level, span of accountability defines the financial statement items for which a manager is accountable.[4] For example, managers can be held accountable for various combinations of their business's income statement and balance sheet. Some managers may be held accountable for revenues only (a sales and marketing manager), for costs only (a manufacturing plant manager), for net profits before interest and taxes (a product division manager), or for return on assets (the manager of a stand-alone business that controls its own balance sheet). We now consider the two most common configurations of financial accountability—**cost center accountability** and **profit center accountability.**

*Cost Center Accountability*   A cost center represents the narrowest span of work-unit accountability encountered in most firms. Managers of cost centers are accountable only for their unit's level of spending. Typically, cost center managers are given cost budgets

---

### Span of Control at GE

In 1981, John Welch assumed control of General Electric. Five years later, he had reorganized its 14 businesses into three "strategic circles": core manufacturing, technology-intensive products, and services. Under Welch's leadership, GE also achieved its target of first or second place in almost all markets worldwide.

   The next, more difficult, step was to streamline the company's communication and decision making processes. Welch first dismantled a layer of middle management so the 14 separate businesses would report directly to him and a few vice chairmen. "Layers hide weakness," claimed Welch. "Layers mask mediocrity. I firmly believe that an overburdened, overstretched executive is the best executive because he or she doesn't have the time to meddle, to deal in trivia, to bother people."

---

*Source:* Nichy, Noel and Charan, Ram, "Speed, Simplicity, Self-Confidence: An Interview with Jack Welch," *Harvard Business Review* (September–October 1989): 112–120.

---

   [4] The concept of span of accountability is equally applicable to nonfinancial goals and performance measures, but we postpone this discussion to later chapters.

and asked to deliver the desired level of goods or service within those spending constraints. To do so, cost center managers need only monitor specific expense lines of their business's profit and loss statement. Most functional units—the mail room, a production plant, R&D labs, or an internal audit staff group—are set up as cost centers.

*Profit Center Accountability*  A profit center manager has a broader span of accountability than a cost center manager. He or she is not only accountable for costs, but also for revenues and, often, for assets as well. Any function or business unit that accounts for its own revenue and expenses on an income statement can be a profit center. For example, an information systems (IS) function can be a profit center if it charges other units for its services, as can a processing plant—as long as it receives revenue for the goods and services provided.

The important implication—one that we explore in detail in Chapter 5—is that the manager of a profit center is asked to make *trade-offs* between costs and revenues to achieve his or her profit goals. Whereas a cost center manager need only focus on minimizing costs (or maximizing outputs for a given level of inputs), a profit center manager with a broader span of accountability must consider the impact of spending levels on revenues and profit. For example, a profit center manager may decide to increase expenses to boost revenue (e.g., by increasing advertising).

Although all profit center managers, by definition, are responsible for an income statement, the span of accountability can differ quite dramatically across different companies and different profit centers. In some profit centers, managers are responsible only for managing revenues, costs, and net profits. In others, managers are also accountable for efficient utilization of assets as recorded on their units' balance sheets. These managers have the widest span of accountability.[5] In essence, they are being held accountable to operate their unit as an integral business. As such, they must not only make trade-offs between costs and revenues, they must also make trade-offs between the costs of the assets they employ and the value that those assets deliver to the business.

## SPAN OF ATTENTION

We have introduced the three structural design levers that senior managers use to organize their businesses: (1) work units—groupings by function or market to drive specialization or market responsiveness, (2) span of control—the subordinates and resources under a manager's direct control, and (3) span of accountability—the range of performance measures for which a manager is accountable to superiors. Now we are ready to make a critical point. These three mechanisms are employed for one primary purpose: to influence **span of attention.** *Span of attention refers to the domain of activities that are within a manager's field of view.* Span of attention defines what an individual will attempt to gather information on and influence. In simple terms, it's what people care

---

[5] Some textbooks refer to balance sheet accountability as an "investment center" to denote accountability for return on investment. This nomenclature is rarely found in practice. Instead, managers use the term profit center as we have defined it above.

about and pay attention to. As we will see in later chapters, managers must be able to influence span of attention at all levels of an organization if they are to have any success in achieving their profit goals and strategies.

Like span of control and span of accountability, span of attention can be narrow or broad. For example, a plant manager with a narrow span of attention may have little interest in any part of the business outside the factory walls. Alternatively, he or she may care very deeply about the level of customer satisfaction associated with products produced in his plant. Similarly, an R&D manager with a narrow span of attention may care little about the growth of the firm—focusing instead only on specific research programs—or, he or she may be very interested in knowing how customer demand is likely to shape technology demands over the next year.

Span of attention is fundamentally different in nature than either span of control or span of accountability. Span of control and span of accountability are top-down concepts. They are determined by superiors. It is, after all, a boss who determines the reporting relationships for his or her subordinates and performance dimensions on which those subordinates will be evaluated. Span of attention, by contrast, comes from *within an individual manager,* because all employees and managers must form their own judgments about what they believe to be important. Span of attention, however, can—and must—be influenced by superiors.

The span of attention for any individual manager is determined by the three levers that we have introduced so far: (1) the work unit to which the manager belongs, (2) the people and functions under the manager's direct control, and (3) the performance measures for which the manager is held accountable to superiors. Let us consider briefly how each level influences span of attention.

***Work Unit Design ⇒ Span of Attention***   In general, people pay a great deal of attention to the work of their own unit, but relatively little attention to work that is outside their field of view. As we have discussed, work units are groups of people brought together to concentrate on functional specialization or market responsiveness. People in the unit work toward shared goals. These goals may be to introduce the latest and best technology for radio products worldwide (functional specialization), to serve government customers in Eastern Europe (market focus), or to process accounting transactions for the entire business as efficiently as possible (functional specialization). Attendance at trade shows, meetings, reports, and hallway discussions are all determined by the type of work and goals assigned to the unit to which an individual belongs.

***Span of Control ⇒ Span of Attention***   Span of control is a powerful determinant of the range of activities that is within a manager's field of view. Managers use the resources under their direct control—people, functions, and business units—to achieve their business goals. They must think carefully about how to deploy those resources effectively. To do this, managers are forced to devote attention to the needs of subordinates who report to them. Goals must be set, resources must be allocated, performance must be monitored, and progress must be evaluated. These activities, and the many face-to-face meetings, telephone calls, and e-mails that are necessary to support a superior-subordinate relationship, require a significant amount of attention.

***Span of Accountability*** ⟹ ***Span of Attention***   Span of attention is influenced by span of accountability because of one simple fact: managers pay attention to what they are measured on. As the old saying goes, "What gets measured, gets managed." If senior managers want a subordinate to devote all his energies and attention to increasing sales, they will make that manager accountable only for achieving revenue goals. If senior managers want attention directed at making trade-offs between marketing expenditures and increased revenues, then a manager will be held accountable for net profit as defined on an income statement. If senior managers want subordinates to focus their energies on the most productive use of assets, then a return-on-net-assets measure will be employed, holding the unit managers accountable for performance on both the income statement and balance sheet.

## Span of Attention and Organizational Design

Shaping span of attention is one of the key objectives of organizational design. Structure is one of the primary tools that managers use to ensure that people are concentrating on the right things—day-in and day-out—as they face many competing demands for their time. Span of attention determines who worries about what. Profit goals and strategies can only be achieved if managers are able to motivate subordinates to devote sufficient time and attention to critical tasks. Span of attention—as determined by work unit assignments, span of control, and span of accountability—is a critical ingredient in the formula of success.

Span of attention is at the core of the concepts of centralization and decentralization. A **centralized organization** is designed so that unit managers have narrow spans of attention. Why? In centralized organizations, senior managers want to ensure that subordinates do not become distracted by information and events that could pull their attention away from maximizing efficiency through specialization. Units are typically grouped by functional specialty, and unit managers are accountable for narrow subsets of the income statement as defined by their cost center responsibilities. The coordination of individual functions and business activities is reserved for higher level managers. Thus, in a centralized organization, accountability for trade-offs among income statement and balance sheet accounts rests at the top of the organization, where the individual functions come together to form profit centers.

**Decentralized organizations,** by contrast, are designed so that managers have wide spans of attention. Decentralized organizations are essential when business strategy demands quick and agile responsiveness to customers and markets. In a decentralized organization, business units are market-based, with employees of the unit interacting directly with customers and markets. Accountability for trade-offs among key income statement and balance sheet accounts is delegated low in the organization. Low-level unit managers run profit centers. They make trade-offs to maximize competing objectives across a wide array of activities. Spans of control are also wide, with many individuals and a broad resource base reporting to individual managers.

## CHAPTER SUMMARY

Managers must decide how to organize their businesses to achieve profit goals and strategies. The functioning of an organization depends on work and information flows. The design of work units, spans of control, and spans of accountability are the main structural tools to influence and direct organizational attention to ensure that everyone is working toward shared goals.

However, organization structure—as discussed in this chapter—is a static concept until we introduce the information flows that are necessary to support work flows and accountability. Information about plans, goals, and results must be created and transmitted. Information about customers, markets, competitors, and best practices must be collected, stored, and disseminated. Above all, managers must ensure consistent and reliable information channels to allow everyone in the business to work together and learn together as they strive to achieve shared business goals. This is the topic of the next chapter.

# CHAPTER

## 4

# Using Information for Performance Measurement and Control

Information is essential to all well-managed businesses and nonprofit organizations. The amount and quality of information available to managers of any organization is a good barometer of organizational health. Managers of organizations that have too little information do not have the means to effectively communicate goals and are forced to make decisions on the fly—by intuition. Managers of organizations that are capable of processing relevant information quickly can plan for the future, communicate direction efficiently, and capitalize more effectively on emerging problems and opportunities.

One of the primary purposes of performance measurement and control is to allow **fact-based management**—management that moves from intuition and hunches to analysis based on hard data and facts. (As Sherlock Holmes said, "It is a capital mistake to theorize before one has data.") In Part II of this book, which follows this chapter, we study the techniques and analyses that allow managers to use performance measurement and control information as a tool for fact-based management.

**Information** can be defined in many ways. A dictionary definition would refer to information as the *communication or reception of intelligence or knowledge*. An entire field of knowledge known as **cybernetics** is devoted to the study of information and its use in feedback processes. Feedback information of various types is used to control animate and inanimate systems, including biological, mechanical, electrical, and organizational systems. It is on this last category—control of organizational systems—that we will focus in this chapter and the remainder of the book.

In terms of achieving profit goals and strategies, Figure 4–1 outlines key information flows that are required for effective management.

Inside an organization, we usually think of information flowing *to managers* to inform them about the operations of their businesses. For example, budget variances are reported to managers for follow-up and action; productivity data is collected and reported to managers to allow the monitoring of significant trends; and order backlogs are reported to give managers assurance that key goals are being met. In terms of implementing strategy, the information is of two types: information about progress in achieving goals, and information about emerging threats and opportunities. Both of these types of information provide **feedback**—information about actual events or outcomes that

**FIGURE 4–1   Information Needs of Top Managers in Achieving Profit Goals and Strategies**

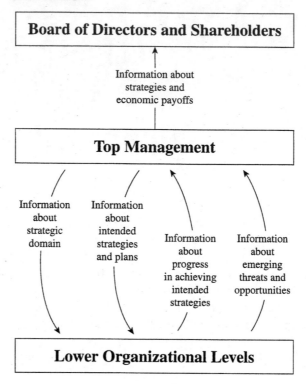

*Source:* Adapted from Simons, *Levers of Control,* 6.

can be compared with expectations or standards. This information is essential to allow managers to conduct and update SWOT analyses based on changing competitive dynamics and internal capabilities.

In addition to feedback, however, information must also flow from managers *to employees* to serve a number of purposes. First, managers must inform employees throughout the organization about the market segments and types of activities to which they are willing to commit resources. Will Boston Retail expand into men's clothing? Will a music recording company focus on classical music, new age, or both? Will an auto supply business cater to original-equipment manufacturers or repair centers? Second, managers must communicate clearly the intended strategy of the business. How it will create value and differentiate itself from competitors? What is the nature of the value that will be created for customers? Will it compete by price or differentiate itself on some other dimension? Employees must have a clear understanding of how top managers have made these choices.

Third, managers must communicate plans, goals, and milestones. How much profit must be generated in the third quarter? What are management's expectations in terms of revenue and market-share growth? How many new stores must be opened next year to hit the business plan goals? This information flow is critical to give employees a clear understanding of the short-term goals of the business so they can contribute to achieving these goals.

Finally, managers must communicate these same strategies and performance goals to *superiors and external parties* whose support is needed to implement the strategy of the business. These external parties may include banks or other lenders who supply capital on a short-term basis, stockholders and investment analysts who provide long-term equity capital to the firm, and suppliers and partners who play important roles in the manufacture and distribution of products and services. We also must not forget the board of directors. Managers must communicate their plans and strategies to their boards for approval and ratification.

In the remainder of this chapter, we introduce three important topics related to the choices that managers must make in using information effectively for performance measurement and control:

1. Trade-offs inherent in choosing to measure either organizational inputs, processes, or outputs as defined by the organizational process model
2. Implications in choosing to use management information for decision making, control, or learning
3. Conflicts in the use of this management information for achieving profit goals and strategies

## ORGANIZATIONAL PROCESS MODEL

Performance measurement and control information can be understood only by reference to some model of underlying organizational processes. In other words, managers must understand the processes by which inputs are converted to outputs. All organizational processes can be decomposed into (1) inputs such as information, material, energy, labor, and support services that are needed to create a product or service, (2) a transformation process that consumes these inputs to create or sustain something of value, and (3) outputs in the form of intermediate or final products or services. This chain is pictured in Figure 4-2.

Consider these examples:

- A clerk at Boston Retail opens a box of incoming sweaters, applies price tags, updates inventory records, and arranges the merchandise on display racks. The *inputs* to her work are the sweaters, tags, and her effort, as well as the storeroom and physical display space. The transformation *process* includes the application of tags, updating of records, and movement of goods from the storeroom to the store shelves. The *output* is the availability of fresh, sorted, and priced merchandise ready for sale.
- An automobile assembly line accepts parts, energy, and computer instructions as *inputs* and transforms these inputs through a *process* as each automobile proceeds down the

**FIGURE 4-2    Inputs-Process-Outputs Model**

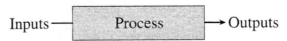

line to have fixtures and engines installed. At the end of the line, a complete automobile emerges as *output*.

- A division manager studies an income statement for the past month. She focuses on the *inputs* or resources consumed by her division (such as materials, depreciation—as a proxy for capital utilization—and overhead costs), the efficiency of the *processes* by which these resources were transformed into product (e.g., gross margin ratio), and the *outputs* (such as sales and inventory).

This basic inputs→process→outputs model is generic, so we could easily create examples for a machine, a factory, an individual worker, a team, or an entire business. The principles are the same: absorb inputs, transform them through productive processes, and create outputs of value (either as inputs to downstream organizational processes or as products or services delivered to customers).

In all of these cases, managers are responsible for ensuring that (1) inputs are appropriate to the tasks at hand and are adequate in quality and quantity, (2) the transformation process is efficient, and (3) the outputs meet specifications. To meet these responsibilities, managers can measure and monitor inputs, processes, and outputs in both nonfinancial and financial terms. Examples of some nonfinancial and financial internal measures are shown in Table 4–1 for:

- development of a new product (inputs include customer ideas, engineering designs, prototyping, and production setups)
- order processing (inputs include sales and marketing campaigns, order-entry clerical labor, and computer processing)
- parts manufacture (inputs include externally sourced components, energy, machine processing capability, and direct and supervisory labor)

For a manager to gain control over any of these processes, however, knowledge about inputs, processes, and outputs is often not enough. How would you respond if

**TABLE 4–1** Examples of Nonfinancial and Financial Measures

| | INPUT MEASURES | PROCESS MEASURES | OUTPUT MEASURES |
|---|---|---|---|
| *Non-Financial Measures for:* | | | |
| (a) New Products | # of engineering hours | # of product delivery milestones achieved | # of new products introduced |
| (b) Order Processing | # of telephone answering staff | Order completion time | # of orders processed |
| (c) Parts Manufacture | # of components meeting specifications | Setup time | % of units meeting standard |
| *Financial Measures for:* | | | |
| (a) New Products | Labor and material $ | $ cost of prototyping | % of sales $ from new products |
| (b) Order Processing | Clerical labor $ | $ cost of backorder handling | $ cost per order processed |
| (c) Parts Manufacture | $ cost of components | Setup $ cost, cost of rework | $ cost per unit |

someone said that production for the week was 11,642 units? Was this good or bad? You could not tell, of course, unless you had a standard or benchmark as a point of reference. Your answer would differ depending on whether the performance expectation was 11,000 units or 12,750 units.

To *gain control* through a cybernetic process, therefore, we must add two additional ingredients beyond an understanding of inputs, processes, and outputs. We also must have (1) a standard or benchmark against which to compare actual performance and (2) a feedback channel to allow information on variances to be communicated and acted upon. These two critical additions to the cybernetic control model are illustrated in Figure 4–3.

An output **standard** or **benchmark** is a formal representation of performance expectations. **Ex ante** performance standards (those set in advance) may be created by reference to efficiency or effectiveness criteria for any measurable data—cost accounting data, quality specifications, budgets and profit plans, productivity data, and so on.

With preset standards at hand, a manager can assess how well inputs have been transformed into outputs. The Boston Retail store manager may compare the 162 items that the sales clerk stocked on the shelf during a two-hour period against a standard of 75 items per hour. This comparison indicates either a high level of effort (relative to past experience) or an unusually efficient worker. The shift supervisor in the auto assembly plant may look at a report that shows the number of automobiles produced on his shift as compared with the number produced during each shift over the past week. A shortfall will cause him to investigate further to understand the reasons. Similarly, the division manager compares the actual profit performance of her division against budgeted profit to ascertain the magnitude of any deviations.

However, having a performance standard or benchmark is, in itself, not sufficient. There must be a way of *using* the data—comparing outputs with standards and using the resulting **variance information** to change the inputs or process to ensure that performance standards will be met in the future. Thus, the second ingredient is a feedback channel coupled with an understanding of how adjustments to inputs and process are likely to influence outcomes.

Feedback is the return of variance information from the *output* of a process to the *input* or *process* stages so that adjustments can be made to maintain desired levels of performance or control the stability of a system (Figure 4–3). We all use feedback systems when we watch the speedometer of our cars (output information) and compare this

**FIGURE 4–3  Cybernetic Feedback Model**

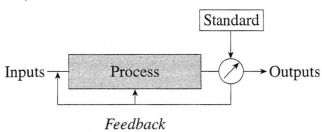

information with posted highway speed signs (pre-set standards) to determine whether we need to accelerate or slow down to keep the car moving at our desired speed (process adjustment). An automatic speed control equipped on many automobiles automates this process and frees our attention from having to constantly monitor the speedometer. The thermostat in our homes, or any number of automatic controllers in a production line, operate in similar ways. (Anticipating a discussion later in the book, what do you think the effect of these cybernetic feedback systems is on return on management effort?)

Feedback information—the backbone of performance measurement and control systems—can be used in many ways. The manager at Boston Retail can use feedback information about one clerk's superior performance to learn how other clerks may do their jobs better; the assembly line's shift supervisor can discuss information about production shortfalls with the foremen to understand what remedial steps have been taken; and the division manager can order cuts on maintenance spending to try to meet profit-plan targets.

## THE CHOICE OF WHAT TO CONTROL

If you look again at the diagram in Figure 4–3, you will notice that a manager might choose to gather information about (1) inputs, (2) the process itself, or (3) outputs. In fact, a manager can, and must, choose among these three categories to determine *where* he or she will devote attention in attempting to ensure that goods and services are produced in accordance with expectations.

For example, to satisfy herself that the sales clerk is working diligently in stocking the shelves, the Boston Retail store manager has two options: she can actually watch the clerk work to see if she is working at an appropriately energetic level, or she can later monitor the outcome of the clerk's efforts—by counting the number of sweaters placed on the shelves and observing if quality of the display meets expectations.

The assembly plant supervisor also has two choices: to count the number of finished automobiles as evidence that the process is proceeding according to plan, or to continually monitor the inputs and the process itself to ensure that automobiles are being assembled without delay. The choice between gathering information on inputs, process, or outputs is fundamental to the performance-control process. How, then, should managers choose?

As a starting point, we can state that *information about inputs is necessary, but rarely sufficient, for control.* For example, managers pay a great deal of attention to the quality of people who are hired and trained, to the nature and quality of material inputs, and to the level of parts inventories. This is especially true when inputs are costly relative to the value of outputs, such as the use of rare metals in electronics or diamonds in jewelry products. However, having high-quality inputs will not guarantee a good product or service. To ensure that these valuable inputs are transformed into high-quality outputs, *managers must focus their performance measurement and control activities on either the transformation process itself or the outputs being produced.*

Assuming that a manager knows the nature of desired outputs (as we shall discuss shortly, this is not always the case), there are four criteria that must be considered in making this choice: (1) technical feasibility of monitoring and measurement, (2) understanding of cause and effect, (3) cost, and (4) desired level of innovation.

## 1. Technical Feasibility of Monitoring and Measurement

In considering the *technical feasibility* of monitoring and measurement, managers must determine whether it is even possible to monitor a process directly or, alternatively, to measure its outcomes. In some cases it is possible to observe processes; in others, it is not. Watching an assembly line worker is not difficult. Nor is visiting a McDonald's location to ensure that service and cleanliness standards are being met. However, watching a mid-level manager as she goes about her tasks—attending meetings, answering telephone calls, visiting with customers, preparing plans and budgets—is impractical. Similarly, some outputs—production units, invoices processed, linear feet of pipe—are possible to quantify and measure. Others, such as goodwill or research productivity, are much more difficult to measure.

A *manager can choose to monitor process directly only if it is possible to observe production or service processes in action.* Watching a sales clerk stock the shelves of a retail store is easy and will lead to the desired outcome of a fully stocked merchandise array. The retail store manager can easily observe the work of the store clerk to ensure that it is progressing satisfactorily. However, the division manager reading an income statement cannot observe the many intricate processes that go into creating the inflows and outflows reflected on the income statement. It is just not possible to be everywhere at once—observing supplies being ordered, products being created, bills being paid, facilities being used, and all the myriad activities that underlie the financial statements. Instead, because she cannot physically observe processes, she must focus on outputs.

The flip side of the same coin is that a *manager can choose to monitor outcomes only if it is possible to measure production or service outputs accurately.* For example, a daily sales report provides accurate quantitative data about the success of each salesman. The sales report is a sufficient indicator of the efforts and contribution of individual salespeople. However, what would the daily output report look like for a research scientist? In this case, it is not possible to measure outputs accurately (at least on a daily timetable), and other approaches must be adopted.

Thus, in some instances, managers may not have a choice about what types of information to receive. They may be forced to focus on either processes or outputs because information on the other variable is simply unavailable.

## 2. Understanding of Cause and Effect

The second criterion relates to the *understanding of cause and effect* in the chain of activities that leads to outputs. Even if it is possible to monitor processes directly, a manager may not understand the actions that lead to the desired outcomes. In a parts-assembly operation for electronic test equipment, for example, the relationship between cause and effect is clear. If parts are supplied in the proper quantity and quality, and if workers install and test those parts according to carefully laid-out procedures, a fully functioning piece of electronics equipment will be built. Based on engineering drawings, development of test procedures, the training of workers, and the successful manufacture of many similar units, managers can have high confidence that following the specified process will lead to the desired outcomes. Thus, managers can easily gather information to ensure that processes are operating according to instructions.

Consider, by contrast, attempts to secure a major construction contract to build a large commercial building. A team of salespeople work on the deal for more than a year—developing relationships, compiling cost and bid data, and working with architects and mortgage brokers. The complexity of the project precludes a complete ex ante understanding of the actions and behaviors that will lead to the desired outcome—winning the bid. Too many possibilities are uncertain. Managers and employees of the construction firm must decide how to increase the chance of winning the bid as circumstances unfold. Procedure manuals specifying the exact steps to be undertaken for each contingency are not possible. In this case, even though gathering information about actions and behaviors may be feasible, senior managers cannot have any confidence that following a set of prespecified activities will lead to success. Gathering information in attempts to monitor process, therefore, is wasted effort if the causal link to desired outputs is not well understood.

The same problem occurs in monitoring any creative work—that of a research scientist, software programmer, architect, or orchestra leader. *If a manager does not understand the cause-and-effect relationship between the transformation process and desired outcomes, monitoring processes is not feasible as the primary means of control.* Thus, even though it may be possible to directly observe the work of a research scientist in his lab, it is not feasible to monitor that behavior to ensure successful discovery efforts. The cause-and-effect relationship between the researcher's efforts and the discovery of new products is not well understood and cannot, therefore, be modeled or predicted with any degree of accuracy.

### 3. Cost

Notwithstanding the limitations described above, in many situations managers may reasonably choose to monitor *either* processes *or* outputs. Often, both are observable. In these circumstances, we must analyze the *relative cost* of generating information about processes or outputs. Cost in this instance has two components: (1) the costs of generating and processing information and (2) lost opportunity or damages resulting from *not* generating information. The latter cost depends on the importance of securing the desired outcomes.

As an example, consider the plight of a sales manager who wishes to gather information on the activities of a sales representative. He can choose to gather information on the adequacy of the sales process by accompanying the sales rep on all his weekly visits or he can review outputs by perusing a weekly sales report. Which of these two options will he pick? In this instance, using the sales report is much more economical of the manager's time, and this alternative will be chosen. This example is typical—monitoring outputs is usually less time consuming than monitoring process. *All things being equal, therefore, managers will choose to monitor outputs to conserve their time and attention.*

In some instances, however, the important cost is not the cost of monitoring; it is related to the cost of *not monitoring* a critical process. Consider NASA managers responsible for the launch of a space shuttle. They may choose to monitor either the process of launch controllers working step-by-step through authorized procedures or they may measure only the output—whether or not the launch was successful. In this instance, because of the high cost of a launch failure to the space program, it is a safe bet that managers will choose to measure processes very carefully. As a general principle, *whenever safety or quality is a critical criterion of effectiveness, managers will choose to gather information about, and monitor directly, the transformation process itself.*

## 4. Desired Level of Innovation

After analyzing relative cost, there is one last consideration—often the most important from a managerial perspective—in choosing whether to monitor process or outputs: the effect on innovation. Which choice—monitoring process or monitoring outputs— yields the most innovation? The least innovation?

Start with the choice that yields the least innovation. Standard operating procedures, job descriptions, and manuals specify in great detail how a task is to be performed. Supervisors can look over their employees' shoulders to ensure that they are doing what is expected, and information on conformance to policies and procedures can be collected regularly. By telling people *what to do* and ensuring that they do just that, we limit freedom of action. People are precluded from experimenting; they cannot innovate and try new things. Therefore, *if managers desire to limit innovation, they will choose to control processes carefully by standardizing work procedures.*

Why would managers want to limit innovation? There are often important reasons related to quality, efficiency, and safety. When quality is an important consideration, there is always the risk that employees may introduce poor quality inputs, or service may not be conducted at the desired level of performance. Thus, fast-food franchisors like Burger King always insist on detailed written policies that specify minimum quality levels for key ingredients and standardized procedures and cooking times for preparing food. Corporate managers do not want to leave it up to local employees to experiment with these critical ingredients of competitive success.

When we think of efficiency in a large-scale semi-automated plant, we can understand why it may sometimes not be optimal to have assembly line employees tinkering with parts of the production line. In the absence of specialized training and/or specialized structures (autonomous teams or cells), managers leave this task to engineers and production-control specialists who can optimize across the entire line. Henry Ford, who invented the moving assembly line, used standardization of process to transform the production of automobiles from a craft industry into the highly efficient, mass-production industry that we know today.

Similarly, when speed—time to market—is an important competitive variable, managers may wish to standardize development processes to drive efficiency in the roll-out of new products. Thus, in many high-technology businesses, internal processes are standardized around product "platforms" for a full range of products. Enhancements and next-generation products can be rolled out quickly by minor modifications to the standardized product platforms.

Finally, the control of process becomes important where safety is critical to success—and the costs of failure are high. We have mentioned already the potential cost of failure at a NASA space shuttle launch. The same principle holds, for example, in the operation of a nuclear reactor. How significant are the costs of failure and a reactor meltdown? How much leeway for innovation and experimentation would you want managers to give nuclear plant operators? For this reason, where safety is critical, managers always limit discretion and innovation by installing very tight process controls.

**Total Quality Management** (TQM) is a popular approach that represents the standardization and streamlining of key operating processes to ensure high levels of quality and/or low defect rates. Under TQM methods, prescribed steps are followed to streamline and routinize key processes. By following TQM methods (the seven steps of quality), the potential for error and waste can be minimized.

Controlling process tightly assumes that senior managers know best—or at least have a broader perspective than the workers whose discretion is being limited. However, this is not always the case. The more competitive and fast moving the marketplace, the more important it becomes to give employees the freedom to experiment. If, instead of constraining initiative, managers wish to empower employees to exercise their energies in creating value, then managers must give workers the freedom to experiment. *For maximum innovation, managers do not focus on process, but instead focus on monitoring outputs.*

By controlling output rather than process, subordinates are free to create solutions and opportunities that managers had not previously contemplated. Employees are held accountable for output goals, but they are encouraged to experiment with inputs and processes to configure the transformation process in a way that best meets local market conditions. As a result, services can be tailored to meet the needs of specific customers. Process flows can be redesigned to streamline the transformation process.

Of course, there is risk in innovation. If people are to experiment, they must be allowed to make mistakes. Yet, some errors can be extremely costly. Employees may fail to meet customer expectations; they may squander resources; they may damage the business's reputation for quality. An important agenda for later chapters of this book, therefore, is understanding how to capture the benefits of innovation while, at the same time, controlling these inevitable strategic risks.

### When All Else Fails

In rare circumstances, it may not be possible to obtain reliable information on *either* process *or* outputs. Processes may be poorly understood or unobservable. Outputs may be ill-defined or created at remote locations that are not easily susceptible to information gathering and oversight. In these exceptional cases, a manager must rely on other—mostly informal—means of control. For example, forest rangers commonly work alone in the wilderness areas for periods of several months. It is neither possible to observe their behavior nor to measure the value of their outputs as they engage in activities to further the mission of the Forest Service.

In these rare instances, managers have no choice but to rely primarily on the *control of inputs,* coupled with a high degree of training and indoctrination. Employees must be carefully selected, trained, and indoctrinated with the values and objectives of the organization. In some religious orders, for example, missionaries work in remote geographic locations. Because their work cannot be directly monitored or measured, they are sent out to the field only after careful selection, training, and indoctrination at the seminary. The same is true for expatriate managers of large multinational firms. These individuals are often selected because of their understanding and allegiance to the goals of the home office and then sent abroad—away from the direct oversight of their bosses—to supervise the activities and instill core values in foreign-based subsidiaries.

Table 4–2 summarizes the factors that managers must consider in determining whether to devote their attention to controlling inputs, processes, or outputs.

## USES OF INFORMATION

Having discussed how managers choose among alternatives for collecting information on inputs, processes, or outputs, we must now consider what they should do with it. What is the purpose for gathering and analyzing this information? Management information can be used for a variety of purposes—planning, coordination, motivation, evaluation, and education. For our purposes, these differing uses can be categorized into five broad categories.

Information for:

- Decision making
- Control
- Signaling
- Education and learning
- External communication

We examine each of these uses in turn.

**TABLE 4–2** Factors in Determining Whether to Control Inputs, Processes, or Outputs

| CONTROL INPUTS WHEN: | CONTROL PROCESSES WHEN: | CONTROL OUTPUTS WHEN: |
|---|---|---|
| • It is impossible to monitor processes or outputs (i.e., monitor inputs as a last resort) | • Processes can be observed and/or measured | • Outputs can be observed and/or measured |
| • Cost of input is high relative to value of outputs (e.g., precious metals in computer chips) | • Cost of measuring/monitoring process is low | • Cost of measuring/monitoring outputs is low |
| • Quality and/or safety is important | • Standardization is critical for safety and/or quality | |
| | • Cause-and-effect relationships are understood | • Cause-and-effect relationships may not be well understood |
| | • Proprietary processes or process enhancements can result in strategic advantage | • Freedom to innovate is desired |

## Information for Decision Making

Managers routinely rely on information to *improve decision processes.* For example, a request for an increase in head count may cause managers to study profit plans and other performance data to ascertain what the effects are likely to be on the cost structure of the business. Before making their decision, managers are interested in understanding how additional employees (an increase in the level of inputs) will affect service processes and outputs. Similarly, a decision to add a new line to a production facility may hinge on an analysis of performance data that provides insight into the economics and profitability of the business. In each of these cases, information about cause-and-effect relationships is used to bring economic facts to bear on the decision.

Managers use information for decision making in two broad categories: (1) information for planning and (2) information for coordination. **Planning** is the process of setting aspirations through performance goals and ensuring an adequate level and mix of resources to achieve those goals. In simple terms, **plans** are a road map for the business.

---

### Dell Computers

Dell Computer Corporation was founded in 1984 by 19-year-old Michael Dell, with the innovative concept of selling custom-built PCs directly over the telephone. After going public in 1988, Dell Computer's revenue grew at 67% and earnings at 63% annually. By 1992, the company posted $2 billion in sales, and sales for 1993 were expected to reach $3 billion. However, in the second quarter of 1993, the company announced its first loss.

What happened? The astounding growth had outpaced performance measurement and control systems. The turn of bad luck began in November 1992 with the abrupt resignation of the chief financial officer. Then, Dell Computer lost $38 million in the second quarter of 1992 due to aggressive foreign exchange dealings. Finally, in May 1993, the launch of a series of new laptop computers, based on the unexpectedly outdated 386 chip, was canceled. For fiscal 1993, Dell reported a net loss of $36 million, or $1.06 a share, despite a 42% increase in sales to $2.8 billion. The company took a $91.4 million charge to earnings for inventory writedowns, the laptop problems, and restructuring.

Explaining its loss to the financial markets, the company said that management control systems and infrastructure had not kept pace with the tripling in sales. Management was overextended, and coordination problems between marketing and production left overvalued inventory in the warehouse. Dell was forced to renegotiate its debt agreements with its bankers to avoid default.

An analyst commented on Dell's problems: "Without [performance management and control] systems behind you, you can grow yourself into bankruptcy."

---

*Sources:* A. Osterland, "Dell: Nice Quarter, but . . . ," *Company Watch,* March 15, 1994, 20; and L. Kehoe, "Dell Stock Hit by Gloomy Second Quarter," *Financial Times,* July 15, 1993, 24; Palmer, Jay, "Dell Computer: Goodbye, Buzzards," *Barron's* 74, Issue 42, October 17, 1994, 22–24.

As we shall see in Part II of the book, performance measurement and control systems play a central role in mapping future direction by giving managers quantitative information for setting goals and the ability to price out their plans.

**Coordination** refers to the ongoing ability to integrate disparate parts of a business to achieve objectives. As businesses become more complex, coordination becomes both more important and more difficult. The outputs of one unit are often the inputs to another unit (for example, when the output of the customer order department is input to the purchasing department). In any customer-focused business, the work of marketing, sales, production, and distribution must be coordinated like a complex jigsaw puzzle. Customers must receive current information about new product offerings; manufacturing capabilities must be sufficient to fulfill demand; and internal administrative functions must be structured and staffed to adequately support the business. Information on inputs, processes, and outputs for many different work units and functions is critical to line up and coordinate these resources.

## Information for Control

Managers use information for **control** when they use feedback to ensure that inputs, processes, and outputs are aligned to achieve organizational goals. Managers most commonly use feedback information for control purposes to motivate and evaluate employees. (The principles are equally applicable to inanimate objects such as a machine.)

Profit plans and variance information play a critical role in the **ex post evaluation** of performance by comparing actual effort and outcomes against expectations. Profit plans and performance goals often provide important benchmarks of accomplishment. Income statements and performance reports provide the actual data on performance. These feedback data can be used to evaluate the performance of individuals and the businesses for which they work.

Information in the form of output goals, such as profit plan goals or performance targets, can be a powerful tool to motivate employees to adjust inputs, processes, and outputs to achieve organizational goals. Such motivation may be either **extrinsic**—the anticipation of tangible rewards such as money or promotion as an incentive for performance—or **intrinsic**—internally generated inducements for performance arising from such feelings as personal accomplishment. As we shall discuss later, both extrinsic and intrinsic motivation are influenced directly by performance measurement and control techniques.

We must remember, however, that the use of information for control is inextricably linked to assumptions that managers make about human behavior in organizations. In Chapter 1, we set out assumptions that guide the analysis of this book. We assume that people are multifaceted in their response to the opportunities that are offered by organizations: they want to contribute and achieve, be rewarded and recognized for their accomplishments, do what is right, and have some opportunity to innovate and exercise their creative capacities.

Yet, these same opportunities that release human potential create risk. Some employees may not share the goals of management, or they may actively work in their own self-interest to the detriment of the firm. Others, although well meaning, may be ill-equipped to make the correct choice when faced with difficult trade-offs and unyielding pressures for performance.

Managers need to be aware of the risks that they are creating so they can adequately control and manage these risks. Assessing and calibrating these danger signals relies on special information and risk analysis techniques. Information is needed to diagnose potential risks and highlight problem areas. Information about operations risk, asset impairment risk, business risk, and franchise risk must be collected and reported regularly to managers. We will examine this further in later chapters.

## Information for Signaling

Information is used for **signaling** when managers send cues throughout the organization about their preferences, values, and the type of opportunities that they want employees to seek and exploit. The use of information for signaling is predicated on a simple fact that we will rely on later in the book: everyone watches what the boss watches. Employees throughout the organization are looking for cues as to what is important and where they should be focusing their energy and attention. To avoid embarrassment and ensure that their actions are those desired by top management, employees will try to understand what information is important to their superiors. What pieces of information and what types of reports do their bosses focus on? What do they do with this information? What types of information do superiors ignore, even though it is routinely produced?

By focusing systematically on certain types of information, and ignoring other information, all managers send strong signals to their employees about their preferences and values and the types of opportunities that they want people to focus on. A manager's behavior in studying and processing information—as observed by subordinates who are challenged to explain data and discuss its meaning—becomes a powerful indicator of what is important and what will be rewarded.

## Information for Education and Learning

Information is also used for *education and learning*—to train individual managers and employees and to enable the entire organization to understand changes in the internal and external environment that might affect it. For example, the information contained in performance measurement and control systems is important in educating managers on the economics of their business and the drivers of revenue, cost, and performance. All managers progress through developmental stages in which they become increasingly skilled in managing their businesses. Working with performance measures and control data—to plan and coordinate the business, to motivate and evaluate subordinates, and to signal preferences and priorities—is a powerful way for employees to learn how to leverage scarce resources to achieve their objectives. Employees are forced to study the relationship of outputs to inputs, and to understand the key drivers of the firm's profit goals and strategies.

Information can also be important in supporting organizationwide learning. Profit plans and performance measurement data, for example, can inform managers about the effects of changes in the competitive environment. This information may be used subsequently for planning and control, or it may be used to alert managers of pending opportunities or problems in the business and the need to remain vigilant.

---

### Ritz-Carlton: Using Information Systems to Better Serve the Customer

The Ritz-Carlton Hotel Company and Four Seasons Hotels are the two dominant brands in luxury hotels in North America. Ritz-Carlton senior executives believed that it would be extremely difficult to grow through geographic expansion or by competing head-on with Four Seasons. Therefore, Ritz-Carlton managers decided to focus on finding new ways of using information to differentiate their service. The aim was to build seamless, customer-driven service systems that could anticipate a guest's needs and preferences and, at the same time, react instantly to correct any service error or satisfy any complaint.

Ritz-Carlton developed a systematic process for capturing the unique preferences of each of its customers. When staff members engage in conversations with guests, they listen for comments such as, "I really appreciate it when the beds are made and the bathroom is clean when I come back from breakfast." Staff members also note when guests like extra pillows or an unusual beverage. The guest service coordinator collects the guest preferences and enters this information into a database for all Ritz-Carlton guests. Any service problem experienced by a guest is also entered into the database.

The Ritz-Carlton guest information system enables Ritz-Carlton to provide a unique level of personalized service—consistent across its properties—which is a distinct competitive advantage for this luxury hotel.

*Source:* Norman Klein, W. Earl Sasser, and Thomas Jones, "The Ritz-Carlton: Using Customer Information Systems to Better Serve the Customer," Harvard Business School Case No. 395–064, Rev. May 4, 1995.

---

## Information for External Communication

The previous discussion has focused on the use of performance measurement and control information inside the firm. There is one important additional use of this information—for **external communication** to constituents who have a vested interest in the direction and success of the firm.

These constituents fall into three groups: providers and potential providers of capital (lenders, stockholders, and investment analysts), providers and potential providers of goods and services (suppliers and business partners), and existing and potential customers. Each of these groups wants to know about the future prospects of the firm for different reasons. Lenders, owners, and analysts want to understand the business strategy so they can evaluate the likelihood of its success and the amount of economic value that the firm is likely to generate. Suppliers and business partners are interested in the ability of the firm to honor its commitments—both in the short and the long term. Customers want to know if the firm will be able to support its products and services in the future.

Managers use profit plans and performance information to communicate this information externally. Numbers speak louder than words to investors, suppliers, and customers. In meetings with stockholders, lenders, analysts, business partners, and important customers, managers refer to and share business plans and current performance data.

We discuss how managers use profit plans and performance information to communicate externally in later chapters.

## CONFLICTS IN THE USE OF MANAGEMENT INFORMATION

As we move through the analyses of this book and learn how to use information effectively for performance measurement and control, we must be sensitive to the unit of analysis. The same information may be used quite differently for different accountability units. As described in the previous chapter, an accountability unit might be a machine, an individual, a department, a division, or a business.

Imagine that a manager is working with productivity numbers—say number of units produced per week. He or she might take weekly production data related to an individual machine and use it for *decision making* (Do we have enough excess capacity to accept this new order?), *control* (Is the machine operating within specifications?), or for *learning* (Have the new resin pellets allowed us to increase the throughput on this

---

### Communicating Profit Plan Targets at Guidant

Guidant Corporation was created in 1994 when pharmaceutical giant Eli Lilly & Company decided to spin off all its medical-devices divisions into one stand-alone company. Guidant designs, produces, and distributes medical products, including pacemakers, defibrillators, catheters, and devices for minimally invasive surgery. In December 1994, Lilly sold 20% of Guidant's stock in the market in an initial public offering, and in September 1995, the remaining 80%.

Guidant top managers believed that communicating and meeting profit-plan targets was critical to build their reputation in the capital markets. Top managers wanted to demonstrate that they understood the competitive forces and could outperform their industry. They believed that the best way to show that they had mastered the situation was to share very specific profit plans with the investment community that detailed expected performance for each line of the plans, including sales, cost of goods sold, operating expenses, R&D expenses, and expected profits.

In each quarterly presentation to analysts, top managers compared actual results to date and expected year-end figures with their original profit plan. Any difference was thoroughly explained to demonstrate their control of the situation and build their reputation as a team that delivered on their promises. Investors have handsomely rewarded Guidant's capability to meet its profit plan by doubling its stock price in less than a year, ahead of its competitors.

*Source:* Robert Simons and Antonio Dávila, "Guidant Corporation: Shaping Culture Through Systems," Harvard Business School Case No. 198–076, 1998.

machine?). In this example, because the machine is inanimate, there is no conflict between the various uses of information.

Now take exactly the same productivity information—weekly production data—and relate it to an individual worker. Now—when the accountability unit is a human being—we must separate how the information is used by the individual for decision making and how the same information is used for control by the manager responsible for that person's performance. Focus first on the employee. The production worker can use weekly productivity information for decision making (When should the line be stopped to change over to a new run?), for control (How should I budget my time to increase my productivity?), for education (Which parts of this information should I share with others to teach or compare?), and for learning (How does the output of this new production technique compare with previous periods?).

The picture is complicated, however, because the same productivity information will also be used by superiors for motivation and control of the employee's work effort. In this case, the performance information will be used for setting goals, communicating expectations, and judging performance. For the first time, there is a serious potential for conflict.

Conflict arises because of the different biases introduced into information by the manager as he or she attempts to use it to achieve multiple purposes. To motivate workers, the manager may desire to *inflate* performance goals to challenge workers and thereby ensure that they exert maximum effort. However, the workers may know that any improvements in production methods created by workers, through innovation or hard work, may cause their performance goals to be ratcheted upward—more effort will be expected in the future. Therefore, the workers may have an incentive to *understate* actual performance. At the same time, the boss will want to use the information for early warning if key processes go out of control. To be effective as early warning, however, the manager will want to receive variance information based on relatively *low performance standards* to ensure that feedback information is sent early. The manager will also want to use this same performance information for decision making (Should this machine be overhauled?) and learning (Has this worker created a new way of configuring the machine that reduces scrap?). For these uses the manager would like the information to be as *accurate* as possible—with no distortion for motivational or early warning purposes.

This simple example illustrates that when information is applied to the control of an individual or a team, inevitable conflicts are introduced because information has the potential to affect individual and team performance goals and rewards. A fundamental distinction must be made, therefore, between the use of information for the measurement and control of *people* and the use of the same information for the measurement and control of inanimate objects or *business units*. The same information (for example, productivity figures) can be used to assess the performance of a department (a work unit) or of the manager who is responsible for running that work unit. However, whenever information is used to evaluate the performance of individuals, it is subject to distortion.

**TABLE 4–3** Potential Distortion and Bias in Performance Information Use

| PURPOSE OF PERFORMANCE INFORMATION | INFORMATION BIAS DESIRED BY MANAGERS |
| --- | --- |
| Decision making | None. Attempt to gather most-accurate information for planning and control purposes. |
| Motivation | Inflate performance expectations to create stretch targets for employees. |
| Early warning | Lower minimum-acceptable performance standards to expose variables that may require remedial action. |
| Evaluation | Adjust reported performance for factors outside a subordinate's control. |
| External communication | Lower performance expectations to be sure that goals can be achieved and credibility maintained. |

Table 4–3 summarizes some of the conflicts and biases that are inherent in the use of management information for differing purposes. We will discuss this topic more fully later.

## CHAPTER SUMMARY

Information for performance measurement and control is essential to the effective functioning of organizations. Managers use this information to communicate goals up, down, and across their organizations, and later to monitor performance against those goals.

Using information requires choices about what to monitor and measure. Managers can focus their attention on inputs, processes, and outputs based on factors such as measurability, cost, understanding of cause and effect, and desired levels of innovation. Management information can be used for various purposes: decision making, control, signaling, education and learning, and external communication. As we shall see in later chapters, these different uses require different techniques and design principles.

In the past, performance measurement and control information has suffered from a number of deficiencies: Information was often too limited in scope; information was too aggregated and general to be of much use for effective decision making and control; information was late; and information was unreliable.[1]

Today, with better information technology and a better understanding of how to use performance measurement and control systems effectively, these limitations have been largely overcome. In the remainder of the book, we outline the tools, techniques, and processes that allow effective managers to use performance measurement and control information to implement strategy.

---

[1] Henry Mintzberg, *Impediments to the Use of Management Information* (New York: National Association of Accountants, 1975).

# PART II

# Creating Performance Measurement Systems

# CHAPTER
## 5
# Building a Profit Plan

Profit plans are the principal tools that managers use to price their business and operating plans, make trade-offs between different courses of action, set performance and accountability goals, and evaluate the extent to which business performance is likely to meet the expectations of different constituents.

The terms profit plan and budget are often used interchangeably. A **budget** refers to the resource plans of any organizational unit that either generates or consumes resources. The term profit plan is reserved for units that generate profits—stand-alone business units that generate and are held accountable for both revenues and expenses. Thus, managers might refer to the budget of the maintenance department (which generates expenses, but no revenues), or to the budget of the sales-order department (which generates revenues without full accountability for expenses), or to the profit plan of a financial services business (which has full accountability for sales, operating expenses, and profit).

Regardless of terminology, the preparation of profit plans and budgets follows a consistent pattern in most organizations. Several months before the beginning of each fiscal year (the normal twelve-month operating cycle of the business), managers develop their profit plans or budgets. The objectives of this planning process are threefold:

- *To translate the strategy of the business into a detailed plan to create value.* This process requires managers to agree on assumptions, evaluate strategic alternatives, and arrive at a consensus regarding a business strategy and its ability to satisfy the demands of different constituencies.
- *To evaluate whether sufficient resources are available to implement the intended strategy.* Companies need resources to finance their current operations (operating cash) and to invest in new assets for future growth (investment cash).
- *To create a foundation to link economic goals with leading indicators of strategy implementation.* To implement strategy successfully, financial goals must be linked with key business input, process, and output measures.

To build a profit plan, managers need to answer three different questions relating to the economics of their business.

First, managers must ask, does the organization's strategy create economic value? Strategies may sound attractive when described by proponents in bright words and colorful phrases, but strategies need to be translated into accounting numbers to evaluate how they actually create value. Does it pay to invest in a new strategic opportunity? How attractive are different strategic alternatives? Boston Retail has been successful with its line of clothing for women college students. However, the fashion market continually evolves, creating new opportunities and eliminating ideas that move out of fashion. The strategy has to adapt to these changes if the firm is to continue to create economic value and survive.

Second, managers must ask, does the organization have enough cash to fund the strategy and remain solvent throughout the year? All companies need cash to pay their suppliers, but cash may be in short supply if there is a lag between the sale of goods or services and the collection of cash from customers. In some industries, supermarkets for example, companies collect cash from customers before they need to pay their suppliers; however, this is the exception. Most companies need to plan cash flow carefully to estimate cash reserves and potential borrowing requirements.

Finally, managers must ask, does the organization create enough value to attract the financial resources that it needs to fund long-term investment in new assets? Growth requires productive assets, and acquiring those assets requires investors who are willing to lend resources to a company. Investors will only commit their money to a company if they are likely to receive an adequate return. Boston Retail is expanding and it needs to attract additional financial resources to grow. Before it can convince investors to provide capital to the company, Boston Retail needs to show an attractive return on investment.

## THREE WHEELS OF PROFIT PLANNING

To answer the above questions and design a profit plan, three distinct analyses must be performed. Figure 5–1 shows the three cycles that managers must analyze to build a profit plan: the **profit wheel,** the **cash wheel,** and the **ROE wheel.** In the following sections we look in detail at each of these "wheels." Although we introduce each wheel separately, Figure 5–1 illustrates that these wheels are interlocking like a set of mechanical gears — all three wheels turn simultaneously. Adjusting or changing any assumption or number on any of the wheels causes a change in all the other variables. The wheels move in lockstep like the gears of a mechanical clock.

The foundation of profit planning is built upon **assumptions** about how the future will look. Will the market grow over the next year? How will customers respond to our new product offering? What will competitors do to try to capture market share? Will we be able to expand our manufacturing capabilities to support new growth opportunities? What if we increase our level of advertising? Managers need to agree on assumptions such as these to create a profit plan.

Sometimes, top managers already possess most of the relevant information needed to prepare a profit plan. If so, assumptions can be established at the top and communicated down the organization. However, information is usually dispersed more widely throughout the organization: Sales people often know best what specific customers desire; production managers have information on how to reduce costs and increase quality; the purchasing department is in the best position to understand suppliers' relationships; top management has the organizational and industry perspective to assess opportunities and threats. Accordingly, to incorporate all this information, the *profit planning process* must span the whole organization and involve frequent interactions among different hierarchical levels and departments.

**FIGURE 5–1    Three Wheels of Profit Planning**

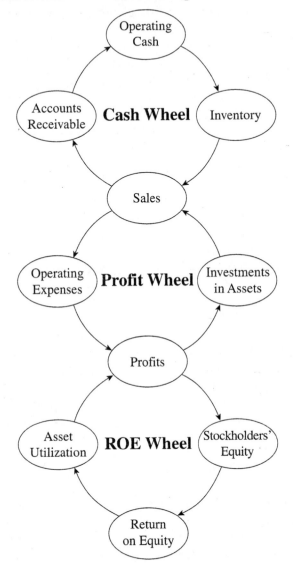

*Source:* Robert Simons, "Templates for Profit Planning," Boston: Harvard Business School Case 9-199-032, 1998.

The profit plan provides information on the economic resources available to the company and helps managers evaluate the trade-offs facing them. Different strategies require different investments. For Boston Retail, the investment plan for opening new clothing stores in New York is not the same plan needed to add furniture to the product line. Perhaps managers would like to invest in all of these alternatives, but resources are limited and managers are forced to make trade-offs. It is not easy to choose: Some managers at Boston Retail may favor geographical expansion, whereas others may prefer to diversify into furniture.

By the end of the profit planning process, people throughout the organization have agreed on the direction of the company. Knowing where the company is going facilitates coordination among the various departments. For example, if the profit plan reflects the introduction of a new product line, employees know that they must include the necessary resources in their own plans to support the success of the new initiative.

In many instances, the profit plan is also used to set performance goals. Managers are held accountable for the achievement of targets defined in the profit plan. As discussed briefly in the previous chapter, when the profit plan is later used for performance evaluation, a tension emerges. If the manager knows that the information disclosed as part of the profit planning process will be used for ex post evaluation, he or she may attempt to build slack into profit plan targets to increase the probability of a favorable evaluation. The undesirable side effect of this biasing behavior is distorted information, which may impede strategy implementation. Because of the inherent conflict between information sharing and performance evaluation, some companies tend to downplay the role of the profit plan as a performance evaluation tool, especially when lower-level managers possess important market and competitive information that must be shared to allow the business to adapt to changing conditions.

## THE PROFIT WHEEL

As all students of accounting know, value creation is measured by profit.[1] Without building a profit plan, managers cannot evaluate whether their intended strategy will generate value for shareholders. Moreover, without a profit plan, managers cannot estimate the economic impact of different strategic alternatives and, as a result, lack adequate information to decide among different courses of action.

The profit plan *summarizes the expected revenue inflows and expense outflows for a specified future accounting period* (typically one year). The outcome of this planning process is a financial document that uses the familiar format of an income statement. To build a profit plan, managers must analyze the profit wheel for the upcoming operating period. Usually, managers go back and forth, iteratively projecting sales, operating expenses, profits, and required investment in assets before the profit plan is acceptable (see Figure 5–2). Then, they work on the cash wheel and the ROE wheel to make sure that sufficient resources will be available to implement the profit plan. If there are not enough resources, they must go back to the profit wheel and repeat the planning process all over again.

### Foundations of a Profit Plan

The starting point for any profit plan is a set of assumptions about the future. These assumptions describe the consensus among managers about how various markets—customer, supplier, and financial—will evolve in the future. The profit plan also reflects

---

[1] We defer to Chapter 8 a discussion of the relationship between economic value added and accounting income. For the purposes of this chapter, we consider accounting income as a measure of economic value created by the firm.

**FIGURE 5–2    The Profit Wheel**

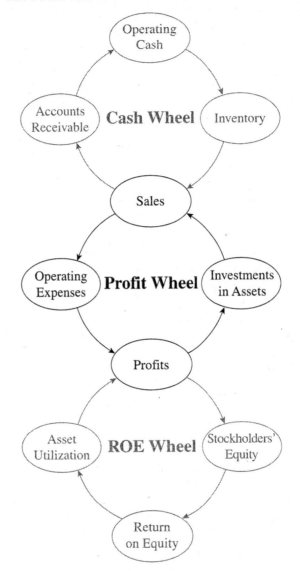

managers' beliefs about *cause-and-effect relationships.* For example, managers may decide to increase the level of advertising if they believe that it will cause a significant increase in the level of sales. Similarly, they may invest in training for their employees if
they believe that this expenditure will improve customer service or increase quality. Finally, the profit plan captures the commitment of managers to an intended strategy. For
example, the merger between Chemical Banking Corporation and Chase Manhattan
Corporation reflected the belief of managers in these two businesses that the banking industry had untapped economies of scale that the new company could capture.

Arriving at consensus often requires intensive interaction among managers. Different perspectives on market competition require sharing information and building a common view about the future of the company. Exhibit 5–1 shows the foundations for building Boston Retail's profit plan for 20X2: actual results of 20X1 with key assumptions for 20X2.

We next review the five steps in creating a profit plan using the profit wheel as illustrated in Figure 5–2.

## Step 1: Estimate the Level of Sales

Most companies start building their profit plan by estimating the level of future sales. This is a logical starting point for two reasons: revenue growth is a major determinant of profit, and the level of operating expenses is often a function of sales volume. Projecting sales is a mixture of art and science; estimating sales volume accurately requires predictions about the impact of external factors and estimates of the effect of internal decisions, such as R&D spending, advertising, and investment in new assets. Sales forecasts are typically generated from sales force estimates, customer surveys, or from a jury of executives or other experts.[2] A good forecast also includes some measure of forecast error, perhaps in the form of a range. For both external and internal factors, a great deal of judgment is required.

To predict sales accurately, companies need to consider many of the external variables that we reviewed in Chapter 2 as part of the analysis of competitive market dynamics, including:

- Macroeconomic factors
- Government regulation
- Competitor moves
- Customer demand

External factors are often outside management's control, but estimating their impact is critical to all companies. For example, estimated car sales depend on predicted prospects for the economy. If potential car buyers are confident about their future income, they are more likely to purchase a new car. Similarly, projected sales for highly regulated European gas and electric utilities depend very much on the prices that are likely to be allowed by the government. The significant influence of macroeconomic factors and political decisions on the level of sales explains why managers pay so much attention to this information.

Competitors' actions and changes in customers' needs are also largely outside managers' control. However, understanding both factors are critical to defining the strategy of the company and designing the profit plan. Managers spend a lot of time evaluating competitors' actions, predicting changes in customers' demands, and judging how the company can capitalize on these events to gain competitive advantage in the marketplace.

In addition to these external factors, internal decisions also have a major impact on the expected level of sales. This is why we illustrate a circular **profit wheel:** sales

---

[2] Steven Nahmias, *Production and Operations Analysis,* (Chicago: Irwin, 1997), 60.

## EXHIBIT 5–1
## Boston Retail
## 20X1 Operating Results with Key Assumptions for 20X2

|  | 20X1 ACTUAL (IN THOUSANDS OF DOLLARS) | KEY ASSUMPTIONS FOR 20X2 |
|---|---|---|
| *Income Statement* | | |
| Sales | $9,200 | 10% sales growth |
| Costs of goods sold | 4,780 | same % of sales as 20X1 |
| Gross margin | 4,420 | |
| Wages and salaries | 1,530 | 4% growth |
| Rent and facilities | 840 | 5% growth |
| Advertising | 585 | same % of sales as 20X1 |
| Administrative expenses | 435 | same % of sales as 20X1 |
| Interest | 72 | estimated at 65 |
| Depreciation | 57 | add depreciation of new assets |
| Training | 38 | 2.5% of wages and salaries |
| Other | 54 | 4% growth |
| Profit before taxes | 809 | |
| Income tax | 283 | 35% of profit |
| Net profit | $ 526 | |

| KEY BALANCE SHEET FIGURES | DECEMBER 31, 20X1 | KEY ASSUMPTIONS FOR 20X2 |
|---|---|---|
| *Assets* | | |
| Cash | $ 208 | Cash will stay at same % level of cash expenses |
| Accounts receivable | 255 | Accounts receivable at same % level of sales |
| Inventory | 985 | Inventory at same % of cost of goods sold |
| Property, plant, and equipment | 1,854 | Property, plant, and equipment increases by new investment |
| Other assets | 325 | Other assets up by 50% |
| Total assets | $3,627 | |
| *Liabilities* | | |
| Accounts payable | $ 209 | Accounts payable at same % of cost of goods sold |
| Bank loan | 1,180 | Pay back debt of $100,000 |
| Stockholders' equity | 2,238 | |
| Total liabilities and stockholders' equity | $3,627 | |

generate profits that are reinvested in assets to generate more sales. Over time, almost every decision in a company impacts the level of sales. However, managers consider most carefully those decisions that have direct influence on sales during the current planning period, such as:

- Mix and pricing of product categories
- Marketing programs
- New-product introductions and product deletions
- Changes in product quality and features
- Manufacturing and distribution capacity
- Customer service levels

Managers have discretion—indeed the responsibility—to set these variables to reflect the agreed strategy. In fact, strategy provides the criteria for consistency in all these decisions.

Based on their analysis of the above factors, managers at Boston Retail estimate that sales volume will grow by 10% in the next year. Exhibit 5–1 illustrates that they are estimating 20X2 sales to be $10,120,000 ($9,200,000 × 110%).

---

### Predicting Sales in an Uncertain World

With rapid product introductions and a proliferation in the number and variety of products offered, manufacturers and retailers are finding it increasingly difficult to accurately predict which of their products will sell and which will not. The accuracy of these estimates affect production plans and the level of expenditure for support functions. If they predict that sales will be higher than actual demand, managers will be left with excess inventory that must be marked down and potentially sold at a loss. If actual demand exceeds sales estimates, then the business will lose potential revenue and damage customer satisfaction as customers are frustrated by an out-of-stock item.

Companies have responded to this challenge in a variety of ways. Dell Computer Corporation has successfully developed a capability to respond extremely quickly to actual customer demand. In 1997 it kept only 12 days' worth of sales in inventory. Other companies have taken steps to dramatically reduce the number of products they sell to simplify the forecasting process.

In the highly volatile fashion skiwear industry, Sport Obermeyer developed a new way to improve the accuracy of its sales forecasts. It had always relied on a committee of company experts to estimate demand and used the average of the committee's predictions to forecast sales volumes for each of its new parkas. Sport Obermeyer analyzed the forecasts for specific product items and found that the *variance* among the individual forecasts of committee members for a product was almost a perfect predictor of forecast accuracy. Using this new insight, it moved the production of the "accurate forecast" items (i.e., low variance among individual forecasts) to China, which required much longer lead times for production, and it delayed the production of its high-variance-forecast items until some initial sales data from early in the season became available. Sport Obermeyer's new forecast system significantly reduced excess inventory costs and stock-outs to retailers.

*Source:* Steven Nahmias, *Production and Operations Analysis* (Chicago: Irwin), 81.

## Step 2: Forecast Operating Expenses

After the expected level of sales is determined, the next task for managers is to estimate operating expenses. To make this estimate, different categories of operating expenses must be analyzed differently.

The first category of operating expense is **variable costs.** As the name suggests, *variable costs vary proportionally with the level of sales or production outputs.* Variable costs are typically estimated as a percentage of sales. To do so, managers must assume that the cause-and-effect relationships between inputs and outputs are constant over the relevant range of sales. That is, an increase in sales volume is assumed to lead to a proportional increase in the usage of inputs. Raw materials is an example of a variable cost in a manufacturing firm. If sales volume of a particular product increases by 10%, we can expect the level of raw material inputs to increase by 10%. Interest expense to cover short-term loans in a bank is another example of a variable cost. The more short-term loans that the bank makes to its customers, the more interest it earns (revenue), but also the more interest it pays to borrow that money (variable costs).

In forecasting variable costs, managers must determine the actual percentage number that relates each category of variable costs to sales. For example, managers may determine that material costs can be set at 24% of sales, labor costs at 18%, energy costs at 4% of sales, and so on. In most cases, a lower cost percentage is preferred (unless reducing variable costs forces higher fixed costs). There are several ways in which variable costs can be reduced as a percentage of sales:

- Taking advantage of economies of scale (e.g., installing one large machine in place of three smaller, less-efficient machines) and economies of scope (such as combining distribution channels for different products to eliminate redundant or underutilized resources)
- Improving operating efficiencies (for example, **re-engineering** or streamlining work flows to do the same work with fewer resources)
- Bargaining with suppliers to negotiate lower prices
- Redesigning products to lower their cost of production
- Increasing prices[3]

The second category of operating expenses is **nonvariable costs.** As the name implies, *nonvariable costs do not vary directly with the level of sales.* However, it would be a mistake to think that they do not vary at all (thus, we avoid calling them fixed costs). These costs are typically large and have become a higher percentage of the operating expenses of most companies in recent years. Nonvariable costs are of three types:

- ***Committed (or engineered) costs.*** Some expenses are determined by previous management decisions and, therefore, are not subject to discretion during the current profit planning period. Depreciation is usually a committed cost because it depends on past investment decisions and company accounting policies. The salaries of managers, engineers, and long-term employees are normally also committed costs, as is the cost of a long-term lease.

---

[3] This alternative reduces variable costs in percentage terms because sales revenue — the denominator — goes up.

- *Discretionary costs.* In contrast to committed costs, the planned level of discretionary expenditures is open to significant debate during the planning process—and subsequent adjustment during the operating period. These are expenses that can be increased or decreased at will, almost without constraints. Advertising, employee training, and research programs are examples of discretionary expenses. Managers can invest as much as they wish if sufficient cash is available. However, managers usually use some guiding criteria to estimate level for these expenses. Some companies choose to set the level of discretionary expenditures by treating them as variable costs. For example, advertising expense is often set as a percentage of sales. Alternatively, managers may set expenditure levels based on industry practice or their assessment about the resource requirements needed to support the intended strategy or specific strategic initiatives. For example, if a business is differentiating its products based on exceptional service, it needs to invest more on employee training than a competitor that competes on low prices and minimal services.

- *Activity-based indirect costs.* The final set of operating expenses are *indirect costs.* Indirect costs cannot be traced directly to a product or service, but change with the level of specific underlying support activities. Examples of activity-based indirect costs include supervision, material handling, and billing costs. Traditionally, these types of cost have been described as "fixed." However, recent developments in cost accounting show that these expenses are not constant, as the word "fixed" implies. They may look fixed, especially if part of the expenses are committed, but their consumption varies with the level of some underlying activity. Most overhead costs, including administrative expenses, fall into this category. To estimate them, managers must identify indirect **cost drivers**—those activities that consume indirect resources. Increases in these cost drivers (for example, increases in customer order complexity or material handling) can be traced to growth in indirect expense levels, such as increased handling, setup, and shipping costs. If cost driver activities can be decreased, then managers can plan to save some money by using fewer resources to perform this activity. Using this approach—known as activity-based budgeting—managers authorize the supply of resources based on anticipated demand for cost driver activities.[4]

## Step 3: Calculate Expected Profit

The difference between expected sales and expected operating expenses determines the amount of economic value that the company is expected to generate in the profit planning period. To assess this value, managers often estimate **NOPAT,** which stands for Net Operating Profit After Taxes, or **EBIAT,** which represents Earnings Before Interest and After Taxes.

These accounting estimates reveal the amount of resources generated during the accounting period that are potentially available for distribution to lenders and owners. Lenders, like banks, have a fixed claim on the profits of the business. They receive interest payments proportional to the amount of financial resources that they lend to the company. Given the expected levels of debt, managers can forecast the expected interest cost by multiplying the expected amount of debt on their balance sheet by the interest rates negotiated with the debt holders (adjusted for income tax effects).

**Profit,** also called **earnings** or **net income,** is the residual economic value *after* interest expense and income taxes (both of which are nondiscretionary payments).

---

[4] Activity-based costing is a topic covered in management accounting courses. It is outside the topic coverage of this book. For more information on activity-based budgeting, see Robin Cooper and Robert S. Kaplan, *Cost & Effect* (Boston: Harvard Business School Press), chap. 15.

Profit is the financial measure of the economic value that is available for distribution to the residual claimants—equity holders—or for reinvestment in the business. Profit is the most important number in evaluating the financial performance of any company.

### Step 4: Price the Investment in New Assets

When managers have agreed on expected sales, operating expenses, and profit numbers, they have created the most important part of a profit plan: the expected income statement. However, the process of translating strategy into economic value does not end there. To finish the profit plan, managers must look at the required level of investment in new assets, including working capital such as inventory and accounts receivable.

As the recursive profit wheel shows, the predicted level of sales is itself determined by the level of assets available to generate those sales. Therefore, managers must decide the levels and types of investments that are required to support desired sales (and strategies). At this point in the process, assumptions about the levels and types of assets needed to support the profit plan must be backed up by an **asset investment plan.** The investment plan is another important tool to implement strategy.

There are two main types of assets for which managers must consider investment: *operating assets* and **long-term assets.** (The cash wheel that we study in the next section is used to determine the investment in operating assets needed by the company.) The proposed investment in long-term productive assets is called the **capital investment plan.** A capital investment plan must reflect and support the intended strategy because it often commits the company to a limited set of strategic alternatives. For example, in the late 1970s, Intel Corporation decided to invest resources in the design and production of microprocessors and to reduce its focus on commodity computer memories. Intel's capital investment plan included resources to develop microprocessors and to build manufacturing facilities. The plan reflected management's new strategy and ensured that sufficient resources would be in place to make that strategy a reality.

Exhibit 5–2 presents the 20X2 asset investment plan for Boston Retail, assuming no major changes in strategy. Anticipated growth in the business will require larger balances in accounts receivable ($26,000) and inventory ($98,000), although these requirements will be partially financed by an increase in accounts payable ($21,000). Some store displays also must be replaced and updated. Two capital initiatives are also planned: (1) a new computerized accounting system that will integrate purchasing, inventory record keeping, and SKU (stock keeping unit) management, and (2) an expansion of the warehouse to accommodate the increase in business.

Before we finish our brief introduction to the asset investment plan, we must mention how companies assess whether any single capital investment proposal is financially attractive. The most common investment evaluation technique is net present value. Finance books discuss this technique in depth because it is a basic tool in the finance toolbox. Any investment proposal that is included in the capital investment plan should meet these financial criteria or be included for compelling strategic reasons. We will have more to say about this in Chapter 7, when we discuss in detail how to create a capital investment plan.

---

**EXHIBIT 5–2**
**Asset Investment Plan for Boston Retail**

| | NEW ASSETS NEEDED FOR 20X2 (THOUSANDS OF DOLLARS) |
|---|---|
| *Working Capital* | |
| Increase in accounts receivable | $ 26 |
| Increase in inventory | 98 |
| Increase in accounts payable | (21) |
| *Long-Term (Depreciable) Assets*[a] | |
| New computerized management system | 60 |
| Store displays | 80 |
| Warehouse expansion | 120 |
| Total investment in new assets during 20X2 | $363 |

---

[a] *For simplicity, assume that long-term assets have an average life of five years; all investments in long-term assets are made in January.*

## Step 5: Close the Profit Wheel and Test Key Assumptions

The feedback loop among all the components of the profit wheel suggests that the profit planning process is not linear. Managers must go back and forth among the variables in the profit plan to ensure that it reflects the strategy and is attractive from an economic point of view. Of course, an electronic spreadsheet such as Excel can be used to link and integrate this process.

When managers have arrived at an acceptable expected profit, they usually perform a **sensitivity analysis** based on changes in sales or other key profit plan variables. The objective of a sensitivity analysis is to estimate how profit might change when underlying assumptions about the competitive environment or other predictions embedded in the base profit plan prove to be under- or overstated. Managers often develop three different scenarios: worst-case scenario, most likely scenario, and best-case scenario. Sales, operating expenditures, and capital acquisition plans are estimated for each scenario. For example, utility companies usually project at least three scenarios based on the severity of winter weather. The most likely scenario is an average winter based on typical temperatures for the region. The other two scenarios are based on the effects of an unusually mild winter and an unusually cold winter. For each scenario, utility companies build a profit plan, test its viability, and prepare action plans based on predicted outcomes of that scenario.

Exhibit 5–3 on pages 90–91 shows the profit plan for Boston Retail. Boston Retail managers have performed a sensitivity analysis by constructing two additional profit plans: one for a better-than-expected market growth rate of 15% (sales = $10,580,000), and another with a worse-than-expected market with no growth (sales = 20X1 sales = $9,200,000). These sales alternatives are illustrated at the top of the exhibit.

---

### Sensitivity Analysis at Allied Signal

Lawrence Bossidy, CEO of Allied Signal, has strong opinions about profit planning: "One of the first things that struck me when I came here was that it was more or less accepted practice that you put a plan together and then missed it. We don't need meaningless targets. We need an operating plan that recognizes that underlying assumptions are often wrong and that provides options when that happens.

"Good finance people are the ones who can help give real meaning to operating plans. When you say you're going to get a 6% improvement in productivity, they're the ones who are supposed to ask where, What are the projects? When are they going to be done? How much money are they going to be providing? If we're going to grow by 5%, they ask the tough questions: Where are we going to grow? What products are going to grow by 5%? How are we going to get price increases? Good financial involvement is critical in constructing a sound operating plan; it really drives at the particulars."

*Source:* Noel M. Tichy and Ram Charan, "The CEO as Coach: An Interview with Allied Signal's Lawrence A. Bossidy," *Harvard Business Review* 73 (March–April 1995): 68–78.

---

## CASH WHEEL

Before a profit plan can be accepted as feasible, managers must forecast whether the company will have enough cash to operate (cash wheel) and whether the return to investors is sufficiently attractive (ROE wheel). If either of these critical constraints is not met, then managers must go back to the drawing board and adjust the profit plan.

The cash wheel (Figure 5–3 on page 92) illustrates the operating cash flow cycle of a business: Sales of products and services to customers generate accounts receivable, which are eventually turned into cash; this cash is used to produce inventory, which in turn can be used to generate more sales. However, depending on the nature of the business, considerable time can elapse between the moment that the company disburses cash to purchase inventory and pay operating expenses until it receives cash from customers for goods and services received. During this period of time, the company may have to borrow from lenders to cover its ongoing operating and capital expenses.

Looking at the cash wheel, we can understand why a company may need more or less operating cash, depending on its industry and its strategy. High levels of inventory require more operating cash to finance the inventory. Similarly, if credit terms to customers are 60 days instead of 30 days, the company needs to borrow more from the bank to cover its cash outflows during the additional 30 days. Conversely, a company can reduce its operating cash by delaying payments to its suppliers, usually by negotiating better credit terms.

## EXHIBIT 5–3
### Boston Retail
### Profit Plan for 20X2 Based on Existing Six Stores
### (in thousands of dollars)

|  | 20X1 ACTUAL | KEY ASSUMPTIONS FOR 20X2 |
|---|---|---|
| Sales | $9,200 | 10% sales growth |
| Costs of goods sold | 4,780 | same % of sales as 20X1 |
| Gross margin | 4,420 |  |
| Wages and salaries | 1,530 | 4% growth |
| Rent and facilities | 840 | 5% growth |
| Advertising | 585 | same % of sales as 20X1 |
| Administrative expenses | 435 | same % of sales as 20X1 |
| Interest | 72 | estimated at 65 |
| Depreciation | 57 | add depreciation of new assets |
| Training | 38 | 2.5% of wages and salaries |
| Other | 54 | 4% growth |
| Profit before taxes | 809 |  |
| Income tax | 283 | 35% of profit |
| Net profit | $ 526 |  |

| KEY BALANCE SHEET FIGURES | DECEMBER 31, 20X1 | KEY ASSUMPTIONS FOR 20X2 |
|---|---|---|
| *Assets* |  |  |
| Cash | $ 208 | Operating cash not less than 150 |
| Accounts receivable | 255 | Accounts receivable at same % level of sales |
| Inventory | 985 | Inventory at same % of COGS |
| Property, plant, and equipment | 1,854 | Property, plant, and equipment increases by new investment |
| Other assets | 325 | Other assets same |
| Total assets | $3,627 |  |
| *Liabilities* |  |  |
| Accounts payable | $ 209 | Accounts payable at same % of COGS |
| Bank loan | 1,180 | Pay back debt of $300,000 |
| Stockholders' equity | 2,238 |  |
| Total liabilities and stockholders' equity | $3,627 |  |

| 20X2 PROFIT PLAN | 20X2 PROFIT PLAN (OPTIMISTIC SCENARIO 15% GROWTH) | 20X2 PROFIT PLAN (PESSIMISTIC SCENARIO NO GROWTH) |
|---|---|---|
| $10,120 | $10,580 | $9,200 |
| 5,258 | 5,497 | 4,780 |
| 4,862 | 5,083 | 4,420 |
| 1,591 | 1,591 | 1,591 |
| 882 | 882 | 882 |
| 644 | 673 | 585 |
| 478 | 500 | 435 |
| 65 | 65 | 65 |
| 109 | 109 | 109 |
| 40 | 40 | 40 |
| 56 | 56 | 56 |
| 997 | 1,167 | 657 |
| 349 | 408 | 230 |
| $    648 | $    759 | $   427 |

DECEMBER 31, 20X2

| | | |
|---|---|---|
| $    302 | $    361 | $   184 |
| 281 | 293 | 255 |
| 1,083 | 1,133 | 985 |
| 2,005 | 2,005 | 2,005 |
| 325 | 325 | 325 |
| $ 3,996 | $ 4,117 | $3,754 |
| $    230 | $    240 | $   209 |
| 880 | 880 | 880 |
| 2,886 | 2,997 | 2,665 |
| $ 3,996 | $ 4,117 | $3,754 |

**FIGURE 5–3** The Cash Wheel

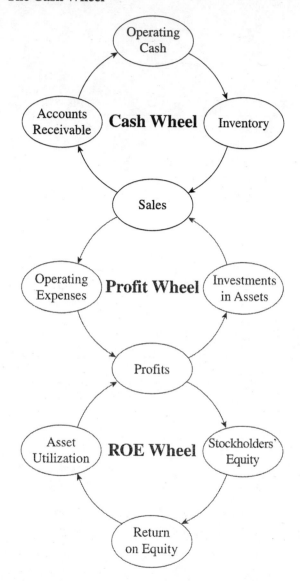

Forecasting cash needs is important for all businesses because companies have limited cash reserves and borrowing capacity. If managers project that the cash needed to operate the business exceeds cash reserves and maximum borrowing capacity, then the *profit plan is not feasible* and must be reworked. For example, fast-growing companies need a lot of cash to finance increases in working capital (inventory and accounts receivable) and the purchase of new productive assets such as machinery and equipment. However, existing debt may limit their borrowing capacity. If a company's borrowing capacity is limited to $500,000 and its profit plan requires $700,000 investment in new assets, then the profit plan is not feasible. To overcome this constraint, managers must choose to either revise their profit plan by reducing growth or, alternatively, they can consider issuing new equity to increase their cash reserves.[5]

The basic technique for computing the cash wheel is quite simple. The most intuitive way to estimate cash requirements is to forecast cash inflows and cash outflows for each specific time period. To estimate the operating cash required during a period of time, managers project the cash that they will receive—in most cases, from customers—and the cash that they will disburse—in paying suppliers, operating expenses, and for committed costs such as interest and lease payments. The basic formula is the following:

$$\begin{array}{c} \text{Operating cash} \\ \text{needed during a period} \end{array} = \begin{array}{c} \text{Cash received} \\ \text{from customers} \end{array} - \begin{array}{c} \text{Cash paid to suppliers} \\ \text{and operating expenses} \end{array}$$

This is the method that most of us employ when budgeting our personal finances to determine whether we have sufficient cash flow to support our rent and car payments.

You may remember from your financial accounting course the name of this cash flow method: it is the **direct method.** Companies often use the direct method to estimate cash requirements for short periods of time—a day, a week, or a month. For each period, managers estimate cash that will be collected (cash inflows) and cash that will be paid out (cash outflows). If cash inflows are larger than cash outflows, then the cash on hand increases. If, however, the opposite holds—cash outflows exceed inflows—the company's cash position gets worse. Sometimes, companies must make very detailed cash forecasts—even daily—if managers project that they may hit or exceed their fixed borrowing limit.

Exhibit 5–4 shows Boston Retail's cash plan for 20X2 broken down by the four quarters of the year. The analysis indicates a small cash shortfall in quarter one, which must be covered by bank borrowing.

To estimate cash needs over longer periods of time—to tie in with the monthly, quarterly, or yearly profit plan projections—companies generally use the **indirect method** (this method should also be familiar from your financial accounting class). To use the indirect method, managers start with their projected income as shown on the profit plan and follow four steps to estimate their cash needs.

## Step 1: Estimate Net Cash Flows from Operations

A simple technique to estimate *operating cash flow* is to use a measure known as **EBITDA,** which stands for Earnings Before Interest, Taxes, Depreciation, and Amortization. It is a rough calculation of nonaccrual—or cash-based—operating earnings that

---

[5] The sustainable growth rate of any business is defined as

$$\text{Sustainable growth rate} = \text{ROE} \times (1 - \text{Dividend payout ratio})$$

where the dividend payout ratio is

$$\text{Dividend payout ratio} = \frac{\text{Cash dividends paid}}{\text{Net income}}$$

Interested readers can refer to any standard finance textbook for a full discussion of the implications and use of this formula.

**EXHIBIT 5–4**
**Boston Retail**
**Quarterly Cash Plan for 20X2**
**(Prepared by estimating cash inflows and outflows)**

|  | FIRST QUARTER | SECOND QUARTER | THIRD QUARTER | FOURTH QUARTER | TOTAL |
|---|---|---|---|---|---|
| Cash at the beginning of the quarter (cash balance at least 200) | $ 208 | $ 200 | $ 200 | $ 200 | $ 208 |
| *Cash Inflows* |  |  |  |  |  |
| Cash received from customers | 1,470 | 2,631 | 2,400 | 3,594 | 10,095 |
| Borrowing required | 288 | (58) | (100) | (130) | — |
| Total cash inflows | $1,758 | $2,573 | $2,300 | $3,464 | $10,095 |
| *Cash Outflows* |  |  |  |  |  |
| Cash paid to suppliers | 818 | 1,359 | 1,274 | 1,885 | 5,336 |
| Cash expenses | 526 | 1,052 | 864 | 1,315 | 3,757 |
| Investment in new assets | 260 | — | — | — | 260 |
| Tax payments | 87 | 87 | 87 | 87 | 348 |
| Pay back debt | 75 | 75 | 75 | 75 | 300 |
| Total cash outflows | $1,766 | $2,573 | $2,300 | $3,362 | $10,001 |
| Total cash flows | $ (8) | — | — | $ 102 | $ 94 |
| Cash at the end of the quarter | $ 200 | $ 200 | $ 200 | $ 302 | $ 302 |

can be computed readily from an income statement. The calculation starts with accrual-based profit—taken directly from the profit plan—and adds back (1) depreciation, which does not require an outlay of cash, and (2) interest and tax expenses, which represent nonoperating expenditures.

## Step 2: Estimate Cash Needed to Fund Growth in Operating Assets

EBITDA is a rough measure that ignores any changes in working capital needed to operate the business. For example, cash may be used up (or provided) by changes in inventory levels and accounts receivable balances. These changes in working capital will either reduce (or increase) cash balances on hand.

Experience in any business will provide good data on the level of working capital needed to fund a business. From past experience, Boston Retail managers know that they must invest approximately $165,000 in inventory, $40,000 in accounts receivable, and $25,000 in store displays for each store. They also know that suppliers will finance approximately $35,000 of this amount through accounts payable. Therefore, adding a new store will mean an investment in working capital of almost $200,000, which will require cash either from cash reserves on hand or from borrowing.

For 20X2, managers anticipate that the increasing scale of operations will require an additional $103,000 of working capital. This amount must be subtracted from operating cash flow calculated as EBITDA. At Boston Retail, the calculation of operating cash flow using EBITDA for 20X2 is shown in Exhibit 5–5.

We can see that managers expect to have approximately $1,068,000 of operating cash flow available to fund growth, repay debt, pay financing costs and taxes, and distribute any dividends to shareholders. If opening a new store requires approximately $200,000 in working capital, the business will have enough free cash from operations (after tax payments and interest) to open three new stores, assuming it does not use its cash for debt repayment, dividends, or other types of investment.

## Step 3: Price the Acquisition and Divestiture of Long-Term Assets

Different strategies and initiatives will require different levels of investment and cash. At Boston Retail, the investment plan for 20X2 (Exhibit 5–2) suggests that the new computer system, warehouse expansion, and store displays will require $260,000. This

**EXHIBIT 5–5**
**Boston Retail**
**Cash Plan for 20X2**
**(Prepared using EBITDA)**

|  | 20X2 |
|---|---|
| Cash at the beginning of the year | $  208 |
| *Cash from Operating Activities* | |
| Profit after taxes | 648 |
| Tax payments | 349 |
| Interest payments | 65 |
| Add: depreciation and other noncash expenses | 109 |
| EBITDA | 1,171 |
| *Changes in Working Capital* | |
| Decrease (increase) in accounts receivable | (26) |
| Decrease (increase) in inventory | (98) |
| Increase (decrease) in accounts payable | 21 |
| Cash flow from operating activities | 1,068 |
| *Cash from Investment Activities* | |
| Investment in new assets | (260) |
| *Cash from Financing Activities* | |
| Pay back debt | (300) |
| Additional borrowing required | — |
| Tax payments | (349) |
| Interest payments | (65) |
| Total cash flows | 94 |
| Cash at the end of the year | $  302 |

anticipated need for cash will reduce the increase in cash on hand from $1,068,000 to $808,000.

### Step 4: Estimate Financing Needs and Interest Payments

The final step in the calculation of cash flow by the indirect method is to subtract the amount of cash needed for (or generated by) financing and income tax. Financing demands on cash flow include dividends, interest expense, and repayment of debt principal. In 20X2, managers at Boston Retail plan to repay $300,000 of their debt and anticipate paying $349,000 in estimated tax payments. In addition, they will pay $65,000 in interest costs. These deductions reduce estimated cash flow as follows:

| | |
|---|---:|
| Operating cash flow (from Exhibit 5–5) | $1,068 |
| Asset purchases | (260) |
| Tax payments | (349) |
| Debt repayment | (300) |
| Interest payments | (65) |
| Increase in cash | 94 |
| Cash on hand—beginning of year | 208 |
| Cash on hand—end of year | $ 302 |

When all is said and done, the indirect method yields exactly the same result as the direct method (compare Exhibits 5–4 and 5–5 as a quick check). The primary difference lies in the fact that the indirect method can be calculated quickly from existing monthly, quarterly, or yearly financial-statement estimates. The direct method requires a detailed, and often laborious, estimate of cash inflows and outflows.

Cash flow analysis often will indicate the need for external funds in the form of either debt or equity to support the proposed profit plan. Managers must choose among available sources of external financing (equity, short-term debt, long-term debt, or some combination of these instruments) and choose funding sources that match financial risk with business risk.

## Ensuring Adequate Cash Flow

In contrast to the profit plan, in which the time horizon is typically one year, cash flow projections often focus on much shorter time periods. The difference between cash inflows and cash outflows during the operating cycle is estimated for most businesses at least monthly. For highly seasonal industries such as ski manufacturing or boat building, cash flow balances must be calculated weekly or even daily during critical periods when available cash may not be sufficient to keep the business solvent. In these industries, a bank may be willing to lend the *average* cash requirements for a business, but the important question is whether the bank will advance the *maximum* cash shortfall that the company needs over the business cycle.

For example, ski manufacturers receive most of their cash from customers—retail ski stores—during the winter ski season when retail customers are purchasing new equipment, however, manufacturers disburse most of their operating cash for the production and distribution of skis at least five months earlier. As a result, these businesses need the most borrowing at the beginning of the season, when they have used up all their cash to manufacture inventory but have not yet received any cash from customers. Estimating the *aggregate* or average difference between cash inflows and cash outflows over the entire year will not reveal the shortfall that occurs before the ski season begins. Managers in these companies may pay a lot of attention to weekly cash requirements during the few critical months before the start of the season.

The cash wheel highlights the fact that all businesses have a significant amount of resources tied up in accounts receivable, inventory, and other working capital accounts. As a result, managers must work diligently to accelerate the flows around the cash wheel, thereby freeing up cash for investment, financing, or operations growth.

*CFO Magazine* conducted a survey of large public companies in 32 industries to learn how effectively managers were able to turn working capital into cash. In their sample, the average company earned $4.2 billion in revenue and generated roughly 9 cents of cash flow for every dollar of sales. On average these companies collected from customers every 50 days, paid suppliers every 33 days, and turned inventory 11 times per year. For the largest companies in the sample, the authors of the survey noted a "rule of 30": they collect bills in 30 days, pay bills in 30 days, and turn inventory in 30 days.

Although all companies can benefit from managing the cash wheel more efficiently, the savings for large companies can be truly significant. For example, Owens Corning recovered $175 million from managing its working capital more effectively; General Motors set a goal for 1997 to find $10 billion in working capital savings.[6]

## ROE WHEEL

Businesses that earn the most profit will be better off: They will have more resources to invest in future opportunities; they will be able to pay higher dividends to investors; their stock price will be higher; and their cost of debt will be lower. Thus, profit can be considered both a constraint and a goal: A minimum level of profit is necessary for survival (a constraint), but more is always better than less (a goal).

Both stock price and dividend payments depend on a business's ability to generate profits from the investments that stockholders make in the business. In the most basic sense, when a stockholder invests $100 in a firm, the managers of the firm use the $100 to purchase assets, which are then deployed to earn profit for the benefit of the stockholder. The critical measure, therefore, is the amount of profit that managers are able to generate from the $100 investment entrusted to them. If the business generates $20, profit can be measured in two ways. First, the business could report a $20 profit—an absolute measure of success. Alternatively, managers could calculate the return on shareholders' investment by comparing the profit output ($20) with the investment input ($100). In this case, the return on the stockholder investment of $100 would be 20%—a ratio.

---

[6] S. L. Mintz and C. Lazere, "Inside the Corporate Cash Machine," *CFO Magazine,* June 1997, 54–62.

---

### Cash Flow Analysis at Chicago Central & Pacific Railroad

Chicago Central & Pacific Railroad was a privately held, highly leveraged regional freight railroad. In 1987, when revenue growth did not keep up with capital spending, the company declared bankruptcy under Chapter 11 legislation. The company was rescued when the senior lender agreed to provide additional operational funding.

The new management team decided to focus attention throughout the business on cash flow by developing a simple direct-cash-flow report according to *Statement of Financial Accounting Standards 95*. Direct-cash-flow reporting would, managers believed, show the company's ability to service debt, quantify the consequences of operating managers' decisions, and simplify variance analysis.

Chicago Central already had a daily cash balance report, but more information was required to understand the sources of cash inflows and outflows for investing, financing, and operating activities. For example, determining direct cash flows from costs related to track improvement was difficult because there was a timing difference between when costs were charged to a project in the books and when actual cash was disbursed. Another challenge was accounting for services that a wholly-owned subsidiary purchased from Chicago Central, as well as for the revenue that this subsidiary collected from other railroads through an "interline accounting" system used in the industry.

With the new system, managers were better aware of the capital spending limits imposed upon them by loan obligations. They also learned that cash collected through interline accounting was 1.5 times greater than regular customer revenue but twice as slow in arriving as cash collected directly from customers.

*Source:* Kevin R. Trout, Margaret M. Tanner, and Lee Nicholas, "On Track with Direct Cash Flow," *Management Accounting* (July 1993): 23–27.

---

Investors in a firm monitor their investment returns carefully—and hold top managers accountable for these returns—so it is not surprising that the single most important measure for investors is **return on investment** (or **ROI**). ROI is a *ratio measure* of the profit output of the business as a percentage of financial investment inputs. This accounting measure is one of the single best surrogates for overall financial performance.[7]

If we adopt the perspective of managers—those entrusted by shareholders to generate profit—then the appropriate internal measure for return on investment is **return on equity (ROE).** The shareholders' equity portion of the balance sheet shows the total original investment by stockholders, plus accumulated business profits that accrue to stockholders' benefit (less, of course, any dividends paid out). Thus, the objective for any manager is to use the equity investment of the firm wisely—for the benefit of stockholders.

---

[7] We introduce alternative measures, such as EVA, in Chapter 8.

As with the profit wheel and the cash wheel, we can work systematically around the ROE wheel to determine if the profit plan is adequate to meet expectations (see Figure 5–4).

### Step 1: Calculate Overall Return on Equity

Return on equity (*ROE*) is calculated as follows:

$$ROE = \frac{\text{Net Income}}{\text{Shareholders' Equity}}$$

**FIGURE 5–4    The ROE Wheel**

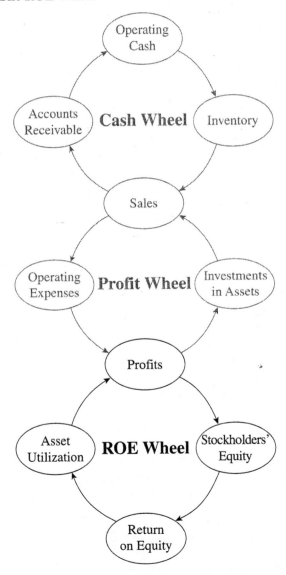

If we assume that senior managers wish to maximize this measure (which is a safe assumption because top managers' performance bonuses are often tied either directly or indirectly to this measure), we must ask ourselves how senior managers cascade this measure down to the organization hierarchy so that lower-level employees will also work to increase ROE.

To answer this question, we can decompose ROE into its component parts. The basic arithmetic decomposition of this measure was devised by Donaldson Brown, who developed his techniques as chief financial officer at Dupont about 1915 and later introduced the techniques to General Motors.[8] ROE can be broken as follows:

$$ROE = \frac{\text{Net Income}}{\text{Shareholders' Equity}}$$

$$= \frac{\text{Net Income}}{\text{Sales}} \times \frac{\text{Sales}}{\text{Shareholders' Equity}}$$

The first term (net income ÷ sales) is a ratio measure of **profitability.** It answers the question, How much profit will we generate for each dollar of sales? This information comes directly from the profit wheel. The second term (sales ÷ stockholders' equity) is a ratio measure as well, but one that is useful only for senior managers, because middle- and lower-level managers do not manage stockholders' equity per se. Rather, managers lower in the business are allocated funds to acquire *assets,* which in turn are used to generate sales and profits. Thus, it is helpful to expand the second term of the equation one step further as follows:

$$ROE = \frac{\text{Net Income}}{\text{Sales}} \times \frac{\text{Sales}}{\text{Assets}} \times \frac{\text{Assets}}{\text{Shareholders' Equity}}$$

$$= \text{Profitability Ratio} \times \text{Asset Turnover Ratio} \times \text{Financial Leverage Ratio}$$

The first term (net income ÷ sales) remains the same—a profitability measure. The second term (sales ÷ assets) is now a ratio measure of **asset turnover.** This ratio answers the question, How many sales dollars will we generate for each dollar that is invested in assets of the business? The objective for any manager is to maximize the sales created by the firm's asset base (assuming, of course, that incremental sales generate profits—not losses). The final term (assets ÷ stockholders' equity) focuses on **financial leverage** by asking, What percentage of total assets employed are to be funded by stockholders and what percentage by debt? To the extent that the asset-to-equity ratio is greater than 1, assets will be funded by debt extended by bondholders, banks, and other creditors of the business. A **leveraged business** is one that relies on a high percentage of debt to fund the productive assets employed in the business.

---

[8] H. T. Johnson and R. S. Kaplan, *Relevance Lost: The Rise and Fall of Management Accounting* (Boston: Harvard Business School Press, 1987), 86, 101.

For Boston Retail, we can plug profit plan numbers from Exhibit 5–3 into the formula to assess projected profitability, asset turnover, and leverage.

$$
\begin{aligned}
ROE &= \frac{\text{Net Income}}{\text{Sales}} \times \frac{\text{Sales}}{\text{Assets}} \times \frac{\text{Assets}}{\text{Shareholders' Equity}} \\[2mm]
&= \frac{648}{10{,}120} \times \frac{10{,}120}{3{,}996} \times \frac{3{,}996}{2{,}886} \\[2mm]
&= 0.064 \quad \times \quad 2.5 \quad \times \quad 1.4 \qquad = 0.225^{*} \\[2mm]
&= \begin{array}{c}\text{Profitability} \\ \text{Ratio}\end{array} \times \begin{array}{c}\text{Asset} \\ \text{Turnover} \\ \text{Ratio}\end{array} \times \begin{array}{c}\text{Financial Leverage} \\ \text{Ratio}\end{array}
\end{aligned}
$$

*(\* difference due to rounding)*

We can see that the business is projected to earn 6.4% net income on sales with asset turnover of 2.5 and a leverage ratio of 1.4. The combination of these three indicators yields ROE of 22.5%.

## Step 2: Estimate Asset Utilization

Within a business, unit managers (division or profit center managers) are often accountable for a variant of ROE known as **ROCE**, which stands for **return on capital employed.** The breakdown of *ROCE* follows the same pattern as above:

$$
ROCE = \frac{\text{Net Income}}{\text{Sales}} \times \frac{\text{Sales}}{\text{Capital Employed}}
$$

In the ROCE ratio, **capital employed** refers to the assets within a manager's direct span of control. (See Chapter 3 for a discussion of span of control.) Some companies define capital employed as total assets controlled by a manager minus noninterest-bearing liabilities (for example, accounts payable). These assets typically include accounts receivable, inventory, and plant and equipment. In other cases, some corporate-level assets, such as unamortized goodwill, are also allocated to profit centers to be included in the "capital" that is employed to generate revenue and profit. Different businesses define ROCE in different ways, so care must be taken in using this ratio to understand precisely what managers are including in the denominator.

The detailed decomposition of ROCE provides important additional information about the effective utilization of capital and assets. We can decompose ROCE into a systematic view of many parts of the business's operations. Figure 5–5 depicts this decomposition. Like branches of a tree, we can pursue each component of the ratio to obtain greater detail and potential insight.

At Boston Retail, managers can take the asset-utilization ratios shown and break them down into more detailed projections relating to individual parts of the business.

Some of the more popular asset-utilization measures that are derived from the ROCE Tree are (using 20X1 asset balances for simplicity):

$$\text{Working Capital Turnover} = \frac{\text{Sales}}{\text{Current Assets} - \text{Current Liabilities}}$$

$$\text{Accounts Receivable Turnover} = \frac{\text{Net Sales on Credit}}{\text{Average Net Receivables}}$$

$$\text{Inventory Turnover} = \frac{\text{Cost of Goods Sold}}{\text{Average Inventory}}$$

$$\text{Fixed Asset Turnover} = \frac{\text{Sales}}{\text{Property, Plant, and Equipment}}$$

These turnover ratios show how efficiently managers have used each category of asset (working capital, accounts receivable, inventory, and fixed assets) to generate sales

**FIGURE 5–5    ROCE Tree**

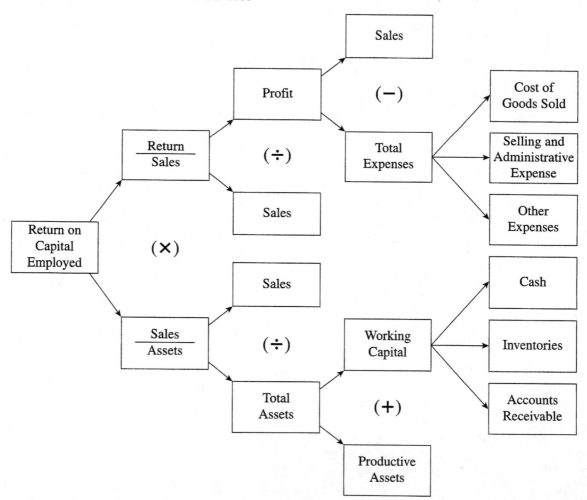

and, ultimately, profit. Generally, a higher number is preferred, indicating that managers have used the assets entrusted to them to maximum advantage. Once ROCE and detailed asset-utilization ratios have been estimated, managers assess the use of the resources under their stewardship.

### Step 3: Compare Projected ROE
### with Industry Benchmarks and Investor Expectations

Once overall expected ROE is calculated, managers must compare it to some benchmark or standard to see how it stacks up against competitors and investor expectations. Managers are sensitive to the ROE expected by investors, analysts, and others who monitor the financial performance of their firm. High returns on investment lead to high stock prices and to the willingness of investors to commit additional financial resources to support the growth of the firm. Low returns cause the opposite result. Therefore, managers typically know—through discussion with analysts and company directors—the ROE that is anticipated from the performance of their business. The returns generated by other similar businesses provide an easily calibrated yardstick.

For Boston Retail, managers might compare their ROE with other publicly traded fashion retailers such as The Limited, GAP, and Nike, whose comparative figures for 1997 are as follows:

|  | ROE | PROFITABILITY | ASSET TURNOVER | FINANCIAL LEVERAGE |
|---|---|---|---|---|
| The Limited | 10.6% | 2.4% | 2.1 | 2.1 |
| Gap | 33.7% | 8.2% | 1.9 | 2.1 |
| Nike | 25.2% | 8.7% | 1.7 | 1.7 |
| Boston Retail | 22.5% | 6.4% | 2.5 | 1.4 |

As with the cash wheel, if the expected ROE is not sufficiently high to meet expectations, it is back to the drawing board to find ways to increase profit or make better use of existing assets.

## Key Financial Measures

Based on our analysis of the principal components of the profit, cash, and ROE wheels, we can summarize the primary financial measures for any business:

- sales
- profit or net income
- cash flow
- investment in new assets
- return on equity (or ROCE)
- net income ÷ sales = profitability
- sales ÷ assets = asset turnover

For Boston Retail, we can recap the profit plan calculations for 20X2 as follows:

- sales = $10,120,000
- profit or net income = $648,000
- cash flow = $1,068,000 operating; $94,000 net (after interest, taxes, new investment, and debt repayment)
- investment in new assets = $260,000
- return on equity = 22.5%
- profitability = 6.4%
- asset turnover = 2.5

## USING THE PROFIT WHEELS TO TEST STRATEGY

Boston Retail is contemplating two different strategies for the future. One strategy is to expand into New York state. The increase in sales volume needed to support this strategy will force the company to move to mass production. The other strategy is to limit geographical expansion but diversify into furniture. The profit plan will change depending on which of these strategies is followed because each strategy has different underlying economics. Exhibit 5-6 shows the assumptions underlying both strategies.

Managers must use the three wheels to evaluate the economics and internal consistency of each of these strategies. Implementing either strategy requires the allocation of scarce resources among the various business opportunities open to a company. Resource allocation decisions commit the long-term future of an organization, so they are important decisions to determine the competitive position of the organization. Therefore, resource allocation decisions are often hotly debated inside companies. Agreement is not an easy task because different division managers will often champion different investment opportunities. If a company invests in a certain product line, it is simultaneously deciding not to invest in alternative product lines. This is always difficult for managers who believe in the prospects of the alternatives that are turned down.

The first step is to use the profit wheel to prepare a profit plan for each of the alternatives, based on the assumptions in Exhibit 5-6. Each alternative generates different levels of profit.

The next step is to use the cash wheel analysis to ensure that cash will be adequate to fund these initiatives. In this case, both strategies generate cash over a one-year period. However, the expected cash inflow from sales might lag the cash outflows linked to the increase in operating and long-term assets. Therefore, Boston Retail managers should estimate cash requirements for periods shorter than a year. For geographical expansion, if most of the investment in new assets were to happen early in the year, Boston Retail might need to borrow money from the bank.

Exhibits 5-7, 5-8, and 5-9 present the profit plans and cash flow analyses for each of the competing strategies.

The final step is to compare the ROE for each of the alternatives. For Boston Retail, ROE (using average equity) is 27% for the geographical expansion ($701 ÷ $2,588) and 29.5% ($775 ÷ $2,625) for the product-line expansion strategy.

---

## EXHIBIT 5-6
### Boston Retail
### Assumptions Underlying Alternative Strategies

---

#### ALTERNATIVE 1: GEOGRAPHICAL EXPANSION INTO NEW YORK STATE

---

*Description of Intended Strategy*

Open three stores in New York state at the beginning of the year

*Additional Investment in New Assets*

$120,000 in fixed assets per new store (five years' straight-line depreciation schedule)
Same investment in working capital as existing stores
$20,000 in advertising per new store

*Operating Results*

Sales per store expected to be the existing average
Cost structure as in existing stores (% of sales)

---

#### ALTERNATIVE 2: ADDING A NEW PRODUCT LINE

---

*Description of Intended Strategy*

Introduce premium outdoor furniture product line in Boston Retail's three biggest stores

*Additional Investment in New Assets*

$25,000 per store (five years' straight-line depreciation schedule)
Same investment in working capital as existing product line
$10,000 in advertising per store carrying furniture

*Operating Results*

Expected increase in sales per store with furniture of 20%
Expected gross margin as clothing line
Administrative costs up by 15%
Wages and salaries up by 10%
Additional cost structure as existing business (% of sales)

---

However, economic criteria alone are not enough to fully assess each strategic alternative. Recall our discussion in Chapter 2. Profit plans may look attractive but actually deplete the core competencies of the firm, or be at odds with the current market position of the company. During the 1980s and early 1990s, for example, Apple Computer showed impressive economic performance, but the company was using up its advantage built over the previous years without creating new competitive advantage. The result was continuous economic problems in the 1990s. For Boston Retail, we could ask ourselves: Are both of these strategic alternatives consistent with Boston Retail's competencies? (We cover performance measurement and control systems related to this question in Chapter 10.)

## EXHIBIT 5–7
### Boston Retail
### Profit Plan for 20X2 Based on Alternative Strategies
### (in thousands of dollars)

|  | 20X1 ACTUAL | 20X2 PROFIT PLAN | 20X2 PROFIT PLAN (GEOGRAPHICAL EXPANSION) | 20X2 PROFIT PLAN (PRODUCT-LINE EXPANSION) |
|---|---|---|---|---|
| Sales | $9,200 | $10,120 | $13,800 | $11,132 |
| Costs of goods sold | 4,780 | 5,258 | 7,170 | 5,784 |
| Gross margin | 4,420 | 4,862 | 6,630 | 5,348 |
| Wages and salaries | 1,530 | 1,591 | 2,387 | 1,750 |
| Rent and facilities | 840 | 882 | 1,322 | 882 |
| Advertising | 585 | 644 | 704 | 673 |
| Administrative expenses | 435 | 478 | 718 | 550 |
| Interest | 72 | 65 | 97 | 72 |
| Depreciation | 57 | 109 | 181 | 124 |
| Training | 38 | 40 | 59 | 43 |
| Other | 54 | 56 | 84 | 62 |
| Profit before taxes | 809 | 997 | 1,078 | 1,192 |
| Income tax | 283 | 349 | 377 | 417 |
| Net profit | $ 526 | $ 648 | $ 701 | $ 775 |

**KEY BALANCE SHEET FIGURES**

|  | 12/31/20X1 | 12/31/20X2 | | |
|---|---|---|---|---|
| *Assets* | | | | |
| Cash | $ 208 | $ 302 | $ 200 | $ 255 |
| Accounts receivable | 255 | 281 | 382 | 309 |
| Inventory | 985 | 1,083 | 1,478 | 1,192 |
| Property, plant, and equipment | 1,854 | 2,005 | 2,293 | 2,065 |
| Other assets | 325 | 325 | 325 | 325 |
| Total assets | $3,627 | $3,996 | $4,678 | $4,146 |
| *Liabilities* | | | | |
| Accounts payable | $ 209 | $ 230 | $ 313 | $ 253 |
| Bank loan | 1,180 | 880 | 880 | 880 |
| Additional borrowing | | | 546 | |
| Stockholders' equity | 2,238 | 2,886 | 2,939 | 3,013 |
| Total liabilities and stockholders' equity | $3,627 | $3,996 | $4,678 | $4,146 |

**EXHIBIT 5–8**
**Boston Retail**
**Quarterly Cash Plan for 20X2 for Alternative Strategies**
**(Prepared by estimating cash inflows and outflows)**

| STRATEGIC ALTERNATIVE 1 **GEOGRAPHICAL EXPANSION INTO NEW YORK** | FIRST QUARTER | SECOND QUARTER | THIRD QUARTER | FOURTH QUARTER | TOTAL |
|---|---|---|---|---|---|
| Cash at the beginning of the quarter (cash balance at least 200) | $ 208 | $ 200 | $ 200 | $ 200 | $ 208 |
| *Cash Inflows* | | | | | |
| Cash received from customers | 1,911 | 3,588 | 3,273 | 4,901 | 13,673 |
| Borrowing required | 758 | 15 | (24) | (203) | 546 |
| Total cash inflows | 2,669 | 3,603 | 3,249 | 4,698 | 14,219 |
| *Cash Outflows* | | | | | |
| Cash paid to suppliers | 1,136 | 1,930 | 1,844 | 2,649 | 7,559 |
| Cash expenses | 752 | 1,504 | 1,236 | 1,880 | 5,372 |
| Investment in new assets | 620 | — | — | — | 620 |
| Tax payments | 94 | 94 | 94 | 94 | 376 |
| Pay back debt | 75 | 75 | 75 | 75 | 300 |
| Total cash outflows | 2,677 | 3,603 | 3,249 | 4,698 | 14,227 |
| Total cash flows | (8) | — | — | — | (8) |
| Cash at the end of the quarter | $ 200 | $ 200 | $ 200 | $ 200 | $ 200 |

| STRATEGIC ALTERNATIVE 2 **PRODUCT-LINE EXPANSION INTO FURNITURE** | FIRST QUARTER | SECOND QUARTER | THIRD QUARTER | FOURTH QUARTER | TOTAL |
|---|---|---|---|---|---|
| Cash at the beginning of the quarter (cash balance at least 200) | $ 208 | $ 200 | $ 200 | $ 200 | $ 208 |
| *Cash Inflows* | | | | | |
| Cash received from customers | 1,591 | 2,894 | 2,640 | 3,954 | 11,079 |
| Borrowing required | 388 | (77) | (93) | (218) | — |
| Total cash inflows | 1,979 | 2,817 | 2,547 | 3,736 | 11,079 |
| *Cash Outflows* | | | | | |
| Cash paid to suppliers | 908 | 1,509 | 1,440 | 2,091 | 5,948 |
| Cash expenses | 565 | 1,129 | 928 | 1,411 | 4,033 |
| Investment in new assets | 335 | — | — | — | 335 |
| Tax payments | 104 | 104 | 104 | 104 | 416 |
| Pay back debt | 75 | 75 | 75 | 75 | 300 |
| Total cash outflows | 1,987 | 2,817 | 2,547 | 3,681 | 11,032 |
| Total cash flows | (8) | — | — | 55 | 47 |
| Cash at the end of the quarter | $ 200 | $ 200 | $ 200 | $ 255 | $ 255 |

**EXHIBIT 5–9**
**Boston Retail**
**Cash Plan for 20X2**
**(Prepared using EBITDA)**

| | STRATEGIC ALTERNATIVE 1 GEOGRAPHICAL EXPANSION INTO NEW YORK 20X2 | STRATEGIC ALTERNATIVE 2 PRODUCT-LINE EXPANSION INTO FURNITURE 20X2 |
|---|---|---|
| Cash at the beginning of the year | $  208 | $  208 |
| *Cash from Operating Activities* | | |
| Projected income after taxes | 701 | 775 |
| Tax payments | 377 | 417 |
| Interest payments | 97 | 72 |
| Add: depreciation and other noncash expenses | 181 | 124 |
| EBITDA | 1,356 | 1,388 |
| *Changes in Working Capital* | | |
| Decrease (increase) in accounts receivable | (127) | (54) |
| Decrease (increase) in inventory | (493) | (207) |
| Increase (decrease) in accounts payable | 104 | 44 |
| Cash flow from operating activities | 840 | 1,171 |
| *Cash from Investment Activities* | | |
| Investment in new assets | (620) | (335) |
| *Cash from Financing Activities* | | |
| Pay back debt | (300) | (300) |
| Additional borrowing required | 546 | — |
| Tax payments | (377) | (417) |
| Interest payments | (97) | (72) |
| Total cash flows | (8) | 47 |
| Cash at the end of the year | $  200 | $  255 |

## CHAPTER SUMMARY

The profit plan describes business strategy in economic terms. Because of the importance of the profit plan as a management tool to *test* and *communicate* strategy, managers typically invest substantial time and effort to develop, negotiate, and design the profit plan for the coming year. Managers use the profit plan to assess the ability of different strategies to generate value and to estimate whether sufficient resources will be available to implement the chosen strategy. Managers at Boston Retail are considering two alternative strategies. The first alternative is to diversify geographically into New

York state. Alternatively, the company may move into furniture. The profit plan depicts the economic implications of these alternatives and allows managers to assess the merits of each strategy.

The process of building a profit plan allows managers to share information about competitive market dynamics and internal strengths and weaknesses. Each person in the company may have different information about what is happening in the market and, accordingly, different beliefs about what is the best future direction for the company. By sharing information, managers *learn* from the experience of others and generate valuable additional insights.

Every profit plan is subject to the constraints imposed by the profit wheel, the cash wheel, and the ROE wheel. Within these constraints, managers still have freedom to design profit plans as they see fit. Building a profit plan is an exercise in creativity—testing ideas, testing assumptions, and testing strategy. Yet, even if everyone in the organization accepts the stated strategy, each person may understand it differently. The profit plan forces managers to make explicit their assumptions about what the company's strategy means.

As we will see in chapters to follow, the profit plan plays other critical roles in every business: in setting performance goals for employees, in communicating expectations to the investment community, and in allowing the evaluation of the performance of individual businesses and managers. A profit plan may look like a simple document, but it is an essential foundation for driving any high-performing business forward.

# 6

# Evaluating Strategic Profit Performance

In the previous chapter, we studied how strategies are translated into profit plans. In this chapter, we review the analytic techniques that managers use to monitor their business's success in achieving those profit goals and strategies.

In any business, managers must go through a series of steps to gain an understanding of the sources of strategic profitability. This is essentially a diagnostic function—tracking the progress of organizational achievements against preset performance goals and strategies. To perform this analysis, we revisit many of the themes introduced previously in the book—strategy implementation, profit wheel analysis, span of accountability, and the use of information for decision making and control.

To analyze profit performance, we must consider two different types of measures: effectiveness measures and efficiency measures.

- **Effectiveness** refers to the extent to which an activity achieves desired outcomes. Effectiveness answers the question: Did we achieve what we set out to do? Thus, measures of effectiveness focus on the comparison of actual results with preset expectations or standards.
- **Efficiency,** by contrast, refers to the level of resources that were consumed to achieve a certain level of output. Measures of efficiency answer the question: How many resources were used to achieve the actual outputs? Thus, efficiency variances focus on ratios of inputs to outputs.

To analyze profit performance, the three conditions enumerated in Chapter 4 must be present:

1. Ability to measure outputs—Managers cannot evaluate how well a business unit or manager has performed unless they are able to quantify outputs. Therefore, the ability to measure outputs is a prerequisite for evaluating whether a business has achieved its objectives and efficiently used scarce resources in achieving those objectives.

2. Existence of a predetermined standard of performance—Having a measure of output is useless unless a standard or target exists against which to compare actual performance. Telling someone that a business generated $125,000 in weekly sales does not mean much without an appreciation of how much the business was expected to produce. Was the sales target $100,000 (in which case the business did well)? Or was it $200,000 (indicating a disastrous week)?

**3.** Ability to use variance information as feedback to adjust inputs and/or process—Measurement and comparison, by themselves, do little good unless managers can use this variance information to change inputs and processes to either bring operations in line with expectations (i.e., where performance is below expectations), or to attempt to capture and replicate unexpected successes (i.e., where performance exceeds expectations). This implies, of course, that managers understand the causal linkages between inputs, processes, and outputs.

Managers can measure countless outputs and processes in any organization. The key to evaluating *strategic* profit performance is focusing on those accounting variables that inform managers about the success of their strategy. In the remainder of the chapter, we outline the procedures for calculating a series of variances that, in total, yield a complete analysis of strategic profitability. These variances include:

- profit plan variances, in absolute and relative terms
- market share variances
- revenue variances
- product efficiency and cost variances
- variances for nonvariable costs

## STRATEGIC PROFITABILITY

**Strategic profitability analysis** is a tool to evaluate the success of a business in generating profit from the implementation of its strategy. To illustrate the techniques of strategic profitability analysis, we will focus on the financial performance of Shade Tree Furniture—a manufacturer of teak and mahogany outdoor furniture.[1] Boston Retail considered acquiring Shade Tree when managers were debating a diversification move into furniture. Shade Tree follows a differentiation strategy supported by premium pricing. The company invests significant resources in advertising to illustrate the quality features that distinguish its products from competitors. The company sells expensive premium furniture through direct mail advertising in periodicals such as *Architectural Digest* and *The New York Times*. Exhibit 6–1 presents Shade Tree's profit plan and actual results for the year ended 20X1.

By examining Exhibit 6–1, we can see that the profit plan, prepared before the beginning of the fiscal year, estimated $413,000 profit for 20X1. Actual profit was $437,211. What are the implications of this difference for evaluating Shade Tree's strategy?

To answer this question, we must know something about Shade Tree's strategic goals. Assume that the key strategic goals established by senior managers at Shade Tree were the following:

- Market share—Managers estimated the size of the outdoor wooden furniture market to be $430 million (or, equivalently, 1,250,000 units of furniture). For 20X1, Shade Tree managers wanted to capture, in dollar terms, 1% of this market. Because Shade Tree Furniture products are premium priced, the 1% market share in dollar terms is equivalent to 0.80% market share in number of pieces of furniture.

---

[1] We have chosen to illustrate strategic profitability analysis techniques using a manufacturing firm so we can review variances that reflect manufacturing and operational efficiencies, in addition to those variances that would apply to a retail company such as Boston Retail.

**EXHIBIT 6–1**
**Shade Tree Furniture**
**Profit Plan and Actual Performance for 20X1**

|  | PROFIT PLAN 20X1 | ACTUAL INCOME STATEMENT 20X1 |
|---|---|---|
| Sales | $4,300,000 | $4,450,050 |
| Cost of goods sold |  |  |
| Raw materials | 1,595,000 | 1,686,672 |
| Wages | 505,000 | 514,696 |
| Other manufacturing costs | 480,000 | 490,650 |
| Gross margin | $1,720,000 | $1,758,032 |
| Administrative and selling expenses | 505,000 | 488,500 |
| Advertising expenses | 516,000 | 520,700 |
| Interest expense | 64,000 | 76,200 |
| Profit before taxes | $ 635,000 | $ 672,632 |
| Income tax | 222,000 | 235,421 |
| Profit after tax | $ 413,000 | $ 437,211 |

- Gross margin—Shade Tree's premium pricing strategy should be reflected in high gross margin. Gross margin targets for 20X1 were set at 40% of sales.
- Advertising—Budgeted at 12% of sales.
- Cash flow—Managers wanted to be able to generate $300,000 cash flow from operations.
- Return on equity—the goal for 20X1 was set at 18%.

To perform strategic profitability analysis, we revisit the profit wheel concepts that we used in Chapter 5. In our analysis, we pay particular attention to three of the four variables on the profit wheel—sales, operating expenses, and profit. The fourth variable—investment in new assets—is covered in the next chapter.

## Computing Profit Plan Variances in Absolute and Relative Terms

The first step in all profitability analysis is to isolate significant deviations from expectations using **variance analysis.** A variance is the difference between (1) an item estimated on a profit plan or budget prepared prior to the start of an accounting period and (2) the actual income or expense as reflected on accounting statements prepared after the accounting period has ended. Variances are **favorable** (F) if actual profit is higher than planned profit. Conversely, variances are **unfavorable** (U) if actual profit is below planned profit.

The first level of analysis then simply computes the difference between actual profit for year 20X1 and the standards set out in the accountability unit's profit plan or budget that was prepared in late 20X0 (see Exhibit 6–2). In Shade Tree Furniture's case, the profit difference is $24,211 (favorable). Sales revenue is $150,050 over plan. Some other expenses are below plan, such as administrative and selling expenses, which is $16,500 under plan.

## EXHIBIT 6–2
### Shade Tree Furniture
### Profit Plan Variances

| | PROFIT PLAN 20X1 (IN DOLLARS) | PROFIT PLAN 20X1 (IN % OVER SALES) | ACTUAL INCOME STATEMENT 20X1 (IN DOLLARS) | ACTUAL INCOME STATEMENT 20X1 (IN % OVER SALES) | VARIANCE ANALYSIS (IN DOLLARS) | |
|---|---|---|---|---|---|---|
| Sales | $4,300,000 | 100.0% | $4,450,050 | 100.0% | $150,050 | (F) |
| Cost of goods sold | | | | | | |
| Raw materials | 1,595,000 | 37.1 | 1,686,672 | 37.9 | (91,672) | (U) |
| Wages | 505,000 | 11.7 | 514,696 | 11.6 | (9,696) | (U) |
| Other manufacturing costs | 480,000 | 11.2 | 490,650 | 11.0 | (10,650) | (U) |
| Gross margin | $1,720,000 | 40.0% | $1,758,032 | 39.5% | $ 38,032 | (F) |
| Administrative and selling expenses | 505,000 | 11.7 | 488,500 | 11.0 | 16,500 | (F) |
| Advertising expenses | 516,000 | 12.0 | 520,700 | 11.7 | (4,700) | (U) |
| Interest expense | 64,000 | 1.5 | 76,200 | 1.7 | (12,200) | (U) |
| Profit before taxes | $ 635,000 | 14.8% | $ 672,632 | 15.1% | $ 37,632 | (F) |
| Income tax | 222,000 | 5.2 | 235,421 | 5.3 | (13,421) | (U) |
| Profit after tax | $ 413,000 | 9.6% | $ 437,211 | 9.8% | $ 24,211 | (F) |

Managers often use this first level of analysis to describe variances in ratio or percentage terms. Thus, a manager might describe her revenue as "3.5% over plan" or administrative and selling expenses as "3% below budget."

Once simple profit variances are calculated, the business strategy must be tested and validated. The reason for variances must be ascertained so that profit plan performance can be evaluated, corrective action taken, and key insights applied to other aspects of the business.

What should managers at Shade Tree make of the additional $24,000 profit? Although the number is relatively small in both absolute and relative terms, it may conceal large offsetting variances. For example, it could be made up of a $124,000 gain due to growth and a $100,000 loss due to poor products. Further analysis may reveal unexpected changes in revenue, cost of raw materials, and a variety of other factors. Higher profits may be due to efficient use of resources, increased demand for goods and services, or changes in the competitive marketplace. Revenue might differ from expectations due to changes in selling prices or to a change in product mix. Cost savings may be due to a successful experiment in production technology. Even though the net profit change is small, each of these potential explanations must be tested and verified so that strategy can be affirmed or adjusted as necessary.

**Strategic profitability** comprises two components, as defined by the following formula:

$$\text{Strategic profitability} = \text{profit (loss) from competitive effectiveness}$$
$$+ \text{profit (loss) from operating efficiencies}$$

These two terms—competitive effectiveness and operating efficiencies—drive sales and operating expenses, respectively, on the profit wheel. Thus, for purposes of our strategic profitability analysis, we can relabel the profit wheel categories, substituting *competitiveness effectiveness* for sales, and *operating efficiencies* for operating expenses (Figure 6–1).

 Analysis of *competitive effectiveness*—did we achieve what we set out to do?—is applicable primarily to business units that set and implement product market strategy. This includes all stand-alone businesses, as well as any profit center or other unit whose managers are accountable for creating profit through market transactions. The analysis of *operating efficiencies*—how many resources were consumed to achieve the actual

**FIGURE 6–1   Strategic Profitability Analysis Wheel**

outputs?—is applicable to all accountability units that manage the flow of Inputs→Process→Outputs. This includes entire businesses and profit centers. It also includes those units that we discussed in Chapter 3 with narrower spans of accountability, such as functions and cost centers.

## COMPETITIVE EFFECTIVENESS: MARKET SHARE VARIANCES

How well did Shade Tree Furniture implement its strategy? To answer this question, we must probe the effectiveness of the business in attracting customers, marketing its products, and differentiating itself from other competitors in the marketplace.

Effectiveness, by definition, focuses on outputs. *Profit* from competitive effectiveness focuses on how well a business fared against its competitors. It is gauged by two principal output indicators: market share growth and price premium. Market share growth reveals how customers reacted to a business's value proposition. Price premium, reflected in the revenue line of the income statement, reveals the success of a business in extracting value based on differentiation of its goods and services. In the next two sections, we compute market share and revenue variances to provide insight into how well the business performed on these dimensions of strategy.

### Computing Market Share Variances

As part of any profit planning process, revenue goals are established based on analysis of market potential, SWOT, and intended strategies. These same market-based factors provide the foundation for analysis of market share growth.

Two key variables affect profitability attributable to market share:

- increase (or decrease) in profit due to changes in market *size* (i.e., changes in total unit or dollar volume sold in the entire market)
- increase (or decrease) in profit due to changes in market *share* (i.e., changes in percentage of total market served by the business)

Each of these variables is evaluated against the original expectations set out in the profit plan (see Exhibit 6–3).

The formula for unexpected profit due to changes in *market size* is:

Market size variance = Δ market size × planned market share × planned average
contribution margin
= (actual market size in units − predicted market size in units)
× planned market share
× planned average contribution margin

From Exhibit 6–3, we find that the profit change due to increases in the size of the outdoor furniture market was:

$$= (1{,}268{,}293 - 1{,}250{,}000)$$
$$\times 0.80\%$$
$$\times \$220 = \underline{\$32{,}196} \ (F)$$

---

**EXHIBIT 6-3**
**Shade Tree Furniture**
**Revenue Assumptions in 20X1 Profit Plan**

| | ASSUMPTIONS REFLECTED IN 20X1 PROFIT PLAN | ACTUAL DATA FOR 20X1 |
|---|---|---|
| Market size (in $) | $430,000,000 | $436,280,000 |
| Market size (in units) | 1,250,000 | 1,268,293 |
| Market share (in $) | 1.00% | 1.02% |
| Market share (in units) | 0.80% | 0.82% |
| Contribution margin per unit in $[a] | $ 220.00[b] | |
| Contribution margin per unit in %[a] | 51.16% | |

---

[a] Only raw material and wages are variable costs
[b] Calculated from data in Exhibit 6-4

Thus, this calculation reveals that Shade Tree's profit increased by $32,196 because of increases in overall market demand.

Next, we want to probe how successful the company was in capturing its share of this total demand. The formula for profit change due to increases or decreases in *market share* is:

---

### A Common Way to Approximate Market Size Variance

Sometimes, managers do not have access to market size data expressed in unit volumes—that is, the number of pieces of furniture sold. In these cases, using market size expressed in *dollar terms* is usually a sufficient approximation to estimate a market size variance. For example, we can estimate the market size variance using the dollar value of the market as follows:

$$= (\$436,280,000 - \$430,000,000)$$
$$\times 1\%$$
$$\times 51.16\% = \underline{\$32,128} \text{ (F)}$$

For Shade Tree Furniture, estimating market size variance in dollars instead of number of units represents a difference in accuracy of less than 2%. Because this approximation fails to separate the effects of changes in market size (in units) and changes in unit prices, it is accurate only if the actual average unit market price (market size in dollars ÷ market size in units) is close to the expected average unit market price. A simple calculation reveals that the market for outdoor furniture meets this condition:

Expected average market price = $430,000,000 ÷ 1,250,000 = $344.00
Actual average market price = $436,280,000 ÷ 1,268,293 = $343.99

Market share variance = Δ market share × actual market size × planned average
contribution margin
= (actual market share in units − planned market share in units)
× actual market size
× planned average contribution margin

From Exhibit 6–3 we can easily price the profit that was earned because of better-than-expected market share:

$$= (0.82\% - 0.80\%)$$
$$\times 1{,}268{,}293$$
$$\times \$220 = \underline{\$55{,}804} \text{ (F)}$$

By calculating these two market-based variances, we have ascertained that Shade Tree Furniture added $88,000 to its profit due to changes in the market. Part of this increase was due to unexpected growth in the size of the total market ($32,196), and part was due to an increased share of the larger pie ($55,804). Through our analysis, we have learned that the market for outdoor furniture grew more than expected during 20X1,

---

### A Common Way to Approximate Market Share Variance

Again, however, market share data expressed as dollar sales (instead of number of units) may be more readily available. Therefore, managers sometimes estimate market share variance using data expressed in dollars instead of units sold. However, you must remember that this approach mixes the effects of changes in market share with changes in unit prices. Therefore, it is only an approximation—adequate in most situations—but an approximation nonetheless.

$$= (1.02\% - 1.00\%)$$
$$\times \$436{,}280{,}000$$
$$\times 51.16\% = \underline{\$44{,}640} \text{ (F)}$$

The difference that we get by using market share in dollars instead of units is $11,164. This approximation is accurate if actual average unit price (for both the overall market and the company's products) is close to the expected average unit price used to build the profit plan. For Shade Tree Furniture in 20X1, market prices were as expected, but the company's price was $2.11 below plan.[2] This lower-than-expected price makes the approximation of market share using dollars roughly accurate.[3]

---

[2] Expected average price = $4,300,000 ÷ 10,000 = $430 (see Exhibit 6–4 for volume data). Actual average price = $4,450,050 ÷ 10,400 = $427.89.

[3] We can reconcile the difference of $11,164 using the change in prices as follows:

$$\$11{,}164 = [(0.82\% \times \$2.11 \div \$430) - (0.80\% \times \$0.01 \div \$344)] \times 1{,}268{,}293 \times \$220$$

which indicates that Shade Tree Furniture is competing in a market with an attractive future. Moreover, the company captured a higher market share than expected. To understand the implications of this performance indicator, managers need to answer several questions: Did the premium market for outdoor furniture grow more than the rest of the market? Did the company cut prices to achieve growth? Did the sales and marketing department of Shade Tree Furniture perform up to expectations? We consider these questions next.

## COMPETITIVE EFFECTIVENESS: REVENUE VARIANCES

With market share variances as a backdrop, we now evaluate managers' success in generating acceptable levels of revenue. Revenue is a simple accounting term; it equals sales volume in units multiplied by unit price. However, revenue is much more than that. Revenue is the unequivocal measure of the desirability of a value proposition. It is a key indicator of customer acceptance of products and services. In the long term, it is the ultimate measure of customer satisfaction.

### Computing Revenue Variances

Managers are especially interested in two sources of revenue-based profit:

- increase (or decrease) in profit due to changes in prices
- increase (or decrease) in profit due to changes in product mix

Shade Tree Furniture sells both chairs and benches. Assume for simplicity that each type of product costs the same to manufacture—$210—but the chairs are priced at $400 and the benches sell for $500. In its profit plan, Shade Tree Furniture planned to sell 7,000 chairs and 3,000 benches (see Exhibit 6-4). Thus, in the original profit plan, total revenue was estimated at $4,300,000 (7,000 chairs × $400 + 3,000 benches × $500). However, the actual units sold differed from the number of units predicted in the

---

**EXHIBIT 6-4**
**Shade Tree Furniture**
**Information Needed for Calculation of Revenue Variances**

|  | ASSUMPTIONS REFLECTED IN 20X1 PROFIT PLAN | ACTUAL DATA FOR 20X1 |
|---|---|---|
| Number of chairs (units) | 7,000 | 7,050 |
| Revenues from chairs | $2,800,000 | $2,791,800 |
| Number of benches (units) | 3,000 | 3,350 |
| Revenues from benches | $1,500,000 | $1,658,250 |
| Planned contribution margin per unit (chairs) | $190.00 | |
| Planned contribution margin per unit (benches) | $290.00 | |
| Average expected contribution per piece of furniture | $220.00 | $222.21 |

profit plan. During the year, the company actually sold 7,050 chairs and 3,350 benches, and it generated revenues of $2,791,800 for chairs and $1,658,250 for benches, for a total of $4,450,050. We now have the information that we need to calculate basic revenue variances.

The first step in calculating revenue variances is to dig into the company records to find out how much of the profit variance was attributable to changes in selling prices. In our analysis of strategic effectiveness, it is critical to understand the ability of the business to receive price premiums for its products or services. Premium pricing results from effective differentiation and successful market positioning. Premium prices are possible for two reasons: (1) because customers believe that the value they are receiving is worth the higher price, and/or (2) competitive offerings or substitute products are not available at lower prices. Understanding these factors is essential for effective competition.

A favorable sales price variance, or **price premium** (selling prices are higher than profit plan estimates), indicates that managers have been successful in extracting value from the marketplace—either because of product superiority or weakness in competitors' product positions. An unfavorable sales price variance (selling prices are lower than profit plan estimates) suggests the opposite: the business had to lower price to meet competition or customers were unwilling to pay the planned price for the value they were receiving.

The formula for the *sales price variance* is:

Sales price variance = actual total revenue
  − (product #1 standard selling price × product #1 actual volume)
  − (product #2 standard selling price × product #2 actual volume)
  − . . . .
  − (product #n standard selling price × product #n actual volume)

For Shade Tree Furniture, the sales price variance is:

= $4,450,050 − ($400 × 7,050 chairs) − ($500 × 3,350 benches)
= 4,450,050 − 4,495,000
= $44,950 U

Through this calculation, we can see that lower prices reduced profits by just under $45,000. Managers must now investigate why prices had to be lowered. Did Shade Tree Furniture lower its prices to meet competitive pressures? Or, were discounts needed to compensate for weak demand?

The second revenue variance focuses on **product mix.** Product mix describes the percentage of total sales that is generated by each product in a business's product line. For example, a firm may generate 25% of its revenue from product A, 40% from product B, and 35% from product C. Product mix is important because selling prices and manufacturing costs often differ by product. If companies sell more or less of different products—each with different prices and contribution margins—then actual profit will differ from profit plan estimates.

To isolate the effect of product mix variances on profit, we must work with *standard contribution margins.* **Contribution margin** is defined as selling price minus variable costs. For our purposes, we are interested in isolating the profit effects of changes in product mix; therefore, we need to hold changes in variable costs and selling price constant. Thus, it is important to remember to compute product mix variances using standard (i.e., planned) variable costs per unit rather than actual variable costs per unit, which may reflect unanticipated changes in production efficiency. Similarly, we use planned selling prices in the calculation of contribution margin because the effects of changes in selling price changes have already been identified above as part of the sales price variance.

In its profit plan, Shade Tree Furniture planned to generate 65% of its revenue from chairs and 35% from benches. We know that chairs have a planned contribution margin of $190 per unit ($400 − $210), and benches have a planned contribution margin of $290 per unit ($500 − $210). We can calculate the total planned contribution margin as $2,200,000 (7,000 chairs × $190 + 3,000 benches × $290), and average contribution per unit as $220 ($2,200,000 ÷ 10,000 units). Assuming that costs to produce did not differ from the standards reflected in the profit plan (we will relax this assumption shortly), the restated "standard" contribution—using the actual sales mix— was $2,311,000 (7,050 chairs × $190 + 3,350 benches × $290). Average contribution per unit was $222.21 ($2,311,000 ÷ 10,400 units), reflecting a shift to higher-margin benches.

We can now use this information to compute the change in profit due to changes in product mix. The formula for **product mix variance** is:

$$
\begin{aligned}
\text{Product mix variance} &= \Delta \text{ average standard contribution} \times \text{actual unit volume} \\
&= (\text{actual average standard contribution} - \text{planned average} \\
&\quad \text{standard contribution}) \times \text{actual unit volume} \\
&= [(\$2,311,000 \div 10,400) - (\$2,200,000 \div 10,000)] \times 10,400 \\
&= \underline{\$23,000} \text{ (F)}
\end{aligned}
$$

The shift from chairs to benches generated $23,000 additional profit. With this information in hand, managers need to explore the implications of the switch to higher-margin products. Is this the start of a new trend? How can it be accelerated? What are the implications for production, sourcing, and advertising?

## SUMMARY OF COMPETITIVE EFFECTIVENESS VARIANCES

To summarize, then, we have computed four variances related to competitive effectiveness:

| | | |
|---|---:|---|
| Market size | $32,196 | (F) |
| Market share | 55,804 | (F) |
| Sales price | 44,950 | (U) |
| Product mix | 23,000 | (F) |
| Total profit variances due to competitive effectiveness | $66,050 | (F) |

The picture that emerges from this analysis is generally favorable. Profit exceeded plan by $66,050 due to superior competitive effectiveness. Managers must next take this data and probe its implications. The market is growing ahead of expectations. (Q. What factors are causing this increase in overall market demand?) Managers have been able to shift the product mix from chairs to more profitable benches. (Q. How can the business capitalize on this unexpected shift?) Market share is also growing faster than expectations. (Q. What combination of advertising and promotion programs have contributed to this shift?) The one unfavorable variance is due to lower than planned selling prices. (Q. Are managers "buying" market share by lowering prices?) This pricing issue will have to be watched carefully by managers if they want to implement a differentiation strategy focusing on the high-end premium products in the market.

## VOLUME-ADJUSTED PROFIT PLAN

In the previous section, we examined the reasons for changes in operating profit due to the success or failure of the strategy in attracting customers, extracting value, and building market share. Having completed this analysis, we can now take the level of sales volume as given and move on to the next steps in strategic profitability analysis — analyzing the extent to which managers were able to operate the business efficiently.

### Calculating a Volume-Adjusted Profit Plan (or Flexible Budget)

To gain a full understanding of internal operating efficiencies and their effect on profit, it is necessary to recast the original profit plan to reflect the *actual volume* of sales. What we are trying to accomplish in this step is to set revised performance standards for internal efficiencies based on the realized level of production and sales. As discussed in Chapter 5, many of the profit plan estimates were based on forecasts of sales volume. To the extent that sales forecasts proved to be either too high or too low, managers must recalculate the profit plan standards so that variances can be computed accurately.

Exhibit 6–5 shows how this is done by inserting a new column for the *volume-adjusted profit plan* (or budget) between the original profit plan column and the actual profit column. The volume-adjusted profit plan is calculated by multiplying original estimates of sales-based cost variables (e.g., $159.50 of raw material for each chair or bench manufactured) by the *actual* sales volume (now 7,050 chairs and 3,350 benches instead of 7,000 chairs and 3,000 benches as estimated in the original profit plan) to yield a volume-adjusted estimate (in this example, $1,658,800). This new volume-adjusted profit plan is often called a *flexible budget.*

In our analysis of competitive effectiveness, we have already calculated variances due to market size, market share, sales price, and product mix that total $66,050 (F). This amount represents the difference between the original plan (column 1 of Exhibit 6–5) and the volume-adjusted profit plan (column 3). Now, the remaining profit variances due to internal operating efficiencies can be calculated. These are the variances between the volume-adjusted profit plan (column 3) and actual performance (column 5).

A quick look at the columns shows us that if managers had known a year ago that sales would actually be 7,050 chairs and 3,350 benches with lower selling prices, they

**EXHIBIT 6-5**
**Shade Tree Furniture**
**Calculation of Volume-Adjusted Profit Plan**

| | ORIGINAL PROFIT PLAN 20X1 | EFFECTIVENESS VARIANCES EXPLAINED | VOLUME-ADJUSTED PROFIT PLAN 20X1 | ADDITIONAL VARIANCE TO BE EXPLAINED | ACTUAL INCOME STATEMENT 20X1 |
|---|---|---|---|---|---|
| Sales | $4,300,000 | | $4,450,050 | | $4,450,050 |
| − Cost of goods sold | | | | | |
|    Raw materials | 1,595,000 | | 1,658,800 | $(27,872) | 1,686,672 |
|    Wages | 505,000 | | 525,200 | 10,504 | 514,696 |
|    Other manufacturing costs | 480,000 | | 480,000 | (10,650) | 490,650 |
| Gross margin | $1,720,000 | $66,050 | $1,786,050 | $(28,018) | $1,758,032 |
| Administrative and selling expenses | 505,000 | | 505,000 | $ 16,500 | 488,500 |
| Advertising expenses | 516,000 | | 516,000 | (4,700) | 520,700 |
| Interest expense | 64,000 | | 64,000 | (12,200) | 76,200 |
| Profit before taxes | $ 635,000 | $66,050 | $ 701,050 | $(28,418) | $ 672,632 |

would have budgeted a pretax profit of $701,050. Yet, actual profit was $672,632—$28,418 below revised expectations.

## OPERATING EFFICIENCIES: VARIABLE COSTS

Next, we analyze the business's ability to manage variable costs. This analysis is used primarily in manufacturing firms. In Chapter 5, we distinguished between *variable costs* and *nonvariable costs*. You will recall that variable costs are resources (inputs) that vary proportionally with the level of sales (output). In simple terms:

$$\text{Variable costs} = \text{Input volume} \times \text{Cost per unit of input}$$

$$= \text{Output volume} \times \frac{\text{Input volume}}{\text{Output volume}} \times \text{Cost per unit of input}$$

This last expression reveals that variable costs change with (1) output volume, (i.e., sales volume), (2) an efficiency ratio of inputs to outputs, and (3) the prices of input factors. We have already recalculated output volume to reflect actual sales in the previous step, so we need only calculate two additional variances at this point:

- changes in the use of inputs in relation to outputs (*efficiency variance*)
- changes in the unit cost of those inputs (*production spending variance*)

These two variances will reveal why actual variable costs differ from those reflected in the original profit plan: either the costs of inputs are higher or lower than expected, or the efficiency with which inputs were converted to outputs is different from the profit plan.

## Calculating Production Efficiency and Cost Variances (If Applicable)

Exhibit 6–6 gives us information on how changes in production efficiency and input prices affected the profit of Shade Tree Furniture.

First, let's analyze how well the manufacturing operation at Shade Tree Furniture utilized raw materials. As always, the reference point to analyze performance is managers' expectations as reflected in the profit plan. How much raw material did Shade Tree Furniture's managers expect to use to manufacture one piece of furniture? (We assume for simplicity that chairs and benches use the same amount of wood.)

Exhibit 6–6 tells us the answer. Managers expected to use 50 pounds of wood per piece of furniture at a cost of $3.19 per pound. The expected cost of raw material per chair or bench is $159.50. This expected cost is called the *standard cost of raw material.* This amount can be broken down into the *standard cost of wood* and the expected input/output relationship, or *standard efficiency.*

According to the assumptions that managers used to build the profit plan, the cost of materials required for each piece of furniture is $159.50. During 20X1, Shade Tree Furniture sold 10,400 pieces. Therefore, expected cost was 10,400 × $159.50 = $1,658,800 (you can check this number in the volume-adjusted profit plan, Exhibit 6–5). However, actual costs were $1,686,672. A variance of $27,872 must be explained.

### EXHIBIT 6–6
### Shade Tree Furniture
### Data to Analyze Manufacturing Performance

|  | ASSUMPTIONS REFLECTED IN 20X1 PROFIT PLAN | ACTUAL DATA FOR 20X1 |
|---|---|---|
| *Raw Material* | | |
| Efficiency input/output (pounds per piece of furniture) | 50.00 | 51.00 |
| Cost of one pound of wood | $ 3.19 | $ 3.18 |
| Cost of raw material per chair/bench | 50 × $3.19 = $159.50 | 51 × $3.18 = $162.18 |
| *Labor* | | |
| Efficiency input/output (hours per piece of furniture) | 5.00 | 4.90 |
| Wage per hour | $ 10.10 | $ 10.10 |
| Cost of labor per chair/bench | 5.00 × $10.10 = $ 50.50 | 4.90 × $10.10 = $ 49.49 |
| *Total Variable Cost* | $159.50 + $50.50 = $210.00 | $162.18 + $49.49 = $211.67 |

We can analyze the difference between actual performance and expectations using an *efficiency variance* and a *spending variance*. The formula for the **efficiency variance** is:

Efficiency variance = actual units of output
$\qquad\qquad$ × (planned volume of inputs per unit of output
$\qquad\qquad\qquad$ − actual volume of inputs per unit of output)
$\qquad\qquad$ × planned cost of one unit of input

Thus, the efficiency variance for raw materials at Shade Tree Furniture is:

Efficiency variance = actual number of pieces of furniture produced
$\qquad\qquad$ × (planned pounds of wood per piece
$\qquad\qquad\qquad$ − actual pounds of wood per piece)
$\qquad\qquad$ × planned cost of one pound of wood
$\qquad\qquad$ = 10,400 × (50 − 51) × \$3.19 = \underline{\$33,176} (U)

The manufacturing operation at Shade Tree Furniture used more wood per piece of furniture than expected. In other words, the operation was *less efficient* than expected. This underperformance is reflected in an unfavorable efficiency variance of \$33,176. Were product designs more complex to manufacture than expected? Were workers less skilled and, therefore, used more wood for each piece of furniture? Did workers use more wood to meet increasing production demand? Did they have to use more wood because the purchasing department ordered cheaper wood, which resulted in more rejected pieces? These questions need further exploration by managers to understand the reasons for the efficiency variance. Analyzing additional variances may help in answering these questions.

The actual cost of one pound of wood was \$3.18 instead of the planned \$3.19. How did this change affect profits? Calculation of a **spending variance** answers this question. The formula is:

Spending variance = actual units of output
$\qquad\qquad$ × actual volume of inputs per unit of output
$\qquad\qquad$ × (planned cost of one unit of input
$\qquad\qquad\qquad$ − actual cost of one unit of input)

For raw materials at Shade Tree Furniture we have:

Spending variance = actual number of pieces of furniture produced
$\qquad\qquad$ × actual pounds of wood per piece
$\qquad\qquad$ × (planned cost of one pound of wood
$\qquad\qquad\qquad$ − actual cost of one pound of wood)
$\qquad\qquad$ = 10,400 × 51 × (\$3.19 − 3.18) = \underline{\$5,304} (F)

It appears that the purchasing department was able to obtain wood at a somewhat lower cost than expected. However, was it because a lower quality wood was purchased?

Or were market prices for wood lower than planned? Managers can explore the potential reasons for this variance if it appears to be significant to understanding the internal efficiencies of the business.

Efficiency variance and spending variance together explain the difference between the volume-adjusted profit plan and the actual raw material expense as shown on Exhibit 6–5: \$33,176 (U) + \$5,304 (F) = \$27,872 (U).

We can apply the same tools to analyze the performance of Shade Tree's workers. The variance in wages to be explained is \$10,504 (Exhibit 6–5).

$$
\begin{aligned}
\text{Efficiency variance} = \ & \text{actual number of pieces of furniture produced} \\
& \times \text{(planned labor hours per piece} \\
& \quad - \text{actual labor hours per piece)} \\
& \times \text{planned wages per hour} \\
= \ & 10{,}400 \times (5.00 - 4.90) \times \$10.10 = \underline{\underline{\$10{,}504}} \ (\text{F})
\end{aligned}
$$

$$
\begin{aligned}
\text{Spending variance} = \ & \text{actual number of pieces of furniture produced} \\
& \times \text{actual labor hours per piece} \\
& \times \text{(planned wage per hour} \\
& \quad - \text{actual wage per hour)} \\
= \ & 10{,}400 \times 4.90 \times (\$10.10 - 10.10) = \underline{\underline{\$0}}
\end{aligned}
$$

The planned labor cost is called *standard labor cost.* This amount can be broken down into planned wages, or *standard wages,* and labor hours per piece of furniture, called *standard labor efficiency.*

The efficiency variance was favorable; whereas, actual wages were exactly as planned (i.e., standard wages equal to actual wages). We have now analyzed the "wages" variance of \$10,504 on Exhibit 6–5, indicating that Shade Tree Furniture workers produced more pieces per hour than expected (efficiency variance) and their wages were as expected (spending variance).

Production efficiency and cost variances are useful indicators to understand how efficiently any strategy was implemented. Revenue variances tell us about performance in the market, and spending and efficiency variances inform us about how well managers used the internal capabilities of the business.

Comparing this information with competitors can further enhance management's understanding of how they are using internal efficiencies as sources of advantage. This is especially important for businesses following a low-cost strategy. These businesses need lower input prices and/or higher efficiencies (achieved through process innovation, economies of scale, or economies of scope) than competitors. For such businesses, comparing efficiency costs against competitor benchmarks is critical. In some cases, companies have access to information on manufacturing efficiency through industry associations or independent **benchmarking** studies. When this information is not available, companies must rely on continuous improvement in profit plan indicators to ensure sustainable competitive efficiencies.

## OPERATING EFFICIENCIES: NONVARIABLE COSTS

For service companies like Boston Retail, the concept of efficiency variance is rarely used because there are no manufacturing costs that vary directly with outputs. This does not mean that service companies do not care about efficiency in their processes. On the contrary, the profitability of service companies often depends significantly on how efficiently they use their resources. However, the critical resources in service companies tend to be *nonvariable* costs. For these resources—in both manufacturing and service firms—we calculate spending variances.

### Calculating Variances for Nonvariable Costs

The formula for *spending variance* is simply:

$$\text{Spending variance} = (\text{Planned cost} - \text{Actual cost})$$

In Chapter 5, we identified three different types of nonvariable costs:

- committed (or engineered) costs
- discretionary expenses
- activity-based costs

We can apply spending variance analysis to each category.

### Committed Costs

Companies commit to certain expenses for long periods of time. For example, depreciation of a fixed asset is determined for the life of the asset. Similarly, long-term contracts fix lease expenses over several years. Because committed costs are fixed over long periods of time, there should not generally be any variance between expected and actual costs. However, unexpected events can sometimes cause a variation. For example, a long-term lease contract indexed to inflation will show a *spending variance* if actual inflation is different from expected inflation.

For Shade Tree Furniture, the original profit planned reflected $150,000 for the depreciation of machines. This amount was included in "other manufacturing costs" under cost of goods sold. The actual depreciation was $155,000 because an old machine unexpectedly broke down and was replaced by a new one with higher depreciation. The spending variance was:

$$= \$150,000 - \$155,000$$
$$= \underline{\$5,000} \text{ (U)}$$

### Discretionary Expenses

Discretionary expenses are also analyzed using spending variances to compare expected and actual levels of costs. Advertising expense is a discretionary cost because managers can adjust the level of advertising expense almost at will. Shade Tree Furniture planned to spend $516,000 on advertising, but the expense was $520,700. Using the spending variance formula, we can calculate the variance as

$$= \$516,000 - \$520,700$$
$$= \underline{\$4,700} \text{ (U) (Exhibit 6-5)}$$

Can we conclude that the company overspent in advertising? No. An unfavorable variance is not necessarily bad, because the additional advertising expense may have helped increase market share. As discussed in Chapter 3, managers of profit centers are responsible for making *trade-offs* to maximize profits. In certain circumstances, they may choose to increase spending if it will lead to higher profits.

### Activity-Based Costs

Finally, some types of indirect resources are used in ways that vary with cost-driver activities other than manufacturing outputs. For example, if the quality control department checks the first 10 items of each new batch, then quality control expense will vary with the number of batches. Similarly, warehousing costs may vary with the number of shipping orders, or selling costs may vary with the number of customers or customer segments.

Traditionally, management accounting systems have interpreted these expenses as "fixed" and calculated only *spending variances.* However, recent developments in activity-based costing allow a more revealing analysis. In particular, we can now obtain *volume, efficiency,* and *spending variance* information about activity-based costs. The following example illustrates the analysis.

To maintain its premium prices, Shade Tree Furniture Company has a Quality Control Department to ensure that the furniture is of premium quality. For each batch of furniture, the quality department checks a sample to see if the batch meets its high quality standards. If the sample passes the control check then the batch is shipped, but if it fails the quality control check, then the whole batch is sent back for inspection and rework. For 20X1, the budget for the department was $120,000 (included in "other manufacturing costs"). Half of this amount was salaries and other committed costs; the other half was supplies used to perform the quality control tests. Exhibit 6–7 compares expected and actual performance.

For activity-based costs, we can estimate three variances that you should recognize as similar to previous calculations:

- impact on profits due to changes in cost-driver activity (i.e., number of batches)
- impact on profits due to changes in efficiency
- impact on profits due to changes in cost of resources

---

### EXHIBIT 6–7
### Shade Tree Furniture
### Data to Analyze the Performance of the Quality Control Department

|  | ASSUMPTIONS REFLECTED IN 20X1 PROFIT PLAN | ACTUAL DATA FOR 20X1 |
|---|---|---|
| Number of batches | 500 | 490 |
| Amount of supplies per batch (liters) | 1.50 | 1.40 |
| Cost per one liter of supplies | $ 80.00 | $ 80.50 |
| Total cost of supplies | $60,000 | $55,223 |

The quality department planned to use $60,000 in supplies but it actually spent $55,223. Again, we can use variances to get more detail on how the quality department was able to "save" $4,777. The first variance that we compute is due to volume effects. The cost driver for the quality control process is the number of batches.

$$\text{Volume variance} = (\text{planned number of batches} - \text{actual number of batches})$$
$$\times \text{planned liters of supplies per batch}$$
$$\times \text{planned cost of one liter of supplies}$$
$$= (500 - 490) \times 1.50 \times \$80 = \underline{\$1,200} \text{ (F)}$$

Part of the difference between planned and actual costs comes from a lower number of batches. If the quality department processed 10 batches less than expected, then we should expect cost savings of $1,200.

The quality department also used fewer liters of supplies per batch than planned (1.40 liters versus 1.50 liters). The impact of this difference upon profits is an efficiency variance:

$$\text{Efficiency variance} = \text{actual number of batches}$$
$$\times (\text{planned liters of supplies per batch}$$
$$- \text{actual liters of supplies per batch})$$
$$\times \text{planned cost of one liter of supplies}$$
$$= 490 \times (1.50 - 1.40) \times \$80 = \underline{\$3,920} \text{ (F)}$$

Finally, the quality department paid a higher price for supplies than expected. This difference created a spending variance:

$$\text{Spending variance} = \text{actual number of batches}$$
$$\times \text{actual liters of supplies per batch}$$
$$\times (\text{planned cost of one unit of supplies}$$
$$- \text{actual cost of one unit of supplies})$$
$$= 490 \times 1.40 \times (\$80.00 - \$80.50) = \underline{\$343} \text{ (U)}$$

The difference in activity-based costs between planned and actual performance in the quality department is explained by:

| | | | |
|---|---|---|---|
| Volume variance | $1,200 | (F) | |
| Efficiency variance | 3,920 | (F) | |
| Spending variance | 343 | (U) | |
| Total | $4,777 | (F) | ($60,000 − $55,223 on Exhibit 6–7) |

These variances allow managers to evaluate and perhaps further investigate the performance of the quality department. Managers may judge the efficiency variance to be somewhat high. Did quality people find a way to save on supplies to perform quality control procedures? Did savings jeopardize the quality of Shade Tree Furniture products?

## SUMMARY OF OPERATING EFFICIENCY VARIANCES

To summarize, then, we have computed the following variances related to operating efficiencies:

| | | | |
|---|---|---|---|
| Raw materials | Efficiency variance | $33,176 | (U) |
| | Spending variance | 5,304 | (F) |
| Total variance for raw material | | $27,872 | (U) |
| Labor | Efficiency variance | 10,504 | (F) |
| | Spending variance | 0 | |
| Total variance for labor | | $10,504 | (F) |
| Other manufacturing costs | | | |
| Quality department | Volume variance | 1,200 | (F) |
| | Efficiency variance | 3,920 | (F) |
| | Spending variance | 343 | (U) |
| Other manufacturing costs | Spending variance | 15,427 | (U) |
| Total variance other manufacturing costs | | $10,650 | (U) |
| S&A expenses | Spending variance | 16,500 | (F) |
| Advertising expenses | Spending variance | 4,700 | (U) |
| Interest expense | Spending variance | 12,200 | (U) |
| Total variance for nonproduction costs | | $    400 | (U) |
| Total Operating Efficiency Variances | | $28,418 | (U) |

The objective of analyzing operating efficiency variances was to explain the difference between the volume-adjusted profit plan and the actual income statement (Exhibit 6–5). At this point, we know that the difference of $27,872 in raw materials is mainly due to the operation using more wood per piece of furniture than expected ($33,176). We also know that the savings of $10,504 in wages is related to higher productivity and not to changes in wages. The additional cost of $10,650 identified in other manufacturing costs (Exhibit 6–5) is driven by a spending variance of $15,427. Finally, the changes in administrative, selling, advertising, and interest expenses are described as spending variances.

The picture that emerges from this analysis is mixed. The efficiency in using the raw materials was much lower than expected and this reduced profit by $33,176. If this lower efficiency is due to using cheaper raw material (observe the favorable spending variance for raw material), the decision to use such material reduced efficiency more than it saved in raw material costs. Labor wages were lower than expected and people worked more efficiently than planned. Advertising expense was higher than expected; however, sales were also higher and, if any relationship exists between these two numbers, then the extra advertising was worth it.

## INTERPRETING STRATEGIC PROFITABILITY VARIANCES

The analysis of profit performance due to competitive effectiveness and operating efficiencies is now complete. We can summarize the analysis in Exhibit 6–8.

We can see in Exhibit 6–8 that the sum of the variances is exactly the difference between the original profit plan and the actual performance. This is not an accident. In our review of effectiveness and efficiency variances, we systematically examined each of the profit plan assumptions in sequence. This is illustrated in Table 6–1. The left column lists all the variables that were estimated for the original profit plan: market size, market share, selling price, average contribution, input quantities, input prices, and nonvariable costs. Listed across the top of each column are the seven variances that can be computed by comparing the original profit plan with the actual profit as reported on the income statement. Four of these variances are the competitive effectiveness variances, which explain the difference between the original profit plan and the volume-adjusted profit plan. The remaining three variances are the operating efficiency variances, which explain differences between the volume-adjusted profit plan and actual performance.

As we worked across Table 6–1 from left to right and calculated the seven variances identified at the top of each column, we "flipped" one profit plan variable at a time, turning an assumption in the original profit plan from "plan" to "actual." By comparing the difference between plan and actual for that one variable—and holding all other variables constant—we were able to isolate the variance effects. Thus, for example, the market share variance is based on the change in market share (*plan versus*

**TABLE 6–1** Strategic Profitability Analysis "Switches"

| ASSUMPTION IN ORIGINAL PROFIT PLAN | *ORIGINAL PROFIT PLAN* | COMPETITIVE EFFECTIVE VARIANCES | | | |
|---|---|---|---|---|---|
| | | MARKET SIZE | MARKET SHARE | SALES PRICE | PRODUCT MIX |
| Market Size | **Plan vs. Actual** | | Actual | Actual | Actual |
| Market Share | Plan | **Plan vs. Actual** | | Actual | Actual |
| Selling Price | Plan | Plan | **Plan vs. Actual** | | Actual |
| Average Contribution | Plan | Plan | Plan | **Plan vs. Actual** | |
| Input Quantities | Plan | Plan | Plan | Plan | Plan |
| Input Prices | Plan | Plan | Plan | Plan | Plan |
| Nonvariable Costs | Plan | Plan | Plan | Plan | Plan |

**How to use this table:**

The top row indicates the different variances that can be estimated. For example, "market size" is a competitive effectiveness variance, whereas "production efficiency" variance is an operating efficiency variance. The left column lists assumptions in the original profit plan that can adopt two different values (like a "switch"): plan or actual. Changing the "switches" sequentially gives the different variances.

To calculate a variance, choose the variance of interest from the top row and read down the column. The variance calculation focuses on the difference between "plan and actual" for one specific

**EXHIBIT 6–8**
**Shade Tree Furniture**
**Strategic Profitability Analysis**

| | | |
|---|---:|---|
| Expected profit before taxes | $635,000 | |
| Competitive Effectiveness Variances due to: | | |
| Change in market size | 32,196 | (F) |
| Change in market share | 55,804 | (F) |
| Change in price | (44,950) | (U) |
| Change in product mix | 23,000 | (F) |
| Total competitive effectiveness | 66,050 | (F) |
| Expected profit before taxes (volume-adjusted) | $701,050 | |
| Operating Efficiency Variances due to: | | |
| Efficiency in raw materials | (33,176) | (U) |
| Spending in raw materials | 5,304 | (F) |
| Efficiency in wages | 10,504 | (F) |
| Spending in wages | — | (U) |
| Other manufacturing expenses | (10,650) | (U) |
| Administrative and selling expenses | 16,500 | (F) |
| Advertising expense | (4,700) | (U) |
| Interest expense | (12,200) | (U) |
| Total operating efficiencies | (28,418) | (U) |
| Actual profit before taxes | $672,632 | |

| | OPERATING EFFICIENCY VARIANCES | | | |
|:---:|:---:|:---:|:---:|:---:|
| VOLUME ADJUSTED PROFIT PLAN | PRODUCTION EFFICIENCY | PRODUCTION SPENDING | NONVARIABLE SPENDING | ACTUAL INCOME STATEMENT |
| Actual | Actual | Actual | Actual | Actual |
| Actual | Actual | Actual | Actual | Actual |
| Actual | Actual | Actual | Actual | Actual |
| Actual | Actual | Actual | Actual | Actual |
| **Plan vs. Actual** | | Actual | Actual | Actual |
| Plan | **Plan vs. Actual** | | Actual | Actual |
| Plan | Plan | **Plan vs. Actual** | | Actual |

profit plan assumption and sets all other variables in the formula at either actual or plan according to the values shown in the table. For example, the product mix variance calculates the difference between planned contribution margin and actual contribution margin, while setting market size, market share, and selling price to "actual," and holding input quantities, input prices, and nonvariable costs at their "planned" values.

*actual*) times *actual* market size and *planned* contribution (i.e., selling price, average contribution, input quantities, input prices, and nonvariable costs all held at profit plan estimates). The next variance—sales price—holds market size and share at *actual* and computes the difference between actual and expected selling price (i.e., *plan vs. actual*); again, contribution margin and other variables on the profit plan are maintained at the *plan* values to isolate the effect.

One by one, we systematically covered all the variances, moving from the original profit plan in the left column—where all variables were estimates and/or standards (identified as "plan" in Table 6–1)—to the actual income statement at the far right of the table, where all variables reflect actual performance outcomes.[4]

## Searching for Explanations and Initiating Action Plans

Variances in themselves do little to explain the reasons why performance was above or below expectations. Knowing that input prices fell, or that market share increased, is only the first step. We still do not know why. Managers must investigate the reasons for these changes and initiate actions to either rectify problems or take advantage of unforeseen opportunities. We have identified some of the possible causes earlier, but we can recap as follows:

Shade Tree Furniture's profits before income tax during 20X1 were $37,632 better than planned. The company was favored by a larger market and a higher market share, but it suffered a "cost" of $44,950 from reducing its prices. Did the company capture market share by reducing prices and putting its premium image at risk? The company sold a higher portion of benches, which have a bigger margin. Was this shift a one-time event in 20X1, or does it indicate a change in customers' tastes? The most significant variance on our analysis of operational efficiencies is an unfavorable $33,176 in raw material efficiency. Did the increase in sales volume affect production, or did the company hire low-skilled people to save on labor costs? Finally, administrative and selling expenses had a favorable variance. Was it caused by lower prices, or did the company manage its administrative systems differently?

## USING STRATEGIC PROFITABILITY ANALYSIS

Managers formally compare actual performance to profit plan performance at least once a year and typically more often (e.g., monthly or quarterly). Effective managers *manage by exception.* In other words, they devote their scarce attention to understanding and acting upon variances that could imperil the strategy. Measures that are aligned with expectations receive little attention. By focusing on large or strategic variances, managers can quickly focus their attention on those issues that require follow-up action. Thus, strategic profitability analysis is an extremely important tool to increase ROM.

---

[4] John Shank and Neil Churchill introduced the genesis of this approach in their article "Variance Analysis: A Management-Oriented Approach," *The Accounting Review* 5 (1977): 950–57.

Managers use strategic profitability analyses for three purposes: strategic learning, early warning, and performance evaluation.

## Strategic Learning

Variance analysis helps managers ask the right questions and calculate the costs or benefits of deviations from the norm. What was the effect on profits of higher input costs? What was the effect of a larger market share? Large deviations attract managers' attention.

The comparison between expected and actual performance leads managers to review:

- assumptions and standards
- cause-and-effect relationships
- the validity of intended strategy
- the effectiveness and efficiency of strategy implementation

Of course, the strategy of any particular business will influence which strategic profitability variances managers monitor. By way of example, Table 6–2 summarizes possible choices for two competing strategies: differentiation and low cost.

Managers of businesses following a *differentiation* strategy, based on high value-added products or services, will ensure that price variances and mix variances are being computed routinely and monitored carefully; these are key measures of strategic effectiveness for their businesses. By contrast, managers of firms competing by *low price* and high volume must ensure that they have accurate data to routinely calculate market share, internal efficiencies, and input prices. Regardless of strategy, all firms in competitive markets must monitor their discretionary spending habits (spending variances) and ensure that they are accurately informed about changes in the size of the market in which they are competing.

Strategy evolves as managers learn from their actions and incorporate new information revealed by analysis and follow-up. Variance analysis facilitates this learning process.

**TABLE 6–2** Strategic Profitability Variances for Two Competing Strategies

|  | MARKET SIZE | MARKET SHARE | SALES PRICE | SALES MIX | PRODUCTION EFFICIENCY | PRODUCTION SPENDING | DISCRETIONARY SPENDING |
|---|---|---|---|---|---|---|---|
| Differentiation Strategy | ✓ | ✓ | ✓ | ✓ | ❷ | ❷ | ❷ |
| Low-Cost, High-Volume Strategy | ✓ | ✓ | ❷ | ❷ | ✓ | ✓ | ❷ |

✓ = Primary strategic importance
❷ = Important, but not strategic (i.e., unlikely to cause strategy to fail)

---

### Profit Planning in Magazine Production

In magazine production, advertising sales and revenue from reader subscriptions are the two major sources of profit. However, because so much production work is out-sourced (e.g., prepress and printing), managing vendor costs is essential. In the 1980s, a midsized magazine publisher was losing money with 58 cents of every revenue dollar spent on manufacturing and distribution. Due to high indebtedness, the company was also cash-constrained.

To get a better understanding of the drivers of profitability, the publisher introduced a continual profit planning process that integrated financial income projections prepared by the advertising and circulation departments with cost budgets from manufacturing. For the first time, the manufacturing department based their budgets on layout and itemized vendor costs for a typical issue (e.g., number of pages, black and white versus color, editorial versus advertising content, and type of paper). Subsequent variance analysis between the budgets and actual profits revealed some important gaps.

The key problem was in advertising: Managers lacked a realistic sense of costs and revenues in making projections. The official advertising rates were set too low to generate profits; to make matters worse, advertising representatives were selling space in the magazine by discounting rates even further. Furthermore, production vendors essentially dictated their terms with the magazine. With these insights, new practices were introduced. The work supplied by vendors was opened to competitive bidding. Advertising rates were raised, causing advertisers to buy more-valuable ad space. Finally, changing the layout of the magazine with cost requirements in mind lowered the ratio of manufacturing costs to net revenues from 58% to 35%.

---

*Source:* Adapted from Bert Langford, "Take the Guesswork Out of Budgeting," *Folio: The Magazine for Magazine Management* (Special Sourcebook Issue for 1998 Supplement): 172.

---

## Early Warning and Corrective Action

Strategic profitability analysis also warns managers about possible events that may derail intended strategy. Remember how many interdependencies existed among the variables on the profit wheel, cash wheel, and ROE wheel in Chapter 5? If one of those variables fails, it could mean a major threat to the company.

Unforeseen events continually affect any company. Without an early warning system, unexpected events may only be noticed when major consequences are unavoidable. Comparing the profit plan with ongoing performance facilitates early diagnosis of the potential consequences of these unforeseen events. If a particular item deviates from the value in the profit plan, managers can take actions to bring the indicator back on track. Managers can react early to avoid unpleasant "surprises." However, not all surprises are bad. Sometimes, early warning systems allow managers to take advantage of new opportunities in the market.

## Performance Evaluation

Profit plans can also be used for performance evaluation. The comparison between expected and actual performance serves to inform managers about the effort that subordinates have put into achieving the goals described in the profit plan. Setting objectives and evaluating performance against objectives motivates people to put substantial effort into achieving the strategy of the organization. (We will cover this topic in depth in Chapter 11.)

For effective evaluation, managers must use strategic profitability analysis to get a true picture of the reasons for performance. Shade Tree's sales of $4,450,050 exceeded the profit plan estimate of $4,300,000 by a comfortable margin. Our initial reaction might be to praise the efforts of the sales manager and give him a positive performance evaluation. However, as we gather more information from our strategic profitability variances, we may temper or change our initial opinion. For example, as we saw earlier, sales have been favorably affected by growth in the overall market and possibly by favorable moves by competitors.

---

### Strategic Profitability Analysis in the Banking Industry

A recent survey by the Bank Administration Institute showed that banks are struggling to keep pace with emerging needs for tactical and strategic performance information. As a result, they are spending substantial sums (on average $150,000 per $1 billion of assets) to replace or enhance aging information management systems.

The need for new performance measurement and analysis systems reflects the historic shift away from line-of-business management structures based on distinct legal entities (designed to meet banking regulations). Although many banks are executing new strategies that target specific customers and segments, fewer than one in 10 survey respondents generate either full or partial profitability analyses focusing on individual customers or customer segments. Similarly, only 25% of respondents generate product profitability reports.

An aging information systems infrastructure is at the root of the banks' problems. More than 60% of respondents said that their system platforms were more than five years old. Most older financial systems are based on traditional general ledger systems and cannot handle the complicated allocation algorithms and reports required for multidimensional performance analysis. Providing product and customer-segment profitability with these older systems is often next to impossible. Further complicating the picture is the lack of integration among the various components of each banks' performance management systems: general ledger, cost allocation system, funds-transfer pricing system, a reporting system, and a planning/budgeting system.

To address these challenges, banks are investing in new systems. One-third of survey respondents reported that significant new performance-measurement-systems enhancements were underway, with outlays averaging $2 million per bank.

---

*Source:* Adapted from Craig I. Coit and John Karr, "Performance Measurement: Miles Traveled, Miles to Go," *Banking Strategies* 72 (September/October 1996): 68–70.

## CHAPTER SUMMARY

The discussion in this chapter has focused solely on evaluation of performance using financial accounting data. This is appropriate for our analysis of profit plan performance. However, we need to be careful not to forget the importance of intangible resources and nonfinancial measures. These will be covered in depth in later chapters.

The design of a profit plan is the first step in enabling managers to translate their strategy into action. During this process, managers are forced to make assumptions about the viability of the strategy and agree upon its details. Cause-and-effect relationships are hypothesized and strategies are communicated.

Successful strategy implementation requires managers to test their profit plan assumptions to validate strategy. The strategic profitability analysis tools described in this chapter provide that framework. Variance computations allow managers to understand the effectiveness and efficiency of strategy implementation.

Managers use strategic profitability analysis for three purposes:

- Strategic learning—Strategic profitability analysis allows managers to evaluate the adequacy of the intended strategy of the organization and the cause-effect assumptions that underlie the strategy.
- Early warning and corrective action—Analysis of strategic profitability gives managers either assurance that the strategy is on track or, alternatively, early warning that implementation is not proceeding according to plan.
- Performance evaluation—Strategic profitability analysis gives managers the tools to evaluate the success of individual managers in implementing strategy and the success of business units in creating value.

With strategic profitability data in hand, managers can redesign organizational processes or change the standards—even the strategy—to take advantage of changing developments in competitive markets and internal operations. Like all good performance measurement and control system tools, strategic profitability analysis should be used to enhance ROM. Techniques for using this information to enhance management effectiveness is the topic of Part III of this book.

# C H A P T E R

## 7

# Designing Asset Allocation Systems

I n previous chapters, we referred to the importance of developing a coherent plan for the acquisition and allocation of resources to support strategies underlying the profit plan. Procedures must be created to analyze and determine the appropriate level of investment in productive resources needed to support desired strategies.

We defined an asset in Chapter 2 as *a resource, owned or controlled by the business, that will yield future economic benefits.* At this point in our analysis, it is important to emphasize two aspects of this definition. First, managers must make a *decision* to acquire an asset. The right to own or control something of value is gained only for a price. Managers must make a conscious decision to acquire inventory, finance sales with a note receivable, prepay office rent, invest in research to develop a new drug, or acquire a new production machine. Each of these choices to create an asset requires the expenditure of working capital.

Second, the benefits from owning an asset—its value—are realized in the *future:* Inventory will be turned into cash in three months time, a note receivable will be collected in one year, prepaid rent will allow the future use of office space, a new drug will generate sales over the next 15 years, and a new machine will produce products over its 20-year useful life. In all these cases, expending resources today to build up or acquire an asset yields future benefits to the firm.

Two implications flow from this analysis. First, managers need a set of tools to help them decide when it makes sense to commit current resources to acquire assets (and when it does not). Second, these tools must incorporate estimates of the future economic value that an asset can provide and the degree to which future benefits support business strategies. These tools and analyses are the subject of this chapter.

## ASSET ALLOCATION SYSTEMS

The impetus for acquiring new resources can come from many sources. For example, accounting or production data may suggest that cost, quality, or capacity shortfalls require investment in new assets. Emerging new technologies or markets may stimulate investigation of the benefits of acquiring additional productive assets to support new strategic initiatives. Table 7–1 illustrates some of the types of information that may cause managers to consider upgrading existing assets or investing in new assets. Managers in accounting, marketing, production, engineering, or division management may

**TABLE 7–1**  Sources and Types of Information That Stimulate Requests for Allocation of Assets

| INFORMATION ABOUT | DISCREPANCY | EVIDENCE | SOURCE |
|---|---|---|---|
| Costs | too high | input costs have risen | accounting data |
| | | prices have fallen | marketing |
| | may be lowered | analytic study or model | production or engineering |
| Quality | inadequate | competitive improvement | marketing |
| | | customer need | marketing |
| | | prices have fallen | marketing |
| | may be improved | analytic study or model | engineering |
| Capacity | insufficient | sales > capacity | marketing |
| | | forecast > capacity | marketing |
| | | planned new-product introduction | engineering development marketing division management |

*Source:* Adapted from J. Bower, *Managing the Resource Allocation Process* (Boston: HBS Press, 1996; originally published 1970): 53.

obtain this information from customers, accounting data, analytic models, or production plans.

In small businesses, these types of information will be gathered and processed informally. As businesses grow larger, however, formal systems become critical in identifying the need for new assets and in helping managers decide how to allocate scarce financial resources. An **asset allocation system** is the set of formal routines and procedures designed to process and evaluate requests to acquire new assets. It is sometimes known as a **capital budget** or *capital investment plan.* These systems, like the profit plans to which they are linked, typically work on a calendar cycle—that is, formal proposals for asset acquisitions are created once a year. The timing of this process is designed to ensure that proposals are formally evaluated and approved prior to actually committing to spend any money.

Asset allocation systems provide a number of benefits. First, they provide a *framework* and set of categories into which asset proposals can be grouped. We can think of this framework as a set of buckets lined up according to defined categories. Sorting asset acquisition proposals into different buckets forces managers to be explicit about the type of value that they expect each asset to provide and the economic viability of the proposal. For example, the decision to install a new multimillion-dollar paper making machine would be put in a different category or bucket than the decision to replace the aging sprinkler system in a warehouse.

Second, asset allocation systems include *analytic tools* that can be tailored to different types of assets. The analysis of the net benefits of a sprinkler system is different than the analysis of the net benefits of a paper making machine. With proposals sorted into the correct bucket, decision makers can apply different decision tools to each category.

Finally, and most importantly, asset allocation systems provide *guidelines* that help managers throughout the organization understand how their proposals relate to the strategy of the business. Acquiring assets often involves the analysis and judgment of several, if not many, people. These systems can be used to communicate what types of assets are needed (and not needed) to support new and ongoing strategic initiatives.

The decision to allocate assets to a business can be extremely consequential. For example, a decision to build a plant in a new country, change core production technologies, or acquire a new distribution system can commit a business to a course of action for many years. Acquiring any asset involves choice, and future options may become more limited after choices are made.

Because of the sometimes large sums of money involved, and the often irrevocable commitments, there are few other decisions in organizations in which decision making authority is so carefully prescribed. Businesses invariably impose limits on the discretion of any individual manager to authorize or commit to the acquisition of assets. These limits are a function of span of accountability and position in the organizational hierarchy. The former affects the *type of assets* for which the manager has authority to commit; the latter affects the *amount of money* that a manager can commit.

Unlike double-entry bookkeeping systems, asset allocation systems are not designed according to generally accepted rules of practice. There are no GAAP (generally accepted accounting principles) for the design of asset allocation systems. Instead, managers must tailor these systems to their preferences, based on their performance measurement and control needs. Nevertheless, there are generalizable design principles that can serve as guidelines for any manager as he or she attempts to design systems to guide in the acquisition and allocation of assets.

## Limits on Asset Allocations

Given the variety and unpredictability of requests for new assets, senior managers must provide some type of guidance to subordinates about what kind of assets to acquire. In practice, however, it makes little sense to specify in detail the types of assets that are desirable. In a large business, senior managers cannot know when machines should be replaced or when new technology indicates the need to upgrade equipment. There is too much that is unknown to senior managers, especially as unanticipated problems and opportunities emerge. Because senior managers can never possess the amount of specific knowledge that is known by lower-level managers, information about the need for new assets is typically gathered and created at lower organizational levels.

Therefore, rather than specifying in detail the types of assets that are desirable, senior managers typically specify limits on the types of capital expenditures that will be approved. Within these boundaries, managers are then free to exercise their initiative and judgment concerning the types of assets that they would like to acquire to achieve

---

### Investment Strategy at Coke and Pepsi

Roberto Goizueta, the legendary CEO of Coca-Cola Company, left work at 4:30 most afternoons to spend time with his family. Yet, Coke's market value grew from $4.3 billion when he took over in 1981 to $180 billion by 1997. How did he do it? Goizueta delegated day-to-day management of most details of the business, except for resource allocation. Roberto Goizueta understood that resources had to be allocated to those investments that would enhance shareholder value, and he spent a good deal of his time evaluating how best to deploy Coca-Cola's assets.

During Goizueta's tenure, Coke invested heavily in soft drink infrastructure and brand building. The company divested the capital-intensive and low-return bottling operations into Coca-Cola Enterprises, which allowed Coke to remove these assets from its balance sheet while still retaining nominal control of these strategic assets through its 49% ownership of the company. Contrast Goizueta's investment strategy with PepsiCo, which continued to invest in its restaurant franchises (Kentucky Fried Chicken, Taco Bell, and Pizza Hut) and snack food businesses. In 1997 and 1998, Pepsi decided to embrace some of Coke's investment strategies. It spun off its capital-intensive and low-margin restaurant businesses and announced plans to do the same with its bottling operations.

*Sources:* Adapted from John Huey, "In Search of Roberto's Secret Formula," *Fortune,* December 29, 1997, 230–234, and Patricia Sellers, "How Coke is Kicking Pepsi's Can," *Fortune,* October 28, 1996, 70–84.

---

their business goals. Asset allocation constraints are especially important for expenditures that are large in magnitude or that relate to the strategic priorities of the business.

To create these boundaries, senior managers communicate limits on the type of assets that are suitable for potential acquisition. Senior managers do so by specifying *minimum constraints* that must be considered when proposing assets for potential acquisition. For example, a common means of specifying financial limits for potential new assets is to stipulate the *minimum* ROI that is acceptable. Asset allocation guidelines may stipulate that new asset proposals will not be considered unless they can generate *at least* 18% ROI. This guideline is not designed to tell managers what types of assets to acquire; instead, it tells them what types of assets should not be acquired—those earning less than 18% ROI.

## Policies and Procedures

Understanding how to use asset allocation systems is important, both for those submitting proposals to acquire assets and for those responsible for approving proposals. Individuals making proposals must present information to communicate the need for the asset they wish to purchase. Resources are inevitably scarce, and each proposal will be competing against others for scarce funding resources. Thus, managers proposing to acquire specific assets must attempt to make the best possible case in support of their proposal.

Those responsible for ratifying asset acquisition proposals and allocating funding must also have a set of tools that will help them choose among competing alternatives. Some proposals should be accepted, but others must be rejected because of constraints in either capital or management attention. All proposals, whether good or bad, will have proponents—or champions—who may argue vigorously for the need to expend resources to support important initiatives. Good analysis is the key to responding to these requests in a way that reflects the intended strategy of the business.

Therefore, asset allocation procedures should specify a process by which proposals are evaluated and approved. These procedures typically set out:

1. the *analyses* needed to document a request,
2. the *process* by which proposals will be gathered together and reviewed by top managers, and
3. a *time frame* each year during which managers will consider formal requests for new assets. This time frame should dovetail with the approval of the profit plan to ensure that adequate resources will be available to support strategic initiatives. (See the "Investment in Assets" variable in the profit wheel diagram of Chapter 5.)

### Span of Accountability

Senior managers should communicate policies regarding who has authority to approve the acquisition of assets. As mentioned above, the ability of a manager to acquire assets is directly related to his or her span of accountability. Managers with narrow spans of accountability—such as cost center or functional managers—are usually accountable for managing to a cost budget. Their performance measures do not typically encompass balance sheet assets (e.g., ROA or ROCE). Because cost center managers are not accountable for balance sheet assets, they are not given the authority to unilaterally acquire assets for their functional units without the approval of higher-level managers. For example, a cost center manager in charge of a function such as information technology is held accountable for delivering a specified level of information service utilizing a fixed level of resources. The chief information officer (CIO) is given a spending budget and held accountable for providing a satisfactory level of networked information services within those resources. Requests to purchase additional servers and network equipment to enhance this service must be approved higher in the organization by a manager with a wider span of accountability.

By contrast, business managers with wide spans of accountability will have relatively wide latitude and authority to acquire assets. Business unit managers are accountable for profit performance and, often, for managing the level of balance sheet assets to deliver that profit. Their performance measures can (and should) encompass balance sheet accounts such as working capital and ROCE. Therefore, profit center managers are often given the right—subject to defined spending limits—to acquire and dispose of assets to achieve these objectives.

### Spending Limits

Spending limits, defined according to managerial position and span of accountability, are a common way of limiting discretion. When asset acquisition proposals fall outside a manager's spending limit and/or span of accountability, those proposals must be sent higher in the organization for approval. Thus, asset allocation spending limits may take some variation of the following form based on hierarchical position:

---

### Asset Allocation Authority at SKF

SKF Ab, headquartered in Gothenburg, Sweden, is the world's largest manufacturer of industrial rolling bearings, accounting for a fifth of the $20 billion world market. Its production is organized worldwide, although 65% of its manufacturing still comes from western Europe. To reduce this imbalance, the group is investing $629 million in new plants in growth markets such as the United States, Poland, India, Malaysia and South Korea, as well as five joint ventures in China.

SKF's asset allocation structure has been designed to balance central control and local decision-making. Most capital investment decisions within existing country markets, such as plant extensions, require only the approval of the country manager and do not need to be referred to the financial director in Sweden. Within each local subsidiary, however, the project's economic value must be proven using standard cash flow and payback measures.

SKF's treasury function supports line management's decisions by providing access to capital for investments in specific geographical territories. Treasurers are located regionally, except for areas of high currency volatility (e.g., Asia and South America), which have been recentralized to the group treasury at the Swedish headquarters.

*Source:* Adapted from Tim Burt, "Own Words: Tore Bertilsson, SKF," *Financial Times,* November 5, 1997, and Peter Marsh, "Change of Culture at SKF," *Financial Times,* August 25, 1997, 17.

---

| Hierarchical Position | Authority to Commit to Asset Acquisitions |
|---|---|
| Board of Directors | All asset acquisitions above $1 million must be approved by the Board |
| President and CEO | up to $1 million |
| Executive vice president | up to $500,000 |
| Business unit president | up to $200,000 |
| Functional vice president | up to $50,000 |

Under this type of spending limit rule, approval for increasingly large asset commitments is referred higher in the organization to those with wider spans of accountability. This decision rule ensures that all large, consequential, asset acquisition decisions are reviewed at senior-executive levels to ensure that they align with top management's strategy and do not commit the business to courses of action that are inappropriate or too risky.

Another approach, which often complements spending limits, stipulates different approval paths depending on the strategic implications of the investment. Under this approach, top managers define (1) asset investment categories into which proposals must be sorted and (2) a separate approval process for each category of investment. Usually, approval of strategic investments is reserved for top management; approval of investments to enhance existing operations is delegated to lower-level managers. We consider this approach next.

## SORTING ASSETS BY CATEGORY

Consider the diversity of asset and capital expenditures that might be considered in any business: the purchase of new machinery, the renewal of existing computer equipment, the redesign and remodeling of a distribution facility, and the installation of a new telephone network. Managers responsible for allocating resources need some way to make sense of this diversity.

Managers must have a consistent way of categorizing projects so that the correct analytic tools and decision criteria can be applied to each bucket. Different businesses will create different classification schemes to meet their unique circumstances. The appropriate categories will be determined by the industry in which a firm competes and the types of technology that it employs. For example, the classification criteria will be different in a knowledge-intensive software developer as compared with a capital-intensive steel mill. In most businesses, however, the projects and/or initiatives fall into three general classes, each of which has different criteria for evaluation:

*(1) Assets to Meet Safety/Health/Regulatory Needs*   The acquisition of certain assets is necessary to protect the safety and health of employees, or to protect the local environment. Others are necessary to comply with new local, state, and federal regulations. These expenditures are either mandated by law or necessary to protect health and safety, so a formal cost/benefit justification is not required. These expenditures cannot be deferred or rejected—they are an unavoidable cost of doing business. Therefore, for this category of assets, analysis will focus on the most cost-effective way to comply with health, safety, or regulatory needs.

*(2) Assets to Enhance Operating Efficiency and/or Increase Revenue*   To compete successfully over time, production and information processing capacity must be maintained and overhauled, resulting in expenditures for replacement software and machinery, and the renewal and repair of existing capacity. Sometimes, new assets based on superior technologies can be acquired to reduce cost and/or improve reliability and quality (e.g., construction of a new state-of-the art manufacturing line). These types of expenditures are necessary to maintain efficient productive capacity but can often be deferred for limited periods if managers so choose.

Incremental investments in production, distribution, and internal processing capabilities may also offer the promise of increased revenue. For example, removing production bottlenecks in a manufacturing plant may allow the business to ship more product to meet excess demand. In a bank, faster turnaround of loan applications may allow more loans to be booked each quarter. Specialized techniques for economic analysis must be applied to this category of assets.

*(3) Assets to Enhance Competitive Effectiveness*   Certain assets must be acquired, or capital expenditures made, to fund the strategy of the business. For these assets, project proposals must be compared with strategic goals to determine how important each asset is to meeting the strategic imperatives of the business. These assets might include, for example, acquiring a new distribution network or constructing a new plant in a country where the business does not have any manufacturing capability. Also included in this category are ventures and acquisitions that take the business into new product markets.

Because of their strategic impact and substantial cost, these assets must be subject to a series of tests to ensure that they respond to the strategic and financial goals of the business. These decisions are typically reserved for the highest levels of management because the dollar magnitude can be large and the payoffs uncertain.

## EVALUATING ASSET ACQUISITION PROPOSALS

In this section, we review the different analytic techniques for evaluating asset acquisition proposals. We begin with the most straightforward decisions—those relating to safety, health, and regulation—and work up to the most consequential decisions—those relating to major commitments that irrevocably set the strategic course of the business.

### 1. Evaluating Assets Acquired to Meet Safety/Health/Regulatory Needs

This is the most straightforward category. As noted above, there is little choice or decision regarding these assets. Reputable businesses, and managers of those businesses, must ensure that ongoing operations do not endanger the health or safety of employees and local communities. Ventilation systems, fire alarm and escape systems, emergency evacuation systems, and many other resources must be devoted to ensuring the welfare of employees. In addition, businesses must make all necessary investments to comply with laws and regulations—handicap access must be provided, toxic emissions must be cleaned, and waste chemicals must be disposed of safely.

The only analysis required for these expenditures is to ensure that (1) the assets being purchased are suitable to the task and (2) the business is receiving the best value relative to the features and/or benefits that are provided. Engineering studies and comparison of features versus cost will give managers the necessary information to make these decisions.

---

### Pennsylvania Power and Light

In the early 1990s, Pennsylvania Power & Light Company was considering how to upgrade an antiquated, 1970s-era, fluorescent lighting system in a 17,775 square-foot drafting area. Not only was it expensive to maintain ($12,745 annually), but it was hurting employees' productivity and health through the glare and eyestrain that it produced. A new lighting system, more focused on lighting employees' individual workstations, would cost the company $48,882, but management estimated that it would be paid for in just 73 days and generate an average ROI of 501% annually. Under the new system, which had fewer components, maintenance costs dropped by 76%, drafter productivity percentage (measured in the days to complete a drawing) increased by 13.2%, and energy consumption dropped by 69%. The investment showed an annual cost benefit of $244,929. Worker morale also increased, with an initial 25% drop in sick leave.

---

*Source:* Adapted from Dana Dubbs, "Retrofit Chalks up 501% ROI Through Higher Productivity and Lower Costs," *Facilities Design & Management* (April 1991): 39.

Approvals for this category of investment can be delegated to individual business unit managers. Top-level corporate managers do not need to review or ratify these decisions unless the cost is unusually high, thereby affecting cash flow and/or profit plan and ROE estimates.

## 2. Evaluating Assets to Enhance Operating Efficiency and/or Increase Revenue

The decision to invest in upgrades and improvements for existing operations is usually discretionary. In other words, doing nothing is a viable option. This is the same type of decision many of us make in deciding whether or not to buy a new car. Should we trade up to a newer model with improved features and lower maintenance costs, or should we save our money and make do with our old car for one more year? For these types of decisions, choosing not to invest—at least in the short term—is a viable alternative.

In a business, this type of investment must stand on its own merits. The decision to acquire an asset to enhance efficiency or increase revenue can be delegated to individual business-unit managers. However, in delegating this decision, it becomes the responsibility of those managers to demonstrate that the economic benefits of acquiring the new asset exceed the cost. In essence, the question to be asked is, Will the increase in future cash flows justify the current outlay of resources to acquire or upgrade the asset?

Managers use three analytic techniques to estimate the benefits of investing in assets to improve operational efficiency: payback, discounted cash flow, and internal rate of return.

### Payback

The most common and intuitive cash flow evaluation technique estimates the time period required for an investment to pay for itself from incremental cash flows. **Payback** is calculated as total acquisition cost (an outflow of cash) divided by the amount of the periodic inflow of cash (or cash saving) that the asset is expected to generate. For long-lived assets, the resulting ratio is usually expressed in years. Thus,

$$\text{Payback in Years} = \frac{\text{Total Cash Outlay to Acquire Asset}}{\text{Annual Cash Inflow or Savings During Each Year of the Asset's Life}}$$

Recall from Chapter 5 that Boston Retail was planning to invest in a new computerized management system to integrate sales records, inventory management, purchase orders, and the accounting general ledger. The cost for this system was $60,000. Management estimated that the system would reduce bookkeeping and auditing costs by $10,000 a year and allow the business to lower inventory levels, which would save an additional $5,000 a year in financing costs. The payback for this investment can be calculated quickly as:

$$\text{Payback in Years} = \frac{\$60,000}{\$15,000}$$
$$= 4 \text{ years}$$

Thus, managers estimated that the investment would "pay for itself" in four years.

If cash flows are irregular—for example, if the annual cash savings were estimated to be $6,000, $12,000, $17,000, $20,000, and so on—then payback is calculated simply by adding up the yearly cash savings to determine the year (or month) in which the total savings eclipse the original outlay.

---

### Break-Even Time in Product Development

In the early 1990s, companies such as Hewlett–Packard Company began to use break-even time to assess the performance of their new-product development efforts.[1] Break-even time revealed the number of months before a new product paid back the money that the company had invested in it. The "clock" was set to zero when the product development project was started. During development, the company invested money until the product was launched; then it began to earn profits that progressively paid back the investment. When the profits generated equaled the investment, the product reached its break-even time. (See figure.)

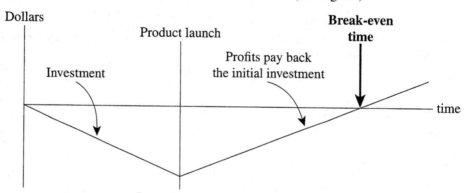

The break-even metric provided very useful information to evaluate the product development process. Long break-even times suggested that products were not as successful as expected and that the company was running the risk of not recouping its investment. Short break-even times provided a good indication that the product development process was efficient and effective.

However, in some companies, senior executives also used this information to evaluate the performance of product development managers. In these cases, product development managers were tempted to game the measure. To reduce break-even time as much as possible, for example, they could select new products that were simple modifications of existing products. These "new" products required very little investment and their success was assured if the original product was already established. Therefore, break-even time was minimized but, paradoxically, the company risked depleting its innovation capabilities as revolutionary products were avoided.

---

[1] For a complete description of the application of HP's break-even time measure, see Charles H. House and Raymond L. Price, "The Return Map: Tracking Product Teams," *Harvard Business Review* 69 (January/February, 1991): 92–100.

Payback calculations are quick and intuitive and are used in almost all businesses. This simple calculation tells managers when they will recoup their investment. Payback reveals the business's exposure to cash drain and the period of time for which it would have a cash deficit related to the project. When cash is scarce, this information is critically important.

A payback calculation, however, does not consider the time value of money. Thus, in dividing current dollars by future dollars, the numerator and denominator of the payback calculation may be stated in currencies of different values. In other words, managers may be dividing apples and oranges. Moreover, the payback calculation ignores the economic benefits received *after* the initial payback period. So, although payback provides important information in terms of *cash flow exposure,* it does not do a good job evaluating the true economic returns from the investment. For this, we need discounted cash flow analysis.

### Discounted Cash Flow

A more sophisticated approach considers not only net cash flows over the entire life of the investment, but also recognizes that future cash flows are worth less than current cash flows. The basic starting point for discounted cash flow analysis is construction of a cash flow time line, as illustrated in Exhibit 7–1. If we stay with Boston Retail's analysis of a computerized reporting system, managers have estimated that the benefits will accrue over a seven-year period (with no residual value).

At this point, we could add up the cost savings over the seven-year period ($15,000 × 7 years = $105,000) and compare this with the initial cash outlay ($60,000) to discover that the project will save the business $45,000. However, this simple summation does not take into account the eroding effects of time on the value of future cash flows.

Therefore, the next step is to use a calculator or discount table to restate the future cash flows into their current dollar equivalents. If managers believe that money will decrease in value by 10% per year, a calculator or present value table can be consulted to find the discount factor for each of the next seven years (the current outlay of $60,000

---

## EXHIBIT 7–1
### Cash Flow Time Line

| | COST SAVINGS | | | | | | |
|---|---|---|---|---|---|---|---|
| INITIAL INVESTMENT JANUARY 1 20X2 | YEAR 1 12/31 20X2 | YEAR 2 12/31 20X3 | YEAR 3 12/31 20X4 | YEAR 4 12/31 20X5 | YEAR 5 12/31 20X6 | YEAR 6 12/31 20X7 | YEAR 7 12/31 20X8 |
| $−60,000 | $15,000 | $15,000 | $15,000 | $15,000 | $15,000 | $15,000 | $15,000 |

**EXHIBIT 7–2**
**Discounted Cash Flow Time Line**

|  | INITIAL INVESTMENT JANUARY 1 20X2 | COST SAVINGS | | | | | | |
|---|---|---|---|---|---|---|---|---|
|  |  | YEAR 1 12/31 20X2 | YEAR 2 12/31 20X3 | YEAR 3 12/31 20X4 | YEAR 4 12/31 20X5 | YEAR 5 12/31 20X6 | YEAR 6 12/31 20X7 | YEAR 7 12/31 20X8 |
|  | $-60,000 | $15,000 | $15,000 | $15,000 | $15,000 | $15,000 | $15,000 | $15,000 |
| Discount Factor | 0 | 0.909 | 0.826 | 0.751 | 0.683 | 0.621 | 0.564 | 0.513 |
| Current Value Equivalent | $ 60,000 | $13,635 | $12,390 | $11,265 | $10,245 | $ 9,315 | $ 8,460 | $ 7,695 |

does not need to be restated because a dollar today is worth exactly one dollar). We can use this information to restate the cash flows for each future year into current-value equivalents (Exhibit 7–2).

By taking the sum of the seven discounted future savings ($13,635 + 12,390 + .... + $7,697 = $73,005) and comparing this amount with the initial investment of $60,000, we see that the true savings is not $45,000, as originally calculated, but instead a more modest $13,005. This summation of discounted cash flows is known as the **net present value** (NPV) of the investment. Stated in current dollars, Boston Retail will be better off by $13,000 if it goes ahead with the investment.

Obviously, the accuracy of a discounted cash flow analysis depends not only on the accuracy of cash flow estimates, but also on the assumed level of the discount rate. At a 10%

**EXHIBIT 7–3**
**Calculation of Repayment of $60,000 Bank Loan**
**and Present Value of Future Cash Savings**

| YEAR ENDED DEC 31 | (1) OPENING LOAN BALANCE | (2) ACCRUED INTEREST ON LOAN [(1) × 10%] | (3) CASH SAVINGS FROM INVESTMENT | (4) BANK PAYMENT |
|---|---|---|---|---|
| January 1, 20X2 |  |  |  |  |
| 20X2 | $60,000 | $6,000 | $15,000 | $15,000 |
| 20X3 | 51,000 | 5,100 | 15,000 | 15,000 |
| 20X4 | 41,100 | 4,110 | 15,000 | 15,000 |
| 20X5 | 30,210 | 3,021 | 15,000 | 15,000 |
| 20X6 | 18,231 | 1,823 | 15,000 | 15,000 |
| 20X7 | 5,054 | 505 | 15,000 | 5,560 |
| 20X8 | — | | 15,000 | — |

Net Present Value of Investment @ 10% interest

discount rate, the project shows a positive NPV of $13,000. However, at a 17% discount rate, the NPV turns negative, showing that the value of cash outflows exceeds the present value of cash inflows by $1,150. Of course, if there is no time value to money—if the discount rate is set at 0—then the NPV of the project is $45,000, as we computed earlier.

Although it is intuitively appealing to think of discounting as a method for recognizing erosion in the purchasing power of money, in a business setting it is more theoretically correct to think of the discount rate as the rate that managers must pay for the use of the financial resources provided by shareholders and lenders (remember the ROE wheel?). By way of illustration, imagine that Boston Retail borrowed $60,000 from the bank to pay for the new computer system. Interest charges would accrue at 10% per year on the unpaid balance. The loan would be repaid in annual installments of $15,000 until the loan was paid in full. This, in fact, is exactly the cash flow that we worked with previously. The only difference is that we are now assuming that the money is being borrowed from a bank.

We have already calculated the NPV of this investment. Using Exhibit 7–2, we calculated that the value to the business of the $60,000 investment is $13,005. Let's calculate what the value would be if we borrowed the $60,000 from the bank. Exhibit 7–3 shows what happens. In year 1, all of the $15,000 cash savings is paid over to the bank to repay the loan and accrued interest. The business does not retain any of the savings. The same is true in years 2, 3, 4, and 5. In each of these years, none of the cost savings accrue to the business; they are all turned over to the bank. By year 6, however, the loan is almost paid off. Only $5,560 is needed to retire the loan. With this final payment, the remaining cash savings—$9,440 in year 6 and $15,000 in year 7—accrue solely to the benefit of the firm. What is the present value of these two amounts? The answer is revealed in column 8. The present value of the cash savings from the investment after the loan is paid off is $13,000 (with a small difference due to rounding).

| (5) ENDING LOAN BALANCE [(1) + (2) − (4)] | (6) CASH SAVINGS RETAINED [(3) − (4)] | (7) PRESENT VALUE FACTOR | (8) PRESENT VALUE OF CASH SAVINGS RETAINED [(6) × (7)] |
|---|---|---|---|
| $60,000 | | | |
| 51,000 | $ — | | |
| 41,100 | — | | |
| 30,210 | — | | |
| 18,231 | — | | |
| 5,054 | — | | |
| — | 9,440 | 0.564 | $ 5,324 |
| — | 15,000 | 0.513 | 7,695 |
| | | | $13,019 |

We can see, therefore, that the discount rate in our example represents the firm's cost of borrowing money—from both shareholders and lenders. The theoretically correct discount rate for asset acquisition calculations is equal to the business's **weighted average cost of capital (WACC)**.[2] This discount rate represents the minimum rate that must be earned on any investment if it is to generate sufficient returns to pay capital providers (both shareholders and creditors) an amount equal to the returns that they expect to receive based on the risk of their investment and the opportunity cost of capital. Failing to return this amount to shareholders and lenders will cause them to cease investing in the firm, and managers will no longer have access to capital to purchase assets to implement their strategy.

In practice, the actual discount rate used in discounted cash flow calculations can be chosen in a variety of ways; it may be based on precise calculations of WACC or it may be based on a rough approximation of desired ROE. Regardless of how it is established, managers must communicate their chosen discount rate consistently throughout the organization so that everyone preparing asset acquisition proposals can work from the same set of assumptions. This consistency in approach allows managers to compare the NPV of different proposals, confident that the results are not biased by differing discount rate assumptions.

## Internal Rate of Return

In calculating the discounted cash flow, we took the cash flows and discount rate as given and calculated the NPV of the investment—a net dollar amount. This amount represents the economic value of the project after consideration of the opportunity cost of the funds that were used to finance it. A related approach also takes the cash flows as given, but it sets the discounted cash flow (or net present value of the project) equal to zero. The computation then solves for the discount rate that equates these two. In other words, the calculation finds the discount rate where the value of cash inflows exactly equals the value of cash outflows. This technique is known as calculating the *discounted rate of return,* or **internal rate of return (IRR).** This is equivalent to asking: If I put $100 in the bank today and will be repaid $110 in one year's time, what rate of return will I be earning on my money? The answer in this simple example, of course, is 10%. A discount rate of 10% equates the present value of the future $110 cash flow ($110 × 0.909 = $100) with the current investment ($100). For business decisions with streams of multiple cash outflows and inflows, a computer or financial calculator is required to solve IRR problems. In the Boston Retail example, you can use a calculator to find the discounted rate of return for a $60,000 outflow that will repay seven annual payments of $15,000 as 16.3%. Using discount tables you can interpolate this result, because the NPV turns negative between 16% and 17%.

IRR is an appealing measure because it collapses the stream of cash flows into a single intuitive ratio that can readily be compared to ROI, ROE, and other commonly used ratio benchmarks. IRR, however, has several technical deficiencies that are covered in standard finance textbooks. For example, IRR calculations can yield multiple rates of return when cash flows change from inflows to outflows several times during the life of

---

[2] We will discuss weighted average cost of capital more fully in chapter 8.

the project. Also, IRR—because it is a ratio—does not take into account the scale of the investment and the size of the cash flows. Finally, IRR assumes that cash inflows can be invested in other projects that yield the same rate of return as the project under consideration.

***Using IRR as an Investment Hurdle***   Notwithstanding the limitations of IRR, senior managers often use a discounted rate of return or IRR target as a guideline to communicate minimum acceptable investment returns for proposed asset acquisitions. When used as a *communication tool,* the chosen IRR is called the **hurdle rate.** Managers are told in advance that projects not passing this financial hurdle—not earning at least this minimum internal rate of return—will not be approved. For example, a firm may set its hurdle rate at 18%, representing management's judgment of the rate of return that is necessary to maintain the financial performance of the business (based on cost of capital, riskiness of proposed projects, and any safety cushions that are built in to compensate for inaccurate or overly optimistic estimates of cash flows).

The effect of communicating this hurdle rate is to stipulate minimum boundary conditions that must be passed. That is, instead of specifying the desired ROI (e.g., "propose projects with a 20% ROI"), the boundary condition leaves it up to individual employees to find and select appropriate projects. Managers are implicitly saying, "I won't tell you what kinds of projects to propose. Higher returns are preferred to lower returns—find the best opportunities out there. But do not bring us projects with rates of return below 18%."

---

### IRR at United Architects

High IRRs used by U.S. firms as thresholds for new investments (e.g., often above 20%) often penalize the evaluation of new technology projects, especially those with uncertain cash savings. An example of this is computer-aided design and drafting (CADD), which has been a revolution to the architectural and engineering industries. United Architects in Los Angeles was constantly losing bids to competitors, not because of the firm's qualifications or bids, but because of a lack of sophistication in the company's visual presentations. Fred Lake, a project manager, believed that a new CADD system would solve the problem, but he knew that management was under great cost pressure as lowest-bid contracts had replaced the traditional cost-plus contracts. Moreover, CADD systems were expensive—from $60,000 to $500,000. Lake could not convince management to invest in a CADD system because calculations revealed a negative NPV.

Lake finally convinced management to acquire a CADD system by including an estimate of lost contribution margin on failed bids in the NPV calculation. The lost margins were easily quantified as Lake's team had lost three bids in the latest quarter. Quantification of this intangible benefit helped management see the potential benefits of this new technology.

---

*Source:* Adapted from John Y. Lee, "The Service Sector: Investing in New Technology to Stay Competitive," *Management Accounting* 72 (June 1991): 45–48.

Managers can use any or all of these three analytic tools to communicate the types of projects that are likely to be supported for improvement of efficiency or for revenue enhancement. For example, they can stipulate that new projects for upgraded technology equipment must pay for themselves from internally generated funds within three years (payback), that all projects must have a demonstrated positive NPV when a discount rate of 13% is applied (discounted cash flow), or that no proposal will be considered if it cannot generate at least an 18% IRR. In addition, managers often provide other guidelines and "rule of thumb" constraints. For example, managers may impose a limit that cash outlays for productive assets (i.e., property, plant, and equipment) cannot exceed annual depreciation charges, or they may allocate funds for equipment upgrades only when the cost of maintenance exceeds the cost of annual depreciation.

## 3. Evaluating Assets to be Acquired for Competitive Effectiveness

We consider next those substantial assets that are acquired to enhance the competitive position of a business. These are notably different than assets acquired to promote efficiency or boost revenues. Assets for competitive effectiveness are needed to support the strategy of the business; as such, they are nondiscretionary if the strategy is to succeed. However, they are usually large and substantial and often commit the business to a direction that can only be altered with difficulty and at considerable expense. Approval of these projects is reserved for the highest level of management.

At Boston Retail, managers considered two strategic options. The first was to expand the business geographically into New York state. The second was to branch out into a new product line—furniture. In theory, the same cash flow techniques discussed previously—payback, discounted cash flow, and IRR—can be applied to asset acquisition proposals intended to improve competitive position. In practice, however, senior managers treat cash flow analysis for these types of assets with caution for two reasons.

First, the cash flows associated with the acquisition of strategic assets are usually extremely uncertain. The actual cash flows from new stores in New York and/or from a new line of furniture depend on management's success in implementing its strategy. Factors discussed in the SWOT analysis of Chapter 2—competitor tactics, acceptance by customers, the ability to find suitable suppliers, and a multitude of other variables (many of which are outside of management's control)—will determine ultimate cash flows. To put too much emphasis on the cash flow analysis techniques presented earlier would inevitably paint a false sense of reliability given the uncertainty inherent in cash flow estimates.

Second, the strategic value of newly acquired assets is often a function of an interaction or synergy with existing resources and capabilities in a way that makes complete analysis difficult. In strategic asset acquisitions, managers invariably hope to extract value because the whole is greater than the sum of its parts. For example, the acquisition of Medco Containment Services—a retail direct-distribution pharmaceutical network— by Merck & Company—a research pharmaceutical company—was based primarily on the perceived benefits of combining the resources and competencies of these two businesses. Managers at Medco and Merck believed that their businesses would be more valuable if they worked together than if they continued to work apart. Managers of the merged firms are betting that they can achieve economies of scale and scope, generate

incremental revenues from cross-selling, and successfully eliminate the inevitable redundancies in bringing together two separate businesses. However, managers must rely
heavily on their intuition and judgment about the ability of managers to work together,
merge different cultures, and extract this extra value from the investment.

This is not to say that managers do not estimate payback, discounted cash flow,
and rates of return (both discounted and undiscounted) for strategic acquisition proposals. They do and, clearly, they should. The point to be made, however, is that they take
this quantitative information—which is based on highly uncertain assumptions—and
combine it with their best judgment about competitive market dynamics, the prospects
for success, and the ultimate long-term payoff that may accrue as a result of the asset
acquisition. Thus, intuition and hunch play as important a role as economic analysis.

Judgment is influenced by a variety of factors that we touched on in Chapter 2 as
we discussed SWOT, distinctive internal capabilities, market franchises, and the value of
relationships and networks. These factors include:

- Alignment of proposal with existing strategy and/or distinctive capabilities
- Risks in acquiring the asset
- Risks in deciding not to acquire the asset
- Quality of information supporting proposal
- Track record and ability of the people involved
- Feasibility and cost of reversing decision

Let's consider each of these factors in turn.

## 1. Alignment of Proposal with Existing Strategy and/or Distinctive Capabilities

The obvious point of departure for managers considering new assets to enhance competitive effectiveness is the extent to which proposals tie in with intended strategies. In
businesses with smart, motivated people, there is never a shortage of ideas about new
ways to create value. Some of these ideas will build on existing competencies, but many
of these ideas will not fit well with management's intentions and strategy for the future,
especially if managers have been at all unclear about their preferences or range of acceptable investment options.

At Boston Retail, managers believed that expanding into a nearby geographic region aligned well with their existing strategy and the capabilities of the business. A move
into furniture did not appear to do so well on this dimension. Therefore, the decision to
acquire a furniture line would require careful thought and judgment about the additional
capabilities that they would need to build or acquire if the strategy were to succeed.

## 2. Risks in Acquiring the Asset

Every strategic decision creates risk. In acquiring an asset that affects the competitive
effectiveness of a business, managers invariably alter existing business processes and capabilities. At Boston Retail, the move into New York state would require substantially
enhanced distribution facilities to serve a wider geographic area. Would the business be
able to expand its distribution infrastructure quickly enough to respond? If not, the resources invested in expansion might be wasted. Managers need to assess the magnitude
of the risk of failure.

Every investment also creates an opportunity cost. Managers must ask themselves: could funds be utilized more effectively in a competitive project? If no current proposals offer acceptable returns, should excess cash be returned to shareholders or held temporarily in money-market funds?

Market analysis gave Boston Retail managers some understanding of potential competitors in the New York market, but how would these competitors respond to the entry of Boston Retail? Would they retaliate? If so, by what means and how aggressively? Would their tactics change the profitability of planned expansion?

Managing these new stores would require a different organization structure. For the first time, stores would be situated outside Massachusetts. A new management team would have to be created and staffed. New reporting relationships and accountabilities would have to be created. Could they find the right people? Could they develop a good performance measurement and control system to ensure that the new managers worked toward the goals of the business?

Finally, a potentially serious risk in the acquisition of any asset outside the current domain of management expertise is distraction of management attention. Will managers be pulled away from what they know how to do best as they attempt to learn how to manage new types of operations? Managers can easily become stretched too thin and, inadvertently, fail to pay sufficient attention to the core business. Choosing to acquire assets that are outside the business's core competency may drive down ROM.

## 3. Risk in Deciding Not to Acquire the Asset

However, doing nothing also brings risk. A business that stands still will inevitably be overtaken by competitors. If Boston Retail managers choose not to expand into New York state, will another competitor take the opportunity to acquire prime retail space and begin building a competing market franchise? If managers fail to act, other competitors will surely take their place, and opportunities available today may no longer be available to those who follow. As we discussed in Chapter 2, first-movers can often create advantages that are difficult to replicate.

Even in relatively mundane matters, failure to act can ultimately harm the business. At Boston Retail, the current profit plan is predicated on the assumption that a $180,000 warehouse expansion will be approved to support the internal growth of the business. Without the expansion of warehouse capacity, however, predicted growth may be choked as the business struggles with inadequate storage and inventory management systems.

## 4. Quality of Information Supporting Proposal

Substantial amounts of information must be created and analyzed to support the acquisition of assets that affect competitive position. A market analysis, economic forecasts, estimates of cash flows and rates of return, and effects on strategic position can all be presented and analyzed. However, managers must assess, as part of their review, the degree of confidence that they have in the information that is presented to them. In some cases, they will have a great deal of confidence in the accuracy and reliability of the data. This is true, for example, of analyses of past trends based on historical accounting records. In other circumstances, they may have very little faith in the "crystal ball" ability of staff analysts to predict cash flows related to complicated acquisitions, or they may disagree with the assumptions (cash flow, asset value recoverability, discount rates) that underlie the analyses.

At Boston Retail, for example, managers have much more confidence in their ability to predict the economic value created by a move into New York state than they do in their ability to predict the long-term viability and benefit of the new furniture line. Furniture is an area where managers have no direct experience or internal data to draw upon to validate their assumptions. Therefore, they are forced to discount the reliability of information to a greater extent in the decision process.

Also, managers must evaluate the quality of the market analysis and supporting economics. Have staff analysts considered the right variables and interactions? Have they taken account of all the contingencies relating to market dynamics? Have they included brand value? Have they taken account of economies of scope? These and many similar questions must be probed by managers as they attempt to assess the quality of the information that is provided in support of the proposal.

## 5. Track Record and Ability of Champion

Throughout the technical analysis, we must remember that asset acquisition proposals are made by people—who have ambitions, skills, and weaknesses. Any proposal to acquire assets must be evaluated in light of the confidence that senior managers can place in the individuals making the proposal. Every substantial asset acquisition proposal has a *champion*—a person who believes that this asset is an important source of competitive advantage for the business and is willing to argue forcefully for the merits of acquiring it. Depending on the proposal, a champion may be a division manager, a functional vice president, or any other manager who believes that acquiring a resource will produce tangible strategic benefits for the business.

Does the champion have a good track record of achieving what he or she sets out to do? Does this person tend to be too optimistic? Too pessimistic? Do we believe that they will have sufficient resources to utilize the asset effectively? These questions, which can only be answered subjectively based on first-hand knowledge of people in the organization, are critical to establishing the confidence that underlies management judgment about the merits of acquiring a strategic asset.

## 6. Feasibility and Cost of Reversing Decision

Acquiring assets to enhance competitive effectiveness often commits the business to a course of action that will play out over many years. At Boston Retail, the decision to move into New York state or the decision to move into furniture will substantially influence the future course of the business. New facilities must be opened, contracts with new suppliers signed, new staff must be hired, and so on.

In deciding whether or not to make these commitments, managers should always imagine the worst. What if this turns out to have been a bad idea? Can we reverse it, and how much will it cost? One of the critical components of the analysis is a feasible exit plan that can be executed should the contingencies of market dynamics or other events force managers to reverse their decision.

## PUTTING IT ALL TOGETHER

The asset acquisition process is both important and complex. Managers use the process to communicate guidelines, solicit proposals, and weigh and evaluate alternatives. The final decision for nonroutine asset acquisitions is often handled by a committee of senior managers who represent different businesses and functions. Over a series of meetings, proposals are presented, questions asked, and managers deliberate—often acting as judges—in deciding how to allocate scarce capital resources. Requests for large acquisitions—beyond the cash-generating ability of the business—must also be weighed against the availability and cost of financing. Here, the chief financial officer plays a critical role in crafting financing options and alternatives.

We can use the inputs → process → outputs model discussed in Chapter 4 to illustrate the approach that managers use in allocating assets to support competitive effectiveness (Figure 7–1).

The "inputs" are information, people, opportunities, threats, and available resources. These inputs are used by managers throughout the organization to create formal proposals to acquire and allocate new assets in support of strategy or to enhance operational efficiencies. The "process" of developing proposals should rely heavily on the techniques outlined in this chapter: analysis of cost effectiveness (for assets related to safety and regulation), calculation of payback, estimation of discounted cash flow, and computation of discounted rate of return or IRR. The "outputs" of this process—the formal proposals submitted to top managers—can then be separated into appropriate categories and compared against strategic plans and economic standards and criteria. Senior managers can allocate funding to support proposals that meet these criteria and reject or defer those that fail to pass the test. Some proposals may be sent back to subordinates with the request to reconsider, redraft, and alter their proposals and related action plans to meet strategic goals.

The asset acquisition process—although usually separate from the profit planning process—should be timed to support the allocation of resources to implement plans and strategies. Thus, "Investment in Assets" is included as a key variable in the profit wheel diagram of Chapter 5. Usually, profit plans are completed first. Soon after, asset acquisition proposals are reviewed by senior managers to ensure that resources will be sufficient to implement plans. When new proposals are approved or rejected, it is often necessary to go back to the profit wheel and rework profit plans. For example, profit plans

**FIGURE 7–1   The Process of Allocating Assets**

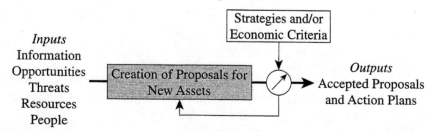

---

### Investment Categories at a Medical Devices Firm

Deciding which new products to develop is a critical decision for many companies, but relying solely on financial analysis may lead a company down the wrong path. Why? New products are often very different from existing ones: They tend to show lower initial financial return; the required investment is higher; the expected levels of sales and costs are more uncertain; and the payback period is longer. Thus, companies may be tempted to underinvest in new products even if, over the long term, they are likely to shape the company's future. To avoid this trap, a medical devices company developed a unique way to analyze new-products decisions.

First, it classified new products into three categories: derivatives, platforms, and breakthroughs. *Derivatives* were new products that incorporated only minor design enhancements. Designing a new interface for a laboratory centrifuge was considered a derivative product. *Platforms* were totally new products that replaced existing ones. A new blood-glucose testing system based on an improved technology, which replaced the system currently being offered, was a platform product. *Breakthrough* products were radically new ideas that would start a new product concept. Syringes with retractable needles, for example, represented a revolutionary new product that would help nurses avoid accidentally hurting themselves.

Then the company allocated a certain amount of money for each category of product, regardless of whether derivatives looked more financially attractive than platforms and breakthroughs. Finally, within each category it then used financial and strategic criteria to decide which products would be funded.

---

that reflect growth in revenue and market share may stimulate asset acquisition proposals for enlarged facilities or new distribution networks. Alternatively, the decision to reject a proposal may require scaling back earlier profit plan goals that were based on the assumption that specific assets would be available to support the strategy.

At Boston Retail, managers worked carefully with the profit wheel analysis developed in Chapter 5 and the strategic considerations discussed in this chapter. On balance, they decided to pursue expansion into New York state. Concerns about ROM, alignment of core competencies, and risk made the acquisition strategy seem undesirable.

## CHAPTER SUMMARY

Acquiring and allocating productive assets is an integral part of achieving profit goals and strategies. Asset allocation systems help managers throughout the organization make effective proposals and give top managers the tools to evaluate the relative merits of each proposal.

The first step in the process is to design a system that allows information about new asset proposals to be gathered, analyzed, and communicated to senior management for consideration. For systems to be effective, managers must:

1.  Communicate limits on the type of assets that are suitable for potential acquisition
2.  Specify a process by which proposals are evaluated and approved
3.  Communicate policies regarding who has authority to approve the acquisition of assets
4.  Categorize projects consistently so that the correct analytic tools and decision criteria can be applied to each bucket

Many firms categorize potential assets into three buckets: assets needed for health/safety/regulation, assets needed to enhance efficiency and/or increase revenue, and assets needed to support strategic initiatives and competitive effectiveness. Each category is subject to different types of analyses.

Designing and using asset allocation systems—like other performance measurement and control systems—is partly art and partly science. Analytic techniques related to cash flow analysis and rate of return analysis play an important role in understanding the economic effects of acquiring new resources. However, as the assets become larger and more strategic, management judgment becomes the determining factor.

# 8

# Linking Performance to Markets

The implementation of profit plans reflects the success of a business in creating value and implementing strategy in competitive markets. In this chapter, we explore how profit plans are linked to those markets and the implications of these linkages for performance measurement and control systems.

In the sections to follow, we discuss two types of markets that affect performance measurement and control systems: markets inside the firm and markets outside the firm. Markets *inside* the firm are created when goods and services are transferred between different business units or divisions of the same firm. In making these transfers, a value must be attached to the flow of these internal goods and services so that the profit plans of each division can properly reflect the value added at each stage of the process. To adjust profit plans appropriately, managers must develop a system of *transfer prices*. We can think of transfer prices as horizontal linkages between the profit plans of different business units in the firm.

Markets *outside* the firm include customer, financial, and supplier markets. These markets are critical to the long-term profitability of the firm. Therefore, measures must be developed to ensure that profit plans are adequately linked to these markets. We will discuss how managers link their profit plans to external markets in this and the next chapter. We can think of the linkage between the profit plan and these external markets as vertical linkages.

## TRANSFER PRICES: MANAGING MARKETS INSIDE THE FIRM

All businesses produce goods and services for eventual sale to third-party customers. In some instances, however, business units sell their products or services to other divisions or business units within the same firm. In these cases, the outputs of one division are inputs for another. For example, an integrated oil company may have three different divisions: (1) exploration and extraction, (2) refining and processing, and (3) retail sales. The exploration and extraction division may choose to sell its crude oil on the open market or transfer it to its sister refinery division. Likewise, the petroleum products produced by the refinery division can be sold on the open market or transferred to the retail division for sale through its retail service stations. In each of these cases the outputs of one division (often called the selling or upstream division) can be transferred internally

**FIGURE 8-1** **Horizontal Flow of Goods/Services Between Autonomous Divisions Within the Same Firm**

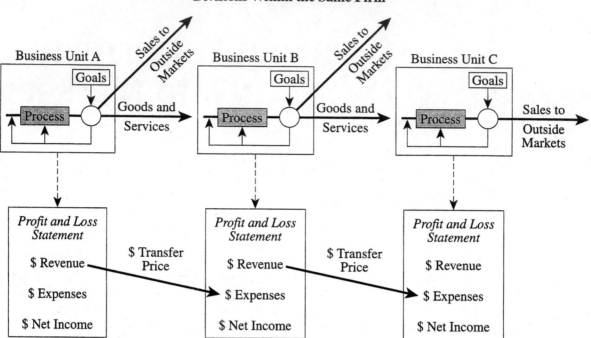

to become inputs for a second division (called the purchasing or downstream division). In these circumstances, managers must consider how to use transfer prices to link these operations through *internal* markets that are created by the horizontal flow of goods inside the firm (Figure 8-1).

A **transfer price** is an *internally set transaction price to account for the transfer of goods or services between divisions of the same firm.* Transfer prices are used to value and coordinate the work flows of interdependent organization units that are each held accountable for financial performance. For example, separate product divisions may each be held accountable for the profit of their respective products. The electronic components produced by one division may be sold to a sister division as inputs to the assembly of consumer radios. Alternatively, the components division may transfer goods to the marketing division for sales and shipment to outside customers. To the extent that the work flows of these separate divisions are interdependent—one transfers goods or services to the other—how should each account for performance?

As we have discussed at length in previous chapters, the profit plan for an individual business unit maps out the expected flows of revenues, expenses, and anticipated levels of profit. A problem arises, however, when the revenues and expenses shown on a business unit's profit plan include product flows to and from sister divisions of the same firm. The prices for these goods and services are not naturally determined by arm's length market transactions—as is normal between independent buyers and sellers—so distortions can be introduced into each business unit's reported revenue, expenses, and profitability.

These distortions can affect both performance evaluation and resource allocation. From the perspective of performance evaluation, the distortion of revenues, expenses, and profits can make it difficult to determine where value is actually being created. For example, if the upstream selling division is receiving too little revenue relative to the value of the products that it transfers to the downstream purchasing division, then upstream's profit will be too low, and downstream's profit will be too high.

This distortion can also be expected to affect resource allocation as individual managers in each of the divisions adjust their profit plans and business activities in response to any perceived distortions in performance evaluation. Managers at the upstream division, for example, will have little incentive to increase the level of sales to the downstream division if they are not receiving full credit for the value of their products. More generally, in cases where internal transfer prices are used, there is substantial risk that unit managers will make decisions that improve their division's profitability (or at least minimize the damaging effects of internal transfers) and, in so doing, lower the overall profit of the firm. To the extent that managers make decisions based on the level of internally set transfer prices, any distortions can affect the willingness of managers to buy goods from or sell goods to sister divisions, to source products internally versus purchasing from outside vendors, to make or buy products, and so on.

On the other hand, it is important to realize that the potential distortions of transfer prices can be mitigated if the profit plan anticipates the effects of these internal transfers and adjusts goals and targets accordingly. In other words, if managers adjust accountability targets based on an anticipated level of internal transfer at some agreed transfer price (even if it is too low or too high), managers will not be penalized for internal transactions at that level.

## TRANSFER PRICING ALTERNATIVES

There are two basic ways of setting transfer prices: at market prices or at prices based on internally generated accounting data.

### Transfer Prices Using Market Data

In many cases, transfers of goods and services between divisions of the same firm can be recorded at *external market prices*. In these cases, the upstream selling division records the transfer as a sale. The associated revenue is set equal to the price that would have been realized if the product (or, in some cases, service) had been sold to an arm's length customer on the outside market. Using the same market-based price, the downstream division records the transfer as an increase in its inventory (which ultimately flows to cost of goods sold). The recorded price is the same price that the division would have had to pay to purchase similar goods or services from an independent supplier on the outside market.

Using external market prices eliminates the potential for distortion resulting from non-arm's length transfers. Prices based on market data reflect the true opportunity cost and market value of the transfer. However, using market prices is possible only when (1) an active market exists for similar goods and services and (2) internal transfer prices based on comparable external market prices can be easily established. This poses little problem for the integrated oil company because highly efficient spot markets exist for all grades of crude oil and refined petroleum products (i.e., active buyers and sellers continually update market prices based on supply and demand). These spot market prices are easily obtained and can be used to set the prices of internal product flows between sister divisions. The same is true for intermediate products that can be purchased from outside vendors by reference to a published price list.

In many instances of internal transfer, however, active markets do not exist to easily price the value of intermediate products transferred between divisions of the same firm. Either the goods are specialized (such as uniquely designed electronic components) or prices cannot be established without obtaining bids from potential suppliers based on exact order quantities and product specifications (e.g., "please quote on this product in this amount").

The advantages—and major disadvantage—of market-based transfer prices are the following:

**Advantages of Market Prices:**
- By mirroring true market prices, prices based on market data allow accurate performance evaluation and minimize the potential for misallocation of resources based on faulty performance measures
- Simple
- Objective, and seen as valid by managers in all divisions
- Provides managers with the sense that they are running their own business

**Disadvantage of Market Prices:**
- For most intermediate goods and services transferred within a firm, market prices are typically not available

## Transfer Prices Using Internal Cost Data

When market prices are not readily available (which is most often the case in practice), managers must rely on internal cost accounting data to establish transfer prices. Transfers among divisions using internal cost data can be priced by several methods: at variable cost, full cost, full cost plus a markup, or, if available, prices that approximate an arm's length market price. The hierarchy of transfer prices is illustrated in Figure 8–2.

### Variable Cost

*Variable cost* of manufacture is the lowest accounting-based transfer price. A variable cost is one that can be traced directly to a product or service and varies directly with output quantities. Variable costs typically include materials, labor, and other direct costs of production. Administrative overheads incurred by the producing division as part of doing business (e.g., indirect costs such as supervision and office rent) are not included in the transfer price. Assuming efficient operations, **variable cost transfer prices** result in revenues (and profits) being understated for the upstream division relative to what

**FIGURE 8–2    Hierarchy of Transfer Prices Using Internal Cost Data**

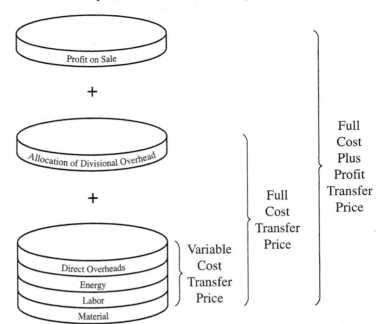

they could have received if they had sold the goods or services on the open market (presuming such a market exists). Correspondingly, the downstream division typically receives goods at a price significantly below a market-based competitive price. Thus, when products are ultimately sold to the customer, the gross margin and profits will reside disproportionately with the downstream division.

Advantages and disadvantages of using variable cost are:

**Advantages of Variable Cost:**
- Simple
- Allows pure marginal-cost decision analysis

**Disadvantages of Variable Cost:**
- Arbitrarily shifts profits from selling divisions to purchasing divisions
- Provides no incentives for the upstream division to manage overheads efficiently or for the downstream division to look elsewhere for sources of supply because of high costs at the upstream division
- Marginal cost may vary over a range of output levels due to economies of larger-scale production
- May limit profit of firm when selling division is at full capacity and is forced to sell its output to its downstream sister division
- The upstream division may refuse to sell to the downstream division in favor of sales to outside parties at prices that include overhead and a margin for profit

- May cause purchasing division to underprice products that are ultimately sold into final customer markets

Because of these limitations, variable cost transfer prices are rarely found in practice.

## Full Cost

A somewhat higher accounting-based transfer price is a **full cost transfer price,** which includes direct costs plus an allocation for the divisional overhead that would normally be covered by the gross profit margin on goods sold to outside customers. Overheads include allocations for a representative portion of manufacturing overheads. Sometimes a portion of selling, general, and administrative overheads are included as well. Full cost is usually calculated using standard costs rather than actual costs to eliminate the possibility of passing along inefficiencies in manufacturing or processing. Full cost transfer pricing is quite common in practice for the following reasons:

**Advantages of Full Cost:**
- Simple — typically calculated by routine cost-accounting methods
- Allows upstream division to recover all its costs
- By charging downstream managers with the overheads that are generated by the upstream division, downstream managers have incentive to monitor the level of costs that are passed on and apply pressure to increase upstream efficiency if costs are excessive. (This pressure may be moderated, however, if the full cost charged by the upstream division is still lower than any alternative cost that the downstream division could obtain from third-party providers.)

**Disadvantages of Full Cost:**
- Subject to inaccuracies of internal cost-accounting allocations
- Fixed costs of the upstream division become variable costs to the downstream division, potentially resulting in the downstream division making decisions that reduce the profitability of the firm (e.g., investing in additional capacity to avoid having to buy from the upstream division even though the upstream division has excess capacity)
- The upstream division may refuse to sell to the downstream division in favor of sales to outside parties at prices that include a margin for profit

## Full Cost Plus Profit

The highest accounting-based transfer price attempts to approach market price by including **full cost plus profit.** In this case the upstream division recovers not only direct costs and overhead, but also some profit on the sale. Markups are most simply calculated as a percentage add-on to the cost of transferred goods. Now, the upstream division and the downstream division share in the final profits on the ultimate sale of the goods in direct proportion to the value that each adds as calculated by the internal accounting system.

**Advantages of Full Cost Plus Profit:**
- Attempts to mirror market prices, which over the long run must include direct costs, overheads, and profits
- Allows upstream division to receive full credit for revenues and profits from sales to internal divisions

**Disadvantage of Full Cost Plus Profit:**
- Unless the downstream division has the right to refuse internal transfers in favor of purchasing from outside suppliers, it can result in the downstream division paying costs that are higher than the value of the products received

## Negotiated Prices

Notwithstanding the virtues of each of these three methods—variable cost, full cost, and full cost plus markup—managers often choose in practice to negotiate among themselves some satisfactory transfer price—in effect, to "split the difference" to ensure that there is equity in the profit plans and results of each of the contributing divisions. This **negotiated transfer price** is usually based on standard direct costs plus some allowance for profit or ROCE.

**Advantage of Negotiated Prices:**
- Perceived fairness among managers who negotiate final prices

**Disadvantages of Negotiated Prices:**
- Time-consuming
- Profit and performance evaluation can be biased by the negotiating skills of the managers representing each of the various divisions

The academic literature has often tried to reconcile the advantages and disadvantages of these different approaches by arguing for the use of a "dual-pricing" system whereby the selling division is credited with market price and the buying division is charged with full cost. Thus, the selling division suffers no revenue disadvantage—and will make no uneconomic decisions—as a result of internal transfers, and the buying division will recognize the cost benefits of sourcing internally rather than going to outside markets. This approach is rarely found in practice. It requires elimination of the accounting profit that is counted twice (once by the selling division upon lateral transfer and once by the buying division upon ultimate sale to customers) and creates ambiguity about what the company is trying to achieve.[1]

## Activity-Based Transfer Prices

Any method based on internal accounting data—variable cost, full cost, or full cost plus profit—is only as good as the data and allocations that support it. Recently, some companies have experimented with activity-based costing methods to develop more-accurate transfer prices. Under this approach, different cost standards are prepared for four different categories of cost: unit-based costs (e.g., direct material), batch-based costs (e.g., setup), product-based costs (e.g., package design), and plant-level costs (e.g., depreciation and insurance). Transfer prices are then charged using two separate approaches. Unit- and batch-level costs are charged based on unit volume—the quantities of products shipped between divisions and the number of batches it takes to produce those

---

[1] Robert G. Eccles, *The Transfer Pricing Problem: A Theory for Practice* (Lexington, Mass.: Lexington Books, 1985), 102–103.

products. Product-based and plant-level costs are charged annually based on planned levels of usage as reflected in profit plans and budgets.[2]

Proponents of this approach argue that it overcomes many of the shortcomings of traditional methods. Advantages and disadvantages are:

**Advantages of Activity-Based Prices:**
- Provides a more-accurate measure of profit performance in each division
- Separates short-term decisions based on batch-level and unit-level costs from long-term decisions based on product- and plant-level costs
- Motivates downstream managers to help selling division managers effectively manage capacity and other plant-level costs

**Disadvantages of Activity-Based Prices:**
- Relatively complicated
- Depends on the accuracy of cost-driven assumptions and availability of reliable data

As this new approach is implemented and tested, managers will be able to evaluate whether the potential benefits outweigh the increased complexity in recordkeeping and potential for disagreement about the reliability of the allocation assumptions.

## TRANSFER PRICING EFFECTS AND TRADE-OFFS

Managers at different levels in a firm often attempt to achieve different objectives through their transfer pricing policies. For example, corporate managers, division managers, and financial staffs may desire the following:[3]

**Corporate Managers Want Transfer Prices to**
- encourage division managers to make decisions that maximize the long-run profitability of the overall firm
- provide information so that managers can make good short-term decisions (such as bids for orders) and long-term decisions (e.g., adding or deleting product lines)

**Division Managers Want Transfer Prices to**
- represent fairly the financial performance of their division
- reflect the impact of good business decisions within their division (e.g., product mix and improved efficiency)
- require downstream division managers to include the full costs associated with the products they are receiving from upstream divisions

**Financial Staffs Want Transfer Prices That**
- are simple and credible, so that they will be used and useful by division managers
- are easy to use and easy to explain

---

[2] For more information on activity-based transfer pricing, see Robert S. Kaplan, Dan Weiss, and Eyal Desheh, "Transfer Pricing with ABC," *Management Accounting* 78 (May 1997): 20–28, and Robin Cooper and Robert S. Kaplan, *Cost & Effect* (Boston: Harvard Business School Press, 1998), Chap. 15.

[3] Kaplan, Weiss, and Desheh, op. cit.

The effects of different transfer pricing policies are illustrated in Exhibit 8–1. Although the profits for the firm as a whole are the same, different transfer pricing methods allocate different amounts of profit between the selling and purchasing divisions.

Overlaid on the choice of transfer price is a decision whether or not divisions should be required to buy and sell from each other or whether either—or both—should have the option of rejecting internal transfers in favor of dealing with arm's length suppliers and customers in external markets. Exhibit 8–2 illustrates what can happen if one or both of the parties is allowed to opt out. In this illustration, the selling division is forgoing profit by selling to its sister division and, if given the chance, may choose not to sell to the purchasing division in favor of more-profitable sales to outside customers. As

## EXHIBIT 8–1
### Effect of Transfer Pricing Policies
### on Divisional Profitability
*Assuming Pricing Has No Effects on Decision Making*

|  | VARIABLE COST | FULL COST | FULL COST PLUS MARKUP | MARKET PRICING |
|---|---|---|---|---|
|  | **SELLING DIVISION** | | | |
| Revenue: | | | | |
| Sales to outside customers [5,000 units @ $100] | $500,000 | $500,000 | $500,000 | $500,000 |
| Sales to Purchasing Division | | | | |
| 2,000 units @ $50 | 100,000 | | | |
| $70 | | 140,000 | | |
| $84 | | | 168,000 | |
| $100 | | | | 200,000 |
|  | 600,000 | 640,000 | 668,000 | 700,000 |
| Cost of goods sold | | | | |
| 7,000 units @ $70 | 490,000 | 490,000 | 490,000 | 490,000 |
| Gross profit–Selling Division | $110,000 | $150,000 | $178,000 | $210,000 |
|  | **PURCHASING DIVISION** | | | |
| Revenue from outside customers | $800,000 | $800,000 | $800,000 | $800,000 |
| Cost of goods sold | | | | |
| 2,000 units purchased from Selling Division | 100,000 | 140,000 | 168,000 | 200,000 |
| Additional value added by Purchasing Division | 350,000 | 350,000 | 350,000 | 350,000 |
|  | 450,000 | 490,000 | 518,000 | 550,000 |
| Gross profit–Purchasing Division | 350,000 | 310,000 | 282,000 | 250,000 |
| Total gross profit for both divisions | $460,000 | $460,000 | $460,000 | $460,000 |

---

**EXHIBIT 8-2**
**Effect of Transfer Pricing Policies**
**on Divisional Profitability**
*Assuming Selling Division Chooses to*
*Sell 1,000 Fewer Units to Purchasing Division*

| | SELLING DIVISION | |
| --- | --- | --- |
| | VARIABLE COST | FULL COST |
| Revenue: | | |
| Sales to outside customers [6,000 units @ $100] | $600,000 | $600,000 |
| Sales to Purchasing Division | | |
| 1,000 @ $50 | 50,000 | |
| 1,000 @ $70 | — | 70,000 |
| | 650,000 | 670,000 |
| Cost of goods sold | | |
| 7,000 units @ $70 | 490,000 | 490,000 |
| Gross profit–Selling Division | $160,000 | $180,000 |
| | **PURCHASING DIVISION** | |
| Revenue from outside customers | $400,000 | $400,000 |
| Cost of goods sold | | |
| 1,000 units purchased from Selling Division | 50,000 | 70,000 |
| Additional value added | 175,000 | 175,000 |
| | 225,000 | 245,000 |
| Gross profit–Purchasing Division | 175,000 | 155,000 |
| Total gross profit for both divisions | $335,000 | $335,000 |

---

a comparison of Exhibit 8–1 and Exhibit 8–2 reveals, if supply shortages affect downstream sales this leads to higher profit for the selling division, but lower overall profit for the firm.

Robert Eccles, who conducted an in-depth study of transfer pricing policies, argues that firms following a strategy of vertical integration to achieve economies of scale and scope are likely to mandate that units within the firm buy and sell from each other—creating the need for a good system of transfer prices because the possibility of dealing with outside parties is removed. Firms following a strategy of unrelated businesses are more likely to leave the choice up to the managers of the individual profit centers.[4] Table 8–1 shows this breakdown in detail.

A special, but important, case arises when products are transferred between business units of the same company located in different countries. As described above, transfer pricing policies determine how much profit each business unit records in its books. If goods and services are transferred across national borders, tax authorities in

---

[4] Adapted from Eccles, pp. 8–9, 57.

**TABLE 8–1** Profit Center Manager's Decision Authority to Choose Between Internal and External Vendors, by Strategic Type

| AUTHORITY | SINGLE BUSINESS VERTICALLY INTEGRATED | | DISTINCT BUSINESSES VERTICALLY INTEGRATED | | UNRELATED BUSINESSES | | TOTAL | |
|---|---|---|---|---|---|---|---|---|
| My decision | 29% | (19) | 35% | (43) | 50% | (48) | 39% | (110) |
| Two-person decision | 20% | (13) | 26% | (32) | 22% | (21) | 23% | (66) |
| Multiple-person decision | 26% | (17) | 18% | (22) | 15% | (14) | 19% | (53) |
| Corporate decision | 20% | (13) | 11% | (14) | 3% | (3) | 10% | (30) |
| Initiated by others | 5% | (3) | 10% | (12) | 10% | (9) | 9% | (24) |
| Total | 100% | (65) | 100% | (123) | 100% | (95) | 100% | (283) |

*Note: Number in brackets represents the number of respondents.*
*Source:* Adapted from Robert G. Eccles, *The Transfer Pricing Problem* (Lexington, Mass.: Lexington Books, 1985), 114.

different countries take great interest in ensuring that the business unit domiciled in their country attracts a sufficient amount of profit for income tax purposes. Accordingly, any attempts by corporate or business executives to evade local income taxes by using transfer prices to shift profits out of high-tax jurisdictions into low-tax countries can result in civil and/or criminal legal action. Thus, when designing international transfer pricing policies, managers must take special care to ensure that their transfer prices fairly replicate the value that is created by each business unit situated in a foreign country.

---

### Transfer Pricing Between Assembly Plants

A company that made hydraulic systems for dump and garbage trucks had two plants. Managers of each plant were measured on their plant's respective profits. One of the plants built the hydraulic systems and the second plant installed them on trucks. The first plant also sold its hydraulic systems to the spare parts market, as well as supplying them to its sister assembly plant. The transfer price for these hydraulic systems was set below the market price for spare parts, reflecting the fact that the original equipment was sold at a lower price than spare parts.

However, this arrangement had unexpected negative consequences. Managers of the hydraulic systems plant were more interested in selling parts to the external market and even competitors than in shipping products to its sister plant. The hydraulic plant manager was constantly praised for his plant's profitability. However, the late and irregular shipments of hydraulic systems to the assembly plant caused constant problems with its customers. Before top management discovered the source of the problem (the artificially low transfer price), the assembly plant manager was blamed for customer complaints.

*Source:* Adapted from James F. Cox, W. Gerry Howe, and Lynn H. Boyd, "Transfer Pricing Effects on Locally Measured Organizations," *Industrial Management* 2 (March 13, 1997): 20.

**TABLE 8–2** Major Trade-Offs in Transfer Pricing Methods[5]

| | TRANSFER PRICING METHOD | | | | |
|---|---|---|---|---|---|
| OBJECTIVE | VARIABLE COST | FULL COST | FULL COST PLUS PROFIT | ACTIVITY-BASED | MARKET PRICE |
| Promotes rational decision making in Selling Division | Poor | Moderate | Better | Better | Best |
| Promotes rational decision making in Purchasing Division | Poor | Better | Better | Better | Moderate |
| Provides accurate product contribution measures | Poor | Moderate | Better | Better | Best |
| Easy to understand | Best | Better | Moderate | Worst | Best |
| Easy to apply | Easy | Moderate | Difficult | Difficult | Varies |

Transfer pricing, as a response to the creation of artificial markets within firms, is inevitably a compromise. Transfer price information, like other information for performance measurement and control, is used for a variety of purposes—decision making, control, coordination, evaluation, and so on. Table 8–2 summarizes the trade-offs managers must make in designing transfer price policies.

Although the theory and mathematics of transfer pricing hold appeal for many academic economists and accountants, in practice, transfer pricing is not a serious problem for most managers to solve. As long as managers are aware of the potential distortions and incentive effects, profit plans can be adjusted ex ante and ex post to reflect internal transfers, and negotiations can easily be conducted between divisions so that no one is unfairly burdened by internal transfers of goods and services.

## LINKING PROFIT PERFORMANCE TO EXTERNAL MARKETS

Now that we have discussed the horizontal linkage of profit plans within the firm, we next consider the vertical linkage of profit plans to external markets.

In Chapter 2, we drew a distinction between corporate strategy and business strategy. You will remember that business strategy is concerned with how to compete in defined product markets. Corporate strategy, by contrast, is concerned with decisions about how to maximize the value of resources controlled by the corporation. These decisions focus primarily on the *allocation* of resources inside the corporation. In single-business firms, all resources are devoted to only one business. In multibusiness firms—firms that are organized to compete in more than one product market—decisions must be made about how to allocate scarce resources across business units to maximize value creation.[6]

---

[5]Adapted from Eccles, p. 267

**FIGURE 8–3   Corporate Performance Flows**

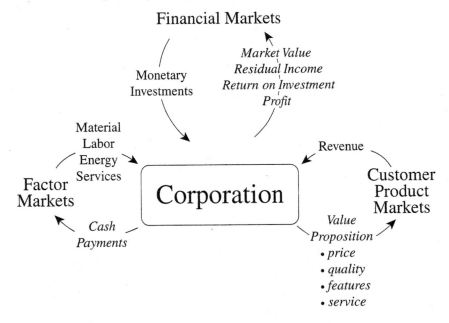

The success of any corporate strategy is reflected in **corporate performance.** *Corporate performance refers to a firm's level of achievement in creating value for market constituents.* Ultimately, corporate performance is determined by the achievement of business goals across the different business units of the firm. High-performing companies create value over time; low-performing companies do not. However, different market constituents seek different types of value. Thus, the creation of value—and corporate performance—can be assessed only from the perspective of major market constituents.

Figure 8–3 presents the flows that must be considered in assessing corporate performance. The key constituents of value creation from a corporate performance perspective are: (1) customers, (2) suppliers, and (3) owners and creditors. All three groups transact with the firm through markets. That is, customers buy (and sometimes resell) goods and services through product markets; suppliers sell products and services to the firm through factor markets; and, owners and creditors buy and sell ownership claims— shares of stock in the company—or debt instruments through financial markets.

## Corporate Performance from the Perspective of Customer Markets

Customers in all competitive product markets face choices; they can choose among several different product or service offerings to meet their needs. Thus, managers of each firm that competes in a defined product market will attempt to develop a unique

---

[6] This section is reprinted from Robert Simons, "Corporate Performance," *Handbook of Technology* (Boca Raton, Fla.: CRC Press, 1999), Chap. 17.4.

**value proposition** to attract customers in given market segments and generate profitable sales. *A value proposition refers to the mix of product and service attributes that a firm offers to customers in terms of price, product features, quality, availability, image, buying experience, and after-sales warranty and service.* Customers and potential customers must perceive that a business's value proposition offers superior value and performance or they will choose to buy from a competitor.

To ensure an adequate flow of revenue and profit, managers must ensure that (a) their firm's products and services are meeting customer needs and expectations, (b) their value proposition is sufficiently differentiated from competitors, and (c) revenues exceed the cost of creating and delivering the value proposition. Managers monitor their value proposition in the marketplace by focusing on key customer-value measures. Customer-value measures can be either financial—expressed in monetary units such as dollars—or nonfinancial—expressed in units, counts, or quantities. Some of the more popular measures (to be covered in depth in the next chapter) are:

**Financial Measures:**

- Revenue, or Revenue Growth—This measure indicates customer willingness to purchase a firm's goods and services.
- Gross Profit Margin—Gross profit margin (sales revenue minus the direct and indirect costs of producing those goods or services) reflects the willingness of customers to pay premium prices in return for perceived value in the firm's products and services.
- Warranty Expenses and/or Product Returns—These measures provide insight into product quality and the extent to which products meet customer expectations concerning features and attributes.

**Nonfinancial Measures:**

- Market Share or Market Share Growth—Market share is a measure of customer acceptance relative to competitive offerings in the marketplace. Market share is calculated as the sales of the firm (revenue) divided by total sales of all competitors in a defined market.
- Customer Satisfaction—These measures reflect customer perceptions of value and the extent to which products or services have met expectations. These data are typically collected through survey techniques administered by telephone or mail after sales of goods and services.
- Referrals—This measure of customer loyalty is calculated by gathering data on the source of new business and maintaining a tally of new business generated by referrals.

## Corporate Performance from the Perspective of Factor Markets

Any corporate strategy—strategy that attempts to maximize the value of resources controlled by the corporation—must rely on the resources provided by factor markets. These suppliers provide critical resources such as labor, contract services, materials, energy, and leased land and buildings.

However, suppliers think of value in a very different way than customers and owners. They are not investing in the firm or making a purchase decision that may have long-term consequences. Instead, they are selling their own goods and services to the firm in exchange for the promise of a cash payment under defined terms (such as net 30 days). Thus, the primary performance measure for suppliers is the promptness and reliability of payment for goods and services received.

In terms of supplier value, the applicable measures that managers monitor relate to liquidity—cash flow and days outstanding in accounts payable. As discussed in Chapter 5, managers of all businesses must project and manage cash balances carefully to ensure that cash on hand is sufficient to meet obligations as they become due.

## Corporate Performance from the Perspective of Financial Markets

From stockholders' perspective, corporate performance is reflected in increases in the monetary value and financial return of their investment. For publicly traded companies, this value can be measured in daily changes in the stock price of the firm. For privately held companies, increases in value can only be assessed with certainty at the time when shares of the company change hands.

Managers must ensure that the financial returns created by the sustained profitability of their business are meeting the expectations of owners and potential owners. In competitive financial markets, there are always alternatives for investment funds. Thus, the economic performance of a firm—as reflected in its stock price—must be sufficient to attract new investment and induce existing stockholders to maintain their ownership position. To assess value creation from a financial market perspective, managers commonly monitor four financial measures of increasing aggregation that focus on corporate performance: profit, ROI, residual income, and market value.

### Financial Value Measures

*Profit* as disclosed on a firm's income statement is the cornerstone of business performance from an investor's perspective. Profit is the residual amount that is retained by the business after subtracting all expenses from the revenues earned during that accounting period.

$$\text{Accounting profit} = (\text{Revenues for the Period}) - (\text{Expenses for the Period})$$

Profit is a measure of how much of the revenue received from customers for goods and services is available for reinvestment in the business or distribution to owners. Note, however, that profit as a stand-alone measure does not take into account the level of investment needed to generate that profit. Thus, it is impossible to evaluate the economic performance of a business that earns $100 profit without knowing whether the investment needed to generate that profit was $500 or $1,000.

*Return on Investment* remedies this problem by considering explicitly the underlying level of financial investment. ROI for any period is calculated as the ratio of accounting profit divided by the investment that was needed to create that income.

$$ROI = \frac{\text{Accounting Profit}}{\text{Investment in Business}}$$

ROI takes account of the investment made by owners to support profits, so higher levels of profit for a given level of investment can be expected to yield higher financial returns for investors and increased market values. As discussed in Chapter 5, common variations of this measure used within firms are ROE, ROA, and ROCE—all of which use internal balance sheet data to compute return measures.

In designing ROI- or ROCE-type measures, managers must make two decisions. First, they must decide what balance sheet items to include in the asset base, or denominator. At a minimum, working capital—cash, accounts receivable, and inventory—should be included. In addition, other productive assets such as buildings and equipment can also be included. This decision will depend on the use to which the measure is being put. If ROCE is being used to evaluate the performance of a *business,* then all productive assets should be included. If ROCE is being used to evaluate the performance of a *manager,* then only those assets within a manager's span of control will typically be included in the calculation.

The second decision concerns the best valuation method for depreciable assets. Should they be stated at net book value (net of accumulated depreciation), gross book value (before depreciation), or replacement cost? Choosing net book value is simple and ties in with generally accepted financial accounting policies. However, this approach suffers from the fact that ROI will increase monotonically over time as depreciation erodes the value of the denominator. Gross book value remedies this problem, but it may provide incentives for managers to shrink the denominator by shedding productive assets that are still useful but fully depreciated. Replacement cost is an effective alternative but is often difficult to compute with accuracy because of the estimates that are inevitably necessary.

Considerable care must be exercised in interpreting ratios that rely on balance sheet data. All readers of financial statements should understand that accountants are often forced to make trade-offs between accurate figures on the balance sheet and accurate figures on the income statement. For example, to measure performance in the income statement figures as accurately as possible, managers may adopt a LIFO inventory accounting policy. In so doing, however, there is no choice but to settle for out-of-date historical cost data on the balance sheet. (We will have more to say about this shortly.)

*Residual Income* is a measure of value creation that goes one step further than ROI by considering how much profit investors *expect* to earn from their capital. **Residual income** is a measure of how much additional profit remains for (1) investment in the business or (2) distribution to owners after allowing for normal (expected) returns on investment. It is calculated by subtracting the normal cost of capital used in the business, calculated at current market rates, from accounting profit.

$$\text{Residual Income} = \text{Accounting Profit} - \text{Charge for Capital Used to Generate Profit}$$
$$= \text{Accounting Profit} - (\text{Value of Assets Used to Generate Profit}$$
$$\times \text{Expected Rate of Return on Those Assets})$$

Although residual income is an old concept, some firms have begun to make further refinements to transform residual income into a calculation known as *economic value added.* This technique is discussed in detail in the next section. Positive residual income correlates with increases in the market value of the firm because positive residual income indicates that a business is accumulating net resources at a rate greater than is needed to satisfy the providers of capital. The firm should, therefore, be in a position to grow and increase future cash flows (or pay out an abnormally high level of dividends to owners).

*Market Value*   represents the highest, most aggregate, measure of value creation because it represents the value of ownership claims in the business as priced by financial markets. **Market value** is the price at which shares in the company trade on the open market. For publicly traded companies, market value is priced daily on a per share basis and reported in the financial press. The total market value of a company, or **market capitalization,** is calculated as the product of the total number of ownership shares outstanding times the price per share.

Total market value = Number of Ownership Shares Outstanding × Price per Share

For example, the market value of The Gap is equal to $15.3 billion (calculated as 268 million shares outstanding × $57 per share).

Market value fluctuates with investor perceptions of the level and timing of expected future cash flows of the business. Market value can be expected to increase for companies in which investors believe that future cash flow growth will be positive. These expectations of value, as priced in current stock prices, are reflected in a calcula-

---

## Top U.S. Market Value Added Firms

Fortune magazine published the following ranking by market value added of the 200 largest U.S. firms (as measured by market capitalization):

| MVA RANK | | | | MARKET VALUE ADDED | ECONOMIC VALUE ADDED | CAPITAL | RETURN ON CAPITAL | COST OF CAPITAL |
|---|---|---|---|---|---|---|---|---|
| 1998 | 1997 | 1993 | COMPANY | ($ MILLIONS) | ($ MILLIONS) | ($ MILLIONS) | (IN %) | (IN %) |
| 1 | 2 | 5 | General Electric | $195,830 | $1,917 | $59,251 | 17.3% | 13.8% |
| 2 | 1 | 2 | Coca-Cola | 158,247 | 2,615 | 10,957 | 36.3 | 12.1 |
| 3 | 3 | 12 | Microsoft | 143,740 | 2,781 | 8,676 | 52.9 | 14.2 |
| 4 | 5 | 4 | Merck | 107,418 | 1,921 | 23,112 | 23.2 | 14.5 |
| 5 | 4 | 24 | Intel | 90,010 | 4,821 | 21,436 | 42.7 | 15.1 |
| 6 | 8 | 9 | Procter & Gamble | 88,706 | 587 | 24,419 | 15.2 | 12.8 |
| 7 | 7 | 11 | Exxon | 85,557 | (412) | 88,122 | 9.4 | 9.9 |
| 8 | 11 | 16 | Pfizer | 83,835 | 1,077 | 15,220 | 19.9 | 12.1 |
| 9 | 6 | 3 | Philip Morris | 82,412 | 3,524 | 43,146 | 20.2 | 11.9 |
| 10 | 10 | 6 | Bristol-Myers Squibb | 81,312 | 1,802 | 14,627 | 25.3 | 12.5 |

*Source:* Adapted from Shawn Tully, "America's Greatest Wealth Creators," *Fortune,* (November 9, 1998): 194.

tion known as **market value added,** which is the excess of current market value over the amount of capital (i.e., adjusted book value) provided to the firm:

$$\text{Market Value Added} = \text{Total Market Value}$$
$$- \text{Capital Provided by Owners and Lenders}$$

## ECONOMIC VALUE ADDED

The concept of residual income has been advocated by accountants for a long time, and its calculation is quite straightforward: the cost of capital is subtracted from accounting profit to determine how much is left over for reinvestment or distribution to owners. Recently, there has been a movement—especially in North America—to elaborate the concept of residual income into a calculation known as **economic value added** (EVA).[7] EVA adjustments attempt to transform accounting income (revenue minus expenses) into a number that more closely approximates economic income (cash flows in excess of the opportunity cost of capital). This calculation is similar to residual income but is distinguished by (1) a series of adjustments to eliminate potential distortions of accrual accounting and (2) the inclusion of both debt and equity sources of capital in the calculation of cost of capital.

### Adjustments to Eliminate the Distortions of Accrual Accounting

Generally accepted accounting principles require managers to account for transactions on an *accrual basis*. Accrual accounting adjustments transfer costs and revenues between accounting periods. This is done for two reasons: (1) to better match costs with revenues and (2) to ensure a conservative calculation of profit when there is uncertainty about the timing of future revenues or costs.

For some categories of accruals—such as recording accounts payable for unpaid invoices—there is little dispute about the desirability of shifting costs to the correct accounting period. However, there are other accruals that accountants make for matching purposes or for reliability purposes that can potentially distort the economic income of a business. EVA calculations attempt to undo these adjustments to (1) generate a profit number that more closely represents economic cash flows and (2) restate the balance sheet to reflect the true value of resources used to generate income.

All accrual adjustments can be reversed for EVA calculations, but the following adjustments are the most common and capture most of the potential distortions of accrual-based accounting:

*LIFO Inventory*    To match cost of goods sold with revenues, companies must choose an inventory accounting policy. Most U.S. companies choose LIFO (last-in, first-out) accounting to reduce income and thereby minimize income taxes. In this accounting method, the most recent product costs ("last in") are matched against current revenue

---

[7] Consultants Stern Stewart & Company have trademarked "EVA" as their name for residual income and "MVA" as their acronym for market value added.

(they are the "first out" for matching purposes), with the desirable result that cost of goods sold on the income statement most closely approximates current purchase prices. An unfortunate side effect of LIFO accounting, however, is the fact that the balance sheet inventory figure is often seriously understated, reflecting product costs that are many years out of date. (The "first-in" product costs can sit on the balance sheet until all inventory is liquidated—literally forever!)

Accordingly, for EVA purposes, the value of the inventory account on the balance sheet is adjusted to *current cost* to more accurately reflect the true value of working capital under the control of management. In addition, any distortion to income due to the reduction of inventory stockpiles and the consequent liquidation of LIFO "layers" (i.e., matching of current revenues with very old prices recorded on the balance sheet) is reversed.

*Deferred Tax Expense*   Many people think that "income tax expense" on a company's income statement shows the amount of income taxes a company is required to pay to the government. This is not true. Instead, accountants require companies to record a different—generally higher—tax expense based on *book income*. The difference between what a company records on its income statement as tax expense and what it actually pays the tax authorities reflects *a timing difference*—that is, accruals are recognized at different points in time for book and tax purposes. The most common timing difference is due to choices in depreciation accounting. For example, many companies choose a straight-line method of depreciation for their bookkeeping to best match revenues with expenses; however, for the calculation of taxable income, companies often adopt some method of accelerated depreciation to minimize taxable income and reduce current tax liabilities. Thus, accounting policies—and net income—differ under the book and tax calculations.

Accountants believe that the taxes saved today because of differences in depreciation policies will have to be paid tomorrow. As a result, *tax expense* on an income statement is based on *book income* (e.g., using straight-line depreciation), not on the income that is calculated on a company's income tax return (using accelerated depreciation). The difference between the taxes actually paid and the amount that would have been paid under the company's accrual assumptions is recorded as a deferred tax liability on the balance sheet. For EVA calculations, the current year's income tax expense attributable to the accrual of deferred taxes is added back to income. Similarly, deferred taxes payable on the balance sheet are considered part of the capital of the firm.

*Amortization of Goodwill*   Accountants account for the difference between the purchase price of a company and its identifiable net assets as goodwill. For example, if Company A purchased Company B for $400 million, and the net assets of Company B (assets minus liabilities) were valued only at $300 million, the balance of $100 million would be shown on the purchaser's balance sheet as an asset—"goodwill"—and amortized over some period up to 40 years. Over each of the future 40 years, some portion of the goodwill would be amortized against income, thereby reducing it. For EVA purposes, the goodwill accrual must be adjusted in two ways. First, the reduction in income due to the amortization of goodwill in the current period is added back to income.

Second, to the extent that accumulated amortization has eroded goodwill, the balance sheet is restated to reflect the full purchase price of the acquisition (not only the value of identifiable tangible assets) so that managers are held accountable for generating returns on the full value of the assets employed.

***Research and Development Expense***   Any asset, by definition, represents the present value of future cash flows. If it cannot generate future cash flows, it cannot be classified as an asset. One of the hotly debated issues in accounting over the years is how to account for R&D expenditures. Are they assets or expenses? Some argue that managers invest in research and development for the sole purpose of developing new products and processes that will generate future cash flows. According to this reasoning, R&D expenditures should be capitalized as an asset to be expensed against revenues of future periods. Accountants, however, are suspicious that the amounts spent on R&D may not be fully recoverable in future periods. They argue that some R&D expenditures are inevitably wasted, because experimentation by nature implies trial and error. Therefore, rather than permitting managers to record R&D expenditures as assets—and amortize them over the lives of new products and processes—accountants in the U.S. require managers to expense all R&D expenditures in the current period (this practice differs in other countries).

The EVA calculation reverses this thinking. R&D expenditures are put back on the balance sheet as assets and amortized over some estimated life (typically five or 10 years). This has the effect of increasing income by the amount of the R&D expense (less any amount associated with its amortization over time) and increasing the value of the asset or capital base recorded on the balance sheet.

## Adjustments to Calculate the Cost of Capital

The next set of calculations summarize the investment base used to generate profit. The cost of capital for EVA is generally calculated by including all forms of financing—both equity and debt. Thus, the investment base closely mirrors what would be used for a standard ROA calculation—that is, by including all of the major accounts on the right side of the balance sheet, we are actually arriving at the value of assets on the left side of the balance sheet.

Once the value of debt and equity are identified (or alternatively, the value of assets employed), the WACC is calculated. For example, if a firm was financed 60% by equity and 40% by debt, the cost of equity financing was 16%, and the after-tax cost of debt financing was 8%, then the WACC would be calculated as follows:

| | | | | |
|------|------------|---|--------|----------|
| Debt | $ 400,000 | × | 8% = | $ 32,000 |
| Equity | 600,000 | × | 16% = | 96,000 |
| | $1,000,000 | | | $128,000 |

Equivalently, the rate itself can be calculated directly as:

$$(0.40 \times 0.08) + (0.60 \times 0.16) = \underline{12.8\%}$$

Of course, multiplying this rate (12.8%) by the total amount of debt and equity ($1,000,000) yields an identical $128,000 as the cost of capital.

The following example for a publicly traded biotechnology company will illustrate the effects of these adjustments. The objectives of this calculation are (1) to compute the true value of assets under management's control (which equals exactly the capital base of the firm), (2) to calculate the expected return on those assets based on WACC, and (3) to subtract expected returns from actual profit (after EVA adjustments) to calculate the residual income.

To make these calculations, the following information is needed. This information would be contained in the footnotes of an annual report or, for a smaller business unit or private company, would be available to managers inside the firm.

1. Inventories are stated at the lower of cost or market. Cost is based on the LIFO method. Replacement cost of year-end inventory would be $5,600 higher than the amount reported on the balance sheet. Replacement cost of year-end inventory for the prior year would be $4,800 higher than the amount reported on the previous year's balance sheet.

2. Deferred taxes are due to timing differences in the calculation of depreciation for tax purposes and book purposes.

3. Goodwill results from the purchase of a subsidiary in 20X1, in which the excess of cost over identifiable net asset value equaled $200,000, which is being amortized over 10 years.

4. Research and development costs, related to the investment in prototypes and test machinery for the next generation of product, are being expensed as incurred. Over the life of the firm, $600,000 of R&D expenditures have been written off.

5. The WACC is 12%.

With this information in mind, refer to Exhibit 8–3 for a summary of the analysis to adjust net income and balance sheet accounts for EVA purposes. [*Note:* The top of Exhibit 8–3 presents four columns for the adjustment of balance sheet accounts. The first column is the original accrual balance sheet at 12/31/20X1 with assets equal to liabilities. The next column represents the EVA adjustments. The final two columns represent "Net Operating Assets" and "Adjusted Capital Base," respectively, as computed under EVA. Net Operating Assets total $1,330,600 in net debits (assets minus current liabilities). The Adjusted Capital Base also equals exactly $1,330,600 in net credits (equity plus long-term liabilities). Every line item on the original balance sheet (either a debit or a credit in column one) can be traced across—after adding or subtracting for any EVA adjustments—to either the Asset (debit) or Capital Base (credit) column. Thus, the debits and credits from the original balance sheet stay in balance.]

After making the adjustments shown in Exhibit 8–3, the calculation of EVA is straightforward:

1. Assets = Capital Employed = $1,330,600
2. Expected Return = $1,330,600 × 12% = $159,700
3. EVA = $326,800 − $159,700 = $167,100

Thus, Bio Techno has earned $167,100 more than its cost of capital.

EVA has proven attractive to companies for several reasons. First, it focuses managers on generating returns in excess of the cost of the capital entrusted to them. Positive EVA should result in the creation of wealth and an increase in value for the firm.

## EXHIBIT 8–3
## Bio Techno Company
### Balance Sheet and Income Statement
### Year Ended December 31, 20X1

|  | 12/31/20X1 | SIMPLIFIED EVA ADJUSTMENTS* | NET OPERATING ASSETS (ASSETS MINUS LIABILITIES) | ADJUSTED CAPITAL BASE (DEBT AND EQUITY CAPITAL) |
|---|---|---|---|---|
| *Assets* |  |  |  |  |
| Cash | $ 280,000 |  | $ 280,000 |  |
| Accounts receivable | 420,000 |  | 420,000 |  |
| Inventory | 300,000 | $ 5,600 (1) | 305,600 | $ 5,600 |
| Plant & equipment | 250,000 |  | 250,000 |  |
| Accumulated depreciation | (140,000) |  | (140,000) |  |
| Goodwill | 180,000 | 20,000 (3) | 200,000 | 20,000 |
| Capitalized R&D |  | 475,000 (4) | 475,000 | 475,000 |
|  | $1,290,000 |  |  |  |
| *Liabilities & Shareholders' Equity* |  |  |  |  |
| Accounts payable | $ 145,000 |  | $ (145,000) |  |
| Income tax payable | 45,000 |  | (45,000) |  |
| Other current liabilities | 270,000 |  | (270,000) |  |
| Long-term notes payable | 120,000 |  |  | 120,000 |
| Deferred income taxes | 105,000 | 105,000 (2) | — | 105,000 |
| Common stock | 305,000 |  |  | 305,000 |
| Retained earnings | 300,000 |  |  | 300,000 |
|  | $1,290,000 |  | $1,330,600 | $1,330,600 |

Note that ROE for Bio Techno would be calculated as $160,000 ÷ $605,000 = 26.4%—a number somewhat higher than the returns suggested by the EVA analysis. Second, because EVA is not a ratio, it reduces the risk of managers shrinking the asset base (denominator) to bolster ROA or ROCE measures (managers can still increase residual income by reducing the asset base, but the effect of shrinking assets is less pronounced under EVA).

However, EVA does not work well in all companies. As with ROI-type measures, EVA demands that all assets be valued accurately. This remains problematic for knowledge-intensive businesses or any business with intangible resources that do not appear on the balance sheet. EVA is also difficult to calculate for any business that must allocate large-scale production and corporate assets among many different business units. Also, EVA does not work well for financial institutions that must set aside a prescribed amount of capital for regulatory purposes.

EVA has also been criticized as a myopic measure that fails to consider the industry and competitive context in which the firm competes. EVA measures the company's

**EXHIBIT 8–3** *(Continued)*

| Income Statement | | EVA ADJUSTMENTS* | EVA Income |
|---|---|---|---|
| Revenue | $5,200,000 | | $5,200,000 |
| Cost of goods sold | 2,930,000 | | 2,930,000 |
| | 2,270,000 | | 2,270,000 |
| Inventory holding gain | | 800 (1) | 800 |
| Selling & administration expenses | 1,780,000 | | 1,780,000 |
| Research & development | 175,000 | 115,000 (4) | 60,000 |
| Amortization of goodwill | 20,000 | 20,000 (3) | — |
| Interest expense | 10,000 | 10,000 (5) | — |
| | 1,985,000 | | 1,840,000 |
| Income before taxes | 285,000 | | 430,800 |
| Income tax expense—Current | 100,000 | 4,000 (5) | 104,000 |
| —Deferred | 25,000 | 25,000 (2) | — |
| Net income | $ 160,000 | | $ 326,800 |

* *Explanation of Adjustments: [balance sheet adjustments are made simultaneously to both the asset (a debit) and the capital base (a credit)]*
*(1) $5,600 is added back to inventory for EVA purposes and added to the capital base. $800 is added to income to adjust for the increase in the LIFO reserve.*
*(2) The deferred income tax reserve is transferred to the capital base. The increase in deferred taxes for the current year is added back to income.*
*(3) Accumulated amortization is added back to goodwill on the balance sheet and net income is increased by the amount of the current year's amortization.*
*(4) Accumulated R&D expenses ($600,000) are added back as an asset, less $125,000 accumulated amortization. An amortization schedule indicates that $60,000 of this should be amortized in 20X1.*
*(5) Because interest is included in the charge for WACC, interest expense (after-tax) is added back to avoid double counting.*

ability to earn more than its cost of capital, but it fails to consider how the company has performed relative to its competitors. Shedding underperforming business, repurchasing shares, and slashing costs may increase a company's short-term share price and EVA, but these actions do not necessarily create sustainable wealth.[8]

One might ask why EVA has taken hold in the 1990s, when accountants have had no luck over many generations in selling the idea of residual income. Part of the answer may be in EVA's ability to bring accrual accounting closer to economic cash flows. However, a deeper answer may lie in the extended bull market of the 1990s, during which stock prices have increased dramatically and unceasingly. Investors have come to count on capital appreciation and higher market values as a matter of course. It proved quite hard to sell residual income as a surrogate for market value added during the period 1966 to 1981, when inflation-adjusted stock prices were either falling or flat.

## LINKING EXTERNAL MARKETS AND INTERNAL OPERATIONS: BACK TO THE PROFIT PLAN

We have discussed the key performance measures that managers monitor to ensure that they are meeting the expectations of investors, customers, and suppliers. Often, however, these external parties want to understand more details about the prospects of the

[8] Gary Hamel, "How Killers Count," *Fortune*, (June 23, 1997): 74.

---

## The Shell Business Model

Top executives wanted Shell Oil Company's 21,000 employees to understand what drives value for the shareholder. With $30 billion in revenue and four major operating companies, Shell managers decided to use performance measurement to communicate the economics of the business.

The Shell Business Model now routinely reports the following indicators:

| | |
|---|---|
| Revenue Growth | Overall Market Value |
| ROI | EVA |

CEO Philip Carroll reported, "It is not a program that lets me sit at a computer and figure out what the East Chicago revenue is going to be. Rather, it influences the way I can discuss and evaluate the changing business strategies of the business units. We think of it as a financial beacon that supports decision making in a very rigorous way."

---

*Source:* Adapted from Joel Kurtzman, "Smart Managing: Is Your Company Off Course?" *Fortune,* February 17, 1997, 128.

---

firm before they invest, purchase products, or deliver services. Managers need a way of communicating their goals to external markets. Financial markets will be interested in knowing the long-term economic prospects of the firm—based on an evaluation of the likelihood of success of its competitive strategy. Important customers who must make critical sourcing decisions will be interested in understanding the commitment of the business to support its products in the future and its ability to deliver promised goods and services according to specifications. Key suppliers who are asked to be partners in the value-creation process will be interested in the mix of activities the firm is investing in and their role in those activities.

Profit plans are the critical link used by managers to link business strategy with value creation. Figure 8–4 shows the pivotal role of the profit plan in linking the creation of economic value with the strategic goals of the organization.

Profit plans are the principal tools that managers use to price their business and operating plans, make trade-offs between different courses of action, set performance and accountability goals, and evaluate the extent to which business performance is likely to meet the expectations of different constituents. Examples of the types of strategic decisions that are reflected in a firm's profit plan include the following:

**FIGURE 8–4   A Profit Plan Links Economic Value Creation
with Strategic Goals**

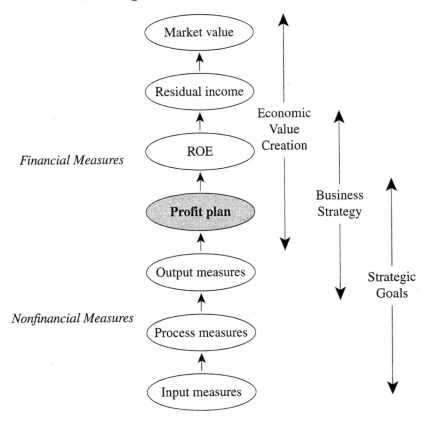

**Revenue**
1. Number of products in product portfolio
2. Mix and type of products
3. Price points of products (a function of features, quality, and competitive products)
4. Changes in any of the above, including
   (a) new-product introductions
   (b) product deletions

**Cost of Goods Sold**
1. Cost of features
2. Cost of quality
3. Efficiency of internal processes
   - production scale and batch sizes
   - economies of purchasing
   - economies of distribution
   - capacity
4. Customization

5. Investment in R&D
6. Investment in plant and equipment (through depreciation)

**Gross Margin**
1. Sustainability of business
2. Success of pricing strategy
3. Market acceptance of product-differentiation strategy

**Selling, General, and Administrative Expenses**
1. Level of support services
2. Outsourcing

**Profit**
1. Attractiveness of business for future investment
2. Willingness of stockholders to invest resources

**FIGURE 8–5    Using Profit Plan Goals to Communicate with External Markets**

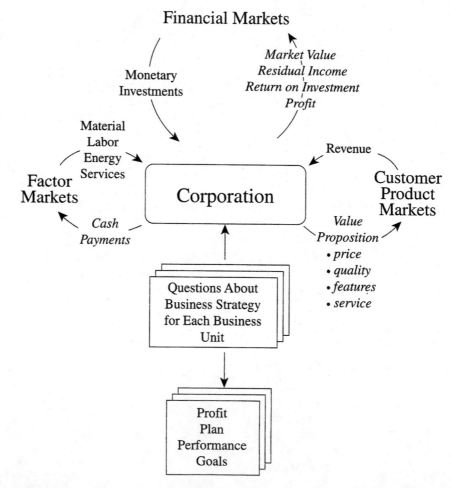

Managers use profit plans to communicate—to analysts, customers, suppliers, and others interested in the prospects of the firm—the strategic choices that have been made and the level of aspirations that have been set as goals (Figure 8–5). This communication—using accounting numbers—can be extremely effective in helping managers reduce the uncertainty of key constituents regarding the prospects and strategy of the firm.

## CHAPTER SUMMARY

Profit plans and other performance indicators are linked to markets inside the firm and outside the firm. Any firm that chooses to transfer goods and service internally between autonomous divisions must rely on transfer prices and adjust the profit plans of the divisions involved. Although there are multiple ways of setting transfer prices, there is no simple solution to the transfer pricing problem. Trade-offs among transfer pricing policies must be understood. In the final analysis, success depends on reasonable managers sitting down and negotiating differences so that the firm can benefit from their actions.

Managers must also understand the linkage between internal operations and external markets. These linkages affect capital markets, customer markets, and supplier markets. To communicate effectively with these markets, managers must know how to use accounting-based tools such as profits plans, ROE and residual income measures, and EVA.

In the next chapter—Building a Balanced Scorecard—we study how to extend this analysis beyond financial accounting numbers by building performance measurement systems that focus on intangible resources: key customers, internal processes, and learning and growth.

# 9

# Building a Balanced Scorecard

The emergence of new information technologies and the opening of global markets has changed many of the fundamental assumptions of modern business. No longer can companies gain sustainable competitive advantage solely by deploying tangible assets. The information-age environment for both manufacturing and service organizations requires new capabilities for competitive success. The ability of a company to mobilize and exploit its intangible assets has become decisive in creating and sustaining competitive advantage.[1]

Intangible resources and assets enable an organization to

- develop customer relationships that build loyalty
- serve new customer segments and markets
- introduce innovative products and services
- produce customized high-quality products and services at low cost and with short lead times
- mobilize employee skills for continuous improvements in process capabilities, quality, and response times

In the past, as companies invested in programs and initiatives to build their capabilities, managers relied solely on financial accounting reports. Today, however, the financial accounting model must be expanded to incorporate the valuation of the company's intangible and intellectual assets. As discussed in earlier chapters, these intangible assets include valuable product and service franchises, motivated and skilled employees, distinctive internal capabilities, and satisfied and loyal customers.

If intangible assets and company capabilities could be valued accurately and reliably on a balance sheet, organizations that enhance these assets and capabilities could communicate this improvement to employees, shareholders, creditors, and other constituencies. Conversely, when companies deplete their stock of intangible assets and capabilities, the loss in value could be reflected immediately on the income statement. Unfortunately, difficulties in placing a reliable financial value on intangible assets—like the value of new-product pipelines, process capabilities, employee skills, customer loyalties, and customer databases—will likely preclude them from ever being recognized on a business's balance sheet. Yet, these are precisely the assets and capabilities that are critical for success in today's competitive environment.

---

[1] Hiroyuki Itami, *Mobilizing Invisible Assets* (Cambridge, Mass.: Harvard University Press, 1987).

**FIGURE 9–1**  **Translating Vision and Strategy: Four Perspectives**

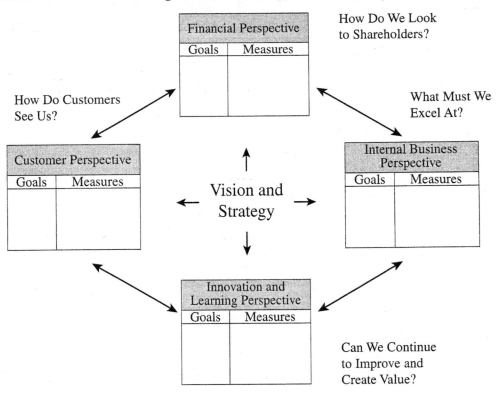

## THE BALANCED SCORECARD

The **balanced scorecard** communicates the multiple, linked objectives that companies must achieve to compete based on their intangible capabilities and innovation. The scorecard translates mission and strategy into goals and measures, organized into four different perspectives: financial, customer, internal business process, and learning and growth (see Figure 9–1).

Managers can build a balanced scorecard by following a logical four-step sequence.

### Step 1: Develop Goals and Measures for Critical Financial Performance Variables

The balanced scorecard retains the **financial performance perspective** discussed in previous chapters because financial measures are essential in summarizing the economic consequences of strategy implementation. Financial performance measures indicate whether the implementation of plans and initiatives is contributing to profit improvement. As discussed in previous chapters, financial objectives can be measured by operating profit, ROCE, and EVA. Additional financial objectives can relate to any variable on the profit wheel, the cash wheel, or the ROE wheel.

For Boston Retail, the financial goals are set out in the profit plan that we developed in Chapter 5. In particular, Boston Retail set a stretch goal to increase sales and operating income by 150% over the next five years—an ambitious target for a mature, largely saturated industry such as apparel retailing.

## Step 2: Develop Goals and Measures for Critical Customer Performance Variables

In the **customer perspective** of the balanced scorecard, managers identify the customer and market segments in which the business desires to compete. Targeted segments could include both existing customers and potential customers. Then, managers develop measures to track the business unit's ability to create satisfied and loyal customers in these targeted segments.

Studies have shown that businesses with satisfied, loyal customers become significantly more profitable over time. Loyal customers typically increase the amount of their purchases, cost less to serve, refer new customers to the business, and are willing to pay a price premium for products or services that they trust. Thus, a 5% increase in customer loyalty can produce profit increases from 25% to 85%.[2]

The customer perspective typically includes several core or generic measures that relate to customer loyalty. These core outcome measures include customer satisfaction, customer retention, new customer acquisition, customer profitability, and market and account share in targeted segments (see Figure 9–2).

**FIGURE 9–2   Customer Perspective: Core Outcome Measures**

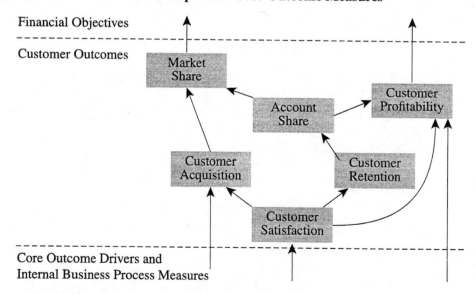

*Source:* Adapted from Robert S. Kaplan and David P. Norton, "Linking the Balanced Scorecard to Strategy," *California Management Review* (Fall 1996).

---

[2] Frederick Reichheld and W. Earl Sasser, Jr. "Zero Defections: Quality Comes to Services," *Harvard Business Review* (September–October, 1990).

Although these customer measures appear to be generic across all types of organizations, they can and should be customized to the targeted customer groups from whom the business expects its greatest growth and profitability. That is, customer satisfaction, customer retention, customer loyalty, and market share should be measured only for those customer or market segments for which the organization desires to be a dominant provider of goods and/or services.

Some common customer-based measures can be developed as follows:

### Customer Satisfaction[3]

- Measuring customer satisfaction can take the form of familiar market research tools such as customer response cards and questionnaires.
- Customer satisfaction can also be measured through letters of complaint, feedback from field sales and service representatives, and "mystery shopper" programs. These sources of customer feedback often give a deeper understanding of customer satisfaction issues.

### Customer Retention

- Monitoring the average duration of a customer relationship can detect problems with the value proposition. Are new customers defecting because they were the wrong customers for this product or service? Are long-term customers leaving because of changes in quality, a better price elsewhere, or a combination of both?
- Surveying defecting customers to understand where defectors go and why they left provides critical feedback on the validity of the firm's strategy.

### Customer Loyalty

- Measuring the number of new customers referred by existing customers can quantify the degree of customer loyalty to a firm. A customer must be highly satisfied before recommending a firm to others.
- Measuring the "depth of relationship" with customers can also provide insight into customer loyalty. For example, a fast-food restaurant chain could measure how much of an average customer's weekly food budget was captured. A luxury-item retailer could measure how often good customers make purchases at their stores versus competitors' stores.

As we have discussed in previous chapters, an effective strategy is based on a unique value proposition the business delivers to attract and retain customers in its targeted segments. Although value propositions vary across industries and across different market segments within industries, there are a common set of attributes that organize the value propositions in most industries. These attributes fall into three categories (see Figure 9–3):

- product/service attributes
- customer relationship
- image and reputation

Let's consider each briefly.

*Product and service attributes* of a value proposition encompass desirable product or service features, price, and quality. For companies competing on operational

---

[3] James Heskett et al., "Putting the Service-Profit Chain to Work," *Harvard Business Review* (March–April 1994): 164–174.

**FIGURE 9–3   Customer Perspective: Linking Unique Value Propositions to Core Outcome Measures**

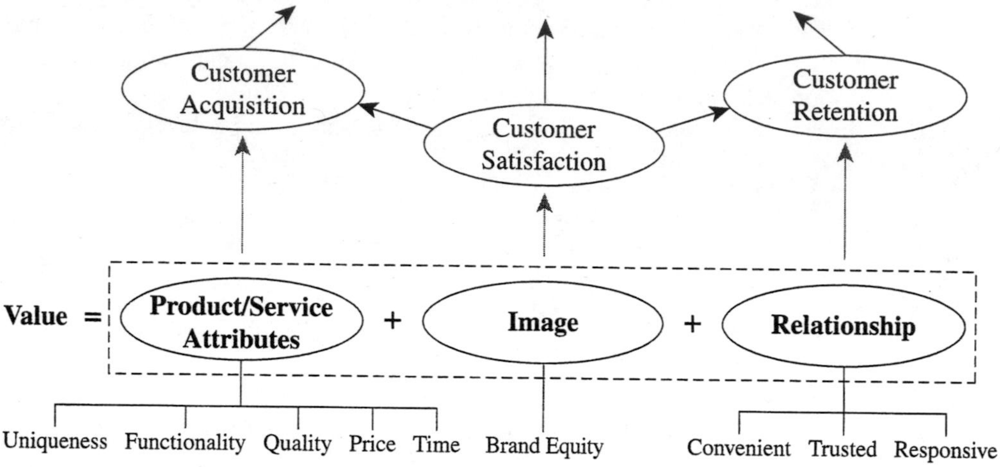

Source: Adapted from Kaplan and Norton, "Linking the Balanced Scorecard to Strategy," p. 62.

excellence, for example, critical performance measures might include the price of the product relative to competitors, the quality perceived by customers (such as defect rates and field failures), and timeliness (such as lead times and on-time delivery). Other companies, competing on uniqueness or particular product features, will choose to measure those product attributes that create value in a different way for their particular customer segment. For example, size is a critical performance variable for implantable medical devices, disk drives, and computer chips. For electronic instruments, accuracy might be highly valued. For automobiles, acceleration, braking capabilities, and engine performance might be dimensions that determine customer preferences. Depending on the value proposition, measures can be developed for each of these critical performance attributes.

The *customer relationship* dimension of a value proposition includes the delivery of the product or service to the customer, including response and delivery time, and how the customer feels about the buying experience. Many companies perform detailed customer surveys or "mystery shopper" programs to assess the quality of the relationship between the customer and the company.

The *image and reputation* dimension of the value proposition enables a company to calibrate and measure the value of its franchise. Advertising and marketing research companies employ techniques to measure the strength of a brand name. These measures can be used to track the effectiveness of the strategy in building franchise value. Other examples of image and reputation measures include the price premium earned by a product compared with an unbranded competitive offering and the willingness of retailers to stock the product because of the consumer demand generated by a strong brand.

Boston Retail could generate a variety of measures for its customer value proposition using all three components of the value equation—product attributes, customer relationship, and brand image—as follows:

## Product Attributes

### 1. Price Benefits

- Average unit retail price (an indicator of a successful product mix)
- Total dollar sales at discounted prices (an indicator of failed merchandise categories)

### 2. Fashion and Design

- Average annual sales growth in "strategic merchandise" (key items that best exemplify the image Boston Retail is attempting to convey)
- Average mark-up achieved (an indicator of well-received merchandise design and fashion)

### 3. Quality

- Return rate (an indicator of the consumer's satisfaction with the quality of the product)

## Customer Relationship

### 1. Availability

- Out-of-stock percentage on strategic merchandise
- Data, collected by responses on a "What do you think?" card solicited from each customer, asking about satisfaction with the availability of size and color on selected items

### 2. Shopping Experience

- "Mystery shopper" audits (An independent, third-party shopper was hired to purchase selected items at each Boston Retail location and evaluate the experience according to criteria established for the "perfect shopping experience.")

## Brand and Image

- Market share in strategic merchandise categories
- Premium price earned on branded items (If Boston Retail is successful in communicating an attractive brand image, it should command a higher price over unbranded or generic items of comparable product characteristics and quality.)

Managers at Boston Retail decided that their core customer outcome measures should include market share, account share (e.g., share of wardrobe), and satisfaction for customers in its targeted segment (18- to 30-year-old, college-educated females). Information on market and account share was not available from public sources. Therefore, Boston Retail engaged a market research firm to conduct surveys to estimate its performance with this targeted customer segment.

## Step 3: Develop Goals and Measures
## for Critical Internal Process Performance Variables

In the **internal business process perspective,** managers identify the critical internal processes for which the organization must excel in implementing its strategy (see Figure 9–4). The internal business processes dimension represents the critical processes that enable the business unit to

- deliver the value propositions that will attract and retain customers in targeted market segments, and
- satisfy shareholder expectations regarding financial returns.

Thus the internal business process measures should be focused on the internal processes that will have the greatest impact on customer satisfaction and achieving the organization's financial objectives.

Each business will have a unique set of processes for creating value for customers and producing superior financial results. The **internal value chain** model provides a handy template that companies can use to customize for their own objectives and measures in their internal business process perspective of the scorecard. The generic value chain model encompasses three principal business processes (see Figure 9–4):

1. innovation processes
2. operations processes
3. post-sales service processes

### Innovation Processes

In the **innovation process,** managers research the needs of customers and then create the products or services that will meet those needs. Companies identify new markets, new customers, and the emerging and latent needs of existing customers. Then, companies design and develop new products and services that enable them to reach these new markets and customers.

As part of the innovation process, managers perform market research to identify the size of the market and the nature of customers' preferences and price sensitivity for the targeted product or service. As organizations deploy their internal processes to meet these customer needs, accurate information on market size and customer preferences becomes vital to effective resource allocation.

Managers at Boston Retail chose to focus their innovation efforts on *fashion leadership.* Thus, they measured this objective with two key measures:

### FIGURE 9–4    The Internal Value Chain

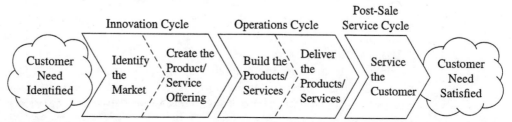

*Source:* Adapted from Kaplan and Norton, *The Balanced Scorecard* (Boston: Harvard Business School Press, 1996), p. 96.

- number of key items in which Boston Retail was first or second to the market
- percentage of sales from items newly introduced into stores

## Operations Processes

The **operations process,** the second major step in the internal value chain, represents those processes that produce and deliver existing products and services to customers. The operations process starts with receipt of a customer order and finishes with delivery of the product or service to the customer. These processes stress efficient, consistent, and timely delivery of existing products and services to existing customers.

The operations process has historically been the focus of most organizations' internal measurement systems. Today—as always—operational excellence and cost reduction remain important goals. However, as the internal value chain in Figure 9–4 shows, such operational excellence may be only one component—and perhaps not the most decisive component—in the internal value chain.

Existing operations tend to be repetitive. Therefore, scientific management techniques can be readily applied to control and improve production and delivery processes. Traditionally, these operating processes have been monitored and controlled by financial measures such as standard costs, budgets, and efficiency variances. Over time, however, excessive focus on narrow financial measures such as labor efficiency, machine efficiency, and purchase price variances has sometimes led to dysfunctional actions, such as:

- keeping labor and machines busy building inventory not related to current customer orders
- switching from supplier to supplier to chase cheaper purchase prices (but ignoring the costs of poor quality and uncertain delivery times)[4]

In recent years, the influence of the TQM and time-based competition practices of leading Japanese manufacturers has led many companies to supplement their traditional cost and financial measurements with measurements of quality and cycle time.[5]

*Quality Measures*   Almost all organizations today have quality initiatives and quality programs in place. Measurement is a central part of any quality program. Therefore, most organizations are already familiar with a variety of process-quality measurements, including:

- process parts-per-million (PPM) defect rates
- yields (ratio of good items produced to good items entering the process)
- scrap

---

[4] Robert Kaplan, "Limitation of Cost Accounting in Advanced Manufacturing Environments," Chap. 1 in Robert S. Kaplan, ed., *Measures for Manufacturing Excellence* (Boston: Harvard Business School Press, 1990).
[5] Many references could be cited here. A representative sample includes C. Berliner and J. Brimson, "CMS Performance Measurement," Chap. 6 in *Cost Management for Today's Advanced Manufacturing* (Boston: Harvard Business School Press, 1988); C. J. McNair, W. Mosconi, and T. Norris, *Meeting the Technology Challenge: Cost Accounting in a JIT Environment* (Montvale, N.J.: Institute of Management Accountants, 1988); and R. Lynch and K. Cross, *Measure Up! Yardsticks for Continuous Improvement* (Cambridge, Mass.: Basil Blackwell, 1991).

- rework
- returns
- percentage of processes under statistical process control

Service organizations should also identify any defects in their internal processes that could adversely affect costs, responsiveness, or customer satisfaction. They can then develop customized measures of quality shortfalls. One bank, for example, developed an index to indicate the defects in its internal processes that lead to customer dissatisfaction. The index included items such as:

- long waiting times
- inaccurate information given to customers
- access denied or delayed
- request or transaction not fulfilled
- financial loss for customer

*Cycle Time Measures*  Many customers place a high value on short and reliable lead times, measured as the time elapsed from when they place an order until the time when they receive the desired product or service. Accordingly, the value proposition delivered to targeted customers often includes short response time for the delivery of goods and services as a critical performance attribute.

Manufacturing companies generally have two ways of offering short and reliable lead times to customers. One way is to have efficient, just-in-time (JIT), short-cycle order fulfillment that can respond rapidly to customer orders. The other way is to produce and hold large stocks of finished-goods inventory so that any customer request can be met by shipments from inventory stocks. Rapid response through JIT processes potentially enables the company to be a low-cost and timely supplier. The second way—based on large inventory stocks—can lead to high inventory carrying and obsolescence costs, as well as an inability to respond quickly to orders for nonstocked items (because the manufacturing processes are typically busy building inventories for normally stocked items). When manufacturing companies attempt to shift away from high inventories (producing large batches for "just-in-case" inventory) to the JIT approach, reducing cycle or throughput times of internal processes becomes a critical internal process objective.

Cycle or throughput times can be measured in different ways. The start of the cycle can correspond to the time that

1. a customer order is received
2. a production batch is scheduled
3. raw materials are ordered for the order or production batch
4. production on the order or batch is initiated

Similarly the end of the cycle can correspond to the time that

1. production of the order or the batch has been completed
2. an order or batch is in finished goods inventory, available to be shipped
3. an order is shipped
4. an order is received by the customer

The choice of starting and ending points is determined by the scope of the operating process for which cycle-time reductions are being sought. The broadest definition, corresponding to an *order fulfillment cycle,* starts the cycle with receipt of a customer order and ends when the customer has received the order. A much narrower definition, aimed at improving the *flow of physical material* within a factory, could correspond to the time between when a batch is started into production and when the batch has been fully processed. Whatever definition is used, the organization should continually measure cycle times and set goals for employees to reduce total cycle times.

Several organizations use a metric called manufacturing cycle effectiveness (*MCE*), defined as:

$$MCE = \frac{\text{Processing Time}}{\text{Throughput Time}}$$

This ratio is less than 1 because throughput time, the denominator, can be broken out as follows:

$$\frac{\text{Throughput}}{\text{Time}} = \frac{\text{Processing}}{\text{Time}} + \frac{\text{Inspection}}{\text{Time}} + \frac{\text{Movement}}{\text{Time}} + \frac{\text{Waiting/Storage}}{\text{Time}}$$

To emphasize the importance of reducing throughput time, this equation can be rewritten as:

$$\text{Throughput Time} = \text{Value-added Time} + \text{Nonvalue-added Time}$$

where *value-added time* equals processing time plus the times during which work is actually being performed on the product, and *nonvalue-added time* represents the time the part is waiting, being moved, or being inspected.

Although JIT production processes and the MCE ratio were originally developed for manufacturing operations, they are just as applicable to service companies. If anything, eliminating waste time in a service delivery process is even more important than in manufacturing companies. Consumers are increasingly intolerant of being forced to wait in line for service delivery. In many service companies, studies have indicated that customers experience long cycle times for service, despite actual processing time being quite low. As a result, some automobile rental companies and hotel chains have now automated all aspects of check-in and check-out, enabling repeat customers to bypass all waiting in line when accessing the service and upon completion of the service delivery process.

Thus, companies attempting to deliver products and services on demand to targeted customers can set objectives to have MCE ratios approach 1, thereby dramatically shortening lead times to customer orders.

*Cost Measures*    Amidst all the attention to process time and process quality measurements, one might lose sight of the cost of these internal processes. Traditional cost accounting systems measure the expenses and efficiencies of individual tasks, operations, or departments. However, these systems fail to measure costs at the *process level of analysis.* Today, with activity-based cost systems, managers can obtain accurate cost measurement of their business processes. Activity-based cost analysis enables organizations to obtain process cost measurements that, along with quality and cycle-time

In addition to the profit plan goals established in Chapter 5, Boston Retail established two critical objectives for its operating processes: (1) sourcing leadership and (2) merchandise availability. It measured these two objectives with two measures each, as shown below:

**Sourcing Leadership**
- Percentage of items returned to vendors because of quality problems
- Vendor performance rating (incorporating dimensions of vendors' quality, price, and lead time)

**Merchandise Availability**
- Out-of-stock percentage on selected key items
- Inventory turnover on selected key items (a "compensating" measure to ensure that high in-stock performance was achieved by excellent supplier and distribution performance, not by holding excess inventories)

measurement, provide important parameters to track the effectiveness and efficiency of important internal business processes.

In summary, some aspects of quality, time, and cost measurements will likely be included as critical performance measures in any organization's internal business process perspective on its balanced scorecard.

## Post-Sale Service Processes

The third and final stage in the internal value chain is customer service after the original sale or delivery of service. The **post-sale service process** includes warranty and repair activities, treatment of defects and returns, and the administration of payments, such as credit card processing. Some companies have explicit strategies to offer superior post-sale service. For example, companies that sell sophisticated equipment or systems may offer training programs for customers' employees to help them use the equipment or system more effectively. They may also offer rapid response to failures and downtime. Newly established automobile dealerships, like Acura and Saturn, have earned reputations for offering dramatically improved customer service for warranty work, periodic car maintenance, and car repairs. A major element in their value proposition is responsive, friendly, and reliable warranty and service work. Accordingly, these companies measure customer satisfaction each time a customer has his or her car serviced by the dealer.

Another aspect of post-sale service can include the invoicing and collection process. Companies with extensive sales on credit or with branded credit cards will likely apply cost, quality, and cycle-time measurements to their billings, collection, and dispute resolution processes. Several department stores offer value propositions that include generous terms under which customers can exchange or return merchandise. As with the car dealer, these companies can measure the satisfaction of key customers with returns policies and billings and collections.

Companies that deal with hazardous chemicals and materials illustrate a special case of post-sale service. These companies may introduce critical performance measures associated with the safe disposal of waste and byproducts from the production process. For example, one distributor of industrial chemicals developed after-sale disposal services for used chemicals, freeing its customers from this expensive task, which is fraught with liability and subject to intense governmental scrutiny by agencies such as the Environmental Protection Agency and the Occupational Safety and Health Administration. This company measures the percentage of customers that uses its recycling program. This measure signals to the company's employees the importance of soliciting this business and delivering post-sale service in a reliable, cost-effective manner.

For many companies, excellent community relations may also be a strategic objective to ensure the continuing right to operate production facilities. Accordingly, these companies often set post-sale service objectives for environmental performance. Measures such as waste produced during production processes may be more significant for their impact on the environment than for their slight increase in production costs. All of these activities add value to the customers' use of the company's product and service offerings.

We have now reviewed the innovation, operations, and after-sale service components of the internal value chain. The analysis reveals two fundamental differences between traditional and balanced scorecard approaches to performance measurement. Traditional approaches attempt to monitor and improve *existing* business processes. These approaches may go beyond just financial measures of performance by incorporating quality and time-based metrics—but they still focus on improving existing processes. The balanced scorecard approach, by contrast, can identify entirely *new processes* at which the organization must excel to meet customer and financial objectives. For example, as part of a balanced scorecard analysis, the organization may realize that it must develop a process to anticipate customer needs or one to deliver new services that customers value. The balanced scorecard internal business process objectives highlight these processes—several of which it may not be currently performing.

The second departure of the balanced scorecard approach is to incorporate *innovation processes* into the internal business process perspective. Traditional performance measurement systems focus on the processes of delivering today's products and services to today's customers. However, the drivers of long-term financial success may require the organization to create entirely new products and services that will meet the emerging needs of current (and future) customers. The innovation process is, for many companies, a more powerful driver of future financial performance than the short-term operating cycle. The ability to manage successfully a multiyear product-development process or to develop a capability to reach entirely new categories of customers may be more critical for future economic performance than managing existing operations efficiently, consistently, and responsively. The internal business process perspective of the balanced scorecard can incorporate objectives and measures for the innovation cycle as well as the operations cycle.

## Step 4: Develop Goals and Measures for Critical Learning and Growth Performance Variables

The fourth balanced scorecard perspective—**learning and growth**—identifies the infrastructure that the organization must build to create long-term growth and improvement. The customer and internal business process perspectives identify the factors most critical for current and future success. However, businesses are unlikely to be able to meet their long-term targets for customers and internal processes using today's technologies and capabilities. Intense global competition requires companies to continually improve their capabilities for delivering value to customers and shareholders.

Organizational learning and growth come from three principal sources: people, systems, and organizational procedures. The financial, customer, and internal business process objectives on the balanced scorecard will typically reveal large gaps between existing capabilities and those required to achieve targets for breakthrough performance. To close these gaps, businesses must invest in training employees, enhancing information technology and systems, and aligning organizational procedures and routines. These objectives are articulated in the learning and growth perspective of the balanced scorecard. As in the customer perspective, employee-based measures can include quantitative outcome measures based on surveys to measure employee satisfaction, employee retention, employee training, and employee skills. Information systems capabilities can be measured by the availability and responsiveness of accurate, critical, customer and internal process information to front-line employees. Organizational procedures can examine alignment of employee incentives with overall organizational success factors and measure rates of improvement in critical customer-based and internal processes.

Studies across multiple industries have shown that employee and customer satisfaction closely track one another.[6] This "satisfaction mirror" occurs for a number of reasons: Positive encounters with customers lead to higher levels of employee job satisfaction, which in turn engender greater employee loyalty. As employee loyalty increases, so does average employee tenure. Over time, employees get to know their job and their customers better. As a result, they can deliver higher levels of service to their customers, potentially at a lower cost. Better service reinforces employee satisfaction, creating a virtuous cycle. Measuring employee skills (through testing and training) and empowerment (evaluating the extent to which employees are given authority to correct customer problems, information systems to support their interactions with customers, etc.) are essential to maintaining the virtuous cycle.

## Step 5: Use the Balanced Scorecard to Communicate Strategy

As we have discussed, the balanced scorecard retains important financial measures. Financial measures alone, however, are insufficient for guiding and evaluating how companies create *future* value through investment in customers, employees, processes, and innovation. Financial measures tell the story of tangible assets; the balanced scorecard provides a window into the value created by intangible assets.

---

[6] James Heskett, W. Earl Sasser, and Leonard Schlesinger, *The Service Profit Chain* (New York: The Free Press, 1997): 101.

Using the balanced scorecard, top managers can measure how effective their business units are in creating value for current and future customers, building and enhancing internal capabilities, and investing in people, systems, and procedures necessary to improve future performance. The balanced scorecard captures critical value-creation activities that escape traditional income statements and balance sheets. While retaining an

---

### Balanced Scorecard and Strategic Alignment at Cigna

Cigna International Property & Casualty Company applied the balanced scorecard approach as part of its strategic transformation. It took President Gerald Isom and his management team three months to define the four categories of the scorecard: financial, external (customer), internal (business processes), and learning and growth. Isom made it clear that these measures would now be used to define and achieve Cigna's vision of becoming a specialist insurer with financial results in the top 25% of the commercial insurance industry. The plethora of nonfinancial measures was totally new to Cigna managers. According to Isom, in the past the entire focus was on the financial numbers. There was insufficient attention devoted to outcomes or to understanding critical performance variables. To communicate strategy down the three levels of the organization, Isom asked the company's three divisions and 20 business units to devise their own balanced scorecards, which were to be constantly reviewed.

Cigna's balanced scorecard enabled business units to align their business plans with corporate strategy. For example, Cigna set premium growth as an objective at the corporate level, but profitable growth required different plans in each business unit. Some business units chose to measure increases in premiums from new producers (brokers and agents), whereas others measured premiums from new segments or premiums from new products. Cigna also wanted strong relations with brokers and agents. Again, different business units implemented measures appropriate to their circumstances: more flexible underwriting in one unit, faster underwriting decisions in another, a broader array of services in a third, more price competitiveness in a fourth, and so on.

Employees received "position shares," whose face value of $10 per share was to be adjusted according to balanced scorecard performance. At the beginning of the year, employees received a certain fixed number of position shares (based on their job level), and additional shares were awarded as a bonus during the year. This system allowed the heads of strategic business units to reward any employee who influenced the unit's performance measure.

Cigna executives can check business unit performance anytime on the corporate information system. Although each business unit has its own target, all units rate themselves using the same 1 to 5 scale numerical system, enabling easy comparisons. Underperforming units are flagged with yellow or red. Constant feedback is reinforced by the fact that the score of each unit is available to the others.

---

*Source:* Adapted from Bill Birchard, "Cigna P&C: A Balanced Scorecard," *CFO* (October 1996): 30–34.

interest in short-term performance—via the financial perspective—the balanced score-card clearly reveals the value drivers for superior long-term financial and competitive performance.

Well-designed scorecards enable both financial and nonfinancial measures to be part of the information system for employees at all levels of the organization. Front-line employees can see the financial consequences from their decisions and actions; senior executives can understand the drivers of long-term financial success. The balanced scorecard represents a translation of a business unit's mission and strategy into tangible goals and measures. The four perspectives of the scorecard permit a balance (1) between short- and long-term objectives, (2) between external measures—for shareholders and customers—and internal measures of critical business processes, innovation, and learning and growth, (3) between desired outcomes and the performance drivers of those outcomes, and (4) between hard objective measures and softer, more subjective measures.

Many people think of measurement as a tool to control behavior and to evaluate past performance. However, the measures on a balanced scorecard should be used in a different way. Balanced scorecard measures should be used to articulate the strategy of the business, to communicate this strategy to employees, and to help align individual, organizational, and cross-departmental initiatives to achieve common goals. Used in this way, the scorecard does not strive to keep individuals and organizational units in com-pliance with a preestablished plan. Rather, the balanced scorecard should be used as part of a larger management system for communication, information sharing, and learning.

The multiplicity of measures on a balanced scorecard may seem confusing, but properly constructed scorecards, as we will see, contain a unity of purpose; all the mea-sures are directed toward achieving an integrated strategy.

## TESTING THE LINKAGE OF MULTIPLE SCORECARD MEASURES TO A SINGLE STRATEGY

The multiple measures on a properly constructed balanced scorecard should consist of a linked series of goals and measures that are both consistent and mutually reinforcing. In other words, the balanced scorecard should be viewed as the instrumentation for a *single* strategy. The integrated system of scorecard measures should incorporate the complex set of cause-and-effect relationships among the critical variables that describe the trajec-tory and the flight plan of the strategy. The linkages should incorporate both outcome measures and performance drivers.

### Cause-and-Effect Relationships

Good measurement systems should make the relationships among goals and measures explicit so they can be managed and validated. The chain of cause and effect should per-vade all four perspectives of a balanced scorecard. For example, ROCE may be a score-card measure in the financial perspective. The driver of this financial measure could be repeat and expanded sales from existing customers, the result of a high degree of loy-alty. Customer loyalty is included on the scorecard (in the customer perspective) be-cause it is expected to have a strong influence on ROCE, but how will the organization achieve customer loyalty? Analysis of customer preferences may reveal that on-time delivery of orders is highly valued by customers. Thus, improved on-time delivery is expected to lead to higher customer loyalty, which, in turn, is expected to lead to higher financial performance. Therefore, both customer loyalty and on-time delivery are incorporated into the customer perspective of the scorecard.

The process continues by asking what internal processes must the company excel at to achieve exceptional on-time delivery. To achieve improved on-time delivery, the business may need to achieve short cycle times in operating processes and high-quality internal processes, both factors that could be scorecard measures in the internal perspective. How do organizations improve the quality and reduce the cycle times of their internal processes? By training and improving the skills of their operating employees, an objective that would be a candidate for the learning and growth perspective. In this manner, an entire chain of cause-and-effect relationships can be established as a vertical vector through the four balanced scorecard perspectives:

| | |
|---|---|
| *Financial* | ROCE |
| | ⇑ |
| *Customer* | Customer Loyalty |
| | ⇑ |
| | On-Time Delivery |
| | ⇑              ⇑ |
| *Internal Business Process* | Process Quality   Process Cycle Time |
| | ⇑              ⇑ |
| *Learning and Improvement* | Employee Skills |

Thus, a properly constructed balanced scorecard should tell the story of the business unit's strategy. It should identify and make explicit the sequence of hypotheses about the cause-and-effect relationships between outcome measures and the performance drivers of those outcomes.

## Performance Drivers

A good balanced scorecard should have a mix of outcome measures and performance drivers (i.e., critical input and process measures). Outcome measures without performance drivers do not communicate how the outcomes are to be achieved. They also do not provide early warning about whether the strategy is being implemented successfully. Conversely, performance drivers based on inputs and processes alone—such as cycle times and PPM defect rates—enable the business unit to achieve short-term operational improvements. However, these measures fail to reveal whether the operational improvements have been translated into expanded business with existing and new customers, and, eventually, into enhanced financial performance. Thus, a good balanced scorecard should have an appropriate mix of outcomes (lagging indicators) and performance drivers (leading indicators) of the business unit's strategy. In this way, the scorecard translates the business unit's strategy into a linked set of measures that define the long-term strategic objectives, as well as the mechanisms for achieving those objectives.

## Strategic Measures

Most organizations today already have hundreds, if not thousands, of measures to keep themselves functioning and to signal when corrective action must be taken. However, most of these measures are not drivers of a business's competitive success. They are necessary for ongoing operations, but they do not define or measure success in achieving key strategic goals.

A simple example clarifies this point. Many aspects of our bodily functions must perform within fairly narrow operating parameters if we are to survive. If our body temperature departs from a normal 1°–2° window (away from 98.6° F or 37° C), or our blood pressure drops too low or escalates too high, we have a serious problem for our survival. In such circumstances, all our energies (and those of skilled professionals) are mobilized to restore these parameters back to their normal levels. However, under normal circumstances, we do not devote much energy to optimizing our body temperature and blood pressure. Being able to control our body temperature to within 0.01° of the optimum will not be one of the strategic success factors that will determine whether we become a chief executive of a company, a senior partner in an international consulting firm, or a tenured professor. Other factors are much more decisive in determining whether we achieve our unique personal and professional objectives. Are body temperature and blood pressure important? Absolutely. If these measurements fall outside predetermined limits, we have a major problem that we must attend to and solve immediately. Although these measurements are *necessary*, they are not *sufficient* for the achievement of our long-run goals.

The balanced scorecard is a complement, not a replacement, for an organization's other performance measurement and control systems. The measures on the balanced scorecard are chosen to direct the attention of managers and employees to those factors where high performance levels can be expected to lead to competitive breakthroughs. Although the cockpit of a Boeing 747 has hundreds of gauges and dials, the pilot monitors only a handful of these gauges actively—using that information to balance the critical performance variables of the aircraft relative to its destination. The other indicators are essential only if a basic function fails to perform and a warning buzzer sounds. Like body temperature and blood pressure, they are hygiene factors. In a business, hygiene factors are not the basis for competitive breakthroughs. If these factors do not meet acceptable standards, they can prevent the organization from meeting its objectives—but they are not the foundation for successful strategy.

For example, in the 1980s, product and process quality of many Western companies were so poor compared with their Japanese competitors that the companies had to put quality improvements at the top of their priorities. After years of hard and diligent work, many U.S. companies have achieved excellent quality and are now at parity with their foreign competitors. At this point, quality has been neutralized as a competitive factor. Of course, companies need to maintain existing quality and continue to make continuous improvements, but quality is no longer a critical factor for determining strategic success. In such a situation, quality is monitored diagnostically, and the company needs to find other dimensions in its value proposition to distinguish itself from competitors. These other dimensions are at the core of the balanced scorecard.

## FOUR PERSPECTIVES: ARE THESE SUFFICIENT?

The four perspectives of the balanced scorecard should be considered as a template, not a straitjacket. No mathematical theorem exists to prove that four perspectives are both necessary and sufficient. The owners and capital contributors to the organization appear on every scorecard through goals and measures in the financial perspective. Customer measures also appear on every scorecard (in the customer perspective) because customers are essential for meeting the financial goals. Goals and measures for employees appear on the balanced scorecard when outstanding performance along this dimension will lead to breakthrough performance for customers and shareholders.

Companies rarely use fewer than four perspectives but, depending on industry circumstances and a business unit's strategy, one or more additional perspectives may be needed. For example, some managers incorporate the interests of other important stakeholders, such as suppliers and the community. When strong supplier relationships are part of the strategy leading to breakthrough customer and/or financial performance, then outcome and performance driver measures for supplier relationships should be incorporated within the organization's internal business process perspective. When outstanding environmental and community performance is a central part of a company's strategy, then objectives and measures for that perspective also become an integral part of a company's scorecard.[7]

## CHAPTER SUMMARY

In rapidly changing, highly competitive global markets, companies succeed by investing in and managing their intangible assets and capabilities. Functional specialization must be integrated into customer-based business processes. Mass production and delivery of standard products and services are being replaced by flexible, responsive, and innovative products and services that can be customized to targeted customer segments. Innovation in products, services, and processes must be created by highly trained employees, superior information technology, and aligned organizational procedures.

As organizations invest in acquiring these new intangible capabilities, their success cannot be motivated or measured solely by the traditional financial accounting model. The balanced scorecard integrates measures at the core of implementing strategy. While retaining key financial measures, the balanced scorecard introduces the drivers of future financial performance. These drivers—encompassing customer, internal business process, and learning and growth perspectives—are derived from an explicit and rigorous translation of the organization's strategy into tangible goals and measures.

---

[7] See comments of D. W. Boivin, President and COO Novacor Chemicals, "Using the Balanced Scorecard," letter to the editor, *Harvard Business Review* (March–April 1996): 170.

# PART III

## Achieving Profit Goals and Strategies

# 10

# Using Diagnostic and Interactive Control Systems

To achieve financial and nonfinancial goals, managers must rely on the efforts and initiative of employees. Employees throughout the organization must understand the business's strategy and their role in achieving strategically important goals. As businesses grow larger, communication of strategic goals and measures becomes both more important and more difficult. Managers face increasing demands on their time and must use their scarce resources wisely. Using performance measurement and control systems effectively becomes critical to success.

Step back in time to the initial start-up of Boston Retail. The founders had an idea that they believed could be built into a successful business. At first, they rented one retail store and started as most entrepreneurs do—by doing everything themselves. They tested their value proposition, focusing on the youthful college fashion market. Feedback from customers was encouraging. The entrepreneurs worked diligently to build up the scale of the business and attract a loyal customer base. Early profits were plowed back into the business and additional resources were acquired—new store furnishings, warehouse facilities, and additional inventory. A few temporary employees were hired to help out in the evenings and during the busy holiday seasons.

In the day-to-day operation of the store, all important decisions were reserved for the founders. They were always on hand and could be consulted for any issues that required a judgment call. The owners signed all checks and monitored carefully the flow of inventory, paperwork, and cash receipts to ensure that all receipts were safely deposited in the bank, all inventory was properly handled, and all sales transactions were accurately recorded. Because of their constant oversight, few errors occurred and those that did were caught early and rectified.

As Boston Retail prospered, additional stores were opened and new employees were hired to staff the stores. The founders tried, as much as possible, to give new employees the training and information needed to effectively perform their jobs. However, as time passed, it became increasingly difficult to directly monitor the work of the employees. The business had grown too large and dispersed. The founders were experiencing limits as to what they could accomplish single-handedly. There were now too many employees and too many stores to watch everything themselves; besides, the entrepreneurial founders wanted to devote more of their time to pursuing expansion opportunities. If the business was to continue its profitable growth, the founders would have to change their focus. For the first time in the history of the young company, success would

**FIGURE 10–1    Two Levers of Control: Diagnostic and Interactive Control Systems**

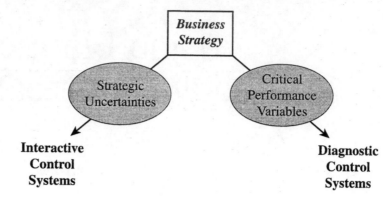

*Source:* Adapted from Simons, *Levers of Control,* p. 7.

be determined by the founders' ability to effectively *communicate* strategy to employees and *control* strategy implementation.

To understand how to communicate and control strategy effectively, we differentiate between two different types of control systems: diagnostic control systems and interactive control systems. Managers rely on both types of systems, but for different purposes. Diagnostic control systems are used as levers to communicate critical performance variables and monitor the implementation of intended strategies. Interactive control systems are used to focus organizational attention on strategic uncertainties and provide a lever to fine-tune and alter strategy as competitive markets change (Figure 10–1).

We should, however, make a critical point at the outset of our analysis. The difference between diagnostic and interactive control systems is not in their technical design features. A diagnostic control system may look identical to an interactive control system. The distinction between the two is solely in the way that managers *use* these systems. For example, the same profit planning system or balanced scorecard can be used *either* diagnostically *or* interactively. As we shall see, this choice has profound implications for maximizing ROM and the effective implementation of strategy.

## DIAGNOSTIC CONTROL SYSTEMS

When driving your car, the speedometer is part of a diagnostic control system. You can use information from the dial on your dashboard to compare your actual speed with the posted speed limit. If there is a significant deviation, you can accelerate or slow down to bring the car in line with the desired speed of travel.

Many of the control systems in businesses operate in much the same way. For example, managers set annual profit plan and balanced scorecard goals and then receive monthly statements that report actual accomplishments for the period. Variance analysis highlights significant differences. If any deviations threaten the achievement of key goals, managers can initiate actions to get things back on track.

We define **diagnostic control systems** as the *formal information systems that managers use to monitor organizational outcomes and correct deviations from preset standards of performance.*[1] Any formal information system can be used diagnostically if it is possible to (1) set a goal in advance, (2) measure outputs, (3) compute or calculate performance variances, and (4) use that variance information as feedback to alter inputs and/or processes to bring performance back in line with preset goals and standards. Diagnostic control systems are the prototypical cybernetic feedback systems described in Chapter 4.

Although profit plans are a common diagnostic control system, managers can use most performance measurement and control systems diagnostically, including:

- balanced scorecards
- expense center budgets
- project monitoring systems
- brand revenue/market share monitoring systems
- human resource systems
- standard cost-accounting systems

## Why Use Control Systems Diagnostically?

Managers must be selective about which control systems they should personally monitor. After all, there are literally thousands of measures in any organization that could be reported to senior managers. Managers cannot review and monitor every possible measure. To understand how managers choose among these systems, we must discuss the two principal reasons for using a system diagnostically: to implement strategy effectively and conserve scarce management attention.

### Implementing Strategy

Managers are interested primarily in monitoring diagnostic control systems that report variance information about **critical performance variables**—*those factors that must be achieved or implemented successfully for the intended strategy of the business to succeed.*[2] In essence, diagnostic control systems are the top-down monitoring tools for implementing strategy as plan (Figure 10–2). They link strategy with critical performance goals and targets and monitor their successful implementation. Without diagnostic control systems, managers could neither communicate nor implement strategy effectively in large complex organizations.

Because of the importance of these systems, managers must ensure that (1) critical performance variables have been analyzed and identified, (2) appropriate goals have been set, and (3) feedback systems are adequate to track performance.

### Conserving Attention

When driving for long distances, watching the speedometer and constantly adjusting the accelerator can be tiring. This activity consumes energy and attention. Thus, automobile

---

[1] Robert Simons, *Levers of Control* (Boston: Harvard Business School Press, 1995): 59.
[2] For a full discussion of critical performance variables, see Chapter 11.

FIGURE 10–2 Linking Strategy to Diagnostic Control Systems

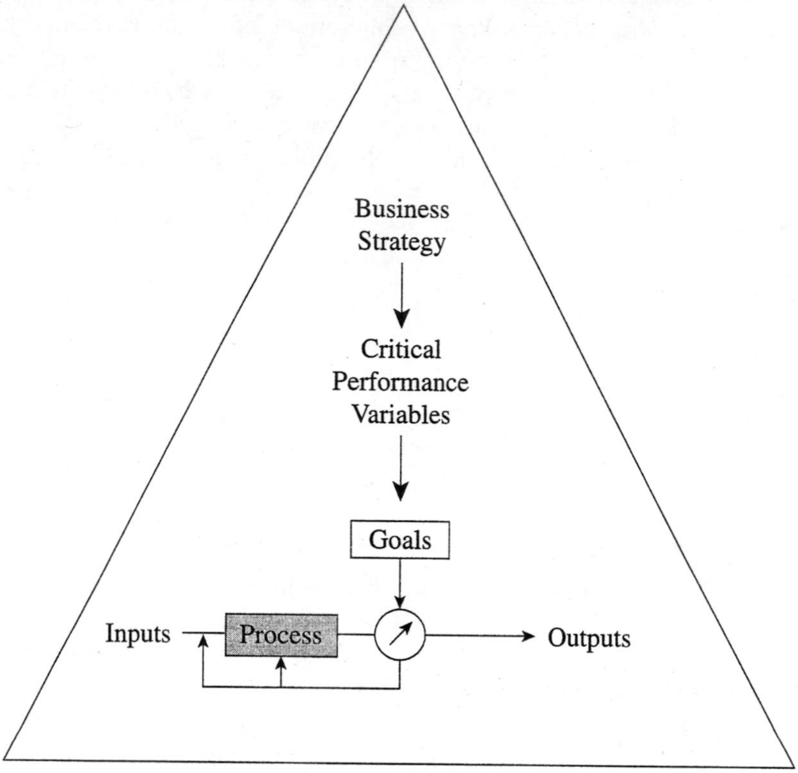

*Source:* Adapted from Simons, *Levers of Control,* p. 63.

companies offer automatic speed controls that automate this diagnostic process. You can set the desired speed, and the computer keeps the automobile's speed within tight bounds. The speed controller frees up your attention to concentrate on other things (daydreaming, talking with your spouse, or worrying about your next appointment).

In organizations, managers can do the same thing with performance measurement and control systems. They can use them to put the organization on automatic pilot. Instead of constantly monitoring a variety of internal processes and comparing results with preset targets and goals, managers receive periodic exception reports from staff accountants. If everything is on track, the reports can be reviewed quickly and managers can move on to other issues. If, on the other hand, significant deviations are identified, then—and only then—do managers need to invest the time and attention to investigate the cause of the deviation and initiate appropriate remedial actions. This process is called *management by exception.*

## Using Diagnostic Control Systems Effectively

Using the automatic speed control in your car conserves attention, but you must know how to use the device effectively. Just as the automobile driver must know how to set the device's speed and adjust it from time to time, so, too, must business managers know how to set key targets and make adjustments as circumstances warrant.

To operate diagnostic control systems effectively, managers must ensure that they devote sufficient attention to five areas: setting goals, aligning performance measures, designing incentives, reviewing exception reports, and following up significant exceptions.

***1. Setting and Negotiating Goals***   Performance goals are the hallmark of diagnostic control systems. They are critical to the effective implementation of strategy because they define where subordinates should devote their energy. Because of the importance of goal setting, managers must personally ensure that goals are appropriate both in terms of desired direction and level of achievement.

When making a long trip in your car, you must initially set the target speed, but then you do not need to adjust it for long periods. In a similar way, managers need only set critical performance goals infrequently—usually once per year. If these goals are properly set, they should not require any additional adjustment or attention. Managers can monitor progress during the operating period by a quick scan of exception reports.

***2. Aligning Performance Measures***   Diagnostic control measures define the span of accountability—that is, the performance variables for which a manager is accountable. Therefore, if managers wish to rely on diagnostic control systems for assurance that strategy is on track, they must ensure that performance measures truly reflect strategic goals and priorities. Techniques such as balanced scorecards are important to assure that these measures align correctly with intended strategy. Again, this need only be done infrequently, but it is extremely important.

***3. Designing Incentives***   The speed control in your car is powered by an internal electrical system. Diagnostic control systems in a business must also be powered up by some energy source. Managers who wish to maximize their ROM use formula-based incentives as a way of powering up, or motivating, goal achievement. Bonuses, promotions, and merit increases can be made contingent upon performance reported in diagnostic control systems. Then, incentives provide extrinsic motivation so that managers do not have to monitor the day-to-day activities of subordinates to be sure that they are working toward desired goals. Diagnostic performance measures and formulas that link rewards with results are sufficient to keep everyone focused on strategy implementation.

***4. Reviewing Exception Reports***   With diagnostic control systems in place, managers can review monthly and quarterly exception reports as soon as they are released to gain confidence that strategy implementation is on track. If measurement systems and incentives are well-designed and aligned, this review can be conducted very quickly and efficiently, thereby increasing ROM. Managers need only scan reports for evidence of large, significant exceptions, or indications that problems may be looming.

***5. Following Up Significant Exceptions***   Although managers use diagnostic control systems to conserve attention, when a significant deviation appears, they must initiate action quickly to get things back on track. Subordinates are monitoring the same

## The Budget Brigade

In an article in *Financial Executive,* managers at The Interpublic Group of Companies (IPG)—a New York-based advertising organization—described their profit planning and budgeting process:

> Complete reviews of each system's business and financial results begin with the budget process in December. The managements of [our three major businesses] meet with the financial and operating managers of every local agency. The managements of all three agency systems then make presentations to IPG in an agreed-on format, which includes a mission statement, business outlook and business strategy, such as new business opportunities. Every year, we give each agency goals for revenue, profit margin, operating profit and net-income growth, based on IPG objectives and historical performance, and we provide salary guidelines and headcount goals. At the budget meetings, we work with the management of each agency system to ensure the goals and guidelines are realistic and achievable.
>
> We also review financial-trend data on a consolidated basis with each agency's management, emphasizing major markets and problem markets. Each review covers cash, dividends, receivable management, capital-expenditure requirements and technology needs. When we finish going over the budgets with the agencies, we consolidate the reviews so we can present them to the board of directors every February, along with our corporate-earnings target and our plans for achieving it.
>
> Each April and September, IPG holds follow-up or update meetings with the agency systems' management to measure performance against budget and objectives. These are thorough and frank reviews of the agency's business and client relationships, designed to ensure agency management is fully aware of business trends, new business opportunities, cash and capital requirements and possible merger or acquisition candidates. These update meetings are crucial to the overall management process and enable IPG to interact with the operating and financial managers of the agencies and keep the lines of communication open, which is so vital in a global business.

*Source:* Thomas J. Volpe and Alan M. Forster, "Ruling With A Firm Hand," *Financial Executive* 11 (January/February, 1995): 43–47.

measures as their bosses (remember, these measures define span of accountability and potential reward incentives), so remedial steps may have already been taken to rectify problems by the time the superior picks up the exception in a diagnostic report. Managers then need only initiate brief discussions to confirm that problems have already been identified and resolved.

## Risks in Using Diagnostic Control Systems

Putting the business on automatic pilot and powering up the system through performance measures and incentives is not without risk, just as putting your car on speed control introduces special risks. All managers who use diagnostic control systems must guard against the following:[3]

---

[3] These risks are enumerated in Simons, *Levers of Control,* pp 81–84.

***Measuring the Wrong Variables***   Setting your car's automatic speed control keeps the vehicle at the right speed but gives no assurance that the car is pointed in the right direction. It does little good to get the speed right if you are traveling south when you want to go north. Similarly, misaligned control systems in businesses can do more harm than good. As the old saying goes, "What gets measured, gets managed." Attention is limited, and people must make choices about where they will spend their time. Sometimes, misaligned diagnostic measures can cause the strategy to go off track.

- In the late 1980s, Dun & Bradstreet's Credit Services Division was accused of overcharging clients. Diagnostic control system measures caused this problem. Measures and incentives rewarded salespeople for increasing sales of subscription units regardless of a client's actual usage patterns. As a result, salespeople failed to inform clients of their true usage patterns in an attempt to sell them more units than they needed.[4]

***Building Slack into Targets***   When performance is a function of achieving preset goals, employees will naturally want to increase the probability of meeting those goals. One way of doing this, of course, is to start with a relatively easy goal. Accordingly, employees may try to build slack into their performance targets. If managers do not compensate for this tendency by ensuring that goals are set at challenging levels, it can lead to serious problems.

- In the 1980s, General Motors measured quality defects on a scale of 1 to 100. To the dismay of plant managers, cars were coming off the assembly line with an average of 45 defects, causing quality scores to fall to a dismal 55 points. To make scores look better, managers changed the rating scale so that scores would now be compared to a target of 145 points. Quality did not improve, but scores under the new system generally exceeded 100, which seemed more acceptable than scores of 50 or 60. During this time, continuing quality problems eroded GM's franchise with customers.[5]

***Gaming the System***   Bonuses tied to diagnostic measures release energy and creativity. People will generally work hard to achieve what they are measured on. However, this energy may focus on ways of enhancing the measure, even if increasing the measure does not lead to advancement of the underlying goal or strategy. This misdirected effort is called gaming.

- To build customer focus, IBM sales representatives were awarded sales commissions for all the IBM products sold in their districts, even if these sales were made by independent retailers. As a result, some reps spent their time traveling around their districts trying to identify retail sales for which they could claim bonus credits. The time spent searching for credits—which was completely unproductive—could have been better spent trying to sell new products to new customers.[6]

---

[4] J.L. Roberts, "Credit Squeeze—Dun & Bradstreet Faces Flap Over How It Sells Reports on Business," *Wall Street Journal* (March 2, 1989): A1.

[5] M. Keller, *Rude Awakening: The Rise, Fall, and Struggle for Recovery of General Motors* (New York: Morrow, 1989): 29–30.

[6] Robert Simons and Hilary Weston, "IBM: Make It Your Business," Harvard Business School Case No. 90–137 (1990).

Other common distortions when relying on diagnostic control systems for goal achievement include:

- *Smoothing*—This occurs when an individual alters the timing and/or recording of transactions to show better performance. This may happen, for example, when a manager has achieved the maximum bonus in one accounting period. Rather than book additional sales that are not eligible for additional bonus in the current period, he or she may defer booking the new revenue until the next accounting period to apply those sales to next period's bonus goal.
- *Biasing*—Managers bias information when they attempt to report only good news (e.g., goals that have been achieved) or to hide or downplay bad news (goals that have been missed).
- *Illegal acts*—Sometimes, performance pressures can cause someone to violate laws or organizational policies in an attempt to increase diagnostic measures and achieve related bonuses.[7]

The negative side effects of diagnostic control systems are pervasive but well known. Whenever people are rewarded for achieving performance targets and left alone to figure out how to do this, there is always the risk some may stray out of bounds. In Chapter 1, we described the organizational blocks that can cause well-intentioned people to stray from the path of doing what they know to be right and ethical. Diagnostic control systems and their related incentives create many of the pressures and temptations that are at the root of this dysfunctional behavior. This tension creates a dilemma for managers. On the one hand, managers are forced to rely on diagnostic control tools to motivate goals achievement and allow high ROM. On the other hand, the same tools inevitably risk dysfunctional behavior from employees who might respond inappropriately to pressure or temptation to bend the rules.

Whenever diagnostic control systems are used for evaluation and reward, managers must install good control systems and be alert for the underlying organizational pressures that may cause well-intentioned people to bend the rules to distort diagnostic measures. We study how to design and use these control systems in Chapters 12 and 13.

## INTERACTIVE CONTROL SYSTEMS[8]

With diagnostic control systems in place, top managers have effectively put their organization on automatic pilot. If goals, measures, and incentives are properly aligned, the business is like a heat-seeking missile focused intently on achieving profit goals and strategies. These systems give managers the freedom to concentrate on growing the business, enhancing profitability, and positioning products and services in rapidly changing markets.

---

[7] Jacob G. Birnberg, Lawrence Turpolec, and S. Mark Young, "The Organizational Context of Accounting," *Accounting, Organizations, and Society* 8 (1983): 111–29.

[8] The remainder of this chapter draws upon ideas, examples, and concepts enumerated in Simons, *Levers of Control*, Chapter 5.

In the previous section, we used an automobile speed control as an analogy for the management by exception that is the hallmark of diagnostic control systems. However, managers need a different kind of control system to grow the business and search for new ways of positioning products and services in dynamic markets. They need a system more like the one used by the National Weather Service to search for and identify patterns of change. Ground stations all over the country monitor temperature, relative humidity, barometric pressure, and wind velocity and direction. Satellites and aircraft provide additional information about emerging storm patterns. All of this information is fed into a central location where data is gathered and analyzed to predict the likely affects of changing conditions. Based on predicted changes, action plans are adjusted (should we delay our trip?) and preparations can be made for impending threats (do we need to evacuate low-lying shore areas in advance of a strengthening hurricane?).

## Strategic Uncertainties

For managers of any business, **strategic uncertainties** are the *emerging threats and opportunities that could invalidate the assumptions upon which the current business strategy is based.* Uncertainty, in general, results from a difference between the amount of information required to perform a task and the amount of information possessed by the organization.[9] Strategic uncertainties relate to *changes* in competitive dynamics and internal competencies that must be understood if the business is to successfully adapt over time. By definition, strategic uncertainties are unknowable in advance and emerge unexpectedly over time.

New technologies may undermine the business's ability to create value, changes in population demographics may decrease the need for specific goods and services, predatory pricing by competitors may put the existing value proposition at risk, product defects may scare away customers, and changes in government policy or regulation may unexpectedly remove vital protection or subsidies. Sometimes, these unexpected changes may also bring opportunities. Changing tariff structures may open up new markets, the unexpected exit of a competitor from the market may offer a chance to serve new customers, or another business may inquire about the possibility of forming a joint venture. Any of these events—either good or bad—may necessitate adjustment of the current strategy and value proposition.

Questions must be asked constantly about how to realign the strategy to take advantage of these emerging opportunities or deflect unexpected threats. Senior managers must energize the entire organization around these issues. Effective managers know that people can be extremely creative and can turn almost any threat or opportunity to advantage—if they can just focus the organization on these uncertainties.

Strategic uncertainties are different than critical performance variables. The critical performance variables enumerated in balanced scorecards or other diagnostic control systems are determined by analysis and embedded in plans and goals. Strategic uncertainties, by contrast, trigger a search for new information and meaning, rather than a

---

[9] Jay R. Galbraith, *Organization Design* (Reading, MA: Addison-Wesley, 1977): p. 36.

**TABLE 10–1** Distinction Between Critical Performance Variables and Strategic Uncertainties

|  | CRITICAL PERFORMANCE VARIABLES | STRATEGIC UNCERTAINTIES |
|---|---|---|
| Recurring questions | What must we do well to achieve our intended strategy? | What changes in assumptions could alter the way we achieve our vision for the future? |
| Focus on | Implementing intended strategy | Testing and identifying new strategies |
| Driven by | Goal achievement | Top management unease and focus |
| Search for | Efficiency and effectiveness | Disruptive change |

*Source:* Adapted from Simons, *Levers of Control,* p. 95.

cursory checkup to ensure that plans are on track. Strategic uncertainties focus on questions rather than answers. Table 10–1 summarizes the main differences between the two concepts.

## Interactive Control Systems

The challenge for managers in any medium- or large-scale business is finding ways to focus everyone in the organization on these strategic uncertainties. To do so, they rely on a simple but universal fact: *everyone watches what the boss watches.*

To signal where they want people to pay attention, senior managers choose to use one or more control systems in a highly interactive way. **Interactive control systems** *are the formal information systems that managers use to personally involve themselves in the decision activities of subordinates.* Simply stated, interactive control systems are the hot buttons for senior managers. They provide the information that the boss pays a lot of attention to and are used to create an ongoing dialogue with subordinates.

We must now repeat the important point that we made in the introduction to this chapter. Interactive control systems are not defined by their technical design features. Instead, they are defined by how senior managers *use* these systems. Top managers pore over reports as soon as they are received and later use the information to challenge the thinking and action plans of subordinates. Senior managers use the interactive control system to spark information searches throughout the entire organization. This intensive use and focus stands in stark contrast to the management by exception that defines diagnostic control systems.

Figure 10–3 illustrates how an interactive control system focuses organizational attention and stimulates the emergence of new strategies over time.

*Business strategy,* in the upper left corner of Figure 10–3, reflects how the business currently creates value for customers and differentiates its products and services from competitors. Management's vision for the future—how it sees the business evolving in the marketplace—gives rise to specific *strategic uncertainties.* These are the issues and questions that keep managers awake at night. Depending on the current strat-

**FIGURE 10-3    Using the Interactive Control Process for Learning**

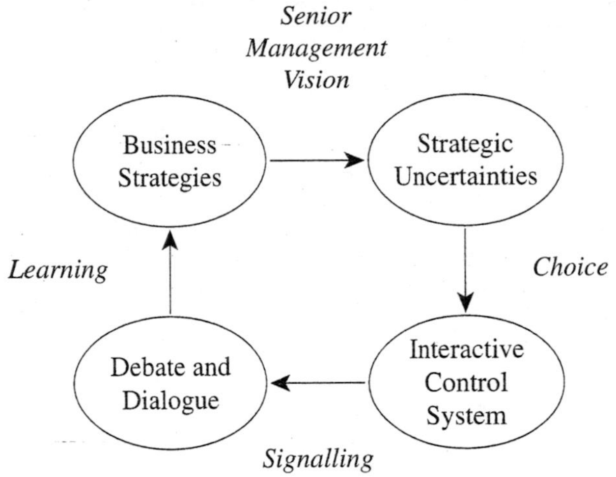

Source: Adapted from Simons, *Levers of Control,* p. 102.

egy and management's vision for the future, strategic uncertainties may relate to changes in customer preferences, competitor actions, new technology, government regulation, or any number of potential threats and opportunities.

To focus the organization on these strategic uncertainties, managers chose one (or more) performance measurement and control system and use it in a highly *interactive* way. Data from the system is used to challenge subordinates and their action plans and force them to attempt to make sense of rapidly changing conditions. This choice signals unequivocally what is important. Remember, everyone watches what the boss watches. In anticipation of the inevitable questioning from their bosses as new data is released, subordinates throughout the business work diligently to gather as much data as they can to be able to respond to questions and suggest action plans that respond to changing circumstances. Interactive *debate and dialogue* takes place at all levels of the organization as new information is studied and analyzed.

This ongoing discussion highlights the need for changing ways of doing things, changing the value proposition, or even changing aspects of the business strategy. The debate and dialogue forces organizational learning, which, in Figure 10-3, loops back to the adjustment of strategy. Thus, *emerging strategy* can be an indirect result of bottom-up action plans and experimentation.

Senior managers at Pepsi describe how they use an interactive control system that reports weekly market share data:

Pepsi's top managers would carry in their wallets little charts with the latest key Nielsen figures. They became such an important part of my life that I could quote them on any product in any market. We would pore over the data, using it to search for Coke's vulnerable points where an assault could successfully be launched, or to explore why Pepsi slipped a fraction of a percentage point in the game. . . . The Nielsens defined the ground rules of competition for everyone at Pepsi. They were at the epicenter of all we did. They were the non-public body counts of the Cola Wars. . . . The company wasn't always this way. The man at the front of the table made it so.[10]

A senior manager at Pepsi described how this interactive control system affected the behavior of managers throughout the business:

> No matter where I was at any time of the day, when the Nielsen flash came out, I wanted to be the first to know about it. I didn't mind a problem, but I hated surprises. The last thing I'd want was Kendall [Pepsi's CEO] calling for an explanation behind a weak number without having had the chance to see it myself. I'd scribble the details down on the back of an envelope or whatever else was convenient. Within an hour, some sixty or seventy people at Pepsi also would get the results and begin to work on them.[11]

The discussions surrounding interactive control systems are always face-to-face, involving operating managers directly. Meetings are used to brainstorm and use every possible piece of data to collectively make sense of changing circumstances. The debate focuses on new information, assumptions, and action plans.

The pressure to use a control system interactively is created quite simply by the regular and recurring attention of the highest levels of management. In face-to-face meetings, senior managers probe subordinates to explain any unforeseen changes in their business and offer suggested action plans. This pressure cascades from the top of the organization to the bottom. In response, through a series of interlocking meetings, the new information and learning flows upward, from the bottom of the organization to the top (see Figure 10–4).

In Chapter 2, we discussed how strategies can emerge spontaneously in organizations as employees experiment and replicate small successes in their attempts to create value. This is strategy as emerging *patterns of action*. Interactive control systems provide the principal means by which managers can guide this otherwise serendipitous process. Many of the best strategies come from unexpected ideas that originate with employees close to customers and markets. At Pepsi, a local experiment eventually laid the groundwork for a new strategy:

> We fought hard for a meager 7 percent share against Coke's 37 percent. It was hardly a contest. Out of sheer desperation, Larry Smith . . . urged an advertising effort more powerful than Pepsi's lifestyle approach. Not wanting to tamper with our hugely successful Pepsi Generation campaign, Pepsi advertising executives and [our advertising agency] resisted. Undaunted, Smith hired his own advertising agency in Texas and dispatched his vice president of marketing to help put together something that would represent a radical departure from what we or any other company had ever done before. The result amounted to one of the most devastating advertising and promotional campaigns ever devised. The Texas agency called it the "Pepsi Challenge."

By focusing attention on strategic uncertainties, managers can use the interactive control process to guide the search for new opportunities, stimulate experimentation and rapid response, and maintain control over what could otherwise be a chaotic process.

---

[10] John Sculley, *Odyssey: Pepsi to Apple: A Journey of Adventure, Ideas, and the Future* (New York: Harper & Row, 1987): 6–7.

[11] Sculley, p. 6.

**FIGURE 10–4   Top-Down Pressure: Bottom-Up Strategy**

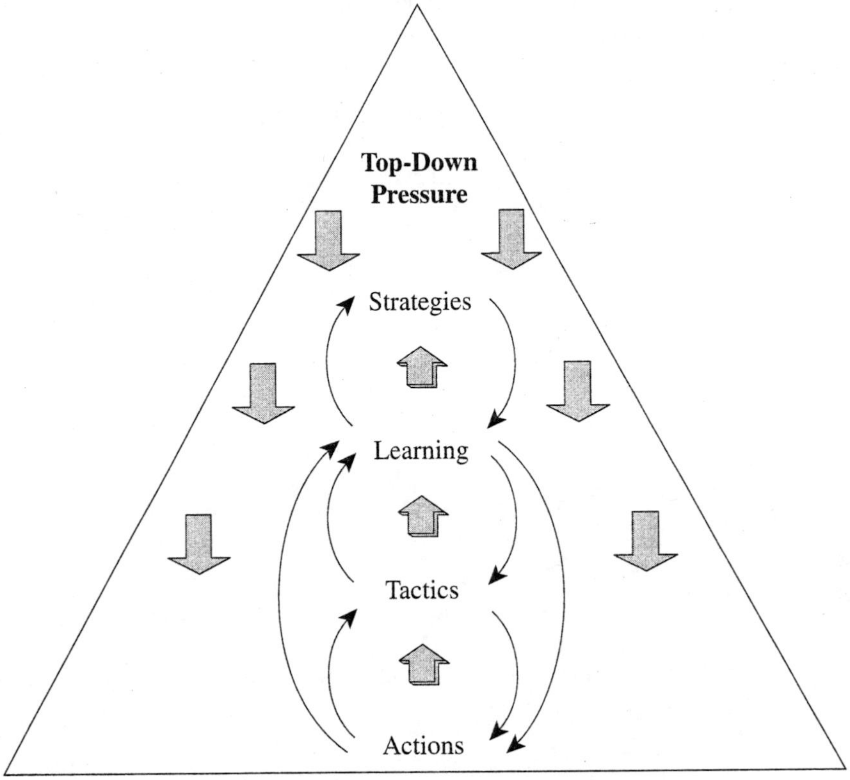

*Source*: Adapted from Simons, *Levers of Control,* p. 99.

Over time, the debate and dialogue that are the hallmarks of interactive control systems allow a business to adapt and renew its strategy:

> We treated each Challenge as a major event, a battle to be fought in our long-term war against Coke. Weeks before a Challenge would debut, we would begin quality tests on the product. If it failed to measure up, we would improve its taste so that a subgoal of the contest was to upgrade the overall quality of our product.[12]

## Design Features of Interactive Control Systems

An interactive control system is not a unique type of control system; any control system can be used interactively by senior managers if it meets certain requirements. For example, managers might choose to use a profit planning system interactively, or a market share monitoring system (like the Nielsen data used at Pepsi), a project monitoring system, or a balanced scorecard. There are countless other systems in any organization that could be used interactively as well.

---

[12] Sculley, pp 43–44, 49.

By way of example, we can look at the U.S. healthcare industry, where senior managers in different firms use *one* of the following five control systems interactively based on their business strategy and unique strategic uncertainties:[13]

- *Profit planning systems* are used interactively when strategic uncertainties relate to the development and protection of new products and markets (e.g., highly innovative consumer products).
- *Project management systems* that report information about the discovery and integration of new technology projects are used interactively in businesses where changes in product technology are strategic uncertainties (e.g., high technology medical devices).
- *Brand revenue budgets* that report revenue, market share, and shipment data by brand or product category are used interactively in businesses where strategic uncertainties relate to extending the attractiveness of mature products (e.g., branded consumer goods such as hair coloring).
- *Intelligence systems* that report information about social, political, and technical business issues are used interactively when there is significant uncertainty concerning changes in regulation and government policy (e.g., prescription drug companies).
- *Human resource systems* that report information on skill inventories, manpower planning, and succession planning are used interactively when strategic uncertainties relate to acquiring new skills to meet competitive needs (e.g., in new and/or rapidly growing businesses).

Figure 10–5 illustrates how these system choices are determined by strategy and strategic uncertainties.

For a system to be eligible for use as an interactive control system, four criteria must be satisfied:

1. *The information contained in an interactive control system must be simple to understand.* If debate and dialogue are to be productive, everyone must be working from the same data and have faith in its accuracy. Managers cannot afford to waste their time arguing about the validity of complex algorithms or calculations that determine how data is compiled. The market share indicators used by managers at Pepsi satisfy this condition. They provide simple and unambiguous data; there is little uncertainty or debate about how the numbers were constructed or their internal validity.

2. *Interactive control systems must provide information about strategic uncertainties.* This condition is at the heart of why interactive control systems are so important— they focus attention unerringly throughout the organization. Everyone watches what the boss watches. Accordingly, it is critical that an interactive control system collect data on the strategic uncertainties of the business. Determined by a business's unique strategy, these uncertainties may relate to customers, technology, government regulation, or any number of other factors that are critical underpinnings of the current value proposition and strategy.

3. *Interactive control systems must be used by managers at multiple levels of the organization.* Managers use control systems interactively to stimulate subordinates to search for, analyze, and discuss new information. Thus, for any system to be used interactively, the information system must be available widely and used by a broad array of subordinate managers. This condition is met by a profit plan; it is not met by a long-range strategic plan that does not leave the executive suite.

---

[13] Robert Simons, "Strategic Orientation and Top Management Attention to Control Systems," *Strategic Management Journal* (Vol. 12, 1991): 49–62.

4.  *Interactive control systems must generate new action plans.* An interactive control system focuses attention on patterns of change. Just as the National Weather Service predictions are used to change action plans, the critical questions asked over and over again by senior business managers using an interactive control system must be: (1) What has changed? (2) Why? and—most importantly— (3) What are we going to do about it? Interactive control systems are used above all else to adjust emerging strategy on a real-time basis.

**FIGURE 10–5   Interactive Control System Choices: A Function of Strategy and Strategic Uncertainties**

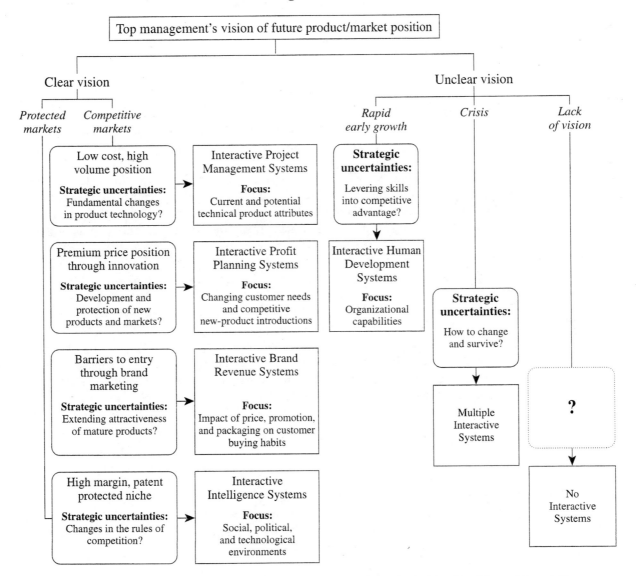

**TABLE 10–2** Factors Affecting the Design and Choice of Interactive Control Systems

| STRATEGIC UNCERTAINTY | IF UNCERTAINTY IS *HIGH*, THEN INTERACTIVE CONTROL SYSTEM | IF UNCERTAINTY IS *LOW*, THEN INTERACTIVE CONTROL SYSTEM |
|---|---|---|
| Technological Dependence | Focuses on emerging new technologies | Focuses on changing customer needs |
| Regulation and Market Protection | Focuses on sociopolitical threats and opportunities | Focuses on competitive threats and opportunities |
| Value Chain Complexity | Uses accounting-based measures | Uses input/output measures |
| Ease of Tactical Response | Uses short planning horizon | Uses long planning horizon |

*Source:* Adapted from Simons, *Levers of Control,* p. 112.

## Choosing Which System to Use Interactively

Given the many systems in an organization that could be used interactively, we can analyze the factors that influence which systems managers select. At least four factors influence the choice of systems to which managers devote their attention (see Table 10–2):

*Technological Dependence*   The more a business is dependent on a specific technological base (such as an aircraft manufacturer), the more critical it becomes for managers of that business to protect their competitive advantage by focusing attention on new ways of applying technology. Managers use interactive project-management systems in these circumstances to focus the organization on emerging technologies and their potential effects on the current strategy of the business. Failure to do so can result in technological obsolescence, as occurred with Encyclopedia Britannica's failure to anticipate the effects of CD-ROM technology on the delivery of encyclopedia information.

Conversely, when technological dependence is low (e.g., household cleaning products), customers are not locked into any one product or product concept. In these cases, senior managers focus organizational attention on finding ways of responding to changing customer needs through new products or marketing programs. In these circumstances, interactive brand-revenue systems or interactive profit-planning systems that can model business trade-offs are often used.

*Regulation*   Managers operating in regulated or semiregulated industries, such as public utilities and research-based pharmaceutical companies, must pay special attention to public sentiment, political pressures, and emerging regulations that could affect their businesses. For these firms, interactive intelligence systems are essential for gathering data to understand and influence the complex social, political, and technical environment of their businesses. Accordingly, managers make these systems interactive to force everyone in the organization to continually scan the environment for signs of impending change in regulations or political processes.

*Complexity of Value Creation*   Managers of businesses with complex value chains— for example, businesses that compete through product innovation in multiple markets such as high-technology consumer electronics—must monitor complex trade-offs across product lines and markets. In these businesses, R&D, production, distribution, and marketing tend to be linked in complex and dynamic ways. Accounting-based measures, such as interactive profit-planning systems, are effective tools for building business models that highlight how changes in one variable are likely to affect the business.

In contrast, managers of businesses with stable, well-understood value chains—for example, mature consumer brands such as Coca Cola—have fewer complex trade-offs to manage. Their businesses are relatively simple. They can, therefore, reduce the level of complexity by focusing attention on simpler input and output measures, such as brand volume and market share. Therefore, these businesses often use brand-revenue budget systems interactively.

***Ease of Tactical Response***   Finally, if copying a competitor's tactics is relatively easy (e.g., the cola wars between Pepsi and Coke), the planning horizon will be extremely short. Tactical responsiveness becomes the key to competitive success. In these circumstances, interactive brand-revenue systems give rapid feedback about the effects of pricing, promotion, and packaging tactics. Conversely, if emulating the strategic initiatives of competitors is difficult due to technological or market constraints (e.g., automobile manufacturing), planning horizons will be substantially longer and interactive project-management systems or interactive profit-planning systems will be more effective.

To test these predictions, consider Johnson & Johnson, which competes with premium-price products and a high level of product innovation. Managers at Johnson & Johnson use their profit planning system interactively to focus attention on the development and protection of new products and markets. Periodically during the year, Johnson & Johnson managers reforecast the predicted effects of competitive tactics and new product rollouts on their profit plans for the current and following year. They also adjust five- and 10-year plans.[14]

Reference to Table 10–2 suggests that their choice of an interactive profit-planning system fits their strategy and strategic uncertainties. The technological dependence of the business is relatively *low*, suggesting that the interactive system should focus on changing customer needs, and there is *little* government regulation in most parts of its business, so the system can be designed to focus on competitive threats and opportunities. Also, the emphasis on innovation and product diversity results in *high* complexity, suggesting the appropriateness of accounting-based measures to monitor trade-offs, and the relative *ease* of tactical response by competitors indicates the need for a planning horizon longer than weeks but shorter than years.

## Choosing How Many Control Systems to Use Interactively

Any medium- to large-size business has a multitude of formal performance measurement and control systems—profit planning systems, budgeting systems, cost accounting systems, balanced scorecards, project monitoring systems, and so on. Most of these systems are used diagnostically. At the extreme, if there are (*n*) control systems in a

---

[14] Robert Simons, "Codman & Shurtleff: Planning and Control System," Harvard Business School Case No. 187–081, 1987.

business, managers will generally use only *one* of these systems interactively and $(n - 1)$ of those systems in a diagnostic, management-by-exception way. Managers choose to use only one system interactively for three reasons: economic, cognitive, and strategic.

*Economic*   Management attention is a scarce and costly resource. By definition, interactive control systems demand frequent management attention throughout the organization and, therefore, exact high opportunity costs by diverting attention from other tasks.

*Cognitive*   The ability of individuals to process large amounts of disparate information is limited. Decision makers suffer from information overload as the amount and complexity of information increases. Attempting to focus intensively on too many things simultaneously risks information overload, superficial analysis, a lack of perspective, and potential paralysis. Thus, effective managers avoid asking subordinates to focus on multiple interactive systems (except during periods of organizational crisis, during which top managers will make *all* control systems interactive for short periods to help redefine strategy).[15]

*Strategic*   The last reason is also the most important. Managers use a control system interactively to activate learning about strategic uncertainties and generate new action plans. Interactive control systems are primarily signaling and communication devices. Using multiple systems interactively diffuses the signal about what is important. Clarity of communication demands focus.

## Interactive Control Systems and Formal Incentives

All control systems must be aligned carefully with incentives. As we discussed in previous sections, the rewards and bonuses tied to the achievement of diagnostic control system goals are generally set by formulas. These formula-based incentives allow managers to "power up" their diagnostic control systems. Recall also, however, that these same formula-based incentive systems can lead to various types of "gaming" behaviors— building slack into targets, smoothing, and biasing of information.

If managers want to use a control system interactively to stimulate information sharing and learning, incentives are necessary but must be designed differently. Linking incentives with predetermined formulas will not work. If formula-based incentives are used, people may attempt to game the system and withhold information, thereby subverting the desired learning.

Incentives for interactive control systems must, therefore, be designed to reward an individual's innovative efforts and contribution. This can only be done by *subjective* assessment. Subjective rewards—relying on the personal judgment of superiors—allow managers to recognize innovative behavior that is difficult to specify in advance and to assess the contribution and effort of individuals in the interactive process. Only subjec-

---

[15] See Simons, "Strategic Orientation and Top Management Attention to Control Systems," 1991, for a discussion of the role of interactive control systems during periods of organizational crisis.

tive rewards provide the flexibility to reward creativity in the face of unanticipated threats and opportunities.

Subjective rewards yield three outcomes that help stimulate organizational learning:

1. Rewarding contribution and effort provides incentives for employees to *make their efforts visible* to their superiors. To demonstrate their contributions, employees will be motivated to communicate information about emerging problems and opportunities to their bosses, as well as to report how they have responded. In this way, they can demonstrate their competence, creativity, and effort through information sharing, analysis, and action planning. Of course, this upward communication feeds the learning process that can lead to better understanding of competitive markets and potential new action plans.

2. Rewarding contribution and effort, rather than results, *reduces information biasing* that is a constant concern in diagnostic control systems. Because rewards are not mechanically tied to uncontrollable events that could affect performance expectations, employees are more likely to share both good news and bad news.

3. Rewarding contribution subjectively demands that superiors have the ability to calibrate the efforts of subordinates accurately. To do so, superiors must themselves have a *sound understanding* of the business environment, decision context, array of possible decision alternatives, and potential outcomes of decisions not taken. Without this knowledge, it is impossible to allocate rewards fairly. However, superiors can only gain this knowledge from a deep understanding of the business and its changing competitive environment. Superiors must, therefore, invest a good deal of their own time and attention to really learn about the business and its changing dynamics.

This last condition also reminds us why most rewards in organizations are based on pre-set formulas. Although subjective rewards promote learning and information sharing (which are undeniably good), they also demand a disproportionate investment of time up and down the hierarchy. This investment is justified for interactive control systems that focus on strategic uncertainties; but for diagnostic processes where goals are clear, ROM is maximized by using formulas to automate the implementation of approved plans.

## Contingencies

There is one special case relating to profit plans that we should mention before we leave this topic. Managers who wish to use a profit plan interactively face a special problem. As we have discussed at length, profit planning systems are a key diagnostic tool for coordination and control. Financial goals must be communicated in all businesses to meet basic obligations to shareholders. Yet, managers at some companies — like those at Johnson & Johnson — may wish to use their profit planning system interactively to stimulate learning about trade-offs among R&D, new-product introduction, advertising, and so on. The question arises, how can a profit plan be used *both* diagnostically and interactively at the same time?

Managers who wish to use their profit plans interactively solve this dilemma by adding contingency buffers to the profit plan to protect key diagnostic targets. These contingencies provide a cushion that allows managers to reforecast profits during the year as part of an interactive process, while at the same time they ensure that key targets are not jeopardized. For example, managers may set a $10 million profit goal for the upcoming year. This target would typically be monitored in a diagnostic fashion, and incentives would be tied by formula to the achievement of this profit plan goal.

If, however, senior managers want to use the profit plan interactively, they can add an additional contingency line that will hold business managers accountable for an initial target of $11 million, with a $1 million contingency fund that can be drawn upon if the business is unable to meet their targets. Monthly meetings will discuss achievement against the profit plan, reasons for unexpected changes, revised estimates based on new-product rollouts and competitor actions, and proposed action plans. As discussed above, bonuses and incentives related to profit plan achievement will be available subjectively.

By mutual agreement, profit plan targets can be adjusted during the year and the contingency can be drawn down if needed to protect the key target of $10 million. Incentives will be determined subjectively based on innovative efforts to expand and seize new opportunities to meet the $11 million goal; the contingency fund can be used as a buffer if necessary to ensure that at least $10 million is achieved.

## RETURN ON MANAGEMENT

In taking charge of a business, one of the most important tasks for managers is to find ways to leverage their time and attention effectively. In Chapter 1, we defined *ROM* as:

$$ROM = \frac{\text{Amount of Productive Organizational Energy Released}}{\text{Amount of Management Time and Attention Invested}}$$

To maximize the impact of their efforts, managers must find ways to increase the numerator and decrease the denominator. They must use all the tools and techniques at their disposal to release productive organizational energy. One of the keys for any manager who wishes to maximize ROM is to understand what he or she must do *personally* and what can be *delegated* to staff assistants. Diagnostic control systems act as *attention-conserving* devices for senior managers: they allow the business to operate without constant monitoring and, thereby, increase ROM. Therefore, much of the work in diagnostic control systems can be delegated to staff specialists and accountants. In contrast, interactive control systems are *attention enhancers*. Senior managers assume primary responsibility for interpreting the data contained in these systems. The interpretation of data in interactive control systems is not delegated. Staff groups are used primarily as facilitators in the interactive process.

Table 10–3 provides a recap of the roles and responsibilities for operating managers and staff groups in designing and using diagnostic and interactive control systems.

Diagnostic control systems are critical to the implementation of strategy, so target setting and follow-up are not delegated. Managers should personally set or negotiate performance goals and receive periodic exception reports to ensure that strategy is on track. However, these systems typically require significant expertise to design and substantial resources to maintain. Therefore, profit planning systems, balanced scorecards,

**TABLE 10-3** Control System Tasks for Managers and Staff Groups Using Diagnostic and Interactive Control Systems

|  | MANAGERS | STAFF GROUPS |
|---|---|---|
| **Diagnostic Control Systems** | Periodically set or negotiate performance targets<br>Receive and review exception reports<br>Follow up significant exceptions | Design and maintain systems<br>Interpret data<br>Prepare exception reports<br>Ensure integrity and reliability of data |
| **Interactive Control Systems** | Choose which system to use interactively<br>Schedule frequent face-to-face meetings with subordinates to discuss data contained in system<br>Demand that operating managers throughout the organization respond to information contained in the systems | Gather and compile data<br>Facilitate interactive process |

*Source:* Adapted from Simons, *Levers of Control*, p. 170.

and strategic profitability analysis can all be designed and managed by staff experts. Managers should supply key assumptions and set targets, but staff groups can interpret data, do the necessary calculations and variance analyses, and send exception reports to managers for review. With this allocation of duties, the ROM of operating managers can be greatly increased.

Interactive control systems require special care in their design and use. Only top managers can decide which control systems they desire to use interactively, based on their vision of the future for the business and their personal sense of strategic uncertainties. Effective managers will insist on face-to-face meetings with subordinates to discuss data, assumptions, and action plans. They will demand that managers throughout the organization respond to the questions raised by the new data. The role of staff groups should be carefully constrained to gathering and compiling data and facilitating the interactive process. Managers should be careful not to allow staff groups to intrude in the interactive process so that paperwork and forms become more important than face-to-face dialogue and action planning. The overriding objective should be to keep the interactive system simple and accessible to operating managers to ensure that it is used by managers throughout the organization.

## BUILDING BLOCK SUMMARY

Appendix 10-1 highlights the essential features of diagnostic and interactive control systems.

**APPENDIX 10–1** Building Block Summary for Diagnostic and Interactive Control Systems

---

#### DIAGNOSTIC CONTROL SYSTEMS

| | |
|---|---|
| **WHAT** | feedback systems that monitor organizational outcomes and correct deviations from preset standards of performance<br><br>*Examples:* profit plans and budgets<br>goals and objectives systems<br>balanced scorecards<br>project monitoring systems<br>brand-revenue monitoring systems<br>strategic planning systems |
| **WHY** | to allow effective resource allocation<br>to define goals<br>to provide motivation<br>to establish guidelines for corrective action<br>to allow ex post evaluation<br>to free scarce management attention |
| **HOW** | set standards<br>measure outputs<br>link incentives to goal achievement |
| **WHEN** | performance standards can be preset<br>outputs can be measured<br>feedback information can be used to influence or correct deviations from standard<br>process or output is a critical performance variable |
| **WHO** | senior managers set or negotiate goals, receive and review exception reports, follow up significant exceptions<br>staff groups maintain systems, gather data, and prepare exception reports |

---

#### INTERACTIVE CONTROL SYSTEMS

| | |
|---|---|
| **WHAT** | control systems that managers use to involve themselves regularly and personally in the decision activities of subordinates<br><br>*Examples:* profit planning systems<br>balanced scorecards<br>project management systems<br>brand revenue systems<br>intelligence systems |
| **WHY** | to focus organizational attention on strategic uncertainties and provoke the emergence of new initiatives and strategies |
| **HOW** | ensure that data generated by the system becomes an important and recurring agenda in discussions with subordinates<br>ensure that the system is the focus of regular attention by managers throughout the organization<br>participate in face-to-face meetings with subordinates<br>continually challenge and debate data, assumptions, and action plans |
| **WHEN** | strategic uncertainties require search for disruptive changes and opportunities |
| **WHO** | senior managers actively use the system and assign subjective, effort-based rewards<br>staff groups act as facilitators |

---

*Source:* Adapted from Simons, *Levers of Control*, pp 179–180.

## CHAPTER SUMMARY

In Part II of this book, we reviewed the design principles and technical features of different types of profit planning, performance measurement, and control systems. In this chapter, we introduce an additional dimension—how managers *use* those systems. This choice is about allocating attention—both their own and, by implication, the attention of the managers who report to them.

Diagnostic control systems are the management-by-exception systems that define span of accountability. If designed properly, these systems give top managers assurance that the goals of each work unit will be achieved. Diagnostic control systems are powered up by formal incentives and bonuses that are set in advance by formula.

Interactive control systems supply signals for people to infer what is important in allowing the business to reposition itself over time. Interactive control systems absorb a great deal of management attention, but it is attention well spent, because it is leveraged throughout the whole organization and allows high ROM. Using a control system interactively forces the entire organization to focus on strategic uncertainties—those assumptions about competition and distinctive competencies that keep the boss awake at night.

In tandem, diagnostic control systems and interactive control systems work together to allow the implementation of today's strategy, while at the same time allowing the organization to position itself for tomorrow's changing marketplace.

# Aligning Performance Goals and Incentives

We have reviewed in detail how to design performance measurement and control systems. Now, we must explore more carefully the impact of these systems on the employees who work in organizations. It is, after all, these employees who will ultimately determine the success or failure of any strategy implementation.

In this chapter, we cover design principles that form the foundation for effective performance goals and incentives. We must consider issues related to the creation of goals, the design of performance measures and targets, and the role of incentives on motivation. Designing performance goals and incentives is like building a house. You start with a series of concepts and a rough idea of what the end product should look like. Then, you make a myriad of choices. The architect reviews plans and discusses design alternatives. The builder discusses options concerning fixtures and trims. The painter offers you more choices for colors, papers, and special effects.

Whether building a house or establishing business goals, we must keep several questions in mind:

- What are we trying to accomplish?
- What are the trade-offs—including costs—explicit in our choices?
- What fundamental aspects of design apply in all circumstances, and what aspects are contingent upon specific strategies and objectives?

## THE NATURE OF PERFORMANCE GOALS

In any business, managers are interested—above all else—in how to use goals to implement strategy. Recall our definition of strategy from Chapter 2: strategy focuses on the *choices* that must be made to create value for customers and differentiate products and services. However, successful strategy implementation requires *communicating* these strategic choices to hundreds or thousands of employees. Each individual employee requires guidance about how he or she can contribute. Performance goals provide that guidance. *A goal is a formal aspiration that defines purpose or expected levels of achievement.* Goals specify the *ends* that managers wish to achieve and the *means* by which to achieve them. They communicate to people what it is that managers expect them to do and how they should allocate their time and attention among competing demands.

## Goals, Objectives, and Targets

Many companies make a distinction between goals, objectives, and targets. For example, *goals* may relate to general aspirations, such as:

- introduce a new line of sailboats for the cruising market
- improve production efficiency
- become profitable

**Objectives** or *targets* are more specific. They incorporate measurement standards and time frames against which to gauge progress and success. For example,

- have six firm orders in hand for a new 32-foot cruising sailboat in the next nine months
- reduce the cost of waste and scrap by 10% each quarter over the next year
- earn 15% return on sales in the next year

In practice, there is little consistency in how firms use the terms goals, objectives, and targets. Some firms use goals and objectives as outlined above, but other firms reverse this order, with objectives relating to general aspirations and goals encompassing specific measurable targets that support those objectives.

We will not attempt to say which ordering is preferable. The important point is that goals and objectives can be made actionable only when *measurement* is attached to any set of aspirations. Therefore, in this chapter we focus on understanding how managers create and define business goals—aspirational directions—and how they calibrate, communicate, and support those goals through performance measures and incentives. Thus, we will adopt the term **performance goal** to denote *a desired level of accomplishment against which actual results can be measured.*

## Purpose of Performance Goals

Financial goals such as maximizing profit, cash flow, or ROCE cannot—by themselves—supply the necessary guidance to implement strategy. Financial goals do not tell employees how to create value for customers or how to differentiate products and services. Without the *clarity of purpose* that performance goals provide, employees may choose very different ways of generating financial returns. One employee may attempt to cut costs at the expense of customer service, whereas another may boost expenses to build customer loyalty. With everyone pulling in different directions, any strategy is bound to fail.

Moreover, it is important to remember that strategies are only hypotheses: they are assumptions and expectations about cause and effect written down in plans and balanced scorecards. To bring strategies to life, managers must use specific performance goals to communicate business direction to subordinates. Because all employees pay attention to what they are measured on, individuals throughout the organization will attempt to infer the strategy of the business from their performance goals and measures (Figure 11–1).

For example, the manager of a retail chain might be held accountable for different performance goals depending on the strategy of the business. With a growth strategy, he might be accountable for increasing sales revenue per store and opening three new stores in Texas. Alternatively, if the business is following a low-cost strategy, the manager might be held accountable for reducing expenses or for keeping prices below

### FIGURE 11–1    Inferring Strategy from Performance Measures

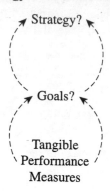

competitors. Each of these *measures* (revenue growth, store openings, expense reduction, price versus competition) will communicate a different set of *priorities* and allow subordinates to *infer* the strategic direction that top managers wish to follow.

Let's revisit Boston Retail. Assume that managers have decided to open three new stores in New York state. Under this strategic alternative, we can recap the key data from the profit plan that we developed in Chapter 5 (See Exhibit 11–1).

By studying the profit plan, it is clear what needs to be done—a vigorous attempt must be made to get the new stores on line and boost revenue by $3.6 million while at

---

### EXHIBIT 11–1
### Boston Retail
### Profit Plan Goals for Expansion Strategy

|  | 20X1 ACTUAL | 20X2 WITH EXISTING STORES | 20X2 WITH ADDITION OF N.Y. STORES | INCREASE DUE TO ADDITION OF N.Y. STORES |
|---|---|---|---|---|
| Sales | $9,200 | $10,120 | $13,800 | $3,680 |
| Cost of goods sold | 4,780 | 5,258 | 7,170 | 1,912 |
| Gross margin | 4,420 | 4,862 | 6,630 | 1,768 |
| Wages | 1,530 | 1,591 | 2,387 | 796 |
| Rent | 840 | 882 | 1,322 | 440 |
| Advertising | 585 | 644 | 704 | 60 |
| Administration | 435 | 478 | 718 | 240 |
| Interest | 72 | 65 | 97 | 32 |
| Depreciation | 57 | 109 | 181 | 72 |
| Training | 38 | 40 | 59 | 19 |
| Other | 54 | 56 | 84 | 28 |
| Total Expenses | 3,611 | 3,865 | 5,552 | 1,687 |
| Profit before tax | $ 809 | $ 997 | $ 1,078 | $ 81 |

the same time holding down expenses. The owner/president of Boston Retail can set additional performance goals for the manager of the new store, such as:

- hire all new staff by June 1
- launch grand opening on Labor Day weekend
- generate $650,000 revenue in first six months

These performance goals and measures allow systematic and clear communication of what he wants the manager to focus on. Relying exclusively on verbal communication is not enough.

Another reason that performance goals are important is tied to the clarity of communication discussed above. The communication of unambiguous performance goals frees up top management attention to focus on other things, allowing high ROM. Recall our discussion of Chapter 4 in which we enumerated the purposes for which managers use information:

- to improve decision making
- to motivate and evaluate the efforts of subordinates
- to signal preferences about activities and opportunities to pursue
- to promote education, training, and learning
- to communicate to external constituencies

Performance goals play a critical role in enhancing ROM for each of these purposes. Goals, by their nature, signal the preferences of top managers — what is important and where people should be dedicating their time. Moreover, performance goals provide a disciplined approach to management that is the essence of management training: how to run a business successfully and achieve your agendas by working through other people. Goals serve as a reference point for all key decisions. When goal achievement is linked to bonuses and promotions, they provide managers with motivational tools. Finally, performance goals can be shared with stockholders and analysts, when appropriate, to communicate the prospects of the business.

## Critical Performance Variables

How do managers select performance goals? In earlier chapters of this book, we studied profit plans, ROE and residual income, and balanced scorecards. Obviously, managers can choose among many performance goals. However, only some of these goals will be *truly* critical to the implementation of their strategy. These are called *critical performance variables* — factors that must be achieved or implemented successfully for the intended strategy of the business to succeed. Managers must identify the critical performance variables for their particular business.

There are two steps in determining critical performance variables for any business. The first is to work deductively to identify potentially important performance drivers. For any strategy, **performance drivers** are variables that either (1) influence the probability of successfully implementing the strategy (an effectiveness criterion) or (2) provide the largest potential for marginal gain over time (an efficiency criterion).

The second step is to identify the critical performance variables from among this list of performance drivers. To do this, managers must ask themselves, If I transported

**FIGURE 11–2   Fear of Failure Determines Critical Performance Variables**

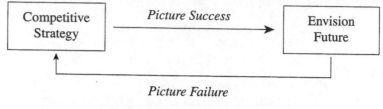

= **Critical Performance Variables**

myself five years forward in time to discover that my business strategy had *failed,* what would I point to as the reasons for this failure? These are the *critical* performance variables—those factors relating to competitive dynamics that are important enough to cause the strategy to fail (Figure 11–2). Depending on the business, these critical performance variables could relate to customer needs, implementing new technology, building new competencies, or the ability to access new markets.

Whatever the critical performance variables for any specific business, the acid test is simple: Any performance variable that could cause the strategy to fail should be on the short list for strategic performance goals.

## SELECTING PERFORMANCE MEASURES

To ensure that performance goals are achieved, managers must design *measures* for desired outcomes. *A* **measure** *is a quantitative value that can be scaled and used for purposes of comparison.* Performance measures may be either financial or nonfinancial. *Financial measures* are stated in monetary terms, usually drawn from a business's accounting systems. Revenue and profit are examples of financial measures. *Nonfinancial measures* are quantitative data created outside the formal accounting system. Weight of scrap metal is quantitative—it can be measured numerically—but, because it is not expressed in dollars and cents, it is classified as a nonfinancial measure.

To determine if a measure is suitable to support a performance goal, it must be subjected to three tests.

### Test 1: Does It Align with Strategy?

Measures tell people what is important. If an employee is being measured on customer satisfaction, he is able to infer what is important. If he is being measured on cost reduction, he is likely to infer something different.

The first test of a good measure, then, is to ask the question: If I looked at the measures for which an employee is accountable, could I accurately infer the goals that senior managers want that person to focus on? For example, what would you infer as the goals for a plant employee accountable for the following measures:

- $ cost/unit
- monthly scrap expense
- setup time in hours

---

### Incentive Problems at the Internal Revenue Service

Congressional investigations of alleged taxpayer abuse by the Internal Revenue Service uncovered some flaws in the IRS's performance goals. The study of the tax agency's examination division found that IRS employees were improperly driven by dollar-collection goals. For example, the annual job performance evaluations of three-fourths of IRS group managers were based on such statistics as "dollars assessed on taxpayers per work-hour." This system led IRS employees to perform overly aggressive and sometimes illegal activities to meet seizure quotas.

According to IRS Commissioner Charles Rossotti, a more balanced approach measuring customer satisfaction, inventory management, and case "quality" was being considered, but any new system would not go into effect for two or three years. In the interim, he predicted that IRS managers would be "very unclear about what they're supposed to do and what they're not supposed to do."

---

*Source:* Adapted from Judith Bruns, "IRS Chief Promises Changes, But Not Overnight," *Dow Jones Newswires Capital Markets Report,* May 1, 1998; Jacob Schlesinger, "IRS to Review Property Seizures for Wrongdoing," *Wall Street Journal,* July 13, 1998, A3; and Stephen Barr, "IRS Report Says Agents Pursued Assets of Sick, Dying Taxpayers," *Washington Post,* July 11, 1998, A9.

---

Would your answer change if the same plant employee were accountable for:

- quality failures
- customer-order fulfillment time
- new-product quality satisfaction

Each of these sets of measures tells a different story in terms of priorities, goals, and, ultimately, business strategy. Good measures allow employees to infer and understand intended business strategy.

### Test 2: Can It be Measured Effectively?

Ideally, measures should be objective, complete, and responsive (Figure 11–3).

## Nature of Measures

An **objective measure** can be independently measured and verified. For example, revenue or cost of goods sold are objective measures because they can be verified by independent auditors. Because objective measures are derived from clear formulas, there is little ambiguity about their meaning or the results that are desired. By contrast, *subjective* measures cannot be independently measured and verified. Instead, they rely on the personal judgment of superiors. The work of an employee can be rated subjectively based on a boss's observation of the salesperson at work. However, the boss must have good information so that he or she can make an informed judgment. In addition, trust must be high, because the subordinate must have confidence that the subjective judgment is fair and will be used appropriately.

**FIGURE 11–3   Nature of Measures**

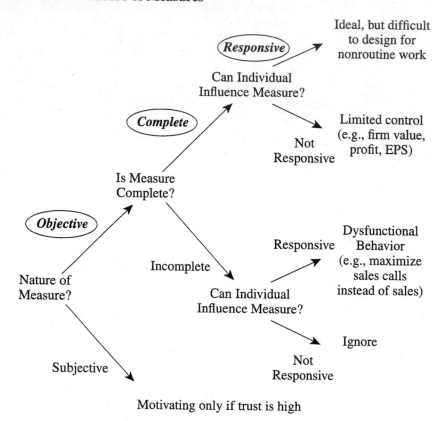

*Source:* Adapted from Simons, *Levers of Control,* p. 77.

Measures also vary according to their degree of completeness and responsiveness. A **complete measure** captures all the relevant attributes of achievement; a **responsive measure** reflects actions that a manager can directly influence. For example, to measure the rate of progress in driving from Boston to Vancouver, car speed as recorded on the speedometer would provide a responsive, but incomplete, measure. The driver can accelerate or decelerate to influence the measure, but it is incomplete because it does not take into account the number and duration of stops.

In a business, share price is often considered to be a complete measure of top management performance because all managerial actions are eventually reflected in share price.[1] However, share price also reflects economic conditions such as interest rates and other factors outside the control of top managers. Therefore, it is not fully responsive to their actions. On the other hand, profit or ROE measures are responsive to the actions of

---

[1] Share price may not be a complete measure in any single period because it may fail to capture the future period effects of management's decisions, especially if managers have private information that is not available to shareholders or financial analysts.

top managers. However, these measures are less complete because they do not reflect the future value of long-term decisions, such as investing in new technologies.

To increase the responsiveness of performance measures, lower-level employees are usually measured only on those activities within their span of control. However, highly responsive measures sometimes create risk. People may engage in behaviors that increase the measure but that do little to increase the overall value of the firm. For example, a manager might choose to measure the number of sales calls made each week by her salesmen. Using this responsive measure, salespeople can easily increase the number of calls per day, if they disregard the potential for sales at each stop. The measure fails the test of completeness.

Objective, complete, and responsive measures—the upper path of Figure 11–3— can often be achieved for lower-level jobs at the plant floor level or at a front-line customer service desk. For higher-level managerial jobs, however, finding the right balance between objectivity, completeness, and responsiveness requires careful thought and design on the part of managers. Measures—if poorly designed—bring unintended consequences described in the previous chapter, including gaming (attempting to manipulate the measure without achieving the underlying goal), smoothing (adjusting accounting accruals to alter the timing of revenues and expenses between periods), and biasing (reporting only favorable data and suppressing unfavorable data). For example, to encourage efficiency in their customer service operation, managers of a credit card company measured employees on (1) the number of calls answered per day and (2) talk time. Goals and rewards depended on increasing the former and decreasing the latter; and employees did just that. Unfortunately, when a customer asked a difficult question that would take a lot of time to answer, employees merely transferred the call to another department. This gaming behavior achieved high scores on the measures but left customers frustrated and angry.

## Test 3: Is the Measure Linked to Value?

As described in earlier chapters, all organizational processes can be segregated according to the *Inputs→Process→Outputs* model. We can measure any number of input variables (information, energy, labor, materials, etc.), process variables (cycle time, quality, usage rates, and so on), or output variables (efficiency and effectiveness).

In our discussion of the balanced scorecard, we made an important distinction between measures that are *leading* indicators of success and those that are *lagging* indicators of success. In building a house, for example, a *lagging* indicator of success—one that tells the story after the fact—might be the profit that you realize in selling the house five years after its completion, perhaps as contrasted with other similar-sized houses. A high resale value indicates that the house was well constructed, aesthetically pleasing, and located in a desirable neighborhood. In this case, profit on sale would be a good lagging indicator of your success in building a good house. In a business setting, break-even time for a new-product introduction would be an example of a lagging indicator.

However, when you are building the house, you probably do not want to wait five years to find out if your house is any good. Instead, you might look at *input* indicators, such as published ratings of neighborhood desirability, the reputation of the architect with whom you will work, and testimonials from other clients who have hired the builder you are considering. In addition, you can also rely on *process* indicators: visiting the site often, checking on critical construction details before they are hidden by finishing walls, monitoring costs to ensure that construction is within your overall budget constraints, and ensuring that top quality fixtures are being installed. These are *leading* indicators.

In business, managers may choose to measure leading variables, such as employee training, process quality controls, and work-in-process costs, as well as lagging variables, such as profit or customer satisfaction. To rely on leading indicators, however, we must remember the critical assumptions about cause-and-effect relationships that we discussed in Chapter 4. Assume a situation where managers believe that highly trained employees (A) cause high levels of customer satisfaction (B), which in turn leads to repeat sales (C), which leads to profit. This could be modeled as follows:

$$A \Rightarrow B \Rightarrow C \Rightarrow \text{Profit}$$

$$\text{where } A = \text{employee training}$$

$$B = \text{customer satisfaction}$$

$$C = \text{repeat sales}$$

How much confidence do we have that any or all of these variables lead to economic value? Profit—the lagging indicator—is likely to be highly correlated with economic value. The more profit the business makes, the more economic value it creates, but is the same equally true for the other three variables?

As we move from right to left, our confidence in the ability of the variable to create economic value decreases. Repeat sales (C) *probably* leads to more profit, but not necessarily. Certain customers, because of their buying habits, lot size, or discounts, may in fact generate losses. Customer satisfaction (B) *may or may not* lead to increased profit. Even though our customers are satisfied, they may still choose to buy from a competitor if that competitor's current product offering more closely meets their current needs. Finally, with employee training, (A), the link to economic value becomes even more tenuous. Although it is probably a good thing to have well-trained employees, it may be *difficult to prove* that training expenditures will generate economic value for the firm—especially when choices must be made about the different types of training to be offered, and employee turnover is high.

Thus, when designing performance measures, output measures (that is, lagging indicators) give the highest confidence that economic value is being created. Input and process measures (i.e., leading indicators) are valid only if managers are confident that they understand cause-and-effect relationships.

(In addition to these three tests of a good measure, the reader may wish to revisit the discussion of Chapter 4 where we describe criteria for choosing to monitor inputs, processes, or outputs. These criteria include technical feasibility of monitoring, understanding of cause and effect, cost, and the desired level of innovation.)

---

### Changing Performance Measures in the Public Sector

U.S. government agencies have been revamping their diagnostic control systems to ensure that they are measuring the right performance variables.

The U.S. Coast Guard, for example, used to measure the number of inspections and certifications performed by its officers. However, it realized that its primary goal was to save lives and it should, therefore, measure its performance by reductions in the marine fatality rate. The main culprit in marine accidents is human error, not equipment failures, which were previously the subject of the inspections. Focusing on sectors with the highest death rates, like the towing industry, the Coast Guard began helping them change the training for new workers, who are most vulnerable to mishaps. In five years, using fewer people at lower cost, the Coast Guard reduced the fatality rate in the towing industry from 91 per 100,000 to 27 per 100,000.

The Federal Emergency Management Agency (FEMA) also took a new tack in its performance measurement. Instead of concentrating on handing out checks and warm blankets after a disaster, it believed that the more buildings that survived a catastrophe, the less aid the agency would have to provide. It began measuring the level of flood insurance in flood-prone areas and the number of inspections in high-risk areas to help local authorities strengthen building codes. As a result of implementing this change in measurement, FEMA has seen reductions in the amount of aid spent per disaster.

The National Oceanic and Atmospheric Administration (NOAA) used to measure the number of weather predictions as a performance indicator. In an effort to improve the effectiveness of its short-term warning and forecast services, it now measures the lead time for tornado warnings. Deploying a new Doppler radar system, NOAA increased the national average for warning time from seven to nine minutes—a short but critical edge for people in the path of a dangerous storm.

*Source:* Adapted from Douglas Stanglind, "What Are You Trying to Do?" *U.S. News & World Report* (March 3, 1997), 36–37.

## How Many Measures for Each Employee?

To implement strategy effectively, people throughout a business must focus their energies on a small number of variables that are truly critical to success. To be effective as communication devices, managers must use measures to focus attention. As we all know, what gets measured, gets managed.

An important design decision for managers, therefore, is deciding how many measures to assign to each subordinate. As a rule of thumb, effective managers provide focus and impact by insisting that individuals be accountable for no more performance measures than they can recall from memory. How many measures is that?

Professor George Miller gave us the answer in the 1950s in his famous article: "The Magic Number Seven, Plus or Minus Two."[2] Think of all the things in our life that are configured in sevens:

- digits of a telephone number
- days of the week
- notes on the musical scale
- colors in the rainbow
- wonders of the world

In business,

- seven steps of quality
- seven "S" analysis
- seven habits of highly effective people

Why seven? Because individuals can remember, recall, and work creatively with seven bits of information. With 10 or more bits of information, individuals suffer from information overload. Moreover, if people are asked to do too many things concurrently, no single initiative will receive enough attention to assure success. Using this rule of thumb, managers should assign no more than seven to nine performance goals to any single individual. Of course, as managers cascade goals and measures down their organizations, different people will be accountable for different measures. This is to be expected as measures are aligned with specific job responsibilities.

## SETTING THE PERFORMANCE BAR

As part of any goal setting process, managers must choose the target or desired level of achievement. Consider the following historical performance data for the Cambridge store of the Boston Retail chain:

|  | 20X0 | 20X1 | 20X2 |
|---|---|---|---|
| Sales goal | $1,300 | $1,550 | *$1,450 or $1,550 or $1,750?* |
| Actual sales | $1,275 | $1,450 | |

What is the correct sales goal or target for 20X2? Should the sales goal be set at last year's actual ($1,450) or some higher amount? If higher, by how much should the performance goal be increased? To answer this question, several factors must be considered; foremost is the importance of any given performance goal to the successful implementation of business strategy. For example, a business strategy may require successfully introducing a new product line to generate an incremental boost in revenue of $50,000 in the first quarter, $75,000 in the second quarter, and $100,000, in both the

[2] George A. Miller, "The Magic Number Seven, Plus or Minus Two: Some Limits in Our Capacity for Processing Information," *The Psychological Review* 63 (1956): 81–97.

third and fourth quarters. If failure to meet these performance goals could jeopardize the successful implementation of the strategy, then there is little choice about the right level.

### Benchmark Comparisons

In each facet of business operations—material acquisition, production, logistics, marketing, R&D, distribution, customer service, and corporate support—some firms or business units do a better job than others. To set performance goals effectively, managers need to know which firms set the standard for the most effective utilization of resources. Then, they must calibrate their own efforts against this "best of class" yardstick. This technique is called *benchmarking*.

For example, the chief financial officer may wish to know what the "best of class" standard is for transaction processing (for example, the number of clerical staff needed to process 10,000 transactions per month), financial statement preparation (e.g., the number of days elapsed between the month-end close and the distribution of monthly financial statements), and information technology (e.g., the optimum level of IT expenditure for each 1,000 employees). To answer these questions, a study can be conducted to determine which firms do the best job on these dimensions and what their relative levels of efficiency and effectiveness are on various indicators. These studies are often conducted by consultants who specialize in this type of work. Gathering this type of information provides top managers with data that can be used to calibrate performance goals related to the effective and efficient use of resources within their own firm.

Businesses with multiple production or distribution sites can also benchmark best *internal* practices by collecting data and comparing performance across units. For example, McDonald's collects statistics from all franchisees on the amount of each sales dollar spent on labor, food, nonfood supplies, and so forth. These data are compiled and

---

### John Browne at British Petroleum

John Browne, CEO of The British Petroleum Company, commented on how to motivate people to excel at learning:

> To get people to learn, you need to give them a challenge. Setting a target is crucial even if you don't actually know whether it's fully achievable—because in times of rapid change, you have to make decisions and get people to step outside the box.

> One process that we employ to promote learning and drive performance is not that unusual. It involves understanding the critical measures of operating performance in each business, relentlessly benchmarking those measures and their related activities, setting higher and higher targets, and challenging people to achieve them.

> We've worked with the managers of each business unit to create an annual performance contract that spells out exactly what they're expected to deliver, and we review their progress quarterly.

*Source:* Steven E. Prokesch, "Unleashing the Power of Learning: An Interview with British Petroleum's John Browne," *Harvard Business Review* 75 (September–October 1997): 146–168.

FIGURE 11–4    **Relationship Between Motivation and Goal Difficulty**

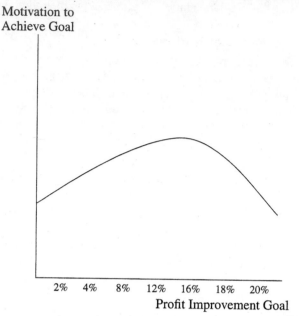

sent out to all McDonald's franchisees to enable then to benchmark their individual operations.

## Motivating Effort

In thinking about the motivational effects of performance goals, two issues must be addressed. First, how do aspirational goals affect individual work habits? In other words, how do individuals respond to goals that are either easy or difficult? The second question is, Who should be involved in setting the performance bar? Is this something reserved for senior managers, or should subordinates be involved in jointly setting the goals and targets that will affect them?

## Level of Difficulty

Behavioral research suggests that individual creativity and initiative can be maximized when people are under some reasonable amount of pressure to perform; remove the pressure, and performance and creativity slow to a more relaxed pace.[3] Therefore, performance goals should be challenging, but not perceived as either too easy or unreasonably difficult. An increase in profit of 4% may be relatively easy to achieve; an increase in profit of 25% may be extremely difficult.

As shown in Figure 11–4, if a goal is too easy to achieve — say 4% — people will not be challenged and the motivational effects will be dampened. As the goal is made

---

[3] For a review of the literature relating to goal difficulty and performance, see chap. 2 in Edwin A. Locke and Gary P. Latam, *A Theory of Goal Setting and Task Performance* (Englewood Cliff, N.J.: Prentice–Hall, 1990).

more difficult, effort increases. Many individuals rise to the challenge and stretch to find ways of meeting the goal. At 15%, employees are working at their full potential to do whatever it takes to get the job done. A certain point is reached, however, where the goal seems unreasonably difficult, and, at this point, individuals begin to give up. They believe that achieving the goal is either impossible or not worth the effort. We see in Figure 11–4 a tailing off in motivation and effort as the goal passes 18%.

### Deciding Who Should Participate in Setting Goals

The previous discussion about goal difficulty begs the question, Who should participate in setting the difficulty level of performance goals? Should this be a top-down process, driven entirely by superiors who establish goals and hand them down to subordinates for implementation? Or, should subordinates have some say in the level of goals that affects them?

Recent research has looked at the degree of employee participation in planning and budgeting processes. Researchers were trying to understand why some organizations encouraged subordinates' participation in these future-looking processes, whereas others imposed top-down objectives for the coming year without input from subordinates.

The results of these studies suggest that the desire for information sharing explains a big portion of the puzzle. When organizations face uncertain environments and the information that may be relevant to address these changes is dispersed throughout the organization, then the planning and budgeting processes are used interactively with intense participation. This participation helps people exchange information and better understand the changes that are happening around them. As a result, performance improves.

On the other hand, companies in stable environments do not need to exchange information about profit plan goals because managers at the top already know what to expect in the future. In these cases, the planning and budgeting processes are not used to exchange information but to challenge people in the organization to achieve challenging objectives and ensure that the objectives are met.[4]

Thus, the decision about who should participate in setting performance goals depends on managers' beliefs about where the relevant information is located in the organization. If managers believe that the information needed to set performance goals is dispersed widely throughout the organization, then a participative style is appropriate. If information is held at the top, then little consultation is needed.

The decision on who should participate in setting performance goals also depends greatly on the assumptions that managers make about human behavior in organizations. For example, in the typical model of human behavior used in economics, subordinates are viewed as rational, self-interested, utility-maximizing individuals who typically are risk averse and dislike effort. These "agents" work under hire for "principals"—the owners or superiors who have the power to set performance goals for subordinates,

---

[4] Leslie Kren, "Budgeting Participation and Managerial Performance: The Impact of Information and Environmental Volatility," *The Accounting Review* 67 (1992): 511–526; Peter Brownell and Alan S. Dunk, "Task Uncertainty and Its Interaction with Budgeting Participation and Budget Emphasis: Some Methodological Issues and Empirical Investigation," *Accounting, Organizations and Society* 16 (1991): 693–703.

evaluate their efforts, and dispense rewards. In this view, the problem is to minimize the tendency of the agent to engage in behaviors that are not in the best interests of the principal (or boss). Part of the solution for the so-called agency problem is to design top-down contracts (that is, goals) and enforcement mechanisms (i.e., performance measures and control systems) linked to rewards and punishments. In this view, subordinates are *not* invited to participate in setting goals because it is expected that subordinates will attempt to bias the goal-setting process in their favor to minimize future effort.

An alternative view, prevalent in organization behavior, is that most individuals inherently enjoy achievement for its own sake and will become self-motivated to achieve the goals of the organization if they (1) believe the goal is legitimate and (2) become committed to the goal through a process that includes their input and participation. Thus, subordinates are invited to participate in goal setting to increase commitment and, ultimately, motivation.

Which of these views is correct? There is probably a little truth in each, and managers will make different choices depending on what the goal-setting process is designed to achieve, who possesses relevant information, and the level of trust in the organization.

## Multiple Purposes of Performance Goals

The goal-setting process is complicated because performance goals are used simultaneously for a variety of purposes. Performance goals are used for communicating strategy and motivation, as described above, but also for planning and coordination, early warning of potential problems, and ex post evaluation of managers and businesses.

Performance goals are important for *planning and coordination* to ensure (1) adequate levels of resources and (2) workflow coordination among interdependent units. Plans must be coordinated and discrepancies worked out in advance. For example, the production department needs to know the marketing department's sales estimates so that it can plan for adequate capacity. If the production department can build 1,500 units per month at full capacity, it will make a big difference if the marketing department's sales forecast calls for 1,200 units per month or 1,800 units per month.

Performance goals also provide managers with standards that can act as *early warning* signals when operations begin to run off track. Performance goals, by their nature, are established before work actually occurs. As the work unfolds, shortfalls and problems can be identified by comparing actual results with the performance goals. Shortfalls on key indicators provide diagnostic early warning indicators for managers to investigate problems and develop remedial actions.

Finally, performance goals are often an important ingredient in ex post *evaluation* of accomplishment. Managers and their units are judged on the extent to which they met, exceeded, or fell short of their performance goals.

Using performance goals for all of these purposes—motivation, planning and coordination, early warning, and evaluation—invites problems because the level of the goal must be adjusted to best serve each different purpose. For example:

- For *planning and coordination*, performance goals should be set at levels that represent management's best judgment about the *most likely* levels of output. To secure and dedicate scarce production resources, it is important that accurate predictions are reflected in performance goals and operating plans.

- For *motivation,* managers may wish to *stretch* performance levels to create pressures for extra performance. For example, a performance increment of 10% may be added to the "best-guess" goal in the hope of motivating better performance.

- For ex post *evaluation,* managers may wish to adjust the original performance goals by *factoring out unforeseen or uncontrollable events* that were outside the manager's span of attention. Although managers predicted selling 1,600 units per month to a major customer, should they be held accountable for lower sales due to a lightning strike that disabled the factory of that customer?[5]

In practice, managers are aware of these tensions and walk a fine line in choosing performance goals that are a compromise in meeting these conflicting objectives. Therefore, when setting performance goals, managers must use their judgment to find the right balance between information accuracy and motivational impact.

## ALIGNING INCENTIVES

In general, there are two ways of motivating people to work toward the goals of an organization. The first occurs when people believe that goals are legitimate and, therefore, exert effort willingly to achieve them. This is "intrinsic" motivation—motivation from within. Intrinsic motivation occurs naturally when people voluntarily join benevolent organizations such as churches, synagogues, and charities where they believe inherently in the goals of the organization. Effort is given willingly because individuals believe in the mission that institution is pursuing. Economists call this the "first-best" solution to motivation.

Managers can enhance intrinsic motivation in a variety of ways. First, as discussed in Chapter 1, they can emphasize the positive ideals and beliefs of the business so that employees want to contribute to its overall mission. In other words, they can make people proud of where they work. Second, they can involve subordinates in the goal-setting process to increase the likelihood that subordinates will see the goals as legitimate. If subordinates are included in the process of setting goals—asked to provide input and information—they are more likely to feel that the goals are legitimate and work more diligently to achieve them. (The risk, of course, is that if given the chance, individuals may attempt to lower expected achievement levels to make goals more attainable and predictable.) Also, managers can communicate the cause-and-effect linkages that underlie the current strategy so that employees can understand better their roles in helping the organization achieve its goals.

The second way that business managers can ensure attention to goal achievement is through a formal **incentive**—that is, a reward or payment that is expected to motivate performance. Financial incentives are an essential element in the design of most performance measurement systems. These mechanisms create "extrinsic motivation"—motivation from outside. To enhance extrinsic motivation, financial performance awards—typically in the form of bonuses—can be linked explicitly to the achievement of goals

---

[5] M. Edgar Barrett and Leroy B. Fraser, "Conflicting Roles in Budgeting for Operations," *Harvard Business Review* 55 (1977): 137–146.

and targets. This is done either by paying a percent of profits or by linking bonuses to the achievement of predetermined outcomes.

For example, a salesman may earn a 7% commission on all revenue with no upside limit: sell more, earn more. This approach might also be used for a division manager who is paid a fixed percentage of division profits. Although this approach is sensible for some employees such as salesmen, it becomes problematic when multiple products and multiple goals—financial and nonfinancial—must be balanced. Thus, if a manager's performance goals include EVA, market share, product quality, and customer satisfaction, it would not be prudent to pay incentives only as a percentage of profit—ignoring the other goals.

Thus, incentives for managers are usually tied to predetermined levels of accomplishment against specific goals or outcomes. If a key target is hit (e.g., increase market share in Europe to 5%), then a bonus is paid. With this approach, goals can be set at varying levels of achievement to reflect the benchmarking data, strategic imperatives, and motivational effects discussed in previous sections.

There are three major design decisions that must be made in designing contingent incentives: (1) the bonus pool, (2) the allocation formula, and (3) the type and mix of incentives.

---

### Performance Pay Pitfalls at Lantech

Lantech was a small (325 employees, 1995 revenues of $65 million), privately held Kentucky-based manufacturer of machines that wrap retail shipments in plastic film. In the late 1970s managers tried to introduce incentive-based pay by asking workers to rate their peers' performance; the resulting tension among workers killed the plan. The next attempt a decade later was to give each of the company's five manufacturing divisions a bonus based on the profit generated by that division, which could comprise as much as 10% of a divisional employee's regular pay.

As the company's founder Pat Lancaster recalled, "By the early Nineties, I was spending 95% of my time on conflict resolution instead of on how to serve our customers." The problem was that Lantech's divisions were so interdependent that it was difficult to determine how to fairly allocate costs and revenues for determining bonuses. Instead of working harder to increase the company profits, employees tried to rig the division profit numbers in their favor. The goal of managers in each division was to gain revenue from other divisions and hand off as much cost as possible. This behavior was costly both in excess inventory (as one division tried to ship as much as possible to other divisions) and technological delay (it took several years to decide to purchase an expensive crane for the shop floor because no one could agree on cost allocations). The ultimate silliness was an argument over whether to allocate the cost of toilet paper by gender.

CEO Lancaster eventually replaced the performance-based system with a profit-sharing system based on salary.

---

*Source:* Adapted from Peter Nulty, "Incentive Pay Can Be Crippling," *Fortune* (November 13, 1995): 235.

## The Bonus Pool

The term "incentive" implies that individuals are paid more when performance exceeds some base or threshold. In other words, higher performance generates higher pay; lower performance, lower pay. Although this seems simple enough, the mechanics can become quite complicated and, in all cases, require careful design.

**Bonus** incentives, defined as additional rewards or payments for successful achievement of a task, are usually paid out of a **bonus pool**—a pot of money that is reserved for the payment of incentive and recognition awards. This pool is typically determined by reference to business or corporate-level performance. For example, 15% of annual corporate profits may be set aside in a bonus pool to fund incentive payments.

The bonus pool for Boston Retail may be computed as:

| | |
|---|---:|
| Revenue | $9,200,000 |
| Pretax profit before bonuses | 952,000 |
| Percent reserved for bonus pool | 15% |
| Bonus pool to be allocated among designated employees | 143,000 |
| Pretax profit after bonuses | 809,000 |

## The Allocation Formula

Once the bonus pool has been determined, the next decision is the allocation of the bonus pool to individuals. There are generally three categories of performance that can be used to allocate bonuses: individual performance, business performance, and corporate performance. For example, a manager at General Electric may receive bonus compensation based on his personal goal achievement, the performance of the lighting business of which he is a member, and the performance of the overall corporation.

For any manager, a decision must be made about how to allocate weights across these three performance variables. In general, *the wider the span of control of an individual manager within a single business, the higher the weight given to business performance relative to personal performance.* Also, the more the business interacts with other business units in the same corporation, the higher the weight given to corporate performance relative to either types of performance. For example, consider the following alternative weighting schemes:

| | MANAGER A | MANAGER B |
|---|:---:|:---:|
| Corporate Performance | 20% | 40% |
| Business Performance | 20% | 40% |
| Individual Performance | 60% | 20% |
| | 100% | 100% |

Manager A's weighting scheme—which gives a relatively high weight to individual performance—is likely to be more appropriate for a lower-ranking employee with a narrow span of control. Manager B's weighting scheme, by contrast, gives primary weight to corporate and business performance and may be appropriate for a senior-level business manager operating a unit that has significant interactions with other units in the corporation.

Within each of these percentages, a further decision must be made about how to calculate the actual amount of the payment. For example, if 40% is allocated to business performance and 20% to personal goal, how do we assess levels of achievement? There are two basic methods: by formula and by subjective judgment.

A formula may be of the following type:

| | |
|---|---|
| If profit $= X$, | then bonus $= Y$ |
| If $X <$ profit $< X + 10\%$, | then bonus $= Y + \$20,000$ |
| If $X + 10\% \leq$ profit $< X + 20\%$, | then bonus $= Y + \$50,000$ |
| If profit $\geq X + 20\%$, | then bonus $= Y + \$75,000$ |

Formula-based allocation systems have two distinct advantages. First, there is no ambiguity about what results are desired or how they will be measured. Thus, employees are clear about what they will be rewarded for. Second, and related to the first, bonus allocation schemes can be set infrequently—typically once per year—and do not then require much attention from managers. Thus, a formula-based allocation system allows high ROM—set the goal, determine the bonus formula, and then concentrate on other things, confident that employees are pursuing the goals that are mirrored in the bonus calculation.

The other alternative is to allocate performance rewards based on subjective evaluation of performance. To do this, managers must use their knowledge, experience, and judgment to determine the contribution of a subordinate. This requires not only a high degree of trust, but also a large investment of time on the part of the boss, who must gather sufficient information to determine the performance of the subordinate. Subjective evaluation is a hallmark of the interactive control systems described in the previous chapter.

Payout formulas can be based on any of the goals discussed to date: profit, cash flow, and ROCE, as well as balanced-scorecard goals such as market share, new-product development, and personal goals such as mentoring and training. Sometimes, compensating goals may be created to try to overcome the limitations of specific measures and goals that we have discussed in earlier chapters. For example, if an important goal is to increase ROCE, senior managers may wish to devise a payout formula that will pay increasing rewards as ROCE increases. There is risk here, however, because there are two ways of increasing any ratio. The first—and desired outcome—is to increase the numerator—net income. But there is also a second way—decreasing the denominator. Thus, there is some risk that, to increase their bonus compensation, managers may be motivated to underinvest in assets or even sell off assets that have future value to the business.

To compensate for this risk, managers can create a payout matrix like the one shown in Figure 11–5. In this matrix, bonus formula payouts are increasing in both ROCE and asset growth, thereby eliminating the incentive for managers to shrink the denominator. The message is now straightforward—increase returns on capital and grow the size of the business.

---

### Eli Lilly Links Compensation to EVA

The pharmaceutical giant Eli Lilly & Company is among a number of companies that have linked senior management compensation to EVA. Lilly decided in 1994 to use EVA as a performance measure for two reasons: EVA aligns well with shareholder value and it forces managers to focus critically on capital expenditures. The pharmaceutical business is highly capital-intensive, so EVA reinforces the concept that managers are accountable for ROCE.

In the past, executive pay at Lilly had been tied to sales and net income, but Lilly found that these measurements did not correlate well to shareholder value. By rewarding managers who deliver continuous, year-to-year improvements in EVA, Lilly hopes that managers will be motivated to continue to raise shareholder value.

Lilly adopted a top-down approach to rolling out EVA. Although lower-level employees do not have their compensation tied to EVA, they know what drives senior officers' bonuses, resulting in a rapid change in attitudes toward capital throughout the business. To promote greater understanding of EVA among employees, Lilly has run stories about EVA in employee publications, and managers talk with their employees about how EVA works. Lilly estimates that teaching EVA concepts to managers requires several days. Implementing this scheme outside the United States requires significantly more training.

Lilly decided to pay bonuses based on EVA calculated at the corporate level, rather than business-unit EVA, for two reasons: Lilly was experiencing a significant reorganization into global business units at the time (and introducing a new compensation system might overwhelm employees), and Lilly wanted to avoid the possibility of individual business-unit managers making decisions that suboptimized corporate EVA.

Lilly also recognized that, because EVA is calculated annually, managers may make shortsighted decisions without regard for long-term shareholder value. For example, lowering the asset base and depleting inventory would increase EVA in one year but leave Lilly with nothing to sell in the following year. To guard against this kind of behavior, Lilly pays out only a portion of a manager's EVA bonus and places the rest in a "bonus bank." Managers can withdraw from the bonus bank only if EVA improves annually. On the other hand, if a manager makes an investment in year one that reduces EVA in year three, Lilly deducts money from the bonus bank. There are no annual caps on EVA bonuses, reducing the potential for distortion to avoid bonus limitation rules.

---

*Source:* Adapted from Justin Martin, "Eli Lilly Is Making Shareholders Rich. How? By Linking Pay to EVA," *Fortune* (September 9, 1996): 173.

**FIGURE 11–5  ROCE Matrix**

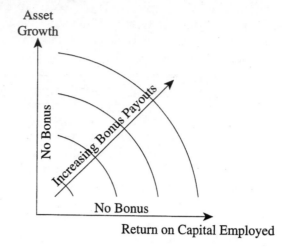

## Types and Mix of Incentives

The final design decision concerns what types of incentives to provide to employees to recognize their achievements. We normally think of bonuses as cash payments, but in fact there is a wide range of options concerning the types of financial incentives that can be provided. In addition to cash, some of the more common are:

- gifts and prizes
- deferred cash payments
- awards of company stock
- grants of options for the future purchase of company stock

We can think this array of incentives as analogous to assets on a balance sheet. On a balance sheet, we start with the most liquid asset—cash—and then progress through a listing of other assets, ranked in order of decreasing liquidity. With incentives, we start with liquid incentives—cash payments—and then move through other categories that move further away from cash: gifts and prizes, deferred cash payments, stock awards, and the granting of stock options.

The incentive value of cash is clear. However, other incentives may provide additional benefits. Gifts and prizes can often be used to great effect as ways of celebrating accomplishment. For example, the ceremonial awarding of a trip to Hawaii in recognition of outstanding accomplishment may create more excitement among employees than the payment of a $3,000 cash bonus. Public recognition is a powerful motivator (just ask any university professor!). This technique—public recognition and rewards—is used extremely effectively by many direct-selling companies such as Mary Kay Cosmetics.

Incentives that have longer-term payouts—for example, deferred cash payments—may force managers to think more carefully about the trade-offs between the short term and the long term in their decision making. For example, the payment of cash bonuses based on sales revenue growth may be deferred for a 12-month period to reflect adjustments for uncollectable customer accounts. Thus, a salesperson who might be inclined to generate quick revenue by selling goods or services to customers with poor credit ratings would think twice about this practice because any bad debts would reduce his or her ultimate bonus payment.

Finally, we may choose to offer payment of incentives in terms of stock or stock options. Stock ownership helps motivate employees to make decisions and act in ways that will enhance shareholder value and, therefore, stock price. Employee incentives are aligned with those of the stockholders. Stock options add an additional dimension. An option is the right to purchase stock at a specified price (known as the strike price). As an incentive payment, we might give employees stock options valued at today's current share price. Holders of these options may choose, at any time in the future, to exercise their right to buy shares in the company at the strike price. Of course, the options only have value if the price of the company's stock rises.

For example, as a bonus, we may give a manager 10,000 stock options valued at today's closing stock price of $23 per share. If share price falls to $20, then the manager is holding worthless options—no rational person would pay $23 to buy a share that is only worth $20. However, if the share price rises to $40, then the manager may choose to purchase the 10,000 shares at the strike price of $23 per share for $230,000. He or she could either hold them or immediately sell them on the open market for $400,000, thereby generating a gain of $170,000. The effect of this award, of course, is to give managers the incentives to do whatever is within their power to increase share price.

It will come as no surprise that stock awards and stock options are among the most popular forms of incentive compensation when stock markets are rising. During the 1990s—the longest U.S. bull market in history—stock awards and options have flour-

---

### Compensating Pilots at Southwest Airlines

In most airline companies, pilots are paid a flat salary. This salary rewards the valuable inputs that pilots bring to the company, that is, their skills and abilities to fly airplanes. This salary structure assumes that selecting the right pilots, paying competitive wages, and giving them a flight schedule for the year will result in the desired level and quality of flight service.

However, not all companies think the same way. In 1995, pilots at Southwest Airlines Company, agreed to give up salary increases for the next five years in exchange for 1.4 million shares in the company per year at a predefined price. The move was not only good for the cash flow of the company, it also acknowledged that pilots bring more than just flying skills to their job: They bring leadership, customer service, and reputation through their daily actions. By accepting a stake in the equity of Southwest, the pilots gained a stake in the long-term performance of the company. Southwest not only rewarded the input that pilots brought (their skills) but also gave them a piece of the output, so that they would act in line with Southwest's ultimate objectives.

---

*Source:* Adapted from Thomas P. Flannery et al. *People, Performance & Pay.* The Hay Group. (New York: The Free Press, 1996): 112.

ished. A 1997 survey suggests that 45% of large companies with option plans grant stock options to all their employees. In contrast, only 10% did so in 1994.[6] By contrast, from 1966 to 1981, when the stock market actually declined in inflation-adjusted terms, there was little interest in this type of compensation.

## EXECUTIVE COMPENSATION AT FORD MOTOR COMPANY

Ford's executive compensation plan illustrates how one company links management and stockholder interests and ties compensation to the achievement of profit goals and strategies.[7] Many large U.S. companies follow similar compensation schemes.

Like all successful companies, Ford must offer competitive compensation to attract and retain talented top managers. Each year, Ford's board of directors commissions an outside consultant to survey executive compensation in the worldwide auto industry and at major U.S. companies. After adjusting the results for company size, performance, reputation, and business complexity, Ford sets its compensation levels to match the average compensation levels reported from the survey.

Ford then divides compensation into two categories: annual compensation and long-term compensation. Annual compensation includes salary and annual bonuses; long-term compensation includes stock options and outright grants of company common stock. Annual bonuses are based on a formula to reward individual or group performance over the past year. Ford ties annual bonuses to EVA by setting the bonus pool for a given year at 6% of pretax residual income. Residual income is computed by taking pretax accounting income and subtracting a cost of capital equal to 10% of capital employed in the business.

Recognizing that decisions made by Ford's executives will affect the company for many years, Ford ties long-term compensation to the achievement of long-term goals and stock price. Stock options and stock grants (the right to receive a prespecified number of shares of stock) are the primary elements of Ford's long-term compensation. Ford's stock-option awards vest (that is, are irrevocably transferred to recipients) over ten years, motivating executives to remain with the company and focus on long-term stock performance.

Depending on market conditions, stock options may not always align executive incentives with shareholder incentives. For example, if an executive's incentives are "out-of-the-money" (i.e., current stock price is lower than option price), then the executive might be motivated to make risky decisions in the hope of boosting performance and stock price. To balance this risk, Ford also makes outright stock grants to its executives as part of their long-term compensation. By owning stock (and not just stock options), executives are fully invested in the downside risk of their decisions. In 1994, the Ford board of directors set goals for all Ford executives at the vice president level and above to own Ford common stock worth a specified multiple of their salary. By 1998, most key managers had achieved this goal.

---

[6] Gretchen Morgenson, "Stock Options Are Not a Free Lunch," *Forbes* (May 18, 1998): 213. In the survey, a large company was defined as one with 5,000 or more employees.

[7] Ford Motor Company Proxy Statement, April 14, 1998.

Ford awards stock grants on a retrospective basis. For example, in 1992 and in 1994, each executive received a number of "contingent stock rights" that were awarded depending on how well Ford met goals in the following areas over a five and three year period, respectively:

| 1992–1996 | 1994–1996 |
|---|---|
| Product quality and worldwide acceptance (35%) | Product quality and worldwide acceptance (35%) |
| Cost reduction (25%) | Corporate ROE (25%) |
| Product programs (25%) | Product programs (25%) |
| Relationship with employees (15%) | Relationship with employees (15%) |

Each quarter, Ford's top 5,200 managers receive reports on their progress toward these goals.[8]

In 1997, Ford's board of directors evaluated the extent to which managers had achieved goals in each of these areas. They concluded that Ford achieved 80% of these goals in the 1992–1996 period and 83% of its goals in the 1994–1996 period. As a result, Ford executives received in stock the same percentage, respectively, of their 1992 and 1994 contingent stock rights.

In 1998, Ford's board of directors continued its balanced scorecard approach to performance goals and incentives by linking future stock-grant awards to goals in the following areas:

- ROE versus nonoil Fortune 50 companies
- product programs
- customer satisfaction
- selected internal financial measures
- product quality
- relationship with employees

## CHAPTER SUMMARY

Setting performance goals and incentives is a key and vital responsibility of management. All managers must set goals for subordinates and for the functions and businesses that they manage. At higher management levels, failure to set goals is a failure of leadership. As Philip Selznick has argued,

> The failure . . . to set goals stems partly from the hard intellectual labor involved, a labor that often seems but to increase the burden of already onerous daily operations. In part, also, there is the wish to avoid conflicts with those in and out of the organization who would be threatened by a sharp definition of purpose, with its attendant claims and respon-

---

[8] Alex Taylor III, "The Gentlemen at Ford Are Kicking Butt," *Fortune* (June 22, 1998): 75.

sibilities. Even business firms find it easy to fall back on conventional phrases, such as that "our goal is to make profit," phrases which offer little guidance in the formulation of policy.[9]

As this quote suggests, setting goals is not easy. It is a skill that must be acquired, combining knowledge of the technical aspects of performance measurement with a grasp of the process flows that are required to cascade performance goals through the organization. Because performance goals and their related incentives determine success (and failure) for individuals, this topic cannot be satisfactorily considered without consideration of the interaction of goals and measures with human behavior.

---

[9] Philip Selznick, *Leadership in Administration* (New York: Harper & Row, 1957): 62–64.

# 12

# Identifying Strategic Risk

C ompeting in any industry entails risk. However, the more aggressive and fast-paced the business and its management, the greater the potential for a misstep. In this chapter, we consider the different types of strategic risks that can imperil the firm. Then, we illustrate how to use the risk exposure calculator—a diagnostic tool to identify organizational pressure points that could cause these risks to rise to dangerous levels. Finally, we discuss the conditions that could cause individual employees to willfully expose the business to risk.

After identifying the sources of strategic risk, we study the control tools and techniques that managers employ to manage these risks.

## SOURCES OF STRATEGIC RISK

A dictionary defines risk as "the possibility of suffering harm or loss."[1] In a business setting, managers must be sensitive to conditions that can cause specific categories of risk to become dangerous. These conditions are a function of the business strategy chosen by top managers.

To effectively manage their business, all managers must assess **strategic risk,** which is *an unexpected event or set of conditions that significantly reduces the ability of managers to implement their intended business strategy.* Figure 12–1 highlights the focus of our analysis. Business strategy—at the center of the figure—is our starting point. Working outward from the center, we consider three basic sources of strategic risk that potentially affect every business: operations risk, asset impairment risk, and competitive risk. If the magnitude of any of these risks becomes sufficiently large, the firm becomes exposed to franchise risk.

### Operations Risk

**Operations risk** results from the consequences of a breakdown in a core operating, manufacturing, or processing capability. All firms that create value through manufacturing or service activities face operations risk to varying degrees. Things can (and do) go wrong in the operating core of the business. Defective products can be shipped, maintenance can be neglected leading to breakdowns, customer packages can be lost, and transactions can be erroneously processed. Any operational error that impedes the flow

---

This chapter is reprinted with permission from Robert Simons, "Identifying Strategic Risk," Harvard Business School Note No. 199-031, 1998. Copyright © 1998 by the President and Fellows of Harvard College.

[1] *The American Heritage Dictionary of the English Language,* 3rd ed. (Boston: Houghton Mifflin, 1992).

**FIGURE 12–1    Sources of Business Risk**

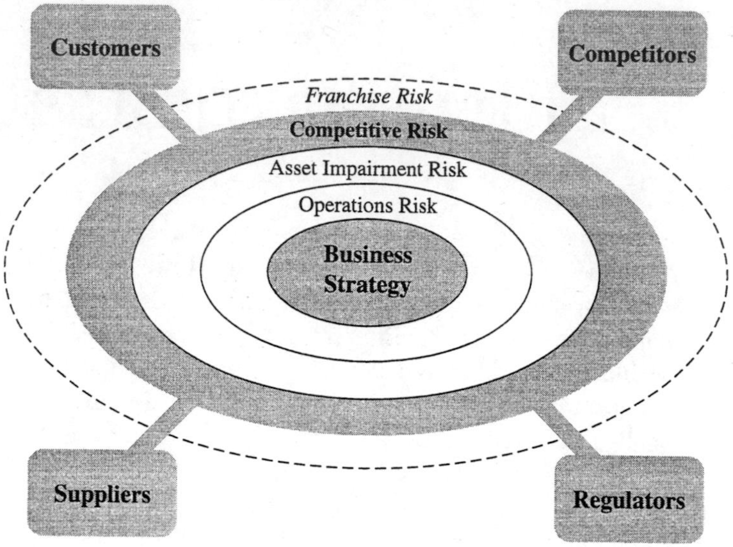

of high-quality products and services has the potential to expose the firm to loss and liability.

Operations risk becomes a strategic risk in the event of critical product or process failures. In a food or drug manufacturer, for example, operations risk is encountered if a toxic substance is inadvertently mixed in with a product formulation. For a financial institution, operations risk is encountered if trades are not executed properly or if a transactions clearing system fails. Fidelity Investment Company, for example, processes more than one million transactions each day in its mutual funds business. With more than $400 billion invested, customers expect their transactions to be processed promptly and accurately. Any failure of processing technology would be devastating to the business.

Basic business strategy affects any firm's exposure to operations risk. For example, AOL has followed an aggressive growth strategy, lowering its prices and providing free access software to capture market share from competitors. However, failures in the ability of its server network to handle growing demand, caused by insufficient modem and network processing capacity, resulted in lawsuits and embarrassing public scrutiny of its service capability. In the food-products industry, Odwalla, a manufacturer of bottled apple juice, attempted to differentiate its products through superior freshness and flavor. To ensure maximum flavor, managers made a strategic decision not to pasteurize their juice. Unfortunately, the operations risk resulting from this strategy led to severe consequences when the company inadvertently shipped tainted products that resulted in sickness and death. Operations risk exposed the business to criminal charges, lawsuits, and loss of confidence by consumers. The company's survival was placed in jeopardy.[2]

---

[2] Pam Belluck, "Juice Maker Pleads Guilty and Pays $1.5 Million in Fatal Poisoning Case," *The New York Times* (July 24, 1998): A12.

In most industries, there are some competitors who knowingly choose strategies in which the safety and/or quality of operations are critical to success—thereby assuming significant operations risk. This is true for an electric utility that chooses to generate power using nuclear power, instead of purchasing bulk power from another provider. The strategy of entering the generation business—backward integrating—coupled with the decision to generate power using nuclear energy rather that fossil fuels, increases operations risk significantly.

In high technology businesses, where certain aspects of operations are "mission critical" to the implementation of strategy, any error or downtime can be sufficiently serious to threaten the viability of the business. We have discussed already the substantial operations risk at large financial institutions like Fidelity Investments. Consider the operations risk at the John F. Kennedy Space Center. Any failure in operations can imperil the safety of the space shuttle and its crew. Because managers rely on complex technologies, NASA has assumed significant operations risk.

The consequences of operations risk are often triggered by employee error. Most of these errors are unintended and/or accidental. Occasionally, however, employees may consciously decide to cut corners in quality or safety to meet performance targets or receive bonuses. For example, the horrific nuclear accident at Chernobyl in the former Soviet Union was caused by operators and managers who intentionally falsified performance indicators to ensure that they would achieve production targets and earn desired bonuses.

### Applying the Inputs → Process → Outputs Model

Applying the inputs → process → outputs model is critical for identifying and controlling operations risk, especially when technology failure can lead to inefficiencies and breakdowns.

Analyzing operations according to the inputs → process → outputs model provides guidance about what key processes should be standardized and controlled tightly to assure safety and quality. This is a first step in the assessment of operations risk. As discussed in Chapter 4, standardization and scalability are appropriate for critical internal processes that lie at the core of a business's operations. The inputs → process → outputs model should be used in all critical parts of the value chain to identify points where system errors could damage key operations or impair important assets. Standardization and practices such as TQM based on best practice, benchmarking, and engineering studies can then be used to ensure that inefficiencies and breakdowns do not create significant operating risks for the business.

## Asset Impairment Risk

Moving outward from the core of Figure 12–1, the second source of strategic risk is **asset impairment risk.** An asset is a resource owned by the firm to generate future cash flows. An asset becomes *impaired* when it loses a significant portion of its current value because of a reduction in the likelihood of receiving those future cash flows. Like other risks, asset impairment risk is largely a function of the way that managers have chosen to compete.

Asset impairment can become a strategic risk if there is deterioration in the financial value, intellectual property rights, or the physical condition of assets that are important for the implementation of strategy.

## Financial Impairment

Financial impairment results from a decline in the market value of a significant balance sheet asset held for resale or as collateral. An asset becomes impaired when the future cash flows accruing to the firm are no longer sufficient to support the asset's balance sheet valuation (computed as the NPV of those future cash flows). For example, firms holding significant Mexican assets found those assets impaired when the government devalued the peso in late 1994. Russian assets became impaired in the same way in 1998. In both of these cases, currency devaluation decreased the expected value of future cash flows. Similarly, the value of a long-term bond portfolio may sink dramatically with a rise in market interest rates (which increases the discount rate used in the NPV calculation).

All firms that sell goods or services on credit face the possibility that accounts receivable—a financial asset on the balance sheet—will prove uncollectable. *Credit risk* occurs when a creditor becomes bankrupt or insolvent and is unable to pay contractual obligations as they become due. All businesses that extend payment terms are exposed to credit risk, although some strategies expose the business to more credit risk than others. Managers must balance risk and reward as they choose the conditions and terms under which they are willing to grant credit. Most businesses can increase sales and revenues if managers are willing to offer more liberal credit terms to customers who are poor credit risks. Long payback periods coupled with low levels of collateral increase the risk and cost of default. Alternatively, managers can minimize credit losses by turning away sales on account, but at the cost of forgone revenue. Similarly, they can insist on marketable collateral to secure loans or withhold the legal transfer of title until payment is made in full.

Depending on the strategy of the firm, creditors may be individuals, businesses, or even governments. At the extreme, a business may be exposed to risk at the national level (called *sovereign risk*) when a foreign government becomes unable or unwilling to repay its debts. Sovereign risk is greatest, of course, when a business follows a strategy that results in significant cross-border financial exposure in politically unstable countries. Instability in Indonesia and other Asian countries in 1998 increased sovereign risk for many firms.

Financial trading firms—those that routinely buy and sell financial securities—often enter into agreements to buy or sell assets on specified dates in the future. These agreements are called forward contracts. Such firms are exposed to a special type of credit risk known as *counterparty* risk—the risk that the other party to the agreement may be unable to honor its contractual obligation due to insolvency or inability to deliver what was promised. This risk can become substantial if a large number of transactions and forward contracts are concentrated with a small number of counterparties or if failures of specific financial institutions lead to a general market insolvency.

For financial trading businesses such as banks, retail stockbrokers, and mutual funds, specific business strategies determine how much financial impairment risk the business is exposed to. Firms following high-risk strategies often hold unhedged assets such as global derivatives and other highly leveraged securities whose value can change rapidly and erratically. More conservative competitors may choose strategies that limit their financial impairment risk: they eschew highly leveraged instruments in favor of more easily controlled investments.

Financial impairment is often due to unpredictable changes in financial market variables. However, like operations risk, assets may sometimes become impaired by the willful actions of employees. Consider these examples:

- A bank vice president wished to improve the asset position of her balance sheet at year-end. Accordingly, she sold a portfolio of mortgage loans to a friendly bank. She did not inform anyone of the agreement to repurchase the mortgage portfolio in six months.
- A bond trader lost $1 million on currency market trades. He instructed accounting personnel to post the loss to a suspense account. He explained that he would offset the loss against an open position that was guaranteed to generate a sizable profit.

In cases such as these, employees expose a business to asset impairment risk in their attempts to achieve performance targets a nd/or cover up previous losses.

Manufacturing and service firms are not immune from financial impairment risk. When excess cash is invested in short-term financial assets, any business may be exposed to financial impairment risk. For example, managers of industrial or consumer-products companies may be tempted to bolster their short-term profitability by taking unhedged financial positions that pay off if financial markets move in predicted directions. As a result of this type of gamble, Procter & Gamble lost millions of dollars in highly leveraged derivative positions. This financial speculation also caused the much publicized municipal insolvency of Orange County, California in the mid 1990s.

---

### Bank Lending Risks

Employees sometimes decide to step out of bounds to take advantage of certain situations. The manager of a bank's branch did precisely this. One of his customers was a construction company that was having problems obtaining a loan from other banks. The bank officer agreed to give the company a loan if, in exchange, the construction company did some work at his house for free. Apparently, the bank officer thought that this was a mutually satisfactory arrangement: the company received the credit that it was looking for, and he was able to have his house remodeled. The bank officer then decided to use the same approach with two other customers, also in the construction sector, who approached the bank for loans. In due course, the regional manager noticed the increased credit risk that the branch was taking with these customers and decided to investigate. He quickly discovered the reasons for their credit approvals and fired the branch manager.

## Impairment of Intellectual Property Rights

For many companies today, intangible resources such as intellectual property and proprietary customer information are far more valuable than the tangible assets on the firm's balance sheet. Many software and Internet firms are good examples. The huge market value of firms such as Microsoft Corporation, Amazon.com, and Netscape Communications is not a function of the size of their balance sheets, but rather reflects the estimated value of future cash flows related to their intangible intellectual resources. Similarly, the value of ethical drug manufacturers such as Merck & Company and Pfizer resides primarily in their research capabilities, patents, and trade secrets.

For these firms, the potential for loss or impairment of these intellectual property rights creates significant strategic risk. Impairment may be due to unauthorized use of intellectual property by competitors (e.g., patent infringement), unauthorized disclosure of trade secrets to a competitor or third party (such as leaking of proprietary computer code, manufacturing procedures, or formulas), and failure to reinvest in intellectual capital as asset quality deteriorates over time (e.g., failure to upgrade information-based assets or invest in employee training).

## Physical Impairment

Assets can also become impaired by the physical destruction of key processing or production facilities. This impairment may be due to fire, flood, terrorist action, or other catastrophe. Managers whose business depends on large-scale data centers must ensure that processing can be switched to backup facilities without significant loss of operating capacity. Risk managers are typically responsible for ensuring adequate coverage for insurable physical destruction risks and the implementation of fail-safe backup plans to protect against mission-critical processing failures.

# Competitive Risk

So far, we have considered strategic risks due to defective transaction flows (operations risk) and impaired value of significant balance sheet assets and intangible resources (asset impairment risk). The third source of strategic risk has to do with the risks inherent in market competition. **Competitive risk** results from changes in the competitive environment that could impair the business's ability to successfully create value and differentiate its products or services. Examples of competitive risks that could impair the ability of a business to create value include the actions of *competitors* in developing superior products and services (for example, compact disks displacing vinyl records); changes in *regulation* and public policy (e.g., regulators requiring electric utilities to sell off their generation facilities); shifts in *customer* tastes or desires (such as fashion fads); and changes in *supplier* pricing and policies (e.g., preferential pricing for "super" retailers) (Figure 12–1).

Competitive risk, by definition, is faced by all businesses that compete in dynamic markets. Regardless of the industry in which a business competes, so long as it has active competitors and demanding customers, it is exposed to competitive risk. The five-forces analysis, covered in Chapter 2, provides a starting point to consider the direction from which these risks can emanate:

- Intense rivalry from existing competitors can change the basis of value creation.
- Demanding customers may choose to switch suppliers.
- Suppliers may choose to limit availability or increase the cost of critical inputs.
- New competitors may enter the industry with new technologies and products.
- Substitute products or services may become available with superior costs or attributes.[3]

Managers must be constantly alert to the risk that they will fail to anticipate and react to these competitive risks quickly, thereby allowing the rules of the competitive game to turn against them. However, competitive risk can also be created by the actions of employees. Employees can inadvertently damage the franchise in their attempts to maximize short-term profit. These kinds of risk are created when employees act inappropriately in dealing with customers, suppliers, and competitors. For any given strategy, a series of questions can reveal those employee behaviors that could imperil the strategy.

***Customers:*** *What employee actions could drive customers away?*
- A small consulting firm competed by offering specialized services to an elite group of demanding clients. Employees in a branch office provided consulting services to the competitor of a large and important client. As a result of a perceived conflict of interest, the large client severed relationships with the firm.

***Suppliers:*** *What employee actions could cause important suppliers to stop supplying the firm?*
- A beer distributor relied on a national brewer for the majority of its business. Employees became complacent and allowed relationships with the supplier to deteriorate. Because of poor service, the brewer awarded distribution rights to a competing wholesaler.

***Substitute Products:*** *What employee actions could cause customers to switch to competing products or services?*
- To obtain commission bonuses in an electronic-instrumentation business, salespeople pushed obsolete products that were stockpiled in inventory. Customers wishing to purchase the latest technology placed orders with new suppliers who were trying to build market share.

***New Entrants:*** *What employee actions could cause new competitors to enter the industry?*
- In a cable television business, abuses in customer service caused regulators to increase competition by licensing new competitors.

Interactive controls systems are essential to monitor competitive risks in a culture that could potentially create barriers to impede the free flow of information about emerging threats and opportunities.

---

[3] Michael E. Porter, *Competitive Strategy* (New York: The Free Press, 1980).

## Franchise Risk

Unlike the three sources of risk enumerated above (operations, asset impairment, and competitive risk), franchise risk is not in itself a *source* of risk. Instead, it is a *consequence* of excessive risk in any one of the three basic risk dimensions. **Franchise risk** occurs when the value of the entire business erodes due to a loss in confidence by critical constituents. Franchise risk occurs when a problem or set of problems threatens the viability of the entire enterprise. In the worst case, customers stop buying a business's products or services because they lose confidence in the company's ability to deliver what it has promised. However, loss of confidence by other constituents—suppliers, regulators, or business partners—can be equally devastating (Figure 12–1).

Loss of confidence in either a brand or the entire corporation—the hallmark of franchise risk—can result from any of the risks previously enumerated. Consider the following examples:

- *Operations risk*—After a well-publicized fatal crash in Florida, AirTran Holdings (formerly ValuJet Airlines) managers were unable to restore public confidence that flight operations and safety procedures at the airline were adequate. The market share of other discount-fare regional competitors also eroded as the public lost confidence in the safety and reliability of low-cost operators.
- *Asset impairment risk*—During the savings and loan crisis, the public lost confidence that besieged banks, reeling from losses in real estate collateral, had sufficient resources to repay depositors. The "run on the banks" that occurred at several institutions required federal agencies to step in and guarantee deposits as a means of restoring confidence.
- *Competitive risk*—The disastrous slide in market share at Apple Computer, reflecting competitive forces and eroding technological leadership, caused many in the industry to lose confidence in Apple's ability to support its products. As a result, software suppliers declined to invest in Apple applications and customers abandoned Apple computers in favor of competitors' products.

Franchise risk—sometimes known as *reputation risk*—occurs when business problems or actions negatively affect customer perceptions of value in using the business's goods or services. The intrinsic value of a business (i.e., its value proposition) is based on customers' willingness to pay for a known set of attributes and quality. Any significant breakdown in operations, impairment of assets, or erosion of competitive strength can negatively influence public perception and drive away customers.

For any firm operating in a competitive market, reputation is critical to the ongoing ability to create value. When customers have a choice about which firms' products to buy, reputation risk must be a major concern for managers. Franchise risk is acute, however, for any firm that depends on its reputation for integrity as a critical competitive resource in attracting and maintaining customers. For example, public accounting firms, defense contractors, airlines, and pharmaceutical firms (among many others) hold a public franchise that depends fundamentally on the public's faith in the integrity and trustworthiness of their business. What are the effects of a story that appears in the morning newspaper describing how managers of a mutual fund have been manipulating published figures to deceive investors? How long will the franchise of that business last? A damaged reputation can destroy the franchise—and ultimately the business—literally overnight.

## Restaurant Risk Management

Dining out in restaurants is a significant part of the modern lifestyle, with patrons' concerns ranging from the politeness of service to safety implications from widely publicized outbreaks of foodborne bacteria. Because of these factors, Debra Smithart, CFO of Brinker International, a $1.2 billion casual-dining company with 600 restaurants, decided to establish an internal audit function to address risk issues. "When we did our own risk audit, we realized we had business risks in areas that you couldn't financially engineer or where you couldn't go out and buy something to protect yourself."

She then decided to automate and build in preventive processes in all the group's operations, even if this meant involving financial personnel in nonfinancial areas. Restaurant managers' bonuses were changed to reflect how well they controlled losses, and accident costs were reported on restaurants' monthly financial statements. Cash registers were modified to identify every transaction in more than 140 ways; kettle designs were changed to prevent hot water burns. The company examined every possibility for preventing any contamination by *e. coli* bacteria because no insurance could be bought for such an occurrence and operational cleanliness measures were not foolproof. Accordingly, Brinker's auditors visited slaughterhouses before deciding on which suppliers would be willing to work with them to develop testing procedures.

Brinker's management team also assumed responsibility in managing potential risks to its reputation. Customer complaints were answered by top management within 24 hours. In 1993, when a polo accident put the chairman and CEO Norman Brinker in a (temporary) coma, the board of directors appointed an interim successor within two days. The company received kudos from the press not only for its management of the potential succession crisis, but also for its response two years later to a fire that burned down a restaurant in Jackson, Mississippi: Brinker found every employee another job (mostly in other Brinker restaurants).

*Source:* Adapted from Stephen Barr, "Redefining Risk," *CFO* (August 1996): 61–66.

---

Many of the pitfalls of risk management can be avoided if early warning systems are in place to warn managers of impending problems. Diagnostic exception reports that focus on key indicators can alert managers if risk levels are unacceptable. Examples of some common risk indicators are:

**Operations Risk**
- system downtime
- number of errors
- unexplained variances
- unreconciled accounts
- defect rates/quality standards
- customer complaints

**Asset Impairment Risk**
- unhedged derivatives on balance sheet
- unrealized holding gains/losses
- concentration of credit or counterparty exposure (e.g., total debt due from specific financial institutions)
- default history
- dropoff in product sales

**Competitive Risk**
- recent product introductions by competitors
- recent regulatory changes
- changes in consumer buying habits reported in trade journals
- changes in distribution systems

**Franchise Risk**
- customers/bids lost to competitors
- unfavorable news coverage
- pending lawsuits/legal actions
- system downtime
- competitor business failure

## ASSESSING INTERNAL RISK PRESSURES

We have now outlined the types of strategic risk that all firms potentially face. Managers must assess their exposure to these risks based on their specific business strategy.

Now we move to the second step of the analysis by attempting to understand how strategic risks may be exacerbated by the context in which the organization operates. Based on a variety of factors, firms competing in the same product markets may be exposed to very different levels of risk. The **risk exposure calculator** (illustrated in Figure 12–2) analyzes the pressure points inside a business that can cause strategic risks to "blow up" into a crisis. Some of these pressures are due to *growth,* some are due to management *culture,* and some are due to *information management.* Collectively, these forces can "surprise" managers in the form of operating errors, impairment of assets, and crises of customer confidence.

The risk exposure calculator is a diagnostic tool to estimate the magnitude and type of "pressures" that might lead to a substantial failure or breakdown. As suggested by Figure 12–2, the nine pressure points that we discuss are additive. One pressure feeds upon the other. If the pressure builds too high, operations risk, asset impairment risk, and competitive risk can cause irreparable damage. Let's look at each of the pressure points in turn.

### Risks Pressures Due to Growth

Growth is a fundamental goal of most high-performing businesses. Yet, success in achieving market-driven growth can bring risk for three reasons. The first reason relates to the *unrelenting pressure for performance* that is a hallmark of high-growth compa-

**FIGURE 12–2   The Risk Exposure Calculator**

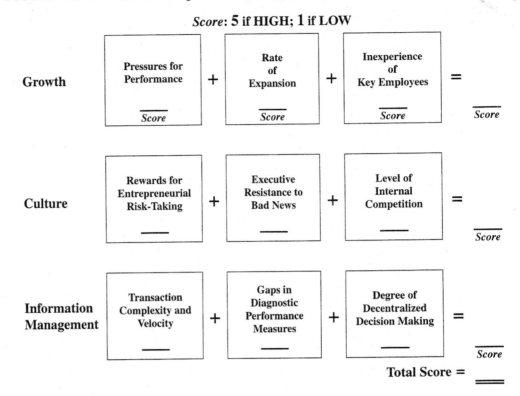

*Score*: **5** if HIGH; **1** if LOW

nies. High-growth companies typically have very high performance expectations for their managers and employees. Goals are set at demanding levels. Employees are informed that they are expected to deliver results (or else risk punishment or possible replacement). Incentive rewards and bonuses are linked directly and explicitly to performance. Under these circumstances, some people may feel intense pressure to succeed at all costs and may, therefore, engage in behaviors that invite risk. They may, for example, take unacceptable credit risks by selling goods and services to customers with poor credit ratings; they may cut corners to speed operations; or, they may be tempted to bend revenue-recognition rules to book profits before full completion of a sale. If pushed hard enough, some employees may even consider misrepresenting their true performance to cover up any temporary shortfalls.

*Rapidly expanding scale of operations* is another sign of successful growth. Successful companies grow bigger. However, rapidly increasing scale can also bring undesirable levels of risk. Resources become strained to the limit as people and systems work beyond their normal capacity. Infrastructures designed for a small operation quickly become inadequate. New production, distribution, and service facilities must be brought on line and integrated into overall operations. As a result of rapidly expanding operations, mistakes and breakdowns may occur. Operations errors are likely to creep into the system. New customer accounts may increase credit risk. Product or service quality may suffer, increasing franchise risk.

Growth also means hiring large numbers of new people to staff operations. Competitive advantage cannot be achieved by waiting until all the right people are in place before launching new products and services. Sometimes, in the rush to staff new positions, background checks may be waived and minimum performance standards and educational qualifications may be lowered. Newly hired employees may lack adequate training and experience and, as a result, not fully understand their jobs. *Decreasing experience* can, therefore, result in increased possibility for inadvertent error. Bad business decisions may expose the firm to asset impairment risk and franchise risk.

These risks are increased significantly when a business *lacks consistent values.* Consistent and strong core values are an essential foundation in any highly competitive business. In new, start-up businesses that have not had time to allow consistent values to emerge and take hold, managers and employees may make very different assumptions about organizational purpose and acceptable behaviors. In larger, more-diversified businesses, different business units within the same firm may have very different core values. This occurred, for example, when General Electric—an industrial company—purchased and attempted to manage Kidder Peabody, a financial brokerage firm. The core values in these businesses were so different that it was difficult to communicate a consistent set of corporate-wide beliefs about acceptable risks and behaviors. What was seen as an acceptable credit or operations risk in one business was completely unacceptable in another business, and vice versa. Confusion about values and beliefs invites individuals under pressure to engage in behaviors that increase risk—especially impairment risk and franchise risk.

These three pressure points—unrelenting drive for performance, expanding scale of operations, and decreasing experience and shared values—operate together in an additive fashion to increase the possibility of *errors of omission and commission.* Quite simply, people under pressure make mistakes. An **error of omission** occurs when an employee inadvertently omits to perform an action that is necessary to protect the franchise and/or assets of the business. An **error of commission** occurs when an employee purposefully follows a course of action that increases risk, impairs assets, or otherwise endangers the business.

Paradoxically, it is success and growth that create the potential for errors of omission and commission. Performance pressure, increasing size, and the hiring of new people generally indicate a healthy, vibrant company. Yet, these same forces can easily become catalysts for significant risk and error.

## Risks Pressures Due to Culture

The culture of an organization—determined by its history and top-management leadership style—is the second major cause of risk pressures in many businesses. For example, many organizational cultures encourage *entrepreneurial risk taking.* Individuals are motivated to be as creative as possible in finding and creating market opportunities. Although this is usually healthy, there is always the danger that individuals may pursue or create opportunities that significantly increase strategic risk. In a culture of entrepreneurial risk taking, investments may be made in risky assets, deals may be struck with counterparties who have a limited ability to honor their contracts, commitments may be made that are difficult to fulfill, or employees may engage in behaviors that damage the reputation of the business.

Culture also influences the willingness of subordinates to inform superiors about potential risks in the business. Early warning signs about impending problems are often evident to employees who are in day-to-day contact with operations, customers, suppliers, and competitive markets. Too often, however, this critically important early warning information is not communicated upward to senior managers. In some organizations, this reluctance arises from a well-founded *fear in bearing bad news.* In businesses where senior managers have a low tolerance for dissent, or are known for "shooting the messenger," information barriers are inevitable. People become afraid to voice their concerns for fear of sanction or other personal repercussions. As a result, the communication of early warning information breaks down, and top managers can be caught off guard when problems surface unexpectedly.

Additionally, some cultures foster a spirit of *internal competition,* which brings a unique set of issues relating to risk. In these cultures, top managers often knowingly foster a sense of competition among subordinates vying for bonuses and/or promotion. Private information often brings power and rewards to the holder, so individuals jealously guard information. This tendency is exacerbated in a culture where advancement is perceived as a zero-sum game. To advance their own careers, employees may increase business risk by gambling with business assets, credit exposure, and firm reputation in attempts to enhance short-term performance. Unfortunately, the payoffs and costs from these behaviors are asymmetric. If the gamble pays off, the individual is rewarded with large bonuses and promotions. If the gamble results in a substantial loss for the firm, however, the worst that can happen to the employee is losing his or her job. The business is forced to absorb the sometimes significant financial or reputation loss.

These three cultural factors—entrepreneurial risk taking, fear of bearing bad news, and internal competition—feed off each other to create forces that lead to *incomplete management information.* In organizations where these pressures are intense, managers may, as a result, be uninformed about dangers that lurk in their businesses. Employees will take unwarranted risks, hold back bad news, and resist sharing information. Accordingly, managers may unknowingly increase performance pressures and ramp up the scale of the business with little understanding of the potential risks.

## Risks Pressures Due to Information Management

The final category of risk is due to information management, which can create risk in several ways. First, *transaction velocity*—created by high transaction volume and increased processing speed—can increase the possibility of operations risk. In 1991, for example, Fidelity Investments processed 250,000 transactions per day; by 1998, the business processed more than one million transactions per day. If information technology had failed to keep pace with this intense increase in processing demand, operational errors would have been inevitable. Accordingly, Fidelity has made massive investments in technology to ensure that support is adequate as the business grows. Still, operations risk is a continuing concern for Fidelity's managers. America Online, by contrast, suffered the consequences of information processing risk related to increased transaction velocity when its processing infrastructure was unable to keep pace with increased demand.

*Transaction complexity* also increases risk. As transactions become more complex, fewer people may fully understand the nature of these transactions and how to control them. Crossborder agreements in international operations, creative financing of customer purchases, and elaborate consortium arrangements can all produce highly complex contracts. Without full understanding of contractual obligations and the nature of contingent cash flows, asset impairment risk increases substantially. The increase in complexity due to highly leveraged derivative financial products (i.e., financial instruments whose value fluctuates based on changes in the values of other underlying assets) has caused more than one well-managed firm to sustain substantial losses.

*Gaps in diagnostic performance measures* also increase risk. If managers are unaware of potential problems, they cannot take remedial action to contain the risk. All types of risk need appropriate diagnostic systems to track current risk levels and serve as warning indicators. Operations risk indicators, financial and credit risk indicators, and systems that provide early warning about changes in competitive risk and franchise risk should be in place (we discuss these indicators later in the chapter). These diagnostic indicators often require specialized information processing systems that can consolidate information across dispersed operations; if these systems are fragmented or inadequate to supply information about problems, the consequences of risks can become greatly magnified.

Finally, highly *decentralized decision making* can increase risk. In decentralized businesses, individuals are encouraged to make decisions autonomously and create opportunities without constant monitoring and oversight by superiors. As we discussed in Chapter 3, this structural configuration is appropriate when top managers wish to focus attention and decision making on local markets. Because of the freedom created by decentralized structures, however, fewer operating rules and constraints are likely to be imposed on operating managers. Consequently, they may be able to engage in activities that increase risk without requiring approval from corporate-level managers. Moreover, when several separate businesses within the same firm are acting independently, understanding the aggregation of risk across business units becomes important. For example, aggregating credit risk across several businesses in the same firm may be important if those businesses are all making risky loans to the same customer. By decentralizing credit approval, the concentration of credit risk is greatly magnified.

These three pressure points—transaction complexity and velocity, gaps in diagnostic performance measures, and decentralized decision making—can lead to lapses in diagnostic information and *inefficiencies and breakdowns* in transaction processing. Such inefficiencies and breakdowns can, in turn, significantly increase operations risk, asset impairment risk, and franchise risk.

The nine pressure points listed in Figure 12–2 provide a window into a business to calibrate the potential for significant risk and loss due to employee or management error, systems breakdown, and bad information. Once identified, managers can estimate the magnitude of the strategic risk exposure and ensure that organizational attention is devoted to controlling significant risks.

## MISREPRESENTATION AND FRAUD

So far in this chapter, we have discussed strategic risks and the pressures that heighten these risks. However, there is one special case—misrepresentation and fraud—that must be considered separately. Sometimes, because of the pressures identified previously, managers and/or employees may knowingly subject the firm to unacceptable levels of risk. Employees may misrepresent their performance (or that of their business) or misappropriate company assets. Bad decisions can be covered up and expose the firm to loss of valuable assets. In most instances, the amounts involved are small. Sometimes, however, these actions have severely damaged—or even destroyed—the businesses in which these people worked.

In Part I of this book, we made some heroic assumptions about the inherent nature of people in high-performing organizations: we assumed that individuals want to contribute, achieve, innovate, do competent work, and will choose to do what is right based on socialized personal values (learned through family and religious teaching, laws, organizational norms, and so on). However, we also identified organization blocks that can overturn these tendencies and lead to dysfunctional behaviors: confusion about how to contribute, temptation and pressures, conflicting demands with too few resources, and fear of failure. We must now confront the consequences of these organizational blocks.

In all too many of these cases, senior managers were unaware of the risks to which employees had exposed the business. Employees had either covered up their actions (to the extent they had contravened stated policies) or failed to report information to superiors that would have given early warning about potential problems. The destruction of Barings Bank by trader Nick Leeson was a chilling reminder to all managers of the types of risks that they must guard against.

Accordingly, we must analyze the forces that can cause individuals to willfully misrepresent or alter data, engage in fraud, or otherwise expose the business to unacceptable levels of risk.

### A Dangerous Triad

Generally, people employed by business and nonprofit organizations do not start out to do bad things. Most often—even in blatant cases of misrepresentation and fraud—an individual starts down a "slippery slope," starting with a small misdeed that, over time, gains momentum and grows in magnitude. Soon, the subterfuge becomes too large for the employee to control. The risk that employees may engage in wrongful acts that expose the business to risk—including misrepresentation and fraud—is greatest *if three conditions exist simultaneously*. These three conditions—pressure, opportunity, and rationalization—are illustrated in Figure 12–3. As we shall discuss, all three conditions are necessary before most individuals will start down the slippery slope.[4]

---

[4] These prerequisites for fraud have been eloquently described by Peter A. Humphery, vice president at Fidelity Investments, in his presentations on risk management.

**FIGURE 12–3    A Dangerous Triad**

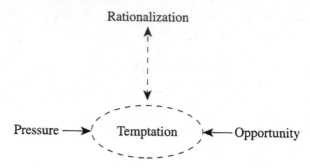

## 1. Pressure

The pressures to achieve profit goals and strategies are intense in any high-performing organization. The risk calculator highlights many of these pressures. Sometimes, the combination of extrinsic and intrinsic forces will create pressure to manipulate accounting records and/or misuse company assets for personal gain. Extrinsic pressures are due largely to the *performance goals and incentives* that were the subject of the previous chapter. As we discussed there, high-performing organizations are typically high-pressure organizations. Employees are often under significant pressure to meet difficult performance goals. Success in meeting these performance goals can bring substantial financial rewards, including salary increases, bonuses, and possible promotion. Pressure to meet goals may be enhanced by the desire for recognition of success—by superiors, subordinates, and peers. Correspondingly, failure to meet performance goals can often result in loss of prestige, reduction in compensation, and, sometimes, dismissal. Together, the potential for rewards and the fear of failure can create a high level of pressure to succeed, sometimes at all costs.

Pressures to bend the rules or otherwise misuse company assets or resources for personal gain can also be due to *personal problems* that originate outside the workplace. Debts, addictions, or other personal crises may create severe pressures to engage in fraud or misrepresentation to take advantage of an employer or misappropriate company assets.

## 2. Opportunity

The second necessary condition for willful error and fraud is *opportunity*. Even if someone is under great pressure to bend the rules to achieve performance goals and/or misappropriate assets, they can only engage in wrongful acts if the opportunity to do so exists. In other words, they must have access to valuable assets and/or be able to manipulate accounting and performance measurement systems to their advantage so that their actions are undetected. Thus, control systems must be sufficiently flawed that any misdeeds will not be detected.

We must remember from Chapter 1, however, one of the fundamental tensions of management: there is too much opportunity and too little management attention. Employees are surrounded with opportunity, especially in high-innovation organizations that rely on the creativity of empowered employees. Yet management attention is limited; there is simply not enough time or attention to monitor all the activities of every employee.

When performance pressure is coupled with opportunity to use company assets for personal gain or inflate performance measures, a dangerous situation is created. Any individual in these circumstances will feel *temptation*—temptation to secure rewards and/or use weaknesses in control systems to their advantage. Notwithstanding this great temptation, however, there is one additional prerequisite that must occur before most people will engage in wrongful acts or misdeeds that put the company at risk. They must believe that what they are doing is not really creating risk for themselves or the business.

## 3. Rationalization

Employees—even those experiencing great temptation and pressure—are unlikely to succumb and engage in wrongful actions unless they can find rationalizations for their aberrant behavior. Employees know the difference between right and wrong and typically will not engage in actions that contravene generally accepted moral codes of our society. A variety of studies has shown that when employees engage in damaging or unethical behaviors, they will do so only if they can justify their actions with one or more of the following excuses:

- The action is not "really" wrong—Employees may convince themselves that many other people do similar things, and/or the action is not serious enough to warrant concern. For example, an auditor may routinely underreport the hours worked by subordinates in an attempt to meet client budget targets.
- The likelihood of being caught is small—Because people often have the opportunity to manipulate company records to cover up their acts, they often believe that they will never be found out. Thus, they may have little fear that their behavior will ever be discovered.
- The action is in the organization's best interest—Employees may convince themselves that misrepresenting performance or manipulating data can advance the firm's interest. For example, an employee may lie to a government investigator because she believes that the investigator is an "enemy" of the business and is trying to hurt it.
- If exposed, senior management would condone the behavior and protect the individuals involved—To the extent that employees believe they are working to protect or further the company's interests, then their rationalization often takes the next logical step. They convince themselves that if they are caught and forced to explain what they did and why they did it, their superiors would understand, support them, and stand by them.[5]

Managers of all high-performing businesses—where there is typically a great deal of both performance pressure and freedom—must ensure that employees cannot easily fall back on these rationalizations.

All three of these conditions—pressure, opportunity, and rationalization—must be present before employees or managers can be expected to abuse their access to infor-

---

[5] Saul W. Gellerman, "Why 'Good' Managers Make Bad Ethical Choices," *Harvard Business Review* 64 (1986): 85–90.

mation or assets for personal gain. If only two of the three prerequisites are present, there is unlikely to be significant risk. For example, opportunity and pressure without rationalization will cause most employees to avoid actions that they know to be wrong,

---

### Corporate Fraud at Kurzweil Applied Intelligence

Senior executives at Kurzweil Applied Intelligence, a manufacturer of voice-recognition software, were able to commit fraud despite the scrutiny of its auditors, directors, and the underwriter of its August 1993 initial public offering. Most astonishing was how this could happen under the reign of CEO Bernard Bradstreet, characterized by former Harvard M.B.A. classmates as conservative and clean-living. Some observers suggested that Bradstreet's increasing personal expenses might have pressured him to boost the value of his 35% stake in the company. Others concluded that Bradstreet was so obsessed with posting six consecutive quarters of improving results, so that he could take the company public, that he would stop at nothing.

Kurzweil posted its first profit of $110,000 on revenues of $10.5 million in 1991. During that time, Bradstreet allowed the company to book several transactions a few days prior to customer shipment to meet quarterly goals. By 1992, the accrual rules were further relaxed and some sales were booked as much as two weeks early. By the following year, the treasurer testified that "the whole [revenue recognition] policy basically went out the window and we did whatever was necessary to book the revenue."

A turning point came at the end of 1992, when Kurzweil's sales vice president pressured a sales representative to close $220,000 in sales to meet a quarterly goal. The sales rep forged his customers' signatures on a bogus order with the full knowledge of the vice president. As part of Kurzweil's annual audit, its accountants sent confirmation letters to these customers. Again, the sales representative forged his customers' signatures on the auditor's forms. Kurzweil booked similar questionable transactions in 1993. In August 1993, Kurzweil went public at $10 per share and a market capitalization of $68 million.

As the next yearly audit approached in early 1994, the treasurer ordered her staff to purge files of compromising materials. The scheme was detected in April 1994, when an auditor uncovered an invoice for nine months of storage for products that were supposedly shipped to customers. After reexamining Kurzweil's books, auditors found that at least $6.3 million of 1994's $18.4 million in sales should not have been booked.

Kurzweil's CEO, sales vice president, treasurer, accounting staff, and most of the sales force were fired. The treasurer received immunity from prosecution in exchange for her testimony. The CEO and sales vice president were tried, convicted, and sentenced to jail.

---

*Source:* Adapted from Mark Maremont, "Anatomy of A Fraud," *Business Week* (September 16, 1996): 90–94.

even in the face of temptation. Their conscience will intervene. Similarly, rationalization and opportunity by themselves are unlikely to lead to problems if there are no external or internal inducements to bend the rules. Why take any risks if there are no pressing reasons? Finally, pressure and rationalization—a potentially dangerous combination—can be contained effectively if employees do not have the opportunity to engage in actions that could put the business at risk. Control systems and safeguards must be sufficient to deny unauthorized access to accounting records and/or valuable assets.

Thus, to control the risks that employees may engage in willful misrepresentation or fraud, managers must remove at least *one* of the three prerequisites. We discuss how effective managers do this in the next chapter.

## LEARNING WHAT RISKS TO AVOID

Unfortunately, the most common, but painful, way of learning about risk is to suffer the consequences firsthand. For example, the manipulation of revenue numbers to hit performance targets can cause acute embarrassment and even lawsuits. The reputation damage can be substantial. If misstatements are material, financial statements must be restated and the indiscretion must be reported to regulatory authorities (and will likely be picked up by the business press). In these cases, two results are almost certain. First, the managers involved in the indiscretion will be disciplined—probably fired along with their superiors, who will be held accountable for poor leadership and oversight. Second, top managers will install new controls—clearly specifying the consequences to those who are tempted to cross the line—to ensure that this damaging behavior will never happen again.

*Vicarious learning* occurs when managers witness a failure or mishap in another business and realize that the same thing could easily happen in their own business ("There, but for the grace of God, go I"). For example, when brokerage firm Kidder Peabody & Company and Barings PLC were fatally damaged because of the unsupervised activity of individual traders, managers of similar Wall Street firms rushed to install new control systems in an attempt to avoid the actions that had caused the demise of these businesses.[6]

To determine strategic risk, a look at failures can be revealing. One technique—followed by a successful U.S. construction company—is to annually review all projects that have *failed*—that is, those that were significantly over budget or failed to meet client expectations. A series of intense meetings is then devoted to discussing the causes for these failures and attempting to learn from them to ensure that they will not recur. Thus, over time, managers have learned that there are certain types of projects that do not fit their core competencies and should be subject to special controls and management attention. For example, they have learned that they have a poor track record at successfully building sewage treatment plants and have, accordingly, declared these types of projects out-of-bounds.

---

[6] John R. Dorman, "Brokerage Firms Take Action to Detect Potential Rogue Trades in Their Midst," *The Wall Street Journal* (November 29, 1995): Cl.

## CHAPTER SUMMARY

Strategic risk comes in many different forms. Managers must assess the nature of the risks facing their business based on the ways that they have chosen to compete in the market. The primary forms of risk are operations risk, asset impairment risk, and competitive risk. If any of these risks becomes severe, the franchise of the entire business may be at stake.

There are nine pressure points that managers should analyze in determining the potential level of risk inside their businesses. These pressures are due to growth, culture, and information management. In combination, these pressure points can lead to errors, incomplete management information, and inefficiencies and breakdowns.

Risk often leads to adverse consequences because of the actions or inactions of employees. Most often, these actions are inadvertent. Sometimes, however, they may be willful. Whatever the cause, employee actions are more likely to cause risk when pressure is high inside the organization.

Individual employees may sometimes create risk by engaging in wrongful acts—either misrepresentation or fraud. This is most likely if three conditions exist: (1) pressure to bend the rules, (2) opportunity to access valuable assets and/or manipulate accounting records, and (3) rationalization that these actions are "not really wrong."

In the next chapter, we discuss how to control strategic risks. Managing risk effectively means utilizing specialized control tools and techniques. All managers must understand how to control these risks, because nothing less than the survival of the business may be at stake.

# 13
# Managing Strategic Risk

In the previous chapter we identified various types of risk, their linkage with business strategy, and the pressure points that aggravate exposure to risk or increase the possibility of loss. In this chapter, we discuss how managers can proactively manage these risks as they work to achieve profit goals and strategies.

Much of the risk that we have described is created by management's use of aggressive performance goals and incentives to get the organization up to speed, just like a driver who steps hard on the gas pedal. In this chapter we look at another set of systems—the brakes that managers employ to control businesses operating at high speeds. High-performing businesses need good brakes, just like high-performing cars. Cars have brakes for two reasons. First, and most obvious, they allow the driver to slow the car down and stop safely. However, cars have brakes for another reason. They give the driver the confidence to go very fast. Imagine a high-performance racing car on a speedway. The driver can operate at top speeds only if he knows that he can rely on excellent brakes to control the car on tight turns. Like the fastest cars, managers of high-performing businesses need the best brakes to control strategic risks that are an inevitable consequence of driving their businesses to their maximum potentials.

Strategic risks are managed primarily by communicating effective boundaries—both business conduct and strategic—and installing good internal control systems. Boundary systems are designed to communicate risks to be avoided and to remove any ability to rationalize actions that could expose the firm to undesirable levels of risk. Internal control systems are designed to protect assets and to remove the opportunity for inadvertent error or willful wrongdoing in transaction processing and performance measurement. Together, these two systems supply the necessary control to ensure that accidental or willful error does not harm the ability of the firm to create value for customers, stockholders, and employees.

## BELIEFS AND BOUNDARIES

Empowered employees—those who are asked to make decisions and assume responsibility for their work—must make choices every day about how to create value. They must balance tensions between profit, growth, and control, tensions between short-term and long-term goals, and tensions between self-interest and the desire to contribute to organizational success. If properly managed, these tensions can result in innovation that enhances the value and strategy of the firm. Think back over the past 10 years to all the innovations that businesses have brought to market and the new markets that individuals have created: cellular telephones, global-positioning satellite systems, derivative financial products, the Internet, and geographical expansion in China and eastern Europe. The list goes on and on. The potential for people to identify and create opportunities in changing markets is virtually limitless.

Sometimes, however, as we discussed in the previous chapter, people may pursue opportunities in a way that actually harms the firm. They may pursue opportunities that do not align with the intended strategy of the business. They may attempt to take advantage of a loophole in the law that causes the firm embarrassment when reported in the press; they may engage in insider trading to personally benefit from knowledge of an upcoming business transaction; or they may decide to ship substandard products in the mistaken belief that no one will be hurt by their actions. Whenever employees are asked to make choices, good brakes are needed to ensure that a business does not crash and burn.

To ensure that employees engage in the right type of activities, managers must first inspire commitment to a clear set of core values. **Core values** *are the beliefs that define basic principles, purpose, and direction.* Often rooted in the personal values of the founders, core values provide guidance about responsibilities to customers, employees, local communities, and stockholders. They explicitly define top management's views on trade-offs such as short-term performance versus long-term responsibilities. Core values provide guidance to employees where rules and standard operating procedures alone cannot suffice.

We know from work in organizational behavior that inspirational leaders (1) articulate a vision that addresses the values of the participants, (2) allow each individual to appreciate how he or she can contribute to the achievement of that vision, (3) provide enthusiastic support for effort, and (4) encourage public recognition and reward for all successes.[1] Employees will go the extra mile and work diligently for the best interest of organizations to which they are committed and proud. For example, commitment to mission and purpose allows successful nonprofit and charitable organizations to attract talented individuals at little or no cost. Without commitment to organizational purpose, people will not be able to fully participate in the decisions that affect growth and profitability.

In small companies, communication of core values can be accomplished informally. As organizations become larger, however, managers must formalize this process by articulating and communicating *formal* beliefs systems. **Beliefs systems** *are the explicit set of organizational definitions that senior managers communicate formally and reinforce systematically to provide basic values, purpose, and direction for the organization.*[2] Using the mission statements and credos discussed in Chapter 2, managers attempt to give all employees who work for the business a sense of pride and purpose. Core values and statements of purpose are actively communicated to provide a compass for action. This is strategy as perspective—one of the four Ps of strategy.

---

[1] John P. Kotter, *A Force for Change* (New York: The Free Press, 1990): 63.
[2] Robert Simons, *Levers of Control*, 34.

Managers should never delegate the preparation of missions and credos. Managers should take every opportunity—both written and verbal—to personally reinforce core values and their importance. To increase ROME, however, the work of distributing documents, designing educational programs, and conducting organizational surveys to test awareness can, and should, be delegated to staff groups.

Because missions and credos are designed to appeal to all levels of the organization—from truck drivers to company presidents—they must be written at high levels of abstraction and generality. Therefore, they can never be specific enough to tell people facing difficult choices how to compete or how to choose appropriate actions in novel situations. These inspirational beliefs are typically too vague to provide much concrete guidance. How, then, can managers avoid those specific employee actions that could expose the business to risk?

In Chapter 4, we discussed two basic ways of controlling human behavior. The first is to tell people *what to do*—to dictate which opportunities to pursue and to specify in detail how to create value and overcome obstacles along the way. This is the "command and control" approach followed by the military in its tactical operations. Mission and objectives are defined by the highest level of command. Surveillance and intelligence data are fed to field commanders, giving them a unique view of emerging threats and opportunities. Tactical and strategic decisions are restricted to those with the proper authority. Commanders issue explicit orders that subordinates are expected to follow faithfully.

In a business that relies on empowered employees to continually innovate, the military model does not work very well. As we discussed, telling people what to do drives out innovation and creativity. Strict orders about how someone must do their job precludes creative experimentation in attempting to find new approaches and ways of doing things. Unlike the military, specific knowledge about threats and opportunities, as well as new ideas about products and markets, is widely dispersed throughout the organization; it is not all in the hands of business "commanders." It is just not possible to transmit all of the knowledge possessed by employees—who are closest to markets and customers—back to senior managers.

The second possibility for controlling human behavior, again covered in detail in Chapter 4, is to hold people *accountable for outcomes* and leave it up to their initiative and creativity to figure out how to do their jobs most effectively. This is the approach used by managers who wish to rely on their subordinates to help them implement strategy in rapidly changing, highly competitive markets. However, it is precisely this approach that carries the most risk. Employees may make widely different assumptions about the types of opportunities to pursue. They may engage in activities that are wasteful or do not support the current business strategy. Sometimes, they may engage in activities that put the business at risk. It is in these circumstances—when individuals are accountable for high levels of performance *and* asked to be creative—that managers need the best brakes.

Managers of high-performing businesses face a dilemma in deciding how to control the opportunity-seeking behavior of employees. On the one hand, opportunism is at the heart of innovation in highly competitive markets. In these fast-moving markets, managers must encourage subordinates to constantly search for new ideas and new ways of creating value. On the other hand, this same opportunism poses considerable risk. Employees may choose to pursue or create an opportunity that exposes the business to consequences that senior managers would choose to avoid.

Therefore, in high-performing businesses, managers must go one step beyond missions and inspirational beliefs. They must also install brakes by communicating clearly to all employees the behaviors and opportunities that are off-limits. In other words, managers must tell subordinates what *not to do* and then encourage them to innovate and seek all possible opportunities—to drive as fast as possible—within those clearly defined boundaries.

The idea of imposing limits or boundaries on opportunistic behavior is not new. This concept is deeply rooted in the Ten Commandments of the Judeo-Christian experience:

1. You shall have no other gods.
2. You shall not make any graven images and bow down.
3. You shall not take the name of the Lord in vain.
4. Keep the Sabbath holy—You shall do no work on that day.
5. Honor your father and mother.
6. You shall not kill.
7. You shall not commit adultery.
8. You shall not steal.
9. You shall not bear false witness against your neighbor.
10. You shall not covet anything that is your neighbor's.

The Ten Commandments do not tell people what to do; they decree what *not* to do. They create boundaries that clearly delineate behaviors that are off-limits.

This turns out to be a simple, but extremely powerful, principle for all business managers. Ask yourself the question, If managers want their employees to be innovative, creative, and entrepreneurial, are they better to tell them *what* to do, or what *not* to do? What happens if managers tell employees what to do? Quite simple, they do it. They arrive at work, follow orders and procedure manuals, and go home at night. But are they likely to innovate? Will they be entrepreneurial and creative? The answer, of course, is no.

Instead, to implement strategy, effective managers inspire their employees to maximum effort and innovation by (1) creating shared beliefs and mission, (2) setting challenging goals, (3) linking incentives to accomplishment, and (4) *declaring certain actions off-limits*. Then—and only then—can employees respond creatively, but safely, to the opportunities they encounter, limited only by their abilities and imagination.

The relationship of beliefs and boundaries to business strategy, which we will explore in the remainder of this chapter, is illustrated in Figure 13–1.

## BUSINESS CONDUCT BOUNDARIES

Based on a business's unique strategy, boundary systems communicate specific *risks to be avoided*. The most basic **business conduct boundaries** are those that define and

**FIGURE 13–1   Two Additional Levers of Control: Beliefs Systems and Boundary Systems**

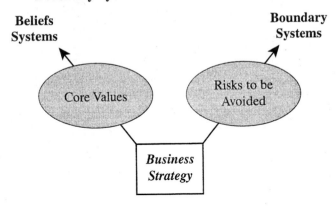

Source: Adapted from Simons, *Levers of Control*, p. 7.

communicate standards of business conduct for all employees. These are commonly called *codes of business conduct*. Like the Ten Commandments, codes of business conduct are stated in negative terms; they specify actions that are forbidden. Off-limit behaviors typically include:

- conflicts of interest—such as, employees are forbidden from owning a significant stake in a business that supplies goods or services to the business
- activities that contravene anti-trust laws—for example, employees are forbidden from colluding to fix prices with competitors
- disclosure of confidential company information—employees are forbidden from revealing private company information to anyone not entitled to know it
- trading in company securities based on nonpublic information—for example, employees are forbidden from buying or selling shares of the company in anticipation of market price reactions when private information becomes available to the public
- illegal payments to government officials—such as, employees are forbidden from making any payments in contravention of local laws to expedite services or receive preferential treatment

More than 75% of medium and large companies—defined as those with net worth in excess of $100 million—have formal codes of business conduct.[3] Some of these proscriptions are aimed at any employee who might be tempted to engage in a wrongful activity for personal enrichment. Other activities are illegal under statute, and it is clear why managers would forbid them. Managers must remember, however, that employees may sometimes be tempted to engage in harmful or unethical activities if they believe that what they are doing is helping the company achieve its goals or protecting the business from adverse consequences. For example, a respected senior vice president of an electric utility company was caught lying under oath to state regulators in a public

---

[3] Robert B. Sweeney and Howard L. Siers, "Survey: Ethics in Corporate America," *Management Accounting* 71 (1990): 34–40.

hearing. He did so not for personal gain, but because he believed that the regulators' line of inquiry could be harmful to the company's legitimate interests.[4]

In their zeal to achieve performance goals and/or protect the company, well-meaning employees sometimes make decisions that can damage the long-term health of the business. The utility vice president was fired, but in the ensuing public scandal, the CEO was also forced to resign. It took a new CEO several years to repair the damage to the company's reputation and restore trust with the regulators.

The Ten Commandments remind all of us of lines that must not be crossed as we attempt to deal with the pressures and temptations that are an inevitable part of daily life. Pressure and temptation can also be substantial in high-performing businesses. Surveys have repeatedly revealed that a majority of managers and employees feel pressure at some time in their careers to compromise personal standards of integrity to achieve company goals.[5] For example, a 1997 study on the sources and consequences of workplace pressure found that more than half (56%) of the 1,300 managers and employees surveyed felt immense pressure at work to act unethically. Sixty percent of survey participants believed that pressure had increased noticeably in the past five years.[6]

As we discussed in the previous chapter, people are more likely to succumb to pressure and temptation if they can find reasons to rationalize their own behavior. Managers of all high-performing businesses—where there is typically a great deal of both performance pressure and freedom—must ensure that employees cannot fall back easily on these rationalizations. Unambiguous codes of conduct must be used as a communication device to eliminate ambiguity about how employees are expected to respond in the face of pressure and temptation.

The need for codes of business conduct is especially critical in any business whose strategy is built upon trust and a reputation for quality and integrity. Managers of these businesses must install business conduct boundaries to protect their franchise. Such businesses include consumer products companies that market health products (e.g., Johnson & Johnson), food manufacturers (General Mills), pharmaceutical companies (Merck), automobile manufacturers (Ford), and countless others. In these companies, any employee action that could undermine a reputation for integrity in the marketplace is potentially catastrophic to the value of its franchise. Shipping tainted product, lying about product attributes, failing to follow required safety testing—any action that could compromise health or safety jeopardizes the trust that is the foundation of these competitive franchises.

A damaged reputation can do serious, sometimes irreparable, harm to the ability of the business to implement its strategy. Think of the consequences when the news media picked up the story that ValueJet was cutting corners on safety checks, or when managers at Denny's restaurants were accused of discrimination in its hiring practices.

---

[4] Ken Goodpaster, "Witness for the Corporation," Harvard Business School Case No. 384–135, 1983.

[5] Archie B. Carroll, "Managerial Ethics: A Post-Watergate Review," *Business Horizons* 18 (1975): 75–80.

[6] Alison Boyd, "Employee Traps—Corruption in the Workplace," *Management Review* 86 (1997): 9. The survey was sponsored by the American Society of Chartered Life Underwriters and Chartered Financial Consultants, and the Ethics Officer Association.

Franchise risk (i.e., reputation risk) is particularly acute for any firm that relies on its reputation for trust and integrity to secure new business. Strategy consulting firms and auditors, for example, invariably set strict codes of business conduct concerning misrepresentation and confidentiality of client data. There is good reason for this. Imagine how long McKinsey & Company or PricewaterhouseCoopers could retain their market franchises if clients suspected that key strategic data, gathered during a consulting assignment or audit, was being leaked to competitors. Their franchise—and their ability to attract and retain clients—would be significantly impaired. Accordingly, in these firms any activity that could jeopardize their reputation for integrity is declared off-limits.

Similarly, professions that depend on public trust always insist upon compliance with a code of business conduct as a condition of membership. Accountants, lawyers, physicians, and other professions diligently safeguard their reputation by codifying rules of professional conduct. These boundaries articulate the types of behavior that could damage the image of the profession and, therefore, must be avoided by its members. For example, the Standards of Ethical Conduct for Management Accountants state in part that members must:

- avoid actual or apparent conflicts of interest and advise all appropriate parties of any potential conflict
- refrain from engaging in any activity that would prejudice their ability to carry out their duties ethically
- refuse any gift, favor, or hospitality that would influence or would appear to influence their actions
- refrain from either actively or passively subverting the attainment of the organization's legitimate and ethical objectives
- recognize and communicate professional limitations or other constraints that would preclude responsible judgment or successful performance of an activity
- refrain from engaging in or supporting any activity that would discredit the profession[7]

In a survey of profit center managers to investigate the types of situations that lead people to engage in unethical activities, managers reported that they were more likely to manipulate profit figures when competitive environments were highly uncertain.[8] In terms of installing brakes, managers must understand that the *greater the performance pressures and temptations in their business, the greater the need for business conduct guidelines.* Many of the recent frauds and control breakdowns—such as Barings Bank and Kidder Peabody—have been caused by intense performance goals coupled with lucrative incentive performance bonuses. In the trading environments in which money managers and equity traders work, there is always the risk that loosely supervised traders will engage in unethical activities to increase their bonus payouts. In these situa-

---

[7] Institute of Management Accountants (formerly National Association of Accountants), "Statement on Management Accounting: Standards of Ethical Conduct for Management Accountants," Statement No. 1C (New York, 1983).

[8] Kenneth A. Merchant, "The Effects of Financial Controls on Data Manipulation and Management Myopia," *Accounting, Organizations, and Society* 15 (1990): 297–313.

tions, managers must install codes of business conduct that stipulate—in no uncertain terms—the types of behavior that are forbidden. Managers must reduce ambiguity and make it difficult for employees to rationalize dangerous behaviors.

The techniques that we studied in previous chapters—profit plans, balanced scorecards, diagnostic and interactive control systems, performance goals and measures, and incentives—are the tools that managers use to implement strategy. However, they are also precisely the means by which performance pressures and temptations are created. This pressure is generally healthy, because performance pressure breeds innovation. (As a counterpoint, consider how little innovation exists in business settings with no performance pressure, such as protected industries, monopolies, or any government agency that does not face market pressures.) But the harder that managers step on the gas pedal, the more important it becomes to have confidence in the quality and robustness of the business's brakes and boundary systems.

## Incentives for Compliance

Like any other control system, rewards and punishments must be aligned with business conduct boundaries, but how should incentives be designed? Is a carrot or stick approach most appropriate for enforcing adherence to boundaries of behavior? (Readers with children will implicitly know the answer to this question.)

In most business situations, there is little reason to reward employees for acting with integrity. Managers should expect nothing less than complete integrity from all subordinates. In fact, the vast majority of employees will, as a matter of personal principle, choose to do what is right without the need for explicit incentives or rewards. To reward integrity would incur costs without any increase in organizational performance.

Therefore, instead of rewarding good behavior, managers generally choose to punish the rare, but significant, instances of noncompliance. For sanctions to be effective, the threat of punishment must be communicated as an inherent part of the business conduct guidelines. Employees must understand that violating these guidelines is grounds for disciplinary action up to and including dismissal. Managers must be clear that sanctions will be enforced on a "no exceptions" basis. In strategy consulting firms, for example, divulging confidential client information brings automatic dismissal with no chance of reprieve. At PricewaterhouseCoopers, the well-known official accountants responsible for tallying the votes for the annual Academy Awards, the rules for staff members are unambiguous: "Discuss the tally with anyone besides your supervisor, and you're fired."[9] Moreover, managers often choose to make an example of people who, through their actions, put the business franchise at risk, so that there can be no mistake about the type of behaviors that are unacceptable.

## Business Conduct Boundaries and Organizational Freedom

Like brakes on a car, boundary systems in organizations can be thought of as either constraining (i.e., bringing the car to a stop) or liberating (allowing the car to travel at high

---

[9] Ed Brown, "The Most Glam Job in Accounting," *Fortune* (March 31, 1997): 30.

speed). We have discussed the constraint side of the coin, but we must now turn the coin over to see the other side. In a perverse way, constraint provides the freedom in which creativity can flourish.

Imagine a situation in which you start a new retail sales job at a Boston Retail store. Your first morning on the job, your new boss tells you that there are no rules: "Just do whatever it takes to satisfy a customer," he says. On your first day on the job, you accept a return from a customer who purchased the item two months ago. Later, the store manager berates you and tells you not to accept any returns beyond a 30-day limit. The next day, you do something else—in this case, telling a customer to try a nearby competitor for a desired item that your store does not carry. Again, your boss is disapproving and admonishes you never to do that again. And so on . . . one incident follows the next: when you try something new, the boss is often upset. Soon, you avoid any behavior that could expose you to the risk of embarrassment and sanction. Because you are unsure about the boundaries of acceptable behavior, innovation comes to a halt.

Compare this to another situation in which, on your first day, you are given a sales manual with clear rules as to what is *not* acceptable—return policies, customer service, and so on. After studying the guidelines to ensure familiarity with all store policies, you are confident that you can engage in any practice or innovation that does not contravene a stated policy. Now, when your boss tells you to "do whatever it takes to satisfy a customer," you have the confidence to be creative within a defined sphere of activity. Like the Ten Commandments, once the rules are understood and internalized, they do not seem onerous. The guidelines do not substantively infringe on important freedoms because there is still so much opportunity to act independently and create value for customers *within the stated boundaries.*

Effective business conduct boundaries are often very simple. At Sears, incoming CEO Arthur Martinez has led the drive to replace 29,000 pages of policies and procedures with two very simple booklets called "Freedoms" and "Obligations." Says Martinez, "What you want to preserve are the great qualities of a corporation. Some would define that as tradition, a sense of integrity, or doing what's right. We're trying to tell our managers what they're responsible for, what freedoms they have to make decisions, and where to turn for help. But we don't want to codify every possible situation."[10]

Business conduct boundaries are a powerful way for managers to communicate their beliefs about the importance of integrity. Such guidelines can empower employees to refuse to do what they believe to be wrong—even if ordered to do so by a superior. Mid-level supervisors are themselves often under intense performance pressures and can apply pressure on subordinates to bend the rules to ensure that key diagnostic targets are achieved (e.g., "let's not book that expense until the start of the new fiscal year"). Business conduct boundaries, if published and communicated widely, provide an incontestable defense against these misguided overtures by superiors.

Appendix 13–1 on page 297 summarizes the essential features of beliefs systems and boundary systems.

---

[10] Patricia Sellers, "Sears: In With the New," *Fortune* (October 16, 1995): 98.

## INTERNAL CONTROLS

Beliefs systems and boundary systems delineate core values and proscribed behaviors, but management must still guard against both willful violations and unintentional errors in company processes (that is, errors of omission and commission). Data from profit statements, ROI and EVA measures, balanced scorecards, and other measurement systems can be relied upon only if managers have faith in the accuracy of the numbers. However, managers of every business must confront the possibility that errors can creep into accounting and measurement systems. Errors can occur in many ways: untrained staff may process transactions incorrectly, or experienced employees may make unintentional errors in the rush of day-to-day work demands. In rare but potentially costly cases, employees may misappropriate company assets for personal gain and then falsify accounting records to avoid detection.

Because of these inevitable risks, managers of even the smallest business must install controls and safeguards to ensure that all transaction information (e.g., sales receipts) is accounted for properly and that employees are denied the opportunity to inappropriately divert assets to personal use. These systems and procedures are called *internal controls,* which are defined as *the policies and procedures designed to (1) ensure reliable accounting information and (2) safeguard company assets.*

Internal controls can be segregated into three categories of safeguards: **structural safeguards, system safeguards,** and **staff safeguards** (see Figure 13–2). Each of these safeguards is essential in any business where a manager or owner delegates custody of assets and/or the processing of accounting transactions to subordinates.

## Structural Safeguards

Structural safeguards—the first category of internal controls—are designed to ensure clear definition of authority for individuals handling assets and recording accounting transactions. Structural safeguards encompass the following:

*Segregation of Duties*   The cardinal rule of internal control is that one person should never handle all aspects of a transaction involving valuable company assets. In particular, the *accounting* for assets should be done by someone other than the person who has *physical custody* of those assets. **Segregation of duties** requires one person to check or reconcile the work of another. Then, if someone makes an error (or purposely misstates a transaction), the second person will catch the inconsistency when he or she reconciles accounting records with assets on hand or transaction receipts.

Most employee frauds are perpetrated when an individual has access to either cash or securities *and* the ability to record accounting transactions for those assets. Without segregation of duties, an unscrupulous person could manipulate accounting records (e.g., post transactions to the wrong account) to hide the misappropriation of funds. Lack of basic segregation of duties allowed Nick Leeson to make unauthorized security trades and hide his trading losses by making false entries in the accounting records at Barings Bank. Over time, his fraud destroyed a 200-year-old institution.

**FIGURE  13–2    Internal Controls: The Foundation of Every Business**

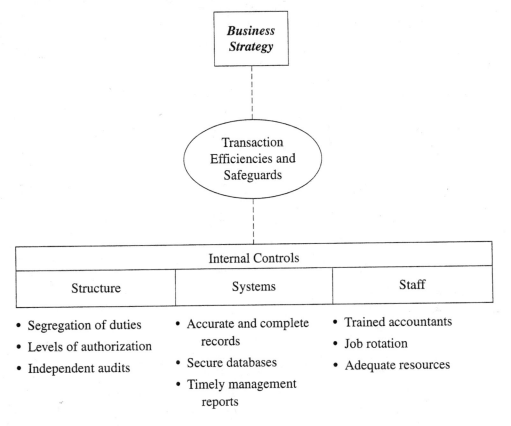

- At Boston Retail, one person deposits daily check receipts in the bank; a second person reconciles bank deposits with check receipt records to ensure that all receipts have been properly deposited.

***Defined Levels of Authorization***   This principle requires that an individual's access to company funds be commensurate with their level of responsibility, thereby limiting exposure to error or fraud.

- At Boston Retail, check-signing authority permits store managers to sign checks up to $500. Checks for larger amounts must be signed by a company officer.

***Physical Security for Valuable Assets***   Valuable assets subject to theft should always be protected by vaults, gates, and locked storerooms. Access to these assets should be restricted to those employees accountable for any loss. Many companies, for example, hold bearer bonds in bank vaults. The bank is typically given instructions to open the vault only if two designated company officials are present so that each official can independently verify that bonds are properly handled and accounted for.

When valuable assets cannot be easily counted and reconciled, direct surveillance becomes necessary to ensure that individuals are adequately safeguarding the assets. Thus, highway toll collectors are watched by camera surveillance in their toll booths.

- At Boston Retail, cash receipts are collected every two hours and deposited in a locked safe in the back of each store.

*Independent Audit*   All firms should use external auditors—certified public accountants (called chartered accountants in Commonwealth countries)—to examine the integrity of the firm's internal controls. As part of their review, auditors examine asset security and the integrity of accounting information. Their findings are reported to senior managers and the board of directors, who are responsible for correcting deficiencies.

The board of directors is ultimately responsible to shareholders for the integrity of internal controls. In larger companies, directors typically choose their most experienced members to form an audit committee to oversee the work of the independent auditors.

- Boston Retail employs a respected accounting firm to audit its financial statements and annually review the adequacy of its internal controls. As part of their review, the auditors provide recommendations to management on how to improve internal controls.

## Systems Safeguards

Systems safeguards are designed to ensure adequate procedures for transaction processing, as well as timely management reports. Systems safeguards encompass the following:

*Complete and Accurate Record Keeping*   Procedures must ensure that all transactions are recorded accurately and promptly in the accounting records. Accounting data becomes worthless for management purposes if it is not accurate and timely. To allow verification and reconciliation of data, there must be an adequate trail of documents (or electronic entries) so that it is possible to track each transaction back to its source. Thus, it should be possible to trace a customer payment back to an accounts receivable statement, which in turn can be traced back to a sales invoice and shipping record.

- Boston Retail's controller balances the general ledger each month and reconciles the bank account and accounts receivable ledger to ensure that all double-entry accounting transactions are accurate.

*Restricted Access to Information Systems and Databases*   Integrity of accounting data can only be assured if access to information systems is restricted to those who have a legitimate right to change or view accounting transaction records. In an electronic age, this requires secure databases that prevent unauthorized access or tampering. Several years ago, Citibank's computer systems were infiltrated by a hacker based in Moscow. Using illicitly obtained access codes, he was able to shift money among bank accounts. Passwords, data encryption, and internal verification routines are necessary to ensure the integrity of information.

- The ability to access accounting systems and to process adjustments in each of Boston Retail's stores is limited by password to the store manager. Passwords are changed monthly.

***Timely Management Reporting***   Managers should receive accounting and control reports soon after the data is processed. If reports are not timely, feedback may be too late to act upon, and the business may be vulnerable to losses and/or poor management decisions based on faulty information.

- The founders at Boston Retail receive an income statement and balance sheet by the eighth working day after each month's end. In addition, they receive sales figures from each store on a weekly basis (daily during the critical holiday season). Bank reconciliations are reviewed monthly.

## Staff Safeguards

Staff safeguards are designed to ensure that accounting and transaction-processing staff have the right level of expertise, training, and resources. Staff safeguards encompass the following:

***Adequate Expertise for Accounting and Control Staff***   The design and operation of good internal controls requires significant technical expertise. This expertise is offered by accounting professionals such as certified public accountants (CPAs) and certified management accountants (CMAs), who are trained in the design of effective internal control systems.

- Managers at Boston Retail are struggling with a decision regarding the possible replacement of the firm's controller, who was hired when the business was small. The increasing complexity of growing operations has outstripped his skills and abilities. The founders have engaged an accounting search firm to identify a candidate with professional accounting certification to assume a newly created position of vice president finance.

***Rotation in Key Jobs***   If an employee is hiding accounting irregularities, an independent person who is asked to take over that job for a period of time will usually discover the discrepancies. Accordingly, it is good practice to insist that employees with access to critical accounting records take regular vacations. During their absence, someone else should assume their responsibilities. The $1.1 billion fraud at Daiwa Bank was concealed when an employee, with access to company bonds, sold the bonds to cover his trading losses. Because he had entered false accounting transactions to cover his trail, he did not take an extended vacation for more than 11 years. Why? He could not afford the risk that someone would take over his work and discover the irregularity. During this time, senior management praised his dedication to the company.[11]

- Managers at Boston Retail rely on their auditors to verify the probity of the accounts. Because of the business's small size, they believe that it is impractical to rotate employees between key accounting jobs.

***Sufficient Resources***   Internal controls cost money. Accounting professionals must be hired, systems installed, and clerical staff trained to perform reconciliations and checks.

---

[11] Jathon Sapsford et al., "How Daiwa Bond Man in New York Cost Bank $1.1 Billion in Losses," *The Wall Street Journal* (September 27, 1995): A6.

Segregation of duties requires two people to perform a job that could be done by one person alone. Yet, the additional work of reconciliation and checking does nothing to increase the output efficiency of the business; it only provides assurance that assets are secure and information is accurate.

Accounting firms have reported a greatly increased number of material errors and frauds over the past decade as many firms have reengineered their internal processes. Reengineering and downsizing often eliminate redundancy and middle management positions that would otherwise provide an independent check of transaction processing accuracy. Accordingly, great care must be taken to ensure that internal controls remain adequate as businesses streamline processes to become more efficient.

- The founders at Boston Retail have devoted additional staff resources to internal controls after their bank manager told them how a business similar to theirs was forced into bankruptcy by the misappropriation of more than $1 million by a dishonest employee who was stealing money to cover gambling debts.

## Responsibility for Internal Controls

Internal controls guard against errors of all kinds. Good internal controls provide the checks and balances to assure managers that errors will not creep into critical operating systems and unauthorized actions will not be allowed to impair assets. They also deny the opportunity to anyone who might be tempted to misrepresent data or misappropriate assets. Although essential in any business, internal controls are especially important where operations risk and asset impairment risk interact with rapid growth. In these situations, errors of omission and commission are both more likely and more costly.

Business managers typically spend little time either designing or overseeing internal control systems. Instead, they delegate this responsibility to trained accountants and auditors. Managers should be aware, however, that if there is ever a significant financial or operating loss due to poor internal controls, they must shoulder the responsibility. Because internal control systems are essential for the security of assets and the integrity of performance information, managers are accountable for ensuring these controls are in place. Thus, business managers must be sure that sufficient resources are devoted to operating these controls effectively.

In large firms, failures in internal controls can lead to financial loss, embarrassment, and, sometimes, the end of promising careers. (Look at the front page of *The Wall Street Journal* to see how many business failures are due to failed internal controls.) In small start-up entrepreneurial firms, inadequate internal controls are sometimes enough to propel the business into bankruptcy. As a result of these risks, large public accounting firms are increasingly refusing to audit businesses with weak internal controls or those where they believe that managers may choose to circumvent controls because of performance pressures.[12]

---

[12] Elizabeth McDonald, "More Accounting Firms Are Dumping Risky Clients," *The Wall Street Journal,* (April 25, 1997).

## Assumptions Underlying Internal Controls

Appendix 13–2 on page 298 analyzes the assumptions that are critical to the effective functioning of internal control systems. A self-assessment tool is also provided in the appendix for you to test your own beliefs about the nature of human activity in organizations and the implications of these assumptions for effective internal controls. Appendix 13–3 on page 300 summarizes the essential features of internal control systems for reference purposes.

## STRATEGIC BOUNDARIES

Beliefs systems, business conduct boundaries, and internal controls deal primarily with the risks that people will make errors or the wrong choices in balancing profit, growth, and control. However, there is another kind of risk that is just as dangerous for long-term profitability and growth—the risk of wasting scarce resources on initiatives that do not support the business's strategy. Does it make sense, for example, to have the managers of an electric utility spend their time trying to build a database business for libraries? Or, for a consumer products company to attempt to run an airline or hotel business? If managers constantly encourage people to look for new opportunities, how can they ensure that subordinates will not waste their time pursuing initiatives that senior managers have no desire or intention of supporting? The dilemma comes back to one of the basic tensions of high-performance organizations: there are too many promising opportunities in the market and too little management attention to go around. The worst thing that managers can do in these situations is to sprinkle a little attention and resources over so many opportunities that no single initiative gains sufficient momentum and resources to allow success.

The basic principle underlying strategic boundaries is straightforward and should be familiar from our earlier discussion. Because managers cannot anticipate all the opportunities that employees can identify or create, it does not make sense to try to enumerate in detail *how* individuals throughout the business should create value in the marketplace. Let them exercise their initiative and creativity to figure out the best way of responding to customer needs and/or configuring internal processes for maximum efficiency and effectiveness. However, managers must recognize that unfocused initiatives can waste both financial resources and management attention—both scarce resources. Therefore, to ensure that individuals throughout the organization are engaged in activities that support the basic strategy of the business, senior managers should state what types of business opportunities should be avoided, thereby drawing a "box" around the opportunities that individuals are encouraged to exploit. The resulting **strategic boundaries** implicitly define the desired *market position* for the business.

More than fifty years ago, Chester Barnard, an influential management theorist, wrote, "The power of choice is paralyzed in human beings if the number of equal opportunities is large. . . . Limitation of possibilities is necessary to choice. Finding a reason why something should *not* be done is a common method of deciding what should be done. The processes of decision . . . are largely techniques for narrowing choice." [13]

Consider the following strategic boundaries that managers of different businesses have installed to focus opportunity-seeking behavior:

- Jack Welch, CEO of General Electric, communicated clearly to all employees that he will not support investment in any business that cannot attain a number one or number two competitive position in its market.

- A large computer company developed a matrix of all anticipated business opportunities that might be pursued during the coming planning cycle. Opportunities were then color coded as "green space" or "red space." Green space represented opportunities that were to be pursued aggressively; those colored red were declared off-limits.

- Automatic Data Processing, the largest U.S. payroll processing company, maintained a list of key requirements for investment in any business opportunity. The requirements related to revenue and growth potential, competitive position, product attributes, and management strength. Failure to meet the necessary minimum requirements for any of these "hurdles" resulted in divestment of the business.

- During Chrysler's dramatic turnaround, CEO Lee Iacocca decided to refocus the firm's resources on North American auto and truck manufacturing. All European, African, and nonautomobile businesses were declared off-limits. As a result, international and tank businesses were sold off, and the firm exited its leasing business.

Each of these examples illustrates how managers used strategic boundaries to communicate direction and maximize their ROM. Effective managers want to make all organizational energy as productive as possible by ensuring that people are devoting their full attention to implementation of intended strategy. At the same time, senior managers do not want to spend all their time looking over the shoulders of subordinates to ensure that initiatives fit with the strategic direction. Therefore, based on their unique strategy—how they want to create value for customers and differentiate their products and services—effective managers specify the opportunities that do not align with the strategy and declare them off-limits.

---

### Strategic Boundaries at Microsoft

Even Bill Gates, founder and CEO of Microsoft—and one of the world's richest men—is clear in terms of business opportunities that are off-limits:

> To be very clear, we are not going to own any telecommunications networks—phone companies, cable companies, things like that. We're not going to build hardware—the computer makers and consumer electronics companies will do that. We're not going to do system integration or consulting for corporate information systems . . . . I don't think companies like Andersen Consulting or EDS will see us as competing in that domain.

*Source:* Brent Schlender, "What Bill Gates Really Wants," *Fortune* (January 16, 1995): 40.

---

[13] Chester I. Barnard, *The Functions of the Executive* (1938; reprint, Cambridge, Mass.: Harvard University Press, 1968): 14.

Consider a bank that attempted to implement a new strategy focusing on private banking services for wealthy individuals. Senior managers segmented their market to focus resources on clients who could generate at least $5,000 in recurring annual net revenue. Existing clients who did not meet this profile were to be pruned so that all energy could be focused on the target market segment. In a meeting with branch managers to discuss the implementation of the new strategy, a branch manager asked, "What happens if an individual who we will never see again walks into my branch and wants to do a one-time foreign exchange transaction that will generate fees of $2,000? Do you really want me to send that customer away?"

The answer to the question was "Yes!" Above all else, senior managers wanted to avoid the myriad day-to-day distractions that could sap organizational attention from the new strategy. Managers worried that each transaction might look attractive on its own merits, but at the end of the day, employees would have been so distracted that they failed to devote enough attention to the clients who were critical to the new strategy. Each decision to pursue an opportunity—as good as that short-term opportunity might appear—has costs in terms of drawing away scarce attention. When attempting to implement a clear strategy, these "opportunity costs" are extremely high, but they may not be obvious to employees faced with what appears to be an easy way to create some short-term value.

Harold Geneen, the legendary CEO of ITT, described how he created a strategic boundary that forbade work on any initiative having to do with the development of computers:

> The road you don't take can be as important in your life as the one you do take. In the very early sixties, when computers were seen as the wave of the future, many of our engineers, particularly those in Europe, were eager to surge into this new, phenomenal field. Our German company, which was far ahead of the others in computer development, outbid IBM and won a contract to build a computerized reservation system for Air France. We lost $10 million on that contract. I called a halt to further computer development.
>
> I withstood a great deal of pressure at the time to enforce my early prohibition against the development of general-purpose computers at ITT. Not only our engineers but our investment advisors favored computer development. Everyone who could was going into computers, they said. The mere announcement would send our stock up, they promised. I stood firm.[14]

## Communicating Strategic Boundaries

Managers usually find it relatively easy to define what they want their organization to achieve in terms of high quality, excellent customer service, superior products, and new markets. However, effective managers know that attempting to be all things to all people in every market is a surefire recipe for lackluster profitability and growth. Choices must be made—in fact, *choice is the essence of strategy*. If there is no choice, there is no strategy.

---

[14] Harold Geneen, *Managing* (New York: Avon Books, 1984): 219–220.

---

### Strategic Boundaries at Daimler-Benz

Jürgen Schrempp, chairman of Daimler-Benz, the holding company of Mercedes, has built a reputation as a tough manager since he took over in May 1995. At the time, Daimler-Benz was a diverse conglomerate with businesses from cars to aerospace, electronics, and software development. Several divisions were reporting losses and ROCE was dismal.

When Schrempp took over the conglomerate, he started by focusing management attention on those businesses where it had a competitive advantage and sold off the rest. For the divisions that Daimler-Benz kept, he established a cutoff point: for a business to stay inside Daimler-Benz, it would have to earn at least 12% return on its capital employed. Divisional managers would be required to meet this target if they wanted to keep their position. In addition, he negotiated with unions an incentive program for each of the 140,000 employees based on their contribution to the overall performance of the company.

---

*Source:* Adapted from *Fortune* (November 10, 1997): 144–152.

---

The hard work of strategy is deciding what *not* to do. Effective strategic boundaries clarify and communicate strategic choice in terms of desired market position. In small firms, this communication can be informal. At Boston Retail, the communication was simple: We will not support any products that we would not own and wear ourselves.

As businesses grow larger and more dispersed, however, the communication must be formalized. Senior managers must be willing to bear direct scrutiny of their choices regarding strategic boundaries and the opportunities that are to be left behind. For example, the following strategic boundaries are often communicated as part of a formal planning process:

*1. Minimum Levels of Financial Performance*   Employees throughout the business are informed about the minimum financial requirements that are prerequisites for continued investment in a business. Recalling our discussion of the profit wheel, cash wheel, and ROE wheel, key financial indicators can include, for example:

- revenue potential
- profit and profitability
- asset utilization ratios
- cash flow and payback

*2. Minimum Sustainable Competitive Position*   Employees throughout the firms should know in advance the types of market positions that senior managers will not support. Jack Welch will not fund any business that cannot reach a number one or number two share position. In a smaller entrepreneurial business, managers may insist that no business opportunity be funded unless it can sustain a critical growth rate.

*3. Products and Services That Do Not Draw on Core Competencies*    Successful managers understand their business's distinctive competencies and seek to exploit these capabilities. Strategic boundaries enumerate the types of products and services that do not exploit core competencies so that employees can avoid opportunities that will distract attention from the core strengths and strategy of the business.

*4. Market Positions and Competitors to be Avoided*    In many industries, certain competitors with powerful resources and deep pockets dominate segments of the market (e.g., Microsoft in operating systems). Managers of smaller firms know that they cannot win an open battle with these competitors. Often, managers will set strategic boundaries that warn employees to avoid market positions that will result in head-on competition with these competitors.

It is important to understand that strategic boundaries such as those listed above stipulate necessary—but not sufficient—conditions for investing in or continuing to support a business opportunity. If a boundary condition is met, this does not imply that top managers will necessarily support the initiative—only that it has passed the basic hurdle. Before any final decision to commit resources, managers must apply the analytic techniques covered earlier in the book (SWOT analysis, asset allocation analysis, profit wheel analysis, and balanced scorecard analysis) to ascertain whether investment is justified.

## Boundary Systems and Staff Groups

Boundaries—both business conduct and strategic—are established by senior managers who are in a unique position to appreciate the risks that derive from innovation and high-performance strategies. To ensure that these boundaries achieve their desired effect, however, managers must rely on staff groups for two critical tasks: communication and monitoring.

Staff specialists are usually assigned responsibility for codifying codes of business conduct (often with the help of legal counsel) and distributing them widely on a periodic basis. Managers should review drafts to be sure they are adequate and insist on modifications based on past or anticipated franchise risks. In addition, dedicated staff specialists often set up procedures whereby recipients of business conduct guidelines are required to periodically sign a document confirming that they understand the guidelines and are abiding by them.

Information contained in these codes of conduct and planning guidelines is communicated regularly, and feedback is received by staff specialists for processing. Deviations can be acted upon, and it is here that staff groups serve a second important role— as policemen. Some firms employ special staff members known as *ombudsmen,* who are responsible for receiving formal complaints dealing with potential infringement of codes of business conduct. These staff groups follow up on all leads and allegations and ensure that the business franchise is not being compromised by the actions of any employee.

Strategic boundaries are different. These boundaries are at the heart of establishing market positions. They implicitly define strategy. Therefore, strategic boundaries are invariably set by top managers, not by staff assistants. However, staff groups can be given

**TABLE 13–1** Tasks for Managers and Staff Groups in Communicating Beliefs and Boundaries

|  | MANAGERS | STAFF GROUPS |
|---|---|---|
| *Beliefs Systems* | Personally prepare substantive drafts of beliefs statements<br>Communicate message and importance | Facilitate awareness and communication through distribution of documents, education programs, and organizational surveys |
| *Boundary Systems* | Personally prepare strategic boundaries<br>Review business conduct boundaries compiled by staff groups<br>Mete out punishment personally to offenders | Prepare business conduct boundaries<br>Communicate both strategic and business conduct boundaries<br>Educate organization about important boundaries<br>Monitor compliance |

*Source:* Adapted from Simons, *Levers of Control*, p. 170.

responsibility to communicate the types of strategic initiatives that top managers will not support—minimum levels of financial performance, minimum sustainable competitive position, and products, service, and markets to be avoided. Most commonly, these boundaries are formalized and distributed as part of an annual strategic-planning process. Staff groups are also asked to police compliance with these boundaries to ensure that no one is surreptitiously pursuing opportunities that have been declared off-limits. Harold Geneen described how he relied on staff assistants to monitor compliance with his strategic boundary forbidding work on computers:

> Others continued to work on computer development for us on the sly. When I learned of this, I hired two very competent engineers and gave them a special assignment which lasted for several years: to roam at will through our worldwide engineering and new products laboratories and to root out, stamp out, and stop all incipient general-purpose computer projects by whatever code name they were called; and if they were given any trouble to call us at headquarters and we would stamp them out for them.[15]

Table 13–1 provides a summary of the roles and responsibilities for operating managers and staff groups in designing and using beliefs systems and boundary systems.

## Risks in Setting Strategic Boundaries

As stated previously, the hard work of strategy is not in specifying what you want to do, the hard work is deciding and communicating what you do *not* want to do. Managers find it easy to use broad generalizations for strategy that focus on such things as "excel-

---

[15] Geneen, p. 220.

lence" or "delighting customers." No one is likely to object or disagree with these expansive strategy statements contained in mission statements or other beliefs systems.

On the other hand, it is much more difficult to specify "we will turn away a customer who cannot generate $5,000 in annual fee revenue," or "we will not fund any products that cannot be mass-produced." With these types of statements there can be no ambiguity in specifying the types of opportunities to avoid. In setting strategic boundaries, managers are forced to make explicit their choices in guiding the strategic direction of the business.

However, there is also significant risk in specifying in stark terms the opportunities that are to be avoided without periodically revisiting that decision. History is littered with businesses where managers were slow in seeing changes in their competitive environments and, accordingly, did not adjust their strategic boundaries in a timely fashion. Wang Computers, for example, maintained a clear strategic boundary that it would not compete in any part of the computer market where IBM was a dominant player. During its formative years, this strategic boundary allowed Wang to build a profitable niche franchise in the dedicated word-processing market, where IBM had chosen not to compete. However, as technology evolved, Wang failed to adjust its strategic boundary. Advancements in hardware and software allowed personal computers to host word-processing software, and Wang's fortunes declined rapidly, resulting ultimately in bankruptcy.

The implication is not that strategic boundaries are inappropriate. They are *essential* to achieve maximum performance potential, but any static strategy is doomed to failure over time. The brakes must be adjusted periodically to ensure that they are properly aligned with changes in technology, industry dynamics, and new ways of creating value in the marketplace.

## CHAPTER SUMMARY

Effective managers attempt to eliminate opportunities that could bring unwanted levels of risk. To do so, managers should communicate formal beliefs and business conduct boundaries. Beliefs and core values—enumerated in missions, credos, and statements of purpose—are the essential foundations for any high-performance organization. Boundary systems linked to clear, enforceable sanctions are especially important when difficult performance goals are set and rewards are linked tightly to performance. It is in these challenging circumstances that individuals may be tempted to bend the rules to achieve difficult targets.

Also, managers of all businesses, large and small, install internal controls—the formal procedures that protect assets and the integrity of management information. Internal controls provide the checks and balances to ensure that errors of omission and commission cannot slip undetected into the transaction processing stream. Effective structural safeguards (such as segregation of duties), system safeguards (e.g., accurate record keeping and documentation), and staff safeguards (for example, adequate expertise and rotation in key jobs) limit the possibility that someone might make an unintentional error—or worse—that could expose the business to risk.

Finally, managers often impose boundaries on strategic activity. The objective of strategic boundaries is to limit the areas in which employees will look for opportunities and commit scarce resources. To ensure adequate controls on creativity and entrepreneurial activities, managers must also communicate the types of behaviors and opportunities that do not align with the strategy and are, therefore, off-limits. Like boundaries on business conduct, the focus is on enumerating how the business will *not* compete and the kinds of opportunities that subordinates must *avoid.*

Creating boundaries involves choice—but choosing is the essence of strategy. It is often uncomfortable for managers to take the risks of declaring clear intentions, but it is the only sustainable path to effectively balancing profit, growth, and control.

**APPENDIX 13–1**  Building Block Summary for Beliefs Systems
and Boundary Systems

| BELIEFS SYSTEMS | |
|---|---|
| **WHAT** | explicit set of beliefs that define basic values, purpose, and direction, including how value is created, level of desired performance, and human relationships |
| **WHY** | to provide momentum and guidance to opportunity-seeking behaviors |
| **HOW** | mission statements<br>vision statements<br>credos<br>statements of purpose |
| **WHEN** | opportunities expand dramatically<br>top managers desire to change strategic direction<br>top managers desire to energize workforce |
| **WHO** | senior managers personally write substantive drafts<br>staff groups facilitate communication, feedback, and awareness surveys |

| BOUNDARY SYSTEMS | |
|---|---|
| **WHAT** | formally stated rules, limits, and proscriptions tied to defined sanctions and credible threat of punishment |
| **WHY** | to allow individual creativity within defined limits of freedom |
| **HOW** | codes of business conduct<br>strategic planning systems<br>asset acquisition systems<br>operational guidelines |
| **WHEN** | Business Conduct Boundaries: when reputation costs are high<br>Strategic Boundaries: when excessive search and experimentation risk dissipating the resources of the firm |
| **WHO** | senior managers formulate with the technical assistance of staff experts (e.g., lawyers) and personally mete out punishment<br>staff groups monitor compliance |

*Source:* Adapted from Simons, *Levers of Control,* p. 178.

---

**APPENDIX 13–2** Behavioral Assumptions About Internal Controls

---

Successful managers understand the importance of hiring the right people—those who have natural drives to achieve, contribute, and act with integrity. However, businesses often create confusing tensions and conflicting motivations. Performance pressures, unclear accountabilities, and temptation sometimes cause good people to engage in behaviors that can damage the business.

Internal controls are designed to catch unintentional errors and discourage behaviors that could lead to misappropriation of assets and fraud. In designing these systems, managers must understand the assumptions that accountants make about the interaction of human behavior and internal controls.[16] If any of these assumptions prove false, then internal controls may be rendered ineffective. You can test your own beliefs regarding these assumptions by completing Table 13–2 on the opposite page. The assumptions underlying internal control systems are the following:

1. *Individuals have inherent moral weaknesses; therefore, internal controls are necessary to safeguard assets and ensure reliable information.* Although managers may believe the best of people—that they want to contribute, achieve, and do right for the business—internal controls assume the worst. This is not to say that everyone will do careless work or take advantage of a situation to steal assets or enter false information. However, internal controls are designed for the exception—those rare, but potentially costly, situations where an individual may fall victim to temptation or pressure.

2. *By the threat of exposure of wrongdoing, an effective internal control system will deter an individual from committing fraud.* Designers of internal controls assume that people will not steal if they risk being caught.

3. *An independent individual will recognize and report irregularities that come to his or her attention.* This assumption—that a second person will uncover and report irregularities—is critical to effective segregation of duties. If irregularities, once discovered, are not reported to senior management, then any independent check will be useless.

4. *Asking someone to assist in defrauding a business is so risky that the probability of collusion between two or more people is low.* Internal control systems assume that employees will report the errors or misbehavior of others. However, if individuals collude to steal assets—for example, if the individual who controls inventory colludes with the person who accounts for that inventory—then no system of internal control can be relied upon to reveal those irregularities.

5. *Formal titles and accountability, as shown on an organization chart, determine who has power in the organization.* Designers of internal control systems assume that power and influence come from the top of the organization. Accordingly, subordinates will pass information about control weaknesses and irregularities up to their bosses.

6. *Records and documentation provide proof of actions and transactions.* Internal controls rely on documents and electronic records for evidence of actual transactions. If documents and records prove to be false or inaccurate, then there can be no assurance that transactions were recorded properly.

7. *There is no inherent conflict between performance goals and the production of reliable information.* Accountants assume that both of these goals—high levels of performance and reliable information—can be achieved simultaneously in organizations.

---

[16] Douglas R. Carmichael, "Behavioral Hypotheses of Internal Control," *The Accounting Review* 45 (April 1970): 235–245. Although this article is almost 30 years old, these behavioral assumptions still underpin all internal control systems.

**TABLE 13–2** Assumptions Underlying Internal Controls

These are the common assumptions underlying internal controls in organizations.[a] Do you agree or disagree with each?

1. Individuals have inherent moral weaknesses; therefore, internal controls are necessary to safeguard assets and information.
   - ☐ I agree
     **But I would qualify this assumption as follows:**
   - ☐ I disagree

2. By threat of exposure of wrongdoing, an effective internal control system will deter fraud.
   - ☐ I agree
     **But I would qualify this assumption as follows:**
   - ☐ I disagree

3. An independent individual will recognize and report irregularities.
   - ☐ I agree
     **But I would qualify this assumption as follows:**
   - ☐ I disagree

4. The probability of collusion to commit fraud between two or more people is low because asking someone to assist in collusion is too risky.
   - ☐ I agree
     **But I would qualify this assumption as follows:**
   - ☐ I disagree

5. Formal titles and accountability are the primary source of power in organizations.
   - ☐ I agree
     **But I would qualify this assumption as follows:**
   - ☐ I disagree

6. Records and documentation provide proof of actions and transactions.
   - ☐ I agree
     **But I would qualify this assumption as follows:**
   - ☐ I disagree

7. There is no inherent conflict between performance goals and the production of reliable information.
   - ☐ I agree
     **But I would qualify this assumption as follows:**
   - ☐ I disagree

[a] Adapted from Douglas R. Carmichael, "Behavioral Hypotheses of Internal Control," *The Accounting Review* 45 (April 1970): 235–245.

**APPENDIX 13–3** Building Block Summary for Internal Control Systems

| INTERNAL CONTROL SYSTEMS | |
| --- | --- |
| **WHAT** | systems that safeguard assets from theft or accidental loss and ensure reliable accounting records and financial information systems |
| **WHY** | to prevent inefficiency in transaction processing, flawed decisions based on inaccurate data, and fraud |
| **HOW** | Structural Safeguards<br>  segregation of duties<br>  defined levels of authorization<br>  restricted access to valuable assets<br>  independent internal-audit function<br>  active audit committee of the board<br>Systems Safeguards<br>  complete and accurate record keeping<br>  restricted access to information systems and databases<br>  relevant and timely management reporting<br>  adequate documentation and audit trail<br>Staff Safeguards<br>  adequate expertise and training for all accounting, control, and internal-audit staff<br>  rotation in key jobs<br>  sufficient resources |
| **WHEN** | at all times in all businesses |
| **WHO** | staff professionals (trained accountants, independent auditors)<br>managers usually should not spend much time designing or reviewing the details of internal controls |

*Source:* Adapted from Simons, *Levers of Control,* p. 181.

# 14

# Levers of Control
# for Implementing Strategy

I n this final chapter, we recap and summarize the performance measurement and control system tools that are available to managers as they work to achieve their profit goals and strategies. In so doing, we can draw an analogy between a manager and a physician. The physician—through training, internship, and experience—is expected to (1) know how to diagnose the health of a patient, (2) understand the range of treatments and medications that are available for any problems, and (3) possess the skill to apply those treatments and remedies to ensure the ongoing health of the patient. For any manager, his or her business is the patient. Like the physician, the manager is expected to know how to diagnose the health of a business, understand the array of performance measurement and control tools that are available to achieve desired goals, and possess the skill to apply those solutions in different circumstances.

In the sections to follow, we organize the performance measurement and control system tools covered so far in the book into a coherent model called the **levers of control.** Then, we illustrate how a manager, like a physician, can diagnose an organization to determine when and how to apply these levers in differing circumstances to achieve specific profit goals and strategies.

## LEVERS OF CONTROL[1]

We have now laid out basic assumptions, built a "tool chest" of performance measurement and control techniques, and illustrated how top managers can use these tools to achieve specific objectives. Each control system or technique was differentiated as much as possible to highlight its unique characteristics and attributes. Now that we have considered each separately, an important proposition can be stated: Control of business strategy is achieved by *integrating the four levers* of beliefs systems, boundary systems, diagnostic control systems, and interactive control systems. The power of these levers in implementing strategy does not lie in how each is used alone, but rather in how they complement each other when used together. The interplay of positive and negative forces creates a dynamic tension between opportunistic innovation and predictable goal achievement that is necessary to stimulate and control profitable growth.

---

[1] The first two sections of this chapter draw from Chapter 7 of Robert Simons, *Levers of Control: How Managers Use Innovative Control Systems to Drive Strategic Renewal* (Boston: Harvard Business School Press, 1995).

## Using the Levers of Control to Guide Strategy

Before focusing on the dynamics of the four levers of control, we must revisit the nature of the strategy process. As discussed in Chapter 2, strategy can be described as a plan, a pattern of actions, a product-market position, or a unique perspective. To be effective, the levers of control must recognize the roles of each of these types of strategy.

To aid in the analysis, consider briefly the distinction between intended strategies, emergent strategies, and realized strategies.[2] *Intended strategies* are the plans that managers attempt to implement in a specific product market based on analysis of competitive dynamics and current capabilities. These are the strategies that managers want to achieve. *Emergent strategies,* by contrast, are strategies that emerge spontaneously in the organization as employees respond to unpredictable threats and opportunities through experimentation and trial and error. These are the strategies that were unplanned. **Realized strategies** are the outcome of both streams—that is, what actually

**FIGURE 14–1 Relationship Between Levers of Control and Realized Strategies**

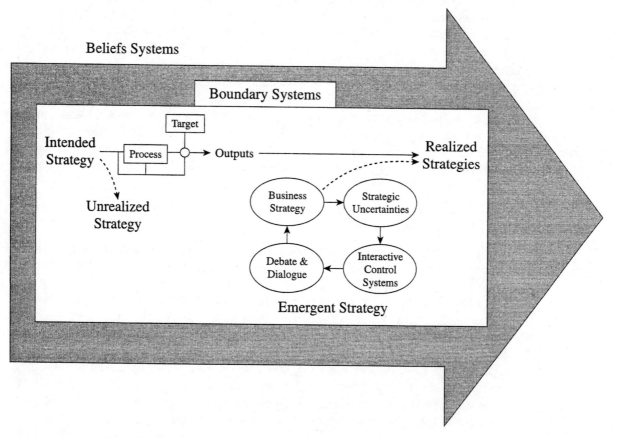

*Source:* Adapted from Simons, *Levers of Control,* p. 154.

[2] Henry Mintzberg, "Patterns in Strategy Formation," *Management Science* 24 (1978): 934–48.

happened. Realized strategies are the combination of intended strategies that were actually implemented and unplanned emergent strategies that occurred spontaneously. This distinction will prove to be important in understanding how the levers can be used to control business strategy (see Figure 14–1).

Diagnostic control systems are the essential management tools for transforming intended strategies into realized strategies: they focus attention on goal achievement for the business and for each individual within the business. Diagnostic control systems relate to *strategy as a plan.* Diagnostic control systems allow managers to measure outcomes and compare results with preset profit plans and performance goals. Without diagnostic control systems, managers would not be able to tell if intended strategies were being achieved.

Some intended strategies, however, may go unrealized; goals may be set inappropriately or circumstances may change, making goal achievement either impossible or less desirable. Some intended strategies are never implemented because unanticipated roadblocks are encountered or resources are insufficient. Again, diagnostic control systems are needed to monitor these situations.

Interactive control systems are different than diagnostic control systems. They give managers tools to influence the experimentation and opportunity-seeking that may result in emergent strategies. At the business level, even in the absence of formal plans and goals, managers who use selected control systems interactively are able to impose consistency and guide creative search processes. These systems relate to *strategy as patterns of action.* Tactical day-to-day actions and creative experiments can be welded into a cohesive pattern that responds to strategic uncertainties and may, over time, become realized strategy.

The beliefs systems of the organization inspire both intended and emergent strategies. Management's vision, expressed in mission statements and credos, motivates organizational participants to search for and create opportunities to accomplish the overall mission of the firm. These systems relate to *strategy as perspective.* Beliefs systems appeal to the innate desires of organizational participants to belong and contribute to purposive organizations. The beliefs systems create direction and momentum to fuse intended and emergent strategies together and provides guidance and inspiration for individual opportunity-seeking.

Boundary systems ensure that realized strategies fall within the acceptable domain of activity. Boundary systems control *strategy as position,* ensuring that business activities occur in defined product markets and at acceptable levels of risk. Without boundary systems, creative opportunity-seeking behavior and experimentation can dissipate the resources of the firm. Boundary systems make explicit the costs that will be imposed on participants who wander outside the boundaries to engage in proscribed behaviors. Table 14–1 summarizes the relationship between the four levers of control and strategy.

## Dynamic Interplay of Forces

Strategic control is not achieved through new and unique performance measurement and control systems, but through beliefs systems, boundary systems, diagnostic control sys-

**TABLE 14–1** Relating the Four Levers of Control to Strategy

| CONTROL SYSTEM | PURPOSE | COMMUNICATES | CONTROL OF STRATEGY AS |
|---|---|---|---|
| Beliefs Systems | Empower and expand search activity | Vision | Perspective |
| Boundary Systems | Provide limits of freedom | Strategic domain | Competitive position |
| Diagnostic Control Systems | Coordinate and monitor the implementation of intended strategies | Plans and goals | Plan |
| Interactive Control Systems | Stimulate and guide emergent strategies | Strategic uncertainties | Pattern of actions |

*Source:* Adapted from Simons, *Levers of Control,* p. 156.

tems, and interactive control systems working together to control both the implementation of intended strategies and the formation of emergent strategies. The dynamic energy for controlling strategy derives from inherent tensions among and within these systems (see Figure 14–2). Two of the control systems—beliefs systems and interactive control systems—motivate organizational participants to search creatively and expand opportunity space. These systems create intrinsic motivation by creating a positive informational environment that encourages information sharing and learning. Beliefs systems and interactive control systems are the positive systems—the yang of Chinese philosophy. The other two systems—boundary systems and diagnostic control systems—are used to constrain search behavior and allocate scarce attention. These systems rely on extrinsic motivation by providing explicit goals, formula-based rewards, and clear limits to opportunity-seeking. Boundary systems and diagnostic control systems are the negative systems—the opposing yin.

As noted earlier, each system is *used* in different ways to leverage scarce management attention and maximize ROM. Diagnostic control systems conserve management attention; interactive systems amplify management attention. Beliefs and boundary systems ensure that core values and rules of the game are understood by everyone in the organization.

Strategic control is achieved, therefore, when the tension between creative innovation and predictable goal achievement is transformed into profitable growth. This tension implies that managers of effective organizations must know how to achieve both high degrees of learning and high degrees of control.

The levers of control are capable of reconciling the tensions between innovation and efficiency. Boundary systems are weighted heavily to control and limits. However, they also reflect learning, because past mistakes and the tactical moves of competitors dictate the adjustment of business conduct and strategic boundaries. Diagnostic control systems clearly emphasize control and efficiency, but setting goals, measuring outcomes, remedying variances, and assigning rewards involve elements of innovation and learning. It is mostly single-loop learning, but, occasionally, double-loop learning

**FIGURE 14–2    Levers of Control**

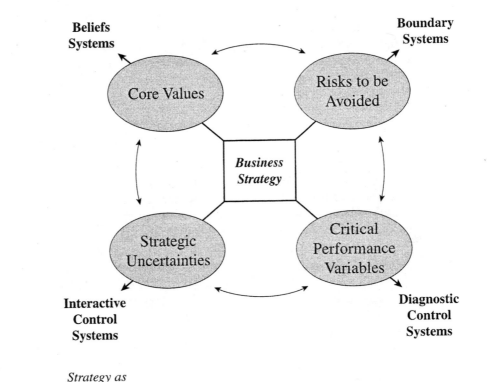

*Source:* Adapted from Simons, *Levers of Control*, p. 159.

occurs.[3] Interactive control systems also involve both control and learning, although learning and innovation dominate as senior managers use the interactive control process as a catalyst to force the organization to monitor changing market dynamics and motivate debate about data, assumptions, and action plans. Over time, the information and learning generated by interactive control systems can be embedded in the strategies and goals that are monitored by diagnostic control systems.

Not only is there an interplay of motivational forces between the four systems, there is also a tension of motivational forces within each system. Boundary systems, for

---

[3] Chris Agyris and Donald A. Schön, *Organizational Learning* (Reading, Mass.: Addison-Wesley, 1978): 18–20.

example, are powered by both direct threats of punishment and innate desires to do right. Diagnostic systems are motivated by wealth-enhancing economic rewards and innate desires to achieve and be recognized by others. Interactive systems are powered by the personal intervention of senior managers, as well as participants' innate desires to innovate and create.

For any organizational participant at any point in time, countervailing forces are at work. The creative tensions between learning and control, between guidance and proscription, between motivation and coercion, and between rewards and punishment become the yin and yang—the dynamic forces that simultaneously foster both stability and change.

## LEVERS OF CONTROL AND HUMAN BEHAVIOR

Managers of any high-performing business know that people are the key to success. Finding, hiring, training, and motivating innovative, opportunity-seeking, entrepreneurial employees is the only way to achieve and sustain competitive advantage in dynamic markets. However, we must also remember the organizational blocks that we identified in Chapter 1. These blocks can easily inhibit the release of productive energy from even the best employees. The organizational blocks to human potential are due primarily to people (1) being unsure of the purpose of the organization and how they can contribute, (2) being subject to pressure and temptation, (3) lacking focus and/or resources, (4) lacking opportunity to innovate, and (5) fearing to challenge the status quo. The levers of control can be used to overcome these blocks if managers are clear about the assumptions they are making about human behavior in organizations.

Assumptions about human behavior entail real risks, risks that flow from the assumptions themselves and risks that the assumptions are wrong. This is the Type I and Type II error problem familiar to students of statistical inference. A Type I error occurs when we reject a hypothesis that is true; a Type II error occurs when we accept a hypothesis that is false.

Suppose that a manager must choose between two models of human behavior and treat subordinates accordingly. The first model postulates that subordinates are honest, hardworking, and fulfill their commitments to the best of their abilities. In this model, subordinates represent potential to be unleashed. The second model views subordinates as inherently dishonest, lazy, and eager to avoid work that involves effort. In this model subordinates require careful monitoring and control.

If a manager chooses the first model when, in fact, subordinates are honest and hardworking, then the manager can unleash the potential of subordinates, who will respond to the opportunity that is provided to them to achieve and contribute.

If a manager chooses the second model when subordinates are actually hardworking and honest, then a Type I error has been made. In this case, subordinates will be denied the opportunity to participate in key decisions for fear that their self-interested behavior will be detrimental to the firm. As subordinates recognize the lack of trust, they will become unwilling to commit and work toward the goals of the organization. Gaming or other dysfunctional behavior will result. Thus, the Type I error becomes a self-fulfilling prophecy that blocks the contribution of subordinates and may lead to negative consequences for the firm.

On the other hand, if the manager believes the first model to be true when subordinates are in fact lazy and adverse to effort, a Type II error has been committed. The actions (or inactions) of the manager will provide an opportunity for subordinates to shirk and potentially misappropriate assets. In this case, the lack of controls and monitoring will allow the self-interested behavior of subordinates to displace organizational goals.

These examples, although clearly stylized and simplistic, illustrate the potential cost and pitfalls of incorrectly specifying human behavior. The assumptions a manager makes about human behavior are critical to the choices that must be made to control strategy.

Of course, there is evidence of both models of behavior in most organizations. Humans value contribution and commitment but also exhibit traits of self-interest. In the absence of leadership and purpose, individuals will inevitably become self-interested and work for their own benefit with little regard to the goals of the organization. Therefore, effective controls must deal with both models.

The model of human behavior adopted in this book reconciles these two views by assuming that people desire (1) to achieve and contribute, (2) to do right, and (3) to create and innovate. We assume lapses in these behaviors are due primarily to organizational blocks, rather than a misspecification of the basic nature of people working inside organizations.

Table 14–2 illustrates the links between these assumptions and managerial action. The first column specifies key behavioral assumptions; the second column lists the organizational blocks that often hinder human potential in organizations. The final two columns provide remedies—both in managerial actions and the levers of control.

Our model of human behavior assumes that people desire to contribute but that organizations often make it difficult for individuals to understand the larger purpose of their efforts or how they can add value in a way that matters. Effective managers recognize these organizational blocks and try to remove them by actively communicating core

**TABLE 14–2** Human Behavior, Organizational Blocks, and the Levers of Control

| ORGANIZATION MAN/WOMAN DESIRES TO | ORGANIZATIONAL BLOCKS | MANAGERIAL SOLUTIONS | RELEVANT CONTROL LEVER |
|---|---|---|---|
| Contribute | Unsure of purpose | Communicate core values and mission | Beliefs systems |
| Do right | Pressure or temptation | Specify and enforce rules of the game | Boundary systems |
| Achieve | Lack of focus or resources | Build and support clear targets | Diagnostic control systems |
| Create | Lack of opportunity or afraid of risk | Open organizational dialogue to trigger learning | Interactive control systems |

*Source:* Adapted from Simons, *Levers of Control,* p. 173.

values and mission. In small organizations, this can and should be done informally whenever senior managers interact with subordinates. In larger organizations, managers must rely on formal systems (i.e., beliefs systems) to inspire organizational commitment and reduce organizational blocks.

Our model assumes that people desire to act in accordance with the moral codes of our society but that temptations and pressures always exist in organizations, which may lead to cutting corners, diverting assets, or otherwise choosing courses of action that are in conflict with stricter codes of behavior. Managers try to remove these blocks by clearly specifying and unambiguously enforcing the rules of the game. Some behaviors are never tolerated. The firing of the manager who inflated his or her expense report by $100 is a familiar story in many organizations. This action signals that the consequences of stepping over ethical and moral boundaries, even in small ways, are severe and non-negotiable. In larger organizations, managers must rely on formal boundary systems to ensure that these boundaries are communicated and understood.

Our model assumes that people desire to achieve, both for tangible economic benefits and because the satisfaction from achievement can be an end in itself. Unfortunately, organizations can make achievement and the resulting sense of accomplishment difficult. Individuals may not be given the opportunity to focus their energies in ways that permit goals to be achieved and recognized. Often, resources are not available to allow people to rise to their potential. Effective managers attempt to remove these blocks by communicating clear targets and providing the necessary resources for achieving those targets. As organizations grow larger, managers use diagnostic controls to achieve these ends.

Finally, our model assumes that individuals want to innovate and create but that organizations often stifle this innate desire. Individuals either are denied the opportunity to experiment or fear the organizational risks that accompany challenges to the status quo. Effective managers remove these blocks by opening up channels for organizational dialogue and encouraging a learning environment that values dissent and new ideas. When organizations are small, this can be done informally. As organizations grow larger, interactive control systems are the necessary catalyst for learning, experimentation, and information sharing.

Assumptions about human nature are at the core of using the levers of control effectively. Use Table 14–2 to test your own assumptions of human behavior. Do you agree with the assumptions that underlie this theory? If not, what are your assumptions concerning human behavior? What are the implications of your behavioral assumptions for strategy formation and implementation? For empowerment? What are the effects of Type I and Type II errors if your assumptions are incorrect? For any manager, confronting and reconciling unstated assumptions of human behavior are the starting points for realizing human potential in organizations.

## APPLYING THE LEVERS OF CONTROL

Now that we have recapped how the levers of control can be used to implement strategy and release productive energy, we will illustrate in the final two sections how managers can use these levers to achieve profit goals and strategies in two different contexts. Performance measurement and control systems are not created equal, and their application at any given point in time depends — like the physician — on diagnosing the life cycle of the business and applying the right control tools and techniques. In the first example, we review how the levers of control can be applied over time as the firm grows and matures. In the second example, we review how newly appointed managers can use the levers of control to take charge of a business and implement their agendas and strategies.

## Levers of Control and Organizational Life Cycle

As businesses evolve and grow over time, they progress through a series of predictable life cycle stages. The levers of control must be phased in over the life cycle of the firm to effectively balance profit, growth, and control. As we shall see, the ability to apply the levers of control at the appropriate stage of a business's growth is essential to building a sustainable franchise.

Managers who run small entrepreneurial firms, such as Boston Retail in its early years, can and should control the 4Ps of strategy informally. Formal information systems, with their requirements for staff experts, technology support, and management training, are not necessary. Core values can be communicated effectively by the actions of the founders and reinforced through day-to-day discussions about what they believe to be important. Risks to be avoided can also be communicated easily as the owners learn firsthand — through actions of employees or watching other firms — what kinds of behavior can put the business at risk. Critical performance variables — both financial and nonfinancial — can be monitored informally, without reliance on formal reports and measures. Information about strategic uncertainties can be gathered from a variety of informal sources: customers, trade shows, suppliers, and competitors. This information consists largely of trade gossip and news of emerging developments in the industry. Internal controls can be minimal and yet still be adequate to meet the requirements of auditors and bankers. Any weaknesses in controls can be compensated by the owner's careful scrutiny of most transactions.

As the business grows larger, however, these informal processes become inadequate. Regular face-to-face contact with employees is reduced due to time pressures. More people, more locations, more customers, and more products all pull top managers in too many directions. As a result, it becomes increasingly difficult for managers to communicate information about strategies and plans to employees. It also becomes increasingly difficult for top managers to stay informed about progress in meeting goals and become aware of emerging threats and opportunities.

Breakdowns in control are often the first sign of problems. Errors, bad decisions, missed opportunities, and confusion slowly sap the energy of the organization. Profit margins erode and competitive position worsens. For the business to survive, the informal controls — once sufficient — must now be formalized.

We next discuss three stages in the life cycle of a typical firm: start-up, rapid growth, and maturity. To achieve profit goals and strategies over the different life cycle stages of the firm, managers must learn how to integrate the techniques and tools that we studied in this book. Figure 14–3 presents a simplified view of how the levers of control can be successfully implemented as a business grows and matures.

**FIGURE 14–3** **Introduction of Control Systems over the Life Cycle of a Business**

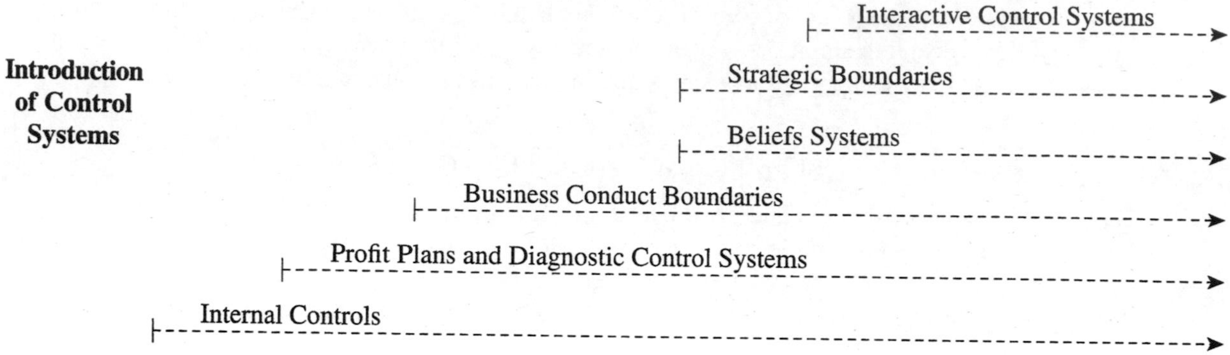

Introduction of Control Systems

Interactive Control Systems ⟶

Strategic Boundaries ⟶

Beliefs Systems ⟶

Business Conduct Boundaries ⟶

Profit Plans and Diagnostic Control Systems ⟶

Internal Controls ⟶

| Life Cycle | Small Start-up | Growing | | Mature |
|---|---|---|---|---|
| Organization Structure | Informal | Functional Specialization | Market-Based Profit Centers | Product/Regional/Customer Groupings |

*Source:* Adapted from Simons, *Levers of Control,* p. 128.

## Stage 1: Start-Up

In the first stage in any organization's evolution—the start-up period—an intimate sense of purpose pervades the business: commitment is achieved by a sense of enthusiasm about the new product or service. Key measures revolve around revenue growth and cash flow as the business struggles to survive. If the value proposition finds appeal in the marketplace, additional employees are hired to bring products and services to a broader market. Threats and opportunities are acted on quickly as people share ideas and action plans. Everyone pulls together by sharing roles and responsibilities to get the job done.

During the early years of an entrepreneurial firm, there is little need for formal control systems. In even the smallest firm, however, managers must install internal control systems to ensure that assets are secure and accounting information is reliable.

> *At Boston Retail, internal control systems have been put in place by the firm's accountant. The system of internal controls is reviewed and tested each year as part of the annual audit conducted by a firm of independent CPAs hired by the board of directors.*

As discussed previously, as the firm prospers and grows, sooner or later it becomes too large to manage informally. Communication between hierarchical levels and geographic locations becomes increasingly difficult. The founders are no longer able to involve themselves in all key decisions. Without effective performance measures and controls, inefficiencies build and market opportunities are missed.

To sustain growth, entrepreneurs must first install effective profit plans to support management needs for decision making and control. Other diagnostic control systems linked to critical performance variables must also be established, and incentives should be tied formally to the achievement of diagnostic targets. Top managers can then rely on exception reports and strategic variance analysis to monitor the achievement of key outputs and profit plan targets.

As managers introduce these new systems, however, they must also be aware of the risks that they are creating. The imposition of formal performance-evaluation systems linked to incentive rewards has increased the likelihood that some employees might cut corners or misuse company assets. Accordingly, effective managers soon install clear business-conduct boundaries to proscribe behaviors that could expose the firm to business risk.

---

*Managers at Boston Retail have built profit plans and set cash flow and ROE objectives. They have established goals for a limited number of nonfinancial performance variables such as store openings and market share. They have used their profit plans to communicate with bankers, shareholders, and important customers. They have analyzed the sources of profitability to ensure that the implementation of their strategy is on track. These plans and goals represent the financial and nonfinancial milestones to be achieved over the coming year.*

---

## Stage 2: Rapid Growth

As the pace of growth increases, new offices are opened and new product lines are launched. To reduce redundancy and increase efficiency, managers create functional work units, each with its own area of specialization. Manufacturing, R&D, marketing, and finance are set up as separate cost centers. Top managers set detailed performance goals, budgets, and incentives for the functional managers who report to them and monitor these systems carefully.

With increasing specialization, efficiencies improve and gross margins increase, allowing both growth and profitability. Unfortunately, the success in driving functional efficiency throughout the business begins to stifle the creativity and initiative that were the hallmarks of the original entrepreneurial business. With narrow specialization and tight functional performance goals, employees find it increasingly difficult to respond creatively to local market conditions. The business begins to lose its vitality and its ability to adapt quickly to market threats and opportunities.

To restore responsiveness and growth at this critical juncture in a firm's life cycle, senior managers must decentralize decision making by creating decentralized accountability structures, such as market-based profit centers. Under the new decentralized structure, profit center managers must be given considerable freedom to run their own businesses to meet local customer needs. They are now responsible for setting business strategy, staffing, and acquiring assets to support local R&D, production, and marketing of their products and services. With empowered profit center managers and an increased focus on local markets, the firm regains its ability to respond quickly to threats and opportunities. Growth again takes hold.

With so much independence in the hands of autonomous profit center managers, however, several additional controls are now needed. First, top managers must create and communicate their core values using formal beliefs systems. Mission and vision statements must be created and communicated to motivate, empower, and supply direction. These formal beliefs systems become critical in instilling shared values among increasingly dispersed employees. Second, managers must clarify and communicate strategic boundaries. With increased delegation of decision rights comes the risk that subordinates will squander scarce resources on opportunities that do not support the overall strategy of the business. Top managers must, therefore, declare certain activities off-limits to avoid distraction, bad investments, and failed projects. Third, accounting measures must focus not only on profitability (i.e., net income as a percent of sales), but also on the assets used to generate those profits. Thus, ROCE and residual income (e.g., EVA) become key measures for evaluating managers and their decentralized businesses. These measures should be augmented by balanced scorecards to communicate corporate strategy and strategic initiatives throughout the business.

---

*The founders of Boston Retail have attempted to define the values and direction of the business by asserting uniqueness, providing prestige to group membership, and using the mission as a symbol to define what the organization represents. Top managers have articulated their core values and beliefs in a simple mission statement:*

> Boston Retail Clothing was founded to offer young-at-heart customers
> the best in fashion, value, and fun. Our employees work together as a team
> to listen, learn, and serve to the very best of our ability.
> We will not sell products that we would not be proud to own and wear ourselves.
> We anticipate fashion trends and ensure that our products lead the way.

*The founders have also communicated a concise, yet clear, boundary as part of their mission statement:* "We will not sell products that we would not be proud to own and wear ourselves." *By communicating clearly the types of market opportunities that will not be supported, managers hope to be successful in ensuring that Boston Retail's business stays focused on the fashion market that is at the core of its value proposition. Other opportunities, even those that could generate short-term profit, are to be passed over.*

---

## Stage 3: Maturity

The business is now large, mature, and complex—perhaps a Fortune 500 company traded on the New York or NASDAQ stock exchanges. The company has several divisions and competes in multiple product markets. To align span of control, span of accountability, and span of attention, managers group together the disparate business units to form larger market-based sectors, grouping similar businesses by product, region, or customer. New staff groups are created to manage the increasingly important planning systems and to design new asset allocation systems to allocate scarce resources among businesses. Staff specialists ensure that strategic criteria are consistent across the corporation and that appropriate financial hurdles are being consistently met.

In the large, mature firm, senior managers must learn how to rely on the opportunity-seeking behavior of subordinates for innovation and new strategic initiatives. At this point, managers should make one or more control systems interactive. These interactive control systems signal where debate and learning should occur. As a result of top management's interest, the entire organization focuses on strategic uncertainties and their potential effects on the implementation of strategy. Staff groups assist in gathering and facilitating information flows, but, to avoid unneeded bureaucracy, the role of staff groups is carefully constrained.

The transition from one life cycle stage to another, outlined briefly, is not always smooth. In the absence of effective performance measurement and control systems, organizations will often drift into a crisis that can imperil managers, employees, and ultimately the entire business. In some cases, the crisis leads to the hiring of new executives, who are asked to make fundamental changes and restore the business to profitable growth. We can consider this situation next.

## TAKING CHARGE OF A BUSINESS

At any point during the life cycle of a business, a new top manager may be hired to take over—either to replace existing managers who failed to achieve profit goals and strategies, or as a result of normal succession planning (i.e., retirement of the previous top manager). In some cases, the mandate of the new managers will be to continue a trajectory of profitable growth. In other cases, they will be hired to turn the business around and restore profitability and growth. To take charge and implement their strategic agenda effectively, managers must know how to use the levers of control. Table 14–3 summarizes how these levers can be used to drive either strategic turnaround or strategic renewal.[4]

### Using the Levers of Control to Drive Strategic Turnaround

If the business has failed to achieve profit goals and strategies in the past, the board of directors or executive committee will expect a new manager to turn the business around quickly and set it on a new course of profitable growth. A new manager must act with determination to change routines and strategies that had previously caused the business to underperform. In these circumstances, a new manager can use the levers of control to (1) overcome organizational inertia, (2) communicate the substance of the new agenda, (3) establish implementation timetables and targets, and (4) ensure continuing attention

---

[4] For a complete discussion of how newly-appointed managers use the levers of control, see Robert Simons, "How New Top Managers Use Control Systems as Levers of Strategic Renewal," *Strategic Management Journal 15* (1994): 169–189.

**TABLE 14–3** How Newly Appointed Managers Use the Levers of Control

| PURPOSE | STRATEGIC TURNAROUND | STRATEGIC RENEWAL |
|---|---|---|
| *First Twelve Months:* | | |
| 1. Overcome organizational inertia ↓ | Formalize and communicate strategic boundaries | Use diagnostic controls to:<br>• Link bonuses to financial targets<br>• Raise minimum performance levels for financial targets |
| 2. Communicate substance of new agenda ↓ | Formalize new strategy and communicate through new mission statements (beliefs systems)<br>Use diagnostic control systems in presentations to superiors | Issue planning guidelines to subordinates outlining new strategic initiatives |
| 3. Establish implementation timetable and targets ↓ | Based on commitments made to superiors, fix accountability targets with subordinates<br>Link diagnostic control system targets to critical performance variables | Use diagnostic control system targets to teach and test new agenda<br>Link diagnostic control system targets to critical performance variables |
| 4. Ensure continuing attention through incentives ↓ | Alter bonus incentives to be subjectively determined based on allegiance to new strategic agenda | Alter bonus incentives to be formula-based and linked to new, more-demanding financial targets<br>Institute business conduct boundaries in response to control system manipulation |
| *Second Twelve Months:* | | |
| 5. Focus organization learning on strategic uncertainties associated with vision for the future | Begin using one control system interactively to signal priorities and motivate debate and dialogue | Begin using one control system interactively to signal priorities and motivate debate and dialogue |

*Source:* Adapted from Simons, *Levers of Control,* p. 150.

through incentives. A new manager can use the levers of control to accomplish these objectives as follows:

**To Overcome Organizational Inertia**

- Strategic boundaries can be crafted and communicated to inform employees that the old strategy and assumptions will no longer be tolerated.

**To Communicate the Substance of the New Agenda**

- A new manager can draft and communicate a new mission and statement of core values to give employees a renewed sense of purpose and direction.
- New managers taking charge can use performance goals to communicate to superiors (that is, the board of directors) the level of achievement that can be expected and the timeframe in which profit goals and strategies will be achieved.

**To Establish Implementation Timetables and Targets**

- To drive this sense of urgency through the organization, managers can use diagnostic control system goals and targets to communicate to subordinates what is expected of them and the timeframe in which they must achieve key objectives.
- To ensure the implementation of strategic objectives, managers can link diagnostic control system targets to the critical performance variables that underly the strategy (i.e., those performance variables that could cause the new strategy to fail).

**To Ensure Continuing Attention Through Incentives**

- To gain allegiance to the new agenda, bonus compensation can be determined subjectively, based on the new top manager's perception of the commitment and allegiance of each subordinate to support and work toward the new strategic agenda.

## Using the Levers of Control to Drive Strategic Renewal

The issues are different—but no less difficult—for a manager taking over a successful business. He or she will likely want to introduce new strategic initiatives to allow the business to adapt to changing competitive realities. At the same time, because of the success of previous management in achieving profit goals and strategies, employees may be complacent and resist the changes desired by the new manager.

Yet, if a company is to succeed in the future and adapt to changing market conditions, strategic renewal will be necessary. As in the case of strategic turnaround, managers can use the levers of control to: (1) overcome organizational inertia and create a sense of urgency, (2) communicate the new agenda for strategic renewal, and (3) establish implementation timetables and targets.

**To Create a Sense of Urgency**

- A new manager can break complacency and create a sense of urgency by raising minimum levels of achievement for diagnostic goals and targets—often by benchmarking leading firms in similar industries.
- In addition, management bonuses can be linked by formula to financial targets and critical performance variables that support new strategic initiatives.

**To Communicate the New Agenda for Strategic Renewal**

- New managers can communicate expectations using top-down performance goals and balanced scorecards.
- Managers can then use the goal-setting process to review and revise the bottom-up goals and initiatives submitted by subordinates. This process can be used to teach subordinates about the new agenda and then test the adequacy of their understanding and response.

**To Establish Implementation Timetables and Targets**

- To support these actions, managers must ensure that diagnostic control systems are adequate to monitor progress in achieving the new profit goals and strategies. If they are deficient, new systems can be installed.

## Focusing on Strategic Uncertainties

Regardless of the mandate of any new top manager—that is, strategic turnaround or strategic renewal—after the new agenda is in place, he or she will want to focus the attention of the entire organization on the strategic uncertainties related to the new strategy. Therefore, top managers can make one or more control systems interactive. These interactive control systems will be used throughout the organization to monitor changes in competitive dynamics and communicate new developments back to senior management. Over time, interactive control systems will allow managers to guide and focus organizational attention and debate so that creative experiments can be welded into a cohesive pattern of action that responds to emerging threats and opportunities.

## ACHIEVING PROFIT GOALS AND STRATEGIES

To achieve profit goals and strategies, managers must manage the inherent tensions found within all high-performing organizations. These are the tensions between:

- profit, growth, and control
- intended and emergent strategies
- unlimited opportunities and limited attention
- self-interest and the desire to contribute

Managers must know how to use various performance measurement techniques in combination with the levers of control to overcome these blocks and manage these tensions.

Effective top managers use the levers of control to inspire commitment to the organization's purpose, to stake out the territory for experimentation and competition, to coordinate and monitor the execution of today's strategies, and to stimulate and guide the search for strategies of the future. Managing the tension between creative innovation and predictable goal achievement is the key to profitable growth.

The levers of control, coupled with the performance measurement techniques of Part II—profit planning, variance analysis, corporate performance measures, balanced scorecards, and resource allocation systems—allow managers to effectively take charge and manage a business. Taken as a whole, these performance measurement tools and control systems provide the motivation, measurement, learning, and control that allow efficient goal achievement, creative adaptation, and profitable growth over the life cycle of the firm.

# PART IV
## Case Studies

# CASE 1   ATH Technologies, Inc.: Making the Numbers

---

**Instructions:**

   This case describes the evolution of an innovative, entrepreneurial firm in the medical technology industry. The successes—and difficulties—of the business are due in large part to management's attempts to design and use formal control systems to achieve profit and performance goals.

   The case is structured in five chronological sections: (1) the founding of the company, (2) growth phase, (3) push to profitability, (4) refocus on process, and (5) takeover by new management. At the end of each section, you will be asked a series of questions about how managers should use control systems to overcome the problems that they encounter. Write your brief answer in the space provided before proceeding to the next section. In this way, you can evaluate your understanding of the applicable techniques to balance profit, growth, and control.

---

## I. The Founding of ATH Technologies, Inc.

In 1986, Dr. Charles Casper and John Frost founded ATH Technologies, Inc. to develop, manufacture, and sell a new medical imaging product. Dr. Casper (47), a radiologist, had trained at Johns Hopkins medical school and, after a research fellowship at Harvard Medical School, joined a private practice in Florida. Casper specialized in the use of imaging systems for the medical practice. Over time, he had experimented with different procedures, such as ultrasounds and x-ray, until he became interested in a new technology based on sending electronic impulses through electrodes attached to the skin and observing how these impulses changed as they went through the body. Together with John Frost—an engineer who specialized in digital imaging for medical applications—Casper perfected the technology, reducing its cost and improving its resolution.

   Both founders anticipated a significant market potential for their product. Relatively low cost combined with improved image quality made it a very attractive alternative for applications where other imaging systems were prohibitively expensive to use. With these expectations, they convinced a group of doctors to invest in the venture. The company started with $2,433,118 in paid-in capital.

   In 1987, ATH Technologies, Inc. received regulatory approval to market its first product—an imaging system to work in conjunction with minimally invasive surgical procedures. Building on this initial success and after a detailed sales and profit projection over a five year period, a deal was struck with Alumni Capital Partners, a venture capital firm, which agreed to invest $5,813,407 to support the launch of the new product. The business plan anticipated the introduction of new products with increased image resolution and a broader range of applications to pull the company into profitability by the end of 1990.

---

*Doctoral Candidate Antonio Dávila and Professor Robert Simons prepared this case as the basis for class discussion rather than to illustrate either effective or ineffective handling of an administrative situation.*

During this period, all the cash of the business would be invested in product development, production tooling, and marketing.

The product was launched in December 1987 and gained a toehold in the marketplace. Additional managers, scientists, and marketing personnel were hired. Some were given equity positions in the company in lieu of fully competitive salaries. As expected, the investment in product development and manufacturing processes absorbed all the cash that the business generated. In 1988, the venture capital firm organized another round of financing, bringing other venture capital firms into the company which invested $5,339,518. At this point, the board comprised 60% inside directors and 40% outsiders.

During 1989, the company improved the product and a new generation was developed. That same year, the founders received an offer to sell the company to Scepter Pharmaceutical, Inc. (a pseudonym), a $5 billion pharmaceutical and medical products company that wished to increase its presence in this market segment. The offer seemed attractive to all the parties involved. The venture capital firms would be able to cash out profitably, Scepter would add a new and successful product to its product line, and ATH would have access to cash to finance faster growth. The business could add more people, expand facilities, and buy new equipment to take advantage of the market opportunity for its product.

ATH was acquired by Scepter in early 1990 for an initial payment of $60 million to existing shareholders. In addition, there was an "earn-out" clause whereby Scepter would pay, on a pro rata basis, an additional $24 million if the new products currently under development were approved by the FDA; $25 million if an independent study proved that the ATH's technology was superior to other existing technologies; and $90 million over a three year period starting in December 1992 if sales growth and earnings goals were met (**Exhibit 1** describes the earn-out structure). ATH's ten equity-holding managers who chose to stay with Scepter could receive between $1 million and $5 million additional pay-out from the sale of the company.

**Questions:**

1. Does the "earn-out" structure focus on the right performance goals?

_____

_____

_____

_____

- Should Scepter Pharmaceutical put additional controls on this entrepreneurial firm?

_____

_____

_____

_____

### EXHIBIT 1:   Structure of the Earn-Out Payments

|  | SALES GOALS | BONUS | EARNINGS GOALS | BONUS |
|---|---|---|---|---|
| 1992 Results | $42 million | $10 million | $5 million | $10 million |
| 1993 Results | $76 million | $15 million | $17.5 million | $15 million |
| 1994 Results | $110 million | $20 million | $24 million | $20 million |

## EXHIBIT 2:    Financial Performance, 1986–1989

|  | 1986 | 1987 | 1988 | 1989 |
|---|---|---|---|---|
| Net Sales | 4,860 | 181,721 | 863,514 | 2,757,505 |
| Gross Margin | (141,047) | (352,754) | (588,652) | 173,228 |
| Marketing & Sales | 19,312 | 197,916 | 817,831 | 1,520,309 |
| Research & Development | 517,294 | 880,219 | 1,449,702 | 2,196,694 |
| Net Income (Loss) | (800,294) | (2,051,149) | (3,619,093) | (4,527,684) |
| Cash and S.T. Investments | 666,634 | 3,919,634 | 5,415,265 | 1,200,682 |
| Other Current Assets | 85,426 | 430,118 | 805,051 | 1,169,266 |
| Net Fixed Assets | 314,585 | 870,966 | 1,102,068 | 1,293,682 |
| Total Assets | 1,243,645 | 5,414,026 | 7,609,829 | 3,976,769 |
| Long Term Debt | — | — | — | — |
| Common Stock | 2,433,118 | 8,246,525 | 13,586,042 | 13,586,042 |
| Retained Earnings | (1,317,942) | (3,369,091) | (6,988,184) | (11,515,868) |
| Headcount (year-end) | 17 | 41 | 65 | 95 |

2. If you were President of ATH Technologies, how would you communicate and motivate employees to achieve profit and performance goals?

_____

_____

_____

_____

- What are the appropriate performance goals for employees to focus on?

_____

_____

_____

- How would you communicate and control events and employee actions that could put business objectives at risk?

_____

_____

_____

_____

3. What are the best financial measures to assess ATH Technologies' performance? Why?

_____

_____

_____

_____

## II. Growth Phase: 1990–1991

After the acquisition by Scepter in 1990, the original ATH management team (Charles, John, and the other managers hired from 1986 through 1990) decided to stay with the business. They were given a great deal of autonomy to manage the newly acquired business. Corporate managers at Scepter Pharmaceutical believed that the culture of this entrepreneurial start-up was fragile, and could be destroyed by forcing the use of bureaucratic planning and control techniques on this small company. In addition, any attempt to meddle in the decision making authority of the founding managers could be construed as impeding the ability of ATH to meet its earn-out goals.

The overriding objective of ATH senior managers—and their corporate-level counterparts at Scepter Pharmaceutical—was to acquire market share through new product development and aggressive marketing efforts. Charles, John, and the other senior managers made it clear how important it was to build ATH's acceptance and franchise. Senior managers talked about the importance of market share in their frequent, informal management meetings, and pored over weekly shipment data to learn how they were faring in the competitive marketplace. Market share targets were not formally linked to the compensation of individual managers. Instead, annual bonuses were to be established subjectively, based on the perceived contribution of each individual to the success of the business.

When the FDA approved the new generation of products in 1991, the first installment of the earn-out was paid. However, the study of the competitiveness of the technology had shown that a new technology developed in Europe could challenge ATH's position. Therefore, this portion of the earn-out was not paid. Unfortunately, profit performance for 1990 and 1991 proved to be very disappointing (see **Exhibit 3**). Although sales revenue had increased dramatically, losses had mounted precipitously. The plan had been to build market share while holding—at worst—a break-even profit position. In fact, 1990 and 1991 had generated $25 million in losses. Part of this was due to the heavy investment in development

| EXHIBIT 3: | Financial Performance, 1986–1991 | | | | | |
|---|---|---|---|---|---|---|
| | 1986 | 1987 | 1988 | 1989 | *1990* | *1991* |
| Net Sales | 4,860 | 181,721 | 863,514 | 2,757,505 | *6,482,616* | *11,974,093* |
| Gross Margin | (141,047) | (352,754) | (588,652) | 173,228 | *(396,400)* | *1,686,298* |
| Marketing & Sales | 19,312 | 197,916 | 817,831 | 1,520,309 | *2,771,004* | *6,495,618* |
| Research & Development | 517,294 | 880,219 | 1,449,702 | 2,196,694 | *4,255,999* | *6,842,274* |
| Net Income (Loss) | (800,294) | (2,051,149) | (3,619,093) | (4,527,684) | *(9,289,664)* | *(15,653,681)* |
| Cash and S.T. Investments | 666,634 | 3,919,634 | 5,415,265 | 1,200,682 | *(279,080)* | *279,672* |
| Other Current Assets | 85,426 | 430,118 | 805,051 | 1,169,266 | *4,678,726* | *5,790,307* |
| Net Fixed Assets | 314,585 | 870,966 | 1,102,068 | 1,293,682 | *3,885,097* | *6,681,805* |
| Total Assets | 1,243,645 | 5,414,026 | 7,609,829 | 3,976,769 | *8,466,257* | *12,941,357* |
| Long Term Debt | — | — | — | — | *12,331,608* | *31,670,492* |
| Common Stock | 2,433,118 | 8,246,525 | 13,586,042 | 13,586,042 | *13,586,042* | *13,586,042* |
| Retained Earnings | (1,317,942) | (3,369,091) | (6,988,184) | (11,515,868) | *(20,805,532)* | *(36,459,214)* |
| Headcount (year-end) | 17 | 41 | 65 | 95 | *221* | *252* |

costs, which were expensed directly. If senior management wanted to meet the requirements for the final $90 million earn-out payment, they needed to turn around the bottom line for 1992.

**Questions:**

1.  How would you evaluate the performance of ATH Technologies, Inc. during the growth period?

    _____

    _____

    _____

    •  What is the strategy of the business?

       _____

       _____

       _____

    •  How should performance be measured and analyzed?

       _____

       _____

       _____

    •  Which additional measures would you use to implement the strategy?

       _____

       _____

       _____

    •  What are the characteristics of a good measure?

       _____

       _____

       _____

2.  If you were President of ATH Technologies, what would you do to focus the attention and efforts of your employees?

    _____

    _____

    _____

3.  What is your assessment of ATH Technologies' financial performance? Using the measures you chose, what are your expectations for its future financial performance?

    _____

    _____

    _____

## III. Push to Profitability: 1992

In early 1992, Charles Casper and his management team decided to launch a comprehensive program "Push to Profitability." The program was established to motivate employees to reach the financial goals set for 1992. The message was straightforward: *The division must break even in 1992. If the objective was accomplished, each employee would receive a cash bonus of 20% of their salary and an all expenses paid trip for two to Hawaii.* In addition, top management kept on the pressure for sales growth.

Graphs were posted throughout the facilities showing the weekly level of sales, costs and profitability. Each month souvenirs from Hawaii were distributed to remind people of the reward ahead. Employees became really focused on the financial performance of the company and they worked hard to increase sales and cut costs—especially discretionary costs.

"Push to Profitability" accomplished its motivational objective. The results for 1992 outstripped expectations: sales quadrupled and profits were $7.083 million (**Exhibit 4**).

The trip to Hawaii in the first week of March 1993 was a resounding success. Everybody enjoyed the opportunity to relax and celebrate their achievement, and praised the division management for organizing such a celebration.

Unfortunately, the euphoria was not to last. As product shipments increased and costs were cut, customer complaints and product returns had increased even more sharply. These problems did not go unnoticed. The Federal Drug Administration (FDA), the government regulatory agency charged with regulating the manufacture and distribution of medical products, paid a surprise visit to the division's manufacturing plant a week after the Hawaii trip to investigate the dramatic increase in product defect returns experienced in the first quarter of 1993.

On March 28, 1993, Charles Casper looked in panic at the FDA report received that morning. The FDA had issued a "Warning Letter" listing over 150 quality and compliance irregularities. If the division did not improve its processes to meet the regulatory demands, it would be barred from selling its core medical products.

When Charles first received the letter, he could not believe it. The same people who had been so thankful and committed had put the division at the brink of disaster!! Everyone in the company was aware of what this letter meant—the FDA would likely shut down the entire operation!

**Questions:**

1. How did managers at ATH Technologies, Inc. achieve their profit and performance goals during 1992?

_____

_____

_____

_____

_____

- What role did control systems play in ATH's success and problems?

_____

_____

_____

_____

- How could top management have avoided the actions by employees that lead to the FDA investigation?

_____

_____

_____

_____

| EXHIBIT 4: | Financial Performance, 1986–1992 (thousands of dollars) | | | | | | |
|---|---|---|---|---|---|---|---|
| | 1986 | 1987 | 1988 | 1989 | 1990 | 1991 | 1992 |
| Net Sales | 5 | 182 | 864 | 2,758 | 6,483 | 11,974 | 49,144 |
| Gross Margin | (141) | (353) | (589) | 173 | (396) | 1,686 | 29,690 |
| Marketing & Sales | 19 | 198 | 818 | 1,520 | 2,771 | 6,496 | 10,927 |
| Research & Development | 517 | 880 | 1,450 | 2,197 | 4,256 | 6,842 | 5,371 |
| Net Income (Loss) | (800) | (2,051) | (3,619) | (4,528) | (9,290) | (15,654) | 7,083 |
| Cash and S.T. Investments | 667 | 3,920 | 5,415 | 1,201 | (279) | 280 | (912) |
| Other Current Assets | 85 | 430 | 805 | 1,169 | 4,679 | 5,790 | 13,388 |
| Net Fixed Assets | 315 | 871 | 1,102 | 1,294 | 3,885 | 6,682 | 5,419 |
| Total Assets | 1,244 | 5,414 | 7,610 | 3,977 | 8,466 | 12,941 | 17,973 |
| Long Term Debt | — | — | — | — | 12,332 | 31,670 | 27,048 |
| Common Stock | 2,433 | 8,247 | 13,586 | 13,586 | 13,586 | 13,586 | 13,586 |
| Retained Earnings | (1,318) | (3,369) | (6,989) | (11,517) | (20,808) | (36,462) | (29,387) |
| Headcount (year-end) | 17 | 41 | 65 | 95 | 221 | 252 | 356 |

- What are the possible consequences of these events on the company's reputation?

 

2. If you were the President of ATH, what would you do to get the business back on track?

 

## IV. Refocus on Process: 1993–1994

Senior managers at ATH Technologies Inc. devoted the second quarter of 1993 to address each of the issues mentioned in the "Warning Letter." In May 1993, Casper called an emergency Management Offsite meeting with all top ATH managers to develop action recommendations to avoid similar events in the future. The conclusions reached at the meeting were:

1. Develop a Vision and Belief system where quality, customer value and investment for the future are emphasized. No explicit mention of financial performance was to be included. (See **Exhibit 5**).
2. Develop a more balanced incentive system aligned with the company's new vision and beliefs. John Frost was in charge of designing a balanced set of measures including product innovation, quality, and customer satisfaction that could be used as the basis for the bonus program for 1994. In addition, a task force would be set up to educate each employee in the division on the measures developed.
3. Modify the bonus program for 1993 to include some non-financial measures. In particular, it was decided that if the earn-out goals for Income Before Taxes were met in absolute terms, employees

would earn up to 16% of their salary; if earn-out goals for Income Before Taxes as a percentage of sales were achieved, there would be an additional 8% bonus; and there would be 6% bonus subjectively decided by the department manager of each employee (see **Exhibit 6**).

By November 1993 John Frost came up with proposed measures centered around delivering value to the customer and the associated bonus scheme (also reproduced in **Exhibit 6** below). These customer measures were believed to reflect the underlying processes that drove the performance of ATH Technologies. Employees were educated and informed about their evolution. The four customer measures he proposed were:

- **Product Defects:** number of units that do not meet our customer's quality requirements divided by the total number of patients treated.
- **Customer Contact Errors:** number of order entry, shipping and telephone responsiveness errors divided by the total number of orders taken.
- **Backorders:** total number of orders received for backordered product divided by total number of orders taken.
- **New Product Delays:** the number of months that new product/enhancement release goals are not achieved.

By the end of 1993, every single issue in the FDA's "Warning Letter" had been resolved. In addition, 80% of the sales and earnings goals for the 1993 "earn-out" were met and the corresponding payment was made.

In 1994, the new bonus scheme was implemented. The maximum bonus for customer focused quality measures was 10%, representing a maximum of 2.5% for improvement in each of the four customer measures described above. The response of the employees was again impressive and they reached the maximum bonus in every single dimension except backorders (see **Exhibit 7**).

In December 1994, the stockholders of ATH Technologies Inc. received their final payment in the "earn-out" scheme. Because goals were not fully met, they received 50% of the sales-related bonus and 70% of the earnings-related bonus. **Exhibit 8** shows the financial results at December 31, 1994.

## Questions:

1. Why did senior managers introduce a vision and belief statement?

_____

_____

_____

2. Why did managers at ATH Technologies Inc. change their performance measures?

_____

_____

_____

_____

- John Frost includes both process and output measures. Why? What is he trying to accomplish?

_____

_____

_____

**EXHIBIT 5:    Vision and Beliefs of ATH Technologies Inc.**

**VISION**

*Our ultimate accountability is to our patients, who live better lives because we continually set the standard for diagnostic excellence with our electronic imaging products.*

**BELIEFS**

*Customer Orientation*

My job is to understand and satisfy my customer's needs.

*Quality*

The care of each patient depends on the quality of the products and services I deliver.

*Performance*

My work is important to the health of each patient, I strive to continually improve what I do and I am recognized for how well I do it.

*People*

I am empowered, I communicate, and I share responsibility for my career development.

*Investment in the Future*

I am accountable to ensure appropriate resources are applied to meet customer needs.

*Balance*

I have support to balance my personal and professional life.

*Alignment*

Our success depends on my commitment to teamwork and to creating and maintaining alignment.

**EXHIBIT 6:    Bonus Scheme for 1993 and 1994**

**Bonus Program 1993**

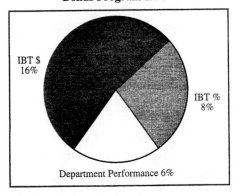

**Bonus Program 1994**

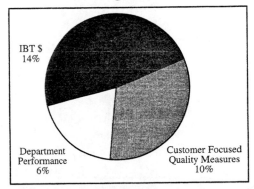

## EXHIBIT 7: Performance Improvement 1994

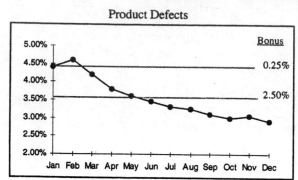

Product Defects

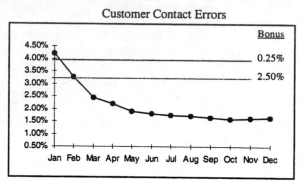

Customer Contact Errors

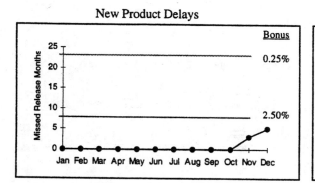

New Product Delays

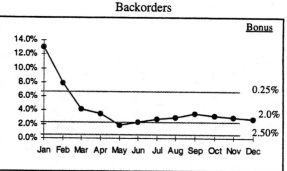

Backorders

## EXHIBIT 8: Financial Performance, 1986–1994 (thousands of dollars)

|  | 1986 | 1987 | 1988 |
|---|---|---|---|
| Net Sales | 5 | 182 | 864 |
| Gross Margin | (141) | (353) | (589) |
| Marketing & Sales | 19 | 198 | 818 |
| Research & Development | 517 | 880 | 1,450 |
| Net Income (Loss) | (800) | (2,051) | (3,619) |
| Cash and S.T. Investments | 667 | 3,920 | 5,415 |
| Other Current Assets | 85 | 430 | 805 |
| Net Fixed Assets | 315 | 871 | 1,102 |
| Total Assets | 1,244 | 5,414 | 7,610 |
| Long Term Debt | 0 | 0 | 0 |
| Common Stock | 2,433 | 8,247 | 13,586 |
| Retained Earnings | (1,318) | (3,369) | (6,989) |
| Headcount (year-end) | 17 | 41 | 65 |

- He also includes ratio and ordinal measures. What are the advantages and problems of each type?

  _____
  _____
  _____
  _____

- Why did John Frost include departmental performance in the bonus scheme?

  _____
  _____
  _____

3. What are the risks for ATH Technologies going forward? How should these risks be monitored and controlled?

   _____
   _____
   _____
   _____

## V. New Management: 1995–1996

During the first quarter of 1995, growth came to a halt. Products had been loaded to customers during the last quarter of 1994 to meet the earn-out goals. More ominously, sales in Europe were declining after a competitor introduced a substitute product based on laser technology to obtain images of the body. Some doctors considered this to be a superior technology. In eight years, ATH's technology had become mature and new competitors had entered

| 1989 | 1990 | 1991 | 1992 | 1993 | 1994 |
|---|---|---|---|---|---|
| 2,758 | 6,483 | 11,974 | 49,144 | 71,836 | 100,765 |
| 173 | (396) | 1,686 | 29,690 | 45,436 | 62,972 |
| 1,520 | 2,771 | 6,496 | 10,927 | 17,019 | 19,226 |
| 2,197 | 4,256 | 6,842 | 5,371 | 9,770 | 10,554 |
| (4,528) | (9,290) | (15,654) | 7,083 | 16,493 | 22,877 |
| 1,201 | (279) | 280 | (912) | 2,644 | 6,423 |
| 1,169 | 4,679 | 5,790 | 13,388 | 20,425 | 26,660 |
| 1,294 | 3,885 | 6,682 | 5,419 | 8,385 | 7,236 |
| 3,977 | 8,466 | 12,941 | 17,973 | 31,577 | 40,836 |
| 0 | 12,332 | 31,670 | 27,048 | 21,162 | 0 |
| 13,586 | 13,586 | 13,586 | 13,586 | 13,586 | 15,770 |
| (11,517) | (20,808) | (36,462) | (29,387) | (14,710) | 5,855 |
| 95 | 221 | 252 | 356 | 619 | 636 |

the market. The focus on growth, cost cutting, and profitability had blind-sided managers to new emerging technologies.

Senior managers began to leave the division after cashing the earn-out. Dr. Casper left in March 1995 and John Frost a month later.

Janet Isabella, a Harvard MBA with significant financial and international experience at Scepter, was brought in to replace the departing executives. She soon realized that the business could not realistically expect to maintain sales at the prior year's level. Accordingly, she asked each department head to reduce costs to 90% of their 1994 level. All incremental spending was focused on new product development in an attempt to regain technological leadership.

By mid 1995 it became clear to everyone at ATH Technologies that the 14% bonus based on achieving income before taxes targets could not be met. The attention of employees was instead devoted to the customer measures (10% of bonus) and departmental objectives (6% of bonus). Customer satisfaction measures were renamed to focus attention on improving rather than avoiding mistakes:

### Customer Focused Quality Measures

| __Old Label__ | | __New Label__ |
|---|---|---|
| Product Defects | | Product Quality |
| Customer Contact Errors |  | Customer Service |
| Backorders | | On Time Shipments |
| New Product Delays | | New Releases |

### EXHIBIT 9: Financial Performance, 1986–1996 (thousands of dollars)

| | 1986 | 1987 | 1988 | 1989 |
|---|---|---|---|---|
| Net Sales | 5 | 182 | 864 | 2,758 |
| Gross Margin | (141) | (353) | (589) | 173 |
| Marketing & Sales | 19 | 198 | 818 | 1,520 |
| Research & Development | 517 | 880 | 1,450 | 2,197 |
| Net Income (Loss) | (800) | (2,051) | (3,619) | (4,528) |
| Cash and S.T. Investments | 667 | 3,920 | 5,415 | 1,201 |
| Other Current Assets | 85 | 430 | 805 | 1,169 |
| Net Fixed Assets | 315 | 871 | 1,102 | 1,294 |
| Goodwill & Trademarks | n/a | n/a | n/a | n/a |
| Total Assets | 1,244 | 5,414 | 7,610 | 3,977 |
| Long Term Debt | 0 | 0 | 0 | 0 |
| Common Stock | 2,433 | 8,247 | 13,586 | 13,586 |
| Retained Earnings | (1,318) | (3,369) | (6,989) | (11,516) |
| Headcount (year-end) | 17 | 41 | 65 | 95 |

During 1995, the business met the product quality requirements to obtain the ISO 9000 quality certification (2.5% bonus) and the customer service target (2.5% bonus), but completely missed the targets for the other two Customer Focused Quality measures. Most departments met their department goals, but product development teams missed most of the new product release goals and they received the lowest bonus at ATH.

Two new products were introduced in January 1996. But by February, several doctors reported serious problems with both products and they were withdrawn from the market, leaving the division with old products in a fast changing market. Internal compliance investigations revealed that corners had been cut by development staff to meet product release targets. Meanwhile, the new technology was taking over the US market. **Exhibit 9** shows the latest financial statements available.

**Questions:**

1. Why did ATH Technologies experience problems with its new products? What role did measurement and control systems play in these problems?

_____

_____

_____

2. How should Janet Isabella design and use performance management and control systems to implement her agenda and take charge of the situation?

_____

_____

_____

- What are the critical performance drivers of success going forward?

_____

| 1990 | 1991 | 1992 | 1993 | 1994 | 1995 | 1996 |
|---|---|---|---|---|---|---|
| 6,483 | 11,974 | 49,144 | 71,836 | 100,765 | 100,181 | 60,054 |
| (396) | 1,686 | 29,690 | 45,436 | 62,972 | 59,249 | 34,900 |
| 2,771 | 6,496 | 10,927 | 17,019 | 19,226 | 18,055 | 17,172 |
| 4,256 | 6,842 | 5,371 | 9,770 | 10,554 | 12,074 | 8,573 |
| (9,290) | (15,654) | 7,083 | 16,493 | 22,877 | 6,185 | (1,234) |
| (279) | 280 | (912) | 2,644 | 6,423 | 72,449 | 304 |
| 4,679 | 5,790 | 13,388 | 20,425 | 26,660 | 24,773 | 11,897 |
| 3,885 | 6,682 | 5,419 | 8,385 | 7,236 | 5,952 | 1,267 |
| n/a | n/a | n/a | n/a | n/a | 95,549 | 88,076 |
| 8,466 | 12,941 | 17,973 | 31,577 | 40,836 | 201,020 | 102,784 |
| 12,332 | 31,670 | 27,048 | 21,162 | 0 | 66,000 | (5,548) |
| 13,586 | 13,586 | 13,586 | 13,586 | 15,770 | 116,995 | 124,123 |
| (20,808) | (36,462) | (29,387) | (14,710) | 5,855 | 670 | (15,025) |
| 221 | 252 | 356 | 619 | 636 | 670 | 289 |

 

- What variables should be measured?

 

- How easy or difficult should goals be?

 

- How should financial expectations be set and communicated?

 

3. How can she use control systems to scan the competitive environment to ensure that the business is not again surpassed by new technology?

 

4. What events or employee actions could put business objectives at risk? How would you ensure that these risks are adequately communicated and controlled?

 

5. How would you measure and evaluate Scepter's decision to purchase ATH Technologies in 1990?

# CASE 2  J Boats

A visitor, strolling along the picturesque harbor of Newport, Rhode Island, might wish to visit the corporate headquarters of J Boats, Inc.—one of America's most successful and famous boat-builders. Each year, over 100,000 people around the world sailed on one of their boats. More than 65 American and international yacht brokers marketed the company's products, emphasizing design innovations which set the industry standard for quality and performance.

In addition to the production plant in Rhode Island, J Boats were built to precise design specifications in factories in eight countries: Argentina, Australia, Brazil, England, France, Italy, Japan, and South Africa. By 1996, the company had produced over 8,500 sailboats, ranging in size from 22′ to 52′. The smallest sailboat cost approximately $20,000 and the largest in excess of $500,000. Production methods were complex, combining sophisticated resin infusion technologies and careful hand-crafting. Building a large yacht could take up to six months in large production facilities employing 500 people.

Over the years, J Boats had won many awards including:

- "Boat of the Year" (*Sail* magazine, *Sailing World, Cruising World*—8 different J Boat designs had earned this distinction in the last 7 years
- "Boat of the Decade" (*Sail* magazine)—awarded to J/24 design
- American Sailboat Hall of Fame—J/24 one of 5 boats originally inducted

In a 1991 article devoted to the people and technologies at the forefront of American competitiveness, *Fortune* magazine named the performance sailboats built by J Boats as one of the 100 best products manufactured in America.

J Boats enjoyed an enviable worldwide reputation. . . . yet, few people realized that the company was managed and operated by just five individuals.

"The garage was 28′ long with a workbench at one end and the door was 9′ wide," Rod Johnstone, co-founder of J Boats explained. "It was no accident that the boat was 24′ by 8′11″—it was the largest boat that would fit in there." Rodney Johnstone had designed his new boat, "Ragtime," in the Fall of 1974 with the idea of creating a fast, comfortable offshore sailboat that he could race with his wife, Lucia, and their five children. He built the boat in his garage with the help of family and friends starting in December 1974, and launched it in May 1976.

With a masters degree in history, Rod had worked as a teacher, a yacht broker, a nuclear submarine construction planner, an advertising salesman for a yachting newspaper, and the head of a sailing school. Each job had brought him back to the love he had learned from his father—sailboats. Rod had built his first sailboat model in his ninth grade shop class. He had been at it ever since.

"We won the first six races we ever sailed," said Rod of the initial success of his new boat. When his brother Bob first sailed with him on the boat in July 1976, they got only second place. "We thought it was a great disaster at the time, but it brought me back to earth."

*Professor Robert Simons prepared this case as the basis for class discussion rather than to illustrate either effective or ineffective handling of an administrative situation.*

Rod made further improvements to the boat. Over Labor Day weekend, Bob came aboard once more and, with his wife Mary, along with Rod and Lucia, as crew, steered "Ragtime" to a resounding victory. After a season of finishing first in all but two of twenty races, the Johnstones had clearly demonstrated that a family crew could go out and win sailboat races.

By midsummer of 1976, at the urging of friends and competitors who wanted a boat just like "Ragtime," Rod decided to produce the boat commercially.

At that time, Rod's elder brother Bob was working as the marketing vice-president for AMF/Alcort, a diversified manufacturer of sporting products including Sunfish and Paceship sailboats and Harley Davidson motorcycles. Also a history major, Bob Johnstone had developed considerable marketing and business expertise in his early career with Quaker Oats—first as a plant manager and subsidiary CEO in Columbia and Venezuela, and later as a product group manager for pet foods in Chicago. As he stated with a wry smile, "I'm the guy who invented cheese flavored burgers for dogs."

After 17 years with Quaker Oats, Bob left to start his own small company—Naturescapes—which designed and marketed photomurals (wall size landscape photographs which could be applied to interior walls like wallpaper). Bob outsourced production of his photomurals to a printing company that specialized in outdoor billboards. He ran this business from his home with the help of his wife, Mary, who took over the business when he joined AMF/Alcort in 1975 to bring marketing expertise to their sailboat division.

One of Bob's first initiatives at AMF was to commission consumer research to investigate the sales potential for higher performance boat designs in the recreational boat market. He learned that there was a significant opportunity for a family-oriented, high performance sailboat in the 24' range. Bob lobbied hard inside AMF to have senior corporate executives consider building and marketing his brother Rod's new 24' design, or something similar. But to no avail. "At that time, Harley motorcycles were losing out to Yamaha's by 10–20 m.p.h., so I couldn't get anyone excited about 1 knot more speed in a sailboat."

In February 1977, Bob resigned his position at AMF to join Rod as an equal partner in the production of the new 24' boat. In May of that year, Rod and Bob Johnstone incorporated their new company—"J Boats"—and adopted the distinctive *J* logo that Rod had designed in the darkroom of the yachting newspaper where he was then working as an ad salesman. With any luck, they hoped in their first year to sell 250 boats called "J/24s" using the one that Rod had designed and built in his garage as the production mold.

### Formative Decisions

The success of the J Boats business venture would be determined by decisions that the Johnstone brothers made in their first year of operations. These decisions were influenced by potential demand for Rod's boat design, the limited resources of the fledgling company, and lessons that Bob had learned in marketing pet food and photomurals.

### Manufacturing

I knew that dogs loved cheese, and I figured that we could really grab the market with a cheese flavored product. We calculated that it wouldn't cost more to make, so we should be able to get more margin through price.

When we introduced the cheese flavored dog burgers, they really took off, reaching $30 million a year and becoming one of the top five new grocery products. We had a winner. We cranked up all our plants, but within a month, we were out of capacity.

This taught me a critical lesson. I said to myself, 'I don't ever want to be in a situation again where I come up with a great product and I don't have the capacity to meet demand.' This led to a unique manufacturing strategy, first with Naturescapes and then with J Boats.

With twenty orders in hand from local sailors, Bob and Rod Johnstone needed to ramp up production quickly to build their new boats. They could do it themselves by setting up a production plant and hiring semi-skilled workers, or they could subcontract production. Based on Bob's experience at Quaker Oats and Naturescapes, they chose the latter course.

"When we asked who was the best boat builder in New England, the answer kept coming back—Everett Pearson." Everett Pearson was well known to both Rod and Bob Johnstone. In 1957, at age 26, Everett had started Pearson Yachts, which he sold seven years later to Grumman Aircraft. Shortly thereafter, Pearson formed a partnership with Neil Tillotson to concentrate on manufacturing fiber reinforced plastics (fiberglass). He was known as the best in the business, and Rod had great confidence in his technical production capabilities,

When Everett sold Pearson Yachts, he was under a five year non-compete clause, so Tillotson-Pearson specialized in fiberglass manufacturing outside the boat building industry. In those early years, Everett learned the importance of design specifications from his Navy and industrial customers, building test torpedoes, cooling towers, fan blades, tanks, plating facilities, and lighting poles. Everett learned the hard way—after customers rejected some early batches because the resin content was off by 3%. This was at a time when no one in the boating industry was paying any attention to technical specifications for fiberglass production—they didn't even know the meaning of the word. The boat builders were just slopping resin into a mold or—worse—spraying in fibers with a chopper gun.

Everett loves the technology. He is constantly experimenting and innovating with fiberglass and epoxy technologies. Every three years he comes up with a new idea that sets the standards for the rest of the industry.

In the fall of 1976, Rod invited Everett Pearson to see his new boat. Everett sat on the boat for an hour, asked questions about its design and construction details, and agreed on the spot to build it for J Boats. Their informal agreement, reproduced as **Exhibit 1,** governed their relationship from 1977 to the present. As the business grew and prospered, the agreement was never changed or updated.

**Distribution**    Bob Johnstone had learned a second important lesson from his previous work life, this time concerning the importance of distribution networks.

I learned that you must rely on established distribution networks. When I was starting up Naturescapes, I thought that I could go "direct" and bypass the retailers. I took out big ads in decorator magazines for my photomurals and shaved my prices by two-thirds because I didn't have to give mark-ups to distributors or wallpaper outlets. I rented a large postal box and checked it every day. . . . I waited two weeks for my first order to come in. It was a disaster.

I realized then that you must have a professional dealer network to succeed.

Using his knowledge of the marine dealer trade acquired at AMF, Bob worked aggressively to sign independent yacht dealers for J Boats. Dealers were asked to stock at least one new boat at all times and to market and promote the boat in their geographical territory. Dealers received discounts of approximately 20% off retail price as compensation for their services. By the end of 1977, J Boats was represented by 45 dealers in North America and was expanding globally with licensing agreements in Argentina, Australia, Brazil, and the U. K.

In their first year, the Johnstone brothers had hoped to sell 250 boats. As 1977 drew to a close, J Boats had sold 750 boats at an average price of $8,500. (**Exhibit 2** provides a picture of the J/24.)

## J Boats, Inc. Today

By 1996, J Boats had achieved a strong competitive position in the recreational boating market. Most production boat builders who had dominated the market in the 1970s had gone out of business because of undistinguished products, poor profitability, or inability to weather economic downturns.

J Boats had followed the successful launch of the J/24 design with more than 25 new sailboat designs allowing the company to sell more than 8,500 boats ranging from 22′ to the newly introduced 52′ luxury cruiser—the J/160. Now the most popular keelboat in the world, more than 5,200 J/24s had been built by TPI (Tillotson-Pearson, Inc.) as well as eight other licensed builders around the world. No current large-scale competitor (e.g., Beneteau, Hunter, Catalina) had been able to build a comparable brand franchise associated with one-design performance and quality. **Exhibit 3** provides illustrative details of four of the eleven boat models currently in production.

The fundamentals of the business remained unchanged. J Boats designed and marketed the new boats, TPI (or a licensed international builder) produced each boat to exacting J Boat specifications, and a network of 65 independent dealers around the world (45 in the U.S. and 20 abroad) sold them into the local boating markets.

**Working with the Builder**    On each new boat design, J Boats worked in partnership with TPI to build a superior product at a price that would be attractive in the market. TPI priced the initial design specifications provided by J Boats using standard quantity and price estimates for materials, labor, and fully allocated overheads. Since initial cost estimates were inevitably too high, managers at J Boats and TPI then worked together to find ways to reduce manufacturing costs to ensure that the ultimate retail price for the boat would be competitive.

TPI then constructed hull and deck "plugs"—full size models—from plywood and fiberglass. Translating the design from paper to the plug took considerable skill and cost—approximately the same as the retail price of one boat (e.g., $100,000 for a 32′ boat). When completed and smooth, the plug was used to form a durable hull mold. The mold could then be used as the foundation to lay-up the composite fiberglass hull for each boat built in the factory.

J Boats was responsible for the cost of building the plug; TPI was responsible for the cost of building the production molds and maintaining them through the production life of each boat design. For each new boat model, plug costs were normally charged back to J Boats on a pro rata basis over 20 hulls. TPI assumed responsibility for all production as well as product warranty claims and repairs.

For each boat delivered to a dealer, TPI received the agreed manufacturing cost (standard materials, labor, and overhead) plus a fixed mark-up (set at 22% of full manufacturing cost)[1] to cover interest, administrative expenses, and profit. Building boats for J Boats accounted for approximately 40% of TPIs overall business. The remainder of its business came from the manufacture of fiberglass products such as windmill blades for electricity generation, subway cars, and high technology swimming pools used by professional athletes.

---

[1] Actual percentage figures have been disguised to preserve confidentiality.

**Marketing and Sales**  In addition to boat design and equipment specifications, J Boats assumed responsibility for:

- working with builders to ensure quality and adherence to specifications
- hiring and firing worldwide sales dealers
- advertising in national sailing periodicals and supporting national boat shows
- conducting sailing demonstrations, attending regattas, and referring customer inquiries to dealers in the customer's area
- assembling orders received from dealers and forwarding them to the builder
- assigning hull numbers and production slots
- providing technical support to owners and to owner class associations

For this work, J Boats earned a fee averaging over 10%[2] of the net price invoiced by TPI to the dealer. J Boats supplied dealers with suggested retail prices calculated to allow dealers to earn a margin in line with industry standards (typically 15% to 20%). After-sales service was provided directly to the customer by the dealer and/or TPI, with J Boats refereeing when necessary on disputed customer claims.

After the sale of each boat, J Boats stayed in touch with owners by means of Class Associations — owners groups which sponsored newsletters, regattas, and exchanged information about buying, selling, modifying, and enhancing the boats. For newer boat models which might initially have fewer than 100 owners, J Boats undertook to write the newsletters and do the mailings themselves. As more boats were sold and classes grew larger, administration of the class association was transferred to owners. J Boats ensured that one of the Johnstone's was represented on the class association executive board to monitor closely any proposed changes in racing rules that might affect specifications and allowable equipment when racing.

**The Founders**  Bob Johnstone explained the importance of product innovation to the success of the business,

> This is a crazy business. It is difficult to maintain volume. You must be very creative and fast moving with a new idea. You can buy good production, accounting, and sales people. But the key to life and death in our business — like any other — is new products and new product strategies.
>
> There seem to be two successful strategies in the boat business — like other recreational products. Either you go for the cheapest product, like Catalina and Hunter, and try to attract people who are entering the sport for the first time. Or you have the best performing brand and try to become the "Rossignol" of sailing. We are clearly in the second category. No one was pursuing this strategy in sailing before J Boats came along. Most builders were in an unprofitable middle ground in terms of pricing and quality, offering mostly styling changes each year.
>
> Our job is to get people excited about buying new boats and get dealers excited about selling them. Responsibilities for each of us flow with what needs to be done, not with formal titles. At the boat shows, we're all selling; in the summer, we're all sailing and showing off our new products. Unlike our competitors, our ads don't showcase the designer, or the builder, or even J Boats as our signature. Everything that we do and say is focused on a single boat identified by the *J* trademark — that's what the customer is really interested in and what we're trying to sell. Unfortunately, you can't reflect the value of the tremendous goodwill surrounding our brand on a balance sheet.

Following almost twenty successful years designing sailboats for J Boats, Rod Johnstone reflected on the design side of the business,

---

[2] Actual percentage figures have been disguised to preserve confidentiality.

Designing boats is part art and part science. Nothing is clear cut in boat design, especially when you are dealing with interactions of wind and water on a keel, rudder, mast, hull, and sails. But neither is boat design merely intuition—it is careful observation and synthesis of data, combined with experience. Over many years and boat designs, I have been able to predict how a boat will function after compensating for the difference in technical engineering standards and what a good builder is actually capable of doing.

Aesthetics are also very important—how a boat looks and feels. We have a simple rule, we will not create and build a boat that we would not want to own ourselves. It's that simple.

**Management Succession**    In 1987, Bob and Rod Johnstone turned over the day-to-day management of the business to their sons: Jeffrey (one of Rod's 3 sons) took over as president, and Stuart and Drake (two of Bob's 3 sons) took over as vice president and sales manager respectively. Jeff, Stuart, and Drake—all avid sailors like their fathers—had cofounded a successful sailing school known as J World. Leveraging the J Boat brand name, the school used J Boat sailboats to teach both novice sailing and advanced racing skills. With his father's flair for design, Rod's son Alan also joined the business to assume responsibility for product development and help in new boat designs. In 1990, Stuart moved to Europe to build the business on a more global scale. He later returned to the U.S. with a part-time role in the business, continuing to promote the brand and offer support at boat shows and regattas. When Drake left the business in 1993 to pursue a graduate degree in business, Jeff and Al managed operations alone for two years before hiring Jim Johnstone (Bob and Rod's nephew) as sales coordinator.

In 1996, Rod and Bob Johnstone (now 59 and 62 respectively) remained the sole shareholders of J Boats, Inc. Rod worked out of his home in Connecticut to supply fresh boat designs to the business. Bob, now based in Maine, focused on marketing, advertising, and new product strategies. Jeff, Jim, and Al ran the business day-to-day. All five members of the family met every month or so at J Boats Newport offices to discuss ongoing projects and business issues.

Jeff Johnstone (age 35), president of J Boats, described the business from his vantage point,

We have a very clear market niche. If you did a survey and asked people what is the first word that comes to mind when they hear J Boats—they would answer performance.

This is both an opportunity and a problem for us. Experienced sailors look for performance because they know that good design and ease of handling translate into both more safety and more fun. They understand our boats and the quality that we build in. But we have much more trouble in the cruising and entry-level markets. Cruisers think that we only build racing boats. For example, if we run an ad showing the interior of one of our new cruising boats, we typically get a very poor response. The racers are not interested and the cruisers have typecast us as builders of racing boats.

Similarly, novices don't understand the trade-offs between quality and price, nor do they have the experience to understand what performance means. Our boats are better built and cost more—we shoot to have our base price roughly equivalent to the "sail away" price of our competitors (e.g., their price includes sails and instruments). So, our boats typically cost 15% - 20% more.

I do worry that, if anything, we are innovating too much. Through the 1980s, we typically introduced one new model per year. Now we are introducing boats much more frequently—due in part to our desire to prevent competitors from capitalizing on our innovations. When we introduce a significant innovation like the retractable bow sprit in our 35' J/105, we want to get other size models to market quickly before competitors copy us.

## Day-to-Day Management and Control

**Project Management**    The energy of the five members of J Boats was primarily directed to new, ongoing design and marketing projects. As Bob Johnstone explained, "Each of us is currently devoting our efforts to one project. I'm focusing on marketing the J/42 which we launched last year; Rod is designing a new 30′ racing boat to push the envelope in terms of flat-out speed and performance; Al is working on the J/32 which will be an inexpensive entry boat for the cruising market; and Jeff is busy with customers interested in the J/160, our 52′ luxury yacht. Meanwhile, Jim is trying to keep the order book full."

In many ways, each boat design was treated as a separate company, with a defined life cycle. Each project went through concept discussions among the J Boats management team. Then, design drawings were prepared, studied, and modified; intensive targeted marketing campaigns were developed; start-up production was followed closely in the plant; and a full manufacturing line was eventually developed. Jeff explained,

> In the boating industry in general, a new boat model typically has a three year production cycle. Lots of splash in the first year of new product introduction, which spills over a bit into the second year. By the second year, dealers are putting lots of pressure on the builder to advertise because they are sitting on a lot of unsold stock. At the end of the second year, the builder may remodel or restyle the boat to try to inject some new life into it. The model is usually dead by the end of the third year.

> We tend to invest in our boat models for much longer—we hope to build boats that will be in demand five or ten years from now. We keep building as long as there is sufficient demand, although at a certain point there are enough boats in the used market to satisfy demand for any specific model. And one thing that you never want to do is to compete with yourself in the used boat market. Who wants to pay $80,000 for a new boat when they can buy a used one for $45,000?

Managers at J Boats spent a lot of time attempting to understand how population demographic trends were likely to impact the recreational boating market. The Johnstones reviewed commissioned studies on barriers to the wider acceptance of sailing as a sport (cost, time, and image), the effects of an aging population on boat demand (more leisure time, desire for family activities, and increased interest in active, athletic pursuits) and cost concerns (limited resources coupled with high expenses). Much of the internal debate within J Boats centered on how to deliver new and exciting products that could pull people into a family-centered lifetime activity. As Rod stated,

> I spend my nights worrying about what is possible in terms of sailboat performance and cost. What turns us on that's not available on the market? Who would want something like this? Would people buy it? We work really hard at attempting to identify who our customer is in every market . . . why he or she will be interested in our product and how much they will be willing to pay. It's very hard to predict the future in terms of peoples' time and dreams.

Monthly management meetings were highly interactive as team members contributed ideas and concerns about each of the active projects. Each member of the management team contributed ideas on design, marketing, and production based on their personal sailing experience and market intelligence they had picked up at trade shows, from customers and dealers, and at local regattas where they showcased their newest designs.

**Financial Planning**    Jeff Johnstone assumed primary responsibility for financial business planning. The major accounting tools that Jeff relied upon were

- production forecasts for each of the 11 current (and planned) boats in production (see **Exhibit 4**)
- cash flow projections based on estimated fee revenue from builders and planned design, marketing, and administrative expenses
- analysis of tooling costs (i.e., building plugs and production molds) for new production models
- quarterly income statement and balance sheet (see **Exhibit 5**)

Boat building was inherently a cyclical business. In good times, the recreational boating market was typically strong, but in lean times people postponed discretionary leisure purchases. Furthermore, during each year there was significant uncertainty about how many customer orders would be received and how many boats of each model should be built for dealer inventories. Cash flow could be severely pinched as cash receipts lagged production.

Customers were required to make a 5% deposit at the time they placed an order. Three to six months later, when a boat was built and ready to be shipped, the customer was required to pay the balance due. The dealer remitted this money—net of dealer sales commission—to TPI. From these funds, TPI then paid J Boats its fee. Customers could cancel orders up to three weeks before the start of production without penalty.

Acutely aware of the cash flow constraints of a cyclical business, Jeff Johnstone had restructured the cash flows so that customer deposits in excess of those required by the builder would be paid directly to J Boats. Only when the boat was completed and shipped, would the deposit—recorded in J Boats' accounts as a liability—be deducted from the fee revenue paid by TPI to J Boats. But, as Jeff Johnstone admitted,

> Financial planning is our weak point. We get so caught up on each of our projects, that it's been frustrating to not be able to step back each week to look at strategy and planning—especially from a financial perspective. We get really pumped up about the creative, entrepreneurial side, but we're not good at coming up with solid budget numbers and running the business based on those numbers. We run the business side by the seat of our pants.
>
> In our monthly meetings, we are very project oriented. We all get involved in the details. What should the seatback distance be? Which equipment should be standard and which should be optional? What size winches should we put on? We don't spend enough time taking a hard look at the numbers. We assume that if the product succeeds, the numbers will work out.

**Cost Control**     The informal relationships with TPI had served J Boats well. But they were not without tensions. The relationship was based on trust—the original agreement (**Exhibit 1**) was testament to that. As Jeff and Alan discussed,

> TPI passes their cost right back to us. After we agree on a price for a particular boat, they do not share either unexpected efficiencies or cost overruns with us. Each part of their operation has a supervisor who has an understandable desire to set standard costs to make sure that their department comes in under budget. We really need to stay on top of this detail stuff. We find, for example, that if we want to add a hand rail to a design, TPI tells us that it will cost $50 and three hours labor. If we come back nine months later and say that we want to eliminate the same hand rail, they want to take out $50 material cost and only one hour of labor.
>
> It becomes essential to have a good understanding of the politics and how things work at the plant. We often have to get everyone around a table—purchasing, Everett, heads of production and QC, and key manufacturing guys—to go through the economics with them, so that they understand how their cost will impact customer acceptance and the ultimate sales potential of a particular boat. At the end of the day, if they want to sell our boats, they have to bring in reasonable pricing.
>
> Staying on top of cost is really important. That's why you see most boat builders driving Chevrolet's instead of BMWs. Most builders have no idea what their costs are. That can cause us problems when a builder like C&C comes into the market with a boat that is priced too low. He's out of busi-

ness in a couple of years, but it creates false expectations in the market about what a boat should cost.

**Relationship with Dealers**    Similar issues were common in relationships with dealers, who were the prime contact for current and potential owners of J Boat products. As Bob Johnstone stated,

> If we had more aggressive, focused dealers, we could be three or four times bigger. A good example is J Boats Chesapeake, which links in with a J World sailing school so that people learn about performance and our boats. This dealership showcases various models of our boats—and only J Boats, organizes cruises and regattas for owners and potential owners, manages a "J Club" time-share program that permits people to sail before owning, and generates a lot of interest (and sales). By contrast, the average dealer does not have much in stock to show a customer, doesn't attempt to generate the excitement that will attract new sailors, and carries a number of competing brands in an attempt to be "all things to all people."

## Decisions

On a spring day in 1996, Jeffrey Johnstone, Al Johnstone, and Jim Johnstone were actively at work in their second floor offices on Newport's Thames Street. Jeffrey Johnstone was on the telephone with the purchasing managers at TPI. At issue were changes to port cover finishes on the seventh hull of the new J/160—flagship of the new line of high performance sprit boats.

Next door, Alan was immersed in final details of the new J/32. Due to be launched in two months time, this was the first J Boat whose lines were not drawn by his father, Rodney. Alan had designed this boat to offer an entry level yacht in the small cruiser market. Attempting to keep the introductory pricing below $100,000, Alan had been working carefully with TPI to select hardware and equipment suppliers which could offer satisfactory quality at lower prices.

Jim Johnstone was on the telephone with a dealer who was inquiring when he could promise a potential customer delivery on a new J/105. Jim looked at the chart on his wall which showed all J Boat models currently in production, available hull numbers, and lead times. Jim informed the dealer that production was sold out through August. The best that he could do would be to promise late August delivery of hull #157.

Later that morning, Rod and Bob would arrive for one of their monthly board meetings. Jeff Johnstone looked over the agenda for the meeting. Three projects would absorb most of their time: the new J/160 and J/32 which were now in start-up production, and the early design details of the J/100 concept boat. In addition, several issues would require resolution:

1. Tooling Costs—The tooling costs (i.e., building the hull plugs) for the J/160 and J/32 had exceeded $350,000. In the past, these costs had been expensed as incurred. Jeff was considering capitalizing this amount and writing it off over the expected life of the design. He wondered if doing this was one way to get some of the intangible value of the business on to the balance sheet.

2. Licensing—A well-known nautical clothing manufacturer had introduced a line of clothing which featured J Boats proprietary *J* logo. They were advertising heavily in a variety of national sailing and fashion magazines without any attempt at securing a licensing agreement. In the past, J Boats had informally allowed other companies to use their logo in apparel and gift items if it was done in good taste and advertisements were placed in J Boat class magazines. Jeff wondered what action to take against the national clothier and how to capture the value of the *J* trademark that was being used by other smaller businesses without permission.

3.  Discontinuing the J/92 — TPI was again putting pressure on J Boats to reduce the number of active models to concentrate volume in fewer designs and reduce production switch over costs. Sales of the J/92 had been ebbing as competitors introduced boats with similar features. The economics for TPI were clear — discontinuing the model would avoid both the TPI costs of maintaining the mold and the cost of setting up production to build just a few boats. On the other hand, existing owners interested in growing the class association would be upset if J Boats was no longer willing to build J/92s.

As 1996 drew to a close, J Boats had completed its twentieth year in the recreational boating industry. The future looked bright, but all five members of the company realized the desirability of an orderly management succession as the business was handed over to the next generation. Additionally, the Johnstones wondered if and how the company should anticipate an altered business relationship with another builder in the event that TPI were sold when Everett Pearson retired in the next few years. In thinking about the future, several issues would require careful consideration:

*   How could J Boats create additional value by leveraging its brand franchise?
*   Should the successful working relationship with TPI be formalized? If so, how?
*   Would an infusion of capital by new investors allow J Boats to create dealer franchises modeled on the success of J Boats Chesapeake?
*   How could J Boats' rudimentary financial planning and reporting be recast to fully reflect and capture the value of the brand franchise that the Johnstones had built over twenty years?
*   What critical performance indicators should the Johnstones monitor to ensure the success of their strategy?

Looking back over twenty years, Rodney Johnstone summed up "success" as the answer to three questions:

1.  Did we make any money?
2.  Did we create something that we are proud of?
3.  Did we have fun doing it?

His brother Bob stated simply, "Over the past twenty years, we've had a gas!"

**EXHIBIT 1**   **Contract with Builder Tillotson Pearson, Inc.**

October 17, 1977

TO: Robert L. Johnstone          Everett Pearson
    J BOATS, INC.,                TILLOTSON PEARSON, INC.

The purpose of this memorandum is:

1. To outline and formalize the "modus operandi" of a relationship which to this point has been extremely successful. Our intent is to insure the continued success and profitability of both TILLOTSON PEARSON as a builder and J BOATS, INC. as the exclusive marketer and designer of the J/24 and other boats.

2. J BOATS is responsible at its expense for boat design, selection and management of dealers worldwide, order entry detail and priority advertising, promotion, marketing strategy, and the J/24 Class Association.

3. TILLOTSON PEARSON is responsible at its expense for tooling, boat construction, providing production facilities and its financing, employee selection and training, and maintenance of mutually agreed upon quality standards, optimum materials purchasing efficiencies, shipping and delivery.

4. J BOATS and TILLOTSON PEARSON work together on determining price/value trade-offs on boat price, options, and accessories. Consequently, these prices are established by mutual consent.

5. J BOATS receives deposits from dealers and credits TILLOTSON PEARSON with the balance beyond the $500 per boat royalty (J/24) established. If the deposit is received by TILLOTSON PEARSON, or if no deposit is received, then TILLOTSON PEARSON will credit J Boats with the $500 per boat royalty. Boats are sold with certified check in advance, or COD via bonded commercial carrier with certified check payment prior to delivery to customer upon arrival. Variations from this procedure are cleared through TILLOTSON PEARSON by dealers in advance of boat delivery. Consequently, TILLOTSON PEARSON assumes the risk of non-collection.

6. TILLOTSON PEARSON agrees to make every attempt to produce the J/24's at a rate consistent with the results of J BOATS' sales effort, both parties realizing there will be peaks and valleys in demand; and the aim will be to arrive at a production level that can be reasonably uniform over an extended period of time. J BOATS agrees to make every attempt to generate a market demand, giving TILLOTSON PEARSON adequate notice of any impending slow-down so that work force adjustments can be made.

7. TILLOTSON PEARSON is responsible for warranty work and manufacturer's liability and agrees to maintain product liability insurance to cover the latter in amounts agreeable to both parties. However, it should be pointed out that there is no insurance available for design errors. TILLOTSON PEARSON agrees to include J BOATS as an additional insured and will provide J BOATS with evidence of such coverage.

8. J BOATS is the proprietor of the J/24 design. TILLOTSON PEARSON has made substantial investment in time, money, and manufacturing facilities to produce the J/24 and hopefully other J BOAT models, and J BOATS has made substantial investment in sales efforts and design and in advertising. The effort has been and it is hoped will continue to be a cooperative effort

*Exhibit 1   Continued*

fair to each party in every way. It is TILLOTSON PEARSON's desire and intent to be the sole producer of this product, committing whatever facilities and finances are necessary to do the job.

9. If J BOATS for some reason finds TILLOTSON PEARSON to be an unsatisfactory supplier and wants to make some other arrangements for producing the boats, they will give TILLOTSON PEARSON 180 days' notice before reducing or terminating production, and TILLOTSON PEARSON agrees to sell tooling for the J/24 and all special production equipment to J BOATS at total cost plus 20%, and if TILLOTSON PEARSON should for any reason want to discontinue making the product, the same conditions would apply. See Note (1) below.

10. If there are locations that TILLOTSON PEARSON cannot adequately service from its present facilities, it will provide facilities in other agreed locations or assist in every way possible on a reasonable cost basis whoever is selected to build the boats in any new location.

11. TILLOTSON PEARSON may not assign this agreement or sub-contract to build J BOATS designs to others without the written approval of J BOATS. Nor will TILLOTSON PEARSON modify the construction or equipment provided and agreed upon without first obtaining the approval of J BOATS.

12. J BOATS agrees that it will not contract similar designs to other builders without first allowing TILLOTSON PEARSON the opportunity to be the builder. And, TILLOTSON PEARSON agrees that it will not build sailboat designs which, in the opinion of J BOATS, are in competition with J BOATS, particularly in the 20 to 35 foot range, without first obtaining the written consent of J BOATS.

13. The above should relieve any anxieties that either party may have about our very promising venture. TILLOTSON PEARSON is concerned with what J BOATS might do with marketing or design leverage for other builders who are anxious to duplicate the J/24 success. J BOATS is concerned about capricious or opportunistic pricing, cost reduction which adversely affects quality, or building agreements with competitors. Continued mutual growth can only come from a concentrated and undistracted effort on behalf of both parties, operating with the mutual confidence that has existed to date.

14. This replaces any previous agreement, written or oral, on the subject between J BOATS, INC., Rodney S. Johnstone, Robert L. Johnstone, and Everett Pearson. When signed by both parties, this constitutes a binding agreement. Please sign and return one copy.

NOTE    (1): The cost of the master plugs or any one complete set of tooling used to manufacture a boat and its component parts shall not exceed the retail selling price of one standard boat, less sails.

Agreement signed this _____2nd_____ day of ____November____ 1977.

Robert L. Johnstone (signed)                    Everett A. Pearson (signed)
        J BOATS, INC.                              TILLOTSON PEARSON, INC.

**EXHIBIT 2** International J/24, The World's Most Popular One-Design Keelboat, Selected for the I.Y.R.U. Nations Cup and the Choice for Sailing Fun by More Than 50,000 Sailors of All Ages.

**EXHIBIT 3   Sample of Boats Currently in Production**

# International J/24

The most popular keelboat class worldwide, with more than 50,000 people sailing in 5,000+ boats in over 100 fleets in more than 30 countries. The J/24's success is its versatility. Equipped with offshore hatches and lifelines, the whole family can get involved. Four berths, cooler, sink, and place for a stove, it's a pocket cruiser or world-class racer.

| | |
|---|---|
| LOA | 24'0" |
| LWL | 20'0" |
| Beam | 8'11" |
| Draft | 4'0" |
| Displacement | 3,100 lbs. |
| Sail area (total) | 261 sq. ft. |

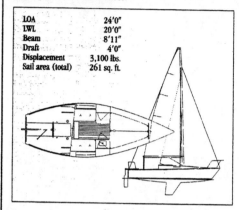

# J/92

At Sail Expo '93, *Sailing World* Magazine's panel of experts and designers awarded the J/92 "Overall Boat of the Year" among all sailboats including multi-hulls. Subscribers came to the same conclusion for the first time in history, making the J/92 the "Reader's Choice." If you're looking for a 30-footer, J/92 will bring you years of sailing joy.

| | |
|---|---|
| LOA | 30'0" |
| LWL | 25'10" |
| Beam | 10'0" |
| Draft-Standard/Shoal | |
| | 5'11"/4'11" |
| Displacement | 5,500 lbs. |
| Ballast | 2,275 lbs. |
| Sail area (total) | 470 sq. ft. |
| Auxiliary | 9 H.P. |

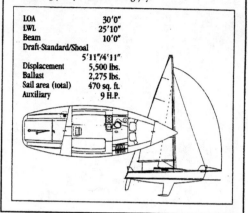

# J/105

Now numbering more than 100 with a one-design class organization, the J/105 is superb. Ever see a husband and wife in their 50s sail a 35-footer under spinnaker through a Wood's Hole (Massachusetts) passage against the current, gybing three times on the narrow doglegs among the rocks, swirling eddies, tugs, ferries, and other summer traffic?

| | |
|---|---|
| LOA | 34'6" |
| LWL | 29'6" |
| Beam | 11'0" |
| Draft-Standard/Shoal | |
| | 6'6"/5'6" |
| Displacement | 7,750 lbs. |
| Ballast | 3,400 lbs. |
| Sail area (total) | 577 sq. ft. |
| Auxiliary | 20 H.P. |

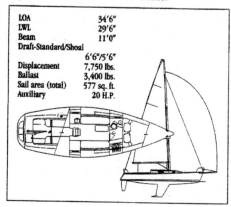

# J/160

**NEW!**

The J/160 is the ultimate in a passagemaking cruiser, with a comfortable three-stateroom layout and capabilities of 7.9 knot speeds upwind with VMGs of 6.1 knots under small jib. Equipped with a 9-foot-long retractable carbon-fiber sprit for asymmetric spinnakers and optional carbon rig, the J/160 will do 9 knots, wind or not.

| | |
|---|---|
| LOA | 52'7" |
| LWL | 46'5" |
| Beam | 14'5" |
| Draft-Standard/Shoal | |
| | 8'8"/6'9" |
| Displacement | 26,000 lbs. |
| Ballast | 11,000 lbs. |
| Sail area (total) | 1,376 sq. ft. |
| Auxiliary | 88 H.P. |

| | |
|---|---|
| Designer | Rod Johnstone |

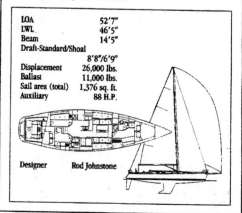

**EXHIBIT 4    1996 Production Forecast**
**As at April 1996**

| J/BOAT MODEL | SOLD IN 1995 | 1996 | | |
| --- | --- | --- | --- | --- |
| | | PROJECTED | SOLD TO DATE | NEED TO SELL |
| J/22 | 20 | 30 | 20 | 10 |
| J/24 | 20 | 10 | 5 | 5 |
| J/80 | 34 | 35 | 21 | 14 |
| J/92 | 10 | 0 | 0 | 0 |
| J/32 | 0 | 20 | 9 | 11 |
| J/100 | 0 | 5 | 0 | 5 |
| J/105 | 34 | 45 | 30 | 15 |
| J/110 | 10 | 5 | 5 | 0 |
| J/120 | 23 | 25 | 18 | 7 |
| J/42 | 10 | 15 | 12 | 3 |
| J/130 | 11 | 6 | 2 | 4 |
| J/160 | 2 | 10 | 10 | 0 |

*Note: Actual figures have been disguised to preserve confidentiality.*

---

### EXHIBIT 5   J Boats, Inc., 1996 Financial Statement Structure

**Balance Sheet Categories:**

| *Assets* | | *Liabilities & Equity* | |
|---|---|---|---|
| Cash | 6% | Accounts payable | 11% |
| Accounts receivable | 18 | Customer deposits | 15 |
| Inventory—Demonstrator boats | 67 | Accrued expenses | 7 |
| Furniture and equipment | 9 | Common stock | 20 |
| | | Retained earnings | 47 |
| | 100% | | 100% |

**Income Statement Categories:**

Revenue:

| | |
|---|---|
| Royalties from TPI | 51% |
| Royalties from international builders | 19 |
| Other | 4 |
| Sales of demonstrator boats | 26 |
| | 100 |

Expenses:

| | |
|---|---|
| Tooling costs | 17 |
| Cost of demonstrator boats sold | 23 |
| International royalty expenses | 4 |
| Salaries, wages, and benefits | 18 |
| Advertising | 6 |
| Boatshow expenses and promotions | 5 |
| Travel | 3 |
| Office, general, and administrative expenses | 5 |
| Interest expense | 1 |
| | 82 |
| Net Income before tax | 18% |

*Note: All figures have been disguised to preserve confidentiality.*

# CASE 3   MCI Communications: Planning for the 1990s

I've lived in a lot of companies that try bottom-up strategic planning, and it's hell. It always fails. We do it strictly top-down at MCI. The people with the vision and the comprehensive knowledge of the business are the only ones with a broad enough perspective to determine company strategy. Management buy-in is a critical step in the process, but it is just as important that we go in there with a plan and that we run the meetings. We are the ones who are always focused on the longer term and that is where the focus must be maintained when discussing strategy.

These words were spoken by Orville Wright, vice chairman and co-CEO of MCI Communications Corporation. By the fall of 1989, Orville Wright and Bill McGowan, MCI's founder, chairman, and co-CEO, presided over the second largest U.S. carrier in the $50 billion-a-year long-distance communications market. The corporation provided an expanding array of voice and data transmission services domestically and abroad. From 1980 to 1989, MCI's revenues grew from $234 million to over $6.5 billion, while its earnings increased more than 30-fold, from under $19 million to over $600 million. **Exhibit 1** provides an historical summary of the company's financial performance and **Exhibit 2** highlights non-financial measures of growth (i.e., market share, head count, and installed capacity).

This case describes the evolution of strategic planning at MCI during the 1980s and discusses top management's philosophy with regard to that process.

## Strategy Setting at MCI

**The Early 1980s**   Since the company's founding in 1968, MCI had evolved through several distinct "business lives." Each phase centered around a different top priority that engaged the core management team in an almost single-minded fashion. The early business goals tended to be extremely specific and relatively short term. They included: lobbying for a license to compete with the AT&T monopoly, raising venture capital to build a network, litigating against AT&T to receive interconnections, lobbying for FCC (Federal Communications Commission) approval of new service offerings, and increasing market share in the traditional domestic long distance market to raise network utilization to an affordable level. Throughout the 1960s and 1970s, the company's survival was uncertain, forcing MCI's leaders to take a relatively short-term, opportunistic approach to management.

In the early 1980s, even as MCI reached a more comfortable financial position, conventional strategic planning activities were still non-existent. The first focus on strategy came in 1981 with the hiring of Brian Thompson as Senior Vice President of Corporate Development. His first task was to push the company's planning horizon out into the future.

When Thompson hired MCI's first director of strategic planning, he told the new director that "if you ever write a strategic plan, you will be fired." At the time, the development of written, detailed strategic plans was considered antithetical to the company's culture and management style. MCI's top management did not like formal systems and they did not like to put things in writing. They developed and managed their strategy on a daily basis. The strategy and operating budgets were skeletal and simple. Because of the extremely rapid pace of change in the industry—in terms of both regulatory developments and technological advancements—detailed annual planning and multi-year strategic planning were considered useless exercises. Management believed that such activities would actually be detrimental to one of MCI's main competitive advantages: its ability to make decisions in a changing environment and act on them more quickly than anyone else.

CEO Bill McGowan and Orville Wright (President and Chief Operating Officer during the mid 1980s) continually discussed MCI's future and personally set MCI's strategic direction, adjusting it on an ad hoc basis as they identified new developments and opportunities in the market. Bill McGowan was the charismatic, tenaciously optimistic visionary who set the company's course; Orville Wright played a critical role in filling in the detail in McGowan's vision and translating it into a set of guidelines for the rest of the organization. Both men were involved in enough of the major operating decisions to refine the vision and personally guide its achievement. The two-man team was assisted by a small core of hand-picked managers who had worked with McGowan long enough and closely enough to understand his vision and appreciate his style.

MCI's informal and sometimes chaotic management style and its leaders' opportunistic approach to strategy worked phenomenally well throughout the 1970s and the first half of the 1980s. Frequent management meetings seemed to provide the necessary level of communication and coordination among the corporate staff and the top line managers.

**1984: Decentralization**   In 1984, in an effort to bring MCI closer to its customers and to manage its local interconnection costs, top management divided MCI into 7 business units along the exact geographic lines of the newly independent regional Bell operating companies.[1] To achieve the complete decentralization that they sought, top management transferred almost all functions from headquarters to the field and gave the seven new division presidents absolute control. McGowan filled the new top posts with members of his core headquarters management team—regardless of their backgrounds and management experience. This assured that the new small, stand-alone MCI businesses would be run by the best qualified individuals, those with the broadest understanding of McGowan's vision. But the decentralization also left virtually no senior management at headquarters.

Throughout the end of 1984 and all of 1985, the decentralization gradually stretched MCI's unstructured system to its limits. The geographic distance put an end to the frequent management meetings (which were replaced by regular electronic mail correspondence) and reduced the level of informal communications among MCI's best brains and key decision makers. Moreover, field managers were given so much autonomy that redundancies in effort and inconsistencies in service offerings began to emerge across business units. Two other factors magnified the control and communications problems: (1) Wright's retirement in late 1985 (he remained vice chairman of the board), and (2) MCI's sheer size. At the end of 1985, MCI employed more than 12,000 people, versus 6,300 just three years earlier.

---

[1] In August 1982, based on antitrust violations, the Justice Department ordered AT&T to divest the regional Bell operating companies. The divestiture became effective on January 1, 1984. Starting in 1984, MCI had to negotiate with all seven "Baby Bells" independently, as their customer, for local interconnection to its own residential and commercial customers.

**1986 and Early 1987: Crisis**    In the fall of 1986, a bundle of problems befell the company all at once. In the third quarter of 1986, revenues declined for the first time and earnings dwindled to almost nothing. By the fourth quarter, MCI management laid off 15% of its staff and took a large write down, resulting in a fourth quarter loss per share of $.09.[2] Meanwhile, the stock price plummeted from its January high of $13.30 to $6.00 per share and the company took on an additional $1 billion in long term debt (bringing the year-end total to $2.8 billion) to weather the storm. To make matters worse, McGowan suffered a heart attack in December 1986 and underwent a heart transplant in April 1987. He did not return full-time until September. MCI's good fortune appeared to have run its course. The resulting trauma brought into question MCI's entire strategic direction, its management systems, and its financial viability.

In McGowan's absence, Orville returned from semi-retirement to run the business. By December 1986, it was clear to both top management and the rank and file that MCI's current strategy, whether it was articulated or not, was not working. (See **Exhibit 1.**)

**1987: The Beginning of Formal Strategy Setting**    Top management considered Orville Wright to be the key person in transforming the role of strategy at MCI. Orville recalled his thoughts and the steps he took in 1987, following McGowan's heart attack:

At the beginning of 1987, when I came back full time as acting-CEO, I sensed that management no longer had a uniform view of where the company was headed. The extreme decentralization had confused managers and Bill's heart attack had demoralized them. Employees seriously doubted whether top management knew where they were heading. In fact, the employee survey done in 1986 specifically identified employees' discomfort with the planning process and our apparent lack of direction. I decided that we had to re-examine the soul and direction of the company and put a strategy in writing. This step was a big deal for a company that had always thrived on ambivalence.

We did a very detailed top to bottom industry analysis and asked some very difficult questions: are we in the right business? . . . should we sell it? . . . milk it? . . . become a niche player? . . . and so on. From January through May of 1987, I spent a good 40 to 50 hours with the Management Committee and the director of Corporate Development. [At the time, the Management Committee, or "MC," consisted of the CEO, Chief Operating Officer Bert Roberts and MCI's three executive vice presidents.] Between our meetings, the Corporate Development staff did most of the research, forecasting, and other analytical work. By May, after several heated arguments, the Management Committee put a 1988–92 strategy on paper. The strong consensus and commitment that formed among the five of us proved invaluable later on, when we presented the plan to the rest of the organization.

In June and July, we held three full-day meetings with the top twenty-three people in the company which included the MC, division presidents, and all senior vice presidents. The Management Committee presented our draft plan to the seven division presidents and all the senior vice presidents and opened up the floor for discussion. Ideas and opinions were thrown around and there was a lot of heated arguing. People were really knocking heads.

This was the first time that top line management was brought in on the strategy setting process. I headed the meetings and maintained control over the discussions, but I encouraged managers to present their ideas and arguments. The tone was "speak now or forever hold your peace."

We finally reached a general consensus among the group of twenty-three and everyone eventually committed to one direction for the company. It's important to note that we did not actually modify our original strategy in any significant way. The five of us on the Committee—particularly

---

[2] The 1986 losses were due primarily to an asset write-down of over $480 million and additional restructuring costs of $150 million, both booked in December of 1986.

Bert—were strongly committed to the 1988 plan and argued vehemently in its defense, and we had the knowledge and analyses to support our arguments.

I don't think the meetings would have been as effective if Bill had been around, because people were so used to his setting the firm's direction without soliciting their input. Bill was very used to that as well. The positive results of that first series of meetings helped me to persuade Bill of the value of formal management buy-in. We had never sought it before.

After the series of meetings, the Corporate Development staff, with the MC's final approval, summarized the agreed-upon strategy in a 10-page written report. In addition to a one-page summary of corporate strategy, the report separately addressed functional strategies for marketing, finance, network/support, and public policy. **Exhibit 3** represents the summary page of the report. The report's quantitative goals for 1988 (the report projected financials out through 1992) served as input to the annual business plan and budget, which were developed in the fall of 1987. Beyond providing extremely ambitious growth targets for particular market segments and network usage, however, the strategy did not guide the budgeting process; its elements were too broad and "too positive" to aid managers in prioritizing specific expenditures and opportunities. In the words of one manager, "I'm not concerned with the ambiguity in the strategy. I'm used to dealing with all 'priority-ones.'"

After the strategy was finalized, Chief Operating Officer Roberts began to promote it aggressively through an elaborate communications campaign designed to reach both internal and external constituencies. He created a video called "Strategic Direction" (management still disliked the word "plan" because it implied inflexibility). The video tapes were circulated throughout the company and supplemented with both letters to employees and speeches made by Bert. The objectives of the aggressive communication campaign were to (1) assure employees that top management had a strategy; (2) to win rank and file commitment to that strategy; and (3) to show the linkage between the corporate strategy and individuals' own performance objectives. The result was the revival of MCI's "can-do" underdog culture.

**1988 and 1989: The Evolution of the Strategy Setting Process** Although the 1987 process described above was not considered the beginning of an annual strategic planning program, the process was repeated in 1988. The content as well as the process underwent little change other than becoming slightly more specific.

In the beginning of 1989, Orville Wright and Executive Vice President Brian Thompson (who oversaw the development and planning functions at that time) modified the strategy setting process for 1990. The rationale for the change was based on two premises: first, the minimal change in strategy that occurred from 1987 to 1988 indicated that a zero-based process was excessive, at least for the time being; and second, the rapid pace of MCI's expansion suggested that more input from Marketing and division management would be beneficial.

In the previous two years, the Corporate Development staff had prepared and presented the Management Committee's draft strategy without formal input in advance from individuals outside the MC. In February 1989, however, the MC decided on an issue-oriented approach to strategy setting. Wright and Thompson drew up a short list of what they considered the most important strategic issues. They then appointed line management task forces—led by the division presidents—to develop position papers on each issue.

From February through April 1989, the Corporate Development staff assisted the 8 or 10 task forces in their research efforts but was not responsible for composing their recommendations. In the late spring, the task forces presented their findings and recommendations to the MC. The Committee and the Corporate Development staff then selectively incorporated those findings into their own draft of the corporate strategy. Although the MC draft rejected the recommendations of some of the task forces, the Committee had all of the task force leaders present their findings at the June meeting and opened the floor for discussion. The size of the June sessions—which was still comprised of the MC, the seven division presidents, and all senior vice presidents—had grown to nearly thirty people. (See **Exhibit 4**)

The primary purpose of the June meetings remained the same: to foster a sense of participation and team spirit and to get management buy-in on the MC's strategic plan. Orville again encouraged managers to challenge the plan, so that differences could be resolved before the strategy was worked into the annual business plan and before it was communicated to the rest of the organization. As in the previous two years, the MC did not revise their draft in any significant way during the management discussions. But because various division presidents and functional senior vice presidents had each already had input into specific parts of the plan, they felt a much stronger sense of involvement and ownership than they had in the past. All managers interviewed by the case writers—at corporate and division levels—described the 1989 strategy setting effort as a substantial improvement over 1987 and 1988: controversial issues were discussed more effectively; non-MC executives were more involved; and the resultant strategy, summarized in a 12-page report, was more specific. **Exhibit 5** represents the strategy as summarized for the multi-media internal communications campaign. Again, the longer confidential version addressed the main functions individually.

**Top Management's Philosophy and Observations**   Several members of top management shared their thoughts on Orville Wright's top-down philosophy and MCI's strategy setting process:

Bert Roberts, Chief Operating Officer:

> In 1989, we knew the general strategic direction to follow, but we needed to better refine our existing strategy in a few key issue areas. Task Forces were effective in addressing the issues, because we needed the personal involvement of our senior line managers. They knew the issues best and they were responsible for making the strategies work. However, it is important that the top management group make the final decision on including Task Force recommendations in the strategy. Top down direction at the broad strategy level is absolutely critical.

Dan Akerson, Executive Vice President and Chief Financial Officer:

> I agree with Bert about the value of top-down strategic planning. Bottom-up sounds great for public relations and for recruiting MBAs, but it doesn't work that well from a practical point of view. The strategic planning process is a very closely held process in our company. The strategic issues and concerns were identified by the Corporate Development staff in conjunction with the Management Committee. Subsequently, key line and staff senior management were asked to work on the identified issues for general discussion and modification at the general strategy session.
>
> The general strategy sessions are critical for a couple of reasons: First, to solicit input from a range of functions and people; and, second, to get "buy in" by the senior management of the company. Generally, there are only minor modifications to the tactics underlying the identified strategic issues.

Although this is a top-down process, we believe that once the strategy has been agreed upon, it should be openly communicated to our employees and shareholders. In fact, we stated our corporate goals in the 1987 Annual Report. This may be a bit too open in that it gives an awful lot of insight to our competitors; but then, we've always erred on the side of candor. Our employees particularly appreciate the openness which I think binds us all to a common cause.

### Dick Liebhaber, Executive Vice President:

A strategic plan should not be the result of something, it should be what we want to happen. Complete consensus is not absolutely necessary. The objective of the June sessions is for everyone simply to understand what we're trying to do. If one of my subordinates does not agree, well, that's interesting. I'll listen. But if I'm not persuaded, he may have a problem. I'm talking about the broad picture now. My managers must decide for themselves *how* to achieve our goals. This organization still thrives on diversity and risk takers. A lot of the prioritizing happens after the broad strategy is set, when we are developing the annual business plan each fall and even during the year. Our strategy is broad enough to accommodate changes in the business plan.

### Jeff Ganek, Director of Corporate Development:

On a scale of 1 to 100, with 100 being completely top down, our strategic plan would score about 90. But as Orville has told you, it is critical to hold open meetings with top line management and hear out their views. Thanks to those meetings, line management believes their role in strategy setting relative to the role of the Corporate Development staff is very large. That perception makes it easier to get them to buy-in. The value of the new more formal process is in the verbal exchange it triggers, not the ultimate document. We're a very verbal company.

MCI is a combination of top down direction and decentralized decision-making. So, although the strategic plan is extremely top down, it is important to realize that it is not a bible that answers all of a manager's questions, and it does not eliminate the need to make difficult decisions on a daily basis. There are contradictions intentionally built in to the plan. Conflicting claims on resources, for example, force managers to make trade-offs all the time. The strategy does not tell managers what not to do; the language is all positive and it's very ambitious.

### Ron Spears, Midwest Division President, provided a perspective from outside corporate headquarters:

Top managers at the operating divisions have always had tremendous leeway on how the business is run day-to-day and month-to-month. But up through 1986, the few truly strategic decisions were made by Orville Wright and Bill McGowan, usually based on McGowan's instincts. That was appropriate, because we were a much smaller company with a very simple goal: get as big as possible as fast as possible.

In 1987, when Bill was recovering from his heart attack, Orville called the first strategy meetings. They were more than an annual strategic planning exercise. We were there to decide if we were in the right business. Maybe it took 25 of us to make up for one Bill McGowan in answering the really big questions.

Orville came in to that first meeting with a bunch of questions and assumptions, not answers. So we had real input for the first time. I think that when Bill heard about the strategy session, he probably thought it was a waste of time. Even the second time round, in 1988, it was clear to me that Bill didn't see too much value in the process.

The most recent strategy sessions this past summer were the best ever. The process had really improved, primarily because of the "pre-session" Orville held in March. At that meeting, we formed issue-based task forces and then during the spring worked with Corporate Development to prepare for the big June meeting. Due to the task forces, there was more input from outside of corporate. We had better quality material to discuss. But, at the end of the day, if Bill and Bert didn't agree with you, you could still get knee-capped.

With a room full of strong personalities, getting buy-in is a painful process. It means being prepared to listen to different views and different numbers. We're not necessarily a great consensus company. But we get general agreement around the major issues with a healthy level of confrontation.

I think the strategy sessions, especially the task force work, are useful drills. But, in my mind, to improve the process, we need another session of just the Management Committee and division presidents—about 15 people—before or after the whole group of 35 meets. With all the senior vice presidents and staff people present, there are just too many people in the room to hold a manageable open discussion. Some of them are very functionally oriented anyway, so they don't have an opinion on 75% of the issues outside their function. Also, the group will probably reach 40 people this June [1990]. In a group that large, you can't talk about sensitive topics such as specific acquisition plans because of confidentiality concerns. We need a forum for a more in-depth discussion of strategy.

Everything Bill preached 10 years ago came true—the role of information technology, globalization, and so on. The implications of what he has said are now pretty clear to us. We have built a cadre of senior managers that really understand what MCI can become. The big questions now are the "how." We may not all have Bill's instinct and sense of timing, but we can make the calls. Now that the general strategic direction has been set by 3 or 4 people, there are about 15 or 20 of us involved in the strategic thought process and specifics. We used to say people are important at MCI, and now we really believe it.

**Strategy-Setting for the 1990s**  No one in top management was certain of how their strategy setting process would look several years down the road. In fact, they did not give it much thought because they had no interest in institutionalizing management procedures. Those interviewed by the case writers still did not consider the three-year-old planning process an annual event.

In January 1990, however, corporate management began to reevaluate the process followed in 1989 in order to decide what modifications to make in MCI's strategy-setting process for 1991. Jeff Ganek and Executive Vice President Brian Thompson had already met with Orville Wright and Bert Roberts on several occasions to explore options. Thompson, who had lead responsibility for the 1990 cycle, explained his concerns:

In 1990, MCI faces a changing environment and new challenges. With revenues of more than $7 billion and a strong financial base, MCI is now a leading, worldwide provider of telecommunications services. Our market is globalizing and customers are becoming increasingly sophisticated. Competition remains intense. All competitors are deploying similar technologies, which are evolving quickly.

These trends may call for a very substantial change in our strategy. MCI must understand what it will take to be cost competitive in the 1990s. And, we must consider how we can differentiate MCI from the competition in the future.

Our current planning process is not necessarily designed to produce such changes. In the past three years, the process has really been one of refining an existing strategy. It worked wonderfully—it was exactly what we needed.

MCI has been successful because we're quick to move and willing to make big moves. The wrong process could inhibit our ability to do that. The 1990 Strategy Cycle must be structured to address these challenges.

## EXHIBIT 1    MCI Financial History: 1980–1988

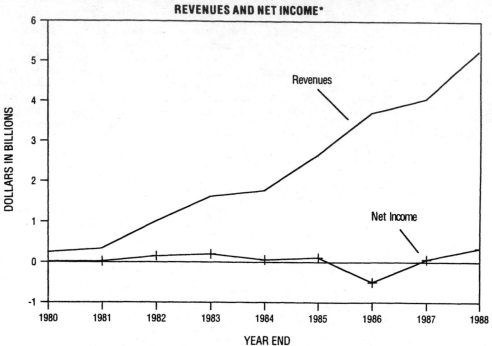

**REVENUES AND NET INCOME***

*NOTE: Figures for 1980 and 1981 are based on year end March 31 (not December 31).

### EXHIBIT 2    Historical Growth

|      | EMPLOYEES | BILLABLE CALLS (MILLIONS) | CIRCUIT MILES (MILLIONS) |
|------|-----------|---------------------------|--------------------------|
| 1980 | 1,545     |                           |                          |
| 1981 | 1,952     |                           |                          |
| 1982 | 6,342     | 437                       | 85                       |
| 1983 | 8,052     | 774                       | 113                      |
| 1984 | 8,756     | 1,232                     | 156                      |
| 1985 | 12,445    | 1,760                     | 322                      |
| 1986 | 13,650    | 2,812                     | 485                      |
| 1987 | 14,236    | 3,627                     | 703                      |
| 1988 | 17,596    | 5,360                     | 811                      |
| 1989 | 19,000    | 7,500                     | 1,152                    |

## EXHIBIT 3   MCI Strategy (Excerpt from 1987 Strategy Meeting Summary)

o  COMPETE IN ALL INTEREXCHANGE SERVICES MARKETS, INCLUDING ALL SERVICES AND GEOGRAPHIC
   AREAS, DOMESTIC AND INTERNATIONAL.

o  GROW FASTER THAN THE MARKET WITH THE OBJECTIVE OF ACHIEVING ▇ BILLION REVENUES IN
   1992 AND ▇ BILLION IN 1997 BY DIFFERENTIATING THROUGH PRODUCT OFFERINGS,
   FLEXIBILITY AND PRICE.

o  IMPROVE THE NETWORK BY INCORPORATION OF MORE REDUNDANCY INTELLIGENCE AND AUTOMATION
   ACHIEVING RELIABILITY AND QUALITY COMPARABLE OR BETTER THAN OUR COMPETITORS BY 1990.

o  IMPROVE OPERATING AND CAPITAL EFFICIENCY WITH THE LONG-TERM OBJECTIVE OF BEING THE
   LOW COST PROVIDER BY TIGHT CONTROL ON EXPENSES, REDUCTION OF CAPITAL INVESTMENTS AND
   REDUCTION OF DEBT.

o  OPPOSE MODIFICATION OF CONSENT DECREE ESPECIALLY RBOC ENTRY INTO LONG DISTANCE,
   PROMOTE STABLE PRICES AND LOWER ACCESS CHARGES BY STRONG REPRESENTATION OF OUR
   RATIONALE FOR COMPETITION TO LEGISLATIVE AND REGULATORY BODIES BOTH STATE AND FEDERAL

o  ACHIEVE POSITIVE CASH FLOW IN 1989, INCREASE PROFITABILITY WITH THE OBJECTIVE OF A
      OPERATING MARGIN IN 1992 BY INCREASING REVENUE, CONTROLLING OPERATING EXPENSES
   AND CAPITAL INVESTMENT.

o  IMPROVE CUSTOMER SATISFACTION WITH THE OBJECTIVE OF BEING THE PREMIER SERVICE COMPANY
   BY PROVIDING BETTER TOOLS AND INFORMATION TO THE SERVICE ORGANIZATION AND BY
   INCREASED TRAINING.

MCI CONFIDENTIAL

## EXHIBIT 4   Organizational Chart of Participants in Strategy Sessions

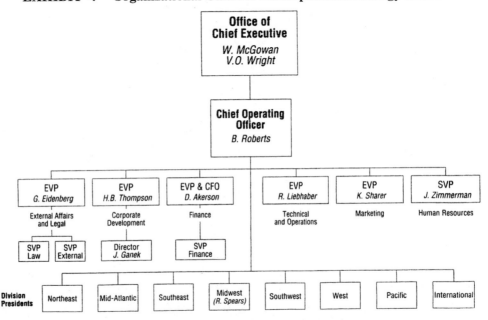

**EXHIBIT 5 MCI Strategies for the 1990s**

Leadership
Growth
Profitability
Quality

**Compete in All Markets**
Pursue Information Services Markets

**Establish Global Presence**
Strategic Overseas Investments
Foreign Partnerships
Transnational Company Focus

**Exceed Twice Market Growth Rate**
Full Product Range
Unsurpassed Sales and Service

**Premier Service Provider**
Superior Quality
Responsive Service

**Leading Technical Reliability and Quality**
Redundancy, Intelligence, Automation
Highest Operating Standards

**Maintain Industry Low-Cost Position**
Organizational Efficiency
Invest in Automation

**Increase Profitability and Cash Flow**

**Advocate Fair Competition**

**Positive Employment Environment**

**MCI**

# CASE 4  Asea Brown Boveri

On August 10, 1987, following six weeks of highly secret negotiations and special directors meetings in Västerås, Sweden and Zürich, Switzerland, a simultaneous news conference was called in Stockholm and Baden, Switzerland. Within minutes, the stunning details of the largest cross-border merger in European history flashed across newswires throughout the world: the two giants of the European electrical equipment industry—Asea AB of Sweden and BBC Brown Boveri Ltd. of Switzerland—would merge to create Asea Brown Boveri (ABB).

The new ABB would become the world's largest competitor in power generation, transmission and distribution; in addition, the combined company would be a leading world supplier of process automation systems, robotics, high speed locomotives and environmental and pollution control equipment. Asea's 65,000 employees would be combined with BBC's 85,000 employees to create a company comprising 850 separate legal entities operating in 140 countries. In 1988, its first year of combined operations, the new company's pretax income would be US$ 536 million on sales of US$ 17.8 billion.

Asea's chief executive officer, Percy Barnevik, (age 46 at the time of the merger) would assume the position of president and chief executive officer of ABB. Thomas Gasser (age 54 at the time of the merger) would become deputy chief executive officer. These men faced the challenge of building a new company on the foundation of two companies that had spent almost a century facing each other as arch rivals.

## Creating the New Company

The announcement of the proposed merger was greeted with considerable optimism, with BBC's shares rising 10% in Zurich and Asea's advancing 15% in Stockholm. Asea was seen as contributing superior current profit performance, sophisticated management controls and marketing aggressiveness, while BBC brought a strong order book, $4 billion in cash and marketable securities, and technical expertise. Barnevik's strong leadership also provided analysts with reasons to be bullish. "He's Europe's Jack Welch," said one, repeating an oft-made comparison.

**Reshaping the Organization**   ABB would start operating as a merged company on January 1, 1988. With only $4\frac{1}{2}$ months to make preparations, Barnevik believed strongly that there could be no honeymoon period, and decided to initiate all the needed changes within the first year. "Sales had to be kept up," he said, "and it was important not to get internally preoccupied. We didn't want people to become paralysed by uncertainty."

The week after the merger announcement, Barnevik selected five key managers from each company to form a ten person top level work group. Breaking this group into task forces, he charged them with analyzing how the operations of Asea and BBC could best be fitted together. Within two months, the main features of the new organization had been agreed upon—a new matrix structure that defined 40 business areas, grouped into business segments on one hand and integrated on a national basis through local holding companies on the other hand.

**Staffing the New Structure** In late October, Barnevik announced that he wanted the new organization operational by Christmas, and that meant filling hundreds of key management positions. To ensure that this process was perceived as fair, he had the personnel directors from Asea and BBC cross-interview and make recommendations on almost 500 senior level managers from the two companies. As part of the process, Thomas Gasser and Percy Barnevik personally interviewed over 100 key managers each.

The criteria for those selected for top jobs were demanding: they had to be risk-takers, team players, leaders, and motivators. In Barnevik's words,

> We sought people capable of becoming superstars—tough-skinned individuals who were fast on their feet, had good technical and commercial backgrounds, and had demonstrated the ability to lead others. . . . For the merger to work, it is essential that we have managers who are open, generous, and capable of thinking in group terms.[1]

**Communicating Objectives and Priorities** With the new team in place, Barnevik initiated a major program to communicate ABB direction and priorities. In January 1988 he convened a meeting of ABB's top 300 managers in Cannes to explain his management philosophy, operating policies, and to set corporate targets.

Over three days, Barnevik set the agenda for the organization, illustrating concepts and priorities with data contained in 198 overhead transparencies. He also emphasized the importance of the "policy bible"—a 21 page booklet that described the new organizational relationships, the commitment to decentralization and strict accountability, and the company's approach to change. He then asked the 300 managers to translate this message into their local languages and convene similar interactive forums with their own organizations so the message would reach another 30,000 ABB people worldwide within sixty days.

**Building Reporting Systems** Barnevik knew that the new organization could not work without a uniform reporting system that could provide managers with accurate and timely information on sales, orders, margins, and other data vital to decision making. When outsiders predicted that such a system could take as long as three years to design and implement in a company as large and complex as ABB, Barnevik and the development team set out to have it in place by August 1988 (in time for the 1989 budget). When the new system (dubbed Abacus) was unveiled on schedule, Barnevik hosted a champagne party for the development team and their spouses.

**Rationalizing Operations** The information provided by the new Abacus system was vital to Barnevik's plans to exploit economies in a global enterprise. After analyzing manufacturing costs in all markets, teams of business area managers began discussions on how to increase economies of scale and scope by designating certain plants as specialized production

---

[1] Jules Arbose, "ABB: The New Energy Powerhouse," *International Management,* June 1988.

sources for major products around the world. They also introduced other cost savings measures such as component outsourcing, overhead cuts, and inventory reduction. Each business area manager was also responsible for identifying best practices among its participating companies and ensuring the learning was transferred.

**Acquiring New Companies**    The substantial amount of cash that BBC brought to the merger, supplemented by the resources squeezed from the new organization through rationalization and tighter controls, allowed Barnevik to begin an acquisition program that would restructure the industry. ABB's expansion strategy was rooted in Barnevik's strong belief that the long-term slide in new power generation capacity would reverse itself soon to meet growing demand. Further, because 95% of all past electrical generation contracts in European Community countries had been won by strong national companies, Barnevik believed that new orders would be awarded only to companies that had a strong local presence. These twin beliefs were behind a massive acquisition/joint venture program designed to make ABB "an insider not an invader" in major national markets throughout Europe.

In Germany, Barnevik acquired AEG's steam turbine business and entered a nuclear reactor joint venture with Siemens; in Italy, he signed a joint venture agreement with Finmeccanica; in UK, he created a partnership to acquire BREL the former British Rail Engineering Limited, and linked up with Rolls Royce. In all, ABB acquired or entered into joint ventures with over 40 companies within 18 months of the announcement of the merger.

By early 1989, Barnevik's attention turned to the huge United States market, and negotiations to acquire Westinghouse's power distribution and transmission business as well as the publicly-traded Combustion Engineering group. By 1990, with Westinghouse and Combustion Engineering acquisitions complete, ABB employed 215,000 people in 1,300 wholly-owned subsidiaries around the world and generated US $27 billion in revenues (see **Exhibit 1**). Barnevik reflected on the blistering pace of ABB's acquisitions:

> This is an industry that hasn't changed much in 40 years. I wouldn't say that [ABB's acquisition of all these national companies] is ideal, but you have to move when the industry is moving. . . . If it works it gives us a hell of a competitive edge.

**Industry Reaction**    This frenetic action in ABB during the late 1980s triggered a major restructuring of the electrical industry throughout Europe. In response to ABB's actions, competitors began reorganizing themselves. Britain's GEC formed a joint venture with Alsthom-Jeumont of France to become Europe's number two power equipment company behind ABB, pushing Germany's Siemens, the long time industry leader, into third place.

Writing in an internal publication, General Electric's Senior Vice President of International Operations, Paulo Fresco, reflected the feelings of many in the industry:

> The lights are going out all over Europe, and the buccaneers have been turned loose. Among them is Percy Barnevik—this Swede with a beard who swings from country to country like the actor Errol Flynn, cutting deals and forming alliances. . . . A convalescing GE power system may find him the most formidable adversary it has ever faced.

## Percy Barnevik: ABB's New Leader

Percy Barnevik was a quiet spoken, bearded man with strong views and a clear vision of his company's future. Throughout his youth in Uddevalla, on the rocky Swedish coast, Percy had worked after school and on weekends in his father's print shop, learning the values of hard work and teamwork. After earning his economics degree at the Gothenburg School of Economics, he spent two years as a post graduate student at Stanford University.

After working in data processing for Sweden's Johnson Group for three years, Barnevik joined the machine tool company Sandvik in 1969, becoming group controller. In 1975 he was given the opportunity to manage Sandvik's U.S. affiliate, and over the next four years his effectiveness in that position caught the eye of Asea's board of directors which hired Barnevik in 1980 to run Asea. His success in rejuvenating the plodding Asea in the early 1980s made him the leading candidate for the top job at ABB.

Even to many of his top managers, Barnevik remained an enigmatic figure. He was clearly European in his origins, yet had been influenced by his American education and management experience, and was truly global in his perspective; he understood technology and was strongly committed to its development, yet remained uncompromisingly marketing oriented; he believed passionately in his long term vision for ABB and encouraged managers to develop bold strategies to achieve it, yet he insisted that they also achieve their short term results; and while his personal style was informal and unassuming, he could also be intolerant and blunt. But even those who did not quite understand him, inevitably respected him.

Three characteristics typified Barnevik's personal management style: (1) a strong work ethic, (2) constant communication, and (3) decisiveness. These values were imprinted on the new company he helped to create. Barnevik operated not only at the level of broad strategy, but developed an impressive feel for the details of ABB's ongoing operations. Barnevik believed strongly in setting clear individual targets and providing managers with feedback on their performance. He tracked key current issues and problems and followed up with individual managers who were expected to be able to answer his incisive questions.

Barnevik travelled constantly, and estimated he was on the road 200 days a year. Yet he insisted that while he may often be out of town, he was never out of touch. In his plane or company car, he was frequently on the telephone with key managers worldwide. With his dry sense of humor he pointed out: "I travel a lot, but I'm normally in my office two days a week—Saturday and Sunday."

The intensive travel underscored Barnevik's belief in the importance of constant communication with the organization. "A leader must first be a teacher," he said. Barnevik believed strongly that everyone must understand the corporate philosophy and objectives and the reasons behind them. On virtually all his trips, he took a large brief case filled with transparencies. His presentations, using two overhead projectors simultaneously and reciting the numbers displayed from memory, were legendary within ABB.

Barnevik believed that ABB managers must expand their jobs and make more decisions. This pressure on managers to decide—and decide quickly—was perhaps the personal characteristic that he had imprinted most indelibly on ABB. His philosophy had been repeated over and over to his team:

> Nothing is worse than procrastination . . . When I look at ten decisions I regret, there will be nine of them where I delayed . . . Better roughly and quickly than carefully and slowly."

He also promoted his "7-3 formula," which reinforced the notion that it was better to make decisions quickly and be right seven out of ten times than to waste time trying to achieve the perfect solution. "Take the initiative and decide—even if it turns out to be the wrong thing. The only thing we cannot accept is people who do nothing." But decisions had to be based on a sound understanding of the business, and on Barnevik's team, sloppy analysis or superficial knowledge were unacceptable. To emphasize that point, he had banned the phrase "I think" at meetings. ("Either you know or you don't," he said.)[2]

## Managing the New Company

By early 1989, eighteen months after the merger was announced, Barnevik shifted his focus from putting the new company together to making it work effectively.

**The Organizing Principles**    The complex new organization was built on twin principles of (1) decentralization of responsibility and (2) individual accountability. Barnevik explained:

> The only way to structure a complex, global organization is to make it as simple and local as possible. ABB is complicated from where I sit. But on the ground, where the real work gets done, all of our operations must function as closely as possible to stand-alone operations. Our managers need well-defined sets of responsibilities, clear accountability, and maximum degrees of freedom to execute.

> We are fervent believers in decentralization. When we structure local operations, we always push to create separate legal entities. Separate companies allow you to create real balance sheets with real responsibility for cash flow and dividends. With real balance sheets, managers inherit results from year to year through changes in equity.

> ABB is a huge enterprise. But the work of most of our people is organized in small units with P&L responsibility and meaningful autonomy. Our operations are divided into nearly 1,200 companies with an average of 200 employees. These companies are divided into 4,500 profit centers with an average of 50 employees.[3]

**The Matrix Organization**    Barnevik used the organizing principles of decentralization and accountability as a foundation for his strategic vision of a world class competitor built on strong national companies. The way he and his management team chose to do this was through the matrix structure that was put in place immediately following the merger. As Barnevik saw it:

> ABB is an organization with three internal contradictions. We want to be global and local, big and small, radically decentralized with centralized reporting and control. If we resolve those contradictions, we create real organizational advantage.

> You want to be able to optimize a business globally — to specialize in the production of components, to drive economies of scale as far as you can, to rotate managers and technologists around the world to share expertise and solve problems. But you also want to have deep local roots everywhere you operate — building products in the countries where you sell them, recruiting the best local talent from the universities, working with the local government to increase exports. If you build such an organization, you create a business advantage that's damn difficult to copy.

> The matrix is the framework through which we organize our activities. It allows us to optimize our business globally and maximize performance in every country in which we operate.[4]

---

[2] Jonathan Kapstein and Stanley Reed, "Preaching the Euro-Gospel: ABB Redefines Multinationalism," *Business Week,* July 23, 1990, p. 36.
[3] William Taylor, "The Logic of Global Business: An Interview with ABB's Percy Barnevik," *Harvard Business Review,* March–April 1991, 91–105.
[4] William Taylor, *op. cit.*

Exhibit 2 presents a schematic outline of the matrix structure in use at ABB. ABB was organized into 1,300 separate operating companies (listed at the top of each column in **Exhibit 2**); each company was a legal entity incorporated and domiciled in one of the 140 countries in which ABB operated. Each operating company had a president and management board. These 1,300 operating companies were managed by region. Thus, a company manager would focus his or her efforts on the operations of that business in one country and be responsible for:

- customer-based regional strategies
- regional results and profitability
- day-to-day management of individual profit centers
- human resource development within the regional unit
- relationships with local governments, communities, labor unions, and the media.

Examples of operating companies were ABB Power Generation Inc., North Brunswick, New Jersey, (building power plants) and ABB Fläkt Oy, based in Helsinki, Finland (building environmental protection systems).

Company managers reported in turn to a regional manager who was typically responsible for all the operating companies within a specific country. Gerhard Schulmeyer, for example, one of eleven executive vice presidents, was responsible for 110 ABB operating companies in the United States, including ABB Power Generation Inc. Bert-Olof Svanholm, another executive vice president, was responsible for the 30 ABB companies operating in Finland, including ABB Fläkt Oy.

The other dimension of the matrix (the vertical axis of **Exhibit 2**) reflected the second clustering of activities of the enterprise into 65 Business Areas (or BAs). Each Business Area represented a distinct worldwide product market. The power transmission activities of ABB, for example, were classified into seven BAs:

- Cables
- Distribution Transformers
- High Voltage Switchgear
- Electric Metering
- Network Control and Production
- Power Systems
- Power Transformers

Each Business Area was the responsibility of a BA manager accountable for:

- worldwide results and profitability
- development of a worldwide strategy
- R&D and product development
- worldwide market allocation and sourcing
- price strategy and price coordination between countries
- purchasing coordination
- product and production allocation
- transfer of know-how in design, production, and quality
- acquisitions and divestments

Each Business Area manager reported in turn to one of the eleven executive vice presidents responsible for individual business segments (i.e., clusters of related Business Areas).

At the risk of oversimplifying, Business Area managers were responsible for developing worldwide product and technology strategies. Regional managers were responsible for executing these strategies based on the unique needs of local markets. **Exhibit 3** illustrates this concept.

The two dimensional reporting matrix—with regional responsibilities running along one dimension and product responsibilities along the other—required two bosses for each operating manager.

Josef Dürr, president of ABB High Voltage Switchgear Ltd., Zurich, explained,

> Our organization seems difficult for an outsider to understand; I will draw you a picture (see **Exhibit 4** for Dürr's diagram).
>
> My company is part of the power transmission business here in Switzerland. Going up the regional part of the matrix, I report directly to Willy Roos who is responsible for all of the various power transmission businesses based in Switzerland. Willy in turn reports to Ed Somm who is responsible for all ABB businesses—power transmission and others—in Switzerland. Somm is an executive vice president and one of the eleven members of the group executive management.
>
> On the BA dimension, I report directly to Anders Larsson who sits in Sweden. Anders is responsible for businesses like mine—high voltage switchgear—all around the world. Anders Larsson reports to Göran Lindahl, who is the executive vice president in charge of the power transmission segment of the business worldwide.
>
> Thus, I am directly responsible to both Roos and Larsson. I have to coordinate my strategies and targets with each of them, be prepared to answer their individual concerns, and be accountable to both for my performance.
>
> But each of them also answers to two masters. Roos reports to Somm (regional manager responsible for Switzerland) and to Lindahl (business segment manager responsible for power transmission worldwide).
>
> Larsson, who sits in Sweden and runs the Swedish switchgear company, reports to Anders Narvinger (regional segment manager responsible for all transmission businesses in Sweden) and Lindahl (power transmission segment).
>
> Have I confused you?

The eleven executive vice presidents who formed the group executive management served as the critical integrating link in the matrix structure. Typically each individual assumed responsibility for one or more business segments as well as several regions. **Exhibit 5** illustrates the responsibilities of each of the eleven men.

Göran Lindahl, 46, one of the executive vice presidents, explained how it all worked,

> Our strategy is to be global with technology and local in our customer orientation. My business does US$ 5.5 billion in annual sales. The business operates 132 factories in 34 countries. That sounds huge doesn't it? But you need to understand that the power transmission business is made up of 750 different profit centers, each with its own P&L. The average profit center generates only $7 million in sales with 45 people.
>
> I have global responsibility for power transmission. That means I am concerned with long term strategy for the business: product planning, new technologies, acquisitions, and divestments.
>
> If I find overcapacity in a product line, I will suggest closing one or more factories. Do you think that you will ever find a manager of a local company suggesting we close down a piece of his business?

The local manager is there to be close to the customer, to execute the strategy. If you look at this slide I use in my presentations (**Exhibit 6**), you will see the concept I am talking about. The Business Areas are concerned primarily with top-down strategy setting as shown by the left arrow. The BAs secondary concern is with actual operations. By the same token, if you look at the right arrow—the bottom-up one—the situation reverses. The regional companies have major responsibility for operations and secondary involvement in strategy. But the difference is one of degree. The distinction is not black and white.

The center of the chart illustrates that budgets and plans are the key link in this company between strategy and operations.

**The ABACUS System**    The centrality of budgets and plans in Lindahl's presentation chart underlined the importance that ABB executives attached to their management systems in executing their strategy. A computer-supported reporting system named "ABACUS" provided the ongoing information required for oversight and complex decision making. Barnevik explained,

> We have the glue of transparent, centralized reporting through a management information system called ABACUS. Every month, ABACUS collects performance data on our 4,500 profit centers and compares performance with budget and forecasts. The data are collected in local currencies but translated into U.S. dollars to allow for analysis across borders. The system also allows you to work the data. You can aggregate and disaggregate results by business segments, countries, and companies within countries.
>
> We look for early signs that businesses are becoming more or less healthy. On the tenth of every month, for example, I get a binder with information on about 500 different operations—the 50 Business Areas, all the major countries, and the key companies in key countries. I look at several parameters—new orders, invoicing, margins, cash flows—around the world and in various business segments. Then I stop to study trends that catch my eye.
>
> Let's say the industry segment is behind budget. I look to see which of the five Business Areas in the segment are behind. I see that process automation is way off. So I look by country and learn that the problem is in the United States and that it's poor margins, not weak revenues. So the answer is obvious—a price war has broken out. That doesn't mean I start giving orders. But I want to have informed dialogues with the appropriate executives.

## Implementation

While many admiring articles had been written about the transformation that Barnevik had begun in ABB, the big question in most observers' minds was whether he and his top management team could make the demanding management principles and sophisticated organization structure work effectively. Could Barnevik reconcile the three dilemmas ("we want to be global and local, big and small, radically decentralized with centralized control") that he had built into this organization? Could he achieve the mission that he and his top managers had set out for ABB (see **Exhibit 7**).

As Barnevik himself acknowledged, "Now comes the crucial test. We have to prove that these new alliances are capable of delivering the advantages that we planned."

**EXHIBIT 1**

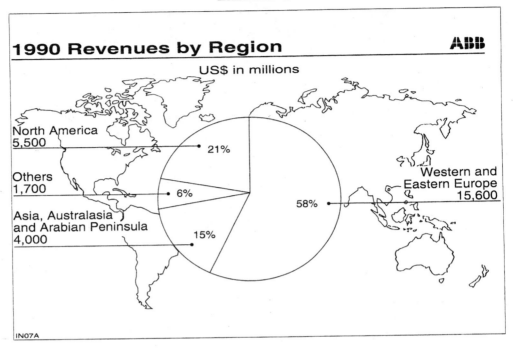

**EXHIBIT 2**

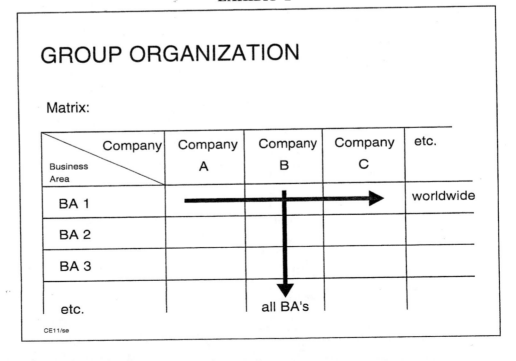

## EXHIBIT 3

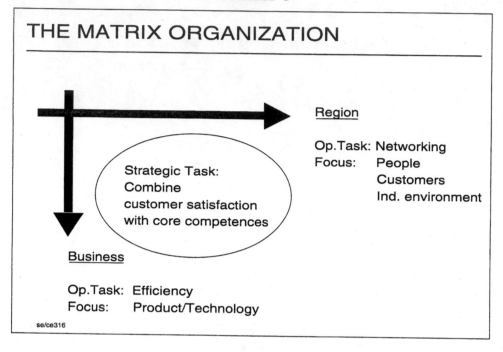

THE MATRIX ORGANIZATION

**Region**

Op.Task: Networking
Focus:      People
               Customers
               Ind. environment

Strategic Task:
Combine
customer satisfaction
with core competences

**Business**

Op.Task:  Efficiency
Focus:      Product/Technology

se/ce316

## EXHIBIT 4

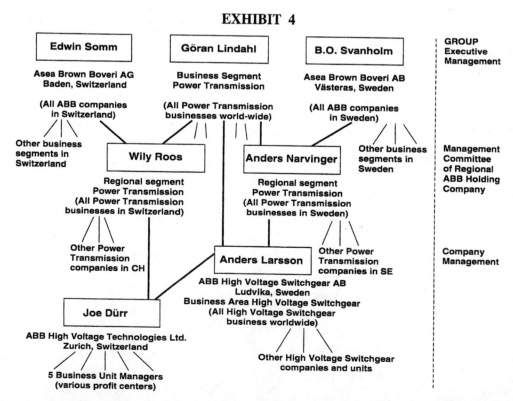

| | | | |
|---|---|---|---|
| **Edwin Somm** | **Göran Lindahl** | **B.O. Svanholm** | **GROUP** Executive Management |

Asea Brown Boveri AG
Baden, Switzerland

Business Segment
Power Transmission

Asea Brown Boveri AB
Västeras, Sweden

(All ABB companies
in Switzerland)

(All Power Transmission
businesses world-wide)

(All ABB companies
in Sweden)

Other business
segments in
Switzerland

**Wily Roos**

**Anders Narvinger**

Other business
segments in
Sweden

Management
Committee
of Regional
ABB Holding
Company

Regional segment
Power Transmission
(All Power Transmission
businesses in Switzerland)

Regional segment
Power Transmission
(All Power Transmission
businesses in Sweden)

Other Power
Transmission
companies in CH

**Anders Larsson**

Other Power
Transmission
companies in SE

Company
Management

**Joe Dürr**

ABB High Voltage Switchgear AB
Ludvika, Sweden
Business Area High Voltage Switchgear
(All High Voltage Switchgear
business worldwide)

ABB High Voltage Technologies Ltd.
Zurich, Switzerland

5 Business Unit Managers
(various profit centers)

Other High Voltage Switchgear
companies and units

# EXHIBIT 5

**Group Executive Management** | **Corporate Staffs\*** | **Business Segments** | **Business Areas** | **Other Business Areas** | **Regions**

## A. Bernborn

Regions: Latin America, Africa and Arabian Penins., West/South Asia, Southeast Asia, Northeast Asia, Australia/New Zealand, Japan

## E. Somm

Other Business Areas: Communication and Information Systems, Superchargers, Other Activities Switzerland

Regions: Switzerland

## B.-O. Svanholm

Business Segment: Transportation

Business Areas: Main Line Rolling Stock, Mass Transit Vehicles, Railway Maintenance, Complete Rail Systems, Signalling, Fixed Railway Installations

Other Business Areas: District Heating, Service, Other Activities Sweden

Regions: Sweden, Finland, Denmark, Iceland, Spain, Portugal

## E. Bielinski / G. Lundberg

Business Segment: Power Plants

Business Areas: Gas Turbine Power Plants, Utility Steam Power Plants, Industrial Steam Power Plants, PFBC, Hydro Power Plants, Nuclear Power Plants, Power Plant Control, Fossil Combustion Systems, Fossil Combustion Services

## G. Lindahl

Business Segment: Power Transmission

Business Areas: Cables and Capacitors, Distribution Transformers, Electric Metering, HV Switchgear, Network Control, Power Systems, Power Transformers, Relays

Other Business Areas: Power Lines and General Contracting

## P. Barnevik CEO

Business Segment: Environmental Control

Business Areas: ABB Fläkt Group, Industrial Processes, Indoor Climate, Gadelius, Service, Components, Cooling, New Ventures, Resource Recovery

## T. Gasser Deputy CEO

Corporate Staffs\*

## S. Carlsson

Business Segment: Power Distribution

Business Areas: LV Apparatus, LV Systems, Installation, MV Equipment, Distribution Plants

Other Business Areas: Telecommunications, Motors, Robotics

Regions: Norway, United Kingdom, Ireland, France, Benelux countries

## G. Schulmeyer

Corporate Staffs\*

Business Segment: Industry

Business Areas: Metallurgy, Process Automation, Drives, Process Engineering, Marine, Oil and Gas, Instrumentation, Semiconductors

Other Business Areas: Other Activities USA

Regions: USA, Canada

## L. Thunell

Corporate Staffs\*

Business Segment: Financial Services

Business Areas: Treasury Centers, Leasing Financing, Insurance, Trading and Trade Finance, Stockbrokerage Investment Management, Other Financial Services

Other Business Areas: Energy Ventures

## E. von Koerber

Corporate Staffs\*

Other Business Areas: Installation Material, Other Activities Germany

Regions: Germany, Italy, Austria, Eastern Europe, Greece

## C. Tidmon

Corporate Staffs\*

Other Business Areas: Integrated Circuits

EXHIBIT 6

# The Matrix Organization

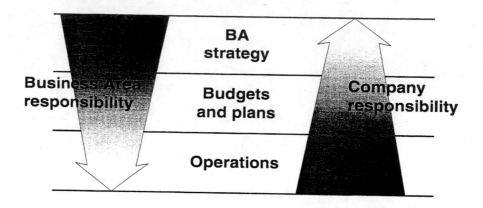

**Power Transmission Segment**

EXHIBIT 7    ABB's Mission, Values, and Policies

**B**    **ABB's Mission**

Worldwide economic growth requires dependable and efficient electric power. ABB is committed to help meet this need by promoting energy efficiency, higher productivity, and quality in all its activities. With its advanced technologies and environmentally sound and will make economic growth and improved living standards a reality for all nations throughout the world.

Our desire to increase the value of our products is based on continuous technological innovation and on competence and motivation of our employees. Our mission is to be a global leader and to act like one. We will be the most competitive, competent, technologically advanced, and quality-minded electrical engineering company in our fields of activity.

ABB's worldwide leadership position, our presence as a domestic company in key markets, our commitment to research and development, and the motivation of our personnel provide the basis for achieving enhanced customer value and ensuring long-term benefits to our employees and shareholders. As a good corporate citizen, ABB is aware of and fulfills its obligations to society in general, and to our communities in particular.

Everyone in ABB is committed to this mission and the intrinsic values underlying it.

# CASE 5   ABB: Accountability Times Two (A)

Helsinki, Finland

Kalle Mattila, president of ABB Strömberg Industry Ltd., sat at his desk wondering what bonus formula to suggest for his own remuneration during tomorrow's meeting with Thorolf Damén and Matti Ilmari.

Mattila had taken over as president on March 1, 1991 with a mandate to improve profitability: this was his first time through the ABB budget process as a company president. Key figures[1] for the nine months ended September 30, 1991 were as follows:

|  | ACTUAL (MILLIONS U.S.) | BUDGET (MILLIONS U.S.) |
|---|---|---|
| Orders | $31.5 | $26.0 |
| Revenues | 20.3 | 21.5 |
| Earnings after financial items | 0.4 | 1.5 |
| Trade receivables | 5.3 | 4.8 |
| Inventories[2] | 6.1 | 5.8 |
| Employees | 111 employees | 110 employees |

ABB Strömberg Industry Ltd. delivered equipment and systems for industry and rail transportation. Business operations were divided into five profit centers: traction, signalling, robots, industrial products, and turbochargers. ABB Strömberg manufactured its own equipment and resold equipment produced by other ABB companies. The business had been performing poorly, but prospects were improving. The State Transport Authority of South Australia had recently chosen ABB Strömberg squirrel cage motor drives for 50 new diesel electric passenger rail cars. The drives would be manufactured in Finland and delivered between 1991 and 1995. Similar drives had now been in service in Adelaide, the state capital, for more than 5 million kilometers. The company had also received recent orders for a (1) new automatic train control system from the Finnish State Railways (to be carried out between 1990 and 1996), (2) portal robots for the shaft factory of Oy Sisu-Auto Ab in Hämeenlinna, and (3) the delivery of pedestrian trucks to the Finnish Army.

---

[1] all figures have been disguised to protect confidentiality

[2] ABB used the "completed contract" method of accounting for sales revenue and work in progress. Accordingly, sales were not removed from inventory until the job was complete and shipped.

*Professor Robert Simons prepared this case as the basis for class discussion rather than to illustrate either effective or ineffective handling of an administrative situation.*

Like all ABB company managers, Mattila reported to two bosses: (1) a Business Area manager responsible for the product market worldwide and (2) a regional manager responsible for the performance of all ABB companies in a particular country or geographical region. For Mattila, his two bosses were (1) Thorolf Damén, located in Italy, who was responsible for the drives Business Area worldwide, and (2) Matti Ilmari, located in Helsinki, who was responsible for all ABB companies in Finland.

Mattila faced two sets of preliminary performance targets for 1992—one set handed down by Damén and one set handed down by Ilmari—which ultimately would have to be reconciled. There were substantial differences in the two sets of figures.

Mattila looked again at the anticipated results for the remainder of 1991. Then, he laid his calculation down beside the two sheets of paper that he had originally received from Damén and Ilmari and scanned the three sets of figures:

| | 1991 PROJECTED ACTUALS | DAMÉN'S 1992 BUSINESS AREAS TARGETS | ILMARI'S 1992 COUNTRY TARGETS |
|---|---|---|---|
| Orders | $38.0 | $44.0 | $40.5 |
| Revenues | 27.5 | 38.0 | 35.0 |
| Earnings after financial items | 0.6 | 2.5 | 1.6 |
| Trade receivables | 5.7 | 6.2 | 4.9 |
| Inventories | 8.3 | 10.0 | 9.1 |
| Employees | 111 employees | 110 employees | 115 employees |

From frequent meetings and conversations with both men, Mattila knew they each had different priorities for the coming year. Damén wanted to build worldwide market share and was concerned that the Finnish operation was not aggressive enough in finding orders or in manufacturing efficiency. If the operation did not improve its profitability, Damén hinted the factory might be closed and production moved to another country.

Ilmari, on the other hand, was under pressure from Bert-Olof Svanholm, the executive vice president responsible for Finland, to improve working capital efficiency. This objective had been included in Ilmari's personal goals for 1992. Ilmari was also feeling pressure from local labor representatives, one of whom sat on the management board of ABB Strömberg Industry Ltd., to expand employment as production volume increased.

No company budget could be submitted to executive group management for approval without joint agreement from the company president and his or her two direct superiors—in this case Ilmari and Damén. In rare cases, executive vice presidents had to step in to mediate disagreements between Business Area and country managers, but this intervention was seldom necessary since ABB managers knew that individuals who failed repeatedly to negotiate consensus would be replaced.

In a joint discussion just the day before, Ilmari, Damén, and Mattila had agreed on a budget that reconciled, as far as possible, the competing demands for results with available resources and business opportunities. The negotiated 1992 budget for ABB Strömberg Industry Ltd. was as follows:

| | |
|---|---|
| Orders | $43.0 |
| Revenues | 38.0 |
| Earnings after depreciation and interest | 2.0 |
| Trade receivables | 6.5 |
| Inventories | 8.4 |
| Employees | 110 |

ABB's bonus scheme provided financial incentives to its top Business Unit managers by rewarding good performance against budget targets. Bonus schemes were generally designed to be simple and flexible: two parameters—earnings after financial items and order intake—were generally believed to be sufficient indicators of performance, although qualitative objectives (e.g., special projects, management development) were often included in bonus calculations.

Bonus schemes for individual managers were negotiated with superiors as part of the budget-setting process. Top ABB managers believed that a bonus formula defined in advance of the budget-setting process would invite "tactical budgeting" by lower level managers who might attempt to bias budget targets to increase the probability of receiving a favorable bonus outcome. More importantly, this annual negotiation process—which managers were expected to take seriously—was a good opportunity to discuss objectives and priorities, and the intersection of Regional and Business Area interests.

The bonus scheme negotiated for each manager was tailored to the difficulty of the task. Managers who presented very ambitious targets, for example, usually had their bonus pay-out geared so that they would receive some financial recognition even if the targets were not achieved. Thus, the bonus formula for some managers might provide payouts when results reached 85% of budget, with maximum payout at 130% of budget. In another case, the starting point for bonus payout may be 95% of budget with an open-ended bonus. A third manager could receive bonus payouts at 75% of budget with a ceiling on payout set at 110% of budget targets.

The compensation package for a typical company president within ABB might be as follows:

| | |
|---|---|
| Salary | 100% |
| Bonus | |
| • quantitative formula based on order intake and earning after financial items (starting point 85% of budget, ending point 110%) | 20% |
| • qualitative bonus for successful implementation of specific programs or initiatives | 10% |

Mattila was due to meet the next day with Ilmari and Damén to negotiate his bonus scheme formula for 1992. He looked again at the 1991 projected results, the original targets provided by each man, and the final negotiated budget figures. He wondered what formula and payout levels to suggest at tomorrow's meeting . . .

# CASE 6  ABB: Accountability Times Two (B)

"The way we allocate markets can sometimes cause tensions. Business Area managers are responsible for two types of allocations. The first allocation is of customer markets around the world to individual ABB companies. These companies are then responsible for staying close to their customers in those regions. The second allocation is of productive capacity to individual ABB companies to achieve economies of scale in production and economies of scope in technology.

"But conflicts can arise when one ABB company is allocated the rights to produce a product and another ABB company is allocated the right to market products in a given country.

"For example, the market for electricity transmission and distribution (T & D) in the United States is very large. Our ABB companies in the U.S. have a lot of experience in transmission and distribution projects, and have therefore been allocated the right to serve this market directly by the Business Area manager responsible for power transmission.

"On the other hand, gas-insulated switchgear is a much more complex product. The worldwide market is small enough that our Business Area managers have decided to consolidate all gas-insulated substation component production in Switzerland. This allows us to focus our technology and achieve economies of scale. As a result, if a project arises to build a complex substation in the U.S., most of that work will be handled by the company that I run here in Switzerland.

"But I have a problem. One of my sales managers, who is based here in Switzerland, has built up excellent customer contacts with U.S. utility executives. By providing technical support on switchgear installations, he developed a relationship with Hardy Construction Co., a construction firm that was actively building power plants in the U.S.

"A power plant project came up for bid in England and Hardy Construction decided to go for it. The bidding was confidential and my company, ABB Switzerland, provided technical support to Hardy on the high voltage gas-insulated substation component. Then, Hardy asked us to participate in the proposal for substations and T & D work. The request to participate was really due to the personal alchemy between the project manager at Hardy and my Swiss sales engineer.

"Because Hardy Construction is located in the United States, ABB U.S. was the company that submitted the formal bid, even though ABB U.S. would do only a small part of the electrical installation. The majority of the ABB participation related to the gas-insulated substation; and Switzerland is the only company capable of doing that work.

"However, to be candid, we didn't really believe that Hardy Construction would be successful on the bid. We were investing our effort mainly to build relations for future work with Hardy.

"But, what do you know, Hardy won the bid. They will be building the plant in Britain with our substation forming a critical part of the installation. My company in Switzerland will be supplying the gas-insulated switchgear, protection controls, auxiliaries, line terminals, and batteries. This is a large job that will form approximately fifteen percent of my annual revenues for next year.

"The problem arises because the plant is being built in Britain: all substation work for British customers has been allocated to the ABB Swedish company; they are responsible for selling all substation work into Britain and staying close to British customers. The reason for this allocation is that, although we produce all high voltage gas-insulated substation components here in Switzerland, most low voltage substations are produced in Sweden.

"I know that the Swedish ABB company manager will want to follow ABB policy allocation rules and run the project himself, even though he and his people have not been involved. He will want us to build the substation components and then transfer it to him using internal transfer prices. He will then in turn sell it to Hardy for installation in Britain.

"At ABB, market prices are used for all internal transfer pricing. We keep costing and pricing procedures separate. In transactions between Group companies located in different countries, the arms' length principle is applied, regardless of the underlying costs. In this case, we would transfer the substation to the Swedish company at the contract price less a negotiated allowance for the administrative work performed by the Swedish company.

"As a result, our net margin on the work will be reduced by 2 to 4 percent and my targets will be adversely affected. As you know, 50% of my bonus depends on hitting targets for the Swiss company that I run; 25% is a function of worldwide Business Area goals (which include the performance of the Swedish company and other similar companies around the world); and 25% depend on how well I do on my personal goals.

"More important, however, is that I remain responsible for the equipment installation of this substation. That means that all communication between our people here in Switzerland who are building the station and the customer must go through a project manager sitting in Sweden.

"One of the tenets of ABB is that the responsibility of each manager in the matrix must be defined precisely. Therefore, the Swedish company *should* get the job because that's what the market allocation rules say. On the other hand, our whole business is built around being both global and local so that we can truly excel in both technology and customer orientation.

"As president of the Swiss company, I have a responsibility to my company. I want to say to the people in Sweden, 'don't be stubborn. Don't give more priority to ABB internal allocation rules than to our mutual concern with the customer. Let us handle this work directly and you stay out of it.'

"How hard do you think I should push? If they don't agree in Sweden, should I push it up? To whom: my Business Area manager or my regional manager? How do you think they will react? You may have heard the working rule around here:

> If two managers cannot agree, escalate the issue up to your bosses for a decision. If you cannot agree a second time, go to your bosses again for a decision. But if you cannot agree a third time, both managers will be replaced!

**CASE 7** Asea Brown Boveri: The ABACUS System

A t 11:00 A.M. on November 12, 1991, Sune Carlsson, executive vice president of ABB Asea Brown Boveri, picked up his telephone to speak with Ken Blom, business controller:

"Are the ABACUS October reports out yet?"

"The release clearance has not yet come over the screen."

"Why don't you phone them and find out when we can pull the preliminary results out of the data base. I want to see the results on France as soon as possible."

"The data should be released sometime this afternoon. I'll check and telephone you back."

Sune Carlsson was one of eleven executive vice presidents who formed the executive committee of giant ABB Asea Brown Boveri. Formed in 1988 with the merger of Asea AB of Sweden and BBC Brown Boveri of Switzerland, Asea Brown Boveri termed itself a "multi-domestic" company. ABB produced electrical equipment and other technology-driven products in over 140 countries around the world by competing in over 60 distinct worldwide product markets. ABB employed 215,000 people around the world and generated annual revenues in excess of US$27 billion.

Carlsson, 50, had joined Asea AB in his native Sweden in 1965 holding different positions such as planning manager in the motor division and manager of the fork lift truck division. In 1977, Carlsson became executive vice president of Asea responsible for production and later also for power plants, power distribution, and industrial equipment. In January 1988, with the merger of Asea and Brown Boveri, Carlsson was appointed executive vice president of ABB responsible for five Business Areas (BAs) related to power distribution as well as the Business Areas for robotics, motors, and telecommunications. Because ABB was organized using a matrix structure, Carlsson also assumed responsibility for specific countries: Norway, France, United Kingdom, Ireland, and Benelux countries (see **Exhibit 1** for a summary of Carlsson's responsibilities).

Carlsson described how he used the ABACUS system:

With our matrix structure, we always have two people looking at every part of the business. The Business Area managers take a high level, strategic perspective by managing the worldwide implications of the businesses they run. The country managers focus on execution at the regional level by staying close to their customers and markets. The integration of the matrix takes place at the executive committee where the executive vice presidents are typically responsible for both specific Business Areas and countries.

I wear two hats: on one hand, I am a segment manager responsible for worldwide performance of nine BAs; each of these Business Areas will be active in many countries around the world. On the other hand, I am also responsible for seven countries; each of those countries will have factories from many Business Areas located there.

I use ABACUS to manage these businesses and countries. When the performance reports come out monthly, I spend at least one full day reviewing figures. In addition, I spend a lot of time studying these figures when traveling.

I use ABACUS almost every day. The system has evolved into an excellent data base. I pull out trend data and search for negative deviations. In most cases, you can see where good figures are coming from. It is more important to react quickly to bad figures. I can quickly compare the performance of, say, our six motor factories in Europe to see if we have any problems. A segment manager has a higher level view than the managers who sit in the six countries where those factories are located.

Ken Blom, my controller, and I spend a lot of time pulling out specialized information to focus on specific questions: at any time, it may be cash flows, asset utilization, inventories, or investments. We both have terminals on our desks and use them a lot.

I like to pick information from the data base before it is published. I focus intensely on orders, revenues, earnings, and employees by Business Area and by country. I ask Ken to get this information a little faster every month.

## Asea Brown Boveri Accounting and Communication System

The ABACUS system was the "glue" of corporate reporting that allowed the ABB matrix structure to function. ABACUS was designed around four key objectives:

1. decentralized collection and verification of data with easy data entry by reporting unit;
2. fast and secure transmission and processing of data;
3. high level of flexibility for report generation;
4. immediate availability of pertinent reports.

ABACUS had been designed with special features for input handling, data base management, consolidation, report generation and information retrieval.

**Input Handling** The smallest unit of management at ABB was the profit center. A profit center was defined as:

> Any self-contained unit that is responsible for its own product development, production, and sales as well as for its own results and asset/liability management. A profit center must be able to measure performance.

ABB had over 4,000 profit centers worldwide. Profit centers were grouped together to form Business Area Units (i.e., separate legal entities) which were domiciled in specific countries and competed in identifiable product markets. For management accountability and oversight purposes, Business Area Units were grouped into one of 65 Business Areas (worldwide product markets) and in turn into eight Business Segments (for which executive vice presidents were responsible). For example,

| | |
|---|---|
| Power transmission | (Business Segment) |
| High voltage switchgear | (Business Area) |
| Gas insulated switchgear | (Business Unit with four profit centers) |

Business Area Units were located in approximately 1,300 ABB companies around the world. Each of these ABB companies was provided with Personal Computer (PC) software to input and verify data to the ABACUS host system.

Access to ABACUS was limited. Two levels of passwords were required to gain access to the PC ABACUS system installed at ABB companies: a password to sign on to the

Corporate Management System and an additional password to sign on to the ABACUS system. Passwords were changed frequently.

The ABACUS system was designed to gather monthly performance data and information necessary for annual budget preparation and updated forecasts. Performance data concerning orders received, revenues, gross margins, period costs, net earnings, and headcount were entered in the ABACUS system by control staff specialists at each operating company within 10 to 14 days of each month end (see **Exhibit 2** for a monthly reporting timetable; see **Exhibit 3** for sample data entry format).

Reconciliation routines within the PC software ensured the internal consistency of data (e.g., the computer would not allow further data entry if revenues did not reconcile between Business Areas and the ABB company).

In addition to numerical data, management comments were required on the progress of the business and explanations for deviations from budget and forecast. All comments throughout the world were required to be written in English. Comments were entered separately for each Business Area Unit within an ABB company so comments could later be consolidated either by Business Area or by country.

During 1991, approximately 1.4 million items of information (80 megabytes) were reported; during 1992, this amount was expected to grow to nearly 2 million items of information (110 megabytes).

Once data were complete and reconciled, the PC ABACUS system transmitted the data over owned and Infonet international lines to ABB's main data processing center located in Västerås, Sweden and, later, on to corporate headquarters in Zurich (**Exhibit 4**). All data in the ABACUS system, both numerical and text, were encrypted by a random algorithm generator prior to transmission to ensure security and prevent unauthorized access.

**Data Base Management (see *Exhibits 5* and *6* for a schematic overview)**   The data received in Västerås were decoded (part of the transmission included secret codes to inform the host computer about the encryption algorithm generated for the transmission) and stored in memo files. When memo data files from around the world were complete, they were consolidated by Business Area and country and stored in the ABACUS main hierarchical data base. Transmission from all ABB companies around the world was coordinated tightly to ensure receipt of all data to meet consolidation timetables.

The Corporate Control department, located at ABB headquarters in Zurich, Switzerland, kept a close watch on data receipt on the day that all ABB subsidiaries were due to transmit their data on ABACUS. On an hourly basis, controllers checked to see what data were still outstanding. By approximately 11:00 A.M. Zurich time, all data were received and consolidated in the main data base. During the morning, the telephone was ringing constantly as managers around the world asked when they could access the data.

At 11:00 A.M., the order was given to begin moving data from the main data base to a second data base—the report generator. At noon, a message was sent out over the network which appeared on PC screens at ABB locations around the world: ABACUS consolidated reports were available for downloading and review.

**Report Generation and Information Retrieval**   Within hours of releasing the information, the majority of important users around the world had downloaded reports for analysis and printing.

The report generator was really two data bases: a 300 megabyte ad hoc or inquiry data base that allowed managers to collect tailored data to answer specific questions (e.g., how much did we spend on consultants in my Business Area over the past six months?) and an 1,800 megabyte data base that produced pre-generated reports.

Reports were routinely generated in the following levels of detail:

1. Corporate consolidation
2. Executive vice president reports
3. Business Area reports
4. Business Unit reports
5. Company reports
6. Corporate control reports
7. Corporate staff reports

Access to reports and the ad hoc data base was restricted by authority and responsibility levels. Company managers, for example, had access to data for their own company and the profit centers within the company; they did not have access to data for other companies. Business Area managers had access to data on all the Business Area Units within their Business Area, but did not have access to other Business Areas. Executive vice presidents had access in detail to the Business Units, Business Areas, and countries (i.e., companies) for which they were responsible; in addition, each had access to broader corporate results.

Data from the data base could be used in three ways. First, data could be extracted in preconfigured reports that provided financial and statistical information as well as management comments. Second, tailored data could be compiled by the mainframe computer and extracted from the ad hoc report data base to answer specific inquiries or for special studies. Third, data could be downloaded from the data base to individual PCs at any ABB location; this data could then be used in spreadsheets or graphical display programs as desired.

In all cases, data were transmitted (encrypted) from the data base to the remote PC and printed at a dedicated printer on site.

**Investment in ABACUS**   From August 1988, when ABACUS was introduced, until 1991, ABB had invested approximately $5.5 million in ABACUS, broken down as follows:

|  | $ MILLIONS |
|---|---|
| Initial investment (1988) |  |
|     Mainframe systems | $3.0 |
|     PC systems | .4 |
|     Documentation | .5 |
|     Data-communication routines | .1 |
|  | $4.0 |
| Upgrading and finetuning (1989–91) | 1.5 |
|  | $5.5 |

## A Perspective from Corporate Control

The Corporate Control group was located at ABB headquarters in Zurich. Percy Barnevik, ABB's chief executive officer, insisted that corporate staff groups be as small as possible.

When Barnevik was named chief executive officer at Asea in 1980, he promptly cut head office staff from 1,700 people to less than 200. After the merger of Asea AB and BBC Brown Boveri Ltd., Barnevik issued the ultimatum that two-thirds of all corporate staff had to find work for themselves within ABB operating companies or be cut. After 60 days, the corporate staff at headquarters had shrunk to only 100 people.

The Corporate Control group at headquarters comprised 20 people with responsibility for corporate accounting and consolidation, external financial reporting, budget coordination, and maintenance of the ABACUS system. The department was under the joint direction of two senior vice presidents: Jean-Pierre Dürig and Tomas Ericsson. Dürig and Ericsson had run the corporate control groups at BBC Brown Boveri and AB Asea respectively prior to the merger.

In response to questions from the casewriter, Jean-Pierre Dürig and Tomas Ericsson explained ABACUS from their perspective:

> The matrix structure in such a large group would have been absolutely impossible ten or fifteen years ago because we did not have the ability to create information data bases to support the two levels of oversight.

> The data base allows us to cut the data any way we want: we can extract performance indicators by company, by region, and by worldwide-product line. Every month, the data are compiled and issued simultaneously in a variety of different ways for managers with different responsibilities.

> The data base is used most heavily by Business Segment and Business Area managers since this is the only way they can compile and access information about the units under their responsibility. Company managers always have legal entity reporting to fall back on.

Q.   What sort of discipline is needed to run a system like this?

> We absolutely insist on consistency. We can not waste time in discussions about what the underlying calculations are. We must be sure, for example, that everyone is using the same definition for earnings. The worst scenario is to have Percy Barnevik challenging managers based on data from the ABACUS system and to have managers responding with local data that no one else has seen before.

> Because ABACUS is so critical to our ability to operate, we insist that everyone must respect some hard and fast rules:
> * people shall not report twice—the only official reporting channel is ABACUS;
> * you shall not force managers to report earlier than the ABACUS deadline or in a separate format;
> * you shall not comment on things that are obvious, e.g., do not write, "we are on budget";
> * no one should get advance information out of the system—access to reports and data must be quickly and simultaneously accessible to corporate management, business controllers, business area controllers, etc.

> ABB is a multi-domestic company. With over 200,000 employees around the world, language could be a serious barrier. ABB has two language requirements: first, all managers must be fluent in English and use only English for their corporate reporting; the second language is the ABACUS system.

Q.   How are expectations about performance set at ABB?

> Each Business Area creates a worldwide strategic plan which is cleared directly with Percy Barnevik. Corporate staff groups do not get involved in this process. Based on these plans, the executive group—Barnevik and the 11 executive vice presidents—agree on targets for each Business Area and for each region. Targets at this level are based on return on capital employed (ROCE), profit, and growth.

Targets are then transmitted through the organization on a top-down basis. Each executive vice president must break down his overall target and parcel it out to the Business Areas and regions under his responsibility. In this phase, Business Area and regional targets have to be reconciled for each Business Area unit. Targets handed down by both Business Areas and regions relate to new orders, revenues, profits, and headcount. If a manager receives two sets of targets that are in conflict, he or she must negotiate with two bosses to iron out the difference and get agreement on expectations for the coming year.

Q. But how can a manager be simultaneously accountable to both a product line boss and a regional boss?

They have no choice but to figure out how to do it. Individual performance assessment is a function of the evaluation of both bosses and there must be joint agreement from both superiors before an individual can be promoted. This ensures equal influence by both the regional managers and the Business Area managers. One of Percy Barnevik's favorite expressions is, "what gets measured, gets done" and everyone is measured from two different perspectives—regional performance and business area performance.

Q. What are managers accountable for?

We use the Du Pont formula to break ROCE (Return On Capital Employed) down into subcomponents using this chart (see **Exhibit 7**). They are held accountable for performance on all of these dimensions.

Q. How is the budget set?

The budget process is basically bottom up. Based on the top-down targets provided by regional and Business Area managers, Business Area Unit managers respond with proposed budgets. These come in by early November after negotiation between Business Area superiors and regional superiors. By December, the overall budget has been approved in total and in its details.

Q. Is the budget changed during the year?

Absolutely not! There is a very strong commitment to achieve the budget. Explanations for shortfalls are not accepted. Rather than listening to explanations, the discussion always focuses on what the manager will do to get back on track.

Managers in this company are expected to be business controllers. Remember, Percy Barnevik is an old controller himself. He knows the value of the control function of management. Everyone must understand that decentralization requires greater accountability and control. At ABB we insist on five rules to improve "controller mentality" in our managers. Profit center managers must:

1. receive clear objectives and provide firm budget commitments;
2. follow up variances with high frequency (weekly, monthly);
3. analyze deviations—demand actions; develop a high sense of urgency;
4. demand budget achievement within the period—no "hockey sticks";
5. go into details from time to time:
   - personal involvement in bigger projects
   - push capital reductions at a detailed level
   - check pricing, discount routines.

There is a clear understanding that failing managers must improve or be replaced.

Q. What is the relevant time frame?

Our budget period is one year. The following year's objectives are set only for the key figures.

Q.   How do you define profit?

The key concept for us is net margin, defined as

$$\frac{\text{Sales price} - \text{full cost}}{\text{Sales price}} \times 100 = \text{Net Margin}$$

Our net margin for 1990 was 1% on our total revenues. Is this poor performance? To decide, you must first understand that our full cost concept includes:

- all direct costs
- all overheads including administration, engineering, and applied research and development
- calculated interest (see **Exhibit 8**)
- calculated depreciation (see **Exhibit 9**)
- provisions for currency, country, and all other risks

We allocate *all* corporate costs, including Business Area administration to operating units so that we have complete accountability at the profit center level. The only exception is corporate R&D (approximately 2% to 3% of total R&D) which attempts to track emerging technology that does not fit in the current portfolio of any Business Area. The profit centers, therefore, have the accumulation of total costs for full absorption in cost rates.

This policy has three effects. First, with all costs allocated, you can understand what it means to operate on very thin margins. From day one, Percy Barnevik has insisted that we don't take on any loss work, no matter what the extenuating circumstances. And that means no loss on a full cost basis.

Second, because of the full allocation principle, the accuracy of allocations is critically important. Managers really care. We spend a lot of time in each of our operations analyzing the drivers of cost and using activity-based cost systems to get allocations as accurate as possible.

Third, all staff units at the center must be able to demonstrate they are adding real value at a competitive cost. This has streamlined our support operations tremendously. The printing shop was spun off with a management buy-out and now operates as an independent company. Catering was disbanded and we now obtain competitive bids. Our fleet of buses and transport vehicles was sold off. And on and on . . .

Technically, of course, direct costing and full costing produce the same net profit figure at the corporate level. But direct costing is especially risky in a decentralized business. The cost calculation changes the behavior of profit center managers.

During negotiations with customers, our managers must calculate the profit potential of each order. Using direct cost calculations, the profit margin may be 40%; using full cost calculations, the profit margin may be 5%. Under which of these calculations is a manager more likely to give away 2% in tough negotiations with a customer?

Q.   Are you planning any changes to ABACUS?

We are always shortening the information deadlines. We want to create a sense of urgency in reporting so that the information can be acted upon rather than be just an historical record. If the data are due on the 12th of the month, we turn around preliminary information on orders, revenues, profits, and headcount by the 13th and final data by the 16th. But we are always looking for ways to compress the time frame.

ABACUS now has reasonable flexibility. Any ratio can be pulled out and an executive vice president can compare his own performance with anyone in the group. But we have just commissioned a study to look at ways to upgrade ABACUS in terms of processing efficiency and user friendliness. Because the design of the system is several years old and based on mainframe technology and hierarchical data bases, the system is not as responsive and flexible as we would like.

The system is excellent for historical reporting and variance analysis. The next question is how much we should be willing to spend to make it as good as the latest software packages that run much smaller applications. These new applications, designed to be run on smaller machines, can do fantastic things in terms of color and graphics. But by now you appreciate the scale and scope of our information needs. Last year alone, we spent $2 million to maintain and operate the ABACUS system, exclusive of the cost of accounting, consolidation, and internal transmission.

We would like to turn this data base system into a real Executive Information system. Executives like Ed Somm, Sune Carlsson and Göran Lindahl are comfortable using their PCs to go directly into the data base—often using a modem at home. But now the data have to be downloaded into PCs and then analyzed using local software to produce graphical output. An Executive Information system should be capable of producing this output directly and should make retrieval even easier.

The current system is menu- and table-driven, so adding new companies or Business Areas into the system is no problem. To design new reports is also not a problem. However, the data must of course exist in the data base. The type of data to be collected is defined by corporate management in accordance with our controlling philosophy. We are very restrictive here, not collecting a lot of details—in order not to burden the reporting companies.

The system is built to meet the requirements from our matrix. We need to control both Regions/Countries/Companies and Business Areas/Business Units. The mainframe system is also designed to allow monitoring of corporate results by managers at the center. Furthermore, all reporting units are required to report at the same time and with the same content as regards the chart of accounts. Some users see this as a limitation in the system, but if it is a limitation, that limitation falls back on our controlling philosophy, not on the system itself.

## ABACUS in Action

At 1:15 P.M. on November 12, Göran Lindahl, executive vice president, walked in to the office of Walter Gugolz, business controller for the power transmission segment. The discussion at the executive committee meeting the previous week, attended by Percy Barnevik and the 11 executive vice presidents, had focused on ways of improving operating efficiency throughout ABB. Factory utilization and throughput times were discussed at length.

Lindahl wanted to discuss with Gugolz what type of data could be collected to analyze the efficiency of the seven Business Areas under Lindahl's responsibility.

Lindahl and Gugolz decided to start with one Business Area—power transformers—to see what the data looked like.

Sitting at the personal computer in his office, Gugolz used his password to sign on to the ABACUS system. He then quickly used the FOCUS editor to write the commands to access data in the ad hoc data base. In five lines, he instructed the central computer to select the performance data he needed for all locations that were coded as components of the power transformer Business Area.

With the data now loaded in files in his personal computer hard disk, Gugolz switched to the Interactive Chart Utility software package and created the commands to generate three bar charts. Each chart printed out on the printer in his office.

Lindahl and Gugolz examined the charts (see **Exhibits 10, 11,** and **12**). Under ABACUS restrictions, no manager had access to data for operations not under his or her control. Company and country managers, therefore, had access only to the performance data for their own company or country. They could not access these comparative data themselves. Lindahl instructed Gugolz to send out copies of the charts to all the company managers. As Lindahl explained:

I have found in the past that it is extremely effective to select several variables to measure each month and send out the comparative charts to all the managers whose operations are being compared. I don't even have to say anything. Those managers will fight like crazy not to be low man on the ranking.

At 1:30 P.M. on November 12, Ken Blom had extracted from ABACUS the October figures that Sune Carlsson wanted on French operations. At 3:00 P.M. Carlsson sent a fax letter to the manager of the French motor company pressing for action plans to remedy a shortfall in profits and unusually high inventory levels. The letter highlighted the deficient figures and contrasted them with budget commitments and with more recent updates that promised improved performance.

The closing sentence of the letter left little doubt of Carlsson's expectations:

"The current level of performance is unacceptable. I will not accept excuses. When I arrive next week, be prepared to discuss in detail your steps to improve profit to agreed levels and to reduce inventory by 16% within three months."

Carlsson explained the purpose of the memo to the casewriter,

This memo is demanding action, with no excuses. I know this letter will scare them a bit, but when I go to France next week, we will discuss markets, sales, technology, and customers. This type of communication is not really indicative of the way we run our business. But, at the end of the day, ABB managers are paid to produce good figures.

**EXHIBIT 1   Carlsson's Reporting Responsibilities**

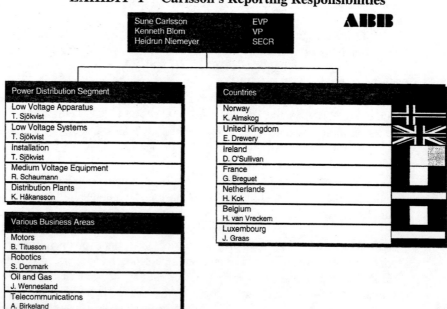

**EXHIBIT 2   Monthly Reporting Timetable**

**ABB**
ASEA BROWN BOVERI

*ACCOUNTING AND REPORTING GUIDELINES*

| 9. | MONTHLY REPORTING | | | Page 2 | |
|---|---|---|---|---|---|

| 9.1 | Timetable | | | | |
|---|---|---|---|---|---|
| | | 9012 | 9101 | 9102 | 9103 |
| | INPUT | 14 Jan | 12 Feb | 12 Mar | 11 Apr |
| | OUTPUT[a] | | | | |
| | Preliminary | 15 Jan | 13 Feb | 13 Mar | 12 Apr |
| | Final | 17 Jan | 15 Feb | 15 Mar | 16 Apr |
| | | 9104 | 9105 | 9106 | 9107 |
| | INPUT | 14 May | 12 Jun | 10 Jul | 13 Aug |
| | OUTPUT[a] | | | | |
| | Preliminary | 15 May | 13 Jun | 11 Jul | 14 Aug |
| | Final | 17 May | 17 Jun | 15 Jul | 16 Aug |
| | | 9108 | 9109 | 9110 | 9111 |
| | INPUT | 11 Sep | 10 Oct | 12 Nov | 11 Dec |
| | OUTPUT[a] | | | | |
| | Preliminary | 12 Sep | 11 Oct | 13 Nov | 12 Dec |
| | Final | 16 Sep | 15 Oct | 15 Nov | 16 Dec |

Note the restricted monthly reporting for periods 9101, 9103, 9106, 9107 and 9109. Only orders received with production and total costs have to be reported (CM020-046, BM010-056 and LM).

It is of utmost importance that all reporting deadlines are respected since any delay at the input stage affects the output timetable.

Timetable for 9112 will be distributed at the end of 1991.

| 9.2 | Forms |
|---|---|

The forms to be used for monthly reporting are denominated

CM—Company specification Monthly
CT—Comments by company/subgroup
BM—Business area specification Monthly
LM—Large orders Monthly

[a]Predefined reports/ABACUS databases

4.  REPORTING — ACTUAL                                    CS-C0 91-08-30

**EXHIBIT 3**   **Sample Data Entry Format**

**ABB**
ASEA BROWN BOVERI

*ACCOUNTING AND REPORTING GUIDELINES*

| 9. | MONTHLY REPORTING | | | | | Page 3 | |
|---|---|---|---|---|---|---|---|

| Company code | Period | Reporting type | Reporting time | | | Date | |
|---|---|---|---|---|---|---|---|
| | | A | M | | | | CM1/2 |

| COMPANY SPECIFICATION MONTHLY | | Reporting code CM | Value[a,b] |
|---|---|---|---|
| **ORDERS RECEIVED:** | | | |
| Orders received............................ | Third Party | 020 | |
| Orders received, other regions......... | ABB Group | 031 | ................................ |
| Orders received, own region............ | ABB Group | 032 | ................................ |
| Orders received............................ | | 039 | ................................ |
| Production costs............................ | | 043 | ................................ |
| Total costs................................... | | | ................................ |
| | | | |
| **REVENUES:** | | | |
| Revenues..................................... | Third Party | 069 | ................................ |
| Revenues, other regions................. | ABB Group | 071 | ................................ |
| Revenues, own region.................... | ABB Group | 072 | ................................ |
| Revenues..................................... | | 099 | ................................ |
| Production costs............................ | | 198 | ................................ |
| GROSS RESULT............................ | | 199 | ................................ |
| Sales and administration costs......... | | 228 | ................................ |
| CALCULATED RESULT.................... | | 299 | ................................ |
| | | | |
| Operating earnings after depreciation.... | | 399 | ................................ |
| | | | |
| Dividend income............................ | ABB Group | 415 | ................................ |
| | | | |
| Earnings after financial items............ | | 499 | ................................ |
| | | | |
| Income before taxes....................... | | 599 | ................................ |
| | | | |
| **EMPLOYEES** (Recalculated to full-time employees) | | | |
| Number of employees at end of period; | | | |
| Employees (excl. apprentices and temp employees | | | |
| on site.................................... | | 730 | ................................ |
| Apprentices................................. | | 732 | ................................ |
| Temporary employees on site............. | | 733 | ................................ |
| TOTAL NUMBER OF EMPLOYEES........ | | 738 | ................................ |

[a] Normally thousands of local currency
[b] For periods 9101, 9103, 9106, 9107 and 9109 only the codes CM020-048 have to be filled in.

4.   REPORTING — ACTUAL

CS-C0 91-08-30

**EXHIBIT 4   PC/ABACUS Data Transmission Worldwide**

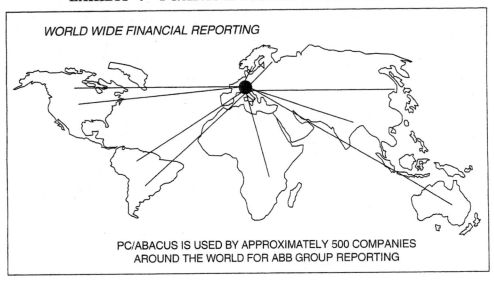

WORLD WIDE FINANCIAL REPORTING

PC/ABACUS IS USED BY APPROXIMATELY 500 COMPANIES
AROUND THE WORLD FOR ABB GROUP REPORTING

**EXHIBIT 5   A Schematic Overview of ABACUS Data Transmission**

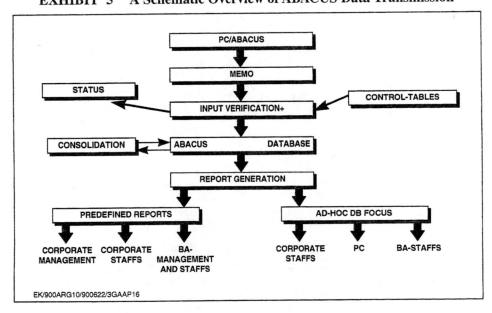

EK/900ARG10/900622/3GAAP16

**EXHIBIT  6    A Schematic Overview of the ABACUS Processing System**

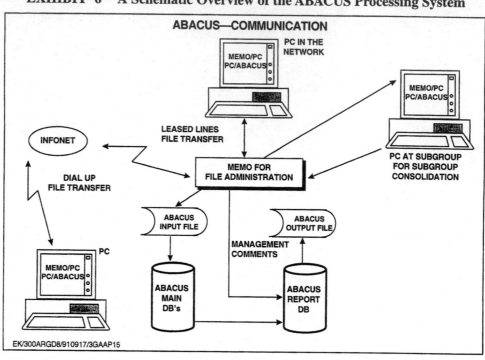

**EXHIBIT  7    Calculation of Return-on-Capital Employed (ROCE)**

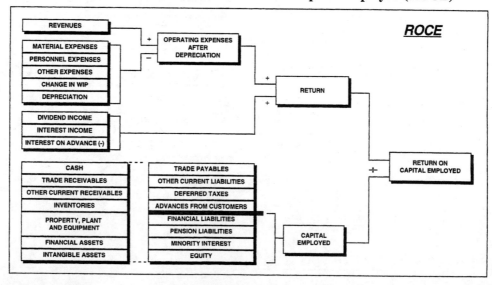

# EXHIBIT 8  Calculated Interest

**7.  CALCULATED INTEREST**

**7.1  The concept of calculated interest**

**7.1.1  Application**

Use of calculated interest is prescribed for cost accounting and related reports, viz.

- Internal income statement
  - calculation model
  - cost centre accounting

Calculated interest is applicable on the capital tied up in operating assets (see section 7.3 below). In no way is calculated interest affected by the actual financing structure of a company (debt/equity ratio and corresponding actual interest expenses).

**7.1.2  Purpose of calculated interest**

The concept of calculated interest aims at:

a) Determining results and margins in which capital costs for the entire capital invested in operations are accounted for

b) Expressing results and margins for the basic operational activities not affected by financial decisions and constraints specific to a company or a period. As a consequence, an objective assessment of the industrial/sales performance of different units is possible at the level of both
  - cross-comparisons between companies
  - inter-period comparisons for the same company (or BA)

By using an interest based on the market rate—normally higher than the inflation rate—the following is envisaged:

- secure the capital invested in operations against inflation (maintenance of substance).
- earn a real interest (given by the difference of market rate and inflation).

**7.  CALCULATED INTEREST**

**7.1.3  Calculated interest in high inflation countries**

In all companies in high inflation regions for which USD accounting is prescribed, particular procedures apply (for Latin America contact BRLAM/Sao Paulo).

**7.2  Determination and use of interest rates**

**7.2.1  Market rate**

The market rate is to be derived from the average local lending rates companies would have to pay when procuring new capital. In the exceptional cases where market rates lie under the inflation rate (measured by the **Consumer Price Index**), the "market" rates shall not be set below the %-change of CPI.

The market rate is to be applied on all assets and liabilities (except items of tangible fixed assets). For details consult Table 7.3.4.

**7.2.2  Real rate**

The real rate is obtained by excluding the inflation rate from the market rate. In low inflation countries the real rate (r) may be calculated by subtracting the inflation rate from the market rate. Otherwise the following more precise formula applies:

$$r = \frac{\text{market rate} - \text{inflation rate}}{1 + (\text{inflation rate}/100)}$$

**Note:**  Above formula is equal to the one used in former text but expressed in a simplified manner.

The real rate is to be applied on the items of tangible fixed assets only. For details consult Table 7.3.4.

**7.2.3  Decision on applicable interest rates**

The same interest rates shall be used within one country (preferably to be set by the country holding). The interest rates set by the main company/holding in a country shall also prevail for subsidiaries of other regions in the specific country.

389

*Exhibit 8 Continued*

| 7. | CALCULATED INTEREST | | | Page 6 |

**7.3.4 Calculation and functional allocation of calculated interest**

| Operating Assets | Valuation Basis | Interest Rate (1) | Allocation to the Function |
|---|---|---|---|
| Trade receivables (2) | B | m | sales° |
| Other current receivables (e.g., advances to suppliers) | B | m | material*° |
| inventories: | | | |
| material | B | m (3) | material |
| work in progress | P | m | other product costs |
| finished goods (of own manufacture) | P | m | sales |
| standard goods for resale | B | m | sales |
| construction in progress | ½ R (4) | r | according to |
| machinery and equipment | ½ R (4) | r | use by |
| buildings | ½ R (4) | r | functions |
| land | R (5) | r | |
| **Deductible capital** | | | |
| Trade payables | B | m | material,° sales** |
| Pension liabilities (6) | B | m | according to the number of employees per function |
| Advances from customers | B | m | revenues |

*If advances, otherwise distribution by function concerned.
**In case of standard goods for re-sale.
°If specifically assignable to an order to be shown under special direct costs in cost calculation and reported under other production cost in reporting of the internal income statement.

| 1. | GENERAL ACCOUNTING PRINCIPLES | CS-CO 91-10-07 |

---

| 7. | CALCULATED INTEREST | | Page 7 |

**Abbreviations:**

| B | = | Book value (adjusted according to ABB guidelines) |
|---|---|---|
| P | = | Incurred Production costs (see this binder, part 6) before calculation of interest on item itself. |
| R | = | Replacement Value (see this binder, part 8, section 8.4.2) |
| m | = | market rate |
| r | = | real rate |

**Notes:**

1) The *market rate* (= m) is applied on monetary or historical values (trade receivables, inventories, the deductible items and advances) as they refer to items exposed to inflation.

   The *real rate* (= r) is applied on items the cost of which include already the effect of inflation. This applies particularly to items of tangible fixed assets for which amortization (= calculated depreciation) is based on replacement values adjusted for inflation.

2) Includes bills of exchange (not discounted). Please note that for the *discounted bills of exchange,* the discount is a normal operational cost to be included in the function sales.

3) In countries with high inflation rates, use of replacement values for material in calculation fulfills the criterion of substance maintenance—accordingly the *real rate* is applicable (avoidance of double counting of inflation by using the market rate). The same applies to companies which in the internal income statement value the material consumption at replacement value (Next In First Out Principle).

Please also refer to Note 1, second paragraph, above.

| 1. | GENERAL ACCOUNTING PRINCIPLES | CS-CO 91-10-07 |

# EXHIBIT 9  Calculated Depreciation

**8. DEPRECIATION**

**8.4  Calculated depreciation**

Calculated depreciation represents an important feature of ABB's *cost calculation system*. Calculated depreciation reflects the amount which is necessary for preserving the production capacity of a company. Accordingly, calculated depreciation is based on continually updated replacement values and the calculated service life of each asset.

**8.4.1  Calculated service lives**

Uniform calculated service lives valid for all ABB group companies are set for main categories of machinery, equipment and buildings. *See details in Table 8.5.*

**8.4.2  Calculated depreciation basis—machinery and equipment**

The *replacement value* of an asset is the basis for determining calculated depreciation. It corresponds to the hypothetical acquisition cost of an equivalent *new item* at the date of valuation.

To achieve a uniform calculation of the replacement value in all companies, the following rates apply:

a)  The replacement value is to be determined based on an indexation of the original acquisition value. Companies shall use as index

   • a representative price index (e.g., machine price index for machinery)

   or (if such index is not available)

   • the consumer price index.

For machinery and EDP-equipment the yearly indices changes are to be adjusted by an aging coefficient (see 8.4.2.1 below).

Special cases:

b)  Items having acquisitions costs in excess of USD 1 million may be assessed individually based onto price of comparable new item on the market.

---

**8. DEPRECIATION**

c)  A one-time individual assessment—for all types of items—may also be necessary in case of significant and singular events such as

   • Change of taxes, import tariffs

   • A permanent reorientation of a company toward manufacture of smaller goods (oversized equipment may be reassessed on the base of adequate alternative machines; an investment appraisal must prove profitability of maintaining old equipment)

   • Take over of used equipment

**8.4.2.1  Use of aging coefficient**

In case a price index is used for establishing the yearly replacement value for machinery and EDP-equipment, a correction with an aging factor is permissible. This adjustment covers the effect of comparatively higher efficiency of new equipment available on the market.

The following adjustment per year is applicable:

|  |  | Aging Coefficient |
|---|---|---|
| machinery (excluding EDP): | 2% → | 98% of index change |
| EDP-equipment: | 5% → | 95% of index change |

**Formula for annual calculation of replacement value**

$$R_n = R_{n-1} \times f \times c$$

where:

$R_n$ = Replacement value of new year

$R_{n-1}$ = Replacement value of former year

$f$ = Price index factor (e.g., change of price index = 12% per year → $f = 1,12$)

*Exhibit 9   Continued*

ASEA BROWN BOVERI

*ACCOUNTING AND REPORTING GUIDELINES*

| 8. | DEPRECIATION | | | | Page 7 |

**Examples:**

| | | $R_{n-1}$ | Price Index Change | Aging Coefficients | $R_n$ |
|---|---|---|---|---|---|
| a) | machinery | 1'000 | 4% | 0,98 | 1'019 |
| b) | machinery | 1'000 | 40% | 0,98 | 1'372 |
| c) | EDP | 1'000 | 4% | 0,95 | 988 |
| d) | EDP | 1'000 | 40% | 0,95 | 1'330 |

Calculations:

| a) | $R_n$ | = | 1'000 x 1,04 x 0,98 |
|---|---|---|---|
| b) | $R_n$ | = | 1'000 x 1,40 x 0,98 |
| c) | $R_n$ | = | 1'000 x 1,04 x 0,95 |
| d) | $R_n$ | = | 1'000 x 1,40 x 0,95 |

**8.4.3   Calculated depreciation basis—buildings**

The replacement value will be derived from the market value of the building, i.e., the price a third party would pay taking into account the intended purpose the building was built for and its current physical condition.

An adjustment of the market price of buildings will be done annually as part of the reassessment of real estate by the cost/profit center responsible for the real estate administration of a company/region. In intervals of not more than five years, the values have to be reassessed by external experts.

**8.4.4   Calculated depreciation method**

The following rules apply:

a)   All items are to be depreciated according to the *straight-line* method.

b)   Depreciation is to be continued with the same percentage rate (based on updated replacement values) after the prescribed depreciation period if equipment remains in use (exception: for capitalized tools and molds, fixtures and furniture, calculated depreciation shall be discontinued after the prescribed depreciation period).

---

**EXHIBIT 10    Power Transformers Business Area Performance Data**

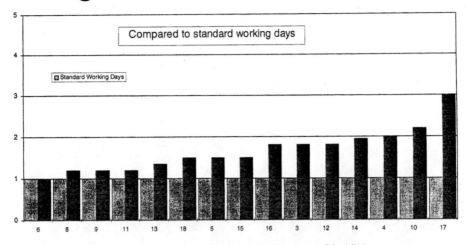

# BA Power Transformers
# Through-Put-Time

(Plant names have been replaced by numbers to preserve confidentiality)

**EXHIBIT 11   Power Transformers Business Area Performance Data**

# BA Power Transformers
# MVA/Squaremeters

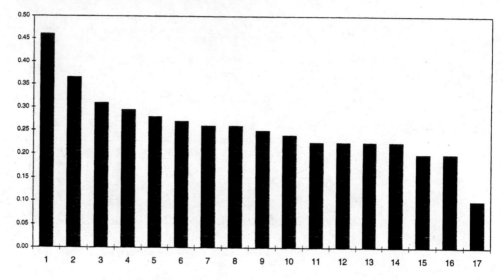

(Plant names have been replaced by numbers to preserve confidentiality)

**EXHIBIT 12    Power Transformers Business Area Performance**

# BA Power Transformers
# Revenues per Employee (KUSD)

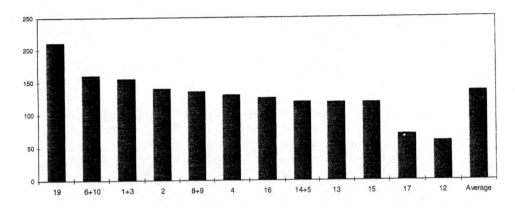

(Plant names have been replaced by numbers to preserve confidentiality

## CASE 8    Roy Rogers Restaurants

It was 8:00 p.m. when Frank Martinez, vice president of franchising for Roy Rogers Restaurants, finally left for home after his second day of meetings in March 1988 with the Franchisee Advisory Council. Although the decision to hold council meetings monthly, rather than biannually, imposed many new demands on himself and his managers, Martinez was encouraged to see a strong rapport developing between the Roy Rogers staff and the franchisees. Attendance at the meetings was increasing, and franchisees were expressing enthusiasm for the company's plans to expand the Roy Rogers system. Martinez was convinced that a successful partnership of Roy Rogers and the franchisees was necessary if the division was to meet the profit growth goal set by Roy Rogers' parent, the Marriott Corporation.

As he left the office, Frank Martinez recalled his conversation with Jack Towle, a major franchisee, who had approached him after the meeting with a request to eliminate the salad-bar concept when he built his next Roy Rogers restaurant. Towle, who was Roy Rogers' third-largest franchisee, operated 16 units in major Baltimore locations. Towle was also one of a small number of franchisees who was expected to play a critical role in the company's new growth strategy; he had recently signed a development agreement to build 34 new units by the end of 1992. As Frank Martinez picked up the phone to inform Ed Bradford, Roy Rogers' vice president and general manager, of Jack's request, he wondered how the organization should respond to an issue with such major implications for both the company and the interests of the 50 other franchisees.

### Marriott Corporation

Roy Rogers Restaurants (often referred to within the company and in advertising as Roy's) was a subsidiary of the Marriott Corporation, a Washington, D.C.-based company which was founded in 1927 by J. Willard Marriott. From its beginnings as a small root beer stand, Marriott had grown to $6.5 billion dollars in sales in 1987, with operations and franchises in 50 states and 24 countries. The company was in three principal businesses: lodging, comprised of both hotel operations and lifecare retirement communities; contract food services for businesses, hospitals, educational institutions, and airlines; and restaurants, comprised of family-oriented and fast-food restaurants as well as highway travel plazas. As a corporation, Marriott was well-known for its expertise in applying creative financing strategies to its real estate development activities. **Exhibits 1** and **2** contain the company's 1987 financial statements and provide sales and income data by business sector.

In its restaurant segment, Marriott operated or franchised more than 1,100 restaurants in 24 states. Its largest chain, Big Boy, was sold in 1987 to a major franchisee. The approximately 220 company-owned units operating at the time of the sale were expected to be converted to a new restaurant concept. Roy Rogers, a fast-food chain serving hamburgers, fried chicken, and roast beef sandwiches, had both franchises and company-owned facilities located primarily in the Middle Atlantic states. Marriott's smallest chain in the restaurant segment was Hot Shoppes, which operated approximately 15 units in the Washington, D.C. area.

Marriott also operated a large number of highway restaurants and merchandise outlets located in travel plazas on 14 turnpikes. The restaurant facilities at the travel plazas included Big Boy and Roy Rogers Restaurants, as well as the fast-food restaurants of competitors such as Burger King. As of 1988, all of these units, including those of the competitors, were operated by Marriott's Travel Plazas Division rather than by the specific chain of which they were a part.

**The Fast-Food Industry**   The fast-food industry was comprised largely of restaurant chains, primarily franchises, that served hamburgers, chicken, pizza, sandwiches, or ethnic food such as Mexican or Chinese dishes. Franchising is explained in **Appendix A**. Chains serving hamburgers as their primary product offering dominated this industry, with approximately 31,511 units and $25.2 billion in sales as of 1986. Fast-food restaurants typically offered restaurant seating or takeout dining, including drive-through service. Takeout service was the most popular, with 60% to 65% of all fast food purchased for takeout consumption. Fast-food dining had become a habit in American life, with nine out of ten people over the age of 12 eating in a fast-food restaurant regularly.[1] Nevertheless, competition within the fast-food segment of the restaurant market had become fierce as the hamburger market matured, particularly with the entry of untraditional competitors such as supermarkets, convenience stores, and producers of prepackaged products suitable for microwave cooking. **Exhibit 3** summarizes information about major competitors in the fast-food industry in 1988.

One industry analyst identified several factors that distinguish the successful restaurant ventures from the failures.[2] First, the individual restaurant or chain must have a standard of product quality that is acceptable to the consumer. Of equal importance is the restaurant's ability to standardize its concept so that customers can predict what their dining experience will be like well before they enter the restaurant. The ability to franchise successfully is also important, because franchising provides for more rapid growth than company operations typically can manage. The most successful chains tend to be marketing-driven organizations that strive to attain the critical mass of advertising needed to establish a strong presence in the target market. Finally, the caliber of a firm's management, both in the various functional areas and in the restaurant facilities themselves, greatly affects the firm's ability to respond to changing industry trends. The ability to compete on these many dimensions becomes particularly important as a market segment matures and growth opportunities become more limited.

Competitors in the hamburger segment of the fast-food industry employed a number of strategies to prepare for the anticipated decline in hamburger demand. Most diversified their offerings with breakfast and other special menus and developed new concepts such as drive-through-only units and home delivery; many attempted to develop international markets for their products. Yet several other factors exacerbated the pressures facing the industry.[3] The

---

[1] The Naisbitt Group, *The Future of Franchising: Looking 25 Years Ahead to the Year 2010* (Washington, D.C.: International Franchise Association, 1986), p. 1.

[2] Daniel R. Lee, "Why some Succeed Where Others Fail," *Cornell Hotel and Restaurant Administration Quarterly* (November 1987), pp. 33–34.

[3] Sidney J. Feltenstein, "Fast Food Businesses Must Adjust to Trends," *Marketing News*, September 25, 1987, p. 22.

first was changing demographics. By the late 1980s, the aging of the baby boom generation (people born between 1945 and 1970) in the United States, and the increase in the elderly population were already having a significant impact on the industry's labor pool and the character of its customer base. Fast-food chains needed to develop product and service offerings, as well as employment opportunities, that would meet the needs of an aging society. In addition, experts pointed out that many localities had become saturated with fast-food restaurants, with the result that suitable prime real estate either was not available or was quite costly to acquire. The cost of media advertising programs had also risen dramatically, making it increasingly difficult for smaller chains without scale economies to afford this traditional tool for increasing customer awareness. Last, because American consumers remained health conscious, they would continue to demand innovative product offerings that were both convenient and nutritious.

In discussing these trends, Ed Bradford, Roy Rogers' vice president and general manager, pointed out the dilemma facing many fast-food restaurant systems:

> While we must continue to develop new product offerings in anticipation of changing consumer preferences, consumers also expect us to offer them a dining experience which is both enjoyable and easily replicable throughout the system. Firms in this business must balance the pressures for innovation with the need to retain the integrity of the service concept which is at the core of their strategy.

Although the many pressures facing the industry were expected to limit opportunities for new national fast-food chains to enter the market, regional competitors like Roy Rogers were expected to enjoy some competitive advantage because of their ability to react quickly to trends, exploit relationships with local real estate developers, and develop niche strategies well-suited to geographically limited markets.

## Roy Rogers Restaurants

The Roy Rogers Restaurant system had a strategic mission that emphasized hamburger and chicken products, a family orientation, and a high-price/high-value perception. The system was named for Roy Rogers, a country-and-western singer in the 1950s, best known for his TV and feature-film appearances with his wife, Dale Evans, and his horse, Trigger. Although he had retired in the mid-1970s, he remained active in the entertainment industry and continued to make himself available to attend grand openings of new Roy Rogers units and other special company events.

Two of the Roy Rogers system's unique features were its salad bar and its Fixin's Bar, a condiment bar located in the middle of the store at which customers could add tomatoes, lettuce, pickles, and other condiments to their sandwiches. At the end of 1986, chicken and hamburgers were the most popular products in Roy Rogers Restaurants in terms of sales revenues, accounting for just over 45% of all sales. Drinks, french fries, cole slaw, and roast beef accounted for another 40% of sales. Salads typically accounted for about 5% of sales. With 345 company-owned and 214 franchised units as of 1987, Roy Rogers was thirteenth in revenues among the top fast-food franchises.[4] Following the arrival in 1986 of Ed Bradford, vice president and general manager, and Frank Martinez, vice president of franchising, the Roy Rogers management team had developed a plan to double the system within five years. **Exhibit 4** shows the organization Ed Bradford had created by 1988. The division hoped to

---

[4] Andrew Kostecka, "Restaurant Franchising in the Economy," *Restaurant Business,* March 20, 1988, p. 194.

add 100 company units and 202 franchised units by 1992; the latter objective required the addition of 45 new franchisees.

Like most franchises, Roy Rogers had a highly competitive selection process for its franchisees. Applicants, whether individuals or partnerships, were expected to complete a document summarizing their personal data, business experience, and independently verified statements of their personal assets, as well as to provide a plan for financing and managing the franchise. Prospective franchisees were expected to have a combined net worth of $500,000 or more, exclusive of their principal residences and personal property, with at least $150,000 in liquid assets available for investment. According to company statistics, 1% of the applicants succeeded in becoming franchisees. In addition to financial qualifications, applicants were evaluated on the basis of their previous restaurant experience, community standing, business accomplishments, and other factors such as character and motivation. Individual owners and operating partners (who were required to have at least a 50% equity position in their partnership) were expected to devote substantially all of their time to the franchise.

Franchisees with the resources to develop multiple sites were attractive applicants to franchisors like Roy Rogers, whose strategy emphasized rapid growth of their system. These franchisees were selected not only for their financial resources and operating experience but also for their expertise in local real estate markets and for the organizational structure they had in place to manage multiple units. Frank Martinez described the situation as follows:

> Franchisors facing pressure to increase profitability and market share constantly struggle with the question of whether they should constrain the growth of their system by adhering to the pure franchise form of single-unit ownership. While single-unit owners have strong incentives to provide the on-site supervision necessary to maintain the quality of their operations, more time and resources may be required to integrate them into the franchise system. On the other hand, franchisees with the resources to develop multiple sites may be able to integrate new units into the system more rapidly, although they may be less effective as managers because they do not have an operating role in their units.

Since there were only a small number of franchisees with the resources and expertise required to operate multiple units, there was considerable competition within the franchisor community to secure multisite development agreements with them. The current population of 51 Roy's franchisees was comprised primarily of individual owner-operators of single or multiple units, with only eight out of the group organized as operating-investment partnerships and three organized as limited partnerships.

Franchises were awarded for a period of 20 years and could be acquired either by constructing a new restaurant or, in selected instances, by purchasing an existing company-owned or franchised facility. When matching franchisees to areas chosen for development, Roy Rogers tried to honor the geographical preferences of franchisees; however, they were expected to relocate if no local sites were available. The Franchise Agreement did not include a guarantee of territorial exclusivity. Other franchises or company-owned restaurants could be established within the same territory if Roy Rogers so desired.

The initial fee to acquire a Roy Rogers franchise was $25,000, plus an option fee of $5,000 for the first unit. The total investment required, and income of a typical franchised unit are summarized in **Exhibits 5** and **6**. Roy's received ongoing monthly royalties of 4% of gross sales from each franchisee as well as the franchisee's commitment to expend 5% of gross sales per month for advertising. Other fast-food chains charged initial franchise fees ranging from $15,000 to $40,000, and royalty fees ranging from 2% to 6% of gross sales.

Some competitors also exacted fees of $20,000 to $50,000 for technical services related to the opening of a new unit and training of personnel. As of 1988, McDonald's, the recognized industry leader, charged an initial franchise fee of $22,500 but did not charge any technical fee.

The Roy Rogers Franchise Agreement contained detailed provisions regarding the location, design, operation, and sale of franchised units. (A summary of the Roy Rogers Franchise Agreement is presented in **Appendix B**.) One of the essential elements of the contract, which was relevant to Jack Towle's request to discontinue the salad bar, was the requirement that the franchisee serve only the menu items specified by the company and follow all company specifications regarding the content, weight, preparation, and variety of products offered. Franchisees were visited approximately every two months by a Roy's franchise consultant, who inspected each operation for compliance with the system and assisted franchisees in making improvements. As of 1988, there were nine franchise consultants, each of whom had responsibility for approximately 25 restaurants. Since uniformity in both quality specifications and the variety of product offerings was considered quite important to the integrity of the system, any deviations from the standard concept were considered serious infractions deserving of close monitoring by management. Although the company tried to be constructive in helping franchisees to rectify performance deficiencies or contract violations, the Franchise Agreement could be terminated if problems were not corrected within a reasonable period of time.

While the company recognized the importance of preserving the Roy Rogers system, management also recognized the need to encourage innovation among the franchisees. As Frank Martinez explained:

> While we do have a well-funded, in-house research and development effort, we also recognize that our franchisees have a great deal to contribute to the Roy Rogers organization. After all, they are entrepreneurs, many of whom have invested a good percentage of their personal wealth and careers in the Roy Rogers system. They also tend to have a unique perspective on the business, which comes from their daily contact with the customers, the suppliers, and the work force. While we want our franchisees to challenge us, to question the status quo, we also want them to see the benefits of working through the organization to accomplish change. Our task as a franchisor is to harness their dedication, creativity, and entrepreneurial spirit in a way which can benefit both the individual franchisees and the system as a whole.

One of the programs the company had introduced to manage the testing and implementation of new ideas was its Product Testing Policy (PTP). In the past, franchisees with suggestions for new products or operational improvements had simply submitted their suggestions to Roy's management for approval to introduce the new concept at their facility. While many ideas had been rejected because they were not sufficiently well-developed or were incompatible with the company's strategy, the franchisees had not been given timely feedback about the reasons certain ideas were not selected for further evaluation. While the company viewed its role in managing the research and development (R&D) process as consistent with its mandate to preserve the integrity of the system, some confusion had existed among the franchisees as to whether Roy's was truly committed to innovation. The new PTP represented an attempt to define the roles of the franchisee and Roy Rogers management in the product development process, while providing a mechanism for objective, timely evaluation of new ideas.

To initiate the PTP, the franchisee submitted a Product Test Request describing the new product idea or proposed operational improvement. The proposal was circulated within

Roy Rogers to the managers of franchising, marketing, and R&D. If the concept was deemed appropriate for further study, the company and franchisee jointly developed a plan for testing the new idea and judging its success. Although the new idea could be tested by either the company R&D department or the franchisee, the franchisee was encouraged to carry out the test whenever feasible. Franchisees received no royalties or other remuneration for ideas they proposed that subsequently were selected for commercial development. Nevertheless, franchisees were quite receptive to the PTP and felt it improved communication and forced some necessary discipline and thoughtful analysis in judging new products.

**The Jack Towle Organization**   With 16 Roy Rogers units operating in urban Baltimore locations, Jack Towle was the third-largest Roy Rogers franchisee. He had been a franchisee for about six years. His units were quite successful, with average sales of $1,300,000 each, 30% higher than the typical Roy Rogers restaurant. Jack Towle was unique among Roy Rogers franchisees in that he owned a number of restaurant franchises with multiple firms. While the Towle franchise contract with Roy Rogers prohibited him from purchasing franchises involving food offerings similar to Roy's, the various franchisors nevertheless did compete with one another for access to the Towle real estate holdings in Baltimore. The Towle organization had considerable expertise in local real estate development and based its franchise development decisions on the profitability of the franchise and the nature of the working relationship with the franchisor. In order to secure the original contract with the Towle organization, Roy Rogers had agreed to reduce the standard royalty payment from 4% to 3% of gross sales for all of Jack Towle's units.

The Towle organization was one of a small percentage of franchisees with whom Roy Rogers had signed franchise development agreements. In 1987, Towle had agreed to develop 34 new units by the end of five years, resulting in a total of 50 units in operation by 1992. Towle had several Roy Rogers Restaurants under construction at the time that he approached Frank Martinez with the request to discontinue the salad bar at the newest facility.

### The Salad Bar Issue

When Jack Towle had approached Frank Martinez at the Franchisee Advisory Council (FAC) meeting, he had argued his case by pointing out that there were circumstances unique to his locations that warranted modification of the system. Towle had explained that the new facility being planned was going to be situated in a business district with considerable lunchtime traffic. From past experience Towle recognized that adequate seating was important to urban customers when selecting a fast-food restaurant for lunch. Since salads sales typically represented only 5% of a unit's business, Towle had concluded that it would be preferable to eliminate the salad bar in the unit being planned and replace it with six additional seats. With customer turnover at lunchtime occurring approximately every 12 minutes, Towle felt that the number of customers who would benefit from the additional seating capacity would outweigh those who could not order salad. Furthermore, with an average customer check estimated at $3.34, Towle felt his unit's revenues and profits would improve if the additional seating succeeded in attracting incremental lunchtime traffic. While the typical check of a salad-bar customer was higher, at $3.85, Towle estimated that only 2.5% of the salad-bar customers would be lost if the salad bar were not available.

As he contemplated possible responses to Towle's request, Frank Martinez was well aware that the Franchise Agreement was unequivocal in prohibiting individual franchisees from modifying the system. The agreement stated: "Franchisee agrees to serve the menu items specified by Franchisor, [and] to follow all specifications and formulas of Franchisor as to contents and weight of products served.[5]" Yet Martinez also knew that other factors had to be considered.

A major concern was the effect of a refusal on Jack Towle's motivation to develop future Roy Rogers franchises. While Martinez felt that Towle would honor his contractual obligation to meet the established development timetable, he was far less certain whether Towle would choose his most attractive sites for the new Roy Rogers facilities. Without Jack Towle's local contacts, it would be difficult and potentially costly for Roy Rogers to gain access to the desirable locations in the Baltimore market. Since rapid franchise development was essential to the firm's strategy, Martinez did not wish to take any action that would prohibit him from becoming the franchisor of preference to this important franchisee.

Yet Frank Martinez conceded that he had an important obligation to protect the interests of the 50 other franchisees as well as the company-owned Roy Rogers operations. Uniformity of product offerings was an essential component of the franchising concept, and he wondered whether allowing Jack Towle to eliminate the salad bar from a restaurant in a major urban location would dilute the consumer's image of Roy Rogers in a way that would harm the entire system. Since the value of an individual franchise depended largely on the success of the system as a whole, Martinez knew that any action he took with respect to Jack Towle's facilities would have important implications for both the company and the individual franchisees.

Martinez also found himself concerned about the precedent that would be set by allowing a franchisee to deviate from the standard menu. Since there were several other franchisees who had signed development agreements or who owned multiple units, many of them could approach Roy Rogers for concessions if they discovered that Jack Towle had been allowed to deviate from the terms of the contract. The FAC meetings provided numerous opportunities for the franchisees to meet and share information, so it was inevitable that the company's handling of this problem would become a topic of conversation within the franchisee community. Furthermore, Martinez had already made some concessions during the original contract negotiations with Jack Towle, and he did not want Towle to develop the impression that the terms of the Franchise Agreement could easily be waived.

As he dialed Ed Bradford's number from his car telephone while on the way home, Frank Martinez was far from certain what he should recommend.

## Appendix A

**Franchising**    The term *franchise* refers to a contract between two entities, one of whom, the franchisor, has a product or service and a system for setting up and operating a business to sell it. The opportunity to replicate this system and to market the product, with its recognized trademarks, has some economic value for which a prospective franchisee is willing to pay a fee. This fee ordinarily consists of an initial payment plus an ongoing percentage of gross revenues or other fees based on the sale of goods or services to the franchisee. Franchise systems in which the franchisor functions as a supplier, with an independent sales relationship with the franchisee, are referred to as product or trade name franchises. Examples of this type of franchise are automobile sales dealerships or gasoline service

---

[5] Roy Rogers Franchise Agreement, 1987 version, p. 12.

stations. Systems in which franchisees gain access to an entire business concept, marketing and operating plans and standards, as well as to continuing assistance from the franchisor, are called business format franchises. It is this latter type of franchise, of which Roy Rogers is an example, that is expected to contribute most to franchising's growth in the next decades. There is also a third type of franchising, called conversion franchising, in which established businesses become franchise outlets for established companies. The conversion franchisees pay fees to the franchise organization in the form of annual fixed fees and royalties in exchange for advertising support and other services. The Century 21 real estate company is a well-known example of this type of franchise.

Franchise business now accounts for approximately one-third of all retail sales in the United States, more than $590 billion dollars, and is expected to account for half of all retail sales by the year 2000.[6] Although franchising is most prevalent in the fast-food restaurant and lodging businesses, franchises offering such diverse services as housekeeping, automobile maintenance, and videocassette rentals have also emerged and are contributing to franchising's dramatic growth. Franchise businesses are notable for dramatically low failure rates as compared with independent businesses. Approximately 97% of the franchises started in a given year are still in operation 12 months later, compared with 62% of independent businesses. After 10 years, 90% of the franchises remain in operation, as compared with 18% of the independent businesses.[7] Because of these impressive result, franchising is often described as a way of capturing many of the advantages of entrepreneurship while minimizing the risks.

In its purest form, franchising involves the purchase of a single-unit operation by an individual who invests his or her personal assets in the franchise and agrees to act as the full-time owner/manager of the facility. In addition to single-unit franchisees, franchisors also may recruit individuals and firms with substantial experience and financial resources who have an interest in developing and operating multiple units in a particular geographical area. A franchisor may also award a master franchise contract, in which he or she sells the right to develop franchises in an entire territory to a middleman, who in turn sells the individual units.

Whatever its structure, the relationship between the franchisor and franchisee is delineated in quite specific terms in the franchise contract, which is negotiated well before a unit opens for business. These agreements typically contain standards for site selection and design, operations, marketing, and sale of the facility. One of the critical factors distinguishing the franchisor-franchisee relationship from that of an employer and employee is the fact that the franchisee is considered the owner of the unit and, therefore, has the right to sell the franchise provided he or she can locate a qualified buyer. Franchise contracts typically allow the franchisor considerable latitude in approving prospective purchasers as well as terminating the franchise contracts of those operators who fail to adhere to the performance standards established for the franchise system, although this latitude is increasingly being restricted by the courts. A summary of the Roy Rogers Franchise Agreement has been included as **Appendix B**.

Franchise offerings must adhere to regulatory standards established by the Federal Trade Commission and various state governments. Franchisors must provide prospective franchisees with a Uniform Franchise Offering Circular (UFOC), whose purpose is to

---

[6] Howard Reill, "Business Barometer," *Restaurant Business,* March 20, 1988, p. 2.
[7] Ibid.

provide extensive background on the franchisor's management team, the franchise concept and contract, and the financial position of the firm. The regulatory agencies scrutinize the financial data contained in the UFOC to ensure that no guarantees of financial performance are offered. This regulatory oversight came about in response to the fraudulent practices that became public during the franchising boom in the 1960s. Many investors were lured into purchasing franchises that, in fact, were pyramid schemes in which a franchisee's income was generated not by selling a product, but rather by recruiting new franchisees.

## Appendix B

### Casewriter's Summary of the Franchise Agreement

**Franchise Option Agreement**   The construction and development of a **Roy Rogers** facility preceded the signing of the Franchise Agreement and were governed by a separate document called the Option Agreement. Following approval of an application, the first-time franchisee paid a $5,000 option fee and submitted a written Site Approval Package that included a basic layout of the facility, aerial photographs, a marked map, a demographic analysis, a financing plan, and three-year cash flow projections. The Real Estate Department at **Roy Rogers** evaluated each site request and notified the franchisee of whether construction could proceed. Multiple submissions could be required before a site was finally selected.

   **Roy Rogers** supplied the general building plans for each new facility; franchisees were expected to retain local architects who could modify the plans to comply with local building codes. Franchisees were required to submit any such changes for review as well as to provide copies of all required permits. Franchisees independently negotiated to purchase or lease the land on which the facility was to reside.

   Once construction was underway, franchisees purchased the necessary equipment and provided **Roy Rogers** with documentation that the equipment conformed to the company's specifications. Although franchisees were free to purchase the equipment wherever they chose, **Roy Rogers** made available a list of qualified vendors whose products the company had already inspected.

**The Franchise Agreement**   The actual Franchise Agreement was typically executed within 30 days of a unit's opening, although technically it could be signed up to 180 days prior to opening. Upon opening the initial franchise fee of $25,000 was paid to the company. Typically, 12 to 18 months elapsed between the approval of a franchisee and the opening of a new facility. The facility approval process was similar for franchisees planning to renovate and convert existing restaurant buildings.

   Franchisees were expected to adhere to a strict timetable in opening units for business. Those who fell behind schedule in opening their restaurant could be charged a monthly fee of $3,000 until the unit became operational or, where applicable, until the agreement could be terminated and a replacement located. Both owners and lessees were required to pay the company an ongoing royalty fee of four percent (4%) of gross revenues once the unit became operational.

   **Financing**   As reflected in **Exhibit 5**, the total cost of building and equipping a new facility ranged between $976,000 and $1,374,000. Costs were somewhat lower for conversions or leasings. Franchisees were permitted to obtain some outside financing, provided the debt to total capital ratio for the franchise project did not exceed 65%.

**Advertising and promotion** Franchisees were expected to contribute to regional advertising and promotion campaigns as well as to devote a specific percentage of their gross receipts to local advertising efforts. The franchise agreement specified a minimum monthly contribution of 5% of gross sales for regional and local advertising expenditures combined. Of this total expenditure, a minimum of 1% of gross revenues were required to be spent on local marketing. The company could increase these spending requirements beyond the contractually established percentages only after obtaining the approval of two-thirds of the franchisees. Franchisees conducted local marketing programs independently; however, they were expected to secure **Roy Rogers'** approval of their annual plans, including any promotional materials to be used.

The regional advertising programs were directed by the Marketing Department at **Roy Rogers**. In designing these programs, the company was not required to ensure that a particular facility benefited directly from the funds it had contributed. The company also was not required to secure the franchisees' approval of the plans or of any materials to be used.

**Roy Rogers** contributed a maximum of $7,500 from the regional advertising pool for expenses associated with the Grand Opening of a franchise. Should **Roy Rogers**, the film star after whom the franchise system was named, attend a Grand Opening or other special event at a restaurant, the franchisee was expected to pay for any expenses associated with his visit.

**Opening the unit** **Roy Rogers** was contractually obligated to make the services of its franchise consultant available to a franchisee opening a new unit. The franchise consultant offered guidance concerning the many tasks involved in opening a new unit and provided training for the franchisee's employees. The franchise consultant was also free to requisition the services of other **Roy Rogers** personnel whose assistance may be required to ensure a successful opening.

**Training** The manager and assistant managers of each unit were required to complete the **Roy Rogers** training program before beginning work. Franchisees were required to absorb the costs of any training programs that the company deemed necessary to address deficiencies in the operation of a unit. They also were required to conduct training on-site for all employees using standard programs developed by **Roy Rogers**.

**Operations** Franchisees were expected to adhere to the company's Operating Manual, which described the many performance, quality, and design standards that constituted the **Roy Rogers** system. Company representatives had the authority to enter the restaurant unit without notice to verify that required procedures were being followed.

The Operating Manual contained standards regarding the cleanliness and maintenance of the equipment and facility. Those who failed to operate the restaurant in a manner required to obtain the highest health classification awarded by local authorities could be required to pay the costs of remedial training for the employees. The Operating Manual specified the days and hours during which each facility was required to operate and the uniforms to be worn by the employees. Franchisees were required to renovate the restaurant building, equipment, and signs at least once every five years to comply with the current image of the system. Furthermore, they were expected to carry out any modifications to the system that the company initiated during the period of the agreement. Signs of the type specified by the company were required to be placed prominently near the unit.

Company specifications concerning the restaurant menu were quite stringent. As part of the Franchise Agreement, the franchisee agreed to serve all of the menu items specified by the company, to follow all specifications regarding the contents, weight, and preparation of the food products, and to sell only products approved by **Roy Rogers.** The company provided the franchisee with the names of approved suppliers whose products conformed to specifications. Although franchisees were free to purchase supplies from any vendor they chose, they were required to submit new vendors' samples or product specifications for a qualifying evaluation. Sale of alcohol and display of entertainment devices such as video games or slot machines were prohibited unless approved by the company. The agreement also contained a provision that any taxes associated with the operation of the facility were to be paid promptly so the operation of the facility would not be jeopardized.

**Financial reporting**   Franchisees were required to submit weekly sales reports by telephone and written sales reports to headquarters within 10 days of the end of each calendar month. Monthly written operating statements were expected to follow the preliminary reports within 25 days after the end of each month. A balance sheet and operating statements were submitted at the end of each fiscal year. **Roy Rogers** could require that these reports be prepared by independent auditors and could visit the franchise without notice to inspect the financial statements and supporting documentation. The **Roy Rogers** Operating Manual contained detailed specifications for the formats of any reports to be used.

**Trademarks**   The trademarks owned by **Roy Rogers** included all "words, symbols, insignia, devices, designs, Trade Names, Service Marks, and rights in distinctive designs of buildings and signs" used to identify restaurants licensed to use the system and its products and services.[8] Franchisees were prohibited from using the trademarks, any variations, or any names confusingly similar to the trademarks, in a manner not approved by **Roy Rogers.** They also were prohibited from taking any steps to claim ownership of the trademarks. Trademarks of other firms could not be used at a **Roy Rogers** facility without the company's approval.

**Noncompete provision**   The franchisee and its key employees ordinarily were prohibited from taking part in any food business similar to **Roy Rogers,** located within a specific mile radius of their unit, for 18 months following the termination of the agreement. (Ownership of less than 1% of the stock of a public corporation in a similar business was allowed.) While operating the franchise, they were expected to avoid any outside activities that would prevent them from devoting full-time effort, i.e., 40 hours per week, to the business.

**Relationship between franchisor and franchisee**   The franchisee was prohibited from holding itself out as an agent, legal representative, partner, subsidiary, joint venturer, or employee of **Roy Rogers.** The franchisee had no legal authority to enter into any binding agreements on the company's behalf. No fiduciary relationship existed between the franchisee and the company.

**Sale or transfer of interest**   Under the terms of the Franchise Agreement, **Roy Rogers** had the right to transfer or sell all or some of its rights and obligations as franchisor to another individual or entity. Because the franchisee had been selected for his or her individual business skills, financial resources, and personal character, however, he or she was not allowed to sell, transfer, or mortgage any interest in the franchise without the company's consent. Franchisees who violated this important element of the agreement could have their franchises terminated without notice.

**Roy Rogers** was permitted to require that a franchisee offer to sell his or her interest to the company before making it available to other interested parties. In addition, franchisees

---

[8] ROY ROGERS UNIT FRANCHISE AGREEMENT, Standard Form, October 28, 1987, p. 16.

could not offer the unit for sale to another party on more favorable terms than the company received. Franchisees were prohibited from advertising for prospective purchasers unless the company permitted them to do so. Prospective acquirers were expected to undertake the application process described earlier to ensure their fitness to operate the business. **Roy Rogers** received $3,000 to cover any legal and training expenses associated with the transfer. In addition, the original franchisee remained secondarily liable for all obligations relating to the franchise for a period of 24 months following the sale to the new franchisee.

Franchisees could organize as corporations only under circumstances prescribed by **Roy Rogers**. Such corporations could not sell any of their shares in a public offering, nor could any shares be transferred without the company's approval. The operating partner of the franchise was required to retain 51% of the shares of the corporation holding the franchise. Violation of these requirements constituted grounds for terminating the franchise.

The Franchise Agreement also contained provisions for transferring the franchise in the event of death or permanent incapacity of the franchisee.

**Termination of franchise** There were several performance-related reasons for which a franchise could be terminated without notice. Some of the more important were as follows: (1) in the event of bankruptcy or insolvency; and (2) in the event that a plan of liquidation or reorganization was filed, whether or not the plan subsequently was approved by the courts. The franchise agreement specifically noted that the franchise could not be deemed an asset in any reorganization or bankruptcy proceeding.

The franchise could be terminated following a grace period for a number of performance-related reasons as well. Franchisees who failed to perform according to the terms of the agreement were given written notice of their deficiencies. Within the next 30 days, they were required either to resolve the problems cited or to show progress in correcting them. A franchisee could be terminated following written notice if he or she was more than 10 days late in making his or her required royalty or advertising payments to **Roy Rogers**. Other reasons for which a franchise could he terminated with notice included significant health and safety violations, failure to satisfy a legal judgment within 30 days after it became final, falsification of reports to the company, ceasing to do business at the unit, or loss of possession or lease of the property on which the unit was located. A franchisee who received three or more notices regarding the same or similar deficiencies within a 12-month period could have his or her agreement terminated without notice.

**EXHIBIT 1   Marriott Corporation's Balance Sheet, January 1, 1988 and January 2, 1987**

|  | 1987 | 1986 |
|---|---|---|
| **Assets** | | |
| Current assets | | |
| Cash and temporary cash investments | $ 15.6 | $ 26.7 |
| Accounts receivable | 493.6 | 450.7 |
| Due from affiliates | 125.8 | 98.2 |
| Inventories, at lower of average cost or market | 186.5 | 171.3 |
| Prepaid expenses | 97.6 | 81.0 |
| Total current assets | $ 919.1 | $ 827.9 |
| Property and equipment | 469.5 | 348.3 |
| Building and improvements | 323.6 | 402.9 |
| Leasehold improvements | 1,064.9 | 874.4 |
| Furniture and equipment | 680.0 | 591.8 |
| Construction in progress | 690.2 | 537.3 |
|  | $3,228.2 | $2,754.7 |
| Accumulated depreciation and amortization | (650.1) | (547.3) |
|  | $2,578.1 | $2,207.4 |
| Investments in and advances to affiliates | 495.1 | 484.5 |
| Assets held for sale | 501.2 | 386.4 |
| Intangible assets | 528.5 | 403.2 |
| Other assets | 348.5 | 269.9 |
|  | $5,370.5 | $4,579.3 |
| **LIABILITIES AND SHAREHOLDERS' EQUITY** | | |
| Current Liabilities | | |
| Accounts payables | $ 508.6 | $ 440.8 |
| Accrued payroll and benefits | 225.0 | 211.9 |
| Other payables and accrued liabilities | 342.7 | 331.9 |
| Current portion of long-term debt | 46.4 | 32.9 |
| Total current liabilities | $1,122.7 | $1,017.5 |
| Long-term debt | 2,498.8 | 1,662.8 |
| Other long-term liabilities | 212.1 | 193.7 |
| Deferred income | 289.5 | 316.8 |
| Deferred income taxes | 436.6 | 397.5 |
| Shareholders' equity | | |
| Common stock, 147.1 million shares issued | 147.1 | 147.1 |
| Additional paid-in capital | 87.7 | 60.1 |
| Retained earnings | 1,150.2 | 948.9 |
| Treasury stock, at cost, 28.3 and 16.5 million shares, respectively | (574.2) | (165.1) |
| Total shareholders' equity | $ 810.8 | $ 991.0 |
|  | $5,370.5 | $4,579.3 |

**EXHIBIT 2**    Marriott Corporation's Income Statement (Fiscal years ended January 1, 1988, January 2, 1987, and January 3, 1986)

|  | 1987 | 1986 | 1985 |
|---|---|---|---|
|  | ($ IN MILLIONS, EXCEPT PER SHARE AMOUNTS) | | |
| **Sales** | | | |
| Lodging | $2,673.3 | $2,233.1 | $1,898.4 |
| Contract services | 2,969.0 | 2,236.1 | 1,586.3 |
| Restaurants | 879.9 | 797.3 | 757.0 |
| Total sales | $6,522.2 | $5,266.5 | $4,241.7 |
| **Operating Expenses** | | | |
| Lodging | $2,409.4 | $2,017.4 | $1,712.6 |
| Contract services | 2,798.4 | 2,081.2 | 1,467.7 |
| Restaurants | 797.5 | 718.2 | 678.8 |
| Total operating expenses | $6,005.3 | $4,816.8 | $3,859.1 |
| **Operating income** | | | |
| Lodging | $ 263.9 | $ 215.7 | $ 185.8 |
| Contract services | 170.6 | 154.9 | 118.6 |
| Restaurants | 82.4 | 79.1 | 78.2 |
| Total operating income | $ 516.9 | $ 449.7 | $ 382.6 |
| Corporate expenses | $ (74.5) | $ (71.7) | $ (54.2) |
| Interest expense | (90.5) | (60.3) | (75.6) |
| Interest income | 47.0 | 42.5 | 42.9 |
| **Income before income taxes** | $ 398.9 | $ 360.2 | $ 295.7 |
| Provision for income tax | $ 175.9 | $ 168.5 | $ 128.3 |
| **Net income** | $ 223.0 | $ 191.7 | $ 167.4 |
| **Earnings per share** | $ 1.67 | $ 1.40 | $ 1.24 |

**EXHIBIT 3** Fast-Food Restaurant Systems—1986–1987 Systemwide Sales and Units[a]

| RANKING BY SALES | CHAIN NAME (PARENT COMPANY) | 1987 SALES | | | |
|---|---|---|---|---|---|
| | | SYSTEMWIDE-SALES ($ IN MILLIONS) | AVERAGE UNIT VOLUME | COMPANY-OWNED ($ IN MILLIONS) | FRANCHISE-OWNED ($ IN MILLIONS) |
| 1 | McDonald's | $14,300 | $1,433,000 | 4,800 | 9,500 |
| 2 | Burger King (Pillsbury Co., Inc.) | 5,179[b] | 1,092,000[b] | 794[b] | 4,385[b] |
| 3 | Kentucky Fried Chicken (PepsiCo., Inc.) | 4,100 | 659,000 | 1,036[b] | 3,064[b] |
| 4 | Hardee (Imasco, Ltd.) | 3,100 | 878,000[b] | 1,400 | 1,700 |
| 5 | Pizza Hut (PepsiCo., Inc.) | 3,000 | 500,000 | 1,400 | 1,600 |
| 6 | Wendy's | 2,817[b] | 767,000[b] | 992[b] | 1,825[b] |
| 7 | Domino's Pizza | 1,906 | 483,000[b] | 513[b] | 1,393[b] |
| 8 | Taco Bell (PepsiCo., Inc.) | 1,502[b] | 560,000[b] | 825[b] | 677[b] |
| 9 | Arby's (Royal Crown Cola, Inc.) | 1,000 | 541,000[b] | 109[b] | 891[b] |
| 10 | Dunkin' Donuts | 729 | 437,000[b] | 12[b] | 717[b] |
| 11 | Little Ceasar's | 725 | 464,000[b] | 176[b] | 549[b] |
| 12 | Jack in the Box (Foodmaster, Inc.) | 655 | 750,000[b] | 512 | 143 |
| 13 | Roy Rogers (Marriott Corp.) | 568[b] | 1,000,000[b] | 328[b] | 240[b] |
| 14 | Church's | 580[b] | 390,000[b] | 418[b] | 162[b] |
| 15 | Popeyes (A. Copeland Interests) | 460 | 663,000[b] | 80 | 380 |

*Source: Adapted from* "Restaurant Franchising in the Economy," Restaurant Business, *March 20, 1988, p. 194.*
[a] *Data include international operations.*
[b] *Estimated by* Restaurant Business Magazine.

| | 1987 UNITS | |
| --- | --- | --- |
| SYSTEMWIDE | COMPANY-OWNED | FRANCHISE-OWNED |
| 9,911 | 3,151 | 6,760 |
| 5,179 | 794 | 4,385 |
| 7,522 | 1,901 | 5,621 |
| 2,912 | 963 | 1,949 |
| 6,163 | 2,863 | 3,300 |
| 3,848 | 1,259 | 2,589 |
| 4,279 | 1,109 | 3,170 |
| 2,682 | 1,473 | 1,209 |
| 1,848 | 202 | 1,646 |
| 1,669 | 29 | 1,640 |
| 1,820 | 441 | 1,379 |
| 897 | 639 | 258 |
| 583 | 344 | 239 |
| 1,486 | 1,072 | 414 |
| 730 | 112 | 618 |

**EXHIBIT 4  Organization Chart**

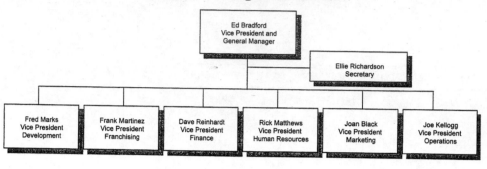

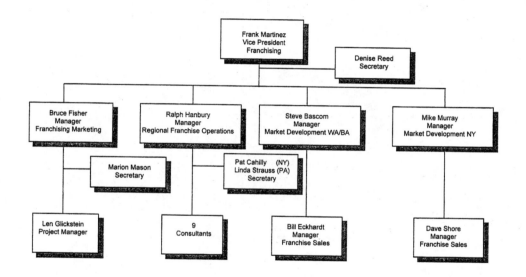

---

**EXHIBIT 5  Cost Structure of a Franchise Unit**

| CAPITAL INVESTMENT | ESTIMATED COST RANGE | |
| --- | --- | --- |
| Facility | $500,000 | $ 550,000 |
| Land | 225,000 | 500,000 |
| Signs, equipment, supplies | 180,000 | 230,000 |
| Inventory | 8,000 | 10,000 |
| Working capital | 25,000 | 40,000 |
| Insurance coverage | 8,000 | 14,000 |
| Franchise fee and option | 30,000 | 30,000 |
| | $976,000 | $1,374,000 |

*Source: Roy Rogers,* Uniform Franchise Offering Circular, *1987 version, p. 26.*

**EXHIBIT 6    Income Statement for a Typical Franchise (Leased Facility)**

|  | AMOUNT | PERCENTAGE TOTAL SALES |
|---|---|---|
| **Sales** | | |
| Gross sales | $1,050,000 | 99% |
| Discount/employee sales | 6,300 | 1 |
| Total sales | $1,056,300 | 100% |
| Cost of goods (food purchase) | 311,500 | 29 |
| Gross profit | $ 744,800 | 71% |
| **Expenses** | | |
| Salaries and benefits | 267,000 | 25 |
| Rent | 97,600 | 9 |
| Paper supplies | 46,400 | 5 |
| Utilities | 41,100 | 4 |
| Interest expense | 29,300 | 3 |
| Equipment depreciation expense | 24,100 | 2 |
| Promotions | 17,800 | 2 |
| Maintenance | 15,000 | 1 |
| Real estate tax | 4,600 | |
| Training | 4,200 | |
| General expenses | 2,200 | |
| Trash removal | 1,900 | |
| Cleaning supplies | 1,800 | |
| Cash register contract | 1,500 | 2 |
| Amortization of franchise fee | 1,250 | |
| Window cleaning | 1,200 | |
| Uniforms | 1,000 | |
| Bookkeeping | 800 | |
| Office supplies | 800 | |
| Dining room plants | 500 | |
| Roy Rogers' name fee | 300 | |
| Exterminator | 200 | — |
| | $ 560,850 | 53% |
| **Royalties/Other Fees** | | |
| Royalties | 42,000 | 4 |
| National advertising | 42,000 | 4 |
| **Total Royalties/Other fees** | $ 84,000 | 8% |
| **Profit before Tax** | 99,950 | 10 |
| Income tax | 49,975 | 5 |
| **Net income** | $ 49,975 | 5 |

**CASE 9**  Codman & Shurtleff, Inc.: Planning and Control System

"This revision combines our results from January to April with the preliminary estimates supplied by each department for the remainder of the year. Of course, there are still a lot of unknown factors to weigh in, but this will give you some idea of our preliminary updated forecast."

As the Board members reviewed the document provided to them by Gus Fleites, vice president of Information and Control at Codman & Shurtleff, Roy Black, president, addressed the six men sitting at the conference table, "This revised forecast leaves us with a big stretch. We are almost two million dollars short of our profit objective for the year. As we discussed last week, we are estimating sales to be $1.1 million above original forecast. This is due in part to the early introduction of the new Chest Drainage Unit. However, three major factors that we didn't foresee last September will affect our profit plan estimates for the remainder of the year.

"First, there's the currency issue: our hedging has partially protected us, but the continued rapid deterioration of the dollar has pushed our costs up on European specialty instruments. Although this has improved Codman's competitive market position in Europe, those profits accrue to the European company and are not reflected in this forecast. Second, we have an unfavorable mix variance; and finally, we will have to absorb inventory variances due to higher than anticipated start up costs of our recently combined manufacturing operations.

"When do we have to take the figures to Corporate?" asked Chuck Dunn, vice president of Business Development.

"Wednesday of next week," replied Black, "so we have to settle this by Monday. That gives us only tomorrow and the weekend to wrap up the June budget revision. I know that each of you has worked on these estimates, but I think that the next look will be critical to achieving our profit objective."

"Bob, do you have anything you can give us?"

Bob Dick, vice president of Marketing, shook his head, "I've been working with my people looking at price and mix. At the moment, we can't realistically get more price. Most of the mix variance for the balance of the year will be due to increased sales of products that we are handling under the new distribution agreement. The mix for the remainder of the year may change, but with 2,700 active products in the catalogue, I don't want to move too far from our original projections. My expenses are cut right to the bone. Further cuts will mean letting staff go."

Black nodded his head in agreement. "Chuck, you and I should meet to review our Research and Development priorities. I know that Herb Stolzer will want to spend time reviewing the status of our programs. I think we should be sure that we have cut back to reflect our spending to date. I wouldn't be surprised if we could find another $400,000 without jeopardizing our long-term programs."

*This case was prepared by Professor Robert Simons as the basis for class discussion rather than to illustrate either effective or ineffective handling of an administrative situation.*

"Well, it seems our work is cut out for us. The rest of you keep working on this. Excluding R&D, we need at least another $500,000 before we start drawing down our contingency fund. Let's meet here tomorrow at two o'clock and see where we stand."

### Codman & Shurtleff, Inc.

Codman & Shurtleff, Inc., a subsidiary of Johnson & Johnson, was established in 1838 in Boston by Thomas Codman to design and fashion surgical instruments. The company developed surgical instrument kits for use in Army field hospitals during the Civil War and issued its first catalogue in 1860. After the turn of the century, Codman & Shurtleff specialized in working with orthopaedic surgeons and with pioneers in the field of neurosurgery.

In 1986, Codman & Shurtleff supplied hospitals and surgeons worldwide with over 2,700 products for surgery including instruments, equipment, implants, surgical disposables, fiberoptic light sources and cables, surgical head lamps, surgical microscopes, coagulators, and electronic pain control simulators and electrodes. These products involved advanced technologies from the fields of metallurgy, electronics, and optics.

Codman & Shurtleff operated three manufacturing locations in Randolph, New Bedford, and Southbridge, Massachusetts, and a distribution facility in Avon, Massachusetts. The company employed 800 people in the United States.

In 1964, Codman & Shurtleff was acquired by Johnson & Johnson, Inc. as an addition to its professional products business. Johnson & Johnson operated manufacturing subsidiaries in 46 countries, sold its products in most countries of the world, and employed 75,000 people worldwide. 1985 sales were $6.4 billion with before tax profits of $900 million [**Exhibit 1**].

Roy Black had been president of Codman & Shurtleff since 1983. In his 25 years with Johnson & Johnson, Black had spent 18 years with Codman, primarily in the Marketing Department. He had also worked at Ethicon and Surgikos. He described his job,

> This is a tough business to manage because it is so complex. We rely heavily on the neurosurgeons for ideas in product generation and for the testing and ultimate acceptance of our products. We have to stay in close contact with the leading neurosurgeons around the world. For example, last week I returned from a tour of the Pacific rim. During the trip, I visited eight Johnson & Johnson/Codman affiliates and 25 neurosurgeons.
>
> At the same time, we are forced to push technological innovation to reduce costs. This is a matter of survival. In the past, we concentrated on producing superior quality goods, and the market was willing to pay whatever it took to get the best. But the environment has changed; the shift has been massive. We are trying to adapt to a situation where doctors and hospitals are under severe pressure to be more efficient and cost-effective.
>
> We compete in 12 major product groups. Since our markets are so competitive, the business is very price sensitive. The only way we can take price is to offer unique products with cost-in-use benefits to the professional user.
>
> Since the introduction of DRG costing[1] by hospitals in 1983, industry volume has been off approximately 20%. We have condensed 14 locations to four and have reduced staff levels by over 20%. There have also been some cuts in R&D, although our goal is to maintain research spending at near double the historical Codman level.

---

[1] On October 1, 1983, Medicare reimbursement to hospitals changed from a cost-plus system to a fixed-rate system as called for in the 1983 Social Security refinancing legislation. The new system was called "prospective payment" because rates were set in advance of treatment according to which of 467 "diagnostic-related groups" (or DRGs) a patient was deemed to fall into. This change in reimbursement philosophy caused major cost-control problems for the nation's 5,800 acute-care hospitals which received an average of 36% of their revenues from Medicare and Medicaid.

Chuck Dunn, vice president of Business Development, had moved three years earlier from Johnson & Johnson Products to join Codman as vice president for Information and Control. During his 24 years with Johnson & Johnson, he had worked with four different marketing divisions as well as the Corporate office. He recalled the process of establishing a new mission statement at Codman,

> When I arrived here, Codman was in the process of defining a more clearly focused mission. Our mission was product oriented, but Johnson & Johnson was oriented by medical specialty. On a matrix, this resulted in missed product opportunities as well as turf problems with other Johnson & Johnson companies.

> It took several years of hard work to arrive at a new worldwide mission statement oriented to medical specialty, but this process was very useful in obtaining group consensus. Our worldwide mission is now defined in terms of a primary focus in the neuro-spinal surgery business. This turns out to be a large market and allows better positioning of our products.

> In addition to clarifying our planning, we use the mission statement as a screening device. We look carefully at any new R&D project to see if it fits our mission. The same is true for acquisitions.

## Reporting Relationships at Johnson & Johnson

In 1985, Johnson & Johnson comprised 155 autonomous subsidiaries operating in three health care markets: consumer products, pharmaceutical products, and professional products. **Exhibit 2** provides details of the business operations of the company.

Johnson & Johnson was managed on a decentralized basis as described in the following excerpt from the 1985 Annual Report,

> The Company is organized on the principles of decentralized management and conducts its business through operating subsidiaries which are themselves, for the most part, integral, autonomous operations. Direct responsibility for each company lies with its operating management, headed by the president, general manager or managing director who reports directly or through a Company group chairman to a member of the Executive Committee. In line with this policy of decentralization, each internal subsidiary is, with some exceptions, managed by citizens of the country where it is located.

Roy Black at Codman & Shurtleff reported directly to Herbert Stolzer at Johnson & Johnson headquarters in New Brunswick, New Jersey. Mr. Stolzer, 59, was a member of the Executive Committee of Johnson & Johnson with responsibility for 16 operating companies in addition to Codman & Shurtleff **[Exhibit 3].** Stolzer had worked for Johnson & Johnson for 35 years with engineering, manufacturing, and senior management experience in Johnson & Johnson Products and at the Corporate office.

The senior policy and decision-making group at Johnson & Johnson was the Executive Committee comprising the chairman, president, chief financial officer, vice president of administration, and eight Executive Committee members with responsibilities for company sectors. The 155 business units of the Company were organized in sectors based primarily on products (e.g., consumer, pharmaceutical, professional) and secondarily on geographic markets.

## Five- and Ten-Year Plans at Johnson & Johnson

Each operating company within Johnson & Johnson was responsible for preparing its own plans and strategies. David Clare, president of Johnson & Johnson, believed that this was one of the key elements in their success. "Our success is due to three basic tenets: a basic belief in decentralized management, a sense of responsibility to our key constituents, and a desire to manage for the long term. We have no corporate strategic planning function nor one strategic plan. Our strategic plan is the sum of the strategic plans of each of our 155 business units."

Each operating company prepared annually a five- and ten-year plan. Financial estimates in these plans were limited to only four numbers: estimated unit sales volume, estimated sales revenue, estimated net income, and estimated return on investment. Accompanying these financial estimates was a narrative description of how these targets would be achieved.

To ensure that managers were committed to the plan that they developed, Johnson & Johnson required that the planning horizon focus on two years only and remain fixed over a five-year period. Thus, in 1983, a budget and second-year forecast was developed for 1984 and 1985 and a strategic plan was developed for the years 1990 and 1995. In each of the years 1984 through 1987, the five- and ten-year plan was redrawn in respect of only years 1990 and 1995. Only in year 1988 would the strategic planning horizon shift five years forward to cover years 1995 and 2000. These two years will then remain the focus of subsequent five- and ten-year plans for the succeeding four years, and so on.

At Codman & Shurtleff, work on the annual five- and ten-year plan commenced each January and took approximately six months to complete. Based on the mission statement, a business plan was developed for each significant segment of the business. For each competitor, the marketing plan included an estimated *pro forma* income statement (volume, sales, profit) as well as a one-page narrative description of their strategy.

Based on the tentative marketing plan, draft plans were prepared by the other departments including research and development, production, finance, and personnel. The tentative plan was assembled in a binder with sections describing mission, strategies, opportunities and threats, environment, and financial forecasts. This plan was debated, adjusted, and approved over the course of several meetings in May by the Codman Board of Directors [see **Exhibit 4**], comprising the president and seven key subordinates.

In June, Herb Stolzer travelled to Boston to preside over the annual review of the five- and ten-year plan. Codman executives considered this a key meeting that could last up to three days. During the meeting Stolzer reviewed the plan, aired his concerns, and challenged the Codman Board on assumptions, strategies, and forecasts. A recurring question during the session was, "If your new projection for 1990 is below what you predicted last year, how do you intend to make up the shortfall?"

After this meeting, Roy Black summarized the plan that had been approved by Stolzer in a two-page memorandum that he sent directly to Jim Burke, chairman and chief executive officer of Johnson & Johnson.

Based on the two-page "Burke letters," the five- and ten-year plans for all operating companies were presented by Executive Committee members and debated and approved at the September meeting of the Executive Committee in New Brunswick. Company presidents, including Roy Black, were often invited to prepare formal presentations. The discussion in these meetings was described by those in attendance as, "very frank," "extremely challenging," and "grilling."

## Financial Planning at Johnson & Johnson

Financial planning at Johnson & Johnson comprised annual budgets (i.e., profit plans) for the upcoming operating year and a second-year forecast. Budgets were detailed financial documents prepared down to the expense center level for each operating company. The second-year forecast was in a similar format but contained less detail than the budget for the upcoming year.

Revenues and expenses were budgeted by month. Selected balance sheet items, e.g., accounts receivable and inventory, were also budgeted to reflect year-end targets.

Profit plan targets were developed on a bottom-up basis by each operating company by reference to two documents: (1) the approved five- and ten-year plan and (2) the second-year forecast prepared the previous year.

Chuck Dunn described the budgeting process at Codman & Shurtleff,

> We wrote the initial draft of our 1987 profit plan in the Summer of 1986 based on the revision of our five- and ten-year plan. By August, the profit plan is starting to crystallize; we have brought in the support areas such as accounting, quality assurance, R&D, and engineering, to ensure that they "buy in" to the new 1987 profit and marketing plans.
>
> The first year of the strategic plan is used as a basis for the departments to prepare their own one-year plans for both capital and expense items. The production budget is based on standard costs and nonstandard costs such as development programs and plant consolidations. As for the R&D budget, the project list is always too long, so we are forced to rank the projects. For each project, we look at returns, costs, time expended, sales projections, expected profit, and gross profit percentages as well as support to be supplied to the plants.
>
> The individual budgets are then consolidated by the Information and Control Department. We look very carefully at how this budget compares with our previous forecasts. For example, the first consolidation of the 1986 profit plan revealed a $2.4 million profit shortfall against the second-year forecast that was developed in 1984 and updated in June 1985. To reconcile this, it was necessary to put on special budget presentations by each department to remove all slack and ensure that our earlier target could be met if possible. The commitment to this process is very strong.
>
> We are paying more and more attention to our second-year forecast since it forces us to re-examine strategic plans. The second-year forecast is also used as a benchmark for next year's profit plan and, as such, it is used as hindsight to evaluate the forecasting ability and performance of managers.

The procedures for approving the annual profit plan and second-year forecast followed closely the procedures described above for the review of the five- and ten-year plans. During the early fall, Herbert Stolzer reviewed the proposed budget with Roy Black and the Codman & Shurtleff Board of Directors. Changes in profit commitment from previous forecasts and the overall profitability and tactics of the Company were discussed in detail.

After all anticipated revenues and expenses were budgeted, a separate contingency expense line item was added to the budget; the amount of the contingency changed from year to year and was negotiated between Stolzer and Black based on the perceived uncertainty in achieving budget targets. In 1986, the Codman & Shurtleff contingency was set at $1.1 million.

Stolzer presented the budget for approval at the November meeting of the Johnson & Johnson Executive Committee.

### Budget Revisions and Reviews

During the year, budget performance was monitored closely. Each week, sales revenue performance figures were sent to Herb Stolzer. In addition, Roy Black sent a monthly management report to Stolzer that included income statement highlights and a summary of key balance sheet figures and ratios. All information was provided with reference to (1) position last month (2) position this month (3) budgeted position. All variances that Black considered significant were explained in a narrative summary.

The accuracy of budget projections was also monitored during the year and formally revised on three occasions. The first of these occasions occurred at the March meeting of the Executive Committee. Going around the table, each Executive Committee member was asked to update the Committee on his most recent estimates of sales and profits for each operating company for the current year. Herb Stolzer relied on Roy Black to provide this information for Stolzer's review prior to the March meeting.

The "June Revision" referred to the revised budget for the current year that was presented to the Executive Committee in June. The preparation of this revised budget required managers at Codman & Shurtleff and all other Johnson & Johnson companies to re-budget in May for the remainder of the fiscal year. This revision involved re-checking all budget estimates starting with the lowest level expense center as well as revising the second-year forecast when necessary.

The third review of budget projections was the "November update" which was presented to the Executive Committee at the November meeting concurrently with their consideration of the budget and second-year forecast for the upcoming budget year. The November update focused on results for the 10 months just completed and revised projections for the remaining two months. At Codman & Shurtleff, preparation of the November update involved performance estimates from all departments but was not conducted to the same level of detail as the June revision.

## Corporate View of the Planning and Control Process

David Clare, president of Johnson & Johnson:

> The sales and profit forecasts are always optimistic in the five- and ten-year plans, but this is O.K. We want people to stretch their imagination and think expansively. In these plans we don't anticipate failure; they are a device to open up thinking. There is no penalty for inaccuracies.

> The profit plan and second-year forecast are used to run the business and evaluate managers on planning, forecasts, and achievements.

> We ask our managers to always include in their plans an account of how and why their estimates have changed over time. That is why we use the five- and ten-year planning concept rather than a moving planning horizon. This allows us to revise our thinking over time and allows for retrospective learning.

> If a manager insists on a course of action and we (the Executive Committee) have misgivings, nine times out of ten we will let him go ahead. If we say, 'No,' and the answer should have been, 'Yes,' we say, 'Don't blame us, it was your job to sell us on the idea and you didn't do that.'

> Johnson & Johnson is extremely decentralized, but that does not mean that managers are free from challenge as to what they are doing. In the final analysis, managing conflict is what management is all about. Healthy conflict is about *what* is right, not *who* is right.

> Our Company philosophy is to manage for the long term. We do not use short term bonus plans. Salary and bonus reviews are entirely subjective and qualitative and are intended to reward effort and give special recognition to those who have performed uniquely. The Executive Committee reviews salary recommendations for all managers above a certain salary level, but Company presidents, such as Roy Black, have full discretion as to how they remunerate their employees.

Herbert Stolzer, Executive Committee member,

> The planning and control systems used in Johnson & Johnson provide real benefits. These systems allow us to find problems and run the business. This is true not only for us at Corporate, but also at the operating companies where they are a tremendous tool. Once a year, managers are forced to

review their businesses in depth for costs, trends, manufacturing efficiency, marketing plans, and their competitive situation. Programs and action plans result.

You have to force busy people to do this. Otherwise, they will be caught up in day-to-day activities—account visits, riding with salesmen, standing on the manufacturing floor.

Our long-term plans are not meant to be a financial forecast; rather, they are meant to be an objective way of setting aspirations. We never make those numbers—who can forecast sales five or ten years out with unforeseen markets, products, and competitors? Even the accuracy of our two-year forecast is bad. The inaccuracy is an indication of how fast our markets are changing. Our businesses are so diverse, with so many competitors, that it is difficult to forecast out two years.

I visit at least twice a year with each operating company board. We usually spend the better part of a week going over results, planning issues, strategic plans, and short and long term problems. The Executive Committee, to the best of my knowledge, never issues quantitative performance targets before the bottom-up process begins.

At the Executive Committee meetings, a lot of argument takes place around strategic planning issues. How fast can we get a business up to higher returns? Are the returns in some businesses too high? Are we moving too fast? However, the outcome is never to go back to the operating company and say we need 8% rather than 6%. The challenge has already taken place between the Executive Committee member and the Company Board. If the EC member is satisfied with the answers provided by the Board, that's the end of it.

It happens very rarely that the consolidated budget is unacceptable. Occasionally, we might say, 'We really could use some more money.' However, in the second review, this may not turn up any extra. If so, that's O.K.

Our systems are not used to punish. They are used to try and find and correct problems. Bonuses are not tied to achieving budget targets. They are subjectively determined, although we use whatever objective indicators are available—for example, sales and new product introductions for a marketing vice president.

The key to our whole system is the operating Company presidents. We are so decentralized that they define their own destiny. A successful Company president needs to be able to stand up to pressure from above. He needs to have the courage to say, 'I have spent hours and hours on that forecast and for the long term health of the Company, we have to spend that budget.'

**Clark Johnson, corporate controller,**

At the Executive Committee review meetings, we always review the past five years before starting on the forecast. We look at volume growth rates—sales growth adjusted for inflation—and discuss problems. Then, we compare growth rate against GNP growth. We keep currency translation out of it. We evaluate foreign subsidiaries in their own currency and compare growth against country specific GNP. We are looking for market share by country. On almost any topic, we start with forecast versus past track record.

The Committee never dictates or changes proposals—only challenges ideas. If it becomes clear to the individual presenting that the forecast is not good enough, only that person decides whether a revision is necessary. These discussions can be very frank and sometimes acrimonious. The result of the review may be agreement to present a revision at the next meeting, specific action items to be addressed, or personal feedback to David Clare.

This process cascades down the organization. Executive Committee members review and challenge the proposals of Company presidents. Company presidents review and challenge the proposals of their vice presidents.

**Thursday, May 8, 1986—8:00 P.M.**   Following the Codman & Shurtleff Board meeting to discuss the June budget revision on the afternoon of Thursday, May 8 (described at the beginning of the case), Roy Black, Chuck Dunn, Bob Dick, and Gus Fleites worked into the evening going over the list of active R&D projects. Their review focused on R&D projects that had been included in the original 1986 budget. They searched for projects that could be eliminated due to changed market conditions or deferred to 1987 because of unplanned slowdowns. After discussing the programs and priority of each major project, Roy Black asked Chuck Dunn to have his staff work the next morning to go over the 40 active projects in detail and look for any savings that could be reflected in the June revision of the budget.

**Friday, May 9, 1986—7:45 A.M.**   In addition to Chuck Dunn, four people were seated around the table in the small conference room. Bob Sullivan and Gino Lombardo were program managers who reported to Bill Bailey, vice president of Research. John Smith was manager, Technical Development, of the research facility in Southbridge that specialized in microscopes, fiberoptics, and light scopes. Gordon Thompson was the research accountant representing the Finance Department.

      After coffee was delivered, Chuck closed the door and turned to the others,

> Here's the situation. We are approximately two million short of the June Revision pre-tax profit target. As you know, our sales volume this year has been good—better than budget, in fact—but a few recent unpredictable events, including unfavorable product mix, and that large variance in the cost of specialty European products, are hurting our profit projection.

> This morning, I want the four of you to look at our original spending projections to see where we stand. For example, we know that R&D underspent $200,000 in the first quarter. Therefore, I think we should take it as a starting point that R&D has $200,000 to give up from its 1986 budget. I know that you can argue that this is just a timing difference, but you know as well as I do that, given the record of the R&D department, this money will probably not be spent this year.

> It's time to get the hopes and dreams out of the R&D list. If we roll up our sleeves, we can probably find $400,000 without sacrificing either our 1986 objectives or our long term growth.

> We worked late last night looking at the project list and I think it can be done. I have to meet again today at 2:00 with the Board and I want to be able to tell them that we can do it. That leaves it up to you to sift through these projects and find that money. We're looking for projects that have stalled and can be put on hold, and some belt-tightening on ongoing work.

      After Chuck Dunn had left the group to its work, Gordon led the group through the list of projects. For each project, the group discussed spending to date, problems with the project, and spending needed for the remainder of the year. For each project, Gordon asked if anything could be cut and occasionally asked for points of clarification. On a separate sheet of paper, he kept track of the cuts to which the R&D managers had agreed. He turned to Project 23,

> How about 23? You were planning on a pilot run of 100 prototypes this year. Should that still be included in the schedule?

> Yes, the project is on track and looks promising. I suppose we could cut the run to 50 without sacrificing our objective. Would anyone have a problem with that?

> It's a bad idea. That item has a very high material component and we have a devil of a time getting it at a reasonable price, even for a run of 100. If we cut the volume any more, the unit material cost will double.

> O.K., we'll stick with 100. How about the salesmen's samples? Is there anything there?

> If we reduced the number of samples by a third, we could save $20,000. I suppose I could live with that, but I don't know how that will impact the marketing plan. Let me call Bob Dick and see what he thinks.

Gordon kept a running total of the expense reductions as the morning progressed. Dunn stopped in approximately once an hour to ask how the work was coming.

**Friday, May 9—2:00 P.M.**   Roy Black opened the meeting, "Gus, do you have the revised budget with the changes we've made? What does it look like?"

As Gus Fleites distributed copies of the budget document to the Codman & Shurtleff Board, Chuck Dunn interjected, "Roy, at the moment, we have found $300,000 in R&D. That reflects adjusting our priority list for the rest of the year and cutting the fat out of on-going projects. As for the last $100,000, we are still working on recasting the numbers to reflect what I call our 'project experience factor.' In other words, I think we can find that $100,000 by recognizing that our projects always take longer than originally planned. My people say that we've cut right to the bone on ongoing programs. The next round of cuts will have to be programs themselves, and we know we don't want to do that."

"We've discussed this before," responded Black, "and I think we all agree on the answer. In the past, we have authorized more projects than we can handle and have drawn the work out over too long a time. The way to go is fewer projects, sooner. It's the only thing that makes sense. Our mission is more focused now and should result in fewer projects. It's unfortunate that Bill Bailey is unavailable this week, but we are going to have to go ahead and make those decisions."

As Fleites briefed the Board on the revised budget, Roy Black turned to Bob Dick to discuss inventory carrying costs. "Bob, don't you think that our inventory level is too high on some of our low turnover products? Wouldn't we be better to cut our inventory position and take a higher back order level? With 2,700 products, does it make sense to carry such a large inventory?"

Bob Dick nodded his head in agreement, "You're right, of course, our stocking charges are substantial and we could recover part of our shortfall if we could cut those expenses. But our first concern has to be our level of service to customers."

"Agreed. But perhaps there is room here to provide fast turnaround on a core of critical products and risk back orders on the high-specialty items. The 80/20 rule applies to most of our business. For example, say we offered top service for all our disposables and implants and flagged set-up products for new hospital construction in our catalogue as '90 day delivery' or 'made to order.' We could then concentrate on the fastest possible turnaround for products where that is important and a slower delivery for products that are usually ordered well in advance in any case."

"I think that may be a good tactic. It won't help us for the June revision, but I'll have our market research people look at it and report back next month."

"Good," responded Black, "that just leaves our commercial expenses. We need some donations from each of you. What I am suggesting is that each of you go back to your departments and think in terms of giving up two percent of your commercial expenses. If everyone gives up two percent, this will give us $500,000. In my opinion, we have to bring the shortfall down to $900,000 before we can draw down part of our contingency fund. We're a long way from the end of the year and it's too early to start drawing down a major portion of the contingency."

Black turned to Bob Marlatt, vice president of Human Resources. "Bob, where do we stand on headcount projections?"

"The early retirement program is set to clear our Corporate Compensation Department next month. That should yield 14 headcount reductions. Otherwise, no changes have been made in our projections through the end of the year. I think that we could all benefit from thinking about opportunities to reduce staff and pay overtime on an as-needed basis to compensate."

Black summed up the discussion,

> Well, I think we all know what is needed. Chuck, keep working on that last $100,000. All of you should think in terms of giving up two percent on commercial expenses and reducing non-critical headcount. That means that you will have to rank your activities and see what you can lose at the bottom end. Bob, I think that we should go back and look at our marketing plan again to see if we can make any changes to boost revenues.

> We need to take a revised budget to Stolzer that is short by no more than $250,000. If necessary, I think we can live with drawing down the contingency to make up the difference.

> So, your work is cut out for you. See you back here on Monday. Have a nice weekend! (laughter all around.)

After the meeting, Roy Black reflected on what had transpired, and his role as an operating manager in Johnson & Johnson.

> These meetings are very important. We should always be thinking about such issues, but it is tough when you are constantly fighting fires. The Johnson & Johnson system forces us to stop and really look at where we have been and where we are going.

> We know where the problems are. We face them every day. But these meetings force us to think about how we should respond and to look at both the upside and downside of changes in the business. They really get our creative juices flowing.

> Some of our managers complain. They say that we are planning and budgeting all the time and that every little change means that they have to go back and re-budget the year and the second-year forecasts. There is also some concern that the financial focus may make us less innovative. But we try to manage this business for the long term. We avoid at all costs actions that will hurt us long term. I believe that Herb Stolzer is in complete agreement on that issue.

> It is important to understand what decentralized management is all about. It is unequivocal accountability for what you do. And the Johnson & Johnson system provides that very well.

**EXHIBIT 1    Johnson & Johnson and Subsidiaries, Consolidated Statement of Earnings and Retained Earnings**

| DOLLARS IN MILLIONS EXCEPT PER SHARE FIGURES (NOTE 1) | 1985 | 1984 | 1983 |
|---|---|---|---|
| Revenues | | | |
| Sales to customers | $6,421.3 | $6,124.5 | $5,972.9 |
| Other revenues | | | |
| Interest income | 107.3 | 84.5 | 82.9 |
| Royalties and miscellaneous | 48.1 | 38.0 | 49.4 |
| Total revenues | $6,576.7 | $6,247.0 | $6,105.2 |
| Costs and expenses | | | |
| Cost of products sold | $2,594.2 | $2,469.4 | $2,471.8 |
| Selling, distribution and administrative expenses | 2,516.0 | 2,488.4 | 2,352.9 |
| Research expense | 471.1 | 421.2 | 405.1 |
| Interest expense | 74.8 | 86.1 | 88.3 |
| Interest expense capitalized | (28.9) | (35.0) | (36.9) |
| Other expenses including nonrecurring charges (Note 2) | 50.3 | 61.8 | 99.9 |
| Total costs and expenses | $5,677.5 | $5,491.9 | $5,381.1 |
| Earnings before provision for taxes on income | $ 899.2 | $ 755.1 | $ 724.1 |
| Provision for taxes on income (Note 8) | 285.5 | 240.6 | 235.1 |
| Net earnings | $ 613.7 | $ 514.5 | $ 489.0 |
| Retained earnings at beginning of period | $3,119.1 | $2,814.5 | $2,540.1 |
| Cash dividends paid (per share: 1985, $2.175; 1984, $1.175; 1983, $1.075) | (233.2) | (219.9) | (204.6) |
| Retained earnings at end of period | $3,499.6 | $3,119.1 | $2,824.5 |
| Net earnings per share | $ 3.36 | $ 2.75 | $ 2.57 |

*Continued*

| Segments of Business (Dollars in Millions) | | 1985 | 1984 | 1983 | Percent Increase (Decreased) 1985 vs. 1984 | 1984 vs. 1983 |
|---|---|---|---|---|---|---|
| Sales to customers (2) | | | | | | |
| Consumer— | Domestic | $1,656.0 | $1,588.3 | $1,502.5 | 4.3% | 5.7% |
| | International | 1,118.5 | 1,161.4 | 1,185.3 | (3.7) | (2.0) |
| | Total | $2,774.5 | $1,749.7 | $2,687.8 | .9% | 2.3% |
| Professional— | Domestic | $1,553.9 | 1,429.3 | 1,465.5 | 8.7 | (2.5) |
| | International | 653.1 | 626.1 | 620.3 | 4.3 | .9 |
| | Total | $2,207.0 | $2,055.4 | $2,085.8 | 7.4 | (1.5) |
| Pharmaceutical— | Domestic | $ 780.0 | $ 718.3 | $ 642.5 | 8.6 | 11.8 |
| | International | 659.8 | 601.1 | 556.8 | 9.8 | 8.0 |
| | Total | $1,439.8 | $1,319.4 | $1,199.3 | 9.1 | 10.0 |
| Worldwide total | | $6,421.3 | $6,124.5 | $5,972.9 | 4.8% | 2.5% |
| Operating profit | | | | | | |
| Consumer | | $ 408.7 | $ 323.4 | $ 422.7 | 26.4% | (23.5)% |
| Professional | | 149.2 | 118.7 | 120.0 | 25.7 | (1.1) |
| Pharmaceutical | | 461.1 | 440.4 | 358.4 | 4.7 | 22.9 |
| Segments total | | $1,019.0 | $ 882.5 | $ 901.1 | 15.5 | (2.1) |
| Expense not allocated to segments (3) | | (119.8) | (127.4) | (177.0) | ____ | ____ |
| Earnings before taxes on income | | $ 899.2 | $ 755.1 | $ 724.1 | 19.1% | 4.3% |
| Identifiable assets at year-end | | | | | | |
| Consumer | | $1,616.2 | $1,560.1 | $1,535.9 | 3.6% | 1.6% |
| Professional | | 1,876.1 | 1,717.6 | 1,673.5 | 9.2 | 2.6 |
| Pharmaceutical | | 1,343.8 | 1,024.3 | 996.2 | 31.2 | 2.8 |
| Segments total | | $4,836.1 | $4,302.0 | $4,205.6 | 12.4 | 2.3 |
| General corporate | | 259.0 | 239.4 | 255.9 | ____ | ____ |
| Worldwide total | | $5,095.1 | $4,541.4 | $4,461.5 | 12.2% | 1.8% |

# EXHIBIT 2

 **CHICOPEE**

Chicopee develops and manufactures products for use by other Johnson & Johnson affiliates, in addition to a wide variety of fabrics that are sold to a broad range of commercial and industrial customers. Chicopee's consumer products include disposable diapers for the private-label market segment.

## Codman

Codman & Shurtleff, Inc. supplies hospitals and surgeons worldwide with a broad line of products including instruments, equipment, implants, surgical disposables, fiberoptic light sources and cables, surgical head lamps, surgical microscopes and electronic pain control stimulators and electrodes.

 **CRITIKON**

Critikon, Inc. provides products used in the operating room and other critical care areas of the hospital. Intravenous catheters, infusion pumps and controllers, I.V. sets, filters and devices for monitoring blood pressure, cardiac output and oxygen are among its products.

 **Devro**

Edible natural protein sausage casings made by Devro companies in the United States, Canada, Scotland and Australia are used by food processors throughout the world to produce pure, uniform, high-quality sausages and meat snacks.

## ETHICON

Ethicon, Inc. provides products for precise wound closure, including sutures, ligatures, mechanical wound closure instruments and related products. Ethicon makes its own surgical needles and provides thousands of needle-suture combinations to the surgeon.

**iolab**

Iolab Corporation manufactures intraocular lenses for implantation in the eye to replace the natural lens after cataract surgery, as well as instruments and other products used in ophthalmic microsurgery.

 **JANSSEN** PHARMACEUTICA

Janssen Pharmaceutica Inc. facilitates availability in the U.S. of original research developments of Janssen Pharmaceutica N.V. of Belgium. Its products include SUFENTA, INNOVAR, SUBLIMAZE and INAPSINE, injectable products used in anesthesiology; NIZORAL and MONISTAT i.v. for systemic fungal pathogens; NIZORAL Cream 2% topical antifungal; VERMOX, an anthelmintic, and IMODIUM, an anti-diarrheal.

**Johnson & Johnson** BABY PRODUCTS COMPANY

The Johnson & Johnson Baby Products Company produces the familiar line of consumer baby products, including powder, shampoo, oil, wash cloths, lotion and others. Additional products include educational materials and toys to aid in infant development, SUNDOWN Sunscreen and AFFINITY Shampoo and Conditioner.

**Johnson & Johnson** CARDIOVASCULAR

Johnson & Johnson Cardiovascular manufactures and markets cardiovascular products used in open heart surgery that include HANCOCK Heart Valves, Vascular Grafts, MAXIMA Hollow Fiber Oxygenators, INTERSEPT Blood Filters and Cardiotomy Reservoirs.

**Johnson & Johnson** DENTAL PRODUCTS COMPANY

The Dental Products Company serves dental practitioners throughout the world with an extensive line of orthodontic, preventive and restorative products. The company also provides dental laboratories with a broad line of crown and bridge materials, including the high-strength ceramic CERESTORE system.

**Johnson & Johnson** HOSPITAL SERVICES

Johnson & Johnson Hospital Services Company develops and implements corporate marketing programs on behalf of Johnson & Johnson professional companies. These programs make it easier to do business with Johnson & Johnson and respond to the needs of hospitals, multihospital systems, alternative sites and distributors to reduce costs. Programs include Corporate Contracts and the COACT On-Line Procurement System.

**Johnson & Johnson** PRODUCTS INC.

Johnson & Johnson Products' Health Care Division provides consumers with wound care and oral care products. Its Patient Care Division offers hospitals and physicians a complete line of wound care products. Its Orthopaedic Division markets surgical implants and fracture immobilization products. The company also provides products to the athletic market.

**Johnson & Johnson** ULTRASOUND

Johnson & Johnson Ultrasound specializes in ultrasound diagnostic imaging equipment. This equipment is used in a wide range of medical diagnoses, including abdominal, cardiovascular, gynecologic, obstetric, pediatric, surgical, neonatal and veterinary applications.

*Exhibit 2 Continued*

## McNEIL

McNeil Consumer Products Company

McNeil Consumer Products Company's line of
TYLENOL acetaminophen products includes regular
and extra-strength tablets, caplets and liquid; children's
elixir, chewable tablets, drops and junior strength
tablets. Other products include various forms of
CoTYLENOL Cold Formula, PEDIACARE cough/cold
preparations, SINE-AID, Maximum-Strength
TYLENOL Sinus Medication and DELSYM cough relief
medicine.

 McNEIL
PHARMACEUTICAL

McNeil Pharmaceutical provides the medical profession with prescription drugs, including analgesics,
short and long-acting tranquilizers, an anti-inflamma-
tory agent, a muscle relaxant and a digestive enzyme
supplement.

Ortho Diagnostic Systems INC.

Ortho Diagnostic Systems Inc. provides diagnostic
systems for the clinical and research laboratory
community. Products include instrument and reagent
systems for the blood bank, coagulation and
hematology laboratories as well as immunology
systems and infectious disease testing kits.

ORTHO
ORTHO PHARMACEUTICAL
CORPORATION

Ortho Pharmaceutical Corporation's prescription
products for family planning are oral contraceptives
and diaphragms. Other products include vaginal anti-
bacterial and anti-fungal agents. The Advanced Care
Products Division markets non-prescription vaginal
spermicides for fertility control, in-home pregnancy
and ovulation test kits and an athlete's foot remedy.
The Dermatological Division provides dermatologists
with products for professional skin treatment.

Personal Products

Products for feminine hygiene—STAYFREE Thin
Maxi's, Maxi-Pads and Mini-Pads, STAYFREE SILHOU-
ETTES BODY-SHAPE Maxi's, ASSURE & NATURAL
Breathable Panty Liners, CAREFREE PANTY SHIELDS,
SURE & NATURAL Maxishields, MODESS Sanitary
Napkins, 'o.b.' Tampons and related products—are the
specialty of Personal Products Company. Other
consumer products include COETS Cosmetic Squares,
TAKE-OFF Make-up Remover Cloths and SHOWER TO
SHOWER Body Powder.

## PITMAN·MOORE

Pitman-Moore, Inc. manufactures and sells an extensive line of biological, diagnostic, and pharmaceutical
products for use by veterinarians in treating various
disease entities in the pet animal segment of the
animal health market. Most notable is IMRAB, the only
rabies vaccine approved for use in five animal species.
Pitman-Moore also supplies vaccines and pharmaceuticals for use in food-producing animals and it markets
surgical products of Johnson & Johnson affiliates
applicable to animal health.

## SURGIKOS

Surgikos, Inc. markets an extensive line of BARRIER
Disposable Surgical Packs and Gowns and surgical
specialty products for use in major operative proce-
dures. Other major products include CIDEX Sterilizing
and Disinfecting Solutions for medical equipment,
SURGINE Face Masks and Head Coverings, MICRO—
TOUCH Latex Surgical Gloves and NEUTRALON
Brown Surgical Gloves for sensitive skin.

## TECHNICARE

Technicare Corporation offers physicians products in
four of the most important diagnostic imaging fields—
computed tomography (CT) scanning, nuclear
medicine systems, digital X-ray and the new field of
magnetic resonance (MR).

## VISTAKON

Vistakon, Inc. develops, manufactures and distributes
soft contact lenses. The company provides contact lens
dispensing professionals with daily wear and extended
wear lenses for nearsighted and farsighted persons. It
also is a major supplier of specialty toric lenses for the
correction of astigmatism.

## XANAR INC.

Xanar, Inc. specializes in products for laser surgery.
Laser surgical devices can be used in general surgery
and other surgical specialties to provide an effective,
less invasive alternative to traditional techniques.
Xanar's products include surgical lasers for gynecology,
otolaryngology, dermatology and podiatry.

The following trademarks of Johnson & Johnson and its affiliated
companies appear in this report:

AFFINITY, ASSURE & NATURAL, BAND-AID, BARRIER, BIOCLONE, CAREFREE
PANTY SHIELDS, CERESTORE, CIDEX, COACT, COETS, COMFORT, CoTYLENOL,
DELSYM, DELTA-LITE, DINAMAP, DISPERSALLOY, DISTALITE, ESPREE, ETHILON,
HALDOL, HANCOCK, HISMANAL, IMODIUM, IMRAB, INAPSINE, INNOVAR,
INTERSEPT, JOHNSON'S, JOHNSON & JOHNSON, K-Y, MAGNUM 120, MAXIMA,
MICROLOC, MICRO-TOUCH, MODESS, MONISTAT, NEUTRALON, NIZORAL, 'o.b.',
ORTHO 7/7/7, ORTHO NOVUM, OVUTIME, PDS, PEDIACARE, PROGESTASSAY,
PROLENE, PROXIMATE, REACH, RhoGAM, SEREFREX, SHOWER TO SHOWER,
SIBELIUM, SINE-AID, STAYFREE, STAYFREE SILHOUETTES BODY-SHAPE,
SUBLIMAZE, SUFENTA, SUNDOWN, SUPROL, SURE & NATURAL, SURGINE,
TAKE-OFF, TESLACON, TIMUNOX, TOLECTIN, TYLENOL, VECTRAL, VERMOX,
VICRYL, VISTAMARC, ZOMAX

## EXHIBIT 3

### JOHNSON & JOHNSON
### Partial Organization Chart

<u>D.R. Clare</u>
President - Johnson & Johnson
Chairman - Executive Committee

<u>R.E. Campbell</u>
Vice-Chairman, Executive Committee
Professional/Latin America Sector

<u>V.J. Dankis</u>
Executive Committee

(Responsibility
for 20
operating
companies)

<u>H.G. Stolzer</u>
Executive Committee

<u>S.A. Christie</u>
Company Group
Chairman

- Codman Europe
- Iolab U.S.A.
- Iolab Europe
- J&J Dental Products
- Vistakon U.S.A.

<u>C.B. Chaffey</u>
President -
• Devro Worldwide

- Devro U.S.A.
- Devro Australia
- Devro Canada
- Devro Germany
- Devro Scotland

<u>E. Taylor</u>
President -
• Critikon
Worldwide

- Critikon
U.S.A.

<u>M.J. Murphy</u>
Vice-President
International

- Critikon Canada
- Critikon France
- Critikon Germany
- Critikon U.K.

<u>R.W. Black</u>
President -
• Codman &
Shurtleff
U.S.A.

<u>J.E. Avery</u>
Company Group
Chairman

(Responsibility
for 14
operating
companies)

<u>R.S. Larsen</u>
Company Group
Chairman

- J&J
Ultrasound
- Technicare

## EXHIBIT 4   Board of Directors

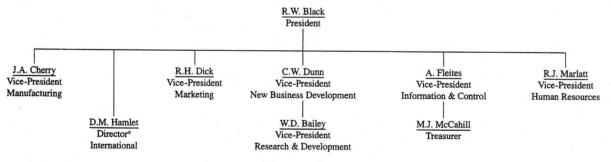

<u>R.W. Black</u>
President

<u>J.A. Cherry</u>
Vice-President
Manufacturing

<u>R.H. Dick</u>
Vice-President
Marketing

<u>D.M. Hamlet</u>
Director[a]
International

<u>C.W. Dunn</u>
Vice-President
New Business Development

<u>W.D. Bailey</u>
Vice-President
Research & Development

<u>A. Fleites</u>
Vice-President
Information & Control

<u>M.J. McCahill</u>
Treasurer

<u>R.J. Marlatt</u>
Vice-President
Human Resources

[a] Not a board member

# CASE 10  Hanson Ski Products

I n early July 1986, Alden (Denny) Hanson, president and chief executive officer of Hanson Ski Products, was preparing for a meeting with his executive committee on the company's current and longer-term financing needs. For one thing, Mr. Hanson wanted to review the plans for fiscal year (FY) 1987.[1] Although the company's bankers had provided a $4.2 million line of credit to meet the year's seasonal cash needs, Denny wanted to recheck his figures to be sure that this credit would be sufficient, particularly since Hanson Ski Products was scheduled to repay stockholder loans of $841,000 in November.

## Company Background

Hanson Ski Products was a leading manufacturer of high-quality ski boots located in Boulder, Colorado. Although it was a relatively new entrant to the market, its revenues ranked among the top 10 ski boot manufacturers worldwide by 1984. Hanson commanded a 20% share of the U.S. market for high-quality ski boots, which was growing at an estimated 10% per year. While the focus of operations was U.S. skiers, the international portion of the company's business was growing faster than the domestic portion. The company expected that in FY 1987, its international revenues would represent about 30% of total sales.

One of the keys to Hanson's successful penetration of this tough market was the unique design of its ski boots. The revolutionary patented rear-entry concept, designed by Chris Hanson, balanced the objectives of comfort and skiing performance sought by the experienced skier. In May 1977, *Fortune* named the specially engineered boot in a world-wide competition "one of the 25 best-designed products available in America." By 1986, Hanson was marketing four models of adult boots, and newer models were continually being added as older models were dropped.

## Past Operating Performance

Hanson Ski Products was founded in 1973. The first year of operations, FY 1974, was devoted to development of boot design and preparation for production. In FY 1975, Hanson shipped 2300 pairs of boots to retailers. By FY 1986, this figure had grown to 85,000 pairs, and revenues had reached $9.8 million (see **Exhibits 1** and **2**).

Hanson management expected net revenues to continue to grow at an impressive rate during FY 1987. Sales projections made early in the planning process had later been revised upward so that it was now expected that net sales would reach $12 million for the year. By FY 1991, Hanson predicted revenues from ski boots would approximate $26 million; beyond that point it was expected that unit volume of sales would only increase proportionately to the overall growth in the market.

---

[1] Fiscal year 1987 at Hanson Ski Products began on April 1, 1986, and ended on March 31, 1987.

*Professor Julie H. Hertenstein and Professor William J. Bruns, Jr. adapted this case from "Hanson Industries, (B)," No. 179-077 and "Hanson Industries," No. 297-066 as the basis for class discussion rather than to illustrate either effective or ineffective handling of an administrative situation. Dates of events and selected financial information have been changed and disguised.*

### The Order Cycle

Hanson's boot business was extremely seasonal and could be broken down into the ordering, shipment, and collection phases. The ordering phase was composed of two parts: the stocking order period and the reorder period. During the stocking order period from March through June, sales representatives conducted an intensive marketing campaign, commencing with the equipment dealers' annual Ski Show held in Las Vegas in March. The timing of this show was important in that it was held just after the end of the previous ski season when both manufacturers and equipment dealers were aware of past equipment sales performance and retail inventory levels. Hanson usually received 25% to 30% of its total orders at this ski show and another 55% to 60% of the orders between April and June, when its sales representatives contacted all dealers who had not attended the show. Discounts ranging from 4% to 12% were offered to customers, and accounts were typically payable on the tenth day of the second or third month following shipment, depending upon the date of their requested shipment. These terms were similar to and slightly tighter than the terms offered by Hanson's competitors.

The reorder period accounted for the remaining 10% to 20% of Hanson's sales and started in July, when dealers reordered to replenish their supplies. A 2% discount was available to these customers for payment by the tenth of the month following shipment.

Sparse snow years affected the order phase in two fiscal years. The first effect was felt almost immediately in the year there was no snow and manifested itself as a reduction in the reorders received. The second and more-pronounced effect was felt during the stocking order period in the following spring. At that time, dealers' inventories were higher than their normal levels, and dealers were wary of placing large initial stocking orders for fear of experiencing two consecutive poor snow years and the consequent falloff in demand.

Shipments began in July, peaked in August, and remained at a high level until December, when they trailed off. The largest part of Hanson's collections of accounts receivable began in December following the shipment phase. In a normal business year, the collection period was about 75 days. However, a poor snow year had the effect of significantly stretching the collection period.

### The Production and Financing Cycle

Manufacturing of the following season's products commenced in January, and production schedules were subsequently modified and adjusted as the shape and size of the order pattern became clearer. A level production policy was adopted for three reasons. Hanson did not want to lay off skilled workers (50% of their 123-person production force) who were key to the manufacture of the ski boots. In addition, the company did not have sufficient physical capacity to turn out an entire year's production after March, when the first orders were received. Finally, management had sufficient confidence in its sales forecasts to manufacture up to 60% of such forecasts in advance of firm orders.

Hanson's seasonal marketing efforts and level manufacturing operations created a substantial financial management challenge. Although by June the company had produced approximately 60% of the year's expected volume of finished boots, it was not until November that most of the year's finished goods inventory was converted to accounts receivable; it was December before the bulk of receivables collections began flowing in.

David Snyder, Hanson's treasurer, typically developed a preliminary cash budget in January, before the start of the fiscal year. On the basis of that projection, he made appropriate arrangements for funding the coming season's cash needs. Based on the results of sales efforts and orders received during the spring, the budget was reviewed in June, and revisions were made as necessary. The proposed final budgets for fiscal year 1987 are shown in **Exhibits 3** and **4**, which also include Snyder's estimates of the balance in each current asset and current liability category at the end of each quarter.

Hanson's management also practiced very tight internal cash management. In fact, Mr. Snyder believed that the optimum target for the firm's cash balances was zero, since Hanson was highly leveraged financially and would have had to pay interest to support any cash balances maintained at the bank. In practice, the cash balances averaged about $100,000.

Despite these efforts to conserve or stretch cash within the firm, Hanson had still found it necessary to arrange substantial short-term loans from banks, finance companies, and from principal stockholders. Although current seasonal financing was being handled exclusively with a group of commercial banks, Hanson had made use of some commercial financing in the past. Commercial financing companies made more frequent audits of the borrower's operations and finances than was typical for the banks and usually levied a higher interest charge. Because of frequent monitoring and higher interest rates, the commercial finance companies felt comfortable in extending a larger amount of funds against inventory and accounts receivable collateral than would normally be true for a commercial bank.

It was the company's goal, however, to move toward exclusive reliance on commercial bank funding, primarily because of the potentially lower cost of such borrowings to Hanson and secondarily because of the higher-quality corporate image it portrayed. In February 1986, Hanson had obtained approval of a $4.2 million revolving line of credit for fiscal 1987 at 3.75% over prime[2] with a group of three banks led by the United Bank of Denver, which was in a good geographical position to maintain day-to-day contact with Hanson. Hanson could draw against this line of credit to the extent of 70% of the cost of inventories and 80% of current accounts receivable.

The banks' reduction of the interest rate charge in FY 1987 was seen by Denny Hanson as an indication of the company's improved credit standing in the eyes of these lenders. That conviction was further strengthened when the banks informed Hanson that the personal guarantees of the major stockholders would not be required as a condition of the 1987 credit line.

As of June 15, 1986, Hanson Ski Products had no plans to issue more stock, and, because of growth, no liquidations of plant or equipment were contemplated. The company had never paid a cash dividend, and it did not plan to initiate dividend payments in fiscal year 1987.

The final element of financial plans for fiscal year 1987 about which Denny Hanson was concerned was the set of loans from shareholders. A total of $841,000 in loans would become due in November 1986. An estrangement had developed between a key shareholder of the group and Mr. Hanson, and only if the loans were paid could Mr. Hanson be sure of maintaining personal control of operations. He hoped the bank line of credit was sufficient to enable the company to pay the loans in full and on time.

---

[2] In July 1986 the prime rate was 8%. The credit line for fiscal 1986 had also been $4.2 million but had carried an interest rate of 4% over prime.

## Questions

1. Using the information in the balance sheet for March 31, 1986 (**Exhibit 2**), and the fiscal year 1987 budgets (**Exhibits 3** and **4**), prepare a projected balance sheet for Hanson Ski Products for March 31, 1987. (To do this, you will need to estimate the size of the commercial bank loan— "Notes-bank"—on that date.) Does your balance sheet tell you whether or not the plans on which the budgets are based are feasible?

2. Project the size of the commercial bank loan at the end of each quarter of FY 1987. Can Hanson stay within the commercial banks' line of credit of $4.2 million? Will the company have sufficient collateral?

3. Prepare quarterly balance sheets for Hanson Ski Products for June 30, 1986; September 30, 1986; and December 31, 1986. What do the four balance sheets you have prepared tell you about the financial structure and strength of Hanson Ski Products?

4. Denny Hanson was particularly concerned that the stockholder loans be paid off in November 1986 when they were due, and he asked Dave Snyder, treasurer, to prepare a cash budget by months for the third quarter of FY 1987 (**Exhibit 5**). Do you see any problems in paying off the loans on time? What could Hanson do to be sure the loans can be paid?

---

### EXHIBIT 1    Hanson Ski Products, Income Statements ($000)

|  | FY 1984 | FY 1985 | FY 1986 |
|---|---|---|---|
| Net sales | $5,753 | $7,671 | $9,776 |
| Cost of goods sold[a] | 3,040 | 4,140 | 5,177 |
| Gross margin | $2,713 | $3,531 | $4,599 |
| Selling, general and administration | 1,585 | 2,109 | 2,519 |
| Product development | 152 | 189 | 260 |
| Operating earnings | $976 | $1,233 | $1,820 |
| Interest expense | 436 | 428 | 507 |
| Income before tax and extraordinary item | $540 | $805 | $1,313 |
| Tax provision | 314 | 468 | 400 |
| Earnings before extraordinary item | $226 | $337 | $913 |
| Extraordinary item tax benefit from utilization of operating loss carryforwards | 314 | 468 | 251 |
| Net earnings | $540 | $805 | $1,164 |
| Earnings per common share: |  |  |  |
| Earnings before extraordinary item | 0.39 | 0.57 | 1.50 |
| Extraordinary item | 0.53 | 0.79 | 0.41 |
| Net earnings | 0.92 | 1.36 | 1.91 |
| Weighted average number of common shares outstanding | 585,889 | 590,566 | 607,761 |

[a] *Depreciation and amortization for 1984, 1985, and 1986 was $341, $396, and $561, respectively.*

---

**EXHIBIT 2   Hanson Ski Products, Consolidated Balance Sheets ($000)**

|  | 3/31/84 | 3/31/85 | 3/31/86 |
|---|---|---|---|
| **Current Assets** | | | |
| Cash | $163 | $81 | $156 |
| Receivables, net | 692 | 1,378 | 1,556 |
| Inventories | 1,352 | 2,104 | 1,729 |
| Prepaid expenses | 99 | 124 | 262 |
| Total current assets | $2,306 | $3,687 | $3,703 |
| **Fixed Assets** | | | |
| Plant, property, and equipment | 1,430 | 1,958 | 3,393 |
| Less accumulated depreciation and amortization | 569 | 836 | 1,255 |
| Total net fixed assets | $861 | $1,122 | $2,138 |
| Other assets | 171 | 191 | 207 |
| Total Assets | $3,338 | $5,000 | $6,048 |
| **Liabilities** | | | |
| Accounts payable | $536 | $967 | $1,586 |
| Notes payable—banks | 1,100 | 2,082 | 1,547[a] |
| Income taxes payable | — | — | 149 |
| Current installments—long-term debt | 109 | 35 | 1,010[b] |
| Total current liabilities | $1,745 | $3,084 | $4,292 |
| Long-term debt | | | |
| Term loan | 1,423 | 1,407 | — |
| Notes payable to banks | 506 | — | — |
| Total | $1,929 | $1,407 | $— |
| **Stockholders' Equity:** | | | |
| Common stock | 1,126 | 1,166 | 1,249 |
| Additional paid-in capital | 105 | 105 | 105 |
| Retained earnings (deficit) | (1,567) | (762) | 402 |
| Total stockholders' equity | $(336) | $509 | $1,756 |
| Total Equities | $3,338 | $5,000 | $6,048 |

[a] *Borrowings under the revolving line of credit were personally guaranteed by the major stockholders and were secured by all of the accounts receivable, inventories, machinery and equipment, furniture, trademarks, and patent rights.*
[b] *Current installments on long-term debt (3/31/86):*

| | |
|---|---|
| *Officers and stockholders* | *$841,000* |
| *Installment purchases* | *169,000* |
| *Capital leases* | *==* |
| | *$1,010,000* |

## EXHIBIT 3    FY 1987 Final Budget (June 15, 1986—$000)

|  | 1st Quarter | 2nd Quarter | 3rd Quarter | 4th Quarter |  |
|---|---|---|---|---|---|
|  | APRIL—JUNE 1986 | JULY—SEPTEMBER 1986 | OCTOBER—DECEMBER 1986 | JANUARY—MARCH 1987 | TOTAL |
| Net revenues | $391 | $5,893 | $4,769 | $832 | $11,885 |
| Cost of goods sold | 344 | 2,630 | 2,176 | 491 | 5,641 |
| Gross margin | $47 | $3,263 | $2,593 | $341 | $6,244 |
| Operating expenses | 779 | 1,204 | 1,256 | 926 | 4,165 |
| Operating income | ($732) | $2,059 | $1,337 | ($585) | $2,079 |
| Tax allowance | — | 432 | 261 | — | 693 |
| Net income (loss) | ($732) | $1,627 | $1,076 | ($585) | $1,386 |

## EXHIBIT 5    Third Quarter FY 1987 Cash Budget by Months ($000)

|  | OCTOBER | NOVEMBER | DECEMBER |
|---|---|---|---|
| Cash receipts | $1,000 | $1,054 | $2,518 |
| Cash outflow |  |  |  |
| For materials, labor, and operating expenses (except for interest) | 830 | 1,065 | 803 |
| Interest | 54 | 56 | 58 |
| Capital expenditures | 69 | 62 | 48 |
| Pay back stockholder loans | — | 841 | — |
| Collateral for bank loans at end of month |  |  |  |
| Receivables | 5,420 | 5,517 | 4,739 |
| Inventory | 1,331 | 1,363 | 1,166 |

**EXHIBIT 4   FY 1987 Cash Budget and Selected Expense and Balance Sheet Items (June 15, 1986; $000)**

|  | 1ST QUARTER APRIL–JUNE 1986 | 2ND QUARTER JULY–SEPTEMBER 1986 | 3RD QUARTER OCTOBER–DECEMBER 1986 | 4TH QUARTER JANUARY–MARCH 1987 |
|---|---|---|---|---|
| Cash receipts | $1,487 | $1,764 | $4,572 | $3,800 |
| Cash outflows |  |  |  |  |
| For materials, labor, and operating expenses (except for interest but including income taxes)[a] | 1,928 | 2,967 | 2,698 | 2,022 |
| Interest | 67 | 110 | 168 | 86 |
| Capital expenditures for fixed assets | 177 | 238 | 179 | 301 |
| Pay back stockholder loans | — | — | 841 | — |
| Depreciation | 143 | 166 | 179 | 195 |
| Assets at end of quarter |  |  |  |  |
| Planned cash balance | 100 | 100 | 100 | 100 |
| Receivables, net | 507 | 4,580 | 4,739 | 1,741 |
| Inventories | 2,808 | 1,690 | 1,166 | 1,869 |
| Prepaid expenses | 241 | 294 | 198 | 283 |
| Other assets | 201 | 247 | 283 | 302 |
| Liabilities at end of quarter |  |  |  |  |
| Accounts payable | 1,849 | 1,717 | 1,755 | 1,664 |
| Income taxes payable | — | — | — | — |
| Current installments long-term debt | 980 | 1,060 | 207 | 189 |
| Notes payable — banks (to be determined) |  |  |  |  |

[a] In general, corporations must pay current year income taxes on a quarterly basis. However, the precise payment requirements are based on a complex set of rules that are different for large or small corporations.

## CASE 11 Walker and Company: Profit Plan Decisions

Ramsey Walker faced important decisions in May 1997 as he walked to his meeting with George and Ted. From what he had learned at business school, he realized that the company should publish fewer titles in fewer segments. Fewer new titles would allow the company to lower its overhead expenses and improve margins. It would also allow the company to publish faster selling books, manage inventory better, and lower the asset base. He believed that the business would benefit by focusing more resources on making Walker and Company books stand out in the marketplace.

Walker and Company was a medium sized book publisher that employed 31 people and 45 commissioned sales representatives. Founded in 1959 by Ramsey's father, Walker was one of only a handful of companies that had survived the last 35 years in the book publishing industry. (**Exhibit 1** presents an organization chart.) Ramsey had taken over the reigns of the business at age 27, upon the death of his father. After managing the business for three years, he had attended business school and earned his MBA in 1997.

> The Monday after my father died, I took over his position as president and publisher of Walker and Company. For a relatively small publisher, the company had an enormously diverse product line and published a huge number of titles: 150 new titles a year across 20 different segments. In all, there were over 1,000 active products.

> I immediately tried to get my hands around the business, but discovered only two things: our cash reserves were rapidly going south; and our most important suppliers—printing companies—were beginning to cut us off. I knew our access to additional capital was virtually nil. I figured we had four to six months before we might have to close our doors.

> We had almost no information about where we were making money or where we were generating cash. As a result, I first spent three months putting together rudimentary profit and loss statements for each product line. We used these as our rationale for cutting back annual new titles from 150 to 100. With fewer new products, we reduced our overhead by 20%. A few months later, we moved our office from fancy Fifth Avenue to the West Village, sold the educational workbook line, and stopped developing new reference books. We then spent 6 months recruiting George Gibson, a well-known, experienced publishing person to build our editorial, marketing and sales expertise. These were radical and difficult changes for a family company that had undergone very little change in its 33 year history.

> The majority of the company (64%) is owned by my two brothers and me. Neither of my brothers works in the business: Sloan is a lawyer at the SEC and Tim is a television producer. And I have accepted a job at K-III Communications Corporation. However, we have a deep attachment to the business. We do not want to see it sold off or closed down. But we do want to see strong financial performance.

Ramsey Walker continued his narrative, attempting to explain the challenges facing the company today, five years after his father died.

> The company recently had a tremendous success. In the fall of 1995, Walker published a book called *Longitude* and it became the company's first international hit. It stayed on *The New York*

*Ramsey Walker, MBA '97, and Professor Robert Simons prepared this case as the basis for class discussion rather than to illustrate either effective or ineffective handling of an administrative situation.*

*Times* hardcover bestseller list for a remarkable four months and on the paperback bestseller list for six months. It was the fastest and biggest selling book in the company's history. It became such a hit that *The New York Times* profiled Walker and Company in its business section. (*Longitude* is the story of a village clockmaker who solved the most pressing navigation problem of the 18th century.)

Based on the amount of press coverage the company is receiving, you might think that the company is rolling in money. In fact, despite the changes I made five years ago, the opposite is true: minimal profits and negative cash flow. I know we need yet another new publishing strategy to succeed in the future: publish fewer books in fewer segments and focus more resources on differentiating those books in the marketplace. While the strategy might be clear, how to implement it is not.

Our greatest shortcoming is our lack of good diagnostic control systems. There are no clear performance targets set from the top, and no one looks at the link between the income statements, balance sheet, and cash flow statement. What we need is a single variable that would link that data together.

I am considering using Return-on-Assets as our primary "critical performance variable." This could act as a proxy for our return-on-investment. We would set ROA goals for the next fiscal year, 1998, at 10%. We know that large publishing companies are achieving 15% ROA. We believe that our business is at least good enough to achieve 10% ROA. In addition, I want to set free cash flow goals based on reducing working capital.

After the changes Ramsey made in 1991, Walker and Company had published 100 new trade books a year in five different editorial segments:

1. **Nonfiction:** Walker published 20 new titles a year in hardcover and paperback covering health, baseball, history, and humor. These books were sold primarily to bookstores and required extensive publicity to pull the books out of the channel. In 1995 and 1996, Walker had enjoyed considerable success in this category with hits such as *Longitude*.

2. **Mystery:** Walker published 20–24 new titles a year in hardcover only. Traditionally, the company had been known for British mysteries, but in recent years it had moved to more "hard-boiled" American mysteries, mostly by male writers. These books were sold primarily to public libraries and a few mystery specialty stores.

3. **Westerns:** Walker published 6–8 new historical western titles a year in hardcover. These books were sold exclusively to public libraries.

4. **Religious and inspirational:** Walker published 14–17 new titles, only in paperback. Walker acquired the rights from other publishers to publish these books in a "large print" format, targeting the aging population with an increasing interest in religious and inspirational issues. These books were sold to religious book retailers and wholesalers.

5. **Children's books:** Walker published 25–30 hardcovers and 5–8 paperbacks. The children's books were sold to both general and specialized retail bookstores, wholesalers, and schools.

The book publishing process at Walker started with the review of manuscripts, followed by careful selection and then a contract with an author. After completion, a manuscript was edited and designed, then printed, bound and sent to the warehouse. The company "pushed" the book into multiple distribution channels and then used advertising and publicity to pull the books into consumer's hands. Walker also licensed "subsidiary rights" to foreign language publishers, movie producers, book clubs, and other licensers.

## Publishing Industry

The worldwide book publishing industry generated $80 billion in revenue during 1996, with over $25 billion accruing to the U.S. market. Books were published for educational and professional markets, as well as for the general public (the "trade" segment). Trade publishers—the category in which Walker and Company competed—were usually classified into one of four categories:

*Large publishers that covered almost all segments:* These included the large media companies such as: Hyperion and Disney Press (Disney); Little Brown (Time Warner); Harper Collins (News Corporation); Simon and Schuster (Viacom); and Bantam Doubleday Dell (Bertellsman). These companies achieved economies of scale in marketing, sales and distribution.

*Medium sized publishers that specialized in one segment:* This segment included Scholastic (children's books) and Thomas Nelson (religious books), among others.

*Small to medium sized publishers that covered a variety of segments:* These companies usually had been publishing for at least 20 years, and were based in New York City—the capital of book publishing. They enjoyed established reputations in the marketplace that allowed them to continue publishing a more general list. Many of these houses had either been bought up or gone out of business in the last twenty years.

*Small and very specialized publishers:* This category included the hundreds or thousands of publishers, most of which had started in the last 5–10 years. They chose one to three very narrow segments and worked to become very good at those segments, i.e. cookbooks for outdoor cooking; new age health; or flyfishing.

## Industry Trends

In contrast to other entertainment businesses like music or films, book publishers issued an enormous number of new titles each year. Approximately 50,000 new book titles were published each year; and a total of 1.2 million titles remained in print (in contrast, 20,000 new CDs and only 170 major feature films were released each year).

With so many books spilling into the marketplace, differentiation was essential to successful strategy. Each publisher had to carefully choose which segments to compete in, and make each book stand out through design, packaging, and publicity efforts. With a huge supply of competing titles, this was an enormously difficult challenge.

As Ramsey Walker stated,

> While the economics of trade books are often unattractive, most people, including the large media companies, stay in the business because of its enormous influence. Books are the greatest source of feature films; they are regularly excerpted and reviewed in magazines and newspapers; and they still form the basis of our educational material. Books influence what we eat, drink, and wear, how we raise children, and care for the sick. They impact how we think and who we vote for. When a public figure wants to get a message out to the public—whether Colin Powell or Bill Gates—their primary vehicle is not electronic; rather, it is good old fashioned paper between two pieces of covered board.

Accordingly, book publishers often placed the creative and intellectual aspects of the trade ahead of economic returns. For editors and publishers alike, it was more of a calling than of a discipline. While these attitudes were changing, change was often slow to come, especially in the smaller houses that did not have the resources for extensive business training.

Meanwhile, the industry was changing dramatically.

**Consolidation**   The book industry had rapidly consolidated in the 1980s and 1990s: the top eight publishers now controlled approximately 40% of the market. Consolidation had occurred in both the retail and wholesale channels. On the retail side, companies such as Barnes & Noble and Borders were pursuing a superstore format; on the wholesale side, Ingram had become the leading wholesaler. These customers had squeezed smaller competitors out of the market or simply bought them up. Customers were now less fragmented and significantly more powerful.

**Hit-Driven and Unpredictable** Like other entertainment businesses, book publishing had become largely hit-driven. A publisher's economic fortunes rose and fell depending on the revenue that each hit book generated. Unfortunately, it was extremely difficult to predict what would become a hit in advance; and it was difficult to repeat the success in the same way a second time. However, hits were necessary to break through the information and entertainment overload bombarding consumers.

**New Distribution Channels** Paradoxically, while books were among the oldest media formats, they had also become among the most successful new businesses on the Internet. *Amazon.com,* listed as one of the top 10 internet sites of 1996, had opened up an efficient way for consumers to access an enormous inventory of books. This new type of distribution channel could not only take market share from existing channels, but might also expand the size of the market to include those who previously could not find or were not interested in books. Other important new channels included warehouse clubs and discount stores.

### *Profit Plan for the Children's Book Line*

Ramsey had already decided to stop publishing Western novels. The line was a distraction of company time for a relatively small return with no upside potential (see **Exhibit 2**). Ramsey had not yet figured out the impact of this decision on the company's profit going forward. He knew, however, that all COGS and one third of operating expenses were variable. The remaining fixed expenses would have to be re-allocated to other lines or reduced.

Now Ramsey was on his way to sit down with George Gibson and Ted Rosenfeld. He wanted to discuss how to manage the children's book line to reach the company's cash flow and profit goals.

George Gibson (46) was president and publisher. George had worked for 25 years in book publishing as a marketing and sales director, subsidiary rights director, and editor. While George did not have extensive training in business or management techniques, he was wonderfully creative and energetic.

Ted Rosenfeld (54) was the chief financial officer. Ted had worked in the book publishing industry for 28 years and had been at Walker for 15 years, originally as controller. Ted focused on the day-to-day financial and logistical operations of the company, including inventory management, setting prices and print runs, managing accounts payable and receivables, shipping, fulfillment, and related personnel. Ted was a graduate of NYU with a major in accounting.

Ramsey had to decide how many new titles to publish in each children's book format for the upcoming year. The decisions regarding product mix in children's books would have a major impact on the future economic performance of the company. Walker published new children's books each year in five different formats:

- Illustrated picture books;
- Photo essays (stories illustrated with photos);
- Black and white illustrated books;
- Informational nonfiction;
- Fiction

After one year, titles became part of the "backlist" but continued to generate sales. Financial results for the year ended May 31, 1997 varied depending on the format (see **Exhibit 3**).

Ramsey's goal for Walker and Company was to achieve $500,000 in free cash flow in 1999 and cumulative $1 million by 2000. At least 50% of that would have to come from the children's book line. He believed that there were two ways of achieving these cash flow goals: increase net income and/or reduce the amount of working capital committed to the business. An emphasis on net income would force more efficient operations. However, achieving more efficient operations would require difficult personnel decisions. Longstanding employees might have to be let go. He also knew that high net income levels—above about 8%—were unrealistic because trade book publishing had never been a high profit margin business.

Ramsey believed that working capital gains could be significant. Some working capital items like inventory had not been managed to maximize cash. Gains would be limited in accounts receivable, however, which could not be collected any faster, and accounts payable, which could not be stretched any longer.

Ramsey also believed that the company should be able to earn 10% ROA. The large publishing companies—those with significant economies of scale—were earning 15%. **Exhibit 4** presents comparative data for other firms in the publishing industry.

To prepare the profit plan for 1998, Ramsey would have to decide exactly how many titles to publish in each format and the effect of that decision on the profit of the children's book line. Ramsey's worksheet for a new product mix decision is shown in **Exhibit 5.** He knew that he would have to analyze a number of financial measures: annual sales growth, profit percent, unit sales, ROA, and expenses. Each measure, however, possessed limitations:

**Annual Sales Growth %:** Did not account for the profitability of different formats or the investment required to generate the sales.

**Profit %:** Did not show the investment required or cash flow impact of generating the profit.

**Average Unit Sales:** Did not show the cost of generating the per title averages. Also, averages could be skewed by one very successful or unsuccessful title.

**Return-on-Assets:** ROA required accurate allocation of expenses and assets which at times could be difficult. Assets consisted primarily of accounts receivables, the inventory of books in the company's warehouse, and "unearned" advances paid to authors. The biggest company asset was inventory. Unearned advances were guaranteed payments made to authors whose books had not yet "earned out" the advance. (Unearned advances could be considered like prepaid expenses.)

**ROI:** It was unclear exactly what to include as "investment." Was it just author advances and the cost of production. Or was it also "investment" in staff and overhead. One way to measure investment would include the total cost of printing the book, plus the guaranteed advance paid to the author.

**Operating Expenses:** Operating expenses were largely fixed or lumpy in nature. At least 10–20 new titles would have to be cut in order to reduce any of the lumpy expenses. For example, the editorial staff head count could not be reduced by just eliminating three or four titles. There had to be a reduction of at least 10–12 titles for each editorial staff reduction. The difficult challenge would be to find the right new title output given the fixed overhead base. Inevitably, there would have to be some expense reductions.

Before he went any further, Ramsey knew that he would have to decide on the number of new titles to be issued in each of the five children's formats, and use that decision to derive a 1998 profit plan for the entire children's book line.

*Required:*

1. Complete Ramsey Walker's profit plan for the children's book line **(Exhibit 5).** What are your working assumptions? Which of these assumptions are critical to your analysis?

2. Review the list of financial performance measures presented above. What measures or calculations should Ramsey use to manage the business? How should those measures be calculated?

3. Based on your analysis, prepare an agenda of the top three action items that Ramsey should discuss with George Gibson and Ted Rosenfeld during their upcoming meeting.

## EXHIBIT 1    Walker and Company Organization Chart

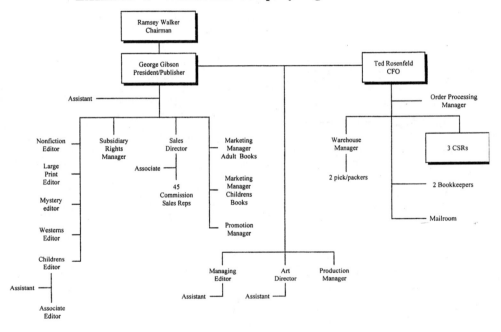

**EXHIBIT 2  Income Statement by Editorial Line For Year Ended May 31, 1997**

|  | TOTAL ACTUAL | LARGE PRINT | ADULT NONFICTION | CHILDREN'S BOOKS | MYSTERY | WESTERN |
|---|---|---|---|---|---|---|
| Gross regular sales | $6,050,677 | $725,425 | $1,990,922 | $2,361,922 | $803,157 | $169,251 |
| Returns | (1,096,488) | (102,844) | (338,380) | (380,587) | (218,462) | (56,215) |
| Net regular sales | 4,954,189 | 622,581 | 1,652,542 | 1,981,335 | 584,695 | 113,036 |
| Special/club sales | 120,330 | 37,064 | 26,146 | 55,049 | 2,071 | 0 |
| Remainder sales | 49,442 | 1,307 | 8,831 | 13,858 | 21,631 | 3,815 |
| **Total net sales** | 5,123,961 | 660,952 | 1,687,519 | 2,050,242 | 608,397 | 116,851 |
| Regular COGS | 1,512,954 | 204,225 | 441,197 | 655,063 | 179,056 | 33,413 |
| Regular royalty | 870,797 | 93,387 | 375,551 | 297,200 | 87,704 | 16,955 |
| Special/club COGS | 88,284 | 17,098 | 22,823 | 47,465 | 898 | 0 |
| Remainder COGS | 150,865 | 1,503 | 26,858 | 40,141 | 67,642 | 14,721 |
| **Total COGS** | 2,622,900 | 316,213 | 866,429 | 1,039,869 | 335,300 | 65,089 |
| **Gross Profit** | 2,501,061 | 344,739 | 821,090 | 1,010,373 | 273,097 | 51,762 |
| **Net subrights income** | 271,813 | 4,609 | 114,990 | 59,662 | 80,771 | 11,781 |
| **Adj. gross profit** | 2,772,874 | 349,348 | 936,080 | 1,070,035 | 353,868 | 63,543 |
| **Expenses:** | | | | | | |
| Editorial | 251,323 | 20,643 | 44,544 | 127,266 | 53,681 | 5,189 |
| Marketing/sales overhead | 226,629 | 16,530 | 40,810 | 156,621 | 12,668 | 0 |
| —direct | 550,470 | 48,465 | 175,416 | 188,856 | 113,599 | 24,134 |
| Cost of free copies | 120,961 | 3,491 | 24,569 | 78,915 | 12,418 | 1,568 |
| Art/production/gen'l edit. | 201,800 | 24,216 | 44,396 | 72,648 | 48,432 | 12,108 |
| Ship/warehouse | 552,797 | 73,886 | 170,090 | 220,826 | 74,550 | 13,445 |
| General and administrative | 712,165 | 106,825 | 156,676 | 284,866 | 135,311 | 28,487 |
| **Total expenses** | 2,616,145 | 294,056 | 656,501 | 1,129,998 | 450,659 | 84,931 |
| **Net trade profit (loss)** | $ 156,729 | $ 55,292 | $ 279,579 | ($59,963) | ($96,791) | ($21,388) |

*Note: Figures have been disguised to preserve confidentiality*

**EXHIBIT 3**   Financial Information for Children's Book Line for Year Ended May 31, 1997

| EDITORIAL FORMAT | PICTURE | PHOTO | B+W | NONFICTION | FICTION | BACKLIST | TOTAL |
|---|---|---|---|---|---|---|---|
| **Income Statement** | | | | | | | |
| Units sold | 44,313 | 23,180 | 12,485 | 22,097 | 7,871 | NA | NA |
| Number of new titles | 5 | 6 | 3 | 7 | 2 | NA | |
| Revenue (including sub rights income) | 388,121 | 222,389 | 137,972 | 198,324 | 66,538 | 1,096,560 | 2,109,904 |
| % Growth from 1995 | 15% | 18% | 7% | −10% | 0% | | |
| COGS | 127,672 | 79,183 | 58,934 | 63,200 | 20,372 | 393,308 | 742,669 |
| Royalties | 58,218 | 33,358 | 20,696 | 29,749 | 9,981 | 145,198 | 297,200 |
| Gross margin % | 52% | 49% | 42% | 53% | 54% | 51% | 51% |
| Editorial expenses | 42,693 | 24,463 | 15,177 | 21,816 | 7,319 | 15,798 | 127,266 |
| Marketing/sales Direct | 34,931 | 20,015 | 12,417 | 17,849 | 5,988 | 65,421 | 156,621 |
| Marketing/sales OH | 34,931 | 20,015 | 12,417 | 17,849 | 5,988 | 97,656 | 188,856 |
| Cost of free copies | 19,406 | 11,119 | 6,899 | 9,916 | 3,327 | 28,248 | 78,915 |
| Art/production/gen'l editorial | 15,525 | 8,896 | 5,519 | 7,933 | 2,662 | 32,113 | 72,648 |
| Shipping/warehousing/ order processing | 38,812 | 22,239 | 13,797 | 19,832 | 6,654 | 119,492 | 220,826 |
| General and administrative | 42,575 | 26,687 | 16,557 | 23,799 | 7,985 | 167,263 | 284,866 |
| Total expenses | 228,873 | 133,434 | 82,783 | 118,994 | 39,923 | 525,991 | 1,129,998 |
| *Profit (loss)* | (26,642) | (23,586) | (24,441) | (13,619) | (3,738) | 32,063 | (59,963) |
| **Balance Sheet** | | | | | | | |
| *Current assets* | | | | | | | |
| Current inventory ($) | 46,932 | 94,398 | 38,589 | 42,574 | 22,100 | 620,000 | 864,593 |
| Unearned author advances | — | 10,000 | — | — | 0 | 20,000 | 30,000 |
| Accounts receivable | 77,624 | 44,478 | 27,594 | 39,665 | 13,308 | 221,331 | 424,000 |
| Total | 124,556 | 148,876 | 66,183 | 82,239 | 35,408 | 861,331 | 1,318,593 |
| *Current Liabilities* | | | | | | | |
| Accounts Payable | 52,348 | 52,074 | 29,257 | 31,732 | 12,742 | — | 178,153 |
| Royalties payable | 23,218 | — | 7,696 | 2,749 | — | | 33,663 |
| Total | 75,566 | 52,074 | 36,953 | 34,481 | 12,742 | | 211,816 |
| *Investment spending* | | | | | | | |
| Plant, paper, printing, binding (outsourced) | 174,494 | 173,581 | 97,523 | 105,774 | 42,472 | | |
| Author advances | 35,000 | 42,000 | 13,000 | 27,000 | 10,000 | | |
| Total investment | 209,494 | 215,581 | 110,523 | 132,774 | 52,472 | | |

**Note:** *Figures have been disguised to preserve confidentiality*

**EXHIBIT 4** **Comparative 1997 Financial Data for Selected Publishing Companies**

| | HOUGHTON MIFFLIN | THOMAS NELSON | MILLBROOK PRESS | PUBLISHING INDUSTRY AVERAGE(a) |
|---|---|---|---|---|
| Market Focus | textbooks; children's; CD-ROMs | Christian; stationery products | children's nonfiction | |
| No. of Employees | 2,550 | 1,250 | 65 | na |
| No. of New Titles Issued (*est.) | 310* | 200 | 200 | na |
| No. of Titles on Backlist (*est.) | 2,750* | 1,100 | 700 | na |
| INCOME STATEMENT | | | | (% of sales) |
| Total Sales ($ millions) | $797.3 | $253.0 | $12.6 | 100.00% |
| Less: Cost of Goods Sold | 362.5 | 138.4 | 6.7 | 50.90% |
| Gross Margin | 434.8 | 114.6 | 5.9 | 49.10% |
| Less: Other Expenses | 328.3 | 89.8 | 6.5 | 49.84% |
| Operating Income | 106.5 | 24.8 | (0.6) | −0.74% |
| BALANCE SHEET | | | | (% of assets) |
| Total Assets ($ millions) | $981.1 | $285.3 | $15.8 | 100.00% |
| Accounts Receivable | 159.5 | 63.3 | 4.9 | 18.11% |
| Inventory | 145.0 | 70.6 | 0.6 | 22.19% |
| Total Current Assets | 324.7 | 185.0 | 9.0 | 56.23% |
| Accounts Payable | 47.6 | 16.7 | 2.3 | 12.41% |
| Total Current Liabilities | 238.7 | 44.8 | 2.5 | 32.38% |
| Free Cash Flow ($ millions) | $73.9 | $4.8 | ($3.7) | na |

(a) Averages of percentages for index of 15 public U.S. book publishers in SIC 2731
Source: Financial data are from public financial statements (recapped in http://globalbb.onesource.com).
Estimates for number of employees and number of titles provided by companies and/or 10 k reports.

**EXHIBIT 5** **Proposed Product Mix and Profit Plan for Children's Book Line —
Year Ending May 31, 1998**

| EDITORIAL LINE | PICTURE | PHOTO | B+W | NONFICTION | FICTION | BACKLIST* | TOTAL |
|---|---|---|---|---|---|---|---|
| **Income Statement** | | | | | | | |
| *Number of new titles* | | | | | | 0 | |
| Sales | | | | | | 1,200,000 | |
| COGS | | | | | | 384,000 | |
| Royalties | | | | | | 180,000 | |
| Gross margin % | | | | | | 53% | |
| Expenses % of sales | | | | | | 47% | |
| Expenses | | | | | | 564,000 | |
| Net income | | | | | | 72,000 | |
| **Balance Sheet — May 31, 1998** | | | | | | | |
| *Current Assets* | | | | | | | |
| Inventory | | | | | | 500,000 | |
| A/R as % of sales (projected) | % | % | % | % | % | 20% | |
| A/R $ | | | | | | 240,000 | |
| Total current assets | | | | | | 740,000 | |
| *Current Liabilities* | | | | | | | |
| A/P as % of sales (projected) | % | % | % | % | % | 0 | |
| A/P $ | | | | | | 0 | |
| Royalties payable | 0 | 0 | 0 | 0 | 0 | 0 | |
| Total current liabilities | | | | | | 0 | |
| **Free Cash Flow (= net income +/− change in net working capital)** | | | | | | | |
| Net income | | | | | | 72,000 | |
| Change in net working capital | | | | | | | |
| Free cash flow | | | | | | | |

* "Backlist" numbers are assumptions based on past performance.
**Note:** Figures have been disguised to preserve confidentiality

## CASE 12  Compagnie du Froid, S.A.

Jacques Trumen, CEO and major shareholder of Compagnie du Froid, S.A., was reviewing the performance of the three regions of the business: France, Italy, and Spain. Evaluating the performance of the regional vice-presidents was not a task that he enjoyed. Jacques had traditionally given each regional manager the same bonus: 2% of corporate profits. Jacques believed that this system avoided arbitrary evaluation criteria and encouraged open and fruitful communication among the regions about new ways of doing business.

The results in 1996 challenged the fairness of this evaluation system. The performance of the Spanish region had been extremely poor and had driven the company's overall profits to their lowest level in 10 years. Jacques thought that it was unfair to have the French and Italian managers pay for the problems of somebody else. But he was not sure how much Andres Molas, the manager of the Spanish division, was to blame for Spain's poor results.

### Compagnie du Froid, S.A.

Founded in 1972 by Jacques Trumen's father, Compagnie du Froid, S.A. had grown steadily over the years to be a major competitor in the summer ice-cream business. It had a dominant position in the coastal tourist areas from Perpignan to Nice and Monaco, the region where it was founded. In 1981, Jacques took over the business and re-directed the company into an aggressive growth strategy. By 1996, the company was a market leader in the eastern part of France, the northeastern coast of Spain, and northern Italy. Jacques kept a watchful eye on the efforts of the three regional managers to expand the operations to other key tourist areas in their regions, but his attention was mainly devoted to the creation of a new business: a year-round ice-cream operation based in Paris.

Jacques believed very much in decentralizing decision making as much as possible. Each region had its own manufacturing, marketing, distribution and sales organization. Regional managers chose distinctive names for new products, the level and mix of advertising, and local suppliers. The central office maintained responsibility for the accounting and financial aspects of the business, development of new products in ice-creams and "specialties" categories, and the sharing of experiences and learning across the regions.

Jacques exercised control of the regions through a profit planning system. The profit plan covered the upcoming fiscal year which began on January 1. In November and December, each region prepared and submitted their initial profit plan to the central office. Jacques used the profit plan to discuss and supervise the expansion strategy of each region and to make sure that enough cash would be generated to support the company's new corporate ventures. The final phase of the profit planning process was a top management meeting which brought together Jacques, the three regional vice-presidents, and the finance and technical officers to discuss new growth opportunities. A lot of time and face-to-face contact was devoted to the profit plan and, once approved, it was the guiding tool to monitor and evaluate performance.

*Doctoral Candidate Antonio Dávila and Professor Robert Simons prepared this case as the basis for class discussion rather than to illustrate either effective or ineffective handling of an administrative situation.*

During the summer months, each region generated a profit statement every two weeks that Jacques reviewed to detect major problems. In addition, Jacques spent a week in each region to "get a feel for the market." At the end of October, another top management meeting occurred to learn from the year's experience and schedule winter activities to prepare for the next season. In early December, Jacques handed bonus checks to the three regional managers.

Top line revenue goals for the upcoming year were established using past growth rates and the market expectations of Jacques and the regional managers. Exchanging knowledge and experiences was a key element in shaping the growth assumptions of the profit plan. For 1996, the expected volume growth was 9% for the French region, 10% for the Spanish region, and 12% for the Italian region.

Since 1992, when Compagnie du Froid introduced its first specialty product—sophisticated ice-cream flavors made with prime quality ingredients, the strategy had been to emphasize these "specialties" that enjoyed higher margins and less intense competition. This strategy became operational through the profit plan: Jacques set ambitious goals for the percentage of sales volume coming from "specialties" for each of the regions.

Standard selling prices and manufacturing costs were based on last year's actuals adjusted for any expected contingencies. Efficiency standards assumed that manufacturing would improve its year-to-year performance based on learning and better equipment.

Finally, Jacques believed that the business should compensate shareholders—himself, his brothers and sisters, and top managers in the company—for the risk of tying up their capital in the business. Thus, he expected a reasonable return on shareholders' investment. His reference point was 18% return-on-investment before taxes.

**Exhibit 1** illustrates the standards used to design the profit plan for one of the three regions.

### France

Jean Pinoux was the manager of the French region. He was promoted to this position in 1994 when Pierre Giraux, the previous manager, took over the lagging Italian operation. Jean had started as a sales representative, then advanced to be responsible for production, and finally became division manager.

Jacques was pleased with Jean's performance (see **Exhibit 2**). His profits were above budget, and sales had increased almost 20% over the previous year. Jean had invested a lot of his time in managing the expansion into the west coast of France, negotiating with new vendors and suppliers, and arranging distribution of the product. If all this effort had paid off in 1996, the profits would have been even higher, but Jacques knew that they would have to wait several years to get the full benefits from this investment.

The performance in the traditional regions of the French market had been a bit disappointing. Market share had slipped from 20% in 1994 to 18% in 1996. Jean Pinoux argued that his frequent trips to the west coast had negatively affected his relationships with distributors in the east coast.

The French region had bought new machines two years ago. While there had been some start-up problems, the machines ran smoothly during 1996 thanks to Jean's manufacturing expertise. The manufacturing operation was staffed with a core group of employees which supervised production and maintained the machines. Most of the workforce was people hired on an hourly basis.

Jean had found a new source of revenue from a personal friend who operated a well known restaurant in Camargue. Over the summer of 1996, Jean's friend had decided to package his meals and distribute them through supermarkets and food stores in the region. He needed refrigerated trucks to deliver his products and Jean agreed to distribute them for a fee. Most of the retail outlets were already visited by Compagnie du Froid's delivery trucks and the incremental cost to the company to provide this service was very low. Jean saw this business opportunity as a simple way to increase revenue. By the end of the summer, he had agreements with two other regional food producers to deliver their products beginning in summer 1997. He planned to work over the winter season on getting more of these deals that were easy and very profitable.

Jacques was surprised by Jean's initiative, but acknowledged that there was a profit potential in the distribution business. He was concerned, however, that distribution was outside Compagnie du Froid's core business and he felt unsure whether to follow this new opportunity (Compagnie du Froid's mission is reproduced in **Exhibit 7**).

## Italy

Pierre Giraux was the manager for the Italian region. He had been in top management positions with Compagnie du Froid for the last 10 years. Previously he had run the French region, but Jacques asked him to take care of the Italian operation because it was not performing adequately. Jacques knew Pierre very well. He was an excellent manager with a very clear sense of the market. Although running the smallest region in the company, Pierre had been the main force in attaining a leadership position in the French market and was a close partner in Jacques' new ventures.

Pierre's performance as manager of the Italian operation had been excellent. He had attained his sales goals and expanded the distribution of the company's products into most of the western Italian coast.

In the manufacturing side, he had suffered from higher wages and lower efficiency than expected. The machines used in Italy had been moved from France when the new equipment was installed in France. The old machines were partly the reason for the lower efficiency, but this expectation had already been incorporated into the profit plan.

**Exhibit 3** shows the performance of the Italian division in 1996.

## Spain

Andres Molas was the manager for the Spanish region. He had been in charge of the Spanish operation since it started in 1982. Andres was the only non-French top manager. His performance had been outstanding until 1996. He had grown the division from scratch and he was very respected for his innovative ideas. For example, last year he had developed a vending machine to sell "specialties". The idea had been so successful that France and Italy were planning to introduce it in 1997. Andres was the most successful manager in introducing new products to the market and the other managers followed some of his marketing ideas.

Unfortunately, 1996 had been problematic for several reasons. (**Exhibit 4** shows the performance of the Spanish region.) New machines, similar to the ones purchased in France, were bought early in the year to increase efficiency, but they did not perform adequately until late August. Technicians from the supplier had to spend several weeks adjusting the machines. Because of these problems, Andres had run out of capacity several times during the year and he had been forced to import product from the French division.

This was the first time that Compagnie du Froid had transferred sales between regions and Jacques had decided to set the transfer price at full cost plus a 5% profit for the manufacturer (see **Exhibit 5**). There was some argument about the policy. Andres was not happy about it because he said that it made his division look bad, but he accepted it as a temporary solution. In addition, the Spanish division had been forced to absorb the expenses of having people travel to France to help fit Spanish containers and packaging to the French production line.

In addition, the market had been very tough that year. Unseasonably cold temperatures had driven tourism down (**Exhibit 6** shows the history of sales and temperature for the various regions). Jacques had developed over time a rule of thumb that a 1°C deviation from the mean summer temperature resulted in a 3% change in volume growth. The 1996 summer temperatures in the coastal zones of Spain had been 1.7°C below average; thus Jacques' rule of thumb predicted volume growth to be only 4.9% rather than the planned 10%. The reaction of a large competitor to lower sales volume had been to lower prices to stimulate demand. Andres had followed with a price cut. Even with total market sales down, Andres decided to keep the level of advertising up to build market share.

### The Bottom Line?

When Jacques finished reviewing all the information, he sat back and began to enjoy an ice-cream. France and Italy had performed well, but Spain's performance had been dismal. Yet, he was unsure how each manager had performed given the circumstances? What did the differences between the profit plan and the actual performance really mean?

Jacques wondered if changes in company policy might be needed. What would happen if he suddenly changed his traditional evaluation system and gave different bonuses to the regional managers? Could he come up with a compensation formula that would be fair? . . . This would be the perfect solution: an evaluation scheme that reflected each manager's performance without the discussions and tensions linked to subjective evaluation. But he was unsure if performance should be linked to (1) the profit plan, (2) strategic goals such as revenue growth, or (3) some overall measure of economic results. Perhaps he should just stay with his traditional method and give each manager a fixed percent of corporate profit.

There were also issues to be resolved about transfer prices. Some of the managers — Andres in particular — had been unhappy with his temporary solution. And Jacques still had not decided what he should say to Jean about his new distribution arrangements.

**EXHIBIT 1    Example of Standards for the 1996 Profit Plan (Spanish Region)**

|  | SPAIN |
|---|---|
| **Standards** | |
| Percentage of volume from specialities | 10% |
| Selling prices (in French Francs) | |
| Ice-cream (per litre) | 14.15 |
| Specialties (per litre) | 26.03 |
| Manufacturing costs (in French Francs) | |
| Dairy (per litre) | 8.35 |
| Other ingredients ice-cream (sugar, flavor, etc., per 100 grams) | 4.83 |
| Other ingredients specialties (sugar, flavor, etc., per 100 grams) | 6.78 |
| Labor (wage per hour) | 26 |
| Labor hours ice-cream (litres per hour) | 107.2 |
| Labor hours specialties (litres per hour) | 11.04 |
| Volume | |
| Dairy ingredients—ice-cream (% of volume) | 72% |
| Other ingredients—ice-cream (grams per litre) | 48 |
| Dairy ingredients—specialties (% of volume) | 93% |
| Other ingredients—specialties (grams per litre) | 73 |

**EXHIBIT 2   French Region, 1996 Results**

| | PROFIT PLAN | | ACTUAL | | VARIANCE |
|---|---|---|---|---|---|
| | Volume ('000) | French Francs ('000) | Volume ('000) | French Francs ('000) | |
| *Sales Data* | | | | | |
| Sales ice-cream (volume in litres) | *4,009* | 57,213 | *4,618* | 64,018 | 6,805 F |
| Sales "specialties" (litres) | *445* | 11,716 | *405* | 10,805 | (911) U |
| Revenue from distribution | | | | 250 | 250 F |
| Total sales | *4,454* | 68,929 | *5,023* | 75,073 | 6,144 F |
| *Cost of Goods Sold* | | | | | |
| Cost ice-cream | | | | | |
| Dairy ingredients (litres) | *2,887* | 25,259 | *3,317* | 29,256 | (3,997) U |
| Other ingredients (100 gr.) | *1,844* | 9,092 | *2,047* | 10,194 | (1,102) U |
| Labor (hours) | *38.29* | 1,187 | *43.56* | 1,400 | (213) U |
| Cost "specialties" | | | | | |
| Dairy ingredients (litres) | *410* | 3,586 | *368* | 3,246 | 340 F |
| Other ingredients (100 gr.) | *316* | 2,217 | *298* | 2,095 | 122 F |
| Labor (hours) | *40.30* | 1,241 | *36.02* | 1,158 | 83 F |
| Contribution margin | | 26,347 | | 27,724 | 1,377 F |
| *Other costs* | | | | | |
| Supervision, energy, maintenance, . . . | | 7,058 | | 7,436 | (378) U |
| Depreciation | | 1,494 | | 1,494 | – |
| Operating margin | | 17,795 | | 18,794 | 999 F |
| *Selling and Administrative Expenses* | | | | | |
| Delivery expenses | | 2,754 | | 2,905 | (151) U |
| Depreciation of trucks | | 1,621 | | 1,633 | (12) U |
| Selling expenses | | 3,451 | | 3,646 | (195) U |
| Advertising | | 3,652 | | 3,424 | 228 F |
| Administrative salaries and expenses | | 2,520 | | 2,591 | (71) U |
| Allocated central office expenses | | 507 | | 618 | (111) U |
| **Profits Before Interest and Taxes** | | **3,290** | | **3,977** | **687** F |
| *Identifiable Assets* | | | | | |
| Cash (average) | | 300 | | 452 | (152) |
| Accounts receivable (average) | | 1,857 | | 2,028 | (171) |
| Plant and equipment (net of Fr. 7,341,000 depreciation) | | 15,081 | | 15,124 | (43) |
| **Total Identifiable Assets** | | **17,238** | | **17,604** | **(366)** |
| *Conditions for tourism* | | | | | |
| Average summer temperature | 29.8 °C | | 29.2 °C | | |

## EXHIBIT 3 Italian Region, 1996 Results

| | PROFIT PLAN | | ACTUAL | | VARIANCE |
|---|---|---|---|---|---|
| | Volume ('000) | French Francs ('000) | Volume ('000) | French Francs ('000) | |
| *Sales Data* | | | | | |
| Sales ice-cream (volume in litres) | 2,452 | 35,095 | 2,480 | 35,538 | 443 F |
| Sales "specialties" (litres) | 272 | 7,142 | 276 | 7,209 | 67 F |
| Total Sales | 2,724 | 42,237 | 2,756 | 42,747 | 510 F |
| *Cost of Goods Sold* | | | | | |
| Cost ice-cream | | | | | |
| Dairy ingredients (litres) | 1,864 | 15,880 | 1,895 | 15,956 | (76) U |
| Other ingredients (100 gr.) | 1,275 | 6,032 | 1,296 | 6,182 | (150) U |
| Labor (hours) | 33.10 | 960 | 36.03 | 1,050 | (90) U |
| Cost "specialties" | | | | | |
| Dairy ingredients (litres) | 259 | 2,206 | 257 | 2,164 | 42 F |
| Other ingredients (100 gr.) | 196 | 1,360 | 197 | 1,375 | (15) U |
| Labor (hours) | 24.24 | 703 | 23.29 | 679 | 24 F |
| Contribution margin | | 15,096 | | 15,341 | 245 F |
| Other costs | | | | | |
| Supervision, energy, maintenance, . . . | | 3,655 | | 3,632 | 23 F |
| Depreciation | | 350 | | 350 | – |
| Operating margin | | 11,091 | | 11,359 | 268 F |
| *Selling and Administrative Expenses* | | | | | |
| Delivery expenses | | 1,054 | | 1,005 | 49 F |
| Depreciation of trucks | | 632 | | 632 | – |
| Selling expenses | | 1,006 | | 1,100 | (94) U |
| Advertising | | 4,250 | | 4,121 | 129 F |
| Administrative salaries and expenses | | 1,785 | | 1,838 | (53) U |
| Rent | | 389 | | 389 | – |
| Allocated central office expenses | | 507 | | 618 | (111) U |
| **Profits Before Interest and Taxes** | | **1,468** | | **1,656** | **188** F |
| *Identifiable Assets* | | | | | |
| Cash (average) | | 300 | | 345 | (45) |
| Accounts receivable (average) | | 1,205 | | 1,142 | 63 |
| Plant and equipment (net of Fr. 10,240,000 depreciation) | | 8,840 | | 8,845 | (5) |
| **Total Identifiable Assets** | | **10,345** | | **10,332** | **13** |
| *Conditions for tourism* | | | | | |
| Average summer temperature | 29.7 °C | | 29.8 °C | | |

## EXHIBIT 4    Spanish Region, 1996 Results

| | PROFIT PLAN | | ACTUAL | | VARIANCE |
|---|---|---|---|---|---|
| | *Volume ('000)* | *French Francs ('000)* | *Volume ('000)* | *French Francs ('000)* | |
| *Sales Data* | | | | | |
| Sales ice-cream (volume in litres) | 3,685 | 52,140 | 3,575 | 49,621 | (2,519) U |
| Sales "specialties" (litres) | 409 | 10,657 | 400 | 10,404 | (253) U |
| Total Sales | 4,094 | 62,797 | 3,975 | 60,025 | (2,772) U |
| *Cost of Goods Sold* | | | | | |
| Cost ice-cream | | | | | |
| Dairy ingredients (litres) | 2,653 | 22,153 | 2,175 | 17,944 | 4,209 F |
| Other ingredients (100 gr.) | 1,769 | 8,543 | 1,450 | 7,047 | 1,496 F |
| Labor (hours) | 34.37 | 894 | 29.21 | 763 | 131 F |
| Cost "specialties" | | | | | |
| Dairy ingredients (litres) | 381 | 3,179 | 362 | 2,987 | 192 F |
| Other ingredients (100 gr.) | 299 | 2,026 | 275 | 1,826 | 200 F |
| Labor (hours) | 37.09 | 964 | 34.73 | 907 | 57 F |
| Contribution margin | | 25,038 | | 28,551 | 3,513 F |
| Other costs | | | | | |
| Supervision, energy, maintenance, . . . | | 6,865 | | 6,930 | (65) U |
| Depreciation | | 1,251 | | 1,251 | – |
| Transfer from France | | | | 6,804 | (6,804) U |
| Operating margin | | 16,922 | | 13,566 | (3,356) U |
| *Selling and Administrative Expenses* | | | | | |
| Delivery expenses | | 2,354 | | 2,424 | (70) U |
| Depreciation of trucks | | 1,321 | | 1,358 | (37) U |
| Subcontracted transportation | | | | 245 | (245) U |
| Selling expenses | | 2,646 | | 2,514 | 132 F |
| Advertising | | 4,500 | | 4,505 | (5) U |
| Administrative salaries and expenses | | 1,985 | | 2,061 | (76) U |
| Rent | | 321 | | 321 | – |
| Allocated central office expenses | | 507 | | 618 | (111) U |
| **Profits Before Interest and Taxes** | | **3,288** | | **(480)** | **(3,768)** U |
| *Identifiable Assets* | | | | | |
| Cash (average) | | 300 | | 312 | (12) |
| Accounts receivable (average) | | 1,352 | | 852 | 500 |
| Plant and equipment | | | | | |
| (net of Fr. 5,341,000 depreciation) | | 15,245 | | 15,478 | (233) |
| **Total Identifiable Assets** | | **16,897** | | **16,642** | **255** |
| *Conditions for tourism* | | | | | |
| Average summer temperature | 30.2 °C | | 28.5 °C | | |

**EXHIBIT 5   1996 Ice-cream Transfers Between France and Spain**

|  | | ICE-CREAM | |
|---|---|---|---|
|  | Cost of ingredients | Cost per litre | Total (in '000 Francs) |
| Volume transferred (in '000 litres) | | | 603 |
| Actual costs (in French Francs) | | | |
|   Dairy Ingredients | 8.82 | 6.34 | 3,823 |
|   Other Ingredients | 4.98 | 2.21 | 1,332 |
|   Labor | 0.30 | 0.30 | 181 |
| Allocated fixed costs (in French Francs) | | | |
|   Other costs | | 1.48 | 892 |
|   Depreciation | | 0.30 | 179 |
|   S&A expenses | | 0.12 | 72 |
| 5% profit margin | | 0.54 | 324 |
| Total transfer price | | **11.29** | **6,803** |

**EXHIBIT 6   Historical Data**

| YEAR | TEMPERATURE (DEGREES CELSIUS) | SALES VOLUME ('000 LITRES) | VOLUME GROWTH |
|---|---|---|---|
| *France* | | | |
| 1982 | 27.7 | 1,344 | |
| 1983 | 29.2 | 1,435 | 6.7% |
| 1984 | 28.4 | 1,484 | 3.4% |
| 1985 | 30.9 | 1,714 | 15.5% |
| 1986 | 32.9 | 2,031 | 18.5% |
| 1987 | 27.3 | 1,984 | −2.3% |
| 1988 | 30.0 | 2,208 | 11.3% |
| 1989 | 30.5 | 2,489 | 12.7% |
| 1990 | 30.8 | 2,761 | 10.9% |
| 1991 | 30.0 | 2,998 | 8.6% |
| 1992 | 29.7 | 3,216 | 7.3% |
| 1993 | 30.3 | 3,445 | 7.1% |
| 1994 | 29.6 | 3,797 | 10.2% |
| 1995 | 29.4 | 4,087 | 7.6% |
| 1996 (budget) | | 4,455 | 9.0% |
| Average | **29.8 °C** | | **9.1%** |

*Exhibit 6    Continued*

| YEAR | TEMPERATURE (DEGREES CELSIUS) | SALES VOLUME ('000 LITRES) | VOLUME GROWTH |
|------|-------------------------------|----------------------------|---------------|
| *Italy* | | | |
| 1986 | 32.2 | 892 | |
| 1987 | 30.4 | 1,036 | 16.1% |
| 1988 | 28.6 | 1,143 | 10.3% |
| 1989 | 31.8 | 1,434 | 25.6% |
| 1990 | 28.1 | 1,508 | 5.1% |
| 1991 | 28.2 | 1,639 | 8.7% |
| 1992 | 29.0 | 1,771 | 8.0% |
| 1993 | 28.3 | 1,872 | 5.7% |
| 1994 | 30.1 | 2,090 | 11.7% |
| 1995 | 30.0 | 2,433 | 16.4% |
| 1996 (budget) | | 2,725 | 12.0% |
| Average | **29.7 °C** | | **12.0%** |
| *Spain* | | | |
| 1982 | 30.8 | 1,069 | |
| 1983 | 31.2 | 1,272 | 18.9% |
| 1984 | 29.0 | 1,402 | 10.2% |
| 1985 | 31.6 | 1,685 | 20.2% |
| 1986 | 29.8 | 1,852 | 9.9% |
| 1987 | 28.3 | 2,006 | 8.3% |
| 1988 | 28.0 | 1,964 | −2.1% |
| 1989 | 27.5 | 2,033 | 3.5% |
| 1990 | 29.9 | 2,231 | 9.8% |
| 1991 | 30.4 | 2,481 | 11.2% |
| 1992 | 31.8 | 2,684 | 8.2% |
| 1993 | 32.4 | 3,036 | 13.1% |
| 1994 | 30.4 | 3,346 | 10.2% |
| 1995 | 31.0 | 3,722 | 11.3% |
| 1996 (budget) | | 4,094 | 10.0% |
| Average | **30.2 °C** | | **10.2%** |

**EXHIBIT 7    Compagnie du Froid S.A. Mission Statement**

**MISSION**

Compagnie du Froid, S.A. exists to offer customers the best in iced summer refreshments. We work as a team to produce and market only premium quality products that are known for innovation, quality, and value. In everything we do, we strive to delight our customers and offer an experience that reflects summer fun and relaxation.

## CASE 13  Texas Eastman Company

T om Wilson, company controller, reflected on the changing role of the accounting department in Texas Eastman Company's new operating environment:

> Traditionally, accounting was the recorder of history, but perhaps we were not directly relevant for the operational decisions taken every day by the departmental managers. We see the need to move accountants physically into manufacturing areas so that they can serve as financial advisors to manufacturing managers. But in order for them to function in this capacity, we need information on a real-time basis. Operators can see hundreds of observations on their processes every couple of hours, but we're issuing cost summaries only every four weeks. We need to break our frame of vision in order to develop more timely and useful information for operating employees.

### Company Background

A visitor is unprepared for a first visit to the Texas Eastman (TEX) chemicals plant in Longview, Texas. No noxious smells or clouds of smoke hang over the 6,000-acre site, and one can almost imagine people fishing in the manmade ponds used as a source of cooling water for the plant (see picture in **Exhibit 1**). The TEX plant is one of six companies in the Eastman Chemicals Division of the Eastman Kodak Company. Summary data on the division appear in **Exhibit 2**.

The Longview plant, established in 1950, produced about 40 chemical and plastic products that were sold to other manufacturers for conversion into construction, industrial, and consumer products. Nearly 9 million pounds of product per day were shipped during 1988. The location in Northeast Texas gave the plant easy access to the East Texas Oil Field for the primary inputs of ethane and propane. Well-served by water, rail, and pipeline transportation, the plant consumed weekly the equivalent of 700 railcars of feedstock—propane and ethane—and 50 railcars of bituminous coal. Employment in 1988 was 2,650 persons. Of these, 1,560 were production workers, and 760 worked in engineering and managerial positions.

**Exhibit 3** shows a simplified diagram of TEX's chemical processes. Feedstock was converted in a cracking plant into ethylene and propylene. These olefin products were then further processed in chemical plants to produce a variety of alcohols, aldehydes, and specialty chemicals and in polyolefin plants to make various forms of plastics and adhesives. Computerized models were used to optimize inputs and outputs as a function of current feedstock costs and the output prices of the plant's products.

### Quality Management Program

The Eastman Chemicals Division made a strong commitment to Total Quality Management in 1983. Because of the strong dollar in the early 1980s, foreign goods were increasing their U.S. market penetration, and customers soon discovered that not only were Japanese and European goods lower in price, they also had higher (more consistent) quality. The automotive industry, feeling the brunt from foreign imports, began to take action by developing its own comprehensive quality programs, such as Ford's Q-1 Program. In addition to internal efforts, the manufacturers began requiring that their suppliers produce delivered goods under Statistical Process Control (SPC).

The Eastman Chemicals Division established its Quality Policy in 1984. The division president articulated the overall Quality Goal, "To be the leader in quality and value of its products and services," and backed this goal with a statement of the 11 principles by which the Quality Goal could be achieved (see **Exhibit 4**). He hoped to instill an intense focus on quality throughout the organization.

The Quality Management Program was built on a "Triangle Model" that included Teamwork, Performance Management, and Statistical Process Control (see **Exhibit 5**). The Teamwork leg, with its roots in the Quality of Work Life, Job Enrichment, and Employee Participation literature, was implemented through Quality Management Teams that permeated the organization. Every person in the plant, from the president down to the lowest-skilled employee, served on at least one Quality Management Team. The teams were linked hierarchically by having members of each Quality Management Team serving on a team at a higher or a lower level of the organization, so that ideas and programs developed at one level could be communicated throughout the organization.

The Performance Management leg was built on B. F. Skinner's behavioral school of psychology and reinforcement. It stressed the need for establishing Key Result Areas (KRA) and developing measures for each KRA. The Performance Management process used seven specific steps:

1. Define the *mission* in terms of the results the organization is expected to contribute.
2. Identify the *key result areas* critical to success in achieving the mission. Key result areas could be financial, safety, or environmental goals, or SPC implementation.
3. Define *measures* for each key result area that indicate how well the unit is performing its mission.
4. Decide how the measures will be *displayed* for monitoring to signal significant changes in measures.
5. Develop *control strategies* that outline a plan of action when significant changes in processes occur.
6. Develop plans to *reinforce* progress and achievements for each measure.
7. Implement *improvement projects* and *allocate resources* where they have the most impact on the key result areas.

The implementation of Statistical Process Control (SPC), the third leg of the Quality Management process, required an even more drastic change in Texas Eastman's operations. Prior to installing SPC procedures, operators were continually monitoring the hundreds of variables, such as temperatures, pressures, humidities, and flow rates, that governed the performance of each chemical process. As any variable moved away from its nominal mean value, operators would tweak the process, attempting to bring the variable back to its standard value. Frequently, this intervention introduced more variation into the final product than if the operators had just left the process alone.

The first step along the route of complete SPC was to define upper and lower control limits for each process variable between which operator intervention should not occur (see **Exhibit 6**). Because no computer capability existed in 1984 for manufacturing operations, the SPC charts had to be plotted by hand and analyzed manually. If an observation was outside the control limit, specific actions were defined to bring the parameter back into control. Runs tests were performed to detect consistent positive or negative biases even while each observation remained within the control limits. Taguchi methods were employed that mathematically modeled operations so that process variation—the distance between the upper and lower control limits—could be reduced even further. But TEX's quality initiatives were limited by the enormous amount of data that had to be collected, analyzed, and stored manually.

### Information Systems

TEX operating personnel had for years been collecting extensive data on operating processes. Operators were assigned to take readings on 180 routes throughout the plant every two to four hours. The data collection process yielded between 30,000 and 40,000 observations on the plant's process parameters (such as temperatures, pressures, flow rates, and tank levels) every 4 hours. These data were entered on preprinted multicolumn worksheets that the operators carried on clipboards as they toured their routes. Clerks entered output data from the worksheets into the daily production report and then sent the process sheets to a nearby warehouse where they were stored in filing cabinets.

Each day, department managers personally reviewed the data collected from operations of the day before. This next-day review, however, conflicted with TEX's current emphasis on quality. The review would frequently detect unfavorable trends in key operating parameters much too late, enabling many pounds of product to be produced with varying product characteristics. Even though only a small fraction of off-spec material might be produced, the variations in product characteristics could create problems for their customers' production processes.

When customers complained about variations in product characteristics, or when TEX people themselves detected unusual variations in products or operations, an engineer would go to the warehouse, occasionally spending many hours locating the relevant worksheets for the particular product or operating department. Once the data were located, the engineer performed an extensive analysis, attempting to learn which parameters might have been outside normal limits. The search and analysis process was tedious, requiring several days or even weeks of work, and occasionally, some of the needed process sheets could not be found in the extensive and often cluttered storage files. Attempts at process improvement were also limited by the availability of operating data only on the paper worksheets in the warehouse storage files.

The first step in providing more accessible information for real-time quality analysis was taken in 1986 with the installation of the Manufacturing & Technical (M&T) System. A stand-alone computer was acquired for manufacturing in order to accumulate and store operating data and perform the statistical analysis. **Exhibit 7** shows the extent of the data collection in the plant by major operating division. About 15% of the observations were updated automatically, about once a minute. The remainder were updated every two to four hours. Because of the SPC analysis, fewer data points were being collected than in 1984.

By 1988, the M&T System had been significantly supplemented by a more general and flexible information system embracing both extensive Digital Equipment Corporation VAX clustered computing and advanced software packages. One package, purchased from an external vendor, monitored those departments equipped with electronic control systems to perform automatic SPC analysis, historic graphs of data, and automatic alarm processing. A second system fed data from daily production reports into the financial control system. The third, using advanced programming techniques, enabled operators to specify which

SPC tests should be performed on the operating data, and if an out-of-control situation were detected, generated a recommended course of action to bring the process back into control. By early 1989, 200 such analytic models had been written. A fourth system provided statistical summaries of operations for individual departments and analysts. The reports included information on shipments and production, process improvements, control limits, historical analyses, and incidence and disposition of customer complaints.

## Existing Accounting System

TEX prepared fully allocated actual cost reports for its operating departments every four weeks. Direct manufacturing and delivery costs were 90% of total costs, manufacturing supervision and clerical costs were 5%, and general factory overhead and support (including computer expenses) represented the remaining 5% of costs. Almost all costs could be traced to individual plants and departments on an actual consumption basis.

An Annual Operating Plan (AOP) was prepared in October and November for the subsequent year. The AOP incorporated all budgets, standards, and plans for the next year. Sales quantities and prices were provided by the marketing department. Each support group provided forecasts of prices for materials, supplies, and utilities. The accounting department then prepared forecasts of departmental and product costs based on this information. The departmental and product cost forecasts became the baseline against which plant performance was measured.

At the end of each four-week reporting period, the accounting department received information about actual departmental costs and production quantities. It multiplied production quantities by variable standard costs and added AOP fixed cost items to obtain a plan unit cost for each product and department. Five variances were computed and reported back to department managers.

1. *Usage Variance*   The effect on Unit Cost of using more or less of an item than planned; measured as the change in input quantity consumed for a given level of output, evaluated at standard prices.

2. *Price Variance*   The effect on Unit Cost of a change in the price of an input, based on actual consumption of each input. Only price variances for labor and for materials and supplies purchased from outside vendors were included in the price variance.[1]

3. *Volume Variance*   The effect on Unit Cost of not operating at the planned capacity utilization. The volume variance reconciled differences in unit costs due to spreading fixed costs over varying volumes.

4. *Change-in-Standard*   The effect of *not* implementing a planned change in operations or of implementing an unplanned change. It represented the difference between the current standard and the planned standard. Any capital authorization with a justification based on cost savings or output increase was always translated into a change in future standards.

5. *Mix Variance*   The effect, in a multiproduct facility, of producing with an actual product mix different from the planned mix, or of producing a nonstandard ratio of formulas for a given product class.

---

[1] No price variance was generated for materials and supplies produced by other Texas Eastman departments, since these variances were already incorporated in those departments' cost sheets. These internal price variances, called Prior Department Variances, however, were shown on the consuming department's cost sheets so that the department manager could consider alternative suppliers or materials if the variance was significant.

The sum of the five variances equaled the difference between total departmental costs and total plan cost. **Exhibit 8** shows the format for a sample Departmental Cost Sheet. At the bottom of the cost sheet, the five variances were split into controllable and non-controllable components:

| *Controllable* | *Non-Controllable* |
|---|---|
| Volume | Volume |
| Change-in-Standard | Change-in-Standard |
| Usage | Price |
| | Mix |

The total volume variance was classified into both controllable and noncontrollable components. Reductions in volume due to shortages of input materials or lack of sales demand were treated as a *noncontrollable variance*. The manager received a *controllable unfavorable* volume variance when the department produced less than demand, and demand was below capacity. The manager received a *controllable favorable* volume variance only when demand was high, and he was able to operate his plant beyond rated capacity.

Controllable change-in-standard variances represented changes in operations under the control of department managers (such as staff levels and material yield changes). In addition to the planned changes in standards resulting from capital expenditures, the standard for any cost element that had experienced a consistently favorable variance during the year would be changed by at least 50% of the annual mean favorable variance.[2] Changes in standards initiated by the accounting department, such as labor rates, depreciation adjustments, and changes in accounting methods were considered department noncontrollable.

The Departmental Cost Sheets were typically issued 12 to 15 days after the close of each four-week reporting period. The accounting department performed analytic studies of the information before its people walked the reports over to explain the results to each departmental manager.

Variances for all operating departments were summarized on Division Cost Summaries for division superintendents and upper management. These summaries included the plant total cost variance as well as controllable variances for each department and division. Finally, a report was issued each period for the president, director of administration, and comptroller that summarized the manufacturing cost of TEX products and gave explanations for significant variances from the AOP.

Pat Kinsey, chief accountant, explained the rationale for the plant's elaborate hierarchy of cost reports:

> The goal of our cost reporting system is to provide to managers on all levels the information they need to manage their areas of responsibility, from the production manager concerned with the efficient operation of the cost centers under his control to the senior members of management who must decide which products to produce and how to allocate company resources. Our system works fine for responsibility accounting and emphasizing controllable variances. But the information is received too late for analyzing the financial consequences from most operating decisions. Our operations personnel must rely on their daily review of key indicators (such as production, yields, and equipment availability) to learn how their operation is performing.

---

[2] The 50% factor reflected a compromise between accounting and operations. Departmental managers were reluctant to incorporate 100% of the gain, since they did not want to risk unfavorable variances in subsequent years.

To understand more clearly the problem of delayed and aggregate financial information, you could think of the department manager as a bowler, throwing a ball at pins every minute. But we don't let the bowler see how many pins he has knocked down with each throw. At the end of the month we close the books, calculate the total number of pins knocked down during the month, compare this total with a standard, and report the total and the variance back to the bowler. If the total number is below standard, we ask the bowler for an explanation and encourage him to do better next period. We're beginning to understand that we won't turn out many world-class bowlers with this type of reporting system.

## The Threebee Company

Steve Briley, department manager of Cracking Plant 3B, had recently devised a supplemental departmental financial report for his operating department:

> The diagram of the cracking process is very simple. We have two inputs of natural gas and energy, and we produce two main products, ethylene and propylene, plus several by-products, such as hydrogen and methane gas. But inside the black box that converts feedstock into propylene and ethylene is an incredibly complex chemical process with thousands of control points, multilevel refrigerants, and recycling intermediate products.
>
> Operators had little information to help them make decisions about tradeoffs among production output, quality, and cost. For example, we could crack gas at higher temperatures and get more conversion of raw material into main and by-products. But this is costly both in terms of achieving the higher temperatures and in wear and tear of the equipment. Also, as we push the cracking plant to maximize the rate of production, it becomes much more difficult to keep quality under control. We face constant tradeoffs among cost, production output, and quality but have virtually no information to point us in the right direction in making these tradeoffs.

Briley took an unconventional approach to solving this problem by creating a fictitious company for his employees and developing a simple financial statement for that company. The Threebee Company was formed in September 1987, and each employee in Plant 3B was issued a share of stock (see **Exhibit 9**). Briley then created an income statement for the Threebee Company (see **Exhibit 10**):

> In preparing the income statement, the quantities for outputs produced and inputs consumed were readily available from the daily production report. I needed to supply prices. I estimated the prices for ethylene and propylene and several by-products (hydrogen, methane, and steam) from nominal market values for these products. It wasn't important to get these prices precisely right, as long as I was in the right ballpark for them. I introduced one wrinkle by recognizing different prices for in-spec and off-spec material. Threebee would earn the full price for ethylene and propylene only if the product was within the upper and lower control limits (set initially at 3 sigma). If product was outside the control limits but still within rated specifications, the product price was set at half the normal price. This 50% discount was a little arbitrary, but I tried to approximate the discounts that final producers might face when selling substandard product. No revenues (zero price) would be earned for material produced outside of specifications.
>
> The basis for the input prices for feedstock and utilities were actual costs, which turned out to be reasonably close to the plant's standard costs. But I would occasionally adjust these costs for additional emphasis. For example, I increased the price of cooling water since the company was starting a conservation drive, and I wanted to encourage operators to be even more thrifty with cooling water.
>
> For equipment costs, I computed a mortgage payment for the capital invested in the department based on a rough estimate of the replacement cost and the company's cost of capital. This figure remained constant in each report, of course, but I wanted the operators to be aware of the cost of the equipment they worked with. I also opened up a loan repayment account to repay any capital expenditures made for product or quality improvements. And I added an additional category, called

Other Costs, as a target for some future cost reduction program. My goal was to start the Threebee Company off in a zero profit condition, after paying the cost of capital, so that even a zero profit would reflect a good return on investment.

Briley encountered some initial skepticism from his colleagues about whether workers would understand or respond to an income statement to evaluate their efforts. He responded:

In my experience, the operators were able and willing to use a new tool, such as this profit statement, as long as they were given sufficient explanation and enough time to grow accustomed to it. Some operators had never worked with an income statement before, and it took some time to explain the concept to them. Fortunately, several of the operators had small businesses on the side, selling crops or raising livestock, and they were familiar with an income statement format. They helped to explain the concept to the others.

More than the details of the income statement, it was the whole change in culture that took some time to get used to. In the past, TEX had never shared financial information with operating people. We just gave the operators specific rules, "do this, don't do that, watch out for this condition," but never told them about the economics of the business they were running.

Once the daily income statement had been designed, data such as actual outputs produced, their quality and the actual quantities of inputs consumed were obtained from the daily production record. With these data, Briley personally prepared the Threebee Company income statement each day:

The operators' first reaction to the income report was surprise about the cost of raw materials and energy consumed in the plant each day. They had no idea about the financial scale of operation of the 3B plant, or how their actions produced large effects on the costs and revenues of the plant. By varying our feedstock inputs, we can shift the ratio of ethylene to propylene production, but that change may require more inputs, decrease total production, and influence the amount of by-product produced. On a cost basis, this may look bad, but if the sales value of the production is greater, the operators can see that the company is better off even though output is down and costs are up.

As operators made suggestions for improving the format or the calculations, Briley soon found himself working 12 hours a day to keep abreast of his normal supervisory responsibilities plus producing the daily Threebee income statement.

When I was away on business, one of the first things the operators wanted me to do when I returned was calculate the profits for the days I missed. They would be disappointed if results were bad during that period because it was too late for them to correct any problems.

Briley's initial goal had been to double the current operating profit of the plant:

Even though I tried to start from a zero profit condition, our September 87 operations were yielding a period (four week) profit of about $200K, mostly because the plant was producing more than standard. I set a goal of achieving a period profit of $400K. If we could hit that figure, I promised to install a new kitchen in the control room for the operators.

We kept charts, updated daily, of daily profits and cumulative profits for the period (see **Exhibit 11**). It only took the operators four periods to achieve the $400K rate of profit, and along the way we broke five new production records for ethylene and propylene. Operators were posting quality statistics every two hours, and quality measures had improved by 50%. Operators had gotten so good at having all material within the 3 sigma limits, we agreed to set a more challenging target by reducing the upper and lower control limits to 2 sigma.

Briley felt satisfied and suspended the program when the higher outputs and quality enabled the $400K profit goal to be achieved. The operators and supervisors had their new kitchen, but they told Briley that they missed the daily calculations. They had enjoyed seeing the daily income statement and the challenge of achieving profit targets. Briley responded:

One of our Threebee Company officers is a computer whiz. He decided to write software so that the daily report could be prepared automatically, using data the operators entered into the system. Now when operators come in each day at 7 A.M. to start their shift, they look first at the profit report for the previous day. When I show up, an operator immediately tells me about yesterday's profits, happy when they had had a good day and disappointed when profits had declined.

Operators and supervisors in the 3B plant were using the information from the daily income statement to make decisions that formerly they were forbidden to make or else they had taken to Briley for approval. Said Briley:

When the company started the Quality Management Program, we had told the operators not to tweak flow rates or change operating conditions without prior approval from their supervisor. They were to hold feed rates and operating conditions constant. Within several periods of operations of the Threebee Company, operators had learned how to tweak the system to *increase* profit; they're taking actions now that they formerly were not allowed to do. They have also learned to focus on a few key items and really keep an eye on those. For example, they found that if propylene quality is good then everything else was working pretty well, so propylene impurities are monitored continuously. They have also narrowed the control limits for many operating parameters to guarantee that the product is never outside the 100% price limits. In fact, they got so good at this, I had to build in a new challenge. I established a Top Grade "Gold" quality region and set a 25% price premium for product falling within the Gold region. My rationale was that the higher quality product could be sold to new outside customers at this higher price.

The operators were also more willing to take action when I wasn't around. For example, one night a hydrogen compressor failed. Normally, repair efforts would have been undertaken on a routine, nonexpedited basis. But the shift supervisor on duty had just seen the value of hydrogen gas from the income report. Knowing the value of the lost output of hydrogen gas, he made an immediate decision to authorize overtime to get the compressor repaired and back on line as soon as possible.

Briley was asked how he used the Period Departmental Cost Reports that he received from the accounting department:

Some data are only available from the Period Report. For example, I don't see daily maintenance records, so we're using budgeted numbers in the Daily Income Statement. The Period Report shows me actual maintenance costs and helps me to calibrate and monitor our maintenance activity. The Period Report also forces us to reconcile between meter readings we take locally and plantwide meterings. Because of metering discrepancies, we need to absorb a pro-rata allocation of deviations between local and plantwide meterings.

Gayle English, a production division superintendent, provided additional comments about the cost reports he received from accounting:

The problem with the period report is that the information comes too late—a cost incurred near the start of a period will not be reported until six or seven weeks later—and results from all the events of that period are aggregated together. As a result, production people often pay little attention to the financial reports since they already know about any chronic problems.

TEX, historically, had shared cost information with departmental managers but was reluctant to disclose information on product profitability. Virtually no financial data had been provided to the operators. With the new report, operators were really surprised about the costs of materials being consumed in the cracking process. Even the costs of small items like filters or half-filled bags of material that they might have been throwing away or discarding surprised them. They never appreciated the cost consequences of things they were doing.

Jerry Matthews, an assistant department superintendent, offered his observations on how the Daily Income Statement changed the roles of the operators:

Initially the work teams were not used to selecting and working on projects. They had to be fed ideas from department managers. But as they got more comfortable with the reports and with the freedom they had, they started to take more initiative. Without having good measures, it would have been difficult to get them interested and involved and to take the ownership for the processes they were controlling. The financial data on costs and profits turned out to be a lot more meaningful to them than just trying to control quantities of steam. It helped them set priorities among different projects. Before, they may have been concentrating on controlling one part of the process that cost only $200/day. Now they can set priorities to focus where their efforts can have the greatest impact.

For example, before we established different prices for in-spec and out-of-spec material, it was hard to mobilize enthusiasm about quality. Occasionally, the cracking department might ship off-spec material to downstream processing plants. Those plants accepted the material but eventually paid a higher price for doing so. They had to perform more purges to get rid of impurities from their chemicals, they might have more rework, and their catalysts would get fouled up sooner. This really ran up the costs of the processing department, but the costs were attributed to that department, not to the supplying department that created the problem. Now, by putting a lower price on off-spec material from the cracking plant, we have everyone's attention.

The daily financial reports have also become a tool for my decision making. I need to decide whether to shut down the plant for maintenance for six days or for eight days. The Daily Income Statement helps me decide whether the additional improvements are worth two more days of shutdown. I can trade off overtime and higher rates of spending during the maintenance period in return for getting the plant back on-line one or two days earlier. When demand falls, I can ask whether it is better to run at a reduced rate or to keep producing at capacity and then shut down for a few days.

Matthews reflected on the changes brought about by the new systems at TEX:

There's so much information out there, and we're still learning how to use it effectively. An operator always has more demands for his time than he can deliver. Which problems should he solve to have the greatest impact? Operators can now see the relative priority of raw material costs versus maintenance costs versus other categories. With the Daily Income Statement, we've "empowered" the operators, making our mission statements about teamwork and ownership real. Doors are opening up; it's mind boggling. It's like giving someone a car who formerly only had a horse. There are new directions and distances we can now consider traveling.

**Accounting Department Reactions**  Jess Greer, a cost analyst in the accounting department, wondered about the changing role for the finance function in the new operating environment of the TEX plant:

There's certainly been a lot of interest in Threebee's Daily Income Statement, and the people seem very enthusiastic about it. In finance, we have been trying to be responsive. Financial information is being used for more and more things. We introduced statistical control limits on some of the variance analysis reports and adjusted standards rapidly to current operating conditions. We're also doing a lot more analytic work on the numbers to explain deviations between actual and standard. The finance people are working much more closely with operations, giving them information that seems to be helping them to manage. But we can clearly do more to improve the delivery of the existing cost system, to make it more timely, and to switch from paper to electronic presentation.

Tom Wilson, company controller, concurred with the need for the finance function to go beyond its traditional role:

Continuous improvement requires very rapid, accurate timely feedback. I don't see how we can maintain our continuous improvement efforts without some kind of daily operating report. Our focus of attention has to be to get cost information to the 1st Level Teams, the people on the line turning the valves that operate the plant.

The senior people in accounting were highly supportive of the Threebee initiative but wondered about its implications for the overall system of financial reporting at TEX. They were uncertain about the consequences if every department developed its own financial summaries. The business people at the top of the organization were used to making decisions based on the Period Cost Reports, and they expected the financial reports for each department to tie in to the results for the plant as a whole. They would not want individual department managers thinking they were doing a terrific job when the plant as a whole was showing poor performance. Among the questions confronting the senior accounting managers were:

> Should there be two systems, the official financial one and one for departmental operations? If each department develops its own financial system, how should the local departmental reports be reconciled with the upper management reports?

## EXHIBIT 1   Texas Eastman's Chemical Plant

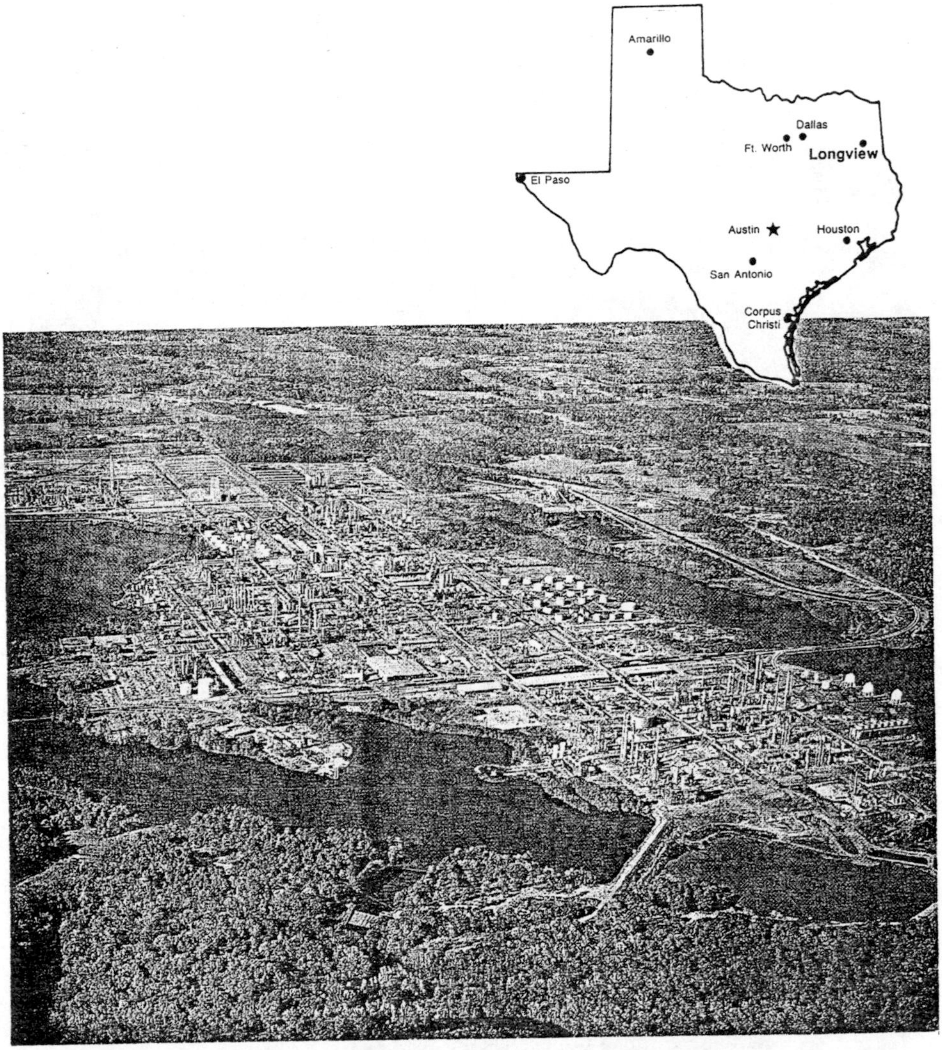

**EXHIBIT 2 EASTMAN CHEMICALS DIVISION:**
**Summary of Operating Results ($000,000)**

|                    | 1988    | 1987    | 1986    |
|--------------------|---------|---------|---------|
| Sales              | $3,033  | $2,600  | $2,378  |
| Operating Earnings | 628     | 388     | 227     |
| Assets             | 2,875   | 2,514   | 2,266   |
| Capital Spending   | 475     | 394     | 314     |

**EXHIBIT 3  Texas Eastman Company Product Flow Diagram**

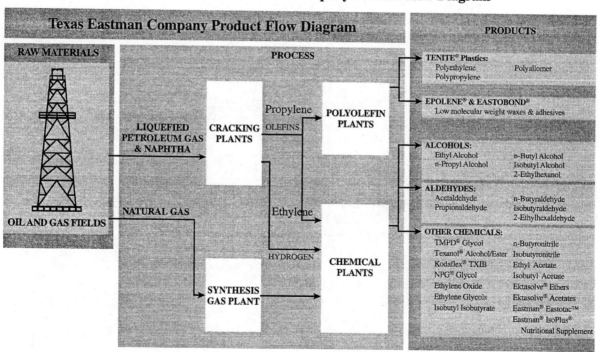

**EXHIBIT 4    Eastman Chemicals Division Quality Policy**

EASTMAN CHEMICALS DIVISION

# QUALITY POLICY

QUALITY GOAL
To be the leader in quality and value of products and services

QUALITY MANAGEMENT PROCESS

• Establish mission, vision, and indicators of performance.
• Understand, standardize, stabilize, and maintain processes.
• Plan, do and reinforce continual improvement and innovation.

OPERATIONAL POLICY

• Achieve process stability and reliability.
• Control every process to the desired target.
• Improve process capability.

PRINCIPLES WHICH SUPPORT AND ENABLE ACHIEVEMENT
OF THE QUALITY GOAL

| | |
|---|---|
| CUSTOMER FOCUS | Emphasize understanding, meeting, and anticipating customer needs. |
| CONTINUAL IMPROVEMENT | Current level of performance can be improved. |
| INNOVATION | Everyone searching for creative process, product, and service alternatives. |
| PROCESS EMPHASIS | Focus on processes as the means to prevent defects and improve results. |
| MANAGEMENT LEADERSHIP | Create an inspiring vision, maintain constancy of purpose, and establish a supportive environment. |
| EMPLOYEE INVOLVEMENT | Every employee participates in decision making and problem solving, along with teamwork among all functional areas and organizational levels. |
| STATISTICAL METHODS | All employees understand the concept of variation and apply appropriate statistical methods to continual improvement and innovation. |
| PERFORMANCE MANAGEMENT | Take pride in work through clear accountabilities, feedback, reinforcement, and removing barriers. |
| EDUCATION AND TRAINING | Encourage learning and personal growth for everyone throughout their career. |
| CUSTOMER AND SUPPLIER RELATIONS | Build long-term partnerships with customers and suppliers. |
| ASSESSMENT | Benchmark against world best and assess performance against the Quality Policy for improvement planning and reinforcement. |

E.W. Deavenport, Jr.
President

Kodak

**EXHIBIT 5** **The Quality Management Triangle**

# THE QUALITY MANAGEMENT TRIANGLE

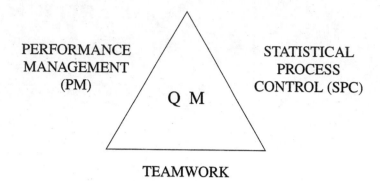

PERFORMANCE MANAGEMENT (PM)

STATISTICAL PROCESS CONTROL (SPC)

Q M

TEAMWORK

**EXHIBIT 6** **The Control Chart: A Basis for Action**

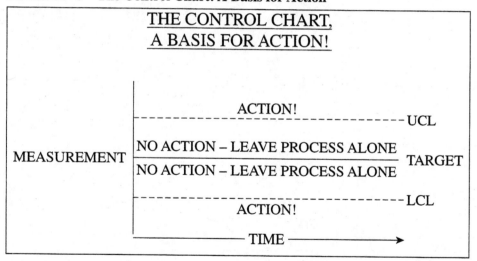

## THE CONTROL CHART, A BASIS FOR ACTION!

MEASUREMENT

ACTION! — — — — — — — — — — — — — — — — — — UCL

NO ACTION – LEAVE PROCESS ALONE

NO ACTION – LEAVE PROCESS ALONE — TARGET

— — — — — — — — — — — — — — — — — — LCL
ACTION!

TIME →

**EXHIBIT 7** **Data Collection Stats**

| DIVISION | NO. OF ROUTES | NO. OF OBSERVATIONS |
|---|---|---|
| Olefin | 27 | 6800 |
| Oxo-Ethylene Products | 51 | 12100 |
| Polyethylene | 28 | 3600 |
| Polypropylene-Eastobond | 30 | 3700 |
| Utilities | 20 | 3100 |
| Supply & Distribution | 8 | 600 |
| TOTALS | 164 | 29900 |

## EXHIBIT 8    Departmental Cost Sheet
Texas Eastman Company
Departmental Cost of Manufacture
Chemical One Mfg. Plant 1

Restricted Information
TEX 7112-01

Sheet No. 98
Third Period
Issued 03/31/89

*Change in Standard*

|  | Actual | Planned | Var. |
|---|---|---|---|
| Period Basis | $1,000* | $2,000 | $3,000* |
| Year-to-Date Basis | 2,000* | 2,000 | 4,000* |

*Production:*

| Period | 80,000 |
|---|---|
| Year | 169,000 |

| | Departmental Cost This Period | | | Departmental Cost This Year | | |
|---|---|---|---|---|---|---|
| | | Var. From Std. | | | Var. From Std. | |
| | Amount | Amount | Unit | Amount | Amount | Unit |
| Raw Materials | $35,000 | $2500 | $.0313 | $ 82,000 | $ 8500* | $.0503* |
| Recoveries | | | | | | |
| Packing Materials | | | | | | |
| Net Materials | 35,000 | 2500 | .0313 | 82,000 | 8500* | .0503* |
| Labor & Benefits | 10,000 | 2000* | .0250* | 26,000 | 2700* | .0160* |
| Mfg. Supplies | 1,200 | 500 | .0063 | 1,900 | 3200 | .0190 |
| Maintenance & Repairs | 8,800 | 1200 | .0150 | 29,000 | 1000 | .0060 |
| Plant Utilities | 5,000 | 1200* | .0150* | 12,000 | 3700* | .0219* |
| Other Expenses | | | | | | |
| Laboratory | | | | | | |
| Plan. & Prod. Records | | | | | | |
| General Plant | | | | | | |
| Depr., Ins., & Taxes | 3,000 | | | 9,000 | | |
| Miscellaneous | | | | 700 | 700* | .0042* |
| Underground Storage | | | | | | |
| Work Done For/By Other | | | | | | |
| Materials Handling | | | | | | |
| Storage and Shipping | | | | | | |
| Waste Treatment | | | | | | |
| Total Conversion Chart | 28,000 | 1500* | .0188* | 78,600 | 2900* | .0172* |
| Total Departmental Cost | $63,000 | $1000 | $.0125 | $160,000 | $11400* | $.0675* |

*Continued next page*

*Exhibit 8    Continued*

| | | Variances | | | |
|---|---|---|---|---|---|
| Cost Summary | Departmental Cost | Usage/ Price | Volume/ Mix | Change in Standard | AOC |
| Period—Amt | $ 63,000 | $   500* | $12,500 | $3,000* | $ 72,000 |
| —Unit | .7875 | .0063* | .1563 | .0375* | .9000 |
| Year—Amt | 160,600 | 14,200* | 15,345 | 4000* | 157,745 |
| —Unit | .9503 | .0841* | .0908 | .0237* | .9223 |

*Variance Analysis*

| | Department Controllable | | | | Department Non-Controllable | | |
|---|---|---|---|---|---|---|---|
| | Chg in Std | Usage | Prod Volume | Price | Chg in Std | Demand Volume | Prod Mix |
| PD | 2,000* | 1,000 | 1,335* | 1,500* | 1,000* | 8,902* | 4,933 |
| YTD | 3,000* | 11,400* | 4,750* | 2,800* | 1,000* | 2,228 | 17,867 |

**EXHIBIT 9    Employee Stock Certificate: 3B Department**

## EXHIBIT 10    Daily Profit Statement for Threebee Company

| SALES | | $/DY | |
|---|---|---|---|
| Steam: +600% | 87,938 lb/hr | 8,416 | |
| +160% | 11,972 lb/hr | 1,068 | |
| −pyro | 24,516 lb/hr | 2,368 | |
| −30% | 11,624 lb/hr | 1,037 | |
| Net | 63,770 | $6,079 | |
| Ethylene: Hi Grade | 776,042 lb/day | 124,167 | |
| Lo Grade | 0 lb/day | 0 | 0% out |
| Waste | 0 lb/day | 0 | |
| Total | 776,042 | $124,167 | |
| Propylene: Hi Grade | 358,280 lb/day | 68,073 | |
| Lo Grade | 32,429 lb/day | 3,081 | 8.3% out |
| Waste | 0 lb/day | 0 | |
| Total | 390,708 | $71,154 | |
| Hydrogen, capacity | 7 lines | $57,708 | |
| Methane, capacity | 9 lines | $5,058 | |
| Heavies | (fixed for nov) | $1,732 | |
| TOTAL SALES | | $265,898 | |

| COSTS | | | |
|---|---|---|---|
| Feedstock: Ethane | 227,865 lb | 6,471 | |
| Propane | 1,595,066 lb | 108,305 | |
| Total | 1,822,930 lb | $114,776 | |
| Maint & Repair | (1987 Avg.) | $4,168 | |
| Utilities: | | | |
| Electricity | 1234 amps | $8,359 | |
| Cooling Water | 4.8 lines | $4,109 | |
| Natural Gas | 3.1 lines | $3,442 | |
| Other (typical) | | $607 | |
| Total Util | | $16,517 | |
| Other Costs | | $45,714 | |
| Total Cost of Goods Sold | | $181,175 | |
| Loan Repayment | | 0 | |
| Mortgage | | $54,946 | |
| TOTAL COSTS | | $236,122 | |
| GROSS PROFIT | | $29,776 | |
| LESS TAXES @ 35% | | $10,422 | |
| NET PROFIT | | $19,354/day | |
| | | (equivalent to $541,923/period profit) | |

**EXHIBIT 11   Daily Profits During Period 4**

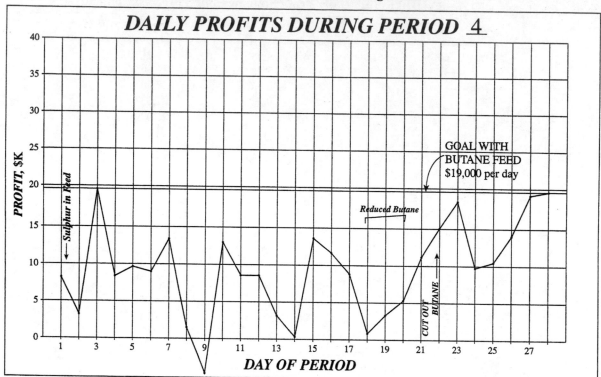

# CASE 14   Burlington Northern: The ARES Decision (A)

ARES will give Operations better control over its assets. We will schedule locomotives and cars more precisely, and get more efficiency and utilization of locomotives and tracks. ARES will also enable us to service our customers better by offering more reliable and predictable deliveries.

*Joe Galassi, executive vice president, Operations*

In July 1990, Burlington Northern's senior executives were deciding whether to invest in ARES (Advanced Railroad Electronics System), an automated railroad control system. ARES, expected to cost $350 million, would radically change how railroad operations were planned and controlled. The potential implications of this investment were so extensive that they affected virtually all parts of the BN organization. Nine years had passed since BN managers had begun to consider whether automated control technology could be applied to the railroad. Yet managers were still divided about whether the ARES project should be continued.

## Company Background

Burlington Northern Railroad was formed in 1970, by the merger of four different railroads. In addition to a vast rail system, the merged company owned substantial natural resources including extensive land grant holdings containing minerals, timber, and oil and gas. In 1989, up to 800 trains per day ran on BN routes (see **Exhibit 1**) generating revenues of $4,606 million and net income of $242 million. Total assets equalled $6,146 million, and 1989 capital expenditures were $465 million (see **Exhibit 2** for recent financial data).

BN's diverse operations and staffs were headquartered in three cities (see **Exhibit 3** for an organization chart). The firm's CEO, COO and corporate functions such as finance, strategic planning, marketing, and labor relations were located in Ft. Worth, Texas. The Operations Department, headquartered in Overland Park, Kansas, was the largest department in BN. It oversaw operating divisions comprising train dispatchers, operators, and their supervisors, and managed support functions such as research and development, engineering, and maintenance. Additional corporate staff functions, such as Information System Services, were located in St. Paul, Minnesota.

## Products, Markets, Competitors, and the Effects of Deregulation

BN's revenues came from seven primary segments: coal, agricultural commodities, industrial products, intermodal, forest products, food and consumer products, and automotive products (**Exhibit 4** contains segment information).

Coal was BN's largest source of revenue, representing about one-third of total revenue. Over 90% of the coal carried by BN originated in the Powder River Basin of Montana and

*Professors Julie H. Hertenstein and Robert S. Kaplan prepared this case as the basis for class discussion rather than to illustrate either effective or ineffective handling of an administrative situation.*

Wyoming. BN had invested heavily in the 1970s to build lines to serve the Powder River Basin. If the U.S. government enacted the anticipated acid rain legislation, demand for the Powder River Basin's low-sulphur coal was expected to increase substantially. Managers also believed that Powder River coal had promising export potential to Japan and other Pacific Rim nations from the west coast ports served by BN.

Coal was carried in unit trains or "sets" (108 cars, each holding 102 tons of coal, powered by 3 to 6 engines). Virtually all of the unit coal traffic was under long-term contract with fewer than two dozen customers. To insure good asset utilization, cycle time was important. A reduction in the average cycle time reduced the number of sets required to carry a given amount of coal, and hence, reduced the capital investment in coal cars, most of which were owned by customers. Thus, unit coal trains never stopped, and the coal business was almost totally predictable. Although sensitive to cycle time, the coal business was not sensitive to arrival time precision as coal could be dumped on the ground without waiting for special unloading facilities or warehouse space. Even electric utilities, however, were becoming aware of just-in-time delivery benefits.

BN's major competition in coal were other railroads, especially the Union Pacific (UP). UP had made substantial investments in heavy duty double track and in new technology, fuel efficient engines for carrying coal. BN management believed UP had excess capacity whereas BN, with its single track lines, was running close to capacity on its coal lines.

Agricultural commodities, primarily grain, was BN's second largest segment. Strategically located to serve the Midwest and Great Plains grain-producing regions, BN was the number one hauler of spring wheat, and the number two hauler of corn. Although grain and coal were both bulk commodity businesses with little competition from trucks, the grain business differed substantially from coal. Demand for grain deliveries was more random since the time of harvest varied from year to year, and export demand for grain also fluctuated with the highly variable market price of grain. Grain traders dealt for the best prices, and long-term arrangements were uncommon. BN managers expected that with the change in economic policies in Eastern Europe (and possibly the Soviet Union), the standard of living in these countries would rise, leading to an increased demand for grain. With its ability to serve both the grain producing regions and west coast and Gulf ports, BN expected this segment of its business to grow significantly in future years.

During the late 1980s, BN changed the marketing of grain transportation through its Certificates of Transportation (COT) program. Under this program, BN sold contracts containing commitments to move carloads of grain within a three-day interval, six months in the future. The COT was helping to eliminate some of the randomness in grain shipments and pricing. BN, though, now had to have cars available reliably for the contracted shipment, or else incur a large penalty for failure to perform. The COT program had been a successful innovation but it put a premium on BN to coordinate and plan its grain operations.

John Anderson, executive vice president for Marketing and Sales, believed that BN's five other commodity businesses had many similarities:

> Although the customers differ, these five businesses all have significant flat or boxcar movements. They have random movement and demand, and are strongly service sensitive. Customers make tradeoffs between price and quality and these businesses all put us into severe competition with trucks.

> Think of a continuum of commodities. At one end of the continuum are commodities that should go by train such as coal or grain. These commodities are heavy and low cost, have low time sensitivity, and come in large lots. At the other end are commodities that should go by truck, such as strawber-

ries, electronics, and garments. These are light and high cost, have extremely high time sensitivity, and come in small lots. In between these two extremes are many commodities where trucks and trains compete vigorously on price and service.

Historically, trucks had taken over the transportation of more and more of the contested commodities. At the end of World War II, about 70% of intercity freight had been shipped by rail. In the post-WW II era, rail's share of intercity shipments was lost, primarily to trucking, and especially in the service sensitive segments. Ed Butt, ARES project director, highlighted the reasons for trucking's inroads:

> Trucks charge as much as two to three times what it would cost for rail service. But trucks go door-to-door, and people will pay for that level of service.

Recent trends in manufacturing, such as just-in-time production systems and cycle time reduction were making trucking's service time advantages even more valuable. Railroads were using their intermodal trailer/container-on-flatcar service to offer door-to-door delivery but still could not offer the reliability of delivery that trucks could obtain on a highway system where drivers could often make up for unexpected delays. As Butt explained:

> We may have peaked at 75% on-time delivery for our general merchandise, and 80% for intermodal. But 75–80% is not good enough for just-in-time service. Trucks are 90–95% and we need to get into that range to attract the just-in-time customers, who are enormously sensitive to consistent reliable deliveries.

**Effects of Deregulation**  The deregulation of both the trucking and railroad industries in 1980 had changed both the railroads' and the truckers' competitive environment. The Motor Carrier Act of 1980 gave truckers much greater freedom in setting rates and entering markets. The Staggers Rail Act of 1980 gave railroads similar freedom in setting their own rates; it also included provisions allowing railroads to own other forms of transportation.

Following deregulation, BN modernized its railroad operations. Richard Bressler, the chairman in 1980, established a research and development department in Operations and hired Steve Ditmeyer to head the group. Numerous new technologies and innovations were considered and, where appropriate, were applied to railroad operations. During the 1980s, railroad productivity increased dramatically: the number of employees declined by 50% while revenue ton miles increased by over two-thirds.

But trucking rates fell significantly after deregulation, putting pressure on the railroads' chief advantage: the low-cost transportation of freight. In 1990, additional regulatory changes permitting trucks to be longer and heavier were under consideration. These changes would enable trucks to further reduce their costs. Dick Lewis, vice president of Strategic Planning, however, recognized:

> In our recent analysis we've been surprised to find that railroads and not trucks are some of our major competition. Since deregulation, intra-railroad competition is increasing and driving down prices at a fearsome rate. [See **Exhibit 5**] Trucks have carved off their own segments fairly solidly. Railroads want to compete in these segments, but they don't, and trucks are pretty secure in them.

## Existing Operations

In 1990 each day up to 800 trains traveled approximately 200,000 train-miles on the 23,356 miles of track on BN routes. The 5,000 junctions created 25 million possible distinct routings, or origin-destination pairs, for the cars that comprised BN trains. Meets and passes— two trains "meeting" on a single track with one of them directed off to a siding so that the other can "pass"—were carefully managed by the railroad's dispatchers. BN managers believed that thousands of meets and passes occurred each day, but were unsure about the precise number; some believed the actual number was as high as 10,000 per day.

A train running off schedule could potentially affect many other trains due to the limited number of tracks—often only one—and sidings in any area. Thus, controlling train operations meant controlling an extensive, complex network of dynamic, interdependent train and car movements.

Trains were controlled by dispatchers, each responsible for a distinct territory. Dispatchers still utilized technology developed around 1920 and little changed since then. A dispatcher was responsible for the 20 or 30 trains operating on his shift in his territory. Operations personnel, however, estimated that a good dispatcher could really only focus on and expedite five to seven trains. The remainder were inevitably treated with less attention and lower priority. At present, dispatcher priority went to scheduling competitive segments like intermodal and merchandise traffic; unit trains carrying coal and grain were not scheduled. Dispatchers had little basis for trading off delaying an intermodal train versus reducing the cycle time for a coal train.

Dispatchers saw information only about their own territories, and not others. Thus, if a delayed train entered a dispatcher's territory, he would be unaware that enough slack existed further down the line to make up all the lost time, and that he should not jeopardize the schedules of his other trains by trying to catch the delayed train up to its schedule. Typically, trains were directed to run as fast as they could and then halted to wait at sidings.

Dispatchers also scheduled maintenance-of-way (MOW) crews. MOW crews would travel to a section of track that needed maintenance and repair. But the crews were not allowed to initiate work on the track until the dispatcher was confident that no train would run down the track during the crew's work period. At present, train arrivals at MOW work sites could be predicted within a 30- to 45-minute window, but for safety reasons, the work crews were cleared off the track much sooner than the beginning of this window.

Dispatchers spent considerable time establishing communications with trains and MOW vehicles. Dispatchers had to search various radio frequencies to establish contact with trains; MOW vehicles often reported long waits until they were able to get through to the dispatcher for permission to get onto the track. In fact, on some occasions, the MOW crew travelled to the maintenance site but were unable to get through to the dispatcher before the maintenance window closed and another train was scheduled to arrive, hence wasting the trip.

Current information about railroad operations was difficult to obtain. For example, to know how much fuel was available, an engineer had to stop the train, get out, and look at the gauge on the tank at the back of the locomotive. Trains refueled nearly every time they passed a fueling station, even if the added fuel was not necessary for the next part of the trip. Further, despite daily maintenance checks of critical components such as brakes, lights, and bells, and scheduled periodic maintenance every 92 days, the only evidence of a locomotive performing poorly came from reports filed by the crew about observable failures or breakdowns. Except for the newest locomotives, no gauges or recording systems monitored conditions that could foreshadow failures such as oil pressure or temperature changes.

Information about the location of cars and trains was also subject to delay and error. Conductors were given instructions about which cars to set out and pick up at each location. Following completion of a set-out or pick-up, the conductor made a written notation. When the train arrived at the next terminal (conceivably hours later), the paper was given to a clerk who entered the data via keyboard to update management data files. Arrivals of trains at stations were recorded by clerks who, if busy, might not observe the actual arrival, thus recording a 12:00 train as 12:15, and then entering this fact at 1:00 to the management data files.

Some executives were exploring the application of modern management science philosophy to improve railroad scheduling. According to Mark Cane, vice president, Service Design:

> There are many potentially useful operations research and artificial intelligence techniques that are not yet being used by the railroad. Decision support technology has made a quantum leap forward, and we are trying to take advantage of it.

Dick Lewis illustrated the contrast between the BN and another highly scheduled transportation company:

> A benchmark company in this area is UPS. UPS has 1200 industrial engineers working for them; BN has only half a dozen.

One view, integrated network management, was being discussed among BN's senior managers. Under this approach, scientifically designed schedules would be generated, broken down into "standards" for each task, plus the appropriate education and incentives would be provided for local operations personnel to cause them to run the railroad to schedule. One operating manager voiced the concerns of many about this approach to railroad train scheduling:

> BN has talked a lot about running a scheduled railroad. However, the real challenge is how to manage the unscheduled, for example, a broken air hose or a broken rail. The problem is that problems do not happen on schedule.

By mid 1990, BN's service design organization had begun to institute a reporting system called the service measurement system. Bands of acceptable performance were established for scheduled trains and compared with actual results. On-time scheduled performance measures became part of the bonus incentive system for non-union operating personnel. Following the institution of the reporting scheme, service showed definite and steady improvement. The percentage of scheduled cars arriving within targeted performance bands jumped from 25% in January 1990 to 58% in June. This suggested to BN managers that service performance could be improved simply by better collection and reporting of performance measures.

## Strategic View of Operations

In late 1989, BN executives undertook a major strategic review to help shape the future. Gerald Grinstein, the chief executive officer of BN, focused the review on answering questions like, "What kind of railroad should we be?" Executives formed eight teams to examine in depth the following areas: operating strategies, customer behavior, information technology, labor, business economics, organizational performance, industry restructuring, and competitive analysis.

Dick Lewis, explained the conclusions reached by this strategic directions project:

> This company, and the railroad industry, face two major challenges: service and capital intensity. We must improve our ability to deliver service. We must reform and reconstitute our service offerings, especially in highly service-sensitive segments. Since World War II, railroads have retrenched

from service sensitive segments. For example, they have stopped carrying passengers and less-than-carload shipments.

If we improve service, the first opportunity created is to increase volume, at the expense of other rail carriers. The second opportunity is to raise prices, but this is more questionable. To be able to raise price requires a *radical* service change, not a marginal one. The change must be radical enough to be perceived by a customer who says, "Wow! That's different!" For example, in our chemical business we recently made such a change. We reduced the average delivery time by more than half, and we also reduced the variability of the delivery time. The shipper found he could get rid of 100 rail cars. That had a measurable value significant enough for the customer to perceive the service improvement. We have subsequently been able to structure an agreement with the shipper to provide financial incentives to BN to further improve the service.

The other side of this equation is that BN must improve utilization of assets. We have high capital intensity, poor utilization of rolling stock, and low asset turnover ratios. Actually, BN is good for the industry, but the industry itself has very poor ratios. Not only are the ratios poor, but the capital requirements for the 1990s are daunting. Just the traditional investments in locomotives, freight cars, and track replacements are daunting. If we can improve utilization of these assets, then we can reduce the capital investment required during the 1990s.

## The ARES Project: The Origins

Steve Ditmeyer, chief engineer-Research, Communications and Control Systems, reached deep into his desk and withdrew a slip of paper with a handwritten note: "Any application to locomotives?" BN's chairman Bressler had written that note in 1981 shortly after Ditmeyer had joined the company, and attached the note to an article on new aircraft instrumentation that promised lowered costs by improving fuel and other operating efficiencies. The note and article eventually filtered down to numerous railroad staffs.

In 1982, BN's R&D department contacted the Collins Air Transport Division of Rockwell International to learn whether aircraft technology could be applied to the rail industry. The two companies agreed to work together to identify workable solutions. By the end of 1983 they discovered that the technology existed to integrate control, communications, and information. An electronics unit, placed in each locomotive, could receive signals from the Department of Defense's Global Positioning System (GPS) satellites, and calculate the train's position to within ± 100 feet, a significant improvement over the existing ± 10–15 mile resolution from existing systems. By calculating its location every second, the train's speed could also be estimated accurately. A communications network could then be developed to carry information back and forth between the train and a control center.

The R&D department managed the early stages of the ARES project, with oversight by the R&D Steering Committee comprised of senior officers of Transportation, Engineering, Mechanical, Operations Services, Marketing and Information Systems. The Board of Directors in July 1985 viewed a demonstration of the proposed technology installed on two locomotives. In August 1985 BN's senior executives agreed to fund a prototype system: equipping seventeen locomotives on BN's Minnesota Iron Range, putting the data segment in place in the Iron Range, and building those elements of the control segment that would permit BN to communicate with and control the locomotives from the Minneapolis control center. The Iron Range was chosen because it was a closed-loop segment of BN's network with a variety of train control systems, and was served only by a limited set of equipment.

By 1986 the ARES project had grown too large to be carried out by the small R&D staff, and Don Henderson was chosen to oversee the formation of a separate ARES team to manage the project's development. Henderson ensured that team members represented various Operations departments that would potentially be affected by ARES: dispatching, mechanical, maintenance-of-way, control systems and communications, freight car management and information system services. The team members worked with their respective departments and with others such as general managers and operating vice presidents to ensure a system that met operational needs and worked in the railroad environment. Operations managers saw ARES as a means to accomplish key goals of service improvements, operating efficiencies and improved capital utilization. Operations incorporated ARES into the strategic plans it prepared and presented to corporate.

The ARES prototype was installed on the Iron Range in 1987. The ARES team, BN field personnel, and system developer Rockwell spent the next several years testing, evaluating, and improving the ARES system.

Under Henderson's guidance, the ARES concept evolved to a full command, control, communications and information system that would enable BN to gain additional control over its operations. ARES, using high speed computing, digital communications, and state-of-the-art electronics, could generate efficient traffic plans, convert those plans into movement instructions for individual trains and MOW units and display those instructions to engine crews. By knowing the position and speed of trains and other equipment on the tracks, ARES could automatically detect deviations from plan or potential problems and communicate these exceptions to control center dispatchers. Dispatchers could determine the corrective action required and use ARES to send and confirm new movement instructions to trains. In many ways, ARES could be considered analogous to the Air Traffic Control system that controlled the aviation industry. ARES eventually came to consist of three segments: Control, Data and Vehicle.

The Control segment received information on train position and speed to produce schedules and to check that vehicles followed proper operating procedures. It warned dispatchers of violations to limits of authority and speed, and produced authorities and checked them for conflict. The Control segment also helped to schedule the MOW crews to get much higher utilization of MOW equipment and labor time. The Control segment displayed for dispatchers the activity in their territories, and supplied information about consists, crews, and work orders for any train.

The Data segment communicated data back and forth between the Control segment and locomotives, MOW vehicles, and track monitoring and control equipment. It made use of BN's existing microwave and VHF radio network.

The Vehicle segment on board each locomotive or MOW vehicle included a display (CRT) to provide information from the Control segment, a keypad to communicate back to the dispatcher, an on-board computer to monitor various aspects of locomotive performance, and a throttle-brake interface that the dispatcher or the on-board computer could activate to stop the train if the crew became disabled, if the train violated its movement authorities, or communication was lost with the ARES system. This segment included a receiver for satellite signals to calculate train position and speed which were then communicated to the Control segment.

The Vehicle segment incorporated an Energy Management System that received information on track profile and conditions, speed limits, power, and car weight to determine a recommended train speed that met service requirements, while minimizing fuel consumption and providing good train-handling characteristics.

The Vehicle segment also included the Locomotive Analysis and Reporting System (LARS). LARS used a number of sensors and discrete signals to monitor the health and efficiency of locomotives and provide early warning signals about potential failures. LARS was expected to permit problematic locomotives to be pulled out of service for maintenance before they failed unexpectedly in a remote region and to provide a database that maintenance people could analyze to prevent future malfunctions.

### The ARES Project: Current Status

By 1989, BN had spent approximately $15 million, cumulatively, on the ARES project. BN managers estimated that Rockwell had spent three times this amount. "Concept validation" had been accomplished through the Iron Range test which had proven that the technology could locate trains under real operating conditions, and could communicate back and forth between the control center and the locomotive. Rolling stock hardware had been tested for robustness and reliability. The Iron Range prototype system was demonstrated not only to numerous groups of BN executives and operating personnel but also to customers, representatives of other railroads, and numerous industry and governmental groups. By late 1989, testing of the prototype was completed. (See **Exhibit 6** for a summary of the development process and **Exhibit 7** for details of further development required for full implementation.)

The ARES team had seen enough from the Iron Range testing to believe that it would enable BN to provide better service, improve asset utilization, and reduce costs. The ARES project that senior executives were evaluating and deciding whether to authorize in 1990 was an integrated command, control, communication and information ($C^3$-I) system for controlling train movements with, according to the ARES staff, "unprecedented safety, precision, and efficiency." According to a document prepared by R&D and project staff members:

> ARES will allow BN to run a scheduled railroad with smaller staffs and more modest [capital] investments than current signaling systems. It will maintain accurate, timely information about train consists and locations. The results will be improved service, with higher revenue potential, and cost reductions. Another important benefit will be the elimination of train accidents caused by violations of movement authority.

The ARES team now requested authorization for the expenditures needed to complete the development of the full operational system and to roll out implementation through the railroad. The ARES team, and its sponsors Don Henderson, vice president-Technology, Engineering and Maintenance and Joe Galassi, executive vice president-Operations, faced several important considerations as they prepared to present this investment for authorization.

First, corporate management was significantly changed from the management that had authorized earlier phases. Four CEOs, including the current executive, Gerald Grinstein, had held office since the 1981 inception of the project. None of the vice presidents who were on the R&D steering committee in 1982 and 1983 was still with the railroad. Of the board members who saw the ARES demonstration in July 1985, only one, the current chairman, remained. Thus, although ARES had undergone a lengthy development process within BN, many who must now support and authorize it were unfamiliar with the choices that had guided its development.

Second, there was a question of whether to propose a full-blown implementation of the ARES project or just an initial phase or two. Presenting the full-blown project would inform top management of the potential range of ARES features and would give them the bottom line for fully installing ARES for the entire railroad: about $350 million. (See **Exhibit 8** for cost breakdown.) Even for a company of the size of BN, this investment was a large amount.

And ARES was a complex project, different from typical railroad investments in modern locomotives, cars, track and ties. According to Henderson:

> We may not do the entire railroad; early implementation at least would inevitably be limited to specific geographic areas. Further, we may or may not implement all of the ARES features; the LARS system and the energy management system are clearly very separable pieces.

Galassi explained the rationale for proposing the entire project:

> We figured that top management would want to have a picture of the total project, rather than being fed a piece at a time for incremental decisions and wondering where the end of the line was.

Finally, there was the issue of how to communicate the ARES benefits and credibly measure their value. Some of the benefits that the ARES team had identified were either difficult to measure because the values were unknown—how much more would a customer be willing to pay for a 1% improvement in service?—or because the railroad did not record and track certain data—how much time was lost by trains waiting for meets and passes? The team firmly believed that if they implemented this innovative technology, they would experience benefits they had not yet even anticipated.

To help measure the variety of benefits from a full-blown implementation of ARES, the team economist, Michael Smith, contracted with a half-dozen outside consultants, each of whom focused on a specific area such as measurement of market elasticity, measurement of LARS effects, measurement of meet/pass efficiency, and improved safety. (See **Exhibit 9** for a summary of each benefit study.) Some benefits could be measured only partially in financial terms; for example, improved safety would reduce damaged equipment and freight by perhaps $20 million per year, although its value in human and political terms was even more significant. According to Steve Ditmeyer:

> ARES reduces the probability of a collision by two orders of magnitude because, in contrast with our existing railroad control system where one failure or a mistake by one person can cause an accident, with ARES no single person or piece of equipment can cause an accident; two must fail simultaneously.

The Strategic Decisions Group (SDG) was hired to help the ARES team integrate the results of the individual consulting studies with other BN data into a single, coherent analysis of benefits. The analysis was conducted using three strategic scenarios supplied by BN's planning and evaluation department: base, focused, and expansion. Using probability distributions of key uncertainties supplied by BN managers, a set of computer models were built to calculate the probability distributions of the net present value of ARES under each of the strategic scenarios.[1] **Exhibit 11** illustrates a representative annual and cumulative after-tax cash flow for the ARES project. The SDG report concluded:

> The potential benefit of ARES is large but highly uncertain. Using the best information currently available, we estimated the gross benefit in the range of $400 million to $900 million, with an expected present value of about $600 million. This benefit should be weighed against a cost of approximately $220 million (present value). . . . The benefits depend greatly on implementation success: The system design must be sound, a strong implementation plan must be developed, and functional groups across the BN system must be committed to using it to full advantage.

---

[1] The cumulative probability distributions of the net present value of ARES benefits under each of the strategic scenarios are shown in **Exhibit 10**.

The ARES team concluded that the primary known benefits of ARES (see **Exhibit 12**) were to be measured in reduced expenditures on fuel, equipment, labor, and trackside equipment; damage prevention; and enhanced revenues. The largest component, revenue enhancements, however, had the most uncertain estimates (see **Exhibit 13**).

## EXHIBIT 1   Burlington Northern Route System

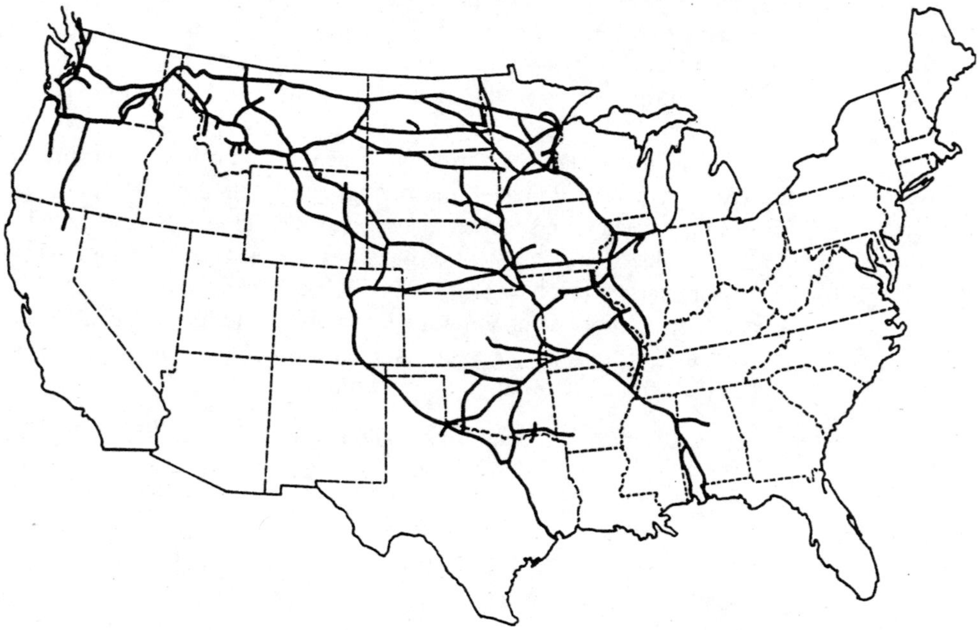

*Source:* Company documents

## EXHIBIT 2    Recent Financial Data ($000)

| | Year Ended December 31, | |
| INCOME STATEMENTS | 1989 | 1988 RESTATED |
| --- | --- | --- |
| Revenues: | | |
|   Railroad | $4,606,286 | $4,541,001 |
|   Corporate and non-rail operations | - | 158,516 |
|     **Total revenues** | **$4,606,286** | **$4,699,517** |
| Costs and Expenses: | | |
|   Compensation and benefits | 1,701,146 | 1,630,283 |
|   Fuel | 327,606 | 288,477 |
|   Material | 319,497 | 341,126 |
|   Equipment rents | 343,436 | 320,900 |
|   Purchased services | 524,845 | 531,555 |
|   Depreciation | 309,206 | 350,948 |
|   Other | 410,266 | 406,459 |
|   Corporate and non-rail operations | 13,748 | 150,869 |
|     **Total costs and expenses** | **$3,949,750** | **$4,020,617** |
| Operating income | 656,536 | 678,900 |
| Interest expense on long-term debt | 270,272 | 292,050 |
| Litigation settlement | - | (175,000) |
| Other income (expense)—net | 4,397 | (32,655) |
| **Income from continuing operations before income taxes** | **390,661** | **179,195** |
| Provision for income taxes | 147,670 | 80,493 |
| **Income from continuing operations** | **$ 242,991** | **$ 98,702** |
| Income from discontinued operations | | |
|   Net of income taxes | - | 57,048 |
| **Net income** | **$ 242,991** | **$ 155,750** |

*Exhibit 2    Continued*

## Balance Sheets ($000)

| | 1989 | 1988 RESTATED |
|---|---|---|
| | *Year Ended December 31,* | |
| **ASSETS** | | |
| Current assets: | | |
| Cash and cash equivalents | $    82,627 | $    83,620 |
| Accounts receivable—net | 430,355 | 685,018 |
| Material and supplies | 133,286 | 157,954 |
| Current portion of deferred income taxes | 119,589 | 98,339 |
| Other current assets | 31,137 | 39,740 |
| **Total current assets** | **$  796,994** | **$1,064,671** |
| Property and equipment—net | 5,154,532 | 5,078,262 |
| Other assets | 196,254 | 187,401 |
| **Total assets** | **$6,147,780** | **$6,330,334** |
| **LIABILITIES AND STOCKHOLDERS' EQUITY** | | |
| Total current liabilities | $1,287,966 | $1,218,757 |
| Long-term debt | 2,219,619 | 2,722,625 |
| Other liabilities | 268,721 | 270,702 |
| Deferred income taxes | 1,277,715 | 1,186,124 |
| **Total liabilities** | **$5,054,021** | **$5,398,208** |
| Preferred stock—redeemable | 13,512 | 14,101 |
| Common stockholders' equity: | | |
| Common stock | 967,528 | 992,405 |
| Retained earnings (deficit) | 131,544 | (20,624) |
| | **$1,009,072** | **$  971,781** |
| Cost of Treasury stock | (18,825) | (53,756) |
| Total common stockholders' equity | **$1,080,247** | **$  918,025** |
| **Total liabilities and stockholders' equity** | **$6,147,780** | **$6,330,334** |

## Capital Expenditures ($000,000)

| | 1989 | 1988 RESTATED |
|---|---|---|
| | *Year Ended December 31,* | |
| Roadway | $297 | $305 |
| Equipment | 154 | 155 |
| Other | 14 | 14 |
| **Total** | **$465** | **$474** |

*Source: 1989 Annual Report*

# EXHIBIT 3    Burlington Northern Organization Chart

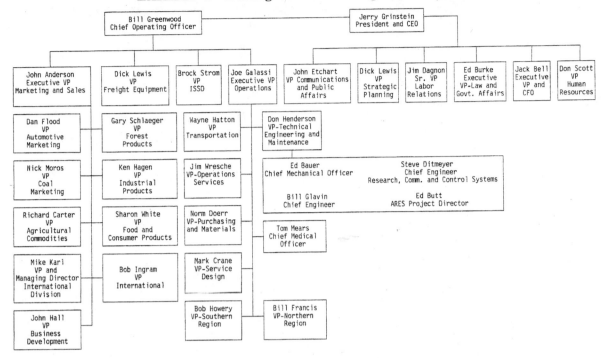

Source:  Company documents

**EXHIBIT 4   Burlington Northern's Seven Business Segments**

| SEGMENT | DESCRIPTION | Revenue (in millions) | | Revenue Ton Miles (in millions) | | Revenue per Revenue Ton Mile (in cents) | |
|---|---|---|---|---|---|---|---|
| | | 1989 | 1988 | 1989 | 1988 | 1989 | 1988 |
| Coal | 90% originates in Powder River Basin | $1,504 | $1,500 | 111,087 | 107,202 | 1.35 | 1.40 |
| Agricultural | Primarily grain; also food and other products | 718 | 743 | 37,443 | 38,167 | 1.92 | 1.95 |
| Industrial Products | 44 major commodities, including chemicals and allied products, primary metal products | 682 | 626 | 26,511 | 23,289 | 2.57 | 2.69 |
| Intermodal | Highway trailers and marine containers moved on specially designed flatcars or double stack cars | 649 | 615 | 21,505 | 20,222 | 3.02 | 3.04 |
| Forest Products | Lumber and wood products; pulp paper and allied products | 480 | 490 | 18,956 | 18,593 | 2.53 | 2.64 |
| Food and Consumer | Food and parts for various finished products industries | 413 | 403 | 15,202 | 14,436 | 2.72 | 2.79 |
| Automotive | Shipment of finished automobiles; evenly divided between domestic and import traffic originating principally from Pacific Northwest ports | 154 | 145 | 1,823 | 1,649 | 8.45 | 8.79 |

*Source: 1989 Annual Report*

**EXHIBIT 5   Railroad Rates and Ton-Mile Revenue**

Grain and Coal Rate Index
Current and Constant Dollars

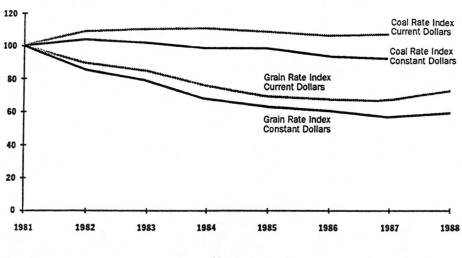

Year

*Exhibit 5    Continued*

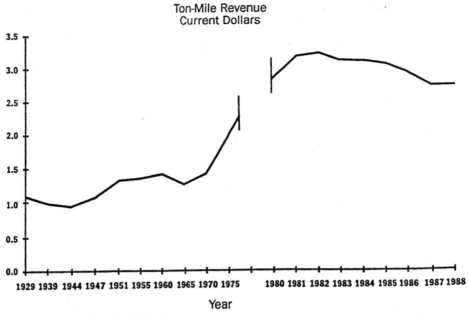

## Ton-Mile Revenue
## Current Dollars

*Source:* Association of American Railroads

**EXHIBIT 6    BN Personnel Involvement in ARES' Design and Implementation**

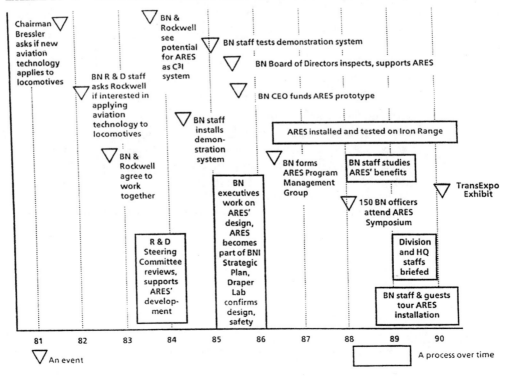

*Source:* Company documents

---

### EXHIBIT 7    Development Required to Implement ARES as of Early 1990

**Scheduling Programs**    Train scheduling programs comprised two modules: the Strategic Traffic Planner (STP) and the Tactical Traffic (or Meet and Pass) Planner. The STP viewed railroad operations globally, for example, determining optimal schedules for the entire railroad system. It could determine whether a late train should be caught up in the current dispatcher's territory, or a subsequent one with more slack. BN had contracted to have STP specifications written, but no computer programs had been written.

The Meet and Pass Planner functioned at a local level. STP schedules were passed to the Meet and Pass Planner. Treating STP schedulers as constraints, the Meet and Pass Planner produced a meet and pass schedule for a dispatcher's shift; the dispatcher revised this schedule, if necessary, and authorized it. Authorized meets and passes were communicated through ARES to the trains as operating instructions, which the engineers carried out. Prototype Meet and Pass Planner computer programs had been written; ARES staff members had tested their functionality and had used them in simulation to evaluate ARES benefits. However, the Meet and Pass Planner had not been tested in the Iron Range nor had it actually controlled trains. ARES staff had identified prototype bugs requiring resolution; they were also concerned whether the meet and pass planning algorithms were the most efficient.

**Energy Management System**    The ARES staff considered Rockwell's original Energy Management System prototype unacceptable; it was not used to provide control input to trains in the Iron Range. Rockwell was reworking the Energy Management System, but it was not yet complete nor ready for testing.

**Locomotive Analysis and Reporting System (LARS)**    The data gathering aspect of LARS had been tested in the Iron Range. However, BN had little experience analyzing these data. They could not evaluate the nature and magnitude of potential savings, due in part to the Iron Range's unique closed-loop where locomotives passed a maintenance station daily instead of every several days as on other portions of the railroad.

**Existing Iron Range Software**    The software used in Iron Range tests was considered prototype software. While it was designed as efficiently as possible, the prototype testing had revealed that greater efficiencies were possible. The production software would further have to be designed to gain greater efficiencies when regulatory restrictions were lifted in the future. Thus, the Iron Range prototype software required redesign before it could be implemented as efficient production software.

---

## EXHIBIT 8    ARES Cost Breakdown

| MAJOR COST CATEGORIES | COST | COMMENTS |
|---|---|---|
| Control Center | ≅$ 80 million | Software development is a major component of this cost. |
| Data Link (Wayside Communications) | ≅$ 80 million | BN planned to replace much of its existing pole line communication network with an ARES-compatible data link regardless of the decision on ARES. However, this conversion had barely begun. |
| On-Board Equipment | ≅$200 million | Roughly $100,000 per road locomotive; less for switch locomotives and MOW vehicles. Of this, LARS = $16,000/locomotive with total costs (including software development) expected to be less than $35 million. Although not expected to exceed LARS, Energy Management System costs had not been estimated in detail. |

LARS and the Energy Management System were generally considered modules separable from the rest of ARES. Beyond these two, however, it was difficult to identify ARES modules that could be implemented independently. For example, sending a movement authority to a train required the control segment to check conflicts with other vehicles' authorities, the data link to communicate the authority to the train, and the on-board equipment to enable the engineer to receive and confirm the authority. Thus, each of these three segments had to be implemented for ARES to operate in any given region. Although not every locomotive had to be equipped, as fewer locomotives in a region were equipped the overall system became less effective since ARES could no longer confirm the location of—and spacing between—all trains. Limiting ARES to a geographic region within BN reduced Data Link and On-Board equipment costs commensurate with track and vehicle reductions, and reduced Control Center costs somewhat.

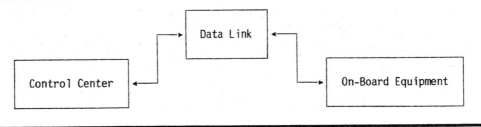

---

---

**EXHIBIT 9**    **Consultant's Studies of ARES Benefits**

---

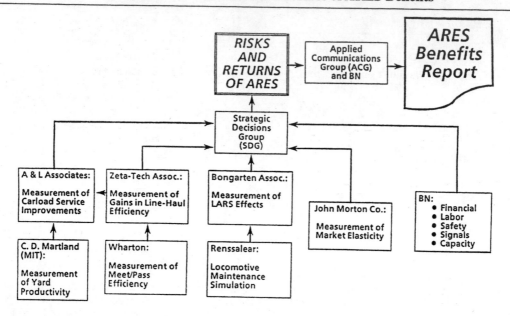

*Source:* Company documents

| CONSULTANT | PURPOSE | APPROACH | RESULTS |
|---|---|---|---|
| A & L Associates | Measure effect of ARES improvements in terminal and line-haul performance on carload service. | Service improvements were modeled for a representative BN section using the Service Planning Model with inputs on existing conditions and expected changes in performance supplied by C.D. Martland, Wharton, and Zeta-Tech. | Reductions in line-haul times and increased terminal performance will decrease total trip times by 7–8% even if scheduled connections and blocking strategies are unchanged. |
| John Morton Company | Measure the increase in traffic expected with an increase in the level of service offered customers in given market/commodity areas. | Questionnaires were distributed to decisionmakers who routinely select modes/carriers for shipping commodities in or across BN territories. A demand elasticity model was constructed using conjoint analysis. The model was calibrated, tested, and sensitivity analyses were conducted to generate demand elasticities for each service attribute. | Perceived performance differences between truck and rail are most dramatic with respect to transit time, reliability, equipment usability, and level of effort. Improving reliability offers greatest leverage for increasing BN's revenues. A 1% improvement in reliability, if, and only if, fully implemented and perceived in the market place could yield a 5% increase in revenues; a 5% improvement in reliability could yield a 20% increase in prices. |

*Exhibit 9    Continued*

| CONSULTANT | PURPOSE | APPROACH | RESULTS |
|---|---|---|---|
| Bongarten Associates | Evaluate the Locomotive Analysis and Reporting System (LARS). | A simulation using actual BN data on train information, trouble reports and repairs tested LARS in four modes: 1) inspection of units committed to shops; 2) examining component status during on-road failures; 3) using prospective diagnostics to schedule additional repairs when locomotive is already committed to the shop; 4) using prospective diagnostics to bring the unit into the shop before a failure occurs. | The two LARS modes which offer the greatest promise are modes 2 and 3; mode 3 offers higher savings but requires development of a prospective diagnostics system. Savings of 3% to 5% were calculated in five areas: departure delay, on-line delay, time off-line, maintenance manhours, and reduced severity of repair due to early detection. |
| Charles Stark Draper Laboratory | Analyze how safe ARES would be, compared to BN's existing train control systems. | Modeling using Markov analysis. | The probability of a train control system-related accident would be reduced by a factor of 100 when ARES is in place. The primary reason for this improvement is that ARES' integrated system architecture provides highly reliable checks and balances that limit the impact and propagation of human errors. |
| Zeta-Tech Associates | Measure gains in line-haul efficiency from Energy Management System (EMS) module and Meet/Pass Planning module. | Recorded actual operating data on 846 trains (55 were selected for detailed analysis) from 16 "lanes" chosen to represent BN's full range of operating conditions, control systems, traffic volumes and mixes. Modeled actual operation to establish baseline fuel consumption and running time; then modeled fuel consumption and running time using (1) EMS module and (2) Meet/Pass Planner. | EMS module produced only 2% net fuel savings and large increases in running times for some trains. Z-T argued this was due to software flaws in algorithm and priorities. Meet/Pass Planner reduced running time for all 846 trains by an average of 21%. For the 55 selected trains, travel time decreased 17% and fuel consumption decreased 2.5%. Reliability increased; the travel time standard deviation also decreased. |
| Wharton | Measure Meet/Pass efficiency and feasibility. | Modeled fuel consumption and running time using various Meet/Pass dispatching algorithms on selected study trains in the 16 lanes evaluated. | ARES can produce meet/pass plans consistent with operating policies which yield travel time and fuel savings in 30 seconds or less; a pacing algorithm produces further fuel savings. |
| C.D. Martland (MIT) | Measurement of yard productivity. | Collected detailed data from several BN yards. Modeled effect of improved reliability of train operations on (1) yard efficiency through improved interface between line-haul, terminal operations, and crew assignments and enhanced capabilities for communications with and supervision of crews; (2) on yard processing times; and (3) on train connection reliability. | Train performance was variable enough to allow considerable room for increased reliability, reducing average yard times about one hour. Modest improvements in terminal efficiency and train connection performance could be achieved through better utilization of terminal crews. Overall ARES could reduce average yard time .5 to 2 hours at major terminals and reduce missed connections by 15 to 17%. |

**EXHIBIT 10** **Cumulative Probability Distributions of ARES Benefits Under Three Scenarios**

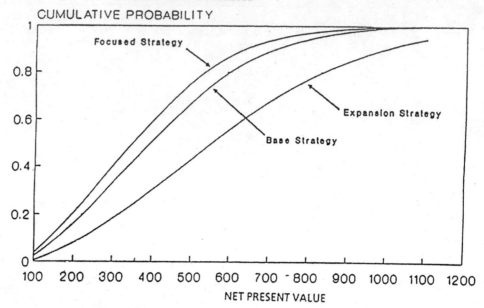

Base (Status Quo ) Strategy Mean = $406 Million
Focused Strategy Mean = $360 Million
Expansion Strategy Mean = $576 Million

*Source:* Company documents

**EXHIBIT 11** **ARES Projected Annual and Cumulative After-Tax Cash Flow**

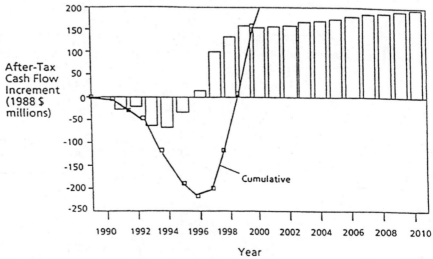

*Source:* Company documents

---

## EXHIBIT 12    Primary ARES Benefits

ARES offers many benefits which enable BN to reach it goals of safe and profitable rail operations. Following is a summary of those benefits.

- Increased rail operations safety results from constant monitoring of wayside signal and detector equipment, train movement, and locomotive health.
- Greater operating efficiency and improved customer service come from operating trains to schedule and handling trains that deviate from schedule, the results of improved traffic planning.
- Improved safety and increased customer service come from real-time position, speed and ETAs for all trains computed continuously and automatically provided to MOW crews and other BN users through existing BN computer systems.
- Improved dispatcher productivity results from automating routine dispatching activities such as threat monitoring, warrant generation, traffic planning, and train sheet documentation.
- Higher effective line capacity is provided by accurate vehicle position information and automatic train movement authorization.
- Improved MOW productivity results from improved traffic planning.
- Improved business management is possible with accurate, current information about the status and performance of operations and equipment.

## KEY POINTS

- The study examined benefits in the following areas and estimates the present value of those benefits:

  - fuel                                                    $ 52 million
  - equipment                                               $ 81 million
  - labor                                                   $190 million
  - trackside equipment and damage prevention              $ 96 million
  - enhanced revenues                                       $199 million
  - TOTAL                                                   $618 million

- To account for uncertainty in these estimates, the study calculated ranges of values for them and probabilities of achieving values within the ranges.
- The factors with the largest potential for delivering benefits are also the most uncertain:
  - ARES' ability to improve transit time and
  - The amount customers are willing to pay for better service.
- Accounting for ranges and probabilities, ARES will make the following mean contribution to net present value for each corporate strategy:
  - focused strategy                                        $360 million
  - base strategy                                           $406 million
  - expansion strategy                                      $576 million
- The probability of ARES earning less than 9% real after-tax rate of return is extremely small.

*Source:* Company documents

**EXHIBIT 13   Price Gain Versus Increased Service Reliability**

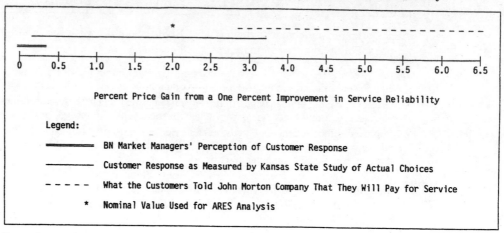

Source: Company documents

# CASE 15   Tennessee Controls: The Strategic Ranking Problem

Tennessee Controls Corporation was founded by two engineers in 1935. The company had grown rapidly due to the successful design and marketing of several technical innovations and by 1990 was a diversified high technology company approaching one billion dollars in annual sales. The founders attributed their success to careful management of the new product choices that inevitably face a growth oriented enterprise.

Although the founders were no longer active in the company, one of their legacies had been the Strategic Ranking Process. Until 1986, the Strategic Ranking Process was a relatively informal process that involved the evaluation of project proposals and culminated in an annual series of meetings to compare, rank, and fund opportunities. This process became increasingly formalized with the creation of a Corporate Planning function in 1986. By 1990 Corporate Planning had grown into a small department with a manager and two analysts.

During 1989, the Corporate Planning Department conceived and developed the Strategic Ranking Index (SRI) which was to be used in the 1990 planning cycle for the first time. Jim Williams, Corporate Planning Manager, described its purpose:

> The problem with making good decisions is the "fuzziness" of the data. This can lead to making subjective rather than objective decisions. What we have done with the SRI is to quantify, as much as possible, the key decision parameters. This can be particularly important when comparing dissimilar alternatives. We're going to set this up like a "war room" where Jim (Jim Wilson, Tennessee Controls President and Chief Executive) can sit in a command chair and call up the details of all projects on a large video screen. I think that having this level of strategic information at his fingertips will give us the ultimate in strategic decision making capability.

The methodology for SRI calculation was formalized in a six-page corporate policy statement (**Appendix 1**).

## The Process Control Division

Located in the foothills of the Appalachian Mountains just outside of Unicoi, Tennessee, the Process Controls Division was the newest and smallest division of Tennessee Controls. The business was started in the late 1960s and had grown to approximately $200 million sales by 1989.

In 1979, a major funding commitment for this business had resulted in the construction of a new, dedicated facility and the recruitment and organization of an engineering and development staff of 200 professionals.

The division was organized as a profit center with functional departments responsible for manufacturing, marketing, and engineering and development. All manufacturing was done in the Unicoi facility. Domestic marketing was accomplished through a national sales force and a distributor network. International sales and marketing were handled through other divisions of the corporation and represented about 30% of total sales.

---

*DBA Candidate Dale Geiger prepared this case under the supervision of Professor Robert Simons as the basis for classroom discussion rather than to illustrate either effective or ineffective handling of an administrative situation.*

The Process Controls Division offered a product line of industrial, programmable, process controllers. These controllers brought the advantages of computer technology to the factory floor by "electrically hardening" the circuitry. Hardening was necessary to prevent electrical noise, factory vibration, dust, and temperature variations from interfering with the computer-like functions of the process controller. Special design requirements of this business also required that, in the unlikely event of failure, the controller "failed safe" to avoid industrial accidents.

Tennessee Controls Corporation's objective for the Process Controls Division had been to develop another major business that would continue the company's tradition of profitable, rapid growth. To date the growth of the division had been satisfactory but its profitability had been disappointing (**Exhibit 1**). The expenses of developing a new site; the recruiting, training, payroll, and benefit costs of the large engineering staff; and the costs of paying distributor discounts in addition to sales force commissions had resulted in disappointing profit levels and the dismissal of the Division Manager in 1989. Using an executive search firm, Judy Starnes was hired in February 1990 as the Division's new Vice President and General Manager.

Judy Starnes, age 39, had an engineering undergraduate education but had spent the majority of her career in brand management at Procter and Gamble. She was chosen for the position because she was thought to be the type of person who could bring complex technologies together while executing the marketing programs necessary to achieve profitability. Her demonstrated ability to turn around unprofitable products was the major reason that the company had broken its tradition of promotion from within.

One of Judy Starnes' first actions was to draft a new mission statement for the Process Control Division. After a two-day retreat with key managers of the division, the following mission was adopted:

> The mission of the Process Controls Division is to apply the talents, knowledge, and skills of our people to make Tennessee Controls the market leader in enabling customers to reap the benefits of industrial control technology.

## The 1990 Strategic Ranking Process Proposals

In September 1990, Starnes was facing her first major resource allocation decision. She was scheduled to present her Division's ranked funding needs the following week at the Corporate Strategic Ranking Meeting. Before she could do that, however, she would have to evaluate the formal funding requests prepared by three of her subordinates. Starnes explained her concerns:

> Any innovative company worth its salt must have a creative backlog: a reservoir of ideas that have the potential of blossoming into major business opportunities. Therefore, we must encourage multiple creative programs during the idea development stage, but we cannot afford to fund all programs to completion. Management must choose only the best opportunities with the maximum likelihood of success.

> From what I've seen, this division has done a great job of generating ideas, maybe too good. I wish we had the resources to fund all of the ideas that made sense. But we just don't have the corporate funding to do an adequate job on more than one, or maybe two, large projects. Even if we had funding, trying to do more would probably swamp the organization and it's important that we execute well on whatever program we choose.

The Sales and Marketing Manager, the Engineering and Development Manager, and the Division Controller each had submitted a proposal for funding during the 1990 cycle. Each proposal represented a distinctly different direction for the Division.

**Proposal 1: Develop New Products For High Volume Market Segment**   Proposed by Steve Gregg, the Division Marketing and Sales Manager, this proposal focused on the low price, high volume segment of the market where Tennessee Controls had competed in the past. Studies of Japanese manufacturers, who tended to be early adopters of new technology, supported the proposition that low-priced controllers with streamlined basic features would soon represent the high growth segment of the business. Gregg felt that aggressive product development in this area would give Tennessee Controls a unique product which could result in domestic market leadership in this segment. This approach would also erect defensible barriers to offshore companies should they decide to market in the United States. (**Exhibit 3** reproduces Gregg's proposal.)

Gregg, age 40, was an electrical engineer with an MBA who had spent his entire career at Tennessee Controls. He had worked in the Process Control Division since 1978, first as a salesman and then as an area sales manager prior to his current assignment which began in 1983. Gregg was highly regarded as an outstanding salesman with deep customer and product knowledge. In 1984, based on projections of market share increases, Gregg had successfully sold corporate management on the dual strategy of using both independent distributors and commissioned salesmen.

**Proposal 2: Develop High Technology Control Systems**   This proposal by Division Engineering and Development Manager, Steve Mowry, argued that the highest profit growth market would be found in products with high technological complexity. Recent trends in the industry had shown that large customers of programmable controllers were interested in networking individual machines into larger systems managed by SCADA (Supervisory Control and Data Acquisition) systems. These systems offered major cost reductions to customers and, because of their complexity and proprietary nature, could command high prices.

As one of the few firms capable of designing such complex systems, Mowry argued that a unique, market leadership position could be obtained in the high end market by a major effort at product development. Delaying funding of the project, Mowry argued, would result inevitably in introduction of a "me too" product at some time in the future. (**Exhibit 4** reproduces Mowry's proposal.)

Mowry, age 48 with a Ph.D. in Electrical Engineering, had been with the Division since its inception and had been in his current job since 1980. Prior to joining the Process Control Division he had held several engineering development positions in other divisions of the company, specializing in power supply design. He had contributed in some fashion to every product development effort of the Division and took great pride in the technical strength of the engineering and development organization which he had played a large role in building.

**Proposal 3: Acquire MDA**   Craig Neirman, the Division Controller, was an advocate of acquiring new products and markets through the purchase of small, high potential businesses. The newest member of the management team, Neirman had come to the Division in 1988 after several assignments in Corporate Control where he had worked on acquisition evaluation. Aged 34, he had joined the company after receiving his Bachelor's and Master's degree in Business Administration from East Tennessee State University.

Neirman had identified the Maryland Data Acquisition Company as a candidate for acquisition. MDA had successfully entered the SCADA market with a DEC computer-based product and had developed a leadership position in the non-hardened market segment. Already profitable with a base of customers, MDA needed capital to finance continued growth and seemed like a natural fit with Tennessee Controls. Risk of failure would be minimized and the opportunities for technical synergy looked good. Furthermore, the existing customer base of MDA would represent good business leads for Tennessee Controls products. (**Exhibit 5** reproduces Neirman's proposal.)

### Ranking The Proposals

Judy Starnes' preliminary work would include the following steps:

1. Review the SRI Calculations as published in the 6-page Corporate Policy PM 2-3-6 (**Appendix 1**).
2. Calculate the Financial Return Index for each proposal using the financial inputs provided by Williams (**Exhibit 2**).
3. Assess the proposals' credibility and risk index from the Proposal Summaries (**Exhibits 3, 4,** and **5**).
4. Calculate the SRI for each proposal.
5. Prepare recommendations to present at the upcoming Strategic Ranking meeting.

As she began to prepare for her corporate presentation, Starnes did not know which of the alternatives would be best for the division. Unfortunately, because the process was brand new, she could not turn to more experienced managers for advice on the calculations. Aware of the importance of the decision for the future of the division and the careers of the three managers involved, she wondered how to best evaluate the quality and credibility of the proposals and their sponsors.

---

# *Appendix 1*

POLICY MANUAL
LEVEL: Corporate
EFFECTIVE: 5/20/90
ORIGINAL: 5/20/90

TCC INTERNAL DATA
REF: No. PM 2-3-6
(Page 1 of 6)

**Subject:**   Strategic Ranking Index
**References:**   1.   Strategic Planning Process: PM No. 2-3-4
              2.   Project Management: PM No. 4-2-1
              3.   Incentive Compensation: PM No. 8-1-1
**Purpose:**   To provide a uniform policy for the calculation and ranking of major development projects within the company.
**Scope:**   All Level 3 business units of TCC including International Subsidiaries.
**Policy:**   All developmental funding requests exceeding US $100,000 must include a documented strategic ranking index to facilitate comparison with other corporate opportunities.

Under normal circumstances, projects submitted for funding should have an overall SRI equal to or greater than 10. Projects with SRI values less than 10 will not be considered unless prior approval is received from a corporate-level officer.

*Appendix 1   Continued*

The required list of supporting documentation shall be updated periodically by Corporate Planning but must include the following at a minimum:

1.  An overall Strategic Ranking Index
2.  A Credibility Index
3.  A Financial Return Index
4.  A Risk Index.

The Overall Strategic Ranking Index is a composite of the other indices, as follows:

$$SRI = \frac{\text{Credibility} \times \text{Financial Return}}{\text{Risk}}$$

The Credibility Index captures the quality of the strategic idea and the adequacy of the resources and planning. As shown in **Attachment 1** the highest scores result when a strong project champion presents a project with strong strategic definition and favorable competitive assessment. Correspondingly, the lowest scores are given to projects with weak champions and poor strategic analysis.

The Financial Return Index is the product of two ratios as shown in **Attachment 2.** The first ratio is the cumulative organization profit through the product life divided by the maximum, cumulative, negative cash flow. This ratio gives a relative, cash-flow-related measure of return on investment.

The second ratio adds a measure of time to the equation by dividing project life by the time to maximum negative cash flow. Life cycle is defined as the time between first NSB (Net Sales Billed) and the time when Net Sales Billed falls to half of its peak level.

The financial projections will be calculated by the Corporate Planning Department based on the Cash Flow Wave diagram shown in **Attachment 3.**

The Risk Index in the denominator of the SRI equation recognizes that high risk is less desirable. The matrix balances product uniqueness and expected market share as shown in **Attachment 4.** The best (lowest) scores are awarded for unique products that can result in Tennessee Controls becoming the market leader. The worst scores are given to copyable products where achievable market share would be less than half that of the market leader.

**Responsibilities:**   The Corporate Planning Manager will provide the basic inputs to the Financial Index ratios based on financial data supplied by the requestor. It is the responsibility of the requesting organization to warrant that the financial data are correct. The Corporate Planning Department is responsible for maintaining and periodically upgrading the Cash Flow Wave model.

It is the responsibility of Level 3 and higher managers to determine the other input indices and to calculate the SRI itself. Adequate backup and explanation should also be provided. Each level of management must assume responsibility for the numbers and recommendations it provides to higher levels. Achievement of projections is to be considered a major input into Key Personnel Award decisions.

> Attachment 1:   SRI Credibility Factor
> Attachment 2:   SRI Financial Return Factor
> Attachment 3:   SRI Cash Flow Wave
> Attachment 4:   SRI Risk Factor.

*Appendix 1    Continued*

**Attachment 1**

# SRI Credibility Index

**Champion Commitment**

Lacks Strong Champion and/or Team

Average Team/Champion

Proven Champion and Team

**Strategic/Marketing Content**

Strong Strategy, Segmentation, Product Definition and Competitive Assess

Some Strategic Analysis: Inadequate on Market Environmental and/or Ignores Significant Strategic Factors

Little/Poor Strategic Analysis: Only Product Plan or "Hipshot" Strategy

Strategy/Marketing Content

Champion Commitment

---

**Attachment 2**

# SRI Financial Return Factor

$$\text{Financial Return Factor} = \frac{\text{Org. Profit Over Product Life}}{\text{Maximum Negative Cash Flow (Cumulative)}} \times \frac{\text{Life Cycle*}}{\text{Years to Maximum Negative Cash Flow}}$$

\* Life Cycle is years between first significant NSB level and time NSB falls to approximately 50% of peak.

---

*Appendix 1    Continued*

**Attachment 3**

# SRI Cash Flow Wave

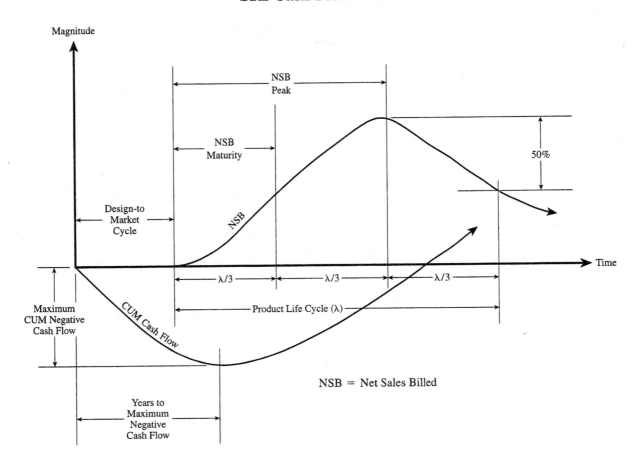

NSB = Net Sales Billed

*Appendix 1    Continued*

**Attachment 4**

# SRI Risk Factor

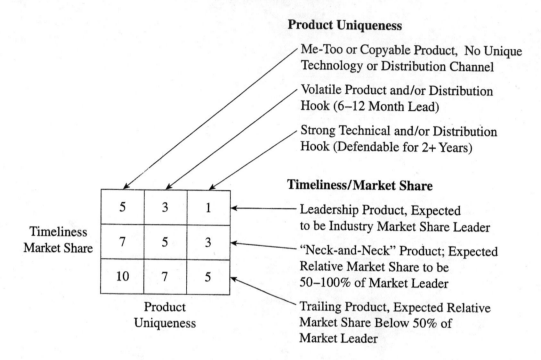

**Product Uniqueness**

Me-Too or Copyable Product,  No Unique Technology or Distribution Channel

Volatile Product and/or Distribution Hook (6–12 Month Lead)

Strong Technical and/or Distribution Hook (Defendable for 2+ Years)

**Timeliness/Market Share**

Leadership Product, Expected to be Industry Market Share Leader

"Neck-and-Neck" Product; Expected Relative Market Share to be 50–100% of Market Leader

Trailing Product, Expected Relative Market Share Below 50% of Market Leader

|  |  |  |
|---|---|---|
| 5 | 3 | 1 |
| 7 | 5 | 3 |
| 10 | 7 | 5 |

Timeliness
Market Share

Product
Uniqueness

---

**EXHIBIT 1    Tennessee Controls Corporation**
Process Control Division Financial Performance

|  | 1988 TOTAL | 1989 | | | | 1989 TOTAL | 88/89 CHANGE |
|---|---|---|---|---|---|---|---|
|  |  | 1ST Q | 2ND Q | 3RD Q | 4TH Q |  |  |
| Net Sales Billed | 173.1 | 34.9 | 49.0 | 55.2 | 58.5 | 197.6 | 24.5 |
| Gross Profit Margin | 61.3 | 13.5 | 15.5 | 17.5 | 18.4 | 64.9 | 3.6 |
| GPM % | 35.4% | 38.9% | 31.6% | 31.7% | 31.5% | 32.8% | (2.6%) |
| General and Administrative | 54.7 | 16.0 | 16.3 | 15.8 | 15.4 | 63.5 | (8.8) |
| Division Profit | 6.6 | −2.5 | −0.8 | 1.7 | 3.0 | 1.4 | (5.2) |
| Profit % | 3.8% | −7.2% | −0.2% | 3.1% | 5.1% | 0.7% | (3.1%) |

## EXHIBIT 2

September 10, 1990

To:      Judy Starnes
From:    Jim Williams, Corporate Planning
Subject: Financial Inputs to SRI Model

Evaluation of forecast data provided by your people has generated the following matrix of financial output that should be used in your SRI Financial Return Index calculation.

As outlined in the Planning Manual, you should next evaluate the risk and credibility criteria, calculate the appropriate SRI Index, and then prepare your recommendations for the SRP Meeting.

Should you wish other forecast data evaluated, please contact me as soon as possible since there is little time left before the Ranking Meeting and I am being swamped by similar requests.

| PROPOSAL: | HIGH VOLUME | SCADA TECHNOLOGY | MDA ACQUISITION |
|---|---|---|---|
| First Sales | 12 Months | 18 Months | Immediately |
| Peak Sales | 10 Years | 5 Years | 15 Years |
| Half-Peak Sales | 15 Years | 15 Years | 25 Years |
| Lifetime Profit | $39.8M | $44.5M | $108.5M |
| Maximum Cumulative Negative Cash Flow Dollars: | $17.0M | $16.4M | $25.0M |
| Maximum Cumulative Negative Cash Flow Years: | 2 Years | 3 Years | 6 Years |

## EXHIBIT 3

September 4, 1990

To:   Judy Starnes
From: Steve Gregg, Marketing and Sales Manager
Re:   The 015 Product Proposal.

When introduced, the 005 and 008 product lines offered state-of-the-art features for a lower price than Allen Bradley or Modicon were charging for older, less capable product.

However, over the last four years, both competitors have provided similar products to the marketplace and our price and performance advantage has dissipated. It is essential to the future of the Division that we regain our role of low cost, high performance supplier to this industry.

*Exhibit 3    Continued*

As you know, we have a difficult time selling into Japan. Their product specifiers very much prefer to buy from Japanese programmable control manufacturers who offer lower-priced products with streamlined features. It is only a matter of time before the Japanese introduce similar attributes into the U.S. programmable control market. Indeed, the only barriers to their entry seem to be the relative size of our market and their lack of distributors.

Responding to this threat is the basis of the proposed 015 product development. Target priced at roughly one-third of our 005 line, this product will deliver roughly equivalent capability in handling smaller applications requiring less than 32 input/output points. The speed of the microprocessor and the enhanced instruction set will make this product particularly attractive in replacing mechanical, drum-timer-type machine controls.

The market potential for the product is large, as shown below. Not only will the product have a price advantage in existing applications, it will open two new markets: the low priced, small I/O market and the drum-timer replacement market.

## Incremental Market Analysis (Units)

|  | YEAR 1 | YEAR 2 | YEAR 3 | YEAR 4 | YEAR 5 | ASSUMED GROWTH RATE |
|---|---|---|---|---|---|---|
| Existing | 60,000 | 69,000 | 79,350 | 91,253 | 104,940 | 15% |
| Served | 70% | 75% | 80% | 85% | 90% | |
| Available | 18,000 | 17,250 | 15,870 | 13,688 | 10,494 | |
| Drum Timer | 30,000 | 33,000 | 36,300 | 39,930 | 43,923 | 10% |
| Low Priced | 30,000 | 39,000 | 50,700 | 65,910 | 85,683 | 30% |
| Total Market | 78,000 | 89,250 | 102,870 | 119,528 | 140,100 | |

Priced at $900 per system with 40% gross margin, these volumes will provide tremendous profitability. The major unknown is the competitors' response. The question is whether they will follow us into this market niche. We believe they are less interested in the low price segment, but nevertheless, I have evaluated the impact of eroding market share if they followed as they did on the 005:

**Assuming Not Followed:**

|  | Year 1 | Year 2 | Year 3 | Year 4 | Year 5 |
|---|---|---|---|---|---|
| TCC Share | 40% | 50% | 55% | 60% | 65% |
| Sales $M | 28.1 | 40.2 | 50.9 | 64.5 | 82.0 |
| Gross Profit $M | 11.2 | 16.1 | 20.4 | 25.8 | 32.8 |

**Assuming Followed:**

|  | Year 1 | Year 2 | Year 3 | Year 4 | Year 5 |
|---|---|---|---|---|---|
| TCC Share | 40% | 50% | 50% | 45% | 40% |
| Sales $M | 28.1 | 40.2 | 46.3 | 48.4 | 50.4 |
| Gross Profit $M | 11.2 | 16.1 | 18.5 | 19.4 | 20.2 |

*Exhibit 3   Continued*

This product is ideally-suited to our distribution and sales network. I think that it could be handled with essentially no change in sales force or sales strategy.

In summary, this product approach is a continuation of our past successful strategy and has the opportunity to add substantially to our business. I feel very strongly that this development should be our number one priority for Strategic Funding this year.

Please let met know if you have any additional questions.

---

## EXHIBIT 4

September 3, 1990

To:     Judy Starnes
From:   Steve Mowry, Engineering
Subject: The SCADA Strategy

Per your request, here is a synopsis of the Supervisory Control and Data Acquisition Strategy.

1. The latest technologies in the business such as CAD-CAM, robotics, flexible manufacturing, etc., all illustrate the need for complex industrial control systems. Emerging applications will network factory floor controllers through some sort of data communication system, most likely using token ring architecture with a MAP protocol. This data buss will then demand sophisticated higher level Supervisory Control and Data Acquisition Systems to efficiently and effectively manage entire factories, systems, or processes.

2. The market potential is huge when you consider the installed base of our existing systems, public utilities, pipelines, refineries, chemical plants, and, in fact, any process-related industry.

3. There is no doubt that there is demand for this function. We have received many requests from customers to "consult" with them on such enhancements and have seen our distributors attempt to provide this higher level control system function.

4. Such higher level functionality allows us to more lucratively price our services. I visualize each job using a base core of high capability next generation controllers and a base core of general SCADA software. Such a base would then be customized for each individual application by a project team that would provide turnkey capabilities. Such a strategy would allow the maximum of value pricing for each individual job and should be extremely profitable.

5. Each job we completed would add to our capabilities' inventory and further extend the base of common software. This would further enhance our profitability and competitive advantage in subsequent similar jobs.

6. I estimate that we could build up a core of software to provide 90% of the functionality with only 10% of the lines of code having to be developed on a custom basis. Competition would have to develop 100%, which makes us unbeatable, pricewise, and at tremendous margin. A suitable control engine is the first prerequisite. We need the speed and processing capability necessary to handle the data acquisition functions.

7. We also need a talented process oriented design and engineering staff. To support this new strategy, I recommend that we hire four individuals from the industries that we initially target. This will give us the inside info on what the customer needs.

8. My forecast assumes that we start with three industries the first year: petrochemical, fine chemical, and food processing. We should then plan to add one industry each year. I have assumed that any industry we pick could generate $10 million sales the first year. This represents less than one major job completion per month. I assumed a reasonably decreasing growth rate in new opportunities

*Exhibit 4    Continued*

within each industry offset by the addition of another new industry each year. I believe that this plan is conservative and may need to be accelerated. I have further assumed that the standard cost of hardware and base software is constant at 30% of sales. The custom component of cost will steadily diminish as we build our expertise and software base through experience. The result is steadily lower cost.

9.  The key is to be first in this business. I hope that this gives you what we need so that we can begin immediately. I have already designated my control engine design team leaders and seek your earliest approval to backfill enough staff so that I can immediately place my most experienced people on this project. I have already been in touch with executive recruiters so as to not delay hiring the industry experts cited above.

## SCADA Forecast Market Detail Buildup

|  | 1991 | 1992 | 1993 | 1994 | 1995 |
|---|---|---|---|---|---|
| Industries Sold To: | 3 | 4 | 5 | 6 | 7 |
| **Sales ($K)** | | | | | |
| 1st 3 Industries | 30,000 | 40,000 | 50,000 | 60,000 | 70,000 |
| 4th Industry | | 10,000 | 13,300 | 16,625 | 19,451 |
| 5th Industry | | | 10,000 | 13,300 | 16,625 |
| 6th Industry | | | | 10,000 | 13,300 |
| 7th Industry | | | | | 10,000 |
| Total | 30,000 | 50,000 | 73,300 | 99,925 | 129,376 |
| **Growth Rate:** | | | | | |
| 1st 3 Industries | | 33% | 25% | 20% | 17% |
| 4th Industry | | | 33% | 25% | 17% |
| 5th Industry | | | | 33% | 25% |
| 6th Industry | | | | | 33% |
| 7th Industry | | | | | |
| Total | | 67% | 47% | 36% | 29% |
| **Custom Cost ($K):** | | | | | |
| 1st 3 Industries | 4,950 | 3,960 | 3,300 | 2,970 | 2,310 |
| 4th Industry | | 1,650 | 1,317 | 1,097 | 963 |
| 5th Industry | | | 1,650 | 1,317 | 1,097 |
| 6th Industry | | | | 1,650 | 1,317 |
| 7th Industry | | | | | 1,650 |
| Total | 4,950 | 5,610 | 6,267 | 7,034 | 7,337 |
| **Summary and Profit Projections ($K):** | | | | | |
| Sales | 30,000 | 50,000 | 73,300 | 99,925 | 129,376 |
| Custom Cost | 4,950 | 5,610 | 6,267 | 7,034 | 7,337 |
| Standard Cost | 9,000 | 15,000 | 21,990 | 29,978 | 38,813 |
| Total Cost | 13,950 | 20,610 | 28,257 | 37,011 | 46,150 |
| Total Cost % | 46.5% | 41.2% | 38.5% | 37.0% | 35.7% |
| Gross Profit | 16,050 | 29,390 | 45,043 | 62,914 | 83,227 |

## EXHIBIT 5

To:   Judy Starnes
From: Craig Neirman

September 1, 1990
Re: MDA Acquisition

The recent corporate openness to acquisition offers a unique opportunity to increase our growth rate. Acquiring MDA provides a proven product line, an existing customer base, and a skilled national sales presence. MDA business is a good platform for future growth.

1.   The Product:

MDA utilizes DEC hardware with MDA proprietary software to handle industrial control problems at the supervisory level. Since their computers are non-hardened, they are not a direct competitor but, instead, are complimentary to our existing strategy.

Data interfaces from our existing product lines to DEC hardware are already in existence although we may want to do some upgrading. Currently, MDA systems installations connect with all of our competitors' equipment as well. In situations where MDA is the primary contractor, MDA is in a position to specify the industrial controller manufacturer and this "pull through" effect has been factored into the pro forma.

A cross section of customers provided by MDA have been interviewed and have established that they have an excellent reputation for meeting commitments and solving problems. MDA also seems to have TCC's same high quality philosophy.

2.   The Customer Base:

MDA has an existing customer base of approximately 200. Roughly half of these represent solid incremental sales opportunities for industrial controls. Their backlog is sufficient to cover their next 4.3 months' sales forecast.

Many of the customer base have bought from MDA more than once. Almost all represent opportunities for repeat business. The growth rate of MDA's sales and customer base has averaged 30% per year for the last three years. My assessment is that this growth rate is sustainable for several more years and, in fact, may have been constrained by their capital limitations.

3.   The Sales Force:

Another intangible but none-the-less significant asset of MDA is their highly aggressive and talented sales force. MDA's philosophy has been to pay salesmen exclusively with a 10% commission and expects the salesmen to be earning $100K per year after two years. Barring unusual circumstances, failure to achieve this level of sales leads to replacement.

This sales force should be more than capable of augmenting our existing sales force. Their skills in systems sales will be extremely useful if and when we develop hardened SCADA controllers of our own.

*Exhibit 5    Continued*

4.   Other Factors:

Additional advantages of the acquisition strategy are as follows:

- We get a proven profit-making business
- We start making profit immediately
- There are other areas of synergism (for example, we think we can achieve major purchase-price reductions in some of their electronic component purchases)
- The DEC representative status should prove useful to some of our contract business
- We can provide economies of scale to reduce administrative costs.

5.   Pro forma is attached.

## PRO FORMA SALES AND PROFIT PROJECTIONS— MDA ACQUISITION ($ Million)

| | *Actual* | *Projected* | *Forecast* | | | | |
|---|---|---|---|---|---|---|---|
| | 1989 | 1990 | 1991 | 1992 | 1993 | 1994 | 1995 |
| MDA Sales | 32.7 | 42.3 | 55.0 | 71.5 | 93.0 | 116.2 | 145.3 |
| Growth % | 33.6% | 29.4% | 30.0% | 30.0% | 30.0% | 25.0% | 25.0% |
| MDA COGS | 18.4 | 25.6 | 33.0 | 41.5 | 52.1 | 63.9 | 78.4 |
| Gr Profit | 14.3 | 16.7 | 22.0 | 30.0 | 40.9 | 52.3 | 66.9 |
| Gr Prof % | 43.7% | 39.5% | 40.0% | 42.0% | 44.0% | 45.0% | 46.0% |
| Mkt/Sales | 5.9 | 7.1 | 9.2 | 12.0 | 15.6 | 19.5 | 24.4 |
| R&D | 4.0 | 4.1 | 5.5 | 7.2 | 9.3 | 11.6 | 14.5 |
| Other G&A | 2.6 | 3.2 | 3.4 | 3.5 | 3.7 | 3.9 | 4.1 |
| PBIT | 1.8 | 2.3 | 3.9 | 7.3 | 12.3 | 17.3 | 23.9 |
| PBIT % | 5.5% | 5.5% | 7.1% | 10.2% | 13.2% | 14.9% | 16.4% |
| **Pull Through Additional Impact** | | | | | | | |
| Pull Through | | | 5.5 | 10.7 | 18.6 | 29.1 | 43.6 |
| % MDA Sales | | | 10.0% | 15.0% | 20.0% | 25.0% | 30.0% |
| STD Cost | | | 1.7 | 3.2 | 5.6 | 8.7 | 13.1 |
| Sales/Mkt | | | 0.6 | 1.1 | 1.9 | 2.9 | 4.4 |
| PBIT | | | 3.2 | 6.4 | 11.1 | 17.5 | 26.1 |
| **Total Impact of Acquisition** | | | | | | | |
| Total Sales | 32.7 | 42.3 | 60.5 | 82.2 | 111.6 | 145.3 | 188.9 |
| Total PBIT | 1.8 | 2.3 | 7.1 | 13.7 | 23.4 | 34.8 | 50.0 |
| PBIT % | 5.5% | 5.4% | 11.7% | 16.7% | 21.0% | 23.6% | 26.5% |

**CASE 16**   Birch Paper Company

> If I were to price these boxes any lower than $480 a thousand, I'd be countermanding my order of last month for our salesmen to stop shaving their bids and to bid full-cost quotations. I've been trying for weeks to improve the quality of our business, and if I turn around now and accept this job at $430 or $450 or something less than $480, I'll be tearing down this program I've been working so hard to build up. The division can't very well show a profit by putting in bids which don't even cover a fair share of overhead costs, let alone give us a profit.
>
> James Brunner, *Manager of Thompson Division*

Birch Paper Company was a medium-sized, partly integrated paper company, producing white and kraft papers and paperboard. A portion of its paperboard output was converted into corrugated boxes by the Thompson Division, which also printed and colored the outside surface of the boxes. Including Thompson, the company had four production divisions and a timberland division that supplied part of the company's pulp requirements.

For several years each division had been judged independently on the basis of its profit and return on investment. Top management had been working to gain effective results from a policy of decentralizing responsibility and authority for all decisions except those relating to overall company policy. The company's top officials believed that in the past few years the concept of decentralization had been successfully applied and that the company's profits and competitive position had definitely improved.

Early in 1975 the Northern Division designed a special display box for one of its papers in conjunction with the Thompson Division, which was equipped to make the box. Thompson's staff for package design and development spent several months perfecting the design, production methods, and materials that were to be used. Because of the box's unusual color and shape, these were far from standard. According to an agreement between the two divisions, the Thompson Division was reimbursed by the Northern Division for the cost of its design and development work.

When the specifications were all prepared, the Northern Division asked for bids on the corrugated box from the Thompson Division and from two outside companies. Each Birch Paper Company division manager normally was free to buy from whatever supplier he wished; on inter-company sales, divisions selling to other divisions were expected to meet the going market price.

In 1975, the profit margins of converters such as the Thompson Division were being squeezed. Thompson, as did many other similar converters, bought the paperboard and linerboard used in making boxes, and its function was to print, cut, and shape the material into boxes.[1] Although it bought most of its materials from other Birch divisions, most of Thompson's sales were made to outside customers. If Thompson got the order from

---

[1] The walls of a corrugated box consist of outside and inside sheets of linerboard and a center layer of fluted corrugating medium.

*Case material of the Harvard Graduate School of Business Administration is prepared as a basis for class discussion. Cases are not designed to present illustrations of either correct or incorrect handling of administrative problems.*

Northern, it probably would buy its linerboard and corrugating medium from the Southern Division of Birch. Thus, before giving its bid to Northern, Thompson got a quote for materials from the Southern Division. Although Southern had been running below capacity and had excess inventory, it quoted the prevailing market price for materials. Southern's out-of-pocket costs for both liner and corrugating medium were about 60% of its selling price. About 70% of Thompson's out-of-pocket costs of $400 per thousand boxes represented the cost of linerboard and the corrugating medium.

The Northern Division received bids on the boxes of $480 per thousand from the Thompson Division, $430 per thousand from West Paper Company, and $432 per thousand from Eire Papers, Ltd. Eire Papers offered to buy from Birch the outside linerboard with the special printing already on it, but it would supply its own inside liner and corrugating medium. The outside liner would be supplied by the Southern Division at a price equivalent to $90 per thousand boxes, and would be printed for $30 per thousand by the Thompson Division. Of the $30, about $25 would be out-of-pocket costs.

Since the bidding results appeared to be a little unusual, William Kenton, manager of the Northern Division, discussed the wide discrepancy in the bids with Birch's commercial vice president. He told the vice president, "We sell in a very competitive market, where higher costs cannot be passed on. How can we be expected to show a decent profit and return on investment if we have to buy our supplies at more than 10% over the going market?"

Knowing that Mr. Brunner had been unable to operate the Thompson Division at capacity on occasion during the past few months, it seemed odd to the vice president that Mr. Brunner would add the full 20% overhead and profit charge to his out-of-pocket costs. When he asked Mr. Brunner about this, the answer he received was the statement that appears at the beginning of the case. Brunner went on to say that, having done the developmental work on the box and having received no profit on that work, he felt entitled to a good markup on the production of the box itself.

The vice president explored further the cost structures of the various divisions. He remembered a comment of the controller at a meeting the week before, to the effect that costs which were variable for one division could be largely fixed for the company as a whole. He knew that in the absence of specific orders from top management Mr. Kenton would accept the lowest bid, which was that of the West Paper Company for $430. However, it would be possible for top management to order the acceptance of another bid if the situation warranted such action. And although the volume represented by the transactions in question was less than 5% of the volume of any of the divisions involved, future transactions could conceivably raise similar problems.

# CASE 17   Polysar Limited

As soon as Pierre Choquette received the September Report of Operations for NASA Rubber [**Exhibits 1 and 2**], he called Alf Devereux, Controller, and Ron Britton, Sales Manager, into his office to discuss the year-to-date results. Next week, he would make his presentation to the Board of Directors and the results for his division for the first nine months of the year were not as good as expected. Pierre knew that the NASA management team had performed well. Sales volume was up and feedstock costs were down resulting in a gross margin that was better than budget. Why did the bottom line look so bad?

As the three men worked through the numbers, their discussion kept coming back to the fixed costs of the butyl rubber plant. Fixed costs were high. The plant had yet to reach capacity. The European Division had taken less output than projected.

Still, Choquette felt that these factors were outside his control. His Division had performed well—it just didn't show in the profit results.

Choquette knew that Henderson, his counterpart in Europe, did not face these problems. The European rubber profits would be compared to those of NASA. How would the Board react to the numbers he had to work with? He would need to educate them in his presentation, especially concerning the volume variance. He knew that many of the Board members would not understand what that number represented or that it was due in part to the actions of Henderson's group.

Pierre Choquette, Alf Devereux, and Ron Britton decided to meet the next day to work on a strategy for the Board presentation.

## Polysar Limited

In 1986, Polysar Limited was Canada's largest chemical company with $1.8 billion in annual sales. Based in Sarnia, Ontario, Polysar was the world's largest producer of synthetic rubber and latex and a major producer of basic petrochemicals and fuel products.

Polysar was established in 1942 to meet wartime needs for a synthetic substitute for natural rubber. The supply of natural rubber to the Allied forces had been interrupted by the declaration of war against the United States by Japan in December 1941. During 1942 and 1943, ten synthetic rubber plants were built by the Governments of the United States and Canada including the Polysar plant in Sarnia.

After the war, the supply of natural rubber was again secure and the nine U.S. plants were sold to private industry or closed. Polysar remained in operation as a Crown Corporation, wholly owned by the Government of Canada. In 1972, by an Act of Parliament, the Canada Development Corporation (CDC) was created as a government-owned, venture capital company to encourage Canadian business development; at that time, the equity shares of Polysar were transferred to the Canada Development Corporation. In 1986, Polysar remained wholly-owned by the CDC; however, in a government sponsored move to privatization, the majority of the shares of the CDC were sold to the Canadian public in the period 1982 to 1985.

Through acquisition and internal growth, Polysar had grown considerably from its original single plant. Polysar now employed 6,650 people including 3,100 in Canada, 1,050 in the U.S., and 2,500 in Europe and elsewhere. The company operated 20 manufacturing plants in Canada, United States, Belgium, France, The Netherlands, and West Germany.

### Structure

The operations of the company were structured into three groups: basic petrochemicals, rubber, and diversified products [**Exhibit 3**].

**Basic Petrochemicals**   Firman Bentley, 51, was Group Vice-President of Basic Petrochemicals. This business unit produced primary petrochemicals such as ethylene as well as intermediate products such as propylene, butadiene, and styrene monomers. Group sales in 1985 were approximately $800 million of which $500 million was sold to outside customers and the remainder was sold as intermediate feedstock to Polysar's downstream operations.

**Rubber**   The Rubber Group was headed by Charles Ambridge, 61, Group Vice-President. Polysar held 9% of the world synthetic rubber market (excluding communist bloc countries). As the largest Group in the company, Rubber Group produced 46% of Polysar sales. Major competitors included Goodyear, Bayer, Exxon, and Dupont.

Rubber products, such as butyl and halobutyl, were sold primarily to manufacturers of automobile tires (six of the world's largest tire companies[1] accounted for 70% of the world butyl and halobutyl demand); other uses included belting, footwear, adhesives, hose, seals, plastics modification, and chewing gum.

The Rubber Group was split into two operating divisions that were managed as profit centers: NASA (North and South America) and EROW (Europe and rest of world). In addition to the two operating profit centers, the Rubber Group included a Global Marketing Department and a Research Division. The costs of these departments were not charged to the two operating profit centers, but instead were charged against Group profits.

**Diversified Products**   John Beaton, 48, was Vice-President of Diversified Products, a group that consisted of the Latex, Plastics, and Specialty Products Divisions. This group was composed of high technology product categories that were expected to double sales within five years. In 1985, the group provided 27% of Polysar's sales revenue.

Bentley, Ambridge, and Beaton reported to Robert Dudley, 60, President and Chief Executive Officer.

### Rubber Group

A key component of Polysar's strategy was to be a leader in high margin, specialty rubbers. The leading products in this category were the butyl and halobutyl rubbers. Attributes of butyl rubber include low permeability to gas and moisture, resistance to steam and weathering, high energy absorption, and chemical resistance. Butyl rubber was traditionally used in inner tubes and general purpose applications. Halobutyl rubber, a modified derivative, possesses

---

[1] Michelin, Goodyear, Bridgestone, Firestone, Pirelli, and Dunlop.

the same attributes as regular butyl with additional properties that allow bonding to other materials. Thus, halobutyls were used extensively as liners and sidewalls in tubeless tires.

Butyl and halobutyl rubber were manufactured from feedstocks such as crude oil, naphtha, butane, propane, and ethane [**Exhibit 4**]. Polysar manufactured butyl rubbers at two locations: NASA Division's Sarnia plant and EROW Division's Antwerp plant.

**NASA Butyl Plant**  The original Sarnia plant, built in 1942, manufactured regular butyl until 1972. At that time, market studies predicted rapid growth in the demand for high-quality radial tires manufactured with halobutyl. Demand for regular butyl was predicted to remain steady since poor road conditions in many countries of the world necessitated the use of tires with inner tubes. In 1972, the Sarnia plant was converted to allow production of halobutyls as well as regular butyl.

By the 1980s, demand for halobutyl had increased to the point that Polysar forecast capacity constraints. During 1983 and 1984, the company built a second plant at Sarnia, known as Sarnia 2, to produce regular butyl. The original plant, Sarnia 1, was then dedicated solely to the production of halobutyl.

Sarnia 2, with a capital cost of $550 million, began full operations late in 1984. Its annual nameplate (i.e., design) production capacity for regular butyl was 95,000 tonnes. During 1985, the plant produced 65,000 tonnes.

**EROW Butyl Plant**  The EROW Division's butyl plant was located in Antwerp, Belgium. Built in 1964 as a regular butyl unit, the plant was modified in 1979/80 to allow it to produce halobutyl as well as regular butyl.

The annual nameplate production capacity of the Antwerp plant was 90,000 tonnes. In 1985, as in previous years, the plant operated near or at its nameplate capacity. The Antwerp plant was operated to meet fully the halobutyl demand of EROW customers; the remainder of capacity was used to produce regular butyl.

In 1981, the plant's output was 75% regular butyl and 25% halobutyl; by 1985, halobutyl represented 50% of the plant's production. Since regular butyl demand outpaced the plant's remaining capacity, EROW took its regular butyl shortfall from the Sarnia 2 plant; in 1985, 21,000 tonnes of regular butyl were shipped from NASA to EROW.

**Product Scheduling**  Although NASA served customers in North and South America and EROW serviced customers in Europe and the rest of the world, regular butyl could be shipped from either the Sarnia 2 or Antwerp plant. NASA shipped approximately one-third of its regular butyl output to EROW. Also, customers located in distant locations could receive shipments from either plant due to certain cost or logistical advantages. For example, Antwerp sometimes shipped to Brazil and Sarnia sometimes shipped to the Far East.

A Global Marketing Department worked with Regional Directors of Marketing and Regional Product Managers to coordinate product flows. Three sets of factors influenced these analyses. First, certain customers demanded products from a specific plant due to slight product differences resulting from the type of feedstock used and the plant configuration. Second, costs varied between Sarnia and Antwerp due to differences in variable costs (primarily feedstock and energy), shipping, and currency rates. Finally, inventory levels, production interruptions, and planned shutdowns were considered.

In September and October of each year, NASA and EROW divisions prepared production estimates for the upcoming year. These estimates were based on estimated sales volumes and plant loadings (i.e., capacity utilization). Since the Antwerp plant operated at capacity, the planning exercise was largely for the benefit of the managers of the Sarnia 2 plant who needed to know how much regular butyl Antwerp would need from the Sarnia 2 plant.

**Product Costing and Transfer Prices**  Butyl rubbers were costed using standard rates for variable and fixed costs.

Variable costs included feedstocks, chemicals, and energy. Standard variable cost per tonne of butyl was calculated by multiplying a standard utilization factor (i.e. the standard quantity of inputs used) by a standard price established for each unit of input. Since feedstock prices varied with worldwide market conditions and represented the largest component of costs, it was impossible to establish standard input prices that remained valid for extended periods. Therefore, the company reset feedstock standard costs each month to a price that reflected market prices. Chemical and energy standard costs were established annually.

A purchase price variance (were input prices above or below standard prices?) and an efficiency variance (did production require more or less inputs than standard?) were calculated for variable costs each accounting period.

Fixed costs comprised three categories of cost. Direct costs included direct labor, maintenance, chemicals required to keep the plant bubbling, and fixed utilities. Allocated cash costs included plant management, purchasing department costs, engineering, planning, and accounting. Allocated non-cash costs represented primarily depreciation.

Fixed costs were allocated to production based on a plant's "demonstrated capacity" using the following formula,

$$\frac{\text{Standard Fixed}}{\text{Cost Per Tonne}} = \frac{\text{Estimated Annual Total Fixed Costs}}{\text{Annual Demonstrated Plant Capacity}}$$

To apply the formula, production estimates were established each fall for the upcoming year. Then, the amount of total fixed costs applicable to this level of production was estimated. The amount of total fixed cost to be allocated to each tonne of output was calculated by dividing total fixed cost by the plant's demonstrated capacity. **Exhibit 5** reproduces a section of the Controller's Guide that defines demonstrated capacity.

Each accounting period, two variances were calculated for fixed costs. The first was a spending variance calculated as the simple difference between actual total fixed costs and estimated total fixed costs. The second variance was a volume variance calculated using the formula:

$$\frac{\text{Volume}}{\text{Variance}} = \left(\frac{\text{Standard Fixed}}{\text{Cost Per Tonne}}\right) \times \left(\left[\begin{array}{c}\text{Actual Tonnes} \\ \text{Produced}\end{array}\right] - \left[\begin{array}{c}\text{Demonstrated} \\ \text{Capacity}\end{array}\right]\right)$$

Product transfers between divisions for performance accounting purposes were made at standard full cost, representing, for each tonne, the sum of standard variable cost and standard fixed cost.

**Compensation**  Employees at Polysar had in the past been paid by fixed salary with little use of bonuses except at the executive level of the company. In 1984, a bonus system was instituted throughout the company to link pay with performance and strengthen the profit center orientation.

## Non-Management Employees

The bonus system varied by employee group but was developed with the intention of paying salaries that were approximately five percent less than those paid by a reference group of 25 major Canadian manufacturing companies. To augment salaries, annual bonuses were awarded, in amounts up to 12% of salary, based on corporate and Divisional performance. Hourly workers could receive annual bonuses in similar proportions based on performance.

All bonuses were based on achieving or exceeding budgeted profit targets. For salaried workers, for example, meeting the 1985 corporate profit objective would result in a 5% bonus; an additional $25 million in profits would provide an additional 4% bonus. Meeting and exceeding Division profit targets could provide an additional 3% bonus.

Using periodic accounting information, Divisional Vice-Presidents met in quarterly communication meetings with salaried and wage employees to discuss divisional and corporate performance levels.

## Management

For managers, the percent of remuneration received through annual bonuses was greater than 12% and increased with responsibility levels.

The bonuses of top Division management in 1985 were calculated by a formula that awarded 50% of bonus potential to meeting and exceeding Divisional profit targets and 50% to meeting or exceeding corporate profit targets.

## Interviews with Rubber Group Vice Presidents[2]

**Pierre Choquette**   Pierre Choquette, 43, was Vice-President[3] of the NASA Rubber Division. A professional engineer, Choquette had begun his career with Polysar in plant management. Over the years, he had assumed responsibilities for product management in the U.S., managed a small subsidiary, managed a European plant, and directed European sales.

> "This business is managed on price and margin. Quality, service, and technology are also important, but it is difficult to differentiate ourselves from other competitors on these dimensions.
>
> "When the price of oil took off, this affected our feedstock prices drastically, and Polysar's worldwide business suffered. Now that prices are back down, we are trying to regroup our efforts and bring the business back to long term health. Polysar will break even in 1985 and show a normal profit again in 1986. Of course, the Rubber Division will, as in the past, be the major producer of profit for the company.
>
> "As you know, this is a continuous process industry. The plant is computerized so that we need the same number of people and incur most of the same overhead costs whether the plant is running fast or slow.
>
> "The regular butyl plant, Sarnia 2, is running at less than capacity. Although the plant should be able to produce 95,000 tonnes, its demonstrated capacity is 85,000. Last year, we produced 65,000. This leaves us sitting with a lot of unabsorbed fixed costs, especially when you consider depreciation charges.

---

[2] Pierre Choquette was interviewed at Harvard Business School in 1985; Doug Henderson was interviewed at Harvard in 1986. Both men were attending the thirteen-week Advanced Management Program that was developed to strengthen the management skills of individuals with potential to become chief executive officers of their companies. In addition to Choquette and Henderson, Polysar had sent Firman Bentley to the program in 1984.

[3] Due to its relatively large size, Rubber Group was the only group with regional vice presidents. Regional responsibilities of the Basic Petrochemicals group and the Diversified Products group were managed by lower-ranking general managers.

"Still, NASA Rubber has been growing nicely. I think that this is in part due to our strong commitment to run the Divisions as profit centers. We have been pushing hard to build both volume and efficiency and I am pleased that our programs and incentives are paying off.

"Our transfers to EROW are still a problem. Since the transfers are at standard cost and are not recorded as revenue, these transfers do nothing for our profit. Also, if they cut back on orders, our profit is hurt through the volume variance. Few of our senior managers truly understand the volume variance and why profit results are so different in the two regions. The accounting is not a problem, but having to continuously explain it to very senior-level managers is. It always comes down to the huge asset that we carry whether the plant is at capacity or not.

"We run our businesses on return on net assets which looks ridiculous for NASA. I worry that if I am not around to explain it, people will form the wrong conclusion about the health of the business. Also, you sometimes wonder if people ascribe results to factors that are outside your control."

**Doug Henderson**    Doug Henderson, 46, Vice-President of EROW Rubber Division, was also a professional engineer. His career included management responsibilities in plant operations, market research, venture analysis and corporate planning, running a small regional business in Canada, and Director of European Sales.

"The Antwerp plant produces about 45,000 tonnes of halobutyl and 45,000 tonnes of regular butyl each year. In addition, we import approximately 15,000 to 20,000 tonnes of regular butyl from Sarnia each year [**Exhibit 6**].

"We inform Sarnia each fall of our estimated regular butyl needs. These estimates are based on our predictions of butyl and halobutyl sales and how hard we can load our plant. The overall sales estimates are usually within ten percent, say plus or minus 8,000 tonnes, unless an unexpected crisis occurs.

"The EROW business has been extremely successful since I arrived here in 1982. We have increased our share in the high growth halobutyl market; the plant is running well; and we have kept the operation simple and compact.

"Looking at our Statement of Net Contribution [**Exhibit 7**], our margins are better than NASA's. For one thing, there is a great surplus of feedstock in Europe and we benefit from lower prices. Also, market dynamics are substantially different.

"We pay a lot of attention to plant capacity. For example, we budgeted to produce 250 tonnes per day this year and we have got it up to 275. We are also working hard to reduce our "off-spec" material as a way of pushing up our yield. If we can produce more, it's free—other than variable cost, it goes right to the bottom line.

"Given these factors, Pierre loves it when I tell him jokingly that our success at EROW is attributable to superb management."

**EXHIBIT 3**

POLYSAR LIMITED
Partial Organization Chart

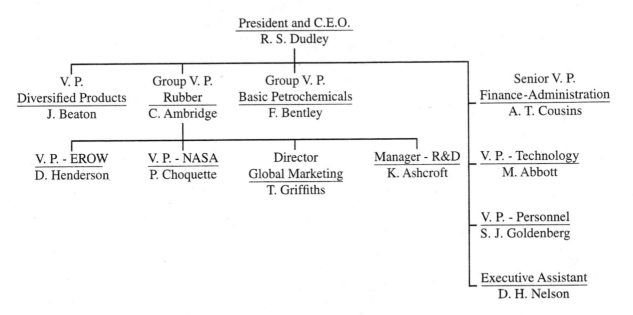

**EXHIBIT 4   Rubber Production Process**

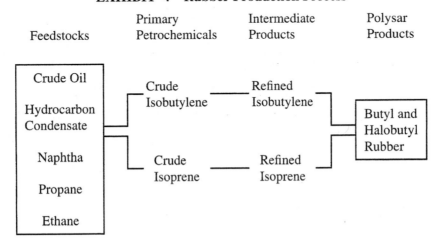

**EXHIBIT 1**
NASA RUBBER DIVISION
Regular Butyl Rubber
Statistics and Analyses
September 1986

| | *9 Months ended September 30, 1986* | | |
| VOLUME—TONNES | ACTUAL ('000's) | BUDGET ('000's) | DEVIATION ('000's) |
|---|---|---|---|
| Sales | 35.8 | 33.0 | 2.8 |
| Production | 47.5 | 55.0 | − 7.5 |
| Transfers | | | |
| to EROW | 12.2 | 19.5 | − 7.3 |
| from EROW | 2.1 | 1.0 | 1.1 |
| PRODUCTION COSTS | ($'000's) | ($'000's) | ($'000's) |
| Fixed Cost—Direct | −21,466 | −21,900 | 434 |
| —Allocated Cash | − 7,036 | − 7,125 | 89 |
| —Allocated Non-Cash | −15,625 | −15,600 | − 25 |
| Fixed Cost to Production | −44,127 | −44,625 | 498 |
| Transfers to/from FG Inventory | 1,120 | 2,450 | −1,330 |
| Transfers to EROW | 8,540 | 13,650 | −5,110 |
| Transfers from EROW | − 1,302 | − 620 | − 682 |
| Fixed Cost of Sales | −35,769 | −29,145 | −6,624 |

*Note: As indicated on p. 1 of the case, financial data have been disguised and do not represent
the true financial results of the company.*

## EXHIBIT 2
NASA RUBBER DIVISION
Regular Butyl Rubber
Statement of Net Contribution
September 1986

| | 9 Months ended September 30, 1986 | | |
| --- | --- | --- | --- |
| | ACTUAL ($'000's) | BUDGET ($'000's) | DEVIATION ($'000's) |
| Sales Revenue—Third Party | 65,872 | 61,050 | 4,822 |
| —Diversified Products Group | 160 | 210 | − 50 |
| —Total | 66,032 | 61,260 | 4,722 |
| Delivery Cost | − 2,793 | − 2,600 | − 193 |
| Net Sales Revenue | 63,239 | 58,660 | 4,579 |
| *Variable Costs* | | | |
| Standard | −22,589 | −21,450 | −1,139 |
| Cost Adjustments | 54 | — | 54 |
| Efficiency Variance | 241 | — | 241 |
| Total | −22,294 | −21,450 | − 844 |
| Gross Margin—$ | 40,945 | 37,210 | 3,735 |
| *Fixed Costs* | | | |
| Standard | −25,060 | −23,100 | −1,960 |
| Cost Adjustments | 168 | 80 | 88 |
| Spending Variance | 498 | — | 498 |
| Volume Variance | −11,375 | − 6,125 | −5,250 |
| Total | −35,769 | −29,145 | −6,624 |
| Gross Profit—$ | 5,176 | 8,065 | −2,889 |
| —% of NSR | 8.2% | 13.7% | − 5.5% |
| *Period Costs* | | | |
| Administration, Selling, Distribution | − 4,163 | − 4,000 | − 163 |
| Technical Service | − 222 | − 210 | − 12 |
| Other Income/Expense | 208 | 50 | 158 |
| Total | − 4,177 | − 4,160 | − 17 |
| Business Contribution | 999 | 3,905 | −2,906 |
| Interest on Working Capital | − 1,875 | − 1,900 | 25 |
| Net Contribution | − 876 | 2,005 | −2,881 |

*Note: As indicated on p. 1 of the case, financial data have been disguised and do not represent the true financial results of the company.*

**EXHIBIT 5**

| POLYSAR | POLYSAR LIMITED — CONTROLLER'S GUIDE | NUMBER 03:02 |
|---|---|---|
| | | PAGE 1 OF 14 PAGES |

| SUBJECT | | NEW | REPLACES |
|---|---|---|---|
| ACCOUNTING FOR INVENTORIES | | X | |
| | | ISSUE DATE Jan. 1/81 | |

| ISSUED BY Director Accounting | AUTHORIZED BY Corporate Controller |
|---|---|

## PURPOSE

To set out criteria and guidelines for the application of the Company's accounting policy for inventories:

> "Inventories are valued at the lower of FIFO (first-in, first-out) cost and net realizable value except for raw materials and supplies which are valued at the lower of FIFO cost and replacement cost."

## SPECIFIC EXCLUSION

This release does not apply to SWAP transactions.

## DEFINITIONS

By-products - one or more products of relatively small per unit market value that emerge from the production process of a product or products of greater value.

Cost system - a system to facilitate the classification, recording, analysis and interpretation of data pertaining to the production and distribution of products and services.

Demonstrated capacity is the actual annualized production of a plant which was required to run full out within the last fiscal year for a sufficiently long period to assess production capability after adjusting for abnormally low or high unscheduled shutdowns, scheduled shutdowns, and unusual or annualized items which impacted either favourably or unfavourably on the period's production. The resulting adjusted historical base should be further modified for changes planned to be implemented within the current fiscal year.

a) Where a plant has not been required to run full out within the last fiscal year, production data may be used for a past period after adjusting for changes (debottleneckings/inefficiencies) since that time affecting production.

b) Where a plant has never been required to run full out, demonstrated capacity could be reasonably considered as "name plate" capacity after adjusting for,

i) known invalid assumptions in arriving at "name plate"
ii) changes to original design affecting "name plate"
iii) a reasonable negative allowance for error.

\* Denotes change from previous issue

---

**EXHIBIT 6**  Schedule of Regular Butyl Shipments from NASA to EROW

| | ACTUAL TONNES | BUDGET TONNES |
|---|---|---|
| 1985 | 21,710 | 23,500 |
| 1984 | 12,831 | 13,700 |
| 1983 | 1,432 | 4,000 |
| 1982 | 792 | 600 |
| 1981 | 1,069 | 700 |

520

**EXHIBIT 7**
EROW RUBBER DIVISION
Regular Butyl Rubber
Condensed Statement of Net Contribution
September 1986

| | *9 Months ended September 30, 1986* |
|---|---|
| Sales Volume — Tonnes | 47,850 |
| | ($'000's) |
| Sales Revenue | 94,504 |
| Delivery Cost | − 4,584 |
| Net Sales Revenue | 89,920 |
| *Variable Cost* | |
| Standard | −28,662 |
| Purchase Price Variance | 203 |
| Inventory Revaluation | − 46 |
| Efficiency Variance | 32 |
| Total | −28,473 |
| Gross Margin — $ | 61,447 |
| *Fixed Cost to Production* | |
| Depreciation | − 4,900 |
| Other | −16,390 |
| | −21,290 |
| Transfers to/from F. G. Inventory | − 775 |
| Transfers to/from NASA | − 7,238 |
| | −29,303 |
| Gross Profit — $ | 32,144 |
| Period Costs | − 7,560 |
| Business Contribution | 24,584 |
| Interest on W/C | − 1,923 |
| Net Contribution | 22,661 |

Notes:  1. *Fixed costs are allocated between regular butyl production (above) and halobutyl production (reported separately).*
2. *As indicated on p. 1 of the case, financial data have been disguised and do not represent the true financial results of the company.*

**CASE 18** Purity Steel Corporation, 1995

"**I**'m no expert in high finance," said Larry Hoffman, manager of the Denver branch for the Warehouse Sales Division of Purity Steel Corporation, to Harold Higgins, general manager of the division, "so it didn't occur to me that I might be better off by leasing my new warehouse instead of owning it. But I was talking to Jack Dorenbush over in Omaha the other day and he said that he's getting a lot better return on the investment in his district because he's in a leased building. I'm sure that the incentive compensation plan you put in last year is fair, but I didn't know whether it adjusted automatically for the difference between owning and leasing and I just thought I'd raise the question. There's still time to try to find someone to take over my construction contract and then lease the building to me when it's finished, if you think that's what I ought to do."

Purity Steel Corporation was an integrated steel producer with annual sales of about $4.5 billion in 1995. The Warehouse Sales Division was an autonomous unit that operated 21 field warehouses throughout the United States. Total sales of the division were approximately $225 million in 1995, of which roughly half represented steel products (rod, bar, wire, tube, sheet, and plate) purchased from Purity's Mill Products Division. The balance of the Warehouse Sales Division volume was copper, brass, and aluminum products purchased from large producers of those metals. The Warehouse Sales Division competed with other producer-affiliated and independent steel warehousing companies and purchased its steel requirements from the Mill Products Division at the same prices paid by outside purchasers.

Harold Higgins was appointed general manager of the Warehouse Sales Division in mid-1994, after spending 12 years in the sales function with the Mill Products Division. Subject only to the approval of his annual profit plan and proposed capital expenditures by corporate headquarters, Higgins was given full authority for his division's operations, and was charged with the responsibility to "make the division grow, both in sales volume and in the rate of return on its investment." Prior to his arrival at division headquarters in St. Louis, the Warehouse Sales Division had been operated in a centralized manner; all purchase orders had been issued by division headquarters, and most other operating decisions at any particular warehouse had required prior divisional approval. Higgins decided to decentralize the management of his division by making each branch (warehouse) manager responsible for the division's activities in his or her geographic area.

In Higgins's opinion, one of the key features of his decentralization policy was an incentive compensation plan announced in late 1994 to become effective January 1, 1995. The description of the plan, as presented to the branch managers, is reproduced in **Exhibits 1, 2, and 3.** Monthly operating statements had been prepared for each warehouse for many years; implementing the new plan required only the preparation of balance sheets for each warehouse. Two major asset categories, inventories and fixed assets (buildings and equipment), were easy to attribute to specific locations. Accounts receivable were collected directly at Purity's central accounting department, but an investment in receivables equal to 35 days'

*Doctoral Candidate Antonio Dávila and Professor Robert Simons prepared this updated case based on an earlier version. Case material of the Harvard Graduate School of Business Administration is prepared as a basis for class discussion and not to illustrate either effective or ineffective handling of administrative problems.*

Copyright © 1997 by the President and Fellows of Harvard College. To order copies or request permission to reproduce materials, call 1-800-545-7685 or write Harvard Business School Publishing, Boston, MA 02163. No part of this publication may be reproduced, stored in a retrieval system, used in a spreadsheet, or transmitted in any form or by any means—electronic, mechanical, photocopying, recording, or otherwise—without the permission of Harvard Business School.

sales (the average for the Warehouse Sales Division) was charged to each warehouse. Finally, a small cash fund deposited in a local bank was recorded as an asset of each branch. No current or long-term liabilities were recognized in the balance sheets at the division or branch level.

At the meeting in December 1994, when the new incentive compensation plan was presented to the branch managers, Higgins had said:

> Howard Percy [division sales manager] and I have spent a lot of time during the last few months working out the details of this plan. Our objective was to devise a fair way to compensate those branch managers who do a superior job of improving the performance in their areas. First, we reviewed our salary structure and made a few adjustments so that branch managers do not have to apologize to their families for the regular pay check they bring home. Next, we worked out a simple growth incentive to recognize that one part of our job is simply to sell steel, although we didn't restrict it to steel alone. But more importantly, we've got to improve the profit performance of this division. We established 5% as the return-on-investment floor representing minimum performance eligible for a bonus. As you know, we don't even do that well for 1994, but our budget for next year anticipates 5% before taxes. Thus, in 1995 we expect about a third of the branches to be below 5%—and earn no ROI bonus—while the other two-thirds will be the ones who really carry the weight. This plan will pay a bonus to all managers who help the division increase its average rate of return. We also decided on a sliding scale arrangement for those above 5%, trying to recognize that the manager who makes a 5% return on a $10 million investment is doing as good a job as one who makes a 10% return on only a half million dollars. Finally, we put a $50,000 limit on the ROI bonus because we felt that the bonus shouldn't exceed 50% of salary, but we can always make salary adjustments in those cases where the bonus plan doesn't seem to adequately compensate a branch manager for his or her performance.

After the telephone call from Larry Hoffman in May 1996, quoted in the opening paragraph, Harold Higgins called Howard Percy into his office and told him the question that Hoffman had raised. "We knew that we probably had some bugs to iron out of this system," Percy responded. "Let me review the Denver situation and we'll discuss it this afternoon."

At a meeting later that day, Percy summarized the problem for Higgins:

> As you know, Larry Hoffman is planning a big expansion at Denver. He's been limping along in an old multistory building with an inadequate variety of inventory, and his sales actually declined last year. About a year ago he worked up an RFE [request for expenditure] for a new warehouse which we approved here and sent forward. It was approved at corporate headquarters last fall, the contract was let, and it's to be completed by the end of this year. I pulled out one page of the RFE which summarizes the financial story [**Exhibit 4**]. Larry forecasts nearly a triple in his sales volume over the next eight years, and the project will pay out in about seven and a half years.

> Here [**Exhibit 5**] is a summary of the incentive compensation calculations for Denver that I worked up after I talked to you this morning. Larry had a very high ROI last year, and received one of the biggest bonuses we paid. Against that background, I next worked up a projection of what his bonus will be in 1997 assuming that he moves into his new facility at the end of the year. As you can see, his ROI will drop from 17.3% to only 7.2%, and even on the bigger investment his bonus in 1997 will go down substantially.

> Finally, I dug out the file on New Orleans where we're leasing the new warehouse that was completed a few months ago. Our lease there is a so-called operating lease, which means that we pay the insurance, taxes, and maintenance just as if we owned it. The lease runs for 20 years with renewal options at reduced rates for two additional 10-year periods. Assuming that we could get a similar deal for Denver, and adjusting for the difference in the cost of the land and building at the two locations, our lease payments at Denver during the first 20 years would be just under $250,000 per year. Pushing that through the bonus formula for Denver's projected 1997 operations shows an ROI of 7.3%, but Larry's bonus would be about 15% less than if he was in an owned building.

"On balance, therefore," Percy concluded, "there's not a very big difference in the bonus payment as between owning and leasing, but in either event Larry will be taking a substantial cut in his incentive compensation."

As the discussion continued, Larry Hoffman and Howard Percy revisited the formula for ROI:

$$\text{Return-on-investment} = \frac{\text{Net Income}}{\text{Investment in Operating Assets}}$$

$$= \frac{\text{Net Income}}{\text{Sales}} \times \frac{\text{Sales}}{\text{Investment in Operating Assets}}$$

$$= (\textit{Return on Sales}) \times (\textit{Asset Turnover})$$

Both wondered whether the proposed bonus plan needed further revision or clarification.

---

## EXHIBIT 1   Branch Managers' Compensation Plan, Warehouse Sales Division

I. *Objectives*

The Warehouse Sales Division has three major objectives:

A.   To operate the Division and its branches at a profit.
B.   To utilize efficiently the assets of the Division.
C.   To grow.

This compensation plan is a combination of base salary and incentive earnings. Incentive earnings will be paid to those managers who contribute to the achievement of these objectives and in proportion to their individual performance.

II. *Compensation Plan Components*

There are three components to this plan:

A.   *Base Salary*

Base salary ranges are determined for the most part on dollar sales volume of the district(s) in the prior year. The higher the sales volume, the higher range to which the manager becomes eligible. The profitability of dollar sales or increases in dollar sales is an important consideration. Actual salaries will be established by the General Manager, Warehouse Sales Division, and the salary ranges will be reviewed periodically in order to keep this Division competitive with companies similar to ours.

B.   *Growth Incentive*

If the district earns a net profit before federal income tax for the calendar year, the manager will earn $1,750 for every $500,000 of increased sales over the prior year. Proportionate amounts will be paid for greater or lesser growth.

C.   *Return-on-Investment Incentive*

In this feature of the plan, incentive will be paid in relation to the size of investment and the return-on-investment. The manager will be paid in direct proportion to his effective use of assets placed at his disposal.

*Exhibit 1   Continued*

The main emphasis of this portion of the plan is on increasing the return at any level of investment, high or low.

III. *Limitations on Return-on-Investment Incentive*

A. No incentive will be paid to a manager whose branch earns less than 5% return-on-investment before federal taxes.

B. No increase in incentive payment will be made for performance in excess of 20% return-on-investment before federal taxes.

C. No payment will be made in excess of $50,000 regardless of performance.

IV. *Calculations on Return-on-Investment Incentive*

**Exhibit 2** is a graphic presentation of this portion of the incentive. Since all possible levels of investment and return-on-investment cannot be detailed on the chart, exact incentive figures cannot be determined. However, a rough estimate can be made by:

A. Finding the approximate level of investment on the horizontal scale.

B. Drawing a line vertically from that point to the approximate return-on-investment percent.

C. Drawing a line horizontally from that point to the vertical scale which indicates the approximate incentive payment.

The exact amount of incentive can be determined from **Exhibit 3** by the following procedure and example.

**Example:**

Investment:        $8,263,750

ROI:        7.3%

Step 1. Subtract 500,000 from the last six digits of investment figures if they are above 500,000.

EXAMPLE: 263,750 is below 500,000; nothing is subtracted.

Step 2. Divide the number from step 1 by 500,000. The result is a percentage.

EXAMPLE: 263,750/500,000 = .5275

Step 3. In the 1% Column in **Exhibit 3**, take the difference between the next highest, investment and next lowest investment.

| EXAMPLE: | Investment | 1% | Difference |
|---|---|---|---|
| | $8,000,000 | $2,100 | |
| | | | $50 |
| | $8,500,000 | $2,150 | |

Step 4. Multiply the result of Step 3 by the result of Step 2 and add to the 1% Column figure for the next lowest investment.

EXAMPLE: $50 × .5275 = $26.37 + $2,100 = $2,126.37

Step 5. Multiply the result of Step 4 by the actual ROI%.

EXAMPLE: $2,126.37 × 7.3 = $15,522.54 Incentive Payment

**EXHIBIT 2  Incentive Payments at Various ROI Percentages**

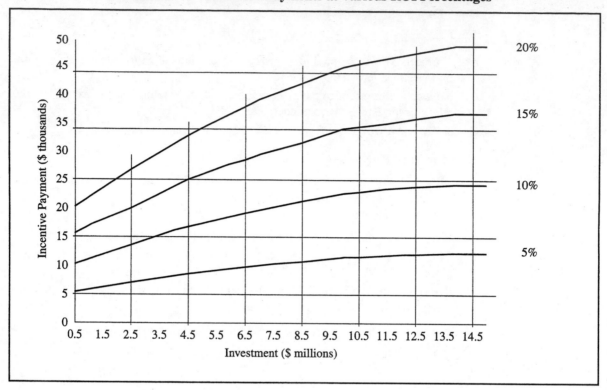

**EXHIBIT 3   Incentive Payments at Various Investments and ROI Percentages**

| INVESTMENT | 1%(a) | 5% | 10% | 15% | 20% |
|---|---|---|---|---|---|
| $   500,000 | 1,045 | 5,225 | 10,450 | 15,675 | 20,900 |
| 1,000,000 | 1,125 | 5,625 | 11,250 | 16,875 | 22,500 |
| 1,500,000 | 1,205 | 6,025 | 12,050 | 18,075 | 24,100 |
| 2,000,000 | 1,285 | 6,425 | 12,850 | 19,275 | 25,700 |
| 2,500,000 | 1,365 | 6,825 | 13,650 | 20,475 | 27,300 |
| 3,000,000 | 1,445 | 7,225 | 14,450 | 21,675 | 28,900 |
| 3,500,000 | 1,525 | 7,625 | 15,250 | 22,875 | 30,500 |
| 4,000,000 | 1,605 | 8,025 | 16,050 | 24,075 | 32,100 |
| 4,500,000 | 1,685 | 8,425 | 16,850 | 25,275 | 33,700 |
| 5,000,000 | 1,750 | 8,750 | 17,500 | 26,250 | 35,000 |
| 5,500,000 | 1,810 | 9,050 | 18,100 | 27,150 | 36,200 |
| 6,000,000 | 1,875 | 9,375 | 18,750 | 28,125 | 37,500 |
| 6,500,000 | 1,935 | 9,675 | 19,350 | 29,025 | 38,700 |
| 7,000,000 | 2,000 | 10,000 | 20,000 | 30,000 | 40,000 |
| 7,500,000 | 2,050 | 10,250 | 20,500 | 30,750 | 41,000 |
| 8,000,000 | 2,100 | 10,500 | 21,000 | 31,500 | 42,000 |
| 8,500,000 | 2,150 | 10,750 | 21,500 | 32,250 | 43,000 |
| 9,000,000 | 2,200 | 11,000 | 22,000 | 33,000 | 44,000 |
| 9,500,000 | 2,250 | 11,250 | 22,500 | 33,750 | 45,000 |
| 10,000,000 | 2,300 | 11,500 | 23,000 | 34,500 | 46,000 |
| 10,500,000 | 2,325 | 11,625 | 23,250 | 34,875 | 46,500 |
| 11,000,000 | 2,350 | 11,750 | 23,500 | 35,250 | 47,000 |
| 11,500,000 | 2,375 | 11,875 | 23,750 | 35,625 | 47,500 |
| 12,000,000 | 2,400 | 12,000 | 24,000 | 36,000 | 48,000 |
| 12,500,000 | 2,425 | 12,125 | 24,250 | 36,375 | 48,500 |
| 13,000,000 | 2,450 | 12,250 | 24,500 | 36,750 | 49,000 |
| 13,500,000 | 2,475 | 12,375 | 24,750 | 37,125 | 49,500 |
| 14,000,000 | 2,500 | 12,500 | 25,000 | 37,500 | 50,000 |
| 14,500,000 | 2,500 | 12,500 | 25,000 | 37,500 | 50,000 |
| 15,000,000 | 2,500 | 12,500 | 25,000 | 37,500 | 50,000 |

*(a) This column is for calculation purposes only. No incentive will be paid for less than 5% ROI.*

**EXHIBIT 4**    Warehouse Sales Division—Denver Branch.
Forecast Additional Sales, Expenses, and After-Tax Profits Due to New Facility
(dollars in thousands)

| | ESTIMATED TO 12/31/95 | 1ST YEAR | 2ND YEAR |
|---|---|---|---|
| Sales dollars | $ 12,300 | 1,565 | 2,620 |
| Gross profit dollars | 2,385 | 245 | 400 |
| Service income | 255 | (125) | (120) |
| Total income | 2,640 | 120 | 280 |
| Less expenses excluding depreciation | (1,645) | (305) | (585) |
| Pre-tax net profit excluding depreciation | 995 | (185) | (305) |
| Additional mill profit | | 65 | 120 |
| | | (120) | (185) |
| Less relocation | | (100) | |
| | | (220) | (185) |
| Less depreciation | | (53) | (53) |
| | | (273) | (238) |
| Less 35% tax | | 96 | 83 |
| Net income | | (177) | (155) |
| Add back depreciation and relocation | | 153 | 53 |
| Annual return of funds | | (24) | (102) |
| Total return over 8 years (in dollars) | | $5,534,549 | |
| Capital expenditures required (in dollars): | | | |
| Land | $ 300,000 | | |
| Building | 2,612,500 | | |
| Equipment | 1,059,650 | | |
| Relocation expense | 100,000 | | |
| Total | | $4,072,150 | |
| Payback period | | 7.3 years | |

| 3RD YEAR | 4TH YEAR | 5TH YEAR | 6TH YEAR | 7TH YEAR | 8TH YEAR |
|---|---|---|---|---|---|
| 5,125 | 7,870 | 11,020 | 15,250 | 18,635 | 22,670 |
| 801 | 1,259 | 1,732 | 2,346 | 2,851 | 3,489 |
| (110) | (100) | (90) | (80) | (80) | (80) |
| 691 | 1,159 | 1,642 | 2,266 | 2,771 | 3,409 |
| (785) | (1,000) | (1,175) | (1,455) | (1,610) | (1,655) |
| (94) | 159 | 467 | 811 | 1,161 | 1,754 |
| 290 | 495 | 625 | 785 | 920 | 1,165 |
| 196 | 654 | 1,092 | 1,596 | 2,081 | 2,919 |
| 196 | 654 | 1,092 | 1,596 | 2,081 | 2,919 |
| (53) | (53) | (53) | (53) | (53) | (53) |
| 143 | 601 | 1,039 | 1,543 | 2,028 | 2,866 |
| (50) | (210) | (364) | (540) | (710) | (1,003) |
| 93 | 391 | 675 | 1,003 | 1,318 | 1,863 |
| 53 | 53 | 53 | 53 | 53 | 53 |
| 146 | 444 | 728 | 1,056 | 1,371 | 1,916 |

**EXHIBIT 5    Return-on-Investment and Incentive Compensation (in dollars)**

| | TOTAL WAREHOUSE SALES DIVISION 1995 ACTUAL | Denver Branch | | |
|---|---|---|---|---|
| | | 1995 ACTUAL | 1997 Projected | |
| | | | OWNED BUILDING | LEASED BUILDING |
| *Investment at Year-end* | | | | |
| Land | $ 5,114,500 | $ 124,500 | $ 300,000 | $ – |
| Buildings (net of depreciation) | 13,950,500 | 324,500 | 2,568,960 | – |
| Equipment (net of depreciation) | 2,722,000 | 32,000 | 1,010,425 | 1,010,425 |
| Subtotal | 21,817,000 | 481,000 | 3,879,385 | 1,010,425 |
| Cash fund | 1,382,500 | 50,000 | 50,000 | 50,000 |
| Accounts receivable | 22,517,500 | 1,241,500 | 1,386,500 | 1,386,500 |
| Inventories | 55,295,500 | 3,132,000 | 3,466,250 | 3,466,250 |
| Total year-end investment | 101,012,500 | 4,904,500 | 8,782,135 | 5,913,175 |
| Investment at start of year | 99,795,500 | 5,263,500 | 8,395,650 | 5,483,150 |
| Average investment during year | 100,404,000 | 5,084,000 | 8,588,895 | 5,698,150 |
| Profit before depreciation & taxes | 4,147,310 | 917,870 | 710,000 | 710,000 |
| Less: depreciation | (648,705) | (40,000) | (92,765) | (49,225) |
| Less: lease payments | (420,565) | – | – | (243,200) |
| Net pre-tax profit | $ 3,078,040 | $ 877,870 | $ 617,235 | $ 417,575 |
| Return on investment | 3.07% | 17.27% | 7.19% | 7.33% |
| *Incentive Compensation* | | | | |
| Sales volume increase (decrease) | | $ (870,000) | $ 1,565,000 | $ 1,565,000 |
| Bonus @ $1,750 per $500,000 | | – | 5,478 | 5,478 |
| ROI bonus: | | | | |
| Base investment | | 5,000,000 | 8,500,000 | 5,500,000 |
| Value for 1% column, **Exhibit 3** | | 1,750 | 2,150 | 1,810 |
| Difference to next base | | 60 | 50 | 65 |
| Interpolated portion | | 10.08 | 8.89 | 25.76 |
| Total value per percentage point | | 1,760 | 2,159 | 1,836 |
| ROI bonus | | 30,392 | 15,515 | 13,453 |
| Total incentive compensation | | $ 30,392 | $ 20,993 | $ 18,931 |

Assumptions used for 1997 projections at Denver:

1. Old facility and equipment sold at the end of 1996, proceeds remitted to corporate headquarters.
2. Depreciation on new facilities in 1997 is $43,540 (60 years, straight line) and $49,225 on equipment (various lives, straight line).
3. Year-end investment in receivables and inventory will approximate 1995 relationship: receivables at 10% of annual sales, inventories at 25% of annual sales.
4. Average total investment assumes that new fixed assets are acquired on December 31, 1996, and that other assets at that date are the same as at the end of 1995.
5. Profit taken from RFE (**Exhibit 4**) as $995,000 less $185,000 first-year decline, less $100,000 relocation expense. Additional mill profit of $65,000 does not reflect on divisional books and was used only at corporate headquarters for capital expenditures evaluation purposes.

**CASE 19** Western Chemical Corporation:
Divisional Performance Measurement

The fact is that we really have not yet figured out the best way to measure and report on the performance of some of our foreign operations. Because of different ownership arrangements and the use of local financing, when we use conventional accounting principles and standards, we often get financial reports that seem to contradict what we believe to be the true results of operations. This creates problems within the company because people who are not familiar with particular operations see the reports and draw erroneous conclusions about how this one or that one is performing relative to others.

Now that you are beginning to get questions from shareholders and analysts about how some of these investments are performing, I realized that Cynthia and I had better brief you on what some of the problems are that we have with division performance measurement.

Stan Rogers, president of Western Chemical Corporation (WCC), was meeting with Samantha Chu, recently appointed director of Investor Relations, and Cynthia Sheldon, who had recently been appointed vice president and controller. Chu had that morning received an inquiry from a well-known chemical industry analyst who had some fairly specific questions about some of the company's investments in Europe and the Far East. When she questioned Sheldon, Cynthia suggested that they meet with Rogers to examine some of the issues that Rogers and Sheldon had been discussing, so that Chu could answer the analyst's requests more accurately.

The information on the financial performance of WCC's foreign operations was prepared by the same accountants who maintained the company's accounts and who prepared its quarterly and annual reports. A single database for all accounting had been established some years earlier in the belief that it could serve all accounting needs of both managers and those external to the company. A common chart of accounts and accounting policies was used throughout the company and in all of its subsidiaries.

A variety of new alliances and ownership arrangements had been used in recent international ventures to speed entry to new international markets and to minimize investment and risk. Because of these, Rogers had become convinced that some of the reports the accountants were preparing about some of the ventures could be quite misleading. It was for that reason that he and Sheldon were already discussing alternative ways to measure divisional performance, and that Sheldon thought Chu should be brought into their discussion before trying to answer the analyst's queries.

### The Company and International Ventures

In 1995, WCC was a 75-year-old, *Fortune 300* chemical company. Its largest business marketed chemicals and chemical programs for water and waste treatment. Additional products and chemical services targeted manufacturing processes where the quality of a customers product could be enhanced. The company was proud of its industry reputation for quality of

*Professor William J. Bruns and Professor Roger Atherton of Northeastern University prepared this case as the basis for class discussion rather than to illustrate either effective or ineffective handling of an administrative situation.*

its solutions to customer problems and exceptional service to customers. WCC had 4,900 employees and operated more than 35 plants in 19 countries. Financial information by geographic area is shown in **Exhibit 1.**

WCC manufactured in many different countries using a variety of ownership arrangements. Some plants were wholly-owned manufacturing sites, and others were operated as joint ventures with local affiliates. Three of these plants were useful illustrations as background for discussing the problems the company faced in measuring the performance of its international ventures. All had been constructed and had come on-stream in the 1991–1993 period.

A chemical plant on the outskirts of Prague in the Czech Republic was operated as a joint venture with a local partner. Total investment in the plant was between $35 and $40 million, including working capital. WCC retained a controlling interest in the joint venture and operated the plant. The company had invested about $5 million in the venture, and the balance of the investment had come from the venture partner and local borrowing.

A similar plant in Poland was 100% owned, and the total capital investment of $40 to $45 million including working capital had been funded by WCC. The venture itself had no external debt.

A third plant in Malaysia was also 100% owned. The plant was built to add capacity in the Pacific region, but the plant was considered part of the company's production capacity serving the global market. WCC had invested approximately $35 million in this Malaysian plant.

## Measuring the Performance of Three International Ventures

Cynthia Sheldon had prepared some exhibits using representative numbers, and she began by explaining the income statement for the venture in the Czech Republic to Samantha Chu.

The first case is Prague. It is pretty much a classic situation. What I have put together here is a basic income statement for the facility for the first three quarters of 1995 (**Exhibit 2**). What this helps to show is how the difference between the ownership structures in Prague and Poland lead to apparent differences in reported income.

This is a nine-month year-to-date income statement for the joint venture. Earnings before interest and taxes of $869,000 is what we would normally report internally for a wholly-owned subsidiary, and that is what would be consolidated. As you proceed down the income statement, there is a charge for interest because we have the ability to leverage these joint ventures fairly highly, anywhere from 60% to 80%. This is interest on external debt—cash going out. We account for it this way because the venture has its own Board of Directors, even though we have management control and retain much of the ability to influence operations, which is not always the case. The fees of $867,000 are coming to WCC under a technical agreement that we have with the joint venture, as a percentage of revenues. In this case, we have put a minority interest line to get down to a net income for WCC. That is the actual income that we would report to the outside world.

We are reporting externally a loss of $646,000 on this business, when in truth, relative to our other businesses which are reported before interest charges and before fees, it is contributing to our corporate income. This report makes it appear that we are operating at a loss of just under $1.2 million, $532,000 of which is the share of our joint venture partner, and our share is the $646,000.

| Stan Rogers described the investment: | In this business WCC has invested, in addition to its technical knowledge and technology, $5 million of its money. In addition, we do not guarantee the debt, which is off balance sheet so far as WCC is concerned. One other way that we can look at these businesses is to look at cash flows to WCC, and cash return on investment to WCC. When we do that, because of the $867,000 in fees which are paid to WCC, |

there is some return. Although the return is small, it is reasonable at this stage of development of a new business. This business, because of the fees, has been in a loss position, but because of the fees it has shown a positive cash return on investment to WCC.

**Sheldon continued:**   Our actual return consists of the fees paid to WCC, or $867,000, and our share of the reported operating losses, for a net income of $221,000. That is the return on our approximately $5 million investment. If the subsidiary were wholly owned with a total investment of approximately $40 million, we would be looking at the $869,000 income before interest and taxes, to which we might decide to apply a tax, on the investment of $40 million. That is how we measure the performance of wholly-owned divisions.

One of the reasons that this report appears as it does was that, a few years ago, then current management decided to work from a single data base and to have one group prepare both the external financial reports and the management reports for internal use. It was a fine decision, except for the fact that the external reporters did not have the interest or ability to report what was actually going on in the affiliates.

Now, let's look at the report for our subsidiary in Poland (**Exhibit 3**). This plant is 100% owned, so we do not report any interest or fees. The total capital investment was funded by the company and totaled about $40 or $45 million including working capital. There is no external debt or minority interest and no fees. The other charges include the amortization of interest that was capitalized during the construction of the plant. The cost of sales includes some profit from materials that are purchased from other plants, but the prices paid are reasonable if you compare them with competitors' prices. This is another interesting problem that we struggle with, since we are probably reporting $2 or $3 million in profits elsewhere because of these plant purchases. But consider how this would look if we were deducting interest on $30 million of debt, and fees of 8% of revenues as we do in the case of the Prague affiliate. We would then be showing a loss from the business of about $3 million. The accountants do not consider this, and their report makes it appear that the business was doing just fine.

**Samantha Chu spoke up:**   Your explanation implies that there must be some other measures of performance that tell you how these plants are performing. What are those?

**Sheldon:**   We use budgets and the original business plans. We look at the performance against those expectations.

**Rogers:**   Also, although we do not monitor cash flows to the degree that we ought to, we have in our head the cash contribution compared to the amounts that we have invested. In the Czech Republic we can look ahead and see that in the future we will have a 35% to 45% cash on cash return. Poland is draining cash out of us at a remarkable rate, and we have not yet figured out a way to stop it. There are still a lot of unresolved business problems. Compared to the original business plan we have not been able to generate the revenues that were forecasted and the costs have been higher. We do not present cash flow reports to our managers, so these analyses all have to be done in our heads. The information we would need to bring this about formally is all available, but we just have not asked anyone to do it.

What we have are three new plants built at about the same time, each having very complex and different financial reporting issues that lead you to have completely different views of the business. Cynthia, show Samantha the report on the plant in Malaysia and what happens when we introduce an economic value added (EVA) approach. . . .

**Sheldon:**   The third plant was built to supply a high margin part of our business. That part of our business is truly a global business in that we can actually ship our product from any of several plants to anywhere in the world. When the decision to build a plant in Malaysia was made we were running out of capacity. We made a strategic decision that we wanted to be located in Malaysia, but this was to be part of our production facilities to serve the global market. We do not usually build a separate plant to supply only the high margin products. The volumes sold and shipped tend to be small, and adding the technostructure of technical service and laboratories to a plant makes the economics somewhat unfavorable unless there are several other units in the same plant producing higher volume products to help carry the costs of these necessary add-ons.

Looking at the column labeled "Region of Manufacture," you can see the sales and profitability of the manufacturing facility in Malaysia (**Exhibit 4**). It sells $12 million worth of product, and you can see that with the costs being what they are, the plant is losing a lot of money. The capital charge that we show is an attempt to get a measure of the economic value added by the plant. As was the case with Poland, this report does not include any interest on the total investment of almost $35 million, or any fees.

The EVA approach uses a 12% capital charge based on the assets employed including working capital including accounts payable and fixed capital. Depreciation is included in cost of sales. I think the way we use EVA is very simple, exactly the way it is employed by other folks, but some get much more sophisticated about allocations, capitalized research and development, and the like. We do not do that.

In addition we have recently started to look not just at "region of manufacture" but also at "region of sale," primarily to get an understanding of whether or not a market is attractive. The second column labeled "Region of Sale" is all product being sold in Southeast Asia even if it is being manufactured outside, so it includes the cost of manufacturing product, shipping it, and delivering it to customers in the region. On that basis the earnings before interest and taxes are about $4 million. If we wanted to get down to economic value added, we would need to deduct taxes and a capital charge and the economic value added would still be negative but not so much so that we could not develop some reasonable strategies to fix it compared to the region of manufacture measure which is pretty daunting.

**Stan Rogers interjected:** There is an incremental layer of complexity here in that this plant is starting to produce for the rest of the world because we are running out of capacity and are using this plant as the swing plant. Those shipments will show up in the Region of Manufacture numbers, but they will not show up in the Region of Sale numbers. We have not yet sorted this out, but my suspicion is that you cannot look at it this way and get an intriguing view—a solid view—of the business. We probably have to look at the whole system and analyze the incremental revenues and costs of the whole business.

The reason why I see this as another iteration of the same or complexity of the same problem, is that in Prague and Poland we had the different corporate structures that led to different accounting treatments of interest and fees, which gave us completely warped views on what was going on in the business. This presents the same challenge but adds the dimensions of region of manufacture and region of sale accounting and the need for total system analysis.

**Samantha Chu broke the silence of the pause which followed:** Have you found a solution to the problem yet?

**Rogers answered:** We understand it. We have not institutionalized a management reporting system that would lead someone who is intelligent but does not understand the background to understand what is really going on. We do not have a management reporting system in place that shows the relative performance of the three plants in a clear manner. On this basis the system does not work.

## *Some Possible Solutions to the Performance Measurement Problem*

Cynthia Sheldon began a discussion of some possible solutions to the division performance measurement problem:

> We are scratching away at a solution, perhaps using the concept of economic value added. We probably will also separate the people who are preparing the managerial reports from those who are concerned with external reporting, even though both groups will be working from the same databases. Until now, when we report to external public relations and to the chairman about the performance of the business, we have used external reporting standards and bases. I have concluded that to get away from that we have to have a separate group engaged with the businesses.

Stan Rogers chimed in:

> From a business standpoint we understand this we think. When we want to do a presentation we will do a one time analysis, pulling the numbers together that we think best reflect the situation. But we do not have a disciplined, repetitious reporting system that produces an analysis of how these businesses are doing in any other way than the way the external reporting system does it. That is an issue of priorities. We just do not have the time or resources to fix the system now. It is not that we do not understand the problem, or that we could not do it. I think we understand the problem, and we understand the intellectual underpinnings of a solution.
>
> I know that does not help you in responding to the analyst's questions today, so you will just have to respond very carefully.

Cynthia Sheldon continued:

> We are really just beginning to use EVA as a tool to get people to understand the issues. There is nothing wrong with using cash flow, return on net assets, and other familiar financial measures. There are always problems with any single financial measure, but right now in order to get people to focus it is easier to have one number and EVA is the most effective single number. We know that in order to make the business viable in our Southeast Asia region we have to go down a path of expanding the business. When you expand, EVA goes down, so if you focus on only that measure you risk saying that I do not want to do that. That is not the right answer. We are already seeing that kind of problem. But at least EVA gets people to focus on the cost of the capital associated with the income that they earn, and it gets more of a sense of cash flow, but we do not rely solely on it.

Stan Rogers summed up his feelings on the division performance measurement problems, echoing some of the conclusions of Sheldon:

> You know, I would say the same thing. There is not a planning department here that thinks about EVA and all that kind of stuff. We probably could use better numbers, but driving the business off any single number probably would not work.

## *Questions*

1.  What is causing the problems in measuring division performance at Western Chemical Corporation?
2.  Are there alternative methods for measuring division performance that would avoid the problems that WCC management is having with the methods that they have been using?
3.  Evaluate the approach to using economic value added (EVA) that WCC management is discussing and using experimentally. What are the strengths and weaknesses of this approach?
4.  How should the performance of divisions of WCC be measured?
5.  What should Samantha Chu tell the analyst if he asks specifically about the investments in the Czech Republic, Poland, and Malaysia?

## EXHIBIT 1 Financial Information by Geographic Area

Western Chemical Corporation (WCC) is engaged in the worldwide manufacture and sale of highly specialized service chemical programs. This includes production and service related to the sale and application of chemicals and technology used in water treatment, pollution control, energy conservation, and other industrial processes as well as a super-absorbent product for the disposable diaper market.

Within WCC, sales between geographic areas are made at prevailing market prices to customers minus an amount intended to compensate the sister WCC company for providing quality customer service.

Identifiable assets are those directly associated with operations of the geographic area. Corporate assets consist mainly of cash and cash equivalents; marketable securities; investments in unconsolidated partnerships, affiliates, and leveraged leases; and capital assets used for corporate purposes.

| Geographic Area Data (in millions) | | | |
|---|---|---|---|
| | 1994 | 1993 | 1992 |
| **Sales** | | | |
| North America | $ 886.9 | $ 915.1 | $ 883.7 |
| Europe | 288.9 | 315.6 | 346.5 |
| Latin America | 72.2 | 66.4 | 60.7 |
| Pacific | 127.7 | 116.7 | 108.2 |
| Sales between areas | (30.1) | (24.4) | (24.6) |
| | $1,345.6 | $1,389.4 | $1,374.5 |
| **Operating Earnings** | | | |
| North America | $181.6 | $216.9 | $211.3 |
| Europe | (10.2) | 41.8 | 48.9 |
| Latin America | 9.3 | 11.4 | 10.0 |
| Pacific | 14.3 | 14.4 | 14.4 |
| Expenses not allocated to areas | (20.3) | (21.6) | (24.3) |
| | $174.7 | $262.9 | $260.3 |
| **Identifiable Assets** | | | |
| North America | $ 485.2 | $ 566.6 | $ 562.2 |
| Europe | 245.2 | 227.4 | 225.5 |
| Latin America | 66.9 | 45.4 | 42.7 |
| Pacific | 147.9 | 126.3 | 124.7 |
| Corporate | 337.0 | 246.7 | 395.5 |
| | $1,282.2 | $1,212.4 | $1,350.6 |

*Exhibit 1    Continued*

Amounts for North America sales in the tabulation above include exports to the following areas:

| (IN MILLIONS) | 1994 | 1993 | 1992 |
|---|---|---|---|
| Latin America | $21.9 | $19.2 | $16.0 |
| All other | 7.3 | 13.0 | 12.0 |

The decrease in operating earnings in 1994 was mainly attributable to the pretax provision of $68 million for consolidation expenses. Of that amount, approximately $34 million was included in European operations.

| EXHIBIT 2    Income from Czech Republic Joint Venture ($ in thousands) | |
|---|---|
| | 9/95 YEAR-TO-DATE |
| Revenues | $11,510 |
| Cost of sales | (9,541) |
| Selling, technical expenses, and administrative expenses | (891) |
| Other income/Other charges | (209) |
| Income before interest and taxes | $    869 |
| Interest | (1,120) |
| Fees | (867) |
| Foreign exchange | (60) |
| Income (loss) | $ (1,178) |
| Minority interest | 532 |
| Taxes | — |
| Net income (loss) | $    (646) |

**EXHIBIT 3 Income from Poland Plant ($ in thousands)**

|  | 9/95 YEAR-TO-DATE |
|---|---|
| Revenues | $32,536 |
| Cost of sales | (28,458) |
| Selling, technical expenses, and administrative expenses | (2,529) |
| Other income/Other charges | (121) |
| Income before interest and taxes | $ 1,428 |
| Interest | — |
| Fees | — |
| Foreign exchange | 34 |
| Income | $1,462 |
| Minority interest | — |
| Taxes | — |
| Net income | $ 1,462 |

**EXHIBIT 4 Income from Malaysia and Southeast Asia ($ in thousands)**

|  | Region of Manufacture | Region of Sale |
|---|---|---|
|  | 9/95 YEAR-TO-DATE | 9/95 YEAR-TO-DATE |
| Revenues | $12,020 | $36,052 |
| Cost of sales | (12,392) | (26,648) |
| Selling, technical expenses, and administrative expenses | (3,775) | (4,845) |
| Other income/Other charges | (685) | (285) |
| Income before interest and taxes | $ (4,832) | $ 4,274 |
| Taxes (40%) | — | (1,710) |
| Net income | $ (4,832) | $ 2,564 |
| Capital charges | (3,600)[a] | (6,686)[b] |
| Economic value added | $ (8,432) | $ (4,122) |

[a] *$30,000 @ 12% = $3,600*
[b] *$110,000 @ 12% × [(36,052 − 12,020) / 102,800] + 30,000 @ 12% = $6,686*

## CASE 20    Chadwick, Inc.: The Balanced Scorecard

The "Balanced Scorecard"[1] article seemed to address the concerns of several division managers who felt that the company was over-emphasizing short-term financial results. But the process of getting agreement on what measures should be used proved a lot more difficult than I anticipated.

Bill Baron, Comptroller of Chadwick, Inc.

### Company Background

Chadwick, Inc. was a diversified producer of personal consumer products and pharmaceuticals. The Norwalk Division of Chadwick developed, manufactured and sold ethical drugs for human and animal use. It was one of five or six sizable companies competing in these markets and, while it did not dominate the industry, the company was considered well-managed and was respected for the high quality of its products. Norwalk did not compete by supplying a full range of products. It specialized in several niches and attempted to leverage its product line by continually searching for new applications for existing compounds.

Norwalk sold its products through several key distributors who supplied local markets, such as retail stores, hospitals and health service organizations, and veterinary practices. Norwalk depended on its excellent relations with the distributors who served to promote Norwalk's products to end users and also received feedback from the end users about new products desired by their customers.

Chadwick knew that its long-term success depended on how much money distributors could make by promoting and selling Norwalk's products. If the profit from selling Norwalk products was high, then these products were promoted heavily by the distributors and Norwalk received extensive communication back about future customer needs. Norwalk had historically provided many highly profitable products to the marketplace, but recent inroads by generic manufacturers had been eroding distributors' sales and profit margins. Norwalk had been successful in the past because of its track record of generating a steady stream of attractive, popular products. During the second half of the 1980s, however, the approval process for new products had lengthened and fewer big winners had emerged from Norwalk's R&D laboratories.

### Research and Development

The development of ethical drugs was a lengthy, costly, and unpredictable process. Development cycles now averaged about 12 years. The process started by screening a large number of compounds for potential benefits and use. For every drug that finally emerged as approved for use, up to 30,000 compounds had to be tested at the beginning of a new product development cycle. The development and testing processes had many stages. The development cycle started with the discovery of compounds that possessed the desirable

---

[1] Robert S. Kaplan and David P. Norton, "The Balanced Scorecard: Measures that Drive Performance," *Harvard Business Review* (January–February 1992).

properties and ended many years later with extensive and tedious testing and documentation to demonstrate that the new drug could meet government regulations for promised benefits, reliability in production, and absence of deleterious side effects.

Approved and patented drugs could generate enormous revenues for Norwalk and its distributors. Norwalk's profitability during the 1980s was sustained by one key drug that had been discovered in the late 1960s. No blockbuster drug had emerged during the 1980s, however, and the existing pipeline of compounds going through development, evaluation and test was not as healthy as Norwalk management desired. Management was placing pressure on scientists in the R&D lab to increase the yield of promising new products and to reduce the time and costs of the product development cycle. Scientists were currently exploring new bio-engineering techniques to create compounds that had the specific active properties desired rather than depending on an almost random search through thousands of possible compounds. The new techniques started with a detailed specification of the chemical properties that a new drug should have and then attempted to synthesize candidate compounds that could be tested for these properties. The bio-engineering procedures were costly, requiring extensive investment in new equipment and computer-based analysis.

A less expensive approach to increase the financial yield from R&D investments was to identify new applications for existing compounds that had already been approved for use. While some validation still had to be submitted for government approval to demonstrate the effectiveness of the drug in the new applications, the cost of extending an existing product to a new application was much, much less expensive than developing and creating an entirely new compound. Several valuable suggestions for possible new applications from existing products had come from Norwalk salesmen in the field. The salesmen were now being trained not only to sell existing products for approved applications, but also to listen to end users who frequently had novel and interesting ideas about how Norwalk's products could be used for new applications.

## Manufacturing

Norwalk's manufacturing processes were considered among the best in the industry. Management took pride in the ability of the manufacturing operation to quickly and efficiently ramp up to produce drugs once they had cleared governmental regulatory processes. Norwalk's manufacturing capabilities also had to produce the small batches of new products that were required during testing and evaluation stages.

## Performance Measurement

Chadwick allowed its several divisions to operate in a decentralized fashion. Division managers had almost complete discretion in managing all the critical processes: R&D, Production, Marketing and Sales, and administrative functions such as finance, human resources, and legal. Chadwick set challenging financial targets for divisions to meet. The targets were usually expressed as Return on Capital Employed (ROCE). As a diversified company, Chadwick wanted to be able to deploy the returns from the most profitable divisions to those divisions that held out the highest promise for profitable growth. Monthly financial summaries were submitted by each division to corporate headquarters. The Chadwick executive committee, consisting of the Chief Executive Officer, the Chief Operating Officer, two Executive Vice Presidents, and the Chief Financial Officer met monthly with each division manager to review ROCE performance and backup financial information for the preceding month.

## *The Balanced Scorecard Project*

Bill Baron, Comptroller of Chadwick, had been searching for improved methods for evaluating the performance of the various divisions. Division managers complained about the continual pressure to meet short-term financial objectives in businesses that required extensive investments in risky projects to yield long-term returns. The idea of a Balanced Scorecard appealed to him as a constructive way to balance short-run financial objectives with the long-term performance of the company.

Baron brought the article and concept to Dan Daniels the President and Chief Operating officer of Chadwick. Daniels shared Baron's enthusiasm for the concept, feeling that a Balanced Scorecard would allow Chadwick divisional managers more flexibility in how they measured and presented their results of operations to corporate management. He also liked the idea of holding managers accountable for improving the long-term performance of their division.

After several days of reflection, Daniels issued a memorandum to all Chadwick division managers. The memo had a simple and direct message: Read the Balanced Scorecard article, develop a scorecard for your division, and be prepared to come to corporate headquarters in 90 days to present and defend the divisional scorecard to Chadwick's Executive Committee.

John Greenfield, the Division Manager at Norwalk, received Daniel's memorandum with some concern and apprehension. In principle, Greenfield liked the idea of developing a scorecard that would be more responsive to his operations, but he was distrustful of how much freedom he had to develop and use such a scorecard. Greenfield recalled:

> "This seemed like just another way for corporate to claim that they have decentralized decision-making and authority while still retaining ultimate control at headquarters."

Greenfield knew that he would have to develop a plan of action to meet corporate's request but lacking a clear sense of how committed Chadwick was to the concept, he was not prepared to take much time from his or his subordinates' existing responsibilities for the project.

The next day, at the weekly meeting of the Divisional Operating Committee, Greenfield distributed the Daniels memo and appointed a three man committee, headed by Divisional Controller, Wil Wagner, to facilitate the process for creating the Norwalk Balanced Scorecard.

Wagner approached Greenfield later that day:

> "I read the Balanced Scorecard article. Based on my understanding of the concept, we must start with a clearly defined business vision. I'm not sure I have a clear understanding of the vision and business strategy for Norwalk. How can I start to build the scorecard without this understanding?"

Greenfield admitted:

> "That's a valid point. Let me see what I can do to get you started."

Greenfield picked up a pad of paper and started to write. Several minutes later he had produced a short business strategy statement for Norwalk (see **Exhibit 1**). Wagner and his group took Greenfield's strategy statement and started to formulate scorecard measures for the division.

Several days later, Greenfield sent Wagner a copy of a memo that he had just received from Dan Daniels. The President had decided that he wanted all the divisions to follow some guiding principles as they developed their scorecards. The memo reiterated Daniels' initial principle that each division should develop the scorecard "that was right for the division." But he wanted all scorecards to use quantitative, objective data. Daniels had heard that several divisions wanted to include measures on customer satisfaction that would be collected from surveys and interviews. Daniels wanted only "hard data" on the scorecard. Opinions measured in surveys may be collected for internal divisional purposes but such information was not to be sent up to corporate headquarters or discussed in Executive Committee reviews of divisional operations. Wagner was not surprised by this restriction. He recalled hearing Executive Committee members, on several occasions, declaring that only "hard data" counted. Wagner thought, as he re-read Daniels' memo, "I guess tough-minded managers at Chadwick don't use 'soft data'."

## Creating Norwalk's Balanced Scorecard

The Scorecard project arrived at a time when Wil Wagner and the two other members of his team already had heavily booked calendars. Several weeks passed before the team could really start to meet and focus on the project. Several more weeks passed before the team could schedule a meeting with the top divisional management of Norwalk. Such a meeting was thought necessary to solicit more information about divisional strategy and key success factors, and to get feedback on the tentative set of measures the project team had formulated.

After many postponements, a one day meeting was scheduled with senior divisional management to comment on the Wagner team's proposed scorecard. This meeting took place only ten days before Greenfield would present the scorecard to the Chadwick Executive Committee at corporate headquarters. Wagner felt that a full day meeting would be necessary to achieve the final consensus so he scheduled the meeting off-site at a hotel, one block from Norwalk's offices. By staying away from office distractions, Wagner hoped that division management could focus on the details of the scorecard design.

Wagner arrived early at the hotel meeting site. He received a message from Greenfield's secretary that the division general manager would be delayed in arriving at the meeting, but that the meeting should start without him. Wagner opened the meeting with 10 top managers (other than Greenfield). He outlined the ground rules established by President Daniels, reviewed Greenfield's strategy statement for Norwalk, and suggested a process to develop and review measures for each of the four perspectives of the Balanced Scorecard.[2] As Wagner finished his opening statement, he was distressed to discover that Mike Hassler, the VP of Marketing, was not present in the room. Wagner learned that Hassler was negotiating a contract with Norwalk's largest distributor and could not join the meeting until 3:00 P.M.

The group of 10 managers started to discuss financial and customer-based measures and Wagner was pleased with the enthusiasm the group was bringing to the task. But after about 25 minutes, the phone in the hotel meeting room rang. Hassler needed to speak with the Sales vice president. Wagner attempted to maintain the momentum of the discussion with the other nine managers, but the telephone conversations going on in the background was clearly distracting the group.

---

[2] The four perspectives described in the article were: financial, customer, internal process, and innovation and learning.

By the end of the day, the phone had rung seven more times to pull managers out of the discussion to take care of company business. Greenfield never showed up. Wagner, however, persisted under the difficult conditions and was able to mobilize the managers in attendance to produce a Balanced Scorecard for the Norwalk Division (see **Exhibit 2**). Wagner briefed Greenfield on the scorecard at a breakfast meeting several days later, prior to Greenfield's appearance at Chadwick Corporate Headquarters.

## EXHIBIT 1  Norwalk Pharmaceutical Division— Business Strategy

1. **Manage Norwalk portfolio of investments**

   - minimize cost to executing our existing business base
   - maximize return/yield on all development spending
   - invest in discovery of new compounds

2. **Satisfy customer needs**
3. **Drive responsibility to the lowest level**

   - minimize centralized staff overhead

4. **People development**

   - industry training
   - unique mix of technical and commercial skills

## EXHIBIT 2  Norwalk Pharmaceutical Division

| FINANCIAL MEASURES | CUSTOMER MEASURES | INTERNAL MEASURES | INNOVATION MEASURES |
|---|---|---|---|
| Net Contribution | Market Share for key markets | Price index for "basket" of formulation | $ Revenue from New Products introduced in last 3 years |
| Working Capital | Customer Complaint Rate | Cost index for technical compounds | |
| Operating Profit After Taxes | | Capital Turnover | |
| | | Inventory turns by product class | |
| | | Gross Margin $ | |
| | | SG&A $ | |

**CASE 21**  Mobil USM&R (A): Linking the Balanced Scorecard

From what I can see, we had a good quarter even though financial results were disappointing. The poor results were caused by unusually warm winter weather that depressed sales of natural gas and home heating oil. But market shares in our key customer segments were up. Refinery operating expenses were down. And the results from our employee-satisfaction survey were high. In all the areas we could control, we moved the needle in the right direction.

B ob McCool, executive vice president of Mobil Corporation's U.S. Marketing and Refining (USM&R) Division, had just commented on first quarter 1995 results.

One executive thought to himself:

This is a total departure from the past. Here was a senior Mobil executive publicly saying, "Hey, we didn't make any money this quarter but I feel good about where the business is going."

### Mobil U.S. Marketing & Refining

Mobil Corporation, headquartered in Fairfax, Virginia, and with operations in more than 100 countries is, with Exxon and Shell, among the world's top three integrated oil, gas, and petrochemicals companies. Mobil's 1995 return-on-capital-employed of 12.8% ranked it 4th among the 14 major integrated oil companies; its 19.1% average annual return to shareholders from 1991 to 1995 was the highest among the 14 major oil companies and exceeded the average annual return on the S&P 500 by more than 2 percentage points. Summary sales and earnings information are shown in **Exhibit 1.**

The corporation consists of five major divisions: Exploration & Producing (the "upstream" business), Marketing & Refining (the "downstream" business), Chemical, Mining & Minerals, and Real Estate. The Marketing & Refining (M&R) Division processes crude oil into fuels, lubricants, petrochemical feedstocks and other products at 20 refineries in twelve countries. M&R also distributes Mobil products to 19,000 service stations and other outlets in more than 100 countries. Total product sales had grown more than 5% per year over the past five years.

The United States Marketing & Refining (USM&R) Division was the fifth-largest U.S. refiner. It operated five state-of-the-art refineries, and its more than 7,700 Mobil-branded service stations sold about 23 million gallons per day of gasoline. This represented a 7% national share (number four in the United States). Mobil's retail network was highly concentrated. In the eighteen states where it sold nearly 95% of its gasoline, Mobil had a 12% market share. Mobil was also the largest marketer of finished lubricants in the United States, with a 12% market share and recent growth rates of about 3%, especially in premium quality blends.

In 1992, USM&R had reported an operating loss from its refining and marketing operations, and ranked 12 out of 13 oil companies in profitability from U.S. marketing and

*Professor Robert S. Kaplan prepared this case as the basis for class discussion rather than to illustrate either effective or ineffective handling of an administrative situation. Mr. Ed Lewis of Mobil's Business and Performance Analysis group provided invaluable assistance.*

refining operations.[1] A profit turnaround started in 1993, and earnings and return-on-assets, which had been depressed in 1991 and 1992, soon exceeded industry averages. Summary financial data of the USM&R Division are presented in **Exhibit 2.**

Until 1994, USM&R was organized functionally. The supply group obtained crude oil and transported it to one of Mobil's refineries. The manufacturing function operated refineries that processed crude oil into products like gasoline, kerosene, heating oil, diesel fuel, jet fuel, lubricants, and petrochemical feedstocks. The product supply organization transported refined petroleum products, through pipelines, barges, and trucks, to regional terminals around the country. The terminal managers received, stored, and managed the extensive inventories of petroleum products and distributed the products to retailers and distributors. The marketing function determined how USM&R would package, distribute, and sell Mobil products through wholesalers and retailers to end-use consumers.

## Reorganization: 1994

In the early 1990s, USM&R faced an environment with flat demand for gasoline and other petroleum products, increased competition, and limited capital to invest in a highly capital-intense business. McCool recalled:

> In 1990 we weren't making any money; in fact there was a half-billion-dollar cash drain. Expenses had doubled, capital had doubled, margins had flattened, and volumes were heading down. You didn't need an MBA to know we were in trouble.

McCool spent the next couple of years attempting to stabilize the business to stop the bleeding.

> We succeeded, but then we had to confront how we could generate future growth.

A climate survey in 1993 revealed that employees felt internal reporting requirements, administrative processes, and top-down policies were stifling creativity and innovation. Relationships with customers were adversarial, and people were working narrowly to enhance the reported results of their individual, functional units. McCool, with the assistance of external consultants, initiated major studies of business processes and organizational effectiveness. Based on the studies, McCool concluded that if USM&R were to grow, it had to make the most of its existing assets and to focus more intensively on customers, giving motorists what *they* want, not what the functional specialists in the organization thought motorists should want.

In 1994, McCool decided to decentralize decision making to managers and employees who would be closer to customers. He reorganized USM&R into 17 Natural Business Units (NBUs) and 14 Service Companies (see **Exhibit 3**). The NBUs included (1) sales and distribution units, (2) integrated refining, sales and distribution units, and (3) specialized product (e.g., distillates, lubricants, gas liquids) and process (stand-alone refinery) units. McCool commented on the need for the reorganization:

> We had grown up as a highly functional organization. We had a huge staff, and they ran the business. We needed to get our staff costs under control. But more important, we had to learn to focus on the customer. We had to get everyone in the organization thinking not how to do their individual job a little bit better, but how to focus all of their energies to enhancing Mobil products and services for customers.

---

[1] Source: "Benchmarking the Integrated Oils, 1995," U.S. Research (Goldman Sachs, July 15, 1996), pp. 83, 85.

Brian Baker, vice president of USM&R, concurred:

> We were a big central organization that had become a bit cumbersome and perhaps had lost touch with the customer. We didn't have the ability to move quickly with new marketing programs in various parts of the country.

USM&R's reorganization occurred simultaneously with a newly developed strategy on customer segmentation. Historically, Mobil, like other oil companies, attempted to maintain volume and growth by marketing a full range of products and services to all consumer segments. The gasoline marketing group had conducted a recent study that revealed five distinct consumer segments among the gasoline-buying public (see **Exhibit 4** for descriptions of the five segments):

- Road Warriors (18%)
- True Blues (16%)
- Generation F3 (27%)
- Homebodies (21%)
- Price Shoppers (20%)

USM&R decided that its efforts should be focused on the first three of these segments (61% of gasoline buyers), and not attempt to attract the price-sensitive but low-loyalty Price Shopper segment that accounted for only 20% of consumers. The new strategy required a commitment to upgrade all service stations so that they could offer fast, friendly, safe service to the three targeted customer segments. It also required a major shift in the role for Mobil's on-site convenience stores (C-stores). Currently, C-stores were snack shops that catered to gasoline purchasers' impulse buying. USM&R wanted to redesign and reorient its C-stores so that they would become a destination stop, offering consumers one-stop, convenient shopping for frequently purchased food and snack items.

## USM&R Balanced Scorecard

The newly appointed business unit managers had all grown up within a structured, top-down, functional organization. Some had been district sales managers, others had managed a pipeline or a regional distribution network. McCool anticipated problems with the transition:

> We were taking people who had spent their whole professional life as managers in a big functional organization, and we were asking them to become the leaders of more entrepreneurial profit-making businesses, some with up to a $1 billion in assets. How were we going to get them out of their historic area of functional expertise to think strategically, as general managers of profit-oriented businesses?

McCool realized that the new organization and strategy required a new measurement system. Historically, USM&R relied on local functional measures: low cost for manufacturing and distribution operations, availability for dealer-based operations, margins and volume for marketing operations, and environmental and safety indicators for the staff group in charge of environment, health, and safety. McCool was unhappy with these metrics:

> We were still in a controller's mentality, reviewing the past, not guiding the future. The functional metrics didn't communicate what we were about. I didn't want metrics that reinforced our historic control mentality. I wanted them to be part of a communication process by which everyone in the organization could understand and implement our strategy. We needed better metrics so that our planning process could be linked to actions, to encourage people to do the things that the organization was now committed to.

Baker also noted the need for new metrics:

> Our people were fixated on volume and margins at the dealer level. Marketing didn't want to lose gasoline dealers. But we didn't have any focus or measurement on dealer quality so we often franchised dealers who didn't sustain our brand image. Also, we drove so hard for short-term profits that when volumes declined, our marketing people attempted to achieve their profit figure by raising prices. You can do that for a while if you have a strong brand, which we have, but you can't sustain this type of action for the long term.

In mid-1993, Ed Lewis, formerly the financial manager for U.S. marketing, was on a special assignment with Dan Riordan, deputy controller of USM&R, to examine the effectiveness of financial analysis for the entire division. They concluded that a lot of excellent financial analysis was being done—plenty of measures, plenty of analysis—but none of it was linked to the division's strategy. In late 1993, Lewis saw an article on the Balanced Scorecard[2] and thought,

> This could be what we are looking for. We were viewed as a flavor-of-the-month operation. Our focus shifted frequently so that if you didn't like what we were doing today, just wait; next month we will be doing something different. Nothing we did tied to any mission. The Balanced Scorecard seemed different. It was a process that tied measurement to the organization's mission and strategy. It could start us on the journey to implement USM&R's new organization and strategy by keeping us focused on where we were heading.

Lewis and Riordan recommended to McCool that USM&R develop a Balanced Scorecard. McCool was receptive since he had heard of the concept in a briefing he had received earlier that year. USM&R's senior management team launched a BSC project in early 1994. They hired Renaissance Solutions, the consulting company founded by David Norton, a co-author of the Balanced Scorecard article, to assist in the process.

A senior-level Steering Committee, consisting of McCool, Baker, the vice presidents of all staff functions, the division controller, and the manager of financial analysis of downstream operations, provided oversight and guidance for the BSC project. The actual project team was led by Lewis and Riordan, assisted by Renaissance consultants.

Starting in January 1994, Lewis and his project team conducted two-hour individual interviews with all members of the leadership team to understand each person's thoughts on the new strategy. The team synthesized the information received from the interviews and, with David Norton facilitating, led several workshops to develop specific objectives and measures for the four Balanced Scorecard perspectives: financial, customer, internal business process, and learning and growth. The workshops always involved active dialogues and debates about the implications of the new strategy. Lewis noted:

> Forcing the managers, during the workshops, to narrow the strategy statements into strategic objectives in the four perspectives really developed alignment to the new strategy. You could just see a consensus develop during the three-month period.

Among the new aspects of the USM&R scorecard was a recognition that the division had two types of customers. The immediate customer was, of course, the extensive network of franchised dealers who purchased gasoline and petroleum products from Mobil. The other customer was the millions of consumers who purchased Mobil products from independent

---

[2] R. S. Kaplan and D. P. Norton, "The Balanced Scorecard—Measures that Drive Performance," *Harvard Business Review* (January–February, 1992).

dealers and retailers. The project team wanted the customer perspective on the scorecard to incorporate strategic objectives and measures for both types of customers.

By May 1994, the project team had developed a tentative formulation of the USM&R scorecard. At that point, they brought in more managers and split into eight sub-teams to enhance and refine the strategic objectives and measures: a Financial team (headed by the VP of Strategic Planning); two Customer teams—one focused on dealers, the other on consumers; a Manufacturing team, focused on measures for refineries and manufacturing cost; a Supply team, focused on inventory management and laid-down delivered cost; an Environmental, Health and Safety team; a Human Resources team; and an Information Technology team. Each sub-team identified objectives, measures, and targets for its assigned area.

The teams also identified when new mechanisms were needed to supply some of the desired measures. For example, the strategy to delight consumers in the three targeted market segments required that all Mobil gasoline stations deliver a speedy purchase, have friendly, helpful employees, and recognize consumer loyalty. At the time, however, no measures existed to evaluate dealer performance on these now critical processes. The consumer-focused customer sub-team developed a Mystery Shopper program in which a third-party vendor purchased gasoline and snacks at each Mobil station on a monthly basis. The shopper scored dealer performance on 23 specific items related to exterior station appearance, service islands, sales area, personnel, and rest rooms. The mystery shopper performance score would be a measure in the customer perspective of USM&R's Balanced Scorecard.

The dealer-focused customer sub-team launched an initiative to support the dealer development strategy. The team developed a tool kit that would help marketing representatives evaluate and work with dealers to improve performance in seven business areas: financial management, service bays, personnel management, car wash, convenience stores, gasoline purchasing, and a better buying experience for customers. The marketing representatives would give a rating to dealers to identify existing strengths and opportunities for improvement. The goal was to increase the profit performance of dealers and wholesale marketers of Mobil products, as measured by Total Gross Profit of dealers and the monthly gross margin from Alternative Profit Centers (APC)—convenience stores and service bays.

By August 1994, the eight sub-teams had developed specific strategic objectives for the four Balanced Scorecard perspectives (see **Exhibit 5**) and selected the initial set of measures for these objectives (see **Exhibit 6**). The process had consumed two to three full-time equivalent weeks from all members of the Executive Leadership Team (McCool and all his direct reports, including the managers of the business units).

Between June and August 1994, while the sub-teams had been refining the strategic objectives and measures, the Steering Committee went through each perspective to identify one or two critical themes. The project team produced a brochure to communicate these strategic themes to all of USM&R's 11,000 employees. In August 1994, USM&R announced its initial Balanced Scorecard and distributed the brochure (see **Exhibit 7**).

## Linking the Balanced Scorecard to NBUs and Servcos

While the USM&R scorecard was still being developed in April 1994, the project team launched pilots to develop business unit scorecards (in the West Coast and Midwest NBUs). Senior management wanted the NBUs to work from the strategic themes established at the USM&R Division level and to translate the division strategy into local, NBU objectives and measures that would reflect the particular opportunities and competitive environment encountered by each NBU. This was part of McCool's belief that NBU managers had to learn to take responsibility for the strategy of their business units.

Ed Lewis, with consultant support, went to the NBUs and replicated the scorecard development process with their personnel:

> We did the interviews, conducted the workshops, and, over a six week period, developed a local scorecard. We used the USM&R scorecard as a guiding light, but that's all it was, a light. When an NBU developed a scorecard, it was their scorecard and they would live by it.

McCool concurred:

> Mobil in the Midwest is not the same as Mobil in New England, or on the West Coast. In each market, the consumer looks at us differently, our competition in each region is different, and the economics of operating in each market are different. I don't want to dictate a solution from Fairfax. We have a basic strategy and set of support programs that we can roll out to each NBU. We do have a few constraints: we want our dealers to operate under a sign that says "Mobil," there's a basic design for the station and for the C-store that we want to share across regions, and we think we have a winning segmentation strategy with fast and friendly service. But if an NBU thinks it has a better driver for success, I'm willing to hear it. I want the NBU head to tell me, here's my business, this is my vision and strategy, and this is how I am going get there from here. Our job in Fairfax is to approve (or disapprove) the strategy and ask what additional resources they might need to get the job done.

Lewis recalled:

> When I first started speaking to NBU managers in the workshops about the C-store focus and measurement, 90% of them thought I was off my rocker. They told me that their business was selling gasoline, not snacks. We told them that the USM&R scorecard was assessing C-store progress through a measure of APC revenues per square foot. Eventually, the NBUs agreed to include this measure on their scorecards so that they would be aligned with the Fairfax scorecard.

> A year later, however, all the NBUs had bought into the C-store strategy. They concurred that developing a new C-store design, and making it a destination stop for consumers, was now a differentiator for the company. They even forced us to change the way we measure C-store sales, from aggregate revenues per square foot to revenues per month (same store sales per period) and gross profit percentage because that's the way the best retailers like 7-11 and Walmart evaluated themselves.

The NBU scorecards, in general, mirrored the USM&R scorecard, though with slightly fewer measures, particularly in the internal perspective since the NBUs were focused on particular functions—such as regional marketing and sales, refining, and distribution—so the full range of internal measures were not relevant to each NBU.[3]

Several of the NBUs devoted a section of their monthly newsletters to Balanced Scorecard information. In the first few issues, the section reviewed a single scorecard perspective, explaining the importance of the perspective, articulating the reasoning behind the specific objectives that had been selected, and describing the measures that would be used to motivate and monitor performance for that perspective. After communicating the purpose and content of the scorecard in the first few issues, the content of the newsletter section shifted from education to feedback. Each issue reported recent results on the measures for one of the perspectives. Raw numbers and trends were supplemented with the human stories on how a department or an individual was contributing to the reported performance. The vignettes communicated to the workforce how individuals and teams were taking local initiatives to help the organization implement its strategy. The stories created role models of individual employees contributing to strategy implementation through their day-to-day activities.

---

[3] See USM&R (B) and (C) (HBS Nos. 197-026 and 197-027) for description of the Balanced Scorecards developed by the New England Sales & Distribution and Lubes NBUs.

### Servco Service Agreements and Balanced Scorecards

The Steering Committee also wanted the servcos to be accountable for their performance. Previously, each staff function operated from the Fairfax headquarters, providing strategy, direction, and services to the field organization. After the reorganization, staff functions were now free-standing service units that had to sell services to the NBUs and get agreement from them on prices and level of service provided. USM&R established buyers committees, consisting of 3 to 5 representatives from the NBUs, to work with each servco. In this way the offerings from every servco would be linked to the mission and strategy of NBUs and to USM&R. Eventually, each servco and its buyers committee agreed on the priorities and prices for the offerings it would provide. Dan Zivny, manager of Finance and Information Services, endorsed the new process:

> Discussions with the buyers committee helped us to communicate to the NBUs about what we do and what our deliverables will be. Previously, the NBUs would complain about the costs and charges for information services. Now the NBUs are part of the process that specifies the outputs we will produce and the prices we will charge.

Several of the servcos began to develop their own Balanced Scorecards.[4] Marty Di Mezza, manager of the Gasoline Marketing servco, noted:

> The service agreement with the buyers committee and our Balanced Scorecard have enabled my organization to become more customer focused. People now realize they have to sell their services and that we have to fit into the entire picture of USM&R.

In addition to developing their own BSC's, key servco people were assigned to collect the data and report on each measure on the USM&R scorecard. Each measure was assigned to a "metric owner" (see **Exhibit 8** for list of metrics and metric owners). For example, DiMezza's Gasoline Marketing organization owned the Mystery Shopper and Dealer Gross Profit metrics. The metric owners verified that the measures appropriately reflected the strategic objectives, and could, based on feedback from the field, make recommendations to the Executive Leadership Team for modified or new measures. People within the metric owner's servco collected the actual data from operations and reported current values of the measures to the metric owner.

### Linking the Balanced Scorecard to Compensation

All salaried employees of USM&R were tied to the Mobil corporate award program. This program was based on performance relative to Mobil's top seven competitors on two financial measures: return-on-capital employed and earnings-per-share growth (see **Exhibit 9**). This program awarded up to a 10% bonus if Mobil ranked #1 on ROCE and EPS growth.

McCool initiated an additional program within USM&R that awarded bonuses up to 20% to managers in each business unit. NBU employees got 30% of the award based on USM&R performance, and 70% based on their NBU performance. Servco employees also got 30% on USM&R performance, 20% on the linkages to other business units, and 50% on their servco BSC. The linkage measures for servcos represented the objectives and results they could influence either in the NBUs or at USM&R.

---

[4] See USM&R (D) (HBS No. 197-028) for description of the Balanced Scorecard developed for the Gasoline Marketing servco.

The bonus plan was part of a new variable pay compensation program. Employees' base pay reference point had been reduced to 90% of competitive market wages. The remaining 10% of compensation could be achieved with average performance on three factors:

- A component based on the two corporate financial performance competitive rankings
- A division component based on the USM&R Balanced Scorecard metrics
- A business unit component based on key performance indicators, from the NBU or servco Balanced Scorecard metrics

An additional 20% of compensation could be received for exceptional performance along these three components. The theory for the variable pay plan was simple: award below average compensation for below average performance, average pay for average performance, and above average pay for above average performance.[5]

McCool wanted each business unit to work with the metric owners to develop its own targets for the scorecard measures. In addition, the BUs assigned a percentage weight associated with achieving this target. This percentage, which summed to 100 across all the targeted measures, would determine the relative contribution of each scorecard measure to the bonus pool. Most business units chose to weight all measures on their scorecards; the remaining one still weighted most of their scorecard measures. Only one business unit put more than a 50% weight on its financial measures.

The business units, beyond establishing targets for each scorecard measure, also assigned a performance factor that represented the perceived degree of difficulty of target achievement (see **Exhibit 10**). The performance factor would be multiplied by the weight assigned to the measure to arrive at a total performance amount, much the way a diving competition is scored (absolute performance on a dive gets weighted by the dive's degree of difficulty). The maximum index score of 1.25 occurred when the target would put the Mobil unit as best-in-class. An average target received a performance factor of 1.00, and a factor score as low as 0.7 would be applied when the target represented poor performance, or was deemed very easy to achieve. The individual business units proposed the performance factors for each measure, but these had to be explained and defended in a review with the Executive Leadership Team and metric owners. Business unit managers also were able to see (and comment on) the targets, weights, and performance factors proposed by the other BUs.

Brian Baker was a strong advocate for the indexed targets:

> Historically, people were rewarded for meeting targets and penalized when they missed a target. So sandbagging targets became an art form around here. I prefer the current system where I can give a better rating to a manager who stretches for a target and falls a little short than to someone who sandbags with an easy target and then beats it.

### Reviewing the Balanced Scorecards

McCool reflected on the experience to date with the Balanced Scorecard:

> It's enabled us to teach the NBU managers about strategy; about lead and lag indicators; and to think across the organization, nor just in functional silos. It's exposed the managers to issues outside their expertise and to understand the linkages they have with other parts of the organization. People now talk about things that are outside their immediate responsibility, like safety, environment, and C-stores. The scorecard has provided a common language, a good basis for communication.

---

[5] In addition, the plan included individual awards, administered within a narrow range, to adjust for performance not captured by the metrics. Business unit managers were awarded a fixed "pot of money" for such individual awards, but this allowance could not be overspent.

We were also fortunate that when Mobil asked us to go to a pay-for-performance plan we could use our scorecard measures. Variable pay plans only work if you have a good set of metrics. Managers accepted the compensation plan based on the scorecard since they believed the measures represented well what they were trying to achieve.

The learning and growth perspective has been the biggest problem. Ultimately, that perspective will be the differentiator for the company, our people's ability to learn and to apply that learning. The good news is at least we now talk about learning, as much as we talk about gross margin. But we are struggling to get good output measures for the learning objective.

McCool commented on the changes in the meetings he conducts with NBU managers:

For a meeting with an NBU manager, like West Coast, I have the manager plus representatives from various servcos, like supply, marketing, and C-stores. And we have a conversation. In the past we were a bunch of controllers sitting around talking about variances. Now we discuss what's gone right, what's gone wrong. What should we keep doing, what should we stop doing? What resources do we need to get back on track, not explaining a negative variance due to some volume mix.

The process enables me to see how the NBU managers think, plan, and execute. I can see the gaps, and by understanding the manager's culture and mentality, I can develop customized programs to make him or her a better manager.

Baker commented on the reviews he recently conducted with the managers of nine NBUs and four Servcos that reported to him:

I went into these reviews thinking they would be long and arduous. I was pleasantly surprised how simple they were. Managers came in prepared. They were paying attention to their scorecards and using them in a very productive way—to drive their organization hard to achieve the targets. How they weighted their measures spoke clearly about their priorities of relative importance up and down the four perspectives.

Basically, there's no way I can understand and supervise all the activities that report to me. I need a device like the scorecard where the business unit managers are measuring their own performance. My job is to keep adjusting the light I shine on their strategy and implementation, to monitor and guide their journeys, and see whether there are any potential storms on the horizon that we should address.

Baker felt that relying on only a single financial measure, like earnings or return-on-capital-employed, was dangerous.

A big shareholder may not care about local business conditions or competitive environments. Just achieve a 12% ROCE, produce the money, and don't tell me about your problems. That's his right as the shareholder, and some people would say, "Those are the rules, and let's set strict earnings objectives for each of our business units and that's it."

But there's another side of me that says to motivate people there are things managers can influence and things they cannot. In a strong market, you can do a bloody bad job and have a great year. And you can do a superb job and fall way short of earnings because the market was so weak. The score-card has several elements that help me understand how well a manager performs against the market. Without the understanding we now have from the scorecard, we would force people to do some pretty bizarre things to make short-term earnings targets, and they could be gone before the problems fall in.

Managers do seem to be using the scorecard for their management processes. They're not just doing it because McCool and I have imposed it on them. It's a system they know that everyone is using; all the other business units are living by the same set of rules. That's incredibly important. Also, the degree of difficulty index allowed them to be more ambitious and aggressive in setting their targets.

McCool concluded:

> In 3 to 4 years, we have come from an operation that was worst in its peer group, draining a half billion dollars a year, to a company that ranks #1 in its peer group, and generates hundreds of millions of dollars of positive cash flow.[6]

> The Balanced Scorecard has been a major contributor. It's helped us to focus our initiatives and to keep them aligned with our strategic objectives. It's been a great communication tool for telling the story of the business and a great learning tool as well. People now see how their daily job contributes to USM&R performance. Our challenge is how can we sustain this performance. We have just seen the tip of the iceberg. I want people to use the scorecard to focus attention on the great opportunities for growth.

**EXHIBIT 1    Mobil Summary Financial Information, 1991–1995 (000,000)**

|  | 1991 | 1992 | 1993 | 1994 | 1995 |
|---|---|---|---|---|---|
| Revenues | $63,311 | $64,456 | $63,975 | $67,383 | $75,370 |
| Operating earnings | 1,894 | 1,488 | 2,224 | 2,231 | 2,846 |
| Capital and exploration expenditures | 5,053 | 4,470 | 3,656 | 3,825 | 4,268 |
| Capital employed at year-end | 25,804 | 25,088 | 25,333 | 24,946 | 24,802 |
| Debt-to-capital ratio | 32% | 34% | 32% | 31% | 27% |
| Rates of return based on: |  |  |  |  |  |
|   Average S/H equity | 10.9% | 8.8% | 13.2% | 13.2% | 16.2% |
|   Industry average |  |  |  | 10.0% | 14.0% |
|   Average capital employed | 9.4% | 7.5% | 10.2% | 10.3% | 12.8% |
|   Industry average |  |  |  | 8.1% | 10.0% |

---

[6] USM&R's 1995 income per barrel of $1.02 greatly exceeded the industry average of $0.65. Global operating return from refining, marketing and transportation operations of 10.1% per dollar of assets was the highest in the industry (up from 8.6% and 5th place in 1994). Source: "Benchmarking The Integrated Oils, 1995," U.S. Research (Goldman Sachs, July 15, 1996) pp. 7, 9.

**EXHIBIT 2**   **U.S. Marketing and Refining: Financial Summary, 1991–1995 (000,000)**

|  | 1991 | 1992 | 1993 | 1994 | 1995 |
|---|---|---|---|---|---|
| Sales and services |  |  |  |  |  |
| Refined petroleum products | $10,134 | $10,504 | $10,560 | $10,920 | $ 2,403 |
| Other sales and services | 3,879 | 3,702 | 3,481 | 3,522 | 3,698 |
| Total sales and services | $14,013 | $14,206 | $14,041 | $14,442 | $16,101 |
| Excise and state gasoline taxes | 2,421 | 2,606 | 2,957 | 3,663 | 3,965 |
| Other revenues | 80 | 118 | 90 | 88 | 108 |
| Total revenues | $16,514 | $16,930 | $17,088 | $18,193 | $20,174 |
| Operating costs and expenses | 16,304 | 17,125 | 16,822 | 17,792 | 19,796 |
| Pretax operating profit | $    210 | $   (195) | $    266 | $    401 | $    378 |
| Income taxes | 94 | (50) | 115 | 160 | 152 |
| Total USM&R earnings | $    116 | $   (145) | $    151 | $    241 | $    226 |
| Special Items | (96) | (128) | (145) | (32) | (104) |
| USM&R operating earnings | $    212 | $    (17) | $    296 | $    273 | $    330 |
| Assets at year-end | $ 6,653 | $ 7,281 | $ 7,248 | $ 7,460 | $ 7,492 |
| Capital employed at year-end | 4,705 | 5,286 | 5,071 | 5,155 | 5,128 |
| Earnings:  gasoline and distillate (cents/gallon) | 3.6 | 0.2 | 3.7 | 4.1 | 4.6 |
| (Industry average) | 3.5 | 2.2 | 4.0 | 3.6 | 2.6 |
| Return on assets | 4.2% | (0.2%) | 5.2% | 4.8% | 5.9% |
| (Industry average) | 7.0 | 4.5 | 7.6 | 6.8 | 4.9 |
| Gasoline market share (top 18 states) |  |  | 11.4% | 11.6% | 11.9% |

**EXHIBIT 3    Natural Business Units (NBUs) and Service Companies (SERVCOs)**

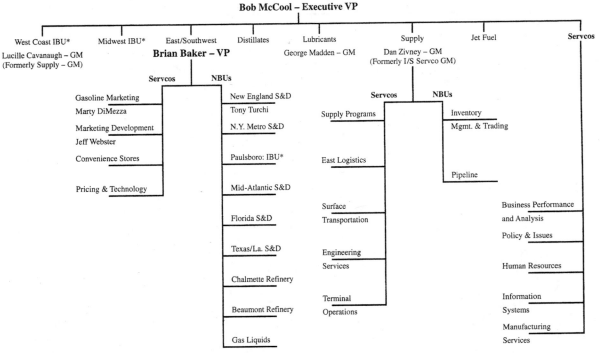

*IBU: Integrated Business Units
    (Refinery, Sales, Distribution)

---

**EXHIBIT 4    Five Gasoline Buyer Segments**

| | |
|---|---|
| **Road Warriors (18%)** | Generally higher-income middle-aged men who drive 25,000 to 50,000 miles a year, buy premium gasoline with a credit card, purchase sandwiches and drinks from the convenience store, will sometimes wash their cars at the carwash. |
| **True Blues (16%)** | Usually men and women with moderate to high incomes who are loyal to a brand and sometimes to a particular station; frequently buy premium gasoline and pay in cash. |
| **Generation F3 (27%)** | (F3—fuel, food, and fast) Upwardly mobile men and women—half under 25 years of age—who are constantly on the go; drive a lot and snack heavily from the convenience store. |
| **Homebodies (21%)** | Usually housewives who shuttle their children around during the day and use whatever gasoline station is based in town or along their route of travel. |
| **Price Shoppers (20%)** | Generally aren't loyal to either a brand or a particular station, and rarely buy the premium line; frequently on tight budgets; the focus of attention of marketing efforts of gasoline companies for years. |

---

## EXHIBIT 5    USM&R Balanced Scorecard Objectives Statement

### Strategic Objectives

<table>
<tr>
<td rowspan="5">FINANCIAL</td>
<td>

**Return on Capital Employed**—Earn a sustained rate of return on capital employed (ROCE) that is consistently among the best performers in the US downstream industry, but no less than the agreed corporate target ROCE of 12%

**Cash Flow**—Manage operations to generate sufficient cash to cover at least USM&R's capital spending, net financing cost, and pro rata share of the Corporate shareholder dividend

**Profitability**—Continually improve profitability by generating an integrated net margin (cents per gallon) that consistently places us as one of the top two performers among the US downstream industry

**Lowest Cost**—Achieve sustainable competitive advantage by integrating the various portions of the value chain to achieve the lowest fully-allocated total cost consistent with the value proposition delivered

**Meet Profitable Growth Targets**—Grow the business by increasing volume faster than the industry average, and by identifying and aggressively pursuing profitable fuels and lubes revenue opportunities that are consistent with the overall division strategy

</td>
</tr>
</table>

<table>
<tr>
<td rowspan="2">CUSTOMER</td>
<td>

**Continually Delight the Targeted Customer**—Identify and fulfill the value propositions for our target consumers (speed, smile, stroke) while maintaining and improving the "price of entry" items

**Improve the Profitability of Our Dealer/Wholesale Marketers**—Improve Dealer/Wholesale Marketer profitability by providing consumer-driven services and products, and by helping develop their business competencies

</td>
</tr>
</table>

<table>
<tr>
<td rowspan="1">INTERNAL</td>
<td>

**Marketing**

    **Product, Service and Alternate Profit Center (APC) Development**—Develop innovative and mutually profitable services and products

    **Dealer and Wholesale Marketer Quality**—Improve the franchise team to a level equal to best-in-class retailers outside the oil industry

**Manufacturing**

    **Lower costs of Manufacturing Faster Than the Competition**—Create a competitive advantage by continuing to increase gross margins and reduce manufacturing expenses faster than the competition

    **Improve Hardware Performance**—Optimize the functioning of our refinery assets through improved yields and decreased downtime

    **Safety**—Strive to eliminate work-related injuries by constantly focusing efforts on improving the safety of our refinery work environment through continued employee education and prevention of workplace hazards

**Supply, Trading, and Logistics**

    **Reducing Laid Down Costs**—Continue to lower supply acquisition and transportation costs to reduce light-products laid-down costs, such that we strive to supply products to our terminals at a cost equal to or better than the competitive market maker

    **Trading Optimization**—Maximize spot market sales realizations from refinery-finished and unfinished light products laid down costs, such that we strive to supply products to our terminals at a cost equal to better than the competitive market maker

    **Inventory Management**—Optimize light products inventories while maintaining satisfactory customer service levels

**Improve Health, Safety, and Environmental Performance**—Be a good employer and neighbor by demonstrating commitment to the safety of all of our facilities and active concern about our impact on the community and the environment

**Quality**—Manage the operations to provide the consumers with quality products supported by quality business processes that are timely and performed correctly the first time throughout the value chain

</td>
</tr>
</table>

*Exhibit 5   Continued*

<table>
<tr>
<td rowspan="5">LEARNING & GROWTH</td>
<td>

**Organizational Involvement**—Enable the achievement of our vision by promoting an understanding of our organizational strategy and by creating a climate in which our employees are motivated and empowered to strive toward that vision

**Core Competencies and Skills**—(a) Integrated view—Encourage and facilitate our people to gain a broader understanding of the marketing and refining business from end to end

       (b) Functional Excellence—Build the level of skills and competencies necessary to execute our vision

       (c) Leadership—Develop the leadership skills required to articulate the vision, promote integrated business thinking and develop our people

**Access to Strategic Information**—Develop the strategic information support required to execute our strategies
</td>
</tr>
</table>

## EXHIBIT 6   Balanced Scorecard

| | OBJECTIVE | MEASURE | FREQUENCY |
|---|---|---|---|
| **FINANCIAL** | **Return on Capital Employed** | ROCE (%) | S |
| | **Cash Flow** | Cash Flow Excl. Div. ($MM) | M |
| | | Cash Flow Incl. Div. ($MM) | M |
| | **Profitability** | P&L ($MM after tax) | M |
| | | Net Margin (cents per gallon before tax) | M |
| | | Net Margin, Ranking out of 6 | Q |
| | **Lowest Cost** | Total Operating Expenses (cents per gallon) | M |
| | **Meet Profitable Growth Targets** | Volume Growth, Gasoline Retail Sales (%) | M |
| | | Volume Growth, Distillate Sales to Trade | M |
| | | Volume Growth, Lubes (%) | M |
| **CUSTOMER** | **Continually Delight the Targeted Consumer** | Share of Segment (%) | Q |
| | | -% of Road Warriors | Q |
| | | -% of True Blues | Q |
| | | -% of Generation F3's | Q |
| | | Mystery Shopper (%) | M |
| | **Improve the Profitability of Our Partners** | Total Gross Profit, Split | Q |
| **INTERNAL** | **Improve EHS Performance** | Safety Incidents (Days Away From Work) | Q |
| | | Environmental Incidents | Q |
| | **Product, Service and APC Development** | APC Gross Margin/Store/Month ($M) | Q |
| | **Lower Costs of Manufacturing Vs Competition** | Refinery ROCE (%) | Q |
| | | Refinery Expense (cents/UEDC) | M |
| | **Improve Hardware Performance** | Refinery Reliability Index (%) | M |
| | | Refinery Yield Index (%) | M |
| | **Improve EHS Performance** | Refinery Safety Incidents | Q |
| | **Reducing Laid Down Cost** | LDC Vs Best Comp. Supply - Gas (cents per gallon) | Q |
| | | LDC Vs Best Comp. Supply - Dist. (cents per gallon) | Q |
| | **Inventory Management** | Inventory Level (MMBbl) | M |
| | | Product Availability Index (%) | M |
| | **Quality** | Quality Index | Q |
| **LEARNING & GROWTH** | **Organization Involvement** | Climate Survey Index | M |
| | **Core Competencies and Skills** | Strategic Competency Availability % | A |
| | **Access to Strategic Information** | Strategic Systems Availability | A |

# EXHIBIT 7    USM&R Brochure of Strategic Theme

**USM&R Strategic Themes ...**

will guide us to our vision and are defined above each graph.

**USM&R Strategic Measures ...**

that will keep us focused on achieving USM&R's strategic themes are explained in the graphs and the bulleted text accompanying them.

## Financially Strong

Reward our shareholders by providing a superior long-term return which exceeds that of our peers.

- Income divided by capital employed including all allocations.

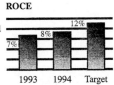

ROCE

## Delight the Customer

Understand our consumers' needs better than anyone and offer them products and services which exceed their expectations.

- The Mystery Shopper program rates how well each of our stations is delivering the "best buying experience."

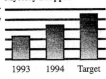

Mystery Shopper

## Win/Win Relationship

Improve Dealer/Wholesale Marketer profitability through customer-driven products and services and by developing their business competencies.

**Dealer/Mobil Gross Profit**

- Total profit earned at Mobil outlets and split between our dealers/ whole-sale marketers and Mobil.

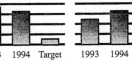

## Safe & Reliable

Maintain a leadership position in safety while keeping our refineries fully utilized.

**USM&R Days Away From Work**    **Manufacturing Reliability Index**

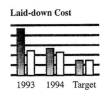

## Competitive Supplier

Provide product to our terminals at a cost equal to or better than the competitive market maker.

- Our cost to deliver product to the terminal vs. lowest cost provider.

**Laid-down Cost**

## Good Neighbor

Protect the health and safety of our people, the communities in which we work, and the environment we all share.

**Environmental Index**

- Composite of:
- reportable releases to air and water
- reportable spills
- community reported incidents.

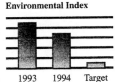

## On Spec On Time

Provide quality products supported by quality business processes that are on time and done right the first time.

- Composite of incidents of:
- product off spec
- order shipped late
- business process errors
- customer complaints
- cost of rework.

**Quality Index**

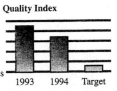

## Motivated & Prepared

Develop and value teamwork and the ability to think Mobil, act locally.

- Survey of employees to measure how people perceive the Mobil workplace environment.

**Climate Survey**

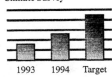

---

# EXHIBIT 8  USM&R Metric Owners

| METRIC OWNER | SERVCO | MEASURES |
|---|---|---|
| Ed Mitchel | Business Performance & Analysis | Financial |
| Jeff Webster | Marketing Development | Share of Segment |
| Marty DiMezza | Gasoline Marketing | Mystery Shopper |
| | | Friendly Serve |
| Borden Walker | Convenience Stores | Alternate Profit Center |
| | | Revenues and Gross Margin |
| Tony Johnson | Manufacturing Services | EHS Performance |
| | | Lower Cost |
| | | Hardware Performance |
| Ted Shore | Supply Programs | Laid Down Cost |
| | | Inventory Level |
| Carol Ellis | Supply Programs | Lubes Quality |
| Chuck Coe | Supply Programs | Fuels Quality |
| Bill Klarman | Human Resources | Organizational Involvement |
| | | Core Competencies |
| Pierre President | Information Systems | Strategic Information Access |

---

# EXHIBIT 9  Corporate Performance Share (CPS)

**Salary Groups 13 - 19 Metrics and Award % (of Reference Salary)**

| EPS Growth Relative Ranking | | | | Seven Major Competitors |
|---|---|---|---|---|
| 2% | 4% | 8% | 10% | Amoco |
| | | | | Arco |
| 2% | 3% | 6% | 8% | BP |
| | | | | Chevron |
| 1% | 2% | 3% | 4% | Exxon |
| | | | | Shell |
| 1%* | 1% | 2% | 2% | Texaco |

ROCE Relative Ranking

*Discretionary

# EXHIBIT 10    Metrics

| Performance Factor |
|---|

| Performance Factor | Qualitative |
|---|---|
| 1.25 | Best In Class |
| 1.20 | |
| 1.15 | Well Above Average |
| 1.12 | |
| 1.09 | |
| 1.06 | Above Average |
| 1.03 | |
| 1.00 | Average |
| 0.90 | |
| 0.80 | Below Average |
| 0.70 | |
| 0.60 | |
| 0.50 | Needs Improvement |
| 0.40 | |

How to think about performance factors

❶ **Objective:**
External Benchmark
1.00 means target equals
the average of competition

1.25 means target equals
the top of the competititve
group

ç **Subjective:**
Internal Benchmark
1.00 means the difficulty of the
target is average

# CASE 22  Citibank: Performance Evaluation

Frits Seegers, President of Citibank California, was meeting with his management team to review the performance evaluation and bonus decisions for the California branch managers. James McGaran's performance evaluation was next. Frits felt uneasy about this one. McGaran was manager of the most important branch in the Los Angeles area, and his financials were impressive. A year ago he would have received "above par" rating with full bonus. But last year, the California Division of Citibank had introduced a new performance scorecard to highlight the importance of a diverse set of measures in achieving the strategic goals of the division. Among the new measures introduced was a customer satisfaction indicator. Unfortunately, James McGaran had scored "below par" on customer satisfaction.

Frits looked at Lisa Johnson, the area manager supervising James McGaran. Frits had read Lisa's comments (**Exhibit 1**). The comments were very positive, but Lisa had not wanted to give a final recommendation until she had discussed it with Frits. She knew that James' case would be watched closely by many managers within the division.

## *The Financial District Branch*

James McGaran was manager of the most important of the 31 branches in the Los Angeles area. Located in Los Angeles's financial district, James's branch had a staff of 15 people, revenues of $6 million, and $4.3 million in profit margin. The customer base was very diverse. Individual customers ranged from people who worked in the financial district with sophisticated retail banking needs to less informed individuals banking for convenience. Business customers were sophisticated buyers who demanded high service quality and knowledgeable employees who could satisfy their financial needs. "Mom and pop" businesses, the dominant segment in other regions, were also present but to a much lesser extent. Competition was intense. Two competitors—Bank of America and Wells Fargo—had offices less than a block away from James's branch.

James joined Citibank in 1985 as assistant branch manager. He had worked in the banking industry since 1977. Within a year, in 1986, he was promoted to manager of a small branch. He progressed quickly through the ranks until 1992 when he was given the responsibility of managing the Financial District office. His performance in this office had exceeded expectations every single year. He had delivered impressive financial results for four years in a row. In 1996, when the division expanded its performance indicators to include non-financial measures, it became apparent that his branch's customer satisfaction ratings did not follow the same pattern as its financial performance.

James reported to Lisa Johnson, Los Angeles area manager. Lisa was a long time employee of Citibank. She joined the company in 1978 in Chicago and moved to California in early 1988. Her area was the biggest in the division and included two regions that had previously been managed separately. Lisa was a hands-on manager who spent a lot of time in the branches supporting the managers and becoming familiar with the events in each branch.

*Doctoral Candidate Antonio Dávila and Professor Robert Simons prepared this case as the basis for class discussion rather than to illustrate either effective or ineffective handling of an administrative situation.*

## New Performance Scorecard

Citibank was a niche player in the California market. It had eighty branches compared with four hundred offices of its biggest competitor. Citibank's strategy in California was to build a profitable franchise by providing relationship banking combined with a high level of service to its customers. Service was delivered face to face (in the branch) or remotely, depending on the wishes of the customers. Customers' service expectations rose in line with their net worth, as did their profitability for the bank. These customers demanded high levels of service with careful personal attention and a broad selection of financial products. Citibank provided a broad array of services including a dense network of ATM machines, 24 hour banking, and home banking.

Financial measures had dominated Citibank's performance evaluation in the past. But top managers in the division felt that these measures were poor vehicles to communicate the high service strategy of the bank. Frits Seegers wanted people in the division to have a broader view of the business and focus their attention on those dimensions that were critical to the long term success of the franchise.

To reflect the importance of non-financial measures as leading indicators of strategy implementation, the California Division developed a Performance Scorecard. It complemented existing financial measures with new measures reflecting important competitive dimensions in the bank's strategy. The initial version was pre-tested in 1995 and, starting in the first quarter of 1996, Performance Scorecard goals and performance data became a central management tool to implement strategy and evaluate performance.

The Performance Scorecard was built around six different types of measures: financial, strategy implementation, customer satisfaction, control, people, and standards (see **Exhibits 2** to **5**).

*Financial measures* were obtained from the regular accounting system and focused primarily on total revenue and profit margin against targets.

*Strategy implementation* measures tracked revenue for different types of target customer segments relevant to the strategy of the branch. James's Performance Scorecard focused primarily on revenues from retail customers—households, businesses, and professionals.

*Customer satisfaction* was measured through telephone interviews with approximately twenty-five branch customers who had visited the branch during the past month. Customer satisfaction scores were derived from questions that focused on branch service as well as other Citibank services like 24 hours phone banking and ATM services. An independent research firm was responsible for administering the survey under the guidance of the division's Relationship Satisfaction department. Given the current strategy of the bank, which focused on customer service as a key differentiator, Frits Seegers considered the customer satisfaction measure as critical to the long term success of his division. He saw it as a leading indicator of future financial performance. If customer satisfaction deteriorated, it was only a matter of time before it showed in the financials.

*Control measures* reported the evaluation by internal auditors on the branch's internal control processes. Branches had to score at least par (defined as 4 on a scale of 1 to 5) to be eligible for any bonus. If the rating was below 4, the branch's business was considered at risk and did not meet the minimum requirements for effective control.

*People and Standards* were non-quantifiable ratings determined subjectively by the branch manager's boss. The "people" measure focused on the proactive efforts of the manager to develop and communicate with subordinates, to encourage area training programs, and to be a role model to more junior people. Standards included an assessment of a manager's involvement in community groups, trade associations, and business ethics.

Each component of the Scorecard was scored independently into one of three rating categories: "below par", "par", or "above par". For those measures that could be measured quantitatively—financial, strategy implementation, customer satisfaction, and control—pre-defined performance thresholds determined where performance fell in this three-level scale. However, ratings related to people and standards lacked an appropriate objective indicator: in these cases performance was determined subjectively by the branch manager's superior.

In addition, the manager's boss gave a global rating for each of the six components of the Scorecard and an overall rating for the branch manager.

## Performance and Incentives

The performance planning process started in October with a negotiation process between Frits Seegers and his area managers. At the end of this initial stage, Performance Scorecard targets for the upcoming year were established for the division and for each area. These targets were cascaded down the organization. Area managers negotiated with branch managers to determine their financial targets and strategy implementation goals for the year. At the end of this process, the targets for branch managers were added up to ensure that they equaled or exceeded the area's targets.

Customer satisfaction and control goals were common to all branches in the division. For customer satisfaction, the 1996 goal was to achieve a rating of at least 80.

Financial, strategy implementation, customer satisfaction, and control targets formed the quantitative basis for *ex post* performance evaluation. Each quarter, area managers received branch information with the actual numbers for each of these measures and a comparison with the quarterly objectives. This information, together with the subjective scores that the area manager gave for the People and Standards ratings, formed the basis for the quarterly and yearly evaluation of branch managers.

Year-end performance evaluation was determined jointly by a team led by Frits Seegers. The team comprised the area managers, including Lisa Johnson, and managers from human resources, quality, and finance. Frits believed that having a team jointly evaluate performance of every branch manager gave consistency to the process throughout the division. It was this team that was now meeting to decide James's performance evaluation for the year.

In addition to other motivational elements associated with the yearly evaluation, a branch manager's bonus was linked to his or her final Performance Scorecard rating. A "below par" rating did not carry any bonus. A "par" rating generated a bonus of up to 15% of the basic salary (for branch managers with a salary in the lower part of the salary bracket, the bonus could reach 20%). An "above par" rating could mean as much as 30% bonus.

Without "par" ratings in *all* the components of the Scorecard, a manager could not get an "above par" rating.

## Performance of the Financial District Branch

Frits reviewed the 1996 performance evaluation forms for James McGaran. His financials were outstanding—20% above target. According to Lisa Johnson, James's branch "had generated the highest revenue and made the greatest margin contribution to the business of any branch in the system." His strategy implementation scores were in the "par" to "above par" range, although Lisa Johnson had given him an "above par" rating in three quarters. James had maintained an "above par" rating in the control scorecard and Lisa Johnson had rated him exceptionally where she had the discretion to do so.

However, customer satisfaction was "below par". A branch obtained a "par" rating if it scored 74 to 79. If customer satisfaction was above 80 or it had improved 6 points with no regression during 2 quarters and it was above the market average (77), then the branch got an "above par" rating.

Lisa and Frits were aware that a strict application of the new policies for performance evaluation meant that James could get at most a "par" evaluation for the year. But James' branch was the largest and toughest branch in the division. He had a demanding clientele and challenging competition. It was difficult to manage such a diverse set of indicators, and the customer satisfaction measure was sometimes hard to reconcile with demonstrated financial performance. James had discussed with Lisa his concerns regarding the adequacy of the survey. Customers rated not only their branch, but also other Citibank services such as ATM's that were out of the control of branch managers. Thus, it was possible that these centralized services were not providing adequate support to the sophisticated customers of James's branch.

Notwithstanding these concerns, James had worked hard to improve the customer satisfaction rating during the last quarter. He had made some changes in his staff to improve the score. One person in the branch was now dedicated to greeting the customer when arriving at the office and helping with any problems that may arise. He also held branch meetings and coached branch employees to focus their attention on improving customer satisfaction.

James gave a lot of importance to his ratings. It was a matter of pride to be "above par" and show that he was able to successfully run the hardest branch in the division. He had felt very disappointed when, in two quarters of the year, his rating had been only par. His branch was difficult and he was delivering the best financial performance in the division. He thought that his efforts deserved an above par rating, even if customer satisfaction was somewhat lagging.

Frits reviewed James's scorecards for each quarter of 1996 (**Exhibit 2** to **5**). His financials were exceptional, but only in the last quarter was he able to pull customer satisfaction to an acceptable level. If the performance evaluation team gave James an "above par" people could think that the division was not serious about its non-financial measures. James had been "below par" in customer satisfaction for all quarters of 1996 and, if this measure was truly important, he should not get an "above par" rating. On the other hand, he deserved the above par given his excellent performance in other dimensions. James was a reference point for a lot of other branch managers.

Frits held the summary scorecard in his hand (**Exhibit 1**) and turned to Lisa Johnson:

"Lisa, I've read over your comments and reviewed James's quarterly scorecards. All that now remains is ticking off the six boxes on this summary form and deciding on an overall performance rating for James . . . What do you recommend?"

## EXHIBIT 1   James McGaran's year-end performance for 1996

| | Below Par | Par | Above Par | YEAR-END PERFORMANCE ASSESSMENT |
|---|---|---|---|---|
| **FINANCIAL** Total     Above plan<br>Revenue    $ 6 million    $604,933<br>Expense    $1.7 million    $88,460<br>Margin    $4.3 million    $693,393 | | | ☐ | James had an exceptional year. The branch grew $56 million or 39% in footings, ranking #1 in the marketplace. Contribution margin was $4.3 million for the year, ranking the branch #1 in the marketplace. Expenses were $88.5 thousand better than plan for the year. Contribution margin improved by 48% from 4Q95 to 4Q96. |
| **STRATEGY IMPLEMENTATION** | | ☐ | | The branch enjoyed strong growth in business, professional, and retail. Citigold began to pick up in the third and fourth quarter. The branch's new household acquisition of 21% was impressive. Annualized attrition was 12% in 1996. James grew balances in all business segments: retail balances improved $2.4 million, Citigold increased $18 million, and business and professional increased $34.8 million. |
| **CUSTOMER SATISFACTION** | ☐ | | | Full-year service scores showed mixed results, 66 1Q, 63 2Q, 54 3Q, 72 4Q. James identified areas of opportunity and put corrective measures in place that allowed him to improve service scores substantially by year-end. |
| **CONTROL**<br>Operating losses    $81,960<br>Fraud losses    $55,920 | ☐ | | | The branch received two "5"s audit ratings in 1996. James is a very conscientious manager and works closely with his SCM to ensure operational compliance all times. Due to the sheer volume of transactions, the branch sustained substantial operating and fraud losses, over $137 thousand full-year. Some of these losses were from prior years, others were beyond branch control. Still, there is room for improvement in this area. |
| **PEOPLE**<br>Performance Management<br>Teamwork<br>Training / Development<br>Employee Satisfaction | | ☐ | | James is an excellent people manager. His Viewpoint results were amongst the best in the Area. He is a team-builder in his branch and motivates his people to go above and beyond. James had minimal turnover in 1996. James is one of the most consistent managers in the Area. His daily meetings are well-planned and productive. He instills focus and discipline in his branch. James is viewed as a team-player in the Area. He is quick to volunteer to help his peers or participate on special projects. James has been working on his MBA and has nearly completed the comprehensive Credit training program. |
| **STANDARDS**<br>Leadership<br>Business Ethics / Integrity<br>Customer Interaction / Focus<br>Community Involvement<br>Contribution to Overall Business | | ☐ | | James has very high standards for himself and those in his employ. He is well respected for his strong leadership skills. He showed sincere concern for his customer service scores and did whatever was necessary to improve customer satisfaction. James and his team are very involved in the local community. James has taken an active role in developing a business network within the community.  He also served as a board member on the American Heart Walk campaign. James's people are also involved in various community groups. |
| **OVERALL EVALUATION** | | | ☐ | This has been an exceptional year for James. From a financial perspective, his branch was rated #1 in the marketplace. His willingness and ability to look outside the box to close a deal are admired and respected. He has done an excellent job refining his management style, becoming one of the most effective leaders and coaches in the marketplace. James is dedicated to the success of the business, as evidenced by his willingness to work weekends, holidays, and during his vacation to ensure customer satisfaction, operational control, and financial growth. James is an outstanding manager. Congratulations on a job well done!! |

Signed by Area Manager: _____

Approved by Regional President: _____

# EXHIBIT 2    James McGaran's Performance Scorecard for the first quarter of 1996

|  | Below Par | Par | Above Par | 1996 RESULTS 1st quarter | 2nd quarter | 3rd quarter | 4th quarter | 1996 GOALS 1st quarter | 2nd quarter | 3rd quarter | 4th quarter |
|---|---|---|---|---|---|---|---|---|---|---|---|
| **FINANCIAL** | | | | | | | | | | | |
| Revenue | | | ✓ | 1,250,094 | | | | 1,134,276 | 1,206,442 | 1,325,692 | 1,416,242 |
| Expense | | ✓ | | 421,430 | | | | 403,586 | 417,972 | 414,900 | 414,900 |
| Margin | | | ✓ | 828,664 | | | | 730,690 | 788,470 | 910,792 | 1,001,342 |
| **STRATEGY IMPLEMENTATION** | | | | | | | | | | | |
| Total Households | | | ✓ | 3,228 | | | | | | | |
| New to bank households | | ✓ | | 257 | | | | | | | |
| Lost to bank households | | | | (93) | | | | | | | |
| Cross-sell, splits, mergers households | | | | 4 | | | | | | | |
| Retail asset balances | | | | $ 5,578 | | | | | | | |
| Market share | | | | 1.8% | | | | | | | |
| **CUSTOMER SATISFACTION** | ✓ | | | Score 66   Goal 80 | | The branch has shown significant and sustained improvement in customer satisfaction. | | | | | |
| **CONTROL** | | | | | | | | | | | |
| Audit | | | | | | | | | | | |
| Legal / Regulatory | | ✓ | | Score 4   Goal 4 | | The branch demonstrates strong operational control. | | | | | |

**PEOPLE**

James is a strong manager. He has inculcated a disciplined sales process and reinforces it with a daily focus on how the business, branch, and individuals are doing vs. goal.

James is currently working on his MBA degree.

James works closely with his staff, coordinating the necessary training programs either in branch or in the class-room. His daily meeting and coaching sessions have allowed him to increase the knowledge and professionalism of his people.

**STANDARDS**

James provides clear and concise direction in his branch. He acts professionally, earning the respect of his staff, colleagues, and customers. James has built a cohesive team and leads by example.
James consistently upholds all bank standards and ensures appropriateness of action for himself and his staff.
Excellent progress in customer interaction.
James proactively develops and implements effective programs to enhance Citibank's image as socially responsible. He and his staff are involved in a number of community groups in Los Angeles.
James makes significant contribution to the business. The branch is currently the highest revenue and margin producer in the market place. James and his team grew revenue by $142.2 million or 16%.

**OVERALL EVALUATION**

James takes complete ownership of his branch and leverages internal and external relationships to grow the business and solve problems. He has demonstrated his ability to consistently outperform the branch's aggressive financial goals.

Signed by Area Manager: _____

**EXHIBIT 3  James McGaran's Performance Scorecard for the second quarter of 1996**

|  | Below Par | Par | Above Par | 1996 RESULTS 1st quarter | 2nd quarter | 3rd quarter | 4th quarter | 1996 GOALS 1st quarter | 2nd quarter | 3rd quarter | 4th quarter |
|---|---|---|---|---|---|---|---|---|---|---|---|
| **FINANCIAL** | | ✓ | | | | | | | | | |
| Revenue | | | | 1,254,876 | 1,486,172 | | | 1,141,612 | 1,213,744 | 1,332,865 | 1,423,454 |
| Expense | | | | 421,430 | 378,959 | | | 403,586 | 436,276 | 436,806 | 437,282 |
| Margin | | | | 833,446 | 1,107,213 | | | 738,026 | 777,468 | 896,059 | 986,172 |
| **STRATEGY IMPLEMENTATION** | | ✓ | | | | | | | | | |
| Total Households | | | | 3,403 | 3,438 | | | | | | |
| New to bank households | | | | 257 | 162 | | | | | | |
| Lost to bank households | | | | (93) | (119) | | | | | | |
| Cross-sell, splits, mergers households | | | | 4 | (7) | | | | | | |
| Retail asset balances | | | | $ 5,578 | $ 5,402 | | | | | | |
| Market share | | | | 1.8% | 1.8% | | | | | | |

**CUSTOMER SATISFACTION** ✓ (Below Par)
Score 63  Goal 80 — The score is down 3 points. James and his team need to work on customer satisfaction.

**CONTROL** ✓ (Above Par)
Audit
Legal / Regulatory — Score 5  Goal 5 — An exceptional score given the size and complexity of the branch.

**PEOPLE** ✓ (Above Par)
Performance Management
Teamwork
Training / Development
Self
Other
Employee Satisfaction

James fosters a strong sense of teamwork, as evidenced by his Viewpoint results and employee satisfaction scores. James maintains very high development standards for himself and his staff.

He is currently working on his MBA degree and should graduate in 1997. James also actively promotes cross-training and self-development.

**STANDARDS** ✓ (Above Par)
Leadership
Business Ethics / Integrity
Customer Interaction / Focus
Community Involvement
Contribution to Overall Business

James is recognized throughout the business as one of California's finest managers. He has demonstrated strong leadership skills and a keen understanding of the business.

The branch, under James's leadership, has made a major contribution to the marketplace. The branch's margin contribution of $1,108M, exceeds the next closest branch by 53%.

**OVERALL EVALUATION** ✓ (Above Par)

James had another exceptional quarter. The branch exceeded its margin goal by 22%. Total margin contribution improved 33%, total footings increased by 9.4%, and revenue increased 18.4%. Congratulations on another outstanding quarter.

Signed by Area Manager: _Johnson_ (signature)

568

# EXHIBIT 4    James McGaran's Performance Scorecard for the third quarter of 1996

## FINANCIAL

| | 1996 RESULTS | | | | 1996 GOALS | | | |
|---|---|---|---|---|---|---|---|---|
| | 1st quarter | 2nd quarter | 3rd quarter | 4th quarter | 1st quarter | 2nd quarter | 3rd quarter | 4th quarter |
| Revenue | 1,254,876 | 1,486,172 | 1,593,690 | | 1,141,612 | 1,213,744 | 1,429,974 | 1,423,454 |
| Expense | 421,430 | 395,216 | 378,458 | | 403,586 | 436,276 | 445,688 | 437,282 |
| Margin | 833,446 | 1,090,956 | 1,215,232 | | 738,026 | 777,468 | 984,286 | 986,172 |

Rating scale: Below Par / Par / Above Par

## STRATEGY IMPLEMENTATION

| | 1st quarter | 2nd quarter | 3rd quarter | 4th quarter |
|---|---|---|---|---|
| Total Households | 3,409 | 3,445 | 3,511 | |
| New to bank households | 257 | 162 | 152 | |
| Lost to bank households | (93) | (119) | (100) | |
| Cross-sell, splits, mergers households | 4 | (7) | 13 | |
| Retail asset balances | $ 5,578 | $ 5,402 | $ 5,437 | |
| Market share | 1.8% | 1.8% | 1.8% | |

## CUSTOMER SATISFACTION

Score  54   Goal  80

Service scores continued to deteriorate in the 3rd. quarter. The branch ran short of one teller and desperately needs another two CBCs to offload the day time traffic in the branch.

## CONTROL

Audit

Legal / Regulatory

Not reviewed this quarter.

## PEOPLE

Performance Management — James has a very focused and disciplined sales process in his branch. His daily sales meetings have become the "model" for the Area.

Teamwork

Training / Development — James is currently working on his MBA degree and participating in the Commercial program.

Self

Other

Employee Satisfaction — Employee satisfaction is high in the branch, as evidenced by James's positive Viewpoint results.

## STANDARDS

Leadership — James is highly respected in the Area as a seasoned manager and leader.

Business Ethics / Integrity

Customer Interaction / Focus — James and his team are very involved in the local community.

Community Involvement — James makes a tremendous contribution to the Area and the business. He has a "can do" attitude and often finds ways to make deals happen despite systems and back-office constraints.

Contribution to Overall Business

## OVERALL EVALUATION

James had another exceptional quarter. Financials improved in all aspects. Expenses were below plan and his contribution margin is the highest in the marketplace.

Signed by Area Manager: _[signature]_

**EXHIBIT 5  James McGaran's Performance Scorecard for the fourth quarter of 1996**

| | Below Par | Par | Above Par | 1996 RESULTS | | | | 1996 GOALS | | | |
|---|---|---|---|---|---|---|---|---|---|---|---|
| | | | | 1st quarter | 2nd quarter | 3rd quarter | 4th quarter | 1st quarter | 2nd quarter | 3rd quarter | 4th quarter |
| **FINANCIAL** | | | | | | | | | | | |
| Revenue | | | | 1,254,876 | 1,486,172 | 1,593,690 | 1,636,056 | 1,141,612 | 1,213,744 | 1,429,974 | 1,580,534 |
| Expense | | | | 421,430 | 395,216 | 378,458 | 456,061 | 403,586 | 436,276 | 445,688 | 454,076 |
| Margin | | | | 833,446 | 1,090,956 | 1,215,232 | 1,179,995 | 738,026 | 777,468 | 984,286 | 1,126,458 |
| **STRATEGY IMPLEMENTATION** | | | | | | | | | | | |
| Total Households | | | | 3,409 | 3,445 | 3,511 | 3,503 | | | | |
| New to bank households | | | | 257 | 162 | 152 | 102 | | | | |
| Lost to bank households | | | | (93) | (119) | (107) | (128) | | | | |
| Cross-sell, splits, mergers households | | | | 4 | (7) | 20 | 18 | | | | |
| Retail asset balances | | | | $ 5,578 | $ 5,402 | $ 5,437 | $ 5,510 | | | | |
| Market share | | | | 1.8% | 1.8% | 1.8% | 1.8% | | | | |

**CUSTOMER SATISFACTION**  Score 72  Goal 80

Congratulations to James and his team for their improvement in service results.

**CONTROL**  Score 5  Goal 5

Audit
Legal / Regulatory

James maintains strong operational control in his branch.

**PEOPLE**

Performance Management
Teamwork
Training / Development
Self
Other
Employee Satisfaction

James is an exceptional performance manager. He communicates clear and concise expectations and manages his people to their best potential.
James is a consummate team player and fosters the same behavior in his branch.
Self and employee development are a priority to James. He is currently working on his MBA degree and is attending comprehensive Credit training program.
James encourages his staff to develop themselves. He also looks for opportunities for them to attend Area or CitiSource training programs.
James enjoys a high level of employee satisfaction, as evidence by his Viewpoint results and low employee turnover.

**STANDARDS**

Leadership
Business Ethics / Integrity
Customer Interaction / Focus
Community Involvement
Contribution to Overall Business

James is highly regarded as an effective leader and coach. His daily sales meetings have become the model for the other branches in the Area.

It's been a difficult year meeting customer expectations in the branch but James and his team have done an outstanding job managing the challenge.
James is very involved in the local community and proactively looks for opportunities for himself and his staff to create an awareness with local groups and establish Citibank and a model corporate citizen.

**OVERALL EVALUATION**

James has done an exceptional job. The branch was rated #1 in the marketplace. It generates the highest revenue and makes the greatest margin to the business. They have done all that while maintaining a 5 rated audits. Exceptional quarter and outstanding year!!

Signed by Area Manager: _Lawrence_

570

# CASE 23   Nordstrom: Dissension in the Ranks? (A)

T he first time Nordstrom sales clerk Lori Lucas came to one of the many "mandatory" Saturday morning department meetings and saw the sign—"Do Not Punch the Clock"—she assumed the managers were telling the truth when they said the clock was temporarily out of order. But as weeks went by, she discovered that on subsequent Saturdays the clock was always "broken" or the time cards were not accessible. When she and several colleagues hand-wrote the hours on their time cards, they discovered that their manager whited-out the hours and accused them of not being "team players." Commenting on the variety of tasks that implicitly had to be performed after hours, Ms. Lucas said, "You couldn't complain, because then your manager would schedule you for the bad hours, your sales per hour would fall, and next thing you know, you're out the door."[1]

Patty Bemis, who joined Nordstrom as a sales clerk in 1981 and quit eight years later, told a similar story:

> Nordstrom recruiters came to me. I was working at The Broadway as Estee Lauder's counter manager and they said they had heard I had wonderful sales figures. We'd all heard Nordstrom was *the* place to work. They told me how I would double my wages. They painted a great picture and I fell right into it. . .
>
> The managers were these little tin gods, always grilling you about your sales. . . . You felt like your job was constantly in jeopardy. They'd write you up for anything, being sick, the way you dressed. . . . The girls around me were dropping like flies. Everyone was always in tears. . . .
>
> Working off the clock was just standard. In the end, really serving the customer, being an All-Star, meant nothing; if you had low sales per hour, you were forced out. . . .
>
> I just couldn't take it anymore—the constant demands, the grueling hours. I just said one day, life's too short.[2]

Despite employee grievances such as those of Lori Lucas and Patty Bemis, top management at the fashion specialty retailer acknowledged no serious problems with its management systems. Jim Nordstrom, co-chairman of the company with his brother John and cousin Bruce, explained management's position in a statement to the press:

> We haven't seen any complaints from the union. . . . If employees are working without pay, breaks, or days off, then it's isolated or by choice.
>
> A lot of them say, "I want to work every day." I have as many people thank us for letting them work all these hours as complain. I think people don't put in enough hours during the busy time. We need to work harder.
>
> A lot of what comes out makes it sound like we're slave drivers. If we were that kind of company, they wouldn't smile, they wouldn't work that hard. Our people smile because they want to.[3]

---

[1] Susan Faludi, "At Nordstrom Stores, Service Comes First—But at a Big Price," *Wall Street Journal,* February 20, 1990, p. A1.
[2] Ibid.
[3] Ibid.

*Hilary Weston prepared this case from public sources under the supervision of Professor Robert Simons as the basis for class discussion rather than to illustrate either effective or ineffective handling of an administrative situation.*

## *Background of the Current Situation*

John W. Nordstrom founded Nordstrom in 1901 as a shoe store. Nearly a century later, by the end of 1989, the company had grown to become the nation's leading specialty retailer of apparel, shoes, and accessories. The company operated 59 department stores in six states and was implementing a national expansion plan that called for store openings in several additional states in the early 1990s. By the end of 1989, sales were approaching $3 billion and Nordstrom enjoyed one of the highest profit margins in its industry.

Nordstrom, which issued shares to the public in 1971, had always been run by members of the Nordstrom family, who still owned roughly half of the company. The third generation of Nordstrom family managers, who had been at the helm since 1970, upheld the management philosophy of the company's founder: offer the customer the best in service, selection, quality, and value.

Superior customer service was Nordstrom's strongest competitive advantage and consequently a major source of its financial success. The retailer had enjoyed nearly 20 years of uninterrupted (primarily double-digit) earnings growth before reporting a decline for the 1989 fiscal year. (**Exhibit 1** provides a history of Nordstrom's financial performance.) With sales per square foot of $380 in 1988,[4] Nordstrom was among the most productive in the industry, generating roughly double the 1988 industry average for specialty retailers of $194 per square foot.[5]

Throughout the 1980s, Nordstrom's salespeople were the envy of the industry in terms of their quality and productivity. The caliber of the company's sales clerks seemed to withstand the pressures of rapid growth as the company's work force expanded geographically and grew from 5,000 employees in 1980 to 30,000 in 1989. The clerks' "heroics" (as they called their exceptional customer service efforts) helped to build the store's alluring image, its extremely strong customer loyalty, and its lofty sales per square foot.

At Nordstrom's, it was common practice for sales clerks, or "Nordies" as they called themselves, to:

- drive to another Nordstrom store to retrieve a desired item in an out-of-stock size or color;
- drive to a customer's home to deliver purchases;
- call up a valued customer to alert her of newly arriving merchandise;
- help a customer assemble a complete outfit by retrieving items from several different departments; and
- write thank you notes to customers for their purchases.

Sales clerks were also known for performing such heroics as changing a customer's flat tire in the store parking lot; paying a customer's parking ticket if his or her shopping time outlasted the parking meter; lending a few dollars to a customer short on cash in order to consummate a purchase; and taking a customer to lunch.

By performing these extraordinary services—which were often performed outside of a sales clerk's scheduled time on the selling floor—sales clerks earned their customers' praise, gratitude, and loyalty. (**Exhibit 2** reproduces a typical customer letter.) In addition to customer loyalty, industrious clerks could earn over $80,000 a year. The average Nordstrom sales clerk earned $20,000 to $24,000 compared to the national average for all retail sales clerks of $12,000 a year.[6]

---

[4] Richard W. Stevenson, "Watch Out Macy's, Here Comes Nordstrom," *New York Times*, August 27, 1989, p. 34.
[5] National Retail Merchants Association, *Financial & Operating Results of Department & Specialty Stores*, 1989 ed.
[6] Faludi, op. cit.

During the 1980s, more and more rivals such as R. H. Macy, Bloomingdales, and Neiman Marcus began to emulate Nordstrom's service-oriented strategy. According to one industry expert:

> All retailers in America have awakened to the Nordstrom threat and are struggling to catch up. Nordstrom is the future of retailing. . . . [It] is the most Darwinian of retail companies today.[7]

At the end of the decade, Nordstrom's much heralded reputation was formally acknowledged with the 1989 National Retail Merchants Association's Gold Medal—considered by many to be the most prestigious award in the industry.[8]

## Policies, Practices, and Measurement Systems

In the mid-1960s, to support its high-service strategy and motivate its salespeople, Nordstrom had introduced an innovative commission system—revolutionary among specialty retail and department stores. Top management combined this incentive compensation system—which was driven by sales per hour (SPH)—with other distinctive policies to guide, motivate, and measure the performance of its sales staff. Although its established set of management systems and policies had proven very effective for over 20 years, problems began to emerge at the end of the 1980s.

**Sales-per-Hour Incentives**   The following account[9] describes the mechanics of Nordstrom's commission-selling system as well as the explicit and implicit ways in which it affected employees:

> Interviews with a dozen current and former Nordstrom employees in California illustrate the contradictory pressures that workers can experience in a system that tries to give equal emphasis to service, profitability, and middle-managerial autonomy.
>
> Most of those interviewed said no manager ever formally told them to go off the clock, an order that would flatly violate state and federal fair labor standards laws. Rather, they said, it becomes clear to most Nordstrom salespeople soon after they are hired that the store's commission-selling program effectively penalizes any salesperson who insists on getting paid for every hour worked.
>
> The reason is that Nordstrom carefully evaluates salespeople on their sales-per-hour ratio. Each employee is given a target SPH ratio—a quota—based on his or her base hourly wage and store department. The actual SPH for the past two weeks—sales minus merchandise returned by customers, divided by hours worked—appears on each paycheck stub.
>
> If the actual SPH is higher than the target SPH, the employee is paid a 6.75% to 10% commission on net sales, depending on the department. If the SPH is below the target, the employee is paid the base hourly wage [roughly $9.00, with variations by department].[10] Failure to meet the target SPH often results in decreased hours or, in some cases, termination. Meeting or surpassing the target SPH means more working hours—including better hours when the shopping is heavier—and a better chance of promotion to a department manager job.
>
> Stories of some Nordstrom workers making $40,000 to $60,000 or more a year thanks to hefty commissions are widespread. But critics of the system say rank-and-file salespeople are often torn in this environment.

[7] Stevenson, op. cit.

[8] Jean Bergmann, "Nordstrom Gets the Gold," *STORES,* January 1990, p. 44.

[9] Bob Baker, "The Other Nordstrom," *Los Angeles Times,* February 4, 1990, p. D1.

[10] Newly hired sales clerks began at an hourly rate of approximately $4.50 and in each of the four quarters of their first year, they received wage increases to bring them up to the maximum base rate for their department, which was roughly $9.00 per hour, depending on the department.

To chalk up the most impressive SPH ratio, salespeople must be on the floor selling. But to carry out the Nordstrom credo of being a "team player" or a "Nordie," they also must be available to run themselves ragged meeting each customer's needs, which can take considerable time. Time also must be spent in routine merchandise stocking, store display activities or attending numerous sales staff meetings. These hours, if formally recorded, lower the SPH.

Initially your feeling is, "I've got to punch in for every minute I'm there," said Joel Kirk, who worked as a salesman and a men's clothing manager for several years in Northern California before leaving Nordstrom last summer to return to college. "Then you find you're at the bottom on SPH, or near it. Then someone nudges you. It's there but it's not said. It's an underlying factor that everyone eventually realizes."

"There is pressure on (department) managers to get people with the biggest SPH into the most hours. You're not told that if you don't (go off the clock) you'll get your hours cut. It becomes an inferred thing. The more you sell per hour, the more hours you get," said Kirk, who spoke on the condition that his real name not be used.

As a result, critics of the system say, people making blue-collar wages and governed by hourly wage laws find themselves having to make time-management decisions usually reserved for white-collar "professionals" who are paid much higher weekly salaries and, in exchange, are expected to work some uncompensated hours.

Nordstrom says to salespeople, "This is your own business, treat it like your own business, but it's not said outright that you're going to have to do all these extra things," said Kirk, who emphasized that he has no hard feelings against the company. "They don't sit you down and say the calling of past customers for new business is important, the thank-you cards are important, taking things to the customer's house is important, running things out to a local tailor when Nordstrom's tailor is backed up is important."

To honor those who thrive, Nordstrom awards its top sellers annual membership in the company's Pace Setters Club, entitling them to 33% discounts on merchandise. The posting of SPH figures creates peer pressure that is regarded by retail analysts as a strong motivator.

However . . . dissident salespeople complain about intense competition between individual salespeople. Often cited is the court case in King County, Washington, where a jury last fall awarded $180,000 to a former Nordstrom saleswoman who claimed that she was wrongfully dismissed because co-workers wrote anonymous letters claiming that she stole from them by falsely crediting herself with their commissions.

**Examples of Compensation Determination:**   The following two examples, one for a sales clerk generating $8,000 in weekly sales and one for a clerk generating $5,000 in weekly sales, illustrate the incentives built in to Nordstrom's SPH compensation system:[11]

**Assumptions:**

- Guaranteed base wage:                              $9.45 per hour
- Hours scheduled per week:                          40
- Sales per hour (SPH) target:                       $140
- Sales per week target:                             40 hrs. $\times$ $140 SPH = $5,600
- Commission rate:                                   6.75% (if sales *exceed* target)
- Overtime pay (O/T) for hours in excess             0.5 $\times$ average regular-time hourly earnings
  of 40 hours/week:

---

[11] These hypothetical examples are based on descriptions of Nordstrom's compensation system provided by multiple public sources, including the Washington State Department of Labor & Industries.

### Example 1

A sales clerk who works 50 hours per week and generates weekly sales of $8,000.

a)  If hours reported     = 40, then
    SPH = $8,000/40      = $200, and
    Weekly earnings      = .0675 × $ 8,000 = $540.

b)  If hours reported     = 50, then
    SPH = $8,000/50      = $160, and
    Weekly earnings      = [.0675 × $8,000] + [premium for 10 hours O/T]
                         = $540 + [10 hours × .5 × $9.45] = $587.25.

As this example illustrates, a sales clerk would earn more for this week's work by reporting overtime hours; however, this option would result in a lower SPH. A low SPH could reduce a clerk's ranking among peers and could work against him or her when the supervisor assigns shifts.[12] As a result, a sales clerk may choose to sacrifice pay in the short term for better shifts and more hours in the future. The higher SPH also may improve a clerk's chances for promotion.

### Example 2

A sales clerk who works 50 hours per week and generates weekly sales of $5,500.

a)  If hours reported     = 40, then
    SPH = $5,500/40      = $137.50 (which is less than target), and
    Weekly earnings      = 40 hours × $9.45 = $378 (no commissions earned).

b)  If hours reported     = 50, then
    SPH = $5,500/50      = $110 (which is less than target), and
    Weekly earnings      = 50 hours × $9.45 + [premium for 10 hours O/T]
                         = $472.50 + [10 hours × .5 × $9.45] = $519.75.

As in the first example, the sales clerk stands to gain financially by reporting all hours worked. If the clerk does so, however, the SPH drops substantially below his or her target level. According to employees' descriptions of the system, a substandard SPH can result in fewer scheduled hours, worse shifts, and—if such performance persists for several pay periods—termination, not to mention stressful peer pressure. Again, employees may opt to work off the clock rather than report all hours.

The lack of a clear distinction between "selling time" and "non-sell" work time exacerbated the pressures on employees. For example, an hour of extra work defined as "non-sell" (e.g., annual stock-taking) by Nordstrom entitled an employee to the guaranteed base wage with no effect on his or her SPH. If the same hour was considered selling time, his or her SPH would be affected negatively. Moreover, the clerk was considered to be fully compensated for all selling hours through commissions (assuming targets were exceeded) and was therefore not entitled to any extra pay for reporting the extra hour worked. (**Exhibit 3** reproduces an internal memo distributed by top management in an effort to clarify its system of differentiating between selling and non-selling time on the job.)

**Additional Elements of the Management System**  Although SPH monitoring was the heart of Nordstrom's distinctive management strategy, the SPH system was complemented

---

[12] Faludi, op. cit.

by other organizational factors. For example, the composition of the sales force was well-suited to the competitive work environment. Nordstrom sales clerks tended to be young, often college-educated people looking for a career in retailing. They were willing to work hard in exchange for the retailer's relatively high salaries and opportunities for rapid advancement.[13] The company's policy of promoting only from within also enhanced the overall level of Nordstrom experience within middle management and helped to motivate ambitious and hard-working employees.

The availability of desirable merchandise in appropriate colors and sizes was critical to Nordstrom's success. Department managers worked closely with buyers and often had direct buying authority. Since the sales-per-hour commission system rewarded turnover, Nordies were committed to working with their department managers to anticipate customer buying patterns and ensuring adequate stock.

Throughout the chain's rapid growth, top management endorsed a decentralized system of operations; department, store, and regional managers were relatively free to make their own decisions.[14] Moreover, they were eligible for bonuses tied to the achievement of their budget goals. Thus, decision-making responsibility and rewards were delegated directly to the front-line salespeople who were closest to the customer. At the same time, however, such decentralization limited top management's control over the application of sales force management systems. Such systems were originally centralized when the organization was much smaller. Without meaningful control over their use, however, these systems—which supported sales force scheduling, compensation, and promotions—could be vulnerable to abuse.

Another aspect of the Nordstrom's work environment that had both positive and negative ramifications was the role of group recognition and peer pressure. At monthly store meetings, managers read aloud customers' letters of praise. Sales staffs responded with applause and cheers. The salespeople who elicited such written praise were honored as "Customer Service All-Stars" and their pictures were usually displayed by the customer-service desk. The All-Stars also received added discounts on clothing and had their efforts documented in their personnel files.[15] The pressure to become an All-Star, however, could result in undesired behavior, such as "sharking"—the term Nordstrom employees used to describe stealing credit for sales made by other staff.

Competition was also promoted on the sales floor via various types of sales contests. For example, a free dinner might be awarded to the employee who generated the most multiple-item sales to individual customers. Such public fanfare helped to keep Nordstrom's sales clerks motivated and its incentive system alive on a day-to-day and hour-to-hour basis. Peer pressure was also strong among management ranks where an elaborate and very public goal-setting process transpired. Every year the company's managers gathered in large meetings where they individually proclaimed their store or departmental goals for the next 12 months. Then, immediately following each announcement, the boss of the particular manager stood up to unveil his or her previously hidden goal for that manager. Again, cheering and howling was a common accompaniment.

One last ingredient that helped to support Nordstrom's sales force management strategy was the use of automation: salespeople were able to track their performance on com-

---

[13] Stevenson, op. cit.
[14] Nordstrom's 1987 Annual Report.
[15] Stevenson, op. cit.

puter printouts available in back offices. The printouts listed individual sales by employee identification number so that clerks could compare their performance to both their own targets and their peers' performance. The ease of access to such information helped employees at all levels to determine precisely their achievement relative to their peers.

Nordstrom management believed their system worked. The company claimed that employees earned one of the highest base pay rates in the industry—as much as $10 an hour—and especially industrious employees could make as much as $80,000 a year. Moreover, Nordstrom's corporate policy of promoting only from within and its policy of decentralization combined to give managers unusual freedom to make decisions that would enhance customer service.[16]

## From a Local Union Dispute to Class Action Suits[17]

In the second half of 1989, the same company policies and compensation systems to which much of Nordstrom's success was attributed became the target of a barrage of employee complaints, union allegations, law suits, and regulatory orders that tainted the company's reputation and blemished its financial performance. By the spring of 1990, the escalating accusations and events remained under dispute and it was not yet clear whether Nordstrom's change of fortune was temporary or long term.

In the summer of 1989, a discontent minority of Nordstrom's sales clerks chose to risk their reputation as "the most helpful and cheerful in the industry" and voice their grievances against the company. Angered by management's actions during contract negotiations, the United Food & Commercial Workers (UFCW) Local 1001 began a publicity campaign against Nordstrom, challenging the legality of the company's labor practices. Local 1001 was based in the state of Washington and represented roughly 1,500 of Nordstrom's nearly 30,000 employees. Local 367 represented another 200 sales clerks in the state. The Washington employees were the only unionized members of the Nordstrom work force; no other Nordstrom employees were unionized.

Representatives of Local 1001 complained that the company coerced employees to work "off the clock" without being paid. They maintained that Nordstrom neither recorded nor compensated employees for all the time they spent performing certain duties that were not directly related to selling—such as delivering packages to customers' homes, attending department meetings, writing thank-you notes to customers, doing inventory work, and general bookkeeping. Moreover, the union claimed that Nordstrom's use of sales per hour as a performance measure—for determining which employees were eligible for commissions (versus hourly wages), which were assigned the most and best shifts, and which were at risk of being fired—implicitly encouraged employees to work off the clock.

In an effort to quantify their claim, Local 1001's union officials distributed back-pay forms to the unionized sales clerks on which they could calculate and submit their individual claims. By late November 1989, the union reported to the press that they had collected $1 million in back-pay claims from several hundred sales clerks.

In November 1989, Local 1001 filed a formal complaint with the Employment Standards Section of the Washington State Department of Labor & Industries. (**Exhibit 4** reproduces the Department of Labor summary of the complaint.) At the same time, members of

---

[16] Ibid.

[17] This section provides a chronological summary of the events that transpired between June 1989 and April 1990 as reported in the press.

the union also voiced their complaints through pamphlets, pickets, and the press, demanding that management reimburse employees the millions of dollars of back pay which they were owed.

Nordstrom management denied the allegations and dismissed them as a union ploy "to drum up support for their cause" at the bargaining table. (Contract negotiations had been at a stalemate since July 1989.) A company spokesperson said that the complaints were unsubstantiated and maintained that the company policy had "always been to pay employees for the time that they've worked."[18]

At the same time, the company was also forced to respond to a variety of charges filed against them by the National Labor Relations Board (NLRB).[19] The NLRB claimed that Nordstrom's bargaining tactics with the UFCW violated federal labor laws and that management had failed to provide the union with requested wage-related data and time card records.

The union complaints triggered a three-month investigation by the Washington State Department of Labor & Industries. On February 15, 1990, the department released its findings, which concurred with several of Local 1001's allegations. The administrative ruling stated that Nordstrom systematically violated state wage and hour laws in its failure both to record all hours worked and to pay sales clerks for performing certain services. The state regulatory agency ordered the company to bolster its record-keeping operations, to pay two years' of back pay to all Washington employees affected by the charge, and to pay employees in the future for time spent on such tasks as deliveries, meetings, and writing thank-you notes. The regulators did not specify the number of employees affected or the dollars involved in the back-pay reimbursements. (**Exhibit 5** reproduces the department's conclusions and its order.)

Local 1001 President Joe Peterson estimated that Nordstrom could be liable for as much as $30 million to $40 million in back-pay claims from its Washington employees alone, and for several hundred million dollars if the union followed through with a nationwide class-action suit on behalf of all Nordstrom employees.[20] By mid-February, the union said it had doubled its November "back-pay" collection and held individual claims totaling over $2 million from roughly 400 sales clerks in Washington, California, and Oregon. According to media reports, the sales clerks who submitted claims worked an average of 8 to 10 hours per week off-the-clock. Peterson asserted, "Nordstrom is doing a disservice to its reputation, employees and stockholders by continuing to deny that they have a culture . . . that requires employees to work without pay."[21]

In response, company co-chairman Bruce Nordstrom affirmed management's intentions to "fully comply with the law" and to review their record-keeping procedures and pay practices for any weaknesses.[22] Management announced that it was refining its time-keeping procedures to correct for any shortcoming. But, at the same time, Bruce Nordstrom denied that there was a "pattern" of abuse and maintained that complying with the law would "not alter our culture nor affect our continued commitment to customer service."[23]

---

[18] Robert Spector, "Union Says Nordstrom Owes Workers Millions," *Footwear News,* November 6, 1989, p. 8.

[19] The National Labor Relations Board (NLRB) is an independent federal agency responsible for enforcing the National Labor Relations Act—a body of federal law that governs relations between labor unions and employers engaged in interstate commerce. In addition to conducting unionization elections, the NLRB investigates, prosecutes and remedies employers' and unions' labor practices that are in violation of the NLR Act. The agency operates out of 52 offices throughout the U.S. and employs nearly 3,000 people. Its leadership (a general counsel and five-member board) are appointed by the president.

[20] George Tibbits, *Financial News* (API newswire), February 26, 1990, time: 13:59 PST.

[21] Blackburn Katia, *Financial News* (API newswire), February 16, 1990, time: 17:21 PST.

[22] Bob Baker, "Agency Orders Nordstrom to Pay Back Wages," *Los Angeles Times,* February 17, 1990, p. D1.

[23] Francine Schwadel, "Nordstrom to Post Its First Decline in Annual Profit," *Wall Street Journal,* February 20, 1990, p. A16.

As part of their efforts to illustrate their good intentions, Nordstrom management vowed to compensate employees for any past errors in its record-keeping and pay practices. To do so, they set up a procedure by which all employees nationwide could submit claims for back pay. The procedure offered employees the opportunity to collect a lump sum payment based on their choice of either length of service or their own detailed individual claims. In the former case, the payment was for $300, $700, or $1,000, depending on an employee's length of service. Initially, this back-pay offer was mailed only to current employees outside of Washington because management had to consult the State Labor & Industries Department and the local union before extending the offer to Washington employees.[24] Management was also designing a process by which former employees entitled to back pay could collect from the company. To fund the back-pay claims program, Nordstrom voluntarily established a $15 million reserve — which had a substantial effect on fourth quarter earnings.[25]

In addition to setting up the back-pay fund, management took steps to improve the existing system and restore its integrity. They first sent a memo to employees detailing company pay policies and reassuring sales clerks that they would be paid for all store meetings, inventory work, and deliveries. They also initiated several procedural changes, including the adoption of sign-out sheets. Under the new system, sales clerks who planned to do extra work at home or on the way home (i.e., deliveries) could punch out on the time clock at the end of their shift but also indicate on the sign-out sheet that they were doing work after hours. The next day they would submit a time sheet showing the amount of extra time worked.

Local 1001 President Peterson argued that this arrangement was placing the burden on employees to keep records, when it was Nordstrom's responsibility.[26] Peterson also criticized another Nordstrom policy: the classification of tasks performed off the sales floor into "selling" and "non-selling" activities. By continuing to classify certain behind-the-scenes tasks as "selling" duties, time spent writing "thank-you" letters and similar activities would remain in the denominator of sales-per-hour performance measures. Consequently, Peterson contended, employees would continue to feel pressure not to report all their hours spent on these tasks.

On February 27, 1990, Nordstrom became the target of another unhappy constituency. Immediately after fourth quarter earnings were released, three individual Nordstrom stockholders filed a suit against the company (for unspecified damages) in Seattle's King County Superior Court. They claimed to have suffered financial losses due to Nordstrom management's failure to disclose adequately their labor problems and the early claims for unpaid work. The suit requested that it be made a class action suit on behalf of Nordstrom's more than 75,000 stockholders.[27] (See **Exhibit 6** for a history of Nordstrom's stock price.)

Within a two-day period, Nordstrom became the target of a second class action suit. On February 28, 1990, UFCW Locals 1001 and 367, together with five individually named plaintiffs employed by Nordstrom filed suit on behalf of approximately 50,000 current and former Nordstrom employees (union and nonunion) nationwide. The lawsuit accused the company of numerous violations of state and federal wage and hour laws and requested that

---

[24] Francine Schwadel, "Nordstrom Creates $15 Million Reserve for Back Wages," *Wall Street Journal,* February 27, 1990, p. A3.

[25]Although the $15 million provision was not made public until late February 1990, it was recorded as an expense against Nordstrom's 1989 fourth-quarter earnings (quarter ending January 31, 1990).

[26] Stuart Silverstein, "Nordstrom to Change Its Timekeeping Procedures," *Los Angeles Times,* February 24, 1990, p. D2.

[27] *Financial News* (newswire), February 27, 1990, time: 20:27 PST.

the King County Superior Court order Nordstrom to improve its record keeping and award damages equal to twice the amount of unpaid wages (plus additional damages determined at trial and attorneys' fees). **Exhibit 7** reproduces the union's alleged "facts." Union officials had decided to launch the suit because they considered Nordstrom's response to the Washington State order, both the policy changes and the $15 million provision for back pay, inadequate.[28]

Reaction to the suit among employees was mixed. Many remained loyal to Nordstrom and came to its defense. Several employee-organized rallies took place outside stores in Seattle and California featuring signs and chants such as "We Love Nordstrom," "My Job is #1," and "I Love Being a Nordie." The demonstrators resented the local unions' assertion that the union spoke for all Nordstrom employees.

Nevertheless, the national publicity elicited by the suit brought into question the image and systems that Nordstrom's competitors had sought to emulate. According to one retail consultant, the company long considered the epitome of retailing excellence and superior service had actually enjoyed an unfair advantage by not paying fully for employees' work. If the apparent means of Nordstrom's success proved true, he believed, other retailers would probably become less eager to replicate the Nordstrom retailing model.

In the spring of 1990, Nordstrom management was defending itself on multiple fronts.

First, on March 16, 1990, Nordstrom's lawyers petitioned the court to void the Washington State Department of Labor & Industries' ruling (dated February 15) on the grounds that the department's investigation and release of findings had violated Nordstrom's constitutional rights to due process and equal protection. (The Labor & Industries Department subsequently filed a counter-claim in defense of its actions.) If Nordstrom and the agency could not resolve their differences directly, the agency would have to take Nordstrom to court to enforce its ruling.

---

[28] *Financial News* (API newswire), February 28, 1990, time: 21:30 PST.

---

**EXHIBIT 1:** **Nordstrom, Inc. and Subsidiaries Ten-Year Statistical Summary ($000, except per share figures)**

|  | 1990 | 1989 | 1988 | 1987 |
|---|---|---|---|---|
| *Operations* | | | | |
| Net sales | $2,671,114 | $2,327,946 | $1,920,231 | $1,629,918 |
| Total costs and expenses | 2,491,705 | 2,129,514 | 1,757,498 | 1,489,679 |
| Earnings before income taxes | 179,409 | 198,432 | 162,733 | 140,239 |
| Net earnings | $ 114,909 | $ 123,332 | $ 92,733 | $ 72,939 |
| Fully diluted earnings per share | 1.41 | 1.51 | 1.13 | .91 |
| *Stores and Facilities* | | | | |
| Company-operated stores | 59 | 58 | 56 | 53 |
| Total square footage | 6,898,000 | 6,374,000 | 5,527,000 | 5,098,000 |

Also, the NLRB maintained their charges that Nordstrom had illegally circumvented the union in communicating with its employees. If the agency could not persuade Nordstrom to settle out of court, it planned to bring its allegations before an administrative judge.

In addition to dealing with state and federal regulatory agencies, Nordstrom remained embroiled in the dispute surrounding both the shareholders' and the union's class action suits against it. In May 1990, *60 Minutes,* the popular CBS news magazine show, televised a 20-minute segment on Nordstrom's incentive systems and related problems.

According to the assistant director of the Washington State Department of Labor & Industries:[29]

> We're looking at what is likely to be the highest wage claim in the history of the state. These are employment practice patterns the company engaged in, not isolated incidents.

### The Jury Was Out

In Nordstrom's 1989 Annual Report, released in March 1990, the company's executive committee summarized its position:

> We are disappointed that there is now litigation regarding the payment of retroactive wages and related issues. Our policy has always been to pay our employees for the work that they perform, and this policy has not changed over the years. Employee initiative and enthusiasm has always been important in servicing the needs of customers, and we appreciate the efforts of our employees. They are the foundation of the Company's success. Some mistakes have been made in compensating our employees, and we are in the process of correcting them. We believe, however, that our sales employees are the highest paid in our industry. And we also believe that they will continue to provide the customer service that they have become known for because they enjoy selling for the Company and because they are rewarded for their efforts through commissions on their sales.

As of April 1990, there were no indications of emerging consensus among Nordstrom's 50,000 current and former employees as to the seriousness of the problem. While

---

[29] Faludi, op. cit.

| 1986 | 1985 | 1984 | 1983 | 1982 | 1981 |
|---|---|---|---|---|---|
| $1,301,857 | $ 958,678 | $ 768,677 | $ 598,666 | $ 512,188 | $ 400,614 |
| 1,214,478 | 886,167 | 694,838 | 550,353 | 468,513 | 364,059 |
| 87,379 | 72,511 | 73,839 | 48,313 | 43,675 | 36,555 |
| $ 50,079 | $ 40,711 | $ 40,239 | $ 27,013 | $ 24,775 | $ 19,655 |
| .65 | .54 | .54 | .38 | .35 | .29 |
| .52 | 44 | 39 | 36 | 34 | 31 |
| 4,727,000 | 3,924,000 | 3,213,000 | 2,977,000 | 2,640,000 | 2,166,000 |

over a thousand employees had mailed in to Local 1001 back-pay claims (averaging $5,000 each),[30] hundreds of other fiercely loyal "Nordies" came to management's defense. Some loyalists expressed their sentiments by signing a petition to decertify the union and some participated in "pro-Nordstrom" rallies.

Confusion around the merits of Nordstrom's management systems and culture was evident in the contradictory claims of outspoken current and former employees. Some of these were negative:

> We have the sworn testimony of a supervisor. He said it was routine in this department that people would come in and do the markdowns in preparation for a sale on their own time, on their day off, off the clock. If they didn't get it done in time, he'd punish them by not scheduling them to work on the first day of the sale. This is no petty violation, and it goes far beyond customer service. It goes right down to the core of the business.[31]

> It was like a snake pit. They'd throw you into the arena, and the strong would survive.[32]

> The system fosters a lot of pettiness and jealousy. . . . It's fear that provides great customer service.[33]

Other comments, however, were positive:

> I've never been asked to work overtime or make deliveries or do anything I didn't feel in my heart I wanted to do for many reasons. And my paycheck reflects that service I give. Everything I do, I'm compensated for in many, many ways.[34]

As the crisis escalated, national newspapers began printing letters to their editors which expressed opinions on the Nordstrom grievances. One letter challenged directly a basic assumption of the union grievance action:

> When I worked at Nordstrom's Anchorage and Spokane stores, I was paid to the minute for all the time I was in the store as an hourly employee. When I was in management, I received a salary and bonus structure that rivaled that of many other professionals. The awards and sales incentives were fair and generous.

> The people dismayed with the long hours required do not grasp a fundamental of retail: The shopkeeper must be available to the customer at the customer's whim, not to suit the employees' or owners' desires.[35]

When confronted by reporter Morley Safer during a *60 Minutes* interview on the problem, Bruce and Jim Nordstrom summarized Nordstrom management's beliefs:

> The system is to have self-empowered people who have an entrepreneurial spirit, who feel that they're in this to better themselves and to feel good about themselves and to make more money and to be successful. That's the system.

> [We have] expectations on our people. And when people apply for a job anyplace, they want to work hard and they want to do a good job. That's their intention. And our intention is to allow them the freedom to work as hard as they want to work.[36]

---

[30] Telephone interview with Joe Peterson, president of UFCW Local 1001, May 16, 1990.
[31] *60 Minutes*, (CBS news documentary on national television), May 6, 1990.
[32] Ibid.
[33] Baker, op. cit.
[34] *60 Minutes*, op. cit.
[35] Letter to the Editor, *Wall Street Journal*, March 14, 1990, p. A19.
[36] *60 Minutes*, op. cit.

**EXHIBIT 2    Sample Customer Letter**

10-23-89

Dear Mr. Nordstrom,

I shopped in your store October 7th. As always it was a fun experience. One of your employees, Anne Smith, was particularly nice. Your store did not have my size in a jacket I loved. Ms. Smith found out that I was from Oregon & wanted the jacket for a party on the 14th. She drove to South Center and picked it up (after work) and I came in later that evening and purchased it. She deserves recognition!

I supervise several employees and recognize outstanding employees when I see them. Ms. Smith went out of her way to see that the

# nordstrom

800 Tacoma Mall
Tacoma, WA 98409-7273
(206) 475-3630

October 31, 1989

Ms. Cheryl Johnson
1321 Lawnridge Ave.
Springfield, OR 97477

Dear Ms. Johnson:

Thank you for your thoughtful letter about the good service you received from Anne Smith in our Individualist department. I'm glad Anne followed through for you and located the jacket you wanted. Customer service is our number one priority at Nordstrom Tacoma Mall and salespeople like Anne help set a positive example for the rest of the store to emulate. It will be my pleasure to share your kind note with Anne and her department manager. I really appreciate your feedback.

Sincerely,

Peter E. Nordstrom
Store Manager

PEN:cam

cc:    Tracy Magnuson, Individualist Manager, Tacoma

*Source:* Washington State Department of Labor & Industries, ESAC Division, Nordstrom Investigation.

**EXHIBIT 3**   International Memo Differentiating "Selling" vs. "Non-Selling" Time

TO:        ALL STORE AND DEPARTMENT MANAGERS
FROM:      THE NORDSTROM FAMILY
SUBJ:      EMPLOYEE COMPENSATION FOR TIME WORKED
DATE:      AUGUST 1, 1989

The following information is offered as a review of some long-standing Company business practices. First of all, the Nordstrom policy of employee compensation is based on the premise that "all employees will be paid for time worked". Although it would be impossible to outline all examples of work activities, we'll attempt to review some common Company practices that warrant employee compensation.

"Hand carries" - merchandise that is picked up by an employee at one store and delivered to another. If done during regular work hours, employee remains on time clock. If effort is made going to and from work, the employee may be entitled to be paid for time over and above their normal commute time. ("Hand carries" that facilitate a personal sale are considered an extension of the selling process and regular "selling-time" would be paid. If the employee has been requested to pick up and deliver merchandise other than for a personal customer, their time would be compensated as "non-sell").

"Home deliveries" - merchandise that is delivered to a customer's home, office, hotel, hospital room, etc. The same criteria as "hand carries" would apply.

Although there are many functions related to each employee's job, listed below are a number of activities that are part of the selling/customer service process. These efforts are to be performed at the work place. Also, when work is performed outside the work place (i.e., at home), then, depending on the circumstances, an employee may be entitled to compensation.

- Time spent locating merchandise from other stores via the telephone.

- Stock assignments, floor moves and work parties, i.e., picking up "dead wood", "singles parties", "running hash", or any other merchandise handling activity.

- Sales promotion activities and customer correspondence, i.e., Thank You notes, addressing sale notices, etc.

- MNS book documentation efforts.

- Customer Service Board, Human Resource Committee, and Safety Committee tasks and activities.

- "Personal Touch" department seminars and activities.

- Employee meetings that are mandatory. In addition, if the meeting is voluntary, then our people should never suffer criticism for not attending.

Again, this partial list does not pretend to encompass all possible job related functions. However, the intent is to reiterate and possibly clarify some compensatory work activities at Nordstrom.

*Source:* Washington State Department of Labor & Industries, ESAC Division, Nordstrom Investigation.

**EXHIBIT 4    Summary of UFCW Local 1001 Complaint**

JOSEPH A. DEAR
Director

STATE OF WASHINGTON
DEPARTMENT OF LABOR AND INDUSTRIES
*General Administration Building   •   Olympia, Washington 98504-0631*
ESAC Division, 406 Legion Way SE
Olympia, Washington 98504 - Phone 586-2236

February 15, 1990

Mr. Wayne Hansen
Lane Powell Moss & Miller
1420 Fifth Avenue, Suite 4100
Seattle, Washington  98101-2338

Dear Mr. Hansen:

On November 21, 1989, The Employment Standards Section of the
Department of Labor and Industries received a complaint from Local 1001
of the United Food and Commercial Workers Union representing the
employees of Nordstrom Inc.  The basis of the complaint was:

1.  Nordstrom employees are required or encouraged to attend
    store, department and group meetings, outside normal work
    hours, without compensation, where the purpose of the meeting
    is to discuss work objectives and other work related topics.

2.  Nordstrom employees are required or encouraged to locate
    merchandise at other stores, either by phone or in person,
    outside of normal work hours, without compensation.  This
    would include, deliveries of merchandise to customers homes,
    called "hand carries."

3.  Employees are required or encouraged to perform stock work
    outside of normal work hours, without compensation.  This
    includes floor moves, sale set-ups, inventory preparation, mark
    downs and ticketing, and other merchandise handling
    activities.

4.  Employees are required or encouraged to write customer
    correspondence including thank-you notes, as well as
    addressing advertising circulars, sales notices, and
    maintaining personal trade books, all outside of normal work
    hours, without compensation.

*Exhibit 4    Continued*

Mr. Wayne Hansen
February 15, 1990



    5.    Employees are required or encouraged to work on "Make
          Nordstrom Special" projects outside of normal work hours,
          without compensation.  This also includes Customer Service
          Book preparation and maintenance, as well as attendance at
          Customer Service Board meetings.

    6.    Employees' overtime rates are not adjusted upward when
          commission payments increase their gross earnings during weeks
          when overtime is worked.

On December 5, 1989, the Department requested certain records from
Nordstrom Inc.  A copy of one of those letters is attached.  The
investigation was assigned to the Seattle Service Location, and was
coordinated by the Regional Supervisor, Cindy Hanson.

On December 11, 1989, the Department met with officials from Nordstrom
Inc., and the company's attorneys.  The majority of the records
requested were provided at that time, with the remaining records being
delivered on December 19, 1989.

Following is an overview of each allegation contained in the complaint;
Nordstrom's position taken regarding the allegation; and the findings
made by the Department.  This overview is based on the complaint and
documents submitted on behalf of the employees (See Exhibit 1); records
provided by Nordstrom (See Exhibit 2); information obtained from the
meeting with Nordstrom officials on December 5, 1989; and various
telephone conversations with Nordstrom and employee representatives.

*Source:* Washington State Department of Labor & Industries, ESAC Division, Nordstrom Investigation.

**EXHIBIT 5**   **Department of Labor & Industries Conclusion and Order**

## II. CONCLUSIONS

Based on the above findings of fact, the Department makes the following conclusions:

1. There is no indication that any of the voluntary meetings referenced in allegation 1 would meet the Department's position on unpaid training time (See Exhibit 3). An example given by Nordstrom at our meeting and the records received indicate that all meetings held are directly related to the employee's jobs. Therefore, the company is in violation of RCW 49.46.020, and RCW 49.46.130, where applicable, for not properly compensating its employees for all time spent in meetings. In addition, Nordstrom has not kept records of this time worked, in violation of RCW 49.46.070 and WAC 296-128-010.

2. Records reviewed indicate employees have made deliveries of merchandise to other stores, in person, outside of normal work hours. Certain hours worked by employees locating and delivering merchandise would be considered hours worked under Chapter 49.46 RCW. Therefore, the company is in violation of RCW 49.46.020, for failing to properly compensate employees for all time worked.

   In addition, Nordstrom has failed to record these hours of work performed by employees as specified in RCW 49.46.070 and WAC 296-128-010(6).

3. Nordstrom has failed to record the actual hours of work performed by cosmetic line managers as specified in RCW 49.46.070, WAC 296-128-010(6). Employees are required to perform inventory duties on their own time and the payment received for these hours worked by cosmetic line managers is not accurate or in accordance with the state overtime provisions as specified in RCW 49.46.130 and WAC 396-128-550.

4. Nordstrom permits the writing of thank-you notes by employees on their own time, without proper compensation, in violation of RCW 49.46.020. Nordstrom has failed to record actual hours of this work performed by employees as specified in RCW 49.46.0709 and WAC 296-128-010.

5. Work performed by employees in preparing Customer Service Books and "Make Nordstrom Special" projects/books is considered time worked. In reviewing the documentation, the

*Exhibit 5   Continued*

department found nothing to substantiate the allegations that employees are encouraged or required to work on "Make Nordstrom Special" projects outside of normal work hours without compensation.

6.  Nordstrom has not paid overtime to employees in violation of the state overtime provisions, as specified in RCW 49.46.130.

### III. ORDER

Based on the above findings of fact and conclusions of law, the Department of Labor and Industries hereby orders Nordstrom Inc. to immediately from this date forward:

1.  Compensate employees for attending various store meetings, when the meeting is held in the interest of the employer or is directly related to the employees' job, pursuant to RCW 49.46.020 and RCW 49.46.130; and to

2.  Comply with record keeping provisions pursuant to RCW 49.46.070, WAC 296-128-010; and to

3.  Compensate employees for all hours of work, pursuant to RCW 49.46.070; and to

4.  Compensate employees for overtime hours worked pursuant to RCW 49.46.130; and to

5.  Retroactively compensate all current and former employees who were not compensated for all hours worked, or who were not properly compensated for overtime hours worked, pursuant to RCW 49.46.020 and RCW 49.46.130.

BY:

Michael Pellegrini
Supervisor of Employment Standards

2·15-90
Date

cc:    Joe Peterson, UFCW Local 1001
       Mark McDermott, Assistant Director, ESAC Division

*Source:* Washington State Department of Labor & Industries, ESAC Division, Nordstrom Investigation.

**EXHIBIT 6**  **Nordstrom Stock Price History**

|      |           | MONTHLY CLOSE ($/SHARE) |
|------|-----------|------------------------|
| 1989 | January   | 32-4/8 |
|      | February  | 31-2/8 |
|      | March     | 33-2/8 |
|      | April     | 33-6/8 |
|      | May       | 34-4/8 |
|      | June      | 31-2/8 |
|      | July      | 35-6/8 |
|      | August    | 41-6/8 |
|      | September | 39-4/8 |
|      | October   | 36-6/8 |
|      | November  | 37-4/8 |
|      | December  | 37-2/8 |
| 1990 | January   | 33-4/8 |
|      | February  | 27-6/8 |
|      | March     | 31-4/8 |

**EXHIBIT 7** **UFCW Local 1001 Complaint for Declaratory and Injunctive Relief, Damages, and Statutory Penalties (Class Action)**

III. <u>FACTS</u>.

11.  Nordstrom and Local 1001 have been parties to a series of collective bargaining agreements, the most recent of which expired on July 31, 1989.  Nordstrom and Local 367 have been parties to a series of collective bargaining agreeemnts, the most recent of which expired on July 31, 1989.  The Unions do not bring the claims herein under these agreements.

12.  Nordstrom has individual employment contracts with its employees, which contracts are formed from company-wide employment policies and practices.  Under these employment contracts, employees are compensated as follows:  Most sales employees are paid an hourly wage for time spent in selling activities ("selling time") and non-selling activities ("non-sell time").  In addition, employees may receive additional wages for selling time in the form of commissions based on sales of goods and services above each employee's sales quota.  Each employee's sales quota is determined by dividing the hourly guaranteed wage rate by the commission rate applicable to the merchandise or services sold.  For example, the sales quota for an employee who is guaranteed $9.75 per hour and has a commission rate of 6.75 percent is $9.75 per hour divided by 0.0675 or $144.44 of sales per hour.  Some sales employees are paid an hourly wage plus a commission on sales of goods and services.  Non-sales employees and some sales employees are paid an hourly wage.

13.  Nordstrom has company-wide policies applicable to all employees, including employees represented by the Unions and unrepresented employees, the terms of which are included in individual employment contracts between Nordstrom and its employees. These policies require payment for all work Nordstrom has permitted to be performed for its benefit, including, but not limited to, the location and acquisition of merchandise from other stores; the delivery of merchandise to a customer's home, office or other location; the performance of various stock assignments; the performance of sales promotion activities, including writing and addressing "Thank You" notes and addressing sale notices to customers; various customer service promotions, including "Make Nordstrom Special" projects, the preparation and maintenance of customer service books, and attendance at customer service board and other company meetings; and various other work activity all for the benefit of Nordstrom.

*Exhibit 7    Continued*

14    14.    Nordstrom has consistently and routinely failed to pay
15    wages to employees represented by the Unions, individual plaintiffs
16    and employees similarly situated, for activities for which
17    compensation is required by individual employment contract or by
18    law, including the activities identified in the preceding paragraph.
19
20    15.    Officers, directors, and responsible managers of Nordstrom
21    knew that employees were performing the work described in paragraph
22    13 above without being paid as required by individual employment
23    contract or by law and yet contined to promote or permit these
24    activities to continue.

1    16.    In failing to pay wages to employees as alleged in
1    paragraphs 13 through 15 above, Nordstrom has acted willfully and
2    with the intent of depriving employees of such wages.
3
4    17.    Nordstrom has failed to keep accurate records of the time
5    worked by employees performing the activities alleged in paragraph
6    13 above.

7    18.    Nordstrom has discouraged employees from submitting claims
8    for compensation for work performed "off the clock" and has
9    subjected employees who submit such claims to reprisal and threat of
10    reprisal.
11
12    19.    Nordstrom has compelled, coerced, or required employees to
13    purchase clothing from Nordstrom to wear while working at stores
14    operated by Nordstrom.

15    20.    Nordstrom has withheld from wages earned by employees the
16    amount of commissions that were paid on merchandise that is
17    subsequently returned, where such merchandise was not sold by the
18    employee against whom the commission was charged.
19

20    21.    By its conduct alleged in paragraphs 13 through 20 above,
21    Nordstrom has irreparably harmed employees represented by the
22    Unions, the individual plaintiffs and other employees similarly
23    situated for which they have no adequate remedy at law.

*Source:* Washington State Department of Labor & Industries, ESAC Division, Nordstrom Investigation.

## CASE 24    Turner Construction Company: Project Management Control Systems

"I received a call this morning from the owner of one of our biggest Philadelphia construction projects, the new Kent Square office tower. The owner wants us to release $500,000 in project savings so that the money will be available to him to reinvest in additional project upgrades. Because the job is now 80% complete, he assumes the unspent contingency reserve is not likely to be needed and should therefore be returned."

G ary Thompson, Turner's Philadelphia Territory General Manager, went on to explain the resulting dilemma:

The project manager and superintendent on the job want to maintain the Construction Contingency for several more months. They want to be financially prepared for potential exposures they've identified.

The contract for this job calls for savings participation. That means that once we release a contingency as savings, we will share it with the owner, in this case keeping 25% for ourselves as additional project earnings and returning 75% to the owner. Our managers are trained to be conservative and have been threatened with their lives to protect our gross earnings on each job. If we release contingency dollars to an owner prematurely, we may never see the money again, regardless of what unforeseen problems and developments happen on that job. Then we are forced to dip into our fee earnings to complete the job.

Because of these pressures, my people have a tendency to want to hold contingencies until the very last minute. But if we wait too long to release the savings, it can threaten our relationship with the client. This timing issue is one of the things I worry about the most; it can really bite you sometimes.

In addition to pressure from the owner, I'm also feeling pressure from division management to release the contingency to earnings. Top management needs to meet Turner's quarterly corporate earnings projection. And because of a loss on a sale of a Turner Development building, corporate called on our division executive VP to try to come up with an additional $200,000 earnings for this quarter. Les Shute—my boss—called me to see how much my territory could contribute.

I've asked Jim Verzella, the project executive on the Kent Square building, to review the project's most recent IOR [Indicated Outcome Report] and talk to the project team to determine how much savings they can comfortably release to the owner at this point. I want to have an answer by the end of the week, when we have the next OAT [Owner, Architect, Turner] meeting with the Kent Square project representative.

Les Shute is coming down at the end of the week for his monthly Territory Review meeting. I need to have an answer for him on what additional amount our territory can book in earnings for this quarter. To be safe, I can tell him I have no additional savings to release as earnings. But I'd rather not have to do that. So, I'll spend a good part of today picking the brains of my five project executives to see how much contingency each of them can release from their current projects. I have to be careful, because once we book earnings, it looks very bad if we fall short of projections in a subsequent quarter—it looks bad to senior management, to our auditors, and ultimately to the stockholders. We never want to release a contingency and then later discover that without the contingency we need to dip into our fee to finish the job.

## Company Background and Structure[1]

During the late 1980s, Turner Construction Company, headquartered in New York City, was the largest general building contractor and construction management company in the U.S. Through its offices in over 35 cities, Turner served virtually all non-residential construction markets, including commercial, hospital, manufacturing, education, hotel, airports, advanced technology, and the public sector. During 1989, Turner managed 550 active projects and completed construction valued at $3.6 billion. Operating income for the construction work completed was $35.6 million. Also in 1989, the company secured $3.2 billion of new business.

Turner's domestic operation was divided into 28 territories, each headed by a territory general manager (TGM). Top management gave each TGM considerable autonomy to run his territory as an independent business and an important role of the TGM was prospecting for new work. Within the decentralized structure, each TGM reported to one of 5 group vice presidents who in turn reported to 3 division executive vice presidents (EVPs) all of whom were members of the Corporate Executive Group. **Exhibit 1** depicts the corporate organizational structure.

Construction operations were managed on a project by project basis. **Exhibit 2** illustrates the composition of a typical project team as well as overall territory structure. A territory's operations manager (TOM), who reported to the TGM, assembled project teams from his territory's staff based on specific project requirements, staff availability, and employee development objectives. (The TOM's function was similar to that of a chief operating officer, while the TGM functioned more like a territory CEO.) Reporting to the TOM were 3 to 6 project executives who each headed 4 or 5 projects at a time. Project executives were assisted by project managers who were assigned to manage each large project.

A typical construction project at Turner lasted 1 to 3 years and was valued at $10 to 25 million. Once awarded a job, Turner management planned and scheduled construction, procured the required materials and manpower, awarded subcontracts, and managed overall operations. Turner typically performed less than 10% of the contracted work using its own staff. Throughout the life of a project, the Turner project team maintained on-going communications with the owner and architect, as well as with a large number of subcontractors and suppliers.

In most cases, Turner negotiated the terms of each contract with the property owner, using its own Estimating staff, subcontractor input, and database of past experience to estimate project costs. The owner usually compensated Turner on a cost-plus basis, up to the guaranteed maximum price ("GMP") stipulated in the contract. Turner's fee for managing the project (i.e., gross earnings) was also stipulated and fixed in the contract. To provide incentives for careful cost management, any savings between the GMP and actual costs were usually shared with the owner according to savings participation terms specified in the contract. Costs in excess of GMP were absorbed exclusively by Turner, reducing project fee earnings.

## Project Management, Financial Control, and the IOR System

**A Project Executive's View**    After meeting with Philadelphia TGM Thompson, the case writer met with Jim Verzella, the Philadelphia project executive in charge of the Kent Square building. When the case writer mentioned the "$500,000 question" currently facing him, Verzella explained its significance and the context of control systems in which it would be resolved:

---

[1] As an aid to the reader, a Glossary of abbreviations used in the case is provided on page 600.

To appreciate how we can find $500,000 for the owner, you first need to understand our IOR [Indicated Outcome Report] system, which was first introduced in the 1920s. Even though Turner builds buildings, our business is really risk management, and the IOR system allows us to do that effectively. The Philadelphia office in particular is very proactive in the way we use the IOR system and other controls. Other companies may have financial tracking systems, but no one spends as much time on it as us.

The IOR is really the heart of our management system at Turner. It raises the flags so that I know what questions to ask. We produce an IOR for every construction project on a quarterly basis, with 6-week updates. The Turner Forecasting System ("TFS") consolidates IORs on a monthly basis, in less detail, at every level up the organization all the way to corporate. The details of the system may appear confusing to an outsider, but it is actually very simple and it assists all of us in doing our jobs. The IOR system is the backbone of most of our other formal reporting systems. (See **Exhibit 3** for a list of the most important management reports and their relationship to the IOR.)

Basically, an IOR is a best efforts prediction at any point in time of the total expected cost and earnings contribution of a completed project. It itemizes the maximum dollar commitment from the owner on the left side of the page and the corresponding dollars that will flow out to subcontractors and suppliers on the right side. Any difference in the two sides represents savings or cost overruns that directly affect our earnings on the completed project.

More specifically, the left side of the IOR—which is based on our original bid and contract—is broken down into expenditures for which reimbursement from the owner is assured (i.e., included in the GMP contract) and those for which it is not yet certain (i.e., scope or other changes not yet approved by the owner). The left side also includes our fee as part of the GMP. The right side of the IOR—called Indicated Cost—separates expenditures to which Turner is committed from expenditures that are anticipated but not yet certain.

I spend roughly two days a month reviewing all my projects' IORs and participating in IOR-related meetings. Although the IOR is formally revised once per quarter, I review informal updates at least once each month. The major risk management decisions that I'm involved with—like the $500,000 one at hand—revolve around that last category of IOR line items, the ones we call contingency holds and exposure holds, or "C-holds" and "E-holds." E-holds are those line item reserves that are earmarked for trade-specific expenditures [plumbing, carpentry, masonry, etc.] that, based on our experience, we believe are very likely to be spent; C-holds are the more general line item reserves that, if all goes well, need not be spent. In addition to the two types of holds, all projects have a Construction Contingency—usually about 2.5% of total project costs—that serves as a bottom line reserve against scope changes and cost increases that are unspecified up front.

The holds and the Construction Contingency represent uncommitted "buffer" dollars that are included in the GMP and are available to absorb reasonable expenses that are difficult to estimate in advance. If not spent, they become savings and are shared with the owner. But, if the holds along with all the other line items are not constantly and carefully monitored, discussed, and revised throughout the life of a project, we cannot proactively manage project earnings. We have to know exactly where the project stands and what is behind those holds to determine what we have left to spend and what we can book as earnings.

I sometimes have to test my staff to see if a contingency reserve is really a C- or an E-hold. They usually want to squirrel everything away as E-holds because they think if we put it as a C-hold, the customer will see it as savings and want to spend it.

Our strategy is to make the owner our partner in managing the project. That's the way to get repeat business, which is very important to us. One of our greatest competitive advantages is our ability to develop and share accurate information with the owner while a project is in progress. We're constantly trying to give an owner an updated end picture of what he'll be spending. The IOR helps us decide when and how to tell an owner whether we expect to realize savings on the project. We can then work together to identify problems and options. That kind of cooperation is the reason that an owner or developer with tens of millions of dollars on the line chooses Turner. Turner doesn't compete solely on price—we're not the cheapest contractors in town. So, we have to show owners that we are expert managers and can spend their money efficiently.

Depending on the experience and demands of an owner, we'll share all or part of the IOR cost detail with him. That helps us to educate the owner and gives him useful information to make decisions on when to intervene and what scope adjustments to request. We actually prefer to work with knowledgeable, involved owners, because they end up making smarter decisions and ultimately being more satisfied with the finished product.

If the numbers in the IOR were not accurate and I could not support them, then dealing with the owner would get messy. It would be difficult to maintain his trust and at the same time negotiate effectively. The key to negotiation is understanding your counterpart [the owner and his project] as well as he knows himself. The detail of the IOR is indispensable in designing creative ways to accommodate owners' demands. For example, once we know where our project risks are, Turner can find a formula for sharing savings that keeps everyone happy. Sometimes that means promising the owner 100% of the first $X in savings, splitting the next $X 50-50, and sharing any additional savings 75-25, with a ceiling on our total take.

Our financial reports must be updated constantly, because the owner's reaction is always negative if we wait too long to give back a considerable savings. Last year, we completed a $20 million project that came in $1 million under the GMP. That sounds like great news, right? But because we didn't release any of the savings until the job was nearly complete, the owners were very upset. They had financing for the whole $20 million and, had we released the savings sooner, they would have spent the $1 million on additional scope development to improve the appearance of the building's facade and lobby. But it was too late by the time we told them they had an extra million dollars to spend.

That brings us back to the $500,000 issue. The Kent Square project is estimated to bill out at $29 million. The job is now 80% complete and our remaining Construction Contingency is $511,000, or 1.8% of total job costs. We also have $328,000 in C-holds and $471,000 in E-holds, with five months to completion. The owner thinks we can release $500,000 from the Contingency because the job has been going so smoothly.

**A Project Manager's View**   Bill Rantanen, the project manager who worked full-time on the Kent Square project, explained how he used the IOR system:

For me, the IOR is a forward-looking project management tool. Our IOR system is more forward-looking than the historical accounting-oriented systems of most of our competitors. It helps my project team anticipate financial and operational problems and avoid surprises. But the reports would be worthless if they were not talked about. The quarterly IOR Review Meetings are a great tool for prompting discussion among my whole team. The team meetings create overlap in knowledge of the job, so that nothing falls through the cracks. Everyone should know what's going on a little bit to their left and a little bit to their right. So, it's critical that activities for the different trades be discussed by team management as a group. We can only get to the C-holds and E-holds after going through the IOR line by line discussing actual and expected costs.

A typical job involves thousands of distinct parts and activities that must fit together precisely in terms of physical positioning on the job site and in terms of scheduling. For example, if carpentry work is falling behind schedule, we may have to arrange to have some overtime work done or we won't be able to start the plumbing according to schedule, and we need money for that; or, if a shipment of metal beams turns out to be a half inch too long, we have to allocate the time and money to cut them down; or, if shipment delays push interior work into a colder time of year, the budget allocation for site heating and electricity could be short by $10,000 a month. So, you see why IORs have to be updated regularly; our exposure is in a constant state of flux. Without the IOR expense and contingency detail, project management would be like writing checks without knowing how much is in the bank account.

The Review meetings also give me a chance to see how everyone is doing—whether my staff is on top of the critical paperwork [e.g., change orders, owner approval letters], and whether the subcontractors are performing up to standards. We can't afford to lose momentum on a job, because time is money. Through the meetings and all the interaction, I'll hear about any problems well before an IOR update is formally published and sent to Corporate.

The IOR meetings are by no means the only type of project management meetings we have; but they are the most forward looking and comprehensive, because the others focus on immediate problems and logistical details. (See **Exhibit 4** for a list of other regular management meetings.)

**The IOR Updating Process**   To understand how a typical IOR was created, the case writer spoke to Philadelphia Senior Cost Engineer Jayne Murphy, who described the IOR updating process:

> The value of the IOR system depends on the quality of the data it contains and the IOR updating process provides the necessary thoroughness. For each quarterly update, we go through an extensive series of discussions and meetings that include all members of a project team. The updating of exposure holds involves a lot of intuition and gut feel and can only be done when you understand the real situation of each project. So, I really have to ask a lot of questions and get a feel for the different projects and teams.

According to Murphy, it took a month or two of detailed work by the estimators and cost engineers to develop the first IOR for a new job. After that, the quarterly updating process took 3 to 4 weeks per project and was coordinated by a cost engineer who usually covered 3 projects at a time. (Cost engineers did not report to the project executive and TOM; instead, they functioned in an independent, quasi-staff capacity. Refer to **Exhibit 2**.) The updating process began with the cost engineer carefully reviewing a variety of document logs to note all new transactions, such as new work orders issued to subcontractors. For answers to specific questions, the cost engineer "made the rounds" among project team members who worked on site. To ask the right questions about the cost of uncompleted work and to interpret team members' assumptions and explanations, the cost engineer had to be familiar with general industry logistics as well as project-specific considerations.

After the cost engineer updated the previous IOR with all easily accessible information, the project's entire management team convened for a formal IOR Review Meeting, which could run all day and into the evening if necessary. The IOR meeting was led by the project executive or project manager and included the project superintendent, project engineer, cost engineer, and accountant. Assistant engineers also attended parts of meetings to review their particular trade (e.g., masonry). In the early stages of a project, a purchasing agent or estimator might also attend. The group walked through the partially updated IOR (40 to 80 pages) on a trade by trade basis. Through this dialogue, the team members explained to the project executive or manager all significant changes in project conditions and "Indicated Cost" and the causes of those changes. Many questions arose and all those present were called on to participate. The cost engineer documented all the agreed upon revisions on his or her partially updated draft. Most of the discussion focused on major variances (versus the previous IOR) and on E-holds, which tended to be more controversial than committed subcontract work and activities that were already in progress.

After incorporating all new information gained from the IOR Review Meeting, the cost engineer prepared a final updated version, reviewed it with the territory's senior cost engineer, requested the team management to sign it, and then sent the new IOR to the TGM for final approval. If the TGM perceived a substantial risk to cost, earnings, or client relations, he would become active in the review process and insist on additional iterations before approving the IOR. Upon approval from the TGM, the IOR was "published" by the territory cost department. Copies of each final IOR went to the project management team, the group vice president, his cost staff, the division executive vice president, and to the corporate cost department. If there were problems with a project, it was not unusual for Al McNeil, Chairman of Turner, to telephone a TGM to discuss details contained in the IOR.

The automated Turner Forecasting System ("TFS") incorporated the summary numbers from every IOR into the monthly territory earnings report and eventually the corporate income statement and corporate earnings projections. See **Exhibit 5** for a flow chart of the entire process.

**The IOR Cover Letter**    Each published IOR was accompanied by a package of summary documents, also prepared by the cost engineer. The three most important were the Financial Summary, the Physical Information Form, and the IOR Cover Letter. Cost Engineer Holly Green described the purpose and contents of the IOR Cover Letter:

> The IOR Cover Letter gives territory and corporate management a concise outline of our financial position on a project. It focuses on the most significant changes in the IOR detail from the prior report and should address the reasons for variations and key assumptions behind them. Because management is not familiar with specific job detail, the cover letter should make sense as a stand-alone assessment of a job's status.

According to Green, the contents of a typical IOR Cover Letter included the following:

- Financial summary of project earnings and volume
- Current earnings-to-cost ratio
- Description and schedule of project milestones
- Description of contract agreement with owner
- Estimated dollar volume of completed project (and explanation of changes)
- Discussion of major changes in earnings
- Discussion of major changes in Direct and Indirect costs
- Breakdown of uncommitted dollars (types of contingencies, unbought items, etc.).

Special attention was devoted in the Cover Letter to an evaluation of the overall level of construction contingency holds (on a trade-by-trade basis, if appropriate), giving consideration to the type of owner, experience of job staff, type of architect and subcontractors, and state of contract documents.

**Senior Management's Views**    Eastern Division Executive Vice President Don Kerstetter:

> The IOR system drives our projections of quarterly earnings as well as reported income to shareholders. If we don't meet those projections, we'll see a response on Wall Street.

> At my level and at corporate, we don't have to review every number in every IOR: the two-page financial summary sheets and the IOR cover letters cover the important issues and reveal the potentially big risks. I look at trends and risks to budgeted earnings. If I see a significant problem, I can dig deeper, right on my terminal, find the source, and then pick up the phone and call the TGM or group VP to discuss it.

> Of course not all cost engineers are equally adept at preparing IOR summaries and cover letters; but I trust the IOR numbers because of all the scrutiny they receive before reaching me. Our company policy of promoting from within and heavily cross-training gives me a high comfort level with the quality of the data. We have a lot of seasoned Turner managers on our projects who—largely because of the IOR system—have learned the Turner way of thinking. The majority of the senior project team has worked at one time in the Cost (IOR) department. So, they've learned a real respect for the cost end of the business.

> Also, there isn't much pressure to play games with the numbers because performance evaluation is a very subjective exercise at Turner. Turner is an open society. Because our bonus system is not tied to project profitability, managers don't hide problems. Bonuses throughout Turner are tied to corporate performance and subjective evaluations of individual contributions. So, managers know they won't be penalized for poor results on a difficult job that they've managed well. They also

know that if they play around with the integrity of the IOR system, project management only becomes more difficult.

Moreover, because the cost engineers who produce the reports don't report to line management, they have no motivation to hide bad news. They walk the job sites and talk with the project teams all the time. Their bosses along with my cost staff attend a lot of project meetings as well. They know how to spot red flags, ferret out the problems and risks on a job, and ask the difficult questions of the project team.

Another reason the system works well is that I have a feel right from the start as to which jobs I should watch closely. When we first authorize a proposal, I can judge how financially risky the job will be. I look at the guaranteed maximum price we have set, the size of the contingency built in to the contract, the type of project, my assessment of owner relations, and the particular people involved. All that information helps me to decide where risk management will be most critical.

In New York, Les Shute chatted with the case writer about his upcoming Monthly Territory Meeting with Gary Thompson:

You could think of my job as just a collection of individual problems. I go back to the IOR when I really need to understand the issues. Philadelphia has had a good year and I haven't needed to look at many IORs in detail. In some of my other territories, I spend a lot of time looking at them.

With the TFS, I try to be a devil's advocate, looking for problems and being suspicious. I get four reports each month—one for each territory. But before these are finalized, I go to each territory and sit down with the TGM and his staff and go over problems and opportunities. A lot of our discussion focuses on the proper level for contingencies.

The IOR and the TFS are really compilations of a whole lot of people's opinions. But you must have a contingency as an escape route. When things are bad, the TGMs will tuck away contingencies and hide good news. That is why it is so important to discuss these things face-to-face. With his boss sitting there, I can look a young cost engineer in the eye and ask, "Can we save $300,000 on this job?" I can read his eyes and I know the answer. When I sit down with Gary and Jayne, I look for the eyes to go from one to the other when I ask the tough questions.

I've asked Gary to give us more earnings this quarter because the company needs it and I know Philadelphia's projects are running well. Of course, those earnings must all be adequately documented for the auditors.

Gary is the only person in Philadelphia that I personally evaluate. He and I set goals for each year and at the end of the year, I write up a one-page evaluation of his performance. The Executive Group uses that as input to debate his contribution and decide on a performance bonus.

I don't think we could run the systems the way we do without executives who have been exposed to all parts of the business and really understand how these costs and contingencies are put together.

## The $500,000 Dilemma

Nearly all of the senior project team, as well as several other executives, were involved in the decision as to what portion of the $500,000 requested should be released to Kent Square. The ultimate decision would be made by the TGM, TOM, and project executive. Verzella, the project executive, explained the status of the decision as well as the decision-making process in general:

I just had a talk with the project manager and project super on Kent Square. They're very concerned about releasing much money. At first, they didn't want to give anything. But we walked through the major E-holds and C-holds and I tried to help them assess the likelihood of actually spending each one. For example, there's talk of a possible local strike in one of the trades. If it occurs, we'll probably have to use overtime labor. I definitely want to hold money for that. Bill Rantanen also has a legitimate need for extra clean-up funds. Whenever there are several different subcontractors working on the same floors within a structure, it inevitably gets messy. You can't keep track of who's account-able for what. So, because of the schedule we're on, we definitely need E-holds for extra clean-up.

We're still discussing a few of the big holds set aside for scope development. The architect on this job tends to submit a constant flow of new drawing and specification changes. Unless the owner will stop signing off on these scope changes, we can't rely on those holds as true buffer reserves. And unless we're confident that our holds are conservative, we cannot afford to release the $500,000 Construction Contingency. I'd be less reluctant if I thought we could go back to the owner later on to pay for any new scope development. But this is a new client for us. I have no idea how likely he is to spend whatever amount we release, and then not have the money to increase the GMP later if we run into unexpected problems. So, should I agree to release the contingency? If I wait too long, the owner may feel we weren't being honest and were hiding it. I know that he wants the $500,000 now to pay down some bridge loans.

Also, if I release the contingency to savings, Les Shute will want me to book our share of it in the territory earnings number. But when a job is 80% complete my confidence level in our IOR estimates is not as high as when the job is 95% complete.

Understanding owner psychology and motives is one of the most important parts of my job for two reasons: first, it helps us to build and maintain good client relationships; and second, it helps me to determine exactly how we share information with each client.

A good partnership helps us to get the owner's cooperation on a timely basis for things like approval letters for scope changes that keep a job running smoothly and on schedule. Over the long run, it preserves Turner's reputation and helps us get repeat business.

To treat owners like partners and build credibility, we want to give them all the facts, including the IOR details. When I have to tell an owner he has no money left to spend, how is he to decide whether to believe me? The IOR provides the detail with which I can explain my thoughts and actions. That means sitting down and explaining to the owner that we have projected savings at the moment but the savings could evaporate the next time we work through the numbers if something unexpected happens.

Owner psychology, style, and priorities are different on every project. There's no text book formula that can tell me what information to share or when to release savings.

I'm now managing six projects. Each owner uses a different method to evaluate contingencies. So, on each project, I have to assess the situation. Is this owner a conservative or a liberal spender? Is he knowledgeable about the construction process and its risks? Does he have untapped financial sources? We also have to size up the architect's style and competence and his relationship with the owner.

One kind of owner comes in, puts the shovel in the ground, says, "Call me when it's all done," and leaves. We're scared stiff of that type of owner. If we don't know what's going through his mind, we may decide not to release any savings until the end.

Take my current hospital project as an example. The owner thinks I'm just squirrelling away money to protect my interests. And he's absolutely right! He's got an architect who hasn't done any draw-ings correctly. And I know the state won't let him spend any more money because he's working from a Certificate of Need. I'm protecting him as much as I'm protecting myself. If I give him money back, he'll spend it, and he has no concept of where his budget is. So I don't consult him on contingency decisions. I'll sit on that contingency and call it whatever I have to, to keep it from the owner!

But I currently have another client at the other extreme. I'd bear my soul to him. I know I can release savings early and get every dime back if we get in a bind later on. He's good for his word and has the financial ability to keep us whole. Most clients fall between these two extreme examples. That's where all the judgement calls come in.

Coming back to the current decision, the bottom line is that I know we can release a portion of the $500,000, but we still need to pin down a number. Before I go back to Gary Thompson, I want to talk with a few other people: my senior cost engineer for her assessment of our exposure on the job; our estimators about some unbought work; and the owner about future scope development. I have a terrific manager on the job; he's great at managing logistics and avoiding cost overruns. So, I don't want to play it safer than necessary. I want to show the owner that we're in control and keep him happy, so we continue to get his business.

The case writers concluded their interviews by getting the perspective of the corporate cost department with regard to the Kent Square owner's request. Bob Meyer, Vice President of Project Management Cost Systems, expressed his opinion:

Some people may think that we spend too much time dealing with the contingency, but I don't think that is true. The time we spend here is really forcing our managers to keep revisiting our strategy with our clients on each job. We keep asking ourselves, "Are we doing the proper evaluation, providing the best product, and the best quality?"

At the end of every job, we produce a final IOR-style cost report that breaks down the whole history of the job in detail—cost per square foot, dollar value of scope development, and so on. That information becomes part of a database our estimators can use for guidance when pricing similar types of jobs. The IOR database allows us to fine tune our strategy: we know that hospital projects usually involve scope changes that cost 3% to 4% of GMP; laboratories and R&D facilities are in the 10% to 15% range.

If you look at the numbers I've circled on the Kent Square IOR (**Exhibit 6**), you will see that we've already released $215,000 of the original Construction Contingency to the owner's savings pool. But I believe that Verzella and Thompson should reconsider the need for maintaining the remaining $511,000. The job is 80% complete and the most recent IOR Financial Summary (**Exhibit 7**) indicates that they still have $328,000 in C-holds and $471,000 in E-holds. It looks like we're in great shape with enough of a buffer, especially given the fact that Gary tends to be relatively conservative in his projections. But it's his call; corporate won't override the decision of a TGM on releasing savings.

If Gary decides to release the $500,000 Construction Contingency, we'd kill two birds with one stone: the owner would get the spending money he is asking for and Turner's 25% share of the savings would help to offset a loss that has been projected elsewhere in the business. Since the job is 80% complete, we could book 25% × $500,000 × 80%—or $100,000—to this quarter's earnings.

Of course, I don't take the releasing of savings to an owner lightly. It should always be done with the owner's complete understanding that if the savings we're estimating today do not materialize at the end of the project, then we expect to be reimbursed by him for the additional scope he requested when he thought he had "savings money" to spend. The problem is that it's difficult to communicate that caveat to owners. It's a particularly delicate matter when you are trying to build a long term relationship with a new client. And the most recent Kent Square Cover Letter (**Exhibit 8**) shows that our relationship with the owner is still in good shape.

## Appendix

### Turner Construction Company: Project Management Control Systems

#### GLOSSARY OF ABBREVIATIONS USED IN CASE

| | |
|---|---|
| C-hold | Contingency-hold (general line item reserves) |
| E-hold | Exposure-hold (reserve for specific expenditures) |
| GMP | Guaranteed Maximum Price (contract ceiling) |
| IOR | Indicated Outcome Report |
| OAT | Owner, Architect, Turner (meeting) |
| TFS | Turner Forecasting System |
| TGM | Territory General Manager |
| TOM | Territory Operations Manager |

# Turner

## EXHIBIT 1

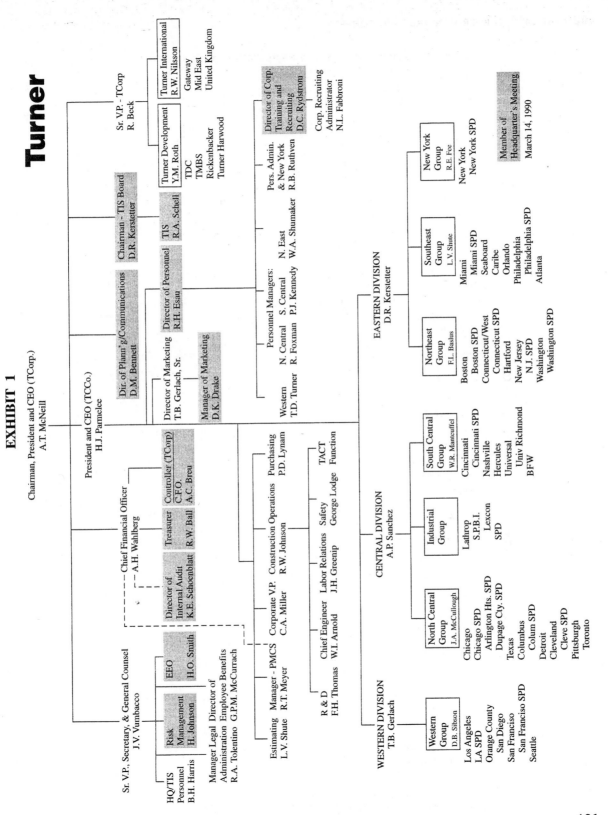

Chairman, President and CEO (TCorp.)
A.T. McNeill

Sr. V.P. - TCorp
R. Beck

Turner International
R.W. Nilsson

Gateway
Mid East
United Kingdom

Turner Development
Y.M. Roth

TDC
TMBS
Rickenbacker
Turner Harwood

President and CEO (TCCo.)
H.J. Parmelee

Dir of Plann'g/Communications
D.M. Bennett

Chairman - TIS Board
D.R. Kerstetter

Director of Personnel
R.H. Esau

TIS
R.A. Schell

Director of Marketing
T.B. Gerlach, Sr.

Manager of Marketing
D.K. Drake

Personnel Managers:
N. Central     S. Central
R. Foxman     P.J. Kennedy

N. East
W.A. Shumaker

Pers. Admin.
& New York
R.B. Ruthven

Director of Corp.
Training and
Recruiting
D.C. Rydstrom

Corp. Recruiting
Administrator
N.L. Fabbroni

Western
T.D. Turner

Chief Financial Officer
A.H. Wahlberg

Director of
Internal Audit
K.E. Schoenblatt

Treasurer
R.W. Ball

Controller (TCorp)
C.F.O.
A.C. Breu

Sr. V.P., Secretary, & General Counsel
J.V. Vumbacco

EEO
H.O. Smith

Risk
Management
H. Johnson

Manager Legal Director of
Administration Employee Benefits
R.A. Tolentino G.P.M. McCurrach

HQ/TIS
Personnel
B.H. Harris

Estimating    Manager - PMCS
L.V. Shute     R.T. Meyer

Corporate V.P.
C.A. Miller

Construction Operations
R.W. Johnson

Purchasing
P.D. Lynam

R & D
F.H. Thomas

Chief Engineer
W.I. Arnold

Labor Relations
J.H. Greenip

Safety
George Lodge

TACT
Function

### WESTERN DIVISION
T.B. Gerlach

Western
Group
D.B. Sibson

Los Angeles
LA SPD
Orange County
San Diego
San Francisco SPD
Seattle

### CENTRAL DIVISION
A.P. Sanchez

North Central
Group
J.A. McCullough

Chicago
Chicago SPD
Arlington Hts. SPD
Dupage Cty. SPD
Texas
Columbus
Colum SPD
Detroit
Cleveland
Cleve SPD
Pittsburgh
Toronto

Industrial
Group

Lathrop
S.P.B.I.
Lexcon
SPD

South Central
Group
W.R. Manteuffel

Cincinnati
Cincinnati SPD
Nashville
Hercules
Universal
Univ Richmond
BFW

### EASTERN DIVISION
D.R. Kerstetter

Northeast
Group
F.L. Baslus

Boston
Boston SPD
Connecticut/West
Connecticut SPD
Hartford
New Jersey
N.J. SPD
Washington
Washington SPD

Southeast
Group
L.V. Shute

Miami
Miami SPD
Seaboard
Caribe
Orlando
Philadelphia
Philadelphia SPD
Atlanta

New York
Group
R.E. Fee

New York
New York SPD

Member of
Headquarter's Meeting

March 14, 1990

## EXHIBIT 2   Territory Organizational Structure

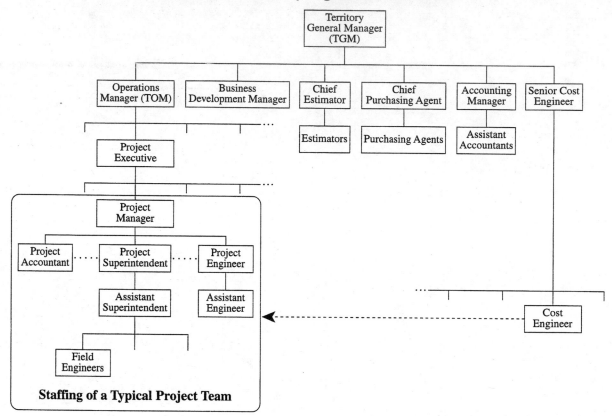

**Staffing of a Typical Project Team**

**EXHIBIT 3    Management Control Reports and Their Relationship to IOR**

| REPORT NAME | RELATIONSHIP TO IOR | FREQUENCY | SCOPE[a] | INTENDED AUDIENCE | PRIMARY TOPIC |
|---|---|---|---|---|---|
| IOR (Indicated Outcome Report) with letter & summary | — | 3 months | project | Territory, group, division, and corporate mgt. | costs, risks, & exposures |
| Operations Report | Output from IOR | monthly | project | Company president | status highlights; problems |
| Job Minutes | Input to IOR | 6 weeks | project | Group & div. mgt. | project logistics, financials, & risks |
| Back Page Report | Input to IOR | monthly | project | Project through div. management | indirect project costs |
| Blue Book Review | Summary of IOR | monthly | project | Owner (client) | costs, risks, exposures |
| Sales Forecasting System | | monthly | territory | Territory through corporate mgt. | prospective projects |
| Turner Forecasting System (TFS) | Output from IOR | monthly | territory through corporate | Div. & corp. management | projection of volume & controllable margin by territory |
| 8-Quarter Report | Adjunct to IOR | monthly | territory through corporate | Division & corp. management | rolling forecast, controllable margin & volume |

[a] *"Scope" refers to the unit addressed in a single report—e.g., a single project, a whole territory, a group, a division, or corporate performance in aggregate. "Territory through corporate" means that reports are successively aggregated at each level in the organization.*

## EXHIBIT 4   Key Management Meetings

| NAME | FREQUENCY | SCOPE[a] | PRIMARY TOPIC | ATTENDEES |
|------|-----------|---------|---------------|-----------|
| IOR Review | 3 months + 6-wk updates | project | project costs & earnings, projected through completion | Core project team[b] and cost engineer |
| Operations Management Meeting (OMM) | 6 weeks | project | major issues re: IOR updates, project logistics, costs, cash flow, profitability, & risk | TOM, sr. cost engineer, core project team, cost acct., & purchasing agent |
| Monthly Minutes | monthly | project | all project logistics & financials in trade-by-trade detail | Core project team only |
| Owner/Architect/ Turner/Subcont. (OATS) Meeting | 4 weeks | project | status update, information sharing & group problem-solving on major issues | Owner's rep, architect, top-level project team |
| Territory Meeting | monthly | territory | general activity & project-specific issues raised by dept. heads & project executives | TGM, TOM, Department heads, & project execs |
| Group VP Meeting | monthly | territory | general activity (inc. financials, new business, personnel, risk, & reserves) | Group VP, div. cost mgr., TOM & project execs |
| Executive Meeting | 6 weeks | company | all co.-wide issues: policies, personnel, sales, earnings, risk | CFO, chief counsel, dept. heads, div. EVPs, & Grp VPs |
| CRC (Contract Review Committee) | weekly | company | authorization of prospective new proposals | Company COO, corporate dept. heads, & division EVPs |

[a] *"Scope" refers to the* broadest *level addressed in a single meeting—e.g., a single project, a whole territory, a group, a division, or corporate performance in aggregate. A "territory in scope" meeting most likely would involve project-specific discussions.*
[b] *Core project team consists of Project Executive and/or Project Manager, Project Superintendent, and Project Engineer.*

**EXHIBIT 5  Turner Project Management Control System**

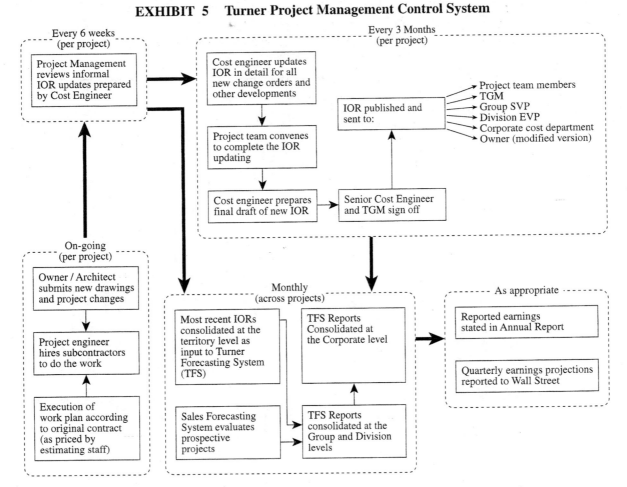

# EXHIBIT 6

Reporting Level - Summary
Report By...Cl-Number
Contract No.: 6125
Report No.: 001

Data Date: 09/30/89
Run Date: 10/25/89
Page No.: 1

*** Indicated Outcome Report ****

Kent Square Tower

|  |  | ESTIMATED COST |  |  |  |  | INDICATED COST |  |  |  |
| --- | --- | --- | --- | --- | --- | --- | --- | --- | --- | --- |
| Budget Codes | Description | Re-Allocated Original Estimate | Approved | Pending | Approx. | Adjusted Estimate | Committed | Uncommitted | Indicated Cost | Savings - Overrun |
| 0200 | SITEWORK | 969,730 | 52,047 | 12,190 | 1,003 | 1,035,570 | 485,348 | 69,847 | 1,055,195 | 19,625 |
| 0300 | CONCRETE | 1,692,310 | 11,982 | 400 | 2,000 | 1,706,692 | 1,658,605 | 46,340 | 1,704,945 | -1,747 |
| 0400 | MASONRY | 1,965,020 | 10,620 |  |  | 1,975,640 | 1,757,243 | 115,000 | 1,872,243 | -103,397 |
| 0500 | METALS | 2,286,240 | 62,746 | 21,877 | 82,000 | 2,452,863 | 2,381,914 | 152,855 | 2,534,773 | 81,910 |
| 0600 | WOOD & PLASTICS |  |  |  |  |  |  |  |  |  |
| 0700 | THERM/MOIST.PROTEC | 623,400 | 450 | 27,142 |  | 650,992 | 396,427 | 57,722 | 454,149 | -196,843 |
| 0800 | DOORS & WINDOWS | 2,184,090 | 1,906 | 33,639 | 2,000 | 2,221,635 | 2,349,812 | 65,483 | 2,415,295 | 193,660 |
| 0900 | FINISHES | 1,290,200 |  | 25,608 | 50,387 | 1,366,195 | 1,343,078 | 142,133 | 1,485,211 | 119,016 |
| 1000 | SPECIALTIES | 50,000 |  |  | 30,000 | 80,000 | 17,160 | 62,840 | 80,000 | 0 |
| 1400 | CONVEYING SYSTEMS | 566,020 | 45,500 | 24,528 |  | 636,048 | 584,485 | 29,528 | 614,013 | -22,035 |
| 1500 | MECHANICAL SYSTEMS | 5,088,800 | 1,213 | 134,079 | 2,237 | 5,226,329 | 4,924,971 | 236,299 | 5,161,270 | -65,059 |
| 1600 | ELECTRICAL | 2,257,600 | 61,934 | 57,545 | 11,872 | 2,388,951 | 2,241,951 | 87,563 | 2,329,514 | -59,437 |
| 3000 | TENANT FIT-OUT | 1,715,430 |  |  | 632,584 | 2,348,014 | 1,777,206 | 570,808 | 2,348,014 | 0 |
| 4000 | ENGINEERING TENANT |  | 24,650 |  | 3,542,670 | 3,567,320 | 2,296,071 | 1,269,550 | 3,565,621 | -1,699 |
| | SUBTOTALS | 20,688,840 | 273,048 | 3,542,536 | 841,825 | 25,656,249 | 22,714,275 | 2,905,968 | 25,620,243 | -36,006 |

DIRECT COST    *** Adjusted Estimate 25,656,249    *** Indicated Cost 25,620,243    -36,006

| 8000 | GENERAL CONDITIONS | 1,716,500 | 15,492 | 266,064 |  | 1,998,056 | 865,423 | 1,130,864 | 1,996,287 | -1,769 |
| | SUBTOTALS | 22,405,340 | 288,540 | 4,118,600 | 841,825 | 27,654,305 | 23,579,698 | 4,036,832 | 27,616,530 | -37,775 |

COST OF WORK    *** Adjusted Estimate 27,654,305    *** Indicated Cost 27,616,530    -37,775

| 8100 | CONTINGENCY | 620,700 | 105,320 |  |  | 726,020 |  | 511,490 | 511,490 | -214,530 |
| 9000 | FEE | 662,000 | 112,010 |  |  | 774,010 | 662,000 | 112,010 | 774,010 |  |
| 9200 | C.F. DISCOUNT | -160,932 |  |  |  | -160,932 |  |  |  | 160,932 |
| 9300 | CONTINGENCY AVAILAB |  |  |  |  |  |  | 39,068 | 39,068 | 39,068 |
| | Total Project Cost | 23,688,040 | 127,608 | 4,335,930 | 841,825 | 28,993,403 | 24,241,698 | 4,699,400 | 28,941,098 | -52,305 |

# EXHIBIT 7

**FINANCIAL SUMMARY**

Report #003   Published: 10/25/89        Data as of: 09/30/89        Engr./Purch. Date:

Contract Name: Kent Square Tower                    Contract No.: 6125
Job Location: Newtown, Pennsylvania                 Territory: Philadelphia
CONTRACT TYPE        A _    C _       CSLT _  CG _    L _     M _      CGS _X
SAVINGS PART         YES X NO _    TCCO. Share: 25% of all savings including Construction Contingency
BASE FEE        Fixed X      OR ___ % Fee on changes 2.88%    GC on Changes 5% markup
TOP CHARGE      YES ____ %    NO X
Special Provisions: Fee is calculated at 2.88% after total changes exceed $500K;
                                General conditions on changes are based on actual expenditures,
        however a 5% mark up is allowed on all changes.

| | CURRENT REPORT | | PREV. RPT. 06/30/89 | | DIFFERENCE | |
|---|---|---|---|---|---|---|
| | SAVINGS | OVERRUN | SAVINGS | OVERRUN | BETTER | WORSE |
| DIRECT COST | 36,006 | | 33,903 | | 2,103 | 0 |
| INDIRECT COST | 1,769 | | 23,034 | | 0 | 21,265 |
| CONTINGENCY | 214,530 | | | | 214,530 | 0 |
| CONTING. POOL | | 39,068 | | | | 39,068 |
| CE DISCOUNT | | 160,932 | | | | 160,932 |
| TOTALS | 252,305 | 200,000 | 56,937 | 0 | 216,633 | 221,265 |
| INDICATED NET | 52,305 | 0 | 56,937 | 0 | 0 | 4,632 |

| | COST OF WORK | | FEE | | COST TO OWNER (VOLUME) | |
|---|---|---|---|---|---|---|
| | This report | Change | This report | Change | This report | Change |
| ORIG. EST. | 23,026,040 | 0 | 662,000 | 0 | 23,688,040 | 0 |
| CHANGES | | | | | | |
| Approved | 288,540 | 106,186 | 0 | 0 | 288,540 | 106,186 |
| Pending | 4,223,920 | 4,085,174 | 112,010 | 112,010 | 4,335,930 | 4,197,184 |
| Approx. | 841,825 | 98,863 | 0 | 0 | 841,825 | 98,863 |
| CE DISCOUNT | (160,932) | (12,364) | 0 | 0 | (160,932) | (12,364) |
| REV. EST. | 28,219,393 | 4,269,859 | 774,010 | 112,010 | 28,993,403 | 4,381,869 |
| IND. SAVG/OVERRUN | (52,305) | 4,632 | | 0 | (52,305) | 4,632 |
| IND. COST | 28,167,088 | 4,274,491 | 774,010 | 112,010 | 28,941,098 | 4,386,501 |

Less Non-Reimbursables    109,300    0
Less "B" Account           20,000    0
Other Adjustments         112,010    112,010

JOB EARNINGS.............   532,700    0

GC ON CHANGES:
        Approved:    $15,492    Pending:    $266,064    Approx.:        $0   Total: $281,556
UNCOMMITTED DOLLARS:            (Exclude Turner Labor and Materials)
        Claim Liab. $           Exposure Holds    471,210       Contingency Holds        320,000
        Unbought $    535,729  Dwgs Exposure                    Unspend Allowances       524,506
TOTAL CLAIMS AGAINST TCCo $              TC CLAIMS AGAINST OWNERS OR OTHERS: $
ASSUMED CLAIM EXPOSURE $                 ASSUMED CLAIM RECOVERY $
OWNER CONTINGENCY:              Estimate                   Remaining
CONSTRUCTION CONTINGENCY       Estimate        $726,020*   Remaining  $511,490*
ALLOWANCE DOLLARS              Original Estimate:  $2,434,530    Indicated  $3,140,952
COST PER SQ. FT.              Original Estimate:   $109.13    Current    $133.91
RETURN OF STAFF (Total Staff)  Original Estimate:   $0.61    Current    $0.70
        (Key Staff)           Original Estimate:            Current
Special Comments: * Includes $185,320 engineering tenant contingency from CE #52

**EXHIBIT 8    Kent Square IOR Cover Letter**

One-Page Excerpt:

```
                                    Kent Square Tower  #6125
                                    Indicated Outcome Report #03
                                    Data Date:  9-30-89
                                    October 27, 1989
                                    Page Three
```

The construction contingency is currently being reported at $511,490. As previously stated $200,000 has been released into the Owner's "Savings Pool." To subsidize trash dumping increases not anticipated $14,520 has also been released from contingency. The original construction contingency of $620,700 has been decreased $214,520 as stated above, and increased $105,320 from the engineering fitout change, CE #52.

In summary this project is progressing smoothly. Physical construction is going well and relatively on schedule. The engineering fitout change (CE #52) has been verbally approved by the Owner, thus TCCo will proceed. The net change produced by CE #52 is $4,010,000:

    1.   Direct Cost .......$3,542,670

    2.   Indirect Cost.........250,000

    3.   Contingency...........105,320

    4.   Fee...................112,010

The engineering fitout change (CE #52) has also extended the project completion date four months to August 1990.

Relationships with the owner , architect  and subcontractors remain good.


                                    Holly Green
                                    PMCS Engineer


Reviewed by Jayne L. Murphy
          Sr. PMCS Engineer
```
```

# CASE 25   Mary Kay Cosmetics: Sales Force Incentives (A)

"The VIP automobile program is our problem child. The cost of all three automobile incentive programs is eating our lunch." These words were spoken in the summer of 1989 by Dick Bartlett, president and chief operating officer of Mary Kay Cosmetics.

In 1984, the company had introduced the VIP (Very Important Performer) car program to motivate its top-performing, non-director beauty consultants (i.e., independent saleswomen). The program, which originally awarded the use of compact size Oldsmobile Firenzas to eligible beauty consultants, was modeled after the company's acclaimed pink Cadillac program, introduced in 1969, for which only director-level consultants were eligible. The pink Buick program, Mary Kay's third program, was also reserved for sales directors, but was based on less difficult performance criteria than the Cadillac program. Under all three car programs, Mary Kay awarded the use of a new car to eligible beauty consultants who sustained the required sales and recruiting levels for the designated number of months. Winners maintained the use of their cars for two years as long as they continued to meet the required sales volumes on a monthly basis. The company bore all the costs associated with leasing the new General Motors cars from ARI Leasing, insuring the cars, and then selling the used ones as consultants returned them.

The car programs had proven to be very effective motivators, helping company sales through a period of market stagnancy in the mid-1980s. Over time, however, the cost of running the programs had escalated substantially. The cost of the VIP program in particular had skyrocketed in the late 1980s, with the number of leased cars approaching 3,000 in early 1989. In addition, there were approximately 1,000 Cadillacs and 1,000 Buicks in force in 1989. The number of car winners as a percentage of the total number of beauty consultants had doubled from 1.25% in 1986 to 2.5% by year-end 1988.

Mary Kay's management now faced the difficult challenge of containing further program cost increases without upsetting the powerful incentive system that was the firm's primary source of growth and success. In addition to reducing total car program costs (especially VIP costs) as a percentage of sales, management was interested in redirecting the dollars behind other elements of its incentive compensation plan for greater cost effectiveness. Also, management wanted to provide reward and recognition for a range of performance levels that was broad enough to meet the varying career interests of current and prospective beauty consultants.

## Company Background

Mary Kay Cosmetics Inc. was an international manufacturer and distributor of premium skin care, hair care, and body care products. Mary Kay products were not available through retail stores. In 1988, its products were sold throughout the United States exclusively by a network of over 175,000 independent (self-employed) women who ranged in status from beauty consultants to national sales directors. (Mary Kay also sold internationally in seven

*Hilary Weston prepared this case under the supervision of Professor Robert Simons as the basis for class discussion rather than to illustrate either effective or ineffective handling of an administrative situation.*

countries.) This sales force met directly with customers in their homes and offices to demonstrate and sell Mary Kay products. The firm's 1,436 company employees worked out of its Dallas headquarters and manufacturing facility and its five regional distribution centers. In 1988, the company's 25th anniversary, Mary Kay Cosmetics achieved record sales of $406 million, up 26% from $326 million in 1987.

The original mission of company founder Mary Kay Ash had been to be a "teaching-oriented" organization that provided women with exceptional opportunities for professional achievement, economic success, recognition, personal development, and independence. The organization had remained true to this goal, but had expanded its mission during the 1980s to include greater emphasis on consumer needs, product innovation, and quality. As revised in 1987, the Mary Kay Mission was "To achieve preeminence in the manufacturing, distribution and marketing of personal care products by providing personalized service, value, convenience and innovative solutions to consumer needs through our independent sales force."

## Company Philosophy

The "Consultant's Guide" book provided to new beauty consultants stated the firm's philosophy as follows:

> From the beginning, the Company has grown based upon the same philosophy: every person associated with the Company, from Chairman Emeritus to the newest recruit, lives by the Golden Rule, "Do unto others as you would have them do unto you" and the priorities of God first, family second, and career third.

In describing the company's commitment to the independent sales force, Chairman Rogers asserted, "Every aspect of the Mary Kay system is aimed at promoting a successful career for the beauty consultants. It's through her succeeding that we all succeed. . . . We're committed to total customer satisfaction; and to the customer, a beauty consultant is Mary Kay."

A director of sales development explained the relationship between the company and its sales force:

> There are five things that all consultants seek. We refer to them as S-T-O-R-M: Satisfaction with a task well done (self-worth); Teamwork (a sense of belonging); Opportunity (to succeed); Recognition; and Money. These five needs are being met through various aspects of our business.

**Company Ownership and Structure**   In 1984, after several years of extraordinary growth, a decline of 14% in sales and 8% in earnings had triggered a sharp drop in the corporation's share price. In December 1985, in response to both the depressed share price and to their own desire to manage for the long term rather than for quarterly earnings, Chairman Mary Kay and her son, Richard Rogers (president and CEO at the time), led a management leveraged buyout for a price of approximately $315 million. Mary Kay and Richard also wished to avoid the impact that public financial reporting could have on sales force attitudes during a sales and stock price decline. Negative attitudes could easily trigger further sales and recruiting declines.

Two years later, in November 1987, Mary Kay assumed the title of chairman emeritus and Rogers, 44, became chairman (retaining his title as CEO). Dick Bartlett, former executive vice president of Marketing, was named president and chief operating officer (COO).

Mary Kay management prided itself on its lean internal staff. President Bartlett placed himself at the bottom of the organization, surrounded by staff support functions. Above him were the four operating divisions—Marketing, Sales, R&D/Manufacturing, and Distribution—which "served" the sales force. Bartlett placed Mary Kay's customer base of 15 to 20 million households at the top of the organizational structure. (**Exhibit 1** depicts the internal organizational structure and **Exhibit 2** shows the hierarchical structure of the sales force as well as the profile of a typical beauty consultant.) Bartlett explained the role of his internal organization and how it operated:

> Our goal is to support the independent sales force of 175,000 beauty consultants, because our sales force is our life blood. Our job in supporting the consultants involves a continual effort to update and improve the quality and selection of our products and to refine our facilities and procedures. We also have to anticipate and respond to the consultants' needs. This all requires creativity and flexibility.
>
> One of my first challenges as president was to break down departmental fiefdoms. I instituted three types of meetings that bring together managers from different departments. The weekly Sales and Marketing meetings are religiously attended by top management. I never miss those meetings. They're where the hot topics are raised and discussed. We've also created what we call "CATS"— Creative Action Teams. These cross-functional temporary task forces are formed on an ad hoc basis whenever any employees identify a specific problem or opportunity which they think they can take on, especially those affecting quality improvement. The purpose of the CATS is to nurture creativity and keep the organization flexible. We track the progress of all CAT projects at our weekly meetings, and employees are usually recognized for successful completion.

The main personal link between the company and the sales force was the group of six regional sales development directors. One of them described his role:

> The job of the six of us is to bridge the gap between the growing sales organization and the company. We picture ourselves as their voice internally. Each of us covers a geographic region containing 700 to 800 sales directors and 30,000 to 40,000 beauty consultants. We wear a lot of hats—information conduit, administrator, motivator, personal and financial advisor, and so on. Also, there's an expectation on the part of each consultant that their own personal considerations will be taken into account. . . . Let's say a woman works all year and misses a director's goal by $18, we'd destroy her if we didn't give her a break. We need to be flexible, so we make those kinds of calls.

## Sales Force Support

In addition to personal contact with the field, Mary Kay Cosmetics employed an elaborate set of tools and programs designed to motivate, recognize, and develop its beauty consultants:

**Communications:**   The company produced a constant flow of written material for the sales force, including a monthly magazine, weekly newsletters, training manuals, and product brochures. It also provided video and audio cassettes (for recruiting, training, and motivating), promotional sales aids, and a telephone hot line for advice and answers. Mary Kay also regularly solicited feedback from consultants and customers by conducting surveys and focus groups. The company used this information to improve existing products and packaging and to develop new products and selling tactics.

**Events:**   Mary Kay sponsored a variety of contests, conferences, and other events for the consultants, which combined all three elements mentioned above—motivation, recognition, and education. The biggest event was the annual seminar, which in 1988 was attended by 25,000 consultants. (The three-day event was divided into four back-to-back identical sessions because of its sheer size.) The seminar was open to all consultants and directors; however, registrants paid their own way to attend and participate in the festivities and training sessions. The climax was a gala awards night in which consultants of all levels were honored and rewarded for their achievements before an applauding crowd of thousands. Rewards ranged from ribbons, jewelry, furs, and luxury trips to the crowning of "queens."

**Sales Force Activities:** Ongoing support within the beauty consultant networks was another important ingredient in the Mary Kay formula for direct selling. Despite the high level of company support, the vast majority of a consultant's interaction was with her unit director and the other 30 to 150 consultants in her unit, and not directly with Mary Kay management, which had no formal control over the sales force.[1]

Because Mary Kay Ash believed that people could be "praised to success," the company fostered a sales force culture based on positive reinforcement and recognition. This was achieved through several means. First, the company did no sales force recruiting; the independent consultants personally chose their own new recruits. This personalized approach increased the likelihood of successful director-consultant relationships. Also, the company provided guidelines to assist the independent sales force in motivating and training its members. For example, the company-suggested Monday unit meetings were the primary forum for the sharing of product information, selling tips, and success stories, as well as group praise. These weekly unit meetings not only served as a support group and training class, but also created peer pressure to succeed. In "Memo," the company's weekly newsletter to directors, and in the *Director's Guide,* the company provided directors with many kinds of creative tips and tools for training and developing their units and conducting effective meetings.

**Recognition and Prizes:** The majority of beauty consultants did not attend the annual seminar or receive cars and other large prizes. All active consultants, however, were motivated to increase their sales and recruiting by a constantly available array of prizes and recognition for incremental progress. Company-sponsored gifts and prizes were offered for achieving sales and recruiting goals and winners' names were listed in *Applause,* Mary Kay's monthly magazine for consultants. In addition, directors, at their own expense and discretion, rewarded their unit members for achieving various milestones. The gifts and prizes handed out by directors to beauty consultants usually took the form of jewelry and other accessories, often with the Mary Kay logo on them, and were usually awarded in front of a group. (**Exhibit 3** lists a representative sampling of the type and cost of directors' gifts to unit members.) For example, upon signing up her first recruit, each consultant received a string of imitation pearls and congratulatory applause at her unit's weekly meeting. At each step in her Mary Kay career, a consultant received additional recognition and status symbols, including "ladder" pins with varying numbers and types of gems, which indicated her level of achievement. (See **Exhibit 4** for the hierarchy of nonfinancial sales force incentives.) Senior Vice President of Sales Bart Bartolacci described the role of recognition as an incentive:

> As Mary Kay herself would say, "A $5 ribbon plus $20 worth of recognition is worth more than a $25 prize." In other words, give them a check, but give it to them on stage. Then they will really respond. I would never take away the recognition element. It would be like putting my head on a chopping block. Some of the women really don't need the money at all, but the recognition is addictive. In fact, the top people in our sales organization motivate their units through recognition, not expensive prizes.

---

[1] The signed agreement between an independent beauty consultant and the company stipulated certain basic guidelines that the consultant was required to follow, such as her legal responsibility to represent the company and its products honestly and accurately. Mary Kay Cosmetics, however, had virtually no management control over the independent contractor sales force.

**Financial Incentives:**   The financial incentives, however, were also considered an indispensable ingredient in the firm's direct selling strategy. According to management, the power and appeal of Mary Kay's incentive system were rooted in the carefully designed combination of compensation, advancement opportunity, prize incentives, and recognition. According to the Mary Kay Marketing Plan (i.e., the incentive compensation and advancement plan), a consultant's income was determined by a very clear and objective method, based on her selling and recruiting activity. No organizational constraints limited the pace at which a consultant could advance her status and increase her income. In 1988, the highest paid sales director earned over $400,000 and roughly 90 others had six-figure incomes. The company, via its beauty consultants, aggressively advertised the Marketing Plan's objectivity and unlimited earning potential to attract new recruits.

The specific components of the plan were based on the following premise, as explained by Sales Group Executive Vice President Barbara Beasley:

> There are three things we want beauty consultants to do: order products, sell products to customers, and recruit new consultants. Recruiting is really the big source of growth because sales per consultant can rise only so much. That puts a limit on both company growth and consultants' earning potential. Moreover, because approximately 70% of consultants drop out each year, we need new recruits just to maintain sales. We currently recruit about 10,000 consultants per month and lose 7,000 per month. I know that turnover rate sounds high. But, in fact, our rate is the lowest in the direct-selling industry, and lower than most retailers' sales staff turnover.

> But a good director must sell as well as recruit. Her best source of new recruits is her customer base. Also, her role as leader, teacher, and motivator involves setting an example for her unit members. We also need the sales directors to stay on top of customers' needs and their reactions to new products because the directors are our strongest tie to the marketplace.

Although all consultants fell into one of two general categories, nondirectors and directors, there were multiple titles within each group. The financial success of the more senior consultants and of directors depended heavily on their ability to recruit new consultants and on the ongoing performance of their recruits.

**Exhibit 5** summarizes the compensation for all levels as described below.

An entry-level beauty consultant's income was the difference between the retail value of the products she sold and the wholesale price (usually 50% of suggested retail) at which she bought products from Mary Kay. A nondirector consultant also received a 4% to 12% commission[2] on the sales of all her personal recruits. Once she had at least five recruits, her title became Team Leader and she could try to qualify for the use of a VIP car.

In order to win the use of a VIP car (a red Pontiac Grand Am) and keep it for the entire awarded period of 24 months, a consultant had to reach and maintain three types of targets over that period: 1) team monthly production volume (i.e., wholesale value of all her recruits' orders); 2) personal monthly wholesale production; and 3) number of active recruits. Each VIP consultant was given a fixed "allowance" she could draw on to make up for shortages in particular months, so that she would not have to relinquish her car because of one or two bad months. The allowance could be increased (and thereby "banked") by performance above the minimum requirements in any given month.

Once a consultant became a sales director (the qualifications were again tied to personal and team production and number of recruits), several additional avenues of income opened up to her. In addition to receiving an 8% to 12% commission on her personal

---

[2] Commissions were based on wholesale orders and the percentage level depended on the number of recruits a consultant had.

recruits' wholesale orders, she received a 9% to 13% commission on the production of the entire unit she directed, which included her recruits' recruits. In addition, she received a sliding-scale monthly bonus of $400 to $2,500 if her unit's total monthly production exceeded $4,000. Thus, if a director's unit achieved the $4,000 threshold, the compensation system rewarded her doubly for the unit's performance. Finally, a director also received a $100 to $400 bonus for each month in which her unit of consultants recruited at least three new active consultants.

As soon as one of a director's unit members became a director herself, the former became a senior sales director. In addition to the sources of director compensation, senior directors also received a 4% commission on the monthly production of all their "offspring" units. If they had eight or more offspring units, the commission increased to 5%.

A national sales director—the highest position in the Mary Kay independent sales force—did not directly work with nondirector beauty consultants. Her compensation was based on the wholesale production of both her first-line and second-line offspring units. She received a commission of 5% to 8% and 2%, respectively, for the two tiers of units.

### History of the VIP Car Program

Between 1983 and 1989, Mary Kay's car programs increased from a base of 1,100 cars on the road to over 5,000 cars. Most of this increase was due to the VIP program, which was introduced in 1984. By mid-1989, VIP cars in force numbered 3,000. The number of VIP car winners had grown rapidly despite increases in program qualification requirements in 1986, 1988, and 1989.

Increased VIP participation was accompanied by several external cost trends:

- The costs to Mary Kay of leasing the cars had increased with interest rates.
- Automobile insurance premiums had escalated faster than both inflation and prices of Mary Kay products.
- General Motors discontinued the Oldsmobile Firenza, reducing the resale value of the one- and two-year-old cars.

All of these trends had contributed in driving up the cost of the VIP program. The cost increase was further magnified by the decline in car "tenure": an increasing proportion of the consultants who had qualified for VIP cars were unable to maintain the required sales and recruiting levels for the 24-month period. As a result, Mary Kay often was forced to reclaim cars that were substantially less than two years old. The newer a car when Mary Kay reclaimed it from a consultant, the greater the disparity between the car's unamortized book value and the (much lower) resale price that Mary Kay received for it. In short, the company absorbed larger losses on cars that were in service for shorter periods of time.

### The Current Challenge

Mary Kay's top management was seeking a broad solution to the rising costs—and corresponding diminishing returns—of its incentive plan, the VIP car program in particular. According to Richard Wiser, vice president of Financial Planning and Analysis:

> Over the last several years, we've watched the cost of the car programs and of commissions creep up relative to sales. [See **Exhibits 6** and **7**.] Car expenses in particular have really jumped up since 1985.
>
> In the past, we've always gone for incremental cost savings. We took a negative approach: we simply raised the program qualification requirements when we wanted to reduce the cost of the program.

Now, we want to be more creative. We have Finance, Marketing, and Sales all working together to identify innovations that would save money for us but, at the same time, keep the sales force morale up and boost the effectiveness of the incentives.

We haven't been getting a bang for our buck from *all* VIP consultants. Unless they are trying to qualify for directorship, many feel no motivation to increase their sales and recruiting efforts above the level needed to maintain the use of their cars. We're not tapping their full potential because we're not rewarding them for achieving it.

President Dick Bartlett continued:

Richard is right. In fact, those VIP consultants who really do want additional income and recognition may rush into directorship prematurely. They may qualify before they have a large, strong team base and sufficient experience. That's bad for everyone. The consultant must fight a frustrating uphill battle to retain her director status. And from our perspective, her unit's size and performance may deteriorate. A weak director hurts unit morale and development. The problem trickles down: when a weak or negligent consultant loses a customer, it's a lost sale for Mary Kay. Customers can't buy our products in retail stores and the customer is not likely to seek out another consultant.

Bartlett and his management team summarized the objectives of the Marketing Plan modifications they sought:

- To improve profit margins by reducing overall beauty consultant compensation (particularly the costs associated with the car programs) as a percent of sales—a ratio that had been escalating yearly.
- To enhance the beauty consultants' career path with more distinct milestones and forms of reward. Bartlett was particularly concerned about two issues that had adversely affected many top performing VIPs:
  (a) Many had worked extra hard to achieve director status but were ill-prepared for the extra demands of continuing director-level performance.
  (b) Many had stagnated at a "maintenance" sales level simply to retain their VIP cars.
- To make cost reductions elsewhere in the Marketing Plan while preserving sales force morale and motivation.
- To minimize the cost to the firm of maintaining low-performing consultants, i.e., those with very few recruits and no indication of ambitious growth goals.

At the conclusion of their interview with the case writers, the managers reemphasized the extreme sensitivity of beauty consultants' actions to changes in the Marketing Plan. They cited an example: in 1984, an announced increase in VIP qualification criteria resulted in an enormous "rush" for VIP status before the effective date of the program change. As a result, the number of VIP car winners temporarily increased dramatically, rather than tapering off as intended. (Refer to **Exhibit 6.**) Moreover, many of those consultants who had rushed to obtain cars had relatively low tenure with Mary Kay. So, they did not have the experience and team strength to maintain their VIP status. As a result, they had to forfeit their cars prematurely, which was demoralizing for them and costly for the firm.

In general, any change in the Marketing Plan that was not well-received by the sales force of over 175,000 beauty consultants could be disastrous to the company: not only would sales drop off in the near term, but the sales force attrition rate could increase and the recruiting rate decrease over the long term. Aware of this danger, management had scheduled the first "Mary Kay Summit Meeting" and invited all national sales directors (the top of the independent sales organization) to be involved in designing changes in the Marketing Plan. Management wanted to bring to the Summit Meeting their own draft plan as a starting point for discussions with the national sales directors.

*Appendix*

Time-Line of Major Changes in the Marketing Plan

| EFFECTIVE DATE | PROGRAM CHANGE |
| --- | --- |
| March 1984: | Introduced the VIP Car Program |
| Objectives: | To stimulate sales and recruiting activity and encourage *consistent* personal performance at the non-director and new director levels |
| Terms: | For Team Leader consultants, directors-in-qualification, and directors who had not reached Cadillac or Buick status. To qualify for the use of a fully insured VIP car (a red Oldsmobile Firenza) a consultant had to have personal recruit team production of $3,000 wholesale per month and personal monthly production of $600 for three consecutive months. These monthly levels had to be maintained for a VIP to retain her title and car. If a VIP depleted her production "allowance," she had to return the car. |
| January 1985: | Began to pay auto insurance for Cadillac and Buick directors |
| Objectives: | To encourage top-performing directors to develop and motivate their personal recruits. |
| Terms: | For each month a Cadillac or Buick director and her personal recruit team achieved the VIP production requirements, Mary Kay would pay for her auto insurance. |
| January 1986: | Increased the VIP qualification requirements |
| Objectives: | To encourage aggressive recruiting; to reduce the program's costs; and to improve the likelihood that VIP qualifiers will have the team base to maintain the VIP monthly production requirements. |
| Terms: | By the end of the three-month qualifying period a consultant had to have 10 (instead of 5) total personal recruits to qualify for the use of a VIP car. |
| January 1986: | Introduced "team credits" for VIPs' and directors' recruiting activity |
| Objectives: | To encourage more aggressive recruiting. |
| Terms: | For each new team member she recruited, a VIP or director could earn an additional credit of $400 or $600 per month (based on the recruit's initial order size) toward the production levels required to retain her car. |
| February 1987: | Restructured director bonus program |
| Objectives: | To increase directors' incentive compensation to better reflect their out of pocket costs of incremental sales. |
| Terms: | Eliminated the $300 monthly bonus for directors with unit volume less than $4,000; changed from a flat $500 monthly bonus for directors with unit volume of $5,000 or higher to a sliding-scale bonus of $500 to $2,500, based on unit volume. |
| July 1987: | Increased requirements for Cadillac and Buick qualification |
| Objectives: | To contain the cost of the directors' car programs. |
| Terms: | To earn the use of a Buick, directors were required to achieve net cumulative unit wholesale volume of $50,000 (instead of $48,000) in two consecutive quarters. To earn a Cadillac, the two-quarter unit production requirement was increased from $72,000 to $75,000. Mary Kay would pay for the auto insurance of all Cadillac and Buick winners (which averaged $600 per year). |

*Appendix    Continued*

| | |
|---|---|
| April 1988: | Increased requirements for VIP qualification |
| Objectives: | To contain the cost of the program. |
| Terms: | Consultants were required to achieve the personal and team monthly production requirements for four (instead of three) consecutive months; and at the end of the qualifying period, they had to have 12 total and 8 active recruits (instead of 10 total and 5 active). |
| May 1988: | Pontiac Grand Am replaced Oldsmobile Firenza as the VIP car |
| Objectives:<br>July 1988: | Change was necessitated when General Motors announced plans to discontinue the<br>Firenza. |
| Objectives: | Increased requirements for Cadillac and Buick qualification |
| Terms | To contain the cost of the directors' car programs. |
| | To earn the use of a Cadillac, directors were required to achieve total net unit wholesale volume of $90,000 (instead of $75,000) over a six-month period, and to earn a Buick, directors must achieve $60,000 (instead of $50,000). Also, the size of co-op lease payments (to be paid by car winners in the months in which they have a production shortfall) was increased. |
| April 1989: | Instituted new eligibility requirement and monthly insurance charges for all car winners |
| Objectives: | To reduce the insurance cost of all car programs. |
| Terms: | Eligibility of new car winners to drive any company-awarded car would be determined by a 12-point system based on each winner's motor vehicle record and accident history. Eligibility would be redetermined annually. Also, effective August 1, 1989, all company-awarded car drivers age 25 or older were assessed a basic monthly $10 underwriting charge; drivers under 25 will be assessed a monthly insurance fee of $20. |
| April 1989: | Increase in requirements for VIP qualification |
| Objectives: | To contain the cost of the VIP car program. |
| Terms: | By the end of the four-month qualification period, consultants had to have 12 total and 10 (instead of 8) active personal recruits. |

**EXHIBIT 1    Mary Kay Organizational Structure**

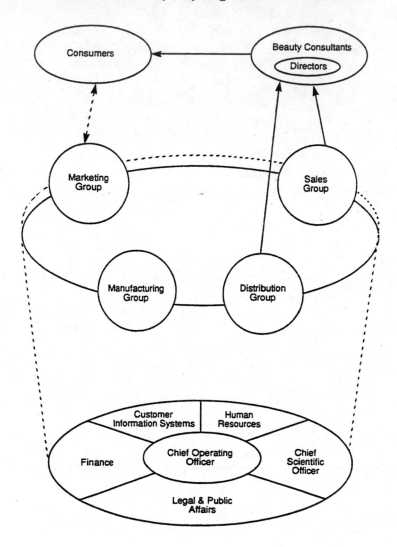

## EXHIBIT 2

## SALES FORCE HIERARCHY

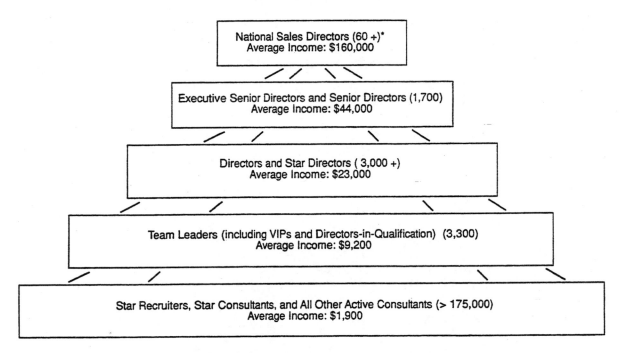

PROFILE OF A TYPICAL BEAUTY CONSULTANT**:

. 24 to 54 years old
. married with children
. holds another job
. has some college education
. lives outside a major urban area
. spends approximately 8 hours per week on Mary Kay work
. earns less than $5,000/year through Mary Kay work
. holds $2,500 to $3,000 worth of inventory (at suggested retail value) in her home

*Numbers in parentheses represent headcounts
**Based on entire sales force. Directors and above, however, do Mary Kay work full-time.

---

### EXHIBIT 3
### Director's Prizes for Unit Members[a]
(Representative Sampling)

| ITEM | COST TO DIRECTOR |
|---|---|
| **Ordered Through Mary Kay Director Supply Department:** | |
| Business card case | $  .50 |
| Checkbook cover | .50 |
| "Ask Me About Mary Kay" luggage tag | .75 |
| Mary Kay pencils (pkg. of 12) | 1.25 |
| Gold money bag | 1.50 |
| Mauve ring binder | 2.75 |
| "Pearls of Sharing" bracelet | 3.00 |
| "Pearls of Sharing" necklace | 5.00 |
| Mary Kay pens (pkg. of 25) | 5.00 |
| "Glamour Face" sweatshirt | 10.00 |
| **Ordered through independent distributors of promotional products and specialty gifts:** | |
| | (all $5 to $20) |
| Mink key rings | |
| Costume jewelry | |
| Picture frames | |
| Wrist watches | |
| Belts | |

---

[a] *These prizes were purchased by directors at their own expense to award to eligible beauty consultants at weekly unit meetings.*

## EXHIBIT 4    Schedule of Non-Financial Incentives for Mary Kay Beauty Consultants[a]

| TITLE OR POSITION | PRIMARY PERFORMANCE CRITERIA | AVAILABLE NONFINANCIAL INCENTIVES AND REWARDS |
|---|---|---|
| Active Beauty Consultant | Order at least $180 of wholesale product each quarter | Ribbons; unit recognition and small prizes |
| Star Consultant | Order at least $1,800 of wholesale product within one quarter | Gold-electroplate ladder pin with add-on gemstones set in silver, quarterly contest prizes |
| Star Recruiter | Personally recruit three or more Active Consultants | Red blazers; special luncheons; Star Recruiter pin |
| Team Leader | Personally recruit five or more Active Consultants | Special buttons and crest for blazer; recognition in *Applause* magazine |
| VIP | Maintain team production of $3,000/month, personal production of $600/month | Special pins; recognition in *Applause* magazine; use of red Pontiac Grand Am |
| Sales Director | Attain a unit size of at least 30 Active Consultants and at least $14,000 wholesale unit production within a four-month, qualification period | Debut ceremony; dozen silk roses; plaque; custom-designed suit; eligibility to win the use of pink Buick or Cadillac |
| Senior Director | Have at least 1 off-spring director (Executive Senior Directors need 5 off-spring) | Special blouse; Pink Buick or Cadillac |
| National Sales Director | Have at least 10 first-line off-spring directors, 8 of whom are senior directors | Top-line Cadillac; Annual Summit Meeting; special suit; President's Circle Awards; "Millionaire Club" recognition |

[a] *This list of awards was supplemented by a continual variety of company-sponsored and director-sponsored contests for specific time periods, as well as personal congratulatory letters from Mary Kay Ash for achievers of various milestones, and lastly, lavish awards and recognition for year-long efforts (before 7,000 people) at the annual Seminar. Contest prizes ranged from calculators and costume jewelry to furniture.*

---

**EXHIBIT 5**   **Mary Kay Marketing Plan**
**(All Sources of Financial Compensation)**

---

| STATUS IN INDEPENDENT SALES ORGANIZATION | COMPENSATION RECEIVED[a] |
|---|---|
| All Consultants: | • Retail mark-up on all personal production (= 100% of wholesale dollar volume less selling expenses) |
| Recruiters, Star Recruiters, Team Leaders, VIPs, and all Directors: | • Retail mark-up on all personal production<br>• 4% to 12% commission on personal recruits' production (i.e., team wholesale volume) |
| All Directors: | • *All* of the above, *plus* . . .<br>• 9% to 13% Director unit commission on total unit production<br>• Production bonus of $400 to $2,500, based on total unit production<br>• Recruiting bonus of $100 to $400, based on number of new active recruits<br>• Life insurance and disability coverage |
| Senior Directors (and Executive Senior Directors): | • *All* of the above, *plus* . . .<br>• 4% (or 5%) commission on wholesale production of off-spring units |
| National Sales Directors: | • *All* of the above, (except Senior Director/Executive Senior Director Commissions), *plus* . . .<br>• 5% to 8% commission on wholesale production of first-line off-spring units<br>• 2% commission on wholesale production of second-line off-spring units<br>• $\frac{1}{2}$% commission on wholesale production of first-line units of second-line directors who became National Sales Directors<br>• Family Security Program |

---

*Note: Mary Kay had an inventory buyback program for any consultant who terminated her Mary Kay career for any reason. Under this program, the company would repurchase any unsold products in the consultant's inventory purchased during the year prior to termination and would reimburse the consultant who elected to return unsold products 90% of her original purchase price for such returned products. Any commissions paid to sales directors on products repurchased by the company were charged back to the directors to whom they were paid based on the company's premise that commissions are earned by sales directors only on products which consultant's buy and resell to the ultimate consumers.*

[a] *Commissions are calculated and paid out on a monthly basis.*

**EXHIBIT 6**

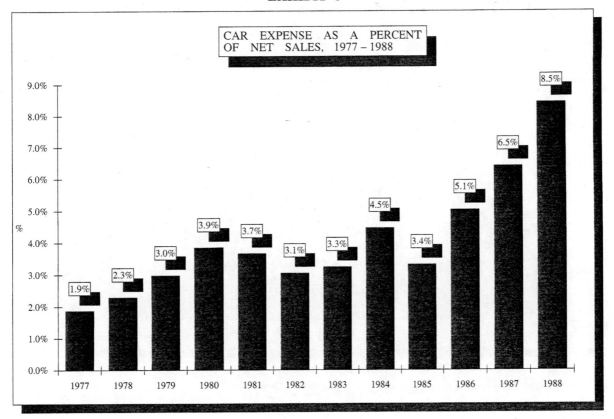

CAR EXPENSE AS A PERCENT OF NET SALES, 1977–1988

## EXHIBIT 7

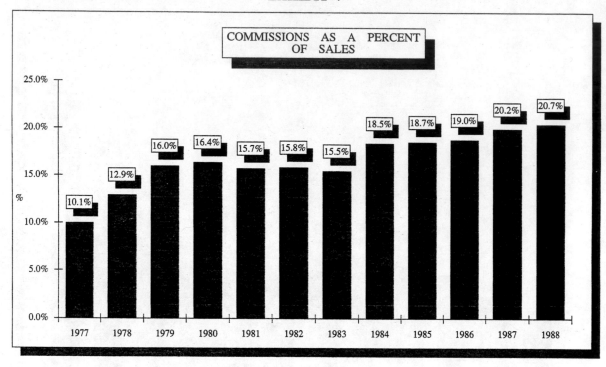

COMMISSIONS AS A PERCENT OF SALES

* Note: The above figures have been disguised to protect the confidentiality of the Company.

**CASE 26**    Duckworth Industries, Inc. —
Incentive Compensation Programs

In early 1992, Mr. John Duckworth, president and controlling shareholder of Duckworth Industries was considering a change in Duckworth Industries' management incentive compensation systems. If implemented the new plan for Duckworth management would, it was hoped, align more closely the interests of management and shareholders. Several industrial firms which were pioneers in value-based management had recently adopted similar management compensation systems. Adopting the new system would keep Duckworth in the vanguard of management incentive compensation planning.

**Background**    Mr. Duckworth was a strong believer in the power of incentives to guide management action. When he was first promoted to a plant management job in the 1950s, Mr. Duckworth took over a plant which had an operating loss of $2.7 million on sales of $9.0 million. He implemented what was then a "state-of-the-art" plan for factory incentives. The plan applied to all supervisors. Achievement of specified goals earned a 15% premium over an individual's base rate of pay. As noted by Mr. Duckworth:

> The more sobering side of the plan consisted of docking supervisors 12% of their base rate when goals were not achieved. Paychecks having a 12% deduction for failure were distributed in bright red envelopes. At that time I was plant manager of the operation, and I got several red pay envelopes. Some 15-18 months after the "12% Club" was profitably and smoothly functioning, the National Labor Relations Board issued a cease and desist order predicated on the fact you cannot tamper with an individual's base pay. Naturally, I complied, but the results were already in — the division was profitable.

Mr. Duckworth founded his own business in 1971. Sales grew from $400,000 in that year to almost $125 million in 1992 (**Exhibit 1**). In 1986, a holding company (Duckworth Industries) was established. It included the original business, Worth Corp., which was a highly profitable producer of proprietary fasteners and adhesives. In 1986, Hospitality Equipment Service was acquired at a purchase price of $5.5 million. In 1988, Hotel Telecom Services was acquired for about $15.0 million. The two newer acquisitions were service businesses rather than manufacturers, and to date had not yet generated satisfactory levels of profitability. In 1992, Duckworth Industries employed 755 people. The structure of the organization is shown in **Exhibit 2.**

**The Six Duckworth Incentive Plans**    Pay for performance was firmly embedded in the corporate culture at Duckworth Industries. In the words of one senior executive, "we put incentives, within reason, behind everything we can."

For plant-level employees, Duckworth had an *attendance* bonus. A 60 cents per hour pay incentive was earned for each pay period during which an employee was never more than 2 minutes late for work.

*This case was prepared as the basis for class discussion rather than to illustrate either effective or ineffective handling of an administrative situation.*

Copyright © 1993 by the President and Fellows of Harvard College. To order copies, call 1-800-545-7685 or write the Publishing Division, Harvard Business School, Boston, MA 02163. No part of this publication may be reproduced, stored in a retrieval system, used in a spreadsheet, or transmitted in any form or by any means — electronic, mechanical, photocopying, recording, or otherwise — without the permission of Harvard Business School.

For plant-level employees up to the shift supervisory level, there was also a *quality* incentive plan (**Exhibits 3** and **4**). Quality measures included many variables such as meeting promised shipment dates and reducing customer complaints of any nature. The quality incentive payment target equaled $100 per employee per month. Performance was often a team effort, and the average employee working under this incentive plan received about $600 per year from it. Employees received a separate check each month for the quality bonus to highlight the importance of quality in the company culture.

All Duckworth employees were participants in a *profit-sharing* plan. At the level of each business unit a profit-sharing pool was created. The pool was equal in size to 15% of pretax profits after a deduction equal to 10% of the beginning-of-year net worth allocated to the business unit. At the end of each year the profit-sharing pool was allocated to employees, pro rata, based on their individual share of total wages and salaries in the business unit. At the Worth business unit profit sharing had grown from about 2% of pay to about 15% of pay in recent years. A plant worker earning $15,000 per year would get $2,250. Information sharing with plant personnel as to profit and margin levels was common at Duckworth, so an estimate of the size of their individual profit sharing allocation could be made by employees as the year progressed.

For all sales and supervisory personnel the company had *individual* incentive plans. These typically afforded an employee the opportunity to earn incentives ranging from 10% to 40% of base pay. The incentive plan targets for a typical customer service representative are included as **Exhibit 5.**

## The Existing Senior Management Incentive Plans

The more senior managers at Duckworth (a group comprised of up to 40 people) all participated in an *annual* incentive compensation plan. A smaller subset of this group also participated in a *long-term* incentive program.

The incentive plans (both annual and long-term) for the senior managers had undergone considerable change in the 1983-1992 decade. Prior to 1990, the *annual* incentive plan would target for each manager a bonus of 20% to 50% of base salary if certain target levels of performance at the business unit level were reached during the year. Typical measures of performance (depending on the manager's area of responsibility) included at least three of the following:

1. Cash flow
2. Sales growth of proprietary products
3. Direct labor variances
4. Inventory turns
5. Accounts receivable (days sales outstanding)
6. Gross margins (less purchase price variances)
7. Special individual projects

In 1990 Duckworth abandoned the narrowly defined annual targets and opted to tie the annual bonus to a matrix built around sales growth and profitability goals. Annually goals for each business unit were set for both sales growth and profitability (**Exhibit 6**). These were determined with reference to the performance levels achieved by various peer group companies (**Exhibit 7**). Individual managers were assigned bonus targets (generally ranging from 25% to 50% of base compensation). Depending on the level of sales growth and profitability achieved, a manager could read directly from the matrix the factor by which his/her target bonus would be multiplied to determine the actual bonus he/she would receive. The incentive compensation matrix for the Worth business unit **(Exhibit 6)** indicated the following: If, in fiscal 1992, a manager working at the Worth business unit had a target bonus of 40%, and the business unit provided a 20% return on assets and 10% sales growth, the manager would receive 1.00 times his/her 40% target bonus. In fact, in 1991 and 1992, business unit managers at Duckworth received the following percentages of their target bonuses from the annual incentive plan.

|                       | 1991 | 1992 |
| --------------------- | ---- | ---- |
| Worth Corp.           | 170% | 0%   |
| Hotel Telecom         | 0    | 24   |
| Hospitality Equipment | 0    | 0    |
| Duckworth Industries  | 90   | 0    |

While Duckworth's annual incentive plan for senior managers covered several dozen employees by 1992, the long-term incentive plan covered fewer participants, particularly in the early part of the decade 1983–1992. In 1983 Duckworth implemented a five-year, long-term management incentive plan. The plan covered only two employees, the then vice president and general manager at Worth (now retired) and the then vice president, sales and marketing at Worth (now president of the Hotel Telecom Services operation). The plan made one payment at the end of five years. It was a phantom stock plan tied to the increase in book value per share multiplied by a performance factor **(Exhibit 8).** The performance factor was determined by several measures including a) the spread separating annual ROE from the sum of the bank prime rate plus two percentage points, b) the annual growth in net book value/share.

According to one of the participants the plan was a horror in complexity, but an attractive feature was that you could have one or two bad years and still get a payment. Because the plan paid only once at the end of five years, it was somewhat like a forced savings plan. "The size of the payment at the end made a meaningful difference in what you could do 'lifestyle'-wise. A check for $150,000 is quite significant when you bring it home. You are willing to make significant personal sacrifices along the way to make it happen."

In 1986 a new long-term management incentive plan was put in place at Duckworth. This plan was broadened to include more managers (15 by 1989) and was designed to begin payments in 1989 after the expiration of the previously described five-year plan. At the start of each year, beginning in 1986, new targets would be established so that incentive payments could be received annually. The business unit management participants in this plan would be awarded a specified percentage of base salary (generally from 25% to 40%) if a Challenge Earnings level of cumulative earnings before interest and taxes (approved by Duckworth's board of directors) was achieved by their business unit during the period. Lesser levels of earnings achievement would produce a proportionately reduced level of award (as shown in **Exhibit 9** for the Worth business unit).

The incentive system established in 1986 continued for four years. The last update was put in place in 1989, and covered the three-year time period ending in 1992.

In fact, between 1989–1992, business unit managers received the following percentages of their target bonuses from the long-term incentive plan.

|                        | 1989 | 1990 | 1991 | 1992 |
| ---------------------- | ---- | ---- | ---- | ---- |
| Worth Corp.            | 112% | 97%  | 92%  | 91%  |
| Hotel Telecom          | —    | 40   | 20   | 0    |
| Hospitality Equipment  | —    | —    | 40   | 45   |
| Duckworth Industries   | 85   | 80   | 75   | 73   |

For the top management team at Duckworth the target and actual bonus payments (measured as a percentage of base salary) are presented as **Exhibit 10.**

## A Proposed New EVA Incentive System

As fiscal 1992 unfolded, both management and Mr. Duckworth (the controlling shareholder) were looking for ways to more closely align the interests of management and shareholders through the incentive plan for senior management. A number of factors had contributed to dissatisfaction with the existing plans. One major factor had to do with operation of the annual incentive plan of Worth in 1992. In many ways Worth's performance in 1992 was improved over that of 1991.

|                                    | Worth Corp. | |
| ---------------------------------- | ----- | ----- |
|                                    | 1991  | 1992  |
| Return on gross performing assets  | 23.6% | 23.9% |
| Sales growth                       | 13.9  | (2.3) |

The return on gross performing assets had increased, but sales had declined slightly (versus a 10% goal and a minimum 5% sales growth requirement to achieve any annual incentive plan payment). The sales decline was caused by the loss of a very large customer buying a product with commodity-type profit margins. Most of the lost sales in 1992 had been replaced by new customers purchasing proprietary products at higher margins. The change in customer mix was good for enhancing long-run shareholder value, but Worth's management failed to achieve any annual incentive bonus as a result of the change given the structure of the existing annual incentive plan (**Exhibit 6**).

Near the close of fiscal 1992 Mr. John Duckworth began reading a book entitled *The Quest for Value* by G. Bennett Stewart. The Stewart book outlined a management incentive plan that promised to link management pay directly to the creation of long-run economic value for shareholders. Implementation of the plan required the services of Stern Stewart & Co., a financial consulting firm.

The economic value-added (EVA) compensation system developed by Stern Stewart would require (1) considerable data analysis and (2) some reorienting in thinking about how to approach the business going forward for Duckworth's senior management. The EVA system was predicated on the following logic:

1.  Economic value for shareholders is created when a firm earns a rate of return on invested capital which exceeds the cost of capital. The economic value-added in a particular year should equal the product of:
    i)  The average capital employed during the year multiplied by
    ii) The spread separating the cost of capital from the return on capital earned during the year.
2.  The economic value-added during a year can be calculated for each business unit. The management of each unit can be directly compensated for their success in adding economic value via a compensation formula that automatically adjusts the baseline for calculating next year's bonus to reflect the actual performance of the prior year.

**The Key Drivers of Economic Value-Added**    **Exhibit 11** shows a calculation of the economic value-added by the Worth division of Duckworth Industries from 1988 through 1992. It also shows the *forecasted* economic value-added for the period 1993–1997.

The key variables in determining the economic value-added by a business unit were:

1.  Net operating profit after taxes (NOPAT)—**Exhibit 11,** Line 9.
    This excludes corporate overhead, and capitalizes R&D expenses and then amortizes them over three years. NOPAT excludes non-economic non-cash charges.[1]
2.  Average capital—**Exhibit 11,** Line 19.
    This excludes construction in progress, and assumes FIFO inventory valuation and the add-back of bad debt reserves. Non-economic non-cash writeoffs are added back to average capital.[2]
3.  Cost of capital—**Exhibit 11,** Line 17.
    This is determined annually for each business unit by using an assumed capital structure and riskiness factor ($\beta$ value) for peer group firms comparable to each business unit. The formula for calculating capital cost was tied to the yield on 30-year Treasury obligations plus a risk premium.

**The Mechanism for Calculating Incentive Compensation**    Stern Stewart recommended a mechanism for linking economic value-added in a business unit during a given year to the incentive compensation paid to management in that year.

*First,* a bonus target was established. At Worth this might equal 37% of base pay (**Exhibit 12,** Line 1). Bonus units (like phantom stock) would be assigned to each manager in an amount such that if the bonus unit was valued at $1.00, the desired level of bonus would be earned by the manager (**Exhibit 12,** Line 3).

*Second,* a baseline EVA level was established (**Exhibit 12,** Line 4). At the end of each year the baseline EVA for the *following* year would change by one-half of the difference between the actual EVA achieved and the baseline EVA for the prior year (**Exhibit 12,** Lines 8–10). This made the system "self-adjusting." If EVA performance improved each year, the new base would click up by one-half the amount of the improvement. If EVA performance deteriorated for several years, the base level would decline so that the targets would not be so far away as to be unreachable in ensuing years.

---

[1] Items such as the one-time writeoff of a divested business would be a non-economic non-cash charge. Items such as depreciation or the amortization of debt discount would be economic non-cash charges.
[2] This was designed to prevent managers from escaping responsibility for poor prior investment decisions by simply divesting the poor performing assets.

*Third,* a base unit value was established for each ensuing year (**Exhibit 12,** Lines 6 and 14). This base unit value defined, to a large degree, how much of the target bonus could be earned by just maintaining the existing level of business performance. If EVA hit exactly the baseline EVA each year, and the base unit value was set at $1.00, then exactly the target bonus would be earned each year. In the case of Worth, after the first year the base unit value dropped to $.80. This meant that simply repeating the EVA baseline performance after 1993 would produce only 80% of the targeted bonus.

*Fourth,* a bonus sensitivity factor (**Exhibit 12,** Lines 7 and 11) was established which could either add to or subtract from the base unit value to create a total unit value. In the Worth example, the bonus sensitivity factor was set at $1,625,000. In any year that EVA varied from the baseline EVA, the amount of the gap was divided by $1,625,000, and the resulting amount (called the *performance* unit value, **Exhibit 12,** Lines 12 and 13) was added to the *base* unit value to determine the *total* unit value (**Exhibit 12,** Line 15). In order to earn one times the target bonus solely from the performance unit factor, management of the business unit had to beat the baseline EVA by the amount of the bonus sensitivity factor.

As indicated in **Exhibit 12,** if Worth hit the forecasted level of EVA in each year, Worth's management would earn the following percentage of their target bonus in each of the next five years.

|  | % OF TARGET BONUS EARNED |
|---|---|
| 1993 | 100% |
| 1994 | 51 |
| 1995 | 122 |
| 1996 | 170 |
| 1997 | 211[3] |

As indicated in **Exhibits 13–16,** if the Hotel Telecom Services and Hospitality Equipment Services business units hit their forecasted level of EVA in each year, Hotel Telecom's and Hospitality Equipment's managements would earn the following percentage of their targeted bonus in each of the next five years (**Exhibits 14** and **16,** Line 15).

|  | *% of Target Bonus Earned* | |
|---|---|---|
|  | HOTEL TELECOM | HOSPITALITY EQUIPMENT |
| 1993 | 45% | 79% |
| 1994 | 99 | 85 |
| 1995 | 69 | 71 |
| 1996 | 66 | 65 |
| 1997 | 62 | 66 |

---

[3] Bonuses up to two times the target bonus were paid immediately. One-third of the amount over this maximum was also paid in cash. Remaining amounts were allocated to a "bonus bank" to be paid out in the future. Negative charges for deteriorating performance reduced the bonus bank. Negative charges could even create a negative balance in the bonus bank which would have to be overcome in order to resume bonus payments in future years.

According to Bennett Stewart, the beauty of the EVA incentive compensation system was that it was "A self-motivated, self-adjusting corporate governance system that linked capital budgeting and strategic investment decisions to the compensation system."

From John Duckworth's perspective, not only were the interests of management and shareholders aligned, but in addition the bogeys for determining bonus compensation would not have to be renegotiated each year. What had been two plans (one annual plan and a long-term plan) could be combined into *one* plan that paid on annual results but was designed to build long-term shareholder value. The system was like a self-winding watch. You set it once and it might keep going, all by itself, for quite some time.

**EXHIBIT 1   Consolidated Financial Statements 1975–1992, Fiscal Years Ended 5/31 ($000)**

| | 1975 | 1980 | 1985 | 1990 | 1991 | 1992 |
|---|---|---|---|---|---|---|
| Net sales | 5,811 | 15,109 | 40,793 | 116,220 | 123,545 | 122,570 |
| Cost of goods sold | 4,294 | 11,164 | 30,142 | 85,875 | 89,865 | 86,720 |
| Selling, gen'l & admin. | 1,231 | 3,199 | 8,638 | 24,610 | 25,080 | 28,800 |
| Operating income | 287 | 746 | 2,013 | 5,735 | 8,595 | 7,050 |
| Investment income | 68 | 177 | 479 | 1,365 | 1,375 | 1,545 |
| Interest expense | 129 | 334 | 902 | 2,570 | 2,390 | 1,635 |
| Profit sharing expense | 55 | 142 | 383 | 1,090 | 1,595 | 1,850 |
| Income before taxes | 172 | 447 | 1,207 | 3,440 | 5,985 | 5,105 |
| Taxes | 50 | 130 | 351 | 1,000 | 1,850 | 1,565 |
| Net income | 122 | 317 | 856 | 2,440 | 4,135 | 3,540 |
| Cash & marketable securities[a] | 1,067 | 2,775 | 7,492 | 21,345 | 24,790 | 26,085 |
| Accounts receivable | 578 | 1,502 | 4,056 | 11,555 | 12,760 | 13,210 |
| Inventory | 572 | 1,487 | 4,014 | 11,435 | 11,380 | 12,995 |
| Less: Lifo reserves | 51 | 131 | 355 | 1,010 | 1,111 | 1,125 |
| Net inventories | 522 | 1,356 | 3,661 | 10,430 | 10,270 | 11,870 |
| Other current assets | 46 | 119 | 321 | 915 | 960 | 990 |
| Total current assets | 2,212 | 5,752 | 15,530 | 44,245 | 48,780 | 52,155 |
| Construction in progress | 25 | 65 | 176 | 500 | 485 | 3,105 |
| Other net PP&E | 799 | 2,076 | 5,605 | 15,970 | 15,450 | 14,330 |
| Other assets[b] | 290 | 753 | 2,032 | 5,790 | 5,735 | 5,685 |
| Total assets | 3,325 | 8,646 | 23,343 | 66,505 | 70,450 | 75,275 |
| Short term debt | 734 | 1,909 | 5,154 | 14,685 | 17,390 | 15,910 |
| Other current liabilities | 1,048 | 2,724 | 7,355 | 20,955 | 19,790 | 23,700 |
| Total current liabilities | 1,782 | 4,633 | 12,510 | 35,640 | 37,180 | 39,610 |
| Long term borrowings | 496 | 1,290 | 3,482 | 9,920 | 8,355 | 7,175 |
| Other liabilities | 63 | 164 | 444 | 1,265 | 1,105 | 1,140 |
| Net worth | 984 | 2,558 | 6,908 | 19,680 | 23,810 | 27,350 |
| Total liab. & net worth | 3,325 | 8,646 | 23,343 | 66,505 | 70,450 | 75,275 |

[a] *Marketable securities were carried at the lower of cost or market. Market exceeded cost by $4,090 in 1990, $7,870 in 1991, and $10,940 in 1992.*
[b] *Other assets included goodwill of $5,130 in 1990, $4,995 in 1991, and $4,855 in 1992.*

**EXHIBIT 2    Organization Chart, Duckworth Industries, Inc., June 1, 1992**

| | John Duckworth<br>President | |
|---|---|---|

**Joseph Nathan**<br>Executive Vice President<br>Chief Operating Officer

**Wade Nimrock**<br>Treasurer

**Kristin Klimsczak**<br>HES V.P. & Gen'l Mgr
- Field Sales
- Power Specialists
- Parts Manager
- Service Manager
- Service Technicians

**Eric Nye**<br>President<br>Hotel Telecom Services

**Andrew Walters**<br>Division Manager
- Field Sales
- Product Engineer
- Parts Manager
- Assembly Technician

**Duncan McFarlan**<br>Branch Manager
- Field Sales
- Wareh./Delivery

**John Kimble**<br>Branch Manager
- Purchasing
- Field Sales
- Wareh./Delivery

**William Kestner**<br>Vice President & General Manager<br>Worth Corp.

**Mark Jefferson**<br>Director Sales/Marketing
- Field Sales
- Marketing
- Clerical

**Robert Davison**<br>V.P. Operations
- Direct Labor
- Operations Mgmt
- Indirect Labor
- Quality Control

**Stephanie Byrne**<br>Director Engineering
- Engineering
- Tool Room

**Douglas Adams**<br>HTS Controller
- Accounting Clerks

**Douglas Healy**<br>HES Controller
- Purchasing
- Wareh. & Ship.
- Accounting Clerks
- Secret./Expediter
- Receptionist

**Guy Peralta**<br>Worth Controller
- Office Manager
- Clerical

| Fiscal Year | — Headcount — | | |
|---|---|---|---|
| | 1993 | 1992 | 1991 |
| Duckworth Industries | 10 | 10 | 12 |
| Worth Corp. | 500 | 485 | 410 |
| HES | 135 | 155 | 170 |
| Hotel Telecom | 110 | 95 | 95 |
| Total | 755 | 745 | 687 |

632

**EXHIBIT 3   Duckworth Corporation, Quality Incentive Bonus Plan, Fiscal Year 1993**

The Quality Incentive bonus plan has been in its current form since FY90 (June of 1989).

As we have improved as a company it is important that our plan be modified to reflect these changes and more accurately represent what the "real world" reflects in terms of total quality performance. After a thorough review of this years' quality performance the following changes are being made to the Quality Incentive bonus plan effective June 1, 1992 (FY93). The monthly complaint ratio and bonus payout levels will be:

| COMPLAINT RATIO | MONTHLY BONUS PAYOUT |
|---|---|
| .6% or less | $100.00 |
| More than .6%, less than 2.0% | $75.00 |
| More than 2.0, less than 3.5% | $50.00 |

As you can see, the lower limits have been changed and the bottom payout of $25 eliminated, but we have increased the top level payout by $25 to $100.00. The total potential maximum yearly payout is now $1,200 compared to $900 with the old plan. This year through the first 11 months we have paid $800 in incentives to each participant. As you can see from the above, superior performance will be rewarded with high-level bonus payouts.

Duckworth quality performance in FY91 improved dramatically to an average **2.7%** complaint ratio with the **last 6 months** of the year averaging **2%.** The revised plan is designed to build on this success and increase our performance to "world class" levels.

The procedure for analyzing, charging responsibility, and tallying total number of complaints by Richard Sterling all remain the same as in the past. The only additional reporting will be a new category recording invoicing errors, such as billing errors or wrong prices on orders. Complete quality is a total system—from the first customer inquiry to billing of parts and all processes in between.

With constant dedication to teamwork, continuous quality improvement and satisfying our **customers requirements,** we are confident that our new goals will be achieved and even surpassed. You are doing it now and we are counting on you to make Duckworth—**Your Company**—The best quality company possible!

William Kestner
Vice President and General Manager

cc:   John Duckworth
     Joseph Nathan

**EXHIBIT 4    Worth Corporation, Quality Incentive Program, FY93 October Results**

| | |
|---|---|
| No. of Shipments | 207 |
| No. of Chargeable Complaints | 4 |
| Complaint Ratio | 1.9% |
| Quality Bonus–October | $75 |
| Quality Bonus–YTD | $300 |

With a record number of shipments, this month had the potential of being a **great quality month,** but we fell short because preventable errors were not caught. Without the large shipment level, the monthly payout would not have been $75.00.

If you look at the customer complaints listed below, you will see that these problems could have been detected by our systems. The key to continued improvement is your using the systems and informing others when the system does not work.

The XXX and YYY complaints are good examples of where the system in place was not followed and resulted in a complaint. The AAA and BBB complaints are examples of where people could have come forth to say the system doesn't adequately detect these kinds of defects.

The tasks of improvement needs to be continually addressed by all. We cannot just let things go on and expect good results. Good results are achieved by good people doing the right things at the right time.

| Type of Complaint | Customer | Complaint |
|---|---|---|
| Manufacturing Process | AAA | Cracked AX47 parts and inventory not rotated. |
| Manufacturing Process | BBB | Cracked AX47 parts and inventory not rotated. |
| Color | YYY | Color significantly off standard (yellow). |
| Label | XXX | Label had wrong code printed. |

Joy Meadow
Quality Assurance Manager

Thomas Spencer
Production Manager

**EXHIBIT 5**   **Worth Corporation, FY93 Incentive Plan for Customer Service Representative; Maximum Award = 10% of average base salary.**

|  | ITEM RESULTS | % OF BONUS | % OF SALARY |
|---|---|---|---|
| **I. Order Accuracy:** | | | |
| 4% maximum potential | | | |
| Accuracy equals percentage of acceptance of orders that have | 98.0% or higher | 40.00% | 4.00% |
| correct pricing and other critical information. This accuracy is | 96.5% | 30.00% | 3.00% |
| tracked by Director of Sales with bonus being paid based on | 95.0% | 20.00% | 2.00% |
| overall FY93 results. | < 95.0% | 0.00% | 0.00% |
| **II. Order Acknowledgement/Turnaround:** | | | |
| 3% maximum potential | | | |
| (effective 9/1/92 — 9 month period) | | | |
| Average number of days (excluding holidays & weekends) from | 2 days or less | 30.00% | 3.00% |
| order placement until printing of order acknowledgement for all | 3 days | 15.00% | 1.50% |
| orders received (except those requiring new part numbers). Results | 4 days | 5.00% | 0.50% |
| to be tracked weekly on late shipments report. | > 4 days | 0.00% | 0.00% |
| **III. Sales Growth:** | | | |
| 3% maximum potential | | | |
| Total net company sales growth over FY92 net sales of $63.5 | $7,000M | 30.00% | 3.00% |
| million | $6,000M | 15.00% | 1.50% |
| | $3,000M | 5.00% | 0.50% |
| | < $3,000M | 0.00 | 0.00% |

**EXHIBIT 6   Duckworth Industries, Inc., Fiscal 1992 Incentive Compensation**

Worth Corporation,

ANNUAL SALES GROWTH %

| RETURN ON GROSS ASSETS % | | 4.90 | 5.00 | 7.50 | 10.00 | 12.50 | 15.00 |
|---|---|---|---|---|---|---|---|
| | | | | | GOAL | | |
| 25.0 | | 0 | 1.74 | 1.81 | 1.88 | 1.95 | 2.03 |
| 24.0 | | 0 | 1.55 | 1.61 | 1.67 | 1.74 | 1.81 |
| 23.0 | | 0 | 1.37 | 1.42 | 1.48 | 1.55 | 1.61 |
| 22.0 | | 0 | 1.20 | 1.25 | 1.31 | 1.37 | 1.42 |
| 21.0 | | 0 | 1.05 | 1.10 | 1.15 | 1.20 | 1.25 |
| 20.0 | GOAL | 0 | 0.91 | 0.95 | 1.00 | 1.05 | 1.10 |
| 19.0 | | 0 | 0.78 | 0.82 | 0.87 | 0.91 | 0.95 |
| 18.0 | | 0 | 0.67 | 0.71 | 0.74 | 0.78 | 0.82 |
| 17.0 | | 0 | 0.57 | 0.60 | 0.63 | 0.67 | 0.71 |
| 16.0 | | 0 | 0.48 | 0.51 | 0.54 | 0.57 | 0.60 |
| 15.0 | | 0 | 0.40 | 0.42 | 0.45 | 0.48 | 0.51 |
| 14.9 | | 0 | 0 | 0 | 0 | 0 | 0 |

Return on Gross Performing Assets will be determined by dividing Operational Cash Flow Earnings (OCFE) into Average Gross Performing Assets (AGPA).

OCFE is net profit adjusted to add depreciation and to eliminate (a) interest expense, (b) acquisition expenses, (c) net investment income, (d) expense or profit relating to LIFO, and (e) gains or losses from the disposition of depreciable assets. All adjustments will be made on an after-tax basis, using Worth Corporation's effective tax rate.

AGPA is a 13-month average of the company's gross book assets, with cumulative depreciation and the LIFO reserve added back, but investment securities and intercompany receivables eliminated.

The Board of Directors reserves the right to adjust the formula and its components, even after the fact, in any way it determines to be appropriate in order to better effectuate the plan and its purpose.

**EXHIBIT 7    ROA/Growth Matrix for Worth Peer Group**

Fasteners/Adhesives

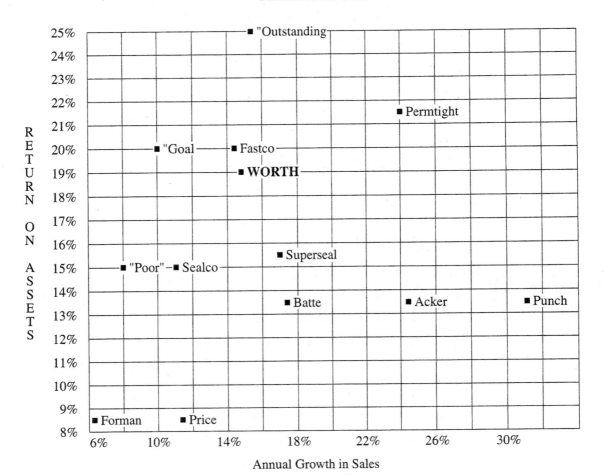

**EXHIBIT 8    Worth Corporation, Inc., Executive Long Term Incentive Plan**

| SUMMARY | 31-MAY-83 | 31-MAY-88 | 5-YR CHANGE |
|---|---|---|---|
| Total shareholders' equity at year end | $8,616,500 | $16,379,000 | |
| Per share, using standard of 500,000 shares | $    17.23 | $    32.76 | |
| Value weighting "Performance Factor" | 0.50 | 1.70 | |
| Weighted share price | $     8.62 | $    55.69 | $47.07 |
| (= Equity per share × performance factor) | | | |
| Per participant | $47.07 × | 3000 shares | = $141,210 |
| In total | | × 2 participants | = $282,420 |

**EXHIBIT 9**    **Worth Division of Duckworth Industries—Management Long-Term Plan *Targets Established* for Successive Three Year Plans versus *Results Achieved***

| PLAN YEARS | CHALLENGE EARNINGS LEVELS (3 YR CUMULATIVE EBIT) | % OF TARGET AWARD EARNED | ACTUAL RESULTS DURING PERIOD |
|---|---|---|---|
| 1986–1989 | $12.0 million | 100% | $13.4 million and 112% |
|  | 10.0 | 50% |  |
|  | 7.5 | 10% |  |
|  | <7.5 | 0% |  |
| 1987–1990 | $20.0 | 100% | $19.3 million and 97% |
|  | 12.5 | 10% |  |
|  | <12.5 | 0% |  |
| 1988–1991 | 28.75 | 100% | $26.1 million and 92% |
|  | 20.0 | 10% |  |
|  | <20.0 | 0% |  |
| 1989–1992 | 33.0 | 100% | $30.1 million and 91% |
|  | 25.0 | 10% |  |
|  | <25.0 | 0% |  |

**Award Determination**    Each Participant will, at the start of a Performance Period, be assigned a Target Award expressed as a percentage of the Participant's average annual base salary to be paid during the Performance Period. The percent of the Target Award earned by each Participant will be based upon the relationship of Performance Period Earnings to various Challenge Earnings Levels specified by the Board for such Performance Period.

The percent of Target Award earned will be awarded on a pro rata basis if the actual results fall between specified Challenge Earnings Levels. If a Participant significantly changes responsibility or positions during the Performance Period, the Board will consider the propriety of an equitable adjustment in the Target Award assigned.

A Participant's award is subject to organizational and environmental constraints affecting Performance Period Earnings. Unforeseen problems (other than those referred to in the next paragraph) or opportunities, as well as peer group performance, will be taken into account during the evaluation process. As soon as practicable after the end of a Performance Period, the Board will determine how successfully objectives were met. The Board will evaluate how unforeseen difficulties, as well as unexpected opportunities, were addressed. To allow recognition for quality of results and level of effort, award amounts may be adjusted (to a maximum of plus or minus 25% of the award) by the Board.

The Plan also recognizes that actions of Participants may be negated or overstated due to the occurrence of certain extraordinary events. Examples of extraordinary events include, but are not limited to, "Acts of God," financial difficulty of a major supplier or customer, unexpected tax law changes and acquisitions, divestitures, mergers or significant structural changes. Should such extraordinary occurrences take place, the Board may adjust the incentive awards (or the various formula components thereof) in any manner reasonably intended to reflect the impact of the extraordinary occurrence.

**EXHIBIT 10   Target and Actual Payments (as a % of Base Salary) for Annual and Long-Term Incentive Compensation Plans**

| | | *1990* | | *1991* | | *1992* | |
|---|---|---|---|---|---|---|---|
| | | TARGET | ACTUAL | TARGET | ACTUAL | TARGET | ACTUAL |
| Manager A | Annual bonus | — | — | 40[a] | 68 | 40[a] | 0 |
| | L.T. Incentive | — | — | 35[a] | 32 | 35[a] | 32 |
| Manager B | Annual bonus | — | — | 25[a] | 35 | 25[a] | 0 |
| | L.T. Incentive | — | — | 25[a] | 23 | 25[a] | 23 |
| Manager C | Annual bonus | 50[a] | 50 | 50[a] | 85 | 50[b] | 0 |
| | L.T. Incentive | 40[a] | 39 | 40[a] | 37 | 40[b] | 0 |
| Manager D | Annual bonus | 25[a] | 25 | 40[a] | 35 | 25[a] | 0 |
| | L.T. Incentive | 25[a] | 24 | 40[a] | 37 | 40[a] | 36 |
| Manager E | Annual bonus | 40[a] | 40 | 40[a] | 68 | 40[a] | 0 |
| | L.T. Incentive | 40[a] | 39 | 35[a] | 32 | 35[a] | 32 |
| Manager F | Annual bonus | — | — | 25[b] | 0 | 25[b] | 6 |
| | L.T. Incentive | — | — | 25[b] | 5 | 25[b] | 0 |
| Manager G | Annual bonus | 40[a] | 40 | 50[b] | 0 | 50[b] | 12 |
| | L.T. Incentive | 40[a] | 39 | 40[b] | 8 | 40[b] | 0 |
| Manager H | Annual bonus | — | — | 25[b] | 0 | 25[b] | 6 |
| | L.T. Incentive | — | — | 25[b] | 5 | 25[b] | 0 |
| Manager I | Annual bonus | 25[a] | 25 | 50[d] | 46 | 50[d] | 0 |
| | L.T. Incentive | 25[a] | 25 | 25[c] | 10 | 60[d] | 44 |
| Manager J | Annual bonus | — | — | — | — | 25[c] | 0 |
| | L.T. Incentive | — | — | — | — | — | — |
| Manager K | Annual bonus | 30[c] | 0 | 30[c] | 0 | 30[c] | 0 |
| | L.T. Incentive | 30[c] | 0 | 30[c] | 12 | 30[c] | 14 |
| Manager L | Annual bonus | 40[c] | 0 | 40[c] | 0 | 50[c] | 0 |
| | L.T. Incentive | 35[c] | 0 | 35[c] | 14 | 35[c] | 16 |
| Manager M | Annual bonus | 50[c] | 0 | 50[c] | 0 | 50[c] | 0 |
| | L.T. Incentive | 50[c] | 0 | 50[c] | 20 | 50[c] | 46 |
| Manager N | Annual bonus | — | — | 35[a] | 60 | 35[a] | 0 |
| | L.T. Incentive | 40[a] | 39 | 40[a] | 37 | 40[a] | 36 |
| Manager O | Annual bonus | 40[a] | 40 | 40[a] | 68 | 40[a] | 0 |
| | L.T. Incentive | 25[a] | 24 | 25[a] | 23 | 25[a] | 23 |
| Manager P | Annual bonus | 20[a] | 20 | 20[a] | 34 | 20[a] | 0 |
| | L.T. Incentive | 20[a] | 19 | 20[a] | 18 | 20[a] | 18 |

[a] *Worth*          *SBU*
[b] *Hotel Telecom Services*          *SBU*
[c] *Hospitality Equipment Services*          *SBU*
[d] *Duckworth Industries*          *SBU*

**EXHIBIT 11  Worth Corporation Summary of Historical and Projected Operating Performance ($000's)**

|  | | History | | | | | Forecast | | | | |
|---|---|---|---|---|---|---|---|---|---|---|---|
| LINE # | | 1988 | 1989 | 1990 | 1991 | 1992 | 1993 | 1994 | 1995 | 1996 | 1997 |
| | **Operating Results** | | | | | | | | | | |
| 1 | Revenue | $47,255 | $54,615 | $57,125 | $65,035 | $63,565 | $69,500 | $76,100 | $83,330 | $91,250 | $99,915 |
| 2 | % Growth | 15.0% | 15.6% | 4.6% | 13.9% | (2.3%) | 9.3% | 9.5% | 9.5% | 9.5% | 9.5% |
| 3 | − Cost of Sales | 34,985 | 40,305 | 41,760 | 46,020 | 42,025 | 47,355 | 51,950 | 56,915 | 62,415 | 68,445 |
| 4 | % Sales | 74.0% | 73.8% | 73.1% | 70.8% | 66.1% | 68.1% | 68.3% | 68.3% | 68.4% | 68.5% |
| 5 | − SG&A | 6,620 | 6,700 | 6,905 | 6,905 | 8,585 | 9,695 | 10,865 | 11,715 | 12,680 | 13,585 |
| 6 | % Sales | 14.0% | 12.3% | 12.1% | 10.6% | 13.5% | 13.9% | 14.3% | 14.1% | 13.9% | 13.6% |
| 7 | − Cash Taxes | $ 2,280 | $ 1,965 | $ 2,615 | $ 3,500 | $ 3,650 | $ 4,225 | $ 4,855 | $ 5,310 | $ 5,785 | $ 6,215 |
| 8 | % Operating Income | 40.4% | 25.8% | 30.9% | 28.9% | 28.2% | 33.9% | 36.5% | 36.1% | 35.8% | 34.8% |
| 9 | **NOPAT** | **$ 3,370** | **$ 5,645** | **$ 5,840** | **$ 8,615** | **$ 9,305** | **$ 8,225** | **$ 8,430** | **$ 9,390** | **$10,370** | **$11,670** |
| | **Capital** | | | | | | | | | | |
| 10 | Net Accounts Receivable | $ 5,310 | $ 4,855 | $ 5,460 | $ 5,525 | $ 6,060 | $ 6,185 | $ 6,760 | $ 7,395 | $ 8,090 | $ 8,850 |
| 11 | Inventory | 2,865 | 2,965 | 3,360 | 3,865 | 4,020 | 4,030 | 4,260 | 4,585 | 4,945 | 5,325 |
| 12 | PP&E | 5,540 | 9,415 | 13,775 | 13,505 | 12,180 | 19,465 | 21,555 | 21,825 | 20,915 | 21,200 |
| 13 | Other Assets | 620 | 350 | 1,455 | 1,565 | 3,765 | 3,210 | 2,450 | 1,800 | 1,245 | 1,185 |
| 14 | − NIBCL's[a] | (10,775) | (9,790) | (11,545) | (10,025) | (13,125) | (9,940) | (10,860) | (12,040) | (13,360) | (14,725) |
| 15 | **Capital** | **$ 3,555** | **$ 7,795** | **$12,505** | **$14,440** | **$12,900** | **$22,945** | **$24,165** | **$23,560** | **$21,830** | **$21,835** |
| | **Operating Analysis** | | | | | | | | | | |
| 16 | NOPAT/Avg Cap (r) | 51.4% | 99.5% | 57.5% | 63.9% | 68.1% | 45.9% | 35.8% | 39.3% | 45.7% | 53.5% |
| 17 | − Cost of Capital (c) | 13.0% | 12.6% | 12.7% | 12.4% | 12.2% | 12.2% | 12.2% | 12.2% | 12.2% | 12.2% |
| 18 | Spread (r − c) | 38.4% | 86.9% | 44.8% | 51.5% | 55.9% | 33.7% | 23.6% | 27.2% | 33.5% | 41.3% |
| 19 | × Average Capital | $ 6,550 | $ 5,675 | $10,150 | $13,470 | $13,670 | $17,925 | $23,555 | $23,865 | $22,695 | $21,830 |
| 20 | **Economic Value Added** | **$ 2,515** | **$ 4,935** | **$ 4,550** | **$ 6,945** | **$ 7,640** | **$ 6,045** | **$ 5,565** | **$ 6,485** | **$ 7,605** | **$ 9,010** |

[a] *Noninterest-bearing current liabilities.*

## EXHIBIT 12   Worth Corporation

### Input Table

| LINE # | | 1993 | 1994 | 1995 | 1996 | 1997 | |
|---|---|---|---|---|---|---|---|
| | **Bonus Pool Characteristics** | | | | | | |
| 1 | Target Bonus | 37% | 37% | 37% | 37% | 37% | |
| 2 | Base Salary (000) | $1,710 | $1,795 | $1,885 | $1,980 | $2,075 | |
| 3 | # of Units (000) | 630 | 660 | 695 | 730 | 765 | |
| | **Bonus Calculation Framework** | | | | | | |
| 4 | Baseline EVA (000) | $6,045 | | | | | |
| 5 | Annual Target Adjustment Factor | 50% | | | | | |
| 6 | Base Unit Value | $1.00 | $0.80 | $0.80 | $0.80 | $0.80 | |
| | **EVA Bonus Sensitivity Factor** | | | | | | |
| 7 | EVA Bonus Sensitivity Factor (000) | $1,625 | | | | | |

### Current Bonus Calculation

| LINE # | | 1993 | 1994 | 1995 | 1996 | 1997 | AVERAGE |
|---|---|---|---|---|---|---|---|
| | **Performance Unit Value** | | | | | | |
| 8 | EVA (000) | $6,045 | $5,565 | $6,485 | $7,605 | $9,010 | $6,940 |
| 9 | − Baseline EVA (000) | $6,045 | $6,045 | $5,805 | $6,145 | $6,875 | $6,180 |
| 10 | = EVA vs Baseline EVA (000) | $ 0 | ($ 480) | $ 680 | $1,460 | $2,135 | $ 760 |
| 11 | / EVA Bonus Sensitivity Factor (000) | $1,625 | $1,625 | $1,625 | $1,625 | $1,625 | $1,625 |
| 12 | = Performance Unit Value | $0.00 | ($0.29) | $0.42 | $0.90 | $1.31 | $0.47 |
| | **Total Unit Value** | | | | | | |
| 13 | Performance Unit Value | $0.00 | ($0.29) | $0.42 | $0.90 | $1.31 | $0.47 |
| 14 | + Base Unit Value | $1.00 | $0.80 | $0.80 | $0.80 | $0.80 | $0.84 |
| 15 | = Total Unit Value | $1.00 | $0.51 | $1.22 | $1.70 | $2.11 | $1.31 |
| | **Current Bonus** | | | | | | |
| 16 | Total Unit Value | $1.00 | $0.51 | $1.22 | $1.70 | $2.11 | $1.31 |
| 17 | # of Units (000) | 630 | 660 | 695 | 730 | 765 | 695 |
| 18 | Current Bonus Earned (000) | $630 | $335 | $850 | $1,240 | $1,620 | $935 |

### Past Bonus If System Had Been In Place Prior 5 Years

| LINE # | | 1988 | 1989 | 1990 | 1991 | 1992 | AVERAGE |
|---|---|---|---|---|---|---|---|
| | **Current Bonus** | | | | | | |
| 19 | Total Unit Value | $1.00 | $2.29 | $1.31 | $2.53 | $2.09 | $1.84 |
| 20 | # of Units (000) | 695 | 720 | 720 | 740 | 530 | 680 |
| 21 | Current Bonus Earned (000) | $695 | $1,645 | $945 | $1,875 | $1,115 | $1,255 |

## EXHIBIT 13 Hotel Telecom Services, Summary of Historical and Projected Operating Performance ($000's)

| LINE # | | History | | | | | Forecast | | | |
|---|---|---|---|---|---|---|---|---|---|---|
| | | 1989 | 1990 | 1991 | 1992 | 1993 | 1994 | 1995 | 1996 | 1997 |
| | **Operating Results** | | | | | | | | | |
| 1 | Revenue | $29,115 | $32,540 | $29,980 | $32,285 | $46,600 | $55,920 | $60,115 | $64,625 | $69,470 |
| 2 | % Growth | NMF | 11.8% | (7.9%) | 7.7% | 44.3% | 20.0% | 7.5% | 7.5% | 7.5% |
| 3 | – Cost of Sales | 20,750 | 24,120 | 22,395 | 24,730 | 36,150 | 43,435 | 46,735 | 50,205 | 54,005 |
| 4 | % of Sales | 71.3% | 74.1% | 74.7% | 76.6% | 77.6% | 77.7% | 77.7% | 77.7% | 77.7% |
| 5 | – SG&A | 5,610 | 5,475 | 5,560 | 5,820 | 7,935 | 9,150 | 9,820 | 10,550 | 11,320 |
| 6 | % of Sales | 19.3% | 16.8% | 18.5% | 18.0% | 17.0% | 16.4% | 16.3% | 16.3% | 16.3% |
| 7 | – Cash Taxes | $ 455 | $ 1,000 | $ 700 | $ 500 | $ 815 | $ 1,060 | $ 1,135 | $ 1,235 | $ 1,325 |
| 8 | % Operating Income | 16.5% | 33.9% | 34.5% | 28.9% | 32.4% | 31.8% | 31.8% | 31.9% | 31.9% |
| 9 | **NOPAT** | **$ 2,300** | **$ 1,950** | **$ 1,325** | **$ 1,230** | **$ 1,700** | **$ 2,275** | **$ 2,425** | **$ 2,640** | **$ 2,825** |
| | **Capital** | | | | | | | | | |
| 10 | Net Accounts Receivable | $ 3,370 | $ 3,240 | $ 3,935 | $ 4,365 | $ 6,115 | $ 7,265 | $ 7,805 | $ 8,385 | $ 9,010 |
| 11 | Inventory | 4,525 | 4,145 | 4,570 | 6,245 | 7,120 | 8,520 | 9,150 | 9,820 | 10,550 |
| 12 | PP&E | 1,365 | 1,250 | 1,355 | 1,525 | 1,520 | 1,405 | 1,395 | 1,255 | 1,085 |
| 13 | Goodwill | 4,395 | 4,395 | 4,395 | 4,400 | 4,400 | 4,400 | 4,400 | 4,400 | 4,400 |
| 14 | Other Assets | 230 | 715 | 1,260 | 1,935 | 290 | 320 | 330 | 345 | 360 |
| 15 | – NIBCL's[a] | (4,720) | (3,860) | (4,630) | (5,490) | (5,575) | (6,985) | (7,505) | (8,085) | (8,685) |
| 16 | **Capital** | **9,170** | **9,890** | **10,891** | **12,975** | **13,870** | **14,920** | **15,570** | **16,115** | **16,710** |
| | **Operating Analysis** | | | | | | | | | |
| 17 | NOPAT/Avg Cap (r) | 22.3% | 20.5% | 12.8% | 10.3% | 12.7% | 15.8% | 15.9% | 16.7% | 17.2% |
| 18 | – Cost of Capital (c) | 13.1% | 13.2% | 12.9% | 12.7% | 12.7% | 12.7% | 12.7% | 12.7% | 12.7% |
| 19 | Spread (r – c) | 9.2% | 7.3% | (0.1%) | (2.4%) | 0.0% | 3.1% | 3.2% | 4.0% | 4.5% |
| 20 | × Average Capital | $10,345 | $ 9,530 | $10,390 | $11,935 | $13,420 | $14,395 | $15,245 | $15,840 | $16,410 |
| 21 | **Economic Value Added** | **$ 950** | **$ 695** | **$ (10)** | **$ (280)** | **$ 0** | **$ 450** | **$ 495** | **$ 630** | **$ 745** |

a Noninterest-bearing current liabilities.

**EXHIBIT 14** **Hotel Telecom Services**

## Input Table

| LINE # | | 1993 | 1994 | 1995 | 1996 | 1997 | |
|---|---|---|---|---|---|---|---|
| | **Bonus Pool Characteristics** | | | | | | |
| 1 | Target Bonus | 38% | 38% | 38% | 38% | 38% | |
| 2 | Base Salary (000) | $905 | $950 | $1,000 | $1,050 | $1,100 | |
| 3 | # of Units (000) | 345 | 360 | 380 | 400 | 420 | |
| | **Bonus Calculation Framework** | | | | | | |
| 4 | Baseline EVA (000) | ($140) | | | | | |
| 5 | Annual Target Adjustment Factor | 50% | | | | | |
| 6 | Base Unit Value | $0.25 | $0.25 | $0.25 | $0.25 | $0.25 | |
| | **EVA Bonus Sensitivity Factor** | | | | | | |
| 7 | = EVA Bonus Sensitivity Factor (000) | $700 | | | | | |

## Current Bonus Calculation

| LINE # | | 1993 | 1994 | 1995 | 1996 | 1997 | AVERAGE |
|---|---|---|---|---|---|---|---|
| | **Performance Unit Value** | | | | | | |
| 8 | EVA (000) | $ 0 | $450 | $ 495 | $ 630 | $ 745 | $465 |
| 9 | − Baseline EVA (000) | ($140) | ($ 70) | $ 190 | $ 340 | $ 485 | $160 |
| 10 | = EVA vs Baseline EVA (000) | $140 | $520 | $ 305 | $ 290 | $ 255 | $300 |
| 11 | / EVA Bonus Sensitivity Factor (000) | $700 | $700 | $ 700 | $ 700 | $ 700 | $700 |
| 12 | = Performance Unit Value | $0.20 | $0.74 | $0.44 | $0.41 | $0.37 | $0.43 |
| | **Total Unit Value** | | | | | | |
| 13 | Performance Unit Value | $0.20 | $0.74 | $0.44 | $0.41 | $0.37 | $0.43 |
| 14 | + Base Unit Value | $0.25 | $0.25 | $0.25 | $0.25 | $0.25 | $0.25 |
| 15 | = Total Unit Value | $0.45 | $0.99 | $0.69 | $0.66 | $0.62 | $0.68 |
| | **Current Bonus** | | | | | | |
| 16 | Total Unit Value | $0.45 | $0.99 | $0.69 | $0.66 | $0.62 | $0.68 |
| 17 | # of Units (000) | 345 | 360 | 380 | 400 | 420 | 380 |
| 18 | Current Bonus Earned (000) | $155 | $360 | $260 | $265 | $ 260 | $260 |

## Past Bonus If System Had Been In Place Prior 4 Years

| LINE # | | 1989 | 1990 | 1991 | 1992 | AVERAGE |
|---|---|---|---|---|---|---|
| | **Current Bonus** | | | | | |
| 19 | Total Unit Value | $1.27 | $0.39 | ($0.68) | ($0.60) | $0.08 |
| 20 | # of Units (000) | 50 | 150 | 325 | 340 | 215 |
| 21 | Current Bonus Earned (000) | $ 60 | $ 60 | ($225) | ($205) | ($78) |

## EXHIBIT 15 Hospitality Equipment Service Co., Summary of Historical and Projected Operating Performance ($000s)

| LINE # | | History | | | | | | Forecast | | | |
|---|---|---|---|---|---|---|---|---|---|---|---|
| | | 1988 | 1989 | 1990 | 1991 | 1992 | 1993 | 1994 | 1995 | 1996 | 1997 |
| | **Operating Results** | | | | | | | | | | |
| 1 | Revenue | $24,770 | $28,670 | $26,555 | $28,525 | $26,720 | $29,220 | $31,410 | $33,765 | $36,300 | $39,020 |
| 2 | % Growth | 49.2% | 15.8% | (7.4%) | 7.4% | (6.3%) | 9.4% | 7.5% | 7.5% | 7.5% | 7.5% |
| 3 | − Cost of Sales | 18,560 | 21,545 | 19,545 | 20,955 | 14,305 | 21,190 | 22,500 | 24,170 | 25,965 | 27,895 |
| 4 | % Sales | 74.9% | 75.1% | 73.6% | 73.5% | 72.2% | 72.5% | 71.6% | 71.6% | 71.5% | 71.5% |
| 5 | − SG&A | 5,765 | 6,100 | 7,240 | 6,495 | 7,135 | 7,065 | 7,480 | 7,950 | 8,455 | 8,985 |
| 6 | % Sales | 23.3% | 21.3% | 27.3% | 22.8% | 26.7% | 24.2% | 23.8% | 23.5% | 23.3% | 23.0% |
| 7 | − Cash Taxes | $ 275 | $ 440 | $ 55 | $ 420 | $ 320 | $ 420 | $ 545 | $ 615 | $ 690 | $ 780 |
| 8 | % Operating Income | 62.0% | 43.0% | (23.7%) | 38.8% | 113.3% | 43.6% | 38.0% | 37.2% | 36.7% | 36.4% |
| 9 | **NOPAT** | **$ 170** | **$ 585** | **($ 290)** | **$ 660** | **($ 35)** | **$ 545** | **$ 885** | **$ 1,035** | **$ 1,190** | **$ 1,365** |
| | **Capital** | | | | | | | | | | |
| 10 | Net Accounts Receivable | $ 2,655 | $ 3,775 | $ 3,075 | $ 3,525 | $ 3,010 | $ 3,660 | $ 6,288 | $ 4,220 | $ 4,530 | $ 4,865 |
| 11 | Inventory | 2,830 | 3,420 | 4,115 | 3,205 | 3,105 | 3,365 | 3,560 | 3,815 | 4,085 | 4,380 |
| 12 | PP&E | 545 | 965 | 815 | 515 | 360 | 950 | 1,160 | 1,370 | 1,580 | 1,790 |
| 13 | Other Assets | 535 | 355 | 335 | 835 | 850 | 675 | 770 | 805 | 805 | 810 |
| 14 | − NIBCL's[a] | (4,295) | (4,845) | (4,095) | (3,250) | (4,045) | (3,295) | (3,520) | (3,805) | (4,110) | (4,440) |
| 15 | **Capital** | **$ 2,270** | **$ 3,675** | **$ 4,250** | **$ 4,825** | **$ 3,280** | **$ 5,355** | **$ 5,900** | **$ 6,405** | **$ 6,890** | **$ 7,400** |
| | **Operating Analysis** | | | | | | | | | | |
| 16 | NOPAT/Avg Cap (r) | 7.8% | 19.7% | (7.3%) | 14.5% | (0.9%) | 12.6% | 15.7% | 16.8% | 17.9% | 19.1% |
| 17 | − Cost of Capital (c*) | 13.4% | 13.4% | 13.4% | 13.4% | 13.4% | 13.5% | 13.5% | 13.5% | 13.5% | 13.5% |
| 18 | Spread (r − c*) | (5.6%) | 6.3% | (20.7%) | 1.1% | (14.3%) | (1.0%) | 2.2% | 3.3% | 4.4% | 5.5% |
| 19 | × Average Capital | $ 2,155 | $ 2,970 | $ 3,960 | $ 4,535 | $ 4,055 | $ 4,315 | $ 5,625 | $ 6,150 | $ 6,645 | $ 7,145 |
| 20 | **Economic Value Added** | **($ 120)** | **$ 185** | **($ 820)** | **$ 50** | **($ 580)** | **($ 40)** | **$ 125** | **$ 205** | **$ 290** | **$ 395** |

**EXHIBIT 16   Hospitality Equipment Service Co.**

## Input Table

| LINE # | | 1993 | 1994 | 1995 | 1996 | 1997 | |
|---|---|---|---|---|---|---|---|
| | **Bonus Pool Characteristics** | | | | | | |
| 1 | Target Bonus | 42% | 42% | 42% | 42% | 42% | |
| 2 | Base Salary (000) | $705 | $740 | $775 | $815 | $855 | |
| 3 | # of Units (000) | 300 | 315 | 330 | 345 | 365 | |
| | **Bonus Calculation Framework** | | | | | | |
| 4 | Baseline EVA (000) | ($310) | | | | | |
| 5 | Annual Target Adjustment Factor | 50% | | | | | |
| 6 | Base Unit Value | $0.25 | $0.25 | $0.25 | $0.25 | $0.25 | |
| | **EVA Bonus Sensitivity Factor** | | | | | | |
| 7 | = EVA Bonus Sensitivity Factor (000) | $500 | | | | | |

## Current Bonus Calculation

| LINE # | | 1993 | 1994 | 1995 | 1996 | 1997 | AVERAGE |
|---|---|---|---|---|---|---|---|
| | **Performance Unit Value** | | | | | | |
| 8 | EVA (000) | ($ 40) | $125 | $205 | $290 | $395 | $195 |
| 9 | − Baseline EVA (000) | ($310) | ($175) | ($ 25) | $ 90 | $190 | ($45) |
| 10 | = EVA vs Baseline EVA (000) | $270 | $300 | $230 | $200 | $205 | $240 |
| 11 | / EVA Bonus Sensitivity Factor (000) | $500 | $500 | $500 | $500 | $500 | $500 |
| 12 | = Performance Unit Value | $0.54 | $0.60 | $0.46 | $0.40 | $0.41 | $0.48 |
| | **Total Unit Value** | | | | | | |
| 13 | Performance Unit Value | $0.54 | $0.60 | $0.46 | $0.40 | $0.41 | $0.48 |
| 14 | + Base Unit Value | $0.25 | $0.25 | $0.25 | $0.25 | $0.25 | $0.25 |
| 15 | = Total Unit Value | $0.79 | $0.85 | $0.71 | $0.65 | $0.66 | $0.73 |
| | **Current Bonus** | | | | | | |
| 16 | Total Unit Value | $0.79 | $0.85 | $0.71 | $0.65 | $0.66 | $0.73 |
| 17 | # of Units (000) | 300 | 315 | 330 | 345 | 365 | 330 |
| 18 | Current Bonus Earned (000) | $235 | $265 | $235 | $225 | $240 | $240 |

## Past Bonus If System Had Been In Place Prior 5 Years

| LINE # | | 1988 | 1989 | 1990 | 1991 | 1992 | AVERAGE |
|---|---|---|---|---|---|---|---|
| | **Current Bonus** | | | | | | |
| 19 | Total Unit Value | $0.71 | $1.10 | ($1.34) | $1.20 | ($0.54) | $0.22 |
| 20 | # of Units (000) | 285 | 525 | 315 | 335 | 255 | 345 |
| 21 | Current Bonus Earned (000) | $205 | $575 | ($425) | $405 | ($140) | $125 |

## CASE 27   Kidder, Peabody & Co.: Creating Elusive Profits

On April 17, 1994 Kidder, Peabody & Co. announced a $350 million pre-tax charge against earnings resulting from the discovery of false trading profits. That same day, the termination of Joseph Jett's employment with the company was made public.

This was the final event of a story that began in November 1991, four months after Joseph Jett joined Kidder, Peabody & Co. During this time, Jett allegedly accumulated trading losses of $85 million dollars, while his profit and loss statement showed $264 million in profits.[1] Notwithstanding these losses, his trading performance had been praised by his supervisors and colleagues, and was reflected in the year-end bonuses awarded to him. The financial world was kept wondering what went wrong and how much Joseph Jett was to blame.

### *Origins*[2]

Kidder, Peabody & Co. was organized in 1865 at 40 State Street in Boston, by Henry Kidder, Francis Peabody, and his brother Oliver Peabody. The three partners had been employed at J.E. Thayer & Brother, founded in 1824, and created their partnership when Nathaniel Thayer decided to retire and turn the business over to them. The company grew during the last part of the 19th century and beginning of the 20th century to become the leading banking house in New England and a major player in the U.S. financial market. In 1868, as New York was eclipsing Boston as the nation's investment banking center, an office was opened at 45 Wall Street. Boston remained the main office until the market crash of 1929.

The firm was hit hard by the debacle of 1929. It survived with the help of several investors who valued the goodwill represented by the Kidder, Peabody name and injected the cash needed to rescue the firm. A new partnership was founded in March 1931 taking over the old Kidder, Peabody & Co. name. Based in New York, its partners were Chandler Hovey, Edwin Webster, and Albert Gordon. The firm survived the difficult thirties and regained its position among the leading investment banking houses by the end of World War II.

By 1985, Kidder, Peabody & Co., with $363 million in capital, was ranked 15th in the industry. Unlike many of its competitors, the firm had funded its growth through accumulated profits which limited its growth opportunities. Competitors were bolstering their capital by issuing shares to the public (e.g., Morgan Stanley), or were being acquired by large corporations (e.g., Salomon Brothers). Finally, in early 1986, 80% of Kidder's equity was sold to General Electric (GE) for $602 million. In 1990, GE increased its ownership to 100%.

---

[1] Source: "Report of Inquiry into False Trading Profits at Kidder, Peabody & Co. Incorporated" by the law firm of Davis Polk & Wardwell, New York, dated August 4, 1994. The investigation team was headed by Gary G. Lynch, a former Director of the SEC's Enforcement Division, and the document is generally referred to as the "Lynch report". Much of the factual information provided is drawn therefrom.

[2] The history of the firm is based on the book "More Than a Century of Investment Banking: the Kidder, Peabody & Co. Story" by Vincent P. Carosso, New York: McGraw-Hill, 1979.

*Doctoral Candidate Antonio Davila and Professor Robert Simons prepared this case as the basis for class discussion rather than to illustrate either effective or ineffective handling of an administrative situation.*

GE Capital Services (GECS), the financial subsidiary of GE to which Kidder, Peabody & Co. reported, was the largest diversified finance company in the United States. Kidder's new financial strength, combined with its investment bank knowledge, promised to make Kidder "a very powerful institution if they integrate people right."[3]

During the first years of the combination, the firm was run by Kidder insiders. But in January 1989, Michael A. Carpenter, a GE executive, was named CEO of Kidder, Peabody & Co.

Carpenter, who previously held the number two position at GECS, had managed leveraged-buyout loans and takeover deals. He had no experience in brokerage but he intended to bring GE's successful management practices to Kidder, driving the investment bank to achieve the number one or number two market position required by GE's chairman Jack Welch. Carpenter's plan for Kidder was:

> "First, to reestablish the firm's total commitment to integrity . . . 'that's numbers 1 to 10'. Second, Kidder was to have a well defined strategy for each business—a GE mandate for all of its businesses. Third, to develop Kidder's people. Fourth, the firm needed to cut overhead, to become 'cost effective.' Fifth was to develop a successful synergy with GE Capital. And sixth was to build a winning culture."[4]

Carpenter's strained relationship with the head of GECS, Gary Wendt, (described as "intense and well known animosity"[5]) constrained his initial enthusiasm to integrate Kidder into GECS and take advantage of the synergies that were still mostly unrealized. During this period, several key managers left the firm seemingly unhappy with the "get-tough moves" of the parent company. Cost cutting had reduced their bonuses despite an increase in Kidder's profits. This drop in bonuses was very noticeable in an industry where bonus pay-outs could be several times the basic salary of a successful employee and competing firms were continuously vying for top performers.

The performance of Kidder, Peabody & Co. under GE's ownership is shown in **Exhibit 1.**

## Organization[6]

With training from MIT and Harvard Business School, Joseph Jett was hired by Kidder, Peabody & Co. in July 1991. At the time he was 33 years old. He had worked previously as a bond trader at Morgan Stanley for two years and at First Boston for eighteen months. In one of them he floundered and was laid off, in the other one he was fired.[7] Jett's job was to trade the long-end market (maturities of ten years or longer) for STRIPS—a type of zero coupon financial instrument[8] related to U.S. Treasury notes and bonds.

Together with Jett, three other traders covered the various segments of the market for zero coupon government instruments. The traders in the zero coupon desk were supervised by the head of the government desk, Melvin Mullin, who had been in that position since June 1988. Mullin was succeeded, at his own recommendation, by Jett in February 1993 when Mullin was appointed head of the derivatives division. **Exhibit 2** presents the relevant organizational structure of Kidder, Peabody & Co.

---

[3] Business Week, May 12, 1986, p. 27.
[4] Fortune, September 5, 1994.
[5] Fortune, September 5, 1994.
[6] This section of the case is based on data from the Lynch report.
[7] "Did He or Didn't He", on *60 Minutes,* aired 2-19-95.
[8] Zero coupon instruments have only one cash flow associated with them at the end of their lives.

The government desk grouped together all the traders involved with government-related instruments. It was part of the Fixed Income Division which employed over 700 people, accounted for the majority of Kidder's earnings, and was responsible for over 90% of Kidder's balance sheet in 1992 and 1993. It employed a large salesforce and had 12 different trading desks each one in charge of a different type of fixed-income instrument: government securities, corporate debt securities, derivative products, municipal securities, and collateralized mortgage obligations.

Edward Cerrullo, a skilled and knowledgeable trader, had headed the Fixed Income Division since 1986. Kidder's new CEO, Michael Carpenter, had little experience in securities' trading and relied heavily on Cerrullo's experience to run the Fixed Income Division. Cerrullo was also a member of Kidder's Board and of several internal committees. He supervised the management tasks of the various desk heads and the trading performance of those desk heads who were also active traders. Jett, at the time he was promoted to head of the government desk, remained an active trader and, accordingly, was supervised directly by Cerrullo.

Cerrullo was assisted by David Bernstein, manager of business development, and by a risk manager responsible for ensuring that the market risk of the various trading positions was properly hedged. Bernstein came from GE where he had worked for twelve years in different financial analysis positions. He joined Kidder in 1988 as Business Unit Controller ("BUC") on the Controller's staff. In September 1991, he moved to the Fixed Income Division as Cerrullo's "right-hand man" to help Cerrullo manage the division. He was respected for his "intelligence and familiarity with financial and administrative issues."[9]

Also under Cerrullo's supervision was the financing or "repo" desk. Its job was to go to the market to execute the trades entered by the traders.

The finance and administration department was headed by Kidder's Chief Financial Officer, Richard O'Donnell, who reported directly to Carpenter. O'Donnell was responsible for formal control reports and procedures of the company and the internal audit function. The operations department or "back office" was also under the umbrella of O'Donnell and included the government clearance area which processed all transactions at settlement date.

### The Government Trading System

U.S. Treasury notes and bonds are financial instruments with the right to a string of cash flows made up of (1) periodic interest payments and (2) the payment of the principal at the end of their lives. However, this cash flow structure is not convenient for some market participants who need an instrument with the equivalent cash flows but where each payment can be traded separately.

To satisfy these market needs, the Federal Reserve Bank of New York (the "Fed") offers the option of exchanging U.S. Treasury notes and bonds for an equivalent set of zero coupon instruments. In other words, it exchanges a single note or bond for a series of instruments representing its cash flow components. These individual components are called "Separate Trading of Registered Interest and Principal of Securities", or STRIPS.

For example, a semiannual bond maturing in 10 years can be exchanged for 21 zero coupon bonds, 20 of them associated with interest payments and 1 with the principal payment (see **Exhibit 3**). This process of converting a bond into separate STRIPS is called

---

[9] The Lynch report, p. 26.

## FIGURE 1 "Changing a dollar for four quarters"

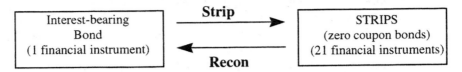

stripping. The Fed also offers the inverse transaction: a market participant can come with the separate STRIPS of a bond and get the full bond. This process is called reconstitution ("recon"). Simply stated, these exchanges are like going to the bank with a dollar and receiving four quarters in return or giving four quarters and getting a dollar back. The Fed routinely offers this service without charge in the same way that a bank would exchange a dollar for four quarters (see **Figure 1**).

Kidder traders in the STRIPS market used a proprietary expert computer system, the *Government Trader System*, to record transactions in this market. Traders only needed to select the trade, specify whether it was a strip or recon and the quantity being traded, and the System updated their inventory position, printed the trade tickets with the transaction's characteristics, informed the financing desk (repo desk) and clearance personnel. The Government Trader System also allowed the trader to scan market prices to detect arbitrage opportunities. Sometimes the value of a stripped bond would be temporarily higher or lower than the complete bond; in these cases the trader could take advantage of the arbitrage opportunity. Usually, STRIPS desks were not high performers because arbitrage opportunities were small and short-lived; most of the income generated came from the sales commissions to execute these trades.

Kidder's proprietary Government Trader System treated a strip—converting a bond into its separate STRIPS—as selling a bond and purchasing STRIPS. For example, the stripping of the 10 year bond described above would be recorded as 22 transactions: selling the bond would represent one transaction and purchasing the 20 zero coupon instruments associated with the interest payments together with the final principal payment would represent the other 21 transactions. These transactions had no counterparty (i.e., buyer or seller) because the Fed was only exchanging one instrument for an equivalent series of instruments (in the same way that an accounting system would not recognize changing a dollar for four quarters). The Government Trader System, recognizing this fact, recorded these transactions as being with Kidder itself.

To increase flexibility, the Government Trader System allowed traders to commit today to a transaction that would take place at a future date (at a price established today). The trader could choose to settle the transaction the next-day ("default" alternative) or at any future date. This forward capability was used at the request of customers or to take advantage of arbitrage opportunities. For example, if a bond was trading cheaper stripped than reconstituted, the trader could take advantage of this arbitrage opportunity by buying STRIPS today and doing a recon—transforming the STRIPS into a bond—the next day. Because arbitrage opportunities were short-lived and the Fed was ready to exchange at any time, most transactions in the STRIP market were done the same day or the next day. Forward strips or recons beyond one day were unusual.

After each transaction, the inventory position of the trader was updated. For example, when a recon was entered—the obligation to deliver STRIPS to get a bond—the trader's "short" position in STRIPS—his deficit position—increased because the Government

Trader System posted the delivery of STRIPS as a sale. At the same time his "long" position in bonds—his outstanding buying position—went up because the trader had increased his stock of bonds. For forward transactions, the effects upon unsettled inventories were equivalent: a forward strip—deliver a bond and get its separate STRIPS—increased the short position on unsettled inventories of bonds (because a bond was being sold) and increased the long position on unsettled STRIPS (that were being bought).

Inventory positions were valued at market price at the end of each trading day (i.e., they were "marked-to-market"). Any change in value was recognized in the trader's daily profit and loss statement. For example, if the price of an instrument went up and the trader had a long position in it—i.e., had the instrument on hand or was committed to buy it at a fixed price—then a profit was recorded; similarly if the trader had a short position on the instrument, then he or she incurred in a loss.

Like all financial instruments, *zero coupon instruments* are valued in the market at the present value of the future cash flow of the instrument. However *interest-bearing bonds and notes* are valued "ex-interest"—the price quoted in the market does not include the interest accrued since the last payment and, thus, does not fully reflect the present value of the future cash flows. When a bond is traded, the seller receives from the buyer the market price of the bond *plus* the accrued interest on the bond since the last interest payment which is not included in the price (see **Exhibit 4**).

This difference in market valuation methods had a special impact on how the Government Trader System accounted for forward settlement transactions. Because strips and recons are "neutral" transactions with no effect on the P&L statement, the System correctly assigned the same value to the bond and its STRIPS at *settlement date*. The value was the market price of the bond ("ex-interest") plus the accrued interest at *settlement date*. But at the *transaction date*, the System valued the STRIPS (which are zero coupon instruments) at their discounted cash flow value (market price), while bonds were valued at their settlement date value. Thus at the *transaction date*, the System recognized a profit (for a recon) or a loss (for a strip) equal to the difference between the value of the STRIPS at the *transaction date* and their value at *settlement date*. This profit or loss disappeared over time to become zero at *settlement date* (see **Figure 2**).

**FIGURE 2    Accounting for future settlement of STRIPS and bonds**

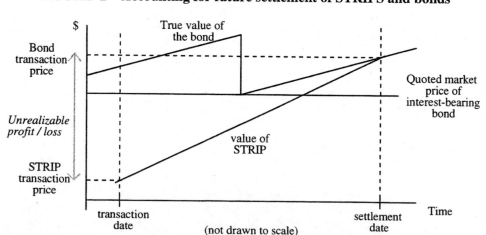

## Trading Strategy

The trading strategy allegedly used by Joseph Jett to generate unrealizable profits was based on the mark-to-market valuation of unsettled positions. According to the Government Trader System, a forward recon to be settled several months into the future produced a sizable profit at the date the transaction was entered. This "unrealizable profit" occurred because of the different valuation methods used by the Government Trading System to value STRIPS and interest-bearing bonds. As discussed above, the unrealized profit was offset over time by small daily losses as the settlement date approached and the computer system updated the value of the STRIP (which was increasing in value as its maturity date drew nearer). But these daily small losses, as well as any other trading losses, could be swamped by the illusory profit generated by entering a new forward recon.

For example, on December 28, 1992 Jett entered a recon of $200 million of 12% bonds maturing in May 2005 to be settled on May 11, 1993. The System showed a profit associated with this transaction of $9.4 million because the long position in bonds (valued at the future settlement date) was $292.9 million while the short position in STRIPS (valued at the transaction date's discounted value) was only $283.5 million.

Many at Kidder believed that, in its strip and recon activities, the Fed behaved as a dumb customer; and where you made money, of course, was on dumb customers.[10] As Jett stated:

> "When you do a strip or recon forward, there is both a buy and a sell of a security, . . . It was puzzling that there was any P&L effect at all. . . . The only reasons [for] P&L consequence is [that the] Fed accept STRIPS at today's yield level for a forward settlement date. . . . [David] Bernstein [the department's manager of business development and Cerrullo's right-hand man] explained it was like doing business with an unsophisticated investor like a municipal defeasance. . . . We all agreed on that."[11]

According to Jett, Cerrullo as well as Mullin, his first supervisor, were aware and informed of his trading strategy. Jett described a successful trading day in a meeting with Cerrullo, O'Donnell, (Kidder's CFO), and general counsel John Liftin:

> "At 9:00 a.m. principal trading rich and I can sell 300 million at a profit level. I enter a strip. Take bond and sell at market. This may put market under pressure. Price falls. Now attractive. I become a buyer. Buy 300 million and enter recon at Fed. My buying pressure creates opposite effect. You can do that all day long. . ."[12]

Forward recons not only had an effect on the profit and loss statement, but they also altered the balance sheet position of each trader. In Joseph Jett's case, the unsettled short position in STRIPS due to forward transactions had grown to be significant as well as its counterpart, the unsettled long position in bonds. Since Cerrullo was concerned about minimizing the balance sheet exposure of the firm, traders were asked to control their asset positions. Keeping his positions at reasonable levels was, perhaps, the most challenging aspect of Jett's trading strategy.

Before September 1993, Kidder's accounting system gave the same treatment to settled (i.e., securities in hand) and unsettled (open transactions) inventories. It reported the *net* position that every trader, and the company as a whole, had in every single financial

---

[10] The Lynch report, p. 34–35.
[11] Institutional Investor, March 1995.
[12] Institutional Investor, March 1995, p. 7.

instrument. Long and short positions on the same financial instrument were netted out by the accounting system irrespective of whether the positions were settled or unsettled. To keep his balance sheet exposure down, Jett compensated his large unsettled positions in forward recons with settled positions in the same bonds and STRIPS. For example, on August 27, 1993, Jett's position in unsettled short STRIPS was $13.2 billion and his unsettled long bond position was $13.4 billion. But, through off-setting settled positions on the same bonds and STRIPS (i.e., inventory on hand)[13], he was able to keep his net position down to $3.9 billion on STRIPS and $9.8 billion on bonds.[14]

In September 1993, Kidder's accounting system was changed. Unsettled positions would now be moved off balance sheet. The past strategy used by Jett to control the size of his balance sheet was no longer possible because settled and unsettled positions were now reported separately and could no longer be netted out. They had to be managed independently. From September 1993 onward, Jett's trading strategy to manage his inventory of unsettled positions could only be based on other unsettled transactions.

To counteract the inventory effect, every forward recon to be settled several months into the future had to be matched with a forward strip in the same bond for a similar dollar amount. But a forward strip, under the Government Trader System, was associated with an unrealized loss. To minimize this loss, Jett used a shorter settlement date for these unsettled strips. (With a shorter settlement date, the loss associated with the different accounting treatments was lower because the discounted cash flow effects were smaller.) As these strips reached their settlement date, they were replaced by a new forward strip with identical characteristics. For example, in December 1993, Jett's average remaining days to settlement for forward recons (generating unrealizable profits) was 43 days, while remaining days to settlement for offsetting forward strips (generating unrealizable losses) was 4 days.[15]

The new trading strategy required the use of both forward recons (to generate unrealizable profits) and forward strips (to keep unsettled inventory down). Because of the snowball effect associated with this profit generating strategy, which required ever larger unsettled forward recon positions, Jett had at times unsettled positions greater than the actual market for the bond he was trading—sometimes as high as 269% of the actual market.[16] As a practical matter, it would have been impossible to settle these positions at settlement date since the clearance personnel would not have been able to purchase the required instruments in the market. They simply did not exist in sufficient quantity. To solve this problem, Jett created next-day settlement transactions on the same instrument to pair-off strips or recons: the clearance personnel received two offsetting transactions that neutralized each other and did not, therefore, require them to go to the market to actually execute the trades. In November 1993, for example, $5 billion of Jett's strip and recon transactions were settled, but $140 billion were paired off.[17]

The effects of the new trading strategy on forward transaction volume are shown in **Exhibit 5** at the end of the case. They also showed up in Jett's personal trading volume and trading mix:

---

[13] By "same bonds and STRIPS", we refer to exactly the same instrument; for example, the 10 years, 8.5% government bond issued August 1991.

[14] The Lynch report, p. 43.

[15] The Lynch report, p. 45.

[16] The Lynch report, p. 42.

[17] The Lynch report, p. 6.

**FIGURE 3   Jett's Personal Trading Volume**

| | JULY TO DECEMBER 1991 (6 MONTHS) | 1992 (12 MONTHS) | 1993 (12 MONTHS) | JANUARY TO MARCH 1994 (3 MONTHS) |
|---|---|---|---|---|
| Trading volume | $25 billion | $273 billion | $1,567 billion | $1,762 billion |
| Trading profit | — | $32.5 million | $151 million | $81 million |
| Trades with counterparties | 78% | 32% | 10% | 5% |
| Trades (strips/recons) with the Federal Reserve | 22% | 68% | 90% | 95% |
| Strips | 10% | 32% | 45% | 47% |
| Recons | 12% | 36% | 45% | 48% |

## The Failure of Internal Controls[18]

Joseph Jett made his first forward recon in November 1991. After several months of poor performance in early 1992, Jett began to show consistent profits. In 1992, his trading profits were $32.5 million, an unheard of record for the STRIPS desk. His bonus was $2 million. In 1993—newly promoted to head of the government desk, but still an actual trader—he generated $151 million in profits, representing 27% of the Fixed Income Division's profits (up from 6% in 1992). His efforts earned him a $9 million bonus and Kidder's "Employee-of-the-Year" award. That same year, Cerrullo was awarded a bonus of $12 million. During the first three months of 1994, Jett's reported profits were $81 million. Exhibit 6 shows Jett's performance over his tenure at Kidder Peabody.

Mullin, Jett's supervisor until he was promoted, reviewed daily reports on the trading activity of all the government desk traders. These reports illustrated the major contribution that Joseph Jett was making to the division's profitability. Mullin's review of Jett's performance in the first half of 1992, when he recommended a substantial raise for Jett, reads:

"Jett's performance in 1992 has been outstanding, after taking some time in the second half of 1991 to grow up the learning curve. Profitability in STRIPS at this time is $8.4 million. This profit level substantially exceeds that of 1991, and on an annualized basis far exceeds our best ever performance in STRIPS.

The level of profitability has been consistent with no month under $1 million; profits have come from intelligent trading activity and close attention to detail. Joseph has worked diligently to become one of the best STRIPS traders in the business."[19]

Mullin did not seem to be knowledgeable of how the unrealizable profits were generated, nor was he aware of the forward recons entered by Jett. Mullin, relying on the computer-generated reports of the Government Trader System, allegedly failed to review information on settlement dates or counterparties that could have guided him in understanding the implications of the trading strategy used by Jett. In October 1992, a review of the government desk done at Cerrullo's request by outside counsel recommended that Mullin review trade tickets. However, Mullin responded that such a review would be impractical

---

[18] This section is based largely on data from the Lynch report.
[19] From the Lynch report, p. 50.

given the volume of trade tickets generated each day. Alternatively, he proposed that he review an exception report. Such a report was never generated.

Cerrullo, Jett's boss since February 1993, believed that "Jett's level of profitability was consistent with asset growth and was attributable to a combination of market-making and arbitrage opportunities in STRIPS."[20] Even when Jett's 1993 profits grew almost five-fold when compared to his 1992 profits, Cerrullo did not go beyond daily P&L reports, risks reports and other Kidder reporting structures to understand where profits—profits that were not generating any cash—were coming from.

Cerrullo said that "he continually monitored Mr. Jett's performance, but that he had to rely on the firm's internal audit reports, which gave no hint of irregularities. . . . that Kidder's accounting and auditing systems gave a reassuring picture of Mr. Jett's trading activity."[21] He believed that "given the liquidity and transparent pricing of the government market, as well as the sophistication of the Government Trader System, adequate systematic controls existed and detailed scrutiny of Jett's trading was unnecessary."[22] Cerrullo said:

> "No numbers I saw ever came close, every single bit of evidence—the inventory reports, the P&L statements, the control reports, the risk management reports—was reinforcing."[23]

**Reports and Reviews**   Kidder, Peabody & Co. had a full accounting and control department to maintain the formal reporting systems and audit the activity of the various desks. This department reviewed all the trading processes, but traders were under no obligation to share their trading strategies with the accounting and control staff. The function of the Business Unit Controller, staffed until September 1991 by Bernstein, was to provide independent accounting and control to the firm. This position was vacant until November 1993 because of lack of a good candidate.

Kidder's internal audit department reviewed Jett's transactions in two different audits. The first one, from January to September 1993, focused on trading practices at the zero coupon desk. The other, from August to September 1993, reviewed the settlement practices in the government clearance area. Neither of these two audits uncovered the true nature of the unrealizable profits. The first audit team was made of inexperienced auditors who relied on Jett's account of his trading strategy without verifying his statements; they deferred to the second audit team to review the settlement process. At the time the second audit team reviewed settlement practices, Jett's trading had not been identified by clearance personnel as a concern and the audit team did not spend time on it. Jett commented on these audits:

> "When a trader is audited, that is the firm's stamp of approval on everything that the trader does."[24]

In May 1993, Charles Fiumefreddo, a member of the Controller's department, was working on a project sponsored by the Inventory Committee to identify forward settlement transactions that could be moved off-balance sheet. The Inventory Committee, comprised of senior executives including Cerrullo (head of the Fixed Income Division), O'Donnell (Chief Financial Officer), and Carpenter (CEO of Kidder Peabody), had become concerned about Kidder's balance sheet asset levels. Kidder's leverage ratio at the end of 1993 was

---

[20] From the Lynch report, p. 13.
[21] New York Times, Tuesday July 26, 1994, p. D1.
[22] From the Lynch report, p. 54.
[23] New York Times, Tuesday July 26, 1994, p. D1.
[24] Newsday, February 19, 1995

about twice that of its nearest Wall Street rival and the company was making efforts to reduce its balance sheet.[25] Generally Accepted Accounting Principles (GAAP) allowed transactions in government securities to be moved off-balance sheet if they were to be settled within one day.

Fiumefreddo identified $1 billion in forward transactions in Jett's ledger. To help him better identify forward transactions in the Government Trader System, Fiumefreddo contacted the analyst who, together with Mullin, had designed the System. Outraged, "Jett called Fiumefreddo and berated him for independently contacting the analyst."[26] Bernstein, Fiumefreddo and Jett met to discuss the matter. Jett and Bernstein discussed a possible P&L distortion that the System could be introducing into forward transactions, but the conclusion was "that Jett's forward reconstitution activity did not generate any P&L distortion."[27]

Jett's outburst at Fiumefreddo was not unusual. Jett was harsh and domineering with subordinates, many of whom were afraid of him. Thus, the junior traders who executed his instructions may have been reluctant to voice their concerns. Jett had a well deserved reputation for firing anyone who questioned his trading methods. In addition, he was seen to be held in increasing esteem by senior management, culminating in the receipt of Kidder's "Employee-of-the-Year" award in January, 1994.[28]

In September 1993, a new management report was generated to monitor forward government transactions that had been moved off balance sheet. This report, called KPPS98, was generated weekly, and received by financial accounting and regulatory accounting staff. Ninety percent of all the transactions and 100% of the dollar volume shown in the report came from Jett's ledger, but accountants argued "that we had no reason as accountants to question how STRIPS trading could generate such large forward positions, and that the volume of forwards were disclosed in balance sheet information reviewed each week by the Inventory Committee."[29]

The financial accounting personnel did, however, inform David Bernstein, Cerrullo's "right hand man", in early December 1993 that part of the increase in Kidder's balance sheet exposure was due to Jett's trading. Jett's trading showed an excess of next-day pair-off transactions (to avoid having large unsettled strips and recons that required actually going to the market). Since next-day pair-off transactions were part of the balance sheet, Bernstein explained to Jett that he "should not enter regular-way pair-offs at months-end when the Fixed Income Division needed to avoid major balance sheet increases."[30]

The repo desk and the government clearance area (back office) were also becoming uneasy about the high number of transactions and the effective cancellation of most of them through pair-offs. Both departments shared their concerns with Bernstein who told them that Jett's trading strategy was legitimate and Cerrullo was aware of it.

Starting January 13, 1994, forward transactions had become so important that the financial accounting personnel disclosed a separate footnote in the weekly balance sheet to inform the Inventory Committee of the size of 'non-regular way' sales (STRIPS). In January 13, 1994 the amount disclosed was $11 billion and one week later it was $25 billion. O'Donnell did not raise any questions regarding the footnote because "the Fixed Income

---

[25] Wall Street Journal, June 15, 1994, p. A1.

[26] From the Lynch report, p. 55.

[27] From the Lynch report, p. 57.

[28] The Lynch report, p. 56 and 66.

[29] From the Lynch report, p. 62.

[30] From the Lynch report, p. 63.

Division remained within its overall inventory limits . . . (and) he relied upon Cerrullo's ability to identify anomalous trading events and positions."[31]

In February 1994, in a routine report to the Market Report Division of the Federal Reserve, the increase in forward positions led to an inquiry by the Fed. When it was found that these transactions had no counter-party, the Fed asked to have them removed from the report to avoid being mislead by the high numbers reported.

During the time that the unrealized profits were generated, two Kidder internal reports showed the actual amount of unrealized profits. These were the Government Credit Exception Report and the Government Security Analysis. The first report was reviewed daily by the credit department. The report showed the strips and recons in two separate accounts, the net of the two accounts being the amount of unrealizable profits. These two accounts were internal accounts ("house accounts"), with no credit limit and the credit personnel never paid attention to them because there was no credit exposure on them.

### Detection

By March 1994, Ed Cerrullo and David Bernstein were surprised by the amazing size of Jett's profits for January and February. He had generated each month as much profit as in all 1992, when his performance was praised by Mullin. By this time, Jett's accumulated profits were approximately $260 million: $350 million of unrealizable profits and $85 million of real trading losses. His trading volume had reached $1.76 trillion and his forward positions exceeded $42 billion in recons and $47 billion in strips.

Bernstein began to investigate carefully. He discovered the forward positions in early March. Bernstein got the insight on the origin of Jett's unrealizable profits through the RACE report. RACE (for "Regulatory Application for Counterparty Exposure") began to be produced in February 1994 by the financial accounting personnel in response to FASB Interpretation 19, which required firms to disclose unrealized P&L effects associated with off-balance sheet instruments.[32] Cerrullo, Bernstein, Jett, and other traders had several meetings to fully understand what was going on. Jett tried several times to explain how his profits were generated, but he failed to convince them of the appropriateness of his trading strategy. His explanations were described as "contradictory and illogical."[33]

Joseph Jett's employment termination with Kidder Peabody was announced on April 17, 1994—the same day that General Electric made public the $350 million pretax charge against earnings resulting from the false profits.

### Who Was to Blame?

Several interpretations have been given to the above described events. In assigning blame, it has been argued that:

> "Jett knew that his forward recons were resulting in unrealizable profits and that he intended to mislead Kidder about his true trading performance. . . . We conclude that Jett's conduct over nearly two and one-half year period can only be explained as the product of a deliberate effort to generate false profits. . . . no one at Kidder other than Jett knew that hundreds of millions of dollars of false profits were embedded in the massive forward reconstitution position maintained by Jett."[34]

[31] From the Lynch report, p. 64.
[32] FASB Interpretation 19 required companies to disclose the gross unrealized P&L associated with off-balance sheet instruments (Lynch Report, p. 78).
[33] From the Lynch report, p. 81.
[34] From the Lynch report, p. 7 to 10.

On the other hand, others believed that Jett acted honestly to capitalize on what he saw as legitimate opportunities:

"Jett had been trained at the Massachusetts Institute of Technology and the Harvard Business School to accept information from computer screens and to act on it. He didn't work in a world of common sense (arbitrage itself, after all, often defies common sense, which is why you need rocket scientists); he worked in cyberspace. If the computer got it wrong, he was going to get it wrong; and if the computer got it wrong in his favor, he would see no reason to ask questions, even when the thing got silly. The Jett story, in other words, is not part of the story of panicked or dishonest traders hiding the slip in the desk."[35]

Jett's lawyer, Kenneth Warner, elaborated on this point of view in an open letter to *The New York Times* on March 7, 1995:

"Joseph Jett and your readers deserve better than your Feb. 28 editorial in which you uncritically adopt Kidder Peabody's position that Mr. Jett 'fooled' the experienced Kidder executives who supervised him.

Government agencies have been investigating this matter for almost a year and no charges, criminal or civil, have yet been filed against Mr. Jett. Moreover, two independent, experienced financial experts retained by CBS's '60 Minutes' to look into the Jett-Kidder controversy concluded during the show's airing Feb. 19 that Mr. Jett committed no fraud.

When experts who examined the financial records believe Mr. Jett, and when government agencies refrain from filing charges, it is difficult to understand how a responsible newspaper can call Mr. Jett 'a rogue.'

Mr. Jett acted openly and did nothing wrong. His trades were contemporaneously reported in Kidder's books and monitored by high Kidder executives. The trades were conducted in compliance with an accounting system established by Kidder long before Mr. Jett's arrival. Mr. Jett left all his earnings in a Kidder account now frozen by Kidder to prevent him from defending himself.

Moreover, after Kidder discharged Mr. Jett and liquidated his trading-desk portfolio, Kidder realized a profit of approximately $8 million on his positions, far from the 'reckless bet' you describe.

Your editorial exemplifies the insidious influence of the propaganda campaign waged against Mr. Jett by Kidder and its parent, General Electric. You have been misled and Mr. Jett has been unfairly pilloried."[36]

Following Jett's dismissal in April 1994, Mullin was fired in August of that same year, and Cerrullo and Carpenter were pressured to resign in July. General Electric decided in November 1994, after reporting a $350 million charge related to Jett's trading and losses associated with mortgage backed securities, to orderly dispose of Kidder's assets. Over two thousand Kidder employees would lose their jobs.

Both Cerrullo and Mullins settled SEC charges against them by paying fines ($50,000 and $25,000 respectively) and agreeing to suspensions from activities in the securities industry (one year for Cerrullo and three months for Mullins). Concerning Jett's supervision, Ed Cerrullo stated:

"Somehow, to single out one supervisor as singularly responsible for a department with 700 or 800 people, $100 billion in assets and $20 billion in daily transactions and earnings of $1 billion is totally unrealistic."[37]

As part of the agreement, neither Cerrullo nor Mullins admitted or denied wrongdoing.

---

[35] Institutional Investor, March 1995, p. 7.
[36] The New York Times, March 7, 1995, p. A18.
[37] Institutional Investor, March 1995, p. 7.

In January 1996, Joseph Jett was named by the SEC in an administrative proceeding over his alleged role in the controversy. The jury began deliberations in June 1996 and was not expected to render a decision until early 1997. An article in *Business Week* proclaimed his innocence:

"In the annals of Wall Street scams, Orlando Joseph Jett holds a special—and contemptible—place. This former Kidder, Peabody & Co. bond trader allegedly masterminded $340 million in phony trades from 1991 to 1994. So badly was Kidder tarnished that its name was dropped when its assets were sold by General Electric Co. to Paine Webber Inc. last year. According to the Securities & Exchange Commission, which is wrapping up administrative proceedings against Jett in New York City, the 38-year old trader was a cunning flimflam artist.

There is only one thing wrong with this picture: There's an awfully good chance that Joseph Jett is an innocent man.

If that sounds ludicrous, it's understandable. For two years, Jett has been pilloried by his former employers and the SEC. His accusers say the former trader secretly abused an 'anomaly' in Kidder's trade-accounting system that recorded 'phantom' profits from stripping and reconstituting Treasury bonds into their interest and principal components. He manufactured phony profits, they say, under the noses of his bosses—and was so good at it that Kidder proudly named him Man of the Year in early 1994. Even now, says Kidder general counsel John Liftin, 'there's no evidence that he has anything resembling a defense.'

But Jett's defense is substantial. He claims that he was using—not abusing—Kidder's computer system and was singled out for blame when the accounting system was changed. Evidence produced at his trial makes a persuasive case that he conducted his trades openly—and even disclosed them to Kidder's internal auditors. And that undermines one of the central tenets of the SEC's case: that Jett was deceptive.

To prove fraud, the SEC must demonstrate intent. As defined in one U.S. Supreme Court ruling, that's a 'mental state embracing intent to deceive, manipulate, or defraud.' The key word is deceive. But documents introduced at the SEC's proceedings against Jett seem to favor him on this crucial point.

Jett's trades were recorded by Jett and other traders in large ledger books, or 'red books' that he kept in plain view on his desk. They were available for anyone to peruse during Jett's frequent absences from the desk. The books undercut the theory that Jett was acting stealthily."[38]

The Lynch report, commissioned and released by General Electric, asked the critical question:

"The obvious question is how the false profits generated by Jett could have gone unnoticed at Kidder for a period of over two years. We conclude that no one provided knowing assistance to Jett's trading abuses. Instead, the story of how Jett's activity remained undetected until near the end of the first quarter of 1994 is primarily one of lax supervision, as well as poor judgments and missed opportunities.

Although we suggest a number of changes in Kidder's supervisory and control procedures, the door to Jett's abuses was opened as much by human failings as by inadequate formal systems. In particular, employees throughout the firm appear to have deferred to the success of the Fixed Income Division and been unwilling to ask hard questions about Jett, the division's rising 'star'."[39]

An additional perspective was provided by the Institutional Investor:

"It's a general manager's responsibility to know what your trading practices are. He should never have had to rely entirely on secondary sources, including the firm's accounting department. You have to rely on your own direct questioning as a manager, no matter how senior you are."[40]

[38] Business Week, July 1, 1996, p. 90.
[39] From the Lynch report, p. 10-11.
[40] Institutional Investor, March 1995, p. 7.

**EXHIBIT 1    Operating Profit of Kidder, Peabody & Co., 1987–1994**

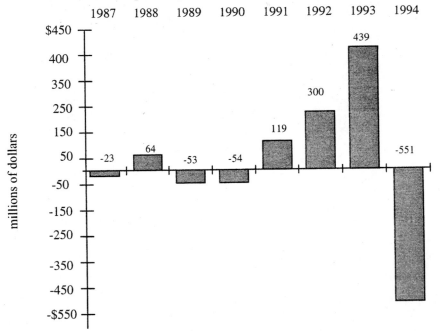

The figure for 1994 includes a one-time charge of $350 million ($210 million after taxes) related to Jett's trading. Approximately $238 million ($143 million after taxes) of the charge are related to prior periods. In addition to the $551 million loss for 1994 shown in the above chart, GECS recognized an additional net loss provision of $868 million related to the exit costs expected to be incurred in connection with Kidder's liquidation.

Source: From information included in General Electric Capital Services, Inc. and General Electric Financial Services, Inc. 10 K reports.

**EXHIBIT 2    Kidder, Peabody & Co., Organizational Chart**

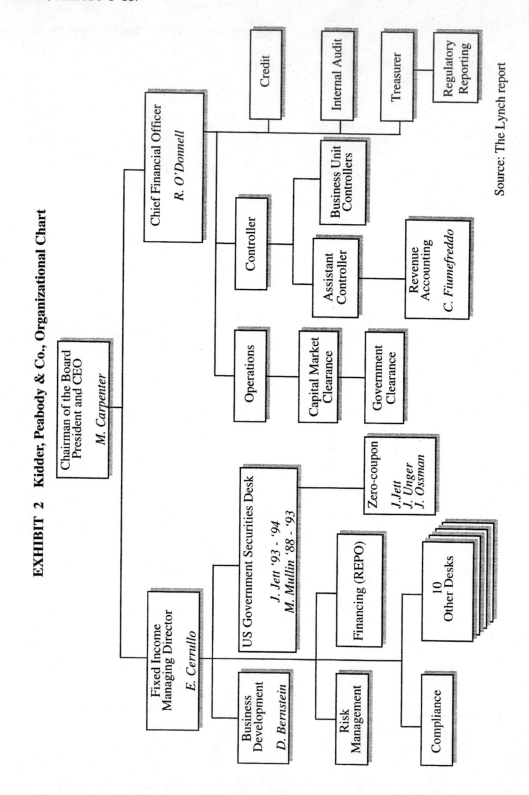

Source: The Lynch report

**EXHIBIT 3    Transforming an Interest-Bearing Bond into a STRIP**

*Cash flow structure of a U.S. Treasury bond.* When a U.S. Treasury bond is purchased, the buyer has the right to the displayed cash flows but cannot trade on them separately unless the bond is stripped. When the bond is stripped,  it is transformed into several instruments, one for each of the original cash flows of the bond. In this example, a 10 year bond with semi-annual interest payments is transformed into 21 separate instruments.

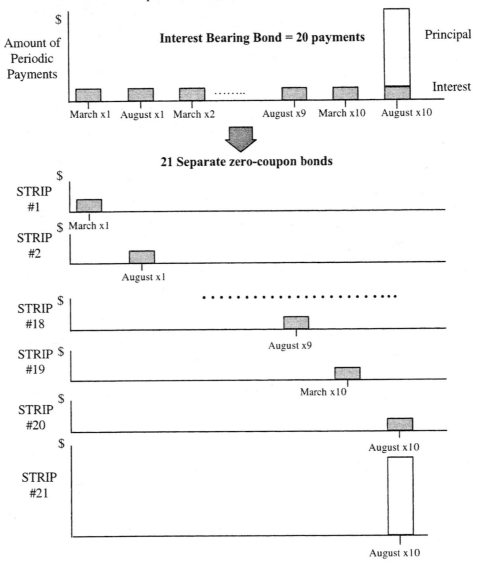

**EXHIBIT 4** **Pricing of Interest-Bearing Bonds and Zero Coupon Bonds
(assuming constant market interest rates over time)**

*Pricing and Market Value of an interest-bearing bond
(Market interest rate = bond rate)*

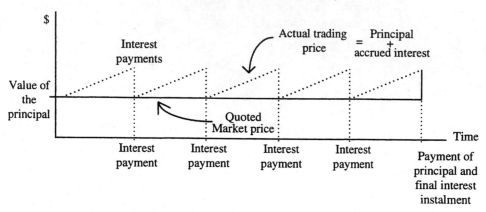

*Pricing and Market Value of a zero coupon bond*

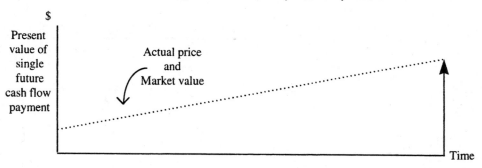

**EXHIBIT  5**   **Jett's Reconstitutions and Stripping—Total Principal Value Traded 1991–1994**

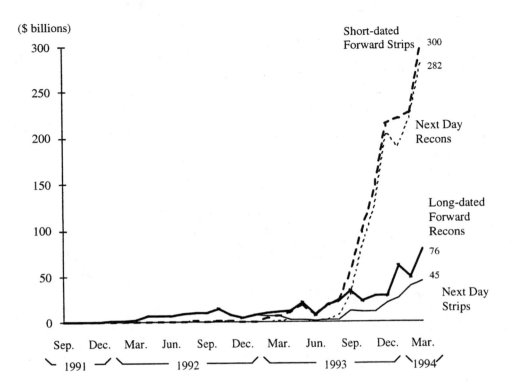

Source: The Lynch Report, p. 46

**EXHIBIT 6    Jett's Performance—Cumulative Results 1991–1994**

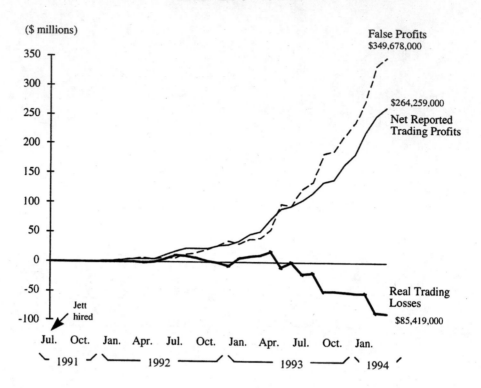

Source: The Lynch Report, p. 39

**CASE 28** Westchester Distributing, Inc. (A)

*From the Law Offices of:*

**CORNELIUS VAN BUREN**
**One Main Street, Suite 200**
**Los Angeles, California 92777**
**FAX 213-555-0553   OFFICE 213-555-0101   MOBILE 213-555-7685**

June 1, 1990

Westchester Distributing, Inc.
13477 San Luis Boulevard
Cosgrove, California 94000
Attn: Elizabeth Jones, Controller

Dear Ms. Jones:

This office represents Wilson Moon. Mr. Moon has requested that I correspond with you regarding a recent transaction between Mr. Moon and Westchester Distributing.

Mr. Moon purchased beer from Westchester but subsequently returned the beer as a result of conversations with Mr. Joe Roberts. Mr. Roberts informed Mr. Moon that he believed Carter Mario and George Pavlov, employees of Westchester, improperly discounted the sale of beer to Mr. Moon. This information was absolutely untrue, and Mr. Moon therefore returned the beer in the interest of avoiding any unfair prejudice to Mr. Mario or Mr. Pavlov. I would like to emphasize that the accusations against the employees have no basis in fact, and I would be happy to discuss the transaction with you at your convenience.

I will also take this opportunity to request that Westchester forward to Mr. Moon the refund for this purchase. Thank you in advance for your anticipated cooperation.

Sincerely,

Cornelius Van Buren

Cornelius Van Buren

CVB/fme
cc: Wilson Moon

"Betty had that look in her eye when she put the letter in front of me" said Vince Patton, referring to Elizabeth Jones, his Vice President of Finance and part-owner of Westchester Distributing. "I knew right away that something serious had happened, but I had no idea that it would cause us all the anguish it did. Even after reading the letter myself, I wasn't quite sure what was going on, but I knew I was going to take somebody out back and shoot 'em. I just didn't know who. It's not every day that an attorney sends us a certified letter because one of our customers wants to return some beer.

"I asked Betty what she knew about the situation, but she didn't know any more than I did. Our next move was to call Joe Roberts and ask him to come upstairs to our offices. Boy, were we in for a surprise.

*Robert J. Boxwell Jr. prepared this case under the supervision of Professor Robert Simons as the basis for class discussion rather than to illustrate either effective or ineffective handling of an administrative situation.*

"Joe came in a little timidly—I think he knew from the tone of my voice on the telephone that something was wrong—and when I gave him the letter and asked him to please explain it, he turned pale and began to tremble a little. He stammered something about trying to protect us, Betty and me, that is, and then he began to cry. Geez, I didn't know what to do. I knew the moment I read the letter that something bad had happened, but I didn't know how bad. Joe crying made me really worried. Betty and I both told Joe to calm down and tell us what happened. I actually considered slapping him to get him to gain his composure like we used to do in the Marines.

"I ended up having to talk to all three of our men before I could feel reasonably comfortable that I had the whole story. It was a real doosey, too.

"It turns out that one of our sales managers together with a salesman were giving a kick-back to a customer to get him to buy some slow-moving beer. They had incentive quotas and were each in line to receive bonuses if quotas were achieved. George was going to win a $500 dollar gift certificate to Nordstrom and Carter was eligible for a cash bonus of fifty cents per case for all Rising Sun Beer sold to new accounts that month. Rising Sun had changed its product label and we were running a joint program with the brewery to move the old bottles through the system as quickly as possible.

"George and Carter gave this one customer a dollar-per-case kickback to take 100 cases. That in itself is a violation of the Alcoholic Beverage Control regulations and could cause us to lose our license for 45 days. Add to that the fact that they reimbursed themselves for the $100 by running through bogus expense reports and falsified broken bottle credits and you can understand why I went through the roof.

"The customer, Mr. Moon, took the 100 cases, but was having a hard time moving them so he started to complain to Carter that he wanted us to take the beer back. Carter promised him three "antique" neon beer signs as a gift if he would keep the beer. These neons are worth about $150 apiece and can be sold easily at flea markets. Carter told George, his sales manager, that Mr. Moon wanted three neons and George started to panic a little bit. He was never too comfortable with the situation in the first place, but George realized that Mr. Moon had them over a barrel and went to Joe Roberts for some help. He told Joe about the kickback and the new demand for the neons and was looking for a way to contain the situation before it got out-of-control any further.

"Joe, our V.P. of Administration, is Betty's and my right-hand man, and we rely on him to handle a lot of the work load, but he really blew this one. Rather than coming right to me he decided to resolve the situation himself. It is obvious that he didn't know the ABC regulations in this area because Westchester is responsible even if the owners are not aware of the violation. As a matter of fact, the ABC would not even hold Carter or George responsible for their individual actions; only the company and its owners are responsible.

"Well, Joe took one neon to Mr. Moon on May 29 and, over lunch, explained to him that this entire situation was bad news and that everybody involved better just forget it ever happened. Mr. Moon blew up, saying that Joe was trying to blame him for something that was not any of his doing. He took the neon and left. Two days later, we got the letter from his attorney."

## Westchester Distributing, Inc.

Vince Patton founded Westchester Distributing in the early 1960s, when the Miller Brewing Company offered him exclusive distribution rights for Westchester County, California. At the time, Vince was the youngest regional manager who had ever worked at the brewery. He had joined the brewery in 1954, following duty in Korea (where he was decorated for bravery and valor) and a brief stint in Law School at UCLA. Earlier, Vince had paid for his education by driving a semi-trailer truck during the day and attending college classes at night. During his eight years with the brewery he established himself as a rising star and top management turned to him when the opportunity arose to find a new distributor for Westchester County. With a $70,000 loan guaranteed by the brewery and four employees, Vince opened Westchester Distributing in 1962.

Vince was a hard charging, get-it-done ex-Marine and college football player who never backed down from a challenge. He pushed his employees to excel at whatever they did and, over the years, developed a group of fiercely loyal Vince Patton fans who were sometimes in awe of him. His employees liked to relate various pieces of Vince Patton folklore. One of their favorite stories related how Vince had a fist fight beside the freeway with one of the local motorcycle gang members who learned the hard way that not every businessman in a suit and tie can be intimidated by a leather jacket.

Elizabeth Jones joined Westchester in 1963, after receiving a degree in mathematics from St. Mary's College. Vince, who had aspired during his adolescence to be a priest, found that Betty shared many of his philosophies; he especially liked her work ethic and devotion to the Company. Over the years Vince came to trust Betty with every aspect of the business, and asked her to join him as a shareholder in Westchester. They were still the only shareholders of the Company.

Over the 27 years that Vince had run Westchester Distributing, the Company earned a reputation for unsurpassed customer service. In an industry where shelf space at the retail level means market share, Westchester drivers and salespeople were generally regarded as the best in Westchester's market. Westchester's major brand, Miller, enjoyed a share of market almost 40% higher than the national average in Westchester's market area.

In 1982, when Westchester's annual volume was approximately 300,000 cases, Westchester entered Miller's annual quality competition. In the annual contest, Miller's top distributors (over 1,000 nationwide) competed for approximately 15 Miller Masters national quality awards, which carried considerable prestige in the industry. The award criteria, which were judged by special Miller auditors who visited each distributor, required documented attention to quality by all employees of a distributor. Westchester won the award in 1982, thus becoming the first small distributor to win the award, and had won the award six of the seven years since 1982, thereby becoming a Miller Grand Master. (Owners of Grand Master distributorships who sold their companies in the 1980s had generally been able to command a 25–50% premium in selling price over comparable non-Grand Masters distributors.)

From 1980 to 1990, Westchester had grown from approximately 250,000 cases per year, $5 million in revenues and 20 employees to approximately 800,000 cases per year, $15 million in revenues, and 60 employees. From a small central office location, the Company operated four warehouses. See **Exhibit 1** for an organization chart.

Vince's attention to detail and his ability to motivate his people had brought recognition to Westchester Distributing. In Vince's words, "All of our people are above average. And then we look for perfection. . . . it drives us all crazy."

**The Beverage Distribution Industry**   According to Vince, "Beverage distribution is a horrible industry to be in. The industry is extremely competitive and sensitive to market share. All breweries are constantly trying to increase their market share and there are always a lot of inexperienced people standing in the wings eager to enter the distribution end of the business. Margins are low, fixed costs relatively high, and demand for products is often dependent on weather conditions. To make sure we never enjoy ourselves, we are constantly reminded that we are nobody's customer. Even our suppliers are our customers. If we don't serve them well, they will find another distributor that will.

"We walk a fine line here at Westchester. My main measure of success is cases-per-stop. When our people arrive at an account, I view it as one might view set-up time in a manufacturing company. I view the number of case orders our salesmen take and our drivers deliver as our run-time. The more cases we sell and deliver to each stop, the more units our set-up cost is spread over. Cases-per-stop is key.

"At the same time, we have to make sure we are devoting the appropriate attention to each of the brands offered by our different suppliers. We have more than 20 suppliers and sell over 150 different packages of product. The Budweiser distributor down the street has only one supplier—Anheuser Busch. But we have to make sure all our suppliers are happy with our service. They all set quotas for us to meet and they would all like to be our sole supplier. But I can't do that! I need as many products as I can get to increase our cases-per-stop up to a point where we are profitable.

"One of our competitors sold out this past summer, and we were able to pick up another 175,000 cases at a good price. We had to do a lot of cajoling to get Miller to allow us to pick up these new suppliers and their products. They agreed to let us do it, but they reserved the right to change their minds if they felt our service to them was suffering at all. We had some early wrinkles to iron out, but things are going well now. Our sales managers are really working hard to learn all the new suppliers' products, promotional programs, and personalities. Most supplier/distributor agreements allow the supplier to discontinue the relationship with 30-day notice. We have been discontinued twice when suppliers were bought by other suppliers, but never have we been discontinued for lack of good service.

"In the beer industry here in the U.S., the big three are Bud, Miller, and Coors. Bud has about 43% of national market share, Miller about 31%, and Coors about 9%. Most Bud distributors distribute only Anheuser Busch products—no waters or juices—and many of Bud's distributorships are owned directly by Anheuser Busch. We are different. Many of the Miller and Coors distributors also distribute imports and are moving toward waters and juices now, too.

Being a distributor for one of the big three has its advantages—namely a solid base and good support from the brewer—but it is by no means a ticket for guaranteed success. Even though Miller is our supplier, we also consider Miller to be our largest customer. We are extremely dependent on Miller for our success. But we're good to Miller and, as a result, they're good to us."

**The ABC**   The California Alcoholic Beverage Control, known in the trade as the "ABC," was established following the repeal of Prohibition to regulate the distribution and sale of alcoholic beverages in the state. The ABC regulations were very strict and penalties for non-compliance often severe.

Section 25600 of the Alcoholic Beverage Control Act stated, in part:

**Free Goods.**   No licensee shall, directly or indirectly, give any premium, gift, or free goods in connection with the sale or distribution of any alcoholic beverage except as provided by rules which shall be adopted by the department to implement this section or except as authorized by this division.

No rule of the department may permit a licensee to give any premium, gift, or free goods of greater than inconsequential value in connection with the sale or distribution of beer. With respect to beer, premiums, gifts, or free goods, including advertising specialties which have no significant utilitarian value other than advertising, shall be deemed to have greater than inconsequential value if they cost more than twenty-five cents ($0.25) per unit, or cost more than fifteen dollars ($15) in the aggregate for all such items given by a single supplier to a single retail premises per calendar year.

With respect to distilled spirits and wines, a licensee may furnish, give, rent, loan, or sell advertising specialties to a retailer provided those items bear conspicuous advertising required of a sign and the total value of all retailer advertising specialties furnished by a supplier directly or indirectly, to a retailer shall not exceed fifty dollars ($50) per brand in any one calendar year per retail premises. The value of a retailer advertising specialty is the actual cost of that item to the supplier who initially purchased it. Transportation and installation costs are excluded. The furnishing or giving of any retailer advertising specialty shall not be conditioned upon the purchase of the suppliers' product. Retail advertising specialties given or furnished free of charge may not be sold by the retail licensee.

Violation of this section of the Act was punishable by loss of license to distribute beer, distilled spirits, and wine.

Many of the regulations of the ABC were designed to protect employees from unscrupulous owners who tried to force employees to bribe customers to take products. As a result, most of the ABC's penalties were directed at the owners of distributorships and the companies themselves rather than at employees who might violate ABC regulations. Consistent with that rationale, the ABC has no provisions to penalize employees who offer "freebies" or kickbacks to customers.

**Beer Delivery, Customer Relations, and Control Systems**   At Westchester Distributing, the majority of customer interaction was performed by three groups of employees: salesmen, drivers, and sales managers.

**Salesmen**   Westchester's ten salesmen visited accounts regularly to take orders that would be delivered the next day. Trucks then departed the next morning with exactly the products that were to be delivered that day. At Westchester, salesmen also worked with customers to develop in-store promotions, optimize shelf space, and merchandise products so that an effective pull environment was attained. Bottler's displays, including neon signs, were an important component in creating effective product demand, and Westchester salesmen were expected to use these displays at their discretion.

At the end of every week, each salesman submitted to the sales managers a daily call report which detailed special calls (i.e., unscheduled customer visits) and entertainment of customers. These reports were reviewed and initialled by both the sales manager and Joe Roberts and then forwarded to Vince Patton.

**Drivers**   Driving a beer truck was "one of the toughest jobs in existence" according to Vince Patton, who spent four years early in his career as a driver. "You have to reach high to pull the cases off the shelves in the truck bays, you have to move 10 or more at a time on a hand truck, price them, store them, and restock all retail shelves, and you have to run, run, run all day long. Our guys move more than 700 cases on a typical day, which is an awful lot of product. And most of our products are in bottles, not cans, meaning the average 24-bottle case weighs about five pounds more than a comparable case of cans."

Bottles break, too, and Westchester's policy was to give credit to customers who found breakage caused by Westchester. Since breakage was sometimes not discovered until cases were opened, it was often difficult to know who actually was responsible for broken bottles. As a practical matter, drivers and salespeople usually reimbursed retailers for broken bottles on the spot and submitted an out-of-pocket expense claim on their weekly expense reports. Broken bottles were not required to be returned to the Westchester warehouse. Broken bottle reimbursement during 1989 amounted to approximately $20,000.

**Sales Managers**    Westchester's three sales managers were the jacks-of-all-trades of the Company. They worked closely with Westchester's many suppliers to ensure that Westchester's service to suppliers (e.g., administering supplier promotional programs or preparing regular monthly reports on sales volume, pricing, etc.) was maintained at the level for which Westchester had become known; they maintained close contact with Westchester's on-site customers (i.e., bars and restaurants where beverages were consumed on the selling establishment's premises) and off-site customers (i.e., liquor stores, supermarkets and other establishments, where beverages were purchased by consumers and carried off the premises for consumption); and they managed the teams of salesmen and drivers who served Westchester's approximately 2,500 on- and off-site customers.

Much of Westchester's customer relations was performed by the three sales managers, since salesmen were often too busy during the course of a day to take time out for lunch or a ball game with a customer. Customer entertainment was usually not elaborate or expensive, but it was expected by customers, especially larger ones. Expenses were usually paid in cash by the sales manager or sales-person, and submitted for reimbursement by the Company.

Sales managers also completed a weekly call report that was submitted for review to Joe Roberts. After review and signature by Roberts, the call reports were forwarded to Vince Patton.

**Internal Controls**    As with many small owner-managed businesses, Westchester Distributing did not have an elaborate system of internal controls. Strict segregation of duties, in particular, was difficult due to the limited number of staff personnel at the Company. To compensate, all cash disbursements were handled directly by Vince Patton and Elizabeth Jones, the sole shareholders of the Company.

With the exception of brief "Standards of Conduct" (**Exhibit 2**)—which employees were required to read and acknowledge by signature each year—formal, written procedures did not exist to guide employees in internal control-related matters. Expense reports were submitted weekly by salesmen and sales managers for reimbursement with their subsequent paychecks. (A blank expense report is reproduced as **Exhibit 3.**) The most frequent items included on these expense reports were lunches and broken bottle credits, both of which usually represented cash outlays by Westchester's employees. Unwritten Company policy was that requests for reimbursement for lunch expenses must be submitted with receipts; salesmen and sales managers usually tore the blank receipts from the bottom of restaurant checks they received when buying lunches for customers and filled in the appropriate amount themselves. Broken bottle credits paid by salespeople were submitted for reimbursement without accompanying receipts.

Joe Roberts, Westchester's Vice President of Administration, reviewed and signed all expense reports before submitting them to Betty Jones for reimbursement. Typical expense reports submitted by salesmen ranged from $20 to $100 per week. Expense reports submitted by sales managers were usually $100 to $150 per week.

Neon beer signs, which were supplied by the breweries for installation in the retail establishments that Westchester served, were stored in Westchester's main warehouse with an assortment of other point-of-sale merchandise. Salespeople, sales managers, merchandisers, and even drivers, at times, all had access to the point-of-sale merchandise and took what they needed to build displays and otherwise promote Westchester's products. Formal inventory records were maintained of neon signs on hand and anyone removing a sign was required to record where it was being used. Point-of-sale merchandise in the warehouse was counted monthly for purposes of reordering. Once a sign was removed from inventory, however, no formal control mechanism existed to account for or reconcile the signs installed at the over 1,000 retail establishments where Westchester had installed displays.

**The Individuals Involved**  Carter Mario, salesman, 39, had been with Westchester since 1982 and earned approximately $40,000 per year. Carter, who had an MBA from a West Coast university, began as a driver after finding the day-to-day pressures of the business world too difficult to handle. Carter's wife, Cindy, was an anesthesiologist at one of the local hospitals.

Many of Carter's accounts, including the West Coast Korean Market, were in the city of Cosgrove close to his home. Carter and Mr. Moon, owner of the Market, had become good friends after Carter had stopped by Mr. Moon's store on his own time to give Mr. Moon some general retailing advice. Of the $100 given to Mr. Moon to induce him to buy the Rising Sun beer, Carter contributed $30, which he recovered by submitting false luncheon receipts on his monthly expense report.

George Pavlov, General Sales Manager, 33, was the son of a former Los Angeles Rams football star. Pavlov's father, George Sr., and Vince Patton were friends. George Sr. called Vince in 1982, when his son was laid off from his job, and asked Vince to give George Jr. an interview if a position opened at Westchester. Two months later, Vince hired George as a draft beer driver, responsible for delivering and installing kegs of beer, which typically weigh 162 lbs.

George was taken under Vince Patton's wing and worked hard at developing his skills and knowledge of the business. Pavlov worked his way up through draft-beer driving to package driving, salesman, assistant sales manager, and became a sales manager in 1989. Of the $100 given to Mr. Moon to induce him to buy the Rising Sun beer, George contributed $70, which he recovered by submitting false lunch receipts and broken bottle claims. George earned approximately $55,000 a year.

Joe Roberts, 36, began his career in the beer industry with one of the big-three brewers after receiving a bachelor's degree in management from Louisiana State University. He joined Westchester in 1984, as Vince and Betty's Vice President of Administration to assist with supplier relations. He was the only Westchester employee in the history of the Company not to be started as a driver. As Vice President of Administration, he was the number three person in the Company. Roberts had removed a neon sign from inventory and given it to Mr. Moon in an attempt to persuade him not to make trouble about the 100 cases that he had been induced to buy.

**Vince's Dilemma**  "This entire kickback situation has put Betty and me in a really sticky situation. The right thing to do seemed obvious at first. We wanted to fire the three of them on the spot. Some of our competitors might tolerate this sort of thing, but I won't. But we're not big enough that we wouldn't miss these guys if they left, especially the managers. You can imagine what three empty seats would do to us. Nevertheless, firing them all was our first reaction—until we thought further.

"Carter Mario had some difficulties with some of the guys in the past, and I don't think he had too many friends here besides George. The truth of the matter is that I had been watching Carter. He was once caught leaving the warehouse with products that had not been signed out—we gave him the benefit of the doubt, but as far as I'm concerned, this is stealing. We also suspected that he was going home in the day for long lunches. Knowing

Carter as I do, however, I worry he will go right to the ABC and tell all if we fire him. And the way the ABC regulations work, Westchester would be closed down for 45 days and Carter Mario would get away scott-free. My 60 people would be out-of-work for a month-and-a-half and the 128 mouths they feed would be affected. For most of these people, I am their total means of support. The Company cannot afford to pay their salaries for a shut-down period and, anyway, why should they be penalized for three people who messed up?

"We couldn't even go to the ABC ourselves, beforehand, and tell them what happened. The regulations are extremely strict because owners have been known to use some major league intimidation tactics on their employees to get them to do illegal acts and then suborn themselves if they got caught. Being up front with the ABC would mean closed doors, no two ways about it.

"How did this happen in the first place? As far as I know, this was an isolated incident, but how can I be sure that this is not the tip of the iceberg? How did we ever let them run through bogus lunches and broken bottle claims? How did we let them give neons as bribes? How could we know how much breakage there is at retail establishments? I have been wrestling with all these things, in addition to managing the assimilation of our newly acquired brands.

"First, I have to decide what to do about these three guys and about the ABC. Carter Mario just sent me this letter to explain his position **(Exhibit 4).** Then, Betty and I will be looking for some assistance on how we can tighten up our internal controls so this kind of thing can't happen again. I dug out this list of internal control principles from an old auditing text **(Exhibit 5),** but I really need some help on where to start."

## EXHIBIT 1 Organization Chart

**Westchester Distributing, Inc.**
**Table of Organization**
**May 1, 1990**

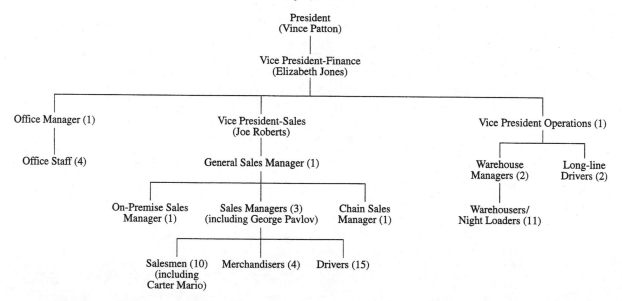

# EXHIBIT 2   Standards of Conduct

Remember, there is a safe way of doing any kind of job. Discover that way for your job and stick to it.

## *Standards of Conduct*

To protect its interests and to assure a productive and safe working environment, every Company must have work rules and set standards of performance and require its employees to comply. The following standards of conduct are examples only; this list is not and should not be construed as the only basis for discipline up to and including discharge:

1. Dishonesty, misrepresentation, or falsification of any Company records such as time cards, application for employment, injury reports, orders, or like documents are prohibited.
2. Gambling, horseplay, fighting, agitating a fight, coercing, intimidating or threatening other employees with bodily harm or injury while on duty or on Company premises are prohibited.
3. Failure to observe and conform to established safety rules or regulations is prohibited.
4. Unauthorized possession of firearms or other weapons or explosives on Company property or while on duty is prohibited.
5. Solicitations and distributions of any kind by an employee, including collecting money from employees, circulating petitions, distributing literature, selling articles or conducting other than Company business during work time are prohibited. "Work time" does not include break or lunch time. The distribution of literature in work areas at any time is prohibited.
6. Theft of Company property, removal of equipment or theft of personal property of others are prohibited.
7. Each employee is expected to meet his financial obligations without involving the Company. Repeated garnishments or attachments are prohibited.
8. Employees must have prior approval of their supervisor before posting or removing any material on official bulletin boards or other Company property. Official materials which have been posted shall not be altered or defaced.
9. Insubordination, refusal to follow instructions or wanton disregard for proper authority will not be tolerated.
10. Willful or negligent damage to Company property or that of customers is prohibited.
11. Visiting the plant outside of working hours is not permitted.
12. All employees shall adhere strictly to all rules and regulations pertaining to our industry as prescribed by the Alcohol Beverage Control Board of the State of California and the Bureau of Alcohol, Tobacco, and Firearms of the United States Treasury Department.
    Copies of the regulations which pertain to your job function will be supplied to you along with this handbook and will be explained fully during your probationary period.
    Any request by a supplier representative or customer for you to violate the State or Federal regulations must be reported to a supervisor immediately.
13. Each employee is expected to report to work on a regular basis and on time. The only exceptions to this policy are for reasons of illness, emergencies or when permission for absence is previously obtained.
    It is your responsibility to insure that your supervisor is notified when you are unable to work for any reason.
    If you fail to return to work following an authorized leave of absence (vacation, sick leave, personal leave, etc.) we will consider you to have voluntarily resigned your employment.
    When required, evidence to substantiate absence from work shall be presented by the affected employee.
14. No personal business is to be conducted during working hours. All personal phone calls will be restricted to emergencies only.
15. No employee is allowed to go home during working hours unless prior arrangements have been made with his or her supervisor.
16. Hourly employees are generally not required to attend after-hour sales meetings. Any such attendance by them at such meetings is entirely voluntary. As a result, they will not be paid for the time spent in such meetings. On rare occasions an hourly employee may be required to attend an after-hour sales meeting. In such case, the employee will be paid for his or her time in attending such meeting.

These rules are not intended to be all inclusive. This list is not intended to suggest that the Company may impose discipline only for violations of these rules, or that an employee may be terminated only for cause. On the contrary, all employees are expressly employed at-will.

# EXHIBIT 3 Expense Report

**Westchester Distributing, Inc.** 191-118

## EXPENSE REPORT
PERIOD ENDING

DEPARTMENT

NAME

ITEMIZE ALL REIMBURSABLE EXPENSES IN APPROPRIATE BLANKS – ITEMIZE ANY NON-REIMBURSABLE EXPENSES ON REVERSE OF LAST COPY.

| DAY | CITY AND STATE | LODGING | TRANSPORTATION AIR, RAIL, ETC. | RENTAL CAR, LIMO, ETC. | LOCAL TAXI, TOLLS & PUB. LIC TRANSIT | AUTO EXPENSES Itemize Below | BUSINESS MEALS Itemize Below BREAKFAST | LUNCH | DINNER | ENTERTAIN-MENT Itemize Below | MISC EXPENSES Itemize Below | DAILY TOTAL |
|-----|----------------|---------|--------------------------------|------------------------|--------------------------------------|-----------------------------|----------------------------------------|-------|--------|------------------------------|-----------------------------|-------------|
| SUN | | | | | | | | | | | | |
| MON | | | | | | | | | | | | |
| TUE | | | | | | | | | | | | |
| WED | | | | | | | | | | | | |
| THU | | | | | | | | | | | | |
| FRI | | | | | | | | | | | | |
| SAT | | | | | | | | | | | | |
| WEEKLY CATEGORY TOTAL $ | | | | | | | | | | | | |

WEEKLY TOTAL OF EXPENSES ◆

NUMBER OF DAYS AWAY FROM HOME

NUMBER OF DAYS AWAY ON PERSONAL AFFAIRS

% OF TOTAL DAYS AWAY FOR PERSONAL AFFAIRS

NATURE OR PURPOSE OF TRAVEL

METHOD OF REIMBURSEMENT
☐ DEDUCT FROM    OR    ☐ MAIL
   MY ADVANCE              TO:

SIGNATURE

APPROVED BY

**ORIGINAL**

## ITEMIZED ENTERTAINMENT AND BUSINESS MEALS

| DATE | NAME OF PERSON(S) ENTERTAINED; COMPANY, TITLE | TIME & PLACE | NATURE & PURPOSE OF ENTERTAINMENT | AMOUNT | % OR $ ALLOCATED TO BUSINESS |
|------|-----------------------------------------------|--------------|-----------------------------------|--------|------------------------------|
| | | | | | |

## ITEMIZED AUTOMOBILE EXPENSES

| DATE | MILEAGE, GAS, PARKING, REPAIRS, ETC. | AMOUNT |
|------|--------------------------------------|--------|
| | | |

## ITEMIZED MISCELLANEOUS EXPENSES

| DATE | ITEMS | AMOUNT |
|------|-------|--------|
| | | |

Source: Company documents.

WilsonJones • Carbonless • MADE IN U.S.A.
44-950N • ® WilsonJones, 1989

WilsonJones® Snap-A-Way® Forms
Carbonless

EXPENSE REPORT 44-950N

674

**EXHIBIT 4**

June 3, 1990

Mr. Vincent Patton
Westchester Distributing, Inc.
13477 San Luis Blvd.
Cosgrove, CA 94000

Dear Mr. Patton:

I know that you and Elizabeth feel that I never had any respect for you, because I found it so difficult to obey some of your many policies. Actually, nothing could be further from the truth. I always had a tremendous amount of respect and admiration for you both.

It is true, however, that these feelings could never be transmitted down to the other members of your management team. I honestly tried to find some reason to admire the other members of your team, but only found them to be individuals whose sole function it was to tell you both what you wanted to hear.

I guess I always felt that you and Elizabeth would sit up behind your locked office doors and draw up scenarios on how you wanted the world to be, and then send me a memo to make it happen. I always wanted one of you to come with me in the field so you could see the real world problems we were experiencing. This never happened, much to my unhappiness.

I am afraid I always thought in the back of my mind, when I would overlook some of your policies, that you would understand. The thought always going through my mind was that it was most important to make your scenario happen, no matter how unreasonable I thought it was. This was a most serious error in judgment on my part. It never crossed my mind that I might be breaking a rule to hurt you or the company.

As I look back over the past five years, I still feel that your company is still the finest firm in the business, and the finest firm I have ever worked for. I think that if we could have found some way to communicate better, we could have avoided any problems.

Very sincerely,
Carter Mario

# EXHIBIT 5

## *Basics of Internal Control*

1. Competent accounting and control staff
2. Division of duties so that:

   - no one person controls complete transaction
   - employees who handle assets do not record asset transactions
   - systems double-check accuracy of transactions and existence of assets

3. Authorizations required for initiating and recording transactions
4. Written procedure manuals
5. Forms and documentation for back-up and review
6. Good accounting system for management information and control
7. Physical security protection for assets and information
8. Bonding of employees who handle assets subject to theft/embezzlement
9. Internal auditing
10. Audits by independent CPAs

## CASE 29  Automatic Data Processing: The EFS Decision

I n November 1988, Lynn Mangum, group vice president of Electronic Financial Services (EFS) and Banking Information Services (BIS), was preparing to write the 1990 Preliminary Strategic Plan for EFS. He had not yet decided whether to prepare a Plan or a recommendation to divest the business unit. In either case, Lynn would have to present his case by the end of the month to Automatic Data Processing's (ADP's) Executive Committee. As he worked late on the night of November 2, he wondered what to recommend. Time was running out.

### The Strategic Planning Process

Corporate management at ADP used its strategic planning system to help strategic business unit (SBU) general managers review their business mix for both pruning and expansion opportunities. The process began each August when Josh Weston and Bill Turner, chief executive officer and chief operating officer respectively, prepared a one-page set of pre-plan guidelines for the head of each SBU. The guidelines posed questions as well as suggestions, to which SBU managers could then respond in preparing their preliminary drafts. **Exhibit 1** represents the one-pager on EFS which Lynn received in early September 1988.

Each SBU general manager responded to the top-down "one-pager" in one of two ways: he either submitted his own one-pager plan to Weston and Turner or discussed the plan with them until they concurred. The general managers' presentations were designed to address their objectives in broad terms, without details on financials or implementation. This preliminary dialogue helped to ensure that the general managers' plans were in line with corporate management's ideas and expectations for the units. The interchange helped to avoid misdirected efforts and unpleasant surprises further along in the process.

The third phase of the strategic planning process was the development of a Preliminary Strategic Plan, which was presented to the Executive Committee in November. This document included a mission statement (usually little changed from year to year), a situation analysis, and strategic objectives, highlighting those areas that represented a change in direction from the current year. Again, the emphasis was on brevity in the written document in order to facilitate a discussion that focused on major strategic issues.

The Executive Committee, which comprised the CEO, chief operating officer, and chief financial officer, met with the head of each SBU separately, signing off on each Preliminary Plan once mutual agreement was reached. Each SBU then developed its final Five-Year Strategic Plan and presented it to the Executive Committee in February (for the fiscal year starting July 1st). The final planning differed from the preliminary version in three ways. First, each major strategic objective originally approved was now supported by a set of 5 to 10 specific programs or agenda items. Second, the final plan included financial projections of revenues, expenses, capital expenditures, and cash flow. Third, the final plan also included specific initiatives to address organizational development needs. After the Strategic Plan was agreed upon, it served as input into the development of the annual Operating Plan for each SBU. (Operating Plans were developed between March 1 and June 1 for the fiscal year starting July 1. They were developed, through three increasingly detailed iterations, in a process analogous to that of the strategic plans.)

### *"The List"*

The 1988 annual report articulated top management's philosophy with regard to managing their existing businesses:

> At ADP, we regularly review the growth potential and strategic importance of each business, each product line, and each client group. Periodically we reduce or dispose of lesser activities which no longer fit strategic objectives. During 1988, for the third consecutive year, we reduced certain product lines equaling about 2% of total revenues. In 1989, we expect similar, selective revenue pruning that will modestly enhance our margins, while obviously reducing our overall revenue growth rate. We are stronger as a result of this pruning and better positioned for the future. . . .

> We now look forward to our 28th consecutive year of publicly reported, double-digit growth . . . in both revenues and earnings—a consistent business achievement that no other publicly held company in the United States has yet accomplished. (See **Exhibit 2** for summary ADP financial statistics.)

At the heart of ADP's corporate philosophy and strategic planning was a list of "Seven Key Requirements for pursuing major service businesses and products." The "List" represented criteria designed to aid SBU general managers in evaluating their businesses and in determining strategic direction. **Exhibit 3** reproduces the complete set of criteria. As **Exhibit 3** illustrates, most of the seven criteria were supported by more specific requirements. The double dots preceding some of the criteria indicate those considered particularly important.

The seven criteria were first formally recorded in the early 1980s, when the List was drafted, refined, and adopted by the Executive Committee. Since the initial adoption, it had undergone no significant changes. Knowledge and use of the List permeated the organization, primarily by way of Senior Management Development Seminars. These one-week, off-site seminars were held three times a year for 60 to 80 managers each year out of the top 200 managers in the corporation. The seminars served as a forum for reinforcing the strategic boundaries while at the same time challenging them. Although the List had not changed significantly, managers attending the seminars were explicitly asked each year whether circumstances had changed such that any of the criteria should be modified or removed. They were also encouraged to review the content of the seminar discussions with their subordinates, thus extending the use of the List to another 400 to 600 managers.

The List had no role in day-to-day management but was frequently referenced in senior executive meetings. In fact, most senior managers could recall the criteria without referring to the written List.

Because no single service business or product could meet *all* of the requirements all of the time, judgment was required in assessing a particular business against the criteria. The difficulty was compounded by the constant changes occurring in the marketplace. Changes in competition, client needs, technology, regulation, and other externalities limited the lasting value of a business assessment made at any particular point in time. The List did, however, suggest to the SBU general managers which sorts of changes could cause the greatest damage to a business's strategic position and therefore deserved regular review.

Although ADP's Mergers & Acquisitions team differed substantially from SBU management in size and function, it also referred to the List regularly. Arthur Kranseler, vice president of Corporate Development, commented on the value of the List to his group:

I keep the List in my briefcase all the time. I don't have to actually take it out anymore, but my staff has copies, and they use it as a checklist in preparing all acquisition reports. . . . When we evaluate an acquisition candidate, we hold up the List and have to make a judgment call. We ask ourselves: Does this business do enough things right? Could we take care of the things they don't do right? We apply the List as rigorously to new lines of business and product lines as to SBUs. The only difference is the size criterion. If we attempt to pursue a small opportunity that deviates from what we do today and know we're good at, then managers see that the pursuit will take a disproportionate amount of their time. We like to avoid low returns on management effort, which we call ROM. We don't have a venture capital laboratory for that kind of thing.

The only negative thing I can say about the List is that it's restrictive on company growth sometimes. We could have been bigger today, but not as strong or profitable without the List.

## Automatic Data Processing, Inc.

Automatic Data Processing, Inc. was founded in 1949 as a manual payroll processing service. In 1988, ADP was the nation's largest independent computing and information services business, with total revenues in excess of $1.5 billion. Employer Services (primarily payroll services), the oldest and largest of ADP's business units, represented about half of total revenues. In the 1960s, ADP began to serve the brokerage industry with back office services and data communications networking. The Brokerage Information Services Group later expanded to include stock quotation and other front office services and now accounted for roughly 20% of company revenues. In 1973, ADP had founded its third major business which serviced auto and truck dealers. Originally founded by the acquisition of two small single-service businesses, Dealer Services now represented roughly 10% of ADP revenues and offered 18 different service applications, including showroom support, repairs scheduling, accounting, inventory management, and factory communications. The fourth largest business was Collision Repair Estimating for the auto insurance industry, entered by a small acquisition in 1980. In addition to the four "core" businesses, ADP operated two much smaller business units, EFS and BIS, which both served financial institutions.

In all four core businesses, ADP held the number one position in market share. Each business offered some combination of computerized recordkeeping or transaction services, and information or database services on an on-going basis. Over the years, the service offerings in each business unit had expanded via both acquisitions (numbering over 100) and internal development and had consistently, year after year, conformed to the List of strategic criteria.

## Electronic Financial Services, Inc. (EFS)

**EFS Lines of Business**   The EFS division, accounting for less than 3% of company revenues, was ADP's youngest business unit. EFS was founded in 1982 with the establishment of a nationwide ATM network that supported automated teller machines for banks and other financial institutions. In 1987, Lynn Mangum, who for over 16 years had risen up through the Banking Information Services division (from operations manager of a $1 million business to general manager of the entire $30+ million business), was put in charge of EFS as well. In 1988, EFS had three major lines of business: in all three product categories, the clients were banks and financial institutions.

In its primary line of business, EFS acted as a third-party processor "driving" the ATMs of individual clients. This included the provision and maintenance of software, on-line database connections used for transaction authorization, and file maintenance. For banks that drove their own ATMs, EFS' second product category provided the "gateway" that linked their data center and local network (if applicable) to a shared network, and switched interbank transactions to the appropriate bank within the shared network. In conjunction with these services, EFS provided settlement information to banks, analogous to the role of a clearinghouse for banks' checks. Lastly, EFS owned and operated The Exchange Network, including its card issuing services and its licensed marketing logo. The Exchange was one of only five national bank debit card networks and boasted 22 million Exchange cardholders. (Debit cards, more commonly known as ATM cards, were issued to bank customers to access automatic teller machines.) EFS maintained on-line connections with all the member banks of the Exchange, switching and processing all network transactions.

In addition to the three main lines of business, EFS had recently introduced its electronic funds transfer (EFT) processing services to the relatively young point-of-sale (POS) marketplace. (POS debit card transactions are generated when debit cards are used to purchase goods at retail locations. A debit card POS transaction differs from a credit card POS transaction in that it immediately debits the cardholder's bank account, rather than billing him monthly for the value of his purchases.) As more and more retailers upgraded their existing POS terminals to accept debit cards in addition to credit cards, debit cards were projected by several industry sources to become a prominent payment vehicle for consumers. EFS was well positioned in this potentially high growth market via newly established relationships with J.C. Penney Systems Services (a driver of 70,000 POS credit card terminals), Interlink (the largest regional POS debit card network), and others. By the start of 1990, EFS expected to have connections with approximately 20,000 debit card POS terminals.

**Financial and Market Position**   In 1988, EFS was the second largest ATM transaction processor in the United States (behind Deluxe Data Systems) and owned the third largest ATM network (behind the Mastercard-owned Cirrus network and the Visa-owned Plus network). Approximately 90% of all ATMs in the country were accessible through EFS gateway connections. The Exchange Network had nearly 1,200 participating institutions who owned or operated over 7,500 ATM locations. According to industry sources, EFS had the highest transaction volume per ATM of any national ATM network. Some sources believed it also boasted the lowest cost per transaction.

Although EFS remained in the red longer than initially anticipated, by 1987 and through late 1988 it enjoyed astounding success which was projected to continue through at least 1990 (see **Exhibit 4**). In 1987, revenues had increased by 10% and pretax profits by 74%. The growth rates for 1988 were 27% and 191% respectively. From 1986 to 1988, the client base had grown at a compound annual rate of 50%, while total transaction volume had increased at a rate of 30%.[1] Net cash flow for the same period had improved from $512,000 to $2.06 million. The business now earned a pretax return on assets in excess of 50%, and its pretax margin, at 15%, was among the highest in the industry. Furthermore, supported by continued client acquisition and an almost perfect client retention record, near-term growth was projected to be in excess of 20% per year. Client breadth enhanced EFS' growth stability: the top 50 clients accounted for only 26% of revenues. Profits were expected to grow even more rapidly than revenues due to economies of scale and to productivity improvements achievable through automation. Five months into the 1989 fiscal year, both revenues and profits were ahead of plan.

---

[1] A significant portion of EFS' growth in 1988 was due to the mid-year acquisition of a large regional ATM network from City National Bank of California.

**Trends and Forecasts in the EFT Industry** Notwithstanding EFS' recent success, an array of market trends had led Lynn Mangum to question the long-term growth potential of the business. In fact, he had expressed his initial concerns in July, four months earlier, in a memo to the Executive Committee. (See **Exhibit 5.**) At that time, with profits increasing dramatically and the threatening trends only beginning to surface, a decision was made to continue managing the business according to plan, to go forward with the strategic planning for 1990, and to "wait and see" how the market developed, keeping a close eye on Lynn's list of concerns. With his Preliminary Strategic Plan due in one week, Lynn still suspected that it was only a matter of time before EFS failed enough of the "tests" on the List to indicate that commitment to the business would not be in ADP's best interests. To help him reassess his suspicions, Lynn referred to the List (**Exhibit 3**), paying close attention to the "double-dot" criteria.

His current concerns echoed those cited in his July memo. First, limits to EFS's revenue potential in the ATM services business were becoming evident. Although industry transaction volume was still growing at a double digit rate, within two years both the number of ATMs and the number of traditional transactions per ATM terminal was expected to level off. Acquisitions would then be the primary means of maintaining 15+% growth in this market, and attractive acquisition candidates were already few in number and high in price.

The uniqueness of EFS' services had also been diminished primarily by its two largest competitors, Cirrus and Plus. The recent growth of these two networks was reducing the need for third party gateway and switching services at the inter-network as well as the interbank level. More and more banks and regional ATM networks were becoming members of the "Big Two" networks through their affiliations with either MasterCard or Visa. The Cirrus and Plus networks now each had so many member banks that they had taken on the quality of neutrality which had once helped EFS to stand apart.

Furthermore, EFS managers described their two main competitors as "rich and illogical," because both Cirrus and Plus had indicated their willingness to compete with price levels yielding no or low profit, tapping their member banks' deep pockets for capital if necessary. Because banks make their money by lending their depositors' funds, the member-banks of the two networks were willing to offer depositor services below cost if those services would enhance their ability to attract depositors. (Some regional ATM network operators had also begun to price "illogically" for the same reasons.) Despite the downward pressure on pricing, EFS still enjoyed a high operating margin because it was the low-cost provider and because most of its service contracts were multi-year. With several major contracts coming up for renewal, however, Mangum worried that competitive bidding could force its transaction fees down.

EFS was also faced with a new breed of client and competition at the regional level. In the recent past, more and more competing banks had agreed to cooperate directly with each other, forming their own regional shared networks and letting the lead bank operate the network. EFS' neutrality and linking capabilities, once a critical source of competitive differentiation when banks did not cooperate directly, was no longer considered a value-added feature. In fact, EFS' ability to compete aggressively for a piece of the value added could become restricted because many of the clients for which it drove terminals and provided gateway services were becoming members of the networks that competed directly with the Exchange.

Moreover, the recent growth of "super-regional" networks such as NYCE in the Northeast and STAR in Southern California—formed when several regionals join forces—

reduced the relative value added of full national coverage. In the mid-1980s, most regional networks covered only a portion of one state; by 1988, however, many regionals were multi-state, meeting an increasing portion of their cardholders' transaction needs without the help of third-party switches to neighboring networks.

The intensified competition was also revealing itself through contractual tactics other than pricing. For example, the super-regional MAC network had blocked EFS' access to its member banks by demanding that those banks not employ EFS to drive their terminals. Ten years earlier, no one in the industry believed that banks would ever cooperate with each other, sharing customer services and information, and jointly operating networks. Now, such cooperation made competing in ATM services not only affordable for individual banks, but also a prerequisite for survival. If direct bank-to-bank communications became increasingly prevalent and sophisticated, the value added by non-bank network operators and gateway services could diminish further.

**The Divestiture Decision**    The question facing Lynn Mangum was what to recommend to the Executive Committee and how strongly to make his pitch. EFS' financial strength had never been better. The division, however, appeared to be showing early signs of deviation from the strategic boundaries imposed by the List.

One option—apart from a continued "wait and see" approach—was to keep EFS within the boundaries by appropriate pruning and by innovative expansion via new lines of business and acquisitions that would meet the seven criteria and fit within the unit's business mission. (See **Exhibit 6** for the EFS Mission Statement.) Once repositioned, EFS could pursue ADP's aggressive growth goals. But the array of feasible growth opportunities was becoming increasingly limited over time, even as the profits continued to grow. A second possibility was to de-emphasize the business, halt new investment, and milk it as a steady-state business while the margins and cash flow remained high. The final option was divestiture. Management would need to determine what method to use to evaluate the milk versus sell decision. Whatever methods were used, management would have to consider a variety of selling scenarios, determining the most opportune time to sell based on the equity markets, the electronic funds transfer (EFT) industry, EFS' financial performance, and various selling strategies.

Lynn wondered whether EFS warranted a significant investment of additional management attention and financial resources. Continued inaction could prove to be costly down the road. But, would he appear a quitter if he recommended divestiture? And what about the generous bonuses (equalling roughly 1/3 of his salary) he was assured, based on EFS profits over the next few years? Lynn knew that ADP top management thought highly of him, but he still wondered what the specific implications of divestiture would be for his career path—within or outside of ADP. His 18 years with ADP had provided an appealing combination of professional challenges and growth, as well as career stability. He hoped the future would offer equally desirable opportunities. At 48 years old, Lynn had a substantial portion of his career still ahead of him.

In considering his options, Lynn reviewed the 1989 Strategic Plan he had presented in January 1988 as well as the one-pager on plans for 1990 (**Exhibit 1**), which he had received just two months earlier. He recalled the difficulty he had in putting together a 1989 plan that adequately addressed EFS' long-term competitive position on all fronts. The List had begun to haunt him back in late 1987 and the one-pager from Weston and Turner rekindled those feelings.

## EXHIBIT 1[a]    EFS "Going-in" Strategic Check List, September 6, 1988

### Product

1.  Dramatically enhance our USP, and eliminate all material competitive disadvantages, at the fastest rate that can be accomplished with our current R&D resources.
2.  Identify and pilot the most proximate, promising concentric circle add-ons to our current product set.

### Automation

1.  Identify and automate all error-prone, repetitive labor, paper, and overlapping steps out of the production stream for ADP and clients.
2.  Complete and install new, automated support systems for real-time monitoring, load balancing, DB maintenance, CRIS, and client billing.
3.  Retool, in System-90 mode, those computer functions and systems that are currently quite inefficient.

### Service

1.  Eliminate virtually all low-grade fever.
2.  Never lose a client for service reasons.
3.  Plan and implement suitable disaster avoidance/recovery procedures for our single-center environment.

### Marketing

1.  Develop at least two major, nontraditional relationships in ever growing mode (7-Eleven, Penney, CATS, AFFN, etc.).
2.  Identify longer term opportunities and potential for ADP dominance in selected niches.
3.  How do we cope with the long-term financial clout, illogical pricing, and competitive threat of Cirrus and Plus (Mastercard and Visa)?

### Organization

1.  Muscle-build the senior management team to create self-sufficiency and depth in every major function, with good backups (including one for you).
2.  Maintain/attain 6:1 spans of control at every level, on way to 8:1 whenever feasible.
3.  Create an even more focused, client/market-driven, time-driven, competitive management culture that is obsessed with growth.

### Financial

1.  Grow revenues and NOI over 20% annually, with rational pricing and high cash flow.
2.  Create an ongoing zero-base culture for planning and analyzing (including database integration and purges to reduce storage costs).
3.  Create periodic memo LOB and product financial statements for zero-base thinking.

---

[a] Definitions of acronyms and terms:

USP = Unique Selling Proposition
DB = database
CRIS = Client Relations Information System
Low-Grade Fever = insufficient attention to detail
LOB = line of business

**EXHIBIT 2   Summary ADP Financial Statistics ($ in millions)**

| FISCAL YEAR | REVENUE | PRE-TAX INCOME | EARNINGS PER SHARE |
|---|---|---|---|
| 1963 | $    1 | X | .01 |
| 1964 | 2 | X | .01 |
| 1965 | 3 | .6 | .02 |
| 1966 | 5 | 1.1 | .03 |
| 1967 | 9 | 2.0 | .04 |
| 1968 | 16 | 3.0 | .05 |
| 1969 | 27 | 4.6 | .06 |
| 1970 | 39 | 6.6 | .09 |
| 1971 | 49 | 9.2 | .11 |
| 1972 | 62 | 12.8 | .14 |
| 1973 | 90 | 16.7 | .17 |
| 1974 | 112 | 20.5 | .20 |
| 1975 | 155 | 27.2 | .25 |
| 1976 | 188 | 35.0 | .31 |
| 1977 | 245 | 6.0 | .39 |
| 1978 | 299 | 54.0 | .46 |
| 1979 | 370 | 64.0 | .54 |
| 1980 | 455 | 76.0 | .64 |
| 1981 | 558 | 90.0 | .74 |
| 1982 | 677 | 106.0 | .83 |
| 1983 | 753 | 115.0 | .92 |
| 1984 | 889 | 133.0 | 1.06 |
| 1985 | 1,031 | 155.0 | 1.22 |
| 1986 | 1,204 | 185.0 | 1.45 |
| 1987 | 1,384 | 222.0 | 1.76 |
| 1988 | 1,549 | 255.0 | 2.20 |
| 1989 est. (?) | 1,700 (?) | 285.0 (?) | 2.50 (?) |

# EXHIBIT 3

*Seven Key Requirements for Pursuing Major Service Businesses and Products* (*Most* must be satisfied to have a good strategy. A poor strategy can seldom succeed, even with excellent execution.)

(1) *Revenue Potential*  Over $50 million of annual *recurring* revenue for an SBU, $20 million for a line of business, and $5 million for a product.

(2) *Growth Potential*  At least a continuing 15% growth rate, preferably over 20%, with good probability (and plans). (This might be less for defensive positions in *existing* business or where ROI is very high.)

(3) *Desirable Competitive Position*

    a. Fragmented current market (exclusive of ADP's position).

    b. ADP in #1 or 2 position (or #3, if fragmented market) with potential to be #1 within five years.

    c. There is no major (deep pockets) illogical players (usually zero profit objectives) whose pricing would likely undermine our profitability.

(4) *Products: Standardized Computer-Related Business Applications (Front and Back Office)*

    a.. Mass-marketable (noncustomized potential for large number of prospects/transactions).

    b.. Mass-producible (noncustomized, near-level production for large number of transactions with limited labor).

    c.. Consistently superior direct client service features and performance, with clear client accountability (see Exhibit B).

    d. Extendable to additional integratable applications, particularly in front-office.

    e.. Influenced by a standardizing "Third Force" (viz—regulations, licensors, peers).

    f. Supported/recommended by influential third forces (viz—banks, CPAs, peers, hardware partners, licensors, trade associations).

    g. Leverages existing client/marketplace relationships (concentric circles).

    h.. Different from competition in noticeable/valuable sustainable ways (UCP/USP) that are not solely dependent upon automation and technology.

(5) *Sustainability of Acceptable Growth in the Market*  Particularly critical for new, nonadjacent business, to earn steady growth and premium pricing.

    a.. Very distinctive product/service position (see Exhibit A).

    b.. Potential and plans for significant client accretion.

    c. Good client life cycle and/or exit barriers. (*Do* consider long-term lock-ins!)

    d. Entry barriers to strong competition. (Long-term client contracts may be relevant.)

    e.. High *net* $ value-added for client (i.e.—client benefit vs. ADP charges) vs. client's other alternatives (see Exhibit A).

    f. Stable client preferences and habits (vs. fickle consumer types).

    g. Lowest cost producer. (Not lowest price seller.)

(6) *Strong Management*  Experience, commitment, focus, capability, credibility, conformity to Key Factors to Success (Exhibit B).

(7) *Promising Financial Potential*

    a.. High-confidence business plan (good trends in margins, growth, lifecycles, ROA).

    b. High confidence risk/reward relationship (no single client dependency).

    c. High product frequency of use/repetitive revenue (stability/predictability).

    d. Clear development checkpoints/contingency plans (and aborts, if warranted).

    e.. Feasible exit plan and absorbable exit cost (if needed).

    f.. Acceptable prospective return (ROI) on prospective investments (including Bow Waves, *all* capital investments, future acquisitions, and cost of money).

    g. Keep client-site hardware off balance sheet, if feasible.

    h. NBE% should seldom exceed processing margin, except where there is a very long client lifecycle . . . in order to provide an adequate return for the risk/difficulty and $ of NBE investment.

**EXHIBIT 4   Automatic Data Processing, Inc.**

| | 1986 | 1987 | 1988 | 1989E | 1990E | '87–88 | '88–90E |
|---|---|---|---|---|---|---|---|
| | | *Fiscal Years Ended June 30* | | | | *Compound Annual Growth Rate (%)* | |
| Clients | 596 | 680 | 799 | 1,212 | 1,450 | 18% | 35% |
| ATMs driven, direct | 1,205 | 1,678 | 2,366 | 2,540 | 2,681 | 41 | 6 |
| Avg. monthly trans-actions (000s) | 5,136 | 6,154 | 9,000 | 13,600 | 16,305 | 46 | 35 |
| Networks accessed | 32 | 37 | 41 | 44 | 47 | 11 | 7 |
| Card base authorized (MM) | 9.5 | 18.9 | 25.1 | 30.2 | 36.3 | 33 | 20 |
| Revenue ($000) | 21,124 | 23,254 | 29,619 | 41,124 | 48,212 | 27 | 28 |
| Gross margin: ($000) | 9,245 | 10,424 | 13,504 | 20,827 | 24,664 | 30 | 35 |
| (as % of Revenue) | 44% | 45% | 46% | 51% | 51% | | |
| Operating profit ($000) | 5,012 | 5,429 | 8,051 | 14,826 | 18,442 | 48 | 51 |
| (as % of Revenue) | 24% | 23% | 27% | 36% | 38% | | |
| Pretax profit ($000) | 1,274 | 2,217 | 4,455 | 10,304 | 13,200 | 101 | 72 |
| (as % of Revenue) | 6% | 10% | 15% | 25% | 27% | | |
| Total net assets ($MM) | 7.47 | 8.3 | 8.91 | 8.9 | 10.23 | 7 | 7 |
| Pretax return on assets | 17% | 27% | 50% | 116% | 129% | | |
| Net cash flow ($000) | 512 | 278 | 2,061 | 6,193 | 6,592 | 641 | 79 |

## EXHIBIT 5

**Interoffice Memorandum**

Electronic Financial Services Division
203 Main Avenue
Clifton, New Jersey 21309-8781
201-210-7100

*ADP*

Date:   July 12, 1988

Subject:   EFS Situation

To:   Bill Turner
      Art Weinbach
      Josh Weston

From:   Lynn Mangum

Attached is a quick summary of the situation surrounding EFS in preparation for further discussion.

LJM:mar
Attachment

## EFS — Summary of Situation

(CONFIDENTIAL)

### Operations/Product Satisfactory

- Any performance problems resolvable
- Product
  - Better than most
  - Missing few features
  - Little true USP (USP as gateway to 44 other networks less valuable as powerful regionals + nationals serve client needs)

### Ability to Grow by Direct Sales

- Still possible (in "mop-up" mode) to attract remaining organizations without card/ATM programs.
- Unlikely that we'll sell much to banks already automated since USP opportunity limited.
- Nontraditional opportunities still around — although many (convenience stores) considering Cash Back at Point of Sale vs. ATMs.

### Threats

- Regionals gobbling locals, expanding "Logo dominance"; *Logo key reason to choose ATM program.*
- Regionals beginning to offer ATM processing (driving and authorization) vs. switching only
  - STAR/NYCE/Yankee 24

  and eliminating layer of service/pricing (MAC has always been processer and is the only switch/processor who prohibits third party processors from bringing ATMs/cards to its network).
- *EFS will retain the majority of its processing business over time* (except for MAC dominated areas) in spite of above, but price pressure will increase.
- EFS revenue from network switching for AFFN, Easy Answer, TX (MATS) and CU24 (Florida CUs) will likely be sustained although value of Easy Answer/TX is diminishing as more powerful regionals make headway.
- "Exchange's" reasonable presence in Florida/California/Massachusetts likely sustainable. With the exception of the possibility of adding Citicorp affiliates, "Exchange" not serious competitor to Plus-CIRRUS. In California, Exchange is strong #2 to STAR and only place where Logo has USP. California presence established by very lucrative *IT* acquisition not likely duplicated. Only similar candidate today is Bass' Exchange in the Pacific Northwest.

Exchange may have window in POS while VISA/M.C. get their act together and implement "Entre" or their own POS debit programs. Overtime, VISA-M.C. likely owners of debit as well as credit card world.

*Exhibit 5   continued*

It's increasingly likely that VISA/Mastercard-CIRRUS/Plus will survive as national networks with regionals disappearing over time (3–5 years) (VISA has standing offer to switch any network for $.02 per transaction). Neither VISA nor Mastercard has current "processing/authorization" capability—rather today they need processors to bring them activity. ADP and the regionals (most using Deluxe) can be the "FDR's" of the debit world—providing profitable processing to big mega switches—gaining few net new clients but benefitting from steady internal transaction growth. Alternative—Mastercard and VISA can offer processing services for themselves and compete directly with regional processors.

Summary

ADP-EFS as a stand alone business will experience ongoing client shrinkage and price pressure which will be somewhat offset by natural transaction growth and limited direct sales. Ability to direct sell to the uncommitted market is still not fully tapped.

ADP-EFS makes a good partner for several relative organizations; in priority they are:

VISA
Mastercard
Deluxe
PNB
EDS

With the possibility of credit card processors covering both debit and credit, the following become additional possibilities:

Tele Check
FDR
Tele Credit
J.C. Penney Systems Service

I believe that our window to capitalize on our value may be disappearing and feel we should begin exploring alternative possibilities as soon as possible.

---

## EXHIBIT 6

### Mission Statement

EFS' mission is to become a premier third party processor of consumer-initiated EFT transactions for financial and nonfinancial organizations. Our business will be distinguished by providing value-added, end-to-end, reliable products, at the lowest cost of operations, for each level of service.

The keystone of EFS success will be working with clients as their "EFT partner/consultant" by providing the total solution for all their EFT needs on either a direct or indirect processing basis.

Strategically, services will include the acquisition, authorization, switching, and gatewaying of traditional and nontraditional transactions within the consumer payment system, as well as the creation of marketable information products resulting from the processing of these transactions. Predominant national market share will be attained through the building of dominant/controlling positions in each of the major U.S. regional markets.

# CASE 30    Hamilton Financial Investments: A Franchise Built on Trust

A s Joe Grahams stood at the podium, Hamilton's senior managers looked up at him expectantly. He concluded his remarks on risk management:

> A thorough understanding of risk comes from business managers understanding their business. If you've been through boom cycles and bust cycles, you know the danger signs. Unless motivation systems are wrong or people are burying their heads in the sand and not paying attention to details, there should be no problem.

Fifteen minutes later, as he crossed 48th street in New York, to return to his office, Joe wondered if further steps were necessary to protect the Hamilton franchise. Hamilton Financial Investments had recently hired a global risk manager—in fact it was Brandon Lamm who had organized the Risk Forum at which he had just spoken. But he was acutely aware of the increasing scrutiny that Hamilton was receiving in both the business and popular press.

Just yesterday, Joe had met with the senior management committee to discuss possible new rules to strengthen the controls on personal trading activities of Hamilton employees. He would have to decide soon on the best course of action.

## Eastern Group, Inc.

The Eastern Group was founded in 1893 by three New York businessmen. The company, then named Lewiston Insurance Co., sold fire, liability, and marine insurance. During the 1920s, Lewiston diversified into life insurance and annuities. In 1949, Danny Everett, a prominent New York banker, took control of the company. Everett wanted to make Lewiston a leading firm in the insurance industry. He first acquired Eastern Company, a well known life insurance company, and renamed the new company the Eastern Group. Everett then engineered a series of mergers and opened offices in the major business centers in Europe. Although Eastern expanded in size, it was still a relatively small firm in the insurance industry.

But in 1962, two months before Everett's retirement, Eastern merged with Atlantic Insurance Company. The merger created one of the largest life insurance companies in the US. Frank Jenkins, who had spent his entire career at Eastern, became CEO of the new company. With Eastern securely atop the life insurance industry, the company expanded into the financial industry. Eastern acquired Jersey International Bank in 1970, Hamilton Financial Investments in 1972, North East Credit Company in 1975, and Xavier Mortgage Bank in 1980. In addition, Eastern made significant investments in the real estate market in the early 1980s. During the 1980s, Eastern's assets grew from $40 billion to $70 billion and revenues from $8 billion to $12 billion.

By 1990, however, Eastern was substantially weakened due to a downturn in the real estate market. A new CEO, Andrew Cavanaugh, led the company through a drastic restructuring named "Focus on 15". Cavanaugh kept only the divisions which were or had

*Doctoral Candidate Antonio Davila and Professor Robert Simons prepared this case as the basis for class discussion rather than to illustrate either effective or ineffective handling of an administrative situation.*

the potential to be in the top 15 in their respective industries. He proceeded to sell the mortgage bank, the liability insurance division, and the marine insurance division. He also reduced the workforce by over 10,000 employees and reorganized Eastern into five subsidiaries. Eastern posted strong earnings in both 1995 and 1996. **Exhibit 1** presents Eastern's balance sheet and **Exhibit 2** Eastern's organizational structure.

## Hamilton Financial Investments

The Hamilton Fund was started in 1959 by a group of New York investors. By 1970, the fund's assets had grown to $100 million. However, with a long-term declining stock market, the early seventies were not a good time for mutual funds. The fund suffered loses in both 1970 and 1971. Hamilton was on the verge of bankruptcy when it was bought by the Eastern Group in 1972. Eastern's CEO, Danny Everett, appointed an experienced investment manager as president of Hamilton, James Wells.

Wells, with the financial backing of Eastern, took several initiatives to ensure the growth of the division. He created Hamilton Research Company (HRC) to serve as an investment advisor to the Hamilton fund. Hamilton also began a process of vertical integration. The division took over back-office account processing functions from the banks and it moved into distribution by selling directly to individuals through advertising and a toll-free telephone line. In addition, Hamilton introduced a money market fund with a check-writing feature that allowed investors the flexibility of a regular bank account.

Wells believed passionately in giving individual investment managers the freedom to manage their funds to their best knowledge and abilities, rather than relying on investment committees to decide the funds' investment strategy. This philosophy allowed fund managers to experiment with different approaches to create value for the investor. Examples of new services included Hamilton Investment Management Services, created in 1975 to provide investment advisory services to large corporate pension clients; a retirement plan for self-employed people introduced in 1976; and Hamilton International, launched in 1977 to attract foreign investment.

By the time Wells retired in 1980, he had diversified into discount brokerage services, introduced 10 new funds, and enhanced distribution channels through a network of walk-in offices. Assets under management equaled $1 billion when Joseph Grahams was appointed as the new president of Hamilton.

Interest rates sky rocketed in the 1980's and, as a result, financial services firms grew rapidly. Hamilton was no exception. Assets under management grew from $1 billion in 1980 to $20 billion in 1987, and the number of Hamilton mutual funds reached 19 in 1989 (from 11 just ten years earlier). In 1988, Hamilton started to distribute its financial services to institutional and corporate customers creating a separate subsidiary to better serve the needs of this segment. To handle the increased volume, new operation centers were opened in Chicago and Los Angeles. By the end of the decade, Hamilton was among the top fifteen companies in the mutual fund industry.

Hamilton continued to grow throughout the nineties. In 1996, the division managed almost 5 million customer accounts. It employed over 5,000 full-time personnel, handling over 84,000 daily customer telephone calls and processing more than 270,000 mutual fund and brokerage transactions each day. Assets under management exceeded $80 billion.

**Exhibit 3 and 4** presents Hamilton's financial position by the end of 1996 as well as significant statistics on its growth.

## *Creating Value for Customers*

Hamilton had two main lines of businesses: mutual funds and brokerage services. **Exhibit 5** presents Hamilton's organizational structure. In addition, the trust bank—Hamilton Management Trust Company—had assets under management of $6.6 billion.

In the mutual fund business—Hamilton's largest—value was created through three key processes: investment management, marketing and sales, and transaction processing.

**Investment Management**   Hamilton's 41 different mutual funds had assets under management of $73.7 billion by the end of 1996. Each fund was designed to meet the needs of a particular segment of investors and they were grouped into six main categories: equity funds that emphasized capital appreciation, equity funds for growth & income, high yield income funds (holding below investment grade debt instruments), taxable fixed income funds, tax free municipal bond funds, and money market funds.

A fund was an investment vehicle where various investors pooled together their financial assets and delegated the management of these assets to a knowledgeable fund manager. The fund issued shares to participating investors who were its owners. Most Hamilton funds sold shares to anyone willing to participate in the fund at any point in time. Investors could redeem their shares in the fund at any time. Prices for fund shares were estimated daily (and in some cases hourly) to allow investors to buy and sell fund shares.

Each fund was an independent company with its own shareholders and board of directors. But the investment decisions and the information required to make these decisions was supplied on a fee basis by Hamilton Research Co. (HRC), the original research and advisory firm set up in 1972. HRC employed all the fund managers as well as the research staff which generated information for investment decisions. HRC was staffed with more than 60 research investment professionals.

**Marketing and Sales**   In addition to fund performance, customer service and a trustworthy reputation were key competitive dimensions in the fund industry. Customers were investing their wealth with the expectation that the fund company would deliver on investment performance and superior service. Advertising was an important vehicle to increase customer awareness and familiarize potential customers with Hamilton's products. But consistently meeting customer expectations was key to building a franchise based on trust.

Hamilton's distribution (i.e., sales) system was tailored to various target market segments. The Retail Group managed $33.4 billion by the end of 1996. This group served individual investors through toll-free telephone access, investor centers (branches), and electronic channels (including Internet). In the retail sector, it was very important to educate the customer who often was not financially sophisticated and may be unaware of the relationship between risk and return. For example, a misinformed customer could invest his life savings in a high risk fund that could, in the short-run, impose unexpected losses on the investor. Customer representatives had to understand the background and objectives of each customer to describe possible investment funds for that person and to inform them about the risks that each investment strategy would have.

Customer representatives were not allowed to recommend specific funds. Instead, they supplied the information that investors needed to make their decisions. Educating the prospective customer was time consuming and not always successful. In booming markets, some customers cared only about the returns, ignoring the risks of the investment process.

Even after the customer representative had correctly informed the customer about the types of funds that best matched his or her investment profile, the customer could still choose to invest in any Hamilton fund.

The Institutional Retirement Group distributed Hamilton's products to corporations, not-for-profit, and government entities. Hamilton was a leading provider of 401-k retirement plans (for profit corporations) and 403-b plans (for not-for-profit organizations). This market was much more sophisticated with institutional customers knowledgeable about the performance trade-offs of their investments. Still, trust played a critical role in these relationships. Customers relied on getting an adequate return, being accurately informed, and having a reliable company taking care of their investment needs.

To fully meet their needs, some customers in the institutional group wanted Hamilton to supply them both with Hamilton products as well as with other investment vehicles supplied by competing fund firms. They wanted to have the flexibility to define their investment strategy without being restricted to Hamilton's products. These demands forced Hamilton to supply competitors' products and be associated with (and suffer the consequences of) problems and failures in other financial institutions.

The Institutional Investment Services Group served financial intermediaries, a distribution channel comprising broker-dealers, banks, investment advisors, and insurance companies. Some private investors liked to manage their investments through financial intermediaries instead of dealing themselves with the fund companies. In dealing with intermediaries, Hamilton was not directly responsible for the relationship with the end customer, but its reputation was at stake because its products and brand were being purchased. A bad investment recommendation from one of these intermediaries could hurt the customer's perception of Hamilton. Similarly, financial problems in one of these distributors could affect Hamilton's reputation if the final customer felt unfairly treated. To limit these problems, the Institutional Services Group had developed demanding acceptance procedures for each intermediary before they were allowed to sell Hamilton's products.

**Transaction Processing**  The last piece in Hamilton's value chain was the back office operation where transactions were processed and cleared, and records were maintained. The mandate of this operation, known as Fund Accounting and Custody Services, was to support high levels of customer service. In addition to performing all the accounting for transactions, Fund Accounting and Custody Services estimated daily the price of the shares of each Hamilton fund, and supplied customers with all the information they needed to assess the performance of their investments. This task was relatively simple for funds with investments in advanced and liquid markets where electronic data transfer made securities' prices readily available. But some Hamilton funds invested in international securities where prices were available only through telephone calls with representatives in those countries. The department had to check the reliability of that information daily to be sure that the fund shares were correctly priced.

Hamilton Systems Company provided the MIS backbone for all Hamilton's operation. It provided the infrastructure and the software to facilitate customer service, investment decisions, and securities' research. People working at the Systems' division were specialists in technology and knowledgeable about financial products and markets.

**Hamilton Brokerage Services**  The second main business operation at Hamilton was a discount brokerage house. It was among the largest brokerage houses on the East coast and was active in the main financial markets in the world. Hamilton also had a brokerage operation in London to serve the European financial markets and another one in Hong Kong to serve the Southeast Asian markets.

As agent for third parties, the Brokerage Group executed trades in most equity, fixed income products, over-the-counter (OTC) markets. Here, as in the fund industry, customer confidence was the most important competitive dimension; without customer trust, any cost or service advantage was worthless. The customers had to be certain that the brokerage house was executing their orders in a timely manner, billing them accurately, and providing adequate information.

In addition to its agent business, the Brokerage Group acted on its own account trading in fixed income, OTC, and foreign exchange markets. When acting as principal, the Brokerage Group was exposed, unless appropriately hedged, to fluctuation in interest and exchange rates and to changes in OTC share values.

## Foundations for Growth

During the 1970's, as the newly-appointed president, James Wells laid Hamilton's foundations for growth. One of the pillars of its success was technology. By the 1990s, Hamilton was spending more than $80 million annually on technology. The continuous investment in infrastructure, new systems and system enhancements allowed Hamilton to have proprietary software to meet customer needs as well as the demands of its research investment professionals. Since the late seventies, Hamilton had state-of-the-art telephone switching capabilities to provide superior customer service. Hamilton was one of the first companies on the East coast to provide 24 hour services, hourly mutual fund price quotes, and to allow same day trading. In addition, Hamilton had its own electronic trading system and calculated daily more than 300 prices for its funds with information coming from all over the world. Technology was such an important part of the company that Hamilton Systems Company had been a separate division reporting directly to Joe Grahams. Its mission was to keep Hamilton at the cutting edge of technology applied to financial markets.

But technology would not be enough without the other pillars of Hamilton's success: innovation, customer service, investment skills, and, more recently, economies of scale. As described above, innovation had been a major driver of Hamilton's growth. It was second only to Fidelity—the industry leader in—introducing a money market fund with checking capabilities and to offer a no-load, open ended fund to invest in tax-free municipal bonds. It was also among the first financial institutions to offer discount brokerage services. Market-focused innovation was emphasized in separate, decentralized units which targeted defined market segments. Innovation defined Hamilton's approach to customer service.

Hamilton could not have prospered, however, unless it was able to deliver sustained, superior performance to investors. Hamilton's culture was shaped by the beliefs of its past president, James Wells, and current one, Joe Grahams. Joe Grahams believed in the personal ability of fund managers to pick stocks to outperform the market. Joe had been a successful money manager himself and learned to appreciate the value of fundamental investment analysis. Fund performance was key. Managers of the funds with the highest returns were praised and their funds attracted new money from customers.

These two characteristics—personal achievement and performance orientation—permeated the organization. Managers at every level were held accountable for their performance and were rewarded handsomely for their achievements. The company was characterized by an entrepreneurial spirit that gave as much freedom as possible at every level in the organization and relied on the abilities of its managers. Unnecessary standardization and bureaucracy were anathema. The entrepreneurial spirit was reinforced by Hamilton's drive for innovation. New products and new businesses, either inside or outside the financial industry, were constantly added. Managers were valued for being action-oriented and for understanding their business. A formal strategic process was never used in the company—it did not convey the sense of action or urgency that was the hallmark of Hamilton's success.

To many in Hamilton, Joe Grahams was larger than life. His reputation permeated the organization and the words, "Joe says . . ." carried special weight. Joe Grahams galvanized the company around performance: he was rarely satisfied. He communicated a sense of urgency to the organization to constantly improve. The culture praised and rewarded outstanding performers and risk-takers. It supported internal competition where reputation was created by beating the best funds in the industry—including other Hamilton funds. Beyond all this, however, was Hamilton's foundation of trust. Hamilton had been able to build and preserve the confidence of its customers for over four decades. **Exhibit 6** includes the Statement of Hamilton's values.

From 1993 to 1996, Hamilton's workforce had grown from 1,400 to over 5,000. The question now was how to ensure that Hamilton continued to deliver on its promise.

## Global Risk Management

During 1994 and 1995, the financial industry had been rocked by the failure of century-old institutions like Kidder, Peabody and Barings Bank. The common theme in all these events was the actions of an isolated person who bent internal control systems to conceal losses until they destroyed well-established firms. At Kidder, Peabody & Co., Joseph Jett, a trader in the government desk accumulated losses of $350 million before his trading scheme was discovered. At Barings, Nicholas Leeson brought down the firm by accumulating losses of over $1 billion trading in the futures market.

These vicarious events convinced Hamilton's top managers that franchise risk rested in the hands of every single employee. Two incidents inside Hamilton reinforced this belief. In March 1994, Hamilton reported to the press incorrect prices on some of its mutual funds. The mistake happened because of an unanticipated problem with a routine systems conversion. The incident, which had no effect whatsoever on fund transactions, generated severe reactions from the press. Hamilton's reputation in the eyes of its customers had been damaged. The second mistake, in December 1994, occurred when Hamilton announced that its initial dividend estimate of $450 million for Hamilton Global Balanced Fund, the company's flagship fund, was incorrect. While the estimation had no financial impact on customers in any way, the size of the mathematical error caused people to question Hamilton's record-keeping abilities. Somebody had mistakenly read a minus sign as a plus sign in preparing the estimate. A headline summarized the incident: "Hamilton's Addition May Subtract From Reputation".

The implications were clear to Hamilton's top managers. "This Cannot Happen Here" could never be an excuse. People had to be aware of the risks they were exposed to and how to manage them. The company needed to manage risk actively. In September 1995, the Corporate Risk Office was created and Brandon Lamm hired.

**The Corporate Risk Office**   In 1994, the Operations Control Steering Committee (OCSC), comprising senior managers from the various divisions, was created with the objective of identifying risks and designing a risk management strategy for Hamilton. The decision was made to staff a risk management structure that encompassed all levels of Hamilton.

Brandon Lamm, 36—an experienced risk manager at GE Capital—joined Hamilton in September 1995 with the objective of coordinating the risk efforts across the company and avoiding incidents that could damage Hamilton's reputation or financial position. The new Global Risk Management office, headed by Lamm, reported to Sidney Schwartz, Hamilton's Chief Financial Officer, and to the Operations Control Steering Committee. Lamm's mandate was to educate, coordinate, monitor, and assist line managers in controlling risk. In addition, Lamm was responsible to the OCSC to identify and report any significant risk that could damage Hamilton or its individual businesses.

In the new structure, each group and business unit had its own risk management department reporting directly to line management and informally through committees and corporate-wide initiatives to Lamm's office. To assist him, Brandon Lamm hired four risk managers to oversee specialized issues: credit risk, market risk, risk systems, and operations control.

Sidney Schwartz, Hamilton's Chief Financial Officer, described the objectives of the Global Risk Office:

> Risk has to be owned by business managers, they have to be aware of the risks in their hands and put in place the appropriate procedures to manage it. The Global Risk Office oversees and coordinates risk initiatives, but we felt that if line managers were to own risk, their risk managers should report to them rather than to the central office.

> The decentralized business culture at Hamilton presents challenges for any corporate function. Business managers are suspicious of any policies that appear to be unneeded bureaucracy. Therefore, in recruiting for the Global Risk Office, we looked for talented professionals that not only possess deep technical expertise and experience, but also the interpersonal skills that are essential to get things done here. The key objectives for the Global Risk Management function are to ensure that we have a high level of awareness about risk management, appropriate controls to manage all types of risk across Hamilton, and timely reporting and escalation of our major risk exposures to senior management.

> Joe, our CEO, asked me once how I would know that we are there. I told him we'll be there when risk management is (1) fully integrated in our culture, (2) business and risk performance is consistently achieved, (3) risk measurement and monitoring activities are highly effective, and (4) Hamilton becomes an industry standard. At that point, risk management resources at the corporate level should be reduced.

Brandon Lamm, Hamilton's Chief Risk Officer, described the role of the Global Risk Management Group:

> I don't believe that there is a standardized model for risk management, especially for a global and complex organization like Hamilton. Here at Global Risk Management, we support senior management and the business units in several ways.

> First, we act as risk consultants providing expertise and advice to individual business units. During the last year we have worked with Hamilton Management Trust Company, with the Systems Group, and with the Human Resources Department. We take a broader view of risk than many institutions. For example, in Human Resources, we identified the risks associated with managing people—from identifying the needs of a position to the recruiting and assimilation process, training and development, and review and rewards procedures.

> Our second role is risk identification and education. Risk identification begins with an annual risk review completed by all business units. Just last month, we finished collecting detailed information on business unit risks—this information will be the basis of future risk initiatives. Regarding

education, we currently have a bi-monthly Risk Forum where business units present their risk management programs and we update the top 50 managers on risk-related issues at Hamilton. The challenge that I am facing now is how to communicate risk awareness to a workforce of 5,000 people.

The final stage is to build the appropriate risk measures and monitoring systems, to define escalation policies and methodologies, and to integrate the efforts across the company. Each business unit will prepare a monthly standard risk report describing risk exposure and losses. We have adopted a broad definition of risk including the traditional financial risk measures—credit and market risk measures—but also including business risk associated with the industry structure and the strategy of the division, operational risk linked to back-office errors, and organizational risk due to a mismatch between our needs and the characteristics of our resources and people.

Hamilton is a very decentralized organization, but top management needs to be informed of any major risk event happening at the business units. The ideal risk management system would centralize monitoring and decentralize management of risk.

Jason Lawrence, President of Hamilton Retail Group, commented on the role of the Corporate Risk Office:

The most important risk is anything that could erode our reputation. In this business all we have is our integrity. We have to communicate to every employee the risks that they face and how important it is to safeguard the value of our brand.

Brandon's role is very important to Hamilton. I see his role as supporting our risk initiatives with the expertise of his department, communicating best practices and experiences across divisions, and developing diagnostic systems to protect our franchise from reputation loss. But, he has to be sensitive to the unique needs of each division and not standardize procedures beyond what is needed.

Dennis McGregor, President of Hamilton Management Trust Company, was the person who, in 1992, started the risk awareness effort at Hamilton. He shared his views about the evolution of risk management inside Hamilton:

The theme that has driven risk management from its inception is thinking about control as an enabler rather than a restraint. A big percentage of our employees have been here for less than two years and do not have the big picture. Risk resides in these operating people who build the franchise reputation every day. Risk has to be individually owned. Top managers in each division should talk about it to show that it is an important theme. The key is to have employees understand the risk at their desks.

Brandon Lamm sat in his new department's conference room with the casewriters. In the eighteen months since he had taken the new position at Hamilton, he had built a risk management department from scratch. He had hired four managers in his department and put in place the structure illustrated in **Exhibit 7.**

You will see on this list the seven key initiatives that I am currently working on (**Exhibit 8**). They are an outgrowth of our Guiding Principles. Overarching these seven initiatives, however, are two main issues concerning me here at Hamilton: decentralization and escalation. This is a highly decentralized culture built on speed and innovation. But part of my mandate is to centralize various aspects of risk measurement and management. This introduces a tension that I must manage carefully.

Let me give you an example. One of the first studies performed by the Corporate Risk Office consolidated counterparty exposure across the various divisions at Hamilton. The results of this study shows that one bank in Singapore handles most of Hamilton's transactions in the Asian emerging markets. Fixed-income funds, equity-funds, brokerage services, and the trust bank channel a significant part of their deals through this institution. None of them exceeded their risk limits when evaluated on their own. It's only when the risk is consolidated that exposure is too high. The problem is that all of our divisions have a high regard for this bank and they rely on its good service and reputation. Asking the divisions to use other intermediaries means increasing their costs. In my first important decision, how far should we go in dictating what these highly successful business managers should do? In Hamilton's decentralized organization, they are not used to being told how to run their business by a newly-appointed corporate risk manager.

The second thing that I have to do is create policies and norms so that individuals escalate problems to senior management in a timely fashion. One of the first things that we did was to gather confidential survey data from each business manager regarding what they saw as potential risk areas. We promised that this information would not be shared outside their respective divisions. The risk profile of the divisions was extremely good. But in one division, bad debts were higher than the industry average, the risks identified were not properly managed, and the analysis was superficial.

I called Bob, the manager of the division, to talk about the situation. He was very cool to me. He argued that the level of bad debts was not high compared to competitors following similar strategies. He said that his people had provided enough information to prove that their risk management practices were fine. Bob added that his staff was working hard to improve several risk management areas that were still a bit weak and that he would contact the Corporate Risk Office whenever he felt that he needed specific support.

I realized during the conversation that Bob had no interest in collaborating with the Risk Office. He did not want us to interfere with his operation. What should we do? We're in a difficult position. On the one hand, if we report to Joe that one of the divisions has bad risk management practices, we will break whatever goodwill we might have with the division managers. On the other hand, we cannot let this problem go unattended. The Corporate Risk Office was created to tackle these kind of issues.

## Protecting the Franchise

On a day-to-day basis, managers throughout Hamilton were forced to make choices — some major, others minor — that had potential implications on the trust that was the foundation of Hamilton's successful franchise. The following section describes three of those situations.

**Condition Yellow**  John Bickerman, Head of Corporate Security, looked at the report in his hands. A background check on Natalie Forrester — a new sales employee in the retail business — revealed that Natalie had overstated her academic credentials. She had indeed graduated from Harvard Business School, as she claimed, but she had not graduated in the top fifteen percent of her class — something that was indicated on her resume.

Hamilton routinely did background checks on new employees and color-coded them as either green, yellow, or red (**Exhibit 9**). Green indicated absence of negative findings; red indicated an undesirable background (e.g., felony record) or misrepresentation in past employment and/or salary data; yellow indicated cause for concern. Hamilton rules forbade managers from continuing the employment of someone with a code red. However, the decision on a code yellow was left up to the individual manager responsible for hiring and/or firing that employee.

John wondered what decision Sid Kester would make. As her boss, Sid had been pleased to hire someone with seven years of sales experience away from a major competitor. Natalie was thought to be high potential. Still, John remembered that Nick Leeson — the rogue trader who brought down Barings — had also overstated his academic accomplishments.

**Risk Adjusted Returns**  A different kind of decision faced Sidney Schwartz, Chief Financial Officer and Brandon Lamm's boss. Brandon had been hired to bring in new ideas, and one of those ideas that Brandon and Sidney discussed related to how business unit performance might be evaluated in a risk-adjusted basis.

The idea behind risk-adjusted performance measurement was to allocate a capital charge to each business unit based on risk and then measure profitability in terms of any surplus or deficit. This concept, also known as "return on risk-adjusted capital" and "economic value added" had been applied by other financial institutions and corporations. Currently, business unit profitability at Hamilton was measured based on operating margin and other traditional income measures. However, earnings generated by business units may not be comparable because the business units assume different levels of risk and capital.

A possible design for an evaluation system would be as follows: each business unit would be charged with an amount of capital that would be determined by its risk exposures and capital fund requirements. The total capital charge allocated to a business unit would incorporate the "worst case" loss given its market, credit, and operational risk, including capital outlays for new investments. The cost of capital would be subtracted from the income of each business unit to come up with the risk adjusted profitability.

Sidney knew that Joe Grahams would like to establish a closer linkage between risk performance and incentive compensation. Allocating capital and measuring risk-adjusted profitability was one way of doing that through the business unit performance measurement process. As Hamilton's CFO, this would also allow him and Joe to review business unit performance to ensure that appropriate returns were being achieved for risks assumed and that capital was used efficiently.

Sidney wondered if and how he should pitch this to Joe. Joe was strong willed and had clear ideas about the power of holding people accountable for their performance. Joe said that he wanted all his key managers to have "skin in the game"—something significant to win or lose based on their performance.

But was this going too far? Joe hated bureaucracy and standardization. He believed strongly in good management judgment and intuition. How would he react to this more mechanical approach? Should it be tied to compensation? Would Joe see it as a useful innovation to keep risk in the minds of all managers, or would it cause the newly created risk management organization to lose its store of initial enthusiasm and goodwill?

---

**FIGURE 1    An Example of the New Evaluation Scheme.**

| ($ MILLIONS) | BUSINESS UNIT A | BUSINESS UNIT B |
|---|---|---|
| Revenue | 100 | 100 |
| Expenses | 80 | 80 |
| Operating Income | 20 | 20 |
| Taxes | 8 | 8 |
| Net Income | $12 | $12 |
| Allocated Capital | $50 | $120 |
| Risk-Adjusted Capital Rate | 12% | 10% |
| Capital Charge | $6 | $12 |
| Adjusted Net Income | $6 | $0 |

**Who Sets the Price?**   On Monday evening at 5:30 Andrea Laura huddled with three colleagues. Laura, president of Hamilton Accounting and Custody Services, would have to make the call within ten minutes. To meet press deadlines, her division was required to report final closing prices on all Hamilton funds within forty minutes of the markets close. The industry standard was accuracy to within $0.01 per share.

The market in Hong Kong had been closed Thursday, Friday, and Monday for the Easter holiday. Therefore, the latest market prices available on the Hong Kong market were from last Wednesday evening. However, the Japanese stock market, which was active on Monday, had fallen by just under two percent at the close. This would certainly have an effect on Hong Kong's opening prices tomorrow.

Laura had to decide whether to estimate the potential fall in value of those Hong Kong stocks to reflect the fall in the Japanese markets. If she did not make the adjustment, sharp-eyed traders could use the old (potentially overstated) prices to sell Hamilton funds when they opened.

This pricing technique was called "fair value pricing". Instead of using the actual closing market prices, fair value pricing used market information to determine the most accurate prices of securities. Hamilton and a few other firms used this system only on special occasions (e.g., when the market was in turmoil) and usually for the Asian markets because of different time zones.

Laura and her colleagues pored over data to assess the exposure on the Hong Kong exchange. Her inclination was to estimate the effects of the Japanese market fall on the Hong Kong securities and adjust downward the prices that she would report to the press in the next few minutes. But she remembered the furor that was created in the financial media when Hamilton had issued prices which later proved to be incorrect. She looked at her watch. It was 5:38.

---

As Joe Grahams crossed 49th street, he wondered what decision would serve Hamilton Investments best. Two new policies were being considered. The first was to ban fund managers from trading in any security in the seven days before or after a Hamilton fund traded in that security. This policy was intended to avoid any criticism that managers were selling securities in their fiduciary role but buying them for their personal interest. The second policy would prohibit fund managers (and all Hamilton employees) from short-selling stocks that Hamilton owned.

The issue of personal trading was brought to the forefront of the mutual fund industry by a portfolio manager who worked for Invesco Funds. He was fired in 1994 after having broken that firm's rules on personal trading by not disclosing some of his personal trades. He was also fined a total of $115,000 and banned for five years from the US securities business by the Securities Exchange and Commission (SEC). That incident prompted an industry panel to establish a new set of guidelines restricting personal trading by fund managers. Examples of recommendations included a ban on investments in initial public offerings, pre-clearance of personal investments and transactions reports, and disclosure to fund share-holders about personal investing procedures. In addition, the SEC and most fund companies began to put greater emphasis on enforcing all personal trading rules.

Hamilton responded by implementing a new policy to restrict the freedom of fund managers when trading for their own account. For the first time, fund managers were forced to execute all their personal trades through Hamilton Brokerage Services. Furthermore, they were also banned from discussing their investment ideas in public; this decision was made after the press bitterly criticized a trader who praised a company in the financial press and some time later decided to sell this company's stock.

However, the financial press had recently expressed the view that Hamilton's policies on personal trading were not tough enough. Some competitors had even criticized Hamilton's policy of allowing fund managers to trade at all, arguing that it put the traders' interest in conflict with shareholders. Grahams hoped that the two proposed policies would eliminate some of that criticism.

But in fact, the rule and practice had always been to put the interest of the shareholders first. Joe Grahams, like James Wells before him, had always encouraged Hamilton investment managers to manage their personal wealth in the stock market if they desired to do so. Many of the managers who came to Hamilton did so because they had a fascination with the market, and had long invested in securities on their own behalf. A personal portfolio was viewed as a way for them to experiment and try new investment strategies, and gain direct experience in the markets.

As he entered the building and crossed the same lobby that Mr. Wells had crossed twenty years ago, he could not help but think of the immense changes in the business. When he had started, he knew everyone by name. Now there were over 5,000 employees around the world.

The real issue was deciding what policies were needed to protect the franchise as Hamilton continued to grow: policies that would not impose unneeded bureaucracy on an organization devoted to performance, innovation and customer service.

**EXHIBIT 1    Statement of Financial Position—The Eastern Group, Inc.**

| (DOLLARS IN MILLIONS) | SEPT. 30, 1996 | SEPT. 30, 1995 |
|---|---|---|
| ASSETS | | |
| Cash and equivalent | 2,518 | 2,256 |
| Investments | 70,524 | 55,265 |
| Accounts receivable | 38,854 | 34,546 |
| Property, plant, and equipment | 254 | 254 |
| Goodwill, intangibles | 4,527 | 3,854 |
| Other assets | 54,795 | 48,598 |
| TOTAL ASSETS | 171,472 | 144,773 |
| LIABILITIES | | |
| Accounts payable | 48,875 | 37,589 |
| Short-term debt | 8,754 | 7,584 |
| Other liabilities | 75,421 | 64,381 |
| Long term debt | 19,823 | 23,561 |
| TOTAL LIABILITIES | 152,873 | 133,115 |
| STOCKHOLDERS' EQUITY | | |
| Preferred stock | 745 | 745 |
| Common stock | 375 | 375 |
| Additional paid in capital | 10,524 | 5,849 |
| Retained earnings | 12,548 | 7,485 |
| Treasury Stock | (5,847) | (3,385) |
| Other Equity | 254 | 589 |
| TOTAL STOCKHOLDERS' EQUITY | 18,599 | 11,658 |
| TOTAL LIABILITIES AND STOCKHOLDERS' EQUITY | 171,472 | 144,773 |

**EXHIBIT 2    Eastern's Organizational Structure.**

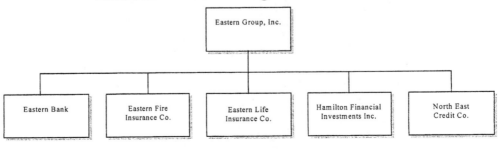

## EXHIBIT 3    Hamilton's Growth and Financial Performance

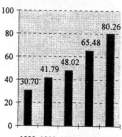

**Assets Under Management**
dollars in billions

22.6% Annual Growth Rate 1996
26.0% Compound Annual Growth Rate
1991-1996

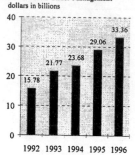

**Retail Assets Under Management**
dollars in billions

14.8% Annual Growth Rate 1996
20.0% Compound Annual Growth Rate
1991-1996

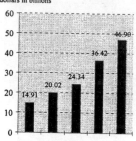

**Institutional Assets Under Management**
dollars in billions

28.8% Annual Growth Rate 1996
31.6% Compound Annual Growth Rate
1991-1996

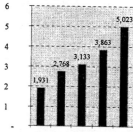

**Total Employees**
in thousands

29.5% Annual Growth Rate 1996
24.8% Compound Annual Growth Rate
1991-1996

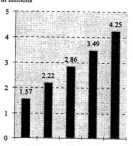

**Mutual Fund Accounts**
in millions

21.7% Annual Growth Rate 1996
28.6% Compound Annual Growth Rate
1991-1996

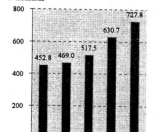

**Brokerage Accounts**
in thousands

15.0% Annual Growth Rate 1996
14.1% Compound Annual Growth Rate
1991-1996

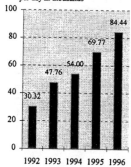

**Telephone Calls**
per day in thousands

21.0% Annual Growth Rate 1996
30.2% Compound Annual Growth Rate
1991-1996

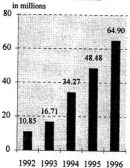

**Mutual Fund Transactions**
in millions

33.9% Annual Growth Rate 1996
53.4% Compound Annual Growth Rate
1991-1996

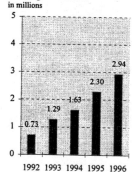

**Brokerage Transactions**
in millions

28.3% Annual Growth Rate 1996
42.4% Compound Annual Growth Rate
1991-1996

**EXHIBIT 4   Consolidated Statement of Financial Condition— Hamilton Financial Investments**

| (DOLLARS IN THOUSANDS) | SEPT. 30, 1996 | SEPT. 30, 1995 |
|---|---|---|
| **ASSETS** | | |
| Cash | 656 | 188 |
| Securities purchased under agreements to resell and cash segregated under regulatory requirements | 483,016 | 334,085 |
| Receivables: | | |
| Due from customers | 523,699 | 437,485 |
| Brokers, dealers and mutual funds | 326,538 | 202,676 |
| Credit card loans | 59,018 | 32,592 |
| Management and investment advisory fees | 34,362 | 34,484 |
| TOTAL RECEIVABLES | 943,617 | 707,237 |
| Invested assets: | | |
| Securities held by broker-dealer subsidiaries, at fair value (cost $69,803 in 1996, $47,382 in 1995) | 60,240 | 40,887 |
| Securities available for sale, at fair value (cost $245,000 in 1996, $239,110 in 1995) | 218,806 | 212,185 |
| Other invested assets, at cost (fair value $11,627 in 1996, $16,614 in 1995) | 9,345 | 11,182 |
| TOTAL INVESTED ASSETS | 288,391 | 264,254 |
| Property and equipment, net | 167,422 | 147,386 |
| Separate account assets, insurance products | 997,145 | 725,347 |
| Other assets | 101,353 | 66,183 |
| TOTAL ASSETS | 2,981,600 | 2,244,680 |
| **LIABILITIES** | | |
| Payable to customers | 815,804 | 628,878 |
| Payable to banks, brokers, dealers and mutual funds | 434,706 | 288,439 |
| Accounts payable and accrued expenses | 182,947 | 160,672 |
| Notes, mortgages and other debt | 117,469 | 111,476 |
| Subordinated debentures | 55,369 | 47,574 |
| Separate account liabilities, insurance products | 996,886 | 724,637 |
| Customer deposits and other liabilities | 69,424 | 49,232 |
| TOTAL LIABILITIES | 2,672,605 | 2,010,908 |
| **STOCKHOLDERS' EQUITY** | | |
| Senior and participating preferred stock: (total liquidating preference amount $267,703 in 1996, $231,779 in 1995) | 82 | 82 |
| Common stock | 63 | 63 |
| Additional paid-in capital | 188,523 | 172,728 |
| Net unrealized appreciation on securities available for sale | 2,910 | 2,022 |
| Retained earnings | 117,417 | 58,877 |
| TOTAL STOCKHOLDERS' EQUITY | 308,995 | 233,772 |
| TOTAL LIABILITIES AND STOCKHOLDERS' EQUITY | 2,981,600 | 2,244,680 |

## EXHIBIT 5    Hamilton's Organizational Structure

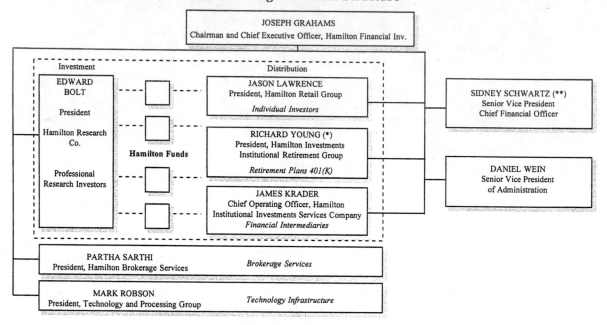

(*)        Dennis McGregor, President of Hamilton Management Trust Company, reports to Richard Young
(**)       Andrea Laura, President of Hamilton Accounting and Custody Services, reports to Sidney Schwartz

## EXHIBIT 6    Hamilton Values

1.  **Employee Respect and Individual Responsibility**
    Our most important asset is our people. We take great pride in hiring the best people available and providing our employees with the resources they need to do their jobs, and an environment where they can learn and grow.

    One of the hallmarks of our management style is individual responsibility. Neither the firm nor any division or subsidiary is managed by a committee.

    Hamilton Investments believes in meritocracy. We reward people who think creatively, take initiative and produce excellent results.

2.  **Quality and Excellence**
    We are committed to providing the highest quality products and services to our customers at all times. This requires listening to and meeting our customers' needs. It also requires careful attention to detail, ongoing analysis and continuous improvement in everything we do.

3.  **Honesty and Integrity**
    Hamilton's business is based on the trust and confidence of our customers. Our reputation is critical to our success. We have a duty to ourselves, our customers and our company to act ethically and honestly in everything we do. This commitment must be met every day by every employee; anything less is unacceptable.

4.  **Teamwork**
    We believe strongly that while individual initiative is important, the greatest success comes when people share ideas and help each other to achieve important business goals.

5.  **Customer Focus**
    Our products and services are consistently driven by total commitment to the needs of our customers.

*Exhibit 6   Continued*

**6. Change and Innovation**

Financial services is a dynamic industry where rapid change is a constant source of challenge and opportunity. We encourage innovation, creativity and flexibility among our people so that we can quickly adapt to changing conditions.

**7. Commitment to Technology**

We value intelligent use of technology because it allows us to innovate, operate more efficiently and improve customer services.

**8. Civic Responsibility**

We are committed to being a good corporate citizen. We allocate a significant portion of our pretax earnings to supporting a wide range of charitable organizations. We also encourage our employees to become involved in community activities that are of interest to them.

## EXHIBIT 7   Schematic of all Positions with Risk Management Responsibilities

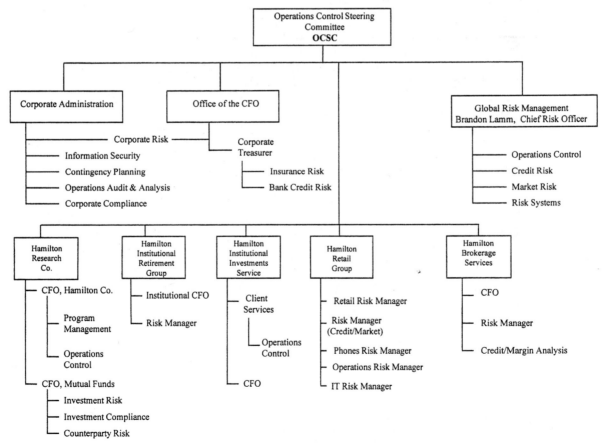

**EXHIBIT 8   Corporate Risk Office: Initiatives and Principles**

### Corporate Risk Office: Key Initiatives

1. Linking performance to incentive compensation.
2. Developing risk measuring and reporting process.
3. Developing risk escalation policies and procedures.
4. Measuring and aggregating counterparty exposures.
5. Establishing best practice frameworks and methodologies.
6. Developing an intranet-based Global Risk MIS.
7. Providing business unit support services.

### Corporate Risk Office
### Guiding Principles for Risk Management

1. Business units are fully responsible and accountable for managing risk, with support from risk professionals providing tools and strategies for effective risk management.
2. We must strive to increase the transparency of risk through measurement and reporting, and communicate exposures through escalation procedures.
3. We should set boundaries to avoid undesirable risk or behavior, as well as limits to manage our risk concentrations.
4. We need to balance our business and control requirements because risk management is a necessary but insufficient requirement for success and survival.
5. Given that we must manage risk on an integrated basis—across different risks, processes, business units, and countries—risk management is everyone's job.

---

### EXHIBIT 9   Guidelines to Establish Personal Risk

---

## Color Code Categories

RED:        Derogatory information that should prevent the extension of an offer of employment, or the continuance of existing employment.

YELLOW:     Derogatory information that may prevent the extension of an offer of employment, or the continuance of existing employment.

GREEN:      Absence of any derogatory information.

## Education Guidelines

Category RED

No attendance at educational facility will be reported as derogatory if attendance is claimed.

Variance in educational major will be reported as derogatory if claimed major is relevant to the position at Hamilton.

Variance in stated degree will be reported as derogatory if materially inaccurate (i.e. B.A. vs. B.S. will not be considered derogatory; B.A. vs M.A. will be considered derogatory).

Degree not awarded will be reported as derogatory if a degree is claimed.

Variance in dates of enrollment which cause a gap of greater than three months (prior 5 years).

Category YELLOW

Variance in educational minor will be reported as derogatory if claimed minor is relevant to the position at Hamilton.

Inability to verify significant information—may appear in any section of the report. All unsuccessful attempts to verify information will be documented in the investigative report. The subject of the investigation and Human Resources will be contacted in order to resolve or explain the situation before this derogatory code is used.

---

## CASE 31　Automation Consulting Services

As they had been doing twice a year for the past six years, the three founding partners of Automation Consulting Services (ACS) convened at Cliff Reed's summer home in Cape Cod in August 1989 to spend a weekend assessing the status of their consulting firm and planning its future. Not surprisingly, they each had come away from their recent tour of ACS' four offices with a long list of questions, concerns, and ideas for change.

Over the years, the semi-annual practice of visiting each office and holding formal meetings with its partners and principals had been an effective way for the three founding partners to identify major problems and new opportunities. This year, however, the three founders sensed that the magnitude of the issues that needed their direct attention had grown out of control. They worried that two days of brainstorming would not be an adequate response to the current challenges of 1989 and those projected for the 1990s.

### Company Background

Clifford Reed, Jack Leland, and Angela Goldberg had founded ACS in 1983 as a technical consulting firm specializing in factory automation for industrial manufacturing firms. ACS advised clients on the development of automation strategy and long-term facilities planning and also provided guidance in the design and implementation of specific automation projects.

From its home base in Boston, ACS had expanded into three additional locations. Offices had been opened in Philadelphia and Detroit in 1985 and 1986, respectively, and ACS had acquired a local partnership in San Jose, California in 1988. By 1989, ACS had a professional staff of 83 consultants and revenues of nearly $26 million. The ACS partnership had tentative plans to open an office in Europe in the near future, with hopes of establishing a client base there before the wave of market changes swept through Europe in 1992.

When Reed, Leland, and Goldberg had first formed their partnership in 1983, demand for automation expertise was growing steadily and their market research indicated that the trend would continue through the 1990s. From the outset, the founders had agreed that revenue growth would be a top priority. They had considered rapid growth an imperative for three main reasons. First, most of their clients and likely prospects were relatively large corporations, often with multiple manufacturing sites; these firms preferred hiring technical consulting firms that could provide the depth and breadth of expertise and geographical coverage to meet all their automation needs. Second, the founders wanted to establish as many client relationships as possible while the market was still young and fragmented in an attempt to build client exit barriers. Third, without a high growth rate, the partnership would not be able to attract, motivate, and retain ambitious junior consultants with the promise of a fast-paced promotion policy and potentially rapid career development. As of the summer of 1989, ACS management had surpassed its aggressive growth goals by doubling revenues in each year of operation, and its founders had no plans to let up the pressure for growth in the near future.

*Hilary A. Weston prepared this case under the supervision of Professor Robert Simons as the basis for class discussion rather than to illustrate either effective or ineffective handling of an administrative situation.*

ACS' phenomenal success was attributable, in part, to the mix of talent and experience embodied in its founders. Cliff Reed was a 10-year veteran engineer from a "Big Three" auto manufacturer, where he had specialized in factory automation. Jack Leland, also an engineer, was a graduate of MIT with eight years of practical experience in manufacturing operations at a high-tech firm before founding ACS. Angela Goldberg was a Harvard MBA, with ten years of experience marketing computers and related equipment to industrial clients.

The three founders—who constituted the Executive Committee—were the only partners with firm-wide responsibilities; all other partners focused only on their own offices. Each of the four offices was headed by a managing partner who was responsible for his or her office's revenues, recruiting efforts, staffing, and client development. The offices varied substantially in size. Each office had 3 to 6 partners as well as from 8 to 31 non-partner professionals. (See **Exhibit 1** for an organizational chart.)

In keeping with the Executive Committee's emphasis on revenue growth, each office was managed as a revenue center, with the partnership as a whole treated as the sole profit center. Each partner's compensation consisted of a share of the firm's total profits in proportion to his share of total revenue generation. (The founders and other managing partners received an additional bonus tied to firm-wide and office-specific revenue growth, respectively.) Expenses were accumulated and monitored on a consolidated firm-wide basis. In addition, each ACS office monitored total hours billed and billability[1] as proxies for office profitability. Revenues, billability, and other performance measures for 1988 are reported, by office, in **Exhibit 2**.

## August 1989: The Executive Committee Retreat

Cliff, Jack, and Angela had not prepared a formal agenda in advance of their two-day retreat. Instead, they began as they had in the past: by discussing their thoughts and concerns, one office at a time, based on their recent tour as well as their individual interactions with the consultants of each office. During this discussion, they kept a running list of priority problems and opportunities, which would serve as the agenda for the second day of their retreat. The following sections highlight the major issues raised on Saturday, August 19.

**The San Jose Office**   The Executive Committee was particularly concerned with the operations of the San Jose office, because it was the only office they had acquired rather than built and molded themselves. The acquisition had been completed less than a year ago. Consequently, the combining of management styles, practices, and personalities was still sorting itself out. To date, all three partners were generally pleased with the acquired staff's skills, experience, and performance.

A recent incident, however, seemed cause for concern. Angela had discovered that one of the San Jose partners, Douglas Crowley, had employed a client billing practice of which she did not approve. Crowley had just completed a project for Powerhouse Inc., a client that needed help in expanding and automating its production capabilities. The project had involved space and equipment planning, mechanical and electrical machine design, and the development of a master plan for increasing production. As was common in ACS' work, Crowley's original proposal and the subsequent contract had stated a price range for the job with a guaranteed price ceiling, rather than a fixed price. As with all clients, Crowley billed

---

[1] Billability refers to the percentage of the professional staff's compensated working time that is charged out to clients—i.e., time that is spent on revenue-generating activities.

Powerhouse monthly. Angela was outraged, however, when she learned from a principal on the project that Crowley had boosted his final bill to Powerhouse to "subsidize" another job that was running over budget.

The principal who informed Angela apparently did not consider Crowley's action a problem. In fact, before seeing Angela's reaction, he told her that "cross-subsidizing" occurred regularly, with Managing Partner Kyle Ross' approval, whenever the costs of a particular job were significantly below the contract price ceiling. "As long as a client's total bill is below the ceiling," the principal claimed, "no one was exploited by cross-subsidizing, and ACS met its revenue target." Angela saw things differently. She wanted to fire Crowley and any others who had engaged in cross-subsidizing. She was particularly angry because Powerhouse, the overcharged client, was a subsidiary of one of her oldest Boston-based clients.

Cliff and Jack agreed with Angela that Crowley's action was clearly not in line with their objective of building long-term client relationships. The founders, however, had never articulated guidelines for partners, in terms of either general business conduct or selling and billing practices. Every partner managed his clients according to his own style and strategy and that of his managing partner. The Executive Committee had never before encountered a major conflict for two reasons: first, at least one of the three founders had been on the team of most of the projects, particularly in the early years; and second, nearly all of the partners except for the three in San Jose had risen through the ACS ranks, and tended to share the same billing practices and client philosophy used by the founders.

The three realized that some type of explicit action or directive might be needed in order to prevent future departures from what they deemed acceptable billing practices. They did not, however, want to overreact and kill the entrepreneurial spirit that had allowed the firm to flourish. An aggressive managing partner like Kyle Ross was the key to ACS' revenue growth. The unwritten rule at ACS had always been local autonomy. The founders believed that this made good business sense, and their managing partners had come to expect substantial independence.

As a result of the California incident, however, Reed, Leland, and Goldberg now questioned the merit of their hands-off management style and wondered what sort of guidance they should provide for the partners and how they should communicate and enforce new policies. They worried that any action that appeared too authoritative could threaten the good working relationships they had with all of the partners. Failure to provide some guidance, however, might expose the firm to serious risks as their operations expanded both in size and geographic reach. In addition to devising appropriate preventive measures, the founders had to decide what, if any, disciplinary action to take with the San Jose consultants directly and indirectly involved in cross-subsidizing. Finally, they also had to decide whether to reveal the billing error to Powerhouse (and other mischarged clients) and whether to return to them a portion of their fees. In principle, all three partners felt they should return the fees, but they did not yet know how many dollars would be involved and they were not sure what explanation to provide to the clients.

**The Detroit Office**    The Detroit office was on the verge of an unforeseen crisis. Within two months, fifty percent of its current client work would be completed and almost no new projects were definitively lined up to fill the void. Nearly half of the office's professional staff would have no billable work. Meanwhile, revenues, profits, and cash flow would dwindle.

ACS had never before faced such a situation because demand for their services had always exceeded supply. The Detroit office relied on a small number of large clients and lacked the client breadth that had developed at the larger, older offices. Instead of compensating for this vulnerability with a business development plan, the Detroit partners had been focusing their attention almost exclusively on three very large existing projects. Two of the three were scheduled to end in the fall of 1989. The anticipated "Phase Two's" had not materialized on either project.

While in the Detroit office the previous week, the Executive Committee had launched a three-point crisis plan: (1) They made arrangements for several Detroit consultants to be assigned temporarily to projects based at the other three offices; (2) they designed a marketing plan to solicit work from existing and new clients; and (3) they transferred a partner with particularly strong selling skills from Boston to Detroit.

The Executive Committee realized that their crisis plan was merely a band-aid. They discussed the client prospecting system that they had tried to install two years earlier. The system, which Angela had heard about from a business school friend in a large consulting firm, was designed to monitor prospecting activity and the probable volume of upcoming work. The system worked as follows:

> Each managing partner would use a chart to keep track of the staffing requirements of all existing and prospective projects. A six-month time line, starting with the current week, would run across the top. Down the left side the partner would list projects grouped into four categories: Ongoing, Sold-but-not-Started, Submitted Proposals, and Prospects. He would then fill in the boxes with the number of junior and senior consultants each project demanded or would demand per week and then sum each column. For bids not yet won, the managing partner would calculate expected staff utilization by applying to each contract an estimated percentage probability of winning it. He could then monitor total projected utilization for each week on the chart and use the chart to run weekly staffing meetings with the other partners. The chart would allow staff meetings to focus on how to hit a particular billability target and where the pressure points were for new client work. The chart could also provide useful information to top management on the activity at individual offices.

In 1987, when the founders had explained the monitoring system to the rest of the partnership, most of the partners had strongly opposed its adoption. The managing partners, whose acceptance was critical, were particularly negative. They had considered the proposed system a time-consuming, bureaucratic activity that would intrude on their freedom to manage their offices autonomously. They had persuaded the founders to abandon the idea based on two arguments:

1. We have always been a decentralized partnership, in our philosophy and in our practices, and there is no evidence in our financial performance that the current arrangements are inadequate; and

2. There is no need for a detailed monitoring system to manage billability levels since we already have the right financial incentive in place for all partners. Managing partners worry about prospecting and billability daily—as do all partners—because the size of their paychecks depends on their annual revenue contribution.

The three founders now discussed how best to revisit the issue with the entire partnership:

Cliff:   This Detroit problem has convinced me that our financial incentives alone are not a fool-proof way to control billability.

Jack:    I agree. But you know that some partners will say the incentive system is just fine, as long as partners apply good judgment. Some of them will point the finger at Margolies [Detroit managing partner] and say he screwed up *despite* the incentive system.

Angela:  Let's try to put aside the issue of blame for now. We need to install some preventative measures so this doesn't happen again. We have to persuade the managing partners to adopt some sort of monitoring system. We may have to agree to let them run it on a decentralized basis to get their cooperation.

Cliff:   But I think the system has to be centralized. Those staffing charts would provide extremely useful information to the three of us. We need to know what sort of prospecting activity is occurring at each office to help us with resource planning for the whole firm. Where should our next office be? What skills should we be recruiting? What sorts of bids are we losing out on? What are our competitors doing? A centralized view of the prospecting charts would also help us to better serve our large multi-site clients—the ones we work with, or could work with, out of more than one office.

Jack:    You're right. But in my opinion, a more basic reason to insist that some form of the reports reaches our desks is that if we don't insist, we have no way of ensuring that everyone is adhering to the system and updating their forecasts on a regular basis.

The discussion then focused on problems of implementation. All three wondered where to begin and how to get the partners to use it. How sophisticated should the tracking system be? Should the system be maintained by partners or should new staff specialists be hired to implement and run the system? How frequently should it be updated? How often should reports be sent to the Executive Committee? Finally, the discussion returned to whether centralized monitoring would really be necessary as long as they had good managers using the data in each office.

**Boston**   Like the two offices discussed above, the Boston office was also confronted by a dilemma that the Executive Committee believed could become a company wide concern. Alan Shapiro, a Boston partner, had recently won a bid to oversee the automation of a university library cataloging and ordering system. ACS had never before served a client in a non-manufacturing business, and one month into the project, ACS' inexperience was revealing itself. Not only was the project running over budget and behind schedule (that had happened before), but it looked like the project team would have to bring in an outside specialist in database management to complete the work promised to the client. ACS had never before "subcontracted" work.

When the proposal for the job had initially been prepared, Angela and Cliff, who jointly managed the Boston office, had been wary about ACS' ability to meet the prospective client's needs. They had decided, however, to let Shapiro make the decision himself as to whether to bid for the job.

Angela identified two issues that the founders had to address—apart from dealing with the specific project. In her words, "First, we must figure out how to guide the firm's strategic direction and expertise so that we are not working on an ad hoc basis, relying on individual partners' decisions to bid for one-time projects. And second, if we are to articulate a strategic direction for the firm, we must determine what it should be with respect to manufacturing versus service sector clients. The service sector is growing rapidly and dramatically increasing its use of technology. But the most effective way to employ the firm's existing skill base—given the sorts of people we have already hired and developed—is to focus on manufacturing."

In addressing the strategy-setting process, Jack commented, "The three of us have always considered ACS to be a consulting firm exclusively for manufacturers, and I think that we have assumed that the partnership both understands and agrees with this focus. Maybe we've been lucky that the firm has maintained its strategic focus as long as it has. It's time we bring the whole partnership together to discuss and draft a long-term plan. The partnership should develop a set of criteria that defines our strategic focus and then each partner would be required to use the criteria as a check list in determining whether a prospective job fit within our core business. If it doesn't, he walks away from the project."

Cliff and Angela agreed with Jack that it was time to think about a longer term strategy and put it down on paper, but they were wary about getting into formal planning and strategic checklists. Cliff also worried, "What if we cannot reach consensus, or if we do not agree with the general consensus among the rest of the partnership? A discussion among all partners could be very time-consuming, especially if we feel our strategy should be reviewed annually. I wonder if this decision as to our future strategy isn't a call we should make ourselves and then just communicate to the other partners?"

**Philadelphia**   Jack Leland, who managed the Philadelphia office, sensed a problem at his office that he suspected ran through the whole firm. He was concerned that the focus on revenues, at the exclusion of expenses, had allowed various expense categories at the office level to creep up and get out of control. (See **Exhibit 3** for firm-wide income statement.)

Jack explained his concern:

> As revenue centers, the offices are not given explicit line-by-line budgets for expenses. So, although the managing partners are given overall expense budgets, they do not really worry about the level of specific expense categories. The number of dollars being spent on recruiting events, office equipment, training, and other "supporting" activities has been creeping up, but we don't have the detailed expense information to react. The limited itemization of costs on the P&L may have been adequate a few years ago, but now there are a lot more things buried in that 15% to 20% called "Other Expenses" that we ought to be monitoring.

The founders discussed the ramifications of converting each office to a profit center so that partners would have incentives to manage costs more closely. Despite the benefits of greater control over costs and profitability, they had concerns about converting ACS offices to profit centers. First, there were the challenges of implementation. They would have to negotiate profit targets with each managing partner. Would the local partners resent this interference with the way they ran their practices? And how much time would the process take?

The switch to office profit centers would also require changes in their incentive plan, which currently rewarded partners based primarily on firm-wide growth and profitability rather than office-specific profits. With compensation tied solely to individual office performance, would partners still be motivated to help other offices and maintain a unified, firm-wide image?

Lastly, as Cliff noted, "It is somewhat of a Catch-22. On the one hand, we don't want to send out new signals that conflict with our basic goal of revenue growth; but on the other hand, as our growth rate inevitably slows down, cost control becomes increasingly important. It will become more difficult to absorb cost increases."

**Day One Wrap-Up**   On Saturday evening, the three founders spent an hour reviewing their notes and jointly summarizing the major issues raised during the day's discussions. Sunday would be spent attempting to develop solutions for these issues. **Exhibit 4** reproduces the outline they developed Saturday evening.

**EXHIBIT 1 Automation Consulting Services**

ACS ORGANIZATION CHART — AS OF JUNE 1989

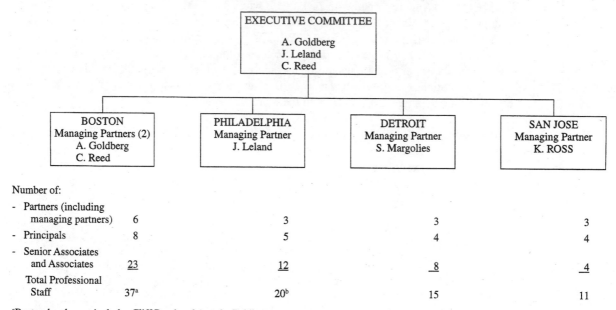

| Number of: | | | | |
|---|---|---|---|---|
| - Partners (including managing partners) | 6 | 3 | 3 | 3 |
| - Principals | 8 | 5 | 4 | 4 |
| - Senior Associates and Associates | 23 | 12 | 8 | 4 |
| Total Professional Staff | 37[a] | 20[b] | 15 | 11 |

[a]Boston headcount includes Cliff Reed and Angela Goldberg.
[b]Philadelphia headcount includes Jack Leland.

**EXHIBIT 2 Automation Consulting Services**

FY 1988: Summary Statistics — By Office

| | BOSTON | PHILADELPHIA | DETROIT | SAN JOSE |
|---|---|---|---|---|
| Revenues | $11,510,560 | $6,240,910 | $4,301,100 | $3,708,000 |
| Billability[a] (annual average) | 80% | 78% | 91% | 82% |
| No. of projects completed during FY | 52 | 24 | 8 | 15 |
| No. of clients served during FY | 29 | 12 | 5 | 11 |

[a] *Billability = (Professional hours billed to clients) ÷ (Total available professional work hours).*

**EXHIBIT 3   Automation Consulting Services**

Fiscal Year 1988: Summary Profit and Loss Statement

| | BOSTON | | PHILADELPHIA | | DETROIT | | SAN JOSE | | TOTAL |
|---|---|---|---|---|---|---|---|---|---|
| Revenues: | $11,510,560 | | $6,240,910 | | $4,301,100 | | $3,708,000 | | $25,760,570 |
| Expenses: | | | | | | | | | |
| Salary and benefits[a] | 3,856,038 | 50% | 2,437,075 | 55% | 1,539,394 | 57% | 1,394,950 | 57% | 9,227,457 |
| Rent and utilities[b] | 1,156,811 | 15 | 443,105 | 10 | 270,069 | 10 | 318,146 | 13 | 2,188,131 |
| Supplies and equipment[c] | 1,311,053 | 17 | 708,967 | 16 | 513,131 | 19 | 391,565 | 16 | 2,924,716 |
| Other[d] | 1,388,174 | 18 | 841,899 | 19 | 378,097 | 14 | 342,169 | 14 | 2,950,789 |
| Total | $7,712,075 | 100% | $4,431,046 | 100% | $2,700,691 | 100% | $2,447,280 | 100% | $17,291,092 |
| Income (pretax) | $3,798,485 | | $1,809,864 | | $1,600,409 | | $1,260,720 | | $8,469,478 |
| Profit Margin (pretax) | 33% | | 29% | | 37% | | 34% | | 33% |

[a] Includes salary, wages, and all benefits of professional and nonexempt staff; excludes distribution of profits to partners
[b] Includes office space, heat and electricity, and telecommunications
[c] Includes stationary, office supplies, computers and leased copiers
[d] Includes graphics services, temp employees, travel and entertainment, subscriptions, on-line databases, library, recruiting support, training materials, and miscellaneous

715

**EXHIBIT 4   Executive Committee Retreat**

**AUTOMATION CONSULTING SERVICES**
AUGUST 19, 1989
**DAY ONE SUMMARY—Prepared by Cliff Reed**

- As our firm's size and experience base continue to grow, the set of opportunities that we can pursue grows exponentially. We need more formal management systems and procedures throughout the practice in order to:

  1) Identify and maintain a unified company strategy and image
  2) Maintain a high and profitable growth rate
  3) Communicate goals and responsibilities to employees
  4) Effectively motivate and monitor performance
  5) Facilitate the sharing of knowledge and ideas among offices

- The executive committee and active partners already have more than enough responsibilities. We must find a way to limit the amount of time that we devote to new management systems and procedures.

- A spirit of entrepreneurship and creativity is our strength and we must maintain that spirit in the future.

- Any new management systems must be consistent with the firm's culture and overall strategy in the signals they send to our employees.

## CASE 32  Becton Dickinson—Designing the New Strategic, Operational, and Financial Planning Process

I n July 1996, Clateo Castellini, chief executive officer of Becton Dickinson, reflected on this year's planning process and reiterated his philosophy:

> Business strategies should be developed and implemented at the business level. The objective of the Strategic, Financial and Operational process is to provide business managers with the criteria to decide how to craft their strategy and how to allocate their resources. It needs to reinforce our strategy of decentralization and top line growth.

The origins of Becton Dickinson's (BD's) strategic planning system could be traced back to 1975, when previous CEO Ray Gilmartin (who left BD in 1994 to become CEO of Merck) introduced a sophisticated planning system to exert tighter control over the strategic direction of the company. The planning system required a strategic profile of each business unit including a clear definition of product markets, analysis of the unit's current competitive position in the industry and a projection of future competitive position under a series of tactical alternatives. This system grew into the Strategic, Operational and Financial, or "SOF," process. Over time, it became a key process to move information up to corporate-level managers where decisions were made. The paperwork evolved to be more detailed and elaborate and, by 1994, when Castellini took charge, the SOF process was deeply embedded in BD's culture.

For two decades, the SOF process had been revised continually to reflect changes in management structure and philosophy. For the 1996 cycle, a new process was established that helped fit the company's new strategy and organization. As before there were both strengths and problems with this new process.

To support his vision and management philosophy, Clateo wanted a fundamental redesign of the SOF process. This would prove to be a difficult task—but critical if Castellini was to change the culture of the company. A blank design template (**Exhibit 8**) is provided for the reader to sketch out a new planning process.

### Background

Becton Dickinson had its roots in a 1897 partnership between Maxwell W. Becton and Farleigh Dickinson to manufacture clinical thermometers. The company's growth through the next 70 years was fueled by the acquisition of other medical supply companies and aggressive efforts to develop and market innovative products.

During the 1980s, top management decided to focus attention on health care and divested all non-healthcare businesses. After restructuring the company, BD's management directed its efforts at making a transition from a more mature U.S. medical supply company to a higher growth global medical technology company. The company's strategy for

*Professor Robert L. Simons, Doctoral Candidate Antonio Dávila and Research Associate Afroze A. Mohammed prepared this case as the basis for class discussion rather than to illustrate either effective or ineffective handling of an administrative situation.*

accomplishing this transition was to introduce differentiated products and devote particular attention to the potential of international markets.

By 1995, BD sales were $2,712 million, 47% coming from outside the U.S. The company produced a broad range of medical products and diagnostic systems for use by health care professionals, medical research institutions, and the general public. **Exhibit 1** presents recent BD financial data, subdivided by geographic and business areas.

**Evolution of Organizational Structure**    The company historically had been U.S. oriented with an international manager overseeing businesses outside the U.S. (even in the early 1990s, international operations were still at times referred as "ex-U.S.") Traditionally, country managers were responsible for sales and marketing efforts in their countries and were compensated for achieving yearly sales and profit targets. They made key decisions, such as whether to introduce particular products in their countries. While manufacturing for most products was done in the United States, BD also manufactured products in Europe, Mexico, Brazil, and Japan with these factories reporting to the appropriate country manager.

In the early 1980s, growth opportunities in Europe and a desire to build a global business convinced top management that the company could no longer allow country managers to make product marketing choices (e.g. a country manager might resist introducing a new product if launch costs would lead to lower country profits). There was also concern about uneven quality and cost standards in European plants. Accordingly, a new structure defined Strategic Business Units (SBUs) across Europe; as a result, the role of country managers in product strategy decisions was diminished. While top management viewed the new organizational structure as beneficial, tensions between European SBU presidents and country managers persisted. Some people believed that, with the new structure, BD was running the risk of weakening its country management capabilities around the world as product line authority was strengthened. There was also concern that worldwide product divisions—headquartered in the United States—would simply reinforce the U.S. view, rather than promoting a global perspective.

By 1993, the organizational structure of the company was built on the foundations of the restructuring of the 1980s. The company was broadly divided into two sectors—Medical Products and Diagnostic Products. The Medical sector encompassed products including hypodermic supplies (syringes and needles), diabetes care products, intravenous catheters, and surgical supplies. The Diagnostic sector produced sophisticated systems for diagnosis of diseases, including instruments for monitoring the health status of patients and devices that identified and tested for organisms causing infectious diseases.

Each sector was headed by a sector president who was responsible for key decisions affecting the U.S., European, Asia-Pacific, and Latin American divisions that comprised the sector. **Exhibit 2** illustrates BD's organizational structure for one sector. Each division had profit and loss (P&L) responsibility and reported financial results directly to the relevant sector president.

In 1994, the company was reorganized into four sectors. The role of the sector president remained pivotal in key decision processes affecting sector divisions and businesses.

**Introduction of Worldwide Teams**    In the mid 1980s, in conjunction with the organization by SBUs and sectors, BD's top managers wanted to achieve greater worldwide coordination. They adopted the concept of transnational management. Under this approach, emphasis was placed on achieving both local responsiveness and global integration. Transnational management stressed the importance of developing new processes and ways of thinking about a company's global business, rather than adopting particular organizational structures. The transnational company would be flexible in organizational form, depending on the needs of the business:

> Some decisions will tend to be made on a global basis, often at the corporate center (most often research priorities and financing decisions, for example); others will be the appropriate responsibility of local management (typically sales and service tasks and labor relations, for instance). But for some issues, multiple perspective are important and shared responsibility is necessary.[1]

To implement the transnational concept, *worldwide teams* were overlaid on BD's existing SBU and sector structure. These teams, formed around the company's major product lines, were led typically by the relevant U.S. divisional president and included the U.S. functional heads for marketing, manufacturing and R&D, key representatives from each of the overseas regions, and the European SBU presidents.

Teams, which met quarterly, were responsible for formulating global business strategy on important issues, including priorities in R&D, manufacturing strategy, capacity and equipment plans, and new product development strategies. The teams were intended to balance global and local needs and provide a mechanism for negotiation and coordination. They did not have P&L responsibility (to avoid giving team leaders, who were typically U.S. division heads, too much power vis-à-vis overseas SBU managers).

Some worldwide teams were sufficiently effective to develop successful new products. Managers reported that these forums encouraged them to think more broadly and also to appreciate the perspectives of different regions and functions. Notwithstanding the important role played by the teams, there were problems with their implementation. First, the worldwide team leaders did not have formal authority over all team members. Second, although the teams had the responsibility for setting worldwide product strategy, they had no direct authority over budgets in the participants' organizations. Finally, while the worldwide teams planned global strategies, implementation depended on divisions whose managers were disciplined by budgets that were developed on a regional or business-unit basis.

Moreover, the commitment to worldwide teams varied greatly across segments of the business. Some of BD's international managers found themselves sitting on several teams, which required a significant amount of time to participate effectively in the activities of each worldwide team. While some teams held regular quarterly meetings and were considered productive forums for problem solving, other teams met rarely.

**Organizational Redesign: 1995**  In 1995, Clateo Castellini introduced a new structure to transform the culture of the company to make it more participative, entrepreneurial, open and self-adaptive. He believed that the existing centralized structure, where too many decisions were made at corporate and sector, had to be replaced by a more decentralized approach where the businesses determined their own strategies and management practices. The four sectors, each with a president at Corporate, were eliminated. No longer would businesses be grouped into sectors. All decisions and resource allocations were to be made at the business level. The sector presidents were re-named senior vice presidents and their responsibilities changed to a mix of businesses and corporate staff departments.

---

[1] Christopher Bartlett and Sumantra Ghoshal, *Managing Across Borders* (Boston: Harvard Business School Press, 1989), p. 208.

Castellini wanted the worldwide business to be the primary vehicle for planning and accountability. Accordingly, the company was organized around five businesses that mirrored BD's major product lines (**Exhibit 3**). Worldwide divisions would now have P&L responsibility. Regions would have sales targets, but the worldwide business teams would be the primary players in crafting strategy.

The role of corporate would be changed. Instead of making key strategy decisions, corporate would provide guiding values and direction to the divisions and ensure cooperation among businesses. Corporate would exist to give the expertise required by businesses to implement the overall direction of the company: corporate staff groups would continue to be responsible for technology planning, business development and strategic planning, interdivisional projects, finance and human resources.

Castellini believed that this new structure would unlock efficiencies to increase sales growth and asset productivity. To further encourage growth, the company began promoting stock ownership programs among BD employees. Clateo also spelled out the characteristics of the kind of company he thought BD needed to become to succeed in a rapidly changing health care industry (see **Exhibit 4**). Finally, Castellini formed six design teams, each led by a top manager, to address the major areas requiring a significant redesign (see **Exhibit 5**).

## Overview of the Old SOF Process: 1975–1993

This section of the case describes the SOF process as it was designed and implemented through 1993 (prior to Castellini taking charge and the subsequent elimination of sectors in favor of worldwide divisions).

The SOF process had, in the past, three primary objectives: (1) strategy review and approval, (2) multi-year financial expectations, and (3) one-year budget development and finalization. It specified a series of dates by which designated strategic issues and financial information were to be analyzed and presented in a "SOF book" for review by sector and corporate management. Top management regarded the strategy development component of the process as a comprehensive means of helping managers identify key strategic choices. Budgets submitted as part of the SOF formed the basis for the company's measurement of operational performance, which was a major determinant of managerial bonus compensation.

Historically, two interlocking sets of SOFs were prepared simultaneously each year by (1) business units, divisions, and regions with responsibility for financial performance; and (2) worldwide teams, with responsibility for setting global strategies for particular product lines. For fiscal year 1993, 31 business units and 17 worldwide teams prepared SOF books.

Business unit and worldwide SOF's had different emphases: *business units* presented information (1) by business, within the U.S., and (2) by geographic area, across businesses, in other regions of the world. In contrast, the SOF prepared by *worldwide teams* analyzed strategic and financial information for a particular business in all parts of the world.

**Structure of the SOF Process**   The SOF process required detailed analysis and presentation of a business unit or worldwide team's competitive situation and strategic response. A typical SOF included the following information:

- Customer analysis and segmentation
- Environmental analysis
- Competitive positioning/industry maturity
- Business strategy
- Marketing, manufacturing, and technology strategies
- Human resource summary
- Risk assessment

**Exhibit 6** outlines the strategic information to be presented in a typical SOF, as delineated by BD's corporate planning department. The SOF also included a section on financial information which differed from business units and worldwide teams. *Business units* submitted profit and loss (P&L) estimates for the next three years, which included data on sales, gross profit, expenses (including research and development, administration, selling) and operating income before taxes. They also submitted detailed budgets for the coming year. These budgets contained quarterly income statements for each SBU, balance sheets, and detailed information on revenue sources, capital expenditures for specific projects, plant productivity, and R&D expenses by project. Division/region presidents were accountable for the financial performance of their business units, as specified in the SOF budget.

*Worldwide teams* had little direct control over financial performance (for which they were not held accountable) and therefore reported much less detailed financial data. The worldwide SOF included an income statement and information on return on net operating assets (RONA). These summary data were gathered across the divisions and regions represented by the team and on a yearly basis.

**Planning Calendar (SOF process)—December to April**   Becton Dickinson's fiscal year extended from October 1 to September 30. The SOF process began in December of the previous year (**Exhibit 7** illustrates the SOF calendar). By February 1, each *business unit* had to submit to sector an estimate of the P&L for the coming year as well as for the following two years. After reviewing these "financial trends", sector presidents gave informal feedback to each business unit as to whether the plan was acceptable.

*Worldwide teams* met in the period January and February to prepare their SOF's. Strategic plans were presented to sector presidents in March.

During March and April, *sector presidents* combined the information submitted to them by business units and worldwide teams to create the overall sector strategy and three-year financial performance expectations. Sector SOF's were then reviewed by the *Strategic Review Committee,* comprising BD's top 15 executives and corporate officers. The *Strategic Management Committee* (SMC), a subset of the SRC, analyzed whether spending was aligned with BD's major strategic initiatives. The *Technology Management Committee* also met in April to review sector strategies and proposed R&D programs.

The April meeting of corporate executives was key in the strategy development. The resource allocation decisions made during the meeting dictated not only the constraints of next year's budget, but also the strategy that businesses could follow. Corporate managers did not see these decisions as constraining business' strategies, but as an opportunity for divisions to prioritize initiatives. Usually, the resource allocation was dependent on the business performance during the current year.

At the end of this first round of interactions between the businesses and top management, each sector and business unit had a clear idea of the company's expectation about financial performance, and received a line-by-line revision to the income statement submitted in February.

**April to September**   Detailed budgets, including plant specific data, were prepared by the business units during April and submitted in May. In June and July, meetings were scheduled with sector presidents to review the proposed budgets.

Intense negotiations between divisional and sector management formed the basis for financial expectations to be incorporated in the July budgets. Divisional staff referred to these meetings as "going to battle". Sector would ask for major expense cuts (e.g. R&D), and business units would argue that their ability to produce "top-line" growth and implement the strategy presented in the SOF document would be seriously jeopardized.

By July, each business unit submitted a SOF document including a complete budget for the upcoming year. The Strategic Review Committee (SRC) met again in August for three days to review the budget submissions and consider the overall financial outlook for the company. Each operating business was reviewed in detail. Based on financial projections for the company as a whole, divisions were given feedback about their actual resource allocations and expected financial performance: this corporate direction was then used to modify budgets.

To the frustration of both divisions and the SRC, cuts in spending were often made at this time. As a result, another iteration was required by the divisions and corporate staff groups in September before the consolidated budget was finalized. The final budget was typically much lower than the initial expectations submitted seven months earlier.

**Performance During the Year**   Budgets were reforecast in December, March, June, and September. Reforecasts were taken seriously by top management and provided a method for the company to have an early estimate of what the year's actual results would be. Reforecasts would then be used to implement measures to correct problems early in the year. Reforecasts did not change agreed budget goals or compensation criteria. Quarterly reforecasts were also used by top sector management to determine performance expectations for the coming fiscal year which were reflected in the new SOF that was being concurrently designed for the upcoming fiscal year. Consequently, some divisions tried to "lowball" the December reforecast with a somewhat pessimistic outlook.

Business units were required to submit actual financial results on a monthly basis to their sector president. These monthly submissions were used to communicate financial results and expectations to the investment community. Business unit managers included extensive comments on the variance between actual, budgeted, and expected results and year-to-year comparisons.

Financial data for strategy centers all over the world were available on a quarterly basis. Only at this point in time could worldwide teams review their performance. Some worldwide teams paid close attention to the financial results of the team and requested team members to submit more detailed information (such as product line sales and profit data) than that provided by the sector controller. In other worldwide teams, however, financial results were not followed closely.

**Incentive Compensation**   BD's incentive compensation for top managers relied heavily on achieving budget goals. For division presidents, achieving targets for operating income before tax (OIBT) was a major determinant of bonus compensation. In addition, top management evaluated the impact of strategies adopted during the year on each business unit's competitive position and organizational effectiveness. Finally, incentive compensation was based on senior management's assessment of the performance of individual division heads. This assessment considered issues such as leadership, judgment, level of effort, and ability to respond to unforeseen events.

The incentive compensation for division presidents before the 1996 reorganization was as follows:

25% sector results (65% operating income before tax vs. budget; 35% strategic goals),

50% business units results (100% operating income before tax vs. budget), and

25% strategic objectives of worldwide teams.

With the reorganization (i.e. elimination of sectors and primary focus on five worldwide divisions), the incentive system was redesigned as follows:

33% worldwide divisions' financial results (measured as the change from previous year's actual results),

33% corporate results (also change from previous year), and

33% achievement of strategic objectives.

**SOF Problems**   The SOF process had been evolving for over 20 years. But both operating and corporate managers perceived several problems in the process:

- It fostered a "command and control" environment between corporate and business units, rather than an open communication regarding the future of the business.
- Too much attention was devoted to developing overarching strategies rather than to the issues and tactics that should be the basis for discussion between corporate and operating managers.
- It encouraged counter-productive negotiation between corporate and business managers. Operating managers felt that corporate executives encouraged optimistic assessments during the strategy formulation process that were later scaled back during the budgeting process.
- Final budgets were cut in September after strategies were approved, yet strategies were not revised to reflect reduced resources available.
- The financial section tended to receive more attention than strategy formulation.
- The process was too detailed and bureaucratic, and the planning cycle was too long and time consuming.
- Approximately two-thirds of the operating units missed their budgeted financial goals each year.

**1996 Design Changes**   In response to these concerns, Jack Fuchs, newly-appointed director of planning, attempted to streamline the SOF process. His goal was to empower the world wide business leaders to take more ownership of the strategy and direction of their businesses.

The first set of changes eliminated the required planning frameworks (e.g., the 5-Forces analysis) and supporting documentation required in the SOF. This change was designed to allow more freedom in the way that business managers analyzed and communicated major strategic issues. The second change was eliminating the communication from corporate to business managers specifying performance expectations for the upcoming planning period. By eliminating this step, it was believed that managers could focus on year-on-year improvement, rather than reacting to an artificial budget goal. Finally, the preliminary (July) and final (September) budget submissions were rolled into one September submission.

Although perceived as a step in the right direction, new problems resulted. First, BD managers and staff were used to working with a detailed highly specified planning process. As a result, businesses and regions suffered from lack of consistent planning approaches and poorly coordinated country, functional, and regional support plans. Also, the roll-up of submitted budgets in September fell significantly short of company goals.

**The Challenge for Jack Fuchs** Clateo Castellini wanted the SOF process redesigned to meet the needs of the new corporate philosophy and strategy. Clateo Castellini created a team, headed by Ed Ludwig, CFO and Senior Vice-President of Finance, to evaluate the process. Working with Jack Fuchs the team enumerated the following "Key Design Principles":

### Key Design Principles

- The planning system should serve *all* "constituents":
  WW Businesses
  Regions and Countries
  Corporate and Executive Committee
  Functions
- Effective planning needs to occur at all levels but be integrated across the enterprise.
- The planning system should provide some *standardized elements (context/timing)* but only that detail required to carry out the task of a particular unit/level.
- Operational control and implementation should be managed at the *lowest possible level.*
- Higher levels of organization should focus more on *integration, portfolio, management, and enterprise planning and measurements.*

In addition, Clateo Castellini had his own objectives that the new SOF process should meet. These were:

- Empower and reduce command and control.
- WW business teams should drive the planning process; (country coordinating plans were necessary as well).
- Plans should be completed at lowest level of control.
- Supply minimum information necessary at levels of organization.
- Planning should emphasize initiatives leading to top-line growth.
- Planning should include non financial (but measurable) goals/initiatives.
- Facilitate ongoing dialog among businesses, Executive Committee, Corporate functions, geographic.

Jack was acutely aware that BD had a unique culture that was reflected in its planning process. Even if it was a time consuming and sometimes tedious process, people at BD were used to devoting time to think about the future and consider the positioning of the company in the market.

Jack knew that the principles articulated by the design team and Clateo Castellini required a major redesign of the SOF process. But it would be a difficult task. He started with a blank page to sketch out his thoughts about the design a new planning process for BD (see **Exhibit 8**).

**EXHIBIT 1** Summary of Financial Data by Geographic and Business Area (thousands of dollars)

|  |  | 1995 | 1994 | 1993 |
|---|---|---|---|---|
| **Revenues** | United States | $1,438,459 | $1,423,060 | $1,371,607 |
|  | Europe | 792,908 | 704,116 | 699,839 |
|  | Other | 481,158 | 432,285 | 393,959 |
|  | Total | $2,712,525 | $2,559,461 | $2,465,405 |
|  | Medical Supplies and Devices | $1,500,075 | $1,421,435 | $1,359,533 |
|  | Diagnostic Systems | 1,212,450 | 1,138,026 | 1,105,872 |
| **Operating Income** | United States | $ 341,277 | $ 264,117 | $ 232,727 |
|  | Europe | 116,229 | 82,040 | 79,453 |
|  | Other | 30,535 | 39,330 | 27,617 |
|  | Total | $ 488,041 | $ 385,487 | $ 339,797 |
|  | Medical Supplies and Devices | $ 330,368 | $ 274,498 | $ 228,337 |
|  | Diagnostic Systems | 157,673 | 110,989 | 111,460 |
|  | Unallocated expenses | (138,463) | (89,328) | (116,903) |
|  | Income before income taxes and cumulative effect of accounting changes | $ 349,578 | $ 296,159 | $ 222,894 |
| **Identifiable Assets** | United States | $1,466,376 | $1,601,569 | $1,613,985 |
|  | Europe | 673,546 | 667,467 | 665,799 |
|  | Other | 419,826 | 431,440 | 412,400 |
|  | Total | $2,559,748 | $2,700,476 | $2,692,184 |
|  | Medical Supplies and Devices | $1,348,860 | $1,433,145 | $1,422,147 |
|  | Diagnostic Systems | 1,210,888 | 1,267,331 | 1,270,037 |
|  | Corporate | 439,757 | 459,057 | 395,381 |
|  | Total | $2,999,505 | $3,159,533 | $3,087,565 |

**EXHIBIT 2  1993 Organizational Structure for Diagnostic Sector**

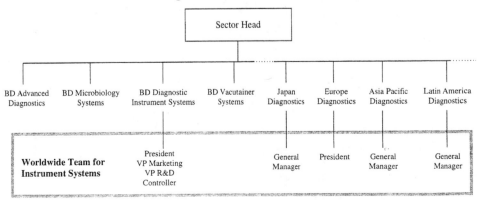

**EXHIBIT 3    Becton Dickinson's Product Line**

Each of Becton Dickinson's five core business areas reflects common success principles. In addition, there are a number of other businesses and technologies that are important. These businesses may become areas for increased focus, or they may become candidates for divestiture, enabling a business to better compete in a specific market. By continuing to concentrate on its strengths, the company will maintain its leadership position well into the future.

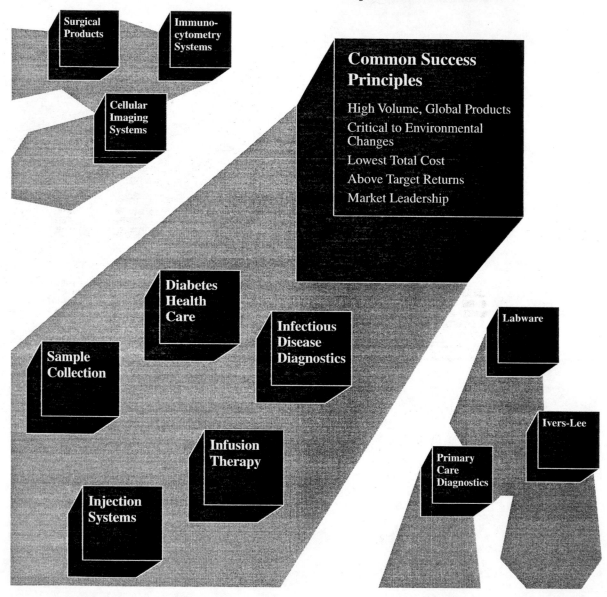

Surgical Products

Immuno-cytometry Systems

Cellular Imaging Systems

**Common Success Principles**

High Volume, Global Products

Critical to Environmental Changes

Lowest Total Cost

Above Target Returns

Market Leadership

Diabetes Health Care

Infectious Disease Diagnostics

Labware

Sample Collection

Ivers-Lee

Infusion Therapy

Primary Care Diagnostics

Injection Systems

**EXHIBIT 4   Desired Characteristics of Becton Dickinson as Articulated by Clateo Castellini**

- Highly Entrepreneurial
- Values The Customer And Is Industry Oriented
- Demonstrates Effective Leadership
- Understands Divisional Responsibilities, But Also Total Company Needs
- Works To Create Shareholders' Value And Assumes Total Responsibility For The Business
- Spartan In Spirit—Modest In Spending, Cares About Shareholders' Money As If It Were Their Own
- Self-motivated and Tenacious—Works Hard And With Dedication And Is Open Minded
- Proud To Belong To The Company—Likes To Invest in BD Shares
- Loves High Quality In Each Detail And In All Activities
- Highly Ethical In Regulatory, Safety, Environmental and Business Practices
- Understands And Appreciates The Value Of People And Of An Organized Team Effort
- Achieves Superior Performance And Personal Style-Fit Drives Professional Progress
- Uses Resources To The Fullest
- We Will Train People On The Above And Will Help People That Do Not Fit To Change Or Move On

**EXHIBIT 5   Design Teams for Organizational Renewal**

| Team | Responsibility |
|---|---|
| Leadership | Define operating philosophy of company and roles/ responsibilities of senior executives |
| Company Activities | Determine how company can add value by strengthening core competencies and inter-business activities |
| Worldwide Businesses-Regions-Countries | Define roles/responsibilities of these with respect to each other |
| Information Planning and Performance Measurement | Determine information needed by each unit (corporate, worldwide businesses, regions) and how performance of each should be measured |
| HR Flow Systems | Define basic philosophy by which we hire, develop, recognize and reward employees |
| Creativity, Innovation, Adaptability | Develop vision of a creative, innovative, adaptive organization and road map to get there |

---

**EXHIBIT 6**    **Division Strategy Center SOF Format**

DESCRIPTION OVERVIEW

---

1. Industry and Served Market Definitions

**Use WW Team Definition**

Each Strategy Center should use the same definition as was developed for the WW Team. Definition should be consistent for all Strategy Centers.

2. Customer Analysis/ Segmentation

The WW Team should develop a customer analysis, including a segmentation scheme. A given Strategy Center might build off of the worldwide approach, but should be sure to adapt to its region. Include:
   1. Medical practice and usage patterns/customer needs
   2. Segmentation

3. Environmental Analysis

Each Strategy Center should adopt the WW analysis to the peculiarities of its own region. Include:
   1. Macro Environment
   2. Porter Model—Key Forces
   3. Competitive Dynamics—Key Competitors

4. Competitive Position Data

Each Strategy Center should provide data for: sales, share of market, market conversion chart (if applicable), relative price and cost. This section is also to include a competitive summary data chart that shows relative competitive positions.

5. Industry Maturity/Competitive Position and Strategic Role

Each Strategy Center should provide a matrix grid as well as its strategic role.

6. Strategy Summary

**Use WW Team Strategy Statement**

Each Strategy Center's profile sheet should use the same WW strategy summary that was developed for the WW Team. A description of the natural period of execution has been provided. Units should use this as a reference, as a self-check, and compare their strategies to this chart.

7. Marketing, Manufacturing, Technology Plans and Key Objectives

Each Strategy Center should include its marketing plan. Manufacturing plans and objectives should be included to the extent they apply to the region. Strategy Centers need not prepare a technology plan if they are part of a WW Team that will submit a WW technology plan. Units not part of a WW Team would need to prepare a technology plan as outlined under Tab 4. This plan is not included in the profile sheet.

Marketing Plan—Target customer segments, how we will position our offering, and the role elements of the marketing mix will play in your strategy.

Manufacturing Plan
   1. Basis of competition
   2. Manufacturing dimensions

Technology Plan
   1. Technology strategy summary

Key Objectives
   1. Critical strategic task and objectives

*Exhibit 6 Continued*

8. Human Resources Summary

Each Strategy Center should provide a summary of its HR Plan. (This year's focus is on workflow.)

9. Risk Assessment

Each Strategy Center should provide a risk assessment for its region. PIMS analysis is strongly suggested, but voluntary.
1. Risk Assessment
2. PIMS Results

10. Financials

Financial submissions will be independent of the "S" and "O" plan. The only financials which will be submitted during the strategy development SOF period are three-year financial trends (Income Statement by Strategy Center) based on the best judgment from Division presidents and Division controllers. The financial trends (projection of FY94-FY96) will be due to the Sectors on February 1. SOF Financials are due with the budget submission on July 8.

## EXHIBIT 7   Overview of the 1993 SOF Planning Calendar

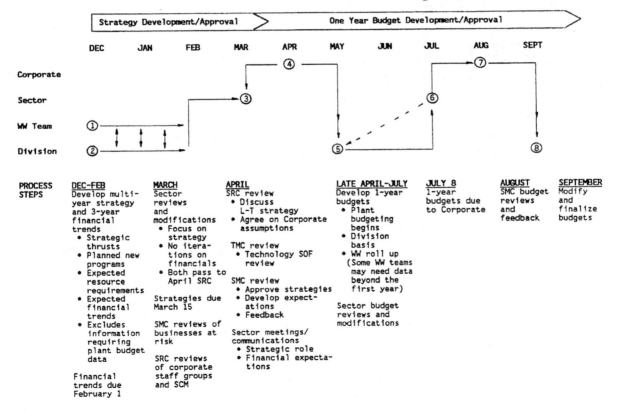

**EXHIBIT 8   Designing the New Planning Process**

| | December | January | February | March | April | May | June | July | August | September | October | November |
|---|---|---|---|---|---|---|---|---|---|---|---|---|
| **CORPORATE MANAGEMENT** | | | | | | | | | | | | |
| I. (a) Information received (from whom?) | | | | | | | | | | | | |
| (b) Action to be taken | | | | | | | | | | | | |
| II. (a) Information sent (to whom?) | | | | | | | | | | | | |
| (b) Purpose | | | | | | | | | | | | |
| **WW DIVISION (Business Team)** | | | | | | | | | | | | |
| I. (a) Information received (from whom?) | | | | | | | | | | | | |
| (b) Action to be taken | | | | | | | | | | | | |
| II. (a) Information sent (to whom?) | | | | | | | | | | | | |
| (b) Purpose | | | | | | | | | | | | |
| **REGIONAL BUSINESS UNITS** | | | | | | | | | | | | |
| I. (a) Information received (from whom?) | | | | | | | | | | | | |
| (b) Action to be taken | | | | | | | | | | | | |
| II. (a) Information sent (to whom?) | | | | | | | | | | | | |
| (b) Purpose | | | | | | | | | | | | |

*Exhibit 8  Continued*

| | December | January | February | March | April | May | June | July | August | September | October | November |
|---|---|---|---|---|---|---|---|---|---|---|---|---|

**FINANCE STAFF**

I. (a) Information received (from whom?)

(b) Action to be taken

II. (a) Information sent (to whom?)

(b) Purpose

**CORPORATE PLANNING STAFF**

I. (a) Information received (from whom?)

(b) Action to be taken

II. (a) Information sent (to whom?)

(b) Purpose

## CASE 33   Guidant Corporation: Shaping Culture Through Systems

"Everyone at Guidant must understand how they create value. And this is only possible if they have a clear vision of Guidant's core values."

These words from Ron Dollens, President and Chief Executive Officer, summarized the challenge facing Guidant's managers as they worked to consolidate Guidant's success as a leader in the high technology segment of the health care industry.

On April 15, 1996, James Cornelius (Chairman of the Board) Ron Dollens (CEO), Keith Brauer (Chief Financial Officer), and Joseph Yahner (Vice President Corporate Resources) spent the morning reviewing the systems put in place to drive Guidant's value system and culture. The four managers agreed that every employee in the organization had to have a clear vision of the risks and opportunities in their hands. Their discussion moved to the issue that concerned them the most: were the systems put in place during the last twelve months shaping the right culture to implement Guidant's intended strategy?

### History

Guidant Corporation designed, produced, and sold medical devices. Products included pacemakers and defibrillators for patients with cardiac problems, catheters used in vascular therapy, and devices for minimally invasive abdominal surgery.

Guidant was created in January 1994 when Eli Lilly, the giant pharmaceutical company, announced the spin-off of five companies from its Medical Devices and Diagnostic Division. These companies had been acquired by Lilly during the 1980s (see **Exhibit 1** for a description of the five companies). Under Lilly, they had been managed as independent entities to preserve the entrepreneurial spirit required in the fast moving healthcare environment. Bringing them together under one roof was expected to generate value by reducing costs through economies of scope in management functions and sales efforts, and by creating competencies common to the medical devices industry.

In early 1994, Guidant top management, comprising former Eli Lilly executives from the Medical Devices and Diagnostic Division, held 55 sessions with investors and analysts in 15 locations in a span of 10 days to present the company to the investment community. In December 1994, 20% of Guidant stock was sold in an initial public offering (IPO). In September 1995, Eli Lilly gave up the other 80% by offering Lilly shareholders the opportunity to exchange Eli Lilly shares for Guidant shares. The results of the spin-off had been remarkable. In December 14, 1994, the date of the IPO, Guidant's shares were priced at $14.50; by March 1996 the price was up to $54 reflecting market capitalization of $3.9 billion (see **Exhibit 2**). It was estimated that the combined value of Eli Lilly and Guidant had moved from $18.3 billion in December 1994 to $35.6 billion by March 1996.

*Doctoral Candidate Antonio Dávila and Professor Robert Simons prepared this case as the basis for class discussion rather than to illustrate either effective or ineffective handling of an administrative situation.*

## Guidant's Three Main Businesses

The new company was organized into three business units: Cardiac Rhythm Management (CRM), Vascular Intervention (VI), and Minimally Invasive Surgery (MIS); and three sales organizations: Western Hemisphere Sales, European Operations, and Pacific Rim Sales. Corporate headquarters was located in Indianapolis, next to Eli Lilly. Jim Cornelius, chairman of the Board, played an active role in the day-to-day management and assumed responsibility for four key support functions (see **Exhibit 4**). Ron Dollens, president and CEO, was responsible for business operations.

The three business units reflected the consolidation of the five original medical devices companies according to similarity of their products. Initially, each business unit had been a self sufficient organization. But Guidant's top management wanted to capture economies of scope and create a common culture by bringing together separate support functions and sharing capabilities across businesses.

Finance and control was kept inside each of the three business units. But Keith Brauer, Guidant's CFO located in Indianapolis, retained strong oversight regarding financial policy issues. Any decision at the business units that required the interpretation of Guidant's financial policies had to be cleared with Brauer.

**Cardiac Rhythm Management (CRM)**   Jay Graf was the president of Cardiac Rhythm Management. The division was the combination of two previous companies: Cardiac Pacemakers, Inc. (CPI) located in St. Paul, Minnesota and Health Rhythm Technologies, Inc. located in Temecula, California. It produced three basic lines of products: cardiac pacemakers, defibrillators, and leads.

*Cardiac pacemakers*   These devices were implanted in the patient's chest and delivered a continuous electrical stimulus to the heart to regulate heartbeat. Once implanted, the life of these devices was 10 years, after which they had to be surgically replaced. By the mid-1990s, pacemaker technologies were considered mature. There was still some room to decrease the size of the device to make it more comfortable, but most of the innovation came from new features that simplified the task of the physician and made the device more flexible. For example, new pacemakers could measure the amount of exercise being performed by the patient to adapt the heartbeat rate. The estimated worldwide market for pacemakers was $2.2 billion and Guidant had a 10% market share. The price of one of these devices was approximately $5,000.

*Defibrillators*   In 1985, CPI introduced the first implantable defibrillator. These devices monitored the heart and delivered a powerful electrical shock when a heart crisis was detected. Only three companies competed in this dynamic market where the size of the device was critical. In the last two years, the size of Guidant's defibrillators had shrunk in stages from 140 cc. to 97 cc., 68 cc., and finally to 59 cc. This reduction not only meant more comfort but, more importantly, it allowed the device to be implanted in the chest closer to the heart thus simplifying surgery and increasing the reliability of the device. The technology was improving so fast that the release of a new defibrillator made existing product inventory obsolete. Worldwide market leadership changed back and forth from competitor Medtronic to Guidant when either of these companies introduced a new defibrillator. The worldwide market was $620 million growing at 10%, twice pacemakers' yearly growth. The price of a defibrillator was approximately $20,000.

*Leads*   Guidant enjoyed a dominant position in the lead market, devices which linked pacemakers and defibrillators to the heart. Innovation was related to the complexity of the lead and implantation techniques. The latest generation allowed implantation through a vein rather than requiring open-chest surgery.

If CRM was to be successful across its entire product line, it needed to be at the cutting edge of technology and aggressively fund growth during the expansion of the market. Guidant managers strived to have sufficient inventory of the latest products at all times to avoid stock-outs (which could represent the loss of a customer to the competition for several generations of the product). However, overstocking was potentially costly since, if the new generation was approved ahead of schedule, the existing product became obsolete. As a result of technological leadership, Guidant wrote off $12.9 million in obsolete inventories in 1995.

**Vascular Intervention (VI)**   Ginger Howard was President of Vascular Intervention. The division, located in Santa Clara, California, was the combination of two of the initial five companies: Advanced Cardiovascular Systems, Inc. (ACS) and Devices for Vascular Intervention, Inc. (DVI).

ACS produced catheters—small tubes to be inserted in the arteries—for interventional cardiology. They comprised dilation catheters (balloons) to open blocked coronary arteries and improve access to heart lesions; guiding catheters to position heart surgery instruments; and a wide line of guide-wires. By late 1995, ACS had three of the top six catheters in the United States in a market estimated to be $2 billion worldwide.

DVI produced atherectomy products. These devices were designed to open blocked coronary arteries by cutting and removing artherosclerotic plaque. The device operated by inserting a catheter into the artery, stabilizing it with a small balloon inside the artery, and then using a cutting tool to remove the plaque that was blocking the artery. DVI had been a leader in the industry, but the introduction by Johnson & Johnson, Inc. of a substitute product based on a new technology in 1993 had led to a significant erosion of market position. DVI sales fell from $80 million in 1994 to $55 million in 1995 and $35 million expected for 1996. Operations were scaled back and resources were redeployed to develop a new product based on the competing technology. In late 1995, Vascular Intervention had launched its first product adopting the new technology in Europe, where regulatory approval could be granted more quickly. In the U.S. the product was still going through the clinical trials associated with the approval process. Regulatory approval was expected during fall 1996.

Price competition in the Vascular Intervention market was intense as the technology became mature and market growth leveled off. Prices had dropped 40% from January 1993 to March 1996. Notwithstanding this fierce competition, the division had been able to maintain margins by focusing efforts in every activity where efficiency could be improved or costs could be cut. Ginger was proud of her division's cost cutting efforts, but she was aware that a singular focus on efficiency could limit the business's ability to innovate and look for new markets. Vascular Intervention was an important provider of cash to fuel technology development in other parts of Guidant, but Ginger believed that continued investment in vascular intervention products was necessary for its own growth and survival.

**Minimally Invasive Surgery (MIS)**   Jay Watkins was the president of MIS, the smallest and fastest growing division of Guidant. The division was the successor of Origin Medsystems, an entrepreneurial start-up founded by Watkins and then acquired by Eli Lilly. MIS product line was created around the emerging laparoscopy market. This new technique allowed physicians to insert small diameter surgical instruments into the abdomen through multiple small incisions. This technique reduced the need for costly open surgery. In some cases, local anesthesia was enough to perform a laparoscopy.

In addition to Origin, the division was also in charge of Compass, an organization created to facilitate the financing and ultimate spin-off of new products developed inside Guidant that did not fit the strategic direction of the company. Gynecare was the first of these ventures. Compass had provided financing, access to venture capital, and managed the new company to its IPO. Guidant retained 31% of Gynecare stock.

## Guidant's Strategy

Shareholder value was key to the thinking of Guidant's top management team. It was at the center of Guidant's definition of strategy (see **Figure 1** below) supported by three key strategic levers.

**1. Global Product Innovation**   Product innovation was the first lever of Guidant's effort to create shareholder value. During 1995, 25 new products were introduced. Forty-five percent of the sales in the second half of 1995 came from products introduced that year. In the three first months of 1996, six products had already hit the market. Guidant used a product family approach to speed product development. A common platform was created to incorporate core features and functions; derivative products could then be rapidly adapted to enhance technological performance and add new features.

The development of a platform took two to three years and involved significant leaps in innovation and technologies. For example, the next platform for defibrillators would include pacemaker capabilities, something that significantly increased the range of potential applications of the device. The strategy of using common parts and freezing requirements early in the process allowed the latest defibrillator to be developed in less than six months, a real breakthrough for the industry.

**FIGURE 1   Guidant's Strategy**

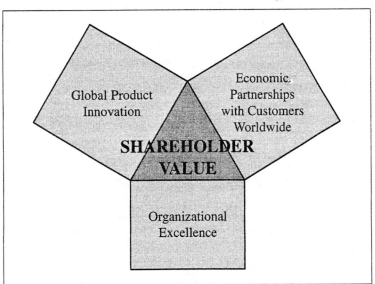

With innovation, however, came risk. In the United States, the Food and Drug Administration (FDA) carefully monitored the products and activities of all companies in the medical devices industry. As described below, new technologies and advances were subject to careful scrutiny. Non-compliance with mandated testing and disclosure regulations resulted in severe sanctions.

**2. Economic Partnerships with Customers Worldwide**    Significant changes were sweeping through Guidant's markets. In the United States, purchasing decisions were being consolidated through powerful Health Management Organizations (HMO's). In all parts of the world, the cost of healthcare was becoming a political issue. To meet these new challenges, Guidant focused on building strong relationships with physicians and healthcare administrators to leverage Guidant's broad product line. In addition, the company was quickly developing a direct salesforce in markets like Japan (second largest healthcare market) and Europe (where Germany was the third largest healthcare market).

In late 1995, the sales function was reorganized to create a common Guidant salesforce. Initially, each business unit had its own salesforce to call on hospitals and healthcare organizations. With the reorganization, a common Guidant salesforce became independent from the business units. All salespeople carried the full Guidant product line. Each business unit retained a reduced marketing department to keep physicians informed about new products and keep in touch with their evolving needs. This organization allowed Guidant to establish closer relationships with its customers, understand better the economics underlying their operations, and gain economic efficiency by eliminating duplication of effort.

In the new structure, the costs of the sales organization were allocated to the business units, which remained profit centers. The sales organization was evaluated on the gross margin of the entire business. One of the potential concerns that the reorganization raised among business managers focused on reduced communication between the independent salesforce and the business units responsible for marketing and new product development. However, top management was confident that the horizontal accountability associated with the new structure would benefit the overall performance of Guidant.

Ron Adler, marketing director of one of Guidant's divisions, spoke with the casewriters:

> "I just spoke with Jacques Lacroix in France. We used to talk on the phone at least once a week to see how things were in Europe, but since the reorganization I speak with him less often. He told me that our sales division in Europe has dropped the prices of AES-90 by 20% to pick up five points in market share. That's good news, but I would prefer if the sales people talk to us before doing something like this. They care about volume. I want to be involved in the day-to-day pricing decisions that affect net profit. Jacques also told me that a French competitor is working on the licensing agreement for a new product. He thought that I knew about it since people in the salesforce have been talking about it for two weeks."

**3. Organizational Excellence**    The third strategic lever was organizational excellence. Top management wanted to create employee commitment to the new Guidant Corporation rather than to each of the five original medical devices companies. Cornelius and Dollens described organizational excellence as "a culture in which all employees function as owners of Guidant." Eight strategic design teams, staffed with cross-functional and cross-divisional people, were formed in September 1995 to develop recommendations on how to leverage Guidant's resources and competencies in the market place. Each team had a core theme to work with:

- Leverage Sales and Distribution
- Build Competence to Ensure Speed to Regulatory Approval
- Optimize Global Presence
- Minimize Risk of Regulatory Actions
- Build Cost-effective Administration
- Leverage Manufacturing Assets
- Create a Stream of Novel Businesses and Products
- Influence Public Policy Important to Our Business

**Shareholder Value**    Since Guidant's IPO in December 1994, the capital markets had been the ultimate judge of Guidant's ability to create shareholder value. Keith Brauer, Guidant's Chief Financial Officer, was very careful to provide analysts and investors with adequate information to translate the successes of the company into shareholder value. Guidant's top managers believed that Wall Street rewarded predictability and they had committed themselves to double Guidant's market value by 1999. They expected to create a strong reputation for Guidant as a reliable company with a management team capable of creating consistent value in the medical devices industry.

Guidant's top managers had also been very explicit in their presentations to analysts about how the company would achieve this challenging goal (see **Figure 2** below). Six specific financial goals (relating to sales growth, profit margins, operating expenses, tax rates, capital investment, and financial leverage) would be the engine to double market value by 1999. Brauer was adamant that business units deliver what the company had promised. He believed that meeting detailed and challenging targets was critical to building Guidant's reputation in the capital markets. (See **Exhibit 3** for the financial statements of the company.)

The emphasis on predictability in every single item on the income statement had been the source of some disagreement between Corporate officers and heads of the business units. In 1995, for example, Vascular Intervention had reported a pleasant surprise—better than

**FIGURE 2    Financial goals**

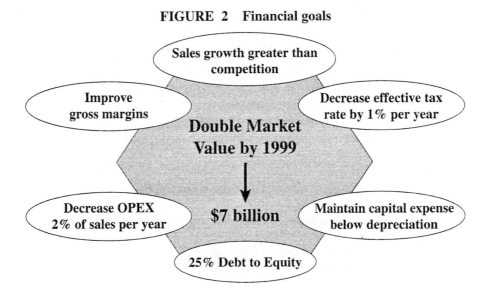

expected profits. The division had succeeded in increasing both sales and net income. But with a larger scale of operations, operating expenses (OPEX) were also above budget. This had caused corporate officers to become concerned since Guidant had explicitly promised analysts to reduce OPEX by 2% per year (see **Figure 2** above). Ginger Howard, President of Vascular Intervention, believed that she had delivered what the market valued most: net income. She argued that she needed the flexibility to make trade-offs in managing her business. She believed that achieving strict targets for every line of the financial statements was not an appropriate demand from Corporate when she had the opportunity to enhance both top-line and bottom-line performance.

## Designing the Systems to Shape Guidant's Culture

To translate the success of Guidant since its IPO into a sustainable position, Jim Cornelius, Ron Dollens, Keith Brauer, and Joe Yahner had developed three types of organizational systems to focus organizational energy around Guidant's strategy: (1) performance measurement systems to drive innovation and value creation, (2) belief systems to communicate core company values, and (3) risk management systems to prevent misbehavior.

Jim Cornelius, together with Keith Brauer, believed that the whole organization should be aware of the financial pressure coming from the market. In turn, challenging financial targets would drive innovation and strategy implementation. However, all the senior managers were aware that too much pressure could be dangerous before Guidant's internal culture was well established.

**1. Measuring Economic Value to Align Incentive Systems**    Guidant's incentive system reached all levels of the organization. Its objective was to align the motivation of employees with the creation of market value and have every person at Guidant benefit from the success of the company.

To measure the progress towards the creation of shareholder value, top management had adopted a new indicator in 1995. "Economic Value Added", a residual income calculation, incorporated income performance and asset intensity to measure performance. It subtracted from profit a capital charge for assets employed:

Residual Income = Net Income − Cost of Capital
= Net Income − (Average Assets − Average Current Liabilities)∗13.5%

By incorporating income statement and balance sheet information, Guidant's top management believed that residual income was a very good internal measure of shareholder value. For 1996, they wanted to communicate this measure down the organization so that people made decisions adopting a shareholders' perspective. By 1997, the goal was to include residual income in the incentives of every employee.

The compensation of the ten senior managers appointed to the Management Committee (see **Exhibit 4**) was heavily linked to Guidant's performance. Cornelius and Dollens believed that, to create a company wide culture, it was critical to link the incentives of the business heads to the global performance of Guidant rather than to the performance of their individual divisions. Accordingly, 10% of their compensation was contingent upon increases in this residual income measure for Guidant and 60% of their compensation linked to stock performance through stock ownership and stock options. To reinforce the creation of a Guidant culture, 365 key management personnel were granted stock options as part of their long term compensation. Cornelius and Dollens expected that this incentive structure would facilitate communication, learning, and mobility across divisions.

For managers reporting to the division presidents, 50% of their bonus was based on improvement of Guidant's residual income and 50% was based on the performance of the division. The residual income bonus would become partially payable if Guidant's year-to-year change in residual income was above -$16 million and would be fully paid if it reached $32 million. Within their respective divisions, division presidents had freedom to design the elements of divisional performance that would be rewarded.

Inside each division, the bonus structure was linked solely to divisional performance. An elaborate system was used to align people with the strategy of the division based on financial and operational indicators (see **Exhibit 5**). Each year, the bonus plan was adapted to the changing needs of the division. For example, at Vascular Intervention there was the "$pot Bonu$ Program" to provide on the spot rewards for exceptional performance. These rewards were proposed by employees, approved by a divisional vice-president, and could be as much as $2,000.

In addition to the bonus based on the divisional performance, Guidant's stock performance also had an impact on all employees' compensation. The company paid an additional 5% in Guidant stock to the employee pension fund. In addition, the company matched 50 cents to the dollar any contribution that an employee made to the retirement plan. The employee's contribution was invested in a diversified fund, but the company's contribution was in Guidant's stock. Joe Yahner, Vice President of Corporate Resources, commented "people really look closely at the stock performance."

Even though the value of Guidant stock was far removed from the actions of lower level employees, the old companies that formed Guidant had traditionally relied heavily on economic incentives and employees had readily accepted the new incentive system. Holding Guidant's stock affected everybody's pocket and reinforced the company-wide culture and supported sharing knowledge across divisions. However, managers understood that the day may come when it would be necessary to fine-tune the incentive system to reflect unit performance more heavily than corporate performance.

**2. Communicating Core Values**   Innovation at Guidant was driven by demanding performance goals. The strategic challenge to move Guidant into its consolidation stage, together with the commitment to double market capitalization by 1999, created pressure throughout the company. But Guidant's top managers believed that blind pursuit of performance goals could undermine the future health of the company. They worried that, under incentive pressures, employees could take actions to improve short-term results with adverse consequences for reputation or even long-term survival of the company.

To reduce the potential for undesirable behavior, Guidant was investing significant effort in the design of management systems to communicate core values. In February 1996, the company distributed among its employees a 32-page Code of Business Conduct designed around Guidant's mission statement and five core values:

*Guidant's Mission Statement*

"Guidant corporation will provide innovative, therapeutic medical solutions of distinctive value for customers, patients and healthcare systems around the world. We will accomplish this in a way that enables our employees to participate as shareholders and provides all of our shareholders with substantial growth and superior performance."

*Guidant's Core Values*

- obligation and dedication to legality and compliance
- integrity and high professional standards
- respect for people
- dedication to quality
- stewardship—the desire of the company to care for the physical and social elements of the communities in which we live and work

Guidant's top management believed these statements were powerful vehicles to remind people what they were working for. For example, the blind pursuit of economic performance might tempt a salesperson to enhance product efficacy claims before receiving full FDA approval. This action would likely go unnoticed and generate sales but could undermine Guidant's reputation. The Mission Statement and Core Values would serve as a firm reminder of the foundation upon which economic value must be created.

**3. Managing Risk** Because of the nature of its products, Guidant worked in a heavily regulated environment. The mandate of the Food and Drug Administration (FDA) was to ensure that health-delivery standards were safe. Mistakes were extremely costly to the agency since they could undermine the confidence of society in the health system. To reduce the chances of mistakes, not only were FDA standards very demanding, but its sanctions for not adhering to the regulations were severe. For example, one of Guidant's competitors had been banned from selling products for one year because of quality problems, while another had operated under an "FDA consent agreement" for 10 years because a manufacturing process change had not been reported to the FDA.

The FDA required detailed information (a 2,000 page report was not uncommon) on the characteristics of new medical device products and their manufacturing process. In the early 1990's, it could take as long as three or four years to gain FDA product approval; by 1996, Guidant's close collaboration and communication with the FDA had reduced this time to 3 to 4 months—an unprecedented milestone for the industry.

FDA regulations required Guidant to inform the agency of any changes in products, manufacturing processes, and sales material. Guidant's managers were responsible for initiating all communications with the FDA and providing the required tests and information.

For products where a new therapy was being developed, the FDA demanded lengthy clinical trials to confirm the therapeutical benefits of the product. The new device had to be tried in a number of patients whose reactions were closely monitored to ensure that the device was delivering what it promised and there were no side effects. When the product was an improvement over an existing one, with no new therapies being developed, the FDA usually was satisfied with engineering trials to prove that the new device behaved similarly or better than the old one. The FDA had to be informed about any change in the manufacturing process that was considered to be significant change. It also had to be consulted when significant changes were made in product claims on product labels or the information package for the physicians.

Decisions on when and how product and labeling changes should be reported to the FDA were scattered throughout the company, involving people in product development, manufacturing, and marketing. Unfortunately, the decision criteria provided by the FDA involved a great deal of personal judgment. Top managers knew that these same people were under the pressure to deliver consistent performance and growth. A single mistake could undermine the trust that the FDA had in Guidant.

To address this important control issue, Guidant had taken several decisions. A new compliance function was created, headed by Michael Gropp, Chief Compliance Officer, reporting directly to Cornelius. This same structure was being duplicated at each of the business units where compliance officers assumed a critical role. A Corporate Audit function was also established to document organizational processes, identify best practices across the company, perform process reengineering, and ensure that internal controls accomplished their objectives. At CPI, a 116-page document, Corporate Compliance Requirements, had been released which specified detailed procedures for 28 key processes, including purchasing, control of nonconforming products, labeling, advertising, and promotion. **Exhibit 6** reproduces a sample page from the Corporate Compliance Requirements. Guidant was also investing $12 million in an integrated SAP computer system to consolidate the administrative system across the company and link all the divisions through it.

Senior managers believed that formal compliance systems were essential to protect Guidant's franchise in the market. The question was how to strike a balance between compliance—by nature a bureaucratic activity—and innovation—one of Guidant's key competitive strengths?

## *The Future*

1995 had been consumed by managing the market pressures of the IPO and making Guidant a solid company. The four men had worked hard to communicate Guidant's story to analysts and investment managers. The market had responded, propelling Guidant stock to a lofty price-earnings multiple.

In their April 15, 1996 meeting, the four managers were evaluating whether the systems put in place would shape the appropriate culture to drive Guidant forward as a successful medical devices company. Keith Brauer, with the input of Ron Dollens, had designed a long range planning system (see **Exhibit 7**). Both managers thought that this system could reinforce Guidant's new culture and force managers to think about the future after the short-term pressures of Guidant's birth.

Jim Cornelius believed that long range planning was a good idea. But he was cautious about going ahead with the system. He was aware that a well-executed planning system required a significant time commitment and possibly an environment stable enough to look two or three years into the future. Furthermore, he was unsure whether this system would constrain strategy definition at the business units where market knowledge resided.

The meeting was wrapping up as the four managers summarized further actions as they moved into the future. Maybe it was a good time to go back to the capital markets with another stock offering. Growth prospects remained strong and the pipeline was full of promising new products that would inevitably compete for scarce funding resources. The future looked bright.

**EXHIBIT 1   The Makeup of Guidant Corporation**

| COMPANY | YEAR PURCHASED BY ELI LILLY | COST[a] | PRODUCT |
|---|---|---|---|
| Advanced Cardiovascular Systems, Co. (ACS) | 1984 | $107 million[b] | Balloon angioplasty catheters, which clear blocked heart arteries. |
| Cardiac Pacemakers, Inc. (CPI) | 1978 | $106 million | Implantable heart pacemakers and defibrillators. |
| Devices for Vascular Intervention, Inc. (DVI) | 1989 | $96 million[c] | Atherectomy catheters which clear clogged heart arteries. |
| Origin Medsystems, Inc. (ORIGIN) | 1992 | $66 million[c] | Devices for minimally invasive surgery. |
| Heart Rhythm Technologies (HRT) | 1992 | — | Catheters that use heat to correct heart rhythm problems. |

*Source:* The Indianapolis Star, *Wednesday, September 14, 1994.*
[a] *The final purchase price of several Lilly device subsidiaries had not been disclosed, because they depend on future financial performance. For those companies, payments disclosed to date are listed.*
[b] *Advanced Cardiovascular Systems' shareholders may have received another 417,000 Lilly shares.*
[c] *Financial cost may be as high as $235 million.*

**EXHIBIT 2   Guidant's Stock Price, December 1994 to April 1996**

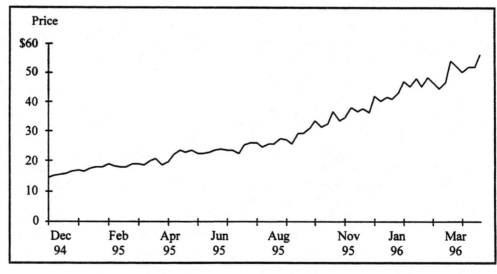

## EXHIBIT 3 Guidant Corporation and Subsidiaries

| | Year Ended December 31 | |
| --- | --- | --- |
| | 1995 | 1994 |
| **Income Statement** (in millions except per share data) | | |
| Vascular Intervention | $ 447.9 | $ 464.5 |
| Cardiac Rhythm Management | 452.4 | 378.6 |
| Minimally Invasive Surgery | 31.0 | 19.3 |
| Net Sales | 931.3 | 862.4 |
| Cost of Sales | 283.4 | 270.9 |
| Gross Profit | 647.9 | 591.5 |
| Research and Development | 134.7 | 130.9 |
| Sales, Marketing, and Administrative | 291.8 | 268.9 |
| Other Expenses — Net | 51.6 | 35.8 |
| Income Before Taxes | 169.8 | 155.9 |
| Income Taxes | 68.7 | 63.8 |
| Net Income | 101.1 | 92.1 |
| Additional net interest — after tax | — | (15.9) |
| Pro-forma net income | $ 101.1 | $ 76.2 |
| **Balance Sheet** (in millions) | | |
| *Current Assets* | | |
| Cash and cash equivalents | $ 3.4 | $ 113.0 |
| Accounts receivable net of allowances $5.7 (1995), $5.4 (1994) | 181.6 | 155.7 |
| Inventories | 124.7 | 120.0 |
| Other Current Assets | 79.3 | 69.1 |
| *Other Assets* | | |
| Property and equipment | 316.4 | 294.8 |
| Goodwill net of allowances $84.7 (1995), $67.1 (1994) | 263.3 | 268.7 |
| Other intangibles, net of allowances $18.9 (1995), $14.2 (1994) | 33.0 | 34.8 |
| Other assets | 55.7 | 47.5 |
| Total Assets | $1,057.4 | $1,103.6 |
| *Current Liabilities* | | |
| Accounts payable | $ 45.8 | $ 36.7 |
| Employee compensation | 63.3 | 46.3 |
| Other liabilities | 99.6 | 140.5 |
| Payables to affiliated companies | | 117.5 |
| Current portion of long-term debt | 70.0 | |

*Continued*

*Exhibit 3 Continued*

| | | |
|---|---|---|
| Noncurrent Liabilities | 394.5 | 498.2 |
| *Shareholders' Equity* | | |
| Common stock, no par value—Authorized shares: 250,000,000 | | |
| Issued and outstanding shares: 1995—71,961,000, 1994—71,860,000 | 192.5 | 192.5 |
| Additional paid-in capital | 146.8 | 64.5 |
| Retained earnings | 102.2 | 7.4 |
| Deferred cost, ESOP | (57.3) | |
| | $1,057.4 | $1,103.6 |

## EXHIBIT 4 Guidant's Organization Structure

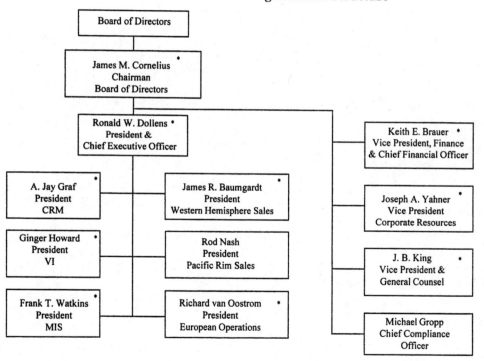

\* Members of the Management Committee

## EXHIBIT 5   Examples of Divisional Incentives for 1996

### Vascular Intervention

| | Performance Range | | | Bonus Pay-out (as percentage of salary) | | |
|---|---|---|---|---|---|---|
| | MINIMUM | TARGET | MAXIMUM | MINIMUM | TARGET | MAXIMUM |
| **Financial Element** | | | | | | |
| Net Revenue Growth | 0% | 10% | 35% | | | |
| | | | | 0% | 10% | 30% |
| Operating Income Growth | 0% | 15% | 35% | | | |
| **Cross-Functional Element** (based on defined *Unit Cost Reduction* and *Key Product Development Milestones*) | | | | 0% | 5% | 10% |
| **Total Bonus** | | | | 0% | 15% | 40% |

### Cardiac Rhythm Management

| | Performance Range | | | Bonus Pay-out (as percentage of salary) | | |
|---|---|---|---|---|---|---|
| | MINIMUM | TARGET | MAXIMUM | MINIMUM | TARGET | MAXIMUM |
| **Financial Element** | | | | | | |
| Sales Growth | 0% | 17% | 25% | | | |
| | | | | 0% | 18.9% | 25% |
| Operating Income Growth divided by number of people | 0% | 15% | 15% | | | |
| **Cross-Functional Element** (based on defined *Product Throughput Reduction* and *Key Product Milestone Compliance*) | | | | 0% | 5% | 10% |
| **Total Bonus** | | | | 0% | 23.9% | 35% |

**EXHIBIT 6   Sample Page from Corporate Compliance Requirements.**

*Section 27.6: U.S. Investigational Device Exemption (IDE) for Significant Risk Devices*

27.6.11   If an investigator is discovered to be out of compliance with the signed agreement, CPI will promptly secure compliance or discontinue shipments of the device to the investigator and terminate the investigator's participation in the investigation. If an investigator's participation has been terminated due to lack of compliance, CPI will also ensure that any investigational devices are returned to CPI unless this action would jeopardize the rights, safety, or welfare of a patient.

27.6.12   CPI will immediately conduct an evaluation of any unanticipated adverse device effect in an investigational device.

27.6.13   If an unanticipated adverse device effect evaluation is determined to present an unreasonable risk to patients, CPI will terminate all investigations or parts of investigations presenting that risk as soon as possible. Terminations will occur no later than five (5) days after the termination decision is made and no later than fifteen (15) days after CPI first received notice of the effect.

27.6.14   CPI will not resume a terminated investigational study without FDA and IRB approval.

27.6.15   CPI will not unduly prolong an IDE study. If investigation data indicates that a premarket approval cannot be justified, CPI will promptly terminate the investigation.

27.6.16   CPI will maintain and consolidate the following accurate, complete and current records relating to the investigation:
  - IDE-related correspondence with other sponsors, monitors, investigators, IRBs, and the FDA;
  - records of shipment, including:
    - name and address of the consignee,
    - type and quantity of device,
    - date of shipment, and
    - model and serial number of the devices shipped;
  - records of disposition which describe the model and serial number of any device:
    - returned to CPI,
    - repaired by the investigational center,
    - disposed of by the investigator or other person, and
    - the reasons for, and methods of, disposal;
  - signed investigator agreements;
  - records concerning adverse device effects (both unanticipated and anticipated);
  - complaints; and
  - any other information required by the FDA.

## EXHIBIT 7   Memo from Keith Brauer

Date: March 14, 1996
To: Distribution
From: Keith Brauer, Chief Financial Officer

*RE: 1996–1999 Long Range Plan Kick-Off*

As you know, the Long Range Plan (LRP) is a strategy/issues driven exercise. This year's LRP represents an opportunity to build on the strategic framework already familiar to Guidant senior management and further utilize our residual income measures.

*LRP Target—Double Market Value by 1999*

Our chairman has challenged the organization to create an LRP that doubles Guidant's market value. Behind this larger goal of doubling market value we have a framework of more specific operating goals related to gross margins, operating expenses, capital spending and so on. It is not expected that each business unit and geography will equally deliver on these more specific operating goals. In some cases, maximum shareholder value is not achieved by meeting *each* goal. However, these goals do represent a vision of what is achievable for the corporation as a whole and we should understand how tradeoffs on these goals impact shareholder value.

*Review Base LRP, Strategic Initiatives ("Upside"), and 15% Price Reduction ("Downside") Scenarios*

In every LRP exercise, there are base-case assumptions and strategies that drive the resulting financials. We would also like to review the strategic initiatives that do not fall within your base plan. These are initiatives that may not be "essential" to your strategy, but represent opportunities to create additional value. We would also like to review a scenario that assumes prices fall 15% below your base case assumption by 1999. This scenario challenges us to re-think the organization to determine how (in this environment), we can maintain a viable business. We will collect financial data for each of these scenarios.

Corporate-wide initiatives and strategic issues are listed below:

*Create additional shareholder value by:*
• Continuing to address and define strategic challenges.
• Aligning efforts (business unit, geographic, and functional) under the Guidant strategic framework.
• Further developing the interaction between business units, geographies and functional areas.
• Building commitment to and understanding of residual income concept.

*Strategic Issues—1996*
• Global Leadership in Implantable Defibrillation.        • Leverage Guidant's Cost Structure.
• Global Leadership in Interventional Cardiology.         • Strengthen Employee Commitment.
• Optimize Pacemaker Market Position.                     • Integrate Investor Relations.

Define Success in Minimally Invasive Surgery.

# FURTHER READING

## Chapter 1: Organizational Tensions to be Managed

1. Argyris, C. 1985. *Strategy, change and defensive routines.* Marshfield, Mass.: Pitman.

2. Argyris, C. 1990. *Overcoming organizational defenses: Facilitating organizational learning.* Needham, Mass.: Allyn and Bacon.

3. Ashforth, B. E., and F. Mael. 1989. Social identity theory and the organization. *Academy of Management Review* 14 (1): 20–39.

4. Deci, E. L., and R. M. Ryan. 1985. *Intrinsic motivation and self-determination in human behavior.* New York: Plenum.

5. Ferris, K. R., and J. L. Livingstone, eds. 1989. *Management planning and control: The behavioral foundations.* Columbus, Ohio: Publishing Horizons, Inc.

6. Herzberg, F. 1966. *Work and the nature of man.* Cleveland, Ohio: World Publishing.

7. Hopwood, A. 1974. *Accounting and human behavior.* Englewood Cliffs, N.J.: Prentice–Hall.

8. Kuhn, R. L., ed. 1988. *Handbook for creative and innovative managers.* New York: McGraw-Hill.

9. Langfield-Smith, K. 1997. Management control systems and strategy: A critical review. *Accounting,* *Organization and Society* 22 (2): 207–232.

10. Leonard-Barton, D. 1995. *Wellsprings of knowledge: Building and sustaining the sources of innovation.* Boston, Mass.: Harvard Business School Press.

11. Lorange, P., M. S. Morton, and S. Ghosal. 1986. *Strategic control systems.* St. Paul, Minn.: West Publishing.

12. Maslow, A. H. 1954. *Motivation and personality.* New York: Harper & Row.

13. McGregor, D. 1960. *The human side of enterprise.* New York: McGraw-Hill.

14. Merchant, K. A., and R. Simons. 1986. Research and control in complex organizations: An overview. *Journal of Accounting Literature* 5: 183–203.

15. Simons, R. 1995. *Levers of control.* Boston: Harvard Business School Press.

16. Simons, R., and A. Dávila. 1998. How high is your return on management? *Harvard Business Review* 76 (1): 70–80.

17. Stevenson, H. H., and J. C. Jarillo. 1990. A paradigm of entrepreneurship: Entrepreneurial management. *Strategic Management Journal* 11: 17–27.

18. Stevenson, H. H., and D. E. Gumpert. 1985. The heart of entrepreneurship. *Harvard Business Review* 63 (2): 85–94.

19. Vancil, R. F. 1973. What kind of management control do you need? *Harvard Business Review* 51: 75–86.

## Chapter 2: Basics for Successful Strategy

1. Andrews, K. R. 1987. *The concept of corporate strategy.* 3rd ed. Homewood, Ill.: Irwin.

2. Burgelman, R. 1996. A process view of strategic business exit: Implications for an evolutionary perspective on strategy. *Strategic Management Journal* 17: 193–214.

3. Collins, J. C., and J. I. Porras. 1994. *Built to last.* New York: Harper Business.

4. Collis, D. J., and C. A. Montgomery. 1998. Creating corporate advantage. *Harvard Business Review* 76 (3): 70–83.

5. Collis, D. J., and C. A. Montgomery. 1997. *Corporate strategy: Resources and scope of the firm.* Chicago: Irwin.

6. Ghemawat, P. 1991. *Commitment: The dynamic of strategy.* New York: Free Press.

7. Itami, H. 1987. *Mobilizing invisible assets.* Boston, Mass.: Harvard University Press.

8. Mintzberg, H. 1987. The strategy concept I: Five Ps for strategy. *California Management Review* 30 (1): 11–24.

9. Mintzberg, H. 1987. Crafting strategy. *Harvard Business Review* 65 (4): 66–75.

10. Mintzberg, H., and J. Waters. 1985. Of strategies, deliberate and emergent. *Strategic Management Journal* 6 (3): 257–272.

11. Porter, M. E. 1980. *Competitive strategy: Techniques for analyzing industries and competitors.* New York: Free Press.

12. Porter, M. E. 1985. *Competitive advantage.* New York: Free Press.

13. Quinn, J. B., and H. Mintzberg. 1991. *Strategy process.* Englewood Cliffs, N.J.: Prentice–Hall.

14. Quinn, J. B. 1980. *Strategies for change: Logical incrementalism.* Homewood, Ill.: Irwin.

15. Rumelt, R. P., D. E. Schendel, and D. J. Teece, eds. 1994. *Fundamental issues in strategy: A research agenda.* Boston, Mass.: Harvard Business School Press.

16. Teece, D. J., G. Pisano, and A. Shuen. 1997. Dynamic capabilities and strategic management. *Strategic Management Journal* 18 (7): 509–533.

17. Wernerfelt, B. 1984. A resource based view of the firm. *Strategic Management Journal* 5 (2): 171–180.

## Chapter 3: Organizing for Performance

1. Baiman, S., Larcker, D. F., and Rajan, M. V. 1995. Organizational design for business units. *Journal of Accounting Research* 33 (2): 205–29.

2. Chandler, A. D., Jr. 1962. *Strategy and structure: Chapters in the history of American industrial enterprise.* Cambridge, Mass.: MIT Press.

3. Bruns, W. J., and J. H. Waterhouse. 1975. Budgeting control and organizational structure. *Journal of Accounting Research* 13: 177–203.

4. Bruns, W. J., Jr., and S. M. McKinnon. 1993. Information and managers: A field study. *Journal of Management Accounting Research* 5: 84–89.

5. Chappe, E. D., and L. R. Sayles. 1961. *The measure of management.* New York: Macmillan.

6. Cyert, R. M., and J. G. March. 1963. *A behavioral theory of the firm.* Englewood Cliffs, N. J.: Prentice–Hall.

7. Galbraith, J. 1973. *Designing complex organizations.* Reading, Mass.: Addison-Wesley.

8. Gordon, L. A., and V. K. Narayanan. 1984. Management accounting systems, perceived environmental uncertainty and organizational structure: An empirical investigation. *Accounting, Organizations and Society* 9 (1): 33–47.

9. Lawrence, P. R., and J. W. Lorsch. 1969. *Organization and environment.* Homewood, Ill.: Irwin.

10. March, J. G., ed. 1988. *Decisions and organizations.* New York: Basil Blackwell.

11. March, J. G., and H. A. Simon. 1958. *Organizations.* New York: Wiley.

12. Miles, R. E., and C. C. Snow. 1978. *Organizational strategy, structure, and process.* New York: McGraw-Hill.

13. Mintzberg, H. 1979. *The structuring of organizations.* Englewood Cliffs, N.J.: Prentice–Hall.

14. Nadler, D. A., and M. L. Tushman. 1997. *Competing by design.* New York: Oxford University Press.

15. Ouchi, W. G. 1977. The relationship between organizational structure and organizational control. *Administrative Science Quarterly* 22: 95–113.

16. Perrow, C. 1986. *Organizations: A critical essay.* 3rd ed. New York: Random House.

17. Thompson, J. 1967. *Organizations in action.* New York: McGraw-Hill.

18. Vancil, R. F. 1979. *Decentralization: Management ambiguity by design.* Homewood, Ill.: Dow Jones-Irwin.

## Chapter 4: Using Information for Performance Measurement and Control

1. Amey, L. R. 1979. *Budget planning and control systems.* Marshfield, Mass.: Pitman.

2. Anthony, R. N. 1988. *The management control function.* Boston: Harvard Business School Press.

3. Anthony, R. N., and V. Govindarajan. 1998. *Management control systems.* 9th ed. Burr Ridge, Ill.: Irwin McGraw-Hill.

4. Ashby, W. R. 1970. *Design for a brain: The origin of adaptive behavior.* London: Chapman and Hall.

5. Barrett, M. E., and L. B. Fraser. 1977. Conflicting roles in budgeting for operations. *Harvard Business Review* 55 (July–August): 137–146.

6. Eccles, R. G. 1991. The performance measurement manifesto. *Harvard Business Review* 69 (1): 131–37.

7. Eisenhardt, K. M. 1985. Control: Organizational and economic approaches. *Management Science* 31 (2): 134–149.

8. Feldman, M. S., and J. G. March. 1981. Information in organizations as signal and symbol. *Administrative Science Quarterly* 26 (2): 171–86.

9. Itami, H. 1977. *Adaptive behavior: Management control and analysis.* Studies in Accounting Research 15. Sarasota, Fla.: American Accounting Association.

10. Lawler, E. E., III, and J. G. Rhode. 1976. *Information and control in organizations.* Santa Monica, Calif.: Goodyear.

11. Locke, E. A., G. P. Latham, and M. Erez. 1988. The determinants of goal commitment. *Academy of Management Review* 13 (1): 23–39.

12. McKinnon, S. M., and W. J. Bruns, Jr. 1992. *The information mosaic.* Boston: Harvard Business School Press.

13. March, J. G. 1994. *A primer on decision making: How decisions happen.* New York: Free Press.

14. Merchant, K. A. 1985. *Control in business organizations.* Marshfield, Mass.: Pitman.

15. Merchant, K. A. 1997. *Modern management control systems: Text and cases.* Upper Saddle River, N.J.: Prentice–Hall.

16. Ouchi, W. G. 1979. A conceptual framework for the design of organizational control mechanisms. *Management Science* 25 (9): 833–48.

17. Thompson, J. D. 1967. *Organizations in action: Social science bases of administrative theory.* New York: McGraw-Hill.

18. Tushman, M., and D. Nadler. 1978. Information processing as an integrating concept in organizational design. *Academy of Management Review* 3 (3): 613–624.

19. Vancil, R. F. 1979. *Decentralization: Managerial ambiguity by design.* Homewood, Ill.: Dow Jones-Irwin.

## Chapter 5: Building a Profit Plan

1. Brownell, P. 1985. Budgetary systems and the control of functionally differentiated organizational activities. *Journal of Accounting Research* 23 (2): 502–512.

2. Brownell, P. 1982. Participation in the budgeting process—When it works and when it doesn't. *Journal of Accounting Literature* 1: 124–53.

3. Govindarajan, V., and A. K. Gupta. 1985. Linking control systems to business unit strategy: Impact on performance. *Accounting, Organizations and Society* 10 (1): 51–66.

4. Kaplan, R. S. 1994. Flexible budgeting in an activity-based costing framework. *Accounting Horizons* 8 (2): 104–109.

5. Hongren, C. T., G. Foster, and S. M. Datar. 1997. *Cost accounting: A managerial emphasis.* 9th ed. Upper Saddle River, N.J.: Prentice–Hall.

6. Emmanuel, C. R., D. Otley, and K. Merchant. 1990. *Accounting for man-*

*agement control.* London; New York: Chapman and Hall.

7. Lorange, P. 1980. *Corporate planning: An executive viewpoint.* Englewood Cliffs, N.J.: Prentice–Hall.

8. Shields, J. F., and M. D. Shields. 1998. Antecedents of participative budgeting. *Accounting, Organizations and Society* 23 (1): 49–76.

9. Simons, R. 1987. Accounting control systems and business strategy: An empirical analysis. *Accounting, Organizations and Society* 12 (4): 127–43.

10. Simons, R. 1987. Planning, control, and uncertainty: A process view. In *Accounting & Management: Field study perspectives,* eds. W. J. Bruns and R. S. Kaplan. Boston: Harvard Business School Press.

11. Steiner, G. A. 1979. *Strategic planning: What every manager must know.* New York: Free Press.

12. Umapathy, S. 1987. *Current budgeting practices in U.S. industry: The state of the art.* New York: Quorum Books.

## Chapter 6: Evaluating Strategic Profit Performance

1. Abarbanell, J. S., and B. J. Bushee. 1998. Abnormal returns to a fundamental analysis strategy. *Accounting Review* 73 (1): 19–45.

2. Barrett, M. E., and L. B. Fraser. 1977. Conflicting roles in budgeting for operations. *Harvard Business Review* 55 (4): 137–146.

3. Garrett, K. 1990. Variance analysis: Uses and abuses. *Accountancy* 106 (1168): 90–91.

4. Hofstede, G. 1968. *The game of budget control.* London: Tavistock.

5. Hunter, K. 1993. Various ways to analyze variance. *Accountancy* 112 (1203): 84–86.

6. Kaplan, R. S. 1994. Flexible budgeting in an activity-based costing framework. *Accounting Horizons* 8 (2): 104–109.

7. Kaplan, R. S. 1983. Measuring manufacturing performance: A new challenge for managerial accounting research. *Accounting Review* 58 (4): 686–705.

8. Kaplan, R. S., and A. A. Atkinson. 1989. *Advanced management accounting.* 2nd ed. Englewood Cliffs, N.J.: Prentice–Hall.

9. Kloock, J., and U. Schiller. 1997. Marginal costing: Cost budgeting and cost variance analysis. *Management Accounting Research* 8: 299–323.

10. Mak, Y. T., and M. L. Roush. 1996. Managing activity costs with flexible budgeting and variance analysis. *Accounting Horizons* 10 (3): 141–146.

11. Mak, Y. T., and M. L. Roush. 1994. Flexible budgeting and variance analysis in an activity-based costing environment. *Accounting Horizons* 8 (2): 93–103.

12. Shank, J. K., and V. Govindarajan. 1993. *Strategic cost management.* New York: Free Press.

13. Shank, J. K., and N. Churchill. 1977. Variance analysis: A management-oriented approach. *The Accounting Review* 5: 950–57.

14. Walsh, F. J., Jr. 1987. Measuring business-unit performance. *Research Bulletin No. 206.* New York: The Conference Board.

15. Shank, J. K., and V. Govindarajan. 1993. *Strategic cost management.* New York: Free Press.

## Chapter 7: Designing Asset Allocation Systems

1. Baldwin, Y. C., and K. B. Clark. 1992. Capabilities and capital investment: New perspectives on capital budgeting. *Journal of Applied Corporate Finance* 5 (2): 67–82.

2. Baldwin, Y. C., and K. B. Clark. 1994. Capital-budgeting systems and capabilities investments in U.S. companies after the Second World War. *Business History Review* 68 (1): 73–109.

3. Boquist, J. A., T. T. Milbourn, and A. V. Thakor. 1998. How do You win the capital allocation game? *Sloan Management Review* 39 (2): 59–71.

4. Bower, J. L. [1970] 1986. *Managing the resource allocation decision.* Boston: Harvard Business School Press.

5. Bromiley, P. 1986. *Corporate capital investment: A behavioral approach.* Cambridge: Cambridge University Press.

6. Haka, S. F., L. A. Gordan, and G. E. Pinches. 1985. Sophisticated capital budgeting selection techniques and firm performance. *The Accounting Review* 60 (4): 651–669.

7. Haka, S. F. 1987. Capital budgeting techniques and firm specific contingencies: A correlational analysis. *Accounting Organizations and Society* 12 (1): 31–48.

8. Hertenstein, J. H. 1988. Introductory note on capital budgeting practices. Boston: Harvard Business School Note 188–059.

9. House, C. H., and R. L. Price. 1991. The return map: Tracking product teams. *Harvard Business Review* 69 (January/February): 92–100.

10. Miller, P., and T. O. Leary. 1997. Capital budgeting practices and complementarity relations in the transition to modern manufacture: A field-based analysis. *Journal of Accounting Research* 35 (2): 257–271.

11. Myers, S. and R. A. Brealey. 1996. *Principles of corporate finance.* 5th ed. New York: McGraw-Hill.

12. Porter, M. E. 1992. Capital disadvantage: America's failing capital investment system. *Harvard Business Review* 70 (5): 65–82.

13. Ross, M. 1986. Capital budgeting practices of twelve large manufacturers. *Financial Management* 15 (4): 15–22.

## Chapter 8: Linking Performance to Markets

1. Alles, M., and S. Datar. 1998. Strategic transfer pricing. *Management Science* 44 (4): 451–461.

2. Bushman, R. M, R. J. Indjejikian, and A. Smith. 1996. CEO compensation: The role of individual performance evaluation. *Journal of Accounting and Economics* 21 (3): 161–193.

3. Chalos, P., and S. Haka. 1990. Transfer pricing under bilateral bargaining. *Accounting Review* 65 (3): 624–641.

4. Cassel, H. S., and V. F. McCormack. 1987. The transfer price dilemma—and a dual price solution. *Journal of Accountancy* 164 (3): 166–175.

5. Dearden, J. 1969. The case against ROI control. *Harvard Business Review* 47 (3): 124–35.

6. Dearden, J. 1987. Measuring profit center managers. *Harvard Business Review* 65 (5): 84–88.

7. Dechow, P. M. 1994. Accounting earnings and cash flows as measures of firm performance: The role of accounting accruals. *Journal of Accounting and Economics* 18 (1): 3–42.

8. Eccles, R. G. 1985. *The transfer pricing problem: A theory for practice.* Lexington, Mass.: Lexington Books.

9. Grabski, S. V. 1985. Transfer pricing in complex organizations: A review and integration of recent empirical and analytical research. *Journal of Accounting Literature* 4: 33–75.

10. Kaplan, R. S., D. Weiss, and E. Desheh. 1997. Transfer pricing with ABC. *Management Accounting* 78 (11): 20–28.

11. Kovac, E. J., and H. P. Troy. 1989. Getting transfer prices right: What Bellcore did. *Harvard Business Review* 67 (5): 148–154.

12. Lev, B. 1989. On the usefulness of earnings: Lessons and directions from two decades of empirical research. *Journal of Accounting Research,* Supplement: 153–92.

13. Luft, J. L., and R. Libby. 1997. Profit comparisons, market prices and managers' judgments about negotiated transfer prices. *The Accounting Review* 72 (2): 217–229.

14. Rappaport, A. 1986. *Creating shareholder value.* New York: Free Press.

15. Reece, J. S., and W. R. Cool. 1978. Measuring investment center performance. *Harvard Business Review* 56 (3): 28–49.

16. Sahlman, W. A. 1997. How to write a great business plan. *Harvard Business Review* 75 (4): 98–108.

17. Swieringa, R. J., and J. H. Waterhouse. 1982. Organizational views of transfer pricing. *Accounting Organizations and Society* 7 (2): 149–165.

18. Stewart, G. 1991. *The quest for value: A guide for senior managers.* New York: Harper Business.

19. Wenner, D. L., and R. W. LeBer. 1989. Managing for shareholder value—from top to bottom. *Harvard Business Review* 67 (6): 52–66.

## Chapter 9: Building a Balanced Scorecard

1. Berliner, C., and J. Brimson. 1988. *Cost management for today's environment.* Boston: Harvard Business School Press.

2. Boivin, D. W. 1996. Using the balanced scorecard: Letters to the editor. *Harvard Business Review* 74 (2): 170.

3. Burgelman, R. 1983. A process model of internal corporate venturing in a diversified major firm. *Administrative Science Quarterly* 28 (2): 223–44.

4. Burgelman, R. 1983. Corporate entrepreneurship and strategic management: Insights from a process study. *Management Science* 29 (12): 1,349–64.

5. Chandler, A. D. 1977. *The visible hand: The managerial revolution in American business.* Cambridge, Mass.: Harvard University Press.

6. Epstein, M., and J. F. Manzoni. 1988. Implementing corporate strategy: From tableaux de bord to balanced scorecards. *European Management Journal* 16: 190–203.

7. Goldratt, E., and J. Cox. 1986. *The goal: A process of ongoing improvement.* Croton-on-Hudson, N.Y.: North River Press.

8. Itami, H. 1987. *Mobilizing invisible assets.* Cambridge, Mass.: Harvard University Press.

9. Heskett, J. L., W. E. Sasser, and L. A. Schlesinger. 1997. *The service profit chain.* New York: Free Press.

10. Hope, T., and J. Hope. 1996. *Transforming the bottom line.* Boston: Harvard Business School Press.

11. Johnson, T. H., and R. S. Kaplan. 1987. *Relevance lost: The rise and fall of management accounting.* Boston, Mass.: Harvard Business School Press.

12. Kaplan, R. S., editor. 1990. *Measures for manufacturing excellence.* Boston, Mass.: Harvard Business School Press.

13. Kaplan, R. S., and D. P. Norton. 1996. *The balanced scorecard: Translating strategy into action.* Boston, Mass.: Harvard Business School Press.

14. Kaplan, R. S., and D. P. Norton. 1996. Using the balanced scorecard as a strategic management system. *Harvard Business Review* 74 (1): 75–85.

15. Kaplan, R. S., and D. P. Norton. 1993. Putting the balanced scorecard to work. *Harvard Business Review* 71 (5): 134–42.

16. Kaplan, R. S., and D. P. Norton. 1992. The balanced scorecard: Measures that drive performance. *Harvard Business Review* 70 (1): 71–79.

17. Lessner, John. 1989. Performance measurement in a just-in-time environment: Can traditional performance measurement still be used? *Journal of Cost Management:* 22–28.

18. Lynch, R. and K. Cross. 1991. *Measure up! Yardsticks for continuous improvement.* Cambridge, Mass.: Basil Blackwell.

19. McNair, C. J., W. Mosconi, and T. Norris. 1988. *Meeting the technology challenge: Cost accounting in a JIT environment.* Montvale, N.J.: Institute of Management Accountants.

## Chapter 10: Using Diagnostic and Interactive Control Systems

1. Austin, R. D. 1996. *Measuring and managing performance in organizations.* New York: Dorset.

2. Argyris, C. and A. Schön. 1978. *Organizational learning: A theory of action perspective.* Reading, Mass.: Addison-Wesley.

3. Birnberg, J. G., L. Turopolec, S. M. Young, and J. W. Buckley. 1983. The organizational context of accounting. *Accounting, Organizations and Society* 8 (2/3): 111–138.

4. Chenhall, R. H., and D. Morris. 1986. The impact of structure, environment, and interdependence on the perceived usefulness of management accounting systems. *The Accounting Review* 61 (1): 58–75.

5. Collins, F., O. Holzmann, and R. Mendoza. 1997. Strategy, budgeting, and crisis in Latin America. *Accounting, Organizations and Society* 22 (7): 669–689.

6. Dent, J. F. 1990. Strategy, organization and control: Some possibilities for accounting research. *Accounting, Organizations and Society* 15 (1/2): 3–24.

7. Keller, M. 1989. *Rude awakening: The rise, fall, and struggle for recovery of General Motors.* New York: Morrow.

8. Levitt, B., and J. G. March. 1988. Organizational learning. *American Review of Sociology* 14: 319–40.

9. Lorange, P., M. S. Scott Morton, and S. Goshal. 1986. *Strategic control.* St. Paul, Minn.: West.

10. McKenney, J. L., M. H. Zack, and V. S. Doherty. 1992. Complementary communication media: A comparison of electronic mail and face-to-face communication in a programming team. In *Networks and organizations: Structure, form, and action,* eds. N. Nohria and R. G. Eccles. Boston: Harvard Business School Press.

11. Mintzberg, H. 1994. *The rise and fall of strategic planning.* New York: Free Press.

12. Nohria, N., and R. G. Eccles. 1992. Face-to-face: Making network organizations work. In *Networks and organizations: Structure, form, and action,* eds. N. Nohria and R. G. Eccles. Boston: Harvard Business School Press.

13. Pascale, R. T. 1984. Perspectives on strategy: The real story behind Honda's success. *California Management Review* 26 (3): 47–72.

14. Sathe, V. 1982. *Controller involvement in management.* Englewood Cliffs, N.J.: Prentice–Hall.

15. Sculley, J. 1987. *Odyssey: Pepsi to Apple . . . A journey of adventure, ideas, and the future.* New York: Harper & Row.

16. Simons, R., and H. Weston. 1990. IBM: Make it your business. Case Study 190–137. Boston: Harvard Business School.

17. Simons, R. 1990. The role of management control systems in creating competitive advantage: New perspectives. *Accounting, Organizations and Society* 15 (1/2): 127–43.

18. Simons, Robert. 1991. Strategic orientation and top management attention to control systems. *Strategic Management Journal* 12: 49–62.

19. Tani, T. 1995. Interactive control in target cost management. *Management Accounting Journal* 6 (4): 399–414.

## Chapter 11: Aligning Performance Goals and Incentives

1. Antle, R., and Smith, A. 1986. An empirical investigation of the relative performance evaluation of corporate executives. *Journal of Accounting Research* 24 (1): 1–39.

2. Baber, W. R. 1985. Budget-based compensation and discretionary spending. *The Accounting Review* 60 (1): 1–9.

3. Baker, G. P., M. C. Jensen, and K. J. Murphy. 1988. Compensation and incentives: Practice vs. theory. *Journal of Finance* 43 (3): 593–616.

4. Bruns, W. J., ed. 1992. *Performance measurement, evaluation, and incentives.* Boston, Mass.: Harvard Business School Press.

5. Carroll, S. J., and H. L. Tosi. 1973. *Management by objectives: Applications and research.* New York: Macmillan.

6. Fama, E. F., and M. C. Jensen. 1983. Separation of ownership and control. *Journal of Law and Economics* 26 (2): 301–25.

7. Goldratt, E. M., and J. Cox. 1986. *The goal.* Revised edition. Croton-on-Hudson, N.Y.: North River Press.

8. Henderson, R. I. 1989. *Compensation management: Rewarding performance.* 5th ed. Englewood Cliffs, N.J.: Prentice–Hall.

9. Hofstede, G. H. 1968. *The game of budget control.* London: Tavistock.

10. Ijiri, Y. 1975. *Theory of accounting measurement.* Studies in Accounting Research 10. Sarasota, Fla.: American Accounting Association.

11. Ittner, C. D., D. F. Larcker, and M. V. Rajan. 1997. The choice of performance measures in annual bonus contracts. *Accounting Review* 72 (2): 231–255.

12. Keating, S. 1995. *Performance measurement in diversified firms: An investigation of the factors affecting performance measurement quality and choice.* D.B.A. dissertation, Boston: Harvard Business School.

13. Kerr, Steven. 1975. On the folly of rewarding A, while hoping for B. *Academy of Management Journal* 18: 769–83.

14. Kohn, A. 1993. Why incentive plans cannot work. *Harvard Business Review* 71 (5): 54–63.

15. Locke, E. A., and G. P. Latham. 1990. *A theory of goal setting and task performance.* Englewood Cliffs, N.J.: Prentice–Hall.

16. Locke, E. A., G. P. Latham, and M. Erez. 1998. The determinants of goal commitment. *Academy of Management Review* 13 (1): 23–39.

17. Merchant, K. A. and J. F. Manzoni. 1989. The achievability of budget targets in profit centers: A field study. *Accounting Review* 64 (3): 539–558.

18. Merchant, K. A. 1989. *Rewarding results: Motivating profit center managers.* Boston: Harvard Business School Press.

19. Milkovich, G. T., and J. M. Newman. 1990. *Compensation.* 3rd ed. Homewood, Ill.: BPI/Irwin.

20. Hopwood, A. 1972. An empirical study of the role of accounting data in performance evaluation. *Journal of Accounting Research* 10 (Supplement): 156–182.

21. Selznik, P. 1957. *Leadership in administration: A sociological interpretation.* New York: Harper & Row.

22. Stedry, A., and E. Kay. 1966. The effects of goal difficulty on performance. *Behavioral Science* 11 (6): 459–70.

## Chapter 12: Identifying Strategic Risk

1. Bernstein, P. L. 1996. *Against the gods: The remarkable history of risk.* New York: Wiley.

2. Bozeman, B., and G. Kingsley. 1998. Risk culture in public and private organizations. *Public Administration Review* 58 (2): 109–118.

3. Chow, C. W., Y. Kato, and K. A. Merchant. 1996. The use of organizational controls and their effects on data ma-

nipulation and management myopia: A Japan versus U.S. comparison. *Accounting Organizations and Society* 21 (2, 3): 175–192.

4. Froot, K. A., D. S. Scharfstein, and J. C. Stein. 1994. A framework for risk management. *Harvard Business Review* 72 (6): 91–102.

5. Gellerman, S. W. 1986. Why 'good' managers make bad ethical choices. *Harvard Business Review* 64 (4): 85–90.

6. Goodpaster, K. 1983. Witness for the corporation. Case Study 284–135. Boston: Harvard Business School.

7. Hellman, T. 1998. The allocation of control rights in venture capital contracts. *Rand Journal of Economics* 29 (1): 57–76.

8. Jackson, S. E., and J. E. Dutton. 1988. Discerning threats and opportunities. *Administrative Science Quarterly* 33 (3): 370–387.

9. MacCrimmon, K. R., and D. A. Wehrung. 1986. *Taking risks: The management of uncertainty.* New York: Free Press.

10. Noreen, E. 1988. The economics of ethics: A new perspective on agency theory. *Accounting, Organizations and Society* 13 (4): 359–369.

11. Osborn, R. N., and D. H. Jackson. 1988. Leaders, riverboat gamblers, or purposeful unintended consequences in the management of complex, dangerous technologies. *Academy of Management Journal* 31 (4): 924–947.

12. Puschaver, L., and R. G. Eccles. 1996. *In pursuit of the upside: The new opportunity in risk management.* Monograph published by Price Waterhouse LLP.

13. Sitkin, S. B., and L. R. Weingart. 1995. Determinants of risky decision-making behavior: A test of the mediating role of risk perceptions and propensity. *Academy of Management Journal* 38 (6): 1,573–1,592.

14. Sitkin, S. B., and A. L. Pablo. 1992. Reconceptualizing the determinants of risk behavior. *Academy of Management Review* 17 (1): 9–38.

## Chapter 13: Managing Strategic Risk

1. Barnard, Chester I. 1938. *The functions of the executive.* Cambridge, Mass.: Harvard University Press.

2. Baruch, H. 1980. The audit committee: A guide for directors. *Harvard Business Review* 58 (3): 174–186.

3. Bowdidge, J. S., and K. E. Chaloupecky. 1997. Nicholas Leeson and Barings Bank have vividly taught some internal control lessons. *American Business Review* 15 (1): 71–77.

4. Carroll, A. B. 1975. Managerial ethics: A post-Watergate review. *Business Horizons* 18: 75–80.

5. Collins, J. C., and J. I. Porras. 1994. *Built to last.* New York: Harper Collins.

6. Dezoort, F. T. 1998. An analysis of experience effects on audit committee members' oversight judgments. *Accounting, Organizations and Society* 23 (1): 1–21.

7. Geneen, H., with A. Moscow. 1984. *Managing.* Garden City, N.Y.: Doubleday.

8. Goold, M. 1991. Strategic control in the decentralized firm. *Sloan Management Review* 32 (2): 69–81.

9. Gorlin, R. A. 1986. *Codes of professional responsibility.* Washington, D.C.: The Bureau of National Affairs.

10. Kendall, R. 1998. *Risk management for executives: A practical approach to controlling business risks.* London: Pitman.

11. McNamee, D. 1997. Risk-based auditing. *The Internal Auditor* 54 (4): 22–27.

12. March, J. D., ed. 1988. *Decisions and organizations.* New York: Basil Blackwell.

13. Merchant, K. 1990. The effects of financial controls on data manipulation and management myopia. *Accounting, Organizations and Society* 15 (4): 297–313.

14. Porter, M. E. 1996. What is strategy? *Harvard Business Review* 74 (6): 61–78.

15. Rich, A. J., C. S. Smith, and P. H. Mihalek. 1990. Are corporate codes of conduct effective? *Management Accounting* 72 (3): 34–35.

16. Simons, R. 1995. Control in an age of empowerment. *Harvard Business Review* 73 (2): 80–88.

17. Simons, R., and A. Dávila. 1998. How high is your return on management? *Harvard Business Review* 76 (1): 70–80.

18. Sweeney, R. B. and H. L. Siers. 1990. Survey: Ethics in corporate America. *Management Accounting* 71 (12): 34–40.

19. Vancil, R. F. 1973. What kind of management control do you need? *Harvard Business Review* 51: 75–86.

20. Watson, T. J., Jr. 1963. *A business and its beliefs: The ideas that helped build IBM.* New York: McGraw-Hill.

## Chapter 14: Levers of Control for Implementing Strategy

1. Christensen, C. M. 1997. *The innovator's dilemma: When new technologies cause great firms to fail.* Boston, Mass.: Harvard Business School Press.

2. Greiner, L. E. 1998. Evolution and revolution as organizations grow. *Harvard Business Review* 76 (3): 55–68. Originally published in 1972.

3. Flamholtz, E. 1995. Managing organizational transitions: Implications for corporate and human resource management. *European Management Journal* 13 (1): 39–51.

4. Hopwood, A. 1974. *Accounting and human behavior.* Englewood Cliff, N.J.: Prentice–Hall.

5. Kuhn, A. J. 1986. *GM passes Ford, 1918–1938: Designing the General Motors performance-control system.* University Park, Penn.: Pennsylvania State University Press.

6. Langfield-Smith, K. 1997. Management control systems and strategy: A critical review. *Accounting, Organizations and Society* 22 (2): 207–232.

7. Senge, P. M. 1990. The leader's new work: Building learning organizations. *Sloan Management Review* 32 (1): 7–23.

8. Simons, R. 1994. How new top managers use control systems as levers of strategic renewal. *Strategic Management Journal* 15 (3): 169–189.

9. Simons, R. 1995. *Levers of control: How managers use innovative control systems to drive strategic renewal.* Boston, Mass.: Harvard Business School Press.

10. Simon, W. L. 1997. *Beyond the numbers.* New York: Van Nostrand Reinhold.

11. Tushman, M. L., W. H. Newman, and E. Romanelli. 1987. Convergence and upheaval: Managing the unsteady pace of organizational evolution. *California Management Review* 29 (1): 29–44.

# GLOSSARY

*Note:* Chapter references refer to the first time that a term is introduced or defined.

**Accountability**   (Chapter 3) the outputs that a work unit is expected to produce and the performance standards that managers and employees of that unit are expected to meet

**Accounting systems**   (Chapter 1) procedures and mechanisms to collect information about the transactions of a business. Account balances are ultimately summarized in financial statements such as balance sheets, income statements, and cash flow statements.

**Activity-based indirect costs**   (Chapter 5) costs that cannot be traced directly to a product or service, but change with the level of underlying support activities

**Asset**   (Chapter 2) a resource owned or controlled by the entity that will yield future economic benefits. Examples include plant, equipment, cash on hand, and inventory.

**Asset allocation system**   (Chapter 7) the set of formal routines and procedures designed to process and evaluate requests to acquire new assets.

**Asset impairment risk**   (Chapter 12) the risk of deterioration in the value of an asset because of a reduction in the likelihood of receiving future cash flows from the asset

**Asset investment plan**   (Chapter 5) summary of investment in operating assets and long-term assets needed to support a profit plan

**Asset turnover**   (Chapter 5) sales divided by assets is a ratio measure of asset turnover. This ratio answers the question, How many sales dollars did we generate for each dollar that was invested in assets of the business?

**Assumptions**   (Chapter 5) the starting point for any profit plan is a set of assumptions about the future. These assumptions describe the consensus among managers about how various markets — customer, supplier, and financial — will look in the future.

**Balanced scorecard**   (Chapter 9) the multiple, linked objectives that companies must achieve to compete based on capabilities and innovation, not just tangible physical assets. It translates mission and strategy into objectives and measures.

**Beliefs system**   (Chapter 13) an explicit set of organizational definitions that senior managers communicate formally and reinforce systematically to provide basic values, purpose, and direction for the organization

**Benchmark**   (Chapter 4) a formal representation of performance expectations based on the demonstrated performance of an exemplary work unit or business

**Benchmarking**   (Chapter 6) a technique used to calibrate an organization's efforts against a "best of class" yardstick

**Bonus**   (Chapter 11) additional reward or payment for successful achievement of a task

**Bonus pool**   (Chapter 11) sum of money reserved for the payment of incentive and recognition awards

**Boundary systems** (Chapter 13) explicit statements embedded in formal information systems that define and communicate specific risks to be avoided. See also *Business conduct boundaries* and *Strategic boundaries*

**Budget** (Chapter 5) resource plans of any organizational unit that either generates or consumes resources

**Business capabilities** (Chapter 2) see *Distinctive capabilities*

**Business conduct boundaries** (Chapter 13) defined standards of business conduct that enumerate forbidden activities and behaviors

**Business goals** (Chapter 1) the measurable aspirations that managers set for a business. Goals are determined by reference to business strategy. Goals may be financial—for example, to achieve 14% return on sales—or nonfinancial—such as to increase market share from 6% to 9%.

**Business strategy** (Chapter 1) how a company creates value for customers and differentiates itself from competitors in a defined product market

**Capital budget** (Chapter 7) see *Asset allocation system*

**Capital employed** (Chapter 5) the assets within a manager's direct span of control. These assets typically include accounts receivable, inventory, and plant and equipment. Sometimes, corporate-level assets, such as unamortized goodwill, are also allocated to profit centers to be included.

**Capital investment plan** (Chapter 5) proposed investment in long-term productive assets

**Cash wheel** (Chapter 5) a model of the operating cash flow through a business. Answers the question of whether the organization has enough cash to remain solvent throughout the year.

**Centralized organization** (Chapter 3) an organization designed so that unit managers have narrow spans of attention. A decentralized organization, by contrast, is designed so that managers have wide spans of attention.

**Committed costs** (Chapter 5) expenses determined by previous management decisions and, therefore, not subject to discretion during the current profit planning period

**Competitive risk** (Chapter 12) changes in the competitive environment that could impair the business' ability to successfully create value and differentiate its products or services

**Complete measure** (Chapter 11) a measure that captures all the relevant attributes of achievement

**Contribution margin** (Chapter 6) selling price minus variable costs

**Control** (Chapter 4) the process of using information to ensure that inputs, processes, and outputs are aligned to achieve organizational goals

**Coordination** (Chapter 4) the ongoing ability to integrate disparate parts of a business to achieve objectives

**Core competencies** (Chapter 2) see *Distinctive capabilities*

**Core values** (Chapter 13) beliefs that define basic principles, purpose, and direction

**Corporate performance** (Chapter 8) a firm's level of achievement in creating value for market constituents (customers, owners and suppliers)

**Corporate strategy** (Chapter 2) the way that a firm attempts to maximize the value of the resources it controls. Corporate strategy decisions focus on where corporate resources will be invested.

**Cost center accountability**   (Chapter 3) the narrowest span of accountability encountered in most firms. Managers of cost centers are accountable only for their unit's level of spending relative to goods or services provided. See also *Profit center accountability*

**Cost drivers**   (Chapter 5) activities that consume indirect resources

**Critical performance variables**   (Chapter 10) factors that must be achieved or implemented successfully for the intended strategy of the business to succeed

**Current assets**   (Chapter 2) cash and other assets that will be turned into cash during the course of an accounting cycle—normally one year

**Customer perspective**   (Chapter 9) one of four balanced scorecard categories. Identifies the customer and market segments in which the business unit desires to compete.

**Cybernetics**   (Chapter 4) the study of information and its use in feedback processes

**Decentralized organization**   (Chapter 3) see *Centralized organization*

**Diagnostic control system**   (Chapter 10) formal information system that managers use to monitor organizational outcomes and correct deviations from preset standards of performance

**Diffusion of attention**   (Chapter 3) the constant switching back and forth between tasks that result in wasted time as employees constantly refocus on a new set of activities

**Direct method**   (Chapter 5) technique to estimate cash flows during a period of time; managers project the cash that they will receive and the cash that they will disburse

**Discounted cash flow analysis**   (Chapter 7) see *Net present value*

**Discretionary costs**   (Chapter 5) expenses that can be increased or decreased at will—almost without constraints

**Distinctive capabilities**   (Chapter 2) special resources and know-how possessed by a firm that give it competitive advantage in the marketplace

**Earnings**   (Chapter 5) see *Profit*

**EBIAT**   (Chapter 5) acronym for earnings before interest and after taxes

**EBITDA**   (Chapter 5) acronym for earnings before interest, taxes, depreciation, and amortization. It is a rough calculation of nonaccrual—or cash-based—operating earnings that can be computed readily from an income statement.

**Economic value added (EVA)**   (Chapter 8) similar to residual income but distinguished by (1) a series of adjustments to eliminate distortions of accrual accounting and (2) the inclusion of both debt and equity sources of capital in the cost of capital

**Economies of scale**   (Chapter 3) reduction in unit costs due to utilization of efficient, large-scale resources and high-volume processing

**Economies of scope**   (Chapter 3) reduction in unit costs due to utilization of the same resources (e.g., distribution channels) across multiple products or activities to increase the throughput for a given fixed amount of that resource

**Effectiveness**   (Chapter 6) the extent to which an activity achieves desired outcomes. Effectiveness focuses on the comparison of actual results with preset expectations or standards.

**Efficiency** (Chapter 6) the level of resources that were consumed to achieve a certain level of output. Efficiency focuses on the ratio of inputs to outputs.

**Efficiency variance** (Chapter 6) the amount by which profit differs from the original profit plan or budget because of unanticipated changes in the level of inputs used to create outputs

**Embedded resources** (Chapter 2) tangible resources that are difficult to acquire and/or replace. Physical plant, distribution channels, and information technology are all embedded assets that represent potential strengths and weaknesses.

**Emergent strategy** (Chapter 2) strategy that emerges spontaneously in the organization as employees respond to unpredictable threats and opportunities through experimentation and trial and error

**Engineered costs** (Chapter 5) see *Committed costs*

**Error of commission** (Chapter 12) error that occurs as a result of an employee knowingly pursuing a course of action that increases risk, impairs assets or otherwise endangers the business

**Error of omission** (Chapter 12) error that occurs as a result of an employee omitting to perform an action that is necessary to protect the franchise or assets of the business

**EVA** (Chapter 8) widely-used acronym for economic value added (Trademarked by consultants Stern, Stewart, & Co.)

**Ex ante** (Chapter 4) set in advance, usually refers to a preset standard

**Ex post evaluation** (Chapter 4) comparing actual effort and outcomes against prior expectations

**External communication** (Chapter 4) informing financial, supplier, and customer markets about the direction and prospects of the firm

**Extrinsic motivation** (Chapter 4) desire to engage in behaviors or actions in anticipation of tangible rewards, such as money or promotion

**Fact-based management** (Chapter 4) management that moves from intuition and hunches to analysis based on hard data and facts

**Favorable variance** (Chapter 6) the amount by which actual profit is higher than planned profit

**Feedback** (Chapter 4) return of variance information from the output of a process to the input or process stages so that adjustments can be made to maintain desired levels of performance or control the stability of a system

**Financial impairment** (Chapter 12) decline in the market value of a significant balance sheet asset held for resale or as collateral

**Financial leverage** (Chapter 5) the ratio of assets to stockholders' equity focuses on financial leverage by asking, "What percentage of total assets employed are funded by stockholders and what percentage by debt?"

**Financial performance perspective** (Chapter 9) one of four balanced scorecard categories. Indicates whether the implementation of company strategy is contributing to profit improvement.

**Five forces** (Chapter 2) systematic analysis of competitive dynamics to determine the nature and intensity of competition. The five forces are customers, suppliers, substitute products, new markets, and competitive rivalry.

**Franchise** (Chapter 2) a business's distinctive ability to attract customers who are willing to purchase the business's products and services based on marketwide perceptions of value. See also *Market franchise*

**Franchise risk** (Chapter 12) risk that the value of the entire business erodes due to a loss in confidence by critical constituents. Also known as reputation risk

**Full cost transfer price** (Chapter 8) transfer price that includes direct costs plus an allocation for the divisional overhead that would normally be covered by the gross profit margin on goods sold to outside customers

**Full cost plus profit transfer price** (Chapter 8) the highest accounting-based transfer price that attempts to approach market price by adding an additional markup to the full cost transfer price

**Function** (Chapter 3) the most basic organization component, comprising a group of managers and employees who specialize in specific work processes

**Functional skills** (Chapter 2) strengths (and weaknesses) in the major functional areas of a business, such as research and development, production and manufacturing, marketing and sales, and administration

**Goal** (Chapter 2) a formal aspiration that defines purpose or expected levels of achievement in implementing the business strategy

**Hurdle rate** (Chapter 7) the minimum internal rate of return that must be achieved before the acquisition of an asset will be approved

**Incentive** (Chapter 11) a reward or payment that is used to motivate performance

**Indirect method** (Chapter 5) technique to estimate cash needs over long periods of time; managers start with their projected income as shown on the profit plan and adjust accruals to reflect actual cash receipts and disbursements

**Information** (Chapter 4) the communication or reception of intelligence or knowledge. It is the critical vehicle for profit planning, performance measurement, and management control.

**Innovation process** (Chapter 9) component of the internal value chain. Represents the "long wave" of value creation.

**Intangible assets** (Chapter 2) Assets that are not physical in nature, such as franchises, copyrights, patents, trademarks, goodwill, valuable licenses (e.g., broadcast rights), and leases.

**Intended strategy** (Chapter 2) planned strategy that managers attempt to implement in a specific product market based on analysis of competitive dynamics and current capabilities

**Interactive control system** (Chapter 10) formal information system that managers use to personally involve themselves in the decision activities of subordinates

**Internal business process perspective** (Chapter 9) one of four balanced scorecard categories. Identifies the critical internal processes at which the organization must excel.

**Internal control systems** (Chapter 1) the set of policies and procedures designed to ensure reliable accounting information and safeguard company assets

**Internal rate of return (IRR)** (Chapter 7) the discount rate applied to any series of cash flows for which the value of the cash inflows exactly equals the value of cash outflows

**Internal value chain** (Chapter 9) model of the set of internal processes, for creating value for customers. Includes identifying the market, creating the product/service offering, building products/services, delivering products/services, and post-sale service.

**Intrinsic motivation** (Chapter 4) desire to engage in behaviors or actions in anticipation of internally-generated rewards such as personal feelings of accomplishment

**Learning and growth perspective** (Chapter 9) one of four balanced scorecard categories. Identifies the infrastructure that the organization must build to create long-term growth and improvement.

**Levers of control** (Chapter 14) the set of beliefs systems, boundary systems, diagnostic control systems, and interactive control systems used by managers to implement intended strategies and guide emergent strategies

**Leveraged business** (Chapter 5) one that relies on a high percentage of debt to fund the productive assets employed in the business to generate revenues

**Long-term assets** (Chapter 5) resources held for an extended period of time, such as land, buildings, and equipment

**Market capitalization** (Chapter 8) market value of the firm calculated as the product of the total number of ownership shares multiplied by the price per share

**Market franchise** (Chapter 2) a business's distinctive ability to attract customers who are willing to purchase the business's products and services based on marketwide perceptions of value. A business is said to "own a franchise" when a brand name itself is an important source of revenue.

**Market skills** (Chapter 2) a business's ability to respond to market needs

**Market value** (Chapter 8) the total value of ownership claims in the business

as priced by financial markets. Represents the highest, most aggregate, measure of value creation. See *Market capitalization*

**Market value added** (Chapter 8) excess of current market value over the amount of capital (i.e., adjusted book value) provided to the firm

**Measure** (Chapter 11) quantitative value that can be scaled and used for purposes of comparison. Measures are necessary to ensure that performance goals are achieved.

**Mission** (Chapter 2) the broad purpose, or reason, that a business exists

**Mission statements** (Chapter 2) Missions (see above) are often written down in formal documents known as mission statements that are designed to communicate the core values of the business and inspire pride in participants

**Negotiated transfer price** (Chapter 8) transfer price based on standard direct costs plus some allowance for profit or return on capital employed

**Net income** (Chapter 5) see *Profit*

**Net present value (NPV)** (Chapter 7) summation of the current value of a series of cash inflows and outflows after adjusting for the time value of money. Also known as *Discounted cash flow analysis*

**NOPAT** (Chapter 5) acronym for net operating profit after taxes

**Nonvariable costs** (Chapter 5) costs that do not vary directly with the level of sales

**Objectives** (Chapter 11) see *Performance goals*

**Objective measure** (Chapter 11) a measure that can be independently verified

**Operations risk** (Chapter 12) risk of a breakdown in a core operating, manufacturing, or processing capability

**Operations process** (Chapter 9) component of the internal value chain. Represents those processes that produce and deliver existing products and services to customers.

**Organizational blocks** (Chapter 1) obstacles that organizations create that inhibit employees from working to their true potential

**Organization chart** (Chapter 3) a diagram of accountability units within an organization. Organization charts are useful visual reference tools because they allow members of the organization to understand how people and resources are grouped and who is responsible for directing activities and receiving accountability information.

**Organizational learning** (Chapter 2) the ability of an organization to monitor changes in its environment and internal processes and adjust its processes, products, and services to capitalize on those changes

**Organizational structure** (Chapter 3) the way in which work units are arranged or put together to form an organization

**Output standard** (Chapter 4) a formal representation of performance expectations

**Payback** (Chapter 7) total acquisition cost of an asset divided by the amount of the periodic (that is, monthly or yearly) inflows of cash (or cash savings) that an asset is expected to generate. Expressed in units of time

**Performance drivers** (Chapter 11) variables that either influence the probability of successfully implementing the strategy or provide the largest potential for marginal gain over time

**Performance goal** (Chapter 11) a desired level of accomplishment against which actual results can be measured

**Performance measurement and control systems** (Chapter 1) the formal information-based routines and procedures managers use to maintain or alter patterns in organizational activities

**Performance measurement systems** (Chapter 1) information systems that managers use to track the implementation of business strategy by comparing actual results against strategic goals and objectives. A performance measurement system typically comprises systematic methods of setting business goals together with periodic feedback reports.

**Planning** (Chapter 4) the process of preparing an economic and strategic road map for a business. Planning provides a framework for setting aspirations through performance goals and ensuring an adequate level and mix of resources to achieve these goals.

**Planning systems** (Chapter 1) recurring procedures to routinely disseminate planning assumptions, gather market information, provide details about relevant analyses, and prompt managers to estimate resource needs and performance goals and milestones

**Plans** (Chapter 4) a road map for the business. See *Planning*

**Position of a business** (Chapter 2) provides the answer to the following two questions: How do we create value for our customers? and How do we differentiate our products and services from those of our competitors?

**Post-sale service process** (Chapter 9) final stage of the internal value chain. Includes warranty and repair activities, treatment of defects and returns, and administration of payments

**Price premium** (Chapter 6) unit price that is higher than profit plan estimate.

Due to effective differentiation and successful market positioning.

**Product mix**   (Chapter 6) percentage of total sales that is generated by each product in a business's product line

**Product division**   (Chapter 3) a separate work unit dedicated to producing and marketing a set of products

**Product market**   (Chapter 2) a defined competitive market for a specific product or category of products

**Product mix variance**   (Chapter 6) the amount by which profit differs from the original profit plan or budget because of unanticipated changes in the sales mix of products with different contribution margins

**Productive assets**   (Chapter 2) assets used to produce goods and services for customers. These assets are usually recorded on a balance sheet.

**Profit**   (Chapter 5) the residual economic value after interest expense and income taxes (both of which are nondiscretionary payments). Based on accounting assumptions, profit is the economic value that is available for distribution to the residual claimants—equity holders—or for reinvestment in the business.

**Profit center accountability**   (Chapter 3) A profit center manager has a broader span of accountability than a cost center manager. He or she is not only accountable for costs, but also for revenues and, sometimes, for assets. See also *Cost center accountability*

**Profit plan**   (Chapter 1) a summary of future financial inflows and outflows for a specified future accounting period. It is usually prepared in the familiar format of an income statement.

**Profit wheel**   (Chapter 5) a model of the flow of operating profit through a busi-

ness. Answers the question of whether the organization's strategy creates economic value

**Profitability**   (Chapter 5) the ratio of net income to sales. Profitability indicates how much profit was generated for each dollar of sales.

**Realized strategy**   (Chapter 14) strategies that were actually implemented. The outcome of intended and emergent strategy.

**Reengineering**   (Chapter 5) streamlining work flows to accomplish the same work with fewer resources

**Regional business**   (Chapter 3) regionally based work units that focus on specific geographic regions

**Residual income**   (Chapter 8) a measure of how much additional profit remains for investment in the business or distribution to owners after allowing for expected returns on investment. See also *Economic value added*

**Resource**   (Chapter 2) a strength of the business embodied in the tangible or intangible assets that are tied semipermanently to the firm

**Responsive measures**   (Chapter 11) a measure that reflects actions that a manager can influence

**Return on capital employed (ROCE)** (Chapter 5) a percentage calculated as the product of net income divided by sales and sales divided by capital employed. See also *Capital employed*

**Return on equity (ROE)**   (Chapter 5) a ratio calculated as net income divided by shareholders' equity

**Return on investment (ROI)**   (Chapter 5) a ratio measure of the profit output of the business as a percentage of financial investment inputs. This accounting measure is one of the single best surrogates for overall financial performance.

**Return on management (ROM)**
(Chapter 1) the amount of productive organizational energy released divided by the amount of management time and attention invested

**Risk exposure calculator** (Chapter 12) a tool to analyze the pressure points inside a business that can cause otherwise manageable risks to "blow up" into a crisis

**ROE wheel** (Chapter 5) a model of the flow of equity capital through a business. Answers the question of whether the organization creates enough value to attract the financial resources that it needs to invest in new assets.

**Segregation of duties** (Chapter 13) key structural aspect of internal control. Ensures that one person never handles all aspects of a transaction involving valuable company assets.

**Sensitivity analysis** (Chapter 5) estimates of profit changes when the underlying assumptions about the environment or other predictions prove to be under or overstated. Companies often develop three different scenarios: worst-case scenario, most likely scenario, and best-case scenario.

**Signaling** (Chapter 4) when managers send cues throughout the organization about their values, preferences, and the type of opportunities that they want employees to seek and exploit

**Span of accountability** (Chapter 3) the range of performance measures used to evaluate a manager's achievements. At a most basic level, span of accountability defines the financial statement items for which a manager is accountable.

**Span of attention** (Chapter 3) the domain of activities that are within a manager's field of view. Span of attention defines what an individual will attempt to gather information on and influence. In simple terms, it's what people care about and pay attention to.

**Span of control** (Chapter 3) how many (and which) subordinates and functions report to a manager. Span of control describes the resources—in terms of people and work units—directly under a manager's control.

**Specialization** (Chapter 3) the focusing of individuals and resources on specific tasks that require expertise, training, and dedicated resources

**Spending variance** (Chapter 6) the amount by which profit differs from the original profit plan or budget because of unanticipated changes in the actual unit cost of inputs

**Staff safeguards** (Chapter 13) internal controls designed to ensure that accounting and transaction processing staff have the right level of expertise, training, and resources

**Standard** (Chapter 4) a formal representation of performance expectations

**Strategic boundaries** (Chapter 13) set of opportunities declared "out of bounds" by senior managers after evaluating a firm's strategy and its unique risks. Implicitly defines the desired market position for the firm.

**Strategic profitability** (Chapter 6) sum of profit (or loss) from competitive effectiveness and the profit (or loss) from operating efficiencies

**Strategic profitability analysis** (Chapter 6) variance analysis techniques to evaluate the success of a business in generating profit from the implementation of its strategy

**Strategic risk** (Chapter 12) unexpected event or set of conditions that significantly reduces the ability of managers to implement their intended business strategy

**Strategic uncertainties** (Chapter 12) emerging threats and opportunities that could invalidate the assumptions upon which the current business strategy is based

**Structural safeguards** (Chapter 13) internal controls designed to ensure clear definition of authority for individuals handling assets and recording accounting transactions

**SWOT** (Chapter 2) an acronym for strengths, weaknesses, opportunities, and threats. A SWOT analysis determines the potential for effective strategy based on an assessment of competitive dynamics (see the *Five forces*) and the resources and capabilities of a business.

**System safeguards** (Chapter 13) internal controls designed to ensure adequate procedures for transaction processing and timely management reports

**Total Quality Management (TQM)** (Chapter 4) a management approach that standardizes and streamlines key operating processes to ensure high levels of quality and/or low defect rates

**Transfer price** (Chapter 8) an internally set transaction price to account for the transfer of goods and services between divisions of the same firm

**Unfavorable variance** (Chapter 6) the amount by which actual profit is below planned profit

**Value proposition** (Chapter 8) the mix of product and service attributes that a firm offers to customers in terms of price, product features, quality, availability, image, buying experience and after-sales warranty and service

**Variable cost transfer price** (Chapter 8) lowest accounting-based transfer price based on only variable costs with no administrative overhead included in the price

**Variable costs** (Chapter 5) costs that vary proportionally with the level of sales or production outputs

**Variance analysis** (Chapter 6) the difference between an item estimated on a profit plan or budget prepared prior to the start of an accounting period and the actual income or expense as reflected on accounting statements prepared after the accounting period has ended

**Variance information** (Chapter 4) the difference between actual outputs and preset standards of performance. Used as feedback for corrective action by managers.

**Weighted average cost of capital (WACC)** (Chapter 7) the average cost of capital calculated by weighting the cost of each source of funds by its proportion of the total market value of the firm. This discount rate represents the minimum rate of return on an investment to meet capital providers' expectations.

**Work unit** (Chapter 3) represents a grouping of individuals who utilize the firm's resources and are accountable for performance

# INDEX